a Wolters Kluwer business

D0472506

GAAP Financial Statement Disclosures Manual

by George Georgiades, CPA

Highlights

CCH's *GAAP Financial Statement Disclosures Manual* provides a complete, quick, and valuable reference source for financial statement disclosures.

Specifically, the Manual contains over 900 examples of realistic sample footnote disclosures to assist in the preparation of financial statements for an audit, a review, or a compilation engagement; facilitates compliance with authoritative pronouncements by integrating the specific disclosure requirements with the sample footnotes; and incorporates all currently effective pronouncements, including those that cover areas of unusual difficulty, such as financial instruments, business combinations, impairment of long-lived assets, income taxes, pensions, accounting changes, variable interest entities, and share-based payment.

The Manual also includes a financial statement disclosures checklist that provides a centralized resource of the required and recommended GAAP disclosures currently in use.

All of the sample disclosures in this Manual, along with the financial statement disclosures checklist, are included on the CD-ROM that accompanies this book.

2007–2008 Edition

2007–2008 *GAAP Financial Statement Disclosures Manual* is current through the issuance of the following pronouncements:

- FASB Statement No. 158, *Employers' Accounting for Defined Benefit Pension and Other Postretirement Plans*
- FASB Interpretation No. 48, *Accounting for Uncertainty in Income Taxes*

- FASB Technical Bulletin 01-1, *Effective Date for Certain Financial Institutions of Certain Provisions of Statement 140 Related to the Isolation of Transferred Financial Assets*
- SOP 06-1, *Reporting Pursuant to the Global Investment Performance Standards*
- EITF Issue No. 06-9, *Reporting a Change in (or the Elimination of) a Previously Existing Difference between the Fiscal Year-End of a Parent Company and That of a Consolidated Entity or between the Reporting Period of an Investor and That of an Equity Method Investee*
- FASB Staff Position No. EITF 00-19-2, *Accounting for Registration Payment Arrangements*
- FASB Staff Position No. FAS 123(R)-6, *Technical Corrections of FASB Statement No. 123(R)*

Unless specifically indicated, the examples provided assume that the most recent financial statements presented are for the year ended December 31, 20X2.

PRACTICE ALERT: On April 28, 2005, the FASB issued for public comment, *The Hierarchy of Generally Accepted Accounting Principles*. This Exposure Draft (ED) proposes to transfer the GAAP hierarchy from the auditing literature issued by the AICPA (i.e., Statement on Auditing Standards No. 69, *The Meaning of "Present Fairly in Conformity with Generally Accepted Accounting Principles"*) to the FASB literature. The FASB proposes to retain the "levels" or "categories" of GAAP already described in the auditing literature, except that the FASB will clarify that FASB Staff Positions and Derivatives Implementation Group issues will receive Level A status. The FASB states in the ED that the guidance proposed would not change current practice. Practitioners should be alert to further developments in this area.

CCH Learning Center

CCH's goal is to provide you with the clearest, most concise, and up-to-date accounting and auditing information to help further your professional development, as well as a convenient method to

help you satisfy your continuing professional education requirements. The CCH Learning Center* offers a complete line of self-study
courses covering complex and constantly evolving accounting and
auditing issues. We are continually adding new courses to the
library to help you stay current on all the latest developments. The
CCH Learning Center courses are available 24 hours a day, seven
days a week. You'll get immediate exam results and certification. To
view our complete accounting and auditing course catalog, go to:
http://cch.learningcenter.com.

Accounting Research Manager™

Accounting Research Manager is the most comprehensive, up-to-
date, and objective online database of financial reporting literature.
It includes all authoritative and proposed accounting, auditing, and
SEC literature, plus independent, expert-written interpretive guidance.

Our Weekly Summary e-mail newsletter highlights the key
developments of the week, giving you the assurance that you have
the most current information. It provides links to new FASB, AICPA,
SEC, PCAOB, EITF, and IASB authoritative and proposal-stage
literature, plus insightful guidance from financial reporting experts.

Our outstanding team of content experts take pride in updating
the system on a daily basis, so you stay as current as possible. You'll
learn of newly released literature and deliberations of current
financial reporting projects as soon as they occur! Plus, you benefit
from their easy-to-understand technical translations.

With **Accounting Research Manager**, you maximize the efficiency
of your research time while enhancing your results. Learn more about

---

* CCH is registered with the National Association of State Boards of Accountancy
(NASBA) as a sponsor of continuing professional education on the National
Registry of CPE Sponsors. State boards of accountancy have final authority on the
acceptance of individual courses for CPE credit. Complaints regarding registered
sponsors may be addressed to the National Registry of CPE Sponsors, 150 Fourth
Avenue North, Nashville, TN 37219-2417. Telephone: 615-880-4200.

* CCH is registered with the National Association of State Boards of Accountancy as
a Quality Assurance Service (QAS) sponsor of continuing professional education.
Participating state boards of accountancy have final authority on the acceptance of
individual courses for CPE credit. Complaints regarding QAS program sponsors
may be addressed to NASBA, 150 Fourth Avenue North, Suite 700, Nashville, TN
37219-2417. Telephone: 615-880-4200.

our content, our experts, and how you can request a FREE trial by
visiting us at **http://www.accountingresearchmanager.com.**

06/07

For questions concerning this shipment, billing, or other customer service matters,
call 1 800 248 3248.

2007–2008

GAAP

FINANCIAL STATEMENT DISCLOSURES MANUAL

GEORGE GEORGIADES, CPA

CCH
a Wolters Kluwer business

This publication is designed to provide accurate and authoritative information in regard to the subject matter covered. It is sold with the understanding that the publisher is not engaged in rendering legal, accounting, or other professional services. If legal advice or other professional assistance is required, the services of a competent professional person should be sought.

—From a *Declaration of Principles* jointly adopted by a Committee of the American Bar Association and a Committee of Publishers and Associations

ISBN: 978-0-8080-9097-7

Printed in the United States of America

Our Peer Review Policy

Thank you for ordering the 2007–2008 *GAAP Financial Statement Disclosures Manual*. Each year we bring you the best accounting and auditing reference guides available. To confirm the technical accuracy and quality control of our materials, CCH voluntarily submitted to a peer review of our publishing system and our publications (see the Peer Review Statement on the following page).

In addition to peer review, our publications undergo strict technical and content reviews by qualified practitioners. This ensures that our books and electronic workpapers meet "real-world" standards and applicability.

Our publications are reviewed every step of the way—from conception to production—to ensure that we bring you the finest guides on the market.

Updated annually, peer reviewed, technically accurate, convenient, and practical—the 2007–2008 *GAAP Financial Statement Disclosures Manual* shows our commitment to creating books and electronic workpapers you can trust.

.ıll *Caldwell, Becker, Dervin, Petrick & Co., L.L.P.*
CERTIFIED PUBLIC ACCOUNTANTS

April 25, 2006

Executive Board
CCH, a Wolters Kluwer business

We have reviewed the system of quality control for the development and maintenance of GAAP Financial Statement Disclosures Manual (2006–2007 Edition), of CCH, a Wolters Kluwer business (the company), applicable to non-SEC issuers in effect for the year ended March 31, 2006, and the resultant materials in effect at March 31, 2006. The design of the system, and compliance with it, are the responsibilities of the company. Our responsibility is to express an opinion on the design of the system, and the company's compliance with that system based on our review.

Our review was conducted in accordance with the standards for reviews of quality control materials promulgated by the Peer Review Committee of the Center for Public Company Audit Firms of the American Institute of Certified Public Accountants. In performing our review, we have given consideration to the following general characteristics of a system of quality control. A company's system for the development and maintenance of quality control materials encompasses its organizational structure and the policies and procedures established to provide the users of its materials with reasonable assurance that the quality control materials are reliable aids to assist them in conforming with professional standards in conducting their accounting and auditing practices. The extent of a company's quality control policies and procedures for the development and maintenance of quality control materials and the manner in which they are implemented will depend upon a variety of factors, such as the size and organizational structure of the company and the nature of the materials provided to users. Variance in individual performance and professional interpretation affects the degree of compliance with prescribed quality control policies and procedures. Therefore, adherence to all policies and procedures in every case may not be possible.

Our review and tests were limited to the system of quality control for the development and maintenance of the aforementioned quality control materials of CCH and to the materials themselves and did not extend to the application of these materials by users of the materials nor to the policies and procedures of individual users.

In our opinion, the system of quality control for the development and maintenance of the quality control materials of CCH was suitably designed and was being complied with during the year ended March 31, 2006, to provide users of the materials with reasonable assurance that the materials are reliable aids to assist them in conforming with those professional standards in the United States of America applicable to non-SEC issuers. Also, in our opinion, the quality control materials referred to above are reliable aids at March 31, 2006.

Caldwell, Becker, Dervin, Petrick & Co., LLP.
CALDWELL, BECKER, DERVIN, PETRICK & CO., L.L.P.

20750 Ventura Boulevard, Suite 140 • Woodland Hills, CA 91364
(818) 704-1040 • FAX (818) 704-5536

About the GAAP Hierarchy

The meaning of the term *generally accepted accounting principles* (GAAP) has varied over time. Originally, GAAP referred to accounting policies and procedures that were widely used in practice. As standard-setting bodies and professional organizations became more involved in recommending preferred practices, the term came to refer more to the pronouncements issued by particular accounting bodies. Today, many different series of authoritative literature exist, some of which are still in effect but are no longer being issued, like APB Opinions and AICPA Accounting Research Bulletins. Others—such as FASB Statements—continue to be issued by accounting organizations.

To better organize and clarify what is meant by GAAP, SAS-69 (The Meaning of "Present Fairly in Conformity with Generally Accepted Accounting Principles") established what is commonly referred to as the GAAP hierarchy. The purpose of the hierarchy is to instruct financial statement preparers, auditors, and users of financial statements concerning the relative priority of the different sources of GAAP used by auditors to judge the fairness of presentation in financial statements. Though the GAAP hierarchy appears in the professional auditing literature, its impact goes beyond its importance to auditors: Preparers, users, and others interested in financial statements must understand the sources of GAAP that underlie those statements.

SAS-69 defines the *GAAP hierarchy* by outlining four categories of established accounting principles. Because these sources of accounting principles arose over five decades and were promulgated by different groups, some conflicts exist among them. The four categories of GAAP correspond to these principles' relative authoritativeness. Higher categories carry more weight and must be followed when conflicts arise. When two or more sources of GAAP within a given level of the hierarchy disagree on a particular transaction, the approach that better portrays the substance of the transaction should be followed.

In addition to these four levels, the GAAP hierarchy recognizes other types of accounting literature that may be useful in resolving financial reporting problems when issues have not been covered in established sources of GAAP.

The figure on the following page displays the four levels of established principles that are supported by authoritative accounting literature, as well as the additional sources of GAAP, and the corresponding CCH coverage.

GAAP Hierarchy CCH Coverage

LEVEL A*

- FASB Statements of Financial Accounting Standards (FAS)
- FASB Interpretations (FIN)
- APB Opinions (APB)
- Accounting Research Bulletins (ARB)

2007 *GAAP Guide Level A*

2007 *GAAP Guide Level A*
2007 *GAAP Guide Level A*
2007 *GAAP Guide Level A*

LEVEL B*

- FASB Technical Bulletins (FTB)
- AICPA Industry Audit and Accounting Guides
- AICPA Statements of Position (SOP)
- FASB Staff Positions

2007 *GAAP Guide Levels B, C, and D*
2006–2007 Engagement Series

2007 *GAAP Guide Levels B, C, and D*
2007 *GAAP Guide Levels B, C, and D*

LEVEL C*

- Consensus Positions of the Emerging Issues Task Force (EITF)
- SEC and FASB Staff Announcements (Topic Ds)
- AICPA AcSEC Practice Bulletins (PB)

2007 *GAAP Guide Levels B, C, and D*
2007 *GAAP Guide Levels B, C, and D*
2007 *GAAP Guide Levels B, C, and D*

LEVEL D*

- AICPA Accounting Interpretations (AIN)
- FASB Implementation Guides (FIG)

2007 *GAAP Guide Levels B, C, and D*
2007 *GAAP Guide Levels B, C, and D*

*All four levels are covered twice monthly in the *GAAP Update Service*.

Other Accounting Literature

- FASB Concepts Statements (CON)
- SEC Rules, Regulations, and Pronouncements
- APB Statements
- AICPA Issues Papers
- International Accounting Standards Committee Statements (2007 *International Accounting/Financial Reporting Standards Guide*)
- GASB Statements, Interpretations, and Technical Bulletins (2007 *Governmental GAAP Guide*)
- Pronouncements of other professional associations and regulatory bodies
- AICPA Technical Practice Aids
- Accounting textbooks, handbooks, and articles

PRACTICE ALERT: On April 28, 2005, the FASB issued for public comment, *The Hierarchy of Generally Accepted Accounting Principles*. This Exposure Draft (ED) proposes to transfer the GAAP hierarchy from the auditing literature issued by the AICPA (i.e., Statement on Auditing Standards No. 69, *The Meaning of "Present Fairly in Conformity with Generally Accepted Accounting Principles"*) to the FASB literature. The FASB proposes to retain the "levels" or "categories" of GAAP already described in the auditing literature, except that the FASB will clarify that FASB Staff Positions and Derivatives Implementation Group issues will receive Level A status. The FASB states in the ED that the guidance proposed would not change current practice. Practitioners should be alert to further developments in this area.

Contents

Part I—Special Financial Statement Topics and Disclosures

Preface

The 2007–2008 *GAAP Financial Statement Disclosures Manual* provides a complete, quick, and valuable reference source for financial statement disclosures. Specifically, the Manual:

- Provides over 900 examples of realistic sample footnote disclosures to assist in the preparation of financial statements for an audit, a review, or a compilation engagement.

- Facilitates compliance with authoritative pronouncements by integrating, in each chapter, the specific disclosure requirements with the sample footnotes.

- Provides sample disclosures that are technically sound, understandable, and comprehensive and that cover a variety of scenarios, from the most common to the most unusual.

- Incorporates all currently effective pronouncements, including those that cover areas of unusual difficulty, such as financial instruments, income taxes, pensions, accounting changes, and going concern.

All of the sample disclosures in the 2007–2008 *GAAP Financial Statement Disclosures Manual* are included on the accompanying CD-ROM. Therefore, once you've identified the disclosure suited to your specific needs, you can simply select it from the CD-ROM, place it into your financial statements, then modify it as necessary.

The Manual is divided into four major parts. Part I, Special Financial Statement Topics and Disclosures, covers major financial accounting and reporting topics. The chapters in Part II, Balance Sheet, are arranged in the order in which the major assets, liabilities, and equity captions ordinarily appear in a balance sheet. For example, assets and liabilities are discussed first in general, then cash and cash equivalents, and so on. Part III, Income Statement, covers the specific elements of "results of operations" that are required to be presented separately under GAAP. Part IV, Statement of Cash Flows, discusses the presentation of specific types of transactions in cash flow statements, alternative formats for presenting the statements, and the disclosure of noncash transactions.

The book is designed for ease of use. You can locate information based either on the disclosure topic or on the disclosure's location in the financial statements. In addition, each chapter is structured as a stand-alone chapter, providing you with all the information you'll need on a specific topic. Each chapter consists of the following parts:

1. **Executive Summary.** This summary provides a clear and concise discussion of the specific financial statement topic or standard.

2. **Authoritative Literature.** This section provides a complete listing of the relevant authoritative pronouncements so that you can access the authoritative information quickly and easily. Authoritative GAAP contained in Levels A and B of the GAAP hierarchy are listed in this section. Also, to the extent that authoritative GAAP in Levels C and D of the GAAP hierarchy require additional disclosures (e.g., certain EITF consensus positions and SOPs), they are listed in this section as well.

3. **Disclosure Requirements.** This section provides a detailed listing of the disclosure requirements mandated by GAAP.

4. **Examples of Financial Statement Disclosures.** This section contains specific examples of disclosures that cover different situations, circumstances, assumptions, and so on. Unless specifically indicated, the examples provided assume that the most recent financial statements presented are for the year ended December 31, 20X2.

The Manual also includes a financial statement disclosures checklist that provides a centralized resource of the required and recommended GAAP disclosures currently in use. It is designed to assist the user in determining whether the required financial statement disclosures have been made.

The 2007–2008 *GAAP Financial Statement Disclosures Manual* is current through the issuance of the following pronouncements:

- FASB Statement No. 158, *Employers' Accounting for Defined Benefit Pension and Other Postretirement Plans*

- FASB Interpretation No. 48, *Accounting for Uncertainty in Income Taxes*

- FASB Technical Bulletin 01-1, *Effective Date for Certain Financial Institutions of Certain Provisions of Statement 140 Related to the Isolation of Transferred Financial Assets*

- SOP 06-1, *Reporting Pursuant to the Global Investment Performance Standards*

- EITF Issue No. 06-9, *Reporting a Change in (or the Elimination of) a Previously Existing Difference between the Fiscal Year-End of a Parent Company and That of a Consolidated Entity or between the Reporting Period of an Investor and That of an Equity Method Investee*

- FASB Staff Position No. EITF 00-19-2, *Accounting for Registration Payment Arrangements*
- FASB Staff Position No. FAS 123(R)-6, *Technical Corrections of FASB Statement No. 123(R)*

The author and publisher welcome comments, suggestions, and recommendations to improve this Manual. These will be considered for incorporation in future revisions of the Manual. Please send your comments to Sandra Lim, sandra.lim@wolterskluwer.com.

Acknowledgments

Thanks are due to the staff at CCH, especially to Sandra Lim, developmental editor, for her efforts in overseeing the production of the manual and to Mei Wang, senior manuscript editor, for bringing this edition to press. The author and publisher also thank Professor Bernard H. Newman, CPA, Ph.D., at Pace University, for his thorough review and comments on the Manual as this year's revision got under way. Also, I thank my wife, Caroline, for her continuous support and encouragement and my sons, Alex and Dmitri, for their inspiration and constant source of energy and joy.

George Georgiades
Laguna Niguel, California

About the Author

George Georgiades, CPA, has more than 26 years of experience in public accounting, including seven years as an audit senior manager with a major international accounting firm. He currently has his own firm and consults exclusively with CPA firms on technical accounting, auditing, and financial statement disclosure issues. In writing this Manual, Mr. Georgiades has capitalized on the extensive experience he has gained from association with clients and with international, national, regional, and local accounting firms. He has been personally involved in more than 600 audit engagements and related financial statements of both small, closely held companies and large, publicly held enterprises. He has personally conducted more than 75 peer reviews, consulting reviews, and inspections. He also brings to the Manual extensive hands-on experience in performing independent technical reviews of financial statements.

Mr. Georgiades is also the author of *Audit Procedures, GAAS Practice Manual,* and the *GAAS Update Service.* He is a member of the American Institute of Certified Public Accountants and the California Society of Certified Public Accountants, and served on the California Society of CPAs' Peer Review Committee.

PART I—
SPECIAL FINANCIAL
STATEMENT TOPICS AND
DISCLOSURES

CHAPTER 1
ACCOUNTING CHANGES AND ERROR CORRECTIONS

CONTENTS

EXECUTIVE SUMMARY

Note: The FASB has issued Statement of Financial Accounting Standards No. 154 (FAS-154), *Accounting Changes and Error Corrections*, which changes the requirements for accounting for and reporting a change in accounting principles. The general accounting for changes in accounting estimates and in the reporting entity did not change under FAS-154. The new Statement supersedes Accounting Principles Board Opinion No. 20 (APB-20), *Accounting Changes*; Statement of Financial Accounting Standards No. 3 (FAS-3), *Reporting Accounting Changes in Interim Financial Statements*; Statement of Financial Accounting Standards No. 73, *Reporting a Change in Accounting for*

> *Railroad Track Structures;* and FASB Interpretation No. 20 (FIN-20), *Reporting Accounting Changes under AICPA Statements of Position.* FAS-154 applies to all voluntary changes in accounting principles and to changes required by an accounting pronouncement in the unusual instance that the pronouncement does not indicate a specific transition method. APB-20 required most voluntary changes in accounting principle to be accounted for by what is commonly referred to as the cumulative effect method. This method required the cumulative effect of the change to be included in the determination of net income of the period of the change. FAS-154 replaces the cumulative effect method for voluntary accounting changes with retrospective application to prior periods' financial statements. "Retrospective application" is the application of a different accounting principle to previously presented financial statements as if that principle had always been used. FAS-154 uses the term "retrospective application" versus "restatement" as used in APB-20; FAS-154 reserves the use of the term "restatement" for corrections of errors in previously issued financial statements. FAS-154 is effective for accounting changes and corrections of errors made in fiscal years beginning after December 15, 2005.

Accounting changes are broadly classified into three categories:

1. Changes in accounting estimates
2. Changes in accounting principles
3. Changes in the reporting entity

Corrections of errors in previously issued financial statements are not accounting changes, but they are covered in the same accounting literature because of their similarity.

Promulgated generally accepted accounting principles (GAAP) identify three accounting methods to account for accounting changes and corrections of errors: (1) current and prospective method, (2) cumulative effect method, and (3) retrospective application to all prior periods presented. These methods are not alternatives—the authoritative literature is specific concerning which method is to be used for each type of accounting change or correction of error.

Changes in Accounting Estimates

A change in an accounting estimate usually is the result of new events, changing conditions, more experience, or additional information, any of which requires previous estimates to be revised. Estimates are necessary in determining depreciation and amortization of long-lived assets, uncollectible receivables, provisions for warranty, and a multitude of other items involved in preparing financial statements.

FAS-154 carries forward the guidance for reporting changes in accounting estimate from APB-20. A change in accounting estimate is accounted for in the period of change if the change affects only that period, or in the period of change and future periods if the change affects both. A change in accounting estimate is not accounted for by restating or retrospectively adjusting amounts reported in financial statements of prior periods or by reporting pro forma amounts for prior periods.

Distinguishing between a change in accounting principle and a change in accounting estimate may be difficult. In some cases, a change in estimate is effected by a change in accounting principle, such as when a depreciation method is changed to reflect a change in the estimated future benefits of the asset or the pattern of consumption of those benefits. Changes in accounting estimates that are inseparable from changes in accounting principles should be accounted for as changes in accounting estimates. Similar to other changes in accounting principle, a change in accounting estimate that is effected by a change in accounting principle is appropriate only if the new principle is justifiable on the basis that it is preferable.

> **Note:** Under FAS-154, a change in depreciation, amortization, or depletion method for long-lived assets should be accounted for as a change in accounting estimate, effected by a change in accounting principle. Therefore, the change may only be made if the new depreciation method is preferable. A change in depreciation method (e.g., from the double declining balance method to the straight-line method) should not be accounted for by retrospective application to prior periods because it constitutes a change in estimate. This is different from APB-20, which previously required that such changes be reported as a change in accounting principle.

Changes in Accounting Principles

An entity may change an accounting principle only if the change is required by a newly issued accounting pronouncement or the entity can justify the use of a different allowable accounting principle on the basis that it is preferable. Common changes in accounting principles include the following:

- Changing the method of pricing inventory (e.g., changing from LIFO to FIFO or from FIFO to LIFO)
- Changing the method of accounting for long-term construction-type contracts
- Adopting a new accounting principle

New rules under FAS-154.   An entity making a change in accounting principle should report that change by retrospective application of the new principle to all periods presented unless it is impracticable to do so. Retrospective application requires the following steps:

1. The cumulative effect of the change to the new principle on periods prior to those presented should be reflected in the carrying amount of assets and liabilities as of the beginning of the first period presented;

2. An offsetting adjustment, if any, should be made to the opening balance of retained earnings for that period; and

3. Financial statements for each individual prior period presented should be adjusted to reflect the period-specific effects of applying the new principle.

If the cumulative effect of applying a change in accounting principle to all prior periods can be determined, but it is impracticable to determine the period-specific effects of that change on all prior periods presented, the cumulative effect of the change should be applied to the carrying amounts of assets and liabilities as of the beginning of the earliest period to which the new accounting principle can be applied. The offsetting adjustment, if any, should be made to the opening balance of retained earnings for that period.

 If it is impracticable to determine the cumulative effect of applying a change in accounting principle to any prior period, the new principle should be applied prospectively as of the earliest date practicable. A change from the first-in, first-out (FIFO) inventory method to the last-in, first-out (LIFO) inventory method when the effects of having been on LIFO in the past cannot be determined is an example of this situation.

Rules prior to FAS-154.   When a change in accounting principle is necessary, it generally is recognized by including the cumulative effect of the change in the net income of the period of change. The cumulative effect of a change in an accounting principle is the total direct effect, less related taxes, that the change has on prior periods (i.e., on retained earnings at the beginning of the period). Accounting for a change in accounting principle through a cumulative effect adjustment involves the following points:

1. Prior-period comparative financial statements are presented as previously reported;

2. The cumulative effect of changing to a new accounting principle is the difference between the amount of retained earnings at the beginning of the period of change and the amount of retained earnings that would have been reported if the change had been applied retroactively; and

3. The cumulative effect of changing to a new accounting principle is included in net income of the period of the change and is shown in the income statement between extraordinary items and net income.

Changes in the Reporting Entity

A change in the reporting entity takes place when the following occurs:

- Presenting consolidated or combined financial statements in place of statements of individual companies
- Changing specific subsidiaries that make up the group of companies for which consolidated financial statements are presented
- Changing the companies included in combined financial statements

FAS-154 carries forward the guidance for reporting changes in the reporting entity from APB-20. An accounting change that results in financial statements that are, in effect, those of a different reporting entity should be retrospectively applied to the financial statements for the new reporting entity.

Correction of Errors

Errors that are discovered in financial statements subsequent to their issuance are reported as prior-period adjustments. Errors result from mistakes in mathematics and in the application of an accounting principle or from misjudgment in the use of facts. Although correcting an error and changing an estimate are similar and are sometimes confused, they differ in that a change in estimate is based on new (revised) information that was previously unavailable. A change from an unacceptable accounting principle to a generally accepted one is considered an error correction for financial reporting purposes.

FAS-154 carries forward the guidance for reporting error corrections from APB-20. An error in financial statements of prior periods that is discovered after those statements are issued is reported as a prior-period adjustment by restating the prior-period financial statements. This requires the following three steps:

1. The cumulative effect of the error on periods prior to those presented (i.e., the period in which the error is discovered and corrected) is reflected in the carrying amounts of assets and liabilities as of the beginning of the first period presented;

2. An offsetting adjustment, if any, is made to the opening balance of retained earnings (or other component of equity or net assets in the statement of financial position) for that period; and

3. Financial statements for each individual prior period presented are adjusted to reflect correction of the period-specific effects of the error.

Authoritative Literature

APB-9   Reporting the Results of Operations

APB-20   Accounting Changes (superseded by FAS-154 for fiscal years beginning after December 15, 2005)

FAS-3   Reporting Accounting Changes in Interim Financial Statements (superseded by FAS-154 for fiscal years beginning after December 15, 2005)

FAS-73   Reporting a Change in Accounting for Railroad Track Structures (superseded by FAS-154 for fiscal years beginning after December 15, 2005)

FAS-111   Rescission of FASB Statement No. 32 and Technical Corrections

FAS-141   Business Combinations

FAS-154   Accounting Changes and Error Corrections

FIN-1   Accounting Changes Related to the Cost of Inventory

FIN-20   Reporting Accounting Changes under AICPA Statements of Position (superseded by FAS-154 for fiscal years beginning after December 15, 2005)

DISCLOSURE REQUIREMENTS

Disclosure Requirements under FAS-154

Changes in accounting estimates. The disclosure requirements for changes in accounting estimates under FAS-154 are as follows:

1. For a change in accounting estimate that affects several future periods (e.g., change in service lives of depreciable assets), disclosure should include the effect of the change on the following for the current period (FAS-154, par. 22):

   a. Income from continuing operations

   b. Net income (or other appropriate captions of change in the applicable net assets or performance indicators)

   c. Related per-share amounts when presented

     (Note: Disclosure of these effects is not necessary for estimates made each period in the ordinary course of accounting, such as for uncollectible accounts or inventory obsolescence, unless the effect of the change in estimate is material.)

2. For a change in accounting estimate that has no material effect in the period of change but is reasonably certain to have a material effect in later periods, a description of the change should be disclosed whenever the financial statements of the period of change are presented (FAS-154, par. 22).

3. If a change in accounting principle effects a change in estimate, the required disclosures detailed below for changes in accounting principles should also be made (FAS-154, par. 22).

Changes in accounting principles. The disclosure requirements for changes in accounting principles under FAS-154 are as follows:

1. The following items should be disclosed in the fiscal period in which a change in accounting principle is made (FAS-154, par. 17):

   a. The nature of and reason for the change in accounting principle, including an explanation of why the newly adopted accounting principle is preferable

   b. The method of applying the change

   c. A description of the prior-period information that has been retrospectively adjusted

   d. The effect of the change on the following for the current period and any prior periods retrospectively adjusted:

     (1) Income from continuing operations

     (2) Net income (or other appropriate captions of changes in the applicable net assets or performance indicator)

     (3) Any other affected financial statement line item

     (4) Any affected per-share amounts

   e. The cumulative effect of the change on retained earnings or other components of equity or net assets in the balance sheet as of the beginning of the earliest period presented

   f. If retrospective application to all prior periods is impracticable, the reasons, and a description of the alternative method used to report the change

   g. If indirect effects of the change in accounting principle are recognized:

> (1) A description of the indirect effects of the change in accounting principle, including the amounts that have been recognized in the current period, and the related per-share amounts, if applicable
>
> (2) Unless impracticable, the amount of the total recognized indirect effects of the accounting change and the related per-share amounts, if applicable, that are attributable to each prior period presented

2. For a change in accounting principle that has no material effect in the period of change but is reasonably certain to have a material effect in later periods, disclosure should be made of the nature of and reason for the change in accounting principle, including an explanation of why the newly adopted accounting principle is preferable, whenever the financial statements of the period of change are presented (FAS-154, par. 17).

3. If an authoritative accounting pronouncement (e.g., new FASB Statement) has been issued but is not yet effective as of the balance-sheet date, and when adopted the company will be required to retroactively restate its financial statements or have a cumulative effect adjustment, the following disclosures should be considered (generally accepted practice and AU 9410.13–.18):

   a. Existence of the authoritative standard

   b. Date the entity must adopt the new standard or, if early adoption is permitted, the date that the entity plans to adopt it

   c. Method of adoption (e.g., retroactive application, cumulative catch-up adjustment)

   d. Impact of the new standard on the reported financial position and results of operations (if the impact has been quantified, the amount must be indicated; if immaterial or not determined, it should be so stated)

Changes in the reporting entity.   The disclosure requirements for changes in the reporting entity under FAS-154 are as follows:

1. Disclosure should include a description of the nature of the change in reporting entity and the reason for it in the period of the change (FAS-154, par. 24).

2. The effect of the change in reporting entity on the following items should be disclosed for all periods presented (FAS-154, par. 24):

   a. Income before extraordinary items

   b. Net income (or other appropriate captions of change in the applicable net assets or performance indicators)

    c. Other comprehensive income

    d. Related per-share amounts

3. For a change in reporting entity that has no material effect in the period of change but is reasonably certain to have a material effect in later periods, disclosure should include the nature of and reason for the change whenever the financial statements of the period of change are presented (FAS-154, par. 24).

Correction of errors. The disclosure requirements for correction of errors under FAS-154 are as follows:

1. The resulting effects (both gross and net of applicable income tax) of prior-period adjustments on the net income of prior periods should be disclosed in the annual report for the year in which the adjustments are made (FAS-154, par. 26; APB-9, par. 26).

2. When single-period financial statements are presented, disclosure should be made of the effect (both gross and net of applicable income tax) of prior-period adjustments on the opening balance of retained earnings and on net income (and on related per-share amounts when presented) of the preceding period (FAS-154, par. 26; APB-9, par. 26).

3. When financial statements for more than one period are presented, disclosure should be made of the effect (both gross and net of applicable income tax) of prior-period adjustments on the opening balance of retained earnings and on net income (and on related per-share amounts when presented) for each of the periods presented (FAS-154, par. 26; APB-9, par. 26).

4. If the financial statements have been restated to correct an error, the following should be disclosed (FAS-154, par. 26):

    a. The fact that previously issued financial statements have been restated

    b. A description of the nature of the error

    c. The effect of the correction on each financial statement line item and any per-share amounts affected for each prior period presented

    d. The cumulative effect of the change on retained earnings or other appropriate components of equity or net assets in the balance sheet, as of the beginning of the earliest period presented

5. If a restated historical, statistical-type summary of financial data for a number of periods (commonly 5 or 10 years) is

presented and prior-period adjustments have been recorded during any of the periods included therein, disclosure is recommended of the restatements in the first summary published after the adjustments (APB-9, par. 27).

Disclosure Requirements If FAS-154 Has *Not* Been Adopted

Changes in accounting estimates. The disclosure requirements for changes in accounting estimates prior to the adoption of FAS-154 are as follows:

1. For an accounting-estimate change that affects several future periods (e.g., change in service lives of depreciable assets, actuarial assumptions affecting pension costs), disclosure should include the effect on income before extraordinary items and net income (and on related per share amounts when presented) of the current period (APB-20, par. 33).

2. For an accounting-estimate change made each period in the ordinary course of accounting for items such as uncollectible accounts or inventory obsolescence, disclosure should be made of the effect, if material, on income before extraordinary items and net income (and on related per share amounts when presented) (APB-20, par. 33).

Changes in accounting principles. The disclosure requirements for changes in accounting principles prior to the adoption of FAS-154 are as follows:

1. For an accounting-principle change that is made in the year in which the change occurs, the following disclosures should be made (APB-20, par. 17):

   a. The nature of the change in accounting principle

   b. The justification for the change in accounting, including a clear explanation of why the newly adopted accounting principle is preferable

   c. The effect of the change on income before extraordinary items and net income (and related per share amounts when presented)

2. For an accounting-principle change that is accounted for as a cumulative effect adjustment, the following disclosures should be made (APB-20, pars. 19-26):

   a. The amount of the cumulative effect should be shown as a separate item in the income statement between the captions "extraordinary items" and "net income" along with the related tax effect (and related per share amounts when presented)

b. The effect of adopting the new accounting principle on income before extraordinary items and on net income (and on related per share amounts when presented) for the period in which the change occurs

c. Pro forma amounts of income before extraordinary items and net income (and related per share amounts when presented) should be shown on the face of the income statements for all periods presented as if the newly adopted accounting principle had been applied during all periods affected

d. If the pro forma amounts cannot be computed or reasonably estimated for individual prior periods, but the cumulative effect on retained earnings at the beginning of the period of change can be determined, the reason for not showing the pro forma amounts by periods should be disclosed

e. If the amount of the cumulative effects of an accounting-principle change on retained earnings at the beginning of the period of change cannot be computed (generally limited to a change from the FIFO inventory method to LIFO), the following disclosures should be made:

— The effect of the change on the results of operations (and on related per share amounts when presented) for the period of change

— The reason for omitting (i) accounting for the cumulative effect and (ii) disclosures of pro forma amounts for prior years

3. For an accounting-principle change that is reported by restating prior years' financial statements, the following disclosures should be made (APB-20, par. 28):

a. The nature of and justification for a change in accounting principle

b. The effect of the change on income before extraordinary items and net income (and on related per share amounts when presented) for all periods presented

4. The following disclosures should be made for a change in the method of depreciation, depletion, or amortization for newly acquired assets while a different method continues to be used for assets of that class acquired in previous years (APB-20, par. 24):

a. Description of the nature of the change in method

    b. The effect of the change in method on income before extraordinary items and net income (and on related per share amounts when presented) for the year in which the change in method occurred

5. If an accounting change is not considered material for the period in which the change occurs, but it is reasonably certain that the change will have a material effect on financial statements of subsequent years, appropriate disclosures should be made whenever the financial statements of the year of change are presented (APB-20, par. 38).

6. If an authoritative accounting pronouncement (e.g., new FASB Statement) has been issued but is not yet effective as of the balance sheet date, and when adopted the company will be required to retroactively restate its financial statements or have a cumulative effect adjustment, the following disclosures should be considered (generally accepted practice):

    a. Existence of the authoritative standard

    b. Date the entity must adopt the new standard or, if early adoption is permitted, the date that it plans to adopt it

    c. Method of adoption (e.g., retroactive application, cumulative catch-up adjustment)

    d. Impact of the new standard on the reported financial position and results of operations (if the impact has been quantified, the amount must be indicated; if immaterial or not determined, it should be so stated)

Changes in the reporting entity. The disclosure requirements for changes in the reporting entity prior to the adoption of FAS-154 are as follows:

1. The following disclosures should be made for a reporting-entity change for the period in which the change has occurred (APB-20, par. 35):

    a. A description of the nature of the change

    b. A description of the reason for the change

    c. The effect of the change on income before extraordinary items and net income (and on related per share amounts when presented) for all periods presented

Correction of errors. The disclosure requirements for correction of errors prior to the adoption of FAS-154 are as follows:

1. For a correction of an error in previously issued financial statements, disclosure should be made of the nature of the error in the period in which the error was discovered and corrected (APB-20, par. 37).

2. For a correction of an error in previously issued financial statements, the effect of the correction of the error on the following should be disclosed in the period in which the error was discovered and corrected (APB-20, par. 37):

   a. Income before extraordinary items

   b. Net income

   c. Related per-share amounts, when presented

3. The resulting effects (both gross and net of applicable income tax) of prior-period adjustments on the net income of prior periods should be disclosed in the annual report for the year in which the adjustments are made (APB-9, par. 26).

4. When single-period financial statements are presented, disclosure should be made of the effect (both gross and net of applicable income tax) of prior-period adjustments on the opening balance of retained earnings and on net income (and on related per-share amounts when presented) of the preceding period (APB-9, par. 26).

5. When financial statements for more than one period are presented, disclosure should be made of the effect (both gross and net of applicable income tax) of prior-period adjustments on the opening balance of retained earnings and on net income (and on related per-share amounts when presented) for each of the periods presented (APB-9, par. 26).

6. If a restated historical, statistical-type summary of financial data for a number of periods (commonly 5 or 10 years) is presented and prior-period adjustments have been recorded during any of the periods included therein, disclosure is recommended of the restatements in the first summary published after the adjustments (APB-9, par. 27).

EXAMPLES OF FINANCIAL STATEMENT DISCLOSURES

 The following sample disclosures are available on the accompanying disc.

Illustrations under FAS-154

Changes in Accounting Estimates

Example 1–1: Change in Depreciable Lives of Property and Equipment—General

It is the Company's policy to periodically review the estimated useful lives of its fixed assets. This review during 20X2 indicated that actual lives for certain asset categories generally were longer than the useful lives used for depreciation purposes in the Company's financial statements. As a result, the Company revised the estimated useful lives of certain categories of property, principally machinery and equipment, effective January 1, 20X2. The effect of this change in estimate was to reduce 20X2 depreciation expense by $100,000, increase 20X2 income from continuing operations by $80,000, and increase 20X2 net income by $60,000.

Example 1–2: Change in Depreciable Lives of Property and Equipment— Specific Reference Made to Average Depreciation Lives

Effective January 1, 20X2, the Company changed its estimates of the useful lives of certain machinery and equipment at its manufacturing plant. The plant's asset depreciation lives that previously averaged ten years were increased to an average of 15 years, while those that previously averaged six to eight years were increased to an average of ten years. The Company made these changes to better reflect the estimated periods during which such assets will remain in service. This change had the effect of reducing 20X2 depreciation expense by $250,000, increasing 20X2 income from continuing operations by $170,000, and increasing 20X2 net income by $120,000.

Example 1–3: Change in Accounting Principle Inseparable from Change in Accounting Estimate—The Change Is Accounted for as a Change in Accounting Estimate

Prior to October 1, 20X2, production and tooling costs were charged to cost of sales based on the estimated average unit cost for Projects A, B, C, and D (the Projects) which, in the aggregate, consist of 100,000 lead-rubber bearings. Effective October 1, 20X2, the Company changed its accounting for cost of sales on the Projects from the average cost basis to the specific-unit cost basis. This change to the specific-unit costing method for the Projects was made in recognition of production rates, existing order base, and length of time required to achieve project deliveries, and, therefore, the resultant increased difficulty, which became apparent in the fourth quarter of 20X2, in making the estimates necessary under the average cost basis method. Because the effect of this change in accounting principle was inseparable from the effect of the change in accounting estimate, the change was accounted for as a change in estimate. As a result, the Company recorded a noncash pretax charge to operations of $500,000 in the fourth quarter of 20X2. The effect of the charge was to decrease 20X2 income from continuing operations by $350,000 and decrease 20X2 net income by $300,000.

Changes in Accounting Principles

Example 1–4: Retrospective Application of a Change in Accounting Principle—Effect on Prior Years Is Determinable and Financial Statements for Prior Periods Retroactively Restated

On January 1, 20X2, ABC Company elected to change its method of valuing its inventory to the first-in, first-out (FIFO) method, whereas in all prior years inventory was valued using the last-in, first-out (LIFO) method. The new method of accounting for inventory was adopted because management believes the FIFO method provides a more meaningful presentation of its financial position because it reflects more recent costs in the balance sheet. Under the current economic environment of low inflation and an expected reduction in inventories and lower production costs, the Company believes that the FIFO cost method also results in a better matching of current costs with current revenues. Comparative financial statements of prior years have been adjusted to apply the new method retrospectively. The following financial statement line items for fiscal years 20X2 and 20X1 were affected by the change in accounting principle.

Income Statement—20X2

	As Computed under LIFO	As Reported under FIFO	Effect of Change
Sales	$3,000,000	$3,000,000	$-0-
Cost of goods sold	(1,130,000)	(1,100,000)	(30,000)
Selling, general, and administrative expenses	(1,000,000)	(1,000,000)	-0-
Income before profit sharing and income taxes	870,000	900,000	30,000
Profit sharing	(87,000)	(96,000)*	(9,000)
Income before income taxes	783,000	804,000	21,000
Income taxes	(313,000)	(322,000)	(9,000)
Net income	$470,000	$482,000	$12,000

* This amount includes a $90,000 profit-sharing payment attributable to 20X2 profits and $6,000 profit-sharing payment attributable to 20X1 profits, which is an indirect effect of the change in accounting principle. The incremental payment attributable to 20X1 would have been recognized in 20X1 if ABC Company's inventory had originally been accounted for using the FIFO method.

Income Statement—20X1

	As Originally Reported	As Adjusted	Effect of Change
Sales	$3,000,000	$3,000,000	$-0-
Cost of goods sold	(1,000,000)	(940,000)	(60,000)
Selling, general, and administrative expenses	(1,000,000)	(1,000,000)	-0-
Income before profit sharing and income taxes	1,000,000	1,060,000	60,000
Profit sharing	(100,000)	(100,000)	-0-
Income before income taxes	900,000	960,000	60,000
Income taxes	(360,000)	(384,000)	(24,000)
Net income	$540,000	$576,000	$36,000

Balance Sheet—12/31/20X2

	As Computed under LIFO	As Reported under FIFO	Effect of Change
Cash	$2,738,000	$2,732,000	$(6,000)
Inventory	320,000	390,000	70,000
Total assets	$3,058,000	$3,122,000	$ 64,000
Accrued profit sharing	87,000	90,000	3,000
Income tax liability	313,000	338,000	25,000
Total liabilities	400,000	428,000	28,000
Paid in capital	1,000,000	1,000,000	-0-
Retained earnings	1,658,000	1,694,000	36,000
Total stockholders' equity	2,658,000	2,694,000	36,000
Total liabilities and stockholders' equity	$3,058,000	$3,122,000	$64,000

Balance Sheet—12/31/20X1

	As Originally Reported	As Adjusted	Effect of Change
Cash	$2,448,000	$2,448,000	$-0-
Inventory	200,000	240,000	40,000
Total assets	$2,648,000	$2,688,000	$40,000

	As Originally Reported	As Adjusted	Effect of Change
Accrued profit sharing	100,000	100,000	-0-
Income tax liability	360,000	376,000	16,000
Total liabilities	460,000	476,000	16,000
Paid-in capital	1,000,000	1,000,000	-0-
Retained earnings	1,188,000	1,212,000	24,000
Total stockholders' equity	2,188,000	2,212,000	24,000
Total liabilities and stockholders' equity	$2,648,000	$2,688,000	$40,000

As a result of the accounting change, retained earnings as of January 1, 20X1 decreased from $648,000, as originally reported using the LIFO method, to $636,000 using the FIFO method.

Statement of Cash Flows—20X2

	As Computed under LIFO	As Reported under FIFO	Effect of Change
Net income	$470,000	$482,000	$12,000
Adjustments to reconcile net income to net cash provided by operating activities:			
Increase in inventory	(120,000)	(150,000)	(30,000)
Decrease in accrued profit sharing	(13,000)	(10,000)	3,000
Decrease in income tax liability	(47,000)	(38,000)	9,000
Net cash provided by operating activities	290,000	284,000	(6,000)
Net increase in cash	290,000	284,000	(6,000)
Cash, January 1, 20X2	2,448,000	2,448,000	-0-
Cash, December 31, 20X2	$2,738,000	$2,732,000	$(6,000)

Statement of Cash Flows—20X1

	As Originally Reported	As Adjusted	Effect of Change
Net income	$540,000	$576,000	$36,000
Adjustments to reconcile net income to net cash provided by operating activities:			
Increase in inventory	(100,000)	(160,000)	(60,000)
Decrease in accrued profit sharing	(20,000)	(20,000)	-0-
Decrease in income tax liability	(72,000)	(48,000)	24,000
Net cash provided by operating activities	348,000	348,000	-0-
Net increase in cash	348,000	348,000	-0-
Cash, January 1, 20X1	2,100,000	2,100,000	-0-
Cash, December 31, 20X1	$2,448,000	$2,448,000	$-0-

Example 1–5: Retrospective Application of a Change in Accounting Principle Is Impracticable

Effective January 1, 20X2, the Company changed its method of valuing a significant component of its inventory from the first-in, first-out (FIFO) method to the last-in, first-out (LIFO) method. Management believes the LIFO method results in a better matching of current costs with current revenues and minimizes the effect of price-level changes on inventory valuations. It was impracticable to determine the cumulative effect of this accounting change and the retroactive application of the LIFO method to prior years, because the Company's accounting records do not provide sufficient information to apply the new method. As a result, the effect of the change has been applied prospectively in 20X2. The effect of the change in 20X2 was to increase cost of goods sold by $750,000, decrease income taxes by $300,000, and decrease net income by $450,000.

Example 1–6: Indirect Effects of Change in Accounting Principle Are Recognized

Effective January 1, 20X2, the Company changed its method of accounting for long-term contracts from the completed contract method to the percentage-of-completion method. The Company believes that the new method more accurately reflects periodic results of operations and conforms to revenue recognition practices predominant in the industry. The effect of this change was to increase 20X2 net income by $800,000. As a result of the change in accounting principle, pension expense for 20X2 has also increased by $145,000.

Example 1–7: Change from Cash Basis to Accrual Basis of Accounting

In previous years, the Company prepared its financial statements on a cash basis of accounting, which is a comprehensive basis of accounting other than GAAP. In 20X2, the financial statements have been prepared on the accrual basis of accounting, in conformity with generally accepted accounting principles. Management also believes that the accrual basis of accounting more accurately reflects the Company's financial position and results of operations. The effect of this change was to increase net income for 20X2 by $375,000. The financial statements for 20X1 have been retroactively restated for the change, which resulted in a decrease of net income for 20X1 of $125,000. Retained earnings has been increased by $150,000 as of January 1, 20X1, for the effect of retroactive application of the new basis of accounting, as follows:

	Increase (Decrease) in Retained Earnings as of January 1, 20X1
Adjustment to record accounts receivable	$500,000
Adjustment to record prepaid expenses and other assets	25,000
Adjustment to record accounts payable	(125,000)
Adjustment to record deferred revenue	(150,000)
Adjustment to record related deferred tax liability on items above	(100,000)
Net increase in retained earnings as of January 1, 20X1	$150,000

Example 1–8: Adoption of New FASB Statement in the Current Year—Prior-Year Financial Statements Not Restated

In 20X2, the Company adopted FASB Statement of Financial Accounting Standards No. [*number*] [(*title*)], which requires [*describe briefly the requirements of the new standard*]. The effect of this change was to [*increase/decrease*] 20X2 income before extraordinary items and 20X2 net income by $[*amount*]. Financial statements for 20X1 have not been restated, and the cumulative effect of the change, totaling $[*amount*], is shown as a one time [*credit/charge*] to income in the 20X2 income statement.

Example 1–9: Adoption of New FASB Statement in the Current Year—Prior-Year Financial Statements Restated

In 20X2, the Company adopted FASB Statement of Financial Accounting Standards No. [*number*] [(*title*)], which requires [*describe briefly the requirements of the new standard*]. The effect of this change was to [*increase/decrease*] 20X2 income before extraordinary items and 20X2 net income by $[*amount*]. The financial statements for 20X1 have been retroactively restated for the change, which resulted in an [*increase/decrease*] in income before extraordinary items and net income for 20X1 of $[*amount*]. Retained earnings as of January 1, 20X1, has been adjusted for the effect of retroactive application of the new Statement.

Example 1–10: Adoption of New FASB Statement in the Current Year—No Material Effect on the Financial Statements

In 20X2, the Company adopted FASB Statement of Financial Accounting Standards No. [*number*] [(*title*)], which requires [*describe briefly the requirements of the new standard*]. There was no material impact on the Company's results of operations or financial condition upon adoption of the new Statement.

Example 1–11: New FASB Statement to Be Adopted in the Future

In December 20X2, the Financial Accounting Standards Board issued Statement No. [*number*] [(*title*)], which requires [*describe briefly the requirements of the new standard*]. The new standard is effective for the year ending December 31, 20X3. The adoption of the new Statement is not expected to have a material effect on the Company's financial position, results of operations, or cash flows.

Or:

The Company is currently evaluating the effect that implementation of the new standard will have on its financial position, results of operations, and cash flows.

Changes in the Reporting Entity

Example 1–12: Financial Statements Currently Consolidated to Include the Accounts of a Previously Unconsolidated Affiliate

Effective January 1, 20X2, the Company began to consolidate into its financial statements the accounts of XYZ Corporation, formerly an unconsolidated affiliate. XYZ Corporation, which primarily manufactures medical equipment, is a venture between the Company and ABC Company of Ohio. The consolidation occurred as a result of revisions of the Stockholders' Agreement between the Company and ABC Company of Ohio. Financial data presented for previous years have not been restated to reflect the consolidation of XYZ Corporation. The consolidation is not material to financial position or results of operations for the periods presented and had no effect on previously reported net income, which included XYZ Corporation on an equity basis.

Example 1–13: Financial Statements Currently Include on the Equity Basis of Accounting the Accounts of a Previously Consolidated Business

On January 1, 20X2, the Company transferred its medical equipment business segment and contributed certain assets and liabilities, totaling $15 million and $4 million, respectively, to a joint venture named Hope Enterprises (a partnership). The Company's equity interest in the joint venture is 35%. As a result, the 20X1 income statement, which included the accounts of the medical equipment business segment on a consolidated basis, has been retroactively restated to reflect adjustment of line items for revenue and costs applicable to the medical equipment business segment transferred to the joint venture and to reflect the losses of this business on the equity basis of accounting. The effect of this change was to increase income before extraordinary items, net income, and other comprehensive income for 20X1 by $489,000, $375,000, and $72,000, respectively.

Correction of Errors

Example 1–14: Correction of Error in Comparative Financial Statements—Error Relates to a Year Not Presented in the Comparative Financial Statements

Retained earnings as of January 1, 20X1, has been reduced by $125,000, net of income tax effect of $75,000, to correct an error made in 20X0 [or a prior year] by including in inventory certain costs totaling $200,000 that should have been expensed to conform with generally accepted accounting principles. The error had no effect on net income for 20X1.

> **Note:** The following table illustrates the correction of error as shown on the face of the Company's statement of retained earnings or statement of stockholders' equity (assume the Company's year-end is December 31 and the error relates to 20X0 or a prior year).

	20X2	20X1
Retained earnings at beginning of year, as previously reported	$3,125,000	$2,625,000
Prior-period adjustment—Error in capitalizing certain inventory costs that should have been expensed in 20X0 (or a prior year)	-0-	(125,000)
Retained earnings at beginning of year, as restated	3,125,000	2,500,000
Net income	700,000	625,000
Retained earnings at end of year	$3,825,000	$3,125,000

Example 1–15: Correction of Errors in Comparative Financial Statements—Errors Relate to First Year Presented in the Comparative Financial Statements and to Prior Year

The Company has restated its previously issued 20X1 consolidated financial statements for matters related to the following previously reported items: sales and accounts receivable; inventory costs and valuation reserves; revisions to the previous policy regarding the capitalization of costs associated with the bulk purchase of inventory; reserves for returns and allowances; unrecorded liabilities; additional bad debt expense; and the related income tax effects. The accompanying financial statements for 20X1 have been restated to reflect the corrections. Also, retained earnings at January 1, 20X1, was reduced by $499,000 as a result of adjustments to sales previously reported and previously unrecorded liabilities in 20X0.

The following is a summary of the restatements for 20X1:

Reduction of previously reported sales, net of related costs of sales	$788,000
Inventory cost adjustments and increase to inventory valuation reserves	310,000
Changes to accounting policy regarding the capitalization of costs associated with the bulk purchase of inventory	243,000

Increase in reserves for returns and allowances	116,000
Unrecorded liabilities	488,000
Additional bad debt expense	281,000
Subtotal	2,226,000
Income tax effect of restatement	(345,000)
Total reduction in 20X1 net earnings	$1,881,000

The effect on the Company's previously issued 20X1 financial statements is summarized as follows:

Balance Sheet as of December 31, 20X1

	Previously Reported	Increase (Decrease)	Restated
Current Assets	$12,298,000	$(2,414,000)	$9,884,000
Other Assets	247,000	(79,000)	(168,000)
Total Assets	17,108,000	(2,493,000)	14,615,000
Current Liabilities	12,569,000	(148,000)	12,421,000
Deferred Tax Liability	51,000	35,000	86,000
Total Liabilities	16,640,000	(113,000)	16,527,000
Stockholders' Deficit:			
Accumulated Deficit— December 31, 20X0	(254,000)	(499,000)	(753,000)
Net Income (Loss) for 20X1	315,000	(1,881,000)	(1,566,000)
Accumulated Deficit— December 31, 20X1	61,000	(2,380,000)	(2,319,000)
Total Liabilities and Stockholders' Deficit	17,108,000	(2,493,000)	14,615,000

Statement of Operations for the Year Ended December 31, 20X1

	Previously Reported	Increase (Decrease)	Restated
Net Sales	$24,871,000	$(1,016,000)	$23,855,000
Cost of Sales	18,162,000	267,000	18,429,000
Gross Profit	6,709,000	(1,283,000)	5,426,000

Selling and Administrative Expenses	5,861,000	838,000	6,699,000
Income (Loss) from Operations	848,000	(2,121,000)	(1,273,000)
Interest Expense	491,000	105,000	596,000
Income (Loss) before Taxes	357,000	(2,226,000)	(1,869,000)
Provision for Income Taxes	42,000	(345,000)	(303,000)
Net Income (Loss)	315,000	(1,881,000)	(1,566,000)

Note: The following table illustrates the correction of errors as shown on the face of the Company's statement of retained earnings or statement of stockholders' equity (assume the Company's year-end is December 31 and the errors relate to 20X1 and 20X0). Also, the balance sheet, the income statement, and the statement of cash flows should clearly indicate in the 20X1 column the word "Restated."

	Number of Shares	Common Stock	Accumulated Deficit	Total Stockholders' Equity (Deficit)
Balance at January 1, 20X1, as previously reported	1,800,000	$18,000	$(254,000)	$(236,000)
Prior period adjustment	—	—	(499,000)	(499,000)
Balance at January 1, 20X1, as restated	1,800,000	18,000	(753,000)	(735,000)
Net loss for 20X1, as restated	—	—	(1,566,000)	(1,566,000)
Balance at December 31, 20X1, as restated	1,800,000	18,000	(2,319,000)	(2,301,000)
Issuance of stock	1,400,000	14,000	—	14,000
Net income for 20X2	—	—	404,000	404,000
Balance at December 31, 20X2	3,200,000	$32,000	$(1,915,000)	$(1,883,000)

*Example 1–16: Correction of Errors in Single-Year Financial
Statements—Errors Relate to Immediately Preceding Year*

The Company's financial statements as of December 31, 20X1, contained the following errors: (1) overstatement of accounts receivable
by $150,000, (2) understatement of accounts payable by $200,000,
and (3) understatement of accrued expenses by $50,000. Retained
earnings as of January 1, 20X2, has been reduced by $275,000 to cor-
rect the aggregate effect of the errors of $400,000, net of their related
income tax effect of $125,000. Had the errors not been made, net
income for 20X1 would have been decreased by $200,000, net of
income tax of $100,000.

> **Note:** The following table illustrates the correction of error as
> shown on the face of the Company's statement of retained earn-
> ings or statement of stockholders' equity (assume the Compa-
> ny's year-end is December 31 and the error relates to 20X1).

	20X2
Retained earnings at beginning of year, as previously reported	$3,500,000
Prior period adjustment—See Note [X]	(275,000)
Retained earnings at beginning of year, as restated	3,225,000
Net income	500,000
Retained earnings at end of year	$3,725,000

Illustrations If FAS-154 Has *Not* Been Adopted

Changes in Accounting Estimates

*Example 1–17: Change in Depreciable Lives of Property and
Equipment—General*

It is the Company's policy to periodically review the estimated useful lives of its fixed assets. This review during 20X2 indicated that
actual lives for certain asset categories generally were longer than
the useful lives used for depreciation purposes in the Company's
financial statements. As a result, the Company revised the estimated
useful lives of certain categories of property, principally machinery
and equipment, retroactive to January 1, 20X2. The effect of this
change in estimate was to reduce 20X2 depreciation expense by
$100,000 and increase 20X2 net income by $60,000.

Example 1–18: Change in Depreciable Lives of Property and Equipment—Specific Reference Made to Average Depreciation Lives

Effective January 1, 20X2, the Company changed its estimates of the useful lives of certain machinery and equipment at its manufacturing plant. The plant's asset depreciation lives that previously averaged ten years were increased to an average of 15 years, while those that previously averaged six to eight years were increased to an average of ten years. The Company made these changes to better reflect the estimated periods during which such assets will remain in service. This change had the effect of reducing depreciation expense by $250,000 and increasing net income by $120,000 in 20X2.

Example 1–19: Change in Both Estimated Lives and Capitalization Policy—Specific Reference Made to Estimated Lives

Traditionally, the Company has deferred certain costs associated with the acquisition of new customer accounts and has amortized the costs over their estimated useful lives. For costs incurred after January 1, 20X1, the estimated useful life of these costs was extended from one year to three years, thereby reducing amortization in 20X1 by $180,000 and increasing 20X1 net income by $100,000. In 20X2, the Company conformed its treatment of other customer acquisition costs that had been previously expensed so that customer acquisition costs are consistently capitalized and amortized over three years. The effect of this change in accounting estimate in 20X2 was to reduce amortization in 20X2 by $150,000 and increase 20X2 net income by $90,000.

Example 1–20: Change in Accounting Principle Inseparable from Change in Accounting Estimate—The Change Is Accounted for as a Change in Accounting Estimate

Prior to October 1, 20X2, production and tooling costs were charged to cost of sales based on the estimated average unit cost for Projects A, B, C, and D (the Projects) which, in the aggregate, consist of 100,000 lead-rubber bearings. Effective October 1, 20X2, the Company changed its accounting for cost of sales on the Projects from the average cost basis to the specific-unit cost basis. This change to the specific-unit costing method for the Projects was made in recognition of production rates, existing order base, and length of time required to achieve project deliveries, and, therefore, the resultant increased difficulty, which became apparent in the fourth quarter of 20X2, in making the estimates necessary under the average cost basis method. Because the effect of this change in accounting principle was inseparable from the effect of the change in accounting estimate, the change was accounted for as a change in estimate. As a result, the Company recorded a noncash pretax charge to operations of $500,000 in the fourth quarter of 20X2. The effect of the charge was to decrease 20X2 net income by $300,000.

Changes in Accounting Principles

Example 1–21: Change in Method of Applying Overhead to Inventory—Cumulative Effect of the Change on Prior Years Is Recorded in the Current Year

Historically, the Company used a single overhead rate in valuing the ending inventory, which had been determined by comparing the total manufacturing overhead expenses for the year with total direct labor costs for the year. In 20X2 the Company performed an extensive study to precisely determine the manufacturing overhead to be applied to specific product lines. As a result, effective January 1, 20X2, the Company changed its method of applying overhead to inventory to more closely reflect the results of this study.

The Company believes that the change in the application of this accounting principle is preferable because it provides a better determination of overhead costs in inventory and, therefore, improves the matching of production costs with related revenues in reporting its operating results. In accordance with generally accepted accounting principles, the cumulative effect of the change for the periods prior to January 1, 20X2, totaling $500,000, after reduction of income taxes of $300,000, has been recorded in the 20X2 income statement. The effect of the change on the current year's net income before cumulative effect of a change in accounting principles is not material.

Pro forma net income for 20X1 is $850,000, assuming the new accounting principle was applied retroactively.

> **Note:** The following table illustrates the cumulative effect of the change as shown at the bottom of the Company's income statement (assume the Company's year-end is December 31 and the latest year presented is 20X2).

	20X2	20X1
Earnings before cumulative effect of a change in accounting principle	$925,000	$730,000
Cumulative effect to January 1, 20X2, of changing overhead recorded in inventory	500,000	-0-
Net earnings	$1,425,000	$730,000

Example 1–22: Change from LIFO to Average Cost Method for Valuing Inventory—Effect on Prior Years Is Determinable and Financial Statements for Prior Periods Retroactively Restated

Effective January 1, 20X2, the Company changed its basis of valuing inventories from the last-in, first-out (LIFO) method to the average cost method. In 20X1 and prior years, the cost of substantially all inventories was determined using the LIFO method. The Company believes that the average cost method of inventory valuation provides a more meaningful presentation of its financial position since this method reflects more recent costs in the balance sheet. Under the current economic environment of low inflation and an expected reduction in inventories and lower production costs, the Company believes that the average cost method also results in a better matching of current costs with current revenues.

The effect of the change in accounting principle was to increase 20X2 net income by $450,000. The change has been applied to prior years by retroactively restating the financial statements presented for 20X1. The effect of the restatement was to increase retained earnings as of January 1, 20X1, by $1,350,000. The restatement decreased 20X1 net income by $305,000.

Note: The following table illustrates the retroactive application of the change as shown on the face of the Company's statement of retained earnings or statement of stockholders' equity (assume the Company's year-end is December 31 and the latest year presented is 20X2).

	20X2	20X1
Retained earnings at beginning of year, as previously reported	$4,725,000	$2,750,000
Cumulative effect on prior years of retroactive restatement for accounting change	-0-	1,350,000
Retained earnings at beginning of year, as restated	4,725,000	4,100,000
Net income	700,000	625,000
Retained earnings at end of year	$5,425,000	$4,725,000

Example 1–23: Change from FIFO to LIFO Method for Valuing Inventory—Effect on Prior Years Is Not Determinable

Effective January 1, 20X2, the Company changed its method of valuing a significant component of its inventory from the first-in, first-out (FIFO) method to the last-in, first-out (LIFO) method. Management believes the LIFO method results in a better matching of current costs with current revenues and minimizes the effect of price level changes on inventory valuations. The cumulative effect of this accounting change for years prior to 20X2 is not reasonably determinable, nor are the pro forma effects of retroactive application of the LIFO method to prior years. The effect of the change in 20X2 was to decrease net income by $800,000.

Example 1–24: Change in Depreciation Method for Newly Acquired Assets

For financial statement purposes, the Company changed to the straight-line method of depreciation effective January 1, 20X2, for all newly acquired property and equipment. Assets acquired before the effective date of the change continue to be depreciated principally by accelerated methods. The Company believes the new straight-line depreciation method will more accurately reflect its financial results by better matching costs of new property over the useful lives of these assets. In addition, the new depreciation method more closely conforms with that prevalent in the industry. The effect of the change was not material to the 20X2 financial results of operations.

Example 1–25: Change in Method of Accounting for Major Maintenance and Repairs Costs

Effective January 1, 20X2, the Company changed its method of accounting for the cost of maintenance and repairs incurred in connection with major maintenance shutdown programs at all its manufacturing plants. These major maintenance costs, which result in plant shutdowns for approximately four to eight weeks, comprise principally amounts paid to third parties for materials, contract services, and other related items. Under the new method, major maintenance costs on projects exceeding $100,000 are capitalized when incurred and then charged against income over the period benefited by the major maintenance shutdown program, usually three years. Prior to this change in accounting method, major maintenance costs relating to plant shutdowns were charged against income when incurred.

The Company believes that the new method of accounting is preferable in that it provides for a better matching of major maintenance costs with future revenues. The Company's management believes that the investment in such major maintenance and repair costs enhances the reliability and performance of its manufacturing plants and, therefore, economically benefits future periods.

The cumulative effect of this accounting change for years prior to 20X2, which is shown separately in the income statement for 20X2, resulted in a benefit of $2 million after related income taxes of $800,000. Excluding the cumulative effect, this change increased net income for 20X2 by $400,000.

Pro forma net income for 20X1 is $1,800,000, assuming the accounting change was applied retroactively.

> **Note:** The following table illustrates the cumulative effect of the change as shown at the bottom of the Company's income statement (assume the Company's year-end is December 31 and the latest year presented is 20X2).

	20X2	20X1
Income before cumulative effect of change in accounting principle	$1,825,000	$1,630,000
Cumulative effect of change in accounting principle	2,000,000	-0-
Net income	$3,825,000	$1,630,000

Example 1–26: Change from the Completed Contract Method to the Percentage-of-Completion Method of Accounting

Effective January 1, 20X2, the Company changed its method of accounting for long-term contracts from the completed contract method to the percentage-of-completion method. The Company believes that the new method more accurately reflects periodic results of operations and conforms to revenue recognition practices predominant in the industry. The effect of this change was to increase 20X2 net income by $600,000. The change has been applied to prior years by retroactively restating the financial statements presented for 20X1. The effect of the restatement was to increase retained earnings as of January 1, 20X1, by $1,000,000. The restatement decreased 20X1 net income by $305,000.

> **Note:** The following table illustrates the retroactive application of the change as shown on the face of the Company's statement of retained earnings or statement of stockholders' equity (assume the Company's year-end is December 31 and the latest year presented is 20X2).

	20X2	20X1
Retained earnings at beginning of year, as previously reported	$4,400,000	$2,900,000
Cumulative effect on prior years of retroactive restatement for accounting change	-0-	1,000,000

	20X2	20X1
Retained earnings at beginning of year, as restated	4,400,000	3,900,000
Net income	650,000	500,000
Retained earnings at end of year	$5,050,000	$4,400,000

Example 1–27: Change in Reporting Period for Subsidiary from Fiscal Year to Calendar Year—The Parent Company's Reporting Period Is a Calendar Year Ending December 31

Effective January 1, 20X2, the Parent Company changed the reporting period of its majority-owned subsidiary XYZ, Inc. from a fiscal year ending November 30 to a calendar year ending December 31. The results of operations of XYZ, Inc. during the period between the end of the 20X1 fiscal year and the beginning of the new calendar year (the stub period) amounted to a net income of $350,000. This amount was credited to retained earnings to avoid reporting more than 12 months results of operations in one year. Accordingly, the 20X2 consolidated operations include the results for XYZ, Inc. beginning January 1, 20X2. The cash activity for the stub period is included in "Other cash activities—stub period, XYZ, Inc." in the Consolidated Statements of Cash Flows.

Example 1–28: Change to Equity Method from Cost Method of Accounting for Investment

During 20X2, the Company bought an additional 25% interest in Bodair Co., thereby increasing its holdings to 40%. As a result, the Company changed its method of accounting for this investment from the cost method to the equity method. Under the cost method, the investment is recorded at cost and dividends are treated as income when received. Under the equity method, the Company records its proportionate share of the earnings or losses of Bodair Co. The effect of the change was to increase 20X2 net income by $437,000 ($.23 per share). The financial statements for 20X1 have been restated for the change, which resulted in an increase of net income for 20X1 of $211,000 ($.12 per share). Retained earnings as of the beginning of 20X1 has been increased by $589,000 for the effect of retroactive application of the new method.

Example 1–29: Change from Cash Basis to Accrual Basis of Accounting

In previous years, the Company prepared its financial statements on a cash basis of accounting, which is a comprehensive basis of accounting other than GAAP. In 20X2, the financial statements have been prepared on the accrual basis of accounting, in conformity with generally accepted accounting principles. Management also believes that the accrual basis of accounting more accurately reflects the Company's financial position and results of operations. The effect of this change was to increase net income for 20X2 by $375,000. The financial statements for 20X1 have been retroactively restated for the change, which resulted in a decrease of net income for 20X1 of $125,000. Retained earnings has been increased by $150,000 as of January 1, 20X1, for the effect of retroactive application of the new basis of accounting, as follows:

	Increase (Decrease) in Retained Earnings as of January 1, 20X1
Adjustment to record accounts receivable	$500,000
Adjustment to record prepaid expenses and other assets	25,000
Adjustment to record accounts payable	(125,000)
Adjustment to record deferred revenue	(150,000)
Adjustment to record related deferred tax liability on items above	(100,000)
Net increase in retained earnings as of January 1, 20X1	$150,000

Example 1–30: Adoption of New FASB Statement in the Current Year—Prior-Year Financial Statements Not Restated

In 20X2, the Company adopted Financial Accounting Standards Board Statement No. [*number*] [(*title*)], which requires [*describe briefly the requirements of the new standard*]. The effect of this change was to [*increase/decrease*] 20X2 income before extraordinary items and 20X2 net income by $[*amount*]. Financial statements for 20X1 have not been restated, and the cumulative effect of the change, totaling $[*amount*], is shown as a one time [*credit/charge*] to income in the 20X2 income statement.

Example 1–31: Adoption of New FASB Statement in the Current Year—Prior-Year Financial Statements Restated

In 20X2, the Company adopted Financial Accounting Standards Board Statement No. [*number*] [(*title*)], which requires [*describe briefly the requirements of the new standard*]. The effect of this change was to [*increase/decrease*] 20X2 income before extraordinary items and 20X2 net income by $[*amount*]. The financial statements for 20X1 have been retroactively restated for the change, which resulted in an [*increase/decrease*] in income before extraordinary items and net income for 20X1 of $[*amount*]. Retained earnings as of January 1, 20X1, has been adjusted for the effect of retroactive application of the new Statement.

Example 1–32: Adoption of New FASB Statement in the Current Year—No Material Effect on the Financial Statements

In 20X2, the Company adopted Financial Accounting Standards Board Statement No. [*number*] [(*title*)], which requires [*describe briefly the requirements of the new standard*]. There was no material impact on the Company's results of operations or financial condition upon adoption of the new Statement.

Example 1–33: New FASB Statement to Be Adopted in the Future

In December 20X2, the Financial Accounting Standards Board issued Statement No. [*number*] [(*title*)], which requires [*describe briefly the requirements of the new standard*]. The new standard is effective for the year ending December 31, 20X3.

The adoption of the new Statement is not expected to have a material effect on the Company's financial position, results of operations, or cash flows.

Or:

The Company is currently evaluating the effect that implementation of the new standard will have on its financial position, results of operations, and cash flows.

Changes in the Reporting Entity

Example 1–34: Financial Statements Currently Consolidated to Include the Accounts of a Previously Unconsolidated Affiliate

Effective January 1, 20X2, the Company began to consolidate into its financial statements the accounts of XYZ Corporation, formerly an unconsolidated affiliate. XYZ Corporation, which primarily manufactures medical equipment, is a venture between the Company and ABC Company of Ohio. The consolidation occurred as a result of revisions of the Stockholders' Agreement between the Company and ABC Company of Ohio. Financial data presented for previous years have not been restated to reflect the consolidation of XYZ Corporation. The consolidation is not material to financial position or results of operations for the periods presented and had no effect on previously reported net income, which included XYZ Corporation on an equity basis.

Example 1–35: Financial Statements Currently Include on the Equity Basis of Accounting the Accounts of a Previously Consolidated Business

On January 1, 20X2, the Company transferred its medical equipment business segment and contributed certain assets and liabilities, totalling $15 million and $4 million, respectively, to a joint venture named Hope Enterprises (a partnership). The Company's equity interest in the joint venture is 35%. As a result, the 20X1 income statement, which included the accounts of the medical equipment business segment on a consolidated basis, has been restated to reflect adjustment of line items for revenue and costs applicable to the medical equipment business segment transferred to the joint venture and to reflect the losses of this business on the equity basis of accounting. The effect of this change was to increase income before extraordinary items, net income, and other comprehensive income for 20X1 by $489,000, $375,000, and $72,000, respectively.

Correction of Errors

Example 1–36: Correction of Error in Comparative Financial Statements—Error Relates to a Year Not Presented in the Comparative Financial Statements

Retained earnings as of January 1, 20X1, has been reduced by $125,000, net of income tax effect of $75,000, to correct an error made in 20X0 [*or a prior year*] by including in inventory certain costs totalling $200,000 that should have been expensed to conform with generally accepted accounting principles. The error had no effect on net income for 20X1.

> **Note:** The following table illustrates the correction of error as shown on the face of the Company's statement of retained earnings or statement of stockholders' equity (assume the Company's year-end is December 31 and the error relates to 20X0 or a prior year).

	20X2	20X1
Retained earnings at beginning of year, as previously reported	$3,125,000	$2,625,000
Prior period adjustment—Error in capitalizing certain inventory costs that should have been expensed in 20X0 (or a prior year)	-0-	(125,000)

	20X2	20X1
Retained earnings at beginning of year, as restated	3,125,000	2,500,000
Net income	700,000	625,000
Retained earnings at end of year	$3,825,000	$3,125,000

Example 1–37: Correction of Errors in Comparative Financial Statements—Errors Relate to First Year Presented in the Comparative Financial Statements and to Prior Years

The Company has restated its previously issued 20X1 consolidated financial statements for matters related to the following previously reported items: sales and accounts receivable; inventory costs and valuation reserves; revisions to the previous policy regarding the capitalization of costs associated with the bulk purchase of inventory; reserves for returns and allowances; unrecorded liabilities; additional bad debt expense; and the related income tax effects. The accompanying financial statements for 20X1 have been restated to reflect the corrections. Also, retained earnings at January 1, 20X1, was reduced by $499,000 as a result of adjustments to sales previously reported and previously unrecorded liabilities in 20X0.

The following is a summary of the restatements for 20X1:

Reduction of previously reported sales, net of related cost of sales	$788,000
Inventory cost adjustments and increase to inventory valuation reserves	310,000
Changes to accounting policy regarding the capitalization of costs associated with the bulk purchase of inventory	243,000
Increase in reserves for returns and allowances	116,000
Unrecorded liabilities	488,000
Additional bad debt expense	281,000
Subtotal	2,226,000
Income tax effect of restatement	(345,000)
Total reduction in 20X1 net earnings	$1,881,000

The effect on the Company's previously issued 20X1 financial statements are summarized as follows:

Balance Sheet as of December 31, 20X1

	Previously Reported	Increase (Decrease)	Restated
Current Assets	$12,298,000	$(2,414,000)	$9,884,000
Other Assets	247,000	(79,000)	168,000
Total Assets	17,108,000	(2,493,000)	14,615,000
Current Liabilities	12,569,000	(148,000)	12,421,000
Deferred Tax Liability	51,000	35,000	86,000
Total Liabilities	16,640,000	(113,000)	16,527,000
Stockholders' Deficit:			
Accumulated Deficit— December 31, 20X0	(254,000)	(499,000)	(753,000)
Net Income (Loss) for 20X1	315,000	(1,881,000)	(1,566,000)
Accumulated Deficit— December 31, 20X1	61,000	(2,380,000)	(2,319,000)
Total Liabilities and Stockholders' Deficit	17,108,000	(2,493,000)	14,615,000

Statement of Operations for the Year Ended December 31, 20X1

	Previously Reported	Increase (Decrease)	Restated
Net Sales	$24,871,000	$(1,016,000)	$23,855,000
Cost of Sales	18,162,000	267,000	18,429,000
Gross Profit	6,709,000	(1,283,000)	5,426,000
Selling and Administrative Expenses	5,861,000	838,000	6,699,000
Income (Loss) from Operations	848,000	(2,121,000)	(1,273,000)
Interest Expense	491,000	105,000	596,000
Income (Loss) before Taxes	357,000	(2,226,000)	(1,869,000)
Provision for Income Taxes	42,000	(345,000)	(303,000)
Net Income (Loss)	315,000	(1,881,000)	(1,566,000)

Note: The following table illustrates the correction of errors as shown on the face of the Company's statement of retained earnings or statement of stockholders' equity (assume the Company's year-end is December 31 and the errors relate to 20X1 and 20X0). Also, the balance sheet, the income statement, and the statement of cash flows should clearly indicate in the 20X1 column the word "Restated."

	Number of Shares	Common Stock	Accumulated Deficit	Total Stockholders' Equity (Deficit)
Balance at January 1, 20X1, as previously reported	1,800,000	$18,000	$(254,000)	$(236,000)
Prior period adjustment	—	—	(499,000)	(499,000)
Balance at January 1, 20X1, as restated	1,800,000	18,000	(753,000)	(735,000)
Net loss for 20X1, as restated	—	—	(1,566,000)	(1,566,000)
Balance at December 31, 20X1, as restated	1,800,000	18,000	(2,319,000)	(2,301,000)
Issuance of stock	1,400,000	14,000	—	(14,000)
Net income for 20X2	—	—	(404,000)	(404,000)
Balance at December 31, 20X2	3,200,000	$32,000	$(1,915,000)	$(1,883,000)

Example 1–38: Correction of Errors in Single-Year Financial Statements—Errors Relate to Immediately Preceding Year

The Company's financial statements as of December 31, 20X1, contained the following errors: (1) overstatement of accounts receivable by $150,000, (2) understatement of accounts payable by $200,000, and (3) understatement of accrued expenses by $50,000. Retained earnings as of January 1, 20X2, has been reduced by $275,000 to correct the aggregate effect of the errors of $400,000, net of their related income tax effect of $125,000. Had the errors not been made, net income for 20X1 would have been decreased by $200,000, net of income tax of $100,000.

Note: The following table illustrates the correction of error as shown on the face of the Company's statement of retained earnings or statement of stockholders' equity (assume the Company's year-end is December 31 and the error relates to 20X1).

	20X2
Retained earnings at beginning of year, as previously reported	$3,500,000
Prior period adjustment—See Note [X]	(275,000)
Retained earnings at beginning of year, as restated	3,225,000
Net income	500,000
Retained earnings at end of year	$3,725,000

CHAPTER 2
ACCOUNTING POLICIES

CONTENTS

EXECUTIVE SUMMARY

An entity's accounting policies are important to understanding the content of its financial statements. Professional standards require the disclosure of significant accounting policies as an integral part of financial statements when the statements are intended to present financial position, cash flows, or results of operations in conformity with generally accepted accounting principles (GAAP). An accounting policy is significant if it materially affects the determination of financial position, cash flows, or results of operations.

The preferable presentation of disclosing an entity's accounting policies is as part of the first note of the financial statements, under the caption "Summary of Significant Accounting Policies" or "Significant Accounting Policies." However, professional standards do recognize the need for flexibility in the matter of formats. Disclosures of accounting policies need not duplicate information presented elsewhere in the financial statements. Therefore, in some instances the accounting-policies note may refer to information that will be found in another note.

Generally, the "Summary of Significant Accounting Policies" note deals with policies and not with numbers. For example, a company may disclose in its summary note the inventory cost method used (e.g., FIFO) and indicate in a separate note the dollar breakdown of raw materials, work-in-process, and finished goods.

Authoritative pronouncements often require an entity to disclose a specific accounting policy. Following are examples of areas of accounting for which policies are specifically required to be disclosed:

- Basis of consolidation
- Depreciation methods
- Inventory methods
- Pension plans
- Cash and cash equivalents
- Recognition of profit on long-term construction contracts
- Recognition of revenue from franchising and leasing operations

Authoritative Literature

APB-22   Disclosure of Accounting Policies

SOP 94-6   Disclosure of Certain Significant Risks and Uncertainties

DISCLOSURE REQUIREMENTS

A company should disclose a description of its significant accounting policies, particularly principles and methods that involve any of the following (APB-22, pars. 8–15):

1. A selection from existing acceptable alternatives
2. The areas peculiar to a specific industry in which the entity functions
3. Unusual and innovative applications of GAAP

In addition, GAAP requires disclosures about the nature of an entity's operations and the use of estimates to prepare financial statements, which are typically included in the first note to the financial statements relating to significant accounting policies. These disclosure requirements are discussed in detail in Chapter 10, "Contingencies, Risks, Uncertainties, and Concentrations."

EXAMPLES OF FINANCIAL STATEMENT DISCLOSURES

The following are examples of the nature of information frequently disclosed in the "Summary of Significant Accounting

Policies," the first note to the financial statements. The following sample disclosures are available on the accompanying disc.

Accounting Period

Example 2–1: Calendar Year—Saturday Nearest December 31

The Company's accounting period ends on the Saturday nearest December 31. The 20X2 and 20X1 years ended on December 28, 20X2, and December 29, 20X1, respectively.

Example 2–2: Fiscal Year—52- or 53-Week Period

The Company's fiscal year is the 52 or 53 weeks ending on the last Saturday in July. The fiscal year ended July 28, 20X2, comprised a 52-week year, and the fiscal year ended July 29, 20X1, comprised a 53-week year.

Example 2–3: Change in Fiscal Year

During 20X2, the Company changed its fiscal year from one ending on the last Sunday in April to one ending on the last Sunday in December. Accordingly, the Company's transition period that ended on December 30, 20X2, includes the 34 weeks from April 29, 20X2, to December 30, 20X2, (Transition 20X2). The Company's full fiscal years include either 52 or 53 weeks. Fiscal 20X2 and 20X1 each include 52 weeks.

The following are selected financial data for Transition 20X2 and for the comparable 34-week period of the prior year:

	December 30, 20X2 (34 weeks)	December 31, 20X1 (34 weeks)
Net sales	$45,000,000	$40,000,000
Cost of goods sold	30,000,000	27,000,000
Gross profit	15,000,000	13,000,000
Selling and administrative expenses	10,000,000	9,000,000
Interest expense	1,000,000	1,000,000
Other income, net	500,000	800,000
Income before income taxes	4,500,000	3,800,000
Income tax expense	2,000,000	1,500,000
Net income	$2,500,000	$2,300,000

Accounts Receivable

Example 2–4: Allowance Method Used to Record Bad Debts—
General Description

The Company uses the allowance method to account for uncollectible accounts receivable. Accounts receivable are presented net of an allowance for doubtful accounts of $425,000 and $365,000 at December 31, 20X2, and December 31, 20X1, respectively.

Example 2–5: Allowance Method Used to Record Bad Debts—
Detailed Description

The Company provides an allowance for doubtful accounts equal to the estimated uncollectible amounts. The Company's estimate is based on historical collection experience and a review of the current status of trade accounts receivable. It is reasonably possible that the Company's estimate of the allowance for doubtful accounts will change. Accounts receivable are presented net of an allowance for doubtful accounts of $940,000 and $790,000 at December 31, 20X2, and December 31, 20X1, respectively.

Example 2–6: Direct Write-Off Method Used to Record Bad Debts

The Company has elected to record bad debts using the direct writeoff method. Generally accepted accounting principles require that the allowance method be used to recognize bad debts; however, the effect of using the direct write-off method is not materially different from the results that would have been obtained under the allowance method.

Example 2–7: Unbilled Receivables

Unbilled receivables represent revenue earned in the current period but not billed to the customer until future dates, usually within one month.

Example 2–8: Long-Term Accounts Receivable

The Company finances certain sales to Latin American customers over two to three years. At December 31, 20X2, and December 31, 20X1, the Company had long-term accounts receivable outstanding of approximately $3,500,000 and $2,300,000, respectively, relating to these sales, which are included in other assets. As of December 31, 20X2, the Company has not experienced any significant change in these receivables; however, the economic and currency related uncertainties in these countries may increase the likelihood of nonpayment. As a result, the Company increased its bad debt reserve at December 31, 20X2.

Example 2–9: Classification of Accounts Receivable with Credit Balances

Accounts receivable with credit balances have been included as a current liability in "Accounts payable" in the accompanying balance sheet.

Advertising Costs

Example 2–10: Advertising Costs Are Expensed as Incurred

Advertising and sales promotion costs are expensed as incurred. Advertising expense totaled $295,000 for 20X2 and $270,000 for 20X1.

Example 2–11: Advertising Costs Are Expensed the First Time the Advertising Takes Place

Production costs of future media advertising are expensed the first time the advertising takes place. Advertising expense totaled $457,000 for 20X2 and $393,000 for 20X1.

Example 2–12: Direct-Response Advertising Costs Are Capitalized and Amortized

Direct-response advertising costs, consisting primarily of catalog book production, printing, and postage costs, are capitalized and amortized over the expected life of the catalog, not to exceed six months. Direct response advertising costs reported as prepaid assets are $275,000 and $350,000 at December 31, 20X2, and December 31, 20X1, respectively. Total advertising expenses were $1,900,000 in 20X2 and $1,600,000 in 20X1.

Example 2–13: Certain Advertising Costs Are Expensed the First Time the Advertising Takes Place and Direct-Response Advertising Costs Are Capitalized

The Company expenses the production costs of advertising the first time the advertising takes place, except for direct-response advertising, which is capitalized and amortized over its expected period of future benefits. Direct-response advertising consists primarily of magazine advertisements that include order coupons for the Company's products. The capitalized costs of the advertising are amortized over the six-month period following the publication of the magazine in which it appears.

> **Note:** This example assumes that the details of advertising costs expensed and capitalized are disclosed in a separate note

to the financial statements. See Chapter 3, "Advertising Costs," for such an illustration.

Capitalization of Interest

Example 2–14: Capitalization of Interest Costs on Borrowings

The Company capitalizes interest cost on borrowings incurred during the new construction or upgrade of qualifying assets. Capitalized interest is added to the cost of the underlying assets and is amortized over the useful lives of the assets. For 20X2 and 20X1, the Company capitalized $450,000 and $525,000 of interest, respectively, in connection with various capital expansion projects.

Cash Equivalents

Example 2–15: Types of Cash Equivalents Specifically Identified

Cash and cash equivalents consist primarily of cash on deposit, certificates of deposit, money market accounts, and investment grade commercial paper that are readily convertible into cash and purchased with original maturities of three months or less.

Example 2–16: Types of Cash Equivalents Described in General Terms

The Company considers deposits that can be redeemed on demand and investments that have original maturities of less than three months, when purchased, to be cash equivalents. As of December 31, 20X2, the Company's cash and cash equivalents were deposited primarily in three financial institutions.

Comprehensive Income

> **Note:** For disclosure examples of comprehensive income, in addition to the ones illustrated below, see Chapter 54, "Comprehensive Income."

Example 2–17: Components of Other Comprehensive Income Disclosed

Comprehensive income consists of net income and other gains and losses affecting shareholders' equity that, under generally accepted accounting principles, are excluded from net income. For the Company, such items consist primarily of unrealized gains and losses on marketable equity investments and foreign currency translation gains and losses. The changes in the components of other comprehensive income (loss) are as follows:

| | Years Ended December 31 | | | |
| | 20X2 | | 20X1 | |
	Pre-Tax Amount	Tax Expense (Credit)	Pre-Tax Amount	Tax Expense (Credit)
Unrealized gain on securities	$650,000	$225,000	$725,000	$265,000
Foreign currency translation adjustments	90,000	31,000	(35,000)	(13,000)
Total other comprehensive income	$740,000	$256,000	$690,000	$252,000

Example 2–18: No Items of Other Comprehensive Income

The Company has no items of other comprehensive income in any period presented. Therefore, net income as presented in the Company's Statement of Operations equals comprehensive income.

Concentrations of Credit and Other Risks

For examples of financial statement disclosures, see Chapter 10, "Contingencies, Risks, Uncertainties, and Concentrations."

Consolidation Policy

> **Note:** For examples of disclosures relating to consolidated and combined financial statements, in addition to the ones illustrated below, see Chapter 9, "Consolidated and Combined Financial Statements."

Example 2–19: Consolidation Policy Specifically Described

The accompanying consolidated financial statements include the accounts of the Company and its majority-owned subsidiary partnerships and corporations, after elimination of all material intercompany accounts, transactions, and profits. Investments in unconsolidated subsidiaries representing ownership of at least 20%, but less than 50%, are accounted for under the equity method. Nonmarketable investments in which the Company has less than 20% ownership and in which it does not have the ability to exercise significant influence over the investee are initially recorded at cost and periodically reviewed for impairment.

Example 2–20: Combined Financial Statements

The financial statements of ABC, Inc. and ZYZ Corp. are combined because each company is owned beneficially by identical sharehold-ers. All significant intercompany accounts and transactions have been eliminated in the combination.

Contingencies

Example 2–21: General Accounting Policy for Contingencies

Certain conditions may exist as of the date the financial statements are issued, which may result in a loss to the Company but which will only be resolved when one or more future events occur or fail to occur. The Company's management and its legal counsel assess such contingent liabilities, and such assessment inherently involves an exercise of judgment. In assessing loss contingencies related to legal proceedings that are pending against the Company or unasserted claims that may result in such proceedings, the Company's legal counsel evaluates the perceived merits of any legal proceedings or unasserted claims as well as the perceived merits of the amount of relief sought or expected to be sought therein.

If the assessment of a contingency indicates that it is probable that a material loss has been incurred and the amount of the liability can be estimated, then the estimated liability would be accrued in the Company's financial statements. If the assessment indicates that a potentially material loss contingency is not probable but is reason-ably possible, or is probable but cannot be estimated, then the nature of the contingent liability, together with an estimate of the range of possible loss if determinable and material, would be disclosed.

Loss contingencies considered remote are generally not disclosed unless they involve guarantees, in which case the guarantees would be disclosed.

Deferred Revenue

Example 2–22: Amounts Billed in Advance

The Company recognizes revenues as earned. Amounts billed in advance of the period in which service is rendered are recorded as a liability under "Deferred revenue."

Earnings per Share

Example 2–23: Basic and Diluted Net Earnings per Share

Basic net earnings (loss) per common share is computed by dividing net earnings (loss) applicable to common shareholders by the weighted-average number of common shares outstanding during the period. Diluted net earnings (loss) per common share is determined using the weighted-average number of common shares outstanding during the period, adjusted for the dilutive effect of common stock equivalents, consisting of shares that might be issued upon exercise of common stock options. In periods where losses are reported, the weighted-average number of common shares outstanding excludes common stock equivalents, because their inclusion would be anti-dilutive.

Environmental Costs

Example 2–24: Environmental Expenditures Expensed or Capitalized

Costs related to environmental remediation are charged to expense. Other environmental costs are also charged to expense unless they increase the value of the property and/or provide future economic benefits, in which event they are capitalized. Liabilities are recognized when the expenditures are considered probable and can be reasonably estimated. Measurement of liabilities is based on currently enacted laws and regulations, existing technology, and undiscounted site-specific costs. Generally, such recognition coincides with the Company's commitment to a formal plan of action.

Example 2–25: Accruals for Environmental Matters Exclude Claims for Recoveries

Accruals for environmental matters are recorded when it is probable that a liability has been incurred and the amount of the liability can be reasonably estimated, or if an amount is likely to fall within a range and no amount within that range can be determined to be the better estimate, the minimum amount of the range is recorded. Accruals for environmental matters exclude claims for recoveries from insurance carriers and other third parties until it is probable that such recoveries will be realized.

Estimates

Example 2–26: General Note Regarding Estimates Inherent in the Financial Statements

Preparing the Company's financial statements in conformity with accounting principles generally accepted in the United States of America ("GAAP") requires management to make estimates and assumptions that affect reported amounts of assets and liabilities and disclosure of contingent assets and liabilities at the date of the financial statements and the reported amounts of revenues and expenses during the reporting period. Actual results could differ from those estimates.

Example 2–27: Significant Estimates Relating to Specific Financial Statement Accounts and Transactions Are Identified

The financial statements include some amounts that are based on management's best estimates and judgments. The most significant estimates relate to allowance for uncollectible accounts receivable, inventory obsolescence, depreciation, intangible asset valuations and useful lives, goodwill impairments, employee benefit plans, environmental accruals, warranty costs, taxes, contingencies, and costs to complete long-term contracts. These estimates may be adjusted as more current information becomes available, and any adjustment could be significant.

Financial Instruments

Note: For disclosure examples of financial instruments, derivatives, and hedging activities and related fair values, in addition to the ones illustrated below, see Chapters 14, "Fair Value Measurements," and 15, "Financial Instruments, Derivatives, and Hedging Activities."

Example 2–28: Fair Value of Financial Instruments Approximates Carrying Amount

The Company's financial instruments are cash and cash equivalents, accounts receivable, accounts payable, notes payable, and long-term debt. The recorded values of cash and cash equivalents, accounts receivable, and accounts payable approximate their fair values based on their short-term nature. The recorded values of notes payable and long-term debt approximate their fair values, as interest approximates market rates.

Example 2–29: Fair Value of Financial Instruments Is Based on Quoted Market Prices or Pricing Models

Fair values of long-term investments, long-term debt, interest rate derivatives, currency forward contracts, and currency options are based on quoted market prices or pricing models using prevailing financial market information as of December 31, 20X2.

Example 2–30: Fair Value of Financial Instruments Is Based on Management's Estimates

The fair value of current assets and liabilities approximate carrying value, due to the short-term nature of these items. There is no quoted market value for the Senior Secured Notes; however, management estimates that, based on current market conditions, such Notes have a fair value of approximately 45% to 55% of the face value of such Notes. Fair value of such financial instruments is not necessarily representative of the amount that could be realized or settled.

Example 2–31: Fair Value of Long-Term Debt Is Estimated Based on Current Rates and Terms Offered to the Company

The fair value of the Company's long-term debt is estimated based on the current rates offered to the Company for debt of similar terms and maturities. Under this method, the Company's fair value of long-term debt was not significantly different from the carrying value at December 31, 20X2.

Example 2–32: Fair Value of Notes Receivable Is Based on Discounted Cash Flows

The fair value of notes receivable, which is based on discounted cash flows using current interest rates, approximates the carrying value at December 31, 20X2.

Foreign Operations

Example 2–33: Company's Future Operations Are Dependent on Foreign Operations

The Company's future operations and earnings will depend on the results of the Company's operations in [*name of foreign country*]. There can be no assurance that the Company will be able to successfully conduct such operations, and a failure to do so would have a material adverse effect on the Company's financial position, results of operations, and cash flows. Also, the success of the Company's operations will be subject to numerous contingencies, some of which are beyond management's control. These contingencies include general and regional economic conditions, prices for the Company's products, competition, and changes in regulation. Because the Company is dependent on international operations, specifically those in [*name of foreign country*], the Company will be subject to various additional political, economic, and other uncertainties. Among other risks, the Company's operations will be subject to the risks of restrictions on transfer of funds; export duties, quotas and embargoes; domestic and international customs and tariffs; changing taxation policies; foreign exchange restrictions; and political conditions and governmental regulations.

Example 2–34: Foreign Currency Adjustments—Functional Currency Is the Foreign Country's Local Currency

The financial position and operating results of substantially all foreign operations are consolidated using the local currencies of the countries in which the Company operates as the functional currency. Local currency assets and liabilities are translated at the rates of exchange on the balance sheet date, and local currency revenues and expenses are translated at average rates of exchange during the period. The resulting translation adjustments are recorded directly into a separate component of shareholders' equity.

Example 2–35: Foreign Currency Adjustments—Functional Currency Is the U.S. Dollar

The Company's functional currency for all operations worldwide is the U.S. dollar. Nonmonetary assets and liabilities are translated at historical rates and monetary assets and liabilities are translated at exchange rates in effect at the end of the year. Income statement accounts are translated at average rates for the year. Gains and losses from translation of foreign currency financial statements into U.S. dollars are included in current results of operations. Gains and losses resulting from foreign currency transactions are also included in current results of operations.

Example 2–36: Foreign Currency Adjustments—Certain Assets and Liabilities Are Remeasured at Current Exchange Rates and Others Are Remeasured at Historical Rates

The U.S. dollar is the "functional currency" of the Company's worldwide continuing operations. All foreign currency asset and liability amounts are remeasured into U.S. dollars at end-of-period exchange rates, except for inventories, prepaid expenses and property, plant and equipment, which are remeasured at historical rates. Foreign currency income and expenses are remeasured at average exchange rates in effect during the year, except for expenses related to balance sheet amounts remeasured at historical exchange rates. Exchange gains and losses arising from remeasurement of foreign currency denominated monetary assets and liabilities are included in income in the period in which they occur.

Going Concern Issues

Example 2–37: Company's Successful Operations Are Dependent on Those of Its Parent

The Company has historically relied on its parent company to meet its cash flow requirements. The parent has cash available in the amount of approximately $83,000 as of December 31, 20X2, and a working capital deficit of $80 million. The Senior Secured Notes in the amount of $65 million have been reclassified because the Company's parent company does not currently have sufficient funds to make the next interest payment (in the approximate amount of $6 million) due in May 20X3. Failure by the parent to make such payment could allow the holders of the Notes to declare all amounts outstanding immediately due and payable. The Company and its parent will need additional funds to meet the development and exploratory obligations until sufficient cash flows are generated from anticipated production to sustain operations and to fund future development and exploration obligations.

The parent plans to generate the additional cash needed through the sale or financing of its domestic assets held for sale and the completion of additional equity, debt, or joint venture transactions. There is no assurance, however, that the parent will be able to sell or finance its assets held for sale or to complete other transactions in the future at commercially reasonable terms, if at all, or that the Company will be able to meet its future contractual obligations.

Impairment of Long-Lived Assets

> **Note:** For disclosure examples of impairment of long-lived assets under FAS-144, *Accounting for the Impairment or Disposal of Long-Lived Assets,* see Chapter 20, "Impairment and Disposal of Long-Lived Assets."

Income Taxes

Example 2–38: C Corporation

Deferred tax assets and liabilities are recognized for the future tax consequences attributable to differences between the financial statement carrying amounts of existing assets and liabilities and their respective tax bases. Deferred tax assets, including tax loss and credit carryforwards, and liabilities are measured using enacted tax rates expected to apply to taxable income in the years in which those temporary differences are expected to be recovered or settled. The effect on deferred tax assets and liabilities of a change in tax rates is recognized in income in the period that includes the enactment date. Deferred income tax expense represents the change during the period in the deferred tax assets and deferred tax liabilities. The components of the deferred tax assets and liabilities are individually classified as current and non-current based on their characteristics. Deferred tax assets are reduced by a valuation allowance when, in the opinion of management, it is more likely than not that some portion or all of the deferred tax assets will not be realized.

Example 2–39: S Corporation

The Company, with the consent of its stockholders, has elected under the Internal Revenue Code to be taxed as an S Corporation. The stockholders of an S Corporation are taxed on their proportionate share of the Company's taxable income. Therefore, no provision or liability for federal income taxes has been included in the financial statements. Certain specific deductions and credits flow through the Company to its stockholders.

This election is valid for [State]; however, [State] law requires a minimum tax of [amount]% on State taxable income. Therefore, a provision and a related liability have been included in the financial statements for [State] income taxes.

Example 2–40: Limited Liability Company

As a limited liability company, the Company's taxable income or loss is allocated to members in accordance with their respective percentage ownership. Therefore, no provision or liability for income taxes has been included in the financial statements.

Example 2–41: Partnership

The Partnership is not a taxpaying entity for federal or state income tax purposes; accordingly, a provision for income taxes has not been recorded in the accompanying financial statements. Partnership income or losses are reflected in the partners' individual or corporate income tax returns in accordance with their ownership percentages.

Example 2–42: Proprietorship

The Proprietorship is not a taxpaying entity for federal or state income tax purposes; accordingly, a provision for income taxes has not been recorded in the accompanying financial statements. Federal and state income taxes of the proprietor are computed on [his/her] total income from all sources.

Example 2–43: Taxes Provided on Undistributed Earnings of Foreign Subsidiaries

The Company's practice is to provide U.S. Federal taxes on undistributed earnings of the Company's non-U.S. sales and service subsidiaries.

Example 2–44: Taxes Not Provided on Undistributed Earnings of Foreign Subsidiaries

A provision has not been made at December 31, 20X2, for U.S. or additional foreign withholding taxes on approximately $10 million of undistributed earnings of foreign subsidiaries because it is the present intention of management to reinvest the undistributed earnings indefinitely in foreign operations. Generally, such earnings become subject to U.S. tax upon the remittance of dividends and under certain other circumstances. It is not practicable to estimate the amount of deferred tax liability on such undistributed earnings.

Example 2–45: Realization of the Deferred Income Tax Asset Is Dependent on Generating Future Taxable Income

Deferred tax assets are reduced by a valuation allowance when, in the opinion of management, it is more likely than not that some portion or all of the deferred tax assets will not be realized. Realization of the deferred income tax asset is dependent on generating sufficient taxable income in future years. Although realization is not assured, management believes it is more likely than not that all of the deferred income tax asset will be realized. The amount of the deferred income tax asset considered realizable, however, could be reduced in the near term if estimates of future taxable income are reduced.

Example 2–46: Tax Credits Accounted for on the Flow-Through Method

Tax credits, grants, and other allowances are accounted for in the period earned (the flow-through method).

Example 2–47: Tax Credits Accounted for on the Deferral Method

Investment tax credits are deferred and included in income as a reduction of income tax expense over the estimated useful lives of the assets that gave rise to the credits.

Example 2–48: Tax Credits Accounted for on the Cost Reduction Method

Investment tax credits are accounted for as decreases of the bases of the assets that gave rise to the credits. The credits are included in income through a reduction of the amount of depreciation expense, which would otherwise be charged to operations, over the estimated useful lives of the assets that gave rise to the credits.

Example 2–49: Company Has Substantial Net Operating Loss Carry-forwards and a Valuation Allowance Is Recorded

The Company recognizes the amount of taxes payable or refundable for the current year and recognizes deferred tax liabilities and assets for the expected future tax consequences of events and transactions that have been recognized in the Company's financial statements or tax returns. The Company currently has substantial net operating loss carryforwards. The Company has recorded a 100% valuation allowance against net deferred tax assets due to uncertainty of their ultimate realization.

Example 2–50: Subchapter S Status Terminated

Before January 1, 20X2, the Company had operated as a C corporation. Effective January 1, 20X2, the stockholders of the Company elected to be taxed under Subchapter S of the Internal Revenue Code. During such period, federal income taxes were the responsibility of the Company's stockholders as were certain state income taxes. As of the effective date of the election, the Company was responsible for Federal built-in-gain taxes to the extent applicable. Accordingly, the consolidated statement of operations for the year ended December 31, 20X2, provides for such taxes. The S corporation election terminated in connection with the consummation of the initial public offering of the Company's common stock on October 10, 20X2.

Example 2–51: Conversion from an LLC to a C Corporation

From the Company's inception in March 19X7 to February 20X2, the Company was not subject to federal and state income taxes since it was operating as a Limited Liability Company (LLC). On February 2, 20X2, the Company converted from an LLC to a C corporation and, as a result, became subject to corporate federal and state income taxes. The Company's accumulated deficit of $4.3 million at that date was reclassified to additional paid-in capital.

Example 2–52: Conversion from Cash Basis to Accrual Basis for Tax Purposes Results in a Deferred Tax Liability

In the current year, the Company converted from a cash basis to an accrual basis for tax purposes in conjunction with its conversion to a C corporation. Due to temporary differences in recognition of revenue and expenses, income for financial reporting purposes exceeded income for income tax purposes. The conversion to an accrual basis along with these temporary differences resulted in the recognition of a net deferred tax liability, and a corresponding one-time charge to expense, of $3.5 million as of December 31, 20X2.

Example 2–53: Subsidiary Files a Consolidated Federal Income Tax Return with Its Parent

The Company files a consolidated federal income tax return with its parent company, but files a separate state income tax return. In accordance with the intercorporate tax allocation policy, the Company pays to or receives from the parent company amounts equivalent to federal income tax charges or credits based on separate company taxable income or loss using the statutory rates.

Intangible Assets

> **Note:** For disclosure examples of intangible assets acquired individually or in connection with business combinations, and related impairment issues pertaining to intangible assets, see the following chapters:
>
> - Chapter 4, "Business Combinations"
> - Chapter 20, "Impairment and Disposal of Long-Lived Assets"
> - Chapter 43, "Intangible Assets"

Inventory

Example 2–54: Inventories Accounted for under FIFO

Inventories are stated at the lower of cost (first-in, first-out basis) or market (net realizable value).

Example 2–55: Inventories Accounted for under LIFO

Inventories are stated at the lower of cost or market. Cost is determined by the last-in, first-out (LIFO) method for all inventories. Market value for raw materials is based on replacement cost and for work-in-process and finished goods on net realizable value.

Example 2–56: Inventory Stated at Standard Cost—Due Consideration Given to Obsolescence and Inventory Levels in Evaluating Net Realizable Value

Inventories are stated at the lower of cost or market. Cost is determined on a standard cost basis that approximates the first-in, first-out (FIFO) method. Market is determined based on net realizable value. Appropriate consideration is given to obsolescence, excessive levels, deterioration, and other factors in evaluating net realizable value.

Example 2–57: Inventories Accounted for under LIFO and FIFO

Inventories, consisting of manufactured products and merchandise for resale, are stated at the lower of cost or market. Manufactured products include the costs of materials, labor, and manufacturing overhead. Inventories accounted for using the last-in, first-out (LIFO) method approximated 60% and 65% of total inventory as of yearend 20X2 and 20X1, respectively. Remaining inventories are generally determined using the first-in, first-out (FIFO) cost method. For detailed inventory information, see Note [X].

Example 2–58: Inventory Valuation Includes Provision for Obsolescence

Inventories are stated at the lower of cost (FIFO) or market, including provisions for obsolescence commensurate with known or estimated exposures. Inventories are shown net of a valuation reserve of $450,000 at December 31, 20X2, and $300,000 at December 31, 20X1.

Example 2–59: Inventory Note Describes Accounting Policy for New Products

Inventories are stated at the lower of cost (determined by the first-in, first-out method) or market (net realizable value). Costs associated with the manufacture of a new product are charged to engineering, research and development expense as incurred until the product is proven through testing and acceptance by the customer.

Example 2–60: Inventory Note Addresses Risk Exposure to Technological Change

Inventories are stated at the lower of cost (FIFO) or market. Inventories consist primarily of components and subassemblies and finished products held for sale. Rapid technological change and new product introductions and enhancements could result in excess or obsolete inventory. To minimize this risk, the Company evaluates inventory levels and expected usage on a periodic basis and records adjustments as required.

Investments

Example 2–61: Short-Term Investments

As part of its cash management program, the Company from time to time maintains a portfolio of marketable investment securities. The securities have an investment grade and a term to earliest maturity generally of less than one year and include tax exempt securities and certificates of deposit. These securities are carried at cost, which approximates market.

Example 2–62: Held-to-Maturity, Trading, and Available-for-Sale Marketable Securities

The Company classifies its debt and marketable equity securities into held-to-maturity, trading, or available-for-sale categories. Debt securities are classified as held-to-maturity when the Company has the positive intent and ability to hold the securities to maturity. Debt securities for which the Company does not have the intent or ability to hold to maturity are classified as available for sale. Held-to-maturity securities are recorded as either short-term or long-term on the balance sheet based on contractual maturity date and are stated at amortized cost. Marketable securities that are bought and held principally for the purpose of selling them in the near term are classified as trading securities and are reported at fair value, with unrealized gains and losses recognized in earnings. Debt and marketable equity securities not classified as held-to-maturity or as trading are classified as available-for-sale and are carried at fair market value, with the unrealized gains and losses, net of tax, included in the determination of comprehensive income and reported in shareholders' equity.

The fair value of substantially all securities is determined by quoted market prices. The estimated fair value of securities for which there are no quoted market prices is based on similar types of securities that are traded in the market. Gains or losses on securities sold are based on the specific identification method.

Example 2–63: Reverse Repurchase Agreements

Securities purchased under agreements to resell (reverse repurchase agreements) result from transactions that are collateralized by negotiable securities and are carried at the amounts at which the securities will subsequently be resold. It is the policy of the Company not to take possession of securities purchased under agreements to resell. At December 31, 20X2, and December 31, 20X1, agreements to resell securities in the amount of $1,300,000 with a three-day maturity and $3,200,000 with a 14-day maturity were outstanding, respectively.

Example 2–64: Accounting Policy Describes the Method of Accounting for Unconsolidated Subsidiaries

The equity method of accounting is used when the Company has a 20% to 50% interest in other entities. Under the equity method, original investments are recorded at cost and adjusted by the Company's share of undistributed earnings or losses of these entities. Nonmarketable investments in which the Company has less than a 20% interest and in which it does not have the ability to exercise significant influence over the investee are initially recorded at cost, and periodically reviewed for impairment.

Life Insurance

Example 2–65: Life Insurance Policies Net of Policy Loans

The Company's investment in corporate owned life insurance policies is recorded net of policy loans in "Other assets" in the Balance

Sheets. The net life insurance expense, including interest expense, is included in "Administrative and general expenses" in the Statements of Operations.

Nature of Operations

Example 2–66: Company Describes Its Primary Products

The Company designs, manufactures, markets, and services test systems and related software, and backplanes and associated connectors. The Company's top five products are (1) semiconductor test systems, (2) backplane connection systems, (3) circuit-board test systems, (4) telecommunications test systems, and (5) software test systems.

Example 2–67: Company Describes the Types of Customers It Has

The Company is a leading global developer, manufacturer, and distributor of hand tools, power tools, tool storage products, shop equipment, under-hood diagnostics equipment, under-car equipment, emissions and safety equipment, collision repair equipment, vehicle service information, and business management systems and services. The Corporation's customers include professional automotive technicians, shop owners, franchised service centers, national accounts, original equipment manufacturers, and industrial tool and equipment users worldwide.

Example 2–68: Company Describes U.S. Geographic Locations Where It Operates

The Company is a leading designer and manufacturer of open-architecture, standard embedded computer components that system designers can easily use to create a custom solution specific to the user's unique application. The Company has operations in New York, New Mexico, Minnesota, North Carolina, and California. The Company's product lines include CPU boards, general purpose input/output modules, avionics interface modules and analyzers, interconnection and expansion units, telemetry boards, data acquisition software, and industrial computer systems and enclosures.

Example 2–69: Company Indicates That Its Operations Are Vulnerable to Changes in Trends and Customer Demand

The Company is a nationwide specialty retailer of fashionable and contemporary apparel and accessory items designed for consumers with a young, active lifestyle. The Company's success is largely dependent on its ability to gauge the fashion tastes of its customers and to provide merchandise that satisfies customer demand. The Company's failure to anticipate, identify, or react to changes in fashion trends could adversely affect its results of operations.

Example 2–70: Company's Operations Are Substantially in Foreign Countries

Substantially all of the Company's products are manufactured in the Dominican Republic, Mexico (under the Maquiladora program), Switzerland, Ireland, and Slovakia. These foreign operations represent captive manufacturing facilities of the Company. The Company's operations are subject to various political, economic, and other risks and uncertainties inherent in the countries in which the Company operates. Among other risks, the Company's operations are subject to the risks of restrictions on transfer of funds; export duties, quotas, and embargoes; domestic and international customs and tariffs; changing taxation policies; foreign exchange restrictions; and political conditions and governmental regulations.

Example 2–71: Company Specifies Percentage of Net Sales Relating to Foreign Operations

Sales to customers outside the United States approximated 35% of net sales in 20X2 and 25% of net sales in 20X1.

New Accounting Pronouncements

Example 2–72: FAS-158, Employers' Accounting for Defined Benefit Pension and Other Postretirement Plans

In September 2006, the Financial Accounting Standards Board issued Statement of Financial Accounting Standards No. 158 (FAS-158), *Employers' Accounting for Defined Benefit Pension and Other Postretirement Plans*. FAS-158 requires employers to fully recognize the obligations associated with single-employer defined benefit pension, retiree healthcare and other postretirement plans in their financial statements. The provisions of FAS-158 are effective for the Company as of the end of the fiscal year ending December 31, 20X3. The Company is evaluating the impact of the provisions of FAS-158 on its financial position, results of operations, and cash flows.

Example 2–73: FAS-157, Fair Value Measurements

In September 2006, the Financial Accounting Standards Board issued Statement of Financial Accounting Standards No. 157 (FAS-157), *Fair Value Measurements*. FAS-157 defines fair value, establishes a framework for measuring fair value in accordance with GAAP, and expands disclosures about fair value measurements. The provisions of FAS-157 are effective for the Company for fiscal years beginning January 1, 20X4. The Company is evaluating the impact of the provisions of FAS-157 on its financial position, results of operations, and cash flows.

Example 2–74: FAS-156, Accounting for Servicing of Financial Assets

In March 2006, the Financial Accounting Standards Board issued Statement of Financial Accounting Standards No. 156 (FAS-156), *Accounting for Servicing of Financial Assets*, which amends the guidance in FAS-140, *Accounting for Transfers and Servicing of Financial Assets and Extinguishments of Liabilities*. Among other requirements, FAS-156 requires an entity to recognize a servicing asset or servicing liability each time it undertakes an obligation to service a financial asset by entering into a servicing contract in certain specified situations. The provisions of FAS-156 are effective for the Company for fiscal years beginning January 1, 20X4. The adoption of FAS-156 is not expected to have a material effect on the Company's financial position, results of operations, or cash flows.

Example 2–75: FAS-155, Accounting for Certain Hybrid Financial Instruments

In February 2006, the Financial Accounting Standards Board issued Statement of Financial Accounting Standards No. 155 (FAS-155), *Accounting for Certain Hybrid Financial Instruments*. FAS-155 amends FAS-133, *Accounting for Derivative Instruments and Hedging Activities*, and FAS-140, *Accounting for Transfers and Servicing of Financial Assets and Extinguishments of Liabilities*. This Statement permits fair value remeasurement for any hybrid financial instrument that contains an embedded derivative that otherwise would require bifurcation. FAS-155 is effective for the Company for all financial instruments acquired or issued after January 1, 20X4. The adoption of FAS-155 is not expected to have a material effect on the Company's financial position, results of operations, or cash flows.

Example 2–76: FIN-48, Accounting for Uncertainty in Income Taxes

In June 2006, the Financial Accounting Standards Board issued FASB Interpretation No. 48 (FIN-48), *Accounting for Uncertainty in Income Taxes—An interpretation of FASB Statement No. 109*. FIN-48 clarifies the accounting for uncertainty in income taxes recognized in an entity's financial statements in accordance with Statement of Financial Accounting Standards No. 109, *Accounting for Income Taxes*. This Interpretation prescribes a recognition threshold and measurement attribute for the financial statement recognition and measurement of a tax position taken or expected to be taken in a tax return. In addition, FIN-48 provides guidance on derecognition, classification, interest and penalties, accounting in interim periods, disclosure, and transition. FIN-48 is effective for the Company in fiscal years beginning January 1, 20X3. The Company is evaluating the impact of the provisions of FIN-48 on its financial position, results of operations, and cash flows.

Example 2–77: FAS-154, Accounting Changes and Error Corrections

In May 2005, the Financial Accounting Standards Board issued Statement of Financial Accounting Standards No. 154 (FAS-154), *Accounting Changes and Error Corrections*, which is a replacement of APB Opinion No. 20, *Accounting Changes*, and FAS-3, *Reporting Accounting Changes in Interim Financial Statements*. FAS-154 requires that a voluntary change in accounting principle be applied retrospectively with all prior-period financial statements presented on the new accounting principle, instead of recording a cumulative effect adjustment within the period of the change, unless it is impracticable to determine the effects of the change on each period being presented. FAS-154 also provides that a correction of errors in previously issued financial statements should be termed a "restatement." This Statement is effective for accounting changes and corrections of errors made in fiscal years beginning after December 15, 2005, and the Company plans to adopt FAS-154 on January 1, 2006. The Company does not expect the adoption of FAS-154 to have a significant impact on its financial statements.

Example 2–78: FAS-123R, Share-Based Payment

In December 2004, the Financial Accounting Standards Board issued Statement of Financial Accounting Standards No. 123 (Revised 2004) (FAS-123R), *Share-Based Payment*. This statement replaces FAS-123, *Accounting for Stock-Based Compensation*, supersedes APB Opinion No. 25, *Accounting for Stock Issued to Employees*, and amends FAS-95, *Statement of Cash Flows*. FAS-123R requires companies to apply a fair-value-based measurement method in accounting for shared-based payment transactions with employees and to record compensation cost for all stock awards granted after the required effective date and for awards modified, repurchased, or cancelled after that date. The scope of FAS-123R encompasses a wide range of share-based compensation arrangements, including share options, restricted share plans, performance-based awards, share appreciation rights, and employee share purchase plans. FAS-123R is effective for the Company on [*date*]. The Company is currently evaluating the effect that FAS-123R will have on its financial position and results of operations.

Example 2–79: FAS-153, Exchanges of Nonmonetary Assets

In December 2004, the Financial Accounting Standards Board issued Statement of Financial Accounting Standards No. 153 (FAS-153), *Exchanges of Nonmonetary Assets*. This Statement eliminates the exception from fair value accounting for nonmonetary exchanges of similar productive assets and replaces it with an exception for exchanges that do not have commercial substance. FAS-153 specifies that a nonmonetary exchange has commercial substance if the future cash flows of an entity are expected to change significantly as a result of the exchange. FAS-153 is effective for nonmonetary asset exchanges occurring in fiscal periods beginning after June 15, 2005. The Company is currently evaluating the effect of this pronouncement on its financial position and results of operations.

Example 2–80: FAS-152, Accounting for Real Estate Time-Sharing Transactions

In December 2004, the Financial Accounting Standards Board issued Statement of Financial Accounting Standards No. 152 (FAS-152), *Accounting for Real Estate Time-Sharing Transactions*. This Statement amends FAS-66, *Accounting for Sales of Real Estate*, to reference the financial accounting and reporting guidance for real estate time-sharing transactions that is provided in AICPA Statement of Position (SOP) 04-2, *Accounting for Real Estate Time-Sharing Transactions*. FAS-152 also amends FAS-67, *Accounting for Costs and Initial Rental Operations of Real Estate Projects*, to state that the guidance for (a) incidental operations and (b) costs incurred to sell real estate projects does not apply to real estate timesharing transactions. The accounting for those operations and costs is subject to the guidance in SOP 04-2. This Statement is effective for financial statements for fiscal years beginning after June 15, 2005. The Company is currently evaluating the effect of this pronouncement on its financial position and results of operations.

Example 2–81: FAS-151, Inventory Costs

In November 2004, the Financial Accounting Standards Board issued Statement of Financial Accounting Standards No. 151 (FAS-151), *Inventory Costs*. This Statement amends Accounting Research Bulletin No. 43, *Restatement and Revision of Accounting Research Bulletins*, Chapter 4. This Statement clarifies that abnormal amounts of idle facility expense, freight, handling costs, and wasted materials (spoilage) should be recognized as current-period charges and not included as part of inventory cost. Also, FAS-151 requires that allocation of fixed production overheads to the costs of conversion be based on the normal capacity of the production facilities. FAS-151 is effective for inventory costs incurred during fiscal years beginning after

June 15, 2005. The Company is currently evaluating the effect of this pronouncement on its financial position and results of operations.

Pension and Other Employee Benefit Plans

Example 2–82: Defined Benefit Pension Plans

The Company has two defined benefit retirement plans that cover substantially all of its employees. Defined benefit plans for salaried employees provide benefits based on employees' years of service and five-year final overall base compensation. Defined benefit plans for hourly paid employees, including those covered by multi-employer pension plans under collective bargaining agreements, generally provide benefits of stated amounts for specified periods of service. The Company's policy is to fund, at a minimum, amounts as are necessary on an actuarial basis to provide assets sufficient to meet the benefits to be paid to plan members in accordance with the requirements of the Employee Retirement Income Security Act of 1974 (ERISA). Assets of the plans are administered by an independent trustee and are invested principally in fixed income securities, equity securities, and real estate.

Example 2–83: Defined Contribution Plan

Certain employees are covered by defined contribution plans. The Corporation's contributions to these plans are based on a percentage of employee compensation or employee contributions. These plans are funded on a current basis.

Example 2–84: Profit-Sharing Plan

The Company has a profit-sharing plan covering most employees with more than two years of service. The Company contributes 5% of earnings before income taxes to the Plan. The company's contributions to the Plan were $325,000 for 20X2 and $215,000 for 20X1.

Example 2–85: Salary Reduction Plan

The Company has a defined contribution, salary-reduction plan that covers all its employees after one year of service. Employees may contribute up to 15% of their salary to the plan and the Company makes a matching contribution of 50%, up to 3% of compensation.

Example 2–86: Postretirement Benefits Other Than Pensions

The Company provides certain postretirement medical, dental, and life insurance benefits principally to most employees. The Company uses the corridor approach in the valuation of postretirement benefits. The corridor approach defers all actuarial gains and losses resulting from variances between actual results and economic estimates or actuarial assumptions. Amortization occurs when the net gains and losses exceed 10% of the accumulated postretirement benefit obligation at the beginning of the year. The amount in excess of the corridor is amortized over the average remaining service period to retirement date of active plan participants or, for retired participants, the average remaining life expectancy.

Property and Equipment and Depreciation Methods

Example 2–87: Basis for Recording Fixed Assets, Lives, and Depreciation Methods

Property and equipment are recorded at cost. Expenditures for major additions and improvements are capitalized, and minor replacements, maintenance, and repairs are charged to expense as incurred. When property and equipment are retired or otherwise disposed of, the cost and accumulated depreciation are removed from the accounts and any resulting gain or loss is included in the results of operations for the respective period. Depreciation is provided over the estimated useful lives of the related assets using the straight-line method for financial statement purposes. The Company uses other depreciation methods (generally accelerated) for tax purposes where appropriate. The estimated useful lives for significant property and equipment categories are as follows:

Vehicles	3 to 10 years
Machinery and equipment	3 to 20 years
Commercial containers	8 to 12 years
Buildings and improvements	10 to 40 years

Example 2–88: Amortization of Leasehold Improvements

Amortization of leasehold improvements is computed using the straight-line method over the shorter of the remaining lease term or the estimated useful lives of the improvements.

Example 2–89: Assets Held under Capital Leases

Assets held under capital leases are recorded at the lower of the net present value of the minimum lease payments or the fair value of the leased asset at the inception of the lease. Amortization expense is computed using the straight-line method over the shorter of the estimated useful lives of the assets or the period of the related lease.

Example 2–90: Construction in Progress and Estimated Cost to Complete Construction of New Facility

The Company is constructing a new facility scheduled to be completed in 20X4, at which time depreciation will commence. As of December 31, 20X2, the Company incurred and capitalized in Construction in Progress $1,600,000. The estimated cost to be incurred in 20X3 and 20X4 to complete construction of the facility is approximately $12 million.

Example 2–91: Review of Carrying Value of Property and Equipment for Impairment

The Company reviews the carrying value of property, plant, and equipment for impairment whenever events and circumstances indicate that the carrying value of an asset may not be recoverable from the estimated future cash flows expected to result from its use and eventual disposition. In cases where undiscounted expected future cash flows are less than the carrying value, an impairment loss is recognized equal to an amount by which the carrying value exceeds the fair value of assets. The factors considered by management in performing this assessment include current operating results, trends and prospects, the manner in which the property is used, and the effects of obsolescence, demand, competition, and other economic factors. Based on this assessment there was no impairment at December 31, 20X2.

Reclassifications

Example 2–92: Items Reclassified Not Specifically Identified

Certain reclassifications have been made to the prior years' financial statements to conform to the current year presentation. These reclassifications had no effect on previously reported results of operations or retained earnings.

Example 2–93: Items Reclassified Specifically Identified

In the current year, the Company separately classified trademarks and copyrights in the Balance Sheets and has included stock-based compensation as selling, general, and administrative expense in the Statements of Operations. For comparative purposes, amounts in the prior years have been reclassified to conform to current year presentations.

Rent Obligation

Example 2–94: Operating Lease Contains Provisions for Future Rent Increases

The Company has entered into operating lease agreements for its corporate office and warehouses, some of which contain provisions for future rent increases or periods in which rent payments are reduced (abated). In accordance with generally accepted accounting principles, the Company records monthly rent expense equal to the total of the payments due over the lease term, divided by the number of months of the lease term. The difference between rent expense recorded and the amount paid is credited or charged to "Deferred rent obligation," which is reflected as a separate line item in the accompanying Balance Sheet.

Reorganization and Re-Incorporation

Example 2–95: Re-Incorporation in a New State

The Company originally was organized under the laws of the state of New York on June 1, 19X9 and was subsequently reincorporated under the laws of the state of Georgia on November 12, 20X1. The name of the company was changed to DEF, Inc. from ABC Corp. on October 15, 20X2. In connection with the re-incorporation of the Company in November 20X1, as approved by the stockholders, the number of authorized shares of the Company's common stock was increased to one hundred million (100,000,000) and each share of common stock was assigned a par value of $.01. The shares outstanding and all other references to shares of common stock reported have been restated to give effect to the re-incorporation.

Example 2–96: Conversion from a Limited Liability Company to a C Corporation

The Company, formerly ABC LLC, converted from a limited liability company to a C corporation on January 1, 20X2. To effect the conversion, the Company formed a new corporation and transferred all of the assets and liabilities into the newly formed entity. The new corporation, XYZ, Inc., simultaneously issued 10,000,000 shares of common stock, with a par value of $0.01 per share, and 15,000,000 shares of Series A redeemable preferred stock in exchange for each existing member's respective percentage ownership interest in ABC LLC. The exchange has been recorded at the Company's historical carrying values on the date of conversion.

Upon conversion to a C corporation on January 1, 20X2, the Company recorded a net deferred tax asset of $450,000, computed based on the difference between the book and tax bases of its assets and liabilities as of that date.

Example 2–97: Emergence from Bankruptcy

Upon emergence from its Chapter 11 proceedings in April 20X2, the Company adopted "fresh-start" reporting in accordance with AICPA Statement of Position No. 90-7 (Financial Reporting by Entities in Reorganization Under the Bankruptcy Code), as of March 31, 20X2. The Company's emergence from these proceedings resulted in a new reporting entity with no retained earnings or accumulated deficit as of March 31, 20X2. Accordingly, the Company's financial information shown for periods prior to March 31, 20X2, is not comparable to consolidated financial statements presented on or subsequent to March 31, 20X2.

The Bankruptcy Court confirmed the Company's plan of reorganization. The confirmed plan provided for the following:

Secured Debt—The Company's $[amount] of secured debt (secured by a first mortgage lien on a building located in Nashville, Tennessee) was exchanged for $[amount] in cash and a $[amount] secured note, payable in annual installments of $[amount] commencing on July 1, 20X3, through June 30, 20X6, with interest at 13% per annum, with the balance due on July 1, 20X7.

Priority Tax Claims—Payroll and withholding taxes of $[amount] are payable in equal annual installments commencing on July 1, 20X3, through July 1, 20X8, with interest at 11% per annum.

Senior Debt—The holders of approximately $[amount] of senior subordinated secured notes received the following instruments in exchange for their notes: (a) $[amount] in new senior secured debt, payable in annual installments of $[amount] commencing March 1, 20X3, through March 1, 20X6, with interest at 12% per annum, secured by first liens on certain property, plants, and equipment, with the balance due on March 1, 20X7; (b) $[amount] of subordinated debt with interest at 14% per annum due in equal annual installments commencing on October 1, 20X3, through October 1, 20X9, secured by second liens on certain property, plant, and equipment; and (c) [percent]% of the new issue of outstanding voting common stock of the Company.

Trade and Other Miscellaneous Claims—The holders of approximately $[amount] of trade and other miscellaneous claims received the following for their claims: (a) $[amount] in senior secured debt, payable in annual installments of $[amount] commencing March 1, 20X3, through March 1, 20X6, with interest at 12% per annum, secured by first liens on certain property, plants, and equipment, with the balance due on March 1, 20X7; (b) $[*amount*] of subordinated debt, payable in equal annual installments commencing October 1, 20X3, through October 1, 20X8, with interest at 14% per annum; and (c) [*percent*]% of the new issue of outstanding voting common stock of the Company.

Subordinated Debentures—The holders of approximately $[*amount*] of subordinated unsecured debt received, in exchange for the debentures, [*percent*]% of the new issue outstanding voting common stock of the Company.

Preferred Stock—The holders of [*number*] shares of preferred stock received [*percent*]% of the outstanding voting common stock of the new issue of the Company in exchange for their preferred stock.

Common Stock—The holders of approximately [*number*] outstanding shares of the Company's existing common stock received, in exchange for their shares, [*percent*]% of the new outstanding voting common stock of the Company.

Example 2–98: Petition for Relief under Chapter 11

On February 13, 20X2, ABC Company (the Debtor) filed petitions for relief under Chapter 11 of the federal bankruptcy laws in the United States Bankruptcy Court for the Western District of Tennessee. Under Chapter 11, certain claims against the Debtor in existence prior to the filing of the petitions for relief under the federal bankruptcy laws are stayed while the Debtor continues business operations as Debtor-in-possession. These claims are reflected in the December 31, 20X2, Balance Sheet as "Liabilities subject to compromise." Additional claims (liabilities subject to compromise) may arise subsequent to the filing date resulting from rejection of executory contracts, including leases, and from the determination by the court (or agreed to by parties in interest) of allowed claims for contingencies and other disputed amounts. Claims secured against the Debtor's assets (secured claims) also are stayed, although the holders of such claims have the right to move the court for relief from the stay. Secured claims are secured primarily by liens on the Debtor's property, plant, and equipment.

The Debtor received approval from the Bankruptcy Court to pay or otherwise honor certain of its prepetition obligations, including employee wages and product warranties. The Debtor has determined that there is insufficient collateral to cover the interest portion of scheduled payments on its prepetition debt obligations. Contractual interest on those obligations amounts to $[*amount*], which is $[*amount*] in excess of reported interest expense; therefore, the Debtor has discontinued accruing interest on these obligations.

Research and Development Costs

Example 2–99: Research and Development Costs Expensed

Research, development, and engineering costs are expensed in the year incurred. For 20X2 these costs were $2,050,000 and for 20X1 they were $1,100,000.

Example 2–100: Product Development Costs Deferred

The Company defers certain costs related to the preliminary activities associated with the manufacture of its products, which the Company has determined have future economic benefit. These costs are then expensed in the period in which the initial shipment of the related product is made. Management periodically reviews and revises, when necessary, its estimate of the future benefit of these costs and expenses them if it is deemed there no longer is a future benefit. At December 31, 20X2, and December 31, 20X1, capitalized product development costs totaled $611,000 and $523,000, respectively.

Example 2–101: Capitalized Costs of Computer Software to Be Sold, Leased, or Otherwise Marketed

Research and development costs are charged to expense as incurred. However, the costs incurred for the development of computer software that will be sold, leased, or otherwise marketed are capitalized when technological feasibility has been established. These capitalized costs are subject to an ongoing assessment of recoverability based on anticipated future revenues and changes in hardware and software technologies. Costs that are capitalized include direct labor and related overhead.

Amortization of capitalized software development costs begins when the product is available for general release. Amortization is provided on a product-by-product basis on either the straight-line method over periods not exceeding two years or the sales ratio method. Unamortized capitalized software development costs determined to be in excess of net realizable value of the product are expensed immediately.

> **Note:** For additional disclosure examples relating to computer software, see Chapter 8, "Computer Software."

Restricted Funds

Example 2–102: Restricted Funds Held by Trustees

Restricted funds held by trustees of $1,300,000 and $900,000 at December 31, 20X2 and 20X1, respectively, are included in other

non-current assets and consist principally of funds deposited in connection with plant closure obligations, insurance escrow deposits,
and amounts held for new plant and other construction arising from
industrial revenue financing. These amounts are principally
invested in fixed income securities of federal, state, and local governmental entities and financial institutions. The Company considers such trustee-restricted investments to be held to maturity. At
December 31, 20X2, and December 31, 20X1, the aggregate fair value
of these investments approximates their amortized costs, and substantially all of these investments mature within one year.

Example 2–103: Investments Restricted for Construction Financing

Restricted investments consist of U.S. governmental obligations
with maturities of more than one year. These investments are carried at fair value and are restricted as to withdrawal for construction financing. Restricted investments are held in the Company's
name and custodied with two major financial institutions.

Example 2–104: Restricted Cash Included in Other Non-Current Assets

At December 31, 20X2, other non-current assets included restricted
cash of $1,200,000 pledged to support a bank credit facility. At
December 31, 20X1, restricted cash balances of $2,450,000 repre-
sented amounts pledged to support bank guarantees issued on several large construction contracts.

Revenue Recognition

*Example 2–105: Sales Recorded When Products Are Shipped, with
Appropriate Provisions for Discounts and Returns*

Sales are recorded when products are shipped to customers. Provisions for discounts and rebates to customers, estimated returns and
allowances, and other adjustments are provided for in the same
period the related sales are recorded. In instances where products
are configured to customer requirements, revenue is recorded upon
the successful completion of the Company's final test procedures
and the customer's acceptance.

Example 2–106: Revenue from Service Contracts

The Company recognizes revenue on service contracts ratably over
applicable contract periods or as services are performed. Amounts
billed and collected before the services are performed are included
in deferred revenues.

Example 2–107: Contract Revenue Recognized on the Percentage-of-Completion Method

The Company recognizes engineering and construction contract revenues using the percentage-of-completion method, based primarily on contract costs incurred to date compared with total estimated contract costs. Customer-furnished materials, labor, and equipment, and in certain cases subcontractor materials, labor, and equipment, are included in revenues and cost of revenues when management believes that the company is responsible for the ultimate acceptability of the project. Contracts are segmented between types of services, such as engineering and construction, and accordingly, gross margin related to each activity is recognized as those separate services are rendered.

Changes to total estimated contract costs or losses, if any, are recognized in the period in which they are determined. Claims against customers are recognized as revenue upon settlement. Revenues recognized in excess of amounts billed are classified as current assets under contract work-in-progress. Amounts billed to clients in excess of revenues recognized to date are classified as current liabilities under advance billings on contracts.

Changes in project performance and conditions, estimated profitability, and final contract settlements may result in future revisions to construction contract costs and revenue.

Example 2–108: Right of Return and Price Protection Exist

Product revenue is generally recognized upon shipment to the customer. The Company grants certain distributors limited rights of return and price protection on unsold products. Product revenue on shipments to distributors that have rights of return and price protection is recognized upon shipment to customers by the distributor.

Example 2–109: Deferral of Certain Revenue and Gross Margins

Product sales are generally recognized upon shipment of product. However, the Company defers recognition of revenues and gross margin from sales to stocking distributors until such distributors resell the related products to their customers. The Company has deferred recognition of gross margin amounting to $4,000,000 and $3,500,000 as of December 31, 20X2, and December 31, 20X1, respectively.

Example 2–110: Warranty Contract Revenue

Warranty contract fees are recognized as revenues ratably over the life of the contract and the contract costs are expensed as incurred.

Example 2–111: Membership Fee Income

Revenue from membership fees is recognized at the end of the membership period (upon the expiration of the refund offer), because membership fees are fully refundable during the entire membership period.

Example 2–112: Revenue from Sales-Type and Operating Leases

Revenue from sales-type leases (primarily with terms of 60 months or greater) is recognized as a "sale" upon shipment in an amount equal to the present value of the minimum rental payments under the fixed non-cancelable lease term. The deferred finance charges applicable to these leases are recognized over the terms of the leases using the effective interest method.

The Company also leases equipment to customers under long-term operating leases (primarily leases with terms of 36 to 54 months), which are generally non-cancelable. Rental revenues are recognized as earned over the term of the lease.

Example 2–113: Revenue Relating to Consignment Method Sales

Revenues are recognized at the time the circuit boards are shipped to the customer, for both turnkey and consignment method sales. Under the consignment method, original equipment manufacturers provide the Company with the electronic components to be assembled, and the Company recognizes revenue only on the labor used to assemble the product.

Example 2–114: Income on Loans

Income on all loans is recognized on the interest method. Accrual of interest income is suspended at the earlier of the time at which collection of an account becomes doubtful or the account becomes 90 days delinquent. Interest income on impaired loans is recognized either as cash is collected or on a cost-recovery basis as conditions warrant.

Example 2–115: Revenue Recognition from Grants

The Company receives employment and research grants from various non-U.S. governmental agencies, and the grants are recognized in earnings in the period in which the related expenditures are incurred. Capital grants for the acquisition of equipment are recorded as reductions of the related equipment cost and reduce future depreciation expense.

Example 2–116: Revenue Is Recognized Only When Specified Criteria Are Met

The Company recognizes revenue only when all of the following criteria have been met:

- Persuasive evidence of an arrangement exists;
- Delivery has occurred or services have been rendered;
- The fee for the arrangement is fixed or determinable; and
- Collectibility is reasonably assured.

Persuasive Evidence of an Arrangement—The Company documents all terms of an arrangement in a written contract signed by the customer prior to recognizing revenue.

Delivery Has Occurred or Services Have Been Performed—The Company performs all services or delivers all products prior to recognizing revenue. Monthly services are considered to be performed ratably over the term of the arrangement. Professional consulting services are considered to be performed when the services are complete. Equipment is considered delivered upon delivery to a customer's designated location.

The Fee for the Arrangement is Fixed or Determinable—Prior to recognizing revenue, a customer's fee is either fixed or determinable under the terms of the written contract. Fees for most monthly services, professional consulting services, and equipment sales and rentals are fixed under the terms of the written contract. Fees for certain monthly services, including certain portions of networking, storage, and content distribution and caching services, are variable based on an objectively determinable factor such as usage. Those factors are included in the written contract such that the customer's fee is determinable. The customer's fee is negotiated at the outset of the arrangement and is not subject to refund or adjustment during the initial term of the arrangement.

Collectibility is Reasonably Assured—The Company determines that collectibility is reasonably assured prior to recognizing revenue. Collectibility is assessed on a customer by customer basis based on criteria outlined by management. New customers are subject to a credit review process, which evaluates the customer's financial position and ultimately its ability to pay. The Company does not enter into arrangements unless collectibility is reasonably assured at the outset. Existing customers are subject to ongoing credit evaluations based on payment history and other factors. If it is determined during the arrangement that collectibility is not reasonably assured, revenue is recognized on a cash basis.

Self-Insurance

Example 2–117: Self-Insured Claims Liability

The Company is primarily self-insured, up to certain limits, for automobile and general liability, workers' compensation, and employee group health claims. Operations are charged with the cost of claims reported and an estimate of claims incurred but not reported. A liability for unpaid claims and the associated claim expenses, including incurred but not reported losses, is actuarially determined and reflected in the balance sheet as an accrued liability. The self-insured claims liability includes incurred but not reported losses of $1,500,000 and $1,745,000 at December 31, 20X2, and December 31, 20X1, respectively. The determination of such claims and expenses and the appropriateness of the related liability is continually reviewed and updated.

Example 2–118: Self-Insured Health Plan Supplemented by Stop-Loss Insurance

The Company has a self-insured health plan for all its employees. The Company has purchased stop-loss insurance in order to limit its exposure, which will reimburse the Company for individual claims in excess of $50,000 annually or aggregate claims exceeding $1,000,000 annually. Self-insurance losses are accrued based on the Company's estimates of the aggregate liability for uninsured claims incurred using certain actuarial assumptions followed in the insurance industry. At December 31, 20X2 and December 31, 20X1, the accrued liability for self-insured losses is included in accrued expenses and approximates $1,300,000 and $900,000, respectively.

Shareholders' Equity

Example 2–119: Stock Split

In June 20X2, the board of directors approved a three-for-two stock split of the Corporation's common stock effected in the form of a 100% stock dividend, which was distributed on September 10, 20X2, to shareholders of record on August 20, 20X2. Shareholders' equity, common stock, and stock option activity for all periods presented have been restated to give retroactive recognition to the stock split. In addition, all references in the financial statements and notes to financial statements, to weighted average number of shares, per share amounts, and market prices of the Company's common stock have been restated to give retroactive recognition to the stock split.

Example 2–120: Stock Repurchase Program

In January 20X2, the Company's Board of Directors approved a stock repurchase program whereby up to 25 million shares of common stock may be purchased from time to time at the discretion of management. As of December 31, 20X2, the Company had purchased 14,200,000 shares at a total cost of $28,500,000. The repurchased shares are held as treasury stock and are available for general corporate purposes.

Example 2–121: Treasury Shares

Common stock held in the Company's treasury has been recorded at cost.

Shipping and Handling Costs

Example 2–122: Shipping and Handling Costs Are Included in Cost of Sales

> **Note:** EITF Issue 00-10, *Accounting for Shipping and Handling Fees and Costs,* indicates that if shipping and handling costs are significant and are **not** included in costs of sales, then disclosure is required of the amount of such costs and the line item in which they are included on the income statement. See Example 2–123 for appropriate disclosure when shipping and handling costs are not included in cost of sales.

The Company's shipping and handling costs are included in cost of sales for all periods presented.

Example 2–123: Shipping and Handling Costs Are Included in Selling, General and Administrative Expenses

> **Note:** EITF Issue 00-10, *Accounting for Shipping and Handling Fees and Costs,* indicates that if shipping and handling costs are significant and are *not* included in costs of sales, then disclosure is required of the amount of such costs and the line item in which they are included on the income statement.

Shipping and handling costs of $785,000 in 20X2 and $692,000 in 20X1 are included in selling, general, and administrative expenses.

Stock Option Plans

Example 2–124: Accounting Requirements of FAS-123/FAS-123R Have Not Been Adopted for Employee Stock Options

FASB Statement of Financial Accounting Standards No. 123, *Accounting for Stock-Based Compensation*, encourages, but does not require, companies to record compensation cost for stock-based employee compensation plans based on the fair value of options granted. The Company has elected to continue to account for stock-based compensation using the intrinsic value method prescribed in Accounting Principles Board Opinion No. 25 (Accounting for Stock Issued to Employees) and related interpretations and to provide additional disclosures with respect to the pro forma effects of adoption had the Company recorded compensation expense as provided in FAS-123 (see Note [X]).

In accordance with APB-25, compensation cost for stock options is recognized in income based on the excess, if any, of the quoted market price of the stock at the grant date of the award or other measurement date over the amount an employee must pay to acquire the stock. Generally, the exercise price for stock options granted to employees equals or exceeds the fair market value of the Company's common stock at the date of grant, thereby resulting in no recognition of compensation expense by the Company.

Example 2–125: Accounting Requirements of FAS-123/FAS-123R Have Been Adopted for Employee Stock Options

The Company has adopted the fair value based method of accounting prescribed in FASB Statement of Financial Accounting Standards No. 123 (*Accounting for Stock-Based Compensation*)/No. 123R (Share-Based Payment) for its employee stock option plans.

Warranty Costs

Example 2–126: Accrual for Warranty Costs Is Made in the Period in Which the Revenue Is Recognized

The Company provides product warranties for specific product lines and accrues for estimated future warranty costs in the period in which the revenue is recognized.

Example 2–127: Accrual for Warranty Costs Is Made When Such Costs Become Probable

Provision for estimated warranty costs is made in the period in which such costs become probable and is periodically adjusted to reflect actual experience.

Example 2–128: Product Warranty Policy and Period Described

The Company warrants its products against defects in design, materials, and workmanship generally for three to five years. A provision for estimated future costs relating to warranty expense is recorded when products are shipped.

Example 2–129: Warranty Costs Are Subject to Significant Estimates

The Company's warranty accruals are based on the Company's best estimates of product failure rates and unit costs to repair. However, the Company is continually releasing new and more complex and technologically advanced products. As a result, it is at least reasonably possible that products could be released with certain unknown quality and/or design problems. Such an occurrence could result in materially higher than expected warranty and related costs, which could have a materially adverse effect on the Company's results of operations and financial condition in the near term.

CHAPTER 3
ADVERTISING COSTS

CONTENTS

EXECUTIVE SUMMARY

In most cases, the costs of advertising should be expensed as incurred or the first time the advertisement occurs. However, there are two exceptions to this general rule:

1. Certain direct-response advertising costs should be capitalized and amortized over the period during which the future benefits or sales are expected to be received. For direct-response advertising where (a) it can be shown that customers responded to a specific advertisement, and (b) there is a probable future economic benefit, only the following two types of costs should be capitalized:

— Incremental direct costs incurred in transactions with independent third parties (e.g., idea development, writing advertising copy, artwork, printing, magazine space, and mailing).

— Payroll and payroll-related costs for employees who are directly associated with the direct-response advertising activities. Items such as administrative costs, rent, and depreciation should not be included in the capitalized advertising costs.

2. Expenditures for advertising costs that are made subsequent to recognizing revenues related to those costs should be capitalized and charged to expense when the related revenues are recognized. For example, some entities assume an obligation to reimburse their customers for some or all of the customers' advertising costs (cooperative advertising). Generally, revenues related to the transactions creating those obligations are earned and recognized before the expenditures are made. Those obligations should be accrued and the advertising costs expensed when the related revenues are recognized.

An entity should periodically assess the realizability of the advertising costs that remain capitalized by comparing the carrying amounts, on a cost-pool-by-cost-pool basis, to the probable remaining future net revenues expected to result directly from such advertising. If the carrying amounts exceed the remaining future net revenues, the excess should be reported as advertising expense of the current period.

Authoritative Literature

SOP 93-7	Reporting on Advertising Costs
EITF 99-17	Accounting for Advertising Barter Transactions
PB-13	Direct-Response Advertising and Probable Future Benefits

DISCLOSURE REQUIREMENTS

The financial statements should include the following disclosures about advertising costs:

1. For direct-response advertising (SOP 93-7, par. 49):
   a. A description of the direct-response advertising reported as assets, if any
   b. The accounting policy being followed
   c. The amortization period

2. For non-direct response advertising costs, whether such costs are expensed as incurred or the first time the advertising takes place (SOP 93-7, par. 49)

3. The total amount charged to advertising expense for each income statement presented, with separate disclosure of amounts, if any, representing a writedown to net realizable value (SOP 93-7, par. 49)

4. The total amount of advertising costs reported as assets in each balance sheet presented (SOP 93-7, par. 49)

5. The amount of revenue and expense recognized from advertising barter transactions for each income statement period presented (EITF 99-17, par. 8). Entities providing advertising in barter transactions that do not qualify for recognition at fair value under EITF 99-17 should disclose for each income statement presented the volume and type of advertising provided and received, such as the number of equivalent pages, number of minutes, or the overall percentage of advertising volume.

EXAMPLES OF FINANCIAL STATEMENT DISCLOSURES

 The following sample disclosures are available on the accompanying disc.

Example 3–1: Advertising Costs Are Expensed as Incurred

Advertising costs are expensed as incurred. Advertising expense totaled $477,000 for 20X2 and $392,000 for 20X1.

Example 3–2: Advertising Costs Are Expensed the First Time the Advertising Takes Place

Production costs of future media advertising are expensed the first time the advertising takes place. Advertising expense totaled $532,000 for 20X2 and $410,000 for 20X1.

Example 3–3: Direct-Response Advertising Costs Are Capitalized

Direct-response advertising costs, consisting primarily of catalog book production, printing, and postage costs, are capitalized and amortized over the expected life of the catalog, not to exceed six months. Direct-response advertising costs reported as "Prepaid assets" are $275,000 and $350,000 at December 31, 20X2, and December 31, 20X1, respectively. Total advertising expenses were $1,900,000 and $1,600,000 in 20X2 and 20X1, respectively.

*Example 3–4: Certain Advertising Costs Are Expensed the First Time
the Advertising Takes Place, and Direct-Response Advertising Costs Are
Capitalized and Written Down to Net Realizable Value*

The Company expenses the production costs of advertising the first
time the advertising takes place, except for direct-response advertising, which is capitalized and amortized over its expected period of
future benefits.

Direct-response advertising consists primarily of magazine
advertisements that include order coupons for the Company's products. The capitalized costs of the advertising are amortized over the
six-month period following the publication of the magazine in
which it appears.

At December 31, 20X2, and December 31, 20X1, capitalized direct-
response advertising costs of $570,000 and $612,000, respectively,
were included in "Other assets" in the accompanying Balance
Sheets. Advertising expense was $5,264,000 in 20X2, including
$432,000 for amounts written down to net realizable value related to
certain capitalized direct-response advertising costs. Advertising
expense was $6,079,000 in 20X1.

Example 3–5: Advertising Barter Transactions

In 20X2 and 20X1, the Company entered into barter agreements
whereby it delivered $1,165,000 and $1,059,000, respectively, of its
inventory in exchange for future advertising credits and other items.
The credits, which expire in November 20X3, are valued at the lower
of the Company's cost or market value of the inventory transferred.
The Company has recorded barter credits of $115,000 and $236,000
in "Prepaid expenses and other current assets" at December 31,
20X2, and December 31, 20X1, respectively. At December 31, 20X2,
and December 31, 20X1, "Other noncurrent assets" include $279,000
and $323,000, respectively, of such credits. Under the terms of the
barter agreements, the Company is required to pay cash equal to a
negotiated amount of the bartered advertising, or other items, and
use the barter credits to pay the balance. These credits are charged
to expense as they are used. During the years ended December 31,
20X2, and December 31, 20X1, approximately $1,080,000 and
$751,000, respectively, were charged to expense for barter credits
used.

The Company assesses the recoverability of barter credits periodically. Factors considered in evaluating the recoverability include
management's plans with respect to advertising and other expenditures for which barter credits can be used. Any impairment losses
are charged to operations as they are determinable. During the years
ended December 31, 20X2, and December 31, 20X1, the Company
charged $250,000 and $425,000, respectively, to operations for such
impairment losses.

Example 3–6: Advertising Policy on Other Companies' Web Sites Pursuant to Contracts Is Explained

The Company expenses the costs of advertising as incurred. Typically the Company purchases banner advertising on other companies' web sites pursuant to contracts which have one-to-three year terms and may include the guarantee of (1) a minimum number of impressions, (2) the number of times that an advertisement appears in pages displayed to users of the web site, or (3) a minimum amount of revenue that will be recognized by the Company from customers directed to the Company's Web site as a direct result of the advertisement. The Company recognizes expense with respect to such advertising ratably over the period in which the advertisement is displayed. In addition, some agreements require additional payments as additional impressions are delivered. Such payments are expensed when the impressions are delivered.

In one case, the Company entered into an agreement for an unspecified number of years. In this case, the Company amortizes as expense the lesser of (1) the number of impressions to date/minimum guaranteed impressions or (2) revenue to date/minimum guaranteed revenue as a percentage of the total payments.

For the years ended December 31, 20X2 and December 31, 20X1, advertising expense totaled approximately $8,325,000 and $9,890,000, respectively.

CHAPTER 4
BUSINESS COMBINATIONS

CONTENTS

EXECUTIVE SUMMARY

Note: The FASB has issued the following two Exposure Drafts (EDs) of proposed accounting standards relating to consolidated financial statements and business combinations:

1. Proposed Statement of Financial Accounting Standards (FAS), *Consolidated Financial Statements, Including Accounting and Reporting of Noncontrolling Interests in Subsidiaries.* The proposed standard would replace ARB No. 51, *Consolidated Financial Statements,* and provides guidance on preparing consolidated financial statements, including the treatment of noncontrolling interests in subsidiaries (i.e., minority interests) in these consolidated statements. The major change in the proposed standard relates to the treatment of noncontrolling interests in subsidiaries, including how a parent is to account for a loss of control in a subsidiary.

2. Proposed Statement of Financial Accounting Standards (FAS), *Business Combinations.* The proposed standard would require the recognition of a business combination at fair value, including recognizing goodwill that pertains to the ownership interest of noncontrolling (minority) shareholders. In addition, professional fees associated with the consummation of a business combination would no longer be capitalized as part of the acquisition cost, but instead be expensed as incurred. FAS-141, *Business Combinations,* will be replaced if this proposed standard is adopted.

Readers should be alert to further developments in this area.

A *business combination* occurs when an entity (including a new entity formed to complete a business combination) acquires:

1. Net assets that constitute a business (commonly referred to as an *asset acquisition*), or

2. Equity interests of one or more other entities and obtains *control* over that entity or entities (commonly referred to as a *stock acquisition*). Control is generally indicated by ownership by one company, directly or indirectly, of over 50% of the outstanding voting shares of another company.

All business combinations should be accounted for using the purchase method. Under the purchase method of accounting, the purchase price should be allocated to the assets acquired and the liabilities assumed as follows:

1. Assets and liabilities should be recorded at their fair values as of the acquisition date, including intangible assets that meet one of the following criteria:

    a. The intangible assets arise from contractual or other legal rights; those rights do not have to be transferable or separable from the acquired entity or from other rights and obligations

    b. The intangible assets can be separated or divided from the acquired entity, and can be sold, transferred, licensed, rented, or exchanged (regardless of whether there is an intent to do so)

2. If the cost of the acquired company exceeds the sum of the amounts assigned to the assets acquired and liabilities assumed, the excess should be recorded as goodwill. An acquired intangible asset that does not meet the criteria in item 1 above should be aggregated and included in the amount recognized as goodwill. Also, the acquiring company should not record as a separate asset any goodwill previously recorded by the acquired company.

3. If the values assigned to the assets acquired and liabilities assumed exceed the cost of the acquired company, that excess (sometimes referred to as negative goodwill) should be allocated as a pro rata reduction of the amounts that otherwise would have been assigned to all of the acquired assets. However, this allocation should exclude the following items:

    a. Financial assets other than equity method investments

    b. Assets to be disposed of by sale

    c. Deferred tax assets

    d. Prepaid assets relating to pension or other postretirement benefit plans

    e. Any other current assets

If any excess remains after reducing those assets to zero, that remaining excess should be recognized as an extraordinary gain.

Authoritative Literature

ARB-43	Chapter 1A, Rules Adopted by Membership
ARB-51	Consolidated Financial Statements
FAS-87	Employers' Accounting for Pensions

FAS-106	Employers' Accounting for Postretirement Benefits Other Than Pensions
FAS-109	Accounting for Income Taxes
FAS-141	Business Combinations
FIN-4	Applicability of FASB Statement No. 2 to Business Combinations Accounted for by the Purchase Method
FTB 85-5	Issues Relating to Accounting for Business Combinations
EITF 95-3	Recognition of Liabilities in Connection with a Purchase Business Combination
EITF 04-1	Accounting For Preexisting Relationships between the Parties to a Business Combination

DISCLOSURE REQUIREMENTS

1. The following disclosures should be made in the period in which a material business combination is completed (FAS-141, par. 51):

    a. The name and a brief description of the acquired entity

    b. The percentage of voting equity interests acquired

    c. The primary reasons for the acquisition, including a description of the factors that contributed to a purchase price that results in recognition of goodwill

    d. The period for which the results of operations of the acquired entity are included in the combined entity's income statement

    e. The cost of the acquired entity and, if applicable, the number of shares of equity interests (e.g., common shares) issued or issuable, the value assigned to those interests, and the basis for determining that value

    f. A condensed balance sheet disclosing the amount assigned to each major asset and liability caption of the acquired entity at the acquisition date

    g. Contingent payments, options, or commitments specified in the acquisition agreement and the accounting treatment that will be followed should any such contingency occur

    h. The amount of purchased research and development assets acquired and written off in the period and the income statement line item in which the amounts written off are aggregated

    i. If the purchase price allocation has not been finalized, that fact and the reasons therefor

2. If material adjustments are made in the current period to the initial allocation of the purchase price recorded in prior periods, the nature and amount of such adjustments should be disclosed (FAS-141, par. 51).

3. If the amounts assigned to goodwill or to other intangible assets acquired are significant to the total cost of the acquired entity, the following disclosures should be made (FAS-141, par. 52):

   a. For intangible assets subject to amortization: the amount, residual value, and weighted-average amortization period, in total and by major intangible asset class

   b. For intangible assets not subject to amortization: the total amount assigned, and the amount assigned to any major intangible asset class

   c. The total amount of goodwill and the amount expected to be deductible for tax purposes

   d. The amount of goodwill by reportable segment, if the combined entity is required to disclose segment information in accordance with FAS-131 (Disclosures about Segments of an Enterprise and Related Information), unless not practical

4. If a series of individually immaterial business combinations were completed during the period are material in the aggregate, the following disclosures should be made (FAS-141, par. 53):

   a. The number of entities acquired and a brief description of those entities

   b. The aggregate cost of the acquired entities, the number of equity interests (e.g., common shares) issued or issuable, and the value assigned to those interests

   c. The aggregate amount of any contingent payments, options, or commitments and the accounting treatment that will be followed should any such contingency occur (if potentially significant to the aggregate cost of the acquired entities)

   d. If the aggregate amount assigned to goodwill or to other intangible assets acquired is significant to the aggregate cost of the acquired entities, the information described in item 3 above should be disclosed

5. If the combined entity is publicly held (optional for nonpublic companies), the following supplemental information should be disclosed for the period in which a material business combination occurs (or if a series of individually immaterial business combinations occur that are material in the aggregate) (FAS-141, pars. 54–55):

   a. Pro forma results of operations for the current period as though the companies had combined at the beginning of the period, unless the acquisition was at or near the beginning of the period

   b. If comparative statements are presented, pro forma results of operations for the immediately preceding period as though the companies had combined at the beginning of that period

   c. On a pro forma basis, at a minimum: revenue; income before extraordinary items and the cumulative effect of accounting changes; net income; and earnings per share

   d. The nature and amount of any material, nonrecurring items included in the reported pro forma results of operations

6. If an extraordinary gain is recognized related to a business combination, the information required by paragraph 11 of APB-30 should be disclosed (FAS-141, par. 56). See Chapter 51, "Extraordinary Items," for further discussion.

7. If a material business combination is completed after the balance-sheet date but before the financial statements are issued, the information in items 1 through 3 above should be disclosed, unless not practicable (FAS-141, par. 57).

8. The following disclosures should be made in the interim financial information of a publicly held entity (optional for nonpublic companies), if a material business combination is completed during the interim period (FAS-141, par. 58):

   a. The name and a brief description of the acquired entity

   b. The percentage of voting equity interests acquired

   c. The primary reasons for the acquisition, including a description of the factors that contributed to a purchase price that results in recognition of goodwill

   d. The period for which the results of operations of the acquired entity are included in the combined entity's income statement

   e. The cost of the acquired entity and, if applicable, the number of shares of equity interests (e.g., common shares) issued or issuable, the value assigned to those interests, and the basis for determining that value

   f. Supplemental pro forma information that discloses the results of operations for the current interim period and the current year up to the date of the most recent interim balance sheet presented (and for the corresponding periods in the preceding year) as though the business combination had been completed as of the beginning of the period being reported on (**Note:** Pro forma information should disclose, at a minimum: revenue; income before extraordinary items and the cumulative effect of accounting changes; net income; and earnings per share)

g. The nature and amount of any material, nonrecurring items included in the reported pro forma results of operations

9. The following disclosures should be made for transfers of net assets or exchanges of shares between entities under common control (FAS-141, pars. D16-D18):

   a. The nature of, and effects on, earnings per share of nonrecurring intercompany transactions involving long-term assets and liabilities

   b. For the period in which the transfer of assets and liabilities or exchange of equity interests occurred:

      — The name and brief description of the entity included in the reporting entity as a result of the net asset transfer or exchange of equity interests

      — The method of accounting for the transfer of net assets or exchange of equity interests

10. The following disclosures should be made if a combined entity plans to incur costs from exiting an activity of an acquired entity, involuntarily terminating employees of an acquired entity, or relocating employees of an acquired entity and the activities of the acquired entity that will not be continued are significant to the combined entity's revenues or operating results or the cost recognized from those activities as of the consummation date are material to the combined entity (EITF 95-3, pars. 13a-b):

    a. For the period in which a purchase business combination occurs:

       — When the plans to exit an activity or involuntarily terminate or relocate employees of the acquired entity are not final as of the balance-sheet date, a description of any unresolved issues, the types of additional liabilities that may result in an adjustment to the purchase price allocation, and how any adjustment will be reported

       — A description of the type and amount of liabilities assumed in the purchase price allocation for costs to exit an activity or involuntarily terminate or relocate employees

- A description of the major actions that make up the plan to exit an activity or involuntarily terminate or relocate employees of an acquired entity
- A description of activities of the acquired entity that will not be continued, including the method of disposition, and the anticipated date of completion and description of employee groups to be terminated or relocated

b. For all periods presented subsequent to the acquisition date in which a purchase business combination occurred, until a plan to exit an activity or involuntarily terminate or relocate employees of an acquired entity is fully executed:

- A description of the type and amount of exit costs, involuntary employee termination costs, and relocation costs paid and charged against the liability
- The amount of any adjustments to the liability account and whether the corresponding entry was an adjustment of the costs of the acquired entity or included in the determination of net income for the period

11. The following disclosures should be made for business combinations between parties with a preexisting relationship (EITF 04-1, par. 8):

a. The nature of the preexisting relationship

b. The settlement amount of the preexisting relationship, if any, and the valuation method used to determine that amount

c. The amount of any settlement gain or loss recognized and its income statement classification

EXAMPLES OF FINANCIAL STATEMENT DISCLOSURES

 The following sample disclosures are available on the accompanying disc. For examples of financial statement disclosures relating to consolidated and combined financial statements, see Chapter 9, "Consolidated and Combined Financial Statements."

Example 4–1: Material Business Combination

In August 20X2, the Company completed the purchase of MBK, Inc., a privately held manufacturer of industrial computer systems and enclosures, by acquiring all of the outstanding capital stock of MBK, Inc. for a total purchase price of $24 million. MBK, Inc.'s results of operations have been included in the consolidated financial statements since the date of acquisition. As a result of the acquisition, the Company is expected to (1) be the leading manufacturer of industrial computer systems and enclosures in Canada and Mexico and (2) reduce costs through economies of scale.

The aggregate purchase price of $24 million consisted of $15 million in cash and common stock valued at $9 million. The value of the 360,000 common shares issued was determined based on the average market price of the Company's common shares over the 2-day period before and after the terms of the acquisition were agreed to and announced.

The following table presents the allocation of the acquisition cost, including professional fees and other related acquisition costs, to the assets acquired and liabilities assumed, based on their fair values:

Cash and cash equivalents	$ 1,000,000
Accounts receivable	4,000,000
Inventories	7,000,000
Other current assets	3,000,000
Property, plant, and equipment	6,000,000
Intangible assets	10,000,000
Goodwill	5,000,000
Total assets acquired	36,000,000
Amounts payable to banks and long-term debt due within one year	(4,000,000)
Other current liabilities	(5,000,000)
Long-term accrued liabilities	(1,000,000)
Long-term debt	(2,000,000)
Total liabilities assumed	(12,000,000)
Net assets acquired	$ 24,000,000

Of the $10 million of acquired intangible assets, $5 million was assigned to registered trademarks that are not subject to amortization and $2 million was assigned to research and development assets that were written off at the date of acquisition in accordance with FASB Interpretation No. 4, *Applicability of FASB Statement No. 2 to Business Combinations Accounted for by the Purchase Method.* Those write-offs are included in general and administrative expenses. The remaining $3 million of acquired intangible assets have a weighted-average useful life of approximately 4 years. The intangible assets that make up that amount include: computer software of $1.6 million (3-year weighted-average useful life), patents of $900,000 (7-year weighted-average useful life), and other assets of $500,000 (5-year weighted-average useful life).

The $5 million of goodwill was assigned to the technology and communications segments in the amounts of $3 million and $2 million, respectively. Of that total amount, $600,000 is expected to be deductible for tax purposes.

The allocation of the purchase price is based on preliminary data and could change when final valuation of certain intangible assets is obtained.

Example 4–2: Supplemental Disclosure of Pro Forma Information

> **Note:** The following supplemental disclosure of pro forma information is required only for publicly-held entities (optional for nonpublic entities). If the pro forma effects are not material, the pro forma information presented below should be replaced with the following sentence: "The pro forma effects of the MBK, Inc. acquisition on the Company's consolidated financial statements were not material."

The following (unaudited) pro forma consolidated results of operations have been prepared as if the acquisition of MBK, Inc. had occurred at January 1, 20X1:

	December 31, 20X2	December 31, 20X1
Sales	$79,000,000	$64,000,000
Net income	8,200,000	3,600,000
Net income per share—Basic	1.86	0.82
Net income per share—Diluted	1.58	0.70

The pro forma information is presented for informational purposes only and is not necessarily indicative of the results of operations that actually would have been achieved had the acquisition been consummated as of that time, nor is it intended to be a projection of future results.

Example 4–3: Exchange of Investment Accounted for on the Equity Method for a Majority Ownership in an Unrelated Entity

On October 15, 20X2, the Company exchanged its 45% interest in Eagle, Co. for 91% of the common stock of Boiler, Co. On that same date, pursuant to a "split-up" of Eagle, Co. structured for tax purposes as a tax-free reorganization under the Internal Revenue Code,

Boiler, Co. received 100% of the machining operations of Eagle, Co. The Company has accounted for this transaction under the purchase method of accounting. Accordingly, the carrying value of the Company's equity investment in Eagle, Co., totaling $8,000,000 at October 15, 20X2, was treated as the purchase price for accounting purposes. The assets acquired by Boiler, Co. included substantially all of the real estate and equipment owned by Eagle, Co. in Cleveland, Ohio and used in the machining and boiler assembly operations and certain other assets and liabilities.

Example 4–4: Exercise of Conversion Option on Preferred Stock Results in Consolidation of Investment Previously Accounted for on the Cost Basis

Prior to 20X2, the Company accounted for its investment in the preferred stock of Oslo, Inc. on the cost basis. Effective October 1, 20X2, the Company exercised its conversion option on its 500,000 shares of Series A 4% Participating Convertible Preferred Stock and as a result is now the record holder of 2,000,000 shares (89%) of the voting stock of Oslo, Inc. The conversion was accounted for using the purchase method of accounting; accordingly, the consolidated results of the Company include the results of Oslo, Inc. since the date of the conversion. Oslo, Inc. is a leading supplier of laboratory instruments and related products.

The unaudited pro forma information that follows was prepared assuming that the conversion had taken place January 1, 20X1. In preparing the pro form a financial information, various assumptions were made; therefore, the Company does not imply that the future results will be indicative of the following pro forma information:

	December 31, 20X2	December 31, 20X1
Sales	$65,000,000	$52,000,000
Net income	6,200,000	2,600,000
Net income per share—Basic	1.16	0.81
Net income per share—Diluted	1.02	0.75

The Company received, prior to the conversion, and recognized as income in 20X2 $1,200,000 in Preferred Stock cash dividends from Oslo, Inc.

Example 4–5: Amount Initially Assigned to Goodwill Subsequently Revised

In October 20X1, the Company acquired XDEG, Inc., a leading provider of health care information products. The Company issued 3,000,000 shares of common stock and 700,000 common stock options, with a total fair value of $35,000,000, in exchange for all outstanding shares of XDEG, Inc. The Company accounted for the acquisition using the purchase method of accounting for business combinations. The purchase price and costs associated with the acquisition exceeded the preliminary estimated fair value of net assets acquired by $10,200,000, which was preliminarily assigned to goodwill.

During 20X2, the Company completed the valuation of the intangible assets acquired in the XDEG, Inc. transaction. Pursuant to the valuation, the Company expensed $4,400,000 of the excess purchase price representing purchased in-process technology that previously had been assigned to goodwill. In management's judgment, this amount reflects the amount the Company would reasonably expect to pay an unrelated party for each project included in the technology. The value of in-process research and development of $4,400,000 represented approximately 37% of the purchase price and was determined by estimating the costs to develop the purchased technology into commercially viable products, then estimating the resulting net cash flows from each project that was incomplete at the acquisition date, and discounting the resulting net cash flows to their present value. The $4,400,000 charge is included as a component of "Other charges" in the accompanying Consolidated Statements of Operations for the year ended December 31, 20X2. Based on the final valuation, the remaining excess purchase price of $5,800,000 was assigned to existing technologies, trade names, and goodwill.

Example 4–6: Additional Purchase Price Payments Subsequently Made for Achieving Specified Levels of Profitability

During 20X2, the Company paid $13 million to the former owners of businesses acquired in previous years. These payments resulted from the acquired businesses having achieved specified levels of profitability during designated periods subsequent to the acquisition. These payments were recorded as additional goodwill.

Example 4–7: Business Combination Pending Government and Shareholder Approval

In November 20X2, the Company signed a definitive agreement to purchase ESY, Inc., a provider of programmable switches. Under the terms of the agreement, between 2,500,000 and 3,000,000 shares of the Company's common stock will be exchanged for all of the outstanding shares and options of ESY, Inc. The agreement is subject to the receipt of certain government approvals and the approval of ESY, Inc.'s shareholders. The deal is expected to be consummated in the first or second quarter of 20X3. The Company expects to account for the acquisition using the purchase method of accounting for business combinations. The historical operations of ESY, Inc. are not expected to be material to the financial position or results of operations of the Company.

Example 4–8: Adjustments Made to Previously Determined Values of Assets Acquired in Business Combination

On September 1, 20X1, the Company acquired the stock of Sibik, Ltd. for $27,000,000. Because Sibik, Ltd. was acquired late in 20X1 and was a complex operation, it required a comprehensive review of asset values and liabilities and a significant part of the evaluation had to take into consideration the integration of Sibik, Ltd. The final assessment of asset values, restructuring the manufacturing and marketing organization, and making other necessary changes was not completed until the second quarter of 20X2. The determination of the final fair values resulted in adjustments, made in 20X2, consisting of changes from initially determined values as of September 1, 20X1, as follows:

Increase in goodwill	$ 1,300,000
Increase in property and equipment	2,100,000
Increase in other assets	400,000
Decrease in inventory	(2,800,000)
Decrease in accounts receivable	(1,000,000)

Example 4–9: Company to Indemnify Prior Owners of Acquired Business for Certain Liabilities

As part of the Company's purchase of certain business operations of Mastol, Inc., the Company agreed to indemnify Mastol, Inc. for certain liabilities that may arise from events that occurred during Mastol's ownership. As this contingency is resolved and if additional consideration is paid, the amount of such payments will be recorded as additional cost of the acquired business and will increase the amount of goodwill recorded for this acquisition.

Example 4–10: Several Individually Immaterial Business Combinations That Are Material in the Aggregate

In the last quarter of 20X2, the Company acquired the following four entities for a total cost of $6,200,000, which was paid primarily in cash:

- Lillo, Inc., based in Victoria, Canada, a leading provider of telecommunications consulting services.
- Fernex Corp., based in Seattle, Washington, a start-up data networking company.
- Drexxel, Inc., based in San Jose, California, a producer of digital networking technology.
- PBC, Ltd., based in Sydney, Australia, a designer and manufacturer of wireless communications networks.

Goodwill recognized in those transactions amounted to $2,300,000 and that amount is expected to be fully deductible for tax purposes. Goodwill was assigned to the communication and technology segments in the amounts of $1,600,000 and $700,000, respectively.

The Company's Consolidated Financial Statements include the operating results of each business from the date of acquisition. In connection with the acquisition of Fernex Corp., the Company may be required to pay certain additional amounts of up to $1,200,000, payable in common stock and to be accounted for under the purchase method, contingent upon the Company achieving certain agreed-upon technology and other milestones.

Example 4–11: Research and Development Costs Acquired in a Business Combination Are Capitalized

In October 20X2, the Company purchased the Chickadee division from Seliga & Co., a provider of data networking products and services in the United States, for $9,000,000 in cash. Chickadee's results of operations have been included in the consolidated financial statements since that date. As a result of the acquisition, the Company is expected to (1) be the leading provider of data networking products and services in the United States and (2) reduce costs through economies of scale. Under the terms of the agreement, the Company purchased the Chickadee division, its accounts and notes receivable and tooling equipment, and assumed certain liabilities. The company also incurred $500,000 of direct, acquisition-related costs, which were capitalized as part of the purchase price.

The purchase price exceeded the fair values of the net assets acquired by $3,200,000. Of this amount, $1,325,000 was assigned to "Purchased in-process research and development," which is being amortized on the straight-line method over the estimated remaining lives of individual projects, ranging from two to five years. The amounts charged to these projects include only costs of materials, equipment, and facilities that the Company deems to have future benefit. The remainder of the excess purchase price, amounting to $1,875,000, was recorded as goodwill and assigned to the technology segment. Of that amount, $300,000 is expected to be deductible for tax purposes.

The following table presents the allocation of the purchase price, including related acquisition costs, to the assets acquired and liabilities assumed based on their fair values at the date of acquisition:

Accounts receivable	$2,250,000
Notes receivable	750,000
Tooling equipment	4,900,000
Purchased in-process research and development	1,325,000
Goodwill	1,875,000
Total assets acquired	11,100,000
Accounts payable	(1,000,000)
Accrued liabilities	(600,000)
Total liabilities assumed	(1,600,000)
Net assets acquired	$9,500,000

Example 4–12: Research and Development Costs Acquired in a Business Combination Are Expensed

"Purchased in-process research and development" expense in the 20X2 Statement of Operations represents the value assigned to research and development projects in a purchase business combination of the Chickadee brand from Seliga & Co. These projects were commenced but not yet completed at the date of acquisition; technological feasibility for these projects has not been established, and they have no alternative future use in research and development activities or otherwise. In accordance with FASB Statement of Financial Accounting Standards No. 2, *Accounting for Research and Development Costs*, as interpreted by FASB Interpretation No. 4, *Applicability of FASB Statement No. 2 to Business Combinations Accounted for by the Purchase Method*, amounts assigned to purchased in-process research and development meeting the above criteria must be charged to expense at the date of consummation of the purchase business combination. In 20X2, a charge of $1,325,000 was recorded for purchased in-process research and development costs in conjunction with this business combination, based on preliminary allocations of purchase price.

Example 4–13: Contingent Future Consideration in Connection With Business Combinations

In connection with certain acquisitions, the Company has agreed to pay additional consideration in future periods, based upon the attainment by the acquired entity of defined operating objectives. In accordance with FASB Statement of Financial Accounting Standards

No. 141, *Business Combinations*, the Company does not accrue contingent consideration obligations prior to the attainment of the objectives. At December 31, 20X2, maximum potential future consideration pursuant to such arrangements, to be resolved over the following six years, is $12 million. Any such payments would result in increases in goodwill.

Example 4–14: Subsequent Event—Business Combination

On January 29, 20X3, the Company completed its acquisition of Corpistat, Inc., a privately held manufacturer of medical diagnostic products. Under the terms of the Purchase Agreement, the Company issued approximately 7,000,000 shares of the Company's common stock and assumed or substituted options to purchase approximately 1,000,000 shares of the Company's common stock, in exchange for all outstanding equity of Corpistat.

The preliminary purchase price of Corpistat was approximately $16,150,000, consisting of the Company's common stock valued at approximately $14,950,000 and assumed or substituted options valued at approximately $1,200,0000, of which $800,000 will be allocated to deferred compensation. The value of the 7,000,000 shares of the Company's common stock issued was determined using the five-day average market price around the measurement date, October 20, 20X2 in accordance with EITF No. 99-12, *Determination of the Measurement Date for the Market Price of Acquirer Securities Issued in a Purchase Business Combination,* and FASB Statement of Financial Accounting Standards No. 141, *Business Combinations.* The value of the 1,000,000 options issued was calculated using a Black-Scholes model with the following assumptions: a volatility of 98.27%, a risk-free interest rate of 2.75%, and an expected life of 4.3 years. The calculation of the preliminary purchase price is subject to refinement.

The following table summarizes the estimated fair values of the assets acquired and liabilities assumed at the date of acquisition. The purchase price allocation herein is based on management's preliminary assessment of the fair value of both the assets acquired and liabilities assumed. The Company is in the process of obtaining a third-party valuation of certain intangible assets; thus, the allocation of the purchase price is subject to refinement.

	January 29, 20X3
Current assets	$15,480,000
Property, plant, and equipment	3,763,000
Other noncurrent assets	1,725,000

Identifiable intangible assets	2,675,000
Goodwill	12,857,000
Total assets acquired	36,500,000
Current liabilities	11,795,000
Other noncurrent liabilities	624,000
Long-term debt	8,731,000
Total liabilities assumed	21,150,000
Net assets acquired	$15,350,000
Deferred compensation component of purchase price	$ 800,000

Of the $2,675,000 of acquired identifiable intangible assets, $2,100,000 was assigned to customer relationships (estimated useful life of 6 years), $382,000 was assigned to developed technology (estimated useful life of 2 to 3 years), and $193,000 was assigned to trade names (estimated useful life of 3 years).

CHAPTER 5
CHANGING PRICES

CONTENTS

EXECUTIVE SUMMARY

Financial statements prepared in conformity with generally accepted accounting principles (GAAP) are based on the assumption of a stable monetary unit. That is, the assumption is made that the monetary unit used to convert all financial statement items into a common denominator (i.e., dollars) does not vary sufficiently over time so that distortions in the financial statements are material. Also, financial statements prepared in conformity with GAAP are primarily historical-cost based (i.e., the characteristic of most financial statement items that is measured and presented is the historical cost of the item).

Over the years, two approaches have been proposed and procedures developed to compensate for changes in the monetary unit and in the value of assets and liabilities after their acquisition. The two approaches are current value accounting and general price-level accounting. Current value accounting substitutes a measure of current value for historical cost as the primary measurement upon which the elements of financial statements are based. General price-level accounting adheres to historical cost but substitutes a current value of the dollar for historical dollars through the use of price indexes. Neither current value accounting nor general price-level accounting is required at the present time. However, procedures are established in the accounting literature for enterprises that choose to develop either general price-level or current value financial statements.

Authoritative Literature

FAS-89   Financial Reporting and Changing Prices

DISCLOSURE REQUIREMENTS

The following are the disclosure requirements for companies that elect to disclose supplementary information on the effects of changing prices (the disclosures are currently voluntary):

1. For each of the five most recent years, disclosures should include (FAS-89, par. 7):

   a. Net sales and other operating revenues

   b. Income from continuing operations on a current cost basis

   c. Purchasing power gain or loss on net monetary items

   d. Increase or decrease in the current cost or lower recoverable amount of inventory and property, plant, and equipment, net of inflation

   e. The aggregate foreign currency translation adjustment on a current cost basis, if applicable

   f. Net assets at year-end on a current cost basis

   g. Income per common share from continuing operations on a current cost basis

   h. Cash dividends declared per common share

   i. Market price per common share at year-end

   j. The Consumer Price Index for all Urban Consumers (CPI-U) used for each year's current cost/constant purchasing power calculations

   k. If the Company has a significant foreign operation measured in a functional currency other than the U.S. dollar, disclosure should be made of whether adjustments to the current cost information to reflect the effects of general inflation are based on the U.S. general price level index or on a functional currency general price level index

2. In addition to the information above, if income from continuing operations on a current cost/constant purchasing power basis differs significantly from the income from continuing operations reported in the primary financial statements, the following additional information should be disclosed (FAS-89, pars. 11-13 and 25):

   a. Components of income from continuing operations for the current year on a current cost/constant purchasing power basis

b. Separate amounts for the current cost or lower recoverable amount at the end of the current year of inventory and property, plant, and equipment

c. The increase or decrease in current cost or lower recoverable amount before and after adjusting for the effects of inflation of inventory and property, plant, and equipment for the current year

d. The principal types of information used to calculate the current cost of (1) inventory; (2) property, plant, and equipment; (3) cost of goods sold; and (4) depreciation, depletion, and amortization expense

e. Any differences between (1) the depreciation methods, estimates of useful lives, and salvage values of assets used for calculations of current cost/constant purchasing power depreciation and (2) the methods and estimates used for calculations of depreciation in the primary financial statements

3. For companies with mineral resource assets (other than oil and gas), such as metal ores or coal, the following additional disclosures are required (FAS-89, par. 14):

a. Estimates of significant quantities of proved mineral reserves or proved and probable mineral reserves (whichever is used for cost amortization purposes) at the end of the year or at the most recent date during the year for which estimates can be made

b. If the mineral reserves include deposits containing one or more significant mineral products, the estimated quantity, expressed in physical units or in percentages of reserves, of each mineral product that is recoverable in significant commercial quantities

c. Quantities of each significant mineral produced during the year

d. Quantity of significant proved, or proved and probable, mineral reserves purchased or sold in place during the year

e. The average market price of each significant mineral product or, for mineral products transferred within the enterprise, the equivalent market price prior to use in a manufacturing process

4. When determining the quantities of mineral reserves to be reported in item 3, the following should be applied (FAS-89, par. 15):

a. If consolidated financial statements are issued, 100% of the quantities attributable to the parent company and 100% of the quantities attributable to its consolidated subsidiaries (whether or not wholly owned) should be included

b. If the company's financial statements include investments that are proportionately consolidated, the company's quantities should include its proportionate share of the investee's quantities

c. If the company's financial statements include investments that are accounted for by the equity method, the investee's quantities should not be included in the disclosures of the company's quantities; however, the company's share of the investee's quantities of reserves should be reported separately, if significant

EXAMPLE OF FINANCIAL STATEMENT DISCLOSURE

The following sample disclosure is available on the accompanying disc.

Example 5–1: Five-Year Comparison of Selected Financial Data Adjusted for the Effects of Changing Prices

The Company is voluntarily presenting certain historical cost/ constant dollar information to indicate the effect of changes in the general price level on certain items that are shown in the primary financial statements based on dollar values determined as of the varying historical dates when the transactions occurred.

Revenues for 20X2 are assumed to have occurred ratably in relation to the change in the Consumer Price Index during the year and are therefore already expressed in average 20X2 dollars. The presentation also shows the gain from decline in purchasing power as a result of net amounts owed. All information shown is in terms of average 20X2 dollars as measured by the Consumer Price Index for all Urban Consumers (CPI-U).

The preparation of these numbers requires the use of certain assumptions and estimates and these disclosures should, therefore, be viewed in that context and not necessarily as a precise indicator of the specific effect of changing prices on the Company's operating results or its financial position. Also, the Company's costs may not change in proportion to changes in the Consumer Price Index.

The following table presents a five year comparison of selected supplementary financial data adjusted for the effect of changes in the general price level.

	Year Ended December 31				
	20X2	20X1	20X0	19X9	19X8
Revenues:					
Historical	$500,000	$450,000	$400,000	$350,000	$300,000
Constant dollar basis	$500,000	$461,000	$411,000	$361,000	$318,000
Income (loss) from continuing operations	$21,800	$15,300	$(5,100)	$(7,200)	$11,700
Gain from decline in purchasing power of net amounts owed	$10,000	$8,000	$9,000	$6,000	$7,000
Excess of increase in specific prices of inventory and property, plant, and equipment over increase in the general price level	$27,500	$23,000	$18,000	$19,000	$8,000
Foreign currency translation adjustment	$(1,400)	$(800)	$(500)	$(400)	$(600)
Net assets at end of year	$200,000	$160,000	$135,000	$120,000	$105,000
Per share information:					
Income (loss) from continuing operations	$2.75	$1.10	$(.24)	$(.70)	$.65
Cash dividends declared	$1.10	$1.00	$.95	$.90	$.87
Market price at year end	$51.50	$41.75	$33.20	$27.90	$25.70
Average consumer price index	314.7	306.9	298.4	289.1	272.4

CHAPTER 6
COMMITMENTS

CONTENTS

EXECUTIVE SUMMARY

Commitments typically involve uncompleted transactions or uncertainties that should be disclosed because of their effect on an entity's financial statements. Commitments include long-term contractual obligations with suppliers or customers for future purchases or sales at specified prices and sometimes at specified levels. The terms of commitments should be disclosed and a provision should be made in the financial statements for any material losses expected to be sustained. Generally accepted accounting principles (GAAP) require disclosure of commitments such as the following:

- To purchase or sell a material amount of inventory at a fixed price
- To restrict dividends
- To limit additional debt or reduce debt by a specified amount
- To enter into significant long-term leases
- To enter into a business combination
- To make material capital expenditures
- To issue shares of capital stock
- To maintain a certain level of working capital

Authoritative Literature

ARB-43   Chapter 3A, Current Assets and Current Liabilities

ARB-43   Chapter 4, Inventory Pricing

FAS-5	Accounting for Contingencies
FAS-13	Accounting for Leases
FIN-14	Reasonable Estimation of the Amount of a Loss
SOP 94-6	Disclosure of Certain Significant Risks and Uncertainties

DISCLOSURE REQUIREMENTS

For large or unusual commitments, the financial statements should disclose (1) a description of the commitment, (2) the terms of the commitment, and (3) the amount of the commitment. Such disclosures apply to the following types of commitments:

- Unused letters of credit (FAS-5, par. 18)
- Obligation to reduce debt (FAS-5, par. 18)
- Obligation to maintain working capital (FAS-5, par. 18)
- Obligation to restrict dividends (FAS-5, par. 18)
- Commitments for major capital expenditures (FAS-5, par. 18)
- Assets pledged as security for loans (FAS-5, par. 18)
- Net losses on inventory purchase commitments (ARB-43, Ch. 4, par. 17)

EXAMPLES OF FINANCIAL STATEMENT DISCLOSURES

The following sample disclosures are available on the accompanying disc. For examples of disclosures of lease commitments in connection with lease arrangements, see Chapter 23, "Leases." For examples of disclosures of commitments in connection with unconditional purchase obligations, see Chapter 46, "Debt Obligations and Credit Arrangements."

Example 6–1: Royalty Commitments

The Company has entered into various license agreements whereby the Company may use certain characters and properties in conjunction with its products. Such license agreements call for royalties to be paid at 5% to 10% of net sales with minimum guarantees and advance payments. Additionally, under one such license, the Company has committed to spend 11% of related net sales, not to exceed $2,000,000, on advertising per year. Royalty expense under these agreements was $1,000,000 in 20X2 and $900,000 in 20X1. Future annual minimum royalty commitments as of December 31, 20X2, are as follows:

20X3	$ 1,200,000
20X4	1,500,000
20X5	1,800,000
20X6	2,500,000
20X7	3,000,000
Thereafter	9,000,000
	$19,000,000

Example 6–2: Milestone Payment Due upon First Product Approval

The Company is obligated to make a milestone payment to Intexts Corp. of $1,200,000 upon the approval of its first product by the FDA or the governing health authority of any other country. This fee can be offset against future royalty payments. In addition, the Company is obligated to pay royalties on its net sales and a percentage of all revenues received from sublicenses relating to the XTS gene therapy technology. Failure to comply with the terms of the License Agreement with Intexts Corp. may cause its termination, which would have a materially adverse effect on the Company.

Example 6–3: License Fee Commitments under License Agreement

The Company entered into an agreement to license software to be incorporated into its data conferencing products. Under the agreement, the Company is obligated to pay annual minimum license fees, ranging from $150,000 to $350,000, through the year 20X6 and the Company may cancel the agreement at any time, provided the Company has paid a minimum of $1,000,000 in connection with the agreement. As of December 31, 20X2, the Company had paid $475,000 of the minimum license fees. In February 20X3, the Company re-negotiated the terms of the contract and paid a lump sum figure of $195,000. Under the terms of this new contract, the Company has no further obligation regarding any fees associated with this licensed software.

Example 6–4: Purchase Contracts

In connection with the EFTX transaction in January 20X1, EFTX and the Company entered into a manufacturing agreement whereby the Company committed to purchase minimum amounts of goods and services used in its normal operations during the first 48 months after the transaction. Future annual minimum purchases remaining under the agreement are $19 million and $22 million for 20X3 and 20X4, respectively. During 20X2 and 20X1, the Company's total purchases under the agreement were $17 million and $13 million, respectively.

Example 6–5: Firm Price Commitment Manufacturing and Supply Agreement

The Company entered into a firm price commitment manufacturing and supply agreement in connection with the acquisition of the F&D trademarks purchased in 20X2. The agreement was entered into with the seller of the trademarks to obtain from the seller tools and other manufacturing resources of the seller for the manufacture of products, upon request by the Company. The manufacturing and supply agreement has created a firm commitment by the Company for a minimum of $4,500,000. A minimum payment of $500,000 on the agreement was due on December 31, 20X2, with three additional payments of $400,000 and five additional payments of $560,000 to follow thereafter, through December 31, 20X6, which is also the date on which the agreement terminates.

Example 6–6: Commitment to Reimburse Supplier for Certain Capital Additions in Connection with Production Agreements

The Company has production agreements, which expire in May 20X9, with Elexix, Ltd. to produce certain specialized products for the Company. The agreements require the Company to reimburse Elexix, Ltd. over the terms of the agreements for specified facility additions, not to exceed $2,500,000, required to manufacture the products. Elexix, Ltd. retains title to the facility additions. Furthermore, if the Company terminates the agreements, it is obligated to pay Elexix, Ltd. for the remaining unreimbursed facility additions. The Company recorded expense of $675,000 and $620,000 under the agreements in 20X2 and 20X1, respectively. The remaining unreimbursed facility additions totaled $710,000 at December 31, 20X2.

Example 6–7: Commitments to Provide Protection Against Price Reductions

The Company has agreements with distributor customers that, under certain conditions, allow for returns of overstocked inventory and provide protection against price reductions initiated by the Company. Allowances for these commitments are included in the Consolidated Balance Sheets as reductions in trade accounts receivable. The Company adjusts sales to distributors through the use of allowance accounts based on historical experience. During 20X2 and 20X1, provisions for these commitments were recorded in the amounts of $3,700,000 and $3,200,000, respectively.

Example 6–8: Commitment to Sell Inventory at a Fixed Price

At December 31, 20X2, the Company has an agreement with a customer to sell a specified minimum number of units of its Eglaze adhesive products over the next 30 months at a fixed price of $10,200,000. The fixed price is equal to approximately 5% above the aggregate selling price at current market prices.

Example 6–9: Obligations to Maintain Working Capital and Financial Ratios, Restrict Dividends and Capital Expenditures, and Borrow Money

The Company has a $10 million revolving bank line of credit that expires in August 20X3. Advances under the line of credit bear interest at the bank's prime rate (8.5% at December 31, 20X2) and are secured by inventories and accounts receivable. Under the terms of the line of credit agreement, the Company is required to maintain certain minimum working capital, net worth, profitability levels, and other specific financial ratios. In addition, the agreement prohibits the payment of cash dividends and contains certain restrictions on the Company's ability to borrow money or purchase assets or interests in other entities without the prior written consent of the bank. There were no borrowings under the line of credit at December 31, 20X2.

Example 6–10: Commitment to Pay Certain Termination Benefits under Employment Agreements

As of December 31, 20X2, the Company had entered into employment agreements with four employees. Under each of the four agreements, in the event employment is terminated (other than voluntarily by the employee or by the Company for cause or upon the death of the employee), the Company is committed to pay certain benefits, including specified monthly severance of not more than $25,000 per month. The benefits are to be paid from the date of termination through May 20X6.

Example 6–11: Future Commitment for Minimum Salary Levels under Employment Contracts

The Company has employment agreements with its executive officers, the terms of which expire at various times through

January 20X3. Such agreements, which have been revised from time to time, provide for minimum salary levels, adjusted annually for cost-of-living changes, as well as for incentive bonuses that are payable if specified management goals are attained. The aggregate commitment for future salaries at December 31, 20X2, excluding bonuses, was approximately $3,500,000.

Example 6–12: Commitments for Construction and Acquisition of Property and Equipment

At December 31, 20X2, the Company had commitments of approximately $12,000,000 for construction and acquisition of property and equipment, all of which are expected to be incurred in 20X3. Also, in connection with an expansion at the Company's manufacturing facility in Boise, Idaho, capital grants from the State totaling $2,500,000 have been approved, $1,000,000 of which had not been received as of December 31, 20X2, and are contingent upon the Company spending approximately $6,000,000 for plant and equipment in Boise.

Example 6–13: Commitment to Maintain Liquid Funds to Secure an Obligation

The Company holds $400,000 in short-term U.S. government money market funds to secure a continuing contractual payment obligation of the Company arising from its acquisition of Axis, Ltd. As a result of this agreement, the Company has classified such funds and the interest earned thereon, totaling $416,000 at December 31, 20X2, as "Restricted investments" under noncurrent assets on the accompanying Consolidated Balance Sheets.

Example 6–14: Commitment to Purchase Capital Stock under Stock Redemption Agreements

The Company has stock redemption agreements with two major stockholders for the purchase of a portion of the common stock from their estates at market value upon death. The Company's commitment under such arrangements, totaling $8,500,000 at December 31, 20X2, is funded by life insurance policies owned by the Company.

Example 6–15: Commitment to Complete Business Acquisition

In December 20X2, the Company announced that it had entered into a definitive agreement to acquire Akcent, Inc., whose products include remote access networking solutions for the small to medium enterprise market segment. The Company expects that the total cash required to complete the transaction will be approximately $13 million, which will be provided from borrowings on the Company's line of credit.

Example 6–16: Letters of Credit—Inventory

At December 31, 20X2, and December 31, 20X1, the Company has outstanding irrevocable letters of credit in the amount of $1,800,000 and $700,000, respectively. These letters of credit, which have terms from two months to one year, collateralize the Company's obligations to third parties for the purchase of inventory. The fair value of these letters of credit approximates contract values based on the nature of the fee arrangements with the issuing banks.

Example 6–17: Letters of Credit—Contracts and Debt Obligations

At December 31, 20X2, standby letters of credit of approximately $2,400,000 have been issued under an agreement, expiring September 30, 20X3. The letters are being maintained as security for performance and advances received on long-term contracts and as security for debt service payments under industrial revenue bond loan agreements. The agreement provides a maximum commitment for letters of credit of $3,500,000 and requires an annual commitment fee of $25,000.

Example 6–18: Letters of Credit—Self-Insurance Program

The Company has letters of credit of $22,000,000 outstanding at December 31, 20X2. The letters are maintained to back the Company's self-insurance program.

Example 6–19: Letters of Credit—Operating Lease, the Terms of Which Have Not Been Finalized

At December 31, 20X2, the Company is committed to enter into an operating lease for manufacturing and distribution facilities, the terms of which have not been finalized. In connection with this commitment, during 20X2, the Company issued on its behalf irrevocable standby letters of credit in the amount of $6,500,000. Upon execution of the lease, the letters of credit will be canceled.

Example 6–20: Bid and Performance Related Bonds

The Company has entered into bid and performance related bonds associated with various contracts. These contracts generally have terms ranging from two to five years. Performance related bonds generally have a term of twelve months. Bid bonds generally have a much shorter term. Potential payments due under these bonds are related to the Company's performance under the applicable contract. The total amount of bid and performance related bonds that were available and undrawn was $5,500,000, excluding restricted cash and cash equivalents of $3,150,000, at December 31, 20X2.

Example 6–21: Customer Financing

Pursuant to certain financing agreements, the Company is committed to provide future financing in connection with purchases of the Company's products and services. The unfunded commitments were $20,700,000 and $18,600,000 at December 31, 20X2 and December 31, 20X1, respectively. Commitments to extend future financing generally have conditions for funding, fixed expiration or termination dates, and specific interest rates and purposes. The Company attempts to limit its financing credit risk by utilizing an internal credit committee that actively monitors the Company's credit exposure.

CHAPTER 7
COMPENSATED ABSENCES

CONTENTS

EXECUTIVE SUMMARY

A company must accrue a liability for employees' compensation for future absences (e.g., vacations, illnesses, holidays) if all of the following conditions are met:

1. The company's obligation relating to employees' rights to receive compensation for future absences is attributable to employee's services already rendered

2. The obligations relate to rights that eventually vest or accumulate

3. Payment of the compensation is probable

4. The amount can be reasonably estimated

If the first three conditions are met but the company cannot reasonably estimate the amount of the accrual, the reasons for not making the accrual should be disclosed in notes to the financial statements.

Authoritative Literature

FAS-43   Accounting for Compensated Absences

DISCLOSURE REQUIREMENTS

Liabilities must be appropriately accrued and reported for employees' compensation for future absences. If the entity has not accrued a liability for compensated absences because the amount cannot be reasonably estimated, that fact should be disclosed in notes to the financial statements (FAS-43, pars. 6, 7, and 15).

EXAMPLE OF FINANCIAL STATEMENT DISCLOSURE

 The following sample disclosure is available on the accompanying disc.

Example 7–1: Company Has Not Accrued a Liability for Compensated Absences Because the Amount Cannot Be Reasonably Estimated

Employees of the Company are entitled to paid vacation and paid sick days depending on job classification, length of service, and other factors. At December 31, 20X2, and December 31, 20X1, the Company had approximately 1,200 employees. Of this total, approximately 1,000 are hourly employees and 200 are salaried employees. Approximately 98% of the Company's hourly employees and 37% of its salaried employees are represented by a number of labor unions. Each union contract contains different provisions for employee-compensated absences. It is not practicable for the Company to estimate the amount of compensation for future absences; accordingly, no liability for compensated absences has been recorded in the accompanying financial statements. The Company's policy is to recognize the costs of compensated absences when actually paid to employees.

CHAPTER 8
COMPUTER SOFTWARE

CONTENTS

EXECUTIVE SUMMARY

Computer Software to Be Sold, Leased, or Otherwise Marketed

Costs incurred internally in creating a computer software product should be charged to expense when incurred as research and development until technological feasibility has been established for the product. Technological feasibility is established upon completion of a detailed program design or completion of a working model. Thereafter, all software development costs should be capitalized and subsequently reported at the lower of unamortized cost or net realizable value. Capitalized costs are amortized based on current and future revenue for each product with an annual minimum equal to the straight-line amortization over the remaining estimated economic life of the product.

The cost of purchased computer software to be sold, leased, or otherwise marketed that has no alternative future use should be accounted for the same as the costs incurred to develop such software internally, as discussed above. If that purchased software has an alternative future use, the cost should be capitalized when the software is acquired and accounted for in accordance with its alternative future use.

Computer Software Developed or Obtained for Internal Use

Accounting literature outlines three stages of software development: (1) preliminary project stage, (2) application development stage, and (3) post-implementation/operation stage. The appropriate accounting for software costs, whether incurred internally or externally, depends on which stage of the software development project these costs are incurred in. In general, costs incurred during the application development stage (e.g., costs incurred for designing the software configuration and interfaces, coding, installation, and testing) should be capitalized and amortized to expense over the software's useful life. Costs incurred during the preliminary project stage (e.g., costs incurred to develop, evaluate, and select alternatives) and costs incurred during the post-implementation and operation stage (e.g., costs incurred for training and application maintenance) should be expensed as incurred.

Software Revenue Recognition

In general, revenue should be recognized from the sale of computer software when all of the following criteria are met:

1. Persuasive evidence of a sale arrangement exists (e.g., a written contract);
2. Delivery of the software has taken place;
3. The software's price is fixed or determinable; and
4. Collectibility of the selling price is probable.

Sale of computer software frequently includes multiple elements such as: enhancements, upgrades, post-contract support (PCS), or other services. If a sale of computer software includes multiple elements, revenue should be allocated to each element based on vendor-specific objective evidence of the fair value of each element. If vendor-specific objective evidence is not available, all revenue should be deferred until such evidence exists or all products and services under the arrangement have been delivered; however, there are exceptions to that general rule. Also, revenue should be recognized under the residual method in some cases. Under the residual method, the fair value of the undelivered elements is deferred; this amount is subtracted from the total selling price for the entire multiple-element arrangement and the difference, attributed to the software elements already delivered, is recognized as revenue.

Authoritative Literature

FAS-2	Accounting for Research and Development Costs
FAS-86	Accounting for the Costs of Computer Software to Be Sold, Leased, or Otherwise Marketed
FIN-6	Applicability of FASB Statement No. 2 to Computer Software
SOP 97-2	Software Revenue Recognition
SOP 98-1	Accounting for the Costs of Computer Software Developed or Obtained for Internal Use
SOP 98-9	Modification of SOP 97-2, Software Revenue Recognition, With Respect to Certain Transactions

DISCLOSURE REQUIREMENTS

1. The following accounting policies for recognizing computer software revenues and costs should be disclosed (Generally accepted practice):

   a. Revenue recognition for each significant type of revenue (e.g., product sales, maintenance and postcontract customer service (PCS), installation and other services, and barter transactions)

   b. Amortization of deferred revenues

   c. Discounts, incentives, and sales returns, and the methods used to develop estimates of significant sales allowances

2. If an entity has capitalized costs incurred for computer software costs to be sold, leased, or otherwise marketed, the following disclosures should be made (FAS-86, par. 11):

   a. Unamortized computer software costs included in each balance sheet presented

   b. The total amount charged to expense in each income statement presented for amortization of capitalized computer software costs and for amounts written down to net realizable value

3. Research and development costs incurred for computer software to be sold, leased, or otherwise marketed should be disclosed either separately or as part of total research and development costs for each period presented (FAS-86, par. 12).

See Chapter 31, "Research and Development Costs," for additional disclosures that may be required about an entity's research and development activities.

EXAMPLES OF FINANCIAL STATEMENT DISCLOSURES

 The following sample disclosures are available on the accompanying disc.

Example 8–1: Software Revenue Recognition

The Company recognizes revenues in accordance with AICPA Statement of Position (SOP) 97-2, *Software Revenue Recognition*, as amended by SOP 98-9 (Modification of SOP 97-2, Software Revenue Recognition, With Respect to Certain Transactions). Revenue from software license agreements is recognized when persuasive evidence of an agreement exists, delivery of the software has occurred, the fee is fixed or determinable, and collectibility is probable. In software arrangements that include more than one element, the Company allocates the total arrangement fee among the elements based on the relative fair value of each of the elements.

License revenue allocated to software products generally is recognized upon delivery of the products or deferred and recognized in future periods to the extent that an arrangement includes one or more elements to be delivered at a future date and for which fair values have not been established. Revenue allocated to maintenance agreements is recognized ratably over the maintenance term and revenue allocated to training and other service elements is recognized as the services are performed. If evidence of fair value does not exist for all elements of a license agreement and post customer support (PCS) is the only undelivered element, then all revenue for the license arrangement is recognized ratably over the term of the agreement as license revenue. If evidence of fair value of all undelivered PCS elements exists but evidence does not exist for one or more delivered elements, then revenue is recognized using the residual method. Under the residual method, the fair value of the undelivered elements is deferred and the remaining portion of the arrangement fee is recognized as revenue.

If the professional services provided are essential to the functionality of the software products or are related to significant production modification, or customization of those products, both the software product revenue and service revenue are recognized using the percentage-of-completion method in accordance with the provisions of AICPA SOP 81-1, *Accounting for Performance of Construction-Type and Certain Production-Type Contracts*. Such contracts typically consist of implementation management services and are generally on a time and materials basis with a few fixed fee contracts entered into in 20X2. The contracts are not subject to renegotiation and range from 5 to 24 months in duration. Revenues and costs are recognized based on the labor hours incurred to date compared to total estimated labor hours for the contract. Contract costs include all direct material, direct labor, and indirect costs related to contract performance. Selling, general, and administrative costs are charged to expense as incurred. Provisions for estimated losses on uncompleted contracts are recorded in the period in which such losses become probable based on the current contract estimates.

Cost of license revenue primarily includes product, delivery, and royalty costs. Cost of maintenance and service revenue consists primarily of labor costs for engineers performing implementation services, technical support, and training personnel as well as facilities and equipment costs.

Example 8–2: Revenue Recognition Policy for Professional Services That Are Not Essential to the Functionality of the Software

The Company's professional services generally are not essential to the functionality of the software. The Company's software products are typically fully functional upon delivery and do not require any significant modification or alteration. Customers typically purchase professional services from the Company to facilitate the adoption of the Company's technology and dedicate personnel to participate in the services being performed, but they may also decide to use their own resources or appoint other professional service organizations to provide these services. Software products are billed separately and independently from professional services, which are generally billed on a time-and-materials or milestone-achieved basis. The Company generally recognizes revenue from professional services as the services are performed. In certain arrangements, the Company offers its professional services in exchange for a fixed fee from the customer. In such arrangements, the Company recognizes revenue under the percentage-of-completion method in accordance with AICPA SOP 81-1, *Accounting for Performance of Construction-Type and Certain Production-Type Contracts*. On these fixed fee professional service arrangements, the Company measures progress to completion based on the ratio of hours incurred to total estimated project hours. The Company believes it is able to reasonably estimate, track, and project the status of completion of a project, and considers customer acceptance as the Company's criteria for substantial completion.

Example 8–3: Product Development Costs of Computer Software to Be Sold, Leased, or Otherwise Marketed Are Expensed

The Company accounts for development costs related to software products to be sold, leased, or otherwise marketed in accordance with FASB Statement of Financial Accounting Standards No. 86, *Accounting for the Costs of Computer Software to Be Sold, Leased, or Otherwise Marketed*. Software development costs are expensed as incurred until technological feasibility has been established, at which time such costs are capitalized until the product is available for general release to customers. To date, the Company's software has been available for general release concurrent with the establishment of technological feasibility and, accordingly, no development costs have been capitalized.

Software development costs incurred and charged to research and development expense totaled $415,000 and $327,000 for the years ended December 31, 20X2, and December 31, 20X1, respectively.

> **Note:** See Chapter 31, "Research and Development Costs," for additional examples of disclosures relating to research and development arrangements.

Example 8–4: Product Development Costs of Computer Software to Be Sold, Leased, or Otherwise Marketed Are Capitalized

Research and development costs are charged to expense as incurred. However, the costs incurred for the development of computer software that will be sold, leased, or otherwise marketed are capitalized when technological feasibility has been established. These capitalized costs are subject to an ongoing assessment of recoverability based on anticipated future revenues and changes in hardware and software technologies. Costs that are capitalized include direct labor and related overhead.

Amortization of capitalized software development costs begins when the product is available for general release to customers.

Amortization is computed as the greater of (1) the ratio of current gross revenues for a product to the total of current and anticipated future gross revenues for the product or (2) the straight-line method over the estimated economic life of the product. Unamortized capitalized software development costs determined to be in excess of net realizable value of the product are expensed immediately.

During the years ended December 31, 20X2, and December 31, 20X1, the Company capitalized product development costs of $4,765,000 and $3,689,000, respectively. During the years ended December 31, 20X2, and December 31, 20X1, amortization of product development costs totaled $357,000 and $346,000, respectively. In addition, in September 20X2, the Company charged $673,000 to operations as a write-down of capitalized computer software costs to their estimated net realizable value.

Example 8–5: Accounting Policy for Costs Incurred to Develop Computer Software for Internal Use

The Company accounts for costs incurred to develop computer software for internal use in accordance with Statement of Position (SOP) 98-1, *Accounting for the Costs of Computer Software Developed or Obtained for Internal Use.* As required by SOP 98-1, the Company capitalizes the costs incurred during the application development stage, which include costs to design the software configuration and interfaces, coding, installation, and testing. Costs incurred during the preliminary project along with post-implementation stages of internal use computer software are expensed as incurred. Capitalized development costs are amortized over various periods up to three years. Costs incurred to maintain existing product offerings are expensed as incurred. The capitalization and ongoing assessment of recoverability of development costs requires considerable judgment by management with respect to certain external factors, including, but not limited to, technological and economic feasibility, and estimated economic life. For the years ended December 31, 20X2, and December 31, 20X1, the Company capitalized software development costs of $1,213,000 and $1,455,000, respectively. As of December 31, 20X2, and December 31, 20X1, net capitalized software costs totaled $3,674,000 and $2,983,000, respectively.

CHAPTER 9
CONSOLIDATED AND COMBINED FINANCIAL STATEMENTS

CONTENTS

EXECUTIVE SUMMARY

Note: The FASB has issued the following two Exposure Drafts (EDs) of proposed accounting standards relating to consolidated financial statements and business combinations:

1. Proposed Statement of Financial Accounting Standards (FAS), *Consolidated Financial Statements, Including Accounting and Reporting of Noncontrolling Interests in Subsidiaries.* The proposed standard would replace ARB

No. 51, *Consolidated Financial Statements*, and provides guidance on preparing consolidated financial statements, including the treatment of noncontrolling interests in subsidiaries (i.e., minority interests) in these consolidated statements. The major change in the proposed standard relates to the treatment of noncontrolling interests in subsidiaries, including how a parent is to account for a loss of control in a subsidiary.

2. Proposed Statement of Financial Accounting Standards (FAS), *Business Combinations*. The proposed standard would require the recognition of a business combination at fair value, including recognizing goodwill that pertains to the ownership interest of noncontrolling (minority) shareholders. In addition, professional fees associated with the consummation of a business combination would no longer be capitalized as part of the acquisition cost, but instead be expensed as incurred. FAS-141, *Business Combinations*, will be replaced if this proposed standard is adopted.

Note: In February 1999, the FASB issued an exposure draft of a proposed Statement of Financial Accounting Standards, Consolidated Financial Statements: Purpose and Policy, that would establish standards for consolidated financial statements of all business enterprises and not-for-profit organizations that control other entities, regardless of the legal form of the controlling or the controlled entities. The most important proposed change is that a controlling entity (parent) would be required to consolidate all entities that it controls (subsidiaries) unless control is temporary. The statement would define control as the "nonshared decision-making ability of one entity to direct the policies and management that guide the ongoing activities of another entity so as to increase its benefits and limit its losses from that other entity's activities." Portions of Accounting Research Bulletin No. 51, *Consolidated Financial Statements*, as amended by FAS-94, *Consolidation of All Majority-Owned Subsidiaries*, would be superseded or amended. In January 2001, the FASB determined that there was not sufficient board member support to proceed with issuing a final standard on consolidation policy. The FASB's board believes, however, that additional guidance on consolidation policy is desirable and has asked the FASB staff to reassess the approach for providing that guidance.

Readers should be alert to further developments in this area.

Consolidated financial statements represent the financial position, results of operations, and cash flows of a parent and its subsidiaries as if the group were a single enterprise. They are prepared by combining all parent and subsidiary accounts and eliminating intercompany balances and transactions. Consolidated financial statements are presumed to present more meaningful information than separate financial statements and must be used in substantially all cases in which a parent directly or indirectly controls the majority voting interest (over 50%) of a subsidiary. However, a majority-owned subsidiary should not be consolidated if control does not rest with the majority owner.

Consolidated financial statements usually are justified on the basis that one of the consolidated entities exercises control over the affiliated group. When there is no such control, combined financial statements may be used to accomplish the same results. For example, a group of companies controlled by an individual shareholder, or a group of unconsolidated subsidiaries that could otherwise not be consolidated, should utilize combined financial statements. Combined financial statements are prepared on the same basis as consolidated financial statements except that no company in the group has a controlling interest in the other.

Consolidated financial statements are prepared primarily for the benefit of creditors and shareholders. Minority interests in net income are deducted to arrive at consolidated net income. Minority interests are theoretically limited to the extent of their equity capital, however, and losses in excess of minority interest equity capital are charged against the majority interest. Subsequently, when the losses reverse, the majority interests should be credited with the amount of minority interest losses previously absorbed before credit is made to the minority interests.

If a parent's and a subsidiary's fiscal years differ by no more than about three months, it is ordinarily acceptable to consolidate the subsidiary using the subsidiary's financial statements for its fiscal year. However, in those circumstances, intervening events or transactions that materially affect the results of operations or financial position should be disclosed or otherwise recognized.

> **Note:** Currently, there are three acceptable alternative presentations of minority interests in the balance sheet: as a liability, as equity, or as a separate "mezzanine" item between liabilities and equity. The "mezzanine" presentation is mandated in SEC filings. However, in June 2005, the FASB issued a proposed Statement of Financial Accounting Standards (FAS), *Consolidated Financial Statements, Including Accounting and Reporting of Noncontrolling Interests in Subsidiaries,* which addresses the presentation of noncontrolling (minority) interests in the balance sheet, among other matters. The proposed standard would replace ARB No. 51 and indicates that non-controlling (minority) interests should be reported in the consolidated balance sheet within equity, separately from the parent stockholder's equity. Readers should be alert to further developments in this area.

Consolidation of Variable Interest Entities

FASB Interpretation (FIN) No. 46, as revised in December 2003, *Consolidation of Variable Interest Entities*, (an interpretation of Accounting Research Bulletin (ARB) No. 51, *Consolidated Financial Statements*), (FIN-46R), addresses consolidation by business enterprises of entities to which the usual condition of consolidation described in ARB-51 does not apply. The general requirement to consolidate under ARB-51 is based on the presumption that an enterprise's financial statements should include all of the entities in which it has a controlling financial interest (i.e., majority voting interest). FIN-46R interprets this general rule to require consolidation of a *variable interest entity* in which the enterprise does not have a majority voting interest but, nevertheless, is subject to a majority of the risk of loss, is entitled to a majority of the entity's residual returns, or both.

What are variable interests?   Variable interests are the investments or other interests that will absorb portions of a variable interest entity's (VIE) expected losses or receive portions of the VIE's residual returns. Examples of variable interests in a VIE include the following:

- Equity investments that are at risk
- Investments in subordinated beneficial interests
- Investments in subordinated debt instruments
- Guarantees
- Derivative interests
- Service contracts
- Leases with a residual value guarantee
- Written put options

When should a VIE be consolidated?   Generally, there are two steps involved with evaluating whether a VIE should be consolidated: (1) determining whether the entity in question is a variable interest entity and (2) determining who is the primary beneficiary. These questions are addressed below.

Is the entity a variable interest entity?   A *variable interest entity*(VIE) is a legal entity (e.g., corporation, partnership, LLP, LLC, trust) that meets any of the following three criteria:

1. *The total equity investment at risk is not sufficient to permit the entity to finance its activities without additional subordinated financial support from other parties.* In other words, the entity's expected losses are greater than the equity investment at risk. There is a rebuttable presumption that an equity investment

of less than 10 percent of the entity's total assets is not sufficient to permit an entity to finance its activities without additional subordinated financial support.

2. *As a group, the holders of the equity investment at risk do not have any of the characteristics of a controlling financial interest.* In other words:

   a. As a group, holders of the equity investment at risk cannot directly or indirectly, through voting rights or similar rights, make decisions about the entity's activities that have a significant effect on the success of the entity; or

   b. As a group, holders of the equity investment at risk have no obligation to absorb the expected losses of the entity; or

   c. As a group, holders of the equity investment at risk do not have the rights to receive the expected residual returns of the entity.

3. The equity investors have voting rights that are not proportionate to their economic interests and the activities of the entity involve, or are conducted on behalf of, an investor with a disproportionately small voting interest.

Who is the primary beneficiary? The enterprise that consolidates a VIE is referred to as the *primary beneficiary* of that VIE. A VIE can have only one primary beneficiary. An enterprise is the primary beneficiary of a VIE if the enterprise has variable interests that will (1) absorb a majority of the VIE's expected losses, (2) receive a majority of the VIE's expected residual returns, or (3) both.

If one enterprise will absorb a majority of a VIE's expected losses and another enterprise will receive a majority of that VIE's expected residual returns, the enterprise absorbing a majority of the losses is considered the primary beneficiary and, therefore, should consolidate the VIE.

Measurement of the VIE's assets, liabilities, and noncontrolling interests. With limited exceptions, an enterprise should initially measure the assets, liabilities, and noncontrolling interests of the newly consolidated VIE at their fair values at the date the enterprise first becomes the primary beneficiary. The following are exceptions to this general rule:

- For VIEs that are under common control with the primary beneficiary, the primary beneficiary should initially measure the assets, liabilities, and noncontrolling interests of the VIE at the amounts at which they are carried in the accounts of the enterprise that controls the VIE.

- When assets and liabilities are transferred from the primary beneficiary to the VIE, the primary beneficiary should initially measure such assets and liabilities at the same amounts at which they would have been measured if they had not been transferred. No gain or loss is recognized on such transfers.

The excess, if any, of (1) the fair value of the newly consolidated assets and the reported amount of assets transferred by the primary beneficiary to the VIE over (2) the sum of the fair value of the consideration paid, the reported amount of any previously held interests, and the fair value of the newly consolidated liabilities and noncontrolling interests should be allocated and reported as a pro rata adjustment of the amounts that would have been assigned to all the newly consolidated assets as if the initial consolidation had resulted from a business combination. On the other hand, any excess of item (2) over item (1) in the preceding sentence should be reported in the period in which the enterprise becomes the primary beneficiary as:

a. Goodwill, if the VIE is a business—a *business* is a self-sustaining integrated set of activities and assets conducted and managed for the purpose of providing a return to investors.

b. An extraordinary loss, if the VIE is not a business.

After initial measurement, the assets, liabilities, and noncontrolling interests of a consolidated VIE should be accounted for in consolidated financial statements as any other majority-owned subsidiary. As such, all intercompany accounts and balances should be eliminated.

Effective dates. An enterprise with an interest in a VIE that has not applied the provisions of FIN-46 as of December 24, 2003, should apply FIN-46R to that VIE as follows:

- *Public entities that are not small business issuers (non-SB):*
  - FIN-46R should be applied no later than the end of the first reporting period that ends after March 15, 2004. For a calendar year-end non-SB filer, this guidance will be effective for its March 31, 2004 quarterly financial statements. This effective date includes those entities to which FIN-46 was previously applied.
  - For entities that were considered special purpose entities (SPE) based on the guidance preceding FIN-46 (e.g., EITF Abstracts, Topic No. D-14, "Transactions Involving Special-Purpose Entities"), FIN-46 or FIN-46R should be applied no later than as of the end of the first reporting period that ends after December 15, 2003. For a calendar

year-end non-SB filer, this guidance will be effective for its December 31, 2003 annual financial statements.

— A non-SB filer that has applied FIN-46 to an entity prior to the effective date of FIN-46R should either continue to apply FIN-46 until the effective date of FIN-46R, or apply FIN-46R at an earlier date.

- *Public entities that are small business issuers (SB):*

  — FIN-46R should be applied no later than the end of the first reporting period that ends after December 15, 2004. For a calendar year-end SB filer, this guidance will be effective for its December 31, 2004 financial statements. This effective date includes those entities to which FIN-46 was previously applied.

  — For entities that were considered special purpose entities (SPEs) based on the guidance preceding FIN-46 (e.g., EITF Abstracts, Topic No. D-14, "Transactions Involving Special-Purpose Entities"), FIN-46 or FIN-46R should be applied no later than as of the end of the first reporting period that ends after December 15, 2003. For a calendar year-end SB filer, this guidance will be effective for its December 31, 2003 annual financial statements.

  — An SB filer that has applied FIN-46 to an entity prior to the effective date of FIN-46R should either continue to apply FIN-46 until the effective date of FIN-46R, or apply FIN-46R at an earlier date.

- *Private entities:*

  — For VIEs created before January 1, 2004, FIN-46R should be applied by the beginning of the first annual period beginning after December 15, 2004. For example, for a calendar year-end private company that has an interest in a VIE initially created on or before December 31, 2003, FIN-46R should be applied starting January 1, 2005.

  — For VIEs created on or after January 1, 2004, FIN-46R should be applied to the VIE immediately.

Disclosures. FIN-46R has created disclosure requirements in addition to the disclosures required by other standards. These additional disclosure requirements are discussed later in this chapter.

Authoritative Literature

ARB-43	Chapter 1A, Rules Adopted by Membership
	Chapter 2A, Comparative Financial Statements
ARB-51	Consolidated Financial Statements (as amended)

FAS-94	Consolidation of All Majority-Owned Subsidiaries
FAS-109	Accounting for Income Taxes
FAS-141	Business Combinations
FIN-46	Consolidation of Variable Interest Entities, (January 2003)
FIN-46R	Consolidation of Variable Interest Entities, (Revised December 2003)
EITF 06-9	Reporting a Change in (or the Elimination of) a Previously Existing Difference between the Fiscal Year-End of a Parent Company and That of a Consolidated Entity or between the Reporting Period of an Investor and That of an Equity Method Investee

DISCLOSURE REQUIREMENTS

Consolidated Financial Statements

Consolidated financial statements should disclose the following:

1. The consolidation policy followed by the company, such as the companies consolidated (ARB-51, par. 5)

2. Material intercompany transactions and accounts, and any profits or losses on assets are eliminated (ARB-51, par. 6)

3. If the consolidated financial statements are prepared using the financial statements of a subsidiary that has a different year-end from the parent, disclosures should be made for intervening events that materially affect financial position or results of operations (ARB-51, par. 4)

4. If an entity is a member of a group that files a consolidated tax return, the entity should disclose the following in its separate financial statements (FAS-109, par. 49):

    a. Aggregate amount of current and deferred tax expense for each statement of operations presented

    b. Amounts of any tax related balances due to or from affiliated entities as of the date of each balance sheet presented

    c. The method used to allocate consolidated current and deferred tax expense to members of the group and the nature and effect of changes in that method during the years for which the disclosures in items a. and b. are presented

Note: The disclosure requirements in item 5 below are prescribed by EITF Issue No. 06-9, *Reporting a Change in (or the Elimination of) a Previously Existing Difference between the Fiscal Year-End of a Parent Company and That of a Consolidated Entity or between the Reporting Period of an Investor and That of an Equity Method Investee.* EITF 06-9 is effective for changes in, or eliminations of, a previously existing difference between an entity's reporting period and that of an equity method investee that occur in interim or annual reporting periods beginning after November 29, 2006. Earlier application is only permitted if an entity has not yet issued its financial statements for the period.

5. If a previously existing difference between the entity's reporting period and that of an equity method investee is changed or eliminated, the disclosures in items 7 through 9 of Part IV, "Accounting Changes—Changes in Accounting Principle," of the Financial Statement Disclosure Checklist should be made (EITF 06-9).

Variable Interest Entities

1. The primary beneficiary of a variable interest entity should disclose the following (unless the primary beneficiary also holds a majority voting interest) (FIN-46R, par. 23):

   a. The nature, purpose, size, and activities of the variable interest entity

   b. The carrying amount and classification of consolidated assets that are collateral for the variable interest entity's obligations

   c. The lack of recourse if creditors (or beneficial interest holders) of a consolidated variable interest entity have no recourse to the general credit of the primary beneficiary

2. An enterprise that holds a significant variable interest in a variable interest entity, but is not the primary beneficiary, should disclose the following (FIN-46R, par. 24):

   a. The nature of its involvement with the variable interest entity and when that involvement began

   b. The nature, purpose, size, and activities of the variable interest entity

   c. The enterprise's maximum exposure to loss as a result of its involvement with the variable interest entity

3. Disclosures required by FAS-140, *Accounting for Transfers and Servicing of Financial Assets and Extinguishments of Liabilities,* about a variable interest entity should be included in the

same note to the financial statements as the information required above (FIN-46R, par. 25).

4. Information about variable interest entities may be reported in the aggregate for similar entities if separate reporting would not add material information (FIN-46R, par. 25).

5. If an enterprise with an interest in a variable interest entity, or potential variable interest entity, created before December 31, 2003 is unable to obtain the information necessary to apply FIN-46R and, as a result, does not apply FIN-46R, the following information should be disclosed (FIN-46R, par. 26):

    a. The number of entities to which FIN-46R is not being applied and the reason why the information required to apply this interpretation is not available

    b. The nature, purpose, size (if available), and activities of the variable interest entities and the nature of the enterprise's involvement with those entities

    c. The reporting enterprise's maximum exposure to loss because of its involvement with the variable interest entities

    d. The amount of income, expense, purchases, sales, or other measure of activity between the reporting enterprise and the variable interest entities for all periods presented (**Note:** If it is not practicable to present that information for prior periods that are presented in the first set of financial statements for which this requirement applies, the information for those prior periods is not required.)

6. If it is reasonably possible that an enterprise will initially consolidate or disclose information about a variable interest entity when FIN-46R becomes effective, the following information should be disclosed in all financial statements initially issued after December 31, 2003, regardless of the date on which the variable interest entity was created (FIN-46R, par. 27):

    a. The nature, purpose, size, and activities of the variable interest entity

    b. The enterprise's maximum exposure to loss as a result of its involvement with the variable interest entity

EXAMPLES OF FINANCIAL STATEMENT DISCLOSURES

 The following sample disclosures are available on the accompanying disc.

Consolidation

Example 9–1: Accounting Policy for Ownership Interests in Investees

The accompanying Consolidated Financial Statements include the accounts of the Company and its majority-owned subsidiary partnerships and corporations, after elimination of all material intercompany accounts, transactions, and profits. Investments in unconsolidated subsidiaries representing ownership of at least 20% but less than 50%, are accounted for under the equity method. Nonmarketable investments in which the Company has less than 20% ownership and in which it does not have the ability to exercise significant influence over the investee are initially recorded at cost and periodically reviewed for impairment.

Example 9–2: Consolidation Policy Specifically Described

Investee companies in which the Company directly or indirectly owns more than 50% of the outstanding voting securities or those in which the Company has effective control over are generally accounted for under the consolidation method of accounting. Under this method, an Investee company's balance sheet and results of operations are reflected within the Company's Consolidated Financial Statements. All significant intercompany accounts and transactions have been eliminated. Minority interests in the net assets and earnings or losses of a consolidated Investee are reflected in the caption "Minority interest" in the Company's Consolidated Balance Sheet and Statement of Operations. Minority interest adjusts the Company's consolidated results of operations to reflect only the Company's share of the earnings or losses of the consolidated Investee company. Upon dilution of control below 50%, the accounting method is adjusted to the equity or cost method of accounting, as appropriate, for subsequent periods.

Example 9–3: Consolidated Statements Include Subsidiaries with Different Year Ends (Parent Company Has a December Year-End)

The Consolidated Financial Statements include the accounts of the parent company and subsidiaries, after elimination of intercompany accounts and transactions. The accounts of certain subsidiaries are consolidated as of November 30 due to the time needed to consolidate these subsidiaries. No events occurred related to these subsidiaries in December 20X2 and December 20X1 that materially affected the financial position, results of operations, or cash flows.

Example 9–4: Change in Reporting Period for Subsidiary from Fiscal Year to Calendar Year—The Parent Company's Reporting Period Is a Calendar Year

Effective January 1, 20X2, the Parent Company changed the reporting period of its majority-owned subsidiary XYZ, Inc. from a fiscal year ending November 30 to a calendar year ending December 31. The results of operations of XYZ, Inc. for the month of December 20X1 (representing the period between the end of its 20X1 fiscal year and the beginning of its new calendar year) amounted to a net income of $350,000. This amount was credited to "Retained earnings" to avoid reporting more than 12 months results of operations in one year. Accordingly, the 20X2 consolidated operations include the results for XYZ, Inc. beginning January 1, 20X2. The cash activity for the stub period is included in "Other cash activities—Stub period, XYZ, Inc." in the Consolidated Statements of Cash Flows.

Note: The following table illustrates the effect on retained earnings as a result of the change in year end of a subsidiary, as reflected in the Consolidated Statement of Stockholders' Equity.

	Common Stock	Additional Paid-in Capital	Retained Earnings	Total
Balances at December 31, 20X0	$500,000	$1,000,000	$2,300,000	$3,800,000
Net income	-0-	-0-	800,000	800,000
Balances at December 31, 20X1	500,000	1,000,000	3,100,000	4,600,000
Net income	-0-	-0-	1,000,000	1,000,000
Dividends	-0-	-0-	(600,000)	(600,000)
Net income for the month ended December 20X1, due to the change in fiscal year-end of a subsidiary	-0-	-0-	350,000	350,000
Balances at December 31, 20X2	$500,000	$1,000,000	$3,850,000	$5,350,000

Example 9–5: Certain Subsidiaries Are Not Consolidated

The Consolidated Financial Statements include the accounts of the Company and all majority-owned subsidiaries, except for certain insignificant subsidiaries, the investments in which are recorded under the cost method because of restrictions upon the transfer of earnings and other economic uncertainties. All significant intercompany accounts and transactions have been eliminated.

Example 9–6: Consolidated Financial Statements Include Less Than 50% Owned Entity

The Consolidated Financial Statements include the accounts of the parent company and its subsidiaries, including XYZ Corp. in which the parent company holds a minority interest. At December 31, 20X2, the parent company owned 26% of XYZ Corp.'s capital stock, representing 78% voting control. All significant intercompany accounts and transactions have been eliminated.

Example 9–7: Change in Ownership in Previously Consolidated Subsidiary Results in Using the Equity Method of Accounting in the Current Period

In 20X0, the Company formed a joint venture with Sycom, Inc. (the Sycom Joint Venture) for the manufacture, distribution, and marketing of leather furniture. The Company originally acquired a 51% interest in the Sycom Joint Venture for $4,000,000 and, accordingly, the joint venture's Financial Statements had been consolidated with the Company's Financial Statements from the acquisition date to December 31, 20X1. Effective January 1, 20X2, the Company sold a 5% interest in the Sycom Joint Venture for $350,000 reducing its interest to 46%. As a result, in 20X2 the Company's investment in the Sycom Joint Venture is being accounted for using the equity method. The deconsolidation of the Sycom Joint Venture had an insignificant effect on the Company's consolidated total assets and net sales as of and for the year ended December 31, 20X2.

Example 9–8: Financial Statements Currently Consolidated to Include the Accounts of a Previously Unconsolidated Affiliate

Effective January 1, 20X2, the Company began to consolidate into its Financial Statements the accounts of XYZ Corporation, formerly an unconsolidated affiliate. XYZ Corporation, which primarily manufactures medical equipment, is a venture between the Company and ABC Company of Ohio. The consolidation occurred as a result of revisions of the Stockholders' Agreement between the Company and ABC Company of Ohio. Financial data presented for previous years have not been restated to reflect the consolidation of XYZ

Corporation. The consolidation is not material to financial position or results of operations for the periods presented and had no effect on previously reported net income, which included XYZ Corporation on an equity basis.

Example 9–9: Consolidation of Newly Formed Entity That Has a Minority Interest

In October 20X2, the Company contributed $2,765,000 in assets to a newly created partnership, Hope Enterprises, L.P. (the Partnership), in exchange for a 79% general partner interest in the Partnership. The contributed assets consisted of certain trademarks that are licensed to the Company pursuant to exclusive long-term license agreements, accounts receivable, property and equipment, and cash. In addition, an outside investor contributed $735,000 in cash to the Partnership in exchange for a 21% limited partner interest. For financial reporting purposes, the Partnership's assets and liabilities are consolidated with those of the Company and the outside investor's 21% interest in the Partnership is included in the Company's Financial Statements as minority interest.

Example 9–10: Presentation of Minority Interest in the Consolidated Financial Statements

Minority interest represents the minority stockholders' proportionate share of the equity of Nostars, Inc. At December 31, 20X2 and December 31, 20X1, the Company owned 22% of Nostars, Inc.'s capital stock, representing 75% voting control. The Company's 75% controlling interest requires that Nostars, Inc.'s operations be included in the Consolidated Financial Statements. The 78% equity interest of Nostars, Inc. that is not owned by the Company is shown as "Minority interest in consolidated subsidiary" in the 20X2 and 20X1 Consolidated Statements of Operations and Consolidated Balance Sheets.

> **Note:** The following table illustrates the presentation of minority interest in the Consolidated Balance Sheets between the liabilities section and the stockholder's equity section. However, currently, there are three acceptable alternative presentations of minority interests in the balance sheet: as a liability, as equity, or as a separate "mezzanine" item between liabilities and equity. The "mezzanine" presentation is mandated in SEC filings. However, in June 2005, the FASB issued a proposed Statement of Financial Accounting Standards (FAS), *Consolidated Financial Statements, Including Accounting and Reporting of Noncontrolling Interests in Subsidiaries*, which addresses the presentation of noncontrolling (minority) interests in the balance sheet, among other matters. The proposed standard would replace ARB No. 51 and indicates that noncontrolling (minority) interests should be reported in the consolidated balance sheet within

equity, separately from the parent stockholder's equity. Readers should be alert to further developments in this area.

	20X2	20X1
Total current liabilities	$15,000,000	$13,000,000
Long-term debt	6,000,000	5,000,000
Deferred income taxes	1,500,000	2,300,000
Minority interest in consolidated subsidiary	1,100,000	1,400,000
Stockholders' equity	7,600,000	6,900,000

Note: The following table illustrates the presentation of minority interest in the Consolidated Statements of Operations as a component of "Other income (expense)."

	20X2	20X1
Net sales	$41,000,000	$37,000,000
Costs and expenses	39,000,000	34,000,000
Operating income	2,000,000	3,000,000
Other income (expense):		
Interest expense	(500,000)	(400,000)
Minority interest in income of subsidiary	(600,000)	(800,000)
Other—Net	200,000	500,000
	(900,000)	(700,000)
Income before income taxes	1,100,000	2,300,000
Income taxes	(450,000)	(900,000)
Net income	$ 650,000	$ 1,400,000

Note: The following table illustrates the presentation of minority interest in the Consolidated Statements of Operations as a separate line item before "Net income."

	20X2	20X1
Net sales	$41,000,000	$37,000,000
Costs and expenses	39,000,000	34,000,000
Operating income	2,000,000	3,000,000

	20X2	20X1
Other income (expense):		
Interest expense	(500,000)	(400,000)
Other—Net	200,000	500,000
	(300,000)	100,000
Income before income taxes and minority interest	1,700,000	3,100,000
Income taxes	(450,000)	(900,000)
Income before minority interest	1,250,000	2,200,000
Minority interest in income of subsidiary	(600,000)	(800,000)
Net income	$ 650,000	$ 1,400,000

Example 9–11: Minority Interest Represents Preferred Shares of a Subsidiary

As of December 31, 20X2, the minority interest balance of $1,250,000 consists of preferred equity securities issued by the Company's subsidiary, XYZ Co. No gain or loss was recognized as a result of the issuance of the preferred securities, and the Company owned substantially all of the voting equity of this subsidiary both before and after the transaction. As of December 31, 20X2, XYZ Co. has outstanding 250,000 shares of Series A Convertible Preferred Stock and 75,000 shares of Series B Preferred Stock with a per-share liquidation preference of $10 plus accrued and unpaid dividends. The dividend rate of Series A and B is 12% per year, payable quarterly, subject to increase if certain financial covenants are not maintained. Series A and B shares are redeemable at the holders' option upon the sale of substantially all of the assets of XYZ Co. The redemption, at the liquidation preference price, would be on September 17, 20X3, or the holders may elect to defer such redemption until October 12, 20X5.

Example 9–12: Parent Company to Spin-Off Previously Consolidated Subsidiary, Resulting in Restatement of Prior Year's Financial Statements

On August 5, 20X2, the Company's Board of Directors approved a plan to spin-off the Company's wholly owned subsidiary, Citrom Specialties, Inc. (Citrom), to the Company's shareholders in the form of a tax-free dividend. The Company has requested and received a ruling from the Internal Revenue Service that this distribution will not be taxable to the Company's shareholders.

The Company's investment in and the results of operations of Citrom are reflected in the Company's Consolidated Financial Statements on the equity method as Citrom is now a temporary investment that the Company anticipates distributing to its shareholders during the year 20X3. Accordingly, the 20X1 Financial Statements have been restated. As a part of the spin-off, approximately $3,000,000 of Citrom's indebtedness to the Company has been contributed as capital. Summary financial information of Citrom consists of the following:

	Year Ended December 31	
	20X2	20X1
Net sales	$33,000,000	$29,000,000
Costs and expenses	35,000,000	30,000,000
Loss before income taxes	(2,000,000)	(1,000,000)
Tax benefit allocated by the parent	250,000	200,000
Net loss	$(1,750,000)	$ (800,000)

	As of December 31	
	20X2	20X1
Current assets	$12,000,000	$10,000,000
Fixed assets	2,000,000	1,500,000
Other assets	3,000,000	2,500,000
Total assets	$17,000,000	$14,000,000
Current liabilities	$11,000,000	$ 8,000,000
Long-term liabilities	4,000,000	3,800,000
Shareholders' equity	2,000,000	2,200,000
Total liabilities and shareholders' equity	$17,000,000	$14,000,000

Included in accounts receivable of the Company at December 31, 20X2, and December 31, 20X1, are net amounts due from Citrom of $650,000 and $475,000, respectively. During the years ended December 31, 20X2, and December 31, 20X1, the Company sold medical products and equipment to Citrom totaling $5,500,000 and $4,900,000, respectively.

Note: The following table shows the restatement of the Company's Financial Statements to reflect the spin-off of Citrom.

	Year Ended December 31	
	20X2	20X1
Consolidated Statements of Operations		
Net sales	$82,000,000	$76,000,000
Costs and expenses	87,000,000	73,000,000

	20X2	20X1
Income (loss) before loss of non-consolidated subsidiary—Citrom	(5,000,000)	3,000,000
Loss of non-consolidated subsidiary—Citrom	(2,000,000)	(1,000,000)
Income (loss) before income taxes	(7,000,000)	2,000,000
Income taxes benefit (expense)	3,000,000	(800,000)
Net income (loss)	$(4,000,000)	$ 1,200,000

	As of December 31	
	20X2	20X1
Consolidated Balance Sheets		
Total current assets	$45,000,000	$43,000,000
Other assets:		
Investment in non-consolidated subsidiary—Citrom	2,000,000	2,200,000

Example 9–13: Consolidated Financial Statements Include Nonhomogenous Operations

The Company's Consolidated Financial Statements include the accounts of Max Credit Corp., a wholly owned finance subsidiary. Business operations of this subsidiary consist primarily of financing certain customer obligations resulting from retail sales of home furnishings, accessories, and related other merchandise charged on credit cards. Summarized financial information of Max Credit Corp. are presented below.

	As of December 31	
	20X2	20X1
Balance Sheets		
Current assets, primarily accounts receivable	$4,500,000	$4,200,000
Property and equipment	400,000	350,000
Other assets	150,000	100,000
Total assets	$5,050,000	$4,650,000
Short-term debt	$1,000,000	$1,200,000
Accounts payable and accrued liabilities	700,000	650,000

	20X2	20X1
Long-term debt	550,000	400,000
Stockholders' equity	2,800,000	2,400,000
Total liabilities and stockholders' equity	$5,050,000	$4,650,000

	Year Ended December 31	
	20X2	20X1
Income Statements		
Revenues	$6,000,000	$5,000,000
Costs and expenses	5,150,000	4,300,000
Income before income taxes	850,000	700,000
Income taxes	450,000	400,000
Net income	$ 400,000	$ 300,000

Example 9–14: Financial Statements Include Certain Allocations from Parent for Certain General and Administrative Expenses

The Company is a majority-owned subsidiary of ABC, Inc. The consolidated financial statements include certain allocations from ABC, Inc. for certain general and administrative expenses such as rent, legal services, insurance, and employee benefits. Allocations are based primarily on the Company's headcount located on ABC, Inc.'s premises in relation to total headcount for all ABC, Inc.'s companies located on the premises. Management believes that the method used to allocate the costs and expenses is reasonable; however, such allocated amounts may or may not necessarily be indicative of what actual expenses would have been incurred had the Company operated independently of ABC, Inc. Amounts due to ABC, Inc. totaled approximately $1,613,000 and $1,397, 000 as of December 31, 20X2, and December 31, 20X1, respectively.

The following table summarizes the expenses allocated to the Company by ABC, Inc. for the years ended December 31, 20X2, and December 31, 20X1:

	Year Ended December 31	
	20X2	20X1
Rent and facilities	$1,115,000	$1,072,000
Legal services	216,000	191,000
Insurance	173,000	162,000
Employee benefits	294,000	289,000

Example 9–15: Gains on Issuance of Stock by Subsidiaries and Affiliates

When a subsidiary sells its stock to unrelated parties at a price in excess of its book value, the Company's net investment in that subsidiary increases. If at that time, the subsidiary is not a newly formed, non-operating entity, nor a research and development, startup or development stage company, nor is there question as to the sub-sidiary's ability to continue in existence, the Company records the increase in its Consolidated Statement of Operations. Otherwise, the increase is reflected as additional paid-in capital in the line item "Effect of subsidiaries' equity transactions" in the Company's Consolidated Statement of Stockholders' Equity.

If gains have been recognized on issuances of a subsidiary's stock and shares of the subsidiary are subsequently repurchased by the subsidiary or by the Company, gain recognition does not occur on issuance subsequent to the date of a repurchase until such time as shares have been issued in an amount equivalent to the number of repurchased shares. Such transactions are reflected as equity transactions, and the net effect of these transactions is reflected in the Consolidated Statement of Stockholders' Equity.

Variable Interest Entities

Example 9–16: Variable Interest Entities—Company Is Assessing the Impact of FIN-46R

The FASB has issued Interpretation No. 46 (FIN-46R) (Revised December 2003), *Consolidation of Variable Interest Entities*. FIN-46R clarifies the application of Accounting Research Bulletin No. 51, *Consolidated Financial Statements*, to certain entities in which equity investors do not have the characteristics of a controlling financial interest or do not have sufficient equity at risk for the entity to finance its activities without additional subordinated financial support from other parties. It separates entities into two groups: (1) those for which voting interests are used to determine consolidation and (2) those for which variable interests are used to determine consolidation (the subject of FIN-46R). FIN-46R clarifies how to identify a variable interest entity and how to determine when a business enterprise should include the assets, liabilities, noncontrolling interests and results of activities of a variable interest entity in its consolidated financial statements.

FIN-46R requires that a variable interest entity is to be consolidated by its "Primary Beneficiary." The Primary Beneficiary is the entity, if any, that stands to absorb a majority of the variable interest entity's expected losses, or in the event that no entity stands to absorb a majority of the expected losses, then the entity that stands to receive a majority of the variable interest entity's expected residual returns.

The consolidation requirements of FIN-46R apply to the Company in the year ended December 31, 2004. If it is reasonably possible that an enterprise will consolidate or disclose information about a variable interest entity when FIN-46R becomes effective, the enterprise is required to disclose in all financial statements initially issued after December 31, 2003, the nature, purpose, size, and activities of the variable interest entity and the enterprise's maximum exposure to loss as a result of its involvement with the variable interest entity.

At December 31, 2003, the Company held the following investments that, for purposes of FIN-46R, will need to be evaluated to determine whether such investments should be consolidated or disclosed as a variable interest entity in the Company's future financial statements:

- Real estate partnerships and joint ventures that are accounted for under the equity method of accounting and have a total carrying value of $12 million on the consolidated balance sheet; the Company's unfunded commitments associated with real estate partnerships and joint ventures were $8.5 million.

- Investment partnerships that are accounted for under the equity method of accounting and have a carrying value of $7.9 million on the consolidated balance sheet; the Company's unfunded commitments associated with investment partnerships were $4.1 million.

- Equity investments that are reported at fair value and have a carrying value of $17.3 million on the balance sheet and private equity investments that are accounted for under the equity method of accounting and have a carrying value of $6.4 million on the balance sheet; the Company's unfunded commitments associated with private equity investments were $1.1 million.

The Company is currently assessing the impact, if any, that the consolidation provisions of FIN-46R may have on the consolidated financial statements.

Example 9–17: Variable Interest Entities—No Impact Is Expected as a Result of FIN-46R

FASB Interpretation No. 46 (FIN-46R) (Revised December 2003), *Consolidation of Variable Interest Entities*, requires that if an enterprise is the primary beneficiary of a variable interest entity, the assets, liabilities, and results of operations of the variable interest entity should be included in the consolidated financial statements of the enterprise. FIN-46R also requires additional disclosures by primary beneficiaries and other significant variable interest holders. As of December 31, 20X3, the Company had variable interests in securitization trusts, which are discussed in Note [X]. These trusts are qualifying special purpose entities, which are exempt from the consolidation requirements of FIN-46R. Therefore, the Company does not expect this Interpretation to have an effect on its consolidated financial statements.

Example 9–18: Variable Interest Entities—Company Has Identified a Potential Variable Interest Entity

FASB Interpretation No. 46 (FIN-46R) (Revised December 2003), *Consolidation of Variable Interest Entities,* requires that if an enterprise is the primary beneficiary of a variable interest entity, the assets, liabilities, and results of operations of the variable interest entity should be included in the consolidated financial statements of the enterprise. The only potential variable interest entity with which the Company is associated is the lessor of a manufacturing facility as disclosed in Note [X]. The Company has guaranteed the residual value of the leased manufacturing facility, with a maximum exposure of $13 million and has guaranteed $18 million of the debt of the lessor from which this facility is leased. The lease, which expires in 20X6 and has two subsequent five-year renewal options, is treated as an operating lease. Rent payments under the lease are determined as LIBOR plus 0.375 percent applied to the initial cost of the facility.

The Company is evaluating whether the lessor is a variable interest entity, whether the Company is the primary beneficiary and, if so, the impact of FIN-46R on financial position and results of operations.

Example 9–19: Variable Interest Entities—Company Is the Primary Beneficiary: Transitional Disclosures and Subsequent Disclosures under FIN-46R

Transitional disclosures—FASB Interpretation No. 46 (FIN-46R) (Revised December 2003), *Consolidation of Variable Interest Entities,* requires that if an enterprise is the primary beneficiary of a variable interest entity, the assets, liabilities, and results of operations of the variable interest entity should be included in the consolidated financial statements of the enterprise. The Company leases an airplane from Aerocrafts, Ltd. The Company believes it is the primary beneficiary and that the lessor is a variable interest entity. Under FIN-46R, the lessor is required to be consolidated in the Company's balance sheet as of December 31, 2004. The airplane will be recorded as an asset and the related debt will be recorded as a liability in the Company's balance sheet. The impact on the Company's future statement of operations will be increased depreciation and interest expense, which will be partially offset by lower rent expense. The Company believes the fair market value of the airplane, based on an independent appraisal, to be approximately $42 million and the related debt to be approximately $33 million at December 31, 2003.

Disclosures after effective date of FIN-46R—The Company has been leasing an airplane from Aerocrafts, Ltd., an entity established for the sole purpose of acquiring and leasing the airplane. Under FIN-46R, Aerocrafts, Ltd. is a variable interest entity and the Company is the primary beneficiary. Therefore, the Company has consolidated the lessor in its consolidated financial statements. The airplane has a carrying amount of $38 million, with related nonrecourse debt of $31 million.

Example 9–20: Variable Interest Entities—Company Has Determined, and Is Disclosing, the Impact of FIN-46R

FASB Interpretation No. 46 (FIN-46R) (Revised December 2003), *Consolidation of Variable Interest Entities*, requires that if an enterprise is the primary beneficiary of a variable interest entity, the assets, liabilities and results of operations of the variable interest entity should be included in the consolidated financial statements of the enterprise. As discussed in Note [X] to the Consolidated Financial Statements, the Company has invested in Max Systems, Inc. ("Max"), a developer of medical diagnostic products. This investment was made in March 20X1 in the form of a $21 million debt instrument. In connection with this investment, the Company has the right to purchase Max for a purchase price that is based on a valuation of Max using a negotiated formula, as defined in the agreement. On July 10, 20X2, the Company entered into a definitive agreement to acquire Max, which represents the Company's exercise of its rights to purchase Max under the agreement. The Company also entered into a commitment to provide non-convertible debt funding to Max of approximately $25 million through the close of the acquisition.

The Company has evaluated its debt investment in Max and has determined that Max is a variable interest entity under FIN-46R. The Company has concluded that it is the primary beneficiary as defined by FIN-46R and, as a result, the Company is required to consolidate Max on January 1, 20X4. To date, the Company has expensed substantially its entire investment in Max as research and development costs, as if such expenses constituted the development costs of the Company.

FIN-46R will require the Company to account for Max as if it had consolidated it since the Company's initial investment in March 20X1. If the Company consolidated Max from the date of its initial investment, the Company would be required to account for the purchase option as a repurchase right. Under FASB Interpretation No. 44 (FIN-44), *Accounting for Certain Transactions Involving Stock Compensation,* and related interpretations, variable accounting is required for substantially all Max employee stock and options because the ending purchase price is primarily derived from a revenue-based formula. Therefore, effective January 1, 20X4, the Company will revalue the stock and options of Max each quarter based on an independent valuation of Max until the completion of the acquisition which is expected in the third quarter of fiscal 20X4.

Consequently, on January 1, 20X4, the Company will record a non-cash cumulative charge based on the adoption of FIN-46R, in the range of $45 million to $75 million (the variable compensation). This will be reported as a separate line item in the Consolidated Statements of Operations, net of tax. The charge will be based on the value of Max employee stock and options and their expected vesting upon FIN-46R adoption pursuant to the independent evaluation, and does not necessarily reflect the value of Max as a whole nor indicate the expected valuation of Max upon acquisition. Subsequent to the adoption of FIN-46R, changes to the value of Max will result in adjustments to the non-cash stock compensation charge based upon the expected vesting of the employee stock and options and will be reflected as operating expenses. These adjustments will be recorded commencing January 1, 20X4 and continue until such time as the acquisition of Max is completed, which is expected to close in the third quarter of fiscal 20X4. These adjustments will be based on changes in the valuation of Max using the negotiated formula. The value computed under the negotiated formula is largely based on revenues derived from specific medical diagnostic products.

Excluding the non-cash stock compensation cumulative charge and any future non-cash variable stock compensation adjustments, the impact of consolidating Max will not materially affect the Company's operating results or financial condition. Other than the investment in Max, the Company does not anticipate that the adoption of FIN-46R will have a material impact on its operating results or financial condition.

Combined Financial Statements

Example 9–21: Combined Financial Statements

The accompanying Combined Financial Statements include the accounts of the following entities, all of which are under common control and ownership:

Or:

The accompanying Combined Financial Statements include the accounts of the following entities because each entity is owned beneficially by identical shareholders:

Name of Entity	Form of Entity
Amishar, Inc.	Corporation
Sandust, L.P.	Partnership
Basin & Sons	Sole proprietorship

All significant intercompany profits, accounts, and transactions have been eliminated in the combination.

> **Note:** The following table presents the individual components of equity if the combined entities have different ownership forms. This may be presented in the equity section on the face of the balance sheet or in a note to the financial statements.

	As of December 31	
	20X2	20X1
Equity		
Stockholders' equity	$1,700,000	$1,500,000
Partners' capital	600,000	700,000
Proprietor's capital	400,000	300,000
Total equity	$2,700,000	$2,500,000

> **Note:** The following table presents the Statement of Changes in Equity accounts if the combined entities have different ownership forms.

	Amishar, Inc. (Corporation)			Sandust, L.P. (Partnership)	Basin & Sons (Proprietorship)
	Common Stock	Additional Paid-in Capital	Retained Earnings	Partners' Capital	Proprietor's Capital
Balances, December 31, 20X0	$100,000	$400,000	$ 700,000	$600,000	$300,000
Net income			400,000	300,000	100,000
Cash dividends			(100,000)		
Partner's withdrawals				(200,000)	
Proprietor's withdrawals					(100,000)
Balances, December 31, 20X1	100,000	400,000	1,000,000	700,000	300,000
Net income			400,000	300,000	400,000
Cash dividends			(200,000)		
Partners' withdrawals				(400,000)	
Proprietor's withdrawals					(300,000)
Balances, December 31, 20X2	$100,000	$400,000	$1,200,000	$600,000	$400,000

CHAPTER 10
CONTINGENCIES, RISKS, UNCERTAINTIES, AND CONCENTRATIONS

CONTENTS

EXECUTIVE SUMMARY

Loss and Gain Contingencies

The following two conditions must be met for a loss contingency to be accrued as a charge to income and disclosed as of the date of the financial statements:

1. It is probable that, at the date of the financial statements, an asset has been impaired or a liability incurred.

2. The amount of loss can be reasonably estimated.

Disclosure is required for loss contingencies not meeting both those conditions if a reasonable possibility exists that a loss may have been incurred.

As a general rule, disclosing loss contingencies that have a remote possibility of materializing is not required. However, loss contingencies that may occur as the result of a guarantee must be disclosed in the financial statements, even if they have a remote possibility of materializing. The accounting and disclosure requirements for guarantees are further disussed below.

Gains from gain contingencies should *not* be credited to income because to do so might result in the recognition of income before it is realized. Gain contingencies, however, should be adequately disclosed in the notes to the financial statements, and care should be exercised in disclosing gain contingencies to avoid misleading implications as to the recognition of revenue prior to its realization.

Accounting for Registration Payment Arrangements. The FASB has issued FASB Staff Position EITF 00-19-2 (FSP EITF 00-19-2), *Accounting for Registration Payment Arrangements*. This FSP specifies that the contingent obligation to make future payments or otherwise transfer consideration under a registration payment arrangement, whether issued as a separate agreement or included as a provision of a financial instrument or other agreement, should be separately recognized and measured in accordance with Statement of Financial Accounting Standards No. 5 (FAS-5), *Accounting for Contingencies*. This FSP further clarifies that a financial instrument subject to a registration payment arrangement should be accounted for in accordance with other applicable generally accepted accounting principles (GAAP) without regard to the contingent obligation to transfer consideration pursuant to the registration payment arrangement. This FSP amends various authoritative literature, notably SAS-133, *Accounting for Derivative Instruments and Hedging Activities*, SAS-150, *Accounting for Certain Financial Instruments with Characteristics of both Liabilities and Equity*, and FASB Interpretation No. 45 (FIN-45), *Guarantor's Accounting and Disclosure Requirements for Guarantees, Including Indirect Guarantees of Indebtedness of Others*.

This FSP is effective immediately for registration payment arrangements and the financial instruments subject to those arrangements that are entered into or modified subsequent to December 21, 2006. For registration payment arrangements and financial instruments subject to those arrangements that were entered into prior to December 21, 2006, the guidance in the FSP is effective for financial statements issued for fiscal years beginning after December 15, 2006, and interim periods within those fiscal years.

Environmental Remediation Contingencies

Companies are subject to a wide range of federal, state, and local environmental laws and regulations. The accrual for environmental remediation liabilities should include incremental direct costs of the remediation effort and costs of compensation and benefits for employees to the extent an employee is expected to devote time directly to the remediation effort.

The measurement of the liability should include (a) the entity's allocable share of the liability for a specific site and (b) the entity's share of amounts related to the site that will not be paid by other potentially responsible parties or the government. The measurement of the liability should be based on the following:

1. Enacted laws and existing regulations and policies
2. Remediation technology that is expected to be approved to complete the remediation effort
3. The reporting entity's estimates of what it will cost to perform all elements of the remediation effort when they are expected to be performed

The measurement may be discounted to reflect the time value of money if the aggregate amount of the obligation and the amount and timing of cash payments for the obligation are fixed or reliably determinable.

Risks, Uncertainties, and Concentrations

Volatility and uncertainty in the business and economic environment result in the need to disclose information about the risks and uncertainties confronted by reporting entities. GAAP requires entities to disclose significant risks and uncertainties in the following areas:

1. *Nature of operations.* Disclosures concerning the nature of operations do not have to be quantified, and relative importance may be described by terms such as *predominantly, about equally,* and *major.*

2. *Use of estimates in the preparation of financial statements.* Financial statements should include an explanation that their preparation in conformity with GAAP requires the application of management's estimates.

3. *Certain significant estimates.* Disclosure regarding an estimate is required when both of the following conditions are met: (a) it is at least reasonably possible that the estimate of the effect on the financial statements of a condition, situation, or set of circumstances that existed at the date of the financial statements will change in the near term due to one or more future confirming events, and (b) the effect of the change would have a material effect on the financial statements.

4. *Current vulnerability due to certain concentrations.* Financial statements should disclose concentrations if all of the following conditions are met: (a) the concentration existed at the date of the financial statements, (b) the concentration makes the enterprise vulnerable to the risk of a near-term severe impact, and (c) it is reasonably possible that the events that could cause the severe impact will occur in the near term.

Authoritative Literature

FAS-5	Accounting for Contingencies
FAS-16	Prior Period Adjustments
FAS-141	Business Combinations
FIN-14	Reasonable Estimation of the Amount of a Loss
SOP 94-6	Disclosure of Certain Significant Risks and Uncertainties
SOP 96-1	Environmental Remediation Liabilities
EITF 03-8	Accounting for Claims-Made Insurance and Retroactive Insurance Contracts by the Insured Entity
FSP EITF 00-19-2	Accounting for Registration Payment Arrangements

DISCLOSURE REQUIREMENTS

Loss and Gain Contingencies

1. The nature and amount of an accrued loss contingency should be disclosed if (a) exposure to loss in excess of the amount accrued exists or (b) disclosure is necessary to keep the financial statements from being misleading (FAS-5, par. 9).

2. If no accrual is made for a loss contingency, or if an exposure to loss exists in excess of the amount accrued, the following disclosures should be made when there is at least a reasonable possibility that a loss or an additional loss may have been incurred (FAS-5, par. 10):

    a. The nature of the contingency

    b. An estimate of the possible loss or range of loss, or a statement that such an estimate cannot be made

3. For losses and loss contingencies that arise subsequent to the date of the financial statements, the following disclosures should be made when it is necessary to keep the financial statements from being misleading (FAS-5, par. 11):

    a. The nature of the loss or loss contingency

    b. An estimate of the amount or range of loss, or possible loss, or a statement that an estimate cannot be made

4. The following disclosures should be made for certain remote loss contingencies relating to guarantees made for outside parties (such as guarantees of indebtedness of others, obligations of commercial banks under stand-by letters of credit, and guarantees to repurchase receivables or other properties that have been sold or assigned) (FAS-5, par. 12):

    a. The nature of the loss contingency

    b. The nature and amount of the guarantee

    c. If subject to estimation, the value of any recovery from other outside parties that could be expected to result

5. Adequate disclosures should be made for unasserted claims or assessments if it is considered probable that a claim will be asserted and there is a reasonable possibility that a loss will arise from the matter (FAS-5, par. 10).

6. Gain contingencies should be adequately disclosed, but care should be exercised to avoid misleading implications about the likelihood of realization (FAS-5, par. 17).

Note: The disclosure requirements in items 7 and 8 below are prescribed by FSP EITF 00-19-2, *Accounting for Registration Payment Arrangements.* FSP EITF 00-19-2 is effective immediately for registration payment arrangements and the financial instruments subject to those arrangements that are entered into or modified subsequent to December 21, 2006. For registration payment arrangements and financial instruments subject to those arrangements that were entered into prior to December 21, 2006, the guidance in FSP EITF 00-19-2 is effective for financial statements issued for fiscal years beginning after December 15, 2006, and interim periods within those fiscal years. Early adoption is permitted as long as financial statements for any period (interim or annual) of the fiscal year have not yet been issued.

7. The following information should be disclosed about each registration payment arrangement or each group of similar arrangements, even if the likelihood of the issuer having to make any payments under the arrangement is remote: (FSP EITF 00-19-2, par. 12):

   a. The nature of the registration payment arrangement

   b. The approximate term of the arrangement

   c. The financial instruments subject to the arrangement

   d. The events or circumstances that would require the issuer to transfer consideration under the arrangement

   e. Any settlement alternatives contained in the terms of the registration payment arrangement, including the party that controls the settlement alternatives

   f. The maximum potential amount of consideration, undiscounted, that the issuer could be required to transfer under the registration payment arrangement, including the maximum number of shares that may be required to be issued

   g. The fact that the terms of the arrangement provide for no limitation to the maximum potential consideration (including shares) to be transferred, if the terms of the arrangement include such provision

   h. The current carrying amount of the liability representing the issuer's obligations under the registration payment arrangement and the income statement classification of any gains or losses resulting from changes in the carrying amount of that liability

8. The following information should be disclosed related to the adoption of FSP EITF 00-19-2 (FSP EITF 00-19-2, par. 21):

   a. The portion of the cumulative-effect adjustment resulting from the recognition and measurement of a contingent liability under FAS-5

b. The portion of the cumulative-effect adjustment resulting from the reclassification of a financial instrument subject to the registration payment arrangement to equity, or the recombination of an embedded derivative

Environmental Remediation Contingencies

1. If accruals for environmental remediation loss contingencies have been recorded in the financial statements, the following information should be disclosed (SOP 96-1, pars. 7.11 and 7.20):

    a. Whether the accrual for environmental remediation liabilities is measured on a discounted basis

    b. The nature and amount of the accrued loss contingency

    c. If any portion of the accrued obligation is discounted, the undiscounted amount of the obligation and the discount rate used

    d. If it is at least reasonably possible that the accrued obligation or any recognized asset for third-party recoveries will change within one year of the date of the financial statements and the effect is material, an indication that it is at least reasonably possible that a change in the estimate will occur in the near term

2. When environmental remediation loss contingencies have not been accrued, or when exposures exist in excess of the amounts accrued, the following information should be disclosed (SOP 96-1, par. 7.21):

    a. A description of the reasonably possible loss contingency and an estimate of the possible loss, or a statement to the effect that such an estimate cannot be made

    b. If it is at least reasonably possible that the estimated contingency will change within one year of the date of the financial statements and the effect is material, an indication that it is at least reasonably possible that a change in the estimate will occur in the near term

3. Entities are also encouraged, but not required, to disclose the following information (SOP 96-1, par. 7.22):

    a. The estimated time frame of disbursements for recorded amounts if expenditures are expected to continue over the long term

    b. The estimated time frame for realization of recognized probable recoveries, if realization is not expected in the near term

   c. The factors that cause the estimates to be sensitive to change with respect to (i) the accrued obligation, (ii) any recognized asset for third-party recoveries, or (iii) reasonably possible loss exposures, or disclosed gain contingencies

   d. If an estimate of the probable or reasonably possible loss or range of loss cannot be made, the reasons why it cannot be made

   e. If information about the reasonably possible loss or the recognized and additional reasonably possible loss for an environmental remediation obligation related to an individual site is relevant to an understanding of the financial position, cash flows, or results of operations of the entity, the following disclosures with respect to the site should be made:

     — The total amount accrued for the site

     — The nature of any reasonably possible loss contingency or additional loss, and an estimate of the possible loss or the fact that an estimate cannot be made and the reasons why it cannot be made

     — Whether other potentially responsible parties are involved and the entity's estimated share of the obligation

     — The status of regulatory proceedings

     — The estimated time frame for resolution of the contingency

4. If an environmental liability for a specific clean-up site is discounted because it meets the criteria for discounting in SOP 96-1 and the effect of discounting is material, the financial statements should disclose the undiscounted amounts of the liability and any related recovery and the discount rate used (SOP 96-1, par. 7.20).

Risks, Uncertainties, and Concentrations

1. The following disclosures are required regarding the nature of the entity's operations (SOP 94-6, par. 10):

   a. A description of the entity's major products or services

   b. The principal markets (e.g., industries and types of customers) for the entity's products or services

   c. The relative importance of each line of business, together with the basis for making that determination (e.g., based on sales, assets, earnings) (This information need not be quantified; instead, relative importance could be conveyed by using terms such as *predominantly, about equally,* or *major.*)

2.   The financial statements or a footnote should include a general statement that the preparation of financial statements requires the use of estimates by management. The following disclosures are required regarding significant estimates used in the determination of the carrying amounts of assets or liabilities or in disclosure of gain or loss contingencies, if (i) it is at least reasonably possible that the effect on the financial statements of the estimates will change within one year of the date of the financial statements due to one or more future confirming events, and (ii) the effect of the change would be material to the financial statements (SOP 94-6, pars. 11 and 13–15):

a.   The nature of the estimate

b.   An indication that it is at least reasonably possible that a change in the estimate will occur in the near term

c.   The factors that cause the estimate to be sensitive to change (this disclosure is encouraged but not required)

d.   If the entity uses risk-reduction techniques to mitigate losses or the uncertainty that may result from future events and, as a result, determines that the criteria described above are not met, the disclosures in items a, b, and c are encouraged, but not required

3.   The following disclosures about concentrations are required if (i) the concentration exists at the date of the financial statements, (ii) the concentration makes the entity vulnerable to the risk of a near-term severe effect, and (iii) it is at least reasonably possible that the events that could cause the severe effect will occur in the near term (SOP 94-6, pars. 21, 22, and 24):

a.   Concentrations in the volume of business transacted with a particular customer, supplier, lender, grantor, or contributor (for purposes of this disclosure, it is always considered at least reasonably possible that any customer, grantor, or contributor will be lost in the near term)

b.   Concentrations in revenue from particular products, services, or fund-raising events

c.   Concentrations in the available sources of supply of materials, labor, or services, or of licenses or other rights used in the entity's operations

d.   Concentrations in the market or geographic area in which the entity conducts its operations (for purposes of this disclosure, it is always considered at least reasonably possible that operations located outside an entity's home country will be disrupted in the near term)

e. For concentrations of labor subject to collective bargaining agreements, the percentage of the labor force covered by a collective bargaining agreement and the percentage of the labor force covered by a collective agreement that will expire within one year

f. For concentrations of operations located outside the entity's home country, the carrying amounts of net assets and the geographic areas in which they are located

4. The following disclosures related to risks for publicly held entities and entities with public accountability are *encouraged* but not required (EITF 03-8, pars. 27–28):

a. Circumstances in which the entity is exposed to risks of future material loss related to torts; theft of, damage to, expropriation of, or destruction of assets; business interruption; errors or omissions; injuries to employees; or acts of nature. A standard form of disclosure is not recommended; however, entities might consider disclosing the following:

— The actual and potential effects of losses from such risks on the entity's historical or planned operations, including exposure to losses from claims, curtailment of research and development or manufacturing, or contraction or cessation of other activities, such as discontinuance of a product line

— Comparison of current insurance coverage by major categories of risk to coverage in prior periods, without necessarily quantifying such coverage or change in coverage

— Recent claims experience

— A description of the reporting entity's risk management programs

b. Circumstances in which the risks in 4a have not been transferred to unrelated third parties through insurance

EXAMPLES OF FINANCIAL STATEMENT DISCLOSURES

The following sample disclosures are available on the accompanying disc. For examples of disclosures of commitments, see Chapter 6, "Commitments." For examples of disclosures of contingencies in connection with unconditional purchase obligations, see Chapter 46, "Debt Obligations and Credit Arrangements."

Loss Contingencies

Example 10–1: General Accounting Policy for Contingencies Disclosed as Part of the Accounting Policies Note to the Financial Statements

Certain conditions may exist as of the date the financial statements are issued, which may result in a loss to the Company but which will only be resolved when one or more future events occur or fail to occur. The Company's management and its legal counsel assess such contingent liabilities, and such assessment inherently involves an exercise of judgment. In assessing loss contingencies related to legal proceedings that are pending against the Company or unasserted claims that may result in such proceedings, the Company's legal counsel evaluates the perceived merits of any legal proceedings or unasserted claims as well as the perceived merits of the amount of relief sought or expected to be sought therein.

If the assessment of a contingency indicates that it is probable that a material loss has been incurred and the amount of the liability can be estimated, then the estimated liability would be accrued in the Company's financial statements. If the assessment indicates that a potentially material loss contingency is not probable, but is reasonably possible, or is probable but cannot be estimated, then the nature of the contingent liability, together with an estimate of the range of possible loss if determinable and material, would be disclosed.

Loss contingencies considered remote are generally not disclosed unless they involve guarantees, in which case the nature of the guarantee would be disclosed.

Example 10–2: No Accrual Is Made for Litigation Because the Likelihood of a Material Adverse Outcome Is Remote

The Company is a defendant in a case that is in the United States District Court in the Northern District of California. The case arose from claims by a former employee that the Company had discriminated against her during her employment at the Company. The suit seeks damages totaling $1,500,000. The Company believes that the claims are without merit and intends to vigorously defend its position. The ultimate outcome of this litigation cannot presently be determined. However, in management's opinion, the likelihood of a material adverse outcome is remote. Accordingly, adjustments, if any, that might result from the resolution of this matter have not been reflected in the financial statements.

Example 10–3: No Accrual Is Made for Potential Liability Because Management Does Not Believe It Is Probable

A former employee of the Company has filed a workers' compensation claim related to injuries incurred in connection with the

September 20X2 fire at the Company's Temecula facility. In the claim, the employee is requesting payment of an additional 50% award of compensation, approximating $450,000, claiming the Company violated a State safety statute in connection with the occurrence of his injury. As of December 31, 20X2, the Company has not recorded a provision for this matter as management intends to vigorously defend these allegations and believes the payment of the penalty is not probable. The Company believes, however, that any liability it may incur would not have a material adverse effect on its financial condition or its results of operations.

Example 10–4: Accrual Is Made but Exposure Exists in Excess of Amount Accrued

The Company is a defendant in a lawsuit, filed by a former supplier of electronic components alleging breach of contract, which seeks damages totaling $750,000. The Company proposed a settlement in the amount of $500,000, based on the advice of the Company's legal counsel. Consequently, $500,000 was charged to operations in the accompanying 20X2 financial statements. However, if the settlement offer is not accepted by the plaintiff and the case goes to trial, the amount of the ultimate loss to the Company, if any, may equal the entire amount of damages of $750,000 sought by the plaintiff.

Example 10–5: Unasserted Claim for Penalties Resulting from Contract Delays

In the ordinary course of business, the Company enters into contracts that provide for the assessment by the Company's customers of penalty charges for delays in the required production capability or completion of contracts. At December 31, 20X2, the Company had not achieved the 50% production capacity specified in a major contract, which also provides for penalties of up to $1,500,000. The Company's management believes that failure to meet the contract's production capacity requirement was caused primarily by customer initiated changes and additional customer requirements after the placement of the order and has informed the customer of the delays caused thereby. No claims for penalties have been made by the customer, and although some uncertainty exists as to whether the final delivery date can be achieved, the Company believes it can fulfill all remaining contractual requirements so that ultimately no penalties will have to be paid.

Example 10–6: Unasserted Claim Relating to Product Defects

In September 20X2, the Company announced that it will conduct an inspection program to eliminate a potential problem with an electrical component supplied to various manufacturers of microwave ovens. The ultimate cost of the repair will not be known until the inspection program is complete, which could have a material effect on the Company's financial condition and results of operations.

Example 10–7: Contingent Liability Resulting from Government Investigation

The Company is currently the subject of certain U.S. government investigations. If the Company is charged with wrongdoing as a result of any of these investigations, the Company could be suspended from bidding on or receiving awards of new government contracts pending the completion of legal proceedings. If convicted or found liable, the Company could be fined and debarred from new government contracting for a period generally not to exceed three years.

Example 10–8: Contingent Liability Relating to Businesses Sold

The Company is contingently liable for obligations totaling approximately $4,000,000 under Industrial Revenue Bond Agreements related to manufacturing plants of businesses that were sold. In November 20X2, the Company was notified that an event of default relating to the nonpayment of $300,000 semi-annual interest installment due October 20X2, by the purchaser of the businesses had occurred. The Company has agreed to loan $300,000 to the purchaser to cure the event of default.

Example 10–9: Contingent Liability Relating to Lease Termination

In September 20X2, the Company notified the developer and landlord of its planned future headquarters in Paramount, California, that the Company intends to terminate the project. The Company had previously entered into a 15-year lease agreement for the new site. Although groundbreaking for the new site has not occurred, the Company anticipates that it will incur lease termination costs. The Company is not able to make a meaningful estimate of the amount or range of loss that could result from an unfavorable resolution of this matter. Consequently, the Company has not provided any accruals for lease termination costs in the financial statements.

Example 10–10: Contingent Liability Relating to Performance and Payment Bonds Issued by Sureties

The Company is contingently liable to sureties in respect of performance and payment bonds issued by the sureties in connection with certain contracts entered into by the Company in the normal course of business. The Company has agreed to indemnify the sureties for any payments made by them in respect of such bonds.

Example 10–11: Contingency Resulting from Default under Lease Agreements

The Company leases certain plant machinery and equipment at its manufacturing facility in Boise, Idaho. As a result of the Company's default under its debt obligations, as more fully discussed in Note [X] to the financial statements, the Company is in default unde these lease agreements. As a result, the lessors have the right to require the Company to prepay the remaining future lease payments required under the lease agreements. Because the lease payments have been made and are expected to be made in a timely manner, the Company does not expect that the lessors will assert this right under these lease agreements.

Example 10–12: Lawsuit Settlement Amount Is Recorded at Present Value of Amount to Be Paid

In October 20X2, the Company settled a legal action brought by a group of employees alleging certain discriminatory employment practices by the Company. Under the settlement, the Company has agreed to provide monetary relief in the amount of approximately $2,500,000, to be paid in installments over a five-year period. The present value of the cost of the settlement and estimated additional legal fees, totaling $1,900,000, have been included in results of operations for 20X2. The current portion of the liability recorded is approximately $500,000 and the remaining $1,400,000 is classified as a noncurrent liability at December 31, 20X2.

Example 10–13: Settlement of Claims Is Not Expected to Exceed Company's Insurance Coverage

Through December 31, 20X2, claims valued at approximately $7,000,000 had been filed against the Company relating to product damage associated with the contamination of a formulated agricultural chemical. Management, based on consultation with its legal counsel, believes that the ultimate settlement of claims for this loss will not exceed its insurance coverage, which totals $15,000,000.

Example 10–14: Company Is without Insurance for Various Risks That Could Adversely Affect the Company's Financial Condition and Operations

Because of the state of the market for insurance in recent years, the Company, and many U.S. corporations, have been unable to obtain insurance for various risks at rates and on terms that they consider reasonable. Consequently, the Company is to a significant degree without insurance for various risks, including those associated with product liability. Although the Company has recorded estimated liabilities for uninsured risks to the extent permitted by generally accepted accounting principles, the absence of various insurance coverages represents a potential exposure for the Company. Therefore, the financial condition and net income of the Company in future periods could be adversely affected if uninsured losses in excess of amounts provided were to be incurred. The portion of liabilities for uninsured losses estimated to be payable after one year is included in "Other noncurrent liabilities" in the accompanying Balance Sheets.

Example 10–15: Company Involved in Arbitration

The Company had been involved in an arbitration entitled *The Company v. ABC, Ltd.* The case was based on the Company's claims that ABC, Ltd. breached noncompetition provisions and other terms of a distribution agreement between the Company and ABC, Ltd.

In October 20X2, the Company was informed that while it had won the case based on the merits of its claims, any recovery of damages was time barred under the terms of the original agreement between the two parties in the dispute. As a result, the Company was required to pay a portion of ABC, Ltd.'s fees and costs related to the arbitration, in the amount of $800,000. The Company expensed these fees and costs awarded to ABC, Ltd. in 20X2. This payment completes the Company's involvement in the matter.

Example 10–16: Litigation Settlement Is Subject to a Confidentiality Agreement

In January 20X2, Stuart Construction Co. (Stuart) filed suit against the Company alleging that the Company had failed to provide coated, welded pipe fittings and joints in accordance with contract specifications for a construction project in the Pacific Grove area. In November 20X2, the parties involved agreed to settle the suit. The financial terms of the settlement are subject to a confidentiality agreement; however, the settlement will not have a material effect on the Company's financial condition or results of operations.

Example 10–17: Company Is Subject to Various Claims and Legal Proceedings in the Ordinary Course of Business That Are Not Considered Material

The Company is subject to various claims and legal proceedings covering a wide range of matters that arise in the ordinary course of its business activities, including product liability claims. Management believes that any liability that may ultimately result from the resolution of these matters will not have a material adverse effect on the financial condition or results of operations of the Company.

Example 10–18: Contingency Resulting from Audit by the Department of Labor

The Company was audited by the Department of Labor in October 20X1. The Department of Labor determined that numerous employees were improperly classified as exempt and should have been classified as non-exempt. As a result, in the year ended December 31, 20X1, the Company recorded an estimated accrual in the amount of $1,500,000 for the past wages that are due for overtime worked. Based on the overtime questionnaires the Company has received from the applicable employees and a revision to the methodology used to calculate overtime pay approved by the Department of Labor, the Company has revised the estimate for this liability to $825,000, of which $675,000 has been paid through December 31, 20X2. The Company is maintaining the remaining accrual, as further claims are probable until the statute of limitations on these claims expires on November 1, 20X4.

Example 10–19: Amount of Future Employer Payroll Taxes Relating to Employees' Stock Options Is Not Known

The Company is subject to employer payroll taxes when employees exercise stock options. The payroll taxes are assessed on the stock option gain, which is the difference between the common stock price on the date of exercise and the exercise price. The tax rate varies depending upon the employees' taxing jurisdiction. The timing and amount of employer payroll taxes is directly related to the timing and number of options exercised by employees, the gain thereon, and the tax rate in the applicable jurisdiction. During the years ended December 31, 20X2 and December 31, 20X1, the Company recorded employer payroll taxes related to stock option exercises of approximately $1,100,000 and $420,000, respectively. Because the Company is unable to predict these employer payroll taxes, the Company is unable to predict what, if any, expense will be recorded in a future period.

Example 10–20: Payments under Registration Payment Arrangement Issued in Conjunction with Financial Instrument Are Probable and Can Be Reasonably Estimated

On January 16, 20X2, the Company issued unsecured promissory notes in the aggregate principal amount of $1,000,000 (the Notes) and warrants to purchase the Company's common stock (the Warrants) to Blue Alliance, Inc. The Notes bear interest at a rate of 11%, mature on July 16, 20X3, and are convertible into 542,000 shares of the Company's common stock at a conversion price of $1.75 per share. The difference between the conversion price and the fair market value of the common stock on the commitment date (transaction date) resulted in a beneficial conversion feature recorded of $590,000. The associated Warrants are exercisable for 270,000 shares of common stock at an exercise price of $1.75 per share. The Warrants, which expire four years after issuance, were assigned a value of $410,000, estimated using the Black-Scholes valuation model. The following assumptions were used to determine the fair value of the Warrants using the Black-Scholes valuation model: a term of four years, risk-free rate of 3.28%, volatility of 100%, and dividend yield of zero. In accordance with EITF Issue No. 00-27, *Application of Issue No. 98-5 to Certain Convertible Instruments*, the values assigned to both the Notes and the Warrants were allocated based on their relative fair values. The discounts on the Notes for the beneficial conversion feature and the Warrants are being amortized to interest expense, using the effective interest method, over the term of the Notes. Total interest expense recognized relating to the beneficial conversion feature and the Warrants discount was $673,000 during the year ended December 31, 20X2.

The holders of the Notes and Warrants have registration rights that require the Company to file a registration statement with the Securities and Exchange Commission (SEC) to register the resale of the common stock issuable upon conversion of the Notes or the exercise of the Warrants. Under EITF Issue No. 00-19, *Accounting for Derivative Financial Instruments Indexed to, and Potentially Settled in, a Company's Own Stock*, the ability to register stock is deemed to be outside of the Company's control. Accordingly, the initial fair value of the Warrants of $410,000 was recorded as an accrued warrant liability in the consolidated balance sheet and is marked to market at the end of each reporting period. At December 31, 20X2, the warrant liability was adjusted to its new fair value of $217,000 as determined by the Company, resulting in a gain of $193,000, which has been reflected in "Interest income and other, net" on the consolidated statement of operations for the year ended December 31, 20X2.

Under the registration rights agreement, the Company has agreed to use its best efforts (1) to file a registration statement for the resale of the common stock issuable upon conversion of the Notes or the exercise of the Warrants and for the registration statement to be declared effective by the SEC by April 1, 20X3, and (2) to maintain the effectiveness of the registration statement through December 31, 20X5 (the term of the agreement). If the registration statement is not declared effective by the SEC by April 1, 20X3, or its effectiveness is not maintained for the specified period, the Company must pay Blue Alliance, Inc., a lump sum amount of $400,000. At December 31, 20X2, the Company determined that the payment of the entire amount of $400,000 is probable and, therefore, recognized a contingent liability for the same amount in the accompanying financial statements.

Gain Contingencies

Example 10–21: Amount of Claim Asserted in Litigation Is Not Specified in the Financial Statement Disclosure

In May 20X2, the Company initiated a legal action against one of its suppliers alleging breach of contract, breach of warranty, and misrepresentation. Management believes, based on the advice of the Company's legal counsel, that the suit could result in a settlement or award by the court in favor of the Company. However, the ultimate outcome of the litigation cannot be determined and no amount has been recognized for possible collection of any claims asserted in the litigation.

Example 10–22: Amount of Claim Asserted in Litigation Is Specified in the Financial Statement Disclosure

On August 10, 20X2, the Company filed suit against Able & Baker Co., its former management consultant and advisory firm. The complaint charges Able & Baker Co. with professional malpractice, negligent misrepresentation, breach of fiduciary duty, breach of contract, and fraud in connection with its advice and services regarding the Company's sale of Hope Enterprises. The complaint seeks $495,000 in compensatory damages, plus prejudgment interest and punitive damages. Able & Baker Co. has included in its answer to the complaint certain "unasserted counterclaims" for fees and expenses incurred by it. A trial date has not been set yet, and no estimate can be made of the amount of the settlement, if any, that will actually be received.

Example 10–23: Gain Not Recognized in the Financial Statements until Received

In December 20X2, a federal court jury found that Dobatek, Inc. infringed on some of the Company's patents and awarded the Company $6,000,000 in damages. Dobatek, Inc. will be required to pay interest on the award amount and legal fees. Should Dobatek, Inc. appeal, the jury verdict or the amount of the damage award could be affected; therefore, the Company will not recognize any award amount in the financial statements until it is received.

Example 10–24: Litigation Settlement Results in Receipt of Award Amount and Gain Recognition

In March 20X2, the Company settled its two year copyright infringement and trade secrets litigation with Britek, Inc. Under the terms of the settlement, Britek, Inc. paid the Company $6,500,000, which was received in full in May 20X2, and the parties have dismissed all pending litigation. The Company recognized a pretax gain, net of related legal fees and other expenses, of $5,300,000 resulting from the settlement, which is included in "Other income" in the 20X2 Consolidated Statement of Operations.

Example 10–25: Insurance Claim Proceeds Are Recorded as Deferred Gain until Final Settlement

In December 20X1, the Company's Vista manufacturing plant in Detroit was extensively damaged as a result of a fire. A $3,000,000 pretax charge was recorded in 20X1 for expected uninsured costs associated with the incident, including deductibles. In 20X2, the Company received interim payments of $14,500,000 on its insurance claim. The Company is in discussions with its insurers as to additional insurance proceeds that the Company believes it is entitled to. Insurance proceeds received under the Company's property damage claim are being deferred pending final settlement of the claim. The Company expects to record a substantial non-recurring gain in 20X3, representing the difference between the property insurance settlement on the plant and the carrying value of the plant at the time of the explosion. The amount of the gain will be dependent on final construction, clean-up expenditures, and the settlement reached with the Company's insurance carriers. As of December 31, 20X2, $14,500,000 has been recorded as a deferred gain and is included in "Other liabilities" in the accompanying Balance Sheet.

Environmental Remediation Contingencies

Example 10–26: Company Has Been Designated as a Potentially Responsible Party and Accrued Estimated Liability on an Undiscounted Basis

The Company has been designated as a potentially responsible party (PRP) by federal and state agencies with respect to certain sites with which the Company may have had direct or indirect involvement. Such designations are made regardless of the extent of the Company's involvement. These claims are in various stages of administrative or judicial proceedings and include demands for recovery of past governmental costs and for future investigations and remedial actions. In many cases, the dollar amounts of the claims have not been specified and, with respect to a number of the PRP claims, have been asserted against a number of other entities for the same cost recovery or other relief as was asserted against the Company. The Company accrues costs associated with environmental matters, on an undiscounted basis, when they become probable and reasonably estimable. As of December 31, 20X2, and December 31, 20X1, the Company has accrued $1,900,000 and $1,600,000, respectively, which represents its current estimate of the probable cleanup liabilities, including remediation and legal costs. This accrual does not reflect any possible future insurance recoveries but does reflect a reasonable estimate of cost-sharing at multiparty sites.

Although the Company's probable liabilities have been accrued for currently, hazardous substance cleanup expenditures generally are paid over an extended period of time, in some cases possibly more than 30 years. Annual cleanup expenditures during 20X2 and 20X1 were approximately $625,000 and $450,000, respectively.

Example 10–27: Accrual for Estimated Environmental Remediation Costs Has Been Discounted

The Company is involved in environmental remediation and ongoing compliance at several sites. At December 31, 20X2, the Company estimated, based on engineering studies, total remediation and ongoing monitoring costs to be made in the future to be approximately $6,500,000, including the effects of inflation. Accordingly, the Company recorded a liability of approximately $4,000,000, which represents the net present value of the estimated future costs discounted at 6%. This is management's best estimate of these liabilities, although possible actual costs could range up to 50% higher. The Company has not anticipated any third-party payments in arriving at these estimates.

Example 10–28: Company Has Not Been Designated as a Potentially Responsible Party but Accrued the Highest Amount in the Range of Potential Loss Because Likelihood of Loss Is Probable

As part of its environmental management program, the Company is involved in various environmental remediation activities. As sites are identified and assessed in this program, the Company determines potential environmental liability. Factors considered in assessing liability include, among others, the following: whether the Company had been designated as a potentially responsible party, the number of other potentially responsible parties designated at the site, the stage of the proceedings, and available environmental technology. As of December 31, 20X2, the Company had identified three sites requiring further investigation. However, the Company has not been designated as a potentially responsible party at any site.

Management has assessed the likelihood that a loss has been incurred at one of its sites as probable and, based on findings included in remediation reports and discussions with legal counsel, estimated the potential loss at December 31, 20X2, to range from $1,500,000 to $2,500,000. As of December 31, 20X2, $2,500,000 had been accrued and is included with "Other accrued liabilities" in the Consolidated Balance Sheets. Although the Company may have a right of contribution or reimbursement under insurance policies, amounts recoverable from other entities with respect to a particular site are not considered until recoveries are deemed probable. No assets for potential recoveries were established as of December 31, 20X2.

Example 10–29: Company Has Not Been Designated as a Potentially Responsible Party but Accrued the Lowest Amount in the Range of Potential Loss Because Likelihood of Loss Is More Likely Than Remote but Not Probable

The Company assesses reasonably possible environmental liability relating to environmental remediation and ongoing compliance at several sites. Such liability is not probable but is more likely than remote. As of December 31, 20X2, while the Company has not been designated as a potentially responsible party at any site, the amount of environmental liability identified that is reasonably possible is in the range of $2,000,000 to $5,500,000. As of December 31, 20X2, the Company accrued $2,000,000 with respect to potential environmental liability. The Company does not expect to incur liabilities at the higher end of the range, based on the limited information currently available.

Example 10–30: Environmental Matter May Result in Increased Operating and Capital Costs to the Company

In 20X2, the State of California made a determination that some of the cement materials stored at the Company's Riverside plant are a Type I waste and requested that the Company apply for a formal permit for an on-site landfill. The Company understands that similar notices were sent to other cement manufacturers in the State. The Company is protesting this determination through legal channels and has received a stay to allow it to demonstrate that current management practices pose no threat to the environment. The Company believes that the State's determination ultimately will be reversed or the Company will receive the needed permit or other adequate relief, such as an agreed order requiring certain additional waste management procedures that are less stringent than those generally required for Type I wastes. If the Company is not successful in this regard, however, like other cement producers in the State, the Riverside plant could incur substantially increased operating and capital costs.

Example 10–31: Accruals for Estimated Future Costs Relate to Divested Operations and Locations No Longer in Operation

The accompanying Consolidated Balance Sheets include accruals for the estimated future costs associated with certain environmental remediation activities related to the past use or disposal of hazardous materials. Substantially all such costs relate to divested operations and to facilities or locations that are no longer in operation. Due to a number of uncertainties, including uncertainty of timing, the scope of remediation, future technology, regulatory changes, and other factors, the ultimate remediation costs may exceed the amounts estimated. However, in the opinion of management, such additional costs are not expected to be material relative to consolidated liquidity, financial position, or future results of operations.

Risks, Uncertainties, and Concentrations

Nature of Operations

Example 10–32: Company Describes Its Primary Products

The Company designs, manufactures, markets, and services test systems and related software, and backplanes and associated connectors. The Company's top five products are semiconductor test systems, backplane connection systems, circuit-board test systems, telecommunications test systems, and software test systems.

Example 10–33: Company Describes the Types of Customers It Has

The Company is a leading global developer, manufacturer, and distributor of hand tools, power tools, tool storage products, shop equipment, under-hood diagnostics equipment, under-car equipment, emissions and safety equipment, collision repair equipment, vehicle service information, and business management systems and services. The Corporation's customers include professional automotive technicians, shop owners, franchised service centers, national accounts, original equipment manufacturers, and industrial tool and equipment users worldwide.

Example 10–34: Company Describes U.S. Geographic Locations Where It Operates

The Company is a leading designer and manufacturer of open-architecture, standard embedded computer components that system designers can easily utilize to create a custom solution specific to the user's unique application. The Company has operations in New York, New Mexico, Minnesota, North Carolina, and California. The Company's product lines include CPU boards, general purpose input/output modules, avionics interface modules and analyzers, interconnection and expansion units, telemetry boards, data acquisition software, and industrial computer systems and enclosures.

Example 10–35: Company Indicates That Its Operations Are Vulnerable to Changes in Trends and Customer Demand

The Company is a nationwide specialty retailer of fashionable and contemporary apparel and accessory items designed for consumers with a young, active lifestyle. The Company's success is largely dependent on its ability to gauge the fashion tastes of its customers and to provide merchandise that satisfies customer demand. The Company's failure to anticipate, identify, or react to changes in fashion trends could adversely affect its results of operations.

Example 10–36: Company's Operations Are Substantially in Foreign Countries

Substantially all of the Company's products are manufactured in the Dominican Republic, Mexico (under the Maquiladora program), Switzerland, Ireland, and Slovakia. These foreign operations represent captive manufacturing facilities of the Company. The Company's operations are subject to various political, economic, and other risks and uncertainties inherent in the countries in which the Company operates. Among other risks, the Company's operations are subject to the risks of restrictions on transfer of funds; export duties, quotas and embargoes; domestic and international customs and tariffs; changing taxation policies; foreign exchange restrictions; and political conditions and governmental regulations.

Example 10–37: Company Specifies Percentage of Net Sales Relating to Foreign Operations

Sales to customers outside the United States approximated 35% of net sales in 20X2 and 25% of net sales in 20X1.

Estimates

Example 10–38: General Note Regarding Estimates Inherent in the Financial Statements

The preparation of the Company's financial statements in conformity with accounting principles generally accepted in the United States of America (GAAP) requires management to make estimates and assumptions that affect reported amounts of assets and liabilities and disclosure of contingent assets and liabilities at the date of the financial statements and the reported amounts of revenues and expenses during the reporting period. Actual results could differ from those estimates.

Example 10–39: Significant Estimates Relating to Specific Financial Statement Accounts and Transactions Are Identified

The financial statements include some amounts that are based on management's best estimates and judgments. The most significant estimates relate to allowance for uncollectible accounts receivable, inventory obsolescence, depreciation, intangible asset valuations and useful lives, employee benefit plans, environmental accruals, taxes, contingencies, and costs to complete long-term contracts. These estimates may be adjusted as more current information becomes available, and any adjustment could be significant.

Example 10–40: Significant Accounting Estimates—Inventory

The Company's provisions for inventory write-downs are based on the Company's best estimates of product sales prices and customer demand patterns, and its plans to transition its products. However, the Company operates in a highly competitive industry that is characterized by aggressive pricing practices, downward pressures on gross margins, and rapid technological advances. As a result of the industry's dynamic nature, it is at least reasonably possible that the estimates used by the Company to determine its provisions for inventory write-downs will be materially different from the actual amounts or results. These differences could result in materially higher than expected inventory provisions and related costs, which could have a materially adverse effect on the Company's results of operations and financial condition in the near term.

Example 10–41: Significant Accounting Estimates—Assets Held for Sale

In October 20X2, in connection with its strategy to reduce debt, the Company decided to sell land and buildings formerly used by a discontinued manufacturing unit. As a result, the Company recorded a non-cash write-down of $1,400,000 to reflect these assets at their estimated fair value of $4,200,000, which is shown as "Assets held for sale" at December 31, 20X2. The charge of $1,400,000 reflects the Company's best estimate of the amount anticipated to be realized on the disposition of the assets. This estimate is based on negotiations with potential buyers and independent parties familiar with valuations of this nature. The amount that the Company will ultimately realize could differ materially from the amount recorded in the financial statements.

Example 10–42: Significant Accounting Estimates—Deferred Tax Assets

Included in the accompanying Balance Sheets at December 31, 20X2, and December 31, 20X1, are deferred tax assets of $2,500,000 and

$2,200,000, respectively, representing tax loss and credit carryforwards. Realization of that asset is dependent on the Company's ability to generate future taxable income. Management believes that it is more likely than not that forecasted taxable income will be sufficient to utilize the tax carryforwards before their expiration in 20X8 and 20X9 to fully recover the asset. However, there can be no assurance that the Company will meet its expectations of future income. As a result, the amount of the deferred tax assets considered realizable could be reduced in the near term if estimates of future taxable income are reduced. Such an occurrence could materially adversely affect the Company's results of operations and financial condition.

Example 10–43: Significant Accounting Estimates—Self-Insured Claims

The Company is primarily self-insured, up to certain limits, for automobile and general liability, workers' compensation, and employee group health claims. The Company has purchased stop-loss insurance, which will reimburse the Company for individual claims in excess of $50,000 annually or aggregate claims exceeding $1,000,000 annually. Operations are charged with the cost of claims reported and an estimate of claims incurred but not reported. A liability for unpaid claims and the associated claim expenses, including incurred but not reported losses, is actuarially determined and reflected in the Balance Sheet as an accrued liability. Total expense under the program was approximately $3,200,000 and $2,900,000 in 20X2 and 20X1, respectively. The self-insured claims liability includes incurred but not reported losses of $1,500,000 and $1,745,000 at December 31, 20X2, and December 31, 20X1, respectively.

The determination of such claims and expenses and the appropriateness of the related liability is continually reviewed and updated. It is reasonably possible that the accrued estimated liability for self-insured claims may need to be revised in the near term.

Other Risks, Uncertainties, and Concentrations

Example 10–44: Company Describes the Risks of the Industry in Which It Operates and Potential Effect on the Company's Operations

The Company participates in a highly volatile industry that is characterized by rapid technological change, intense competitive pressure, and cyclical market patterns. The Company's results of operations are affected by a wide variety of factors, including general economic conditions, decreases in average selling prices over the life of any particular product, the timing of new product introductions (by the Company, its competitors, and others), the ability to manufacture sufficient quantities of a given product in a timely manner, the timely implementation of new manufacturing process technologies, the ability to safeguard patents and intellectual property from competitors, and the effect of new technologies resulting in rapid escalation of demand for some products in the face of equally steep decline in demand for others. Based on the factors noted herein, the Company may experience substantial period-to-period fluctuations in future operating results.

Example 10–45: Company Has Geographic Exposure to Catastrophe Losses

The Company has a geographic exposure to catastrophe losses in certain areas of the country. These catastrophes can be caused by various events, including hurricanes, windstorms, earthquakes, hail, severe winter weather, and fires, and the incidence and severity of catastrophes are inherently unpredictable. The extent of losses from a catastrophe is a function of both the total amount of insured exposure in the area affected by the event and the severity of the event. Most catastrophes are restricted to small geographic areas; however, hurricanes and earthquakes may produce significant damage in large, heavily populated areas. The Company generally seeks to reduce its exposure to catastrophes through individual risk selection and the purchase of catastrophe reinsurance.

Example 10–46: Company Requires No Collateral and Concentrations of Credit Risk Virtually Limited

Financial instruments that potentially subject the Company to concentrations of credit risk consist primarily of cash and cash equivalents and accounts receivable. The Company places its cash and cash equivalents with high quality financial institutions and limits the amount of credit exposure with any one institution. Concentrations of credit risk with respect to accounts receivable are limited because a large number of geographically diverse customers make up the Company's customer base, thus spreading the trade credit risk. At December 31, 20X2, and December 31, 20X1, no single group or customer represents greater than 10% of total accounts receivable. The Company controls credit risk through credit approvals, credit limits, and monitoring procedures. The Company performs credit evaluations of its commercial and industrial customers but generally does not require collateral to support accounts receivable.

Example 10–47: Company Requires Collateral and Has Concentrations in Accounts Receivable

The Company sells its products to distributors and original equipment manufacturers throughout the world. The Company performs ongoing credit evaluations of its customers' financial condition and, generally, requires collateral, such as letters of credit, whenever deemed necessary. At December 31, 20X2, three customers, each of who accounted for more than 10% of the Company's accounts receivable, accounted for 58% of total accounts receivable in aggregate. At December 31, 20X1, four customers, each of who accounted for more than 10% of the Company's accounts receivable, accounted for 52% of total accounts receivable in aggregate.

Example 10–48: Concentrations in Sales to Few Customers

In 20X2, the two largest customers accounted for 30% and 21% of sales. In 20X1, the three largest customers accounted for 32%, 19%, and 18% of sales.

Example 10–49: Concentrations in Sales to Foreign Customers

During 20X2 and 20X1, approximately 38% and 35%, respectively, of the Company's net sales were made to foreign customers. An adverse change in either economic conditions abroad or the Company's relationship with significant foreign distributors could negatively effect the volume of the Company's international sales and the Company's results of operations.

Example 10–50: Company Has Accounts Receivable and Contract Concentrations in Specific Industries

The majority of accounts receivable and all contract work in progress are from engineering and construction clients primarily concentrated in the steel and utility industries throughout the United States. The Company generally does not require collateral, but in most cases can place liens against the property, plant, or equipment constructed or terminate the contract if a material default occurs. The Company maintains adequate reserves for potential credit losses and such losses have been minimal and within management's estimates.

Example 10–51: Company Is Dependent on Few Major Suppliers

The Company is dependent on third-party equipment manufacturers, distributors, and dealers for all of its supply of communications equipment. In 20X2 and 20X1, products purchased from the Company's three largest suppliers accounted for approximately 51% and 65% of product purchases, respectively. The Company is dependent on the ability of its suppliers to provide products on a timely basis and on favorable pricing terms. The loss of certain principal suppliers or a significant reduction in product availability from principal suppliers could have a material adverse effect on the Company. The

Company believes that its relationships with its suppliers are satisfactory; however, the Company has periodically experienced inadequate supply from certain handset manufacturers.

Example 10–52: Risks Associated with Concentrations in the Available Sources of Supply of Materials

Certain components and products that meet the Company's requirements are available only from a single supplier or a limited number of suppliers. The rapid rate of technological change and the necessity of developing and manufacturing products with short life cycles may intensify these risks. The inability to obtain components and products as required, or to develop alternative sources, if and as required in the future, could result in delays or reductions in product shipments, which in turn could have a material adverse effect on the Company's business, financial condition, and results of operations.

Example 10–53: Company Uses Parts and Materials That Are Subject to Industry-Wide Shortages Which Has Forced Suppliers to Allocate Available Quantities

The Company uses numerous suppliers of electronic components and other materials for its operations. Some components used by the Company have been subject to industry-wide shortages, and suppliers have been forced to allocate available quantities among their customers. The Company's inability to obtain any needed components during periods of allocation could cause delays in manufacturing and could adversely affect results of operations.

Example 10–54: Concentrations of Labor Subject to Collective Bargaining Agreement

At December 31, 20X2, the Company had a total of approximately 1,200 employees. Of this total, approximately 1,000 are hourly workers and 200 are salaried. Approximately 98% of the Company's hourly employees and 37% of its salaried employees are represented by a union. The existing union agreement will expire in November 20X3.

Example 10–55: Company Limits the Amount of Credit Exposure Through Diversification

The Company places its short-term investments in a variety of financial instruments and, by policy, limits the amount of credit exposure through diversification and by restricting its investments to highly rated securities.

Example 10–56: Cash in Excess of FDIC Insured Limits

The Company maintains its cash in bank deposit accounts which, at times, may exceed federally insured limits. Accounts are guaranteed by the Federal Deposit Insurance Corporation (FDIC) up to $100,000. At December 31, 20X2, and December 31, 20X1, the Company had approximately $1,250,000 and $1,155,000, respectively, in excess of FDIC insured limits. The Company has not experienced any losses in such accounts.

CHAPTER 11
DEFERRED COMPENSATION ARRANGEMENTS

CONTENTS

EXECUTIVE SUMMARY

Deferred compensation contracts are accounted for individually on an accrual basis. Estimated amounts to be paid under a deferred compensation contract that is not equivalent to a pension plan or a postretirement health or welfare benefit plan should be accrued over the period of an employee's active employment from the time the contract is signed to the employee's full eligibility date. If elements of both current and future services are present, only the portion applicable to the current services is accrued.

If a deferred compensation contract contains benefits payable for the life of a beneficiary, the total liability is based on the beneficiary's life expectancy or on the estimated cost of an annuity contract that would provide sufficient funds to pay the required benefits. The total liability for deferred compensation contracts is determined by the terms of each individual contract. The amount of the periodic accrual, computed from the first day of the employment contract, must total no less than the then present value of the benefits provided for in the contract. The periodic accruals are made systematically over the active term of employment.

If individual deferred compensation contracts, as a group, are in substance a retirement plan, they should be accounted for in accordance with generally accepted accounting principles (GAAP) for pension plans as discussed in Chapter 26, "Pension Plans." Similarly, if individual deferred compensation contracts, as a group, are in substance a postretirement benefit plan other than pensions, they should be accounted for in accordance with GAAP for postretirement benefits as discussed in Chapter 28, "Postretirement Benefits Other Than Pensions."

Authoritative Literature

| APB-12 | Omnibus Opinion—1967 (Deferred Compensation Contracts) |
| FAS-106 | Employers' Accounting for Postretirement Benefits Other Than Pensions |

DISCLOSURE REQUIREMENTS

Authoritative pronouncements require no specific disclosures about deferred compensation contracts or arrangements. However, disclosures similar to those for pension plans and postretirement benefits are found in practice and are considered informative disclosures. The disclosure requirements for pension plans are discussed in Chapter 26, "Pension Plans," and the disclosure requirements for postretirement benefits other than pensions are discussed in Chapter 28, "Postretirement Benefits Other Than Pensions."

EXAMPLES OF FINANCIAL STATEMENT DISCLOSURES

 The following sample disclosures are available on the accompanying disc.

Example 11–1: Present Value of Estimated Future Benefit Payments Are Being Accrued over the Service Period

In March 20X2, the Company entered into a deferred compensation agreement with a key executive. The agreement provides for certain postretirement benefits, contingent on certain conditions, begining in 20X9 and payable over the remaining life of the executive and spouse. The Company accrues the present value of the estimated future benefit payments over the period from the date of the agreement to the retirement date. The Company recognized expense of $141,000 in 20X2 and $102,000 in 20X1 related to this agreement.

Example 11–2: Deferred Compensation Plan Is Funded by Life Insurance Contracts and Provides Guaranteed Interest Rate

The Company has a deferred compensation plan that permits management and highly compensated employees to defer portions of their compensation and earn a guaranteed interest rate on the deferred amounts. The salaries that have been deferred since the plan's inception have been accrued and the only expense, other than salaries, related to this plan is the interest on the deferred amounts. Interest expense during 20X2 and 20X1 includes $103,000 and $68,000, respectively, related to this plan. The Company has included in "Deferred employee benefits" $1,150,000 and $935,000 at December 31, 20X2, and December 31, 20X1, respectively, to reflect its liability under this plan. The Company has established a rabbi trust to finance obligations under the plan with corporate-owned whole-life insurance contracts on the related employees. The Company has included in "Other assets" $1,200,000 and $967,000 at December 31, 20X2, and December 31, 20X1, respectively, which represents cash surrender value of these policies.

Example 11–3: Deferred Compensation Obligation Is Accrued but Unfunded

The Company has two deferred compensation plans for management and highly compensated associates, whereby participants may defer base compensation and bonuses and earn interest on their deferred amounts. Under one plan, a participant may elect to defer a maximum of 100% of his or her compensation. Under another plan, a participant could elect to defer a minimum of 3% of his or her compensation. These deferred compensation plans are unfunded; therefore, benefits are paid from the general assets of the Company. The total of participant deferrals, which is reflected in long-term liabilities, was $823,000 and $554,000 at December 31, 20X2, and December 31, 20X1, respectively. The participant deferrals earn interest at a rate based on U.S. Government Treasury rates. The interest expense related to this plan was $65,000 in 20X2 and $47,000 in 20X1.

Example 11–4: Non-Plan Independent Consultant Stock Options

During the year ended December 31, 20X2, the Company's Board of Directors approved the grant of stock options to an independent consultant to purchase an aggregate of 50,000 shares of its common stock. These options have an exercise price of $11.49 and as of December 31, 20X2, none of these option shares were vested. As a result, the Company has recorded $215,000 in "Deferred compensation," which will be amortized to expense over the three-year vesting period of the options. For the year ended December 31, 20X2, an amount of $36,000 has been amortized to expense. These options were not issued as part of any of the Company's registered Stock Option Plans.

Example 11–5: Restricted Stock Plan

The Company has a Restricted Stock Plan, covering 1,200,000 shares of common stock, whose purpose is to permit grants of shares, subject to restrictions, to key employees of the Company as a means of retaining and rewarding them for long-term performance and to increase their ownership in the Company. Shares awarded under the plan entitle the shareholder to all rights of common stock ownership except that the shares may not be sold, transferred, pledged, exchanged, or otherwise disposed of during the restriction period. The restriction period is determined by a committee that is appointed by the Board of Directors and the period may not exceed ten years. During 20X2 and 20X1, 95,000 shares and 83,000 shares, respectively, were granted with restriction periods of four to six years at market prices ranging from $13.125 to $18.475 in 20X2 and $11.375 to $16.875 in 20X1. The shares were recorded at the market value on the date of issuance as deferred compensation and the related amount is being amortized to operations over the respective vesting period. Compensation expense for the years ended December 31, 20X2, and December 31, 20X1, related to these shares of restricted stock was $375,000 and $290,000, respectively. At December 31, 20X2, the weighted-average grant date fair value and weighted-average contractual life for outstanding shares of restricted stock was $15.03 and 5.2 years, respectively.

Example 11–6: Deferred Compensation Balance and Related Expense Previously Recognized Are Reversed

On July 27, 20X2, Mr. White joined the Company as president, chief executive officer, and a member of the board of directors. On December 29, 20X2, Mr. White resigned his positions with the Company. In July 20X2, the Company granted 1 million shares of stock options to Mr. White at an exercise price of $1.50 below the stock's per share fair value on the date of grant. This grant resulted in the recording of $1.5 million of deferred compensation, which the Company had begun to recognize over the vesting period of the options. All of Mr. White's options expired unvested upon his resignation. Therefore, the remaining deferred compensation balance, as well as the stock compensation expense recorded during the year, were reversed.

CHAPTER 12
DEVELOPMENT STAGE ENTERPRISES

CONTENTS

EXECUTIVE SUMMARY

A *development stage company* is one in which principal operations have not commenced or principal operations have generated an insignificant amount of revenue. A development stage company issues the same basic financial statements as any other enterprise, and such statements should be prepared in conformity with generally accepted accounting principles (GAAP). Accordingly, determining whether a particular cost should be charged to expense when incurred or should be capitalized or deferred should be based on the same accounting standards regardless of whether the enterprise incurring the cost is already operating or is in the development stage.

The financial statements of an entity that is in the development stage should be identified as those of a development stage company. In addition, the statements should include certain disclosures, including cumulative amounts of revenues, expenses, and cash flows from the entity's inception.

Authoritative Literature

FAS-7 Accounting and Reporting by Development Stage Enterprises

FIN-7 Applying FASB Statement No. 7 in Financial Statements of Established Operating Enterprises

SOP 98-5 Reporting on the Costs of Start-Up Activities

DISCLOSURE REQUIREMENTS

The financial statements of development stage companies and related notes should include the following:

1. A balance sheet, including any cumulative net losses reported with a descriptive caption such as "deficit accumulated during the development stage" in the stockholders' equity section (FAS-7, par. 11)

2. An income statement showing (a) amounts of revenue and expenses for each period covered by the income statement and (b) cumulative amounts from the entity's inception (FAS-7, par. 11)

3. A statement of cash flows showing (a) the cash inflows and cash outflows for each period for which an income statement is presented and (b) cumulative amounts from the entity's inception (FAS-7, par. 11)

4. A statement of stockholders' equity showing the following from the entity's inception (FAS-7, par. 11):

   a. For each issuance, the date and number of shares of stock, warrants, rights, or other equity securities issued for cash and for other consideration

   b. For each issuance, the dollar amounts (per share or other equity unit, and in total) assigned to the consideration received for shares of stock, warrants, rights, or other equity securities (dollar amounts should be assigned to any noncash consideration received)

   c. For each issuance involving noncash consideration, the nature of the noncash consideration and the basis for assigning amounts

5. The financial statements should be identified as those of a development stage company and should include a description

of the nature of the development stage activities in which the entity is engaged (FAS-7, par. 12)

6. For the first year the entity is no longer in the development stage, disclosure should be made that in prior years the entity had been in the development stage. (If financial statements for prior years are presented for comparative purposes, the cumulative amounts and other additional disclosures required by items 1–5 above need not be shown.) (FAS-7, pars. 12 and 13)

EXAMPLES OF FINANCIAL STATEMENT DISCLOSURES

 The following sample disclosures are available on the accompanying disc.

Note: Examples 12–1 to 12–6 assume that the entity was formed on July 1, 20X0, and that financial statements for the years ended December 31, 20X2, and December 31, 20X1, are presented. Note that the Statements of Operations, Statements of Stockholders' Equity, and Statements of Cash Flows must be from inception even though Comparative Financial Statements for 20X2 and 20X1 are presented. Details of other note disclosures (e.g., property and equipment, stock options, income taxes) are omitted because they are similar to other businesses.

Example 12–1: Balance Sheets of a Development Stage Enterprise

Prostech Corp.
(A Development Stage Enterprise)
Balance Sheets
December 31, 20X2, and December 31, 20X1

	December 31	
	20X2	*20X1*
Assets		
Current assets:		
Cash and equivalents	$74,353	$250,255
Total current assets	74,353	250,255
Property and equipment, net	2,111	2,439
Other assets	1,065	-0-
Total assets	$77,529	$252,694

	December 31	
	20X2	20X1
Liabilities and Stockholders' Equity		
Current liabilities:		
Accounts payable and accrued liabilities	$68,824	$ 15,460
Total current liabilities	68,824	15,460
Stockholders' equity:		
Preferred Stock—$0.01 par value, 5,000,000 shares authorized, none issued at December 31, 20X2, and December 31, 20X1	-0-	-0-
Common Stock—$.001 par value, 40,000,000 shares authorized, 7,537,319 issued at December 31, 20X2, and 5,979,528 at December 31, 20X1	7,538	5,980
Additional paid-in capital	751,584	675,252
Note receivable for common stock issued	(7,242)	-0-
Deficit accumulated during development stage	(743,175)	(443,998)
Total stockholders' equity	8,705	237,234
Total liabilities and stockholders' equity	$77,529	$252,694

Example 12–2: Statements of Operations of a Development Stage Enterprise

Prostech Corp.
(A Development Stage Enterprise)
Statements of Operations
For the Years Ended December 31, 20X2, and December 31, 20X1,
and the Period from July 1, 20X0, (Inception) to December 31, 20X2

	For the Years Ended December 31		July 1, 20X0, (Inception) to December 31,
	20X2	20X1	20X2
Revenue	$193,500	$ -0-	$243,500
Costs and expenses:			
Cost of sales	-0-	-0-	-0-

	For the Years Ended December 31		July 1, 20X0, (Inception) to December 31,
	20X2	20X1	20X2
Research and development	345,592	283,922	669,514
Selling, general, and administrative	151,315	174,472	345,787
Total costs and expenses	496,907	458,394	1,015,301
Loss from operations	(303,407)	(458,394)	(771,801)
Interest income	4,230	14,396	28,626
Net loss	$(299,177)	$(443,998)	$(743,175)

Example 12–3: Statements of Stockholders' Equity of a Development Stage Enterprise

Prostech Corp. (A Development Stage Enterprise)

Statements of Stockholders & Equity for the Period from July 1, 20X0, (Inception) to December 31, 20X2

	Common Stock		Additional Paid-in Capital	Note Receivable for Common Stock Issued	Deficit Accumulated during Development Stage	Total
	Number of Shares	Amount				
Issuance of Common Stock on July 1, 20X0 for cash at $.12 per share	5,616,528	$5,617	$657,465	$ -0-	$ -0-	663,082
Net loss July 1, 20X0 to December 31, 20X0	-0-	-0-	-0-	-0-	-0-	-0-
Balance at December 31, 20X0	5,616,528	5,617	657,465	-0-	-0-	663,082
Distribution of Common Stock for services at $.05 per share	363,000	363	17,787	-0-	-0-	18,150
Net loss for 20X1	-0-	-0-	-0-	-0-	(443,998)	(443,998)
Balance at December 31, 20X1	5,979,528	5,980	675,252	-0-	(443,998)	237,234
Issuance of Common Stock for cash upon exercise of options at $.05 per share	1,410,000	1,410	69,090	-0-	-0-	70,500
Issuance of Common Stock for cash and note receivable at $.05 per share	147,791	148	7,242	(7,242)	-0-	148
Net loss for 20X2	-0-	-0-	-0-	-0-	(299,177)	(299,177)
Balance at December 31, 20X2	7,537,319	$7,538	$751,584	$(7,242)	$(743,175)	$ 8,705

Example 12–4: Statements of Cash Flows of a Development Stage Enterprise

Prostech Corp.
(A Development Stage Enterprise)
Statements of Cash Flows
For the Years Ended December 31, 20X2, and
December 31, 20X1, and the Period from July 1, 20X0,
(Inception) to December 31, 20X2

	For the Years Ended December 31		July 1, 20X0, (Inception) to December 31,
	20X2	20X1	20X2
Cash Flows from Operating Activities			
Net loss	$(299,177)	$(443,998)	$(743,175)
Adjustments to reconcile net loss to net cash used in operating activities:			
Depreciation	828	300	1,128
Non-cash distribution of common stock	-0-	18,150	18,150
Increase in accounts payable and accrued liabilities	53,364	15,460	68,824
Other, net	(1,065)	-0-	(1,065)
Net Cash Used in Operating Activities	(246,050)	(410,088)	(656,138)
Cash Flows from Investing Activities			
Purchase of property and equipment	(500)	(2,739)	(3,239)
Net Cash Used in Investing Activities	(500)	(2,739)	(3,239)
Cash Flows from Financing Activities			
Proceeds from issuance of common stock upon exercise of options	70,500	-0-	70,500
Proceeds from sale of common stock	148	-0-	663,230

	For the Years Ended December 31		July 1, 20X0, (Inception) to December 31,
	20X2	20X1	20X2
Net Cash Provided by Financing Activities	70,648	-0-	733,730
Net Increase (Decrease) in Cash and Equivalents	(175,902)	(412,827)	74,353
Cash and Equivalents, Beginning of Period	250,255	663,082	-0-
Cash and Equivalents, End of Period	$ 74,353	$250,255	$ 74,353

Example 12–5: Description of Development Stage Operations

Prostech Corp. (Company) was incorporated on July 1, 20X0, in Delaware. Shares of Common Stock of the Company totaling 5,616,528 shares were sold for a total cash consideration of $663,082.

The Company is a development stage entity and is primarily engaged in the development of pharmaceuticals to treat urological disorders. The initial focus of the Company's research and development efforts will be the generation of products for the treatment and diagnosis of prostate cancer. The production and marketing of the Company's products and its ongoing research and development activities will be subject to extensive regulation by numerous governmental authorities in the United States. Prior to marketing in the United States, any drug developed by the Company must undergo rigorous preclinical (animal) and clinical (human) testing and an extensive regulatory approval process implemented by the Food and Drug Administration (FDA) under the Food, Drug and Cosmetic Act. The Company has limited experience in conducting and managing the preclinical and clinical testing necessary to obtain regulatory approval. There can be no assurance that the Company will not encounter problems in clinical trials that will cause the Company or the FDA to delay or suspend clinical trials.

The Company's success will depend in part on its ability to obtain patents and product license rights, maintain trade secrets, and operate without infringing on the proprietary rights of others, both in the United States and other countries. There can be no assurance that patents issued to or licensed by the Company will not be challenged, invalidated, or circumvented, or that the rights granted thereunder will provide proprietary protection or competitive advantages to the Company.

For the year ended December 31, 20X2, revenues of $193,500 were from a research agreement. The Company has no significant operating history and, from July 1, 20X0, (inception) to December 31, 20X2, has generated a net loss of $743,175. The accompanying financial statements for the year ended December 31, 20X2, have been prepared assuming the Company will continue as a going concern. During the year 20X3, management intends to raise additional debt and/or equity financing to fund future operations and to provide additional working capital. However, there is no assurance that such financing will be consummated or obtained in sufficient amounts necessary to meet the Company's needs.

The accompanying financial statements do not include any adjustments to reflect the possible future effects on the recoverability and classification of assets or the amounts and classifications of liabilities that may result from the possible inability of the Company to continue as a going concern.

Example 12–6: Disclosure That Company Was in the Development Stage in Prior Years

> **Note:** Example 12–6 assumes that the Company is considered an operating company in the year 20X3 and that 20X2 was the last year that the Company was in the development stage.

Prostech Corp. (Company) was incorporated on July 1, 20X0, in Delaware and was in the development stage through December 31, 20X2. The year 20X3 is the first year during which the Company is considered an operating company and is no longer in the development stage.

CHAPTER 13
EXIT OR DISPOSAL ACTIVITIES

CONTENTS

EXECUTIVE SUMMARY

A liability for costs associated with exit or disposal activities should be recognized when incurred and measured at its fair value (with limited exceptions). An entity's commitment to an exit or disposal plan, in and of itself, does not create a present obligation that meets the definition of a liability. Examples of costs associated with exit or disposal activities include:

- Contract termination costs (excluding capital leases)
- Costs to consolidate or close facilities
- Costs to relocate employees
- One-time termination benefits provided to terminate employees

The fair value of the liability is the amount at which it could be settled in a current transaction between willing parties (i.e., other than a forced or liquidation transaction). After initial measurement, changes in the liability should be measured using the credit-adjusted risk-free rate that was used to measure the liability initially. The cumulative effect of a change resulting from a revision to either the timing or the amount of the estimated cash flows should be (a) recognized as an adjustment to the liability in the period of the change and (b) reported in the same income statement line item that was used to initially recognize the related costs. Changes due to the passage of time should be recognized as an increase in the carrying amount of the liability and as an expense (e.g., accretion expense).

Costs associated with an exit or disposal activity that does not involve a discontinued operation should be included in income from continuing operations before taxes in the income statement. If a subtotal "Income from Operations" is presented, it should include the amounts of those costs. Costs associated with an exit or disposal activity involving discontinued operations should be included in the results of discontinued operations.

Authoritative Literature

FAS-146   Accounting for Costs Associated with Exit or Disposal Activities

DISCLOSURE REQUIREMENTS

The following disclosures should be made in the period in which an exit or disposal activity is initiated and in any subsequent period until the activity is completed:

1. A description of the exit or disposal activity, including the facts and circumstances leading to the activity and the expected completion date (FAS-146, par. 20)

2. For each major type of costs associated with the activity, e.g., one-time termination benefits, contract termination costs, and other associated costs (FAS-146, par. 20):

   a. The total amount expected to be incurred in connection with the activity

   b. The amount incurred in the period

   c. The cumulative amount incurred to date

   d. A reconciliation of the beginning and ending liability balances showing separately the changes during the period attributable to costs incurred and charged to expense, costs paid or otherwise settled, and adjustments to the liability with an explanation of the reasons for those adjustments

3. The line item in the income statement in which the costs described above are included (FAS-146, par. 20)

4. For each reportable segment (FAS-146, par. 20):

   a. The total amount of costs expected to be incurred in connection with the activity

   b. The amount incurred in the period

c. The cumulative amount incurred to date, net of any adjustment to the liability with an explanation of the reasons for the adjustment

5. If a liability for a cost associated with the activity is not recognized because fair value cannot reasonably be determined, that fact and the reasons for that (FAS-146, par. 20)

EXAMPLES OF FINANCIAL STATEMENT DISCLOSURES

 The following sample disclosures are available on the accompanying disc.

Example 13–1: Various Costs Associated with Exit or Disposal Activities

As a result of the Company's change in strategy and due to a difficult business environment, in July 20X1 the Company announced plans to restructure its operations to rationalize, integrate and align the resources of the Company. This restructuring program includes workforce reductions, closure of excess facilities, and other charges. The expected completion date is September 20X3.

The restructuring program resulted in costs incurred primarily for (1) workforce reduction of approximately 350 employees across certain business functions and operating units and (2) abandoned or excess facilities relating to lease terminations and non-cancelable lease costs. To determine the lease loss, which is the Company's loss after its cost recovery efforts from subleasing a building, certain estimates were made related to the (1) time period over which the relevant building would remain vacant, (2) sublease terms, and (3) sublease rates, including common area charges. If market rates continue to decrease in these markets or if it takes longer than expected to sublease these facilities, the actual loss could exceed this estimate.

A summary of the restructuring and other costs recognized for the years ended December 31, 20X2 and December 31, 20X1 are as follows:

	Workforce Reduction	*Excess Facilities*	*Other Exit Costs*	*Total*
Amounts expected to be incurred	$2,950,000	$1,875,000	$200,000	$5,025,000
Amounts incurred in:				
20X1	$1,950,000	$1,350,000	$ —	$3,300,000

	Workforce Reduction	*Excess Facilities*	*Other Exit Costs*	*Total*
20X2	1,000,000	225,000	200,000	1,425,000
Cumulative amount incurred as of December 31, 20X2	$2,950,000	$1,575,000	$200,000	$4,725,000

The Company expects to incur additional charges of approximately $300,000 during the first half of 20X3, as a result of additional facilities that the Company is planning to vacate as well as other restructuring charges.

At December 31, 20X2 and December 31, 20X1, the accrued liability associated with the restructuring and other related charges consisted of the following:

	Workforce Reduction	*Excess Facilities*	*Other Exit Costs*	*Total*
20X1:				
Charges	$1,950,000	$ 1,350,000	$ -0-	$3,300,000
Payments	(725,000)	(475,000)	-0-	(1,200,000)
Accrued liability at December 31, 20X1	1,225,000	875,000	-0-	$2,100,000
20X2:				
Charges	1,000,000	225,000	200,000	1,425,000
Payments	(870,000)	(630,000)	(200,000)	(1,700,000)
Adjustment	-0-	(50,000)	-0-	(50,000)
Accrued liability at December 31, 20X2	$1,355,000	$ 420,000	$ -0-	$1,775,000

For 20X2, the adjustment of $50,000 to the accrued liability was the result of the Company successfully settling certain contingencies relating to one of its facility leases.

The remaining accrual as of December 31, 20X2 of $1,775,000 consists of $1,600,000 that is expected to be paid during the year ending December 31, 20X3 and $175,000, expected to be paid through various dates by March 31, 20X6.

The restructuring and other related charges are included in the line item "Special charges" in the income statement. The workforce reduction charges relate to the telecommunications business segment. Excess facilities charges and other exit costs relate to the semiconductor segment.

Example 13–2: One-Time Termination Benefits

In December 20X2, the Company decided to cease operations at one of its manufacturing plants in Victorville, California, primarily because that operation never generated a profit. In connection with this activity, the Company determined that it no longer needs the 100 employees who currently work in that location. The Company notified the employees that they will be terminated in 90 days. Each employee will receive as a termination benefit a cash payment of $5,000, which will be paid at the date an employee ceases rendering service during the 90-day period. The Company recognized a liability of $500,000 in December 20X2, which approximates fair value. The entire amount is outstanding at December 31, 20X2. Because of the short discount period, the liability amount of $500,000 recognized is not materially different from its fair value.

The costs are included in the line item "Termination benefits" in the income statement for the year ended December 31, 20X2 and relate to the Company's telecommunications segment.

Example 13–3: Abandoned Leased Facilities

In June 20X2, the Company abandoned its administrative office facilities in Laguna Hills and Newport Beach, CA. Although the Company remains obligated under the terms of these leases for the rent and other costs associated with these leases, the Company made the decision to cease using these spaces on June 30, 20X2, and has no foreseeable plans to occupy them in the future. Therefore, in accordance with FASB Statement of Financial Accounting Standards No. 146, *Accounting for Costs Associated with Exit or Disposal Activities*, the Company recorded a charge to earnings of approximately $575,000 to recognize the costs of exiting the space. The liability is equal to the total amount of rent and other direct costs for the period of time space is expected to remain unoccupied plus the present value of the amount by which the rent paid by the Company to the landlord exceeds any rent paid to the Company by a tenant under a sublease over the remainder of the lease terms, which expire in March 20X8 for Laguna Hills, CA, and April 20X9 for Newport Beach, CA.

CHAPTER 14
FAIR VALUE MEASUREMENTS

CONTENTS

EXECUTIVE SUMMARY

In September 2006, the FASB issued Statement of Financial Accounting Standards No. 157 (FAS-157), *Fair Value Measurements*, which provides guidance for using fair value to measure assets and liabilities and expands disclosures about fair value measurements. FAS-157 applies whenever other standards require or permit assets or liabilities to be measured at fair value; however, it does not expand the use of fair value in any new circumstances.

Prior to FAS-157, the methods for measuring fair value were diverse and inconsistent, especially for items that are not actively traded. FAS-157 clarifies that for items that are not actively traded, such as certain kinds of derivatives, fair value should reflect the price in a transaction with a market participant, including an adjustment for risk. In addition, FAS-157 requires expanded disclosure of the effect on earnings for items measured using unobservable data. Therefore, changes in practice that result from applying FAS-157 relate to the definition of fair value, the methods used to measure fair value, and the expanded disclosures about fair value measurements.

Under FAS-157, fair value refers to the price that would be received to sell an asset or paid to transfer a liability in an orderly transaction between market participants in the market in which the reporting entity transacts. The FASB clarifies the principle that fair value should be based on the assumptions market participants use when pricing the asset or liability. In support of this principle, FAS-157 establishes a fair value hierarchy that prioritizes the information used to develop those assumptions. The fair value hierarchy gives the highest priority to quoted prices in active markets and the lowest priority to unobservable data (e.g., the reporting entity's own data). Under FAS-157, fair value measurements would be separately disclosed by level within the fair value hierarchy.

FAS-157 expands disclosures about the use of fair value to measure assets and liabilities in interim and annual periods subsequent to initial recognition. It does not eliminate or modify the fair value disclosure requirements under other accounting pronouncements (e.g., Statement of Financial Accounting Standards No. 107 (FAS-107), *Disclosures about Fair Value of Financial Instruments*); rather, it encourages entities to combine the fair value information disclosed under FAS-157 with the fair value information disclosed under other such accounting pronouncements.

FAS-157 is effective for financial statements issued for fiscal years beginning after November 15, 2007, and interim periods within those fiscal years. Earlier application is encouraged provided that the reporting entity has not yet issued financial statements for that fiscal year, including any financial statements for an interim period within that fiscal year.

Fair Value Measurement

FAS-157 defines fair value as "the price that would be received Fair Value Measurement to sell an asset or paid to transfer a liability in an orderly transaction between market participants at the measurement date." Key concepts in this definition are (1) the price, (2) the particular asset or liability subject to measurement, and (3) market participants. The following discussion provides additional guidance with respect to these items.

The price. FAS-157 indicates that the basis for a fair value is the price at which a company would sell its asset or the price that it would pay to settle its liability at the measurement date (referred to as the exit price). This assumes that the asset or liability is exchanged in an orderly transaction between market participants in the "principal market" (not a forced liquidation or distressed sale). The principal market is the market in which the company would sell the asset or transfer the liability with the greatest volume and level of activity for the asset or liability. In the absence of a principal market, fair value would be based on the "most advantageous market" for the asset or liability. The most advantageous market is the market in which a company would sell its asset or transfer its liability with the price that maximizes the amount that would be received for the asset or minimizes the amount that would be paid to transfer the liability, considering transaction costs in the respective markets.

The asset or liability subject to fair value measurement. A fair value measurement is for a particular asset or liability and thus should consider attributes specific to the asset or liability. For example, the condition or location of the asset or liability and any restrictions on the sale or use of the asset at the measurement date affect the asset or liability's fair value.

Market participants. Market participants are buyers and sellers in the principal or most advantageous market for the asset or liability that meet the following four criteria:

1. They are unrelated parties, as that term is used in Statement of Financial Accounting Standards No. 57 (FAS-57), *Related Party Disclosures*.

2. They are knowledgeable and have a reasonable understanding about the asset or liability and the transaction based on all available information, including information that might be obtained through due diligence efforts that are usual and customary.

3. They are able to transact (i.e., legally and financially) for the asset or liability.

4. They are willing to transact for the asset or liability (i.e., willing, but not forced or otherwise compelled to do so).

Fair Value at Initial Recognition

When an asset is acquired or a liability is assumed in an exchange, the transaction price represents the price paid to acquire the asset or received to assume the liability (i.e., entry price). In contrast, the fair value of the asset or liability represents the price that would be received to sell the asset or paid to transfer the liability (i.e., an exit price). In many cases, the transaction price equals the exit price and, therefore, represents the fair value of the asset or liability at initial recognition. In determining whether a transaction price represents the fair value of the asset or liability at initial recognition, a company should consider factors specific to the transaction and to the specific asset or liability. Examples of situations in which the transaction price might *not* represent the fair value of an asset or liability at initial recognition are:

- The transaction is between related parties.
- The transaction occurs under duress or the seller is forced to accept the price because of certain pressure (e.g., financial difficulties).

- The unit of account represented by the transaction price is different from the unit of account for the asset or liability that is measured at fair value (e.g., the asset or liability is only one of the elements in the transaction that includes multiple elements).

- The market in which the transaction occurs is different from the market in which the company would sell the asset or transfer the liability (e.g., a retail market versus an interdealer market for a reporting entity that is a securities dealer).

Valuation Techniques

FAS-157 indicates that valuation techniques consistent with the market approach, income approach, or cost approach should be used to measure fair value. Following are brief descriptions of each approach.

Market approach. The market approach uses prices and other relevant information generated by market transactions involving identical or comparable assets or liabilities. This approach often uses market multiples derived from a set of comparables.

Income approach. The income approach uses valuation techniques to convert future amounts to a single discounted present amount. The measurement is based on the value indicated by current market expectations about those future amounts. Examples include present value techniques, option-pricing models (e.g., Black-Scholes-Merton formula), and the multiperiod excess earnings method.

Cost approach. The cost approach is based on the amount that currently would be required to replace the service capacity of an asset (sometimes referred to as "current replacement cost"). The price that would be received from the asset is determined on the basis of the cost to a buyer to acquire or construct a substitute asset of comparable utility, adjusted for obsolescence.

Valuation techniques that are appropriate in the circumstances and for which sufficient data are available should be used to measure fair value. A combination of valuation techniques may be appropriate, and valuation techniques used to measure fair value should be applied consistently. A change in the valuation technique or its application is appropriate if the change results in a measurement that is equally or more representative of fair value in the circumstances. Revisions from a change in the valuation technique or its application are accounted for as changes in accounting estimate in accordance with Statement of Financial Accounting Standards No. 154, *Accounting Changes and Error Corrections*.

Fair Value Hierarchy

The term *inputs* refers to the assumptions that market participants use in pricing the asset or liability. FAS-157 distinguishes between *observable inputs* and *unobservable inputs.* Observable inputs reflect the assumptions market participants would use in pricing the asset or liability based on market data obtained from independent sources. Unobservable inputs reflect an entity's own assumptions about the assumptions market participants would use in pricing the asset or liability. FAS-157 indicates that valuation techniques should maximize the use of observable inputs and minimize the use of unobservable inputs. FAS-157 establishes a fair value hierarchy that prioritizes the inputs used in valuation techniques and creates the following three broad levels, with Level 1 being the highest priority:

- *Level 1 inputs:* Level 1 inputs are quoted market prices in active markets for identical assets or liabilities that are accessible at the measurement date (e.g., equity securities traded on the New York Stock Exchange).

- *Level 2 inputs:* Level 2 inputs are from other than quoted market prices included in Level 1 that are observable for the asset or liability, either directly or indirectly (e.g., quoted market prices of similar assets or liabilities in active markets, or quoted market prices for identical or similar assets or liabilities in markets that are not active).

- *Level 3 inputs:* Level 3 inputs are unobservable (e.g., a company's own data) and should be used to measure fair value to the extent that observable inputs are not available.

Authoritative Literature

FAS-157   Fair Value Measurements

DISCLOSURE REQUIREMENTS

The disclosure requirements in items 1 and 2 below are prescribed by FAS-157, which is effective for fiscal years beginning after November 15, 2007, and interim periods within those fiscal years. Early adoption is permitted as long as financial statements for any period (interim or annual) of the fiscal year have not yet been issued. The disclosure requirements of FAS-157 need not be applied for financial statements for periods presented prior to its initial application.

The quantitative disclosures in items 1 and 2 below should be presented in a tabular format (FAS-157, par. 34). In addition, the entity is encouraged, but not required, to combine the fair value information disclosed in accordance with items 1 and 2 with the fair value information disclosed under other accounting pronouncements (e.g., FAS-107, *Disclosures about Fair Value of Financial Instruments*). The entity is encouraged, but not required, to disclose information about other similar measurements (e.g., inventories measured at market value under Accounting Research Bulletin No. 43, Chapter 4, *Inventory Pricing*), if practicable (FAS-157, par. 35):

1. For assets and liabilities that are measured at fair value on a *recurring basis* (e.g., trading securities) subsequent to initial recognition, the following disclosures should be made for each major category of assets and liabilities for each interim and annual period (FAS-157, par. 32):

    a. The fair value measurements at the reporting date

    b. The level within the fair value hierarchy in which the fair value measurements in their entirety fall, segregating fair value measurements using quoted prices in active markets for identical assets or liabilities (Level 1), significant other observable inputs (Level 2), and significant unobservable inputs (Level 3)

    c. For fair value measurements using significant unobservable inputs (Level 3), a reconciliation of the beginning and ending balances, separately presenting changes during the period attributable to the following:

        (1) Total gains or losses for the period (realized and unrealized), segregating those gains or losses included in earnings (or changes in net assets), and a description of where those gains or losses are reported in the income statement

        (2) Purchases, sales, issuances, and settlements (net)

        (3) Transfers in or out of Level 3 (e.g., transfers due to changes in the observability of significant inputs)

        (Note: This reconciliation disclosure may be presented net for derivative assets and liabilities)

    d. The amount of the total gains or losses for the period in 1c above included in earnings (or changes in net assets) that are attributable to the change in unrealized gains or losses relating to those assets and liabilities still held at the reporting date and a description of where those unrealized gains or losses are reported in the income statement

    e. The valuation techniques used to measure fair value and a discussion of changes in valuation techniques, if any, during the period **(Note: This disclosure item is applicable in annual periods only)**

2. For assets and liabilities that are measured at fair value on a *nonrecurring basis* (e.g., impaired assets) in periods subsequent to initial recognition, the following disclosures should be made for each major category of assets and liabilities for each interim and annual period (FAS-157, par. 33):

    a. The fair value measurements recorded during the period and the reasons for the measurements

    b. The level within the fair value hierarchy in which the fair value measurements in their entirety fall, segregating fair value measurements using quoted prices in active markets for identical assets or liabilities (Level 1), significant other observable inputs (Level 2), and significant unobservable inputs (Level 3)

    c. For fair value measurements using significant unobservable inputs (Level 3), a description of the inputs and the information used to develop the inputs

    d. The valuation techniques used to measure fair value and a discussion of any changes in the valuation techniques used to measure similar assets or liabilities in prior periods **(Note: This disclosure item is applicable in annual periods only)**

EXAMPLES OF FINANCIAL STATEMENT DISCLOSURES

 The following sample disclosures, which are adapted from FAS-157, are available on the accompanying disc.

Example 14–1: Assets and Liabilities Are Measured at Fair Value on a Recurring Basis

The following are the major categories of assets and liabilities measured at fair value on a recurring basis during the year ended December 31, 20X2, using quoted prices in active markets for identical assets (Level 1); significant other observable inputs (Level 2); and significant unobservable inputs (Level 3).

Description	Level 1: Quoted Prices in Active Markets for Identical Assets	Level 2: Significant Other Observable Inputs	Level 3: Significant Unobserv- able Inputs	Total at December 31, 20X2
Trading securities	$105,000	$10,000	$ -0-	$115,000
Available-for-sale securities	75,000	-0-	-0-	75,000
Derivatives	25,000	15,000	20,000	60,000
Venture capital investments	-0-	-0-	10,000	10,000
Total	$205,000	$25,000	$30,000	$260,000

Note: For liabilities, a similar table should be presented.

The following is a reconciliation of the beginning and ending balances for assets and liabilities measured at fair value on a recurring basis using significant unobservable inputs (Level 3) during the period ended December 31, 20X2:

	Derivatives	Venture Capital Investments	Total
Beginning balance	$14,000	$11,000	$25,000
Total gains or losses (realized/unrealized):			
Included in earnings (or changes in net assets)	11,000	(3,000)	8,000
Included in other comprehensive income	4,000	-0-	4,000
Purchases, issuances, and settlements	(7,000)	2,000	(5,000)
Transfers in or out of Level 3	(2,000)	-0-	(2,000)
Ending balance	$20,000	$10,000	$30,000

Note: For liabilities, a similar table should be presented.

	Derivatives	Venture Capital Investments	Total
The amount of total gains or losses for the period included in earnings (or changes in net assets) attributable to the change in unrealized gains or losses relating to assets still held at the reporting date	$7,000	$2,000	$9,000

Gains and losses (realized and unrealized) included in earnings (or changes in net assets) for the period ended December 31, 20X2, are reported in trading revenues and in other revenues as follows:

	Trading Revenues	Other Revenues
Total gains or losses included in earnings (or changes in net assets) for the period ended December 31, 20X2	$11,000	$(3,000)
Change in unrealized gains or losses relating to assets still held at December 31, 20X2	$ 7,000	$ 2,000

Note: In addition, for annual periods, the valuation techniques used to measure fair value and a discussion of any changes in valuation techniques during the period should be disclosed.

Example 14–2: Assets and Liabilities Are Measured at Fair Value on a Nonrecurring Basis

The following are the major categories of assets and liabilities measured at fair value on a nonrecurring basis during the year ended December 31, 20X2, using quoted prices in active markets for identical assets (Level 1); significant other observable inputs (Level 2); and significant unobservable inputs (Level 3):

Description	Level 1: Quoted Prices in Active Markets for Identical Assets	Level 2: Significant Other Observable Inputs	Level 3: Significant Unobservable Inputs	Total at December 31, 20X2	Total Gains (Losses) for the Year Ended December 31, 20X2
Long-lived assets held and used	$ -0-	$ 750,000	$ -0-	$ 750,000	$ (250,000)
Goodwill	-0-	-0-	300,000	300,000	(350,000)
Long-lived assets held for sale	-0-	260,000	-0-	260,000	(150,000)
Total	$-0-	$1,010,000	$300,000	$1,310,000	$(750,000)

Note: For liabilities, a similar table should be presented.

In accordance with the provisions of Statement of Financial Accounting Standards No. 144 (FAS-144), *Accounting for the Impairment or Disposal of Long-Lived Assets,* long-lived assets held and used with a carrying amount of $1,000,000 were written down to their fair value of $750,000, resulting in an impairment charge of $250,000, which was included in earnings for the period. In addition, in accordance with FAS-144, long-lived assets held for sale with a carrying amount of $350,000 were written down to their fair value of $260,000, less cost to sell of $60,000 (or $200,000), resulting in a loss of $150,000, which was included in earnings for the period.

In accordance with the provisions of Statement of Financial Accounting Standards No. 142, *Goodwill and Other Intangible Assets,* goodwill with a carrying amount of $650,000 was written down to its implied fair value of $300,000, resulting in an impairment charge of $350,000, which was included in earnings for the period.

> **Note:** For fair value measurements using significant unobservable inputs (Level 3), a description of the inputs and the information used to develop them should be disclosed. In addition, for annual periods, the valuation techniques used to measure fair value and a discussion of any changes in the valuation techniques used to measure similar assets or liabilities in prior periods should be disclosed.

CHAPTER 15
FINANCIAL INSTRUMENTS, DERIVATIVES, AND HEDGING ACTIVITIES

CONTENTS

EXECUTIVE SUMMARY

Note regarding FAS-155: The FASB has issued Statement of
Financial Accounting Standards No. 155 (FAS-155), *Accounting for Certain Hybrid Financial Instruments*. Under current
generally accepted accounting principles (GAAP), an entity that
holds a financial instrument with an embedded derivative must
bifurcate the financial instrument, resulting in the host and the
embedded derivative being accounted for separately. FAS-155
permits, but does not require, entities to account for financial
instruments with an embedded derivative at fair value thus
negating the need to bifurcate the instrument between its host
and the embedded derivative. FAS-155 extends the requirements of Statement of Financial Accounting Standards No. 133,
Accounting for Derivative Instruments and Hedging Activities,
to interests in securitized financial assets (eliminating the FAS-
133 exemption that previously applied to securitizations). That
is, an entity must now evaluate whether an interest in securitized financial assets contains an embedded derivative. Prior to
FAS-155, this analysis was not required for interests in securitized financial assets.

In addition, FAS-155 clarifies that concentrations of credit risk are not embedded derivatives. Finally, FAS-155 amends Statement of Financial Accounting Standards No. 140, *Accounting for Transfers and Servicing of Financial Assets and Extinguishments of Liabilities*, to remove the prohibition on holding certain derivative financial instruments by a qualifying special-purpose entity (SPE). FAS-155 is effective for financial instruments acquired or issued in fiscal years beginning after September 15, 2006.

Note regarding FAS-156: The FASB has issued Statement of Financial Accounting Standards No. 156 (FAS-156), *Accounting for Servicing of Financial Assets*, which amends the guidance in Statement of Financial Accounting Standards No. 140. Among other requirements, FAS-156 requires an entity to recognize a servicing asset or servicing liability each time it undertakes an obligation to service a financial asset by entering into a servicing contract in any of the following situations:

- A transfer of the servicer's financial assets that meets the requirements for sale accounting

- A transfer of the servicer's financial assets to a qualifying special-purpose entity in a guaranteed mortgage securitization in which the transferor retains all of the resulting securities and classifies them as either available-for-sale securities or trading securities in accordance with Statement of Financial Accounting Standards No. 115, *Accounting for Certain Investments in Debt and Equity Securities*

- An acquisition or assumption of an obligation to service a financial asset that does not relate to financial assets of the servicer or its consolidated affiliates

FAS-156 is effective as of the beginning of an entity's first fiscal year that begins after September 15, 2006. Earlier adoption is permitted as of the beginning of an entity's fiscal year, provided the entity has not issued financial statements.

Note regarding FAS-157: In September 2006, the FASB issued Statement of Financial Accounting Standards No. 157 (FAS-157), *Fair Value Measurements*, which provides guidance for using fair value to measure assets and liabilities and expands disclosures about fair value measurements. FAS-157 applies whenever other standards require or permit assets or liabilities to be measured at fair value; however, it does not expand the use of fair value in any new circumstances.

Prior to FAS-157, the methods for measuring fair value were diverse and inconsistent, especially for items that are not actively traded. FAS-157 clarifies that for items that are not actively traded, such as certain kinds of derivatives, fair value

should reflect the price in a transaction with a market participant, including an adjustment for risk. In addition, FAS-157
requires expanded disclosure of the effect on earnings for items
measured using unobservable data. Therefore, changes in practice that will result from applying FAS-157 relate to the definition of fair value, the methods used to measure fair value, and
the expanded disclosures about fair value measurements.

Under FAS-157, fair value refers to the price that would be
received to sell an asset or paid to transfer a liability in an
orderly transaction between market participants in the market
in which the reporting entity transacts. The FASB clarifies the
principle that fair value should be based on the assumptions
market participants would use when pricing the asset or liability. In support of this principle, FAS-157 establishes a fair value
hierarchy that prioritizes the information used to develop those
assumptions. The fair value hierarchy gives the highest priority
to quoted prices in active markets and the lowest priority to
unobservable data (e.g., the reporting entity's own data). Under
FAS-157, fair value measurements would be separately disclosed by level within the fair value hierarchy.

FAS-157 expands disclosures about the use of fair value to measure assets and liabilities in interim and annual periods subsequent to initial recognition. It does not eliminate or modify the
fair value disclosure requirements under other accounting pronouncements (e.g., Statement of Financial Accounting Standards No. 107, *Disclosures about Fair Value of Financial
Instruments*); rather, it encourages entities to combine the fair
value information disclosed under FAS-157 with the fair value
information disclosed under other such accounting pronouncements.

FAS-157 is effective for financial statements issued for fiscal
years beginning after November 15, 2007, and interim periods
within those fiscal years. Earlier application is encouraged, provided that the reporting entity has not yet issued financial statements for that fiscal year, including any financial statements for
an interim period within that fiscal year.
Additional disclosures that are required under FAS-157 are discussed in Chapter 14, "Fair Value Measurements."

Financial Instruments

A *financial instrument* is defined as cash, evidence of an ownership
interest in an entity, or a contract that meets the following criteria:

1. Imposes on one entity a contractual obligation (a) to deliver
   cash or another financial instrument to a second entity or (b)
   to exchange other financial instruments on potentially unfavorable terms with the second entity, and

2. Conveys to that second entity a contractual right (a) to receive cash or another financial instrument from the first entity or (b) to exchange other financial instruments on potentially favorable terms with the first entity.

Generally accepted accounting principles (GAAP) require all entities to disclose the fair value of their financial instruments and certain information relating to these financial instruments; however, certain disclosures are optional for nonpublic companies that (1) have total assets on the financial statement date of less than $100 million and (2) have no instrument that, in whole or in part, is accounted for as a derivative instrument.

Disclosure of information about significant concentrations of credit risk from an individual counterparty or groups of counterparties for all financial instruments is also required.

For financial instruments recognized at fair value in the balance sheet, the disclosure requirements of FAS-157 also apply. FAS-157 expands disclosures about the use of fair value to measure assets and liabilities in interim and annual periods subsequent to initial recognition. It does not eliminate or modify the fair value disclosure requirements under other accounting pronouncements (e.g., FAS-107, *Disclosures about Fair Value of Financial Instruments*); rather, it encourages entities to combine the fair value information disclosed under FAS-157 with the fair value information disclosed under other such accounting pronouncements. Chapter 14, "Fair Value Measurements," discusses in detail the fair value measurements and disclosures under FAS-157.

Issues relating to transfers and servicing of financial assets are discussed in Chapter 35, "Transfers and Servicing of Financial Assets."

Financial instruments with characteristics of both liabilities and equity. Statement of Financial Accounting Standards No. 150 (FAS-150), *Accounting for Certain Financial Instruments with Characteristics of Both Liabilities and Equity*, establishes standards for issuers of financial instruments with characteristics of both liabilities and equity related to the classification and measurement of those instruments. FAS-150 essentially requires the following three classes of financial instruments previously classified as equity to be classified as liabilities (or assets in some cases):

1. *Mandatorily redeemable financial instruments.* These financial instruments should be classified as liabilities in an entity's financial statements unless the redemption is required to occur only upon the entity's liquidation or termination. A financial instrument issued in the form of shares is mandatorily redeemable if it embodies an unconditional obligation requiring the issuer to redeem the instrument by transferring

its assets at a specified or determinable date or upon an event certain to occur. For example, shares that are required to be redeemed by an entity upon the death of a stockholder (an event certain to occur) are mandatorily redeemable shares.

2. *Obligations to repurchase the issuer's equity shares by transferring assets.* Financial instruments other than outstanding shares that, at inception, meet the following criteria should be classified as liabilities (or as assets in some circumstances): (a) the financial instruments embody an obligation to repurchase the issuer's equity shares, or are indexed to such an obligation and (b) they require, or may require, the issuer to settle the obligation by transferring assets. Examples include forward purchase contracts or written put options on an issuer's equity shares that are to be physically settled or net cash settled.

3. *Certain obligations to issue a variable number of shares.* Financial instruments that embody an unconditional obligation, or financial instruments other than outstanding shares that embody a conditional obligation, which the entity must or may settle by issuing a variable number of equity shares should be classified as liabilities (or as assets in some circumstances) if, at inception, the monetary value of the obligation is based solely or predominantly on any of the following:

   (a) A fixed monetary amount that is known at inception (e.g., a payable to be settled with a variable number of the entity's equity shares).

   (b) Variations in something other than the fair value of the entity's equity shares (e.g., a financial instrument indexed to the S&P 500 and to be settled with a variable number of the entity's equity shares).

   (c) Variations inversely related to changes in the fair value of the entity's equity shares (e.g., a written put option that could be settled net by delivering a variable number of equity shares).

FAS-150 effective date Except as discussed below, FAS-150 is effective for financial instruments entered into or modified after May 31, 2003; for financial instruments entered into previously, FAS-150 is effective at the beginning of the first interim period beginning after June 15, 2003.

- *Mandatorily redeemable financial instruments of nonpublic entities that are not SEC registrants*
  - For financial instruments that are mandatorily redeemable on fixed dates and for amounts that either are fixed or are determined by reference to an external index (e.g.,

interest rate index, currency index), FAS-150 is effective for fiscal periods beginning after December 15, 2004.

— For all other financial instruments that are mandatorily redeemable (e.g., shares redeemable at death, separation, or fair value), FAS-150 is deferred indefinitely pending further FASB action.

• *Certain mandatorily redeemable noncontrolling interests (commonly known as minority interests) of all entities, public and nonpublic*

— For mandatorily redeemable noncontrolling interests that would not have to be classified as liabilities by the subsidiary, under the "only upon liquidation" exception in paragraph 9 of FAS-150, but would be classified as liabilities by the parent in consolidated financial statements, FAS-150 is deferred indefinitely pending further FASB action.

— For other mandatorily redeemable noncontrolling interests that were issued before November 5, 2003, the *measurement* provisions of FAS-150 are deferred indefinitely pending further FASB action, both for the parent in consolidated financial statements and for the subsidiary that issued the instruments that result in the mandatorily redeemable noncontrolling interest. However, the *classification* provisions of FAS-150 are not deferred.

— During the deferral period, all public entities and nonpublic entities that are SEC registrants are required to follow the *disclosure* requirements in paragraphs 26 and 27 of FAS-150.

Derivative Instruments and Hedging Activities

A *derivative instrument* is a financial instrument or other contract with all three of the following characteristics:

1. It has (a) one or more underlyings and (b) one or more notional amounts or payment provisions or both. An *underlying* is a specified interest rate, security price, commodity price, foreign exchange rate, index of prices or rates, or other variable. An underlying may be a price or rate of an asset or liability but is not the asset or liability itself. A notional amount is a number of currency units, shares, bushels, pounds, or other units specified in the contract.

2. It requires no initial net investment or an initial net investment that is smaller than would be required for other types

of contracts that would be expected to have a similar response to changes in market factors.

3. Its terms permit or require net settlement, it can readily be settled net by a means outside the contract, or it provides for delivery of an asset that puts the recipient in a position not substantially different from net settlement.

GAAP require that all derivatives (both assets and liabilities) be recognized in the statement of financial position at fair value. Each derivative instrument is classified in one of the following four categories: (1) no hedge designation, (2) fair value hedge, (3) cash flow hedge, and (4) foreign currency hedge.

Gains and losses on derivative instruments are accounted for as follows:

1. *No hedge designation.* The gain or loss should be recognized currently in earnings.

2. *Fair value hedge.* The gain or loss should be recognized currently in earnings.

3. *Cash flow hedge.* The effective portion of the gain or loss (i.e., change in fair value) on a derivative designated as a cash flow hedge is reported in other comprehensive income (outside net income). The remaining gain or loss, if any, should be recognized currently in earnings. Amounts in accumulated other comprehensive income are reclassified into earnings (net income) in the same period in which the hedged forecasted transaction affects earnings.

4. *Foreign currency hedge.* The gain or loss should be accounted for as follows:

    a. The gain or loss on the hedging derivative or nonderivative instrument in a hedge of a foreign currency-denominated firm commitment and the offsetting loss or gain on the hedged firm commitment should be recognized currently in earnings in the same accounting period.

    b. The gain or loss on the hedging derivative instrument in a hedge of an available-for-sale security and the offsetting loss or gain on the hedged available-for-sale security should be recognized currently in earnings in the same accounting period.

    c. The effective portion of the gain or loss (i.e., change in fair value) on the hedging derivative instrument in a hedge of a forecasted foreign currency-denominated transaction should be reported as a component of other comprehensive income (outside net income) and reclassified into earnings in the same period or periods during which the hedged forecasted transaction affects earnings. The remaining gain or loss on the hedging instrument should be recognized currently in earnings.

d. The gain or loss on the hedging derivative or nonderivative instrument in a hedge of a net investment in a foreign operation should be reported in other comprehensive income (outside net income) as part of the cumulative translation adjustment to the extent it is effective as a hedge.

Authoritative Literature

FAS-107	Disclosures about Fair Value of Financial Instruments (as amended by FAS-133)
FAS-126	Exemption from Certain Required Disclosures about Financial Instruments for Certain Non-public Entities
FAS-133	Accounting for Derivative Instruments and Hedging Activities
FAS-138	Accounting for Certain Derivative Instruments and Certain Hedging Activities
FAS-149	Amendment of Statement 133 on Derivative Instruments and Hedging Activities
FAS-150	Accounting for Certain Financial Instruments with Characteristics of Both Liabilities and Equity
FSP FAS 150-3	Effective Date, Disclosures, and Transition for Mandatorily Redeemable Financial Instruments of Certain Nonpublic Entities and Certain Mandatorily Redeemable Noncontrolling Interests under FASB Statement No. 150, *Accounting for Certain Financial Instruments with Characteristics of Both Liabilities and Equity*
FAS-155	Accounting for Certain Hybrid Financial Instruments
FAS-156	Accounting for Servicing of Financial Assets
FAS-157	Fair Value Measurements
FIN-39	Offsetting of Amounts Related to Certain Contracts

FIN-41	Offsetting of Amounts Related to Certain Repurchase and Reverse Repurchase Agreements
SOP 94-6	Disclosure of Certain Significant Risks and Uncertainties
FSP SOP 94-6-1	Terms of Loan Products That May Give Rise to a Concentration of Credit Risk
EITF 99-2	Accounting for Weather Derivatives
EITF 00-19	Accounting for Derivative Financial Instruments Indexed to, and Potentially Settled in, a Company's Own Stock
FSP EITF 00-19-2	Accounting for Registration Payment Arrangements
EITF 06-7	Issuer's Accounting for a Previously Bifurcated Conversion Option in a Convertible Debt Instrument When the Conversion Option No Longer Meets the Bifurcation Criteria in FASB Statement No. 133, *Accounting for Derivative Instruments and Hedging Activities*

DISCLOSURE REQUIREMENTS

Note: FAS-157 expands disclosures about the use of fair value to measure assets and liabilities in interim and annual periods subsequent to initial recognition. It does not eliminate or modify the fair value disclosure requirements under other accounting pronouncements (e.g., FAS-107, *Disclosures about Fair Value of Financial Instruments*); rather, it encourages entities to combine the fair value information disclosed under FAS-157 with the fair value information disclosed under other such accounting pronouncements. See Chapter 14, "Fair Value Measurements," for additional disclosures of fair value that are required under FAS-157.

Financial Instruments

1. Significant concentrations of credit risk arising from all financial instruments should be disclosed, including the following about each significant concentration (FAS-107, par. 15A; FAS-133, par. 531d):

    a. Information about the activity, region, or economic characteristic that identifies the concentration

b. The maximum amount of loss due to credit risk that, based on the gross fair value of the financial instrument, the entity would incur if parties to the financial instruments that make up the concentration failed completely to perform according to the terms of the contracts and the collateral or other security, if any, for the amount due proved to be of no value to the entity

c. The entity's policy of requiring collateral or other security to support financial instruments subject to credit risk

d. Information about the entity's access to the collateral or other security

e. The nature and a brief description of the collateral or other security supporting those financial instruments

f. The entity's policy of entering into master netting arrangements to mitigate the credit risk of financial instruments, information about the arrangements for which the entity is a party, and a brief description of the terms of those arrangements, including the extent to which they would reduce the entity's maximum amount of loss due to credit risk

2. The following information about fair value of financial instruments should be disclosed either in the body of the financial statements or in the accompanying notes (These disclosures about the fair value of financial instruments are optional for an entity that meets all of the following criteria: (i) the entity is a nonpublic entity, (ii) the entity's total assets are less than $100 million on the date of the financial statements, and (iii) the entity has not held or issued any derivative financial instruments during the reporting period.) (FAS-107, pars. 10 and 14; FAS-133, pars. 531 and 532):

a. Fair value of financial instruments for which it is practicable to estimate fair value (For trade receivables and payables, no disclosure is required when the carrying amount approximates fair value.) In connection with this item:

— When disclosure is made in the accompanying notes, the fair value should be presented together with the related carrying amount in a form that makes it clear whether the fair value and carrying amount represent assets or liabilities and how the carrying amounts relate to what is reported in the balance sheet

— Disclosure should be made in a single note or, if disclosed in more than a single note, one of the notes should include a summary table that contains the

> fair value and related carrying amounts and cross-references to the locations of the remaining disclosures

> b. The methods and significant assumptions used to estimate the fair value of financial instruments

> c. In disclosing the fair value of a financial instrument, the entity should not net that fair value with the fair value of other financial instruments, except to the extent that the offsetting of carrying amounts in the balance sheet is permitted

> d. For financial instruments for which it is concluded that estimating fair value is not practicable, (i) information related to estimating the fair value of the financial instrument (such as the carrying amount, effective interest rate, and maturity) and (ii) the reasons why it is not practicable to estimate fair value

3. For weather derivative instruments within the scope of EITF Issue 99-2, existing GAAP disclosures for financial instruments, such as those required in FAS-107, should also be made (EITF 99-2, par. 11)

4. Entities are *encouraged*, but not required, to disclose quantitative information about the market risks of financial instruments that is consistent with the way an entity manages or adjusts its market risks (e.g., details of current positions, details of activity during the period, a gap analysis of interest rate repricing or maturity dates, and the duration of the financial instruments) (FAS-107, pars. 15C and 15D; FAS-133, par. 531d)

5. Entities are *encouraged*, but not required, to disclose information on how underwriting procedures are designed to control the credit risk that may arise from future payment increases (FSP SOP 94-6-1, par. 8)

Financial instruments with characteristics of both liabilities and equity.   The following are the presentation and disclosure requirements for financial instruments with characteristics of both liabilities and equity:

1. Financial instruments that are required to be presented as liabilities should not be presented between the liabilities section and equity section of the balance sheet (FAS-150, par. 18)

2. Entities that have no equity instruments outstanding but have financial instruments issued in the form of shares, all of which are mandatorily redeemable financial instruments required to be classified as liabilities, should:

a. Describe those instruments as "shares subject to manda-tory redemption" in the balance sheets to distinguish those instruments from other liabilities (FAS-150, par. 19)

b. Present payments to holders of such instruments and related accruals separately from payments to and interest due to other creditors in the statements of cash flows and operations (FAS-150, par. 19)

c. Disclose the components of the liability that would oth-erwise be related to shareholders' interest and other com-prehensive income, if any, subject to the redemption feature; for example, par value and other paid-in amounts of mandatorily redeemable instruments should be disclosed separately from the amount of retained earnings or accumulated deficit (FAS-150, par. 28)

3. For financial instruments with characteristics of both liabili-ties and equity, the following items should be disclosed (FAS150, par. 26):

a. The nature and terms of the financial instruments

b. The rights and obligations embodied in those financial instruments

c. Information about any settlement alternatives in the con-tract

d. The identity of the entity that controls the settlement alternatives

4. For all outstanding financial instruments with characteristics of both liabilities and equity, and for each settlement alterna-tive, the following items should be disclosed (FAS-150, par. 27):

a. The amount that would be paid, or the number of shares that would be issued and their fair value, determined under the conditions specified in the contract if the settle-ment were to occur at the reporting date

b. How changes in the fair value of the entity's equity shares would affect those settlement amounts

c. The maximum amount that the entity could be required to pay to redeem the instrument by physical settlement

d. The maximum number of shares that could be required to be issued

e. That a contract does not limit the amount that the entity could be required to pay or the number of shares that the entity could be required to issue

f. For a forward contract or an option indexed to the enti-ty's equity shares: (i) the forward price or option strike price, (ii) the number of the entity's shares to which the contract is indexed, and (iii) the settlement date(s) of the contract

Derivative Instruments and Hedging Activities

1. The following disclosures should be made for all derivative instruments (and for nonderivative instruments designated and qualifying as hedging instruments) (FAS-133, par. 44):

   a. The entity's objectives for holding or issuing the instruments

   b. The context needed to understand the entity's objectives

   c. The entity's strategies for achieving these objectives

   d. The entity's risk management policy for each type of hedge, including a description of the items or transactions for which risks are hedged

   e. For derivative instruments not designated as hedging instruments, the purpose of the derivative activity

   f. The disclosures for items a through e above should distinguish between:

      — Derivative instruments (and nonderivative instruments) designated as fair value hedging instruments

      — Derivative instruments designated as cash flow hedging instruments

      — Derivative instruments (and nonderivative instruments) designated as hedging instruments for hedges of the foreign currency exposure of a net investment in a foreign operation

      — All other derivatives

   Note: The disclosure requirement in item 2 below is prescribed by FAS-133, *Accounting for Derivative Instruments and Hedging Activities*, as amended by FAS-155, *Accounting for Certain Hybrid Financial Instruments*. The disclosure requirement in item 3 below is prescribed by FAS-155. FAS-155 is effective for all financial instruments acquired, issued, or subject to a remeasurement (new basis) event occurring after the beginning of an entity's first fiscal year that begins after September 15, 2006. Early application is permitted only if (1) it occurs at the beginning of an entity's fiscal year and (2) the entity has not yet issued any interim or annual financial statements for that fiscal year (FAS-155, par. 6).

2. Disclosures should be made that provide information to users of the financial statements to allow them to understand the effects on earnings (or other performance indicators for entities that do not report earnings) of changes in the fair value of hybrid financial instruments measured at fair value under the election and under the practicability exception in paragraph 16 of FAS-133 (FAS-133, par. 44B; FAS-155, par. 4e)

3. Separate disclosures should be made, upon adoption of FAS-155, of the gross gains and losses that make up the cumulative-effect adjustment (resulting from the difference between the total carrying amount of the individual components of the existing bifurcated hybrid financial instrument and the fair value of the combined hybrid financial instrument), determined on an instrument-by-instrument basis (FAS-155, par. 7)

4. The following disclosures should be made for derivative instruments designated and qualifying as *fair value hedging instruments* (as well as for nonderivative instruments that may give rise to foreign currency transaction gains or losses) and for the related hedged items, for each reporting period for which a complete set of financial statements is presented (FAS-133, par. 45):

    a. The net gain or loss recognized in earnings during the reporting period representing (i) the amount of the hedges' ineffectiveness, (ii) the component of the derivative instruments' gain or loss, if any, excluded from the assessment of hedge effectiveness, and (iii) a description of where the net gain or loss is reported in the statement of income or other statement of financial performance

    b. The amount of net gain or loss recognized in earnings when a hedged firm commitment no longer qualifies as a fair value hedge

5. The following disclosures should be made for derivative instruments that have been designated and qualifying as *cash flow hedging instruments* and for the related hedged transactions (FAS-133, par. 45):

    a. The net gain or loss recognized in earnings during the reporting period representing (i) the amount of the hedges' ineffectiveness, (ii) the component of the derivative instruments' gain or loss, if any, excluded from the assessment of hedge effectiveness, and (iii) a description of where the net gain or loss is reported in the statement of income or other statement of financial performance

    b. A description of the transactions or other events that will result in the reclassification into earnings of gains and

losses that are reported in accumulated other comprehensive income, and the estimated net amount of the
existing gains or losses at the reporting date that is
expected to be reclassified into earnings within the next
12 months

c. The maximum length of time over which the entity is
hedging its exposure to the variability in future cash
flows for forecasted transactions excluding those forecasted transactions related to the payment of variable
interest on existing financial instruments

d. The amount of gains and losses reclassified into earnings
as a result of the discontinuance of cash flow hedges
because it is probable that the original forecasted transactions will not occur by the end of the originally specified time period or within the additional period of time
discussed in FAS-133, as amended

6. The following disclosure should be made for derivative
instruments designated and qualifying as hedges of the foreign currency exposure of a net investment in a foreign
operation (as well as for nonderivative instruments that may
give rise to foreign currency transaction gains or losses)
(FAS-133, par. 45):

a. The net amount of gains or losses included in the cumulative translation adjustment during the reporting period

7. The following disclosures should be made as part of reporting changes in the components of other comprehensive
income (FAS-133, pars. 46 and 47):

a. The net gain or loss on derivative instruments designated and qualifying as cash flow hedging instruments
that are reported in comprehensive income should be
displayed as a separate classification within other comprehensive income

b. As part of the disclosures of accumulated other comprehensive income, the following should be disclosed separately:

— The beginning and ending accumulated derivative
gain or loss

— The related net change associated with current-
period hedging transactions

— The net amount of any reclassification into earnings

8. For freestanding derivative financial instruments (e.g., forward sale contract, purchase put or call option, written call
option, etc.) that are indexed to, and potentially settled in, a

company's own stock, the following disclosures should be made (EITF 00-19, pars. 51–53):

a. The pertinent information about the contract, including:

    (1) The forward rate

    (2) The option strike price

    (3) The number of issuer's shares to which the contract is indexed

    (4) The settlement date(s) of the contract

    (5) The issuer's accounting for the contract (i.e., as an asset, liability, or equity)

b. If the terms of the contract provide settlement alternatives, those settlement alternatives should be disclosed, including who controls the settlement alternatives and the maximum number of shares that could be required to be issued to net share settle a contract, if applicable [Note: Paragraph 5 of FAS-129 requires additional disclosures for actual issuances and settlements that occurred during the accounting period—See the disclosure checklist, Part I, "Stockholders' Equity," item 4]

c. The fact that a potentially infinite number of shares could be required to be issued to settle the contract, if a contract does not have a fixed or determinable maximum number of shares that may be required to be issued

d. A contract's current fair value for each settlement alternative (denominated, as relevant, in monetary amounts or quantities of shares) and how changes in the price of the issuer's equity instruments affect those settlement amounts (e.g., the issuer is obligated to issue an additional X shares or pay an additional Y dollars in cash for each $1 decrease in stock price)

e. If contracts that are classified as assets or liabilities meet the definition of a derivative instrument under the provisions of FAS-133, the disclosures that are required by paragraphs 44 and 45 of FAS-133 also are required for those contracts [See the disclosure checklist, Part IV, "Financial Instruments—Derivatives and Hedging Activities," items 1 and 4–6]

f. If contracts have been reclassified into (or out of) equity during the life of the instrument (in whole or in part), disclosures should include:

    (1) Contract reclassifications (including partial reclassifications)

    (2) The reason for the reclassification

    (3)   The impact on the issuer's financial statements

    (4)   The accounting policy for partial reclassifications

g. The disclosures required by paragraph 8 of FAS-129 should be made for any equity instrument in the scope of EITF 00-19 that is (or would be if the issuer were a public company) classified as temporary equity [See the disclosure checklist, Part I, "Stockholders' Equity," item 5]

Note: The disclosure requirements in item 9 below are prescribed by EITF Issue No. 06-7, *Issuer's Accounting for a Previously Bifurcated Conversion Option in a Convertible Debt Instrument When the Conversion Option No Longer Meets the Bifurcation Criteria in FASB Statement No. 133, "Accounting for Derivative Instruments and Hedging Activities."* EITF 06-7 is effective for all previously bifurcated conversion options in convertible debt instruments that no longer meet the bifurcation criteria in FAS-133 in annual or interim periods beginning after December 15, 2006, irrespective of when the debt instrument was entered into. Early adoption is permitted only if financial statements for the period have not yet been issued. Retrospective application in accordance with Statement of Financial Accounting Standards No. 154 (FAS-154), *Accounting Changes and Error Corrections*, is permitted.

9. For previously bifurcated conversion options in convertible debt instruments that no longer meet the bifurcation criteria in FAS-133, the following disclosures should be made (EITF 06-7):

    a. A description of the principal changes causing the embedded conversion option to no longer require bifurcation under FAS-133

    b. The amount of the liability for the conversion option reclassified to stockholders' equity

EXAMPLES OF FINANCIAL STATEMENT DISCLOSURES

The following sample disclosures are available on the accompanying disc. For additional information, see the following chapters in this book:

- Chapter 2, "Accounting Policies," for related additional disclosures, including concentrations of credit risk

- Chapter 6, "Commitments," for related additional disclosures, including letters of credit

- Chapter 10, "Contingencies, Risks, Uncertainties, and Concentrations," for related additional disclosures, including concentrations of credit risk and financial guarantees

- Chapter 14, "Fair Value Measurements," for related additional disclosures of fair value, which are required under FAS-157

- Chapter 35, "Transfers and Servicing of Financial Assets," for related additional disclosures, including transfers of financial instruments

- Chapter 37, "Cash and Cash Equivalents," for related additional disclosures, including cash balances in excess of federally insured limits

- Chapter 38, "Accounts and Notes Receivable," for related additional disclosures, including concentrations of credit risk and transfers of accounts receivable

Note: FAS-157 expands disclosures about the use of fair value to measure assets and liabilities in interim and annual periods subsequent to initial recognition. It does not eliminate or modify the fair value disclosure requirements under other accounting pronouncements (e.g., FAS-107, *Disclosures about Fair Value of Financial Instruments*); rather, it encourages entities to combine the fair value information disclosed under FAS-157 with the fair value information disclosed under other such accounting pronouncements. See Chapter 14, "Fair Value Measurements," for additional disclosures of fair value that are required under FAS-157.

Fair Value of Financial Instruments

Example 15–1: Disclosures about Fair Value of Financial Instruments by a Nonfinancial Entity

The Company uses the following methods and assumptions to estimate the fair value of each class of financial instruments for which it is practicable to estimate such value:

Cash and short-term investments—The carrying amount approximates fair value because of the short maturity of those instruments.

Accounts receivable—The carrying value of accounts receivable approximates fair value due to their short-term nature and historical collectibility.

Long-term investments—The fair values of some investments are estimated based on quoted market prices for those or similar investments. For other investments for which there are no quoted market prices, a reasonable estimate of fair value could not be made without incurring excessive costs. Additional information pertinent to the value of an unquoted investment is provided below.

Accounts payable—The carrying value of accounts payable approximates fair value due to the short-term nature of the obligations.

Long-term debt—The fair value of the Company's industrial bonds is estimated based on the quoted market prices for the same or similar issues or on the current rates offered to the Company for debt of the same remaining maturities. The fair value of the Company's other long-term debt is estimated by discounting the future cash flow using the Company's current borrowing rates for similar types and maturities of debt, except for floating-rate notes for which the carrying amounts were considered a reasonable estimate of fair value.

Foreign currency contracts—The fair value of foreign currency contracts (used for hedging purposes) is estimated by obtaining quotes from brokers.

The estimated fair values of the Company's financial instruments are as follows:

	20X2		20X1	
	Carrying Amount	*Fair Value*	*Carrying Amount*	*Fair Value*
Cash and short-term investments	$1,113,000	$1,113,000	$987,000	$987,000
Accounts receivable	3,218,000	3,218,000	2,946,000	2,946,000
Long-term investments for which it is:				
Practicable to estimate fair value	894,000	894,000	716,000	716,000
Not practicable to estimate fair value	477,000	-0-	412,000	-0-
Accounts payable	(1,171,000)	(1,171,000)	(1,342,000)	(1,342,000)
Long-term debt	(1,561,000)	(1,487,000)	(953,000)	(905,000)
Foreign currency contracts	102,000	102,000	91,000	91,000

It was not practicable to estimate the fair value of an investment representing 14% of the issued common stock of an untraded company; that investment is carried at its original cost of $477,000 and $412,000 at December 31, 20X2 and December 31, 20X1, respectively. Pertinent financial information reported by the untraded company are as follows:

	20X2	20X1
Total assets	$9,818,000	$8,971,000
Stockholders' equity	$5,100,000	$4,539,000
Revenues	$14,676,000	$13,974,000
Net income	$561,000	$398,000

The company determined the estimated fair value amounts by using available market information and commonly accepted valuation methodologies. However, considerable judgment is required in interpreting market data to develop the estimates of fair value. Accordingly, the estimates presented herein are not necessarily indicative of the amounts that the Company or holders of the instruments could realize in a current market exchange. The use of different assumptions and/or estimation methodologies may have a material effect on the estimated fair values.

Example 15–2: Disclosures about Fair Value of Financial Instruments by a Financial Entity

The Company uses the following methods and assumptions to estimate the fair value of each class of financial instruments for which it is practicable to estimate such value:

Cash and short-term investments—For those short-term instruments, the carrying amount is a reasonable estimate of fair value.

Investment securities and trading account assets—For securities and derivative instruments held for trading purposes (which include bonds, interest rate futures, options, interest rate swaps, securities sold not owned, caps and floors, foreign currency contracts, and forward contracts) and marketable equity securities held for investment purposes, fair values are based on quoted market prices or dealer quotes. For other securities held as investments, fair value equals quoted market price, if available. If a quoted market price is not available, fair value is estimated using quoted market prices for similar securities.

Loan receivables—For certain homogeneous categories of loans, such as some residential mortgages, credit card receivables, and other consumer loans, fair value is estimated using the quoted market prices for securities backed by similar loans, adjusted for differences in loan characteristics. The fair value of other types of loans is estimated by discounting the future cash flows using the current rates at which similar loans would be made to borrowers with similar credit ratings and for the same remaining maturities.

Deposit liabilities—The fair value of demand deposits, savings accounts, and certain money market deposits is the amount payable on demand at the reporting date. The fair value of fixed-maturity certificates of deposit is estimated using the rates currently offered for deposits of similar remaining maturities.

Long-term debt—Rates currently available to the Company for debt with similar terms and remaining maturities are used to estimate fair value of existing debt.

Commitments to extend credit, standby letters of credit, and financial guarantees written—The fair value of commitments is estimated using the fees currently charged to enter into similar agreements, taking into account remaining terms of the agreements and the present credit-worthiness of the counterparties. For fixed-rate loan commitments, fair value also considers the difference between current levels of interest rates and the committed rates. The fair value of guarantees and letters of credit is based on fees currently charged for similar agreements or on the estimated cost to terminate them or otherwise settle the obligations with the counterparties at the reporting date.

The estimated fair values of the Company's financial instruments are as follows:

	20X2		20X1	
	Carrying Amount	Fair Value	Carrying Amount	Fair Value
Financial assets:				
Cash and short-term investments	$1,230,000	$1,230,000	$1,565,000	$1,565,000
Trading account assets	2,341,000	2,341,000	2,978,000	2,978,000
Investment securities	5,033,000	5,033,000	5,622,000	5,622,000
Loans	10,236,000	-0-	9,253,000	-0-
Less: allowance for loan losses	(632,000)	-0-	(581,000)	-0-
Loans, net of allowance	9,604,000	9,543,000	8,672,000	8,581,000

	20X2		20X1	
	Carrying Amount	*Fair Value*	*Carrying Amount*	*Fair Value*
Financial liabilities:				
Deposits	11,409,000	11,182,000	10,736,000	10,471,000
Securities sold not owned	618,000	618,000	563,000	563,000
Long-term debt	1,762,0000	1,744,000	1,382,000	1,371,000
Unrecognized financial instruments:				
Commitments to extend credit	(5,608,000)	(5,532,000)	(4,923,000)	(4,892,000)
Standby letters of credit	(674,000)	(674,000)	(532,000)	(532,000)
Financial guarantees written	(418,000)	(410,000)	(323,000)	(307,000)

The Company has determined the estimated fair value amounts by using available market information and commonly accepted valuation methodologies. However, considerable judgment is required in interpreting market data to develop the estimates of fair value. Accordingly, the estimates presented herein are not necessarily indicative of the amounts that the Company or holders of the instruments could realize in a current market exchange. The use of different assumptions and/or estimation methodologies may have a material effect on the estimated fair values.

Financial Instruments with Characteristics of Both Liabilities and Equity

Example 15–3: Adoption of FAS-150, "Accounting for Certain Financial Instruments with Characteristics of Both Liabilities and Equity," Is Not Expected to Have a Material Effect on the Financial Statements

In May 2003, the Financial Accounting Standards Board issued Statement of Financial Accounting Standards No. 150 (FAS-150), *Accounting for Certain Financial Instruments with Characteristics of Both Liabilities and Equity.* FAS-150 addresses certain financial instruments that, under previous guidance, could be accounted for as equity, but now must be classified as liabilities in statements of financial position. These financial instruments include: (1) mandatorily redeemable financial instruments, (2) obligations to repurchase the issuer's equity shares by transferring assets, and (3) obligations to issue a variable number of shares. With limited exceptions, FAS-150 is effective for financial instruments entered into or modified after May 31, 2003, and otherwise is effective at the beginning of the first interim period beginning after June 15, 2003. The Company does not expect that the adoption of FAS-150 will have a material impact on its results of operations and financial position.

Example 15–4: Effect of Adoption of FAS-150, "Accounting for Certain Financial Instruments with Characteristics of Both Liabilities and Equity," Is Described in the Notes to the Financial Statements

In May 2003, the Financial Accounting Standards Board issued Statement of Financial Accounting Standards No. 150 (FAS-150), *Accounting for Certain Financial Instruments with Characteristics of Both Liabilities and Equity.* FAS-150 addresses certain financial instruments that, under previous guidance, could be accounted for as equity, but now must be classified as liabilities in statements of financial position. These financial instruments include: (1) mandatorily redeemable financial instruments, (2) obligations to repurchase the issuer's equity shares by transferring assets, and (3) obligations to issue a variable number of shares. With limited exceptions, FAS150 is effective for financial instruments entered into or modified after May 31, 2003, and otherwise is effective at the beginning of the first interim period beginning after June 15, 2003. The Company adopted the provisions of FAS-150 on January 1, 20X4. As a result of the adoption, the Company's mandatorily redeemable preferred securities have been reclassified from shareholders' equity to liabilities and the payments to the holders of the securities, which were previously recorded as minority interest on the statement of operations, are now recorded as interest expense.

Example 15–5: Mandatorily Redeemable Convertible Preferred Stock Reported as a Long-Term Liability

The Company issued 400,000 shares of mandatorily redeemable Series B Convertible Preferred Stock in March 20X1. Each share has a liquidation value of $10 per share. The liquidation value, plus accrued but unpaid dividends, is payable on March 8, 20X9, the mandatory redemption date. The Company has the option to redeem all, but not less than all, of the shares of Series B preferred stock at any time after six years from the date of issuance for a number of shares of the Company's common stock equal to the liquidation value plus accrued and unpaid dividends divided by the current market price of common stock determined in relation to the date of redemption. Under this option, were the redemption to have taken place at December 31, 20X2, each share would have been converted into 1.081 shares of common stock. In addition, each share of preferred stock is convertible, at any time, at the option of the holder into the right to receive shares of the Company's common stock. Initially, each share was convertible into .732 shares of common stock, subject to adjustment in the event of certain dividends and distributions; a merger, consolidation, or sale of substantially all of the Company's assets; a liquidation or distribution; and certain other events. Were the conversion to have taken place at December 31, 20X2, each share would have been converted into .732 shares of common stock. Holders of preferred stock are entitled to cumulative annual cash dividends of $1 per share, payable quarterly. In any liquidation of the Company, each share of preferred stock is entitled to a liquidation preference before any distribution may be made on the Company's common stock or any series of capital stock that is junior to the Series B preferred stock. In the event of a change in control of the Company, holders of Series B preferred stock also have specified exchange rights into common stock of the Company or into specified securities or property of another entity participating in the change in control transaction.

Effective July 1, 20X2, the Company adopted FASB Statement No. 150, *Accounting for Certain Financial Instruments with Characteristics of Both Liabilities and Equity*. Following adoption of the standard, mandatorily redeemable preferred stock, totaling $4,000,000, is reported as a long-term liability in the balance sheet. As of December 31, 20X2, 1,000,000 preferred stock shares are authorized and 400,000 shares are issued and outstanding.

Balance Sheet Presentation—The following presentation illustrates the reporting of the mandatorily redeemable convertible preferred stock as a long-term liability based on this example.

Liabilities:

Accounts payable	$2,350,000
Short-term debt	900,000
Accrued expenses	500,000
Total current liabilities	3,750,000
Long-term debt	2,500,000
Mandatorily redeemable convertible preferred stock	4,000,000
Deferred income taxes	725,000

Stockholders' equity:

(*Details omitted*)

Derivative Instruments and Hedging Activities

Example 15–6: Description of Objectives and Strategies for Holding and Issuing Derivatives

The Company holds and issues derivative financial instruments for the purpose of hedging the risks of certain identifiable and anticipated transactions. In general, the types of risks hedged are those relating to the variability of future earnings and cash flows caused by movements in foreign currency exchange rates and changes in commodity prices and interest rates. The Company documents its risk management strategy and hedge effectiveness at the inception of and during the term of each hedge. In hedging the transactions the Company, in the normal course of business, holds and/or issues the following types of derivatives:

Forward rate agreements—The purpose of this instrument is to hedge the fair value of firm purchase or sale commitments denominated in foreign currencies and of the net investments in foreign subsidiaries.

Interest rate swaps—The purpose of this instrument is to hedge the fair value of fixed-rate debt and cash flows of variable-rate financial assets.

Futures contracts—The purpose of this instrument is to hedge the fair value of microchips inventory.

Call and put options—The purpose of this instrument is to hedge the cash flows of forecasted sales or purchases of inventory.

The Company holds and issues such derivatives only for the purpose of hedging such risks, not for speculation. Generally, the Company enters into hedging relationships such that changes in the fair values or cash flows of items and transactions being hedged are expected to be offset by corresponding changes in the values of the derivatives. At December 31, 20X2, hedging relationships exist for short-term investments, bond indebtedness, microchips inventory, firm foreign-currency-denominated purchase commitments, and anticipated purchases and sales of microchips inventory.

Derivatives that have been designated and qualify as fair value hedging instruments are reported at fair value. The gain or loss on the derivative instrument as well as the offsetting gain or loss on the hedged item attributable to the hedged risk are recognized in earnings in the current period.

Derivatives that have been designated and qualify as cash flow hedging instruments are reported at fair value. The gain or loss on the effective portion of the hedge (i.e., change in fair value) is initially reported as a component of other comprehensive income. The remaining gain or loss, if any, is recognized currently in earnings. Amounts in accumulated other comprehensive income are reclassified into net income in the same period in which the hedged forecasted transaction affects earnings.

Example 15–7: Fair Value Hedging Instruments

The Company enters into interest rate swaps to convert portions of its fixed rate trust-preferred securities to floating rate securities, its fixed rate long term subordinated debt to floating rate debt and to a lesser degree, certain fixed rate loans to variable rate loans. The fixed rate liability instruments are changed to variable rate instruments by entering into "receive fixed/pay variable swaps" and the fixed rate asset instruments are changed to variable rate instruments by entering into "pay fixed/receive variable swaps."

During 20X2 and 20X1, the Company recognized net gains of $84,000 and $67,000, respectively, from derivative instruments designated and qualifying as fair value hedges. All hedges were highly effective; therefore, the gains, which are included in other income, are attributable to the portion of the change in the fair value of the derivative hedging instruments excluded from the assessment of the effectiveness of the hedges.

Also, during 20X2, a previous hedge on a firm future foreign currency commitment no longer qualified as a fair value hedge, because the hedging relationship was no longer deemed to be highly effective. As a result, a loss of $39,000 was recognized in the 20X2 Statement of Operations.

Example 15–8: Cash Flow Hedging Instruments

The Company uses interest rate swaps to convert floating rate long-term debt to fixed rate debt.

During 20X2 and 20X1, the Company recognized net gains of $72,000 and $59,000, respectively, from cash flow hedges. All hedges were highly effective; therefore, the gains, which are included in other income, are attributable to the portion of the change in the fair value of the derivative hedging instruments excluded from the assessment of the effectiveness of the hedges. Cash flow hedges of forecasted transactions resulted in an aggregate credit balance of $97,000 remaining in accumulated other comprehensive income at December 31, 20X2. The Company expects to transfer approximately $61,000 of that amount to earnings during 20X3 when the forecasted transactions actually occur. All forecasted transactions currently being hedged are expected to occur by 20X4. Also, during 20X2, the Company transferred $41,000 to earnings from accumulated other comprehensive income because a forecasted transaction that was originally expected to occur was cancelled.

Example 15–9: Hedges of Net Investment in Foreign Operation

The Company uses five-year yen denominated debt to hedge its investment in a Japanese manufacturer of semiconductors. The purpose of this hedge is to protect against adverse movements in exchange rates.

Example 15–10: Foreign Currency Hedging Activities

The Company manufactures and sells its products in a number of countries throughout the world and, as a result, is exposed to movements in foreign currency exchange rates. The Company's major foreign currency exposures involve the markets in Western and Eastern Europe, Asia, Mexico, and Canada. The primary purpose of the Company's foreign currency hedging activities is to manage the volatility associated with foreign currency purchases of materials and other assets and liabilities created in the normal course of business. The Company primarily utilizes forward exchange contracts and purchased options with maturities of less than 18 months and currency swaps with maturities up to five years.

The Company enters into certain foreign currency derivative instruments that do not meet hedge accounting criteria. These, primarily, are intended to protect against exposure related to intercompany financing transactions and income from international operations. The fair values of these instruments at December 31, 20X2 were recorded as $3,452,000 in assets and $671,000 in liabilities.

In addition, the Company utilizes purchased foreign currency options, forward exchange contracts, and cross currency swaps which qualify as cash flow hedges. These are intended to offset the effect of exchange rate fluctuations on forecasted sales, inventory purchases, intercompany royalties, and intercompany loans denominated in foreign currency. The fair values of these instruments at December 31, 20X2 were recorded as $2,794,000 in assets and $3,125,000 in liabilities. Gains and losses on these instruments are deferred in other comprehensive income (OCI) until the underlying transaction is recognized in earnings. The earnings impact is reported in either net sales, cost of products sold, or marketing research and administrative expenses, to match the underlying transaction being hedged. Qualifying cash flow hedges that are currently deferred in OCI will be reclassified into earnings as the underlying transactions are recognized. No currency cash flow hedges were discontinued during the year due to changes in expectations on the original forecasted transactions.

Example 15–11: Commodity Hedging Activities

Raw materials used by the Company are subject to price volatility caused by weather, supply conditions, political and economic variables, and other unpredictable factors. To manage the volatility related to anticipated inventory purchases, the Company uses futures and options with maturities generally less than one year and swap contracts with maturities up to five years. These market instruments are designated as cash flow hedges. The mark-to-market gain or loss on qualifying commodity hedges is included in other comprehensive income to the extent effective, and reclassified into cost of products sold in the period during which the hedged transaction affects earnings. Qualifying commodity cash flow hedges that are currently deferred in other comprehensive income will be reclassified into earnings as the underlying transactions are recognized. The mark-to-market gains or losses on non-qualifying, excluded, and ineffective portions of hedges are recognized in cost of products sold immediately. No commodity cash flow hedges were discontinued during the year.

Example 15–12: Description of Derivatives That Have Not Been Designated as Hedges

The Company has the following contracts that have not been designated as hedges:

- Variable rate swap agreement entered into with a major financial institution in which the Company pays a floating rate based on LIBOR and receives a floating rate based on an investment fund index, with payments being calculated on a notional amount. The swap is an overlay to short-term investments and provides diversification benefits. The swap is settled quarterly, marked to market at each reporting date and all unrealized gains and losses are recognized in earnings currently.

- Lumber and other commodity futures designed to manage the Company's consolidated exposure to changes in inventory values due to fluctuations in market prices for selected business units. The Company's commodity futures positions are marked to market at each reporting date and all unrealized gains and losses are recognized in earnings currently. To date, these contract positions have not had a material effect on the Company's financial position, results of operations, or cash flows.

Example 15–13: Policy Describes When Hedge Accounting Is Discontinued

Hedge accounting is discontinued when it is determined that a derivative instrument is not highly effective as a hedge. Hedge accounting is also discontinued when: (1) the derivative instrument expires; is sold, terminated or exercised; or is no longer designated as a hedge instrument because it is unlikely that a forecasted transaction will occur; (2) a hedged firm commitment no longer meets the definition of a firm commitment; or (3) management determines that designation of the derivative as a hedging instrument is no longer appropriate.

When hedge accounting is discontinued, the derivative instrument will be either terminated, continue to be carried on the balance sheet at fair value, or redesignated as the hedging instrument in either a cash flow or fair value hedge, if the relationship meets all applicable hedging criteria. Any asset or liability that was previously recorded as a result of recognizing the value of a firm commitment will be removed from the balance sheet and recognized as a gain or loss in current period earnings. Any gains or losses that were accumulated in other comprehensive income from hedging a forecasted transaction will be recognized immediately in current period earnings, if it is probable that the forecasted transaction will not occur.

Example 15–14: Reporting Changes in the Components of Comprehensive Income

The following is an analysis of the changes in the net gain on cash flow hedging instruments included in accumulated other comprehensive income:

	20X2	*20X1*
Balance at beginning of year	$47,000	$43,000
Net gain for the year	21,000	16,000
Amount reclassified to earnings	(15,000)	(12,000)
Balance at end of year	$53,000	$47,000

> **Note:** See Chapter 48, "Stockholders' Equity," and Chapter 54, "Comprehensive Income," for additional examples of disclosures of reporting changes in the components of comprehensive income.

Concentrations of Credit Risk

> **Note:** For additional sample disclosures relating to concentrations of credit risk, see the following chapters:
> - Chapter 2, "Accounting Policies"
> - Chapter 6, "Commitments"
> - Chapter 10, "Contingencies, Risks, Uncertainties, and Concentrations"

- Chapter 37, "Cash and Cash Equivalents"
- Chapter 38, "Accounts and Notes Receivable"

Example 15–15: Concentrations of Credit and Market Risk Arising from Derivative Instruments

All of the Company's foreign currency exchange and interest rate derivative instruments involve elements of credit and market risk in excess of the amounts recognized in the consolidated financial statements. The counterparties to the financial instruments consist of a number of major financial institutions. In addition to limiting the amounts of the agreements and contracts it enters into with any one party, the Company monitors its positions with and the credit quality of the counterparties to these financial instruments. The Company does not anticipate nonperformance by any of the counterparties.

Example 15–16: Concentration of Credit Risk Virtually Limited and Collateral Is Not Required

Financial instruments that potentially subject the Company to concentrations of credit risk consist primarily of cash and cash equivalents and accounts receivable. The Company places its cash and cash equivalents with high quality financial institutions and limits the amount of credit exposure with any one institution. Concentrations of credit risk with respect to accounts receivable are limited because a large number of geographically diverse customers make up the Company's customer base, thus spreading the trade credit risk. At December 31, 20X2, and December 31, 20X1, no single group or customer represents greater than 10% of total accounts receivable. The Company controls credit risk through credit approvals, credit limits, and monitoring procedures. The Company performs credit evaluations of its commercial and industrial customers but generally does not require collateral to support accounts receivable.

CHAPTER 16
FINANCIAL STATEMENTS:
COMPARATIVE

CONTENTS

EXECUTIVE SUMMARY

The presentation of comparative financial statements enhances the usefulness of annual and interim reports. Although not required, ordinarily it is desirable that financial statements of two or more periods be presented. Footnotes and explanations that appeared on the statements for the preceding years should be repeated, or at least referred to, in the comparative statements to the extent that they continue to be of significance.

It is necessary that prior-year figures shown for comparative purposes be comparable with those shown for the most recent period, or that any exceptions to comparability be clearly identified and described.

Authoritative Literature

ARB-43   Chapter 2A, Comparative Financial Statements

DISCLOSURE REQUIREMENTS

Reclassifications or other changes affecting comparability of financial statements presented should be disclosed (ARB-43, Ch. 2A, par. 3).

EXAMPLES OF FINANCIAL STATEMENT DISCLOSURES

 The following sample disclosures are available on the accompanying disc. For information on disclosures of changes in accounting principles, changes in accounting estimates, changing in the reporting entity, and corrections of errors, see Chapter 1, "Accounting Changes and Error Corrections."

Example 16–1: Reclassifications of a General Nature

Certain amounts in the prior periods presented have been reclassified to conform to the current period financial statement presentation. These reclassifications have no effect on previously reported net income.

Example 16–2: Change in Method of Classifying Cash Equivalents and Restatement of Prior-Year Balances

During the year ended December 31, 20X2, the Company changed the method of classifying cash equivalents and has restated prior-year balances to reflect the change. All highly liquid investments with original maturities of three months or less at date of purchase are carried at cost, which approximates fair value, and are considered to be cash equivalents. These investments were previously classified as marketable securities. All other investments not considered to be a cash equivalent now are categorized separately as investments.

Example 16–3: Reclassification of Reimbursements Received for Out-of-Pocket Expenses

In January 20X2, the Company adopted the accounting requirements of EITF No. 01-14 (formerly Topic No. D-103, *Income Statement Characterization of Reimbursements Received for "Out-of-Pocket" Expenses Incurred*), which concluded that reimbursements received for "out-of-pocket" expenses should be characterized as revenue in the income statement. Under EITF No. 01-14, the Company reclassified prior period numbers to reflect the required adoption. Accordingly, professional services revenues and their related costs increased by $1,250,000 for the year ended December 31, 20X1.

CHAPTER 17
FOREIGN OPERATIONS AND CURRENCY TRANSLATION

CONTENTS

EXECUTIVE SUMMARY

There are two major areas of foreign operations: (1) translation of foreign currency financial statements for purposes of consolidation, combination, or reporting on the equity method and (2) accounting for and reporting foreign currency transactions.

Before an attempt is made to translate the records of a foreign operation, the records should be in conformity with generally accepted accounting principles (GAAP). In addition, if the foreign statements have any accounts stated in a currency other than their own, they must be converted into the foreign statement's currency before translation into U.S. dollars or any other reporting currency. In summary:

1.   Assets, liabilities, and operations of an entity should be expressed in the functional currency of the entity. The functional currency of an entity is the currency of the primary economic environment in which the entity operates.

2.   The current rate of exchange should be used to translate the assets and liabilities of a foreign entity from its functional currency into the reporting currency. The weighted-average exchange rate for the period is used to translate revenue, expenses, and gains and losses of a foreign entity from its functional currency to the reporting currency. The current rate of exchange is used to translate changes in financial position other than those items found in the income statement, which are translated at the weighted average exchange rate for the period.

3.   Gain or loss on the translation of foreign currency financial statements is not recognized in current net income but should be reported in other comprehensive income. If remeasurement

from the recording currency to the functional currency is necessary prior to translation, however, gain or loss on remeasurement is recognized in current net income.

4. The amounts accumulated in the translation adjustment component of stockholders' equity are realized on the sale or substantially complete liquidation of the investment in the foreign entity.

5. The financial statements of a foreign entity in a country that has had cumulative inflation of approximately 100% or more over a three-year period (highly inflationary) must be remeasured into the functional currency of the reporting entity.

6. Gains or losses from foreign currency transactions are recognized in current net income, except for:

   a. Gain or loss on a designated and effective economic hedge of a net investment in a foreign entity

   b. Gain or loss on certain long-term intercompany foreign currency transactions

   c. Gain or loss on a designated and effective economic hedge of a firm, identifiable, foreign currency commitment that meets certain conditions

7. Deferred taxes generally must be provided for the future tax effects of taxable foreign currency transactions and taxable transaction adjustments. However, deferred taxes should not be provided on unremitted earnings of a foreign subsidiary in certain instances.

FASB Statement of Financial Accounting Standards No. 52, (FAS-52) *Foreign Currency Translation,* is the primary source of GAAP for foreign operations and foreign currency translation. However, FAS-52 has been amended by FAS-133, *Accounting for Derivative Instruments and Hedging Activities.* FAS-133 addresses the accounting for freestanding foreign currency derivatives and certain foreign currency derivatives embedded in other instruments. See Chapter 15, "Financial Instruments, Derivatives, and Hedging Activities," for the accounting for freestanding foreign currency derivatives and certain foreign currency derivatives embedded in other instruments.

Authoritative Literature

ARB-43 Chapter 12, Foreign Operations and Foreign Exchange

FAS-52 Foreign Currency Translation (as amended by FAS-133)

FAS-95 Statement of Cash Flows

FAS-109 Accounting for Income Taxes

FAS-130 Reporting Comprehensive Income

FAS-133 Accounting for Derivative Instruments and Hedging Activities

FAS-138 Accounting for Certain Derivative Instruments and Certain Hedging Activities

FIN-37 Accounting for Translation Adjustments upon Sale of Part of an Investment in a Foreign Entity

DISCLOSURE REQUIREMENTS

The following disclosures should be made for foreign operations and currency translation:

1. Significant foreign operations, including foreign earnings reported in excess of amounts received in the United States (ARB-43, Ch. 12, pars. 5–6)

2. The aggregate exchange transaction gain or loss included in the determination of net income should be disclosed as follows (FAS-133, par. 45):

   a. For derivative instruments, as well as nonderivative instruments that may give rise to foreign currency transaction gains or losses, that have been designated and have qualified as *fair value hedging instruments* and for the related hedged items:

      — The net gain or loss recognized in earnings during the reporting period representing (i) the amount of the hedges' ineffectiveness, (ii) the component of the derivative instruments' gain or loss, if any, excluded from the assessment of hedge effectiveness, and (iii) a description of where the net gain or loss is reported in the statement of income or other statement of financial performance

      — The amount of net gain or loss recognized in earnings when a hedged firm commitment no longer qualifies as a fair value hedge

   b. For derivative instruments that have been designated and have qualified as *cash flow hedging instruments* and for the related hedged transactions:

      — The net gain or loss recognized in earnings during the reporting period representing (i) the amount of the hedges' ineffectiveness and (ii) the component of the derivative instruments' gain or loss, if any, excluded from the assessment of hedge effectiveness and a description of where the net gain or loss is reported in the statement of income or other statement of financial performance

— A description of the transactions or other events that will result in the reclassification into earnings of gains and losses that are reported in accumulated other comprehensive income, and the estimated net amount of the existing gains or losses at the reporting date that is expected to be reclassified into earnings within the next 12 months

— The maximum length of time over which the entity is hedging its exposure to the variability in future cash flows for forecasted transactions excluding those forecasted transactions related to the payment of variable interest on existing financial instruments

— The amount of gains and losses reclassified into earnings as a result of the discontinuance of cash flow hedges because it is probable that the original forecasted transactions will not occur

c. For derivative instruments, as well as nonderivative instruments that may give rise to foreign currency transaction gains or losses, that have been designated and have qualified as hedges of the foreign currency exposure of a *net investment in a foreign operation:*

— The net amount of gains or losses included in the cumulative translation adjustment during the reporting period

3. An analysis of the change in the cumulative translation adjustments included as a component of accumulated other comprehensive income, including, at a minimum, the following (FAS-52, par. 31):

a. Beginning and ending amounts of cumulative translation adjustments

b. The aggregate adjustment for the period resulting from translation adjustments and gains and losses from hedges of a net investment in a foreign entity and long-term intercompany balances

c. The amount of income taxes for the period allocated to translation adjustments

d. The amounts transferred from cumulative translation adjustments and included in determining net income for the period as a result of the sale or complete (or substantially complete) liquidation of an investment in a foreign entity

4. Exchange rate changes that occur after the balance-sheet date, including the effects of rate changes on unsettled balances pertaining to foreign currency transactions. If the effects of rate changes cannot be determined, that fact should be disclosed (FAS-52, pars. 32 and 143).

5. The following additional disclosures are optional and should be considered to supplement the required disclosures described above (FAS-52, par. 144):

   a. Mathematical effects of translating revenue and expenses at rates that are different from those used in previous financial statements

   b. Economic effects (such as selling prices, sales volume, and cost structures) of rate changes

EXAMPLES OF FINANCIAL STATEMENT DISCLOSURES

 The following sample disclosures are available on the accompanying disc.

Example 17–1: Foreign Currency Adjustments—Functional Currency Is the Foreign Country's Local Currency

The financial position and results of operations of the Company's foreign subsidiaries are measured using the foreign subsidiary's local currency as the functional currency. Revenues and expenses of such subsidiaries have been translated into U.S. dollars at average exchange rates prevailing during the period. Assets and liabilities have been translated at the rates of exchange on the balance-sheet date. The resulting translation gain and loss adjustments are recorded directly as a separate component of shareholders' equity, unless there is a sale or complete liquidation of the underlying foreign investments. Foreign currency translation adjustments resulted in gains of $425,000 and $366,000 in 20X2 and 20X1, respectively.

Transaction gains and losses that arise from exchange rate fluctuations on transactions denominated in a currency other than the functional currency are included in the results of operations as incurred. Foreign currency transaction losses included in operations totaled $57,000 in 20X2 and $46,0000 in 20X1.

Example 17–2: Foreign Currency Adjustments—Functional Currency Is the U.S. Dollar

The Company's functional currency for all operations worldwide is the U.S. dollar. Nonmonetary assets and liabilities are translated at historical rates and monetary assets and liabilities are translated at exchange rates in effect at the end of the year. Income statement accounts are translated at average rates for the year. Gains and losses from translation of foreign currency financial statements into U.S. dollars are included in current results of operations. Gains and losses resulting from foreign currency transactions are also included in current results of operations. Aggregate foreign currency translation and transaction losses included in operations totaled $138,000 in 20X2 and $114,000 in 20X1.

Example 17–3: Foreign Currency Adjustments—Certain Assets and Liabilities Are Remeasured at Current Exchange Rates While Others Are Remeasured at Historical Rates

The U.S. dollar is the functional currency of the Company's worldwide continuing operations. All foreign currency asset and liability amounts are remeasured into U.S. dollars at end-of-period exchange rates, except for inventories, prepaid expenses and property, plant, and equipment, which are remeasured at historical rates. Foreign currency income and expenses are remeasured at average exchange rates in effect during the year, except for expenses related to balance sheet amounts remeasured at historical exchange rates. Exchange gains and losses arising from remeasurement of foreign currency-denominated monetary assets and liabilities are included in income in the period in which they occur.

Example 17–4: Foreign Currency Hedging Activities

The Company manufactures and sells its products in a number of countries throughout the world and, as a result, is exposed to movements in foreign currency exchange rates. The Company's major foreign currency exposures involve the markets in Western and Eastern Europe, Asia, Mexico, and Canada. The primary purpose of the Company's foreign currency hedging activities is to manage the volatility associated with foreign currency purchases of materials and other assets and liabilities created in the normal course of business. The Company primarily utilizes forward exchange contracts and purchased options with maturities of less than 18 months and currency swaps with maturities up to five years.

The Company enters into certain foreign currency derivative instruments that do not meet hedge accounting criteria. These primarily are intended to protect against exposure related to intercompany financing transactions and income from international operations. The fair values of these instruments at December 31, 20X2 were recorded as $3,452,000 in assets and $671,000 in liabilities.

In addition, the Company utilizes purchased foreign currency options, forward exchange contracts, and cross currency swaps which qualify as cash flow hedges. These are intended to offset the effect of exchange rate fluctuations on forecasted sales, inventory purchases, intercompany royalties, and intercompany loans denominated in foreign currency. The fair values of these instruments at December 31, 20X2 were recorded as $2,794,000 in assets and $3,125,000 in liabilities. Gains and losses on these instruments are deferred in other comprehensive income (OCI) until the underlying transaction is recognized in earnings. The earnings impact is reported in either net sales, cost of products sold, or marketing research and administrative expenses, to match the underlying transaction being hedged. Qualifying cash flow hedges that are currently deferred in OCI will be reclassified into earnings as the underlying transactions are recognized. No currency cash flow hedges were discontinued during the year due to changes in expectations on the original forecasted transactions.

> **Note:** See Chapter 15, "Financial Instruments, Derivatives, and Hedging Activities," for additional examples.

Example 17–5: Analysis of the Change in Cumulative Foreign Currency Translation Adjustments

Accumulated other comprehensive income for 20X2 and 20X1 represents foreign currency translation items associated with the Company's European and South American operations. Following is an analysis of the changes in the cumulative foreign currency translation adjustment account for 20X2 and 20X1:

	Accumulated Other Comprehensive Income— Foreign Currency Translation	
	20X2	*20X1*
Balance at beginning of year	$2,250,000	$1,600,000
Foreign currency translation adjustments	1,317,000	1,100,000
Income tax effect relating to translation adjustments	(540,000)	(450,000)
Amount recognized in operations as a result of the sale of the Company's German subsidiary in 20X2	(625,000)	-0
Balance at end of year	$2,402,000	$2,250,000

> **Note:** See Chapter 48, "Stockholders' Equity," for examples of the change in cumulative foreign currency translation

adjustments as reflected in an entity's statement of stockholders' equity.

Example 17–6: Significant Exchange Rate Changes After the Balance-Sheet Date of December 31, 20X2

On January 13, 20X3, the Brazilian government allowed the value of its currency, the Real, to float freely against other currencies. Between January 13, 20X3, and March 17, 20X3, the Real's exchange rate to the U.S. dollar has declined as much as 44% from the exchange rate on December 31, 20X2. As nearly all the Company's transactions in Brazil are Real-denominated, translating the results of operations of the Company's Brazilian subsidiary into U.S. dollars at devalued exchange rates will result in a lower contribution to consolidated revenues and operating income. Based on the Real exchange rate to the U.S. dollar on March 17, 20X3, the Company's currency translation of the foreign investment in its Brazilian subsidiary from the Real (functional currency) to the U.S. dollar would result in a devaluation of approximately $6 million. Currency devaluations resulting from translating assets and liabilities from the functional currency to the U.S. dollar are included as a component of other comprehensive income (loss) in stockholders' equity.

Example 17–7: Company Discloses Nature of Its Operations in Foreign Countries

Substantially all of the Company's products are manufactured in the Dominican Republic, Mexico (under the Maquiladora program), Switzerland, Ireland, and Slovakia. These foreign operations represent captive manufacturing facilities of the Company. The Company's operations are subject to various political, economic, and other risks and uncertainties inherent in the countries in which the Company operates. Among other risks, the Company's operations are subject to the risks of restrictions on transfer of funds; export duties, quotas, and embargoes; domestic and international customs and tariffs; changing taxation policies; foreign exchange restrictions; and political conditions and governmental regulations.

Example 17–8: Amount of Foreign Earnings Exceeds Amounts Actually Received in the United States

In 20X2 and 20X1, earnings from the Company's French subsidiary totaled $705,000 and $643,000, respectively; dividends received from this subsidiary totaled $500,000 and $400,000 in 20X2 and 20X1, respectively.

Example 17–9: Company Specifies Percentage of Net Sales Relating to Foreign Operations

Sales to customers outside the United States approximated 35% of net sales in 20X2 and 25% of net sales in 20X1. An adverse change in either economic conditions abroad or the Company's relationship with significant foreign distributors could negatively affect the volume of the Company's international sales and the Company's results of operations.

Example 17–10: Concentration in Accounts Receivable from Foreign Customers

As of December 31, 20X2, and December 31, 20X1, approximately 38% and 35%, respectively, of the Company's total accounts receivable were due from four foreign customers.

Example 17–11: Revenues and Long-Lived Assets by Geographic Area

The following table indicates the Company's relative amounts of revenue and the long-lived assets for 20X2 and 20X1 by geographic area:

	20X2		20X1	
	Revenue	*Long-Lived Assets*	*Revenue*	*Long-Lived Assets*
United States	$50,719,000	$14,395,000	$47,611,000	$13,618,000
Europe:				
Germany	7,592,000	2,530,000	7,058,000	2,367,000
France	6,133,000	1,662,000	5,450,000	1,278,000
Italy	5,562,000	2,129,000	4,923,000	1,854,000
Other	4,397,000	1,012,000	3,820,000	1,299,000
Total Europe	23,684,000	7,333,000	21,251,000	6,798,000
Other foreign countries	3,789,000	1,126,000	3,214,000	1,011,000
Total	$78,192,000	$22,854,000	$72,076,000	$21,427,000

Example 17–12: Restrictions on Transfer of Assets of Foreign Operations

The governments and national banking systems of certain countries in which the Company has consolidated foreign affiliates impose various restrictions on the payment of dividends and transfer of funds out of those countries. Additionally, provisions of credit agreements entered into by certain foreign affiliates presently restrict the payment of dividends. The estimated U.S. dollar amount of the foreign net assets included in the Consolidated Balance Sheets that are restricted in some manner as to transfer to the Company was approximately $22 million and $19 million at December 31, 20X2, and December 31, 20X1, respectively.

Example 17–13: Company's Future Operations Are Dependent on Foreign Operations

The Company's future operations and earnings will depend on the results of the Company's operations in [*foreign country*]. There can be no assurance that the Company will be able to successfully conduct such operations, and a failure to do so would have a material adverse effect on the Company's financial position, results of operations, and cash flows. Also, the success of the Company's operations will be subject to numerous contingencies, some of which are beyond management's control. These contingencies include general and regional economic conditions, prices for the Company's products, competition, and changes in regulation. Since the Company is dependent on international operations, specifically those in [*foreign country*], the Company will be subject to various additional political, economic, and other uncertainties. Among other risks, the Company's operations will be subject to the risks of restrictions on transfer of funds; export duties, quotas, and embargoes; domestic and international customs and tariffs; changing taxation policies; foreign exchange restrictions; and political conditions and governmental regulations.

Example 17–14: Deferred Taxes Not Provided on Undistributed Earnings of Foreign Subsidiaries—Amount of Deferred Tax Liability Is Not Disclosed

A provision has not been made at December 31, 20X2, for U.S. or additional foreign withholding taxes on approximately $12 million of undistributed earnings of foreign subsidiaries since it is the present intention of management to reinvest the undistributed earnings indefinitely in foreign operations. Generally, such earnings become subject to U.S. tax upon the remittance of dividends and under certain other circumstances. It is not practicable to estimate the amount of deferred tax liability on such undistributed earnings.

Example 17–15: Deferred Taxes Not Provided on Undistributed Earnings of Foreign Subsidiaries—Amount of Deferred Tax Liability Is Disclosed

The Company has not recorded deferred income taxes applicable to undistributed earnings of foreign subsidiaries that are indefinitely reinvested in foreign operations. Undistributed earnings amounted to approximately $6,000,000 and $5,200,000 at December 31, 20X2, and December 31, 20X1, respectively. If the earnings of such foreign subsidiaries were not definitely reinvested, a deferred tax liability of approximately $1,500,000 and $1,300,000 would have been required at December 31, 20X2, and December 31, 20X1, respectively.

Example 17–16: Deferred Taxes Recorded on Undistributed Earnings of Foreign Subsidiaries

At December 31, 20X2, the accompanying consolidated Balance Sheet includes a deferred tax liability of $300,000 for the estimated income taxes that will be payable upon the anticipated future repatriation of approximately $1,000,000 of undistributed earnings of foreign subsidiaries in the form of dividends.

CHAPTER 18
GOING CONCERN

CONTENTS

EXECUTIVE SUMMARY

Information that raises uncertainty about an entity's ability to continue as a going concern generally relates to the entity's ability to meet its maturing obligations without selling operating assets, undergoing debt restructuring, or revising operations based on outside pressures or similar strategies. If there is substantial doubt about an entity's ability to continue as going concern for a period of time not to exceed one year beyond the balance-sheet date, adequate disclosures should be made in the financial statements. If the substantial doubt about the entity's ability to continue as a going concern is alleviated, disclosures should be made of the conditions and events that initially caused the substantial doubt, their possible effects, and mitigating factors (e.g., management's plans).

Authoritative Literature

SAS-59   The Auditor's Consideration of an Entity's Ability to Continue as a Going Concern

FAS-5   Accounting for Contingencies

DISCLOSURE REQUIREMENTS

1. If, after considering management's plans, a conclusion is reached that there is substantial doubt about the entity's ability to continue as a going concern for a period of time not to exceed one year beyond the balance-sheet date, the financial statements should include the following disclosures (AU 341.10):

    a. Pertinent conditions and events giving rise to the assessment of substantial doubt about the entity's ability to continue as a going concern for a period of time not to exceed one year beyond the balance-sheet date

    b. The possible effects of such conditions and events

    c. Management's evaluation of the significance of those conditions and events and any mitigating factors

    d. Possible discontinuance of operations

    e. Management's plans (including relevant prospective financial information)

    f. Information about the recoverability or classification of recorded asset amounts or the amounts or classification of liabilities

2. When substantial doubt about the entity's ability to continue as a going concern for a period of time not to exceed one year from the balance-sheet date is alleviated, the financial statements should include the following disclosures (AU 341.11):

    a. The principal conditions and events that initially caused the auditor to believe there was substantial doubt

    b. The possible effects of such conditions and events, and any mitigating factors, including management's plans

EXAMPLES OF FINANCIAL STATEMENT DISCLOSURES

The following sample disclosures are available on the accompanying disc.

Example 18–1: Going-Concern Issues Arising from Recurring Losses and Cash Flow Problems

As shown in the accompanying financial statements, the Company has incurred recurring losses from operations, and as of December 31, 20X2, the Company's current liabilities exceeded its current assets by $800,000 and its total liabilities exceeded its total assets by $1,900,000. These factors raise substantial doubt about the Company's ability to continue as a going concern. Management has instituted a cost reduction program that included a reduction in labor and fringe costs. In addition, the Company has redesigned certain product lines, increased sales prices on certain items, obtained more favorable material costs, and has instituted more efficient management techniques. Management believes these factors will contribute toward achieving profitability. The accompanying financial statements do not include any adjustments that might be necessary if the Company is unable to continue as a going concern.

Example 18–2: Going-Concern Issues Arising from Default of Certain Loan Agreements

The Company incurred a loss of approximately $3,200,000 in 20X2 and continued to experience certain decreases in working capital. As a result, the Company is in technical default of certain covenants contained in its credit and loan agreement with its primary lender. In addition, this default has triggered events of default under certain other obligations of the Company, including a $2,000,000 interim capital financing notes and certain promissory notes secured by real estate and equipment. The holders of the interim capital financing notes and promissory notes may, at their option, give notice to the Company that amounts are immediately due and payable. As a result, $10,500,000 of the Company's total long-term debt has been classified as a current liability in the accompanying Balance Sheet at December 31, 20X2.

The Company's default of the loan agreements described above raise substantial doubt about the Company's ability to continue as a going concern. The Company is currently working with all of its lenders to obtain necessary waivers under the terms of the various agreements and is negotiating with its primary lender to stabilize its lender relationships by establishing certain internal operating and management plans. The Company also retained the services of an outside consulting firm to institute and implement all required programs to accomplish management's objectives. The Company is also evaluating the disposal of certain assets, raising new capital for future operations, and selectively increasing certain product prices. However, there can be no assurance that the Company will be successful in achieving its objectives.

The accompanying financial statements have been prepared assuming that the Company will continue as a going concern; however, the above conditions raise substantial doubt about the Company's ability to do so. The financial statements do not include any adjustments to reflect the possible future effects on the recoverability and classification of assets or the amounts and classifications of liabilities that may result should the Company be unable to continue as a going concern.

Example 18–3: Company Has Sufficient Funds to Meet Its Needs over the Next Year but Is Uncertain about Whether It Can Accomplish Its Business Objectives over the Following Years

The Company has sustained recurring losses and negative cash flows from operations. Over the past year, the Company's growth has been funded through a combination of private equity, bank debt, and lease financing. As of December 31, 20X2, the Company had approximately $200,000 of unrestricted cash. On January 12, 20X3, the Company executed an agreement with a group of private investors whereby the Company issued $10,000,000 in convertible subordinated loan notes. The Company believes that, as a result of this, it currently has sufficient cash and financing commitments to meet its funding requirements over the next year. However, the Company has experienced and continues to experience negative operating margins and negative cash flows from operations, as well as an ongoing requirement for substantial additional capital investment. The Company expects that it will need to raise substantial additional capital to accomplish its business plan over the next several years. In addition, the Company may wish to selectively pursue possible acquisitions of businesses, technologies, content, or products complementary to those of the Company in the future in order to expand its presence in the marketplace and achieve operating efficiencies. The Company expects to seek to obtain additional funding through a bank credit facility or private equity. There can be no assurance as to the availability or terms upon which such financing and capital might be available.

Example 18–4: Liquidity Disclosure—Company Discusses Liquidity Issues but Believes Actions It Has Taken Will Enable It to Continue as a Going Concern over the Next Year

At December 31, 20X2, the Company had cash and cash equivalents of $36,300,000, a working capital deficit of $15,693,000 and an accumulated deficit of $67,847,000. Additionally, the Company has incurred losses since its inception as infrastructure costs were incurred in advance of obtaining customers. Subsequent to year end, the Company ceased making payments due under certain operating lease agreements as part of an effort to restructure payment terms.

Management has taken several actions to ensure that the Company will continue as a going concern through December 31, 20X3, including the closing of two data centers, headcount reductions, and reductions in discretionary expenditures. Further, as discussed in Note [X], the Company has entered into an agreement in which it will (1) receive approximately $50 million in additional cash; (2) convert amounts due to ABC, Inc. into equity; and (3) restructure lease payments subsequent to year end. Management believes that these actions will enable the Company to continue as a going concern through December 31, 20X3.

Example 18–5: Company's Successful Operations Are Dependent on Those of Its Parent

The Company has historically relied on its parent to meet its cash flow requirements. The parent company has cash available in the amount of approximately $83,000 as of December 31, 20X2, and a working capital deficit of $80 million. The Senior Secured Notes in the amount of $65 million have been reclassified because the Company's parent does not currently have sufficient funds to make the next interest payment (in the approximate amount of $6 million) due in May 20X3. Failure by the parent to make such payment could allow the holders of the Notes to declare all amounts outstanding immediately due and payable. The Company and its parent will need additional funds to meet the development and exploratory obligations until sufficient cash flows are generated from anticipated production to sustain operations and to fund future development and exploration obligations.

The parent plans to generate the additional cash needed through the sale or financing of its domestic assets held for sale and the completion of additional equity, debt, or joint venture transactions. There is no assurance, however, that the parent will be able to sell or finance its assets held for sale or to complete other transactions in the future at commercially reasonable terms, if at all, or that the Company will be able to meet its future contractual obligations.

CHAPTER 19
GUARANTEES

CONTENTS

EXECUTIVE SUMMARY

FASB Interpretation No. 45, *Guarantor's Accounting and Disclosure Requirements for Guarantees, Including Indirect Guarantees of Indebtedness of Others* (FIN-45), indicates that the issuance of a guarantee obligates the guarantor in two important ways: (1) the guarantor is obligated to perform over the term of the guarantee in the event that the specified triggering events or conditions occur (the noncontingent element) and (2) the guarantor is contingently obligated to make future payments if those triggering events or conditions occur (the contingent element).

FIN-45 indicates that there have been differing interpretations about the disclosures required of guarantors under Statement of Financial Accounting Standards No. 5 (FAS-5), *Accounting for Contingencies,* and about the need for a guarantor to recognize an initial liability for its obligation under a guarantee. Some believed that FAS-5 prohibits the guarantor from initially recognizing a liability for a guarantee issued, unless it is probable that payments will be required under that guarantee. FIN-45 clarifies that a guarantor is required (with certain exceptions) to recognize, at the inception of a guarantee, a liability for the fair value of the obligations it has undertaken in issuing the guarantee. Also, FIN-45 expands the disclosure requirements for guarantees, including indirect guarantees of indebtedness of others (see the "Disclosure Requirements" section below).

Authoritative Literature

FIN-45   Guarantor's Accounting and Disclosure Requirements for Guarantees, Including Indirect Guarantees of Indebtedness of Others

FSP FIN 45-3   Application of FASB Interpretation No. 45 to Minimum Revenue Guarantees Granted to a Business or Its Owners

DISCLOSURE REQUIREMENTS

For each guarantee, or each group of similar guarantees, a guarantor should disclose the following information, even if the likelihood of the guarantor having to make any payments under the guarantee is remote (FIN-45, pars. 13–14):

1. The nature of the guarantee.

2. The approximate term of the guarantee.

3. How the guarantee arose.

4. The events or circumstances that would require the guarantor to perform under the guarantee.

5. The maximum potential amount of future payments, undiscounted, which the guarantor could be required to make under the guarantee (this disclosure is not required for product warranties). With respect to this disclosure item:

   a. If the maximum potential future payments under the guarantee are unlimited, that fact should be disclosed.

   b. If the guarantor is unable to develop an estimate of the maximum potential amount of future payments, the guarantor should disclose the reasons why it cannot estimate the maximum potential amount.

6. The current carrying amount of the liability, if any.

7. The nature of any recourse provisions that would enable the guarantor to recover from third parties any of the amounts paid under the guarantee.

8. The nature of any assets held either as collateral or by third parties that, upon the occurrence of any triggering event or condition under the guarantee, the guarantor can obtain and liquidate to recover the amounts paid under the guarantee. Also, if estimable, the guarantor should indicate the extent to which the proceeds from liquidation of those assets would be expected to cover the maximum potential amount of future payments under the guarantee.

9. For product warranties or for guarantees related to the functional performance of nonfinancial assets owned by the guaranteed party:

   a. The guarantor's accounting policy and methodology used in determining its liability for such product warranties or guarantees, including any liability (such as deferred revenue) associated with extended warranties.

   b. A reconciliation of the changes in the guarantor's aggregate liability for such product warranties or guarantees, showing the following:

      — The beginning balance of the aggregate liability.

      — Aggregate reductions in that liability for payments made (in cash or in kind).

— Aggregate changes in the liability for accruals related to such product warranties or guarantees issued during the period.

— Aggregate changes in the liability for accruals related to preexisting warranties (including adjustments related to changes in estimates).

— The ending balance of the aggregate liability.

Also, the disclosure requirements detailed in items 1 through 9 above should be made for all minimum revenue guarantees in financial statements of annual or interim periods ending after the beginning of the first fiscal quarter following November 10, 2005, regardless of whether they were recognized and measured under FIN-45 (FSP FIN 45-3, par. 7).

EXAMPLES OF FINANCIAL STATEMENT DISCLOSURES

 The following sample disclosures are available on the accompanying disc.

Example 19–1: Guarantee of Third-Party Indebtedness—No Liability Is Recorded

As of December 31, 20X2, the Company is contingently liable as guarantor with respect to $5,400,000 of indebtedness of Extraped, Inc., an entity that is owned by the Company's stockholders. The term of the guarantee is through June 30, 20X4. At any time through that date, should Extraped, Inc. be over 90 days delinquent on its debt payments, the Company will be obligated to perform under the guarantee by primarily making the required payments, including late fees and penalties. The maximum potential amount of future payments that the Company is required to make under the guarantee is $3,000,000.

Example 19–2: Guarantee of Third-Party Indebtedness—Liability Is Recorded

In January 20X2, the Company executed a "Guarantee Agreement" (the Agreement) to guarantee the payment of $500,000 advanced to an affiliate, Steinhart Corp., by Amcor Funding, Inc. The guarantee agreement expires March 31, 20X3. In November 20X2, Steinhart Corp. became insolvent, which triggered an event of default under the terms of the Agreement. At December 31, 20X2, the Company accrued a loss of $500,000 for the full amount of the potential payment that the Company would be required to make under the guarantee. Steinhart Corp. is in the process of liquidating its assets; however, the Company does not expect to recover any of the amounts paid under the guarantee.

Example 19–3: Guarantee of Indebtedness of Joint Venture Obligates Company to Advance Funds to the Joint Venture if Certain Loan Covenants Are Not Met

The Company holds a 25% ownership interest in Stellark, Inc., which has a $7,000,000 line of credit agreement (Agreement) with First Nations Bank. Under terms of the Agreement, the Company is obligated to advance to Stellark, Inc. a maximum of $2,500,000 if its working capital falls below $500,000 or its current ratio is less than 1. Any funds advanced under this Agreement are available to First Nations Bank. In addition, First Nations Bank may have claims against the Company in an amount not to exceed $2,000,000 of any unsatisfied required advances. The term of the guarantee is through April 30, 20X4. At December 31, 20X2, Stellark, Inc. was in compliance with the terms of the Agreement with First Nations Bank.

Example 19–4: Assets Held as Collateral in Connection with Guarantee of Future Lease Payments

In March 20X2, the Company sold The Red Shoe, Inc., a chain of 25 stores located throughout Ohio and Michigan. In connection with this sale, the Company has guaranteed that certain lease payments will be made by the purchasers through December 31, 20X5. The maximum amount of future lease payments guaranteed by the Company totaled $6,800,000 at December 31, 20X2. At December 31, 20X2, the purchasers have set aside $1,000,000 in a trust account for the benefit of the Company, which the Company can obtain to recover any amounts paid under the guarantee. The Company believes that the purchasers will be able to perform under their respective lease agreements and that no payments will be required and no losses incurred under such guarantees.

Example 19–5: Guaranteed Advance and Royalty Payments in Connection with New Joint Venture

In January 20X2, the Company entered into a joint venture agreement with Sapiex Corp. creating a new limited liability company (LLC) in which the Company holds a 50% ownership interest. On December 1, 20X2, the LLC entered into a license agreement expiring December 31, 20X9, with an option for a five-year automatic extension if the LLC pays the licensor $27,000,000 in royalties during the initial seven-year period of the agreement. The license agreement includes guaranteed minimum royalty payments of $17,000,000 payable over the seven-year initial term and $7,500,000 payable over the five-year renewal period, if applicable. The Company is responsible for funding $8,000,000 of the $17,000,000 guaranteed royalty payments. The guarantee payments include a $3,000,000 advance, paid within 15 days after the agreements were executed, and seven minimum guaranteed installments of $2,000,000, due each January 30, starting in 20X3 and ending 20X9. The Company was responsible for funding $2,000,000 of the initial advance and is responsible for funding $750,000 of the first four and $1,000,000 of the next three of seven yearly installments.

Example 19–6: Certain Guarantees Are Denominated in Foreign Currencies and May Vary Based on Fluctuations in Foreign Exchange Rates

The Company has unconditionally guaranteed the repayment of certain loans and related interest and fees for an unconsolidated equity investee. The guarantees continue until the loans, including accrued interest and fees, have been paid in full. The maximum amount of the guarantees may vary, but is limited to the sum of the total due and unpaid principal amounts plus related interest and fees. Additionally, the maximum amount of the guarantees, certain of which are denominated in foreign currencies, will vary based on fluctuations in foreign exchange rates. As of December 31, 20X2, the maximum principal amount guaranteed was approximately $9 million.

The Company may recover a portion of its maximum liability upon liquidation of the investee's assets. The proceeds from such liquidation cannot be accurately estimated due to the multitude of factors that would affect the valuation and realization of such proceeds of a liquidation.

Example 19–7: Company Issued Residual Value Guarantees in Case It Does Not Purchase Leased Property

In connection with various operating leases, the Company issued residual value guarantees, which provide that if the Company does not purchase the leased property from the lessor at the end of the lease term, then the Company is liable to the lessor for an amount equal to the shortage, if any, between the proceeds from the sale of the property and an agreed value. As of December 31, 20X2, the maximum amount of the residual value guarantees was approximately $7.5 million. The Company's management believes that proceeds from the sale of properties under operating leases would exceed the payment obligation and, therefore, no liability to the Company currently exists.

Example 19–8: Indemnification Guarantee to Landlord and Sublessee under Lease Agreements

The Company leases space in certain buildings, including its corporate headquarters building, under operating leases. The Company has standard indemnification arrangements under those leases that require it to indemnify the landlord against losses, liabilities and claims incurred in connection with the premises covered by the Company leases, its use of the premises, property damage or personal injury, and breach of the lease agreement, as well as occurrences arising from the Company's negligence or willful misconduct. The Company also subleases certain space and agrees to indemnify the sublessee for losses caused by the Company's employees on the premises. The term of these indemnification agreements is generally perpetual from the time of execution of the agreement. The maximum potential amount of future payments the Company could be required to make under these indemnification agreements is unlimited. The Company has never incurred costs to defend lawsuits or settle claims related to these indemnification agreements. As of December 31, 20X2, the Company had not accrued a liability for this guarantee because the likelihood of incurring a payment obligation in connection with this guarantee is remote.

Example 19–9: Product Warranties

The Company sells the majority of its products to customers along with unconditional repair or replacement warranties for a full year from the date of purchase. The Company determines its estimated liability for warranty claims based on the Company's experience of the amount of claims actually made. It is reasonably possible that the Company's estimate of the accrued product warranty claims will change in the near term. Estimated costs for product warranties are recognized at the time revenue is recognized.

The following is a reconciliation of the changes in the Company's aggregate product warranty liability for the years ended December 31, 20X2, and December 31, 20X1:

	20X2	20X1
Accrued liability at beginning of period	$2,511,000	$1,350,000
Payments made	(1,096,000)	(722,000)
Costs recognized for warranties issued during the period	1,972,000	1,756,000
Changes in estimates for preexisting warranties	(131,000)	127,000
Accrued liability at end of period	$3,256,000	$2,511,000

Example 19–10: Officers' and Directors' Indemnification Guarantee

The Company's Certificate of Incorporation provides that the Company indemnify its officers and directors for certain events or occurrences that happen by reason of the fact that the officer or director is, was, or has agreed to serve as an officer or director of the Company. The term of the indemnification period is for the officer's or director's lifetime. The maximum potential amount of future payments the Company could be required to make under these indemnification agreements is unlimited; however, the Company has a Director and Officer insurance policy that limits its exposure and enables the Company to recover a portion of any future amounts paid. As of December 31, 20X2, the Company had not accrued a liability for this guarantee, because the likelihood of incurring a payment obligation in connection with this guarantee is remote.

Example 19–11: Guarantee in Connection with Business Sale Agreements

In connection with agreements for the sale of portions of its business, including certain discontinued operations, the Company has typically retained the liabilities of a business that relate to events occurring prior to its sale, such as tax, environmental, litigation, and employment matters. The Company generally indemnifies the purchaser of a Company's business in the event that a third party asserts a claim against the purchaser that relates to a liability retained by the Company. These types of indemnification guarantees typically extend for a number of years. The Company is unable to estimate the maximum potential liability for these types of indemnification guarantees as the business sale agreements do not specify a maximum amount and the amounts are dependent upon the outcome of future contingent events, the nature and likelihood of which cannot be determined at this time. Historically, the Company has not made any significant indemnification payments under such agreements and no amount has been accrued in the accompanying consolidated financial statements with respect to these indemnification guarantees.

Example 19–12: Indemnification of Lenders under Credit Facilities

Under its credit facilities, the Company has agreed to indemnify its lenders against costs or losses resulting from changes in laws and regulations, which would increase the lenders' costs, and from any legal action brought against the lenders related to the use of loan proceeds. These indemnifications generally extend for the term of the credit facilities and do not provide for any limit on the maximum potential liability. Historically, the Company has not made any significant indemnification payments under such agreements and no amount has been accrued in the accompanying consolidated financial statements with respect to these indemnification guarantees.

Example 19–13: Indemnification Guarantee to Customers under Technology License Agreements

The Company licenses technology to certain customers under license agreements that provide for the Company to indemnify the customers against claims of patent and copyright infringement. This indemnity does not apply in the case where the licensed technology has been modified by the customers or combined with other technology, hardware, or data that the Company has not approved. The term of these indemnification agreements is generally perpetual from the time of execution of the agreement. The maximum potential amount of future payments the Company could be required to make under these indemnification agreements is unlimited. The Company has never incurred costs to defend lawsuits or settle claims related to these indemnification agreements. As of December 31, 20X2, the Company had not accrued a liability for this guarantee, because the likelihood of incurring a payment obligation in connection with this guarantee is remote.

Example 19–14: Indemnification Guarantee to Vendors under Technology License Agreements

The Company licenses technology from third parties under agreements that contain standard indemnification provisions that require the Company to indemnify the third party against losses, liabilities, and claims arising from the Company's unauthorized use or modification of the licensed technology. The term of these indemnification agreements is generally perpetual from the time of execution of the agreement. The maximum potential amount of future payments the Company could be required to make under these indemnification agreements is unlimited. The Company has never incurred costs to defend lawsuits or settle claims related to these indemnification agreements. As of December 31, 20X2, the Company had not accrued a liability for this guarantee, because the likelihood of incurring a payment obligation in connection with this guarantee is remote.

CHAPTER 20
IMPAIRMENT AND DISPOSAL
OF LONG-LIVED ASSETS

CONTENTS

EXECUTIVE SUMMARY

Recognition of impairment of long-lived assets generally is required when events and circumstances indicate that an entity will not be able to recover the carrying amount of those assets. The accounting for impaired assets differs depending on whether the company intends to dispose of the asset or continue to use it.

Long-Lived Assets to Be Held and Used

An entity is required to (a) recognize an impairment loss only if the carrying amount of a long-lived asset is not recoverable from its expected undiscounted cash flows and (b) measure an impairment loss as the difference between the carrying amount and fair value of the asset.

An entity should recognize an impairment loss, equal to the amount by which the carrying amount of a long-lived asset exceeds its fair value, if both of the following conditions are met:

1. *The carrying amount of the long-lived asset is not recoverable.* A long-lived asset's carrying amount is not recoverable if it exceeds the sum of the undiscounted cash flows expected to result from the use and eventual disposition of the asset. Estimates of future cash flows used to test the recoverability of a long-lived asset should exclude interest charges that will be recognized as an expense when incurred; and

2. *The carrying amount of the long-lived asset exceeds its fair value.* Quoted market prices in active markets, if available, should be used to measure fair value. If quoted market prices are not available, fair value may be based on the best information available in the circumstances, including present value techniques.

Once the carrying amount of an impaired asset to be held and used has been written down to fair value, that value becomes the asset's new cost basis; restoration of a previously recognized impairment loss is prohibited.

An impairment loss recognized for a long-lived asset to be held and used should be included as a component of income from continuing operations before income taxes.

Long-Lived Assets to Be Disposed Of

An entity is required to record a long-lived asset classified as held for sale at the lower of its carrying amount or fair value less cost to sell, and to cease depreciation. A loss should be recognized for any initial or subsequent write-down to fair value less cost to sell. A gain should be recognized for any subsequent increase in fair value less cost to sell, but not in excess of the cumulative loss previously recognized. In order for a long-lived asset to be sold and to be classified as held for sale, certain specified criteria must be met. Among other things, those criteria specify that (a) the asset must be available for immediate sale in its present condition subject only to usual and customary terms for sales of such assets and (b) the sale of the asset must be probable, and its transfer expected to qualify for recognition as a completed sale, within one year, with certain exceptions. If the criteria for classification as held for sale are met after the balance-sheet date but before issuance of the financial statements, retroactive reclassification of the asset as held for sale at the balance-sheet date is prohibited.

If circumstances arise that would change a plan of sale and an entity, as a result, decides not to sell a long-lived asset previously classified as held for sale, the asset should be reclassified as held and used. The reclassified asset should be measured at the lower of the following:

1. The asset's carrying amount before being classified as held for sale, adjusted for any depreciation and amortization expense that would have been recognized had the asset been continuously classified as held and used, *or*

2. The asset's fair value at the date it is reclassified as held and used.

A gain or loss recognized for a long-lived asset that is classified as held for sale and is not a component of an entity should be included in income from continuing operations before income taxes. A gain or loss on disposal of operations that constitute a component of an entity should be reported as part of discontinued operations, as discussed in Chapter 51, "Discontinued Operations."

A long-lived asset classified as held for sale should be presented separately in the balance sheet. The assets and liabilities of a disposal group classified as held for sale should be presented separately in the asset and liability sections, respectively, of the balance sheet. Those assets and liabilities should not be offset and presented as a single amount.

Long-lived assets to be disposed of other than by sale (e.g., by abandonment, in an exchange for a similar asset, or in a distribution to owners in a spinoff) should continue to be classified as held and used until they are disposed of, and should be accounted for as discussed above under "Long-Lived Assets to Be Held and Used." If a long-lived asset is to be abandoned or distributed to owners in a spinoff together with other assets (and liabilities) as a group, and that disposal group is a component of an entity, then the disposal should be accounted for as discontinued operations as discussed in Chapter 51, "Discontinued Operations."

Authoritative Literature

FAS-142   Goodwill and Other Intangible Assets

FAS-144   Accounting for the Impairment or Disposal of
            Long-Lived Assets

DISCLOSURE REQUIREMENTS

Note: FASB Statement of Financial Accounting Standards No.
157 (FAS-157), *Fair Value Measurements*, expands disclosures
about the use of fair value to measure assets and liabilities in
interim and annual periods subsequent to initial recognition. It
does not eliminate or modify the fair value disclosure requirements under other accounting pronouncements (e.g., Statement of Financial Accounting Standards No. 107 (FAS-107),
Disclosures about Fair Value of Financial Instruments); rather,
it encourages entities to combine the fair value information disclosed under FAS-157 with the fair value information disclosed
under other such accounting pronouncements. See Chapter 14,
"Fair Value Measurements," for additional disclosures of fair
value that are required under FAS-157.

1. For impaired assets to be held and used, the following disclosures should be made in financial statements that include
   the period of the impairment loss (FAS-144, par. 26):

   a. A description of the impaired assets and the facts and cir-
      cumstances leading to the impairment

   b. If not separately presented on the face of the income
      statement, the amount of the impairment loss and the
      caption in the income statement that includes that loss

   c. The method(s) for determining fair value (e.g., quoted
      market price, present value techniques)

   d. If applicable, the business segment in which the impaired
      long-lived asset is reported

2. The following items should be presented separately in the
   balance sheet (FAS-144, par. 46):

   a. Long-lived assets that are classified as held for sale

   b. The assets and liabilities of a disposal group classified as
      held for sale (Note: The assets and liabilities should not
      be offset and presented as a single amount)

3. For a long-lived asset (disposal group) that either has been
   sold or is classified as held for sale, the following disclosures
   should be made in financial statements that include the
   period in which the asset (group) has been sold or is classified as held for sale (FAS-144, par. 47):

   a. A description of the facts and circumstances leading to the expected disposal

   b. The expected manner and timing of the disposal

   c. The carrying amount(s) of the major classes of assets and liabilities included as part of a disposal group, if not separately presented on the face of the balance sheet

   d. The gain or loss recognized and, if not separately presented on the face of the income statement, the caption in the income statement that includes the gain or loss

   e. If applicable, amounts of revenue and pretax profit or loss reported in discontinued operations

   f. If applicable, the segment in which the long-lived asset (disposal group) is reported

4. If an entity decides not to sell a long-lived asset (disposal group) previously classified as held for sale, or removes an individual asset or liability from a disposal group previously classified as held for sale, the following disclosures should be made in the financial statements that include the period of that decision (FAS-144, par. 48):

   a. A description of the facts and circumstances leading to the decision to change the plan to sell the long-lived asset (disposal group)

   b. The effect on the results of operations for the period and any prior periods presented

5. If the criteria for classification of a long-lived asset as held for sale are met after the balance-sheet date, but before issuance of the financial statements, the following information should be disclosed (FAS-144, par. 33):

   a. A description of the facts and circumstances leading to the expected disposal

   b. The expected manner and timing of the disposal

   c. The carrying amount(s) of the major classes of assets and liabilities included as part of a disposal group, if not separately presented on the face of the balance sheet

EXAMPLES OF FINANCIAL STATEMENT DISCLOSURES

 The following sample disclosures are available on the accompanying disc. See Chapter 51, "Discontinued Operations," for examples of reporting discontinued operations.

Note: FAS-157 expands disclosures about the use of fair value to measure assets and liabilities in interim and annual periods subsequent to initial recognition. It does not eliminate or

modify the fair value disclosure requirements under other accounting pronouncements (e.g., FAS-107, *Disclosures about Fair Value of Financial Instruments*); rather, it encourages entities to combine the fair value information disclosed under FAS-157 with the fair value information disclosed under other such accounting pronouncements. See Chapter 14, "Fair Value Measurements," for additional disclosures of fair value that are required under FAS-157.

Example 20–1: Accounting Policy for Impairment of Fixed Assets and Intangible Assets with Finite Lives

Unlike goodwill and indefinite-lived intangible assets, the accounting rules do not provide for an annual impairment test in determining whether fixed assets (e.g., property, plant, and equipment) and finite-lived intangible assets (e.g., customer lists) are impaired. Instead, they require that a triggering event occur before testing an asset for impairment. Examples of such triggering events include a significant disposal of a portion of such assets, an adverse change in the market involving the business employing the related asset, a significant decrease in the benefits realized from an acquired business, difficulties or delays in integrating the business, and a significant change in the operations of an acquired business.

Once a triggering event has occurred, the impairment test employed is based on whether the intent is to hold the asset for continued use or to hold the asset for sale. If the intent is to hold the asset for continued use, the impairment test involves a comparison of undiscounted cash flows against the carrying value of the asset as an initial test. If the carrying value of such asset exceeds the undiscounted cash flow, the asset would be deemed to be impaired. Impairment would then be measured as the difference between the fair value of the fixed or amortizing intangible asset and the carrying value to determine the amount of the impairment. The Company generally determines fair value by using the discounted cash flow method. If the intent is to hold the asset for sale and certain other criteria are met (i.e., the asset can be disposed of currently, appropriate levels of authority have approved sale, and there is an actively pursuing buyer), the impairment test is a comparison of the asset's carrying value to its fair value less costs to sell. To the extent that the carrying value is greater than the asset's fair value less costs to sell, an impairment loss is recognized for the difference. Assets held for sale are separately presented on the balance sheet and are no longer depreciated.

Example 20–2: Accounting Policy for Impairment of Goodwill and Indefinite-Lived Intangible Assets

The Company periodically reviews the carrying value of intangible assets not subject to amortization, including goodwill, to determine whether impairment may exist. FASB Statement of Financial Accounting Standards No. 142, *Goodwill and Other Intangible Assets*, requires that goodwill and certain intangible assets be assessed annually for impairment using fair value measurement techniques. Specifically, goodwill impairment is determined using a two-step process. The first step of the goodwill impairment test is used to identify potential impairment by comparing the fair value of a reporting unit with its carrying amount, including goodwill. The estimates of fair value of a reporting unit, generally the Company's operating segments, are determined using various valuation techniques with the primary technique being a discounted cash flow analysis. A discounted cash flow analysis requires one to make various judgmental assumptions including assumptions about future cash flows, growth rates, and discount rates. The assumptions about future cash flows and growth rates are based on the Company's budget and long-term plans. Discount rate assumptions are based on an assessment of the risk inherent in the respective reporting units. If the fair value of a reporting unit exceeds its carrying amount, goodwill of the reporting unit is considered not impaired and the second step of the impairment test is unnecessary. If the carrying amount of a reporting unit exceeds its fair value, the second step of the goodwill impairment test is performed to measure the amount of impairment loss, if any. The second step of the goodwill impairment test compares the implied fair value of the reporting unit's goodwill with the carrying amount of that goodwill. If the carrying amount of the reporting unit's goodwill exceeds the implied fair value of that goodwill, an impairment loss is recognized in an amount equal to that excess. The implied fair value of goodwill is determined in the same manner as the amount of goodwill recognized in a business combination. That is, the fair value of the reporting unit is allocated to all of the assets and liabilities of that unit (including any unrecognized intangible assets) as if the reporting unit had been acquired in a business combination and the fair value of the reporting unit was the purchase price paid to acquire the reporting unit.

The impairment test for other intangible assets not subject to amortization consists of a comparison of the fair value of the intangible asset with its carrying value. If the carrying value of the intangible asset exceeds its fair value, an impairment loss is recognized in an amount equal to that excess. The estimates of fair value of intangible assets not subject to amortization are determined using various discounted cash flow valuation methodologies. Significant assumptions are inherent in this process, including estimates of discount rates. Discount rate assumptions are based on an assessment of the risk inherent in the respective intangible assets.

Example 20–3: Impairment Loss Recognized as a Result of Change in Policy for Replacing Property and Equipment

Effective June 1, 20X2, management approved a revision to the Company's policy of replacing certain transportation equipment and heavy duty machinery and equipment. Under the revised policy, the Company replaces transportation equipment after eight years, and heavy duty machinery and equipment after ten years. The previous policy was to not replace transportation equipment before they were a minimum of ten years old, and heavy duty machinery and equipment before they were a minimum of twelve years old. As a result of this decision, the Company recognized an impairment loss of $2,115,000 in 20X2 for those transportation equipment and heavy duty machinery and equipment scheduled for replacement in the next two years under the new policy. Depreciable lives were also adjusted effective June 1, 20X2 to reflect the new policy.

Example 20–4: Impairment of Assets Held and Used Recognized as a Result of Strategic Review of Certain Operations

In 20X2, during the course of the Company's strategic review of its diagnostic chemicals kits operations, the Company assessed the recoverability of the carrying value of certain fixed assets which resulted in impairment losses of $1,400,000. These losses reflect the amounts by which the carrying values of these assets exceed their estimated fair values determined by their estimated future discounted cash flows. The impairment loss is recorded as a component of "Operating expenses" in the Income Statement for 20X2.

Example 20–5: Impairment of Assets to Be Disposed of by Sale

In 20X2, the Company adopted a plan to dispose of most of its plant assets, machinery and equipment, and furniture and fixtures relating to its manufacturing facility in Boise, Idaho. The Company expects that the final sale and disposal of the assets will be completed in the year 20X3. In connection with the plan of disposal, the Company determined that the carrying values of some of the underlying assets exceeded their fair values. Consequently, the Company recorded an impairment loss of $1,715,000, which represents the excess of the carrying values of the assets over their fair values, less cost to sell. The impairment loss is recorded as a separate line item ("Impairment charge") in the Income Statement for 20X2. The carrying value of the assets that are held for sale is separately presented in the Balance Sheet in the caption "Assets held for sale," and these assets are no longer depreciated.

Example 20–6: Intangible Assets Impairment Results in Reduction of Amortization Period

In 20X2, the Company recognized $2,600,000 in impairment losses on certain identified intangible assets that are being amortized (primarily trade names and intellectual property) relating to the Company's electronic components operation. Despite the Company's efforts to improve the operations at this division, several internal and external factors have impacted, and are expected to continue to impact, results of operations. As a result, projected future cash flows from this division were determined to be less than the carrying value of the division's long-lived assets. The revised carrying value of the intangible assets was calculated using discounted estimated future cash flows. Management also determined that the useful life of the trade names and intellectual property should be reduced from fifteen to ten years. The residual balance for these intangible assets, $1,300,000, will be amortized over the remaining ten years on a straight-line basis.

Example 20–7: Impairment Write-Down Recognized as a Result of Strategic Review of Certain Operations

In 20X2, during the course of the Company's strategic review of its diagnostic chemicals kits operations, the Company recorded a pretax charge of $3,200,000 ($1,970,000 after tax) relating to the impairment of certain intangible assets held for use when it was determined that future undiscounted cash flows associated with these assets were insufficient to recover their carrying values. The impaired assets principally represent the company's historic ownership interest in product rights and license agreements. The assets were written down to fair value, which was determined on the basis of future discounted cash flows and confirmed by an independent appraisal.

CHAPTER 21
INTEREST COST

CONTENTS

EXECUTIVE SUMMARY

Capitalization of Interest Cost

Interest cost should be capitalized as part of the cost of acquiring or constructing certain assets, such as a plant, a warehouse, or a real estate development. To qualify for interest capitalization, assets need a period of time to get them ready for their intended use, which may be either (1) for sale or (2) for use within the business. However, interest cannot be capitalized in the following circumstances:

1. For inventories that are routinely manufactured or otherwise produced in large quantities on a repetitive basis

2. For qualifying assets acquired using gifts or grants that are restricted by the grantor to acquisition of those assets to the extent that funds are available from such gifts or grants

If a specific borrowing is made to acquire the qualifying asset, the interest rate incurred on that borrowing may be used to determine the amount of interest costs to be capitalized. That interest rate is applied to the average accumulated expenditures for the period to calculate the amount of capitalized interest cost on the qualifying asset. Capitalized interest cost on average accumulated expenditures in excess of the amount of the specific borrowing is calculated by the use of the weighted-average interest rate incurred on other borrowings outstanding during the period.

If no specific borrowing is made to acquire the qualifying asset, the weighted-average interest rate incurred on other borrowings outstanding during the period is used to determine the amount of interest cost to be capitalized. The weighted-average interest rate is applied to the average accumulated expenditures for the period to calculate the amount of capitalized interest cost on the qualifying asset.

In situations involving qualifying assets financed with the proceeds of restricted tax-exempt borrowings, the amount of interest cost to be capitalized should be (1) all interest cost of those borrowings less (2) any interest earned on temporary investment of the proceeds of the borrowings from the date of the borrowing until the specified qualifying assets acquired with those borrowings are ready for their intended use.

Imputed Interest

When a note is exchanged for property, goods, or services in an arm's-length transaction, it is generally presumed that the interest stated on the note is fair and adequate. If no interest is stated or if the interest stated appears unreasonable, the transaction should be valued at the fair value of the note or property, goods, or services, whichever is more clearly determinable. If such fair value is not readily determinable, the transaction should be valued at the present value of the note, determined by discounting the future cash payments under the note by an appropriate interest rate. The difference between the face amount of the note and its present value represents a discount or premium, which should be amortized over the life of the note using the interest method, or a method that approximates the interest method. The discount or premium amount is not an asset or a liability separable from the note that gives rise to it; therefore, the discount or premium should be reported in the balance sheet as a direct deduction from or addition to the face amount of the note.

Authoritative Literature

APB-12	Omnibus Opinion—1967
APB-21	Interest on Receivables and Payables
FAS-34	Capitalization of Interest Cost
FAS-42	Determining Materiality for Capitalization of Interest Cost
FAS-58	Capitalization of Interest Cost in Financial Statements That Include Investments Accounted for by the Equity Method
FAS-62	Capitalization of Interest Cost in Situations Involving Certain Tax-Exempt Borrowings and Certain Gifts and Grants
FAS-95	Statement of Cash Flows
FIN-33	Applying FASB Statement No. 34 to Oil and Gas Producing Operations Accounted for by the Full Cost Method

DISCLOSURE REQUIREMENTS

The following disclosures should be made with respect to interest cost:

1. For an accounting period in which no interest cost is capitalized, the amount of interest cost incurred and charged to expense during the period (FAS-34, par. 21)

2. For an accounting period in which some interest cost is capitalized, the total amount of interest cost incurred during the period and the amount thereof that has been capitalized (FAS-34, par. 21)

3. The amount of interest cost incurred in connection with product financing arrangements (FAS-34, par. 21; FAS-49, par. 9)

4. For notes payable or receivable that require the imputation of interest, disclosures should include (APB-21, par. 16):

   a. A description of the note

   b. The effective interest rate

   c. The face amount of the note

   d. The amount of discount or premium resulting from present value determination

   e. The amortization of the discount or premium to interest

5. The amount of interest paid (net of amounts capitalized) for each period for which a statement of cash flows is presented (FAS-95, par. 29)

EXAMPLES OF FINANCIAL STATEMENT DISCLOSURES

 The following sample disclosures are available on the accompanying disc.

Example 21–1: Interest Cost Capitalized

The Company capitalizes interest cost incurred on funds used to construct property, plant, and equipment. The capitalized interest is recorded as part of the asset to which it relates and is amortized over the asset's estimated useful life. Interest cost capitalized was $315,000 and $268,000 in 20X2 and 20X1, respectively.

> **Note:** The amount of interest cost capitalized may be disclosed as part of the note on property and equipment.

Example 21–2: Interest Cost Charged to Operations

The Company incurred interest cost of $472,000 in 20X2 and $436,000 in 20X1, all of which were charged to operations.

> **Note:** The amount of interest expense charged to operations may be disclosed on the face of the income statement, or as part of the debt footnote.

Example 21–3: Details of Interest Expense, Interest Capitalized, and Interest Paid Provided in a Separate Note

Details of interest cost incurred for the years ended December 31, 20X2, and December 31, 20X1 are as follows:

	20X2	20X1
Interest cost charged to operations	$523,000	$476,000
Interest cost capitalized	91,000	112,000
Total interest cost incurred	$614,000	$588,000

Interest paid during 20X2 and 20X1, net of capitalized interest, amounted to $511,000 and $458,000, respectively.

Example 21–4: Interest Cost Incurred in Connection with Product Financing Arrangement

In 20X2, the Company entered into a product financing arrangement with a vendor for the purchase of $13 million of electronic connectors. Accordingly, this inventory and the related short-term debt have been included in the Balance Sheet at December 31, 20X2. The vendor has also made commitments, on the Company's behalf, to purchase additional amounts of the electronic connectors for delivery in 20X3. The average interest rate on the product financing arrangement was 7.3% at December 31, 20X2. Interest expense incurred and paid under this product financing arrangement totaled $193,000 for 20X2.

Example 21–5: Liability Requires Imputation of Interest

At December 31, 20X2, the Company has included as a liability the present value, computed with an effective annual rate of 10%, of a death benefit related to the termination of an employment contract as a result of the death of the President in 20X2. This termination death benefit will be paid in thirty-six equal monthly installments of $30,000 commencing in April 20X3.

Example 21–6: Notes Receivable Require Imputation of Interest

In March 20X2, the Company received $50,000 in cash and $2,200,000 in notes in full payment of outstanding trade receivables resulting from the reorganization by a major customer, pursuant to a bankruptcy decree. The notes vary in maturity from six months to five years. They include non-interest bearing notes and notes bearing interest at rates of 4% to 6%. The notes are recorded at the present value of the future cash flows, utilizing an imputed interest of 10%, which equals $2,017,000. Notes receivable are due as follows: $418,000 in 20X3, $536,000 in 20X4, $374,000 in 20X5, $318,000 in 20X6, and $196,000 in 20X7.

CHAPTER 22
INTERIM FINANCIAL REPORTING

CONTENTS

EXECUTIVE SUMMARY

Note: The FASB has issued Statement of Financial Accounting Standards No. 154 (FAS-154), *Accounting Changes and Error Corrections*, which changes the requirements for accounting for and reporting a change in accounting principles. The general accounting for changes in accounting estimates and in the reporting entity did not change under FAS-154. The new Statement supersedes Accounting Principles Board Opinion No. 20 (APB-20), *Accounting Changes*; FAS-3, *Reporting Accounting Changes in Interim Financial Statements*; FAS-73, *Reporting a Change in Accounting for Railroad Track Structures*; and FASB Interpretation No. 20, *Reporting Accounting Changes under AICPA Statements of Position*. FAS-154 applies to all voluntary changes in accounting principles and to changes required by an accounting pronouncement in the unusual instance that the pronouncement does not indicate a specific transition method. APB-20 required most voluntary changes in accounting principle to be accounted for by what is commonly referred to as the cumulative effect method. This method required the cumulative effect of the change to be included in the determination of net income of the period of the change. FAS-154 replaces the cumulative effect method for voluntary accounting changes with retrospective application to prior periods' financial statements. "Retrospective application" is the application of a different accounting principle to previously presented financial statements as if that principle had always been used. FAS-154 uses the term "retrospective application" versus "restatement" as used in APB-20; FAS-154 reserves the use of the term "restatement" for corrections of errors in previously issued financial statements. FAS-154 is effective for accounting changes and corrections of errors made in fiscal years beginning after December 15, 2005.

Interim financial reports may be issued quarterly, monthly, or at other intervals, and may include complete financial statements or summarized data. Each interim period should be viewed as an integral part of the annual period. The results for each interim period should be based on the accounting principles and reporting practices generally used by the entity to prepare its latest annual financial statements, with limited exceptions, such as a change in an accounting principle. Also, certain accounting principles may require modification at interim dates so that the interim period's results better relate to the annual results. For example, when interim physical inventory counts are not taken, inventories may be estimated at interim dates using the gross profit method. Similarly, income taxes may be estimated at interim periods to reflect the entity's best estimate of the effective tax rate expected to be applicable for the full year.

The following guidelines should be observed for recognizing revenues and expenses during interim periods:

1. Revenues should be recognized as earned on the same basis as followed for the full year.

2. Costs and expenses that are associated directly with revenue (e.g., material costs, wages and salaries, fringe benefits, manufacturing overhead, and warranties) should be reported in the same period that the related revenue is recognized.

3. All other costs and expenses should be charged against income in the interim period as incurred, or allocated among interim periods based on an estimate of time expired, benefit received, or other activity associated with the periods.

4. Certain costs and expenses are frequently subjected to year-end adjustments even though they can reasonably be approximated at interim dates. Examples of such items include allowances for uncollectible accounts, year-end bonuses, depreciation, and inventory shrinkage. Adjustments for such items should be estimated and assigned to the interim period so that the interim period bears a reasonable portion of the anticipated annual amount.

5. Material extraordinary items, unusual or infrequent transactions, and gains and losses on disposal of a business segment should be recognized in the interim period in which they occur and should not be prorated over the full year.

6. Income taxes should be determined by applying an estimated annual effective tax rate, based on the current year's estimated annual results, to income or loss from continuing operations. The tax effects of extraordinary items, unusual or infrequent items, discontinued operations, and cumulative effects of accounting changes should be recorded in the interim period in which they occur.

Authoritative Literature

APB-28	Interim Financial Reporting
FAS-3	Reporting Accounting Changes in Interim Financial Statements (superseded by FAS-154 for fiscal years beginning after December 15, 2005)
FAS-16	Prior Period Adjustments
FAS-109	Accounting for Income Taxes
FAS-128	Earnings per Share
FAS-129	Disclosure of Information about Capital Structure
FAS-130	Reporting Comprehensive Income
FAS-131	Disclosures about Segments of an Enterprise and Related Information
FAS-132R	Employers' Disclosures about Pensions and Other Postretirement Benefits (Revised 2003)
FAS-141	Business Combinations
FAS-154	Accounting Changes and Error Corrections
FAS-157	Fair Value Measurements
FAS-158	Employers' Accounting for Defined Benefit Pension and Other Postretirement Plans
FIN-18	Accounting for Income Taxes in Interim Periods
FIN-45	Guarantor's Accounting and Disclosure Requirements for Guarantees, Including Indirect Guarantees of Indebtedness of Others
FSP FIN 45-3	Application of FASB Interpretation No. 45 to Minimum Revenue Guarantees Granted to a Business or Its Owners
EITF 06-3	How Taxes Collected from Customers and Remitted to Governmental Authorities Should Be Presented in the Income Statement (That Is, Gross Versus Net Presentation)
EITF 06-7	Issuer's Accounting for a Previously Bifurcated Conversion Option in a Convertible Debt Instrument When the Conversion Option No Longer Meets the Bifurcation Criteria in FASB Statement No. 133, *Accounting for Derivative Instruments and Hedging Activities*

EITF 06-9	Reporting a Change in (or the Elimination of) a Previously Existing Difference between the Fiscal Year-End of a Parent Company and That of a Consolidated Entity or between the Reporting Period of an Investor and That of an Equity Method Investee
FSP FAS 106-2	Accounting and Disclosure Requirements Related to the Medicare Prescription Drug, Improvement and Modernization Act of 2003
FSP EITF 00-19-2	Accounting for Registration Payment Arrangements

DISCLOSURE REQUIREMENTS

General

1. If the company uses estimated gross profit rates to determine the cost of goods sold during interim periods or uses other methods different from those used at annual inventory dates, the following disclosures should be made (APB-28, par. 14):

   a. The method used at the interim date

   b. Any significant adjustments that result from reconciliations with the annual physical inventory

2. When costs and expenses incurred in an interim period cannot be readily identified with the activities or benefits of other interim periods, disclosures should be made about the nature and amount of such costs (**Note:** Disclosure is not required if items of a comparable nature are included in both the current interim period and the corresponding interim period of the preceding year.) (APB-28, par. 15).

3. If revenues of the entity are subject to material seasonal variations, the following disclosures should be made to avoid the possibility that interim results may be taken as fairly indicative of the estimated results for a full fiscal year (APB-28, par. 18):

   a. The seasonal nature of the business activities

   b. Information for 12-month periods ended at the interim date for the current and preceding years (*optional*)

4. Disclosures should be made of the reasons for significant variations in the customary relationship between income tax expense and pretax accounting income, if they are not otherwise apparent from the financial statements or from the nature of the entity's business (APB-28, par. 19; FIN-18, par. 25).

5. Extraordinary items, gains or losses from the disposal of a component of an entity, unusual seasonal results, business combinations, unusual and infrequently occurring transactions, and events that are material to the operating results of the interim period should be reported separately and included in the determination of net income for the interim period in which they occur. (**Note:** See item 3 in the "Additional Disclosures Applicable Only to Publicly Held Companies" section below for disclosures required for public companies with material business combinations.) (APB-28, par. 21).

6. Disclosures should be made about contingencies and other uncertainties that could be expected to affect the fairness of presentation of the interim financial information. (**Note:** Such disclosures should (a) include, but not be limited to, those matters that form the basis of a qualification of an independent auditors' report and (b) be repeated in interim reports until the contingencies have been removed or resolved or have become immaterial.) (APB-28, par. 22).

7. The number of shares issued on conversion, exercise, or otherwise during at least the most recent annual fiscal period and any subsequent interim period presented should be disclosed (FAS-129, par. 5).

8. Total comprehensive income should be disclosed in condensed financial statements (FAS-130, par. 27).

9. If there is a significant difference between total comprehensive income and net income, disclosure of the components of the difference should be considered (FAS-130, par. 125).

10. Unusual or infrequently occurring items that will be separately disclosed in the financial statements for the fiscal year should be separately disclosed as a component of pretax income from continuing operations (FIN-18, par. 17).

11. Accounting policies relevant only to interim reporting should be disclosed (e.g., off-season costs).

Accounting Changes and Error Corrections

Note: The disclosure requirements in items 1 through 11 below are required for entities that have not adopted FAS-154. The disclosure requirements in items 6 through 20 below are required for entities that have adopted FAS-154, which is effective for accounting changes and corrections of errors made in fiscal years beginning after December 15, 2005. Early adoption is permitted for accounting changes and corrections of errors made in fiscal years beginning after June 1, 2005.

1. For changes in accounting principles or reporting entity that result in retroactive restatement of previously issued financial statements, the following items should be disclosed for all periods presented, if not presented on the income statement (APB-28, par. 25; APB-20, pars. 28 and 35):

   a. Nature and justification

   b. Effect on income before extraordinary items and net income (and related per share amounts, if applicable)

2. For corrections of errors that result in the retroactive restatement of previously issued financial statements, the following items should be disclosed in the period in which the error was discovered and corrected (APB-28, par. 25; APB-20, par. 37):

   a. Nature

   b. Effect on income before extraordinary items and net income (and related per share amounts, if applicable)

3. The effect of a change in accounting estimate, including a change in the estimated effective annual tax rate, on income before extraordinary items, and net income (and related per-share amounts, if applicable) should be disclosed if material in relation to any period presented. (**Note:** Disclosure of the effect on income statement amounts is not necessary for estimates made each period in the ordinary course of accounting for certain items [e.g., uncollectible accounts or inventory obsolescence]. However, if the effects are material, then disclosure of the income statement amounts is recommended but not required. In addition, the effect on earnings of a change in estimate that is made in the current interim period should be reported in the current and subsequent interim periods, if material to any period presented. It should continue to be reported in the interim financial information of the subsequent year for as many periods as necessary to avoid misleading comparisons.) (APB-28, par. 26; APB-20, par. 33).

4. The following disclosures about a cumulative effect-type accounting change, other than changes to last-in, first-out (LIFO), should be made in interim financial reports (FAS-3, par. 11, APB-28, par. 27B):

   a. In financial reports for the interim period in which the new accounting principle is adopted, disclosures should be made of:

      (1) The nature of and justification for the change

      (2) The effect of the change on income from continuing operations and net income (and related per-share amounts, if applicable) for the interim period in

which the change is made (**Note:** If the change is made in a period other than the first interim period of a fiscal year, the effect of the change on income from continuing operations and net income [and related per-share amounts, if applicable] for each prechange interim period of the fiscal year should be disclosed. In addition, the restated income from continuing operations, and net income [and related per-share amounts, if applicable] for each prechange interim period of the fiscal year should be disclosed.)

(3) Income from continuing operations and net income (and related per-share amounts, if applicable) computed on a pro forma basis for (i) the interim period in which the change is made and (ii) any interim periods of prior fiscal years for which financial information is being presented (**Note:** If no financial information for interim periods of prior fiscal years is being presented, disclosure should be made, in the period of change, of the actual and pro forma amounts of income from continuing operations, and net income [and related per-share amounts, if applicable] for the interim period of the immediately preceding fiscal year that corresponds to the interim period in which the changes are made.)

b. In year-to-date and last-12-months-to-date financial reports that include the interim period in which the new accounting principle is adopted, disclosures should be made of:

(1) The effect of the change on income from continuing operations and net income (and related per-share amounts, if applicable) for the interim period in which the change is made

(2) Income from continuing operations and net income (and related per-share amounts, if applicable) computed on a pro forma basis for (i) the interim period in which the change is made and (ii) any interim periods of prior fiscal years for which financial information is being presented (**Note:** If no financial information for interim periods of prior fiscal years is being presented, disclosure should be made, in the period of change, of the actual and pro forma amounts of income from continuing operations, and net income [and related per-share amounts, if applicable] for the interim period of the immediately preceding fiscal year that corresponds to the interim period in which the changes are made.)

   c.   In financial reports for subsequent (postchange) interim periods of the fiscal year in which the new accounting principle is adopted, disclosures should be made of the effect of the change on income from continuing operations and net income (and related per-share amounts, if applicable) for that postchange interim period

5.   For changes in accounting principles when neither the cumulative effect of the change nor the pro forma amounts can be computed (principally a change to the LIFO method of inventory pricing), the following disclosures should be made (**Note:** If a change of this type has been made in the first or any other interim period of an entity's fiscal year, the disclosures in item 4 above [except the pro forma amounts for interim periods of prior fiscal years included in item 4a(3) above] should be made.) (FAS-3, pars. 12-13; APB-28, pars. 27C–27D):

   a.   An explanation of the reasons for omitting accounting for the cumulative effect of the change

   b.   An explanation of the reasons for omitting disclosure of pro forma amounts for prior years

6.   Disclosures should be made of any changes in accounting principles or practices from those applied in (APB-28, par. 23):

   a.   The comparable interim period of the prior year

   b.   The preceding interim periods in the current year

   c.   The prior annual financial statements

7.   The cumulative effects of an accounting change or correction of an error that are material to an interim period, but not material to the estimated income for the full fiscal year or to the trend of earnings, should be disclosed separately in the interim period (**Note:** The related amount of applicable income taxes may be disclosed but is not required.) (APB-28, par. 29; FIN-18, par. 71).

8.   The following disclosures should be made in interim financial statements about an adjustment related to prior interim periods of the current fiscal year (FAS-16, par. 15):

   a.   The effect on income from continuing operations and net income (and related per-share amounts, if applicable) for each prior interim period of the current fiscal year

   b.   Restated income from continuing operations and net income (and related per share amounts, if applicable) for each prior interim period

9.   The resulting effects (both gross and net of applicable income tax) of prior-period adjustments on the net income of prior

periods should be disclosed in the interim report for the period in which the adjustments are made (APB-9, par. 26; FAS-154, par. 26).

10. When single-period financial statements are presented, the effect (both gross and net of applicable income tax) of prior-period adjustments on the opening balance of retained earnings and net income (and on related per-share amounts when presented) of the preceding period should be disclosed (APB-9, par. 26; FAS-154, par. 26).

11. When financial statements for more than one period are presented, the effect (both gross and net of applicable income tax) of prior-period adjustments on the opening balance of retained earnings and net income (and on related per-share amounts when presented) for each of the periods presented should be disclosed (APB-9, par. 26; FAS-154, par. 26).

12. The following disclosures should be made for a change in accounting principle in the interim period the change occurs (FAS-154, par. 17):

    a. The nature of and reason for the change in accounting principle, including an explanation of why the newly adopted accounting principle is preferable

    b. The method of applying the change

    c. A description of the prior-period information that has been retrospectively adjusted

    d. The effect of the change on the following for the current period and any prior periods retrospectively adjusted:

        (1) Income from continuing operations

        (2) Net income (or other appropriate captions of changes in the applicable net assets or performance indicator)

        (3) Other affected financial statement line items

        (4) Affected per-share amounts, if applicable

    e. The cumulative effect of the change on retained earnings or other components of equity or net assets in the balance sheet as of the beginning of the earliest period presented

    f. If retrospective application to all prior periods is impracticable, the reasons why, and a description of the alternative method used to report the change

    g. If indirect effects of the change in accounting principle are recognized:

        (1) A description of the indirect effects of the change in accounting principle, including the amounts that

have been recognized in the current period, and the related per-share amounts, if applicable

(2) Unless impracticable, the amount of the total recognized indirect effects of the accounting change and the related per-share amounts, if applicable, that are attributable to each prior period presented

13. For a change in accounting principle that has no material effect in the period of change but is reasonably certain to have a material effect in later periods, disclosures should be made of the nature of and reason for the change in accounting principle, including an explanation of why the newly adopted accounting principle is preferable, whenever the financial statements of the period of change are presented (FAS-154, par. 17).

14. In the fiscal year in which a new accounting principle is adopted, for financial information reported in interim periods after the date of adoption of a new accounting principle, the effect of the change on the following items should be disclosed for the postchange interim periods (FAS-154, par. 18):

   a. Income from continuing operations

   b. Net income (or other appropriate captions of changes in the applicable net assets or performance indicators)

   c. Related per-share amounts, if applicable

15. If a change in accounting principle effects a change in estimate, the disclosures detailed in items 12 through 14 above should be made (FAS-154, par. 22; APB-28, par. 26).

16. For a change in accounting estimate that affects several future periods (e.g., change in service lives of depreciable assets), the effect of the change on the following for the current period should be disclosed (**Note:** Disclosure of these effects is not necessary for estimates made each period in the ordinary course of accounting [e.g., uncollectible accounts, inventory obsolescence] unless the effect of the change in estimate is material.) (FAS-154, par. 22; APB-28, par. 26):

   a. Income from continuing operations

   b. Net income (or other appropriate captions of change in the applicable net assets or performance indicators)

   c. Related per-share amounts, if applicable

17. For a change in accounting estimate that has no material effect in the period of change but is reasonably certain to have a material effect in later periods, a description of the change should be disclosed whenever the financial statements of the period of change are presented (FAS-154, par. 22; APB-28, par. 26).

18. For changes in the reporting entity, the following should be disclosed in the period of the change (FAS-154, par. 24):

    a. Nature and reason for it

    b. Effect on income before extraordinary items, net income (or other appropriate captions of changes in the applicable net assets or performance indicator), and other comprehensive income (and related per-share amounts, if applicable)

19. For a change in reporting entity that has no material effect in the period of change but is reasonably certain to have a material effect in later periods, disclosures should be made of the nature of, and reason for, the change, whenever the financial statements of the period of change are presented (FAS-154, par. 24).

20. If the financial statements have been restated to correct an error, the following should be disclosed (FAS-154, par. 26):

    a. The fact that previously issued financial statements have been restated

    b. A description of the nature of the error

    c. The effect of the correction on each financial statement line item and any per-share amounts, if applicable, affected for each prior period presented

    d. The cumulative effect of the change on retained earnings or other appropriate components of equity or net assets in the balance sheet, as of the beginning of the earliest period presented

Change in, or Elimination of, a Previously Existing Difference between an Entity's Reporting Period and That of a Consolidated Entity or an Equity Method Investee

Note: The disclosure requirements in item 1 below are prescribed by EITF Issue No. 06-9, *Reporting a Change in (or the Elimination of) a Previously Existing Difference between the Fiscal Year-End of a Parent Company and That of a Consolidated Entity or between the Reporting Period of an Investor and That of an Equity Method Investee.* EITF 06-9 is effective for changes in, or eliminations of, a previously existing difference between an entity's reporting period and that of a consolidated entity or an equity method investee that occur in the interim or annual reporting periods beginning after November 29, 2006. Earlier application is permitted only if an entity has not yet issued its financial statements for the period.

1. If a previously existing difference between the entity's reporting period and that of a consolidated entity or an equity method investee is changed or eliminated, the disclosures in items 12 through 15 above under "Accounting Changes and Error Corrections" should be made (EITF 06-9).

Contingencies, Risks, Uncertainties, and Concentrations

Note: The disclosure requirements in items 1 and 2 below are prescribed by FSP EITF 00-19-2, *Accounting for Registration Payment Arrangements*. FSP EITF 00-19-2 is effective immediately for registration payment arrangements and the financial instruments subject to those arrangements that are entered into or modified subsequent to December 21, 2006. For registration payment arrangements and financial instruments subject to those arrangements that were entered into prior to December 21, 2006, the guidance in FSP EITF 00-19-2 is effective for financial statements issued for fiscal years beginning after December 15, 2006, and interim periods within those fiscal years. Early adoption is permitted as long as financial statements for any period (interim or annual) of the fiscal year have not yet been issued. See chapter 10 for a sample disclosure.

1. The following information should be disclosed about each registration payment arrangement or each group of similar arrangements, even if the likelihood of the issuer having to make any payments under the arrangement is remote (FSP EITF 00-19-2, pars. 12 and 16):

   a. The nature of the registration payment arrangement

   b. The approximate term of the arrangement

   c. The financial instruments subject to the arrangement

   d. The events or circumstances that would require the issuer to transfer consideration under the arrangement

   e. Any settlement alternatives contained in the terms of the registration payment arrangement, including the party that controls the settlement alternatives

   f. The maximum potential amount of consideration, undiscounted, that the issuer could be required to transfer under the registration payment arrangement, including the maximum number of shares that may be required to be issued

   g. The fact that the terms of the arrangement provide for no limitation to the maximum potential consideration (including shares) to be transferred, if the terms of the arrangement include such provision

    h. The current carrying amount of the liability representing the issuer's obligations under the registration payment arrangement and the income statement classification of any gains or losses resulting from changes in the carrying amount of that liability

2. The following information should be disclosed related to the adoption of FSP EITF 00-19-2 (FSP EITF 00-19-2, par. 21):

    a. The portion of the cumulative-effect adjustment resulting from the recognition and measurement of a contingent liability under FAS-5

    b. The portion of the cumulative-effect adjustment resulting from the reclassification of a financial instrument subject to the registration payment arrangement to equity or the recombination of an embedded derivative

Fair Value Measurements

Note: The disclosure requirements in items 1 and 2 below are prescribed by Statement of Financial Accounting Standards No. 157 (FAS-157), *Fair Value Measurements*. FAS-157 is effective for fiscal years beginning after November 15, 2007, and interim periods within those fiscal years. Early adoption is permitted as long as financial statements for any period (interim or annual) of the fiscal year have not yet been issued. The disclosure requirements of FAS-157 need not be applied for financial statements for periods presented prior to the initial application.

The quantitative disclosures required in items 1 and 2 below should be presented in a tabular format (FAS-157, par. 34). In addition, the entity is encouraged, but not required, to combine the fair value information disclosed in accordance with items 1 and 2 with the fair value information disclosed in accordance with other items in this checklist. The entity is also encouraged, but not required, to disclose information about other similar measurements (e.g., inventories measured at market value under ARB-43), if practicable. (FAS-157, par. 35)

1. For assets and liabilities that are measured at fair value on a recurring basis subsequent to initial recognition, the following disclosures should be made for each major category of assets and liabilities for each interim period (FAS-157, par. 32):

    a. The fair value measurements at the reporting date

    b. The level within the fair value hierarchy in which the fair value measurements in their entirety fall, segregating fair value measurements using quoted prices in active markets for identical assets or liabilities (Level 1), significant other observable inputs (Level 2), and significant unobservable inputs (Level 3)

c. For fair value measurements using significant unobservable inputs (Level 3), a reconciliation of the beginning and ending balances, separately presenting changes during the period attributable to the following:

(1) Total gains or losses for the period (realized and unrealized), segregating those gains or losses included in earnings (or changes in net assets), and a description of where those gains or losses included in earnings (or changes in net assets) are reported in the statement of income (or activities)

(2) Purchases, sales, issuances, and settlements (net)

(3) Transfers in and (or) out of Level 3 (e.g., transfers due to changes in the observability of significant inputs)

(**Note:** This reconciliation disclosure may be presented net for derivative assets and liabilities.)

d. The amount of total gains or losses for the period in item 1c (1) above included in earnings (or changes in net assets) that are attributable to the change in unrealized gains or losses relating to those assets and liabilities still held at the reporting date and a description of where those unrealized gains or losses are reported in the statement of income (or activities)

e. In the first interim period in the fiscal year in which FAS-157 is initially applied, the valuation techniques used to measure fair value and a discussion of any changes in valuation techniques during the period

2. For assets and liabilities that are measured at fair value on a nonrecurring basis in periods subsequent to initial recognition, the following disclosures should be made for each major category of assets and liabilities for each interim period (FAS-157, par. 33):

a. The fair value measurements recorded during the period and the reasons for the measurements

b. The level within the fair value hierarchy in which the fair value measurements in their entirety fall, segregating fair value measurements using quoted prices in active markets for identical assets or liabilities (Level 1), significant other observable inputs (Level 2), and significant unobservable inputs (Level 3)

c. For fair value measurements using significant unobservable inputs (Level 3), a description of the inputs and the information used to develop the inputs

d. In the first interim period in the fiscal year in which FAS-157 is initially applied, the valuation techniques used to measure fair value and a discussion of any changes in the valuation techniques used to measure similar assets or liabilities in prior periods

Financial Instruments—Derivatives and Hedging Activities

Note: The disclosure requirements below are prescribed by EITF 06-7, *Issuer's Accounting for a Previously Bifurcated Conversion Option in a Convertible Debt Instrument When the Conversion Option No Longer Meets the Bifurcation Criteria in FASB Statement No. 133, "Accounting for Derivative Instruments and Hedging Activities."* EITF 06-7 is effective for all previously bifurcated conversion options in convertible debt instruments that no longer meet the bifurcation criteria in FAS-133 in annual or interim periods beginning after December 15, 2006, irrespective of when the debt instrument was entered into. Early adoption is permitted only if financial statements for the period have not yet been issued. Retrospective application in accordance with FAS-154 is permitted.

1. For previously bifurcated conversion options in convertible debt instruments that no longer meet the bifurcation criteria in FAS-133, the following disclosures should be made (EITF 06-7):

    a. A description of the principal changes causing the embedded conversion option to no longer require bifurcation under FAS-133

    b. The amount of the liability for the conversion option reclassified to stockholders' equity

Guarantees

1. The following information should be disclosed for each guarantee, or each group of similar guarantees, even if the likelihood of the entity having to make any payments under the guarantee is remote (FIN-45, pars. 13–14):

    a. The nature of the guarantee

    b. The approximate term of the guarantee

    c. How the guarantee arose

    d. The events or circumstances that would require the entity to perform under the guarantee

e. The maximum potential amount of future payments, undiscounted, the entity could be required to make under the guarantee (**Note:** This disclosure is not required for product warranties.) With respect to this disclosure item:

   (1) If the maximum potential future payments under the guarantee are unlimited, that fact should be disclosed

   (2) If the entity is unable to develop an estimate of the maximum potential amount of future payments, the entity should disclose the reasons why it cannot estimate the maximum potential amount

f. The current carrying amount of the related liability, if any

g. The nature of any recourse provisions that would enable the entity to recover from third parties any of the amounts paid under the guarantee

h. The nature of any assets held either as collateral or by third parties that, on the occurrence of any triggering event or condition under the guarantee, the entity can obtain and liquidate to recover the amounts paid under the guarantee (In addition, if estimable, the entity should indicate the extent to which the proceeds from the liquidation of those assets would be expected to cover the maximum potential amount of future payments under the guarantee.)

i. For product warranties or for guarantees related to the functional performance of nonfinancial assets owned by the guaranteed party, the following additional items should be disclosed:

   (1) The entity's (guarantor's) accounting policy and methodology used in determining its liability for such product warranties or guarantees, including any liability (such as deferred revenue) associated with extended warranties

   (2) A reconciliation of the changes in the entity's aggregate liability for such product warranties or guarantees, showing the following:

      (i) The beginning balance of the aggregate liability

      (ii) Aggregate reductions in that liability for payments made (in cash or in kind)

      (iii) Aggregate changes in the liability for accruals related to such product warranties or guarantees issued during the period

    (iv) The aggregate changes in the liability for accruals related to pre-existing warranties (including adjustments related to changes in estimates)

    (v) The ending balance of the aggregate liability

> **Note:** The disclosure requirements in item 2 below are prescribed by FSP FIN 45-3, *Application of FASB Interpretation No. 45 to Minimum Revenue Guarantees Granted to a Business or Its Owners,* which is effective for all minimum revenue guarantees in financial statements of interim periods ending after the beginning of the first fiscal quarter following November 10, 2005. Early application is permitted.

2.   The disclosure requirements detailed in item 1 above should be made for all minimum revenue guarantees, regardless of whether they were recognized and measured under FASB Interpretation No. 45 (FIN-45), *Guarantor's Accounting and Disclosure Requirements for Guarantees, Including Indirect Guarantees of Indebtedness of Others* (FSP FIN 45-3, par. 7).

Income Statement Classification

> **Note:** The disclosure requirement in item 1 below is prescribed by EITF Issue No. 06-3, *How Taxes Collected from Customers and Remitted to Governmental Authorities Should Be Presented in the Income Statement (That Is, Gross Versus Net Presentation).* EITF 06-3 is effective in interim and annual periods beginning after December 15, 2006.

1.   For taxes that fall within the scope of EITF 06-3 (e.g., sales tax), if those taxes are reported on a gross basis and are significant, the amounts of those taxes included in interim financial statements should be disclosed for each period for which an income statement is presented (**Note:** This disclosure may be provided on an aggregate basis.) (EITF 06-3).

Pension and Postretirement Benefit Plans

1.   For defined benefit pension plans and other defined benefit postretirement plans of nonpublic entities, disclosures should be made of the total amount of the employer's contributions paid, and expected to be paid, during the current fiscal year, if significantly different from amounts previously disclosed (**Note:** Estimated contributions may be presented in the aggregate for contributions required by funding regulations or laws, discretionary contributions, and noncash contributions.) (**Note:** This disclosure requirement applies

only to nonpublic entities; see the "Additional Disclosures Applicable Only to Publicly Held Companies" section for disclosures that are applicable to publicly held companies.) (FAS-132R, par. 10).

Note: Except for certain nonpublic entities, the disclosure requirements in items 2b–e below are effective for the first interim or annual periods beginning after June 15, 2004. For nonpublic entities that sponsor one or more defined benefit postretirement health care plans that provide prescription drug coverage and have no more than 100 participants, the disclosure requirements in 2b–e below are effective for fiscal years beginning after December 15, 2004. Early adoption is encouraged but not required. Prior to applying the accounting guidance in FSP FAS 106-2, *Accounting and Disclosure Requirements Related to the Medicare Prescription Drug, Improvement and Modernization Act of 2003*, the disclosure requirements in 2a below should be provided.

2. For employers that sponsor single-employer defined benefit postretirement health care plans that provide prescription drug coverage, the following disclosures should be made (FSP FAS 106-2, pars. 20–22):

    a. For periods in which the employer has not yet been able to determine the actuarial equivalency to Medicare Part D under the Medicare Prescription Drug, Improvement and Modernization Act of 2003 (the Act):

        (1) The existence of the Act

        (2) A statement clarifying that measures of the accumulated postretirement benefit obligation (APBO) or net periodic postretirement benefit cost do not reflect any amount associated with the federal subsidy provided by the Act because the employer is unable to conclude whether the benefits provided by the plan are actuarially equivalent to Medicare Part D under the Act

    b. For financial statements for the first period in which the employer includes the effects of the federal subsidy provided by the Act in measuring the APBO and net periodic postretirement benefit cost:

        (1) The reduction in the APBO for the subsidy related to benefits attributed to past service

        (2) The effect of the subsidy on the measurement of net periodic postretirement benefit cost for the current period, including:

      (i) Any amortization of the actuarial experience gain in item (1) above as a component of the net amortization called for by paragraph 59 of Statement of Financial Accounting Standards No. 106, *Employers' Accounting for Postretirement Benefits Other Than Pensions*

      (ii) The reduction in current-period service cost and interest cost on the APBO due to the subsidy

  c. An explanation of any significant change in the benefit obligation or plan assets not otherwise apparent in the above disclosures

  d. Gross benefit payments (paid and expected), including prescription drug benefits

  e. Gross amount of the subsidy receipts (received and expected)

Additional Disclosures Applicable Only to Publicly Held Companies

1. For publicly traded companies that report summarized financial information to their security holders at interim dates (including reports on fourth quarters), the following items, at a minimum, should be reported (**Note:** When summarized financial data are regularly reported on a quarterly basis, the information with respect to the current quarter and the current year-to-date or the last 12 months to date should be provided with comparable data for the preceding year.) (APB-28, pars. 30 and 32; FAS-131, par. 33):

  a. Sales or gross revenues

  b. Provision for income taxes

  c. Extraordinary items (including related income tax effects)

  d. Cumulative effect of a change in accounting principles or practices

  e. Net income

  f. Comprehensive income

  g. Basic and diluted earnings per share data for each period presented

  h. Seasonal revenue, costs, or expenses

  i. Significant changes in estimates or provisions for income taxes

j. Disposal of a segment of a business and extraordinary, unusual, or infrequently occurring items

k. Contingent items

l. Changes in accounting principles or estimates

m. Significant changes in financial position

n. The following information about reportable operating segments (including provisions related to the restatement of segment information in previously issued financial statements):

(1) Revenues from external customers

(2) Intersegment revenues

(3) A measure of segment profit or loss

(4) Total assets for which there has been a material change from the amount disclosed in the last annual report

(5) A description of differences from the last annual report in the basis of segmentation or in the measurement of segment profit or loss

(6) A reconciliation of the total of the reportable segments' measures of profit or loss to the entity's consolidated income before income taxes, extraordinary items, discontinued operations, and the cumulative effect of changes in accounting principles (However, if, for example, an entity allocates items, such as income taxes and extraordinary items to segments, the entity may choose to reconcile the total of the segments' measures of profit or loss to consolidated income after those items. Significant reconciling items shall be separately identified and described in that reconciliation.)

o. The effects of significant events on the interim financial results (**Note:** Entities are *encouraged*, but not required, to disclose this information.)

2. If condensed interim balance sheet information or cash flow data is not presented, significant changes since the last reporting period with respect to liquid assets, net working capital, long-term liabilities, or stockholder's equity should be disclosed (APB-28, par. 33).

3. The following disclosures should be made in the interim financial information if a material business combination is completed during the interim period (FAS-141, par. 58):

a. The name and a brief description of the acquired entity

    b. The percentage of voting equity interests acquired

    c. The primary reasons for the acquisition, including a description of the factors that contributed to a purchase price that result in recognition of goodwill

    d. The period for which the results of operations of the acquired entity are included in the combined entity's income statement

    e. The cost of the acquired entity and, if applicable, the number of shares of equity interests (e.g., common shares) issued or issuable, the value assigned to those interests, and the basis for determining that value

    f. Supplemental pro forma information that discloses the results of operations for the current interim period and the current year up to the date of the most recent interim balance sheet presented (and for the corresponding periods in the preceding year) as though the business combination had been completed as of the beginning of the period being reported on (**Note:** That pro forma information should disclose, at a minimum: revenue; income before extraordinary items and the cumulative effect of accounting changes; net income; and earnings per share.)

    g. The nature and amount of any material, nonrecurring items included in the reported pro forma results of operations.

4. If an entity changes the structure of its internal organization in a manner that causes the composition of its reportable segments to change, the corresponding information for earlier periods, including interim periods, should be restated, unless it is impracticable to do so (**Note:** The entity should also disclose whether it has restated the segment information for earlier periods. If the segment information for earlier interim periods is not restated to reflect the change, the entity should disclose in the year in which the change occurs segment information for the current period under both the old basis and the new basis of segmentation, unless it is impracticable to do so.) (FAS-131, pars. 34–35).

Note: In September 2006, the FASB issued Statement of Financial Accounting Standards No. 158 (FAS-158), *Employers' Accounting for Defined Benefit Pension and Other Postretirement Plans.* This standard amends FAS-87, *Employers' Accounting for Pensions*; FAS-88, *Employers' Accounting for Settlements and Curtailments of Defined Benefit Pension Plans and for Termination Benefits*; FAS-106, *Employers' Accounting for Postretirement Benefits Other Than Pensions*; and FAS-132 (Revised 2003), *Employers' Disclosures about Pensions and Other Postretirement Benefits.* For an employer with publicly traded equity securities, FAS-158 is effective for financial statements with fiscal years ending after December 15, 2006. See item 5 below for the disclosure requirements about defined benefit pension plans and other defined benefit postretirement plans prior to the adoption of FAS-158 and item 6 below for the disclosure requirements after the adoption of FAS-158.

5. The following disclosures should be made about defined benefit pension plans and other defined benefit postretirement plans (FAS-132R, par. 9; APB-28, par. 30k):

   a. For each income statement presented, the amount of net periodic benefit cost recognized, showing separately the following: (1) service cost component, (2) interest cost component, (3) expected return on plan assets for the period, (4) amortization of the unrecognized transition obligation or asset, (5) amount of recognized gains or losses, (6) amount of prior service cost recognized, and (7) amount of gain or loss recognized due to a settlement or curtailment

   b. The total amount of the employer's contributions paid, and expected to be paid, during the current fiscal year, if significantly different from amounts previously disclosed (**Note:** Estimated contributions may be presented in the aggregate for contributions required by funding regulations or laws, discretionary contributions, and noncash contributions.)

6. The following disclosures should be made about defined benefit pension plans and other defined benefit postretirement plans (APB-28, par. 30k; FAS-132R, par. 9; FAS-158, pars. E1s and F3):

   a. For each income statement presented, the amount of net periodic benefit cost recognized, showing separately the following: (1) service cost component, (2) interest cost component, (3) expected return on plan assets for the period, (4) gain or loss component, (5) prior service cost or credit component, (6) transition asset or obligation component, and (7) gain or loss recognized due to a settlement or curtailment

   b. The total amount of the employer's contributions paid, and expected to be paid, during the current fiscal year, if significantly different from amounts previously disclosed (Estimated contributions may be presented in the aggregate for contributions required by funding regulations or laws, discretionary contributions, and noncash contributions.)

EXAMPLES OF FINANCIAL STATEMENT DISCLOSURES

For examples of disclosures relating to accounting changes and error corrections affecting interim periods, see Chapter 1, "Accounting Changes and Error Corrections."

 The following sample disclosures are available on the accompanying disc.

Example 22–1: Quantities and Costs Used in Calculating Cost of Goods Sold on a Quarterly Basis Include Estimates of the Annual LIFO Effect

The quantities and costs used in calculating cost of goods sold for the three months and six months periods ended June 30, 20X2, include estimates of the annual LIFO effect. The actual effect cannot be known until the year-end physical inventory is completed and quantity and price indices developed.

Example 22–2: Seasonal Nature of Operations Due to Normal Maintenance

Although there is no pronounced seasonality in demand for the Company's products, typically the second quarter of the year is the Company's best in terms of profitability. Generally, in the third quarter of the year, plants are closed for the first week of July for scheduled normal maintenance.

Example 22–3: Nature of Operations Affected by Weather and Spending Patterns of Significant Customers

The Company has historically experienced variability in revenues, income before income taxes and net income on a quarterly basis. A significant amount of this variability is due to the fact that the Company's business is subject to seasonal fluctuations, with activity in its second and, occasionally, third fiscal quarters being adversely affected by weather. In addition, budgetary spending patterns of significant customers, which often run on a calendar year basis, have resulted in greater volatility of second fiscal quarter results. Therefore, the results of operations presented for the three months ended March 31, 20X2, are not necessarily indicative of results of operations for the full year.

Example 22–4: Seasonal Nature of Operations Quantified

The Company's business is highly seasonal with between 65% and 80% of sales occurring in the second and third fiscal quarters combined.

Example 22–5: Unusual or Nonrecurring Item

The results of operations for the third quarter of 20X2 include (1) a $798,000 ($483,000 after-tax) nonrecurring charge to address the impairment of existing manufacturing facilities in Carson City, Nevada, and to relocate certain contractual employees to the Company's new facility in Chandler, Arizona; (2) a gain of $1,500,000 ($908,000 after-tax) related to the termination of a license agreement, net of charges for related equipment write-offs and capacity adjustments; and (3) charges of $1,300,000 ($782,000 after-tax) for the settlement of certain environmental litigation.

Example 22–6: Extraordinary Item

In the second quarter of 20X2, the Company's manufacturing facility in Orange, Florida, was severely damaged by an earthquake. After the settlement with the insurer, the Company retired the building and recognized an extraordinary gain of $719,000, net of income taxes of $342,000.

Example 22–7: Significant Change in Income Tax Rate

The effective tax rate for the three-month period ended September 30, 20X2, was 48%, which was higher than the tax rate for the preceding quarters. The higher tax rate is primarily the result of a proposed tax adjustment of approximately $1,200,000 by the Internal Revenue Service.

Example 22–8: Significant Items Affecting Fourth-Quarter Results of Operations Disclosed—Financial Information Is Not Separately Reported for the Fourth Quarter

In the fourth quarter of 20X2 the Company recorded net pretax charges for inventory and related reserves of approximately $3,500,000 and a goodwill write-down of $1,000,000 primarily as a result of changes in customer demand for certain Company products. In addition, the credit for income taxes in the fourth quarter of 20X2 was favorably affected by approximately $1,000,000 as a result of the settlement of tax examinations for earlier years. These adjustments reduced fourth quarter net income per share by $0.10.

Example 22–9: Summarized Quarterly Data

The following sets forth certain unaudited quarterly statements of operations data for each of the Company's quarters for 20X2 and 20X1. In management's opinion, this quarterly information reflects all adjustments, consisting only of normal recurring adjustments, necessary for a fair presentation for the periods presented. Such quarterly results are not necessarily indicative of future results of operations and should be read in conjunction with the audited consolidated financial statements of the Company and the notes thereto.

	Dec. 31, 20X2	Sept. 30, 20X2	June 30, 20X2	March 31, 20X2
Net revenues	$7,014,000	$6,131,000	$5,227,000	$5,101,000
Cost of sales and expenses	3,176,000	3,192,000	3,027,000	2,749,000
Income before income taxes	3,838,000	2,939,000	2,200,000	2,352,000
Income tax expense	1,774,000	1,380,000	1,028,000	1,079,000
Net income	$2,064,000	$1,559,000	$1,172,000	$1,273,000
Basic earnings per share	$.62	$.46	$.35	$.39
Diluted earnings per share	$.59	$.44	$.33	$.36
Net revenues	$5,914,000	$5,331,000	$5,460,000	$6,048,000
Cost of sales and expenses	3,116,000	2,804,000	2,343,000	2,307,000
Income before income taxes	2,798,000	2,527,000	3,117,000	3,741,000
Income tax expense	1,274,000	1,153,000	1,472,000	1,758,000
Net income	$1,524,000	$1,374,000	$1,645,000	$1,983,000
Basic earnings per share	$.53	$.48	$.50	$.61
Diluted earnings per share	$.49	$.44	$.46	$.55

Example 22–10: Pension and Other Postretirement Benefit Plans—Public Entities

Components of net periodic benefit cost for the Company's pension plan are as follows:

	Three Months Ended September 30		Nine Months Ended September 30	
	20X2	20X1	20X2	20X1
Service cost	$1,200,000	$1,100,000	$3,700,000	$3,400,000
Interest cost	1,400,000	1,156,000	3,900,000	3,250,000
Expected return on plan assets	(1,600,000)	(900,000)	(4,200,000)	(3,900,000)
Amortization of prior service cost	240,000	160,000	525,000	260,000
Amortization of net (gain) loss	70,000	(10,000)	90,000	115,000
Net periodic benefit cost	$1,310,000	$1,506,000	$4,015,000	$3,125,000

Components of net periodic benefit cost for the Company's post-retirement benefit plan are as follows:

	Three Months Ended September 30		Nine Months Ended September 30	
	20X2	20X1	20X2	20X1
Service cost	$200,000	$170,000	$700,000	$625,000
Interest cost	400,000	350,000	990,000	695,000
Expected return on plan assets	(150,000)	(190,000)	(315,000)	(420,000)
Amortization of prior service cost	(70,000)	(10,000)	(125,000)	(150,000)
Net periodic benefit cost	$380,000	$320,000	$1,250,000	$750,000

The Company previously disclosed in its financial statements for the year ended December 31, 20X1, that it expected to contribute $4,800,000 to its pension plan and $900,000 to its postretirement benefit plan in 20X2. As of September 30, 20X2, contributions of $3,700,000 and $650,000 have been made to the pension plan and postretirement benefit plan, respectively. The Company presently anticipates contributing an additional $1,500,000 to fund its pension plan in 20X2 for a total of $5,200,000. Also, the Company presently anticipates contributing an additional $450,000 to fund its postretirement benefit plan in 20X2 for a total of $1,100,000.

Example 22–11: Pension and Other Postretirement Benefit Plans—Nonpublic Entities

The Company previously disclosed in its financial statements for the year ended December 31, 20X1, that it expected to contribute $4,800,000 to its pension plan and $900,000 to its postretirement benefit plan in 20X2. As of September 30, 20X2, contributions of $3,700,000 and $650,000 have been made to the pension plan and postretirement benefit plan, respectively. The Company presently anticipates contributing an additional $1,500,000 to fund its pension plan in 20X2 for a total of $5,200,000. Also, the Company presently anticipates contributing an additional $450,000 to fund its postretirement benefit plan in 20X2 for a total of $1,100,000.

CHAPTER 23
LEASES

CONTENTS

EXECUTIVE SUMMARY

A lease that transfers substantially all the benefits and risks inherent in the ownership of property should be capitalized. Such a lease is accounted for by the lessee as the acquisition of an asset and the incurrence of a liability. The lessor accounts for such a lease as a sale (sales-type lease) or financing (direct-financing lease). All other leases are referred to as operating leases and should be accounted for as the rental of property.

The following are the broad classifications of leases under generally accepted accounting principles (GAAP):

Lessees	Lessors
Capital lease	Sales-type lease
Operating lease	Direct-financing lease
	Operating lease

Sales-type and direct-financing leases are the lessor's equivalent for a capital lease by a lessee.

Accounting for Leases—Lessees

A lease should be classified as a capital lease by a lessee if the lease meets at least one of the following criteria:

1. By the end of the lease term, ownership of the leased property is transferred to the lessee.
2. The lease contains a bargain purchase option.
3. The lease term is at least 75% of the estimated remaining economic life of the leased property. This criterion is not applicable when the beginning of the lease term falls within the last 25% of the total estimated economic life of the leased property.
4. At the inception of the lease, the present value of the minimum lease payments is at least 90% of the fair value of the leased property. This criterion is not applicable when the beginning of the lease term falls within the last 25% of the total estimated economic life of the leased property.

If none of these criteria are met, the lessee should classify the lease as an operating lease.

In a capital lease, the lessee should record a capital asset and a lease obligation for the same amount. The amount recorded should be the lesser of (1) the fair value of the leased asset at the inception of the lease, or (2) the present value of the minimum lease payments as of the beginning of the lease term. Once capitalized, the leased asset should be depreciated like any owned asset.

Under an operating lease, the lessee generally should charge the lease payments to rent expense on a straight-line basis over the lease term, even if payments are not made on straight-line basis.

Accounting for Leases—Lessors

A *sales-type lease* is a type of capital lease that results in a profit or loss to the lessor and transfers substantially all the benefits and risks inherent in the ownership of the leased property to the lessee. In a sales-type lease, the fair value of the leased property at the inception of the lease differs from its cost or carrying amount, thereby resulting in a profit or loss to the lessor.

A *direct-financing lease* is a type of capital lease that does *not* result in a profit or loss to the lessor but does transfer substantially all the benefits and risks inherent in the ownership of the leased property to the lessee. In a direct-financing lease, the leased property's book value and fair value are the same; therefore, there is no resulting profit or loss.

A lessor should classify a lease as a sales-type or direct-financing lease, whichever is appropriate, if the lease at inception meets at least one of the four criteria discussed above and *both* of the following criteria:

1. Collection of the minimum lease payments is reasonably predictable.

2. No important uncertainties exist for unreimbursable costs yet to be incurred by the lessor. Important uncertainties include extensive warranties and material commitments beyond normal practice. *Executory costs*, such as insurance, maintenance, and taxes, are not considered important uncertainties.

If none of these criteria are met, the lease should be classified as an operating lease by a lessor.

A sales-type lease should be accounted for by a lessor as follows:

1. The lessor should determine the *gross investment in the lease*, which is (a) the minimum lease payments (net of amounts, if any, included therein for executory costs to be paid by the lessor, together with any profit thereon) plus (b) the unguaranteed residual value accruing to the benefit of the lessor.

2. The present value of the gross investment in the lease should be recorded as a receivable in the balance sheet.

3. The difference between the gross investment in the lease (as determined in item 1 above) and its present value (as determined in item 2 above) should be recorded as unearned income and amortized to income over the lease term by the interest method. (The unearned income is included in the balance sheet as a deduction from the related gross investment.)

4. The present value of the minimum lease payments should be recorded as the sales price. The carrying amount of the leased property, plus any initial direct costs and less the present value of the unguaranteed residual value, should be charged against income in the same period.

A direct-financing lease should be accounted for by a lessor as follows:

1. The lessor should determine the *gross investment in the lease*, which is (a) the minimum lease payments (net of amounts, if any, included therein for executory costs to be paid by the lessor, together with any profit thereon) plus (b) the unguaranteed residual value accruing to the benefit of the lessor.

2. The difference between the gross investment in the lease (as determined in item 1 above) and the carrying amount of the leased property should be recorded as unearned income. The unearned income and any initial direct costs should be amortized to income over the lease term by the interest method.

3. The net investment in the lease (i.e., gross investment as determined in item 1 above plus any unamortized initial direct costs less the unearned income) should be recorded as a receivable in the balance sheet.

For operating leases, the lessor should include the cost of the property leased to the lessee in the lessor's balance sheet as property, plant, and equipment and should be depreciated. Material initial direct costs (those directly related to the negotiation and consummation of the lease) are deferred and allocated to income over the lease term. Rental income should be amortized over the lease term on a straight-line basis, unless some other systematic and rational basis is more representative of the time pattern in which income is earned.

Other Lease Matters

Leveraged leases shall be classified and accounted for in the same manner as nonleveraged leases. A *leveraged lease* is a type of direct financing lease that has certain additional characteristics, principally the involvement of a long-term creditor.

Additional requirements apply to sale-leaseback transactions, leases involving real estate, leases involving and between related parties, leases with governmental entities, money-over-money leases, wrap leases, leases in business combinations, and subleases.

Authoritative Literature

FAS-13	Accounting for Leases
FSP FAS 13-2	Accounting for a Change or Projected Change in the Timing of Cash Flows Relating to Income Taxes Generated by a Leveraged Lease Transaction
FAS-22	Changes in the Provisions of Lease Agreements Resulting from Refundings of Tax-Exempt Debt
FAS-23	Inception of the Lease
FAS-27	Classification of Renewals or Extensions of Existing Sales-Type or Direct Financing Leases
FAS-28	Accounting for Sales with Leasebacks
FAS-29	Determining Contingent Rentals

FAS-91	Accounting for Nonrefundable Fees and Costs Associated with Originating or Acquiring Loans and Initial Direct Costs of Leases
FAS-94	Consolidation of All Majority-Owned Subsidiaries
FAS-98	Accounting for Leases:
	• Sale-Leaseback Transactions Involving Real Estate
	• Sales-Type Leases of Real Estate
	• Definition of the Lease Term
	• Initial Direct Costs of Direct Financing Leases
FAS-109	Accounting for Income Taxes
FAS-140	Accounting for Transfers and Servicing of Financial Assets and Extinguishments of Liabilities—A Replacement of FASB Statement No. 125
FAS-145	Rescission of FASB Statements No. 4, 44, and 64, Amendment of FASB Statement No. 13, and Technical Corrections
FIN-19	Lessee Guarantee of the Residual Value of Leased Property
FIN-21	Accounting for Leases in a Business Combination
FIN-23	Leases of Certain Property Owned by a Governmental Unit or Authority
FIN-24	Leases Involving Only Part of a Building
FIN-26	Accounting for Purchase of a Leased Asset by the Lessee during the Term of the Lease
FIN-27	Accounting for a Loss on a Sublease
FTB 79-10	Fiscal Funding Clauses in Lease Agreements
FTB 79-12	Interest Rate Used in Calculating the Present Value of Minimum Lease Payments
FTB 79-13	Applicability of FASB Statement No. 13 to Current Value Financial Statements
FTB 79-14	Upward Adjustment of Guaranteed Residual Values
FTB 79-15	Accounting for Loss on a Sublease Not Involving the Disposal of a Segment
FTB 79-16(R)	Effect of a Change in Income Tax Rate on the Accounting for Leveraged Leases

FTB 79-17	Reporting Cumulative Effect Adjustment from Retroactive Application of FASB Statement No. 13
FTB 79-18	Transition Requirement of Certain FASB Amendments and Interpretations of FASB Statement No. 13
FTB 82-1	Disclosure of the Sale or Purchase of Tax Benefits through Tax Leases
FTB 85-3	Accounting for Operating Leases with Scheduled Rent Increases
FTB 86-2	Accounting for an Interest in the Residual Value of a Leased Asset:

- Acquired by a Third Party or
- Retained by a Lessor That Sells the Related Minimum Rental Payments

FTB 88-1	Issues Relating to Accounting for Leases:

- Time Pattern of the Physical Use of the Property in an Operating Lease
- Lease Incentives in an Operating Lease
- Applicability of Leveraged Lease Accounting to Existing Assets of the Lessor
- Money-Over-Money Lease Transactions
- Wrap Lease Transactions

EITF 98-9	Accounting for Contingent Rent

DISCLOSURE REQUIREMENTS

Leases—Lessees

Lessees should make the following disclosures:

1. A general description of leasing arrangements, including, but not limited to, the following (FAS-13, par. 16):
   a. The basis on which contingent rental payments are determined
   b. The existence and terms of renewal or purchase options and escalation clauses
   c. Restrictions imposed by lease agreements such as those concerning dividends, additional debt, and further leasing
2. The nature and extent of leasing transactions with related parties (FAS-13, par. 29).

3. For capital leases, the following disclosures should be made (FAS-13, pars. 13 and 16):

    a. For each balance sheet presented, the gross amount of assets recorded under capital leases by major classes according to nature or function and the total amount of accumu lated amortization thereon (this information may be combined with the comparable information for owned assets)

    b. Obligations related to assets recorded under capital leases should be separately identified in the balance sheet as obligations under capital leases, subject to the same considerations as other obligations in classifying them as current and noncurrent liabilities in classified balance sheets

    c. Future minimum lease payments as of the date of the latest balance sheet presented, in the aggregate and for each of the five succeeding fiscal years, with separate deductions from the total for the amount representing executory costs (including any profit thereon), that are included in the minimum lease payments and for the amount of the imputed interest necessary to reduce the net minimum lease payments to present value

    d. The total of minimum sublease rentals to be received in the future under noncancelable subleases as of the date of the latest balance sheet presented

    e. Total contingent rentals actually incurred for each period for which an income statement is presented

    f. Amortization of capitalized leases separately reported on the income statement or presented in a note to the financial statements (the amortization may be combined with depreciation expense, but that fact must be disclosed)

4. For operating leases, the following disclosures should be made (FAS-13, par. 16):

    a. For operating leases having initial or remaining noncancelable lease terms in excess of one year:

    — Future minimum rental payments required as of the date of the latest balance sheet presented, in the aggregate and for each of the five succeeding fiscal years

    — The total amount of minimum rentals to be received in the future under noncancelable subleases as of the date of the latest balance sheet presented

    b. For all operating leases (except for rental payments under leases with terms of a month or less that were not renewed):

    — Rental expense for each period for which an income statement is presented

— Presentation of separate amounts for minimum rentals, contingent rentals, and sublease rental income

5. For seller-lessee transactions, a description of the terms of the sale-leaseback transaction, including future commitments, obligations, provisions, or circumstances that require or result in the seller-lessee's continuing involvement (FAS-98, par. 17).

6. If a sale-leaseback transaction is accounted for by the deposit method or as a real estate financing arrangement, the following disclosures should be made (FAS-98, par. 18):

   a. The obligation for future minimum lease payments as of the date of the latest balance sheet presented in the aggregate and for each of the five succeeding fiscal years

   b. The total of minimum sublease rentals, if any, to be received in the future under noncancelable subleases in the aggregate and for each of the five succeeding fiscal years

Leases—Lessors

Lessors should make the following disclosures:

1. A general description of the lessor's leasing arrangements (FAS-13, par. 23).

2. The nature and extent of leasing transactions with related parties (FAS-13, par. 29).

3. For sales-type and direct-financing leases, the following disclosures should be made (FAS-13, par. 23; FAS-91, par. 25):

   a. The components of the net investment in sales-type and direct-financing leases as of the date of each balance sheet presented, as follows:

      — Future minimum lease payments to be received with separate deductions for (i) amounts representing executory costs, including any profit thereon, included in the minimum lease payments and (ii) the accumulated allowance for uncollectible minimum lease payments receivable

      — The unguaranteed residual values accruing to the benefit of the lessor

      — Initial direct costs for direct-financing leases only

      — Unearned income

   b. Future minimum lease payments to be received for each of the five succeeding fiscal years as of the date of the latest balance sheet presented

   c. Total contingent rentals included in income for each period for which an income statement is presented

4. For operating leases, the following disclosures should be made (FAS-13, par. 23):

   a. The cost and carrying amount, if different, of property on lease or held for leasing, by major classes of property according to nature or function, and the amount of accumulated depreciation in total as of the date of the latest balance sheet presented

   b. Minimum future rentals on noncancelable leases as of the date of the latest balance sheet presented, in the aggregate and for each of the five succeeding fiscal years

   c. Total contingent rentals included in income for each period for which an income statement is presented

5. For leveraged leases, the following disclosures should be made (FAS-13, par. 47):

   a. The amount of related deferred taxes presented separately from the remainder of the net income investment

   b. Separate presentation (in the income statement or in related notes) of pretax income from the leveraged lease, the tax effect of pretax income, and the amount of investment tax credit recognized as income during the period

   c. If leveraged leasing is a significant part of the lessor's business activities in terms of revenue, net income, or assets, the following components of the net investment in leveraged leases should be disclosed:

      — Rentals receivable, net of that portion of the rental applicable to principal and interest on the nonrecourse debt

      — A receivable for the amount of the investment tax credit to be realized on the transaction

      — The estimated residual value of the leased assets (the estimated residual value should not exceed the amount estimated at the inception of the lease, except as provided in FAS-23)

      — Unearned and deferred income consisting of (i) the estimated pretax lease income (or loss), after deducting initial direct costs, remaining to be allocated to income over the lease term and (ii) the investment tax credit remaining to be allocated to income over the lease term

6. Lessors that recognize contingent rental income should disclose (EITF 98-9, par. 13):

   a. The accounting policy for recognizing contingent rental income

b. If contingent rental income is recognized (accrued) prior to achieving the specified target that triggers the contingent rents, the effect on net income of accruing such rents prior to achieving the specified target should be disclosed

Note: The disclosure requirements in item 7 below are prescribed by FSP FAS 13-2, *Accounting for a Change or Projected Change in the Timing of Cash Flows Relating to Income Taxes Generated by a Leveraged Lease Transaction.* FSP FAS 13-2 is effective for fiscal years beginning after December 15, 2006, with early adoption permitted as long as (1) the consensus is applied as of the beginning of the fiscal year and (2) financial statements for any period (interim or annual) of the fiscal year have not yet been issued.

7. The lessor should disclose the following in the fiscal year of adoption of FSP FAS 13-2 as of the most recent statement of financial position or income statement presented (FSP FAS 13-2, par. 14):

a. The nature of the change in accounting principle

b. The cumulative effect of the change on retained earnings in the statement of financial position as of the date of adoption

Leases—Tax Leases

1. If the entity is involved in the sale or purchase of tax benefits through tax leases, the entity should make the following disclosures (FTB 82-1, par. 4):

a. The method of recognizing revenue

b. The method of allocating the income tax benefits and asset costs to current and future periods

2. If unusual or infrequent, the nature and financial effects of sales or purchases of tax benefits through tax leases should be disclosed on the face of the income statement or in a note to the financial statements (FTB 82-1, par. 6).

3. Significant contingencies existing with respect to sales or purchases of tax benefits through tax leases should be disclosed (FTB 82-1, par. 7).

4. If comparative financial statements are presented, disclosures should be made of any changes in the method of accounting for sales or purchases of tax benefits through tax leases that significantly affect comparability (FTB 82-1, par. 7).

5. If a significant variation in the customary relationship between income tax expense and pretax accounting income

occurs as a result of sales or purchases of tax benefits through
tax leases, the estimated amount and nature of the variation
should be disclosed (FAS-109, par. 288).

EXAMPLES OF FINANCIAL STATEMENT DISCLOSURES

The following sample disclosures are available on the
accompanying disc.

Lessees

*Example 23–1: Operating Leases Include Renewal Options, Increases in
Future Minimum Payments, and Payment of Executory Costs*

The Company leases many of its operating and office facilities for
various terms under long-term, non-cancelable operating lease
agreements. The leases expire at various dates through 20X9 and
provide for renewal options ranging from three months to six years.
In the normal course of business, it is expected that these leases will
be renewed or replaced by leases on other properties.

The leases provide for increases in future minimum annual rental
payments based on defined increases in the Consumer Price Index,
subject to certain minimum increases. Also, the agreements generally require the Company to pay executory costs (real estate taxes,
insurance, and repairs). Lease expense totaled $25,500,000 and
$24,700,000 during 20X2 and 20X1, respectively.

The following is a schedule by year of future minimum rental
payments required under the operating lease agreements:

Year Ending December 31	Amount
20X3	$ 27,000,000
20X4	29,500,000
20X5	31,000,000
20X6	33,500,000
20X7	35,000,000
Thereafter	80,000,000
	$236,000,000

Total minimum lease payments do not include contingent rentals
that may be paid under certain leases because of use in excess of
specified amounts. Contingent rental payments were not significant
in 20X2 or 20X1.

Example 23–2: Operating Leases Include Sublease Income

The Company leases corporate office and warehouse facilities, machinery and equipment, computers, and furniture under operating lease agreements expiring at various times through 20X9. Substantially all of the leases require the Company to pay maintenance, insurance, property taxes, and percentage rent ranging from 3% to 12%, based on sales volume over certain minimum sales levels. Effective March 20X2, the Company entered into a sublease agreement for its former ware house facility, which expires in September 20X6.

Minimum annual rental commitments under non-cancelable leases are as follows at December 31, 20X2:

Year Ending December 31	Minimum Lease Commitments	Sublease Income	Net Lease Commitments
20X3	$ 5,196,000	$247,000	$ 4,949,000
20X4	4,962,000	247,000	4,715,000
20X5	4,352,000	247,000	4,105,000
20X6	3,511,000	185,000	3,326,000
20X7	3,793,000	-0-	3,793,000
Thereafter	4,430,000	-0-	4,430,000
	$26,244,000	$926,000	$25,318,000

Rental expense, including common area maintenance, was $5,533,000 and $5,391,000, of which $77,000 and $45,000 was paid as percentage rent based on sales volume, for the years ended December 31, 20X2, and December 31, 20X1, respectively.

Example 23–3: Operating Leases Contain Purchase Option, Contingent Liability, and Restrictive Covenants

The Company has entered into lease agreements relating to certain corporate facilities that would allow the Company to purchase the facilities on or before the end of the lease term in March 20X3 for a specified purchase price. If at the end of the lease term the Company does not purchase the property under lease or arrange a third-party purchase, then the Company would be obligated to the lessor for a guarantee payment equal to a specified percentage of the agreed purchase price for the property. The Company would also be obligated to the lessor for all or some portion of this amount if the price paid by the third party is below 15% of the specified purchase price.

As of December 31, 20X2, the total amount related to the leased facilities for which the Company is contingently liable is $12,000,000. Under the terms of the agreements, the Company is required to maintain restricted investments, as collateral, of approximately $9,500,000 during the remainder of the lease term; this amount is shown as "Restricted long-term deposits" in the Company's Balance Sheet.

The lease agreements also require the Company to comply with certain covenants and to maintain certain financial ratios. As of December 31, 20X2, the Company was in compliance with all ratios and covenants.

Example 23–4: Operating Leases Contain Rent Abatements and Provisions for Future Rent Increases That Are Amortized on the Straight-Line Method over the Lease Term

The Company has entered into several operating lease agreements, some of which contain provisions for future rent increases, rent free periods, or periods in which rent payments are reduced (abated). The total amount of rental payments due over the lease term is being charged to rent expense on the straight-line method over the term of the lease. The difference between rent expense recorded and the amount paid is credited or charged to "Deferred rent obligation," which is included in "Other current liabilities" in the accompanying Balance Sheet.

Example 23–5: Rent Expense Includes Contingent Rent and Sublease Rental Income

The following summary shows the composition of total rental expense for all operating leases:

	20X2	20X1
Minimum rents	$5,200,000	$4,750,000
Contingent rents	2,360,000	2,150,000
Less: Sublease rental income	(470,000)	(450,000)
Net rental expense	$7,090,000	$6,450,000

Contingent rents are based on factors other than the passage of time, primarily percentage of revenues in excess of specified amounts.

Example 23–6: Capital Leases—Future Minimum Lease Payments

The Company leases certain machinery and equipment under agreements that are classified as capital leases. The cost of equipment under capital leases is included in the Balance Sheets as property, plant, and equipment and was $6,943,000 and $6,822,000 at December 31, 20X2, and December 31, 20X1, respectively. Accumulated amortization of the leased equipment at December 31, 20X2, and December 31, 20X1, was approximately $4,720,000 and $4,245,000, respectively. Amortization of assets under capital leases is included in depreciation expense.

The future minimum lease payments required under the capital leases and the present value of the net minimum lease payments as of December 31, 20X2, are as follows:

	Year Ending December 31	Amount
	20X3	$1,250,000
	20X4	975,000
	20X5	820,000
	20X6	745,000
	20X7	620,000
	Thereafter	1,527,000
Total minimum lease payments		5,937,000
Less: Amount representing estimated taxes, maintenance, and insurance costs included in total amounts above		(125,000)
Net minimum lease payments		5,812,000
Less: Amount representing interest		(1,855,000)
Present value of net minimum lease payments		3,957,000
Less: Current maturities of capital lease obligations		(823,000)
Long-term capital lease obligations		$3,134,000

Example 23–7: Components of Property under Capital Leases

Assets recorded under capital leases and included in property and equipment in the Company's Balance Sheets consist of the following at December 31, 20X2, and December 31, 20X1:

	20X2	20X1
Distribution and manufacturing facility	$3,250,000	$3,250,000
Data processing equipment	1,975,000	1,050,000
Furniture and equipment	725,000	536,000
Transportation equipment	347,000	213,000
	6,297,000	5,049,000
Less: Accumulated amortization	(2,514,000)	(2,091,000)
	$3,783,000	$2,958,000

Example 23–8: Sale-Leaseback Transaction Accounted for as an Operating Lease Results in Deferred Gain That Is Being Amortized over the Term of the Lease

In March 20X2, the Company sold certain machinery and equipment for $11,525,000. Under the agreement, the Company is leasing back the property from the purchaser over a period of 15 years. The Company is accounting for the leaseback as an operating lease. The gain of $1,630,000 realized in this transaction has been deferred and is being amortized to income in proportion to rent charged over the term of the lease. At December 31, 20X2, the remaining deferred gain of $1,490,000 is shown as "Deferred gain on property sale" in the Company's Balance Sheet.

The lease requires the Company to pay customary operating and repair expenses and to observe certain operating restrictions and covenants, including restrictions on net worth and dividend payments. The lease contains renewal options at lease termination and purchase options at amounts approximating fair market value as of specified dates in the agreement. For the year ended December 31, 20X2, the total rental expense incurred by the Company under this lease was $1,173,000. The minimum lease payments required by the lease are as follows:

Year Ending December 31	Amount
20X3	$ 1,983,000
20X4	1,621,000
20X5	1,372,000
20X6	1,011,000
20X7	963,000
Thereafter	6,523,000
	$13,473,000

Example 23–9: Sale-Leaseback Transaction Accounted for as an Operating Lease Results in No Gain or Loss

In March 20X2, the Company entered into an agreement with an independent third party to sell and leaseback certain machinery and equipment, which is accounted for as an operating lease. The net carrying value of the machinery and equipment sold was $8,250,000. Because the net carrying value of the machinery and equipment was equal to their sales price, there was no gain or loss recognized on the sale. The lease agreement entered into between the Company and the counterparty was for a minimum lease term of twelve months with three one-year renewal options. For the year ended

December 31, 20X2, the total rental expense incurred by the Company under this lease was $1,025,000.

Example 23–10: Sale-Leaseback Transaction Accounted for as a Financing Arrangement

In April 20X2, the Company completed the refinancing of its headquarters facility under a sale-leaseback arrangement. The facility was sold for $8,230,000, of which $2,300,000 was received in the form of an interest bearing note receivable due in April 20X7, and the remainder $5,930,000 in cash. The cash received was used to pay (1) existing mortgages on the property of $1,425,000, (2) expenses of the transaction of $350,000, and (3) bank debt of $4,155,000. The transaction has been accounted for as a financing arrangement, wherein the property remains on the Company's books and will continue to be depreciated. A financing obligation in the amount of $5,930,000, representing the proceeds, has been recorded under "Financing obligation, sale-leaseback" in the Company's Balance Sheet, and is being reduced based on payments under the lease.

The lease has a term of 12 years for the office and eight years for the warehouse and requires minimum annual rental payments as follows:

Year Ending December 31	Amount
20X3	$1,100,000
20X4	1,128,000
20X5	1,156,000
20X6	1,185,000
20X7	1,215,000
Thereafter	3,216,000
	$9,000,000

The Company has the option to renew the lease at the end of the lease term and the option to purchase the property at the end of the warehouse lease.

Example 23–11: Contingency Resulting from Default under Lease Agreements

The Company leases certain plant machinery and equipment at its manufacturing facility in Boise, Idaho. As a result of the Company's default under its debt obligations, as more fully discussed in Note [X] to the financial statements, the Company is in default under these lease agreements. As a result, the lessors have the right to require the Company to prepay the remaining future lease payments required under the lease agreements. Because the Company has paid the lease payments and all lease payments are expected to be made in a timely manner, the Company does not expect that the lessors will assert this right under these lease agreements.

Example 23–12: Lease Termination Results in Contingent Liability

In September 20X2, the Company notified the developer and landlord of its planned future headquarters in Paramount, California, that the Company intends to terminate the project. The Company had previously entered into a 15-year lease agreement for the new site. Although groundbreaking for the new site has not occurred, the Company anticipates that it will incur lease termination costs. The Company is not able to make a meaningful estimate of the amount or range of loss that could result from an unfavorable resolution of this matter. Consequently, the Company has not provided any accruals for lease termination costs in the financial statements.

Example 23–13: Warrants Issued in Connection with a Lease Agreement

In July 20X1, the Company issued a fully vested, non-forfeitable warrant that entitles the holder to purchase 25,000 shares of the Company's common stock at an exercise price of $10.00 per share, in connection with a lease agreement. This warrant is exercisable through July 20X6. The fair value of this warrant, approximately $375,000, is being expensed over the term of the lease. The fair value of this warrant was calculated using the Black-Scholes option-pricing model. As of June 20X2, this warrant was exercised in full.

In addition, in January 20X1, in connection with an equipment lease line, the Company issued a fully vested warrant that entitles the holder to purchase 110,000 shares of the Company's common stock at an exercise price of $1.50 per share. This warrant is exercisable through January 20X8. The fair value of this warrant, approximately $362,000, is being expensed as a cost of financing over the four-year period of the lease line. The fair value of this warrant was calculated using the Black-Scholes option-pricing model. The warrant was exercised in full during 20X2.

Lessors

Example 23–14: Operating Leases

Operating leases arise from the leasing of the Company's machinery and equipment to retail customers, primarily in the construction industry in the United States. Initial lease terms generally range from 36 to 84 months. Depreciation expense for assets subject to operating leases is provided primarily on the straight-line method over the term of the lease in amounts necessary to reduce the carrying amount of the asset to its estimated residual value. Estimated and actual residual values are reviewed on a regular basis to determine that depreciation amounts are appropriate. Depreciation expense relating to machinery and equipment held as investments in operating leases was $373,000 for 20X2 and $417,000 for 20X1.

Investments in operating leases are as follows at December 31:

	20X2	*20X1*
Machinery and equipment, at cost	$4,373,000	$4,770,000
Lease origination costs	63,000	65,000
Accumulated depreciation	(813,000)	(765,000)
Allowance for credit losses	(50,000)	(90,000)
Net investments in operating leases	$3,573,000	$3,980,000

Future minimum rental payments to be received on noncancelable operating leases are contractually due as follows as of December 31, 20X2:

Year Ending December 31	Amount
20X3	$ 883,000
20X4	645,000
20X5	422,000
20X6	213,000
20X7	105,000
Thereafter	75,000
	$2,343,000

Future minimum rental payments to be received do not include contingent rentals that may be received under certain leases because of use in excess of specified amounts. Contingent rentals were not significant in 20X2 or 20X1.

Example 23–15: Sales-Type Leases

The components of lease receivables for the net investment in sales-type leases are as follows at December 31:

	20X2	*20X1*
Total minimum lease receivables	$4,100,000	$3,600,000
Less: Allowance for uncollectible amounts	(125,000)	(100,000)
Net minimum lease payments receivable	3,975,000	3,500,000
Estimated residual values of leased property	230,000	145,000
Less: Unearned interest income	(710,000)	(625,000)
Net investment in sales-type leases	$3,495,000	$3,020,000
Current portion	$1,300,000	$1,050,000
Long-term portion	2,195,000	1,970,000
	$3,495,000	$3,020,000

Future minimum lease receivables due from customers under sales-type leases as of December 31, 20X2, are as follows:

Year Ending December 31	*Amount*
20X3	$ 852,000
20X4	827,000
20X5	793,000
20X6	602,000
20X7	464,000
Thereafter	562,000
	$4,100,000

Future minimum lease receivables do not include contingent rentals that may be received under certain leases because of use in excess of specified amounts. Contingent rentals were not significant in 20X2 or 20X1.

Example 23–16: Direct-Financing Leases

The components of lease receivables for the net investment in direct financing leases are as follows as of December 31:

	20X2	20X1
Total minimum lease receivables	$5,519,000	$5,837,000
Less: Allowance for credit losses	(80,000)	(143,000)
Net minimum lease payments receivable	5,439,000	5,694,000
Estimated residual values of leased property	3,720,000	2,923,000
Deferred initial direct costs	125,000	150,000
Less: Unearned income	(2,150,000)	(2,410,000)
Net investment in direct financing leases	$7,134,000	$6,357,000
Current portion	$2,760,000	$2,323,000
Long-term portion	4,374,000	4,034,000
	$7,134,000	$6,357,000

Future minimum lease receivables due from customers under direct-financing leases as of December 31, 20X2, are as follows:

Year Ending December 31	Amount
20X3	$1,906,000
20X4	1,619,000
20X5	949,000
20X6	712,000
20X7	233,000
Thereafter	100,000
	$5,519,000

Unearned income on direct financing leases is recognized in such a manner as to produce a constant periodic rate of return on the net investment in the direct-financing lease.

Future minimum lease receivables do not include contingent rentals that may be received under certain leases because of use in excess of specified amounts. Contingent rentals were not significant in 20X2 or 20X1.

Example 23–17: Leveraged Leases

Leveraged lease assets acquired by the Company are financed primarily through nonrecourse loans from third-party debt participants. These loans are secured by the lessee's rental obligations and the leased property. Net rents receivable represent gross rents less the principal and interest on the nonrecourse debt obligations. Unguaranteed residual values are principally based on independent appraisals of the values of leased assets remaining at the expiration of the lease. Leveraged lease investments are primarily related to heavy construction and drilling equipment, with original lease terms ranging from 5 to 15 years.

The Company's investment in leveraged leases consists of rentals receivable net of principal and interest on the related nonrecourse debt, estimated residual value of the leased property, and unearned income. The unearned income is recognized as leveraged lease revenue in income from investments over the lease term.

The Company's net investment in leveraged leases comprises the following at December 31, 20X2, and December 31, 20X1:

	20X2	20X1
Net lease receivables	$ 9,819,000	$8,761,000
Estimated unguaranteed residual values	10,863,000	9,910,000
Less: Unearned income	(10,150,000)	(9,613,000)
Investment in leveraged leases	$10,532,000	$9,058,000
Current portion	$ 2,031,000	$1,754,000
Long-term portion	8,501,000	7,304,000
	$10,532,000	$9,058,000

Deferred tax liability arising from leveraged leases totaled approximately $4,125,000 and $3,234,000 at December 31, 20X2, and December 31, 20X1, respectively.

The following is a summary of the components of income from leveraged leases for the years ended December 31, 20X2, and December 31, 20X1:

	20X2	20X1
Pretax leveraged lease income	$237,000	$151,000
Income tax effect	85,000	73,000
Income from leveraged leases	$322,000	$224,000

Leases with Related Parties

Example 23–18: Company Has a Long-Term Operating Lease with a Related Party

The Company leases its corporate headquarters and warehouse facility from a partnership owned by the two Company shareholders. The lease provides for monthly payments of $32,000, expires in 20X9, and contains a renewal option for an additional seven years. Due to the current economic conditions of the Company, rent was reduced to $32,000 per month from $45,000 per month effective January 1, 20X2. Rent expense incurred and paid to the partnership was $384,000 and $540,000 for 20X2 and 20X1, respectively.

The following is a schedule by year of future minimum rental payments due to the partnership under the operating lease agreement:

Year Ending December 31	Amount
20X3	$ 384,000
20X4	384,000
20X5	416,000
20X6	416,000
20X7	450,000
Thereafter	1,200,000
	$3,250,000

Example 23–19: Company Has a Month-to-Month Operating Lease with a Related Party

The Company leases its administrative offices on a month-to-month basis from a partnership in which the Company's stockholder is a partner. Total rent paid to the partnership was $123,000 and $117,000 for the years ended December 31, 20X2, and December 31, 20X1, respectively.

Example 23–20: Company Discloses the Nature and Extent of Several Long-Term Operating Lease Agreements with Affiliated Entities

The Company leases various manufacturing facilities and equipment from companies owned by certain officers and directors of the Company, either directly or indirectly, through affiliates. The leases generally provide that the Company will bear the cost of property taxes and insurance.

Details of the principal operating leases with related parties as of December 31, 20X2, including the effect of renewals and amendments executed subsequent to December 31, 20X2, are as follows:

Name of Related Party/ Description of Lease	Date of Lease	Term	Basic Annual Rental Amount	Future Minimum Rental Amounts
Hope Realty Trust:				
Land & building—Chicago	12-13-Y1	15 years	$200,000	$1,000,000
Corporate offices	12-22-Y1	15 years	$100,000	$ 500,000
Machinery & equipment	11-30-Y6	10 years	$125,000	$ 625,000
John Jones Family Trust:				
Land & buildings—Atlanta	6-29-Y6	10 years	$150,000	$ 675,000
Furniture & computers	7-01-Y7	10 years	$100,000	$ 550,000
Mack Realty Trust:				
Land & building—Detroit	6-25-Y6	15 years	$200,000	$1,900,000
Corporate offices	12-28-Y6	10 years	$110,000	$ 550,000
Furniture & equipment	1-1-Y7	10 years	$ 80,000	$ 400,000

Rent incurred and paid to these related parties was $1,069,000 and $1,087,000 for the years ended December 31, 20X2, and December 31, 20X1, respectively.

Future minimum lease payments to these related parties as of December 31, 20X2 are as follows:

Year Ending December 31	Amount
20X3	$1,065,000
20X4	1,110,000
20X5	1,150,000
20X6	1,205,000
20X7	1,260,000
Thereafter	685,000
	$6,475,000

CHAPTER 24
LONG-TERM CONTRACTS

CONTENTS

EXECUTIVE SUMMARY

Under generally accepted accounting principles (GAAP), revenues from long-term contracts should be recognized under either the percentage-of-completion method or the completed-contract method. The percentage-of-completion method is appropriate in situations in which reliable estimates of the degree of completion are available, in which case a pro rata portion of the income from the contract is recognized in each accounting period covered by the contract. If reliable estimates are not available, the completed-contract method is used, in which income is deferred until the end of the contract period. The percentage-of-completion and the completed-contract methods are not alternatives; a contractor must use the appropriate method.

Regardless of the revenue recognition method used, an entity should accrue an anticipated loss on a contract whenever it becomes apparent that the total estimated contract costs (i.e., costs incurred to date, plus estimated costs to complete) will materially exceed the total estimated contract revenue.

Generally, four basic types of contracts are encountered in practice:

1. *Fixed-price or lump-sum contracts.* A fixed-price or lump-sum contract is a contract in which the price is not usually subject to adjustment because of costs incurred by the contractor.

2. *Time-and-material contracts.* Time-and-material contracts are contracts that generally provide for payments to the contractor on the basis of direct labor hours at fixed hourly rates and cost of materials or other specified costs.

3. *Cost-type contracts.* Cost-type contracts provide for reimbursement of allowable or otherwise defined costs incurred plus a fee that represents profit.

4. *Unit-price contracts.* Unit-price contracts are contracts under which the contractor is paid a specified amount for every unit of work performed.

Authoritative Literature

ARB-43   Chapter 11, Government Contracts

ARB-45   Long-Term Construction-Type Contracts

SOP 81-1   Accounting for Performance of Construction-Type
and Certain Production-Type Contracts

DISCLOSURE REQUIREMENTS

The following disclosures are required for long-term contracts:

1. The method used to account for long-term contracts (i.e., the percentage-of-completion method or the completed-contract method) (ARB-45, par. 15)

2. Departure from the basic revenue recognition policy for a single contract or group of contracts (SOP 81-1, pars. 25 and 31)

3. The policies relating to combining and segmenting contracts, if applicable (SOP 81-1, par. 21)

4. When the percentage-of-completion method of accounting is used, the method of measuring the extent of progress toward completion should be disclosed (e.g., cost-to-cost, direct labor) (SOP 81-1, pars. 21 and 45)

5. If the completed-contract method is used, the criteria used to determine substantial completion (SOP 81-1, par. 52)

6. The amount of revenue from claims recognized in excess of the agreed contract price (SOP 81-1, pars. 65–67)

7. If the contractor recognizes revenues from claims only when the amounts have been received or awarded, the amounts of such revenues recorded during the period should be disclosed (SOP 81-1, par. 66)

8. The effect of significant revisions in contract estimates (SOP 81-1, par. 84)

9. The amount of advances, if any, offset against cost-type contract receivables (ARB-43, Ch. 11A, par. 22)

10. Provisions for losses on contracts should be disclosed separately as liabilities on the face of the balance sheet, if material (SOP 81-1, par. 89)

11. Provisions for losses on contracts that are material, unusual, or infrequent should be disclosed as a separate component of construction costs on the face of the income statement (SOP 81-1, par. 88)

12. The nature and amount of any large or unusual contract commitments (FAS-5, par. 18)

13. The unbilled costs and fees under cost-type contracts should be shown separately from billed accounts receivable (ARB-43, Ch. 11A, par. 21)

EXAMPLES OF FINANCIAL STATEMENT DISCLOSURES

 The following sample disclosures are available on the accompanying disc.

Example 24–1: General Accounting Policy for Contracts under the Percentage-of-Completion Method

Sales and cost of sales related to long-term contracts are accounted for under the percentage-of-completion method. Sales under fixed-type contracts are generally recognized upon passage of title to the customer, which usually coincides with physical delivery or customer acceptance as specified in contractual terms. Such sales are recorded at the cost of items delivered or accepted plus a proportion of profit expected to be realized on a contract, based on the ratio of such costs to total estimated costs at completion. Sales, including estimated earned fees, under cost reimbursement-type contracts are recognized as costs are incurred.

Profits expected to be realized on contracts are based on the Company's estimates of total contract sales value and costs at completion. These estimates are reviewed and revised periodically throughout the lives of the contracts with adjustments to profits resulting from such revisions being recorded on a cumulative basis in the period in which the revisions are made. When management believes the cost of completing a contract, excluding general and administrative expenses, will exceed contract-related revenues, the full amount of the anticipated contract loss is recognized.

Revenues recognized in excess of amounts billed are classified as current assets under "Contract work-in-progress." Amounts billed to clients in excess of revenues recognized to date are classified as current liabilities under "Advance billings on contracts."

Example 24–2: General Accounting Policy for Contracts under the Completed-Contract Method

Revenues from fixed-price contracts are recognized on the completed contract method. This method is used because the typical contract is completed in three months or less, and financial position and results of operations do not vary significantly from those that would result from use of the percentage-of-completion method. A contract is considered complete when all costs except significant items have been incurred and the installation is operating according to specifications or has been accepted by the customer. Revenues from time-and-material contracts are recognized currently as the work is performed.

Contract costs include all direct material and labor costs and those indirect costs related to contract performance, such as indirect labor, supplies, tools, repairs, and depreciation costs. General and administrative costs are charged to expense as incurred. Provisions for estimated losses on uncompleted contracts are made in the period in which such losses are determined.

Costs in excess of amounts billed are classified as current assets under "Costs in excess of billings on uncompleted contracts." Billings in excess of costs are classified as current liabilities under "Billings in excess of costs on uncompleted contracts."

Example 24–3: Revenue Recognized under Both the Completed-Contract and the Percentage-of-Completion Methods of Accounting

Revenue is recognized on both the completed-contract and the percentage-of-completion methods of accounting. The Company uses the percentage-of-completion method of accounting for all contracts that exceed $1 million in net operating revenues and recognizes such revenue upon incurring costs equal to the lesser of 25% of the contract costs or $500,000. Progress on percentage-of-completion contracts is measured generally by costs incurred to date compared with an estimate of total costs at the project's completion. Provision is made for anticipated losses, if any, on uncompleted contracts.

Example 24–4: Methods of Measuring Percentage-of-Completion Are Described

Revenues from long-term contracts are recognized on the percentage-of-completion method. Percentage-of-completion is measured principally by the percentage of costs incurred and accrued to date for each contract to the estimated total costs for each contract at completion. Certain of the Company's electrical contracting business units measure percentage-of-completion by the percentage of labor costs incurred to date for each contract to the estimated total labor costs for such contract.

The Company also enters into long-term contracts for the manufacture of products. Sales on production-type contracts are recorded as deliveries are made (units-of-delivery method of percentage-of-completion).

Example 24–5: Research and Development Contracts with Anticipated Losses

On a selective basis, the Company may enter into a contract to research and develop or manufacture a product with a loss anticipated at the date the contract is signed. These contracts are entered into in anticipation that profits will be obtained from future contracts for the same or similar products. These loss contracts often provide the Company with intellectual property rights that, in effect, establish it as the sole producer of certain products. Such losses are recognized at the date the Company becomes contractually obligated, with revisions made as changes occur in the related estimates to complete.

Example 24–6: Description of Segmented Contracts

Contracts are segmented between types of services, such as engineering and construction, and, accordingly, gross margin related to each activity is recognized as those separate services are rendered.

Example 24–7: Concentrations of Credit Risk

The majority of accounts receivable and all contract work-in-progress are from engineering and construction clients in various industries and locations throughout the United States. Most contracts require payments as the projects progress or in certain cases advance payments. The Company generally does not require collateral but in most cases can place liens against the property, plant, or equipment constructed or terminate the contract if a material default occurs. Accounts receivable from customers of the Company's Eastern operations are primarily concentrated in the steel and utility industries. The Company maintains adequate reserves for potential credit losses and such losses have been minimal and within management's estimates.

Example 24–8: Accounting for Cost Overruns under Fixed-Price Contracts

Under fixed-price contracts, the Company may encounter, and on certain programs from time to time has encountered, cost overruns caused by increased material, labor, or overhead costs; design or production difficulties; and various other factors such as technical and manufacturing complexity, which must be, and in such cases have been, borne by the Company. Adjustments to contract cost estimates are made in the periods in which the facts requiring such revisions become known. When the revised estimate indicates a loss, such loss is provided for currently in its entirety.

Example 24–9: Details of Contract Receivables Balance

Following are the details of contract receivables at December 31, 20X2, and December 31, 20X1:

	20X2	20X1
Amounts billed:		
Completed contracts	$1,217,000	$1,062,000
Contracts in progress	3,892,000	3,259,000
Retentions	813,000	768,000
	5,922,000	5,089,000
Unbilled	231,000	184,000
	6,153,000	5,273,000
Less: Allowance for doubtful accounts	(197,000)	(239,000)
	$5,956,000	$5,034,000

Of the retentions balance and the unbilled amounts at December 31, 20X2, approximately $613,000 is expected to be collected in the year 20X3, with the balance to be collected in subsequent years as contract deliveries are made and warranty periods expire.

Example 24–10: Details of Costs and Estimated Earnings on Uncompleted Contracts Reconciled to the Balance Sheets

Costs and estimated earnings on uncompleted contracts and related amounts billed as of December 31, 20X2, and December 31, 20X1, are as follows:

	20X2	20X1
Costs incurred on uncompleted contracts	$2,737,507	$2,282,127
Estimated earnings	202,211	158,832
	2,939,718	2,440,959
Less: Billings to date	(2,983,243)	(2,479,998)
	$(43,525)	$(39,039)

Such amounts are included in the accompanying Balance Sheets at December 31, 20X2, and December 31, 20X1, under the following captions:

	20X2	20X1
Costs and estimated earnings in excess of billings on uncompleted contracts	$91,569	$73,794
Billings in excess of costs and estimated earnings on uncompleted contracts	(135,094)	(112,833)
	$(43,525)	$(39,039)

Example 24–11: Allowances for Contract Losses Included in Current Liabilities

Other current liabilities at December 31, 20X2, and December 31, 20X1, include allowances for contract losses and other contract allowances aggregating $600,000 and $900,000, respectively.

Example 24–12: Contract Revenue from Claims Recognized When the Amounts Are Awarded or Resolved

The Company's policy is to recognize contract revenue from claims against customers and others on construction projects only when the amounts are awarded or resolved. Revenues from such claims amounted to $647,000 in 20X2 and $483,000 in 20X1.

Example 24–13: Contract Revenue from Claims Recognized When Realization Is Probable

The Company's policy is to recognize contract revenue from claims against customers and others on construction projects when realization is probable, the amount could be reasonably estimated, and the claim has reasonable legal basis. Claims involve the use of estimates and it is reasonably possible that revisions to the estimated recoverable amounts of recorded claims may be made in the near-term.

Example 24–14: Amounts Recognized from Claims and Pending Change Orders Disclosed and Identified in Balance Sheet Captions

Costs and estimated earnings in excess of billings on uncompleted contracts include unbilled revenues for pending change orders of approximately $590,000 and $417,000 at December 31, 20X2, and December 31, 20X1, respectively; and claims of approximately $370,000 and $223,000 at December 31, 20X2, and December 31, 20X1, respectively. In addition, accounts receivable as of December 31, 20X2, and December 31, 20X1, includes claims and contractually billed amounts related to such contracts of approximately $900,000 and $716,000, respectively. Generally, the customer will not pay contractually billed amounts to the Company until final resolution of related claims.

Example 24–15: Contingent Liability in Respect of Performance and Payment Bonds Issued by Sureties

The Company is contingently liable to sureties in respect of performance and payment bonds issued by the sureties in connection with certain contracts entered into by the Company in the normal course of business. The Company has agreed to indemnify the sureties for any payments made by them in respect of such bonds.

Example 24–16: Change from the Completed-Contract Method to the Percentage-of-Completion Method of Accounting

Effective January 1, 20X2, the Company changed its method of accounting for long-term contracts from the completed-contract method to the percentage-of-completion method. The Company believes that the new method more accurately reflects periodic results of operations and conforms to revenue recognition practices predominant in the industry. The effect of this change was to increase 20X2 net income by $600,000. The change has been applied to prior years by retroactively restating the financial statements presented for 20X1. The effect of the restatement was to increase retained earnings as of January 1, 20X1, by $1,000,000. The restatement decreased 20X1 net income by $305,000.

> **Note:** The following table illustrates the retroactive application of the change as shown on the face of the Company's Statement of Retained Earnings or Statement of Stockholders' Equity (assume the Company's year-end is December 31 and the latest year presented is 20X2).

Statement of Retained Earnings or Statement of Stockholders' Equity

	20X2	20X1
Retained earnings at beginning of year, as previously reported	$4,400,000	$2,900,000
Cumulative effect on prior years of retroactive restatement for accounting change	-0-	1,000,000
Retained earnings at beginning of year, as restated	4,400,000	3,900,000
Net income	650,000	500,000
Retained earnings at end of year	$5,050,000	$4,400,000

CHAPTER 25
NONMONETARY TRANSACTIONS

CONTENTS

EXECUTIVE SUMMARY

Note: In December 2004, the FASB issued Statement of Financial Accounting Standards No. 153 (FAS-153), *Exchanges of Nonmonetary Assets—An Amendment of APB Opinion No. 29.* The guidance in APB Opinion No. 29 (APB-29), *Accounting for Nonmonetary Transactions,* is based on the principle that exchanges of nonmonetary assets should be measured based on the fair value of the assets exchanged, with certain exceptions. Previously, APB-29 provided an exception to the basic fair value measurement principle for exchanges of similar productive assets. That exception required that some nonmonetary exchanges, although commercially substantive, be recorded on a carryover basis (i.e., based on the recorded amount of the asset relinquished). FAS-153 amends APB-29 to eliminate this exception and to replace it with a broader exception for exchanges of nonmonetary assets that do not have commercial substance (i.e., transactions that are not expected to result in significant changes in the cash flows of the reporting entity). The provisions of FAS-153 are effective for nonmonetary asset exchanges occurring in fiscal periods beginning after June 15, 2005. Early application is permitted and companies must apply FAS-153 prospectively. The discussion in this chapter has been updated to reflect the provisions of FAS-153.

As a general rule, accounting for nonmonetary transactions (i.e., exchanges and nonreciprocal transfers that involve little or no monetary assets or liabilities) should be based on the fair value of the assets or services involved and any gain or loss should be recognized. However, a nonmonetary exchange should be measured based on the recorded amount of the nonmonetary assets relinquished (after reduction for any impairment of value), and not on the fair values of the exchanged assets, under any of the following circumstances:

- The fair value of the assets received or relinquished is not reasonably determinable.
- The exchange transaction is essentially to facilitate sales to customers other than the parties to the exchange.
- The exchange transaction lacks commercial substance (i.e., the transaction is not expected to result in significant changes in the cash flows of the reporting entity).

An *exchange* is a reciprocal transfer in which each party to the transaction receives and/or gives up assets, liabilities, or services. Exchanges can be either monetary or nonmonetary, or a combination of both. Nonmonetary exchanges usually are for the mutual convenience of two businesses. An example would be an exchange of inventory for trucking services.

A *nonreciprocal transfer* is a transfer of assets or services in one direction, either from an enterprise to its owners or another entity, or from owners or another entity to the enterprise. Examples of nonreciprocal transfers are as follows:

- Distribution of nonmonetary assets, such as marketable equity securities, to stockholders as dividends
- Distribution of nonmonetary assets to stockholders to redeem or acquire outstanding capital stock of the entity
- Distribution of nonmonetary assets, such as capital stock of subsidiaries, to stockholders in corporate liquidations or plans of reorganization that involve disposing of all or a

significant segment of the business (such plans are variously referred to as *spin-offs, split-ups,* and *split-offs*)

- Distribution of nonmonetary assets to groups of stockholders, pursuant to plans of rescission or other settlements relating to a prior business combination, to redeem or acquire shares of capital stock previously issued in a business combination
- Charitable contributions by an entity
- Contribution of land by a governmental unit for construction of productive facilities by an entity

When a nonmonetary asset is involuntarily converted to a monetary asset, a monetary transaction results, and a gain or loss should be recognized in the period of conversion. The gain or loss is the difference between the carrying amount of the nonmonetary asset and the proceeds from the conversion. Examples of involuntary conversion are the total or partial destruction of property through fire or other catastrophe, theft of property, or condemnation of property by a governmental authority (eminent domain proceedings).

Authoritative Literature

APB-29	Accounting for Nonmonetary Transactions
FAS-109	Accounting for Income Taxes
FAS-153	Exchanges of Nonmonetary Assets
FIN-30	Accounting for Involuntary Conversions of Nonmonetary Assets to Monetary Assets
EITF 99-17	Accounting for Advertising Barter Transactions
EITF 00-8	Accounting by a Grantee for an Equity Instrument to Be Received in Conjunction with Providing Goods or Services
EITF 04-13	Accounting for Purchases and Sales of Inventory with the Same Counterparty

DISCLOSURE REQUIREMENTS

The following disclosures should be made regarding nonmonetary transactions (APB-29, par. 28):

1. The nature of the nonmonetary transaction
2. The basis of accounting for the assets transferred
3. Gains or losses recognized

In addition, gains and losses resulting from involuntary conversions of nonmonetary assets to monetary assets should be reported as either an extraordinary item or an unusual or infrequent item as appropriate (FIN-30, par. 4).

Disclosure should be made in each period's financial statements of the amount of gross operating revenue recognized as a result of nonmonetary transactions for which the entity provides goods or services in exchange for equity instruments issued by the customer (EITF 00-8, par. 10).

In addition, the amount of revenue and costs (or gains/losses) associated with inventory exchanges recognized at fair value should be disclosed (**Note:** For an affected entity, this disclosure should be applied to new arrangements that it enters into in reporting periods beginning after March 15, 2006.) (EITF 04-13, par. 5)

EXAMPLES OF FINANCIAL STATEMENT DISCLOSURES

 The following sample disclosures are available on the accompanying disc.

Example 25–1: Barter Transactions—Inventory Delivered in Exchange for Future Advertising Credits

In 20X2 and 20X1, the Company entered into barter agreements whereby it delivered $1,165,000 and $1,059,000, respectively, of its inventory in exchange for future advertising credits and other items. The credits, which expire in November 20X3, are valued at the lower of the Company's cost or market value of the inventory transferred. The Company has recorded barter credits of $115,000 and $236,000 in "Prepaid expenses and other current assets" at December 31, 20X2, and December 31, 20X1, respectively. At December 31, 20X2, and December 31, 20X1, "Other noncurrent assets" include $279,000 and $323,000, respectively, of such credits. Under the terms of the barter agreements, the Company is required to pay cash equal to a negotiated amount of the bartered advertising, or other items, and use the barter credits to pay the balance. These credits are charged to expense as they are used. During the years ended December 31, 20X2, and December 31, 20X1, approximately $1,080,000 and $751,000, respectively, were charged to expense for barter credits used.

The Company assesses the recoverability of barter credits periodically. Factors considered in evaluating the recoverability include management's plans with respect to advertising and other expenditures for which barter credits can be used. Any impairment losses are charged to operations as they are determinable. During the years ended December 31, 20X2, and December 31, 20X1, the Company charged $250,000 and $425,000, respectively, to operations for such impairment losses.

Example 25–2: Barter Transactions—Advertising Revenues and Expenses

Pursuant to the consensus reached by the Emerging Issues Task Force (EITF) in Issue No. 99-17, *Accounting for Advertising Barter Transactions*, the Company's barter transactions are recorded at the estimated fair value of the advertisements provided, based on recent historical cash transactions. Barter revenue is recognized when the advertising impressions or other services are delivered to the customer and advertising expense is recorded when the advertising impressions or other services are received from the customer. If the Company receives the advertising impressions or other services from the customer prior to its delivery of the advertising impressions, a liability is recorded; and if the Company delivers the advertising impressions to the customer prior to receiving the advertising impressions or other services, a prepaid expense is recorded on the Consolidated Balance Sheets. For the years ended December 31, 20X2, and December 31, 20X1, the Company recognized approximately $4.2 million and $1.9 million of advertising revenues, respectively, and $3.4 million and $1.5 million of advertising expenses, respectively, from barter transactions. The Company has recognized approximately $1.6 million and $1.1 million in prepaid expenses related to barter transactions as of December 31, 20X2 and December 31, 20X1, respectively.

Example 25–3: Notes Receivable Balance Due from Related Parties Is Paid through Forfeiture of Bonuses

As of December 31, 20X1, the Company had notes receivable due from certain executives and officers amounting to approximately $1,500,000. These notes bear interest at rates ranging from 7.25% to 7.85% and have maturities of six months to five years. In 20X2, $625,000 of the notes receivable balance was paid through forfeiture of management bonuses.

Example 25–4: Common Stock Awarded as Compensation

During 20X2 and 20X1, common stock with an aggregate fair market value of $515,000 and $496,000, respectively, was awarded to key executives as compensation.

Example 25–5: Contribution of Subsidiary Stock

During 20X2, the Company's contributions to the Advest Foundation consisted of 55,000 shares of the Company's majority-owned

Plantex subsidiary. A pretax gain of $120,000 was recorded on the donations. The shares contributed to the Advest Foundation had a market value of $425,000, which was recorded as a contribution expense in the accompanying 20X2 Income Statement.

Example 25–6: Distribution of Nonmonetary Assets to Stockholders as Dividends

In 20X2, the Company declared and paid a dividend to its stockholders in the form of shares of common stock of Santorest & Co., whose stock the Company held as an investment. The Company's stockholders received three shares of Santorest & Co. common stock for each share of the Company's stock held. As a result, retained earnings was charged a total of $317,000, which represents the aggregate market value of the shares of Santorest & Co. that were issued as a dividend. In connection with this transaction, the Company recognized a gain of $116,000 in 20X2, which represents the excess of the aggregate market value of the shares of Santorest & Co. issued over the aggregate carrying value of these shares.

Example 25–7: Spin-Off of a Business Segment

In May 20X2, the Company announced plans to spin off its electronic connectors business to shareholders in a tax-free distribution. In August 20X2, the Company's Board of Directors approved the spin-off effective December 31, 20X2, to shareholders of record as of December 17, 20X2, through the issuance of shares in a new legal entity, Electors, Inc. Common shares were distributed on a basis of one share of Electors, Inc. for every five shares of the Company's common stock.

The consolidated financial results of the Company have been restated to reflect the divestiture of Electors, Inc. Accordingly, the revenues, costs, and expenses; assets and liabilities; and cash flows of Electors, Inc. have been excluded from their respective captions in the Consolidated Statements of Income, Consolidated Balance Sheets, and Consolidated Statements of Cash Flows. These items have been reported as "Income from discontinued operations, net of income taxes" in the Consolidated Statements of Income; "Net assets of discontinued operations" in the Consolidated Balance Sheets; and "Net cash flows from discontinued operations" and "Net investing and financing activities of discontinued operations" in the Consolidated Statements of Cash Flows.

As of December 31, 20X2, the net assets of the discontinued segment of $4,289,000 have been charged against the Company's retained earnings to reflect the spin-off. During 20X2, the Company recorded a pretax charge of $615,000 ($483,000 after taxes) for expenses related to the spin-off.

The following table summarizes financial information for the discontinued operations for all periods presented:

	20X2	20X1
Net sales	$8,300,000	$8,750,000
Income before income taxes	$ 211,000	$ 273,000
Net income	$ 107,000	$ 182,000
Current assets	$2,436,000	$2,543,000
Total assets	$8,161,000	$8,615,000
Current liabilities	$2,597,000	$1,796,000
Total liabilities	$3,872,000	$3,978,000
Net assets of discontinued operations	$4,289,000	$4,637,000

Example 25–8: Revenues Recognized under Reciprocal Arrangements

On occasion, the Company has purchased goods or services for its operations from organizations at or about the same time that it licensed its software to these organizations. These transactions are recorded at terms the Company considers to be fair value. For these reciprocal arrangements, the Company considers Accounting Principles Board (ABP) Opinion No. 29, *Accounting for Nonmonetary Transactions*, and Emerging Issues Task Force (EITF) Issue No. 01-2, *Issues Related to the Accounting for Nonmonetary Transactions*, to determine whether the arrangement is a monetary or nonmonetary transaction. Transactions involving the exchange of boot representing 25% or greater of the fair value of the reciprocal arrangement are considered monetary transactions within the context of APB Opinion No. 29 and EITF Issue No. 01-2. Monetary transactions and nonmonetary transactions that represent the culmination of an earnings process are recorded at the fair value of the products delivered or products or services received, whichever is more readily determinable, providing the fair values are determinable within reasonable limits. In determining the fair values, the Company considers the recent history of cash sales of the same products or services in similar sized transactions. Revenues from such transactions may be recognized over a period of time as the products or services are received. For nonmonetary reciprocal arrangements that do not represent the culmination of the earnings process, the exchange is recorded based on the carrying value of the products delivered, which is generally zero.

Revenues recognized under reciprocal arrangements were approximately $4,579,000 in 20X2, of which $2,636,000 involved nonmonetary transactions, as defined above. The Company did not recognize any revenues under reciprocal arrangements in 20X1.

CHAPTER 26
PENSION PLANS

CONTENTS

EXECUTIVE SUMMARY

A *pension plan* may be broadly classified as either a defined benefit plan or a defined contribution plan. A *defined benefit pension plan* is one that contains a pension benefit formula, which generally describes the amount of pension benefit that each employee will receive for services performed during a specified period of employment. A *defined contribution pension plan* provides an individual account for each participant and specifies how contributions to each individual's account are determined.

Generally accepted accounting principles (GAAP) for employers' accounting for pension plans center on the determination of annual pension expense (identified as net periodic pension cost) and the presentation of an appropriate amount of pension liability in the statement of financial position. Net periodic pension cost has often been viewed as a single amount, but it is actually made up of several components that reflect different aspects of the employer's financial arrangements as well as the cost of benefits earned by employees.

A pension plan may be contributory or noncontributory; that is, the employees may be required to contribute to the plan (contributory), or the entire cost of the plan may be borne by the employer (noncontributory). A pension plan may be funded or unfunded; that is, the employees and/or the employer may make cash contributions to a pension plan trustee (funded), or the employer may make only credit entries on its books reflecting the pension liability under the plan (unfunded).

New Requirements under FAS-158

In September 2006, the FASB issued Statement of Financial Accounting Standards No. 158 (FAS-158), *Employers' Accounting for Defined Benefit Pension and Other Postretirement Plans.* This new standard requires employers of business entities with one or more defined benefit plans to: (1) recognize in their balance sheets an asset for a plan's overfunded status or a liability for a plan's underfunded status; (2) measure a plan's assets and its obligations that determine its funded status as of the end of the employer's fiscal year (eliminating the alternative of a measurement date that could be up to three months earlier under prior standards); and (3) recognize changes in the funded status of a plan through comprehensive income in the year in which the changes occur. FAS-158 also amends the disclosure requirements in the notes to the financial statements by requiring information about certain effects on net periodic benefit cost for the next fiscal year that arise from delayed recognition of the gains or losses, prior service costs or credits, and transition assets or obligations. FAS-158 does not change the accounting and reporting by defined contribution and multiemployer plans.

FAS-158 applies to plan sponsors that are public and private companies. The requirement to recognize the funded status of a benefit plan and the disclosure requirements are effective for fiscal years ending after December 15, 2006, for public entities, and for fiscal years that end after June 15, 2007, for all other entities. In addition, nonpublic entities are required to disclose certain information (specified later under "Disclosure Requirements") in the notes to the financial statements for fiscal years ending after December 15, 2006, but before June 16, 2007. The requirement to measure plan assets and benefit obligations as of the date of the employer's fiscal year-end balance sheet is effective for fiscal years ending after December 15, 2008, for all entities. Earlier application is encouraged and retrospective application is not permitted.

Under FAS-158, entities are no longer required to report on their balance sheets an additional minimum pension liability for their underfunded obligations (or any corresponding intangible asset), because the funded status of defined benefit plans will now be fully recognized on their balance sheets.

The discussion in the remainder of this chapter has been updated to reflect the requirements of FAS-158.

Defined Benefit Pension Plans

An entity's *net periodic pension cost* represents the net amount of pension cost for a specified period that is charged against income. Under GAAP, the components of net periodic pension cost are (a) service cost; (b) interest cost on the projected benefit obligation; (c) actual return on plan assets; (d) amortization of any prior service cost or credit included in accumulated other comprehensive income; (e) recognition of net gain or loss, if any; and (f) amortization of any net transition asset or obligation.

Net periodic pension cost is estimated in advance at the beginning of a period based on actuarial assumptions relating to (a) the discount rate on the projected benefit obligation, (b) the expected long-term rate of return on pension plan assets, and (c) the average remaining service periods of active employees covered by the pension plan. At the end of the period, adjustments are made to account for the differences (actuarial gains or losses), if any, between the estimated and actual amounts.

Employers must recognize the funded status of a benefit plan as the difference between the fair value of plan assets and the benefit obligations in their balance sheets. For a pension plan, the benefit obligation is the projected benefit obligation; for other postretirement plans, the benefit obligation is the accumulated benefit obligation. The funded status of all overfunded plans are aggregated and recognized as an asset in the employer's balance sheet. Similarly, the funded status of all underfunded plans are aggregated and recognized as a liability in the employer's balance sheet. The aggregate overfunded amount is presented as a noncurrent asset in the employer's balance sheet, whereas the aggregate underfunded amount is presented as a current liability, noncurrent liability, or combination of the two. The current portion is the amount by which the actuarial present value of the benefits included in the benefit obligation payable in the next 12 months or operating cycle, if longer, exceeds the fair value of plan assets.

In addition, employers recognize, as a component of other comprehensive income, the gains or losses and prior-service costs or credits that arise during the period but are not recognized as components of net periodic benefit cost of the period in accordance with Statement of Financial Accounting Standards (FAS) No. 87, *Employers' Accounting for Pensions*, and FAS-106, *Employers' Accounting for Postretirement Benefits Other Than Pensions*. Adjustments in other comprehensive income are recognized when the gains or losses, prior service costs or credits, and transition assets or obligations are subsequently recognized as components of net periodic pension cost in accordance with FAS-87, FAS-88, *Employers' Accounting for Settlements and Curtailments of Defined Benefit Pension Plans and for Termination Benefits*, and FAS-106.

Measurement date. Business entities are required to measure plan assets and benefit obligations as of the date of the fiscal year-end balance sheet unless:

- The plan is sponsored by a subsidiary that is consolidated using a fiscal period that differs from the parent company (as permitted by Accounting Research Bulletin No. 51, *Consolidated Financial Statements*), or
- The plan is sponsored by an investee that is accounted for by the equity method using a fiscal period that is different from the investor's (as permitted by Accounting Principles Board Opinion No. 18, *The Equity Method of Accounting for Investments in Common Stock*).

In these cases, the business entity must measure the subsidiary's plan assets and benefit obligations as of the date used to consolidate the subsidiary's balance sheet and the investee's plan assets and benefit obligations as of the date of the investee's financial statements used to apply the equity method.

Defined Contribution Pension Plans

A defined contribution pension plan provides for individual accounts for each plan participant and contains the terms that specify how contributions are determined for each participant's individual account. Each periodic employer contribution is allocated to each participant's individual account in accordance with the terms of the plan, and pension benefits are based solely on the amount available in each participant's account at the time of his or her retirement. The amount available in each participant's account at the time of his or her retirement is the total of the amounts contributed by the employer, plus the returns earned on investments of those contributions, plus forfeitures of other participants' benefits that have been allocated to the participant's account, and less any allocated administrative expenses.

The net periodic pension cost of a defined contribution pension plan is the amount of contributions in a period that are made to the individual accounts of participants who performed services during that same period. Contributions for periods after an individual retires or terminates should be estimated and accrued during periods in which the individual performs services.

Settlements, Curtailments, and Termination Benefits

A *settlement* of a pension plan is an irrevocable action that relieves the employer (or the plan) of primary responsibility for an obligation and eliminates significant risks related to the obligation and the assets used to effect the settlement. Examples of transactions that constitute a settlement include (a) making lump-sum cash payments to plan participants in exchange for their rights to receive specified pension benefits and (b) purchasing nonparticipating annuity contracts to cover vested benefits.

Gain or loss on a plan settlement is based on pension plan records that have been updated as of the day before the settlement. If the total pension plan obligation is settled by the employer, the maximum gain or loss is recognized. If part of the pension benefit obligation is settled, the employer must recognize a pro rata portion of the maximum gain or loss. For example, if a settlement results in a 40% reduction of the projected benefit obligation, an employer should recognize only 40% of the maximum gain or loss on the settlement. Gain or loss on a plan settlement is reported as an ordinary gain or loss, unless it meets the criteria of an extraordinary item.

A *curtailment* is a significant reduction in, or an elimination of, defined benefit accruals for present employees' future services. Examples of curtailments are (a) termination of employees' services earlier than expected, which may or may not involve closing a facility or discontinuing a segment of a business, and (b) termination or suspension of a plan so that employees do not earn additional defined benefits for future services.

If the total effects of a plan curtailment result in a loss, the loss is recognized when it is *probable* that the curtailment will occur and the effects of the curtailment can be *reasonably estimated*. If the total effects of a plan curtailment result in a gain, the gain is recognized only when the related employees terminate or the plan suspension or amendment is adopted. Gain or loss on the total effects of a pension plan curtailment is reported as an ordinary gain or loss, unless it meets the criteria of an extraordinary item.

Termination benefits are classified as either special or contractual. *Special termination benefits* are those that are offered to employees for a short period in connection with the termination of their employment. *Contractual termination benefits* are those that are required by the terms of an existing plan or agreement and that are provided only on the occurrence of a specified event, such as early retirement or the closing of a facility.

GAAP require employers to recognize the cost of termination benefits as a loss and corresponding liability. The recognition date depends on whether the benefits are special or contractual. The recognition date on which the employer records the loss and corresponding liability for special termination benefits occurs when (a) the employees accept the offer of the special termination benefits and (b) the amount of the cost of the benefits can be *reasonably estimated*. The recognition date on which the employer records the loss and corresponding liability for contractual termination benefits occurs when (a) it is *probable* that employees will be entitled to the benefits and (b) the amount of the cost of the benefits can be *reasonably estimated*. A loss on termination benefits is reported as an ordinary loss, unless it meets the criteria of an extraordinary item.

Authoritative Literature

FAS-87   Employers' Accounting for Pensions

FAS-88   Employers' Accounting for Settlements and Curtailments of Defined Benefit Pension Plans and for Termination Benefits

FAS-106   Employers' Accounting for Postretirement Benefits Other Than Pensions

FAS-109   Accounting for Income Taxes

FAS-130	Reporting Comprehensive Income
FAS-132R	Employers' Disclosures about Pensions and Other Postretirement Benefits (Revised 2003)
FAS-141	Business Combinations
FAS-158	Employers' Accounting for Defined Benefit Pension and Other Postretirement Plans
EITF 03-2	Accounting for the Transfer to the Japanese Government of the Substitutional Portion of Employee Pension Fund Liabilities

DISCLOSURE REQUIREMENTS

The disclosure requirements for pension plans apply to both public and nonpublic entities. However, with respect to defined benefit pension plans, nonpublic entities are allowed to provide reduced disclosures, if they so elect, regardless of materiality.

Also, companies that have defined benefit pension plans and other postretirement benefit plans may elect to present the required disclosures for their plans in a parallel format in a single note to the financial statements, since most of the disclosures about defined benefit pension plans and postretirement benefit plans are similar.

> **Note:** In September 2006, the FASB issued Statement of Financial Accounting Standards No. 158 (FAS-158) entitled *Employers' Accounting for Defined Benefit Pension and Other Postretirement Plans*. This standard amends FAS-87, *Employers' Accounting for Pensions*; FAS-88, *Employers' Accounting for Settlements and Curtailments of Defined Benefit Pension Plans and for Termination Benefits*; FAS-106, *Employers' Accounting for Postretirement Benefits Other Than Pensions*; and FAS-132 (Revised 2003), *Employers' Disclosures about Pensions and Other Postretirement Benefits*.
>
> For an employer with publicly traded equity securities, the disclosure and recognition provisions of FAS-158 are effective for financial statements with fiscal years ending after December 15, 2006. For an employer without publicly traded equity securities, the disclosure and recognition provisions of FAS-158 are effective for financial statements with fiscal years ending after June 15, 2007. Certain additional disclosures are required for employers without publicly traded equity securities until they apply the recognition provisions of FAS-158. For all employers, the measurement provisions of FAS-158 are effective for financial statements with fiscal years ending after December 15, 2008. Until that time, certain measurement-related disclosures continue to be required.

Defined Benefit Pension Plans—Disclosure Requirements for All Public Entities and for Those Nonpublic Entities That Elect to Voluntarily Provide These Disclosures (Annual Periods)—Prior to the Adoption of FAS-158

The following disclosures, which are applicable prior to the adoption of FAS-158, should be made for defined benefit pension plans:

1. A description of the plan (FAS-132R, par. 5)

2. For each income statement presented, the amount of net periodic pension cost recognized, showing separately the following (FAS-132R, par. 5h):

   a. Service cost component

   b. Interest cost component

   c. Expected return on plan assets for the period

   d. Amortization of the unrecognized transition obligation or asset

   e. Amount of recognized gains and losses

   f. Amount of prior service cost recognized

   g. Amount of gain or loss recognized due to a settlement or curtailment

3. For each balance sheet presented, the funded status of the plan, amounts not recognized in the entity's balance sheet, and amounts recognized in the entity's balance sheet, including the following (FAS-132R, par. 5c):

   a. The amount of any unamortized prior service cost

   b. The amount of unrecognized net gain or loss (including asset gains and losses not yet reflected in market-related value)

   c. The amount of any remaining unamortized, unrecognized net obligation, or net asset existing at the date of initial application of FAS-87

   d. The amount of net pension asset or liability

   e. Any intangible asset and the amount of accumulated other comprehensive income

4. For each balance sheet presented, a reconciliation of the beginning and ending balances of the benefit obligation, with separate disclosure of the following (FAS-132R, par. 5a):

   a. Service cost

   b. Interest cost

   c. Contributions by plan participants

    d. Actuarial gains and losses

    e. Foreign currency exchange rate changes

    f. Benefits paid

    g. Plan amendments

    h. Business combinations

    i. Divestitures

    j. Curtailments

    k. Settlements

    l. Special termination benefits

5. For each balance sheet presented, a reconciliation of the beginning and ending balances of the fair value of plan assets, including the effects of the following (FAS-132R, par. 5b):

    a. Actual return on plan assets

    b. Foreign currency exchange rate changes

    c. Contributions by employer

    d. Contributions by plan participants

    e. Benefits paid

    f. Business combinations

    g. Divestitures

    h. Settlements

6. For each income statement presented, the amount included within other comprehensive income arising from a change in the additional minimum pension liability recognized (FAS-132R, par. 5i)

7. For each balance sheet presented, the following assumptions used in the accounting for the plan (FAS-132R, par. 5j):

    a. The weighted-average assumed discount rates

    b. The weighted-average rates of compensation increase (for pay-related plans)

    c. The weighted-average expected long-term rates of return on plan assets specifying, in tabular format, the assumptions used to determine the benefit obligation and the net benefit cost

8. The following information about plan assets (FAS-132R, par. 5d):

    a. For each balance sheet presented, the percentage of the fair value of total plan assets held in each major category of plan assets, including at a minimum the following categories: (i) equity securities, (ii) debt securities, (iii) real estate, and (iv) all other assets. Also, disclosure of additional asset categories, and additional information about specific assets within a category, is encouraged if that information is considered useful

b. As of the latest balance sheet presented, a narrative description of investment policies and strategies, including: (i) target allocation percentages, or range of percentages, for each major category of plan assets presented on a weighted-average basis, and (ii) other factors that are pertinent to an understanding of the policies or strategies such as investment goals, risk management practices, permitted and prohibited investments including the use of derivatives, diversification, and the relationship between plan assets and benefit obligations

c. As of the latest balance sheet presented, a narrative description of the basis used to determine the overall expected long-term rate-of-return-on-assets assumption, such as: (i) the general approach used, (ii) the extent to which the overall rate-of-return-on-assets assumption was based on historical returns, (iii) the extent to which adjustments were made to those historical returns in order to reflect expectations of future returns, and (iv) how those adjustments were determined

9. For each balance sheet presented, the accumulated benefit obligation (FAS-132R, par. 5e)

10. Until the provisions of FAS-132 (Revised 2003) are adopted in full for domestic and foreign plans, financial statements that exclude foreign plans from the disclosure requirements of items 8 or 9 above, should disclose separately for domestic plans the following (FAS-132R, par. 19):

a. The total fair value of plan assets as of the date of the latest balance sheet presented

b. The overall expected long-term rate of return on assets for the latest period for which an income statement is presented

11. As of the latest balance sheet presented, the benefits expected to be paid in each of the next five fiscal years, and in the aggregate for the five fiscal years thereafter (FAS-132R, par. 5f)

12. The company's best estimate of contributions expected to be paid to the plan during the next fiscal year beginning after the date of the latest balance sheet presented (FAS-132R, par. 5g) (Estimated contributions may be presented in the aggregate for contributions required by funding regulations or laws, discretionary contributions, and noncash contributions)

13. The measurement date used to determine pension benefit information for the plans that make up at least the majority of plan assets and benefit obligations (FAS-132R, par. 5k)

14. The amounts and types of securities of the employer and related parties included in plan assets (FAS-132R, par. 5n)

15. The approximate amount of future annual benefits of plan participants covered by insurance contracts issued by the employer or related parties (FAS-132R, par. 5n)

16. Any significant transactions between the employer or related parties and the plan during the period (FAS-132R, par. 5n)

17. Any alternative amortization method used to amortize prior service costs or unrecognized net gains and losses (FAS-87, pars. 26 and 33; FAS-106, par. 60; FAS-132R, par. 5o)

18. Any substantive commitment, such as past practice or a history of regular benefit increases, used as the basis for accounting for the benefit obligation (FAS-132R, par. 5p)

19. The cost of providing special or contractual termination benefits recognized during the period and a description of the nature of the event (FAS-132R, par. 5q)

20. An explanation of any significant change in the benefit obligation or plan assets not otherwise apparent in the above disclosures (FAS-132R, par. 5r)

21. The disclosures for prior annual periods presented for comparative purposes as a result of applying the provisions of FAS-132 (Revised 2003), should be restated for (a) the percentages of each major category of plan assets held, (b) the accumulated benefit obligation, and (c) the assumptions used in the accounting for the plans (FAS-132R, par. 20) (If this is not practicable, the notes to the financial statements should include all available information and identify the information that is not available)

22. For employers with two or more defined benefit pension plans, if disclosures for plans with assets in excess of the accumulated benefit obligation have been combined with disclosures about plans with accumulated benefit obligations in excess of assets, the following disclosures should be made separately (FAS-132R, par. 6):

    a. The aggregate projected benefit obligation and aggregate fair value of plan assets for plans with projected benefit obligations in excess of plan assets

    b. The aggregate accumulated benefit obligation and aggregate fair value of plan assets for plans with accumulated benefit obligations in excess of plan assets

23. If two or more defined benefit pension plans are combined, the amounts recognized as prepaid benefit costs and accrued benefit liabilities should be disclosed separately (FAS-132R, par. 6)

24. Domestic and foreign defined benefit pension plans may be aggregated unless the benefit obligations of the foreign plans are significant relative to the total benefit obligation and the plans use significantly different assumptions (FAS-132R, par. 7)

Defined Benefit Pension Plans—Disclosure Requirements for All Public Entities and for Those Nonpublic Entities That Elect to Voluntarily Provide These Disclosures (Annual Periods)—After the Adoption of FAS-158

The following disclosures, which are applicable after the adoption of FAS-158, should be made for defined benefit pension plans:

1. A description of the plan (FAS-132R, par. 5)

2. For each income statement presented, the amount of net periodic pension cost recognized, showing separately the following (FAS-132R, par. 5h; FAS-158, par. E1d):

   a. Service cost component

   b. Interest cost component

   c. Expected return on plan assets for the period

   d. Gain or loss component

   e. Prior service cost or credit component

   f. Transition asset or obligation component

   g. Amount of gain or loss recognized due to settlements or curtailments

3. For each balance sheet presented, the funded status of the plans and the amounts recognized in the entity's balance sheet, showing separately the assets and current and noncurrent liabilities recognized (FAS-132R, par. 5c; FAS-158, par. E1c)

4. For each balance sheet presented, a reconciliation of the beginning and ending balances of the benefit obligation, with separate disclosure of the following (FAS-132R, par. 5a):

   a. Service cost

   b. Interest cost

   c. Contributions by plan participants

   d. Actuarial gains and losses

  e.   Foreign currency exchange rate changes

  f.   Benefits paid

  g.   Plan amendments

  h.   Business combinations

  i.   Divestitures

  j.   Curtailments

  k.   Settlements

  l.   Special termination benefits

5.   For each balance sheet presented, a reconciliation of the beginning and ending balances of the fair value of plan assets, including the effects of the following (FAS-132R, par. 5b):

  a.   Actual return on plan assets

  b.   Foreign currency exchange rate changes

  c.   Contributions by employer

  d.   Contributions by plan participants

  e.   Benefits paid

  f.   Business combinations

  g.   Divestitures

  h.   Settlements

6.   For each income statement presented (FAS-132R, pars. 5i and 10A–B; FAS-158, pars. E1e and E1t):

  a.   The net gain or loss and net prior service cost or credit recognized in other comprehensive income for the period pursuant to paragraphs 25 and 29 of FAS-87 and paragraphs 52 and 56 of FAS-106, as amended

  b.   Reclassification adjustments of other comprehensive income for the period

7.   For each income statement presented, the amounts in accumulated other comprehensive income that have not yet been recognized as components of net periodic benefit cost, showing separately the net gain or loss, net prior service cost or credit, and net transition asset or obligation (FAS-132R, pars. 5i and 10C; FAS-158, pars. E1f and E1t)

8.   For each balance sheet presented, the following assumptions used in the accounting for the plan (FAS-132R, par. 5j):

  a.   The weighted-average assumed discount rates

  b.   The weighted-average rates of compensation increase (for pay-related plans)

   c. The weighted-average expected long-term rates of return on plan assets specifying, in tabular format, the assumptions used to determine the benefit obligation and the net benefit cost

9. The following information about plan assets (FAS-132R, par. 5d):

   a. For each balance sheet presented, the percentage of the fair value of total plan assets held in each major category of plan assets, including at a minimum the following categories: (i) equity securities, (ii) debt securities, (iii) real estate, and (iv) all other assets. Also, disclosure of additional asset categories and additional information about specific assets within a category is encouraged if that information is considered useful

   b. As of the latest balance sheet presented, a narrative description of investment policies and strategies, including (i) target allocation percentages, or range of percentages, for each major category of plan assets presented on a weighted-average basis, and (ii) other factors that are pertinent to an understanding of the policies or strategies, such as investment goals, risk management practices, permitted and prohibited investments, including the use of derivatives, diversification, and the relationship between plan assets and benefit obligations

   c. As of the latest balance sheet date presented, a narrative description of the basis used to determine the overall expected long-term rate-of-return-on-assets assumption, such as (i) the general approach used, (ii) the extent to which the overall rate-of-return-on-assets assumption was based on historical returns, (iii) the extent to which adjustments were made to those historical returns in order to reflect expectations of future returns, and (iv) how those adjustments were determined

10. For each balance sheet presented, the accumulated benefit obligation (FAS-132R, par. 5e)

11. Until the provisions of FAS-132 (Revised 2003) are adopted in full for domestic and foreign plans, financial statements that exclude foreign plans from the disclosure requirements of items 9 or 10 above, should disclose separately for domestic plans the following (FAS-132R, par. 19):

   a. The total fair value of plan assets as of the date of the latest balance sheet presented

   b. The overall expected long-term rate of return on assets for the latest period for which an income statement is presented

12. As of the latest balance sheet presented, the benefits expected to be paid in each of the next five fiscal years, and in the aggregate for the five fiscal years thereafter (FAS-132R, par. 5f)

13. The company's best estimate of contributions expected to be paid to the plan during the next fiscal year beginning after the date of the latest balance sheet presented (FAS-132R, par. 5g) (Estimated contributions may be presented in the aggregate for contributions required by funding regulations or laws, discretionary contributions, and noncash contributions)

14. The amounts and types of securities of the employer and related parties included in plan assets (FAS-132R, par. 5n)

15. The approximate amount of future annual benefits of plan participants covered by insurance contracts issued by the employer or related parties (FAS-132R, par. 5n)

16. Any significant transactions between the employer or related parties and the plan during the period (FAS-132R, par. 5n)

17. Any alternative amortization method used to amortize prior service costs or net gains and losses (FAS-87, pars. 26 and 33; FAS-106, par. 60; FAS-132R, par. 5o; FAS-158, pars. C2d, C2h, D2k, and E1h)

18. Any substantive commitment, such as past practice or a history of regular benefit increases, used as the basis for accounting for the benefit obligation (FAS-132R, par. 5p)

19. The cost of providing special or contractual termination benefits recognized during the period and a description of the nature of the event (FAS-132R, par. 5q)

20. An explanation of any significant change in the benefit obligation or plan assets not otherwise apparent in the above disclosures (FAS-132R, par. 5r)

21. For each balance sheet presented, the amounts in accumulated other comprehensive income expected to be recognized as components of net periodic benefit cost over the fiscal year that follows the most recent annual balance sheet presented, showing separately the net gain or loss, net prior service cost or credit, and net transition asset or obligation (FAS-132R, pars. 5s and 10C; FAS-158, pars. E1i and E1t)

22. The amount and timing of any plan assets expected to be returned to the employer during the 12-month period, or operating cycle, if longer, that follows the most recent annual balance sheet presented (FAS-132R, par. 5t; FAS-158, par. E1j)

23. The disclosures for prior annual periods presented for comparative purposes as a result of applying the provisions of

FAS-132 (Revised 2003), should be restated for (a) the percentages of each major category of plan assets held, (b) the accumulated benefit obligation, and (c) the assumptions used in the accounting for the plans (FAS-132R, par. 20) (If this is not practicable, the notes to the financial statements should include all available information and identify the information that is not available)

24. For employers with two or more defined benefit pension plans, if disclosures for plans that have accumulated benefit obligations in excess of plan assets and plans that have plan assets in excess of accumulated benefit obligations are presented on a combined basis, the following disclosures should be made separately with respect to plans that have *projected* benefit obligations in excess of plan assets (FAS-132R, par. 6):

    a. The aggregate projected benefit obligations

    b. The aggregate fair value of plan assets

25. For employers with two or more defined benefit pension or postretirement plans, if disclosures for plans that have accumulated benefit obligations in excess of plan assets and plans that have plan assets in excess of accumulated benefit obligations are presented on a combined basis, the following disclosures should be made separately with respect to plans that have *accumulated* benefit obligations in excess of plan assets (FAS-132R, par. 6):

    a. The aggregate accumulated benefit obligations

    b. The aggregate fair value of plan assets

26. Domestic and foreign defined benefit pension plans may be aggregated unless the benefit obligations of the foreign plans are significant relative to the total benefit obligation and the plans use significantly different assumptions (FAS-132R, par. 7)

27. The following information disclosed separately for pension plans and other postretirement benefit plans (FAS-158, par. 7):

    a. For each annual statement of income presented, the amounts recognized in other comprehensive income, showing separately the net gain or loss and net prior service cost or credit

    b. The amounts disclosed in item a above separated into amounts arising during the period and reclassification adjustments of other comprehensive income as a result of being recognized as components of net periodic benefit cost for the period

  c. For each annual statement of income presented, the net transition asset or obligation recognized as a reclassification adjustment of other comprehensive income as a result of being recognized as a component of net periodic benefit cost for the period

  d. For each annual statement of financial position presented, the amounts in accumulated other comprehensive income that have not yet been recognized as components of net periodic benefit cost, showing separately the net gain or loss, net prior service cost or credit, and net transition asset or obligation

  e. The amounts in accumulated other comprehensive income expected to be recognized as components of net periodic benefit cost over the fiscal year that follows the most recent annual statement of financial position presented, showing separately the net gain or loss, net prior service cost or credit, and net transition asset or obligation

  f. The amount and timing of any plan assets expected to be returned to the business entity during the 12-month period, or operating cycle, if longer, that follows the most recent annual statement of financial position presented

 28. The following transitional disclosures upon implementation of FAS-158:

  a. In the year that the recognition provisions of FAS-158 are initially applied, the incremental effect of applying FAS-158 on individual line items in the year-end balance sheet (FAS-158, par. 20)

  b. In the year that the measurement date provisions of FAS-158 are initially applied, the separate adjustments of both retained earnings and accumulated other comprehensive income from applying FAS-158 (FAS-158, par. 21)

Defined Benefit Pension Plans—Reduced Disclosure Requirements for Nonpublic Entities (Annual Periods)—Prior to the Adoption of FAS-158

The following are the reduced disclosure requirements for defined benefit pension plans of nonpublic entities that are applicable prior to the adoption of FAS-158:

 1. A brief description of the plan (FAS-132R, par. 8)

 2. For each balance sheet presented, the following information about the plan (FAS-132R, par. 8a):

  a. The benefit obligation

b. The fair value of plan assets

c. The funded status of the plan

3. For each income statement presented, the following information about the plan (FAS-132R, par. 8b):

a. Employer contributions

b. Participant contributions

c. Benefits paid

4. The following information about plan assets (FAS-132R, par. 8c):

a. For each balance sheet presented, the percentage of the fair value of total plan assets held in each major category of plan assets, including at a minimum the following categories: (i) equity securities, (ii) debt securities, (iii) real estate, and (iv) all other assets. Also, disclosure of additional asset categories, and additional information about specific assets within a category, is encouraged if that information is considered useful

b. As of the latest balance sheet presented, a narrative description of investment policies and strategies, including: (i) target allocation percentages, or range of percentages, for each major category of plan assets presented on a weighted-average basis, and (ii) other factors that are pertinent to an understanding of the policies or strategies such as investment goals, risk management practices, permitted and prohibited investments including the use of derivatives, diversification, and the relationship between plan assets and benefit obligations

c. As of the latest balance sheet presented, a narrative description of the basis used to determine the overall expected long-term rate-of-return-on-assets assumption, such as: (i) the general approach used, (ii) the extent to which the overall rate-of-return-on-assets assumption was based on historical returns, (iii) the extent to which adjustments were made to those historical returns in order to reflect expectations of future returns, and (iv) how those adjustments were determined

5. For each balance sheet presented, the accumulated benefit obligation (FAS-132R, par. 8d)

6. As of the latest balance sheet presented, the benefits expected to be paid in each of the next five fiscal years, and in the aggregate for the five fiscal years thereafter (FAS-132R, par. 8e)

7. The company's best estimate of contributions expected to be paid to the plan during the next fiscal year beginning after the

date of the latest balance sheet presented (FAS-132R, par. 8f) (Estimated contributions may be presented in the aggregate for contributions required by funding regulations or laws, discretionary contributions, and noncash contributions)

8. For each balance sheet presented, the amounts recognized in the balance sheet, including (FAS-132R, par. 8g):

   a. The net pension prepaid assets or accrued liabilities

   b. The amount of any intangible asset recognized

   c. The amount of accumulated other comprehensive income recognized

9. For each income statement presented, the amount of net periodic benefit cost recognized and the amount included within other comprehensive income arising from a change in the minimum pension liability recognized pursuant to FAS-87, paragraph 37, as amended (FAS-132R, par. 8h)

10. For each balance sheet presented, the following assumptions used in the accounting for the plan (FAS-132R, par. 8i):

    a. The weighted-average assumed discount rates

    b. The weighted-average rates of compensation increase (for pay-related plans)

    c. The weighted-average expected long-term rates of return on plan assets specifying, in tabular format, the assumptions used to determine the benefit obligation and the net benefit cost

11. The measurement date used to determine pension benefit information for the plans that make up at least the majority of plan assets and benefit obligations (FAS-132R, par. 8j)

12. The amounts and types of securities of the employer and related parties included in plan assets (FAS-132R, par. 8l)

13. The approximate amount of future annual benefits of plan participants covered by insurance contracts issued by the employer or related parties (FAS-132R, par. 8l)

14. Any significant transactions between the employer or related parties and the plan during the period (FAS-132R, par. 8l)

15. The nature and effect of significant nonroutine events, such as amendments, combinations, divestitures, curtailments, and settlements (FAS-132R, par. 8m)

16. The disclosures for prior annual periods presented for comparative purposes as a result of applying the provisions of FAS-132 (Revised 2003), should be restated for: (a) the percentages of each major category of plan assets held, (b) the accumulated benefit obligation, and (c) the assumptions used in

the accounting for the plans (FAS-132R, par. 20) (If this is not practicable, the notes to the financial statements should include all available information and identify the information that is not available)

17. For employers with two or more defined benefit pension plans, if disclosures for plans with assets in excess of the accumulated benefit obligation have been combined with disclosures about plans with accumulated benefit obligations in excess of assets, the following disclosures should be made separately (FAS-132R, par. 6):

    a. The aggregate projected benefit obligation and aggregate fair value of plan assets for plans with projected benefit obligations in excess of plan assets

    b. The aggregate accumulated benefit obligation and aggregate fair value of plan assets for plans with accumulated benefit obligations in excess of plan assets

18. If two or more defined benefit pension plans are combined, the amounts recognized as prepaid benefit costs and accrued benefit liabilities should be disclosed separately (FAS-132R, par. 6)

19. Domestic and foreign defined benefit pension plans may be aggregated unless the benefit obligations of the foreign plans are significant relative to the total benefit obligation and the plans use significantly different assumptions (FAS-132R, par. 7)

20. For fiscal years ending after December 15, 2006, but before June 16, 2007, for entities that have not applied the recognition provisions of FAS-158, the following disclosures should be made (FAS-158, par. 14):

    a. A brief description of the provisions of FAS-158

    b. The date that the adoption of FAS-158 is required

    c. The date the employer plans to adopt the recognition provisions of FAS-158, if earlier

Defined Benefit Pension Plans—Reduced Disclosure Requirements for Nonpublic Entities (Annual Periods)—After the Adoption of FAS-158

The following are the reduced disclosure requirements for defined benefit pension plans of nonpublic entities that are applicable after the adoption of FAS-158:

1. A brief description of the plan (FAS-132R, par. 8)

2. For each balance sheet presented, the following information about the plan (FAS-132R, par. 8a):

    a. The benefit obligation

    b. The fair value of plan assets

    c. The funded status of the plan

3. For each income statement presented, the following information about the plan (FAS-132R, par. 8b):

    a. Employer contributions

    b. Participant contributions

    c. Benefits paid

4. The following information about plan assets (FAS-132R, par. 8c):

    a. For each balance sheet presented, the percentage of the fair value of total plan assets held in each major category of plan assets, including at a minimum the following categories: (i) equity securities, (ii) debt securities, (iii) real estate, and (iv) all other assets. In addition, disclosure of additional asset categories and additional information about specific assets within a category is encouraged if that information is considered useful

    b. As of the latest balance sheet presented, a narrative description of investment policies and strategies, including (i) target allocation percentages, or range of percentages, for each major category of plan assets presented on a weighted-average basis, and (ii) other factors that are pertinent to an understanding of the policies or strategies, such as investment goals, risk management practices, and permitted and prohibited investments, including the use of derivatives, diversification, and the relationship between plan assets and benefit obligations

    c. As of the latest balance sheet presented, a narrative description of the basis used to determine the overall expected long-term rate-of-return-on-assets assumption, such as (i) the general approach used, (ii) the extent to which the overall rate-of-return-on-assets assumption was based on historical returns, (iii) the extent to which adjustments were made to those historical returns in order to reflect expectations of future returns, and (iv) how those adjustments were determined

5. For each balance sheet presented, the accumulated benefit obligation (FAS-132R, par. 8d)

6. As of the latest balance sheet presented, the benefits expected to be paid in each of the next five fiscal years, and in the aggregate for the five fiscal years thereafter (FAS-132R, par. 8e)

7. The company's best estimate of contributions expected to be paid to the plan during the next fiscal year beginning after the date of the latest balance sheet presented (FAS-132R, par. 8f) (Estimated contributions may be presented in the aggregate for contributions required by funding regulations or laws, discretionary contributions, and noncash contributions)

8. For each balance sheet presented, the amounts recognized in the balance sheet, including showing separately the benefit assets and current and noncurrent benefit liabilities (FAS-132R, par. 8g; FAS-158, par. E1m)

9. For each income statement presented (FAS-132R, pars. 8h and 10A–B; FAS-158, pars. E1m and E1t):

   a. The net gain or loss and net prior service cost or credit recognized in other comprehensive income for the period pursuant to paragraphs 25 and 29 of FAS-87 and paragraphs 52 and 56 of FAS-106, as amended

   b. Reclassification adjustments of other comprehensive income for the period

10. For each income statement presented, the amounts in accumulated other comprehensive income that have not yet been recognized as components of net periodic benefit cost, showing separately the net gain or loss, net prior service cost or credit, and net transition asset or obligation (FAS-132R, pars. 8h and 10C; FAS-158, pars. E1o and E1t)

11. For each balance sheet presented, the following assumptions used in the accounting for the plan (FAS-132R, par. 8i):

    a. The weighted-average assumed discount rates

    b. The weighted-average rates of compensation increase (for pay-related plans)

    c. The weighted average expected long-term rates of return on plan assets specifying, in tabular format, the assumptions used to determine the benefit obligation and the net benefit cost

12. The amounts and types of securities of the employer and related parties included in plan assets (FAS-132R, par. 8l)

13. The approximate amount of future annual benefits of plan participants covered by insurance contracts issued by the employer or related parties (FAS-132R, par. 8l)

14. Any significant transactions between the employer or related parties and the plan during the period (FAS-132R, par. 8l)

15. The nature and effect of significant nonroutine events, such as amendments, combinations, divestitures, curtailments, and settlements (FAS-132R, par. 8m)

16. For each balance sheet presented, the amounts in accumulated other comprehensive income expected to be recognized as components of net periodic benefit cost over the fiscal year that follows the most recent annual balance sheet presented, showing separately the net gain or loss, net prior service cost or credit, and net transition asset or obligation (FAS-132R, pars. 8n and 10C; FAS-158, par. E1q)

17. The amount and timing of any plan assets expected to be returned to the employer during the 12-month period, or operating cycle, if longer, that follows the most recent annual balance sheet presented (FAS-132R, par. 8o; FAS-158, par. E1r)

18. The disclosures for prior annual periods that are presented for comparative purposes as a result of applying the provisions of FAS-132 (Revised 2003), should be restated for (a) the percentages of each major category of plan assets held, (b) the accumulated benefit obligation, and (c) the assumptions used in the accounting for the plans (FAS-132R, par. 20) (If this is not practicable, the notes to the financial statements should include all available information and identify the information that is not available.)

19. For employers with two or more defined benefit pension plans, if disclosures for plans that have accumulated benefit obligations in excess of plan assets and plans that have plan assets in excess of accumulated benefit obligations are presented on a combined basis, the following disclosures should be made separately with respect to plans that have *projected* benefit obligations in excess of plan assets (FAS-132R, par. 6; FAS-158, par. E1k):

    a. The aggregate projected benefit obligations

    b. The aggregate fair value of plan assets

20. For employers with two or more defined benefit pension or postretirement plans, if disclosures for plans that have accumulated benefit obligations in excess of plan assets and plans that have plan assets in excess of accumulated benefit obligations are presented on a combined basis, the following disclosures should be made separately with respect to plans that have *accumulated* benefit obligations in excess of plan assets (FAS-132R, par. 6; FAS-158, par. E1k):

    a. The aggregate accumulated benefit obligations

    b. The aggregate fair value of plan assets

21. Domestic and foreign defined benefit pension plans may be aggregated unless the benefit obligations of the foreign plans are significant relative to the total benefit obligation and the plans use significantly different assumptions (FAS-132R, par. 7)

22. The following information disclosed separately for pension plans and other postretirement benefit plans (FAS-158, par. 7):

   a. For each annual statement of income presented, the amounts recognized in other comprehensive income, showing separately the net gain or loss and net prior service cost or credit

   b. The amounts disclosed in item a above separated into amounts arising during the period and reclassification adjustments of other comprehensive income as a result of being recognized as components of net periodic benefit cost for the period

   c. For each annual statement of income presented, the net transition asset or obligation recognized as a reclassification adjustment of other comprehensive income as a result of being recognized as a component of net periodic benefit cost for the period

   d. For each annual statement of financial position presented, the amounts in accumulated other comprehensive income that have not yet been recognized as components of net periodic benefit cost, showing separately the net gain or loss, net prior service cost or credit, and net transition asset or obligation

   e. The amounts in accumulated other comprehensive income expected to be recognized as components of net periodic benefit cost over the fiscal year that follows the most recent annual statement of financial position presented, showing separately the net gain or loss, net prior service cost or credit, and net transition asset or obligation

   f. The amount and timing of any plan assets expected to be returned to the business entity during the 12-month period, or operating cycle, if longer, that follows the most recent annual statement of financial position presented

23. The following transitional disclosures upon implementation of FAS-158:

   a. In the year that the recognition provisions of FAS-158 are initially applied, the incremental effect of applying FAS-158 on individual line items in the year-end balance sheet (FAS-158, par. 20)

   b. In the year that the measurement date provisions of FAS-158 are initially applied, the separate adjustments of both retained earnings and accumulated other comprehensive income from applying FAS-158 (FAS-158, par. 21)

Defined Benefit Pension Plans—Disclosure Requirements for Public and Nonpublic Entities (Interim Periods)

Public entities Public entities should disclose the following information in their interim financial statements (FAS-132R, par. 9):

1. For each income statement presented, the amount of net periodic benefit cost recognized, showing separately the following:

   a. Service cost component

   b. Interest cost component

   c. Expected return on plan assets for the period

   d. Amortization of the unrecognized transition obligation or asset

   e. Amount of recognized gains or losses

   f. Amount of prior service cost recognized

   g. Amount of gain or loss recognized due to a settlement or curtailment

2. The total amount of the employer's contributions paid, and expected to be paid, during the current fiscal year, if significantly different from amounts previously disclosed (Estimated contributions may be presented in the aggregate for contributions required by funding regulations or laws, discretionary contributions, and noncash contributions)

Nonpublic entities Nonpublic entities should disclose the total amount of the employer's contributions paid, and expected to be paid, during the current fiscal year, if significantly different from amounts previously disclosed. Estimated contributions may be presented in the aggregate for contributions required by funding regulations or laws, discretionary contributions, and noncash contributions (FAS-132R, par. 10).

Defined Contribution Pension Plans

The following disclosures should be made for defined contribution pension plans:

1. A brief description of the plan (FAS-132R, par. 11)

2. The amount of cost recognized as expense during the period (FAS-132R, par. 11)

3. The nature and effect of significant matters affecting comparability of information for all periods presented, such as a

change in the rate of employer contributions, business combinations, or divestitures (FAS-132R, par. 11)

Multiemployer Pension Plans

The following disclosures should be made for multiemployer pension plans:

1. The amount of employer contributions during the period (amounts attributable to pensions and other postretirement benefit plans may be combined) (FAS-132R, par. 12)

2. A description of the nature and effect of any changes affecting comparability, such as a change in the rate of employer contributions, business combinations, or divestitures (FAS-132R, par. 12)

3. If it is either probable or reasonably possible that an employer would withdraw from a multiemployer plan under circumstances that would give rise to a withdrawal obligation, disclosure of the information required by FAS-5 should be made (FAS-132R, par. 13)

Japanese Employee Pension Fund Plans

The following disclosures should be made for employers with Japanese Employees' Pension Fund (EPF) plans that have accounted for the separation of the "substitutional portion" of the benefit obligation of an EPF in Japan from the corporate portion and the transfer of the "substitutional portion" and related assets to the Japanese government (EITF 03-2, par. 8):

1. The difference between the obligation settled and the assets transferred to the government, determined in accordance with the government formula and displayed as a subsidy from the government

2. Separate from the government subsidy, the derecognition of previously accrued salary progression at the time of settlement

EXAMPLES OF FINANCIAL STATEMENT DISCLOSURES

The following sample disclosures are available on the accompanying disc.

Illustrations under FAS-158: Defined Benefit Plans

Example 26–1: Defined Benefit Pension Plans—Public Entities

The Company sponsors two funded defined benefit pension plans for eligible employees who are 21 years of age with one or more years of service and who are not covered by collective bargaining agreements. Benefits paid to retirees are based on age at retirement, years of credited service, and average compensation. The Company's funding policy is to contribute the larger of the amount required to fully fund the plan's current liability or the amount necessary to meet the funding requirements as defined by the Internal Revenue Code.

In addition, the Company sponsors an unfunded Executive Pension Plan. This plan is nonqualified and provides certain key employees defined pension benefits that supplement those provided by the Company's other retirement plans.

The following table sets forth the benefit obligation, fair value of plan assets, and the funded status of the Company's plans; amounts recognized in the Company's financial statements; and the principal weighted-average assumptions used:

	20X2	20X1
Change in projected benefit obligation:		
Benefit obligation at beginning of year	$27,800,000	$23,200,000
Service cost	1,700,000	1,500,000
Interest cost	1,900,000	2,000,000
Actuarial loss	4,700,000	1,900,000
Divestitures	(100,000)	-0-
Curtailments	(5,800,000)	-0-
Benefits paid	(1,300,000)	(800,000)
Benefit obligation at end of year	$28,900,000	$27,800,000
Change in plan assets:		
Fair value of plan assets at beginning of year	$22,700,000	$18,300,000
Actual return on plan assets	1,200,000	4,500,000
Employer contributions	1,300,000	700,000
Divestitures	(300,000)	-0-
Benefits paid	(900,000)	(800,000)
Fair value of plan assets at end of year	$24,000,000	$22,700,000
Funded status at end of year	$(4,900,000)	$(5,100,000)

Amounts recognized in the balance sheets consist of:

Noncurrent assets	$300,000	$300,000
Current liabilities	(1,500,000)	(1,500,000)
Noncurrent liabilities	(3,700,000)	(3,900,000)
	$(4,900,000)	$(5,100,000)

Amounts recognized in accumulated other comprehensive income consist of the following:

	20X2	20X1
Net loss (gain)	$(1,700,000)	$(1,800,000)
Prior service cost (credit)	500,000	1,600,000
	$(1,200,000)	$(200,000)

The following are weighted-average assumptions used to determine benefit obligations at December 31, 20X2, and December 31, 20X1:

	20X2	20X1
Discount rate	6.75%	7.00%
Rate of compensation increase	5.25%	4.75%

The following are weighted-average assumptions used to determine net periodic benefit cost for the years ended December 31, 20X2, and December 31, 20X1:

	20X2	20X1
Discount rate	7.00%	7.25%
Expected long-term return on plan assets	8.00%	7.75%
Rate of compensation increase	5.50%	5.00%

The Company's expected long-term return on plan assets assumption is based on a periodic review and modeling of the plans' asset allocation and liability structure over a long-term period. Expectations of returns for each asset class are the most important of the assumptions used in the review and modeling and are based on comprehensive reviews of historical data and economic/financial market theory. The expected long-term rate of return on assets was selected from within the reasonable range of rates determined by (1) historical real returns, net of inflation, for the asset classes covered by the investment policy and (2) projections of inflation over the long-term period during which benefits are payable to plan participants.

Components of net periodic benefit cost and other amounts recognized in other comprehensive income are as follows:

	20X2	20X1
Net Periodic Benefit Cost:		
Service cost	$1,700,000	$1,500,000
Interest cost on projected benefit obligations	1,900,000	2,000,000
Expected return on plan assets	(1,800,000)	(1,300,000)
Amortization of prior service cost	100,000	200,000
Amortization of actuarial loss	200,000	-0-
Net periodic benefit cost	2,100,000	2,400,000
Other Changes in Plan Assets and Benefit Obligations Recognized in Other Comprehensive Income:		
Net loss (gain)	100,000	300,000
Prior service cost (credit)	(1,000,000)	(800,000)
Amortization of prior service cost	(100,000)	(200,000)
Total recognized in other comprehensive income	(1,000,000)	(700,000)
Total recognized in net periodic benefit cost and other comprehensive income	$1,100,000	$1,700,000

The estimated net gain and prior service cost for the defined benefit pension plans that will be amortized from accumulated other comprehensive income into net periodic benefit cost over the next fiscal year are $300,000 and $100,000, respectively.

The following table summarizes the Company-sponsored pension plans that have projected benefit obligations in excess of plan assets and the accumulated benefit obligation of the unfunded Executive Pension Plan in which the accumulated benefit obligation exceeds plan assets:

	20X2	20X1
Projected benefit obligation in excess of plan assets:		
Projected benefit obligation	$3,900,000	$4,200,000
Fair value of plan assets	$2,800,000	$2,600,000
Accumulated benefit obligation in excess of plan assets:		
Accumulated benefit obligation	$1,300,000	$1,100,000
Fair value of plan assets	$ -0-	$ -0-

The accumulated benefit obligation for all defined benefit pension plans was $16,100,000 and $14,700,000 at December 31, 20X2, and December 31, 20X1, respectively.

The Company's pension plan weighted-average asset allocations at December 31, 20X2, and December 31, 20X1, by asset category, are as follows:

	Plan Assets at December 31,	
	20X2	20X1
Asset Category		
Equity securities	55%	52%
Debt securities	28	31
Real estate	10	11
Other	7	6
Total	100%	100%

The Company's target asset allocation as of December 31, 20X2, by asset category, is as follows:

Asset Category	
Equity securities	50–70%
Debt securities	30–50%
Real estate	0–20%
Other	0–20%

The Company's investment policy includes various guidelines and procedures designed to ensure assets are invested in a manner necessary to meet expected future benefits earned by participants. The investment guidelines consider a broad range of economic conditions. Central to the policy are target allocation ranges (shown above) by major asset categories.

The objectives of the target allocations are to maintain investment portfolios that diversify risk through prudent asset allocation parameters, achieve asset returns that meet or exceed the plans' actuarial assumptions, and achieve asset returns that are competitive with like institutions employing similar investment strategies.

The investment policy is periodically reviewed by the Company and a designated third-party fiduciary for investment matters. The policy is established and administered in a manner that is compliant at all times with applicable government regulations.

Equity securities include common stock of Ace Ltd. in the amounts of $1,200,000 (5% of total plan assets) and $1,589,000 (7% of total plan assets) at December 31, 20X2, and December 31, 20X1, respectively.

The Company expects to contribute $1,500,000 to its pension plan in 20X3.

The following pension benefit payments, which reflect expected future service, as appropriate, are expected to be paid:

20X3	$1,000,000
20X4	1,050,000
20X5	1,175,000
20X6	1,225,000
20X7	1,315,000
Years 20X8–20Y2	7,325,000

Example 26–2: Defined Benefit Pension Plans—Alternative Reduced Disclosures for a Nonpublic Entity

> **Note:** This example illustrates the alternative reduced disclosures for a nonpublic entity under FAS-158 using the same facts in Example 26–1.

The Company sponsors two funded defined benefit pension plans for eligible employees who are 21 years of age with one or more years of service and who are not covered by collective bargaining agreements. Benefits paid to retirees are based on age at retirement, years of credited service, and average compensation. The Company's funding policy is to contribute the larger of the amount required to fully fund the plan's current liability or the amount necessary to meet the funding requirements, as defined by the Internal Revenue Code.

In addition, the Company sponsors an unfunded Executive Pension Plan. This plan is nonqualified and provides certain key employees defined pension benefits that supplement those provided by the Company's other retirement plans.

	20X2	20X1
Projected benefit obligation at December 31	$ 28,900,000	$ 27,800,000
Fair value of plan assets at December 31	24,000,000	22,700,000
Funded status at end of year	$(4,900,000)	$ (5,100,000)
Amounts recognized in the balance sheets consist of:		
Noncurrent assets	$ 300,000	$ 300,000
Current liabilities	(1,5000,000)	(1,500,000)
Noncurrent liabilities	(3,700,000)	(3,900,000)
	$(4,900,000)	$(5,100,000)

The following are weighted-average assumptions used to determine benefit obligations at December 31, 20X2 and December 31, 20X1:

	20X2	20X1
Discount rate	6.75%	7.00%
Rate of compensation increase	5.25%	4.75%

The following are weighted-average assumptions used to determine net periodic benefit cost for the years ended December 31, 20X2 and December 31, 20X1:

	20X2	20X1
Discount rate	7.00%	7.25%
Expected long-term return on plan assets	8.00%	7.75%
Rate of compensation increase	5.50%	5.00%

The Company's expected long-term return on plan assets assumption is based on a periodic review and modeling of the plans' asset allocation and liability structure over a long-term period. Expectations of returns for each asset class are the most important of the assumptions used in the review and modeling and are based on comprehensive reviews of historical data and economic/financial market theory. The expected long-term rate of return on assets was selected from within the reasonable range of rates determined by (1) historical real returns, net of inflation, for the asset classes covered by the investment policy and (2) projections of inflation over the long-term period during which benefits are payable to plan participants.

Benefit cost	$ 2,100,000	$ 2,400,000
Employer contributions	$ 1,300,000	$ 700,000
Benefits paid	$ 300,000	$ 800,000

The following table summarizes the Company-sponsored pension plans that have projected benefit obligations in excess of plan assets and the accumulated benefit obligation of the unfunded Executive Pension Plan in which the accumulated benefit obligation exceeds plan assets:

	20X2	20X1
Projected benefit obligation in excess of plan assets:		
Projected benefit obligation	$3,900,000	$4,200,000
Fair value of plan assets	$2,800,000	$2,600,000
Accumulated benefit obligation in excess of plan assets:		
Accumulated benefit obligation	$1,300,000	$1,100,000
Fair value of plan assets	$ -0-	$ -0-

The accumulated benefit obligation for all defined benefit pension plans was $16,100,000 and $14,700,000 at December 31, 20X2, and December 31, 20X1, respectively.

The Company's pension plan weighted-average asset allocations at December 31, 20X2, and December 31, 20X1, by asset category, are as follows:

	Plan Assets at December 31,	
	20X2	20X1
Asset Category		
Equity securities	55%	52%
Debt securities	28	31
Real estate	10	11
Other	7	6
Total	100%	100%

The Company's target asset allocation as of December 31, 20X2, by asset category, is as follows:

Asset Category	
Equity securities	50–70%
Debt securities	30–50%
Real estate	0–20%
Other	0–20%

The Company's investment policy includes various guidelines and procedures designed to ensure assets are invested in a manner necessary to meet expected future benefits earned by participants. The investment guidelines consider a broad range of economic conditions. Central to the policy are target allocation ranges (shown above) by major asset categories.

The objectives of the target allocations are to maintain investment portfolios that diversify risk through prudent asset allocation parameters, achieve asset returns that meet or exceed the plans' actuarial assumptions, and achieve asset returns that are competitive with like institutions employing similar investment strategies.

The investment policy is periodically reviewed by the Company and a designated third-party fiduciary for investment matters. The policy is established and administered in a manner that is compliant at all times with applicable government regulations.

Equity securities include common stock of Ace Ltd. in the amounts of $1,200,000 (5% of total plan assets) and $1,589,000 (7% of total plan assets) at December 31, 20X2 and December 31, 20X1, respectively.

The Company expects to contribute $1,500,000 to its pension plan in 20X3.

The following pension benefit payments, which reflect expected future service, as appropriate, are expected to be paid:

20X3	$1,000,000
20X4	1,050,000
20X5	1,175,000
20X6	1,225,000
20X7	1,315,000
Years 20X8–20Y2	7,325,000

Example 26–3: Disclosures about Defined Benefit Pension Plans and Other Postretirement Benefit Plans Are Presented in a Parallel Format in a Single Note to the Financial Statements

The Company and its subsidiaries sponsor numerous defined benefit pension plans and other postretirement benefit plans. The following tables set forth the benefit obligation, the fair value of plan assets, and the funded status of the Company's plans; the amounts recognized in the Company's financial statements; and the principal weighted-average assumptions used:

	Pension Benefits		Postretirement Benefits	
	20X2	*20X1*	*20X2*	*20X1*
Change in benefit obligation:				
Benefit obligation at beginning of year	$1,266,000	$1,200,000	$ 738,000	$700,000
Service cost	76,000	72,000	36,000	32,000
Interest cost	114,000	108,000	65,000	63,000

	Pension Benefits 20X2	20X1	Postretirement Benefits 20X2	20X1
Plan participants' contributions	-0-	-0-	20,000	13,000
Amendments	120,000	-0-	75,000	-0-
Actuarial gain	(25,000)	-0-	(24,000)	-0-
Acquisition	900,000	-0-	600,000	-0-
Benefits paid	(125,000)	(114,000)	(90,000)	(70,000)
Benefit obligation at end of year	$2,326,000	$1,266,000	$1,420,000	$738,000

	Pension Benefits		Postretirement Benefits	
	20X2	20X1	20X2	20X1
Change in plan assets:				
Fair value of plan assets at beginning of year	$1,068,000	$ 880,000	$ 206,000	$ 87,000
Actual return on plan assets	29,000	188,000	(3,000)	24,000
Acquisition	1,000,000	-0-	25,000	-0-
Employer contribution	75,000	114,000	171,000	152,000
Plan participants' contributions	-0-	-0-	20,000	13,000
Benefits paid	(125,000)	(114,000)	(90,000)	(70,000)
Fair value of plan assets at end of year	$2,047,000	$ 1,068,000	$ 329,000	$ 206,000
Funded status at end of year	$ (279,000)	$ (198,000)	$(1,091,000)	$(532,000)
Amounts recognized in the balance sheets consist of:				
Noncurrent assets	$ 64,000	$ -0-	$ -0-	$ 68,000
Current liabilities	(100,000)	(48,000)	(400,000)	(200,000)
Noncurrent liabilities	(243,000)	(150,000)	(691,000)	(400,000)
	$(279,000)	$(198,000)	$(1,091,000)	$(532,000)

Amounts recognized in accumulated other comprehensive income consist of the following:

	Pension Benefits		Postretirement Benefits	
	20X2	20X1	20X2	20X1
Net loss (gain)	$ 83,000	$ 38,000	$ 59,000	$ 60,000
Prior service cost (credit)	260,000	160,000	585,000	540,000
	$ 343,000	$198,000	$644,000	$600,000

The following are weighted-average assumptions used to determine benefit obligations at December 31, 20X2, and December 31, 20X1:

	Pension Benefits		Postretirement Benefits	
	20X2	20X1	20X2	20X1
Discount rate	6.75%	7.00%	7.00%	7.25%
Rate of compensation increase	5.25%	4.75%	N/A	N/A

The following are weighted-average assumptions used to determine net periodic benefit cost for the years ended December 31, 20X2, and December 31, 20X1:

	Pension Benefits		Postretirement Benefits	
	20X2	20X1	20X2	20X1
Discount rate	7.00%	7.25%	7.25%	7.25%
Expected long-term return on plan assets	8.00%	7.75%	8.25%	8.50%
Rate of compensation increase	5.50%	5.00%	N/A	N/A

The Company's expected long-term return on plan assets assumption is based on a periodic review and modeling of the plans' asset allocation and liability structure over a long-term period. Expectations of returns for each asset class are the most important of the assumptions used in the review and modeling and are based on comprehensive reviews of historical data and economic/financial market theory. The expected long-term rate of return on assets was selected from within the reasonable range of rates determined by (1) historical real returns, net of inflation, for the asset classes covered by the investment policy and (2) projections of inflation over the long-term period during which benefits are payable to plan participants.

For measurement purposes, a 10% annual rate of increase in the per capita cost of covered healthcare benefits was assumed for 20X3. The rate was assumed to decrease gradually to 4% for 20X9 and remain at that level thereafter.

Components of net periodic benefit cost and other amounts recognized in other comprehensive income are as follows:

	Pension Benefits		Postretirement Benefits	
	20X2	20X1	20X2	20X1
Net Periodic Benefit Cost:				
Service cost	$ 76,000	$ 72,000	$ 36,000	$ 32,000
Interest cost	114,000	108,000	65,000	63,000
Expected return on plan assets	(107,000)	(88,000)	(21,000)	(9,000)
Amortization of prior service cost	20,000	20,000	30,000	30,000
Recognized net actuarial loss	8,000	2,000	1,000	1,000
Net periodic benefit cost	111,000	114,000	111,000	117,000
Other Changes in Plan Assets and Benefit Obligations Recognized in Other Comprehensive Income:				
Net loss (gain)	45,000	40,000	(1,000)	(15,000)
Prior service cost (credit)	120,000	70,000	75,000	90,000
Amortization of prior service cost	(20,000)	(20,000)	(30,000)	(30,000)

	Pension Benefits		Postretirement Benefits	
	20X2	*20X1*	*20X2*	*20X1*
Total recognized in other comprehensive income	145,000	90,000	44,000	45,000
Total recognized in net periodic benefit cost and other comprehensive income	$ 256,000	$ 204,000	$ 155,000	$ 162,000

The estimated net loss and prior service cost for the defined benefit pension plans that will be amortized from accumulated other comprehensive income into net periodic benefit cost over the next fiscal year are $25,000 and $60,000, respectively. The estimated net loss and prior service cost for the defined benefit postretirement plans that will be amortized from accumulated other comprehensive income into net periodic benefit cost over the next fiscal year are $35,000 and $90,000, respectively.

The Company acquired Massari, Ltd. on December 31, 20X2, including its pension plans. As a result, the Company's plans were amended to establish parity with the benefits provided by Massari, Ltd.

The Company has multiple nonpension postretirement benefit plans. The healthcare plans are contributory, with participants' contributions adjusted annually; the life insurance plans are noncontributory. Accounting for the healthcare plans anticipates future cost sharing changes to the written plan that are consistent with the Company's expressed intent to increase retiree contributions each year by 50% of the excess of the expected general inflation rate over 6%. On December 31, 20X2, the Company amended its postretirement healthcare plans to provide long-term care coverage.

Assumed healthcare cost trend rates have a significant effect on the amounts reported for the healthcare plans. A 1% point change in assumed healthcare cost trend rates would have the following effects:

	1% Point Increase	1% Point Decrease
Effect on total of service and interest cost components	$ 22,000	$ (20,000)
Effect on postretirement benefit obligation	$173,000	$(156,000)

The accumulated benefit obligation for all defined benefit pension plans was $733,000 and $650,000 at December 31, 20X2, and December 31, 20X1, respectively.

The Company's pension plans' weighted-average asset allocations at December 31, 20X2, and December 31, 20X1, by asset category, are as follows:

	Plan Assets at December 31,	
	20X2	*20X1*
Asset Category		
Equity securities	55%	52%
Debt securities	28	31
Real estate	10	11
Other	7	6
Total	100%	100%

The Company's target asset allocation as of December 31, 20X2, by asset category, is as follows:

Asset Category	
Equity securities	50–70%
Debt securities	30–50%
Real estate	0–20%
Other	0–20%

The Company's investment policy includes various guidelines and procedures designed to ensure assets are invested in a manner necessary to meet expected future benefits earned by participants. The investment guidelines consider a broad range of economic conditions. Central to the policy are target allocation ranges (shown above) by major asset categories.

The objectives of the target allocations are to maintain investment portfolios that diversify risk through prudent asset allocation parameters, achieve asset returns that meet or exceed the plans' actuarial assumptions, and achieve asset returns that are competitive with like institutions employing similar investment strategies.

The investment policy is periodically reviewed by the Company and a designated third-party fiduciary for investment matters. The policy is established and administered in a manner that is compliant at all times with applicable government regulations.

Equity securities include common stock of Ace Ltd. in the amounts of $102,000 (5% of total plan assets) and $75,000 (7% of total plan assets) at December 31, 20X2, and December 31, 20X1, respectively.

The Company's postretirement benefit plans weighted-average asset allocations at December 31, 20X2, and December 31, 20X1, by asset category, are as follows:

	Plan Assets at December 31,	
	20X2	*20X1*
Asset Category		
Equity securities	57%	54%
Debt securities	26	29
Real estate	12	8
Other	5	9
Total	100%	100%

The Company's target asset allocation as of December 31, 20X2, by asset category, is as follows:

Asset Category	
Equity securities	40–60%
Debt securities	25–40%
Real estate	0–20%
Other	0–20%

The Company's investment policy includes various guidelines and procedures designed to ensure that assets are invested in a manner necessary to meet expected future benefits earned by participants. The investment guidelines consider a broad range of economic conditions. Central to the policy are target allocation ranges (shown above) by major asset categories.

The objectives of the target allocations are to maintain investment portfolios that diversify risk through prudent asset allocation parameters, achieve asset returns that meet or exceed the plans' actuarial assumptions, and achieve asset returns that are competitive with like institutions employing similar investment strategies.

The investment policy is periodically reviewed by the Company and a designated third-party fiduciary for investment matters. The policy is established and administered in a manner that is compliant at all times with applicable government regulations.

Equity securities include common stock of Beas Ltd. in the amounts of $33,000 (10% of total plan assets) and $25,000 (12% of total plan assets) at December 31, 20X2, and December 31, 20X1, respectively.

The Company expects to contribute $150,000 to its pension plans and $200,000 to its postretirement benefit plans in 20X3.

The following benefit payments, which reflect expected future service, as appropriate, are expected to be paid:

	Pension Benefits	Postretirement Benefits
20X3	$100,000	$125,000
20X4	105,000	130,000
20X5	118,000	140,000
20X6	125,000	150,000
20X7	135,000	175,000
Years 20X8–20Y2	775,000	860,000

Illustrations If FAS-158 Has *Not* Been Adopted: Defined Benefit Plans

Example 26–4: Defined Benefit Pension Plans with No Minimum Liability—Public Entities

The Company sponsors two funded defined benefit pension plans for eligible employees who are 21 years of age with one or more years of service and who are not covered by collective bargaining agreements. Benefits paid to retirees are based on age at retirement, years of credited service, and average compensation. The Company's funding policy is to contribute the larger of the amount required to fully fund the Plan's current liability or the amount necessary to meet the funding requirements as defined by the Internal Revenue Code.

The Company also sponsors an unfunded Executive Pension Plan. This plan is nonqualified and provides certain key employees defined pension benefits that supplement those provided by the Company's other retirement plans.

The Company uses a December 31 measurement date for all its plans. The following table sets forth the benefit obligation, fair value of plan assets, and the funded status of the Company's plans; amounts recognized in the Company's financial statements; and the principal weighted-average assumptions used:

	20X2	20X1
Change in projected benefit obligation:		
Benefit obligation at beginning of year	$27,800,000	$23,200,000
Service cost	1,700,000	1,500,000
Interest cost	1,900,000	2,000,000
Actuarial loss	4,700,000	1,900,000
Divestitures	(100,000)	-0-
Curtailments	(5,800,000)	-0-
Benefits paid	(1,300,000)	(800,000)
Benefit obligation at end of year	$28,900,000	$27,800,000
Change in plan assets:		
Fair value of plan assets at beginning of year	$22,700,000	$18,300,000
Actual return on plan assets	1,200,000	4,500,000
Employer contributions	1,300,000	700,000
Divestitures	(300,000)	-0-
Benefits paid	(900,000)	(800,000)
Fair value of plan assets at end of year	$24,000,000	$22,700,000
Funded status	$(4,900,000)	$(5,100,000)
Unrecognized net actuarial gain	(1,700,000)	(1,800,000)
Unrecognized prior service cost	700,000	1,900,000
Unrecognized net transition obligation	(200,000)	(300,000)
Accrued pension cost	$(6,100,000)	$(5,300,000)
Amounts recognized in the balance sheets consist of:		
Prepaid pension cost included with other assets	$300,000	$300,000
Accrued pension cost included with accrued liabilities	(6,400,000)	(5,600,000)
Net amount recognized at end of year	$(6,100,000)	$(5,300,000)

The following are weighted-average assumptions used to determine benefit obligations at December 31, 20X2, and December 31, 20X1:

	20X2	20X1
Discount rate	6.75%	7.00%
Rate of compensation increase	5.25%	4.75%

The following are weighted-average assumptions used to determine net periodic benefit cost for the years ended December 31, 20X2, and December 31, 20X1:

	20X2	20X1
Discount rate	7.00%	7.25%
Expected long-term return on plan assets	8.00%	7.75%
Rate of compensation increase	5.50%	5.00%

The Company's expected long-term return on plan assets assumption is based on a periodic review and modeling of the plans' asset allocation and liability structure over a long-term period. Expectations of returns for each asset class are the most important of the assumptions used in the review and modeling and are based on comprehensive reviews of historical data and economic/financial market theory. The expected long-term rate of return on assets was selected from within the reasonable range of rates determined by (1) historical real returns, net of inflation, for the asset classes covered by the investment policy, and (2) projections of inflation over the long-term period during which benefits are payable to plan participants.

Components of net periodic benefit cost are as follows:

	20X2	20X1
Service cost—Benefits earned during the period	$1,700,000	$1,500,000
Interest cost on projected benefit obligations	1,900,000	2,000,000
Expected return on plan assets	(1,800,000)	(1,300,000)
Amortization of prior service cost	100,000	200,000
Amortization of actuarial loss	200,000	-0-
Net periodic benefit cost	$2,100,000	$2,400,000

The following table summarizes the Company-sponsored pension plans that have projected benefit obligations in excess of plan assets and the accumulated benefit obligation of the unfunded Executive Pension Plan in which the accumulated benefit obligation exceeds plan assets:

	20X2	20X1
Projected benefit obligation in excess of plan assets:		
Projected benefit obligation	$3,900,000	$4,200,000
Fair value of plan assets	$2,800,000	$2,600,000
Accumulated benefit obligation in excess of plan assets:		
Accumulated benefit obligation	$1,300,000	$1,100,000
Fair value of plan assets	$ -0-	$ -0-

The accumulated benefit obligation for all defined benefit pension plans was $16,100,000 and $14,700,000 at December 31, 20X2, and December 31, 20X1, respectively.

The Company's pension plan weighted-average asset allocations at December 31, 20X2, and December 31, 20X1, by asset category, are as follows:

	Plan Assets at December 31,	
	20X2	20X1
Asset Category		
Equity securities	55%	52%
Debt securities	28	31
Real estate	10	11
Other	7	6
Total	100%	100%

The Company's target asset allocation as of December 31, 20X2, by asset category, is as follows:

Asset Category	
Equity securities	50–70%
Debt securities	30–50%
Real estate	0–20%
Other	0–20%

The Company's investment policy includes various guidelines and procedures designed to ensure assets are invested in a manner necessary to meet expected future benefits earned by participants. The investment guidelines consider a broad range of economic conditions. Central to the policy are target allocation ranges (shown above) by major asset categories.

The objectives of the target allocations are to maintain investment portfolios that diversify risk through prudent asset allocation parameters, achieve asset returns that meet or exceed the plans' actuarial assumptions, and achieve asset returns that are competitive with like institutions employing similar investment strategies.

The investment policy is periodically reviewed by the Company and a designated third-party fiduciary for investment matters. The policy is established and administered in a manner that complies at all times with applicable government regulations.

Equity securities include common stock of Ace Ltd. in the amounts of $1,200,000 (5% of total plan assets) and $1,589,000 (7% of total plan assets) at December 31, 20X2, and December 31, 20X1, respectively.

The Company expects to contribute $1,500,000 to its pension plan in 20X3.

The following pension benefit payments, which reflect expected future service, as appropriate, are expected to be paid:

20X3	$1,000,000
20X4	1,050,000
20X5	1,175,000
20X6	1,225,000
20X7	1,315,000
Years 20X8–20Y2	7,325,000

Example 26–5: Defined Benefit Pension Plans with No Minimum Liability—Alternative Reduced Disclosures for a Nonpublic Entity

> **Note:** This example illustrates the alternative reduced disclosures for a nonpublic entity using the same facts in Example 26–4.

In September 2006, the Financial Accounting Standards Board issued Statement of Financial Accounting Standards No. 158 (FAS-158), *Employers' Accounting for Defined Benefit Pension and Other Postretirement Plans.* This new standard requires employers to (1) recognize in their balance sheets an asset for a plan's overfunded status or a liability for a plan's underfunded status; (2) measure a plan's assets and its obligations that determine its funded status as of the end of the employer's fiscal year (eliminating the alternative of a measurement date that could be up to three months earlier under prior standards); and (3) recognize changes in the funded status of a plan through comprehensive income in the year in which the changes occur. FAS-158 also amends the disclosure requirements in the notes to the financial statements by requiring information about certain effects on net periodic benefit cost for the next fiscal year that arise from delayed recognition of the gains or losses, prior service costs or credits, and transition asset or obligation.

The requirement to recognize the funded status of a benefit plan and the disclosure requirements are effective for fiscal years that end after June 15, 2007, for the Company. The requirement to measure plan assets and benefit obligations as of the date of the Company's fiscal year-end balance sheet is effective for fiscal years ending after December 15, 2008. The Company plans to adopt the provisions of FAS-158 on [*date*].

The Company sponsors two funded defined benefit pension plans for eligible employees who are 21 years of age with one or more years of service and who are not covered by collective bargaining agreements. Benefits paid to retirees are based on age at retirement, years of credited service, and average compensation. The Company's funding policy is to contribute the larger of the amount required to fully fund the plan's current liability or the amount necessary to meet the funding requirements as defined by the Internal Revenue Code.

In addition, the Company sponsors an unfunded Executive Pension Plan. This plan is nonqualified and provides certain key employees defined pension benefits that supplement those provided by the Company's other retirement plans.

The Company uses a December 31 measurement date for all its plans.

	20X2	*20X1*
Projected benefit obligation at December 31	$28,900,000	$27,800,000
Fair value of plan assets at December 31	24,000,000	22,700,000
Funded status	$ (4,900,000)	$ (5,100,000)
Accrued pension cost	$ (6,100,000)	$ (5,300,000)
Amounts recognized in the balance sheets consist of:		
Prepaid pension cost included with other assets	$ 300,000	$ 300,000
Accrued pension cost included with accrued liabilities	(6,400,000)	(5,600,000)
Net amount recognized at end of year	$(6,100,000)	$ (5,300,000)

The following are weighted-average assumptions used to determine benefit obligations at December 31, 20X2, and December 31, 20X1:

	20X2	20X1
Discount rate	6.75%	7.00%
Rate of compensation increase	5.25%	4.75%

The following are weighted-average assumptions used to determine net periodic benefit cost for the years ended December 31, 20X2, and December 31, 20X1:

	20X2	20X1
Discount rate	7.00%	7.25%
Expected long-term return on plan assets	8.00%	7.75%
Rate of compensation increase	5.50%	5.00%

The Company's expected long-term return on plan assets assumption is based on a periodic review and modeling of the plans' asset allocation and liability structure over a long-term period. Expectations of returns for each asset class are the most important of the assumptions used in the review and modeling and are based on comprehensive reviews of historical data and economic/financial market theory. The expected long-term rate of return on assets was selected from within the reasonable range of rates determined by (1) historical real returns, net of inflation, for the asset classes covered by the investment policy, and (2) projections of inflation over the long-term period during which benefits are payable to plan participants.

	20X2	20X1
Benefit cost	$ 2,100,000	$ 2,400,000
Employer contributions	$ 1,300,000	$ 700,000
Benefits paid	$ 300,000	$ 800,000

The following table summarizes the Company-sponsored pension plans that have projected benefit obligations in excess of plan assets and the accumulated benefit obligation of the unfunded Executive Pension Plan in which the accumulated benefit obligation exceeds plan assets:

	20X2	20X1
Projected benefit obligation in excess of plan assets:		
Projected benefit obligation	$3,900,000	$4,200,000
Fair value of plan assets	$2,800,000	$2,600,000
Accumulated benefit obligation in excess of plan assets:		
Accumulated benefit obligation	$1,300,000	$1,100,000
Fair value of plan assets	$ -0-	$ -0-

The accumulated benefit obligation for all defined benefit pension plans was $16,100,000 and $14,700,000 at December 31, 20X2, and December 31, 20X1, respectively.

The Company's pension plan weighted-average asset allocations at December 31, 20X2, and December 31, 20X1, by asset category, are as follows:

| | Plan Assets at December 31, | |
	20X2	20X1
Asset Category		
Equity securities	55%	52%
Debt securities	28	31
Real estate	10	11
Other	7	6
Total	100%	100%

The Company's target asset allocation as of December 31, 20X2, by asset category, is as follows:

Asset Category	
Equity securities	50–70%
Debt securities	30–50%
Real estate	0–20%
Other	0–20%

The Company's investment policy includes various guidelines and procedures designed to ensure assets are invested in a manner necessary to meet expected future benefits earned by participants. The investment guidelines consider a broad range of economic conditions. Central to the policy are target allocation ranges (shown above) by major asset categories.

The objectives of the target allocations are to maintain investment portfolios that diversify risk through prudent asset allocation parameters, achieve asset returns that meet or exceed the plans' actuarial assumptions, and achieve asset returns that are competitive with like institutions employing similar investment strategies.

The investment policy is periodically reviewed by the Company and a designated third-party fiduciary for investment matters. The policy is established and administered in a manner that complies at all times with applicable government regulations.

Equity securities include common stock of Ace Ltd. in the amounts of $1,200,000 (5% of total plan assets) and $1,589,000 (7% of total plan assets) at December 31, 20X2, and December 31, 20X1, respectively.

The Company expects to contribute $1,500,000 to its pension plan in 20X3.

The following pension benefit payments, which reflect expected future service, as appropriate, are expected to be paid:

20X3	$1,000,000
20X4	1,050,000
20X5	1,175,000
20X6	1,225,000
20X7	1,315,000
Years 20X8–20Y2	7,325,000

Example 26–6: Disclosures for a Defined Benefit Pension Plan That Recognizes a Minimum Liability

The Company and its subsidiaries sponsor numerous defined benefit pension plans. The Company uses a December 31 measurement date for all its plans. The following table sets forth the benefit obligation, fair value of plan assets, and the funded status of the Company's plans; amounts recognized in the Company's financial statements; and the principal weighted-average assumptions used:

	20X2	20X1
Change in projected benefit obligation:		
Benefit obligation at beginning of year	$1,266,000	$1,200,000
Service cost	76,000	72,000
Interest cost	114,000	108,000
Amendments	(20,000)	-0-
Actuarial gain	(25,000)	-0-
Benefits paid	(125,000)	(114,000)
Benefit obligation at end of year	$1,286,000	$1,266,000
Change in plan assets:		
Fair value of plan assets at beginning of year	$1,156,000	$ 968,000
Actual return on plan assets	29,000	188,000
Employer contribution	139,000	114,000

Benefits paid	(125,000)	(114,000)
Fair value of plan assets at end of year	$1,199,000	$1,156,000
Funded status	$ (87,000)	$ (110,000)
Unrecognized actuarial loss	83,000	38,000
Unrecognized prior service cost	170,000	225,000
Net amount recognized	$ 166,000	$ 153,000
Amounts recognized in the statement of financial position consist of:		
Prepaid benefit cost	$255,000	$227,000
Accrued benefit liability	(153,000)	(127,000)
Intangible asset	50,000	53,000
Accumulated other comprehensive income	14,000	-0-
Net amount recognized	$166,000	$153,000

The following are weighted-average assumptions used to determine benefit obligations at December 31, 20X2, and December 31, 20X1:

	20X2	20X1
Discount rate	6.75%	7.00%
Rate of compensation increase	5.25%	4.75%

The following are weighted-average assumptions used to determine net periodic benefit cost for the years ended December 31, 20X2, and December 31, 20X1:

	20X2	20X1
Discount rate	7.00%	7.25%
Expected long-term return on plan assets	8.00%	7.75%
Rate of compensation increase	5.50%	5.00%

The Company's expected long-term return on plan assets assumption is based on a periodic review and modeling of the plans' asset allocation and liability structure over a long-term period. Expectations of returns for each asset class are the most important of the assumptions used in the review and modeling and are based on comprehensive reviews of historical data and economic/financial market theory. The expected long-term rate of return on assets was selected from within the reasonable range of rates determined by (1) historical real returns, net of inflation, for the asset classes covered by the investment policy, and (2) projections of inflation over the long-term period during which benefits are payable to plan participants.

Components of net periodic benefit cost are as follows:

	20X2	20X1
Service cost	$ 76,000	$ 72,000
Interest cost	114,000	108,000
Expected return on plan assets	(116,000)	(97,000)
Amortization of prior service cost	35,000	35,000
Recognized actuarial loss	17,000	11,000
Net periodic benefit cost	$126,000	$129,000

The projected benefit obligation, accumulated benefit obligation, and fair value of plan assets for the pension plans with accumulated benefit obligations in excess of plan assets were $263,000, $237,000, and $84,000, respectively, as of December 31, 20X2, and $247,000, $222,000, and $95,000, respectively, as of December 31, 20X1.

The accumulated benefit obligation for all defined benefit pension plans was $733,000 and $650,000 at December 31, 20X2, and December 31, 20X1, respectively.

The Company's pension plan weighted-average asset allocations at December 31, 20X2, and December 31, 20X1, by asset category are as follows:

	Plan Assets at December 31,	
Asset Category	20X2	20X1
Equity securities	55%	52%
Debt securities	28	31
Real estate	10	11
Other	7	6
Total	100%	100%

The Company's target asset allocation as of December 31, 20X2, by asset category, is as follows:

Asset Category	
Equity securities	50–70%
Debt securities	30–50%
Real estate	0–20%
Other	0–20%

The Company's investment policy includes various guidelines and procedures designed to ensure assets are invested in a manner necessary to meet expected future benefits earned by participants. The investment guidelines consider a broad range of economic conditions. Central to the policy are target allocation ranges (shown above) by major asset categories.

The objectives of the target allocations are to maintain investment portfolios that diversify risk through prudent asset allocation parameters, achieve asset returns that meet or exceed the plans' actuarial assumptions, and achieve asset returns that are competitive with like institutions employing similar investment strategies.

The investment policy is periodically reviewed by the Company and a designated third-party fiduciary for investment matters. The policy is established and administered in a manner that complies at all times with applicable government regulations.

Equity securities include common stock of Ace Ltd. in the amounts of $60,000 (5% of total plan assets) and $81,000 (7% of total plan assets) at December 31, 20X2, and December 31, 20X1, respectively.

The Company expects to contribute $150,000 to its pension plan in 20X3.

The following pension benefit payments, which reflect expected future service, as appropriate, are expected to be paid:

20X3	$100,000
20X4	105,000
20X5	118,000
20X6	125,000
20X7	135,000
Years 20X8–20Y2	755,000

The provisions of FASB Statement of Financial Accounting Standards No. 87, *Employers' Accounting for Pensions,* require the Company to record an additional minimum liability of $64,000 and $53,000 at December 31, 20X2, and December 31, 20X1, respectively. This liability represents the amount by which the accumulated benefit obligation exceeds the sum of the fair market value of plan assets and accrued amounts previously recorded. The additional liability may be offset by an intangible asset to the extent of previously unrecognized prior service cost. The intangible assets of $50,000 and $53,000 at December 31, 20X2, and December 31, 20X1, respectively, are included on the line item entitled "Other assets" in the balance sheets. The remaining amounts of $14,000 and $0 are recorded as a component of stockholders' equity, net of related tax benefits of $8,000 and $0, on the line item titled "Accumulated other comprehensive income (loss)" in the balance sheets at December 31, 20X2, and December 31, 20X1, respectively.

Example 26–7: Disclosures about Defined Benefit Pension Plans and Other Postretirement Benefit Plans Are Presented in a Parallel Format in a Single Note to the Financial Statements

The Company and its subsidiaries sponsor numerous defined benefit pension plans and other postretirement benefit plans. The Company uses a December 31 measurement date for all its plans. The following tables set forth the benefit obligation, the fair value of plan assets, and the funded status of the Company's plans; the amounts recognized in the Company's financial statements; and the principal weighted-average assumptions used:

	Pension Benefits		Postretirement Benefits	
	20X2	20X1	20X2	20X1
Change in benefit obligation:				
Benefit obligation at beginning of year	$1,266,000	$1,200,000	$738,000	$700,000
Service cost	76,000	72,000	36,000	32,000
Interest cost	114,000	108,000	65,000	63,000
Plan participants' contributions	-0-	-0-	20,000	13,000
Amendments	120,000	-0-	75,000	-0-
Actuarial gain	(25,000)	-0-	(24,000)	-0-
Acquisition	900,000	-0-	600,000	-0-
Benefits paid	(125,000)	(114,000)	(90,000)	(70,000)
Benefit obligation at end of year	$2,326,000	$1,266,000	$1,420,000	$738,000

	Pension Benefits		Postretirement Benefits	
	20X2	20X1	20X2	20X1
Change in plan assets:				
Fair value of plan assets at beginning of year	$1,068,000	$880,000	$206,000	$87,000

Actual return on plan assets	29,000	188,000	(3,000)	24,000
Acquisition	1,000,000	-0-	25,000	-0-
Employer contribution	75,000	114,000	171,000	152,000
Plan participants' contributions	-0-	-0-	20,000	13,000
Benefits paid	(125,000)	(114,000)	(90,000)	(70,000)
Fair value of plan assets at end of year	$2,047,000	$1,068,000	$ 329,000	$ 206,000
Funded status	$(279,000)	$(198,000)	$(1,091,000)	$(532,000)
Unrecognized net actuarial loss	83,000	38,000	59,000	60,000
Unrecognized prior service cost	260,000	160,000	585,000	540,000
Prepaid (accrued) benefit cost	$ 64,000	$ -0-	$ (447,000)	$ 68,000

The following are weighted-average assumptions used to determine benefit obligations at December 31, 20X2, and December 31, 20X1:

	Pension Benefits		Postretirement Benefits	
	20X2	20X1	20X2	20X1
Discount rate	6.75%	7.00%	7.00%	7.25%
Rate of compensation increase	5.25%	4.75%	N/A	N/A

The following are weighted-average assumptions used to determine net periodic benefit cost for the years ended December 31, 20X2, and December 31, 20X1:

	Pension Benefits		Postretirement Benefits	
	20X2	20X1	20X2	20X1
Discount rate	7.00%	7.25%	7.25%	7.25%
Expected long-term return on plan assets	8.00%	7.75%	8.25%	8.50%
Rate of compensation increase	5.50%	5.00%	N/A	N/A

The Company's expected long-term return on plan assets assumption is based on a periodic review and modeling of the plans' asset allocation and liability structure over a long-term period. Expectations of returns for each asset class are the most important of the assumptions used in the review and modeling and are based on comprehensive reviews of historical data and economic/financial market theory. The expected long-term rate of return on assets was selected from within the reasonable range of rates determined by (1) historical real returns, net of inflation, for the asset classes covered by the investment policy, and (2) projections of inflation over the long-term period during which benefits are payable to plan participants.

For measurement purposes, a 10% annual rate of increase in the per capita cost of covered healthcare benefits was assumed for 20X3. The rate was assumed to decrease gradually to 4% for 20X9 and remain at that level thereafter.

Components of net periodic benefit cost are as follows:

	Pension Benefits		Postretirement Benefits	
	20X2	*20X1*	*20X2*	*20X1*
Service cost	$76,000	$72,000	$36,000	$32,000
Interest cost	114,000	108,000	65,000	63,000
Expected return on plan assets	(107,000)	(88,000)	(21,000)	(9,000)
Amortization of prior service cost	20,000	20,000	30,000	30,000
Recognized net actuarial loss	8,000	2,000	1,000	1,000
Net periodic benefit cost	$111,000	$114,000	$111,000	$117,000

The Company acquired Massari, Ltd. on December 31, 20X2, including its pension plans. As a result, the Company's plans were amended to establish parity with the benefits provided by Massari, Ltd.

The Company has multiple nonpension postretirement benefit plans. The healthcare plans are contributory, with participants' contributions adjusted annually; the life insurance plans are noncontributory. The accounting for the healthcare plans anticipates future cost sharing changes to the written plan that are consistent with the Company's expressed intent to increase retiree contributions each year by 50% of the excess of the expected general inflation rate over 6%. On December 31, 20X2, the Company amended its postretirement healthcare plans to provide long-term care coverage.

Assumed healthcare cost trend rates have a significant effect on the amounts reported for the healthcare plans. A 1% point change in assumed healthcare cost trend rates would have the following effects:

	1% Point Increase	1% Point Decrease
Effect on total of service and interest cost components	$ 22,000	$ (20,000)
Effect on postretirement benefit obligation	$173,000	$(156,000)

The accumulated benefit obligation for all defined benefit pension plans was $733,000 and $650,000 at December 31, 20X2, and December 31, 20X1, respectively.

The Company's pension plans weighted-average asset allocations at December 31, 20X2, and December 31, 20X1, by asset category, are as follows:

	Plan Assets at December 31,	
	20X2	20X1
Asset Category		
Equity securities	55%	52%
Debt securities	28	31
Real estate	10	11
Other	7	6
Total	100%	100%

The Company's target asset allocation as of December 31, 20X2, by asset category, is as follows:

Asset Category	
Equity securities	50–70%
Debt securities	30–50%
Real estate	0–20%
Other	0–20%

The Company's investment policy includes various guidelines and procedures designed to ensure assets are invested in a manner necessary to meet expected future benefits earned by participants. The investment guidelines consider a broad range of economic conditions. Central to the policy are target allocation ranges (shown above) by major asset categories.

The objectives of the target allocations are to maintain investment portfolios that diversify risk through prudent asset allocation parameters, achieve asset returns that meet or exceed the plans' actuarial assumptions, and achieve asset returns that are competitive with like institutions employing similar investment strategies.

The investment policy is periodically reviewed by the Company and a designated third-party fiduciary for investment matters. The policy is established and administered in a manner that complies at all times with applicable government regulations.

Equity securities include common stock of Ace Ltd. in the amounts of $102,000 (5% of total plan assets) and $75,000 (7% of total plan assets) at December 31, 20X2, and December 31, 20X1, respectively.

The Company's postretirement benefit plans weighted average asset allocations at December 31, 20X2, and December 31, 20X1, by asset category, are as follows:

	Plan Assets at December 31,	
Asset Category	20X2	20X1
Equity securities	57%	54%
Debt securities	26	29
Real estate	12	8
Other	5	9
Total	100%	100%

The Company's target asset allocation as of December 31, 20X2, by asset category, is as follows:

Asset Category	
Equity securities	40–60%
Debt securities	25–40%
Real estate	0–20%
Other	0–20%

The Company's investment policy includes various guidelines and procedures designed to ensure assets are invested in a manner necessary to meet expected future benefits earned by participants. The investment guidelines consider a broad range of economic conditions. Central to the policy are target allocation ranges (shown above) by major asset categories.

The objectives of the target allocations are to maintain investment portfolios that diversify risk through prudent asset allocation parameters, achieve asset returns that meet or exceed the plans' actuarial assumptions, and achieve asset returns that are competitive with like institutions employing similar investment strategies.

The investment policy is periodically reviewed by the Company and a designated third-party fiduciary for investment matters. The policy is established and administered in a manner so as to comply at all times with applicable government regulations.

Equity securities include common stock of Beas Ltd. in the amounts of $33,000 (10% of total plan assets) and $25,000 (12% of total plan assets) at December 31, 20X2, and December 31, 20X1, respectively.

The Company expects to contribute $150,000 to its pension plans and $200,000 to its postretirement benefit plans in 20X3.

The following benefit payments, which reflect expected future service, as appropriate, are expected to be paid:

	Pension Benefits	Postretirement Benefits
20X3	$100,000	$125,000
20X4	105,000	130,000
20X5	118,000	140,000
20X6	125,000	150,000
20X7	135,000	175,000
Years 20X8–20Y2	755,000	860,000

Illustrations Applicable under FAS-158 and Prior Standards

Example 26–8: Profit Sharing Plan

The Company has a qualified profit sharing plan that covers substantially all full-time employees meeting certain eligibility requirements. The annual contribution is discretionary as determined by the Board of Directors; however, the contributions cannot exceed 15% of compensation for the eligible employees in any one tax year. The Company's contributions to the plan were $325,000 for 20X2 and $215,000 for 20X1.

Example 26–9: 401(k) Savings Plan

The Company has a 401(k) Plan ("Plan") to provide retirement and incidental benefits for its employees. Employees may contribute from 1% to 15% of their annual compensation to the Plan, limited to a maximum annual amount as set periodically by the Internal Revenue Service. The Company matches employee contributions dollar for dollar up to a maximum of $1,500 per year per person. All matching contributions vest immediately. In addition, the Plan provides for discretionary contributions as determined by the board of directors. Such contributions to the Plan are allocated among eligible participants in the proportion of their salaries to the total salaries of all participants.

Company matching contributions to the Plan totaled $632,000 in 20X2 and $595,000 in 20X1. No discretionary contributions were made in 20X2 or 20X1.

Example 26–10: Money Purchase Pension Plan

The Company sponsors a trusteed defined contribution money purchase pension plan covering substantially all employees meeting minimum age and service requirements and not covered by collective bargaining agreements. Contributions are based on a percentage of each eligible employee's compensation and are at about 10% of each covered employee's salary. The Company's contributions to the plan totaled $346,000 for 20X2 and $271,000 for 20X1.

Example 26–11: Incentive Bonus Plan

The Company has an Incentive Bonus Plan ("Bonus Plan") for the benefit of its employees, including executive officers. The total amount of cash bonus awards to be made under the Bonus Plan for any plan year depends primarily on the Company's sales and net income for such year.

For any plan year, the Company's sales and net income must meet or exceed, or in combination with other factors satisfy, levels targeted by the Company in its business plan, as established at the beginning of each fiscal year, for any bonus awards to be made. Aggregate bonus awards to all participants under the Bonus Plan may not exceed 7% of the Company's net income. The board of directors has the authority to determine the total amount of bonus awards, if any, to be made to the eligible employees for any plan year based on its evaluation of the Company's financial condition and results of operations, the Company's business and prospects, and such other criteria as the Board may determine to be relevant or appropriate. The Company expensed $822,000 in 20X2 and $320,000 in 20X1 in conjunction with the Bonus Plan.

Example 26–12: Deferred Compensation Plan

The Company has a deferred compensation plan (DCP) covering highly compensated employees as defined by the DCP. Under the plan, eligible employees may contribute a portion of their salary on a pre-tax basis. The DCP is a non-qualified plan; therefore, the associated liabilities are included in the Company's December 31, 20X2, and December 31, 20X1, Consolidated Balance Sheets. In addition, the Company has established a rabbi trust to finance obligations under the DCP with corporate-owned life insurance policies on participants. The cash surrender value of such policies is also included in the Company's December 31, 20X2, and December 31, 20X1, Consolidated Balance Sheets. Total expense under the DCP for the years ended December 31, 20X2, and December 31, 20X1, amounted to $427,000 and $319,000, respectively.

Example 26–13: Combined Disclosures of Defined Contribution Pension Plans and Defined Contribution Postretirement Plans

The Company sponsors several defined contribution pension plans covering substantially all employees. Employees may contribute to these plans and these contributions are matched in varying amounts by the Company. Defined contribution pension expense for the Company was $543,000 for 20X2 and $429,000 for 20X1.

Also, the Company sponsors defined contribution postretirement healthcare and life insurance benefit plans. Contributions to these plans were $311,000 in 20X2 and $304,000 in 20X1.

Example 26–14: Union-Sponsored Multiemployer Pension Plans

The Company participates in various multi-employer union-administered defined benefit pension plans that principally cover production workers. Total contributions to these plans were $472,000 for 20X2 and $461,000 for 20X1.

Example 26–15: Liability Resulting from Withdrawal from Multiemployer Pension Plan Is Recognized in the Financial Statements

Effective October 13, 20X2, the Company decided to withdraw its participation in the Glass Workers Industry Pension Plan. As a result, the Company will be required to contribute its share of the Plan's unfunded benefit obligation. The Company's actuaries have advised that the Company's required contribution at the withdrawal date will be approximately $734,000. As a result, a provision for that amount has been charged against earnings in the 20X2 Statement of Operations.

Example 26–16: Company Would Not Have a Material Liability If It Withdrew from Multiemployer Pension Plan

The Company's contributions to union-sponsored, defined benefit, multiemployer pension plans were $511,000 in 20X2 and $473,000 in 20X1. These plans are not administered by the Company and contributions are determined in accordance with provisions of negotiated labor contracts. As of December 31, 20X2, the actuarially computed values of vested benefits for these plans were primarily equal to or less than the net assets of the plans. Therefore, the Company would have no material withdrawal liability. However, the Company has no present intention of withdrawing from any of these plans, nor has the Company been informed that there is any intention to terminate such plans.

Example 26–17: Curtailment and Special Termination Benefits

In January 20X2, the Company offered a limited program of Retirement Enhancements. The Retirement Enhancements program provided for unreduced retirement benefits to the first 150 employees who retired before December 31, 20X3. In addition, each retiring participant could elect a lump-sum payment of $25,000 or a $400 monthly supplement payable until age 62. As of December 31, 20X2, a total of 125 employees applied for retirement under this program. The Retirement Enhancements program represented a curtailment and special termination benefits under FASB Statement of Financial Accounting Standards No. 88, *Employers' Accounting for Settlements and Curtailments of Defined Benefit Pension Plans and for Termination Benefits*. The Company recorded a charge of $2,936,000 in 20X2 to cover the Retirement Enhancements program.

Example 26–18: Interim-Period Disclosures—Public Entities

Components of net periodic benefit cost for the Company's pension plan are as follows:

	Three Months Ended September 30		Nine Months Ended September 30	
	20X2	20X1	20X2	20X1
Service cost	$1,200,000	$1,100,000	$3,700,000	$3,400,000
Interest cost	1,400,000	1,156,000	3,900,000	3,250,000
Expected return on plan assets	(1,600,000)	(900,000)	(4,200,000)	(3,900,000)
Amortization of prior service cost	240,000	160,000	525,000	260,000
Amortization of net (gain) loss	70,000	(10,000)	90,000	115,000
Net periodic benefit cost	$1,310,000	$1,506,000	$4,015,000	$3,125,000

Components of net periodic benefit cost for the company's postretirement benefit plan are as follows:

	Three Months Ended September 30		*Nine Months Ended September 30*	
	20X2	*20X1*	*20X2*	*20X1*
Service cost	$200,000	$170,000	$700,000	$625,000
Interest cost	400,000	350,000	990,000	695,000
Expected return on plan assets	(150,000)	(190,000)	(315,000)	(420,000)
Amortization of prior service cost	(70,000)	(10,000)	(125,000)	(150,000)
Net periodic benefit cost	$380,000	$320,000	$1,250,000	$750,000

The Company previously disclosed in its financial statements for the year ended December 31, 20X1, that it expected to contribute $4,800,000 to its pension plan and $900,000 to its postretirement benefit plan in 20X2. As of September 30, 20X2, contributions of $3,700,000 and $650,000 have been made to the pension plan and postretirement benefit plan, respectively. The Company presently anticipates contributing an additional $1,500,000 to fund its pension plan in 20X2 for a total of $5,200,000. Also, the Company presently anticipates contributing an additional $450,000 to fund its postretirement benefit plan in 20X2 for a total of $1,100,000.

Example 26–19: Interim-Period Disclosures—Nonpublic Entities

The Company previously disclosed in its financial statements for the year ended December 31, 20X1, that it expected to contribute $4,800,000 to its pension plan and $900,000 to its postretirement benefit plan in 20X2. As of September 30, 20X2, contributions of $3,700,000 and $650,000 have been made to the pension plan and postretirement benefit plan, respectively. The Company presently anticipates contributing an additional $1,500,000 to fund its pension plan in 20X2 for a total of $5,200,000. Also, the Company presently anticipates contributing an additional $450,000 to fund its postretirement benefit plan in 20X2 for a total of $1,100,000.

CHAPTER 27
POSTEMPLOYMENT BENEFITS

CONTENTS

EXECUTIVE SUMMARY

Postemployment benefits are benefits provided to former or inactive employees, their beneficiaries, and covered dependents after employment but before retirement. Postemployment benefits may be provided in cash or in kind and may be paid as a result of a disability, layoff, death, or other event. They include, but are not limited to, salary continuation, supplemental unemployment benefits, severance benefits, disability-related benefits (including workers' compensation), job training and counseling, and continuation of benefits such as healthcare benefits and life insurance coverage.

Postemployment benefits should be accrued if they meet all of the following conditions:

1. They relate to services already rendered.

2. The employee's right to be paid postemployment benefits vests or accumulates.

3. It is probable the benefits will be paid.

4. The amount that will be paid can be reasonably estimated.

Postemployment benefits that do not meet all of the above criteria should be accounted for as contingencies; accordingly, they should be:

1. Accrued if (a) information available prior to issuance of the financial statements indicates that it is probable that a liability has been incurred at the balance-sheet date and (b) the amount of the liability can be reasonably estimated.

2. Disclosed (but not accrued) if (a) it is probable a liability exists but the amount of the liability cannot be reasonably estimated or (b) it is reasonably possible, but not probable, that a liability exists.

Authoritative literature does not specifically address how to measure the postemployment benefit obligation. However, the literature does state that companies may refer to the guidance on measuring pension obligations (Chapter 26, "Pension Plans") and obligations for postretirement benefits other than pensions (Chapter 28, "Postretirement Benefits Other Than Pensions"), to the extent similar issues apply to the postemployment benefits.

In addition, authoritative literature does not provide explicit guidance on discounting; therefore, the use of discounting in measuring postemployment benefit obligations is permitted but not required.

Authoritative Literature

FAS-112   Employers' Accounting for Postemployment Benefits

DISCLOSURE REQUIREMENTS

Authoritative literature does not require an entity to disclose the amount of postemployment benefits. However, if the entity has not accrued an obligation for postemployment benefits only because the amount cannot be reasonably estimated, the entity should disclose that fact in the financial statements (FAS-112, par. 7).

EXAMPLES OF FINANCIAL STATEMENT DISCLOSURES

The following sample disclosures are available on the accompanying disc.

Example 27–1: Company Discloses Amount of Postemployment Benefits Charged to Operations

> **Note:** Although authoritative literature does not require that the amount of postemployment benefits be disclosed, such disclosure is considered informative.

The Company provides certain postemployment benefits to eligible former or inactive employees and their dependents during the period subsequent to employment but prior to retirement and accrues for the related cost over the service lives of the employees. These benefits include certain disability and healthcare coverage and severance benefits. Postemployment benefit costs charged to operations in 20X2 and 20X1 totaled $97,000 and $73,000, respectively.

Example 27–2: Company Does Not Disclose Amount of Postemployment Benefits Charged to Operations

> **Note:** Although authoritative literature does not require that the amount of postemployment benefits be disclosed, such disclosure is considered informative.

The Company provides certain postemployment benefits to eligible former or inactive employees and their dependents during the period subsequent to employment but prior to retirement and accrues for the related cost over the service lives of the employees. These benefits include certain disability and healthcare coverage and severance benefits.

Example 27–3: Company Uses Discounting to Measure the Postemployment Benefit Obligation

> **Note:** The use of discounting in measuring postemployment benefit obligations is permitted but not required.

The Company provides certain benefits to former or inactive employees after employment but before retirement and accrues for the related cost over the service lives of the employees. Those benefits include, among others, disability, severance, and workers' compensation. The assumed discount rate used to measure the postemployment benefit liability was 7% at December 31, 20X2, and 6.5% at December 31, 20X1.

Example 27–4: Company Is Self-Insured under Its Postemployment Benefit Plans

The Company is self-insured under its employees' short-term and long-term disability plans, which are the primary benefits paid to inactive employees prior to retirement. Following is a summary of the obligation for postemployment benefits included in the Company's balance sheets at December 31, 20X2, and December 31, 20X1:

	20X2	20X1
Included with "Salaries and related liabilities"	$105,000	$102,000
Included with "Other long-term liabilities"	693,000	607,000
	$798,000	$709,000

Example 27–5: Company Has Not Accrued a Liability for Postemployment Benefits Because the Amount Cannot Be Reasonably Estimated

FASB Statement of Financial Accounting Standards No. 112, *Employers' Accounting for Postemployment Benefits*, requires employers to recognize an obligation for benefits provided to former or inactive employees after employment but before retirement. The Company provides the following postemployment benefits to former and inactive employees: supplemental unemployment benefits, disability-related benefits, and job training and counseling. It is not practicable for the Company to reasonably estimate the amount of its obligation for postemployment benefits; accordingly, no liability for postemployment benefits has been recorded in the accompanying financial statements. The Company's policy is to recognize the costs of such postemployment benefits when actually paid.

CHAPTER 28
POSTRETIREMENT BENEFITS
OTHER THAN PENSIONS

CONTENTS

EXECUTIVE SUMMARY

A *postretirement benefit plan* is one in which an employer agrees to provide certain postretirement benefits to current and former employees after they retire, upon the occurrence of a covered event, such as retirement, death, disability, or termination of employment. Generally accepted accounting principles (GAAP) require the accrual of postretirement benefits in a manner similar to the recognition of net periodic pension cost for pension plans.

A postretirement plan may be broadly classified as either a defined benefit plan or a defined contribution plan. In a *defined benefit postretirement plan*, the benefit may be defined in terms of a specified monetary amount (such as a life insurance benefit) or a specified type of benefit (such as all or a percentage of the cost of specified surgical procedures). A *defined contribution postretirement plan* provides an individual account for each participant and specifies how contributions to each individual's account are determined.

A postretirement benefit plan may be *contributory* (employees may be required to contribute to the plan) or *noncontributory* (the entire cost of the plan is borne by the employer).

Also, a postretirement benefit plan may be *funded* or *unfunded*—that is, the employees and/or the employer may make cash contributions to a postretirement benefit plan trustee (i.e., funded), or the employer may make only credit entries on its books reflecting the postretirement benefit liability under the plan and pay all benefits from its general assets (i.e., unfunded).

New Requirements under FAS-158

In September 2006, the FASB issued Statement of Financial Accounting Standards No. 158 (FAS-158), *Employers' Accounting for Defined Benefit Pension and Other Postretirement Plans*. This new standard requires employers of business entities with one or more defined benefit plans to (1) recognize in their balance sheets an asset for a plan's overfunded status or a liability for a plan's underfunded status; (2) measure a plan's assets and its obligations that determine its funded status as of the end of the employer's fiscal year (eliminating the alternative of a measurement date that could be up to three months earlier under prior standards); and (3) recognize changes in the funded status of a plan through comprehensive income in the year in which the changes occur. FAS-158 also amends the disclosure requirements in the notes to the financial statements by requiring information about certain effects on net periodic benefit cost for the next fiscal year that arise from delayed recognition of the gains or losses, prior service costs or credits, and transition assets or obligations. FAS-158 does not change the accounting and reporting by defined contribution and multiemployer plans.

FAS-158 applies to plan sponsors that are public and private companies. The requirement to recognize the funded status of a benefit plan and the disclosure requirements are effective for fiscal years ending after December 15, 2006, for public entities, and for fiscal years that end after June 15, 2007, for all other entities. In addition, nonpublic entities are required to disclose certain information (specified later under "Disclosure Requirements") in the notes to the financial statements for fiscal years ending after December 15, 2006, but before June 16, 2007. The requirement to measure plan assets and benefit obligations as of the date of the employer's fiscal year-end balance sheet is effective for fiscal years ending after December 15, 2008, for all entities. Earlier application is encouraged and retrospective application is not permitted.

Under FAS-158, entities are no longer required to report on their balance sheets an additional minimum pension liability for their underfunded obligations (or any corresponding intangible asset), because the funded status of defined benefit plans will now be fully recognized on their balance sheets.

The discussion in the remainder of this chapter has been updated to reflect the requirements of FAS-158.

Defined Benefit Postretirement Plans

The entity's primary objectives when accounting for a defined benefit postretirement plan are to (1) charge postretirement benefit costs to operations over the period employee services are rendered and (2) charge liabilities and credit assets when retirement benefits are paid. The annual cost of a defined benefit postretirement plan consists of the following components: (1) service cost; (2) interest cost on the plan's obligation to provide benefits; (3) actual return on plan assets; (4) amortization of any prior service cost or credit included in accumulated other comprehensive income; (5) recognition of net gain or loss, if any; and (6) amortization of any net transition asset or obligation.

Net periodic postretirement cost is estimated in advance at the beginning of a period based on actuarial assumptions such as the discount rate on accumulated benefit obligation, the expected long-term rate of return on postretirement plan assets, and future compensation levels. At the end of the period, adjustments are made to account for the differences (actuarial gains or losses), if any, between the estimated and actual amounts.

Most postretirement benefit plans include healthcare benefits, which require the use of additional unique assumptions such as per capita claims cost (the current cost of providing postretirement health-care benefit at each age at which a participant is expected to receive benefits), and healthcare cost trend rates.

Employers must recognize the funded status of a benefit plan as the difference between the fair value of plan assets and the benefit obligations in their balance sheets. For a pension plan, the benefit obligation is the projected benefit obligation; for other postretirement plans, the benefit obligation is the accumulated benefit obligation. The funded status of all overfunded plans are aggregated and recognized as an asset in the employer's balance sheet. Similarly, the funded status of all underfunded plans are aggregated and recognized as a liability in the employer's balance sheet. The aggregate overfunded amount is presented as a noncurrent asset in the employer's balance sheet. The aggregate underfunded amount is presented as a current liability, noncurrent liability, or combination of the two. The current portion is the amount by which the actuarial present value of the benefits included in the benefit obligation payable in the next 12 months or operating cycle, if longer, exceeds the fair value of plan assets.

Employers also recognize, as a component of other comprehensive income, the gains or losses and prior service costs or credits that arise during the period but are not recognized as components of net periodic benefit cost of the period in accordance with Statement of Financial Accounting Standards (FAS) No. 87 (FAS-87), *Employers' Accounting for Pensions*, and FAS-106, *Employers' Accounting for Postretirement Benefits Other Than Pensions*. Adjustments in other comprehensive income are recognized when the gains or losses, prior service costs or credits, and transition assets or obligations are subsequently recognized as components of net periodic pension cost in accordance with FAS-87, FAS-88, *Employers' Accounting for Settlements and Curtailments of Defined Benefit Pension Plans and for Termination Benefits*, and FAS-106.

Measurement date. Business entities are required to measure plan assets and benefit obligations as of the date of the fiscal year-end balance sheet unless:

- The plan is sponsored by a subsidiary that is consolidated using a fiscal period that differs from the parent company (as permitted by Accounting Research Bulletin No. 51, *Consolidated Financial Statements*), or

- The plan is sponsored by an investee that is accounted for by the equity method using a fiscal period that is different from the investor's fiscal period (as permitted by Accounting Principles Board Opinion No. 18, *The Equity Method of Accounting for Investments in Common Stock*).

In these cases, the business entity must measure the subsidiary's plan assets and benefit obligations as of the date used to consolidate the subsidiary's balance sheet, and the investee's plan assets and benefit obligations as of the date of the investee's financial statements used to apply the equity method.

Defined Contribution Postretirement Plans

A *defined contribution postretirement plan* provides for individual accounts for each plan participant and contains the terms that specify how contributions are determined for each participant's individual account. Each periodic employer contribution is allocated to each participant's individual account in accordance with the terms of the plan, and postretirement benefits are based solely on the amount available in each participant's account at the time of his or her retirement. The amount available in each participant's account at the time of his or her retirement is the total of the amounts contributed by the employer, plus the returns earned on investments of those contributions, plus forfeitures of other participants' benefits that have been allocated to the participant's account, and less any allocated administrative expenses.

A defined contribution postretirement plan may require the employer to contribute to the plan only for periods in which an employee renders services, or the employer may be required to continue making payments for periods after the employee retires or terminates employment. To the extent an employer's contribution is made in the same period as the employee renders services, the employer's net periodic postretirement benefit cost equals the amount of contributions required for that period. If the plan requires the employer to continue contributions after the employee retires or terminates, the employer should make accruals during the employee's service period of the estimated amount of contributions to be made after the employee's retirement or termination.

Settlements, Curtailments, and Termination Benefits

A *settlement* of a postretirement plan is an irrevocable action that relieves the employer (or the plan) of primary responsibility for an obligation and eliminates significant risks related to the obligation and the assets used to effect the settlement. Examples of transactions that constitute a settlement include (1) making lump-sum cash payments to plan participants in exchange for their rights to receive specified postretirement benefits and (2) purchasing nonparticipating insurance contracts to cover the accumulated postretirement benefit obligation for some or all of the participants in the plan.

When a postretirement benefit obligation is settled, the maximum gain or loss to be recognized in income is the net gain or loss remaining in accumulated other comprehensive income plus any transition asset remaining in accumulated other comprehensive income. This maximum gain or loss includes any gain or loss resulting from the remeasurement of plan assets and of the accumulated postretirement benefit obligation at the time of settlement.

A *curtailment* is an event that either (1) significantly reduces the expected years of future service of active plan participants or (2) eliminates the accrual of defined benefits for some or all of the future services of a significant number of active plan participants. Examples of curtailments are (1) termination of employees' services earlier than expected, which may or may not involve closing a facility or discontinuing a segment of a business, and (2) termination or suspension of a plan so that employees do not earn additional benefits for future services.

The prior service cost included in accumulated other comprehensive income associated with the portion of the future years of service that had been expected to be rendered, but as a result of a curtailment are no longer expected to be rendered, is a loss.

Termination benefits are classified as either special or contractual. *Special termination benefits* are those that are offered to employees for a short period in connection with the termination of their employment. *Contractual termination benefits* are those that are required by the terms of an existing plan or agreement and that are provided only on the occurrence of a specified event, such as early retirement or the closing of a facility.

GAAP require the recognition of the cost of termination benefits as a loss and corresponding liability. The recognition date depends on whether the benefits are special or contractual. Special termination benefits should be accrued when (1) the employees accept the offer of the special termination benefits and (2) the amount of the cost of the benefits can be *reasonably estimated*. The recognition date on which the employer records the loss and corresponding liability for contractual termination benefits occurs when (1) it is *probable* that employees will be entitled to the benefits and (2) the amount of the benefits to be provided can be *reasonably estimated*.

Authoritative Literature

FAS-88	Employers' Accounting for Settlements and Curtailments of Defined Benefit Pension Plans and for Termination Benefits
FAS-106	Employers' Accounting for Postretirement Benefits Other Than Pensions
FAS-132R	Employers' Disclosures about Pensions and efits Other Postretirement Benefits (Revised 2003)

FAS-158	Employers' Accounting for Defined Benefit Pension and Other Postretirement Plans
FSP FAS 106-2	Accounting and Disclosure Requirements Related to the Medicare Prescription Drug Improvement and Modernization Act of 2003
EITF 03-2	Accounting for the Transfer to the Japanese Government of the Substitutional Portion of Employee Pension Fund Liabilities

DISCLOSURE REQUIREMENTS

The disclosure requirements for postretirement benefit plans apply to both public and nonpublic entities. However, with respect to defined benefit postretirement plans, nonpublic entities are allowed to provide reduced disclosures, if they so elect, regardless of materiality.

Also, companies that have defined benefit pension plans and other postretirement benefit plans may elect to present the required disclosures for their plans in a parallel format in a single note to the financial statements, because most of the disclosures about defined benefit pension plans and postretirement benefit plans are similar.

> **Note:** In September 2006, the FASB issued Statement of Financial Accounting Standards (FAS-158) No. 158 entitled *Employers' Accounting for Defined Benefit Pension and Other Postretirement Plans*. This standard amends FAS-87, *Employers' Accounting for Pensions*; FAS-88, *Employers' Accounting for Settlements and Curtailments of Defined Benefit Pension Plans and for Termination Benefits*; FAS-106, *Employers' Accounting for Postretirement Benefits Other Than Pensions*; and FAS-132 (Revised 2003), *Employers' Disclosures about Pensions and Other Postretirement Benefits*.
>
> For an employer with publicly traded equity securities, the disclosure and recognition provisions of FAS-158 are effective for financial statements with fiscal years ending after December 15, 2006. For an employer without publicly traded equity securities, the disclosure and recognition provisions of FAS-158 are effective for financial statements with fiscal years ending after June 15, 2007. Certain additional disclosures are required for employers without publicly traded equity securities until they apply the recognition provisions of FAS-158. For all employers, the measurement provisions of FAS-158 are effective for financial statements with fiscal years ending after December 15, 2008. Until that time, certain measurement-related disclosures continue to be required.

Defined Benefit Postretirement Plans—Disclosure Requirements for All Public Entities and for Those Nonpublic Entities That Elect to Voluntarily Provide These Disclosures (Annual Periods)—Prior to the Adoption of FAS-158

The following disclosures, which are applicable prior to the adoption of FAS-158, should be made for defined benefit postretirement plans:

1. A brief description of the plan (FAS-132R, par. 5)

2. For each income statement presented, the amount of net periodic benefit cost for the period, showing separately the following (FAS-132R, par. 5h):

   a. Service cost component

   b. Interest cost component

   c. Expected return on plan assets for the period

   d. Amortization of the unrecognized transition obligation or asset

   e. Amount of recognized gains and losses

   f. Amount of prior service cost recognized

   g. Amount of gain or loss recognized due to a settlement or curtailment

3. For each balance sheet presented, the funded status of the plan, amounts not recognized in the entity's balance sheet, and amounts recognized in the entity's balance sheet, including the following (FAS-132R, par. 5c):

   a. The amount of any unamortized prior service cost

   b. The amount of unrecognized net gain or loss (including asset gains and losses not yet reflected in market-related value)

   c. The amount of any remaining unamortized, unrecognized net obligation or net asset existing at the date of initial application of FAS-106

   d. The net postretirement benefit prepaid assets or accrued liabilities

4. For each balance sheet presented, a reconciliation of the beginning and ending balances of the benefit obligation, with separate disclosure of the following (FAS-132R, par. 5a):

   a. Service cost

   b. Interest cost

    c. Contributions by plan participants

    d. Actuarial gains and losses

    e. Foreign currency exchange rate changes

    f. Benefits paid

    g. Plan amendments

    h. Business combinations

    i. Divestitures

    j. Curtailments

    k. Settlements

    l. Special termination benefits

5. For each balance sheet presented, a reconciliation of the beginning and ending balances of the fair value of plan assets, including the effects of the following (FAS-132R, par. 5b):

    a. Actual return on plan assets

    b. Foreign currency exchange rate changes

    c. Contributions by employer

    d. Contributions by plan participants

    e. Benefits paid

    f. Business combinations

    g. Divestitures

    h. Settlements

6. For each balance sheet presented, the following assumptions used in the accounting for the plan (FAS-132R, par. 5j):

    a. The weighted-average assumed discount rates

    b. The weighted-average rates of compensation increase (for pay-related plans)

    c. The weighted-average expected long-term rates of return on plan assets specifying, in tabular format, the assumptions used to determine the benefit obligation and the net benefit cost

7. The following information about plan assets (FAS-132R, par. 5d):

    a. For each balance sheet presented, the percentage of the fair value of total plan assets held in each major category of plan assets, including at a minimum the following categories: (i) equity securities, (ii) debt securities, (iii) real estate, and (iv) all other assets. Also, disclosure of additional asset categories, and additional information about specific assets within a category, is encouraged if that information is considered useful

b. As of the latest balance sheet presented, a narrative description of investment policies and strategies, including: (i) target allocation percentages, or range of percentages, for each major category of plan assets presented on a weighted-average basis, and (ii) other factors that are pertinent to an understanding of the policies or strategies such as investment goals, risk management practices, permitted and prohibited investments including the use of derivatives, diversification, and the relationship between plan assets and benefit obligations

c. As of the latest balance sheet presented, a narrative description of the basis used to determine the overall expected long-term rate-of-return-on-assets assumption, such as: (i) the general approach used, (ii) the extent to which the overall rate-of-return-on-assets assumption was based on historical returns, (iii) the extent to which adjustments were made to those historical returns in order to reflect expectations of future returns, and (iv) how those adjustments were determined

8. Until the provisions of FAS-132 (Revised 2003) are adopted in full for domestic and foreign plans, financial statements that exclude foreign plans from the disclosure requirements of item 7 above, should disclose separately for domestic plans the following (FAS-132R, par. 19):

   a. The total fair value of plan assets as of the date of the latest balance sheet presented

   b. The overall expected long-term rate of return on assets for the latest period for which an income statement is presented

9. As of the latest balance sheet presented, the benefits expected to be paid in each of the next five fiscal years, and in the aggregate for the five fiscal years thereafter (FAS-132R, par. 5f)

10. The company's best estimate of contributions expected to be paid to the plan during the next fiscal year beginning after the date of the latest balance sheet presented (FAS-132R, par. 5g) (Estimated contributions may be presented in the aggregate for contributions required by funding regulations or laws, discretionary contributions, and noncash contributions)

11. The measurement date used to determine postretirement benefit information for the plans that make up at least the majority of plan assets and benefit obligations (FAS-132R, par. 5k)

12. The assumed healthcare cost trend rate(s) for the next year used to measure the expected cost of benefits covered by the plan (gross eligible charges), a general description of the direction and pattern of change in the assumed trend rates thereafter, together with the ultimate trend rate(s) and when that rate is expected to be achieved (FAS-132R, par. 5l)

13. The effect of a 1% point increase and the effect of a 1% point decrease in the assumed healthcare cost trend rates on (1) the aggregate of the service and interest cost components of net periodic postretirement healthcare benefit cost of the current period and (2) the accumulated postretirement benefit obligation for healthcare benefits as of the latest balance sheet presented (FAS-132R, par. 5m)

14. The amounts and types of securities of the employer and related parties included in plan assets (FAS-132R, par. 5n)

15. The approximate amount of future annual benefits of plan participants covered by insurance contracts issued by the employer or related parties (FAS-132R, par. 5n)

16. Any significant transactions between the employer or related parties and the plan during the period (FAS-132R, par. 5n)

17. Any alternative amortization method used to amortize prior service costs or unrecognized net gains and losses (FAS-87, pars. 26 and 33; FAS-106, par. 60; FAS-132R, par. 5o)

18. Any substantive commitment, such as past practice or a history of regular benefit increases, used as the basis for accounting for the benefit obligation (FAS-132R, par. 5p)

19. The cost of providing special or contractual termination benefits recognized during the period and a description of the nature of the event (FAS-132R, par. 5q)

20. An explanation of any significant change in the benefit obligation or plan assets not otherwise apparent in the above disclosures (FAS-132R, par. 5r)

21. The disclosures for prior annual periods presented for comparative purposes as a result of applying the provisions of FAS-132 (Revised 2003), should be restated for: (a) the percentages of each major category of plan assets held, (b) the accumulated benefit obligation, and (c) the assumptions used in the accounting for the plans (FAS-132R, par. 20) (If this is not practicable, the notes to the financial statements should include all available information and identify the information that is not available)

22. For employers with two or more defined benefit postretirement plans, if disclosures for *underfunded plans* (those that have accumulated postretirement benefit obligations in

excess of plan assets) and *overfunded plans* (those that have plan assets in excess of accumulated postretirement benefit obligations) are presented on a combined basis, the following disclosures should be made separately with respect to plans that are underfunded (FAS-132R, par. 6):

    a. The aggregate accumulated postretirement benefit obligation

    b. The aggregate fair value of plan assets

23. If two or more defined benefit postretirement plans are combined, the amounts recognized as prepaid benefit costs and accrued benefit liabilities should be disclosed separately (FAS-132R, par. 6)

24. Domestic and foreign defined benefit postretirement plans may be aggregated unless the benefit obligations of the foreign plans are significant relative to the total benefit obligation and the plans use significantly different assumptions (FAS-132R, par. 7)

Defined Benefit Postretirement Plans—Disclosure Requirements for All Public Entities and for Those Nonpublic Entities That Elect to Voluntarily Provide These Disclosures (Annual Periods)—After the Adoption of FAS-158

The following disclosures, which are applicable after the adoption of FAS-158, should be made for defined benefit postretirement plans:

1. A description of the plan (FAS-132R, par. 5)

2. For each income statement presented, the amount of net periodic benefit cost for the period, showing separately the following (FAS-132R, par. 5h; FAS-158, par. E1d):

    a. Service cost component

    b. Interest cost component

    c. Expected return on plan assets for the period

    d. Gain or loss component

    e. Prior service cost or credit component

    f. Transition asset or obligation component

    g. Amount of gain or loss recognized due to settlements or curtailments

3. For each balance sheet presented, the funded status of the plans and the amounts recognized in the entity's balance

sheet, showing separately the assets and current and noncurrent liabilities recognized (FAS-132R, par. 5c; FAS-158, par. E1c)

4. For each balance sheet presented, a reconciliation of the beginning and ending balances of the benefit obligation, with separate disclosure of the following (FAS-132R, par. 5a):

   a. Service cost

   b. Interest cost

   c. Contributions by plan participants

   d. Actuarial gains and losses

   e. Foreign currency exchange rate changes

   f. Benefits paid

   g. Plan amendments

   h. Business combinations

   i. Divestitures

   j. Curtailments

   k. Settlements

   l. Special termination benefits

5. For each balance sheet presented, a reconciliation of the beginning and ending balances of the fair value of plan assets, including the effects of the following (FAS-132R, par. 5b):

   a. Actual return on plan assets

   b. Foreign currency exchange rate changes

   c. Contributions by employer

   d. Contributions by plan participants

   e. Benefits paid

   f. Business combinations

   g. Divestitures

   h. Settlements

6. For each income statement presented (FAS-132R, pars. 5i and 10A–B; FAS-158, pars. E1e and E1t):

   a. The net gain or loss and net prior service cost or credit recognized in other comprehensive income for the period pursuant to paragraphs 25 and 29 of FAS-87 and paragraphs 52 and 56 of FAS-106, as amended

   b. Reclassification adjustments of other comprehensive income for the period

7. For each income statement presented, the amounts in accumulated other comprehensive income that have not yet been recognized as components of net periodic benefit cost, showing separately the net gain or loss, net prior service cost or credit, and net transition asset or obligation (FAS-132R, pars. 5i and 10C; FAS-158, pars. E1f and E1t)

8. For each balance sheet presented, the following assumptions used in the accounting for the plan (FAS-132R, par. 5j):

   a. The weighted-average assumed discount rates

   b. The weighted-average rates of compensation increase (for pay-related plans)

   c. The weighted-average expected long-term rates of return on plan assets specifying, in tabular format, the assumptions used to determine the benefit obligation and the net benefit cost

9. The following information about plan assets (FAS-132R, par. 5d):

   a. For each balance sheet presented, the percentage of the fair value of total plan assets held in each major category of plan assets, including at a minimum the following categories: (i) equity securities, (ii) debt securities, (iii) real estate, and (iv) all other assets. Also, disclosure of additional asset categories and additional information about specific assets within a category is encouraged if that information is considered useful

   b. As of the latest balance sheet presented, a narrative description of investment policies and strategies, including (i) target allocation percentages, or range of percentages, for each major category of plan assets presented on a weighted-average basis, and (ii) other factors that are pertinent to an understanding of the policies or strategies, such as investment goals, risk management practices, permitted and prohibited investments, including the use of derivatives, diversification, and the relationship between plan assets and benefit obligations

   c. As of the latest balance sheet date presented, a narrative description of the basis used to determine the overall expected long-term rate-of-return-on-assets assumption, such as (i) the general approach used, (ii) the extent to which the overall rate-of-return-on-assets assumption was based on historical returns, (iii) the extent to which adjustments were made to those historical returns in order to reflect expectations of future returns, and (iv) how those adjustments were determined

10. Until the provisions of FAS-132 (Revised 2003) are adopted in full for domestic and foreign plans, financial statements that exclude foreign plans from the disclosure requirements of item 9 above should disclose separately for domestic plans the following (FAS-132R, par. 19):

    a. The total fair value of plan assets as of the date of the latest balance sheet presented

    b. The overall expected long-term rate of return on assets for the latest period for which an income statement is presented

11. As of the latest balance sheet presented, the benefits expected to be paid in each of the next five fiscal years and in the aggregate for the five fiscal years thereafter (FAS-132R, par. 5f)

12. The company's best estimate of contributions expected to be paid to the plan during the next fiscal year beginning after the date of the latest balance sheet presented (FAS-132R, par. 5g) (Estimated contributions may be presented in the aggregate for contributions required by funding regulations or laws, discretionary contributions, and noncash contributions)

13. The assumed healthcare cost trend rates for the next year used to measure the expected cost of benefits covered by the plan (gross eligible charges), a general description of the direction and pattern of change in the assumed trend rates thereafter, together with the ultimate trend rates and when the rates are expected to be achieved (FAS-132R, par. 5l)

14. The effect of a 1% point increase and the effect of a 1% point decrease in the assumed healthcare cost trend rates on (a) the aggregate of the service and interest cost components of net periodic postretirement healthcare benefit cost of the current period and (b) the accumulated postretirement benefit obligation for healthcare benefits as of the latest balance sheet presented (FAS-132R, par. 5m)

15. The amounts and types of securities of the employer and related parties included in plan assets (FAS-132R, par. 5n)

16. The approximate amount of future annual benefits of plan participants covered by insurance contracts issued by the employer or related parties (FAS-132R, par. 5n)

17. Any significant transactions between the employer or related parties and the plan during the period (FAS-132R, par. 5n)

18. Any alternative amortization method used to amortize prior service costs or net gains and losses (FAS-87, pars. 26 and 33; FAS-106, par. 60; FAS-132R, par. 5o; FAS-158, pars. C2d, C2h, D2k, and E1h)

19. Any substantive commitment, such as past practice or a history of regular benefit increases, used as the basis for accounting for the benefit obligation (FAS-132R, par. 5p)

20. The cost of providing special or contractual termination benefits recognized during the period and a description of the nature of the event (FAS-132R, par. 5q)

21. An explanation of any significant change in the benefit obligation or plan assets not otherwise apparent in the above disclosures (FAS-132R, par. 5r)

22. For each balance sheet presented, the amounts in accumulated other comprehensive income expected to be recognized as components of net periodic benefit cost over the fiscal year that follows the most recent annual balance sheet presented, showing separately the net gain or loss, net prior service cost or credit, and net transition asset or obligation (FAS-132R, pars. 5s and 10C; FAS-158, pars. E1i and E1t)

23. The amount and timing of any plan assets expected to be returned to the employer during the 12-month period, or operating cycle if longer, that follows the most recent annual balance sheet presented (FAS-132R, par. 5t; FAS-158, par. E1j)

24. The disclosures for prior annual periods presented for comparative purposes as a result of applying the provisions of FAS-132 (Revised 2003), should be restated for (a) the percentages of each major category of plan assets held, (b) the accumulated benefit obligation, and (c) the assumptions used in the accounting for the plans (FAS-132R, par. 20) (If this is not practicable, the notes to the financial statements should include all available information and identify the information that is not available)

25. For employers with two or more defined benefit pension or postretirement plans, if disclosures for plans that have accumulated benefit obligations in excess of plan assets and plans that have plan assets in excess of accumulated benefit obligations are presented on a combined basis, the following disclosures should be made separately with respect to plans that have *accumulated* benefit obligations in excess of plan assets (FAS-132R, par. 6):

    a. The aggregate accumulated benefit obligations

    b. The aggregate fair value of plan assets

26. Domestic and foreign defined benefit pension plans may be aggregated unless the benefit obligations of the foreign plans are significant relative to the total benefit obligation and the plans use significantly different assumptions (FAS-132R, par. 7)

27. The following information disclosed separately for pension plans and other postretirement benefit plans (FAS-158, par. 7):

   a. For each annual statement of income presented, the amounts recognized in other comprehensive income, showing separately the net gain or loss and net prior service cost or credit

   b. The amounts disclosed in item a above separated into amounts arising during the period and reclassification adjustments of other comprehensive income as a result of being recognized as components of net periodic benefit cost for the period

   c. For each annual statement of income presented, the net transition asset or obligation recognized as a reclassification adjustment of other comprehensive income as a result of being recognized as a component of net periodic benefit cost for the period

   d. For each annual statement of financial position presented, the amounts in accumulated other comprehensive income that have not yet been recognized as components of net periodic benefit cost, showing separately the net gain or loss, net prior service cost or credit, and net transition asset or obligation

   e. The amounts in accumulated other comprehensive income expected to be recognized as components of net periodic benefit cost over the fiscal year that follows the most recent annual statement of financial position presented, showing separately the net gain or loss, net prior service cost or credit, and net transition asset or obligation

   f. The amount and timing of any plan assets expected to be returned to the business entity during the 12-month period, or operating cycle if longer, that follows the most recent annual statement of financial position presented

28. The following transitional disclosures upon implementation of FAS-158:

   a. In the year that the recognition provisions of FAS-158 are initially applied, the incremental effect of applying FAS-158 on individual line items in the year-end balance sheet (FAS-158, par. 20)

   b. In the year that the measurement date provisions of FAS-158 are initially applied, the separate adjustments of both retained earnings and accumulated other comprehensive income from applying FAS-158 (FAS-158, par. 21)

Defined Benefit Postretirement Plans—Reduced Disclosure Requirements for Nonpublic Entities (Annual Periods)—Prior to the Adoption of FAS-158

The following are the reduced disclosure requirements for defined benefit postretirement plans of nonpublic entities that are applicable prior to the adoption of FAS-158:

1. A brief description of the plan (FAS-132R, par. 8)
2. For each balance sheet presented, the following information about the plan (FAS-132R, par. 8a):
   a. The benefit obligation
   b. The fair value of plan assets
   c. The funded status of the plan
3. For each income statement presented, the following information about the plan (FAS-132R, par. 8b):
   a. Employer contributions
   b. Participant contributions
   c. Benefits paid
4. The following information about plan assets (FAS-132R, par. 8c):
   a. For each balance sheet presented, the percentage of the fair value of total plan assets held in each major category of plan assets, including at a minimum the following categories: (i) equity securities, (ii) debt securities, (iii) real estate, and (iv) all other assets. Also, disclosure of additional asset categories, and additional information about specific assets within a category, is encouraged if that information is considered useful
   b. As of the latest balance sheet presented, a narrative description of investment policies and strategies, including: (i) target allocation percentages, or range of percentages, for each major category of plan assets presented on a weighted-average basis, and (ii) other factors that are pertinent to an understanding of the policies or strategies such as investment goals, risk management practices, permitted and prohibited investments including the use of derivatives, diversification, and the relationship between plan assets and benefit obligations
   c. As of the latest balance sheet presented, a narrative description of the basis used to determine the overall expected long-term rate-of-return-on-assets assumption, such as: (i) the general approach used, (ii) the extent to

which the overall rate-of-return-on-assets assumption was based on historical returns, (iii) the extent to which adjustments were made to those historical returns in order to reflect expectations of future returns, and (iv) how those adjustments were determined

5. As of the latest balance sheet presented, the benefits expected to be paid in each of the next five fiscal years, and in the aggregate for the five fiscal years thereafter (FAS-132R, par. 8e)

6. The company's best estimate of contributions expected to be paid to the plan during the next fiscal year beginning after the date of the latest balance sheet presented (FAS-132R, par. 8f) (Estimated contributions may be presented in the aggregate for contributions required by funding regulations or laws, discretionary contributions, and noncash contributions)

7. For each balance sheet presented, the amounts recognized in the balance sheet, including the net postretirement benefit prepaid assets or accrued liabilities (FAS-132R, par. 8g)

8. For each income statement presented, the amount of net periodic benefit cost recognized as expense (FAS-132R, par. 8h)

9. For each balance sheet presented, the following assumptions used in the accounting for the plan (FAS-132R, par. 8i):

   a. The weighted-average assumed discount rates

   b. The weighted-average rates of compensation increase (for pay-related plans)

   c. The weighted-average expected long-term rates of return on plan assets specifying, in tabular format, the assumptions used to determine the benefit obligation and the net benefit cost

10. The measurement date used to determine postretirement benefit information for the plans that make up at least the majority of plan assets and benefit obligations (FAS-132R, par. 8j)

11. The assumed healthcare cost trend rate(s) for the next year used to measure the expected cost of benefits covered by the plan (gross eligible charges) and a general description of the direction and pattern of change in the assumed trend rates thereafter, together with the ultimate trend rate(s) and when that rate is expected to be achieved (FAS-132R, par. 8k)

12. The amounts and types of securities of the employer and related parties included in plan assets (FAS-132R, par. 8l)

13. The approximate amount of future annual benefits of plan participants covered by insurance contracts issued by the employer or related parties (FAS-132R, par. 8l)

14. Any significant transactions between the employer or related parties and the plan during the period (FAS-132R, par. 8l)

15. The nature and effect of significant nonroutine events, such as amendments, combinations, divestitures, curtailments, and settlements (FAS-132R, par. 8m)

16. The disclosures for prior annual periods presented for comparative purposes as a result of applying the provisions of FAS-132 (Revised 2003), should be restated for: (a) the percentages of each major category of plan assets held, (b) the accumulated benefit obligation, and (c) the assumptions used in the accounting for the plans (FAS-132R, par. 20) (If this is not practicable, the notes to the financial statements should include all available information and identify the information that is not available)

17. For employers with two or more defined benefit postretirement plans, if disclosures for *underfunded plans* (those that have accumulated postretirement benefit obligations in excess of plan assets) and *overfunded plans* (those that have plan assets in excess of accumulated postretirement benefit obligations) are presented on a combined basis, the following disclosures should be made separately with respect to plans that are *underfunded* (FAS-132R, par. 6):

    a. The aggregate accumulated postretirement benefit obligation

    b. The aggregate fair value of plan assets

18. If two or more defined benefit postretirement plans are combined, the amounts recognized as prepaid benefit costs and accrued benefit liabilities should be disclosed separately (FAS-132R, par. 6)

19. Domestic and foreign defined benefit postretirement plans may be aggregated unless the benefit obligations of the foreign plans are significant relative to the total benefit obligation and the plans use significantly different assumptions (FAS-132R, par. 7)

20. For fiscal years ending after December 15, 2006, but before June 16, 2007, for entities that have not applied the recognition provisions of FAS-158, the following disclosures should be made (FAS-158, par. 14):

    a. A brief description of the provisions of FAS-158

    b. The date that the adoption of FAS-158 is required

    c. The date the employer plans to adopt the recognition provisions of FAS-158, if earlier

Defined Benefit Postretirement Plans—Reduced Disclosure Requirements for Nonpublic Entities (Annual Periods)—After the Adoption of FAS-158

The following are the reduced disclosure requirements for defined benefit postretirement plans of nonpublic entities that are applicable after the adoption of FAS-158:

1. A brief description of the plan (FAS-132R, par. 8)
2. For each balance sheet presented, the following information about the plan (FAS-132R, par. 8a):
   a. The benefit obligation
   b. The fair value of plan assets
   c. The funded status of the plan
3. For each income statement presented, the following information about the plan (FAS-132R, par. 8b):
   a. Employer contributions
   b. Participant contributions
   c. Benefits paid
4. The following information about plan assets (FAS-132R, par. 8c):
   a. For each balance sheet presented, the percentage of the fair value of total plan assets held in each major category of plan assets, including at a minimum the following categories: (i) equity securities, (ii) debt securities, (iii) real estate, and (iv) all other assets. Also, disclosure of additional asset categories and additional information about specific assets within a category is encouraged if that information is considered useful
   b. As of the latest balance sheet presented, a narrative description of investment policies and strategies, including (i) target allocation percentages, or range of percentages, for each major category of plan assets presented on a weighted-average basis, and (ii) other factors that are pertinent to an understanding of the policies or strategies, such as investment goals, risk management practices, permitted and prohibited investments, including the use of derivatives, diversification, and the relationship between plan assets and benefit obligations
   c. As of the latest balance sheet presented, a narrative description of the basis used to determine the overall expected long-term rate-of-return-on-assets assumption, such as (i) the general approach used, (ii) the extent to

which the overall rate-of-return-on-assets assumption was based on historical returns, (iii) the extent to which adjustments were made to those historical returns in order to reflect expectations of future returns, and (iv) how those adjustments were determined

5. For each balance sheet presented, the accumulated benefit obligation (FAS-132R, par. 8d)

6. As of the latest balance sheet presented, the benefits expected to be paid in each of the next five fiscal years, and in the aggregate for the five fiscal years thereafter (FAS-132R, par. 8e)

7. The company's best estimate of contributions expected to be paid to the plan during the next fiscal year beginning after the date of the latest balance sheet presented (FAS-132R, par. 8f) (Estimated contributions may be presented in the aggregate for contributions required by funding regulations or laws, discretionary contributions, and noncash contributions)

8. For each balance sheet presented, the amounts recognized in the balance sheet, including showing separately the benefit assets and current and noncurrent benefit liabilities (FAS-132R, par. 8g; FAS-158, par. E1m)

9. For each income statement presented (FAS-132R, pars. 8h and 10A–B; FAS-158, pars. E1m and E1t):

   a. The net gain or loss and net prior service cost or credit recognized in other comprehensive income for the period pursuant to paragraphs 25 and 29 of FAS-87 and paragraphs 52 and 56 of FAS-106, as amended

   b. Reclassification adjustments of other comprehensive income for the period

10. For each income statement presented, the amounts in accumulated other comprehensive income that have not yet been recognized as components of net periodic benefit cost, showing separately the net gain or loss, net prior service cost or credit, and net transition asset or obligation (FAS-132R, pars. 8h and 10C; FAS-158, pars. E1o and E1t)

11. For each balance sheet presented, the following assumptions used in the accounting for the plan (FAS-132R, par. 8i):

   a. The weighted-average assumed discount rates

   b. The weighted-average rates of compensation increase (for pay-related plans)

   c. The weighted-average expected long-term rates of return on plan assets specifying, in tabular format, the assumptions used to determine the benefit obligation and the net benefit cost

12. The assumed healthcare cost trend rates for the next year used to measure the expected cost of benefits covered by the plan (gross eligible charges), a general description of the direction and pattern of change in the assumed trend rates thereafter, together with the ultimate trend rates and when those rates are expected to be achieved (FAS-132R, par. 8k)

13. The amounts and types of securities of the employer and related parties included in plan assets (FAS-132R, par. 8l)

14. The approximate amount of future annual benefits of plan participants covered by insurance contracts issued by the employer or related parties (FAS-132R, par. 8l)

15. Any significant transactions between the employer or related parties and the plan during the period (FAS-132R, 8l)

16. The nature and effect of significant nonroutine events, such as amendments, combinations, divestitures, curtailments, and settlements (FAS-132R, par. 8m)

17. For each balance sheet presented, the amounts in accumulated other comprehensive income expected to be recognized as components of net periodic benefit cost over the fiscal year that follows the most recent annual balance sheet presented, showing separately the net gain or loss, net prior service cost or credit, and net transition asset or obligation (FAS-132R, pars. 8n and 10C; FAS-158, par. E1q)

18. The amount and timing of any plan assets expected to be returned to the employer during the 12-month period, or operating cycle if longer, that follows the most recent annual balance sheet presented (FAS-132R, par. 8o; FAS-158, par. E1r)

19. The disclosures for prior annual periods that are presented for comparative purposes as a result of applying the provisions of FAS-132 (Revised 2003), should be restated for (a) the percentages of each major category of plan assets held, (b) the accumulated benefit obligation, and (c) the assumptions used in the accounting for the plans (FAS-132R, par. 20) (If this is not practicable, the notes to the financial statements should include all available information and identify the information that is not available)

20. For employers with two or more defined benefit pension or postretirement plans, if disclosures for plans that have accumulated benefit obligations in excess of plan assets and plans that have plan assets in excess of accumulated benefit obligations are presented on a combined basis, the following disclosures should be made separately with respect to plans that have *accumulated* benefit obligations in excess of plan assets (FAS-132R, par. 6; FAS-158, par. E1k):

     a. The aggregate accumulated benefit obligations

     b. The aggregate fair value of plan assets

21. Domestic and foreign defined benefit pension plans may be aggregated unless the benefit obligations of the foreign plans are significant relative to the total benefit obligation and the plans use significantly different assumptions (FAS-132R, par. 7)

22. The following information disclosed separately for pension plans and other postretirement benefit plans (FAS-158, par. 7):

     a. For each annual statement of income presented, the amounts recognized in other comprehensive income, showing separately the net gain or loss and net prior service cost or credit

     b. The amounts disclosed in item a above separated into amounts arising during the period and reclassification adjustments of other comprehensive income as a result of being recognized as components of net periodic benefit cost for the period

     c. For each annual statement of income presented, the net transition asset or obligation recognized as a reclassification adjustment of other comprehensive income as a result of being recognized as a component of net periodic benefit cost for the period

     d. For each annual statement of financial position presented, the amounts in accumulated other comprehensive income that have not yet been recognized as components of net periodic benefit cost, showing separately the net gain or loss, net prior service cost or credit, and net transition asset or obligation

     e. The amounts in accumulated other comprehensive income expected to be recognized as components of net periodic benefit cost over the fiscal year that follows the most recent annual statement of financial position presented, showing separately the net gain or loss, net prior service cost or credit, and net transition asset or obligation

     f. The amount and timing of any plan assets expected to be returned to the business entity during the 12-month period, or operating cycle if longer, that follows the most recent annual statement of financial position presented

23. The following transitional disclosures upon implementation of FAS-158:

a. In the year that the recognition provisions of FAS-158 are initially applied, the incremental effect of applying FAS-158 on individual line items in the year-end balance sheet (FAS-158, par. 20)

b. In the year that the measurement date provisions of FAS-158 are initially applied, the separate adjustments of both retained earnings and accumulated other comprehensive income from applying FAS-158 (FAS-158, par. 21)

Defined Benefit Postretirement Plans—Disclosure Requirements for Public and Nonpublic Entities (Interim Periods)

Public entities.   Public entities should disclose the following information in their interim financial statements (FAS-132R, par. 9):

1. For each income statement presented, the amount of net periodic benefit cost recognized, showing separately the following:

    a. Service cost component

    b. Interest cost component

    c. Expected return on plan assets for the period

    d. Amortization of the unrecognized transition obligation or asset

    e. Amount of recognized gains or losses

    f. Amount of prior service cost recognized

    g. Amount of gain or loss recognized due to a settlement or curtailment

2. The total amount of the employer's contributions paid, and expected to be paid, during the current fiscal year, if significantly different from amounts previously disclosed (Estimated contributions may be presented in the aggregate for contributions required by funding regulations or laws, discretionary contributions, and noncash contributions)

Nonpublic entities. Nonpublic entities should disclose the total amount of the employer's contributions paid, and expected to be paid, during the current fiscal year, if significantly different from amounts previously disclosed. Estimated contributions may be presented in the aggregate for contributions required by funding regulations or laws, discretionary contributions, and noncash contributions (FAS-132R, par. 10).

Defined Benefit Postretirement Health Care Plans—All Companies (Interim and Annual Periods)

For employers who sponsor single-employer defined benefit postretirement health care plans that provide prescription drug coverage, the following disclosures should be made (FSP FAS 106-2, pars. 20–22):

1. For periods in which the employer has not yet been able to determine the actuarial equivalency to Medicare Part D under the Medicare Prescription Drug Improvement and Modernization Act of 2003 (the Act):

   a. The existence of the Act

   b. A statement that measures of the accumulated postretirement benefit obligation (APBO) or net periodic postretirement benefit cost do not reflect any amount associated with the federal subsidy provided by the Act because the employer is unable to conclude whether the benefits provided by the plan are actuarially equivalent to Medicare Part D under the Act

2. For financial statements for the first period in which the employer includes the effects of the federal subsidy provided by the Act in measuring the APBO and net periodic postretirement benefit cost:

   a. The reduction in the APBO for the subsidy related to benefits attributed to past service

   b. The effect of the subsidy on the measurement of net periodic postretirement benefit cost for the current period, including:

      (1) Any amortization of the actuarial experience gain in Item 2a as a component of the net amortization called for by paragraph 59 of FAS-106

      (2) The reduction in current period service cost and interest cost on the APBO due to the subsidy

3. An explanation of any significant change in the benefit obligation or plan assets not otherwise apparent in the above disclosures

4. Gross benefit payments (paid and expected), including prescription drug benefits

5. Gross amount of the subsidy receipts (received and expected)

Japanese Employee Pension Fund Plans

The following disclosures should be made for employers with Japanese Employees' Pension Fund (EPF) plans that have accounted for the separation of the "substitutional portion" of the benefit obligation of an EPF in Japan from the corporate portion and the transfer of the "substitutional portion" and related assets to the Japanese government (EITF 03-2):

1. The difference between the obligation settled and the assets transferred to the government, determined in accordance with the government formula and displayed as a subsidy from the government

2. Separate from the government subsidy, the derecognition of previously accrued salary progression at the time of settlement

Defined Contribution Postretirement Plans

The following disclosures should be made for defined contribution postretirement plans:

1. A brief description of the plan (FAS-132R, par. 11)

2. The amount of cost recognized as expense during the period (FAS-132R, par. 11)

3. The nature and effect of significant matters affecting comparability of information for all periods presented, such as a change in the rate of employer contributions, business combinations, or divestitures (FAS-132R, par. 11)

Multiemployer Postretirement Benefit Plans

The following disclosures should be made for multiemployer postretirement benefit plans:

1. The amount of employer contributions during the period (amounts attributable to pensions and other postretirement benefit plans may be combined) (FAS-132R, par. 12)

2. A description of the nature and effect of any changes affecting comparability, such as a change in the rate of employer contributions, business combinations, or divestitures (FAS-132R, par. 12)

3. If it is either probable or reasonably possible that (a) an employer would withdraw from a multiemployer postretirement benefit plan under circumstances that would give rise

to a withdrawal obligation or (b) an employer's contribution to a multiemployer postretirement benefit plan would be increased during the remainder of a contract period in order to maintain a negotiated level of benefit coverage (a "maintenance of benefits" clause), disclosure of the information required by FAS-5 should be made (FAS-132R, par. 13)

EXAMPLES OF FINANCIAL STATEMENT DISCLOSURES

The following sample disclosures are available on the accompanying disc.

Illustrations under FAS-158: Defined Benefit Plans

Example 28–1: Defined Benefit Postretirement Plans—Public Entities

The Company has multiple nonpension postretirement benefit plans. The healthcare plans are contributory, with participants' contributions adjusted annually; the life insurance plans are noncontributory. The accounting for the healthcare plans anticipates future cost sharing changes to the written plan that are consistent with the Company's expressed intent to increase retiree contributions each year by 50% of the excess of the expected general inflation rate over 6%. On December 31, 20X2, the Company amended its postretirement healthcare plans to provide long-term care coverage.

The following tables set forth the benefit obligation, the fair value of plan assets, and the funded status of the Company's plans; the amounts recognized in the Company's financial statements; and the principal weighted-average assumptions used:

	20X2	20X1
Change in benefit obligation:		
Benefit obligation at beginning of year	$ 738,000	$ 700,000
Service cost	36,000	32,000
Interest cost	65,000	63,000
Plan participants' contributions	20,000	13,000
Amendments	75,000	-0-
Actuarial gain	(24,000)	-0-
Acquisition	600,000	-0-
Benefits paid	(90,000)	(70,000)
Benefit obligation at end of year	$ 1,420,000	$ 738,000

	20X2	20X1
Change in plan assets:		
Fair value of plan assets at beginning of year	$ 206,000	$ 87,000
Actual return on plan assets	(3,000)	24,000
Acquisition	25,000	-0-
Employer contribution	171,000	152,000
Plan participants' contributions	20,000	13,000
Benefits paid	(90,000)	(70,000)
Fair value of plan assets at end of year	$ 329,000	$ 206,000
Funded status at end of year	$(1,091,000)	$(532,000)
Amounts recognized in the balance sheets consist of:		
Noncurrent assets	$ 60,000	$ 70,000
Current liabilities	(350,000)	(400,000)
Noncurrent liabilities	(801,000)	(202,000)
	$ (1,091,000)	$ (532,000)

Amounts recognized in accumulated other comprehensive income consist of the following:

	20X2	20X1
Net loss (gain)	$ 59,000	$ 60,000
Prior service cost (credit)	585,000	540,000
	$644,000	$600,000

The following are weighted-average assumptions used to determine benefit obligations at December 31, 20X2, and December 31, 20X1:

	20X2	20X1
Discount rate	7.00%	7.25%

The following are weighted-average assumptions used to determine net periodic benefit cost for the years ended December 31, 20X2, and December 31, 20X1:

	20X2	20X1
Discount rate	7.00%	7.25%
Expected long-term return on plan assets	8.25%	8.50%

The Company's expected long-term return on plan assets assumption is based on a periodic review and modeling of the plans' asset allocation and liability structure over a long-term period. Expectations of returns for each asset class are the most important of the assumptions used in the review and modeling and are based on comprehensive reviews of historical data and economic/ financial market theory. The expected long-term rate of return on assets was selected from within the reasonable range of rates determined by (1) historical real returns, net of inflation, for the asset classes covered by the investment policy and (2) projections of inflation over the long-term period during which benefits are payable to plan participants.

For measurement purposes, a 10% annual rate of increase in the per capita cost of covered healthcare benefits was assumed for 20X3. The rate was assumed to decrease gradually to 4% for 20X9 and remain at that level thereafter.

Components of net periodic benefit cost and other amounts recognized in other comprehensive income are as follows:

	20X2	20X1
Net Periodic Benefit Cost:		
Service cost	$ 36,000	$ 32,000
Interest cost	65,000	63,000
Expected return on plan assets	(21,000)	(9,000)
Amortization of prior service cost	30,000	30,000
Recognized net actuarial loss	1,000	1,000
Net periodic benefit cost	111,000	117,000
Other Changes in Plan Assets and Benefit Obligations Recognized in Other Comprehensive Income:		
Net loss (gain)	(1,000)	15,000
Prior service cost (credit)	50,000	60,000
Amortization of prior service cost	(5,000)	(10,000)
Total recognized in other comprehensive income	44,000	65,000
Total recognized in net periodic benefit cost and other comprehensive income	$155,000	$182,000

The estimated net loss and prior service cost for the defined benefit postretirement plans that will be amortized from accumulated other comprehensive income into net periodic benefit cost over the next fiscal year are $25,000 and $75,000, respectively.

The Company acquired Massari, Ltd. on December 31, 20X2, including its postretirement benefit plans. As a result, the Company's plans were amended to establish parity with the benefits provided by Massari, Ltd.

Assumed healthcare cost trend rates have a significant effect on the amounts reported for the healthcare plans. A 1% point change in assumed healthcare cost trend rates would have the following effects:

	1% Point Increase	1% Point Decrease
Effect on total of service and interest cost components	$122,000	$ (20,000)
Effect on postretirement benefit obligation	$173,000	$(156,000)

The Company's postretirement benefit plans weighted-average asset allocations at December 31, 20X2, and December 31, 20X1, by asset category, are as follows:

	Plan Assets at December 31,	
	20X2	20X1
Asset Category		
Equity securities	57%	54%
Debt securities	26	29
Real estate	12	8
Other	5	9
Total	100%	100%

The Company's target asset allocation as of December 31, 20X2, by asset category, is as follows:

Asset Category	
Equity securities	50–70%
Debt securities	30–50%
Real estate	0–20%
Other	0–20%

The Company's investment policy includes various guidelines and procedures designed to ensure assets are invested in a manner necessary to meet expected future benefits earned by participants. The investment guidelines consider a broad range of economic conditions. Central to the policy are target allocation ranges (shown above) by major asset categories.

The objectives of the target allocations are to maintain investment portfolios that diversify risk through prudent asset allocation parameters, achieve asset returns that meet or exceed the plans' actuarial assumptions, and achieve asset returns that are competitive with like institutions employing similar investment strategies.

The investment policy is periodically reviewed by the Company and a designated third-party fiduciary for investment matters. The policy is established and administered in a manner that complies at all times with applicable government regulations.

Equity securities include common stock of Beas Ltd. in the amounts of $33,000 (10% of total plan assets) and $25,000 (12% of total plan assets) at December 31, 20X2, and December 31, 20X1, respectively.

The Company expects to contribute $200,000 to its postretirement benefit plans in 20X3.

The following benefit payments, which reflect expected future service, as appropriate, are expected to be paid:

20X3	$125,000
20X4	130,000
20X5	140,000
20X6	150,000
20X7	175,000
Years 20X8–20Y2	860,000

Example 28–2: Defined Benefit Postretirement Plans—Alternative Reduced Disclosures for a Nonpublic Entity

> **Note:** Example 28–2 illustrates the alternative reduced disclosures for a nonpublic entity under FAS-158 using the same facts in Example 28–1.

The Company has multiple nonpension postretirement benefit plans. The healthcare plans are contributory, with participants' contributions adjusted annually; the life insurance plans are noncontributory.

	Postretirement Benefits	
	20X2	20X1
Benefit obligation at December 31	$ 1,420,000	$ 738,000
Fair value of plan assets at December 31	329,000	206,000
Funded status at end of year	$(1,091,000)	$ (532,000)

	20X2	20X1
Amounts recognized in the balance sheets consist of:		
Noncurrent assets	$ 60,000	$ 70,000
Current liabilities	(350,000)	(400,000)
Noncurrent liabilities	(801,000)	(202,000)
	$(1,091,000)	$(532,000)

The following are weighted-average assumptions used to determine benefit obligations at December 31, 20X2, and December 31, 20X1:

	20X2	20X1
Discount rate	7.00%	7.25%

The following are weighted-average assumptions used to determine net periodic benefit cost for the years ended December 31, 20X2, and December 31, 20X1:

	20X2	20X1
Discount rate	7.25%	7.25%
Expected long-term return on plan assets	8.25%	8.50%

The Company's expected long-term return on plan assets assumption is based on a periodic review and modeling of the plans' asset allocation and liability structure over a long-term period. Expectations of returns for each asset class are the most important of the assumptions used in the review and modeling and are based on comprehensive reviews of historical data and economic/financial market theory. The expected long-term rate of return on assets was selected from within the reasonable range of rates determined by (1) historical real returns, net of inflation, for the asset classes covered by the investment policy, and (2) projections of inflation over the long-term period during which benefits are payable to plan participants.

For measurement purposes, a 10% annual rate of increase in the per capita cost of covered healthcare benefits was assumed for 20X3. The rate was assumed to decrease gradually to 4% for 20X9 and remain at that level thereafter.

	20X2	20X1
Benefit cost	$111,000	$117,000
Employer contribution	$171,000	$152,000
Plan participants' contributions	$ 20,000	$ 13,000
Benefits paid	$ 90,000	$ 70,000

The Company acquired Massari, Ltd. on December 31, 20X2, increasing the postretirement benefit obligation by $600,000 and related plan assets by $25,000. Amendments during the year to the Company's plans increased the postretirement benefit obligation by $75,000.

The Company's postretirement benefit plans weighted-average asset allocations at December 31, 20X2, and December 31, 20X1, by asset category, are as follows:

	Plan Assets at December 31,	
	20X2	*20X1*
Asset Category		
Equity securities	57%	54%
Debt securities	26	29
Real estate	12	8
Other	5	9
Total	100%	100%

The Company's target asset allocation as of December 31, 20X2,

Asset Category	
Equity securities	50–70%
Debt securities	30–50%
Real estate	0–20%
Other	0–20%

by asset category, is as follows:

The Company's investment policy includes various guidelines and procedures designed to ensure assets are invested in a manner necessary to meet expected future benefits earned by participants. The investment guidelines consider a broad range of economic conditions. Central to the policy are target allocation ranges (shown above) by major asset categories.

The objectives of the target allocations are to maintain investment portfolios that diversify risk through prudent asset allocation parameters, achieve asset returns that meet or exceed the plans' actuarial assumptions, and achieve asset returns that are competitive with like institutions employing similar investment strategies.

The investment policy is periodically reviewed by the Company and a designated third-party fiduciary for investment matters. The policy is established and administered in a manner that complies at all times with applicable government regulations.

Equity securities include common stock of Beas Ltd. in the amounts of $33,000 (10% of total plan assets) and $25,000 (12% of total plan assets) at December 31, 20X2, and December 31, 20X1, respectively.

The Company expects to contribute $200,000 to its postretirement benefit plans in 20X3.

The following benefit payments, which reflect expected future service, as appropriate, are expected to be paid:

20X3	$125,000
20X4	130,000
20X5	140,000
20X6	150,000
20X7	175,000
Years 20X8–20Y2	860,000

Example 28–3: Disclosures about Defined Benefit Pension Plans and Other Postretirement Benefit Plans Are Presented in a Parallel Format in a Single Note to the Financial Statements

The Company and its subsidiaries sponsor numerous defined benefit pension plans and other postretirement benefit plans. The following tables set forth the benefit obligation, the fair value of plan assets, and the funded status of the Company's plans; the amounts recognized in the Company's financial statements; and the principal weighted-average assumptions used:

	Pension Benefits		Postretirement Benefits	
	20X2	*20X1*	*20X2*	*20X1*
Change in benefit obligation				
Benefit obligation at beginning of year	$1,266,000	$1,200,000	$ 738,000	$700,000
Service cost	76,000	72,000	36,000	32,000
Interest cost	114,000	108,000	65,000	63,000
Plan participants' contributions	-0-	-0-	20,000	13,000
Amendments	120,000	-0-	75,000	-0-
Actuarial gain	(25,000)	-0-	(24,000)	-0-
Acquisition	900,000	-0-	600,000	-0-
Benefits paid	(125,000)	(114,000)	(90,000)	(70,000)
Benefit obligation at end of year	$2,326,000	$1,266,000	$1,420,000	$738,000

	Pension Benefits		Postretirement Benefits	
	20X2	20X1	20X1	20X2
Change in plan assets:				
Fair value of plan assets at beginning of year	$1,068,000	$ 880,000	$ 206,000	$ 87,000
Actual return on plan assets	29,000	188,000	(3,000)	24,000
Acquisition	1,000,000	-0-	25,000	-0-
Employer contribution	75,000	114,000	171,000	152,000
Plan participants' contributions	-0-	-0-	20,000	13,000
Benefits paid	(125,000)	(114,000)	(90,000)	(70,000)
Fair value of plan assets at end of year	$2,047,000	$1,068,000	$ 329,000	$ 206,000
Funded status at end of year	$ (279,000)	$ (198,000)	$(1,091,000)	$(532,000)
Amounts recognized in the balance sheets consist of:				
Noncurrent assets	$ 64,000	$ -0-	$ -0-	$ 68,000
Current liabilities	(100,000)	(48,000)	(400,000)	(200,000)
Noncurrent liabilities	(243,000)	(150,000)	(691,000)	(400,000)
	$(279,000)	$(198,000)	$(1,091,000)	$(532,000)

Amounts recognized in accumulated other comprehensive income consist of the following:

	Pension Benefits		Postretirement Benefits	
	20X2	20X1	20X2	20X1
Net loss (gain)	$ 83,000	$ 38,000	$ 59,000	$ 60,000
Prior service cost (credit)	260,000	160,000	585,000	540,000
	$ 343,000	$198,000	$644,000	$600,000

The following are weighted-average assumptions used to determine benefit obligations at December 31, 20X2, and December 31, 20X1:

	Pension Benefits		Postretirement Benefits	
	20X2	20X1	20X2	20X1
Discount rate	6.75%	7.00%	7.00%	7.25%
Rate of compensation increase	5.25%	4.75%	N/A	N/A

The following are weighted-average assumptions used to determine net periodic benefit cost for the years ended December 31, 20X2, and December 31, 20X1:

	Pension Benefits		Postretirement Benefits	
	20X2	20X1	20X2	20X1
Discount rate	7.00%	7.25%	7.25%	7.25%
Expected long-term return on plan assets	8.00%	7.75%	8.25%	8.50%
Rate of compensation increase	5.50%	5.00%	N/A	N/A

The Company's expected long-term return on plan assets assumption is based on a periodic review and modeling of the plans' asset allocation and liability structure over a long-term period. Expectations of returns for each asset class are the most important of the assumptions used in the review and modeling and are based on comprehensive reviews of historical data and economic/financial market theory. The expected long-term rate of return on assets was selected from within the reasonable range of rates deter-mined by (1) historical real returns, net of inflation, for the asset classes covered by the investment policy, and (2) projections of infla-tion over the long-term period during which benefits are payable to plan participants.

For measurement purposes, a 10% annual rate of increase in the per capita cost of covered healthcare benefits was assumed for 20X3. The rate was assumed to decrease gradually to 4% for 20X9 and remain at that level thereafter.

Components of net periodic benefit cost and other amounts rec-ognized in other comprehensive income are as follows:

	Pension Benefits		Postretirement Benefits	
	20X2	*20X1*	*20X2*	*20X1*
Net Periodic Benefit Cost:				
Service cost	$ 76,000	$ 72,000	$ 36,000	$ 32,000
Interest cost	114,000	108,000	65,000	63,000
Expected return on plan assets	(107,000)	(88,000)	(21,000)	(9,000)
Amortization of prior service cost	20,000	20,000	30,000	30,000
Recognized net actuarial loss	8,000	2,000	1,000	1,000
Net periodic benefit cost	111,000	114,000	111,000	117,000
Other Changes in Plan Assets and Benefit Obligations Recognized in Other Comprehensive Income:				
Net loss (gain)	45,000	40,000	(1,000)	(15,000)
Prior service cost (credit)	120,000	70,000	75,000	90,000
Amortization of prior service cost	(20,000)	(20,000)	(30,000)	(30,000)
Total recognized in other comprehensive income	145,000	90,000	44,000	45,000
Total recognized in net periodic benefit cost and other comprehensive income	$ 256,000	$ 204,000	$ 155,000	$ 162,000

The estimated net loss and prior service cost for the defined benefit pension plans that will be amortized from accumulated other comprehensive income into net periodic benefit cost over the next fiscal year are $25,000 and $60,000, respectively. The estimated net loss and prior service cost for the defined benefit postretirement plans that will be amortized from accumulated other comprehensive income into net periodic benefit cost over the next fiscal year are $35,000 and $90,000, respectively.

The Company acquired Massari, Ltd. on December 31, 20X2, including its pension plans. As a result, the Company's plans were amended to establish parity with the benefits provided by Massari, Ltd.

The Company has multiple nonpension postretirement benefit plans. The healthcare plans are contributory, with participants' contributions adjusted annually; the life insurance plans are noncontributory. The accounting for the healthcare plans anticipates future cost sharing changes to the written plan that are consistent with the Company's expressed intent to increase retiree contributions each year by 50% of the excess of the expected general inflation rate over 6%. On December 31, 20X2, the Company amended its postretirement healthcare plans to provide long-term care coverage.

Assumed healthcare cost trend rates have a significant effect on the amounts reported for the healthcare plans. A 1% point change in assumed healthcare cost trend rates would have the following effects:

	1% Point Increase	1% Point Decrease
Effect on total of service and interest cost components	$ 22,000	$ (20,000)
Effect on postretirement benefit obligation	$173,000	$(156,000)

The accumulated benefit obligation for all defined benefit pension plans was $733,000 and $650,000 at December 31, 20X2, and December 31, 20X1, respectively.

The Company's pension plans' weighted-average asset allocations at December 31, 20X2, and December 31, 20X1, by asset category are as follows:

| | Plan Assets at December 31, | |
	20X2	20X1
Asset Category		
Equity securities	55%	52%
Debt securities	28	31
Real estate	10	11
Other	7	6
Total	100%	100%

The Company's target asset allocation as of December 31, 20X2, by asset category, is as follows:

Asset Category	
Equity securities	50–70%
Debt securities	30–50%
Real estate	0–20%
Other	0–20%

The Company's investment policy includes various guidelines and procedures designed to ensure assets are invested in a manner necessary to meet expected future benefits earned by participants. The investment guidelines consider a broad range of economic conditions. Central to the policy are target allocation ranges (shown above) by major asset categories.

The objectives of the target allocations are to maintain investment portfolios that diversify risk through prudent asset allocation parameters, achieve asset returns that meet or exceed the plans' actuarial assumptions, and achieve asset returns that are competitive with like institutions employing similar investment strategies.

The investment policy is periodically reviewed by the Company and a designated third-party fiduciary for investment matters. The policy is established and administered in a manner that complies at all times with applicable government regulations.

Equity securities include common stock of Ace Ltd. in the amounts of $102,000 (5% of total plan assets) and $75,000 (7% of total plan assets) at December 31, 20X2, and December 31, 20X1, respectively.

The Company's postretirement benefit plans' weighted-average asset allocations at December 31, 20X2, and December 31, 20X1, by asset category, are as follows:

	Plan Assets at December 31,	
	20X2	20X1
Asset Category		
Equity securities	57%	54%
Debt securities	26	29
Real estate	12	8
Other	5	9
Total	100%	100%

The Company's target asset allocation as of December 31, 20X2, by asset category, is as follows:

Asset Category	
Equity securities	40–60%
Debt securities	25–40%
Real estate	0–20%
Other	0–20%

The Company's investment policy includes various guidelines and procedures designed to ensure assets are invested in a manner necessary to meet expected future enefits earned by participants. The investment guidelines consider a broad range of economic conditions. Central to the policy are target allocation ranges (shown above) by major asset categories.

The objectives of the target allocations are to maintain investment portfolios that diversify risk through prudent asset allocation parameters, achieve asset returns that meet or exceed the plans' actuarial assumptions, and achieve asset returns that are competitive with like institutions employing similar investment strategies.

The investment policy is periodically reviewed by the Company and a designated third-party fiduciary for investment matters. The policy is established and administered in a manner so as to comply at all times with applicable government regulations.

Equity securities include common stock of Beas Ltd. in the amounts of $33,000 (10% of total plan assets) and $25,000 (12% of total plan assets) at December 31, 20X2, and December 31, 20X1, respectively.

The Company expects to contribute $150,000 to its pension plans and $200,000 to its postretirement benefit plans in 20X3.

The following benefit payments, which reflect expected future service, as appropriate, are expected to be paid:

	Pension Benefits	*Postretirement Benefits*
20X3	$100,000	$125,000
20X4	105,000	130,000
20X5	118,000	140,000
20X6	125,000	150,000
20X7	135,000	175,000
Years 20X8–20Y2	775,000	860,000

Illustrations If FAS-158 Has *Not* Been Adopted: Defined Benefit Plans

Example 28–4: Defined Benefit Postretirement Plans—Public Entities

The Company has multiple nonpension postretirement benefit plans. The healthcare plans are contributory, with participants' contributions adjusted annually; the life insurance plans are noncontributory. The accounting for the healthcare plans anticipates future cost sharing changes to the written plan that are consistent with the Company's expressed intent to increase retiree contributions each year by 50% of the excess of the expected general inflation rate over 6%. On December 31, 20X2, the Company amended its postretirement healthcare plans to provide long-term care coverage.

The Company uses a December 31 measurement date for all its plans. The following tables set forth the benefit obligation, the fair value of plan assets, and the funded status of the Company's plans; the amounts recognized in the Company's financial statements; and the principal weighted-average assumptions used:

	20X2	20X1
Change in benefit obligation:		
Benefit obligation at beginning of year	$738,000	$700,000
Service cost	36,000	32,000
Interest cost	65,000	63,000
Plan participants' contributions	20,000	13,000
Amendments	75,000	-0-
Actuarial gain	(24,000)	-0-
Acquisition	600,000	-0-
Benefits paid	(90,000)	(70,000)
Benefit obligation at end of year	$1,420,000	$738,000

Change in plan assets:

Fair value of plan assets at beginning of year	$206,000	$87,000
Actual return on plan assets	(3,000)	24,000
Acquisition	25,000	-0-
Employer contribution	171,000	152,000
Plan participants' contributions	20,000	13,000
Benefits paid	(90,000)	(70,000)
Fair value of plan assets at end of year	$329,000	$206,000

	20X2	20X1
Funded status	$(1,091,000)	$(532,000)
Unrecognized net actuarial loss	59,000	60,000
Unrecognized prior service cost	585,000	540,000
Prepaid (accrued) benefit cost	$ (447,000)	$ 68,000

The following are weighted-average assumptions used to determine benefit obligations at December 31, 20X2, and December 31, 20X1:

	20X2	20X1
Discount rate	7.00%	7.25%

The following are weighted-average assumptions used to determine net periodic benefit cost for the years ended December 31, 20X2 and December 31, 20X1:

	20X2	20X1
Discount rate	7.25%	7.25%
Expected long-term return on plan assets	8.25%	8.50%

The Company's expected long-term return on plan assets assumption is based on a periodic review and modeling of the plans' asset allocation and liability structure over a long-term period. Expectations of returns for each asset class are the most important of the assumptions used in the review and modeling and are based on comprehensive reviews of historical data and economic/financial market theory. The expected long-term rate of return on assets was selected from within the reasonable range of rates determined by (1) historical real returns, net of inflation, for the asset classes covered by the investment policy, and (2) projections of inflation over the long-term period during which benefits are payable to plan participants.

For measurement purposes, a 10% annual rate of increase in the per capita cost of covered healthcare benefits was assumed for 20X3. The rate was assumed to decrease gradually to 4% for 20X9 and remain at that level thereafter.

Components of net periodic benefit cost are as follows:

	20X2	20X1
Service cost	$36,000	$32,000
Interest cost	65,000	63,000
Expected return on plan assets	(21,000)	(9,000)
Amortization of prior service cost	30,000	30,000
Recognized net actuarial loss	1,000	1,000
Net periodic benefit cost	$111,000	$117,000

The Company acquired Massari, Ltd. on December 31, 20X2, including its postretirement benefit plans. As a result, the Company's plans were amended to establish parity with the benefits provided by Massari, Ltd.

Assumed healthcare cost trend rates have a significant effect on the amounts reported for the healthcare plans. A 1% point change in assumed healthcare cost trend rates would have the following effects:

	1% Point Increase	1% Point Decrease
Effect on total of service and interest cost components	$122,000	$ (20,000)
Effect on postretirement benefit obligation	$173,000	$(156,000)

The Company's postretirement benefit plans, weighted-average asset allocations at December 31, 20X2, and December 31, 20X1, by asset category are, as follows:

	Plan Assets at December 31,	
	20X2	20X1
Asset Category		
Equity securities	57%	54%
Debt securities	26	29
Real estate	12	8
Other	5	9
Total	100%	100%

The Company's target asset allocation as of December 31, 20X2, by asset category, is as follows:

Asset Category

Equity securities	50–70%
Debt securities	30–50%
Real estate	0–20%
Other	0–20%

The Company's investment policy includes various guidelines and procedures designed to ensure assets are invested in a manner necessary to meet expected future benefits earned by participants. The investment guidelines consider a broad range of economic conditions. Central to the policy are target allocation ranges (shown above) by major asset categories.

The objectives of the target allocations are to maintain investment portfolios that diversify risk through prudent asset allocation parameters, achieve asset returns that meet or exceed the plans' actuarial assumptions, and achieve asset returns that are competitive with like institutions employing similar investment strategies.

The investment policy is periodically reviewed by the Company and a designated third-party fiduciary for investment matters. The policy is established and administered in a manner that complies at all times with applicable government regulations.

Equity securities include common stock of Beas Ltd. in the amounts of $33,000 (10% of total plan assets) and $25,000 (12% of total plan assets) at December 31, 20X2, and December 31, 20X1, respectively.

The Company expects to contribute $200,000 to its postretirement benefit plans in 20X3.

The following benefit payments, which reflect expected future service, as appropriate, are expected to be paid:

20X3	$125,000
20X4	130,000
20X5	140,000
20X6	150,000
20X7	175,000
Years 20X8–20Y2	860,000

Example 28–5: Defined Benefit Postretirement Plans—Alternative Reduced Disclosures for a Nonpublic Entity

Note: This example illustrates the alternative reduced disclosures for a nonpublic entity, using the same facts as those in Example 28–4.

In September 2006, the Financial Accounting Standards Board issued Statement of Financial Accounting Standards No. 158 (FAS-158), *Employers' Accounting for Defined Benefit Pension and Other Post-retirement Plans.* This new standard requires employers to (1) recognize in their balance sheets an asset for a plan's overfunded status or a liability for a plan's underfunded status; (2) measure a plan's assets and its obligations that determine its funded status as of the end of the employer's fiscal year (eliminating the alternative of a measurement date that could be up to three months earlier under prior standards); and (3) recognize changes in the funded status of a plan through comprehensive income in the year in which the changes occur. FAS-158 also amends the disclosure requirements in the notes to the financial statements by requiring information about certain effects on net periodic benefit cost for the next fiscal year that arise from delayed recognition of the gains or losses, prior service costs or credits, and transition assets or obligations.

The requirement to recognize the funded status of a benefit plan and the disclosure requirements are effective for fiscal years that end after June 15, 2007, for the Company. The requirement to measure plan assets and benefit obligations as of the date of the Company's fiscal year-end balance sheet is effective for fiscal years ending after December 15, 2008. The Company plans to adopt the provisions of FAS-158 on [*date*]. The Company has multiple nonpension postretirement benefit plans. The healthcare plans are contributory, with participants' contributions adjusted annually; the life insurance plans are noncontributory. The Company uses a December 31 measurement date for all its plans.

	Postretirement Benefits	
	20X2	*20X1*
Benefit obligation at December 31	$(1,420,000)	$(738,000)
Fair value of plan assets at December 31	329,000	206,000
Funded status	$(1,091,000)	$(532,000)
Prepaid (accrued) benefit cost recognized	$ (447,000)	$ 68,000

The following are weighted-average assumptions used to determine benefit obligations at December 31, 20X2, and December 31, 20X1:

	20X2	*20X1*
Discount rate	7.00%	7.25%

The following are weighted-average assumptions used to determine net periodic benefit cost for the years ended December 31, 20X2,and December 31, 20X1:

	20X2	20X1
Discount rate	7.25%	7.25%
Expected long-term return on plan assets	8.25%	8.50%

The Company's expected long-term return on plan assets assumption is based on a periodic review and modeling of the plans' asset allocation and liability structure over a long-term period. Expectations of returns for each asset class are the most important of the assumptions used in the review and modeling and are based on comprehensive reviews of historical data and economic/financial market theory. The expected long-term rate of return on assets was selected from within the reasonable range of rates determined by (1) historical real returns, net of inflation, for the asset classes covered by the investment policy and (2) projections of inflation over the long-term period during which benefits are payable to plan participants.

For measurement purposes, a 10% annual rate of increase in the per capita cost of covered healthcare benefits was assumed for 20X3. The rate was assumed to decrease gradually to 4% for 20X9 and remain at that level thereafter.

Benefit cost	$111,000	$117,000
Employer contribution	$171,000	$152,000
Plan participants' contributions	$20,000	$13,000
Benefits paid	$90,000	$70,000

The Company acquired Massari, Ltd. on December 31, 20X2, increasing the postretirement benefit obligation by $600,000 and related plan assets by $25,000. Amendments during the year to the Company's plans increased the postretirement benefit obligation by $75,000.

The Company's postretirement benefit plans, weighted-average asset allocations at December 31, 20X2, and December 31, 20X1, by asset category, are as follows:

	Plan Assets at December 31,	
	20X2	20X1
Asset Category		
Equity securities	57%	54%
Debt securities	26	29
Real estate	12	8
Other	5	9
Total	100%	100%

The Company's target asset allocation as of December 31, 20X2, by asset category, is as follows:

Asset Category	
Equity securities	50–70%
Debt securities	30–50%
Real estate	0–20%
Other	0–20%

The Company's investment policy includes various guidelines and procedures designed to ensure assets are invested in a manner necessary to meet expected future benefits earned by participants. The investment guidelines consider a broad range of economic conditions. Central to the policy are target allocation ranges (shown above) by major asset categories.

The objectives of the target allocations are to maintain investment portfolios that diversify risk through prudent asset allocation parameters, achieve asset returns that meet or exceed the plans' actuarial assumptions, and achieve asset returns that are competitive with like institutions employing similar investment strategies.

The investment policy is periodically reviewed by the Company and a designated third-party fiduciary for investment matters. The policy is established and administered in a manner so as to comply at all times with applicable government regulations.

Equity securities include common stock of Beas Ltd. in the amounts of $33,000 (10% of total plan assets) and $25,000 (12% of total plan assets) at December 31, 20X2, and December 31, 20X1, respectively.

The Company expects to contribute $200,000 to its postretirement benefit plans in 20X3.

The following benefit payments, which reflect expected future service, as appropriate, are expected to be paid:

20X3	$125,000
20X4	130,000
20X5	140,000
20X6	150,000
20X7	175,000
Years 20X8–20Y2	860,000

Example 28–6: Disclosures about Defined Benefit Postretirement Plans and Pension Plans Are Presented in a Parallel Format in a Single Note to the Financial Statements

The Company and its subsidiaries sponsor numerous defined benefit pension plans and other postretirement benefit plans. The Company uses a December 31 measurement date for all its plans. The following tables set forth the benefit obligation, the fair value of plan assets, and the funded status of the Company's plans; the amounts recognized in the Company's financial statements; and the principal weighted-average assumptions used:

	Pension Benefits		Postretirement Benefits	
	20X2	20X1	20X2	20X1
Change in benefit obligation:				
Benefit obligation at beginning of year	$1,266,000	$1,200,000	$738,000	$700,000
Service cost	76,000	72,000	36,000	32,000
Interest cost	114,000	108,000	65,000	63,000
Plan participants' contributions	-0-	-0-	20,000	13,000
Amendments	120,000	-0-	75,000	-0-
Actuarial gain	(25,000)	-0-	(24,000)	-0-
Acquisition	900,000	-0-	600,000	-0-
Benefits paid	(125,000)	(114,000)	(90,000)	(70,000)
Benefit obligation at end of year	$2,326,000	$1,266,000	$1,420,000	$738,000

	Pension Benefits		Postretirement Benefits	
	20X2	20X1	20X2	20X1
Change in plan assets:				
Fair value of plan assets at beginning of year	$1,068,000	$880,000	$206,000	$87,000
Actual return on plan assets:	29,000	188,000	(3,000)	24,000
Acquisition	1,000,000	-0-	25,000	-0-
Employer contribution	75,000	114,000	171,000	152,000
Plan participants' contributions	-0-	-0-	20,000	13,000
Benefits paid	(125,000)	(114,000)	(90,000)	(70,000)
Fair value of plan assets at end of year	$2,047,000	$1,068,000	$329,000	$206,000
Funded status	$(279,000)	$(198,000)	$(1,091,000)	$(532,000)
Unrecognized net actuarial loss	83,000	38,000	59,000	60,000
Unrecognized prior service cost	260,000	160,000	585,000	540,000
Prepaid (accrued) benefit cost	$64,000	$-0-	$(447,000)	$68,000

The following are weighted-average assumptions used to determine benefit obligations at December 31, 20X2, and December 31, 20X1:

	Pension Benefits		Postretirement Benefits	
	20X2	20X1	20X2	20X1
Discount rate	6.75%	7.00%	7.00%	7.25%
Rate of compensation increase	5.25%	4.75%	N/A	N/A

The following are weighted-average assumptions used to determine net periodic benefit cost for the years ended December 31, 20X2, and December 31, 20X1:

	Pension Benefits		Postretirement Benefits	
	20X2	20X1	20X2	20X1
Discount rate	7.00%	7.25%	7.25%	7.25%
Expected long-term return on plan assets	8.00%	7.75%	8.25%	8.50%
Rate of compensation increase	5.50%	5.00%	N/A	N/A

The Company's expected long-term return on plan assets assumption is based on a periodic review and modeling of the plans' asset allocation and liability structure over a long-term period. Expectations of returns for each asset class are the most important of the assumptions used in the review and modeling and are based on comprehensive reviews of historical data and economic/financial market theory. The expected long-term rate of return on assets was selected from within the reasonable range of rates determined by (1) historical real returns, net of inflation, for the asset classes covered by the investment policy and (2) projections of inflation over the long-term period during which benefits are payable to plan participants.

For measurement purposes, a 10% annual rate of increase in the per capita cost of covered healthcare benefits was assumed for 20X3. The rate was assumed to decrease gradually to 4% for 20X9 and remain at that level thereafter.

Components of net periodic benefit cost are as follows:

	Pension Benefits		Postretirement Benefits	
	20X2	20X1	20X2	20X1
Service cost	$76,000	$72,000	$36,000	$32,000
Interest cost	114,000	108,000	65,000	63,000
Expected return on plan assets	(107,000)	(88,000)	(21,000)	(9,000)
Amortization of prior service cost	20,000	20,000	30,000	30,000
Recognized net actuarial loss	8,000	2,000	1,000	1,000
Net periodic benefit cost	$111,000	$114,000	$111,000	$117,000

The Company acquired Massari, Ltd. on December 31, 20X2, including its pension plans. As a result, the Company's plans were amended to establish parity with the benefits provided by Massari, Ltd.

The Company has multiple nonpension postretirement benefit plans. The healthcare plans are contributory, with participants' contributions adjusted annually; the life insurance plans are noncontributory. The accounting for the healthcare plans anticipates future cost sharing changes to the written plan that are consistent with the Company's expressed intent to increase retiree contributions each year by 50% of the excess of the expected general inflation rate over 6%. On December 31, 20X2, the Company amended its postretirement healthcare plans to provide long-term care coverage.

Assumed healthcare cost trend rates have a significant effect on the amounts reported for the healthcare plans. A 1% point change in assumed healthcare cost trend rates would have the following effects:

	1% Point Increase	1% Point Decrease
Effect on total of service and interest cost components	$ 22,000	$ (20,000)
Effect on postretirement benefit obligation	$173,000	$(156,000)

The accumulated benefit obligation for all defined benefit pension plans was $733,000 and $650,000 at December 31, 20X2, and December 31, 20X1, respectively.

The Company's pension plans, weighted-average asset allocations at December 31, 20X2, and December 31, 20X1, by asset category, are as follows:

	Plan Assets at December 31,	
	20X2	20X1
Asset Category		
Equity securities	55%	52%
Debt securities	28	31
Real estate	10	11
Other	7	6
Total	100%	100%

The Company's target asset allocation as of December 31, 20X2, by asset category, is as follows:

Asset Category	
Equity securities	50–70%
Debt securities	30–50%
Real estate	0–20%
Other	0–20%

The Company's investment policy includes various guidelines and procedures designed to ensure assets are invested in a manner necessary to meet expected future benefits earned by participants. The investment guidelines consider a broad range of economic conditions. Central to the policy are target allocation ranges (shown above) by major asset categories.

The objectives of the target allocations are to maintain investment portfolios that diversify risk through prudent asset allocation parameters, achieve asset returns that meet or exceed the plans' actuarial assumptions, and achieve asset returns that are competitive with like institutions employing similar investment strategies.

The investment policy is periodically reviewed by the Company and a designated third-party fiduciary for investment matters. The policy is established and administered in a manner that complies at all times with applicable government regulations.

Equity securities include common stock of Ace Ltd. in the amounts of $102,000 (5% of total plan assets) and $75,000 (7% of total plan assets) at December 31, 20X2, and December 31, 20X1, respectively.

The Company's postretirement benefit plans, weighted-average asset allocations at December 31, 20X2, and December 31, 20X1, by asset category, are as follows:

	Plan Assets at December 31,	
	20X2	20X1
Asset Category		
Equity securities	57%	54%
Debt securities	26	29
Real estate	12	8
Other	5	9
Total	100%	100%

The Company's target asset allocation as of December 31, 20X2, by asset category, is as follows:

Asset Category	
Equity securities	40–60%
Debt securities	25–40%
Real estate	0–20%
Other	0–20%

The Company's investment policy includes various guidelines and procedures designed to ensure assets are invested in a manner necessary to meet expected future benefits earned by participants. The investment guidelines consider a broad range of economic conditions. Central to the policy are target allocation ranges (shown above) by major asset categories.

The objectives of the target allocations are to maintain investment portfolios that diversify risk through prudent asset allocation parameters, achieve asset returns that meet or exceed the plans' actuarial assumptions, and achieve asset returns that are competitive with like institutions employing similar investment strategies.

The investment policy is periodically reviewed by the Company and a designated third-party fiduciary for investment matters. The policy is established and administered in a manner that complies at all times with applicable government regulations.

Equity securities include common stock of Beas Ltd. in the amounts of $33,000 (10% of total plan assets) and $25,000 (12% of total plan assets) at December 31, 20X2 and December 31, 20X1, respectively.

The Company expects to contribute $150,000 to its pension plans and $200,000 to its postretirement benefit plans in 20X3.

The following benefit payments, which reflect expected future service, as appropriate, are expected to be paid:

	Pension Benefits	Postretirement Benefits
20X3	$100,000	$125,000
20X4	105,000	130,000
20X5	118,000	140,000
20X6	125,000	150,000
20X7	135,000	175,000
Years 20X8–20Y2	755,000	860,000

Illustrations Applicable under FAS-158 and Prior Standards

Example 28–7: Defined Contribution Postretirement Plans

The Company sponsors defined contribution postretirement health-care and life insurance benefit plans. Contributions to these plans were $236,000 in 20X2 and $222,000 in 20X1.

Example 28–8: Combined Disclosures of Defined Contribution Postretirement Plans and Defined Contribution Pension Plans

The Company sponsors several defined contribution pension plans covering substantially all employees. Employees may contribute to these plans and their contributions are matched in varying amounts by the Company. Defined contribution pension expense for the Company was $543,000 for 20X2 and $429,000 for 20X1.

Also, the Company sponsors defined contribution postretirement healthcare and life insurance benefit plans. Contributions to these plans were $311,000 in 20X2 and $304,000 in 20X1.

Example 28–9: Union-Sponsored Multiemployer Postretirement Benefit Plans

The Company participates in various multi-employer, union-administered postretirement benefit plans, which provide for healthcare and life insurance benefits to both active employees and retirees. Total contributions to these plans were $423,000 for 20X2 and $410,000 for 20X1.

Example 28–10: Interim-Period Disclosures—Public Entities

Components of net periodic benefit cost for the Company's pension plan are as follows:

	Three Months Ended September 30		Nine Months Ended September 30	
	20X2	*20X1*	*20X2*	*20X1*
Service cost	$1,200,000	$1,100,000	$3,700,000	$3,400,000
Interest cost	1,400,000	1,156,000	3,900,000	3,250,000
Expected return on plan assets	(1,600,000)	(900,000)	(4,200,000)	(3,900,000)
Amortization of prior service cost	240,000	160,000	525,000	260,000

Amortization of net (gain) loss	70,000	(10,000)	90,000	115,000
Net periodic benefit cost	$1,310,000	$1,506,000	$4,015,000	$3,125,000

Components of net periodic benefit cost for the Company's postretirement benefit plan are as follows:

	Three Months Ended September 30		Nine Months Ended September 30	
	20X2	20X1	20X2	20X1
Service cost	$200,000	$170,000	$700,000	$625,000
Interest cost	400,000	350,000	990,000	695,000
Expected return on plan assets	(150,000)	(190,000)	(315,000)	(420,000)
Amortization of prior service cost	(70,000)	(10,000)	(125,000)	(150,000)
Net periodic benefit cost	$380,000	$320,000	1,250,000	$750,000

The Company previously disclosed in its financial statements for the year ended December 31, 20X1, that it expected to contribute $4,800,000 to its pension plan and $900,000 to its postretirement benefit plan in 20X2. As of September 30, 20X2, contributions of $3,700,000 and $650,000 have been made to the pension plan and postretirement benefit plan, respectively. The Company presently anticipates contributing an additional $1,500,000 to fund its pension plan in 20X2 for a total of $5,200,000. Also, the Company presently anticipates contributing an additional $450,000 to fund its postretirement benefit plan in 20X2 for a total of $1,100,000.

Example 28–11: Interim-Period Disclosures—Nonpublic Entities

The Company previously disclosed in its financial statements for the year ended December 31, 20X1, that it expected to contribute $4,800,000 to its pension plan and $900,000 to its postretirement benefit plan in 20X2. As of September 30, 20X2, contributions of $3,700,000 and $650,000 have been made to the pension plan and postretirement benefit plan, respectively. The Company presently anticipates contributing an additional $1,500,000 to fund its pension plan in 20X2 for a total of $5,200,000. Also, the Company presently anticipates contributing an additional $450,000 to fund its postretirement benefit plan in 20X2 for a total of $1,100,000.

Example 28–12: Disclosure under FASB Staff Position No. 106-2, "Accounting and Disclosure Requirements Related to the Medicare Prescription Drug Improvement and Modernization Act of 2003"

In May 2004, the FASB issued Staff Position No. 106-2 (FAS FSP 106-2), *Accounting and Disclosure Requirements Related to the Medicare Prescription Drug Improvement, and Modernization Act of 2003* (the Act). FAS FSP 106-2 provides guidance on accounting for the effects of a subsidy available under the Act to companies that sponsor retiree medical programs with drug benefits that are at least actuarially equivalent to those available under Medicare. In addition to the direct benefit to a company from qualifying for and receiving the subsidy, the effects would include expected changes in retiree participation rates and changes in estimated health care costs that result from the Act.

The Company believes that its postretirement benefit plan currently provides prescription drug coverage that is at least actuarially equivalent to the new benefit available under Medicare, and it will therefore qualify for the subsidy for an initial period of time after the Act is implemented until actuarial equivalency changes as a result of existing limits on the Company's cost of providing the benefit.

The Company adopted the provisions of FAS FSP 106-2, effective January 1, 20X2. The expected federal subsidy had the effect of reducing the Company's accumulated postretirement benefit obligation by approximately $650,000 as of January 1, 20X2. This reduction is recognized as an actuarial gain and will be amortized over three years. The reduction in the net periodic postretirement benefit cost for 20X2 was $75,000.

CHAPTER 29
QUASI-REORGANIZATIONS AND REORGANIZATIONS UNDER THE BANKRUPTCY CODE

CONTENTS

EXECUTIVE SUMMARY

Quasi-Reorganizations

Under carefully defined circumstances, contributed or paid-in capital generally may be used to restructure a corporation, including the elimination of a deficit in retained earnings. This procedure is called a *quasi-reorganization* or *corporate readjustment*. Such circumstances generally require that the following criteria be met to be eligible to reorganize under quasi-reorganization: (1) the entity must have exhausted all retained earnings; (2) the entire procedure is made known to all persons entitled to vote on matters of general corporate policy, and the appropriate consents to the particular transactions are obtained in advance, in accordance with the applicable law and charter provisions; and (3) the entity must have changed management, lines of business, methods of operations, and such other matters, so that the entity is reasonably expected to have profitable operations based on the restated asset and liability carrying amounts in terms of present conditions. In a quasi-reorganization, a company reduces the carrying amounts of its balance sheet accounts to fair value; the offsetting adjustment should be charged to retained earnings. If the adjustment exceeds the balance in the retained earnings account, any difference should be charged to additional paid-in capital. A new retained earnings account should be established at the effective date of such readjustment, and the effective date generally should be disclosedfor a period of ten years.

Reorganizations under the Bankruptcy Code

The accounting followed by entities reorganizing as going concerns under Chapter 11 of the Bankruptcy Code is similar in many ways to the fresh-start accounting of a quasi-reorganization. However, there are some differences and, therefore, formal reorganizations under the Bankruptcy Code should not be confused with quasi-reorganizations. For example, in a quasi-reorganization, a formal plan to restructure liabilities and debt to creditors is not adopted.

An entity should adopt fresh-start accounting upon its emergence from Chapter 11 if (1) the reorganization value of the assets of the emerging entity immediately before the date of confirmation by the Court is less than the total of all postpetition liabilities and allowed claims and (2) holders of existing voting shares immediately before confirmation receive less than 50% of the voting shares of the emerging entity.

Authoritative Literature

ARB-43	Chapter 7, Capital Accounts
	Chapter 7A, Quasi-Reorganization or Corporate Readjustment
ARB-46	Discontinuance of Dating Earned Surplus
FAS-109	Accounting for Income Taxes
SOP 90-7	Financial Reporting by Entities in Reorganization Under the Bankruptcy Code
PB-11	Accounting for Preconfirmation Contingencies in Fresh-Start Reporting

DISCLOSURE REQUIREMENTS

Quasi-Reorganizations

1. The nature and a description of the quasi-reorganization should be adequately disclosed in the financial statements. After a quasi-reorganization or corporate readjustment, a new retained earnings account should be established and dated to show that it runs from the effective date of the readjustment. This dating should be disclosed in the financial statements until such time as the effective date is no longer deemed to possess any special significance, which is generally not more than ten years (ARB-46, par. 2).

2. Companies that recognize the tax benefits of prior deductible temporary differences and carryforwards in income rather than contributed capital (i.e., companies that have previously adopted FAS-96 and effected a quasi-reorganization that involved only the elimination of a deficit in retained earnings) should disclose the following (FAS-109, par. 39):

   a. The date of the quasi-reorganization

   b. The manner of reporting the tax benefits and that it differs from present accounting requirements for other entities

   c. The effect of those tax benefits on income from continuing operations, income before extraordinary items, and net income (and on related per share amounts, if applicable)

Reorganizations under the Bankruptcy Code

1. Companies that have filed petitions with the Bankruptcy Court and expect to reorganize as going concerns under Chapter 11 should disclose the following (SOP 90-7, pars. 23–31 and 34):

   a. Prepetition liabilities, including claims that become known after a petition is filed, which are not subject to reasonable estimation

   b. Principal categories of claims subject to compromise

   c. The extent to which reported interest expense differs from stated contractual interest

   d. Details of operating cash receipts and payments resulting from the reorganization if the indirect method is used in the statement of cash flows

   e. In the earnings per share calculation, whether it is probable that the plan will require the issuance of common stock or common stock equivalents, thereby diluting current equity interests

2. In the consolidated financial statements of one or more entities in reorganization under Chapter 11 and of one or more entities not in reorganization proceedings, the following disclosures should be made (SOP 90-7, pars. 32–33):

   a. Condensed combined financial statements of the entities in reorganization proceedings

   b. Intercompany receivables and payables of entities in reorganization

3. For companies that have emerged from Chapter 11 under confirmed plans that adopt fresh start reporting, the following disclosures should be made (SOP 90-7, par. 39):

   a. Adjustments to the historical amounts of individual assets and liabilities

   b. The amount of debt forgiveness

   c. The amount of prior retained earnings or deficit eliminated

   d. Significant matters relating to the determination of reorganization value such as:

   — The method(s) used to determine reorganization value and factors such as discount rates, tax rates, the number of years for which cash flows are projected, and the method of determining terminal value

   — Sensitive assumptions about which there is a reasonable possibility of the occurrence of a variation that would significantly affect the measurement of reorganization value

   — Assumptions about anticipated conditions that are expected to be different from current conditions, unless otherwise apparent

4. For companies that have emerged from Chapter 11 under confirmed plans that adopt fresh start reporting and have recorded an adjustment that resulted from a preconfirmation contingency, the following disclosures should be made (PB-11, pars. 8–9):

   a. The adjustment in income or loss from continuing operations of the emerged entity

EXAMPLES OF FINANCIAL STATEMENT DISCLOSURES

The following sample disclosures are available on the accompanying disc.

Quasi-Reorganizations

Example 29–1: Quasi-Reorganization Adopted in Connection with Ownership Change and Restructuring of Operations

In recognition of the change in ownership of the Company and the restructuring of operations, the Company believes that future operations are not burdened with the problems of the past. As a result, the Company believed it to be appropriate to adjust the carrying value of assets and liabilities to their fair value as of January 1, 20X2. Following extensive research and consultations with legal counsel and independent accountants, management recommended, and the Company's Board of Directors approved, a quasi-reorganization to be effective as of January 1, 20X2. Accordingly, all assets and liabilities of the Company have been retroactively restated as of January 1, 20X2, to their fair value, determined as follows:

- Inventories—market value reduced by selling costs and a reasonable profit allowance
- Property, plant, and equipment—recent appraisal values
- Debt due beyond one year—principal and interest payments due beyond one year have been discounted at 10%
- Convertible subordinated debentures—appraisal from an investment banker
- Liability for pension plans—amounts have been discounted at 10%

   Note: The following table illustrates the caption used in the Company's stockholders' equity section to show the dating of retained earnings from the effective date of the quasi-reorganization of January 1, 20X2.

	20X2	*20X1*
Common stock	$20,000	$700,000
Additional paid-in capital	80,000	900,000
Retained earnings since January 1, 20X2, in connection with quasi-reorganization	373,000	-0-
Accumulated deficit (prior to quasi-reorganization)	-0-	(1,325,000)
Total stockholder's equity	$473,000	$275,000

Reorganizations under the Bankruptcy Code

Example 29–2: Petition for Relief under Chapter 11

On February 13, 20X2, ABC Company (the Debtor) filed petitions for relief under Chapter 11 of the federal bankruptcy laws in the United States Bankruptcy Court for the Western District of Tennessee. Under Chapter 11, certain claims against the Debtor in existence prior to the filing of the petitions for relief under the federal bankruptcy laws are stayed while the Debtor continues business operations as Debtor-in-possession. These claims are reflected in the December 31, 20X2, Balance Sheet as "Liabilities subject to compromise." Additional claims (liabilities subject to compromise) may arise subsequent to the filing date resulting from rejection of executory contracts, including leases, and from the determination by the court (or agreed to by parties in interest) of allowed claims for contingencies and other disputed amounts. Claims secured against the Debtor's assets (secured claims) also are stayed, although the holders of such claims have the right to move the court for relief from the stay. Secured claims are secured primarily by liens on the Debtor's property, plant, and equipment.

The Debtor received approval from the Bankruptcy Court to pay or otherwise honor certain of its prepetition obligations, including employee wages and product warranties. The Debtor has determined that there is insufficient collateral to cover the interest portion of scheduled payments on its prepetition debt obligations. Contractual interest on those obligations amounts to $[amount], which is $[amount] in excess of reported interest expense; therefore, the Debtor has discontinued accruing interest on these obligations.

Example 29–3: Emergence from Bankruptcy

Upon emergence from its Chapter 11 proceedings in April 20X2, the Company adopted "fresh-start" reporting in accordance with AICPA Statement of Position No. 90-7, *Financial Reporting by Entities in Reorganization under the Bankruptcy Code*, as of March 31, 20X2. The Company's emergence from these proceedings resulted in a new reporting entity with no retained earnings or accumulated deficit as of March 31, 20X2. Accordingly, the Company's financial information shown for periods prior to March 31, 20X2, is not comparable to consolidated financial statements presented on or subsequent to March 31, 20X2.

The Bankruptcy Court confirmed the Company's plan of reorganization. The confirmed plan provided for the following:

Secured Debt—The Company's $[amount] of secured debt (secured by a first mortgage lien on a building located in Nashville, Tennessee) was exchanged for $[amount] in cash and a $[amount] secured note, payable in annual installments of $[*amount*] commencing on July 1, 20X3, through June 30, 20X6, with interest at 13% per annum, with the balance due on July 1, 20X7.

Priority Tax Claims—Payroll and withholding taxes of $[*amount*]are payable in equal annual installments commencing on July 1, 20X3, through July 1, 20X8, with interest at 11% per annum.

Senior Debt—The holders of approximately $[*amount*] of senior subordinated secured notes received the following instruments in exchange for their notes: (a) $[*amount*] in new senior secured debt, payable in annual installments of $[*amount*] commencing March 1, 20X3, through March 1, 20X6, with interest at 12% per annum, secured by first liens on certain property, plant, and equipment, with the balance due on March 1, 20X7; (b) $[*amount*] of subordinated debt with interest at 14% per annum due in equal annual installments commencing on October 1, 20X3, through October 1, 20X9, secured by second liens on certain property, plant, and equipment; and (c) [*percent*]% of the new issue of outstanding voting common stock of the Company.

Trade and Other Miscellaneous Claims—The holders of approximately $[*amount*] of trade and other miscellaneous claims received the following for their claims: (a) $[*amount*] in senior secured debt, payable in annual installments of $[*amount*] commencing March 1, 20X3, through March 1, 20X6, with interest at 12% per annum, secured by first liens on certain property, plant, and equipment, with the balance due on March 1, 20X7; (b) $[*amount*] of subordinated debt, payable in equal annual installments commencing October 1, 20X3, through October 1, 20X8, with interest at 14% per annum; and (c) [*percent*]% of the new issue of outstanding voting common stock of the Company.

Subordinated Debentures—The holders of approximately $[*amount*] of subordinated unsecured debt received, in exchange for the debentures, [*percent*]% of the new issue outstanding voting common stock of the Company.

Preferred Stock—The holders of [*number*] shares of preferred stock received [*percent*]% of the outstanding voting common stock of the new issue of the Company in exchange for their preferred stock.

Common Stock—The holders of approximately [*number*] outstanding shares of the Company's existing common stock received, in exchange for their shares, [*percent*]% of the new outstanding voting common stock of the Company.

CHAPTER 30
RELATED-PARTY DISCLOSURES

CONTENTS

EXECUTIVE SUMMARY

Note: FASB Interpretation No. 45 (FIN-45), *Guarantor's Accounting and Disclosure Requirements for Guarantees, Including Indirect Guarantees of Indebtedness of Others,* elaborates on the disclosures that an entity should make in its financial statements about its obligations under certain guarantees that it has issued. Some guarantees are issued to benefit entities that meet the definition of a related party (e.g., joint ventures, equity method investees). In those cases, the disclosures required by FIN-45 are in addition to the disclosures required by FASB Statement of Financial Accounting Standards No. 57, *Related Party Disclosures.* See Chapter 19, "Guarantees," for an entity's disclosure requirements for guarantees.

In general terms, *related parties* exist when there is a relationship that offers the potential for transactions at less than arm's-length, favorable treatment, or the ability to influence the outcome of events differently from that which might result in the absence of that relationship. A related party may be any of the following:

- *Affiliate*—An affiliate is a party that directly or indirectly controls, is controlled by, or is under common control with another party.

- *Principal owner*—This is generally the owner of record or known beneficial owner of more than 10% of the voting interests of an entity.

- *Management*—Persons having responsibility for achieving objectives of the entity and requisite authority to make decisions that pursue those objectives. This normally includes members of the board of directors, chief executive officer, chief operating officer, president, treasurer, any vice president in charge of a principal business function (e.g., sales, administration, finance), and any other individual who performs similar policymaking functions.

- *Immediate family of management or principal owners*—Generally, this includes spouses, brothers, sisters, parents, children, and spouses of these persons.

- *A parent company and its subsidiaries*—This is typically an entity that "directly or indirectly has a controlling financial interest" in a subsidiary company.

- *Trusts for the benefit of employees*—Trusts for the benefit of employees include pension and profit-sharing trusts that are managed by, or under the trusteeship of, the entity's management.

- *Other parties*—Other parties include any other party that has the ability to significantly influence the management or operating policies of the entity, to the extent that it may be prevented from fully pursuing its own separate interests. The ability to exercise significant influence may be indicated in several ways, such as representation on the board of directors, participation in policy-making processes, material intercompany transactions, interchange of managerial personnel, or technological dependency.

Common related-party transactions include the following:

- Contracts that carry no interest rate or an unrealistic interest rate
- Nonmonetary transactions that involve the exchange of similar assets
- Loan agreements that contain no repayment schedule
- Loans to parties that do not possess the ability to repay
- Services or goods purchased from a party at little or no cost to the entity
- Maintenance of bank balances as compensating balances for the benefit of another
- Intercompany billings based on allocation of common costs
- Leases to an entity from its principal shareholder

Financial statement disclosure of related party transactions is required by GAAP in order for those statements to fairly present financial position, results of operations, and cash flows.

Authoritative Literature

ARB-43	Chapter 1A, Rules Adopted by Membership
FAS-57	Related Party Disclosures
FIN-45	Guarantor's Accounting and Disclosure Requirements for Guarantees, Including Indirect Guarantees of Indebtedness of Others

DISCLOSURE REQUIREMENTS

The following disclosures should be made for material related-party transactions:

1. The nature of the relationship of the parties involved (FAS-57, par. 2)

2. A description of the transactions, including transactions to which no amounts or nominal amounts were ascribed, for each of the periods for which income statements are presented, and any other information deemed necessary to an understanding of the effects of the transactions on the financial statements (FAS-57, par. 2)

3. The dollar amounts of transactions for each of the periods for which income statements are presented and the effects of any change in the method of establishing the terms from those used in the preceding period (FAS-57, par. 2)

4. Amounts due from or to related parties as of the date of each balance sheet presented and, if not otherwise apparent, the terms and manner of settlement (FAS-57, par. 2)

5. When the company and one or more other entities are under common ownership or management control and the existence of that control could result in operating results or financial position of the company significantly different from those that would have resulted if the company were autonomous, then the nature of the control relationship should be disclosed even though there are no related-party transactions (FAS-57, par. 4)

Also, if guarantees are issued for the benefit of related parties, additional disclosure requirements apply regarding such guarantees. See Chapter 19, "Guarantees," for an entity's disclosure requirements for guarantees.

Disclosures concerning related-party transactions should not be worded in a manner that implies that the transactions were consummated on terms equivalent to those that prevail in arm's-length transactions, unless such representations can be substantiated (FAS-57, par. 3).

EXAMPLES OF FINANCIAL STATEMENT DISCLOSURES

 The following sample disclosures are available on the accompanying disc.

Example 30–1: Advances Made to Related Parties for Expansion and Financing Needs

The Company has made advances to PRC Development, an entity owned by the president and certain officers of the Company, primarily to accommodate expansion and other financing needs of this related entity. Such advances bear interest at rates equal to the

Company's weighted average cost of borrowing, which for the years ended December 31, 20X2, and December 31, 20X1, was 7.25% and 7.75%, respectively. Interest charged to PRC Development for the years ended December 31, 20X2, and December 31, 20X1, was $379,000 and $493,000, respectively.

Example 30–2: Company's Corporate Services Agreement with a Related Entity Provides for Payment of a Fee Based on Company's Net Sales

The Company has a corporate services agreement with Odeyssa, Inc., an entity that is controlled by the Company's chairman of the board of directors and president. Under the terms of the agreement, the Company pays a fee to Odeyssa, Inc. for various corporate support staff, administrative services, and research and development services. Such fee equals 2.2% of the Company's net sales, subject to certain adjustments, and totaled $1,975,000 and $1,836,000 in 20X2 and 20X1, respectively.

Example 30–3: Demand Note Receivable from Stockholder Is Classified as Noncurrent Because Repayment Is Not Anticipated During the Next Year

At December 31, 20X2, and December 31, 20X1, the Company has a note receivable of $295,200 and $268,400, respectively, due from its stockholder that is due upon demand. This note is unsecured and bears interest at 10%. Accrued interest on this note totaled $51,200 and $24,400 as of December 31, 20X2, and December 31, 20X1, respectively, and is included in the note receivable balance. The note receivable has been classified as noncurrent in the accompanying Balance Sheets because repayment is not anticipated during the next year.

Example 30–4: Notes Receivable Balance Due from Related Parties Is Paid through Forfeiture of Bonuses

As of December 31, 20X1, the Company had notes receivable due from certain executives and officers amounting to approximately $1,500,000. These notes bear interest at rates ranging from 7.25% to 7.85% and have maturities of six months to five years. In 20X2, $625,000 of the notes receivable balance was paid through forfeiture of management bonuses.

Example 30–5: Company Is Forgiving Loan Balance Due from an Officer

On May 19, 20X0, the Company loaned $500,000 to Dave Jones, a senior vice president of the Company. Mr. Jones executed an unsecured promissory note in favor of the Company that matures on

May 18, 20X4. In 20X1, the Company forgave a total of $200,000 of outstanding principal amount and $47,000 in accrued interest. In 20X2, the Company forgave a total of $100,000 of outstanding principal amount and $31,000 in accrued interest. The remaining outstanding balance of the loan as of December 31, 20X2, was $205,000, representing $200,000 in principal and $5,000 in accrued interest, and bears interest at a rate of 7.95%.

Example 30–6: Loan Payable to Related Company Is Secured and Subordinated to Bank Debt

In November 20X1, Cubes, Ltd., an entity that is partially owned by a minority shareholder of the Company, loaned $1,000,000 to the Company for working capital and equipment financing. The loan is payable in five annual installments of $200,000, plus applicable interest, beginning November 20X2. Interest accrues at the prevailing prime rate plus 1.75% (9% at December 31, 20X2). The loan is secured by inventory, accounts receivable, and machinery and equipment, and is subordinated to the Company's line of credit with the bank. At December 31, 20X2, and December 31, 20X1, the outstanding balance due was $800,000 and $1,000,000, respectively.

Example 30–7: Loan Covenants Restrict Payment on Shareholder Loan Made to Company

At December 31, 20X2, and December 31, 20X1, the Company's shareholder has advanced $200,000 and $182,000, respectively, to the Company. These loans are represented by three separate demand notes, are unsecured, and carry interest at 10%. Loan covenants and restrictions prohibit the shareholder from receiving any payment on these loans until such time that other loan commitments are satisfied. Accordingly, these shareholder loans are recorded as long-term debt in the accompanying financial statements.

Example 30–8: Financial Services Agreement with a Related Entity Provides for a Fee at Less Than Prevailing Market Rate

GBG Capital Management (GBG), an entity in which an officer of the Company holds a beneficial interest, performs services for the Company as its agent in connection with negotiations regarding various financial arrangements of the Company. In January 20X1, the Company entered into a Financial Services Agreement for five years with GBG pursuant to which GBG has agreed to render financial advisory and related services to the Company for a fee equal to 90% of the fees that would be charged to the Company by unaffiliated third parties for the same or comparable services. Each year, the Company pays GBG an annual $1,000,000 retainer as an advance against payments due pursuant to this agreement and reimburses GBG for its reasonable out-of-pocket expenses. The Company paid fees to GBG totaling $1,500,000 in 20X2 and $1,300,000 in 20X1 relating to several business acquisitions and dispositions made by the Company.

Example 30–9: Company's Consulting Agreement with a Shareholder Provides for Future Payment for a Covenant Not to Compete

For the years ended December 31, 20X2, and December 31, 20X1, consulting service fees in the amount of $326,000 and $302,000, respectively, were paid to Dr. Mark Makhoul, a shareholder. Dr. Makhoul provides consulting services to the Company pursuant to a consulting agreement that terminates on December 31, 20X5 (subject to extension for an additional five-year term) and for which he receives annual payments of $300,000. The Company also reimburses Dr. Makhoul for his out-of-pocket expenses in performing such consulting services. In addition, the Company has agreed to pay to Dr. Makhoul $250,000 for a period of 24 months following the termination of his consulting relationship with the Company in exchange for his agreement not to compete with the Company during this period.

Example 30–10: Company Pays Royalties in Connection with Patents and Licensing Rights Acquired from Related Party

The Company has patents and licensing rights that were acquired from John Teen, the Company's president and major stockholder. As consideration, the Company pays royalties equal to 2.5% of gross sales on all manufactured products covered by the patents and licensing rights. In 20X2 and 20X1, the Company paid royalties of $1,379,000 and $1,243,000, respectively, to Mr. Teen.

Example 30–11: A Director of the Company Is a Partner in the Law Firm That Acts as Counsel to the Company

A director of the Company is a partner in the law firm that acts as counsel to the Company. The Company paid legal fees and expenses to the law firm in the amount of approximately $375,000 in 20X2 and $210,000 in 20X1.

Example 30–12: A Director of the Company Is an Owner in an Insurance Agency That Has Written Policies for the Company

A director of the Company has an ownership interest in an insurance agency that has written general liability policies for the

Company with premiums totaling $136,000 in 20X2 and $122,000 in 20X1.

Example 30–13: Company Purchased Land and Buildings from Directors

During 20X2, the Company purchased land and buildings adjoining one of its plants from two Company directors for $1,250,000. The board of directors unanimously approved the purchase, with the two directors involved in the transaction abstaining.

Example 30–14: Company Sold Building to Chief Executive Officer at a Price That is within the Range of Appraised Values

In 20X2, the Company sold a building to its chief executive officer for $3,750,000 in cash, which was approved by the Company's board of directors. The sales price was in excess of book value, resulting in a gain of $490,000, and was within the range of appraised values. The building had previously been offered for sale to the public for six months.

Example 30–15: Salary Advance Made to Officer as Part of New Employment Contract

During 20X2, the Company made a $100,000 salary advance to Jane Apostol, an officer, as part of a new employment contract that required her to relocate to Los Angeles, California. According to the terms of the contract, Ms. Apostol is required to repay the loan at $20,000 per year for the next five years, beginning in 20X3.

Example 30–16: Related Party Supplies Inventory Materials to the Company

The Company has an agreement with Just, Inc., an entity in which a major stockholder of the Company owns a significant interest, which provides for purchases by the Company of electrical equipment, subassemblies, and spare parts. Purchases from Just, Inc. for 20X2 and 20X1 totaled $2,900,000 and $3,750,000, respectively. Accounts payable to Just, Inc. amounted to $1,010,000 and $1,236,000 at December 31, 20X2, and December 31, 20X1, respectively. In addition, in 20X2 the Company made advance payments to Just, Inc. for future inventory purchases in return for lower prices on certain components. Advance payments of $420,000 were included in prepaid expenses at December 31, 20X2.

Example 30–17: Company Sells a Substantial Portion of Its Products to a Related Entity

The Company sells a substantial portion of its medical instruments products to Horizons, Ltd., an entity in which the Company's vice-president of operations is a majority stockholder. During 20X2 and 20X1, the Company sold approximately $10,400,000 and $8,732,000 of products to Horizons, Ltd. Trade receivables from Horizons, Inc. were $1,923,000 and $1,544,000 at December 31, 20X2, and December 31, 20X1, respectively.

Example 30–18: Related Parties Reimburse the Company for Allocated Overhead and Administrative Expenses

The Company's managed limited partnerships reimburse the Company for certain allocated overhead and administrative expenses. These expenses generally consist of salaries and related benefits paid to corporate personnel, rent, data processing services, and other corporate facilities costs. The Company provides engineering, marketing, administrative, accounting, information management, legal, and other services to the partnerships. Allocations of personnel costs have been based primarily on actual time spent by Company employees with respect to each partnership managed. Remaining overhead costs are allocated based on the pro rata relationship of the partnership's revenues to the total revenues of all businesses owned or managed by the Company. The Company believes that such allocation methods are reasonable. Amounts charged to managed partnerships and other affiliated companies have directly offset the Company's general and administrative expenses by approximately $5,100,000 and $5,400,000 for the years ended December 31, 20X2, and December 31, 20X1, respectively.

Example 30–19: Company Has Several Long-Term Operating Lease Agreements with Affiliated Entities

The Company leases various manufacturing facilities and equipment from companies owned by certain officers and directors of the Company, either directly or indirectly, through affiliates. The leases generally provide that the Company will bear the cost of property taxes and insurance.

Details of the principal operating leases with related parties as of December 31, 20X2, including the effect of renewals and amendments executed subsequent to December 31, 20X2, are as follows:

Name of Related Party/ Description of Lease	Date of Lease	Term	Basic Annual Rental Amount	Future Minimum Rental Amounts
Hope Realty Trust:				
Land & building— Chicago	12-13-Y1	15 years	$200,000	$1,000,000
Corporate offices	12-22-Y1	15 years	$100,000	$500,000
Machinery & equipment	11-30-Y6	10 years	$125,000	$625,000
John Jones Family Trust:				
Land & buildings— Atlanta	6-29-Y6	10 years	$150,000	$675,000
Furniture & computers	7-1-Y7	10 years	$100,000	$550,000
Kilmer Realty Trust:				
Land & building— Detroit	6-25-Y6	15 years	$200,000	$1,900,000
Corporate offices	12-28-Y6	10 years	$110,000	$550,000
Furniture & equipment	1-1-Y7	10 years	$80,000	$400,000

Rent incurred and paid to these related parties was $1,069,000 and $1,087,000 for the years ended December 31, 20X2, and December 31, 20X1, respectively.

Future minimum lease payments to these related parties as of December 31, 20X2, are as follows:

Year Ending December 31	Amounts
20X3	$1,065,000
20X4	1,110,000
20X5	1,150,000
20X6	1,205,000
20X7	1,260,000
Thereafter	685,000
	$6,475,000

Example 30–20: Company Has a Month-to-Month Lease with a Related Party

The Company leases its administrative offices on a month-to-month basis from a partnership in which the Company's stockholder is a partner. Total rent paid to the partnership was $123,000 and $117,000 for the years ended December 31, 20X2, and December 31, 20X1, respectively.

Example 30–21: Companies under Common Control May Experience Change in Operations

The Company's 80% shareholder also controls other entities whose operations are similar to those of the Company. Although there were no transactions between the Company and these entities in 20X2 or 20X1, the 80% shareholder is, nevertheless, in a position to influence the sales volume of the Company for the benefit of the other entities that are under his control.

Example 30–22: Guarantee of Indebtedness of Related Entity—No Liability Is Recorded

As of December 31, 20X2, the Company is contingently liable as guarantor with respect to $5,400,000 of indebtedness of Extraped, Inc., an entity that is owned by the Company's stockholders. The term of the guarantee is through June 30, 20X4. At any time through that date, should Extraped, Inc. be over 90 days delinquent on its debt payments, the Company will be obligated to perform under the guarantee by primarily making the required payments, including late fees and penalties. The maximum potential amount of future payments that the Company is required to make under the guarantee is $3,000,000.

Example 30–23: Liability Is Recorded as a Result of Guarantee of Indebtedness of an Affiliate

In January 20X2, the Company executed a "Guarantee Agreement" (the Agreement) to guarantee the payment of $500,000 advanced to an affiliate, Steinhart Corp., by Amcor Funding, Inc. The guarantee agreement expires March 31, 20X3. In November 20X2, Steinhart Corp. became insolvent, which triggered an event of default under the terms of the Agreement. At December 31, 20X2, the Company accrued a loss of $500,000 for the full amount of the potential payment that the Company would be required to make under the guarantee. Steinhart Corp. is in the process of liquidating its assets; however, the Company does not expect to recover any of the amounts paid under the guarantee.

Example 30–24: Guarantee of Indebtedness of Joint Venture Obligates Company to Advance Funds to the Joint Venture if Certain Loan Covenants Are Not Met

The Company holds a 25% ownership interest in Stellark, Inc., which has a $7,000,000 line of credit agreement (Agreement) with First Nations Bank. Under terms of the Agreement, the Company is obligated to advance to Stellark, Inc. a maximum of $2,500,000 if its working capital falls below $500,000 or its current ratio is less than 1. Any funds advanced under this Agreement are available to First Nations Bank. In addition, First Nations Bank may have claims against the Company in an amount not to exceed $2,000,000 of any unsatisfied required advances. The term of the guarantee is through April 30, 20X4. At December 31, 20X2, Stellark, Inc. was in compliance with the terms of the Agreement with First Nations Bank.

Example 30–25: Shareholders' Stock Purchase Agreement

The Company and the shareholders have established a Stock Purchase Agreement whereby the Company is obligated to purchase, in the event of the death of any shareholder, all of the decedent's outstanding shares. The repurchase price is determined pursuant to a formula provided in the agreement. The Company has purchased insurance on the lives of the shareholders to help meet its obligation under the Stock Purchase Agreement.

Example 30–26: Purchase of Deceased Shareholder's Stock at Fair Value

In March 20X2, the death of a shareholder triggered the Buy/Sell provisions of the Stock Purchase Agreement dated January 1, 20X0. The provisions of the Agreement required the Company to purchase the shareholder's stock at fair market value, with a minimum cash payment of 10%.

The fair market value of the stock, as determined by an independent valuation, was $2,675,000. The Company paid $1,000,000 in life insurance policy proceeds against the purchase price. The remaining balance of $1,675,000 was financed at 10%, representing the current corporate borrowing rate, and is payable in 36 equal monthly installments to the shareholder's estate.

Example 30–27: Sales Commissions Payable to Related Entities

Sales commissions are payable to a company owned by one of the Company's principal stockholders for sales obtained by this related entity. These commissions amounted to approximately $540,000 and $473,000 for the years ended December 31, 20X2, and December 31, 20X1, respectively, of which $145,000 and $132,000 are included in accrued expenses at December 31, 20X2, and December 31, 20X1, respectively.

CHAPTER 31
RESEARCH AND DEVELOPMENT COSTS

CONTENTS

EXECUTIVE SUMMARY

Generally, research and development costs should be charged to expense when incurred rather than recorded as inventory, component of overhead, or otherwise capitalized. However, intangibles purchased from others and the costs of materials, equipment, and facilities acquired or constructed for research and development activities, and that have alternative future uses, should be capitalized and depreciated over their useful lives. Depreciation expense related to such capitalized costs should be considered research and development costs.

Research and development costs acquired in a business combination accounted for under the purchase method should be assigned a portion of the purchase price based on their fair values, if any. The subsequent accounting by the acquiring entity of these research and development assets is that costs assigned to assets with alternative future uses are capitalized and all others are expensed at the date of consummation of the business combination.

If an entity enters into an arrangement with other parties that fund its research and development, the accounting and reporting for research and development costs depend on the nature of the obligation that the entity incurs in the arrangement. The nature of the obligation in such arrangements can be classified in one of the following categories:

1. *The obligation is solely to perform contractual research and development services for others.* In such situations, the research and development costs incurred should be capitalized as inventory and charged to cost of sales when revenue is recognized.

2. *The obligation represents a liability to repay all of the funds provided by the other parties.* In such situations, the entity should estimate and accrue the liability to repay the other parties and charge research and development costs to expense as incurred.

3. *The obligation is partly to perform contractual services and partly a liability to repay some, but not all, of the funds provided by the other parties.* In such situations, research and development costs are charged partly to expense and partly to cost of sales. The portion charged to cost of sales is related to the funds provided by the other parties that do not have to be repaid by the entity. The portion charged to expense is related to the funds provided by the other parties that are likely to be repaid by the entity.

Costs incurred to establish the technological feasibility of computer software to be sold, leased, or otherwise marketed are research and development costs and should be charged to expense when incurred. After technological feasibility has been established, costs incurred for computer software to be sold, leased, or otherwise marketed should be capitalized and amortized on a product-by-product basis. See Chapter 8, "Computer Software," for further discussion.

Authoritative Literature

FAS-2	Accounting for Research and Development Costs
FAS-68	Research and Development Arrangements
FAS-86	Accounting for the Costs of Computer Software to Be Sold, Leased, or Otherwise Marketed
FAS-141	Business Combinations
FIN-4	Applicability of FASB Statement No. 2 to Business Combinations Accounted for by the Purchase Method
FIN-6	Applicability of FASB Statement No. 2 to Computer Software

FTB 84-1   Accounting for Stock Issued to Acquire the Results of
             a Research and Development Arrangement

DISCLOSURE REQUIREMENTS

The financial statements should include the following disclosures:

1. For an entity that accounts for its obligations under a
   research and development arrangement as a contract to perform research and development for others (FAS-68, par. 14):

   a. The terms of significant agreements under the research
      and development arrangement (including royalty
      arrangements, purchase provisions, license agreement,
      and commitments to provide additional funding) as of
      the date of each balance sheet presented

   b. The amount of compensation earned and costs incurred
      under such contracts for each period for which an
      income statement is presented

2. Total research and development costs charged to expense in
   each period for which an income statement is presented
   (FAS-2, par. 13)

3. For research and development assets acquired in a business
   combination accounted for as a purchase and that have no
   alternative future use, the portion of the purchase price that
   has been allocated to research and development and charged
   to expense at the date of consummation of the business combination (FIN-4, par. 5)

4. Research and development costs incurred for computer software to be sold, leased, or otherwise marketed should be disclosed either separately or as part of total research and
   development costs for each period presented (FAS-86, par. 12)

EXAMPLES OF FINANCIAL STATEMENT DISCLOSURES

 The following sample disclosures are available on the
accompanying disc.

*Example 31–1: Research and Development Costs Charged to Expense as
Incurred*

Expenditures for research activities relating to product development
and improvement are charged to expense as incurred. Such expenditures amounted to $546,000 in 20X2 and $612,000 in 20X1.

Example 31–2: Product Development Costs Deferred

The Company defers certain costs related to the preliminary activities associated with the manufacture of its products, which the Company has determined have future economic benefit. These costs are then expensed in the period in which the initial shipment of the related product is made. Management periodically reviews and revises, when necessary, its estimate of the future benefit of these costs and expenses them if it deems there no longer is a future benefit. At December 31, 20X2, and December 31, 20X1, product development costs capitalized totaled $817,000 and $734,000, respectively.

Example 31–3: Contract to Perform Research and Development Services for Others

The Company has two contracts with Panax, Inc. under which it is obligated to perform certain specific research and development activities. The Company receives royalties under the terms of one of the contracts and licensing fees under the terms of the other contract. Under both contracts, Panax, Inc. can require the Company to purchase their interest in the research and development. Also, under certain circumstances, the Company is obligated to use its own funds if the amount of funds provided by Panax, Inc. is not sufficient to complete the research and development effort.

Compensation earned and costs incurred by the Company under these contracts for the years ended December 31, 20X2, and December 31, 20X1, are as follows:

	20X2	20X1
Royalties and other fees earned	$1,385,000	$1,266,000
Costs incurred charged to operations	$1,102,000	$1,014,000

At December 31, 20X2, and December 31, 20X1, the Company's commitments to provide additional funding under these contracts amounted to $517,000 and $433,000, respectively.

Example 31–4: Research and Development Costs Acquired in a Business Combination Are Capitalized

In October 20X2, the Company purchased the Chickadee division from Seliga & Co., a provider of data networking products and services in the United States, for $9,000,000 in cash. Chickadee's results of operations have been included in the consolidated financial statements since that date. As a result of the acquisition, the Company is expected to (1) be the leading provider of data networking products and services in the United States and (2) reduce costs through economies of scale. Under the terms of the agreement, the Company purchased the Chickadee division, its accounts and notes receivable and tooling equipment, and assumed certain liabilities. The company also incurred $500,000 of direct, acquisition-related costs, which were capitalized as part of the purchase price.

The purchase price exceeded the fair values of the net assets acquired by $3,200,000. Of this amount, $1,325,000 was assigned to "Purchased in-process research and development," which is being amortized on the straight-line method over the estimated remaining lives of individual projects, ranging from two to five years. The amounts charged to these projects include only costs of materials, equipment, and facilities that the Company deems to have future benefit. The remainder of the excess purchase price, amounting to $1,875,000, was recorded as goodwill and assigned to the technology segment. Of that amount, $300,000 is expected to be deductible for tax purposes.

The following table presents the allocation of the purchase price, including related acquisition costs, to the assets acquired and liabilities assumed based on their fair values at the date of acquisition:

Accounts receivable	$ 2,250,000
Notes receivable	750,000
Tooling equipment	4,900,000
Purchased in-process research and development	1,325,000
Goodwill	1,875,000
Total assets acquired	11,100,000
Accounts payable	(1,000,000)
Accrued liabilities	(600,000)
Total liabilities assumed	(1,600,000)
Net assets acquired	$ 9,500,000

Example 31–5: Research and Development Costs Acquired in a Business Combination Are Expensed

"Purchased in-process research and development" expense in the 20X2 Statement of Operations represents the value assigned to research and development projects in a purchase business combination of the Chickadee brand from Seliga & Co. These projects were commenced but not yet completed at the date of acquisition; technological feasibility for these projects has not been established, and they have no alternative future use in research and development activities or otherwise. In accordance with FASB Statement of Financial Accounting Standards No. 2, *Accounting for Research and*

Development Costs, as interpreted by FASB Interpretation No. 4, *Applicability of FASB Statement No. 2 to Business Combinations Accounted for by the Purchase Method,* amounts assigned to purchased in-process research and development meeting the above criteria must be charged to expense at the date of consummation of the purchase business combination. In 20X2, a charge of $1,325,000 was recorded for purchased in-process research and development costs in conjunction with this business combination, based on preliminary allocations of purchase price.

CHAPTER 32
SEGMENT INFORMATION

CONTENTS

EXECUTIVE SUMMARY

Generally accepted accounting principles (GAAP) require that public entities report certain information (1) about operating segments in complete sets of financial statements and in condensed financial statements of interim periods and (2) about the segments' principal products and services, the geographic areas in which they operate, and their major customers. Although the disclosures about segments of an entity are not required for *nonpublic* business entities or for not-for-profit organizations, such entities are encouraged to provide the same information as public business entities.

Operating segments are components of an entity that meet all of the following criteria:

1. Engage in business activities from which revenues may be earned and in which expenses may be incurred
2. Operating results are regularly reviewed by the entity's chief operating decision maker (e.g., chief executive officer, chief operating officer, or a group of individuals) for purposes of making decisions about resource allocation and performance evaluation
3. Discrete financial information is available

An entity should report separately information about each operating segment that meets any of the following quantitative criteria:

1. The operating segment's total revenues (both external, such as sales to other entities, and intersegment, such as sales between operating segments) make up 10% or more of the combined revenue of all reported operating segments
2. The absolute amount of the reported profit or loss of the operating segment is 10% or more of the greater (in absolute amount) of (a) the combined reported profit of all operating segments that did not report a loss or (b) the combined reported loss of all operating segments that did report a loss
3. The operating segment's assets are 10% or more of the combined assets of all operating segments

For purposes of the above criteria, two or more operating segments may be aggregated into a single operating segment if the segments have similar economic characteristics and if the segments are similar in each of the following areas:

1. The nature of their products and services
2. The nature of their production processes
3. Their type or class of customers
4. Their distribution methods
5. The nature of their regulatory environment, if applicable, (e.g., banking, insurance)

The following are other situations in which separate information about an operating segment should be reported:

- If total external revenue reported by operating segments constitutes less than 75% of total consolidated revenue, then additional operating segments should be identified as reportable segments (even if they do not meet the quantitative criteria above) until at least 75% of the total consolidated revenue is included in reportable segments.

- Information about other business activities and operating segments that are not reportable should be combined and disclosed in an "all other" category.

- If a prior-year reportable segment fails to meet one of the quantitative criteria in the current reporting period, but management believes the segment to be of continuing significance, then information about that segment shall continue to be presented.

- If an operating segment meets the criteria as a reportable segment for the first time in the current period, prior-year segment information that is presented for comparative purposes should be restated to reflect the new reportable segment as a separate segment, unless it is impracticable.

There may be a practical limit to the number of reportable segments that an entity separately discloses so that segment information does not become extremely detailed. As a practical matter, authoritative literature indicates that as the number of reportable segments exceeds ten, an entity should consider whether a practical limit has been reached.

Authoritative Literature

FAS-131   Disclosures about Segments of an Enterprise and Related Information

FTB 79-4   Segment Reporting of Puerto Rican Operations

FTB 79-5   Meaning of the Term "Customer" as It Applies to Health Care Facilities under FASB Statement No. 14

DISCLOSURE REQUIREMENTS

The following information should be disclosed for each period for which a complete set of financial statements is presented:

1. Factors used to identify the entity's reportable segments, including the basis of organization such as (FAS-131, par. 26):

    a. Differences in products and services

    b. Geographic areas

    c. Regulatory environments

    d. A combination of factors

2.   Types of products and services from which each reportable segment derives its revenues (FAS-131, par. 26)

3.   The amount of profit or loss and total assets for each reportable segment (FAS-131, par. 27)

4.   The following financial information about each reportable segment, if the specified amounts are included in the determination of segment profit or loss reviewed by the chief operating decision maker (FAS-131, par. 27):

   a.   Revenues from external customers

   b.   Revenues from transactions with other operating segments

   c.   Interest revenue (this may be reported net of interest expense if a majority of the segment's revenues are from interest and the chief operating decision maker relies primarily on net interest revenue to assess performance)

   d.   Interest expense

   e.   Depreciation, depletion, and amortization

   f.   Unusual items, as described in APB Opinion No. 30

   g.   Equity in the net income of investees accounted for by the equity method

   h.   Income tax expense or benefit

   i.   Extraordinary items

   j.   Significant noncash items other than depreciation, depletion, and amortization

5.   The following financial information about each reportable segment, if the specified amounts are included in the determination of segment assets reviewed by the chief operating decision maker (FAS-131, par. 28):

   a.   The amount of investment in equity-method investees

   b.   Total expenditures for additions to long-lived assets (other than financial instruments, long-term customer relationships of a financial institution, mortgage and other servicing rights, deferred policy acquisition costs, and deferred tax assets)

6.   An explanation of the measurements used for segment profit or loss and segment assets for each reportable segment, including, at a minimum, the following information (FAS-131, par. 31):

   a.   The basis of accounting for any transactions between reportable segments

   b.   The nature of any differences between the measurements of the reportable segments' profit or loss and the entity's consolidated income before income taxes, extraordinary items, discontinued operations, and cumulative effect of changes in accounting principles

c. The nature of any differences between the measurements of the reportable segments' assets and the entity's consolidated assets

d. The nature of any changes from prior periods in the measurement methods used to determine reported segment profit or loss and the effect, if any, of those changes on the amount of segment profit or loss

e. The nature and effect of any asymmetrical allocations to segments (e.g., an entity might allocate depreciation expense to a segment without allocating the related depreciable assets to that segment)

7. Reconciliations of all of the following items (FAS-131, par. 32):

a. The total of the reportable segments' revenues to the entity's consolidated revenues

b. The total of the reportable segments' profit or loss to the entity's consolidated income before income taxes, extraordinary items, discontinued operations, and cumulative effect of changes in accounting principles (However, if an entity allocates items such as income taxes and extraordinary items to segments, the entity may choose to reconcile the total of the segments' profit or loss to consolidated income after those items.)

c. The total of the reportable segments' assets to the entity's consolidated assets

d. The total of the reportable segments' amounts for every other significant item of information disclosed to the corresponding consolidated amount (e.g., an entity may choose to disclose liabilities for its reportable segments, in which case the entity would reconcile the total of reportable segments' liabilities for each segment to the entity's consolidated liabilities if the segment liabilities are significant)

8. The following items are required to be disclosed on an entity-wide basis, unless they are disclosed as part of the information about reportable segments (Entities that have a single reportable segment must also disclose this information.) (FAS-131, pars. 36-39):

a. Revenues from external customers for each product and service or each group of similar products and services, based on information used to produce the entity's general-purpose financial statements (unless it is impracticable to do so, in which case the entity should disclose that fact)

    b. The following information about geographic areas, based on information used to produce the entity's general-purpose financial statements (unless it is impracticable to do so, in which case the entity should disclose that fact):

      — Revenues from external sources (i) attributed to the entity's country of domicile and (ii) attributed to all foreign countries in total from which the entity derives revenues. If revenues from external customers attributed to an individual foreign country are material, the entity should disclose those revenues separately; the entity should disclose the basis for attributing revenues from external customers to individual countries.

      — Long-lived assets (other than financial instruments, long-term customer relationships of a financial institution, mortgage and other servicing rights, deferred policy acquisition costs, and deferred tax assets) located in (i) the entity's country of domicile and (ii) all foreign countries in total in which the entity holds assets. If assets in an individual foreign country are material, the entity should disclose those assets separately.

    c. The extent of the entity's reliance on a single external customer from which 10% or more of revenues are derived, the amount of revenues earned from each such single customer, and the operating segment reporting the revenue

9. The following information should be disclosed about each reportable segment in condensed financial statements of interim periods (FAS-131, par. 33):

    a. Revenues from external customers

    b. Intersegment revenues

    c. Segment profit or loss

    d. Total assets for which there has been a material change from the amount disclosed in the last annual report

    e. A description of differences from the last annual report in the basis of segmentation or in the basis of measurement of segment profit or loss

    f. A reconciliation of the total reportable segments' profit or loss to the entity's consolidated income before income taxes, extraordinary items, discontinued operations, and cumulative effect of changes in accounting principles (However, if an entity allocates items such as income taxes and extraordinary items to segments, the entity may reconcile the total of the segments' profit or loss to consolidated income after those items.)

10. If an entity changes the structure of its internal organization in a manner that causes the composition of its reportable segments to change, the corresponding information for earlier periods, including interim periods, should be restated, unless it is impracticable to do so. The entity should also disclose that it has restated the segment information for earlier periods. (If the segment information for earlier periods, including interim periods, is not restated to reflect the change, the entity should disclose in the year in which the change occurs segment information for the current period under both the old basis and the new basis of segmentation, unless it is impracticable to do so.) (FAS-131, pars. 34–35)

EXAMPLES OF FINANCIAL STATEMENT DISCLOSURES

 The following sample disclosures are available on the accompanying disc.

Example 32–1: Company Operates in a Single Business Segment and Discloses Entity-Wide Geographic Data and Sales to Major Customers

The Company operates in a single business segment that includes the design, development, and manufacture of electronic surveillance equipment and products for the commercial electronics industry. The following table summarizes the Company's revenues and long-lived assets in different geographic locations:

	20X2	20X1
Revenues:		
United States	$59,820,000	$54,338,000
Singapore	11,341,000	9,102,000
Other foreign countries	20,145,000	17,010,000
Total	$91,306,000	$80,450,000
Long-lived assets:		
United States	$16,764,000	$15,430,000
Singapore	6,450,000	6,020,000
Other foreign countries	1,230,000	1,113,000
Total	$24,444,000	$22,563,000

Geographic area data is based on product shipment destination. Export sales as a percentage of revenues were 40% for 20X2 and 35% for 20X1.

In 20X2 and 20X1, sales to a single customer were 13% and 11% of total sales, respectively.

The geographic summary of long-lived assets is based on physical location.

Example 32–2: Company's Operations Are Classified Into Two Principal Reportable Segments: Domestic and International Operations

The Company manages its operations through two business segments: domestic and international. Each unit sells railroad electronics and related products as well as services to railroads and transit authorities. The international business segment sells the Company's products and services outside the U.S.

The Company evaluates performance based on net operating profit. Administrative functions such as finance, treasury, and information systems are centralized. However, where applicable, portions of the administrative function expenses are allocated between the operating segments. The operating segments do not share manufacturing or distribution facilities. In the event any materials and/or services are provided to one operating segment by the other, the transaction is valued according to the company's transfer policy, which approximates market price. The costs of operating the manufacturing plants are captured discretely within each segment. The Company's property, plant and equipment, inventory, and accounts receivable are captured and reported discretely within each operating segment.

Summary financial information for the two reportable segments is as follows:

	20X2	20X1
United States Operations:		
Net sales	$25,200,000	$22,400,000
Operating income	2,150,000	2,410,000
Assets	15,600,000	14,400,000
Accounts receivable	5,070,000	4,510,000
Inventory	4,250,000	4,325,000
International Operations:		
Net sales	$1,360,000	$1,310,000
Operating income	69,000	31,000
Assets	65,000	59,000
Accounts receivable	171,000	143,000
Inventory	56,000	42,000

	20X2	20X1
Consolidated Operations:		
Net sales	$26,560,000	$23,710,000
Operating income	2,219,000	2,441,000
Assets	15,665,000	14,459,000
Accounts receivable	5,241,000	4,653,000
Inventory	4,306,000	4,367,000

Example 32–3: Company Has Five Operating Segments That Are Aggregated into Three Reportable Segments and Are Reconciled to the Company's Consolidated Amounts

The Company has five principal operating segments, which are the design, manufacturing and marketing of (1) semiconductor test systems, (2) backplane connection systems, (3) circuit-board test systems, (4) telecommunication test systems, and (5) software test systems. These operating segments were determined based on the nature of the products and services offered. Operating segments are defined as components of an enterprise about which separate financial information is available that is evaluated regularly by the chief operating decision-maker in deciding how to allocate resources and in assessing performance. The Company's chief executive officer and chief operating officer have been identified as the chief operating decision makers. The Company's chief operating decision makers direct the allocation of resources to operating segments based on the profitability and cash flows of each respective segment.

The Company has determined that there are three reportable segments: (1) semiconductor test systems segment, (2) backplane connection systems segment, and (3) other test systems segment. The other test systems segment comprises circuit-board test systems, telecommunication test systems, and software test systems; these operating segments were not separately reported as they do not meet any of the quantitative thresholds under FASB Statement of Financial Accounting Standards No. 131, *Disclosures about Segments of an Enterprise and Related Information.*

The Company evaluates performance based on several factors, of which the primary financial measure is business segment income before taxes. The accounting policies of the business segments are the same as those described in "Note 1: Summary of Significant Accounting Policies." Intersegment sales are accounted for at fair value as if sales were to third parties. The following tables show the operations of the Company's reportable segments:

	Semiconductor Test Systems Segment	Backplane Connection Systems Segment	Other Test Systems Segment	Corporate and Eliminations	Consolidated
20X2					
Sales to unaffiliated customers	$19,670,000	$5,458,000	$4,975,000	$-0-	$30,103,000
Intersegment sales	-0-	275,000	-0-	(275,000)	-0-
Net sales	19,670,000	5,733,000	4,975,000	(275,000)	30,103,000
Income before taxes (1)	2,125,000	692,000	531,000	(450,000)	2,898,000
Total assets (2)	10,391,000	3,850,000	2,700,000	6,200,000	23,141,000
Property additions (3)	1,400,000	640,000	150,000	700,000	2,890,000
Interest expense	120,000	74,000	53,000	-0-	247,000
Depreciation and amortization (3)	545,000	280,000	200,000	320,000	1,345,000
20X1					
Sales to unaffiliated customers	$17,840,000	$4,940,000	$4,310,000	$-0-	$27,090,000
Intersegment sales	-0-	210,000	-0-	(210,000)	-0-
Net sales	17,840,000	5,150,000	4,310,000	(210,000)	27,090,000
Income before taxes (1)	1,930,000	584,000	487,000	(400,000)	2,601,000
Total assets (2)	10,110,000	3,725,000	2,574,000	5,900,000	22,309,000
Property additions (3)	1,050,000	420,000	170,000	400,000	2,040,000
Interest expense	113,000	67,000	48,000	-0-	228,000
Depreciation and amortization (3)	510,000	240,000	180,000	290,000	1,220,000

(1) Income before taxes of the principal businesses exclude the effects of employee profit sharing, management incentive compensation, other unallocated expenses, and net interest income.

(2) *Total business assets* are the owned or allocated assets used by each business. *Corporate assets* consist of cash and cash equivalents, marketable securities, unallocated fixed assets of support divisions and common facilities, and certain other assets.

(3) Corporate property additions and depreciation and amortization expense include items attributable to the unallocated fixed assets of support divisions and common facilities.

Information as to the Company's sales in different geographical areas is as follows:

	20X2	20X1
Sales to unaffiliated customers:		
United States	$16,112,000	$13,143,000
Asia Pacific region	5,477,000	6,374,000
Europe	4,993,000	4,065,000
Japan	2,300,000	2,439,000
Other	1,221,000	1,069,000
	$30,103,000	$27,090,000

Sales are attributable to geographic areas based on location of customer. Neither the Company nor any of its segments depends on any single customer, small group of customers, or government for more than 10% of its sales.

Also, because a substantial portion of the Company's sales are derived from the sales of product manufactured in the United States, long-lived assets located outside the United States are less than 10%.

Example 32–4: Company Discloses Sales to Major Customers and the Identity of the Segments Reporting the Sales

> **Note:** This example assumes the same facts as in Example 32–3, except that the Company has sales to major customers, for which disclosure is required of (1) the total amount of sales to the major customer and (2) the identity of the segment reporting the sales.

In 20X2 and 20X1, sales to a customer of the Company's Semiconductor Test Systems segment totaled approximately $4,214,000 (14%), and $3,522,000 (13%), respectively, of the Company's consolidated sales. In 20X2 and 20X1, sales to a different customer of the Company's Backplane Connection Systems segment totaled $3,913,000 (13%), and $3,251,000 (12%), respectively, of the Company's consolidated sales.

Example 32–5: Company Discloses Its Exposure to Economic Conditions in Foreign Countries

The Company has operations in Hong Kong, China, and Brazil. These countries have experienced illiquidity, volatile currency exchange rates and interest rates, and reduced economic activity. The Company will be affected for the foreseeable future by economic conditions in these regions, although it is not possible to determine the extent of the effects.

CHAPTER 33
STOCK-BASED COMPENSATION, STOCK OPTION PLANS, AND STOCK PURCHASE PLANS

CONTENTS

EXECUTIVE SUMMARY

Stock issued to employees may include compensation (compensatory plan) or may not include compensation (noncompensatory plan). A *compensatory plan* is one in which services rendered by employees are compensated for by the issuance of stock. The measurement of compensation expense included in compensatory plans is the primary problem in accounting for stock issued to employees.

Generally accepted accounting principles (GAAP) for stock-based compensation plans are established primarily in Accounting Principles Board Opinion No. 25 (APB-25), *Accounting for Stock Issued to Employees*, FASB Statement of Financial Accounting Standards No. 123 (FAS-123), *Accounting for Stock-Based Compensation*, and FAS-148, *Accounting for Stock-Based Compensation—Transition and Disclosure*. APB-25 is based on the intrinsic value method of accounting. FAS-123 established a method of accounting for stock-based compensation that is based on the fair value of stock options and similar instruments. Adoption of the fair value based method of accounting under FAS-123 is encouraged but not required for all stock-based compensation arrangements with *employees*. However, the fair value based method of accounting under FAS-123 must be adopted as the measurement basis for transactions in which an entity acquires goods or services from *nonemployees* in exchange for equity instruments.

Note: In December 2004, the FASB issued Statement of Financial Accounting Standards No. 123R (FAS-123R), *Share-Based Payment*. This statement replaces FAS-123, *Accounting for Stock-Based Compensation*, supersedes APB Opinion No. 25, *Accounting for Stock Issued to Employees*, and amends FAS-95, *Statement of Cash Flows*. FAS-123R requires companies to apply a fair-value-based measurement method in accounting for shared-based payment transactions with employees and to record compensation cost for all stock awards granted after the required effective date and to awards modified, repurchased, or cancelled after that date. The scope of FAS-123R encompasses a wide range of share-based compensation arrangements, including share options, restricted share plans, performance-based awards, share appreciation rights, and employee share purchase plans. Therefore, pro forma disclosure of the income statement effect is no longer an alternative to financial statement recognition. For further guidance on FAS-123R, see discussion later in this chapter.

APB-25

The essential characteristics of noncompensatory stock options or stock purchase plans are as follows:

1. Substantially all full-time employees meeting limited employment qualifications may participate.

2. Stock is offered equally to eligible employees, but the plan may limit the total amount of shares that can be purchased.

3. The time permitted to exercise the rights is limited to a reasonable period.

4. Any discount from the market price is no greater than would be a reasonable offer of stock to shareholders or others.

Plans that do not have these characteristics are classified as compensatory plans.

Under traditional stock option and stock purchase plans, an employer corporation grants options to purchase shares of its stock, sometimes at a price lower than the prevailing market, making it possible for the individual exercising the option to have at least a potential profit at the time of acquisition. Compensatory plans result in compensation expense on the books of the Company and in compensation income to the recipient. Under APB-25, the cost of compensation is measured by the excess of the quoted market price of the stock over the option price on the measurement date. This is referred to as the *intrinsic value method*. The measurement date is the first date on which the employer knows (1) the number of shares the employee is to receive and (2) the option or purchase price. Usually, the measurement date is the grant date.

Compensation expense related to compensatory plans should be recognized as an expense over the period of employment attributable to the option. If this period is not stated, a reasonable estimate must be made, taking into account the circumstances implied by the terms of the agreement. Stock issued in accordance with a plan for past and future services of an employee is allocated between expired costs and future costs. Future costs are charged to the periods in which the employee performs services. In the event stock options are exercised before the related compensation cost is actually incurred, a deferred or prepaid compensation account is set up. Unearned compensation cost should be written off to the period(s) in which they were actually earned, and any balances at a reporting date should be deducted from stockholders' equity.

FAS-123, as Amended by FAS-148

Under FAS-123, a plan is noncompensatory if it meets the following criteria:

1. Substantially all full-time employees meeting limited employment qualifications may participate.

2. The plan has no option features other than the following:

    a. Employees are permitted a short period of time, not exceeding 31 days, after the purchase price has been fixed to enroll in the plan

    b. The purchase price is based solely on the stock's market price at the date of purchase, and employees are permitted to cancel participation before the purchase date and receive a refund of amounts previously paid

3. The discount from the market price does not exceed the greater of (a) a per-share discount that would be reasonable in a recurring offer of stock to stockholders or others, or (b) the per-share amount of stock issuance costs avoided by not having to raise a significant amount of capital by a public offering. A discount of 5% or less would meet this criterion.

Plans that do not have these characteristics are classified as compensatory plans.

FAS-123 establishes a method of accounting for stock compensation plans that is based on the fair value of employee stock options and similar equity instruments. The method is in contrast to that described in APB-25, which is based on the intrinsic value of equity instruments. Companies are permitted to continue using the method of accounting described in APB-25 but are required to make specific disclosures as if the fair value method of FAS-123 had been used to measure compensation cost.

The general principle underlying FAS-123 is that equity instruments are recognized at the fair value of the consideration received for them. In a transaction with third parties for goods and services, fair value may be the value of the consideration received or the value of the equity instruments issued, whichever is more reliably measurable. Applying this general principle to stock compensation results in the equity instruments being measured and recognized at their fair value and the compensation cost being the excess of that amount over any amount paid by the employee. For example, if an employee pays $10 for a stock option valued at $30, $20 is the amount of compensation attributed to employee services.

The objective of the measurement process described in FAS-123 is to estimate the fair value, based on the stock price at the grant date, of equity instruments to be issued to employees when they have satisfied all conditions required to earn the right to benefit from the instruments. The fair value of an option estimated at the grant date is not subsequently adjusted for changes in the price of the underlying stock or other variables (e.g., changes in volatility, the life of the option, dividends on the stock, or the risk-free interest rate).

Transition requirements under FAS-148. In December 2002, the FASB issued Statement of Financial Accounting Standards No. 148 (FAS-148), *Accounting for Stock-Based Compensation—Transition and Disclosure.* FAS-148 amends FAS-123 to provide three transition alternatives for those companies voluntarily choosing to recognize stock-based employee compensation using the fair-value method. One of these transition methods was specified in FAS-123 and two of the transition methods are new to FAS-148.

The three transition alternatives under FAS-148 are:

1. *Prospective method (the only transition alternative permitted under FAS-123).* Under this transition approach, stock-based employee compensation is recognized using the fair-value method for employee awards granted, modified, or settled after the beginning of the fiscal year in which the fair-value method is first applied. This transition method leads to increasing amounts of compensation expense being recognized in the first few years after the adoption of the fair-value method (the FASB refers to this as the "ramp-up" effect). This is the one method that was permitted under FAS-123, and this transition method will no longer be allowed for changes to the fair-value method made in fiscal years beginning after December 15, 2003.

2. *Modified prospective method.* Under this transition approach, stock-based employee compensation is recognized from the beginning of the fiscal year in which the fair value method is first applied as if that accounting method had been used to account for all employee awards granted, modified, or

settled in fiscal years beginning after December 15, 1994 (the effective date of FAS-123).

3. *Retroactive restatement method.* Under this transition approach, all prior periods presented are restated to reflect what compensation cost would have been if the fair-value method had been used to measure compensation cost for all awards granted, modified, or settled in fiscal years beginning after December 15, 1994 (the effective date of FAS-123). Also, restatement of periods prior to those presented is permitted but not required.

The recognition and measurement provisions of FAS-123 are unaffected by the issuance of FAS-148. However, FAS-148 amends FAS-123 to require more prominent note disclosure of the effect on reported net income of recognizing stock-based employee compensation using the intrinsic value method rather than the fair-value method. Also, FAS-148 extends these required disclosures to interim financial statements. See the "Disclosure Requirements" section below for further detail.

With the exception of the required interim disclosures, the provisions of FAS-148 are effective for fiscal years ending after December 15, 2002. Earlier application is permitted for financial statements for fiscal years ending prior to December 15, 2002, if those financial statements had not yet been issued as of the date FAS-148 was issued. The interim disclosure provisions are effective for interim periods beginning after December 15, 2002.

FAS-123R

In December 2004, the Financial Accounting Standards Board issued Statement of Financial Accounting Standards No. 123R (FAS-123R), *Share-Based Payment*, which is a revision of Statement of Financial Accounting Standards No. 123, *Accounting for Stock-Based Compensation*. In addition to requiring supplemental disclosures, FAS-123R addresses the accounting for share-based payment transactions in which a company receives goods or services in exchange for (a) equity instruments of the company or (b) liabilities that are based on the fair value of the company's equity instruments or that may be settled by the issuance of such equity instruments. FAS-123R focuses primarily on accounting for transactions in which a company obtains *employee* services in share-based payment transactions. The Statement eliminates the ability to account for share-based compensation transactions using Accounting Principles Board Opinion No. 25 (APB-25), *Accounting for Stock Issued to Employees*, and generally requires that such transactions be accounted for using a fair-value-based method. Accordingly, pro forma disclosure is no longer an alternative. Share-based awards to *nonemployees* should continue to be measured and recognized in accordance with FAS-123R and EITF Issue No. 96-18,

Accounting for Equity Instruments That Are Issued to Other Than Employees for Acquiring, or in Conjunction with Selling, Goods or Services.

Measurement basis. A company is required to recognize the goods acquired or services received in a share-based payment transaction when it obtains the goods or as services are received, with a corresponding increase in equity (generally, paid-in capital) or a liability, depending on whether the instruments granted satisfy the equity or liability classification criteria. With limited exceptions, a share-based payment transaction with *employees* should be measured based on the fair value of the equity instruments issued on the grant date or on the fair value of the liabilities incurred. The fair value of a stock option awarded to an employee generally must be estimated using an option-pricing model (e.g., Black-Scholes) that takes into account, at a minimum, the following six variables:

1. The exercise price of the option
2. The expected term of the option, taking into account both the contractual term of the option and the effects of employees' expected exercise and post-vesting employment termination behavior
3. The current price of the underlying share
4. The expected volatility of the price of the underlying share for the expected term of the option
5. The expected dividends on the underlying share for the expected term of the option
6. The risk-free interest rate(s) for the expected term of the option

It should be noted that the aforementioned requirement applies to nonpublic companies as well; however, if a nonpublic company is unable to estimate the expected volatility of the price of its underlying share, it may measure awards based on a "calculated value," which substitutes the volatility of an appropriate index for the volatility of the company's own share price. [**Note:** The "minimum-value" method is no longer acceptable for nonpublic companies.]

Share-based awards to *nonemployees* should be measured and recognized using the fair-value method in accordance with FAS-123R and EITF Issue No. 96-18. Share-based payment transactions with nonemployees should be measured based on the fair value of the equity instruments issued or the fair value of goods or services received, whichever is more reliably measurable.

Awards classified as equity. The compensation cost for an award of share-based employee compensation classified as equity should be recognized over the requisite service period, with a corresponding credit to equity (generally, paid-in capital). The requisite service period is the period during which an employee is required to provide service in exchange for an award, which often is the vesting period.

Awards of share-based employee compensation ordinarily specify a performance condition or a service condition (or both) that must be satisfied for an employee to earn the right to benefit from the award. No compensation cost is recognized for instruments that employees forfeit because a service condition or a performance condition is not satisfied. FAS-123R requires a company to estimate the number of awards that are expected to vest and to revise the estimate as the actual forfeitures differ from the estimate. A company is not permitted to wait to account for the forfeitures as they occur.

In addition, some awards contain a market condition (i.e., awards that become exercisable upon achievement of a preestablished stock price). The effect of a market condition is reflected in the fair value of an award on the grant date. Therefore, compensation cost is recognized for an award with a market condition provided that the requisite service is rendered, regardless of whether the market condition (i.e., targeted stock price) is achieved.

Equity instruments for which it is not possible to reasonably estimate fair value at the grant date. Generally, it should be possible to reasonably estimate the fair value of most equity share options and other equity instruments at the date they are granted. However, in those rare circumstances for which it is not possible to reasonably estimate fair value at the grant date, the equity instrument should (a) be measured at its intrinsic value and (b) remeasured at each reporting date through the date of exercise or other settlement. Compensation cost for each period until settlement should be based on the change in the intrinsic value of the equity instrument in each reporting period. The intrinsic value method should continue to be used for such equity instruments, even if the company subsequently determines that it is possible to estimate the award's fair value.

FAS-123R recognizes that a nonpublic company may not be able to reasonably estimate the fair value of its equity share options because it is not practicable to estimate the expected volatility of its share price. In such circumstances, the company should account for its equity awards based on a value calculated using the historical volatility of an appropriate industry sector index instead of the expected volatility of the company's share price (i.e., "calculated value").

Awards classified as liabilities. FAS-123R requires liability classification for certain equity instruments that would be classified as liabilities under FASB Statement of Financial Accounting Standards No. 150 (FAS-150), *Accounting for Certain Financial Instruments with Characteristics of Both Liabilities and Equity.* Share-based payment awards should be classified as liabilities in the following circumstances:

- If the underlying shares are classified as liabilities
- If the company can be required to settle the award by transferring its cash or other assets to employees rather than by issuing an equity instrument
- For awards with conditions other than market, performance, or service conditions (i.e., awards that may be indexed to a factor in addition to the company's share price, for example an award of options whose exercise price is indexed to the market price of a commodity, such as gold)
- For awards with repurchase features (e.g., puttable shares that give the employee the right to require the employer to repurchase them for cash equal to their fair value) if either of the following conditions is met: (a) the repurchase feature permits the employee to avoid bearing the risks and rewards normally associated with equity share ownership for a reasonable period of time from the date the requisite service is rendered and the share is issued (generally six months), or (b) it is probable that the employer would prevent the employee from bearing those risks and rewards for a reasonable period of time (generally six months) from the date the share is issued

Public companies must measure liabilities at fair value. Nonpublic companies may elect to measure liabilities using fair value (or "calculated value" if a company cannot reasonably estimate the expected volatility of its stock, as previously discussed), or intrinsic value. Regardless of the method used, public and nonpublic companies must remeasure the fair value of the liabilities incurred in share-based transactions with employees at the end of each reporting period through settlement. Changes in the fair value (or intrinsic value for a nonpublic company that elects that method) of a liability incurred under a share-based payment arrangement that occur during the requisite service period should be recognized as compensation cost over that period.

Other pertinent provisions of FAS-123R.   The following are additional relevant provisions of FAS-123R:

1. *Reload options.* A reload feature provides for automatic grants of additional options whenever an employee exercises previously granted options using the company's shares, rather than cash, to satisfy the exercise price. At the time of exercise using shares, the employee is automatically granted a new option (called a *reload option*) for the shares used to exercise the previous option. Reload stock options are treated as new grants; accordingly, the fair value should be determined on the grant date of the reload option.

2. *Contingent features.* A contingent feature of an award that might cause an employee to return to the company either equity instruments earned or realized gains from the sale of equity instruments earned for consideration that is less than fair value on the date of transfer should be accounted for if and when the contingent event occurs (i.e., should not be reflected in estimating the fair value at the grant date).

3. *Modifications of awards of equity instruments.* A modification of the terms or conditions of an equity award should be treated as an exchange of the original award for a new award. In substance, the company repurchases the original instrument by issuing a new instrument of equal or greater value, incurring additional compensation cost for any incremental value. The effects of a modification should be measured as follows:

   a. Incremental compensation cost should be measured as the excess, if any, of the fair value of the modified award over the fair value of the original award immediately before its terms are modified, measured based on the share price and other pertinent factors at that date. The effect of the modification on the number of instruments expected to vest also should be reflected in determining incremental compensation cost.

   b. Total recognized compensation cost for an equity award should at least equal the fair value of the award at the grant date unless at the date of the modification the performance or service conditions of the original award are not expected to be satisfied. Therefore, the total compensation cost measured at the date of a modification should be (1) the portion of the grant-date fair value of the original award for which the requisite service is expected to be rendered (or has already been rendered) at that date plus (2) the incremental cost resulting from the modification.

   c. A change in compensation cost for an equity award measured at intrinsic value should be measured by comparing the intrinsic value of the modified award, if any, with the intrinsic value of the original award, if any, immediately before the modification.

4. *Cancellations and replacements of awards of equity instruments.* Cancellation of an award accompanied by the concurrent grant of a replacement award or other valuable consideration is accounted for as a modification of the terms of the cancelled award. Therefore, incremental compensation cost is measured as the excess of the fair value of the replacement award or other valuable consideration over the fair value of the cancelled award at the cancellation date. A cancellation of an award that is not accompanied by the concurrent grant

of a replacement award or other valuable consideration is accounted for as a repurchase for no consideration. Accordingly, any previously unrecognized compensation cost is recognized at the cancellation date.

5. *Income tax effects.* Tax benefits resulting from income tax deductions in excess of compensation cost recognized for financial reporting are recognized as additional paid-in capital. However, an excess of a realized tax benefit for an award over the deferred tax asset for that award should be recognized in the income statement to the extent that the excess stems from a reason other than changes in the fair value of a company's shares between the measurement date for accounting purposes and a later measurement date for tax purposes. The amount deductible on the company's tax return may be less than the cumulative compensation cost recognized for financial reporting. The write-off of a deferred tax asset related to that deficiency, net of any related valuation allowance, should first be offset to the extent of any remaining additional paid-in capital from excess tax benefits from previous awards accounted for in accordance with either FAS-123 or FAS-123R. The remaining balance, if any, of the write-off of a deferred tax asset related to a tax deficiency should be recognized in the income statement.

6. *Classification of income tax effects in statement of cash flows.* Cash retained as a result of excess tax benefits should be presented in the statement of cash flows as a financing cash inflow. The write-off of deferred tax assets relating to unrealized tax benefits associated with recognized compensation cost should be reflected as an operating cash flow.

7. *Awards to employees by certain related parties.* Share-based payments to an employee by a related party, or other economic interest holder, should be accounted for as compensation by the company, unless the award is for a purpose other than compensation.

Disclosure requirements.   The disclosure requirements of FAS-123R are summarized in a separate section later in this chapter.

Effective dates.   FAS-123R applies to all awards granted after the required effective date. However, it should not be applied to awards granted in periods before the required effective date, except to the extent that prior periods' awards are modified, repurchased, or canceled after the required effective date. The cumulative effect of initially applying FAS-123R, if any, should be recognized as of the required effective date. The effective dates vary for different types of entities. The following is a summary:

- *Public companies that do not file as small business issuers.* FAS-123R is effective for public companies that do not file as small business issuers as of the beginning of the first interim or annual reporting period that begins after June 15, 2005. Therefore, calendar year-end companies will be required to adopt FAS-123R in the third quarter of 2005. However, the SEC adopted a rule that allows public companies that do not file as small business issuers to implement FAS-123R at the beginning of their next fiscal year, instead of the next reporting period, that begins after June 15, 2005.

- *Public companies that file as small business issuers.* FAS-123R is effective for public companies that file as small business issuers as of the beginning of the first interim or annual reporting period that begins after December 15, 2005. Therefore, calendar year-end small business issuers will be required to adopt FAS-123R in the first quarter of 2006.

- *Nonpublic companies.* FAS-123R is effective for nonpublic companies as of the beginning of the first annual reporting period that begins after December 15, 2005. Therefore, calendar year-end nonpublic companies will be required to adopt FAS-123R effective January 1, 2006.

Early adoption of FAS-123R for interim or annual periods for which financial statements or interim reports have not been issued is encouraged.

Transition requirements. As of the required effective date, all public entities and those nonpublic entities that used the fair-value-based method for either recognition or pro forma disclosure under FAS-123 should apply the *modified prospective* transition method. For periods before the required effective date, those entities may elect to apply the modified retrospective transition method. Nonpublic entities that used the minimum-value method in FAS-123 for either recognition or pro forma disclosures are required to apply the prospective transition method as of the required effective date. The following is a summary of the "modified prospective" and "modified retrospective" transition methods:

- *Modified prospective transition.* Under the modified prospective method, companies are required to recognize compensation cost for the portion of awards for which the requisite service has not been rendered (i.e., unvested awards) that are outstanding as of the required effective date as the requisite service is rendered on or after the required effective date. The compensation cost for that portion of awards should be based on the grant-date fair value of those awards as calculated for either recognition or pro forma disclosures under FAS-123. Companies that previously adopted only the pro forma disclosure provisions of FAS-123 are required to recognize compensation cost relating to the unvested portion of those awards in the financial statements beginning with the date on which FAS-123R is adopted, through the end of the requisite service period. Companies should *not* record a cumulative effect of a change in accounting principle to adjust for the difference between the compensation cost recognized under APB-25 and the compensation cost that would have been recognized if the award had been accounted for under FAS-123R since the grant date.

For purposes of the modified prospective transition method, FAS-123R precludes changes to the grant-date fair value of equity awards granted before the required effective date. The compensation cost for those earlier awards should be attributed to periods beginning on or after the required effective date of FAS-123R using the attribution method that was used under Statement 123, except that the method of recognizing forfeitures only as they occur should not be continued. Any unearned or deferred compensation (contra equity accounts) related to those earlier awards should be eliminated against the appropriate equity accounts. Also, if the company's prior policy was to account for forfeitures as they occurred, forfeitures would have to be estimated upon adoption of FAS-123R; in such circumstances, balance-sheet amounts (e.g., additional paid-in capital and deferred tax assets) related to any compensation cost previously recognized in income because of that policy should be eliminated and recognized as the cumulative effect of a change in accounting principles for those awards that are not expected to vest.

Under the modified prospective transition method, the financial statements are unchanged for periods prior to adoption and the pro forma disclosures previously required by FAS-123 for those prior periods will continue to be required to the extent those amounts differ from the amounts in the statement of operations.

- *Modified retrospective transition.* Under the modified retrospective method, companies are allowed to restate prior periods by recognizing compensation cost in the amounts previously reported in the pro forma footnote disclosures under the provisions of FAS-123. Companies are permitted to apply the modified retrospective method either (a) to all prior periods presented for which FAS-123 was effective or (b) to prior interim periods of the year in which FAS-123R is adopted. Under the modified retrospective method, the recognition of compensation cost under FAS-123R is generally the same as the accounting under the modified prospective method discussed previously for (a) awards granted, modified, or settled subsequent to the adoption of FAS-123R, and (b) awards granted prior to the date of adoption of FAS-123R for which the requisite service period has not been completed (i.e., unvested awards).

Nonpublic companies that used the minimum-value method to measure compensation cost under FAS-123 (whether for financial statement recognition or pro forma disclosure purposes) are required to apply FAS-123R prospectively to new awards and to awards modified, repurchased, or cancelled after the required effective date. Those nonpublic companies should continue to account for nonvested awards at the date of initial application using the accounting principles originally applied to those awards (either the minimum-value method under FAS-123 or the provisions of APB-25). This prospective transition method (available only to nonpublic companies that used the minimum-value method) will reduce comparability of the income statements for several years after the date of adoption of FAS-123R.

Authoritative Literature

ARB-43	Chapter 13B, Compensation Involved in Stock Option and Stock Purchase Plans
APB-25	Accounting for Stock Issued to Employees
FAS-123	Accounting for Stock-Based Compensation
FAS-123R	Share-Based Payment
FSP FAS 123R-6	Technical Corrections of FASB Statement No. 123R
FAS-148	Accounting for Stock-Based Compensation— Transition and Disclosure
FIN-28	Accounting for Stock Appreciation Rights and Other Variable Stock Option or Award Plans
FIN-38	Determining the Measurement Date for Stock Option, Purchase, and Award Plans Involving Junior Stock
FIN-44	Accounting for Certain Transactions Involving Stock Compensation
FTB 97-1	Accounting under Statement 123 for Certain Employee Stock Purchase Plans with a Look-Back Option
EITF 00-23	Issues Related to the Accounting for Stock Compensation under APB Opinion No. 25 and FASB Interpretation No. 44
SOP 76-3	Accounting Practices for Certain Employee Stock Ownership Plans
SOP 93-6	Employers' Accounting for Stock Ownership Plans

DISCLOSURE REQUIREMENTS

Stock-Based Compensation Plans

Note: The disclosures below are applicable to entities that have not yet adopted FAS-123 (Revised 2004) (FAS-123R), *Share-Based Payment.* If an entity has adopted FAS-123R, see the disclosure requirements later in this chapter under "Share-Based Payment."

All entities must disclose the following information, regardless of the method used (APB-25 or FAS-123, as amended by FAS-148) to account for employee stock-based compensation arrangements (FAS-123, pars. 46-48; FAS-148, par. 2):

1. The following information in the "Summary of Significant Accounting Policies," or its equivalent:

   a. The method used (either the intrinsic value method or the fair value based method) to account for stock-based employee compensation in each period presented

   b. If the entity has adopted the fair value method, a description of the method of reporting the change in accounting principle for all financial statements in which the period of adoption is presented

   c. If awards of stock-based employee compensation were outstanding and accounted for under APB-25's intrinsic value method for any period for which an income statement is presented, the following information in a tabular format for all periods presented:

      — Reported net income, and basic and diluted earnings per share

      — Stock-based employee compensation cost, net of related tax effects, included in net income as reported

      — Stock-based employee compensation cost, net of related tax effects, that would have been included in determining net income if the fair-value method had been applied to all awards granted, modified, or settled in fiscal periods beginning after December 15, 1994

      — Pro forma net income assuming that the fair-value method had been applied to all awards granted, modified, or settled in fiscal periods beginning after December 15, 1994

      — Pro forma basic and diluted earnings per share assuming that the fair-value method had been applied to all awards granted, modified, or settled in fiscal periods beginning after December 15, 1994

Note: The same tabular disclosures required on an annual basis in item c are required in quarterly reports if any quarter presented includes the effects of stock-based employee compensation accounted for using the intrinsic value method in APB-25.

2. For those entities adopting the fair value method, the following disclosures should be made in the year of adoption when using the retroactive restatement or modified prospective transitional approach:

   a. The transition adjustment, if any

   b. The effect of restatement of intervening periods, if any

3. A description of the stock-based compensation plan, including the general terms of awards, such as vesting requirements, maximum term of options granted, and number of shares authorized for grants of options or other equity instruments

4. For each year for which an income statement is presented, the number and weighted-average exercise prices of options that were:

   a. Outstanding at the beginning of the year

   b. Outstanding at the end of the year

   c. Granted during the year

   d. Exercised during the year

   e. Exercisable at the end of the year

   f. Forfeited during the year

   g. Expired during the year

5. The weighted-average fair value (as of grant date) of options granted during the year (If the exercise price of some options differs from the market price of the stock on the grant date, weighted-average exercise prices and weighted-average fair values of options should be disclosed separately for options whose exercise price (a) equals, (b) exceeds, or (c) is less than the market price of the stock on the date of grant.)

6. The number and weighted-average fair value (as of grant date) of equity instruments other than options (e.g., shares of nonvested stock) granted during the year

7. A description of the method and significant assumptions used during the year to estimate the fair values of options, including (a) risk-free interest rate, (b) expected life, (c) expected volatility, and (d) expected dividends

8. Total compensation cost recognized in the financial statements

9. The terms of significant modifications of outstanding awards

10. The range of exercise prices, the weighted-average exercise price, and the weighted-average remaining contractual life for options outstanding as of the date of the latest balance sheet presented, and for each range:

    a. The number, weighted-average exercise price, and weighted-average remaining contractual life of options outstanding

    b. The number and weighted-average exercise price of options currently exercisable

An entity that grants options under multiple stock-based employee compensation plans should provide the foregoing information separately for different types of awards to the extent that the differences in the characteristics of the awards make separate disclosure important to an understanding of the entity's use of stock-based compensation (FAS-123, pars. 46–48). In addition, disclosure should be made of the accounting policy for recognizing compensation cost for fixed awards with graded (pro rata) vesting—that is, straight-line or the accelerated expense attribution method under FASB Interpretation No. 28 (EITF 00-23, par. 13).

Employee Stock Ownership Plans

The financial statements of a company sponsoring an employee stock ownership plan (ESOP) should disclose the following information:

1. A description of the plan (SOP 93-6, par. 53a)

2. The basis for determining contributions (SOP 93-6, par. 53a)

3. The employee groups covered (SOP 93-6, par. 53a)

4. The nature and effects of significant matters affecting comparability of information for all periods presented (SOP 93-6, par. 53a)

5. For leveraged ESOPs and pension reversion ESOPs, the basis for releasing shares and how dividends on allocated and unallocated shares are used (SOP 93-6, par. 53a)

6. The following accounting policies for blocks of both "old ESOP shares" and "new ESOP shares"(The following disclosures are required if the employer has both old ESOP shares for which it does not adopt the guidance in SOP 93-6 and new ESOP shares for which the guidance in SOP 93-6 is required; *old ESOP shares* are those acquired or held by the plan on or before December 31, 1992.) (SOP 93-6, par. 53b):

    a. The method of measuring compensation

  b. The classification of dividends on ESOP shares

  c. The treatment of ESOP shares for earnings per share computations

7. The amount of plan compensation cost recognized for each period for which an income statement is presented (SOP 936, par. 53c)

8. If the employer does not adopt SOP 93-6 for the old ESOP shares, the following disclosures should be made at the balance-sheet date for both old ESOP shares and new ESOP shares (SOP 93-6, par. 53d):

  a. The number of allocated shares

  b. The number of committed-to-be-released shares

  c. The number of suspense shares held by the ESOP

9. The fair value of unearned ESOP shares at the balance-sheet date for shares accounted for under SOP 93-6 (This disclosure need not be made for old ESOP shares for which the employer does not apply the guidance in SOP 93-6 for those shares.) (SOP 93-6, par. 53e)

10. The existence and nature of any repurchase obligation, including disclosure of the fair value of the shares allocated as of the balance-sheet date that are subject to a repurchase obligation (SOP 93-6, par. 53f)

11. If an employer has, in substance, guaranteed the debt of an ESOP, the employer's financial statements should disclose the following (SOP 76-3, par. 10):

  a. The compensation element and the interest element of annual contributions to the ESOP

  b. The interest rate and debt terms

Share-Based Payment (Disclosure Requirements Under FAS-123R)

Note: The disclosure requirements below are prescribed by FAS-123 (Revised 2004) (FAS-123R), *Share-Based Payment,* which is effective as of (a) the beginning of the first interim or annual reporting period beginning after June 15, 2005, for public entities that do not file as small business issuers—however, the SEC adopted a rule that allows public companies that do not file as small business issuers to implement FAS-123R at the beginning of their next fiscal year, instead of the next reporting period, that begins after June 15, 2005; (b) the beginning of the first interim or annual reporting period beginning after December 15, 2005, for public entities that file as small business issuers—however, the SEC adopted a rule that allows small business issuers to implement FAS-123R at the beginning of their next fiscal year, instead of the next reporting period, that begins after December 15, 2005; and (c) the beginning of the first annual period beginning after December 15, 2005, for non-public entities. Early adoption is encouraged. If an entity has not adopted FAS-123R, see the disclosure requirements above under "Stock-Based Compensation Plans."

The disclosure requirements for FAS-123R are as follows:

1. For an entity with one or more share-based payment arrangements, the following information should be disclosed (FAS-123R, par. 64 and A240-A242; FSP FAS 123R-6, par. 4):

   a. A description of the share-based payment arrangements that includes the following:

      (1) The general terms of awards under the arrangements, such as the requisite service periods and any other substantive conditions (including those related to vesting)

      (2) The maximum contractual term of equity (or liability) share options or similar instruments

      (3) The number of shares authorized for awards of equity share options or other equity instruments

      (4) The method used to measure compensation cost from share-based payment arrangements with employees

   b. For the most recent year for which an income statement is presented, the following:

      (1) The number and weighted-average exercise prices (or conversion ratios) for each of the following groups of share options (or share units):

         (i) Outstanding at the beginning of the year

         (ii) Outstanding at the end of the year

         (iii) Exercisable or convertible at the end of the year

         (iv) Granted during the year

         (v) Exercised or converted during the year

         (vi) Forfeited during the year

         (vii) Expired during the year

      (2) The number and weighted-average grant-date fair value (or calculated value for a nonpublic entity that uses that method or intrinsic value for awards measured pursuant to FAS-123R, pars. 24-25) of equity instruments not specified in item 1b(1) above (e.g., shares of nonvested stock), for each of the following groups of equity instruments:

      (i)   Nonvested at the beginning of the year

      (ii) Nonvested at the end of the year

      (iii) Granted during the year

      (iv) Vested during the year

      (v) Forfeited during the year

c. For each year for which an income statement is presented, the following:

    (1) The weighted-average grant-date fair value (or calculated value for a nonpublic entity that uses that method or intrinsic value for awards measured at that value pursuant to FAS-123R, pars. 24 and 25) of equity options or other equity instruments granted during the year

    (2) The total intrinsic value of options exercised (or share units converted) during the year

    (3) Share-based liabilities paid during the year

    (4) The total fair value of shares vested during the year

d. For fully vested share options (or share units) and share options expected to vest at the date of the latest balance sheet, the following:

    (1) For options (or share units) outstanding:

       (i)   The number of options (or share units)

       (ii) Weighted-average exercise price (or conversion ratio)

       (iii) Aggregate intrinsic value (except for nonpublic entities)

       (iv) Weighted-average remaining contractual term

    (2) For options (or share units) currently exercisable or convertible:

       (i)   The number of options (or share units)

       (ii) Weighted-average exercise price (or conversion ratio)

       (iii) Aggregate intrinsic value (except for nonpublic entities)

       (iv) Weighted-average remaining contractual term

e. For each year for which an income statement is presented (not required for entities that use the intrinsic value method pursuant to FAS-123R, pars. 24–25) the following:

(1) A description of the method used during the year to estimate the fair value (or calculated value) of awards under share-based payment arrangements

(2) A description of the significant assumptions used during the year to estimate the fair value (or calculated value) of share-based compensation awards, including (if applicable):

(i) Expected term of share options and similar instruments, including a discussion of the method used to incorporate the contractual term of the instruments and employees' expected exercise and postvesting employment termination behavior into the fair value (or calculated value) of the instrument

(ii) Expected volatility of the entity's shares and the method used to estimate expected volatility

(iii) If the method used to estimate expected volatility employs different volatilities during the contractual term, the range of expected volatilities used and the weighted-average expected volatility

(iv) For nonpublic entities that use the calculated value method, (a) the reasons it is not practicable to estimate the expected volatility of its share price, (b) the appropriate industry sector index selected, (c) the reasons for selecting the industry sector index, and (d) how historical volatility has been calculated using the industry sector index selected

(v) Expected dividends

(vi) If the method used to estimate fair value employs different dividend rates during the contractual term, the range of expected dividends used and the weighted-average expected dividends

(vii) Risk-free rates

(viii) If the method used to estimate fair value employs different risk-free rates, the range of risk-free rates used

(ix) Discount for postvesting restrictions and the method for estimating it

f. For an entity that grants equity or liability instruments under multiple share-based payment arrangements with employees, the information described in Items 1a–1e separately for different types of awards to the extent that the differences in the characteristics of the awards are important to an understanding of an entity's use of share-based compensation. Examples of separate disclosures for different types of awards include:

(1) The weighted exercise prices (or conversion ratios) at the end of the year for options (or share units) with a fixed exercise price (or conversion ratio) and those with an indexed exercise price (or conversion ratio)

(2) The number of options (or share units) not yet exercisable into those that will become exercisable (or convertible) based solely on fulfilling a service condition and those for which a performance condition must be met for the options (share units) to become exercisable (convertible)

(3) Awards that are classified as equity and those classified as liabilities

g. For each year for which an income statement is presented, the following:

(1) Total compensation cost for share-based payment arrangements recognized in income as well as the total related recognized tax benefit

(2) Total compensation cost for share-based payment arrangements capitalized as part of the cost of an asset

(3) A description of significant modifications, including:

(i) The terms of the modifications

(ii) The number of employees affected

(iii) The total incremental compensation cost resulting from the modifications

h. As of the latest balance sheet date presented, the following:

(1) The total compensation cost related to nonvested awards not yet recognized

(2) The weighted-average period over which the total compensation cost related to nonvested awards not yet recognized is expected to be recognized

i. If not separately disclosed elsewhere, the amount of cash received from exercise of share options and similar instruments granted under share-based payment arrangements

j. If not separately disclosed elsewhere, the tax benefit realized from stock options exercised during the annual period

    k. If not separately disclosed elsewhere, the amount of cash used to settle equity instruments granted under share-based payment arrangements

    l. A description of the entity's policy, if any, for issuing shares upon share option exercise (or share unit conversion), including the source of those shares (i.e., new shares or treasury shares)

    m. If as a result of an entity's policy for issuing shares upon share option exercise (or share unit conversion), an entity expects to repurchase shares in the following annual period, an estimate of the amount (or range, if more appropriate) of shares to be repurchased during that period

    n. Any other information necessary to understand:

        (1) The nature and terms of share-based payment arrangements that existed during the period and the potential effects of those arrangements on share holders

        (2) The effect of compensation cost arising from share-based payment arrangements on the income statement

        (3) The method of estimating the fair value of the goods or services received, or the fair value of the equity instruments granted (or offered to grant), during the period

        (4) The cash flow effects resulting from share-based payment arrangements

    o. Supplemental information that might be useful to investors and creditors, such as a range of values calculated on the basis of different assumptions

      Note: Entities are *encouraged*, but not required, to disclose the supplemental information. Also, the supplemental information should be reasonable and should not lessen the prominence and credibility of the required disclosure information. The alternative assumptions should be described to enable users of the financial statements to understand the basis of the supplemental information.

2. For an entity that acquires goods or services other than employee services in share-based payment transactions, disclosure requirements similar to those in Item 1 above, which are important to an understanding of the effects of those transactions on the financial statements should be provided (FAS-123R, par. 65).

3. For an entity that applies the modified retrospective application method to all prior years for which FAS-123 was effective and does not present all of those years in comparative

financial statements, the effects of any adjustments to the beginning balances of paid-in capital, deferred taxes, and retained earnings for the earliest year presented, to reflect the results of modified retrospective application to those prior years not presented, should be disclosed in the year FAS-123R is adopted.

Note: If an entity applies the modified retrospective application method only to prior interim periods in the year of initial adoption of FAS-123R, there would be no adjustment to the beginning balances of paid-in capital, deferred taxes, or retained earnings for the year of initial adoption (FAS-123R, par. 77).

4. In the period that FAS-123R is adopted, the effect of the change from applying the original provisions of FAS-123 on the following items should be disclosed (FAS-123R, par. 84):

   a. Income from continuing operations

   b. Income before income taxes

   c. Net income

   d. Cash flow from operations

   e. Cash flow from financing activities

   f. Basic and diluted earnings per share

5. For a public entity that has awards under share-based payment arrangements with employees that are accounted for under the intrinsic value method of APB-25 for any period for which an income statement is presented, the following information should be disclosed in tabular format (FAS-123R, par. 84):

   a. Net income and basic and diluted earnings per share as reported

   b. The share-based employee compensation cost, net of related tax effects, included in net income as reported

   c. The share-based employee compensation cost, net of related tax effects, that would have been included in net income if the fair-value-based method had been applied to all awards

   d. Pro forma net income as if the fair-value-based method had been applied to all awards

   Note: Pro forma amounts should reflect the difference in share-based employee compensation cost, if any, included in net income and the total cost measured by the fair-value-based method, as well as additional tax effects, if any, that would have been recognized in the income statement if the fair-value-based method had been applied to all awards.

e. Pro forma basic and diluted earnings per share as if the fair-value-based method had been applied to all awards

> **Note:** Pro forma per-share amounts should reflect the change in the denominator of the diluted earnings per share calculation as if the assumed proceeds under the treasury stock method, including measured but unrecognized compensation cost and any excess tax benefits credited to additional paid-in capital, were determined under the fair-value-based method.

6. A nonpublic entity that used the minimum value method for pro forma disclosures under the original provisions of FAS-123 should not continue to provide those pro forma disclosures for outstanding awards accounted for under the intrinsic value method of APB-25 (FAS-123R, par. 85).

EXAMPLES OF FINANCIAL STATEMENT DISCLOSURES

The following sample disclosures are available on the accompanying disc.

Example 33–1: FAS-123R, Share-Based Payment—Company Is Assessing the Effect of FAS-123R on Its Financial Statements

In December 2004, the Financial Accounting Standards Board issued Statement of Financial Accounting Standards No. 123R (FAS-123R), *Share-Based Payment*, which is a revision of Statement of Financial Accounting Standards No. 123 (FAS-123), *Accounting for Stock-Based Compensation*. In addition to requiring supplemental disclosures, FAS-123R addresses the accounting for share-based payment transactions in which a company receives goods or services in exchange for (a) equity instruments of the company or (b) liabilities that are based on the fair value of the company's equity instruments or that may be settled by the issuance of such equity instruments. FAS-123R focuses primarily on accounting for transactions in which a company obtains *employee* services in share-based payment transactions. The Statement eliminates the ability to account for share-based compensation transactions using Accounting Principles Board Opinion No. 25 (APB-25), *Accounting for Stock Issued to Employees*, and generally requires that such transactions be accounted for using a fair-value-based method. Accordingly, proforma disclosure is no longer an alternative.

Under FAS-123R, the Company is required to recognize compensation cost for the portion of outstanding awards previously accounted for under the provisions of APB-25 for which the requisite service had not been rendered as of the adoption date for this Statement. The Statement also requires companies to estimate forfeitures of stock compensation awards as of the grant date of the award. Because the Company's current policy is to recognize forfeitures as they occur, a cumulative effect of a change in accounting principle will be recognized in income based on the estimate of remaining forfeitures for awards outstanding as of the date FAS-123R is adopted.

FAS-123R permits public companies (and nonpublic companies that used the fair-value method for either recognition or pro forma disclosure under FAS-123) to adopt its requirements using one of the following two methods:

- A "modified prospective" method in which compensation cost is recognized beginning with the effective date (a) based on the requirements of FAS-123R for all share-based payments granted after the effective date and (b) based on the requirements of FAS-123 for all awards granted to employees prior to the effective date of FAS-123R that remain unvested on the effective date; *or*

- A "modified retrospective" method, which includes the requirements of the modified prospective method described above but also permits entities to restate, based on the amounts previously recognized under FAS-123 for purposes of pro forma disclosures, either (a) all prior periods presented for which FAS-123 was effective or (b) prior interim periods of the year in which FAS-123R is adopted.

The Company expects to adopt FAS-123R on [*insert date*]. The Company is currently assessing the final impact of this standard on its consolidated results of operations, financial position, and cash flows. This assessment includes evaluating option valuation methodologies and assumptions, as well as potential changes to the Company's compensation strategies.

Example 33–2: FAS-123R, Share-Based Payment—Company Discloses Adoption of FAS-123R Using the Modified Prospective Transition Method

In December 2004, the Financial Accounting Standards Board issued Statement of Financial Accounting Standards No. 123R (FAS-123R), *Share-Based Payment*, which is a revision of Statement of Financial Accounting Standards No. 123 (FAS-123), *Accounting for Stock-Based Compensation*.

FAS-123R eliminates accounting for share-based compensation transactions using the intrinsic value method prescribed in Accounting Principles Board Opinion No. 25 (APB-25), *Accounting for Stock Issued to Employees*, and requires instead that such transactions be accounted for using a fair-value-based method. The Company has elected to adopt the provisions of FAS-123R effective January 1, 20X2, under the modified prospective transition method, in which compensation cost was recognized beginning with the effective date (a) based on the requirements of FAS-123R for all share-based payments granted after the effective date and (b) based on the requirements of

FAS-123R for all awards granted to employees prior to the effective date of FAS-123R that remain unvested on the effective date.

As permitted under FAS-123, the Company elected to follow Accounting Principles Board Opinion No. 25, *Accounting for Stock Issued to Employees*, and related interpretations in accounting for stock-based awards to employees through December 31, 20X1. Accordingly, compensation cost for stock options and nonvested stock grants was measured as the excess, if any, of the market price of the Company's common stock at the date of grant over the exercise price.

With the adoption of FAS-123R, the Company elected to amortize stock-based compensation for awards granted on or after the adoption of FAS-123R on January 1, 20X2, on a straight-line basis over the requisite service (vesting) period for the entire award. For awards granted prior to January 1, 20X2, compensation costs are amortized in a manner consistent with Financial Accounting Standards Board Interpretation No. 28 (FIN-28), *Accounting for Stock Appreciation Rights and Other Variable Stock Option or Award Plans*. This is the same manner applied in the pro forma disclosures under FAS-123.

Example 33–3: FAS-123R, Share-Based Payment—Company Discloses Adoption of FAS-123R Using the Modified Retrospective Transition Method

In December 2004, the Financial Accounting Standards Board issued Statement of Financial Accounting Standards No. 123R (FAS-123R), *Share-Based Payment*, which is a revision of Statement of Financial Accounting Standards No. 123 (FAS-123), *Accounting for Stock-Based Compensation*.

FAS-123R eliminates accounting for share-based compensation transactions using the intrinsic value method prescribed in Accounting Principles Board Opinion No. 25 (APB-25), *Accounting for Stock Issued to Employees*, and requires instead that such transactions be accounted for using a fair-value-based method. The Company has elected to adopt the provisions of FAS-123R effective January 1, 20X2, under the modified retrospective transition method. All prior-period financial statements have been restated to recognize compensation cost in the amounts previously reported in the Notes to Conslidated Financial Statements under the provisions of FAS-123, *Accounting for Stock-Based Compensation*. The beginning balances of deferred taxes, paid-in capital, and retained earnings for 20X1 have been restated by $1,250,000, $3,275,000, and $2,025,000. respectively, to recognize compensation cost for fiscal years 19X7 through 20X0 in the amounts previously reported in the Notes to Consolidated Financial Statements under the provisions of FAS-123.

Example 33–4: Multiple Share Option Plans—Company Applies FAS-123R

As of December 31, 20X2, the Company has two share-based compensation plans, which are described in detail below. The compensation cost that has been charged against operations for those plans was

$2,940,000 and $2,870,000 for the years ended December 31, 20X2 and 20X1, respectively. The total income tax benefit recognized in the income statement for share-based compensation arrangements was $1,030,000 and $1,010,000 for the years ended December 31, 20X2 and 20X1, respectively. Compensation cost capitalized as part of inventory and fixed assets for 20X2 and 20X1 was $50,000 and $20,000, respectively.

Share Option Plan

The Company's 20X0 Employee Share Option Plan (the Plan), which is shareholder-approved, permits the grant of share options and shares to its employees for up to 8 million shares of common stock. The Company believes that such awards better align the interests of its employees with those of its shareholders. Option awards are generally granted with an exercise price equal to the market price of the Company's stock at the date of grant; those option awards generally vest based on 5 years of continuous service and have 10-year contractual terms. Share awards generally vest over five years. Certain option and share awards provide for accelerated vesting if there is a change in control, as defined in the Plan.

The fair value of each option award is estimated on the date of grant using a lattice-based option valuation model that uses the assumptions noted in the table below. Because lattice-based option valuation models incorporate ranges of assumptions for inputs, those ranges are disclosed. Expected volatilities are based on implied volatilities from traded options on the Company's stock, historical volatility of the Company's stock, and other factors. The Company uses historical data to estimate option exercise and employee termination within the valuation model; separate groups of employees that have similar historical exercise behavior are considered separately for valuation purposes. The expected term of options granted is derived from the output of the option valuation model and represents the period of time that options granted are expected to be outstanding; the range given below results from certain groups of employees exhibiting different behavior. The risk-free rate for periods within the contractual life of the option is based on the U.S. Treasury yield curve in effect at the time of grant.

	20X2	*20X1*
Expected volatility	25%–40%	24%–38%
Weighted-average volatility	33%	30%
Expected dividends	1.5%	1.5%
Expected term (in years)	5.3–7.8	5.5–8.0
Risk-free rate	6.3%–11.2%	6.0%–10.0%

A summary of option activity under the Plan as of December 31, 20X2, and changes during the year then ended is presented below:

Options	Shares	Weighted-Average Exercise Price	Weighted-Average Remaining Contractual Term	Aggregate Intrinsic Value
Outstanding at January 1, 20X2	4,660,000	$4.2		
Granted	950,000	$6.0		
Exercised	(800,000)	$3.6		
Forfeited or expired	(80,000)	$5.9		
Outstanding at December 31, 20X2	4,730,000	$4.7	6.5	$8,514,000
Exercisable at December 31, 20X2	3,159,000	$4.1	4.0	$7,581,600

The weighted-average grant-date fair value of options granted during the years ended December 31, 20X2 and 20X1, was $1.96 and $1.75, respectively. The total intrinsic value of options exercised during the years ended December 31, 20X2 and 20X1, was $2,520,000 and $2,090,000, respectively.

A summary of the status of the Company's nonvested shares as of December 31, 20X2, and changes during the year ended December 31, 20X2, is presented below:

Nonvested Shares	Shares	Weighted-Average Grant-Date Fair Value
Nonvested at January 1, 20X2	980,000	$4.15
Granted	150,000	$6.35
Vested	(100,000)	$3.57
Forfeited	(40,000)	$5.56
Nonvested at December 31, 20X2	990,000	$4.34

As of December 31, 20X2, there was $2,590,000 of total unrecognized compensation cost related to nonvested share-based compensation arrangements granted under the Plan. That cost is expected to be recognized over a weighted-average period of 4.9 years. The total fair value of shares vested during the years ended December 31, 20X2 and 20X1, was $2,280,000 and $2,100,000, respectively.

During 20X2, the Company extended the contractual life of 200,000 fully vested share options held by 10 employees. As a result of that modification, the Company recognized additional compensation expense of $100,000 for the year ended December 31, 20X2.

Performance Share Option Plan

Under its 20X0 Performance Share Option Plan (the Performance Plan), which is shareholder-approved, each January 1 the Company grants selected executives and other key employees share option awards whose vesting is contingent upon meeting various departmental and company-wide performance goals, including decreasing time to market for new products, revenue growth in excess of an index of competitors' revenue growth, and sales targets for the semiconductor segment. Share options under the Performance Plan are generally granted at-the-money, contingently vest over a period of 1 to 5 years, depending on the nature of the performance goal, and have contractual lives of 7 to 10 years. The number of shares subject to options available for issuance under the Performance Plan cannot exceed five million.

The fair value of each option grant under the Performance Plan was estimated on the date of grant using the same option valuation model used for options granted under the Plan and assumes that performance goals will be achieved. If such goals are not met, no compensation cost is recognized and any recognized compensation cost is reversed. The inputs for expected volatility, expected dividends, and risk-free rate used in estimating those options' fair value are the same as those noted in the table above related to options issued under the Share Option Plan. The expected term for options granted under the Performance Plan in 20X2 and 20X1 is 3.3 to 5.4 years, and 2.4 to 6.5 years, respectively.

A summary of the activity under the Performance Plan as of December 31, 20X2, and changes during the year then ended is presented below:

Performance Options	Shares	Weighted-Average Exercise Price	Weighted-Average Remaining Contractual Term	Aggregate Intrinsic Value
Outstanding at January 1, 20X2	2,533,000	$4.4		
Granted	995,000	$6.0		
Exercised	(100,000)	$3.6		
Forfeited	(604,000)	$5.9		

Outstanding at December 31, 20X2	2,824,000	$4.7	7.1	$5,083,200
Exercisable at December 31, 20X2	936,000	$4.1	5.3	$2,340,000

The weighted-average grant-date fair value of options granted during the years ended December 31, 20X2 and 20X1, was $ 1.73 and $1.60, respectively. The total intrinsic value of options exercised during the years ended December 31, 20X2 and 20X1, was $500,000 and $800,000, respectively. As of December 31, 20X2, there was $1,690,000 of total unrecognized compensation cost related to non-vested share-based compensation arrangements granted under the Performance Plan; that cost is expected to be recognized over a period of 4.0 years.

Cash received from option exercise under all share-based payment arrangements for the years ended December 31, 20X2 and 20X1, was $3,240,000 and $2,890,000, respectively. The actual tax benefit realized for the tax deductions from option exercise of the share-based payment arrangements totaled $1,130,000 and $1,010,000, respectively, for the years ended December 31, 20X2 and 20X1.

The Company has a policy of repurchasing shares on the open market to satisfy share option exercises and expects to repurchase approximately 350,0000 shares during 20X3, based on estimates of option exercises for that period.

Example 33–5: Nonpublic Entity Uses the Calculated Value Method under FAS-123R

> **Note:** With a few exceptions as discussed in this Chapter, the disclosure requirements under FAS-123R are substantially the same for public and nonpublic entities. However, for nonpublic entities that use the calculated value method, a nonpublic entity should disclose: (a) the reasons it is not practicable to estimate the expected volatility of its share price; (b) the appropriate industry sector index selected; (c) the reasons for selecting the industry sector index; and (d) how historical volatility has been calculated using the industry sector index selected. The following example illustrates these specific disclosure requirements for nonpublic entities that use the calculated value method. For all other applicable disclosure requirements, see the other examples provided in this chapter.

As permitted under FAS-123R for nonpublic entities, the Company has elected to use the calculated value method to account for the options it issued in 20X2. A nonpublic entity that is unable to estimate the expected volatility of the price of its underlying share may measure awards based on a "calculated value," which substitutes the volatility of an appropriate index for the volatility of the entity's own share price. Currently, there is no active market for the company's common shares. In addition, management has determined that it is unable to reasonably estimate the fair value of the options on the date of grant because the Company has not issued any new common stock for several years and management has not been able to identify a similar publicly held entity that can be used as a benchmark. Therefore, as a substitute for volatility, the Company used the historical volatility of the Dow Jones Internet Commerce index, which is representative of the company's size and industry. The Company has used the historical closing values of that index to estimate volatility, which was calculated to be 30.2%.

Example 33–6: Company Discloses in Its "Summary of Significant Accounting Policies" Its Use of the Intrinsic Value Method under APB-25

> **Note:** This example assumes that the most recent financial statements presented are for the year ended December 31, 20X2, and that the Company continues to account for stock-based employee compensation using the intrinsic value method under APB-25. The illustration assumes that all previous awards were fixed stock options with no intrinsic value at the date of grant. Also, for simplicity, it is assumed that this disclosure is made in the "Summary of Significant Accounting Policies" and reference is made to another note where the additional required detail disclosures are made. Alternatively, the disclosure in this example can be included as part of the note describing more fully the Company's stock based compensation plans and related stock option activity.

At December 31, 20X2, the Company has three stock-based employee compensation plans, which are described more fully in Note [X]. The Company accounts for those plans under the recognition and measurement principles of APB Opinion No. 25, *Accounting for Stock Issued to Employees*, and its related Interpretations. No stock-based employee compensation cost is reflected in net income, as all options granted under those plans had an exercise price equal to the market value of the underlying common stock on the date of grant. The following table illustrates the effect on net income and earnings per share if the Company had applied the fair value recognition provisions of FASB Statement No. 123, *Accounting for Stock-Based Compensation*, to stock-based employee compensation.

	20X2	*20X1*	*20X0*
Net income, as reported	$479,000	$407,000	$348,000
Add: Stock-based compensation included in net income, net of related tax effects	-0-	-0-	-0-

Deduct: Total stock-based employee compensation expense determined under fair value based method for all awards, net of related tax effects	(19,000)	(13,000)	(11,000)
Pro forma net income	$460,000	$394,000	$337,000
Basic earnings per share:			
As reported	$2.70	$2.32	$1.95
Pro forma	$2.59	$2.24	$1.89
Diluted earnings per share:			
As reported	$2.03	$1.76	$1.50
Pro forma	$1.95	$1.71	$1.45

Example 33–7: Single Stock Compensation Plan—Company Applies APB-25

The Company has a Stock Option Plan (Plan) under which officers, key employees, and non-employee directors may be granted options to purchase shares of the Company's authorized but unissued common stock. The maximum number of shares of the Company's common stock available for issuance under the Plan is 10 million shares. As of December 31, 20X2, the maximum number of shares available for future grants under the Plan is 4,200,000 shares. Under the Plan, the option exercise price is equal to the fair market value of the Company's common stock at the date of grant. Options currently expire no later than 10 years from the grant date and generally vest within five years. Proceeds received by the Company from exercises of stock options are credited to common stock and additional paid-in capital. Additional information with respect to the Plan's stock option activity is as follows:

	Number of Shares	*Weighted- Average Exercise Price*
Outstanding at December 31, 20X0	3,378,000	$ 7.49
Granted	630,000	$36.23
Exercised	(472,000)	$ 3.06
Cancelled	(88,000)	$16.38

Outstanding at December 31, 20X1	3,448,000	$13.12
Granted	480,000	$38.35
Exercised	(600,000)	$ 4.59
Cancelled	(203,000)	$23.64
Outstanding at December 31, 20X2	3,125,000	$18.13
Options exercisable at December 31, 20X1	1,152,000	$ 3.66
Options exercisable at December 31, 20X2	1,038,000	$ 6.11

The following tables summarize information about stock options outstanding and exercisable at December 31, 20X2:

	Stock Options Outstanding		
Range of Exercise Prices	Number of Shares Outstanding	Weighted-Average Remaining Contractual Life in Years	Weighted-Average Exercise Price
$ 1.46–$ 5.55	558,000	2.2	$ 2.83
$ 5.62–$11.10	702,000	4.9	$ 7.18
$11.42–$34.75	892,000	6.9	$15.16
$34.85–$60.80	973,000	8.8	$37.51
	3,125,000	6.2	$18.13

	Stock Options Exercisable	
Range of Exercise Prices	Number of Shares Exercisable	Weighted-Average Exercise Price
$ 1.46–$ 5.55	558,000	$ 2.83
$ 5.62–$11.10	376,000	$ 6.16
$11.42–$34.75	70,000	$16.82
$34.85–$60.80	34,000	$37.53
	1,038,000	$ 6.11

The Company has elected to follow APB Opinion No. 25, *Accounting for Stock Issued to Employees,* in accounting for its employee stock options. Accordingly, no compensation expense is recognized in the Company's financial statements because the exercise price of the Company's employee stock options equals the market price of the Company's common stock on the date of grant. If under Financial

Accounting Standards Board Statement No. 123, *Accounting for Stock-Based Compensation*, the Company determined compensation costs based on the fair value at the grant date for its stock options, net earnings and earnings per share would have been reduced to the following pro forma amounts:

	20X2	*20X1*
Net earnings:		
As reported	$3,750,000	$3,195,000
Add: Stock-based compensation included in net income, net of related tax effects	-0-	-0-
Deduct: Total stock-based employee compensation expense determined under fair value based method for all awards, net of related tax effects	(150,000)	(145,000)
Pro forma	$3,600,000	$3,050,000
Basic earnings per share:		
As reported	$1.10	$.80
Pro forma	$1.06	$.76
Diluted earnings per share:		
As reported	$1.06	$.78
Pro forma	$1.02	$.74

The weighted-average estimated fair value of stock options granted during 20X2 and 20X1 was $ 17.71 and $16.95 per share, respectively. These amounts were determined using the Black-Scholes option-pricing model, which values options based on the stock price at the grant date, the expected life of the option, the estimated volatility of the stock, the expected dividend payments, and the risk-free interest rate over the expected life of the option. The assumptions used in the Black-Scholes model were as follows for stock options granted in 20X2 and 20X1:

	20X2	*20X1*
Risk-free interest rate	5.3%	6.6%
Expected volatility of common stock	45.5%	30.5%
Dividend yield	1.4%	1.5%
Expected life of options	6 years	6 years

The Black-Scholes option valuation model was developed for estimating the fair value of traded options that have no vesting restrictions and are fully transferable. Because option valuation models require the use of subjective assumptions, changes in these assumptions can materially affect the fair value of the options, and the Company's options do not have the characteristics of traded options, the option valuation models do not necessarily provide a reliable measure of the fair value of its options.

Example 33–8: Multiple Stock Compensation Plans—Company Applies APB-25

The Company's Omnibus Stock Plan provides for the granting of 15 million shares of common stock for awards of options under the Company's 19X4 Stock Option Plan, the 19X4 Employee Stock Purchase Plan, and the 19X6 Stock Incentive Plan.

Under the 19X4 Stock Option Plan, options to purchase up to 10,500,000 shares of common stock may be granted to officers, employees, and consultants to the Company. The Company may grant options that are either qualified (incentive stock options) or nonqualified under the Internal Revenue Code of 1986, as amended. Options under the Plan will generally vest over a three-year period and the option term may not exceed ten years. Total options granted under this plan amounted to 128,100 in 20X2 and 148,313 in 20X1.

The Company's 19X4 Employee Stock Purchase Plan provides that eligible employees may contribute up to 10% of their base earnings toward the semiannual purchase of the Company's common stock, at a price equal to 85% of the lower of the market value of the common stock on the first and last day of the applicable period. There are limitations on the number of shares that can be purchased in any period. Total shares issued under this plan were 127,082 in 20X2 and 160,906 in 20X1. Because the plan is noncompensatory, no charges to operations have been recorded.

The 19X6 Stock Incentive Plan permits the issuance of options of common stock in the form of incentive stock options, nonstatutory stock options, stock appreciation rights, performance shares, restricted stock, or unrestricted stock to selected employees of the Company. Options under the plan vest over a three-year period. Stock appreciation rights entitle recipients to receive an amount determined in whole or in part by appreciation in the fair market value of the stock between the date of the award and the date of exercise. Performance share awards entitle recipients to acquire shares of stock upon attainment of specified performance goals. Restricted stock awards entitle recipients to acquire shares of stock, subject to the right of the Company to repurchase under certain circumstances all or part of the shares at their purchase price (or to require forfeiture of such shares if purchased at no cost) from the recipient. Restricted shares vest over a five-year period. Unearned compensation, representing the fair market value of the shares at the date of issuance, is charged to earnings over the vesting period. Total options granted under this plan amounted to 760,763 in 20X2 and 1,209,471 in 20X1. No stock appreciation rights or performance shares were granted in 20X2 or 20X1.

In addition to the above plans, the Company's 19X4 Director Stock Option Plan provides for the grant of nonqualified stock options to the Company's nonemployee directors. The total number of shares to be issued under this plan may not exceed 100,000 shares. Options granted under the 19X4 Director Stock Option Plan have an exercise price equal to the fair market value of the common stock on the date of the grant and a term equal to ten years. Total options granted under this plan amounted to 8,055 in 20X2 and 5,310 in 20X1.

Pursuant to FASB Statement of Financial Accounting Standards No. 123 (FAS-123), *Accounting for Stock-Based Compensation*, the Company has elected to account for its stock option plans under the provisions of APB Opinion No. 25, *Accounting for Stock Issued to Employees*. Accordingly, no compensation cost has been recognized for the stock option plans. The Company has evaluated the pro forma effects of FAS-123 and as such, net earnings, basic earnings per common share, and diluted earnings per common share would have been as follows:

	20X2	*20X1*
Net earnings (loss):		
As reported	$(3,686,000)	$1,480,000
Add: Stock-based compensation included in net income, net of related tax effects	-0-	-0-
Deduct: Total stock-based employee compensation expense determined under fair value based method for all awards, net of related tax effects	(67,000)	(60,000)
Pro forma	$(3,753,000)	$1,420,000
Basic earnings per share:		
As reported	$(1.03)	$.47

	20X2	20X1
Pro forma	$(1.05)	$.45
Diluted earnings per share:		
As reported	$(1.03)	$.44
Pro forma	$(1.05)	$.42

The fair value of each option was estimated on the date of grant using the Black-Scholes option-pricing model and the following assumptions:

	20X2	20X1
Risk-free interest rate	5.43%	6.17%
Expected volatility of common stock	35.5%	52.1%
Dividend yield	-0-	1.31%
Expected life of options	10 years	10 years

The following is a summary of the status of all of the Company's stock option plans as of December 31, 20X2, and December 31, 20X1 and changes during the years ended on those dates:

	Number of Shares	Weighted-Average Exercise Price
Outstanding at December 31, 20X0	4,056,000	$25.29
Granted	1,524,000	$45.48
Exercised	(507,000)	$14.09
Cancelled	(55,000)	$23.12
Outstanding at December 31, 20X1	5,018,000	$32.58
Granted	1,024,000	$45.94
Exercised	(370,000)	$16.52
Cancelled	(128,000)	$32.44
Outstanding at December 31, 20X2	5,544,000	$33.96
Options exercisable at December 31, 20X1	340,000	$21.19
Options exercisable at December 31, 20X2	451,000	$23.73

The following tables summarize information about stock options outstanding and exercisable at December 31, 20X2:

	Stock Options Outstanding		
Range of Exercise Prices	Number of Shares Outstanding	Weighted-Average Remaining Contractual Life in Years	Weighted-Average Exercise Price
$ 8.69–$13.56	84,000	0.9	$13.28
$16.56–$24.31	702,000	3.0	$19.09
$25.13–$35.00	2,247,000	6.6	$31.54
$39.75–$45.94	2,511,000	8.1	$45.61
	5,544,000	6.5	$33.96

	Stock Options Exercisable	
Range of Exercise Prices	Number of Shares Exercisable	Weighted-Average Exercise Price
$ 8.69–$13.56	52,000	$13.54
$16.56–$24.31	233,000	$18.40
$25.135–$35.00	99,000	$27.96
$39.75–$45.94	67,000	$43.91
	451,000	$23.73

Example 33–9: Multiple Stock Compensation Plans—Company Applies FAS-123

At December 31, 20X2, the Company has three stock-based compensation plans, which are described below. The Company accounts for the fair value of its grants under those plans in accordance with Financial Accounting Standards Board Statement No. 123 (Accounting for Stock-Based Compensation). The compensation cost that has been charged against income for those plans was $7,900,000 and $6,400,000 for 20X2 and 20X1, respectively.

The Company has a fixed stock option plan, ABC Company Employee Stock Option Plan, under which the Company may grant options to its employees for up to 10 million shares of common stock. The exercise price of each option equals the market price of the Company's stock on the date of grant and an option's maximum term is ten years. Options are granted on January 1 and vest at the end of the third year. The weighted-average estimated fair value of stock options granted during 20X2 and 20X1 was $17.71 and $16.95 per share, respectively. A summary of the status of the Company's fixed stock option plan as of December 31, 20X2, and December 31, 20X1, and changes during the years ending on those dates is presented below:

Fixed Stock Option Plan	Number of Shares	Weighted-Average Exercise Price
Outstanding at December 31, 20X0	4,500,000	$34.29
Granted	900,000	$50.48
Exercised	(700,000)	$27.09
Cancelled	(100,000)	$46.12
Outstanding at December 31, 20X1	4,600,000	$38.58
Granted	1,000,000	$55.94
Exercised	(850,000)	$34.52
Cancelled	(90,000)	$51.44
Outstanding at December 31, 20X2	4,660,000	$42.96
Options exercisable at December 31, 20X1	2,924,000	$35.19
Options exercisable at December 31, 20X2	2,873,000	$41.73

The following tables summarize information about fixed stock options outstanding and exercisable at December 31, 20X2:

	Stock Options Outstanding		
Range of Exercise Prices	Number of Shares Outstanding	Weighted-Average Remaining Contractual Life in Years	Weighted-Average Exercise Price
$25.69–$33.56	1,107,000	3.6	$29.28
$39.56–$41.31	467,000	5.0	$40.09
$46.13–$50.19	1,326,000	6.6	$48.54
$55.75–$60.94	1,760,000	8.5	$57.61
	4,660,000	6.5	$42.96

	Stock Options Exercisable	
Range of Exercise Prices	Number of Shares Exercisable	Weighted-Average Exercise Price
$25.69–$33.56	952,000	$29.54
$39.56–$41.31	325,000	$40.40
$46.13–$50.19	1,199,000	$48.96
$55.75–$60.94	397,000	$55.91
	2,873,000	$41.73

Also, the Company has a performance-based stock option plan, Enterprise 20X2 Stock Option Plan, under which the Company grants selected executives and other key employees stock option awards, whose vesting is contingent upon increases in the Company's market share for its principal product. If at the end of three years market share has increased by at least 5% from the date of grant, one-third of the options under the award vest to active employees. However, if at that date market share has increased by at least 10%, two-thirds of the options under the award vest, and if market share has increased by 20% or more, all of the options under the award vest. The number of shares subject to options under this plan cannot exceed 5 million. The exercise price of each option, which has a ten-year life, is equal to the market price of the Company's common stock on the date of grant. The weighted-average estimated fair value of stock options granted during 20X2 and 20X1 was $19.97 and $24.32 per share, respectively. A summary of the status of the Company's performance-based stock option plan as of December 31, 20X2, and December 31, 20X1, and changes during the years ending on those dates is presented below:

Performance-Based Stock Option Plan	Number of Shares	Weighted-Average Exercise Price
Outstanding at December 31, 20X0	1,635,000	$48.29
Granted	980,000	$55.48
Exercised	(40,000)	$47.09
Cancelled	(42,000)	$50.12
Outstanding at December 31, 20X1	2,533,000	$51.58
Granted	995,000	$60.94
Exercised	(100,000)	$46.52
Cancelled	(604,000)	$51.44
Performance-Based Stock Option Plan		
Outstanding at December 31, 20X2	2,824,000	$55.96
Options exercisable at December 31, 20X1	780,000	$46.19
Options exercisable at December 31, 20X2	936,000	$47.73

As of December 31, 20X2, the performance-based stock options of 2,824,000 outstanding under the Plan have exercise prices between $ 46.52 and $60.94, and a weighted-average remaining contractual life) of 7.7 years. The Company expects that approximately one-third of the nonvested awards at December 31, 20X2, will eventually vest based on projected market share.

The Company's third stock-based compensation plan is an employee stock purchase plan, ABC Company Employee Stock Purchase Plan, under which the Company is authorized to issue up to 10 million shares of common stock to its full-time employees, nearly all of whom are eligible to participate. Under the terms of the Plan, employees can choose each year to have up to 6% of their annual base earnings withheld to purchase the Company's common stock. The purchase price of the stock is 85% of the lower of its beginning-of-year or end-of-year market price. Approximately 75% to 80% of eligible employees have participated in the Plan in the last 3 years. Under the Plan, the Company sold 723,000 shares and 629,000 shares to employees in 20X2 and 20X1, respectively.

For all three plans, the fair value of each option was estimated on the date of grant using the Black-Scholes option-pricing model with the following assumptions:

	Risk-Free Interest Rate	Expected Volatility of Stock	Expected Dividend Yield	Life of Options
20X2				
Fixed stock option plan	6.7%	26%	1.5%	5 years
Performance-based stock option plan	6.9%	26%	1.5%	6 years
Employee stock purchase plan	6.2%	24%	1.5%	1 year
20X1				
Fixed stock option plan	5.7%	24%	1.5%	6 years
Performance-based stock option plan	5.8%	24%	1.5%	6 years
Employee stock purchase plan	5.2%	22%	1.5%	1 year

Example 33–10: Employee Stock Purchase Plan—Company Applies APB-25

The Company's 19X5 Employee Stock Purchase Plan (Plan) is a plan under which employee participants may purchase shares of the Common Stock at 85% of market value on the first or last business day of the twelve-month plan period beginning each January, whichever value is lower. Such purchases are limited to 10% of the employee's regular pay. A maximum aggregate of 1,000,000 shares has been reserved under the Plan, 423,643 of which were available for future purchases at December 31, 20X2. In January 20X3, 82,450 shares were purchased at $ 20.11 per share and in January 20X2, 64,312 shares were purchased at $18.36 per share. The Company applies APB Opinion No. 25 (Accounting for Stock Issued to Employees) and related Interpretations in accounting for the Plan. Accordingly, no compensation cost has been recognized in the accompanying financial statements. Had compensation cost for the Company's employee stock purchase plan been determined consistent with the provisions of Financial Accounting Standards Board Statement No. 123 (Accounting for Stock-Based Compensation), net earnings, basic earnings per common share, and diluted earnings per common share would have been as follows:

	20X2	*20X1*
Net earnings (loss):		
As reported	$2,343,000	$1,375,000
Add: Stock-based compensation included in net income, net of related tax effects	-0-	-0-
Deduct: Total stock-based employee compensation expense determined under fair value based method for all awards, net of related tax effects	(306,000)	(164,000)
Pro forma	$2,037,000	$1,211,000
Basic earnings per share:		
As reported	$1.21	$.79
Pro forma	$1.05	$.70
Diluted earnings per share:		
As reported	$1.16	$.72
Pro forma	$1.01	$.63

The pro forma value of the employees' purchase rights was estimated using the Black-Scholes model and the following assumptions: no dividend yield, an expected life of one year, expected volatility of 36.2%, and a risk-free interest rate of 5.7%. The weighted-average fair value of these purchase rights granted in 20X2 and 20X1 was $ 11.64 and $8.42, respectively.

Example 33–11: Restricted Stock Plan—Company Applies APB-25; Pro Forma Effect under FAS-123 Is Not Disclosed Due to Immateriality

The Company has a Restricted Stock Plan covering 1,500,000 shares of common stock, the purpose of which is to permit grants of shares, subject to restrictions, to key employees of the Company as a means of retaining and rewarding them for long-term performance and to increase their ownership in the Company. Shares awarded under the plan entitle the shareholder to all rights of common stock ownership except that the shares may not be sold, transferred, pledged, exchanged or otherwise disposed of during the restriction period. The restriction period is determined by a committee, appointed by the board of directors, and may not exceed ten years.

The Company accounts for its Restricted Stock Plan under APB Opinion No. 25, *Accounting for Stock Issued to Employees*. During 20X2 and 20X1, 95,000 shares and 83,000 shares, respectively, were granted with restriction periods of four to six years at market prices ranging from $ 13.125 to $18.475 in 20X2 and $11.375 to $16.875 in 20X1. The shares were recorded at the market value on the date of issuance as deferred compensation and the related amount is being amortized to operations over the respective vesting period. During the years ended December 31, 20X2, and December 31, 20X1, unearned compensation charged to operations related to these shares of restricted stock was $375,000 and $290,000, respectively. At December 31, 20X2, the weighted-average grant date fair value and weighted-average contractual life for outstanding shares of restricted stock was $15.03 and 5.2 years, respectively.

The pro forma net income impact under FASB Statement of Financial Accounting Standards No. 123, *Accounting for Stock-Based Compensation*, is not material.

A summary of restricted stock award share activity follows:

	20X2	20X1
Awards available for grant—		
Beginning of year	728,000	186,000
New awards authorized	400,000	725,000
Available awards terminated	(200,000)	(100,000)
Restricted shares awarded	(95,000)	(83,000)
Awards available for grant—		
End of year	833,000	728,000

Example 33–12: Reversal of Deferred Stock-Based Compensation and Additional Paid-in Capital Relating to Employees Who Left the Company

As a result of employees who left the Company during the years ended December 31, 20X2, and 20X1, the Company reversed approximately $329,000 and $415,000, respectively, of deferred stock-based compensation and additional paid-in capital, which represented the unamortized balance of deferred stock-based compensation relating to employees who left the Company.

Example 33–13: Leveraged ESOP

The Company sponsors a leveraged employee stock ownership plan (ESOP) that covers all U.S. employees who work twenty or more hours per week. The Company makes annual contributions to the ESOP equal to the ESOP's debt service less dividends received by the ESOP. All dividends received by the ESOP are used to pay debt service. The ESOP shares initially were pledged as collateral for its debt. As the debt is repaid, shares are released from collateral and allocated to active employees, based on the proportion of debt service paid in the year. The Company accounts for its ESOP in accordance with AICPA Statement of Position No. 93-6, *Employers' Accounting for Employee Stock Ownership Plans*. Accordingly, the debt of the ESOP is recorded as debt and the shares pledged as collateral are reported as unearned ESOP shares in the Balance Sheet. As shares are released from collateral, the Company reports compensation expense equal to the current market price of the shares, and the shares become outstanding for earnings-per-share computations. Dividends on allocated ESOP shares are recorded as a reduction of retained earnings; dividends on unallocated ESOP shares are recorded as a reduction of debt and accrued interest. ESOP compensation expense was $275,000 and $250,000 for 20X2 and 20X1, respectively. The ESOP shares as of December 31, 20X2, and December 31, 20X1, were as follows:

	20X2	20X1
Allocated shares	80,000	40,000
Shares released for allocation	40,000	40,000
Unreleased shares	80,000	120,000
Total ESOP shares	200,000	200,000
Fair value of unreleased shares at December 31	$1,200,000	$1,500,000

Example 33–14: Leveraged ESOP Used to Fund Employer's Portion of 401(k) Plan

The Company sponsors a 401(k) savings plan under which eligible employees may choose to save up to 6% of salary income on a pre-tax basis, subject to certain IRS limits. The Company matches 50% of employee contributions with Company common stock. The shares for this purpose are provided principally by the Company's employee stock ownership plan (ESOP), supplemented as needed by newly issued shares. The Company makes annual contributions to the ESOP equal to the ESOP's debt service less dividends received by the ESOP. All dividends received by the ESOP are used to pay debt service. The ESOP shares initially were pledged as collateral for its debt. As the debt is repaid, shares are released from collateral and allocated to employees who made 401(k) contributions that year, based on the proportion of debt service paid in the year. The Company accounts for its ESOP in accordance with AICPA Statement of Position No. 93-6, *Employers' Accounting for Employee Stock Owner-ship Plans.* Accordingly, the shares pledged as collateral are reported as unearned ESOP shares in the balance sheet. As shares are released from collateral, the Company reports compensation expense equal to the current market price of the shares, and the shares become out-standing for earnings-per-share computations. Dividends on allo-cated ESOP shares are recorded as a reduction of retained earnings; dividends on unallocated ESOP shares are recorded as a reduction of debt and accrued interest.

Compensation expense for the 401(k) match and the ESOP was $325,000 and $305,000 for 20X2 and 20X1, respectively. The ESOP shares as of December 31, 20X2, and December 31, 20X1 were as follows:

	20X2	*20X1*
Allocated shares	85,000	40,000
Shares released for allocation	50,000	45,000
Unreleased shares	75,000	115,000
Total ESOP shares	210,000	200,000
Fair value of unreleased shares at December 31	$850,000	$1,150,000

CHAPTER 34
SUBSEQUENT EVENTS

CONTENTS

EXECUTIVE SUMMARY

There are two types of subsequent events that require consideration:

1. Events that provide additional evidence with respect to conditions that existed at the balance sheet date and affect the estimates inherent in the process of preparing financial statements (Type 1). These events have a direct effect on the financial statements and require adjustment.

2. Events that provide evidence with respect to conditions that did not exist at the date of the balance sheet but arose subsequent to that date (Type 2). These events have no direct effect on the financial statements and should not result in an adjustment; however, disclosure may be required in notes to the financial statements.

Examples of subsequent events that have a direct effect on the financial statements and require an adjustment of account balances in the current year's financial statements, if material, include:

- A customer with an outstanding accounts receivable balance as of the balance-sheet date and that declares bankruptcy in the subsequent period
- The subsequent settlement of a litigation at an amount that is different from the amount recorded in the financial statements
- The subsequent sale of property not being used in operations at a price less than the carrying value in the financial statements
- The subsequent sale of investments at a price less than the carrying value in the financial statements
- Payment of contingent liabilities

The following are examples of subsequent events that do not result in an adjustment of financial statement accounts but may be so significant that they require disclosure for fair presentation of the financial statements:

- Issuance of bonds or equity securities
- Acquisition of a business
- Litigation that arises subsequent to the balance-sheet date
- Uninsured loss of inventories as a result of fire or flood
- Loss of receivables resulting from conditions that arose subsequent to the balance-sheet date
- Interruption of production by natural disaster, governmental action, or labor stoppage
- Decline in market value of inventory as a consequence of government action barring further sale of the client's products
- Significant realized and unrealized gains and losses that result from changes in quoted market prices of securities arising after the balance-sheet date
- Material commitments to purchase property, plant, and equipment
- Material commitments under a long-term lease agreement
- Sale of assets

Authoritative Literature

SAS-1 (AU 560)   Section 560, Subsequent Events

FAS-5   Accounting for Contingencies

DISCLOSURE REQUIREMENTS

In order for the financial statements not to be misleading, appropriate disclosures should be made of subsequent events based on information that becomes available prior to the issuance of the financial statements. An entity should consider supplementing the historical financial statements by providing pro forma data disclosure in the footnotes, giving effect to the subsequent event as if it had occurred as of the date of the financial statements (FAS-5, par. 11; AU 560.05—.07 and 560.09).

EXAMPLES OF FINANCIAL STATEMENT DISCLOSURES

 The following sample disclosures are available on the accompanying disc.

Business Combinations and Joint Ventures

Example 34–1: Business Acquisition—Goodwill Is Expected to Result from the Transaction

On February 15, 20X3, the Company completed the acquisition of Itec for $5 million in cash, subject to adjustment upon finalizing the closing balance sheet. Itec is a Boston-based company and leading supplier of high-density and general-purpose AC/DC converters and ring generators distributed primarily throughout North America. The purchase price will be allocated to the underlying assets and liabilities based on their estimated fair values. The resulting goodwill from this transaction is currently estimated at $1,500,000. The goodwill estimate is preliminary, pending the results of appraisals, an audit, and further financial analysis. For the year ended December 31, 20X2, Itec had sales of approximately $6.3 million and net income of approximately $593,000.

In addition, the Company may pay up to $1,500,000 earnout consideration to Itec's stockholders based on Itec's attaining certain defined operational performance objectives through June 30, 20X4. The source of funds for the acquisition was a combination of the Company's available cash, as well as advances totaling $3 million under its existing credit facility. In connection with the Itec acquisition, the Company amended its credit facility with its primary bank to waive certain requirements and amend certain provisions.

Example 34–2: Business Acquisition—Goodwill Is Not Expected to Result from the Transaction

On January 18, 20X3, the Company entered into a definitive agreement to acquire all of the outstanding capital stock of Communix, a leading supplier of automotive coatings. The agreed purchase price consists of (i) a cash component of $500,000 payable at closing, (ii) a promissory note in the amount of $1 million due one year after closing (and payable in cash or in the Company's common stock at the option of the sellers), (iii) a promissory note in the amount of $2 million due two years after closing (and payable in cash or in the Company's common stock at the option of the Company), and (iv) the issuance of 500,000 shares of the Company's common stock.

The purchase price will be allocated to the underlying assets and liabilities based on their estimated fair values. No goodwill is expected to result from this transaction. For the year ended December 31, 20X2, Communix had sales of approximately $10 million and net income of approximately $1,200,000.

Example 34–3: Joint Venture

On February 1, 20X3, the Company and Medwax commenced operations of SOSP, Inc., a 50/50 joint venture to manufacture and distribute electronic connectors. Concurrent with the formation of the joint venture, the Company contributed assets to the venture with a net book value at December 31, 20X2, of about $500,000 and will provide funds, as needed by the venture, up to $3 million per year through 20X7.

Casualty Loss

Example 34–4: Inventory Destroyed in Fire

In February 20X3, the Company suffered a fire in its main warehouse located in Hillsborough, Virginia. The Company estimates that inventory with a recorded value of approximately $1,200,000 was destroyed. Although the exact amount of the loss is not currently determinable, the Company expects to recover 50% to 75% of the value through insurance proceeds.

Debt/Financing

Example 34–5: New Financing Arrangement

On January 29, 20X3, the Company entered into a Revolving Loan Agreement (the Loan Agreement) with Ace State Bank. The Loan Agreement provides for borrowings through January 31, 20X8 (the Maturity Date). Borrowings will bear interest at the bank's prime rate. The maximum amount that may be outstanding under the Loan Agreement is $20,000,000 through December 31, 20X4. Thereafter, the maximum amount of borrowings that may be outstanding under the Loan Agreement is reduced by $1,000,000 in calendar 20X5 and by $1,000,000 in each of the following calendar years up to the Maturity Date. Under the terms of the Loan Agreement, the Company will pay Ace State Bank $200,000 plus an unused commitment fee during the term of the Loan Agreement. The Company will also pay legal, accounting, and other fees and expenses in connection with the Loan Agreement.

Example 34–6: Issuance of Convertible Subordinated Notes

On January 12, 20X3, the Company executed an agreement with a group of institutional investors whereby the Company issued $12 million in convertible subordinated loan notes. These notes bear an interest rate of 11% per year and mature in 20X5.

Example 34–7: Maximum Borrowing under Line of Credit

In February and March 20X3, the Company borrowed $800,000 under its line of credit for working capital purposes. As a result, the Company has borrowed the maximum amount available under the credit line. The Company is negotiating with the bank to increase its credit line limit by $2,000,000. However, there can be no assurance that the Company will be successful in increasing its credit line.

Inventory

Example 34–8: Commitment to Sell Inventory at Fixed Price

On January 15, 20X3, the Company entered into an agreement with a customer to sell a specified minimum number of units of its Eglaze adhesive products over the next thirty months at a fixed price of $10,200,000. The fixed price is equal to approximately 5% above the aggregate selling price at current market prices.

Leases

Example 34–9: New Operating Lease Agreement

In February 20X3, the Company entered into an operating lease agreement for a manufacturing plant to be constructed in Carson, New Jersey. The total cost of assets to be covered by the lease is limited to $15,000,000. The manufacturing facility is scheduled for completion in June 20X4. Payments under the lease will be determined and will commence upon completion of construction and will continue through the initial lease term of five years. The Company has options to renew the lease for two five-year periods and to purchase the facility at its estimated fair market value at any time during the lease term.

Example 34–10: Contingent Liability Relating to Lease Termination

In March 20X3, the Company notified the developer and landlord of its planned future headquarters in Paramount, California, that the Company intends to terminate the project. The Company had previously entered into a 15-year lease agreement for the new site. Although groundbreaking for the new site has not occurred, the Company anticipates that it will incur lease termination costs. However, the Company is not able to make a meaningful estimate of the amount or range of loss that could result from an unfavorable resolution of this matter.

License Agreement

Example 34–11: License Fee Commitments under License Agreement

In February 20X3, the Company entered into an agreement to license software to be incorporated into its data conferencing products. Under the agreement, the Company is obligated to pay annual minimum license fees, ranging from $150,000 to $350,000 through the year 20X6 and the Company may cancel the agreement at any time, provided the Company has paid a minimum of $1,000,000 in connection with the agreement.

Litigation

Example 34–12: Patent Infringement Lawsuit

On February 13, 20X3, the Company was named as a defendant in a patent infringement suit brought by Pasterine, Ltd., alleging that certain of the Company's products infringe seven patents that Pasterine Ltd. allegedly owns and is seeking a judgment of infringement for each of these asserted patents and other costs. The Company is reviewing the suit and, based on advice from legal counsel, believes that the complaints are without merit. However, no assurance can be given that this matter will be resolved in the Company's favor.

Example 34–13: Sexual Discrimination Lawsuit

In March 20X3, the Company and two principal officers were named as defendants in a lawsuit brought by a former employee alleging sexual discrimination. Management believes that the lawsuit is without merit and the outcome will not have a material adverse effect on the financial position or results of operations of the Company.

Example 34–14: Settlement of Threatened Litigation in Connection with Event Occurring after Year-End

In January 20X3, the Company breached its contract with a supplier by failing to buy a minimum amount of certain specified products for the month of January, which the Company was committed to buy under terms of the agreement. The supplier threatened litigation to enforce the terms of the contract. As a result, on March 29, 20X3, the Company agreed to pay $400,000 to the supplier in an out-of-court settlement. The amount will be charged to operations in 20X3.

Property and Equipment

Example 34–15: Purchase of Assets

On March 4, 20X3, the Company entered into an agreement to purchase a new warehouse and distribution center at a total cost of $4,700,000. The Company opened escrow and made a deposit of $500,000. The purchase price is expected to be financed by the Company's primary bank over five years at an interest rate of 1% above the bank's prime rate.

Example 34–16: Sale of Assets

On January 23, 20X3, the Company sold one of its warehouse and distribution facility for $4,400,000, with an after tax gain of $890,000. The proceeds were used to repay long-term borrowings.

Example 34–17: Sale and Leaseback of Facility

Subsequent to December 31, 20X2, the Company entered into a sale and leaseback agreement with regard to its manufacturing facility in Grand Rapids, Michigan. The transaction has been recorded as a sale with the cash proceeds of $11 million used to repay borrowings of $7.5 million and the remainder used for working capital purposes. The Company recorded a gain of $2.5 million on the sale.

Under the terms of the agreement, the Company has committed to lease a portion of the facility for 12 years. The present value of minimum lease payments at inception of the obligation approximates $4 million.

Related Parties

Example 34–18: Advances Made to Related Parties

In February and March 20X3, the Company made advances totaling $1,200,000 to PRC Development, an entity owned by the president and certain officers of the Company, primarily to accommodate expansion and other financing needs of this related entity. Such advances are unsecured, bear interest at 10%, and are payable in semiannual installments starting April 1, 20X4.

Stockholders' Equity

Example 34–19: Conversion of Debentures into Common Stock

On March 1, 20X3, the holders of the Company's 10% convertible debentures have elected to convert an aggregate of $4,000,000 principal amount of the debentures into 696,520 shares of the Company's common stock.

Example 34–20: Sale of Common Stock

On February 11, 20X3, the Company sold 300,000 shares of its common stock at $10 per share. The proceeds will be used for working capital purposes and to pay off long-term debt of approximately $1,300,000.

Example 34–21: Stock Option Plan

In February 20X3, the Company adopted a Stock Option Plan ("Plan") that provides for the granting of stock options to certain key employees. The Plan reserves 450,000 shares of common stock, including 200,000 shares granted to the president under his employ-ment arrangement. Options under the Plan are to be granted at no less than fair market value of the shares at the date of grant.

Example 34–22: Stock Split

On March 1, 20X3, the Company's board of directors declared a two-for-one stock split of the common stock effected in the form of a 25% stock dividend, to be distributed on or about April 10, 20X3, to hold-ers of record on March 23, 20X3. Accordingly, all references to num-ber of shares, except shares authorized, and to per share information in the consolidated financial statements have been adjusted to reflect the stock split on a retroactive basis.

Example 34–23: Amendment to Certificate of Incorporation to Decrease Number of Authorized Shares

Subsequent to December 31, 20X2, the board of directors approved a proposal to amend the Certificate of Incorporation to decrease the number of authorized shares of common stock from 50,000,000 shares to 5,000,000 shares and to effect a one-for-ten reverse split of common stock whereby each ten shares of common stock will be exchanged for one share of common stock. The Amendment will have no effect on the par value of the common stock.

Example 34–24: Cash Dividend

On January 27, 20X3, the Company declared a cash dividend of $0.07 per share payable on March 3, 20X3, to shareholders of record on February 10, 20X3.

CHAPTER 35
TRANSFERS AND SERVICING
OF FINANCIAL ASSETS

CONTENTS

EXECUTIVE SUMMARY

Note regarding FAS-155: The FASB has issued Statement of Financial Accounting Standards No. 155 (FAS-155), *Accounting for Certain Hybrid Financial Instruments.* Under current generally accepted accounting principles (GAAP), an entity that holds a financial instrument with an embedded derivative must bifurcate the financial instrument, resulting in the host and the embedded derivative being accounted for separately. FAS-155 permits, but does not require, entities to account for financial instruments with an embedded derivative at fair value thus negating the need to bifurcate the instrument between its host and the embedded derivative. FAS-155 also extends the requirements of Statement of Financial Accounting Standards No. 133 (FAS-133), *Accounting for Derivative Instruments and Hedging Activities,* to interests in securitized financial assets (eliminating the FAS-133 exemption that previously applied to securitizations). That is, an entity must now evaluate whether an interest in securitized financial assets contains an embedded derivative. Prior to FAS-155, this analysis was not required for interests in securitized financial assets.

In addition, FAS-155 clarifies that concentrations of credit risk are not embedded derivatives. Finally, FAS-155 amends Statement of Financial Accounting Standards No. 140 (FAS-140), *Accounting for Transfers and Servicing of Financial Assets and Extinguishments of Liabilities,* to remove the prohibition on holding certain derivative financial instruments by a qualifying special-purpose entity (SPE). FAS-155 is effective for financial instruments acquired or issued in fiscal years beginning after September 15, 2006.

Note regarding FAS-156: The FASB has issued Statement of Financial Accounting Standards No. 156 (FAS-156), *Accounting for Servicing of Financial Assets,* which amends the guidance in FAS-140, *Accounting for Transfers and Servicing of Financial Assets and Extinguishments of Liabilities.* Among other requirements, FAS-156 requires an entity to recognize a servicing asset or servicing liability each time it undertakes an obligation to service a financial asset by entering into a servicing contract in any of the following three situations:

1. A transfer of the servicer's financial assets that meets the requirements for sale accounting;

2. A transfer of the servicer's financial assets to a qualifying special-purpose entity in a guaranteed mortgage securitization in which the transferor retains all of the resulting securities and classifies them as either available-for-sale securities or trading securities in accordance with Statement of Financial Accounting Standards No. 115 (FAS-115), *Accounting for Certain Investments in Debt and Equity Securities;* or

3. An acquisition or assumption of an obligation to service a financial asset that does not relate to financial assets of the servicer or its consolidated affiliates.

FAS-156 is effective as of the beginning of an entity's first fiscal year that begins after September 15, 2006. Earlier adoption is permitted as of the beginning of an entity's fiscal year, provided the entity has not issued financial statements.

Note regarding FAS-157: In September 2006, the FASB issued Statement of Financial Accounting Standards No. 157 (FAS-157), *Fair Value Measurements*, which provides guidance for using fair value to measure assets and liabilities and expands disclosures about fair value measurements. FAS-157 applies whenever other standards require or permit assets or liabilities to be measured at fair value; however, it does not expand the use of fair value in any new circumstances.

Prior to FAS-157, the methods for measuring fair value were diverse and inconsistent, especially for items that are not actively traded. FAS-157 clarifies that for items that are not actively traded, such as certain kinds of derivatives, fair value should reflect the price in a transaction with a market participant, including an adjustment for risk. FAS-157 also requires expanded disclosure of the effect on earnings for items measured using unobservable data. Therefore, changes in practice that will result from applying FAS-157 relate to the definition of fair value, the methods used to measure fair value, and the expanded disclosures about fair value measurements.

Under FAS-157, fair value refers to the price that would be received to sell an asset or paid to transfer a liability in an orderly transaction between market participants in the market in which the reporting entity transacts. The FASB clarifies the principle that fair value should be based on the assumptions market participants would use when pricing the asset or liability. In support of this principle, FAS-157 establishes a fair value hierarchy that prioritizes the information used to develop those assumptions. The fair value hierarchy gives the highest priority to quoted prices in active markets and the lowest priority to unobservable data (e.g., the reporting entity's own data). Under FAS-157, fair value measurements would be separately disclosed by level within the fair value hierarchy.

FAS-157 expands disclosures about the use of fair value to measure assets and liabilities in interim and annual periods subsequent to initial recognition. It does not eliminate or modify the fair value disclosure requirements under other accounting pronouncements (e.g., Statement of Financial Accounting Standards No. 107 (FAS-107), *Disclosures about Fair Value of Financial Instruments*); rather, it encourages entities to combine the fair value information disclosed under FAS-157 with the fair value information disclosed under other such accounting pronouncements.

FAS-157 is effective for financial statements issued for fiscal years beginning after November 15, 2007, and interim periods within those fiscal years. Earlier application is encouraged, provided that the reporting entity has not yet issued financial statements for that fiscal year, including any financial statements for an interim period within that fiscal year.

See Chapter 14, "Fair Value Measurements," for additional disclosures that are required under FAS-157.

After a transfer of financial assets (e.g., mortgage receivables), an entity recognizes the financial and servicing assets it controls and the liabilities it has incurred, derecognizes financial assets when control has been surrendered, and derecognizes liabilities when extinguished. A transfer of financial assets in which the transferor has surrendered control over those assets is accounted for as a sale to the extent that consideration other than beneficial interests in the transferred assets is received in exchange. A transferor has surrendered control over transferred assets only if all of the following conditions are met:

1. The transferred assets have been isolated from the transferor (i.e., they are beyond the reach of the transferor and its creditors).

2. Each transferee has the unconditional right to pledge or exchange the transferred assets it received; or, if the transferee is a qualifying special purpose entity (SPE), each holder of the SPE's beneficial interests has the unconditional right to pledge or exchange the beneficial interests it received.

3. The transferor does not maintain effective control over the transferred assets either (a) through an agreement that entitles and obligates the transferor to repurchase or redeem the transferred assets before their maturity or (b) through the ability to unilaterally cause the holder to return specific assets, other than through a cleanup call.

If a transfer of financial assets does not meet the criteria for a sale as described above, the transferor and transferee should account for the transfer as a secured borrowing with pledge of collateral.

Factoring arrangements are a means of discounting accounts receivable on a non-recourse, notification basis. Accounts receivable are sold outright, usually to a transferee (the factor) that assumes the full risk of collection, without recourse to the transferor in the event of a loss. Debtors are directed to send payments to the transferee. Factoring arrangements that meet the criteria for a sale as described above should be accounted for as sales of financial assets because the transferor surrenders control over the receivables to the factor.

Authoritative Literature

FAS-107	Disclosures about Fair Value of Financial Instruments
FAS-115	Accounting for Certain Investments in Debt and Equity Securities
FAS-140	Accounting for Transfers and Servicing of Financial Assets and Extinguishments of Liabilities
FAS-155	Accounting for Certain Hybrid Financial Instruments
FAS-156	Accounting for Servicing of Financial Assets
FAS-157	Fair Value Measurements
FTB 01-1	Effective Date for Certain Financial Institutions of Certain Provisions of Statement 140 Related to the Isolation of Transferred Financial Assets
SOP 01-6	Accounting by Certain Entities (Including Entities with Trade Receivables) That Lend to or Finance the Activities of Others
SOP 03-3	Accounting for Certain Loans or Debt Securities Acquired in a Transfer

DISCLOSURE REQUIREMENTS

Transfers of Financial Assets

The following disclosures should be made for transfers of financial assets (FAS-140, par. 17; FAS-156, par. 4h):

1. If the entity has entered into repurchase agreements or securities lending transactions, its policy for requiring collateral or other security

2. If the entity has pledged any of its assets as collateral that are not reclassified and separately reported in the balance sheet, the carrying amount and classification of those assets as of the date of the latest balance sheet presented

3. If the entity has accepted collateral that it is permitted by contract or custom to sell or repledge, the following disclosures should be made as of the date of each balance sheet presented:

   a. The fair value of the collateral

   b. The portion of that collateral that it has sold or repledged

   c. Information about the sources and uses of that collateral

4. If it is not practicable to estimate the fair value of certain assets obtained or liabilities incurred in transfers of financial assets during the period, a description of those items and the reasons why it is not practicable to estimate their fair value

5. If the entity has securitized financial assets during any period presented and accounts for that transfer as a sale, the following disclosures should be made for each major asset type (e.g., credit card receivables, automobile loans, mortgage loans):

    a. The accounting policies for initially measuring the interests that continue to be held by the transferor, if any, and servicing assets or servicing liabilities, if any, including the methodology (whether quoted market price, prices based on sales of similar assets and liabilities, or prices based on valuation techniques) used in determining their fair value

    b. The characteristics of securitizations (a description of the transferor's continuing involvement with the transferred assets, including, but not limited to: servicing; recourse; and restrictions on interests that continue to be held by the transferor) and the gain or loss from sale of financial assets in securitizations

    c. The key assumptions used in measuring the fair value of interests that continue to be held by the transferor and servicing assets or servicing liabilities, if any, at the time of securitization, including at a minimum: quantitative information about discount rates; expected prepayments including the expected weighted-average life of prepayable financial assets; and anticipated credit losses, if applicable

    d. Cash flows between the securitization SPE (special purpose entity) and the transferor, unless reported separately elsewhere in the financial statements or notes, including: proceeds from new securitizations; proceeds from collections reinvested in revolving-period securitizations; purchases of delinquent or foreclosed loans; servicing fees; and cash flows received on interests that continue to be held by the transferor

6. If the entity has interests that continue to be held by the transferor in securitized financial assets or servicing assets or servicing liabilities relating to assets that it has securitized, at the date of the latest balance sheet presented, the following disclosures should be made for each major asset type (e.g., credit card receivables, automobile loans, mortgage loans):

a. The accounting policies for subsequently measuring those interests, including the methodology (whether quoted market price, prices based on sales of similar assets and liabilities, or prices based on valuation techniques) used in determining their fair value

b. The key assumptions used in subsequently measuring the fair value of those interests, including at a minimum: quantitative information about discount rates; expected prepayments including the expected weighted-average life of prepayable financial assets; and anticipated credit losses, including expected static pool losses if applicable

c. A sensitivity analysis or stress test showing the hypothetical effect on the fair value of those interests (including any servicing assets or servicing liabilities) of two or more unfavorable variations from the expected levels for each key assumption that is reported under b above independently from any change in another key assumption, and a description of the objectives, methodology, and limitations of the sensitivity analysis or stress test

d. For the securitized assets and any other financial assets that it manages together with them:

   (i) The total principal amount outstanding, the portion that has been derecognized, and the portion that continues to be recognized in each category reported in the balance sheet, at the end of the period

   (ii) Delinquencies at the end of the period

   (iii) Credit losses, net of recoveries, during the period

   (iv) Average balances during the period (this disclosure item is encouraged, but not required)

For loans or debt securities ("loans"), with evidence of deterioration of credit quality since origination, acquired by completion of a transfer for which it is probable, at acquisition, that there is an inability to collect all contractually required payments receivable, the following disclosures should be made (SOP 03-3, pars. 14 and 16):

1. Description of how prepayments are considered in the determination of contractual cash flows and cash flows expected to be collected

2. Separately for both those loans that (i) are accounted for as debt securities and (ii) are not accounted for as debt securities (as of each balance sheet presented):

   a. Outstanding balance and related carrying amount at the beginning and end of the period

    b.   Amount of accretable yield at the beginning and end of the period, reconciled for additions, accretion, disposals of loans, and reclassifications to or from nonaccretable difference during the period

    c.   For loans acquired during the period: (i) contractually required payments receivable, (ii) cash flows expected to be collected, and (iii) fair value at the acquisition date

    d.   For loans for which the income recognition model is not applied in accordance with paragraph 6 of SOP 03-3: (i) carrying amount at the acquisition date for loans acquired during the period and (ii) carrying amount of all loans at the end of the period

  3. For loans that are not accounted for as debt securities:

    a.   Amount of expense recognized in accordance with paragraph 8(a) of SOP 03-3, for each period for which an income statement is presented

    b.   Reductions of the allowance recognized in accordance with paragraph 8(b)(1) of SOP 03-3, for each period for which an income statement is presented

    c.   Amount of allowance for uncollectible accounts at the beginning and end of the period, for each period for which a balance sheet is presented

Servicing of Financial Assets and Liabilities

The disclosure requirements in items 2 through 4 and 8 below are prescribed by FAS-140, *Accounting for Transfers and Servicing of Financial Assets and Extinguishments of Liabilities,* as amended by FAS-156, *Accounting for Servicing of Financial Assets.* The disclosure requirements in items 5 through 7 below are prescribed by FAS-156. FAS-156 is effective on a prospective basis in the first period ending in the first fiscal year that begins after September 15, 2006. Early adoption is permitted as of the beginning of an entity's fiscal year, providing the entity has not yet issued annual or interim financial statements for any period of that fiscal year. If an entity has not adopted FAS-156, the disclosure requirements in item 1 below apply.

  1. The following disclosures should be made for all servicing assets and servicing liabilities (FAS-140, par. 17e; FAS-140, Q&A, No. 100):

    a.   The amounts of servicing assets or liabilities recognized and amortized during the period

    b.   The fair value of recognized servicing assets and liabilities for which it is practicable to estimate that value, and the method and significant assumptions used to estimate the fair value

c. The risk characteristics of the underlying financial assets used to stratify recognized servicing assets for purposes of measuring impairment in accordance with FAS-140

d. If the predominant risk characteristics of the underlying financial assets used to stratify recognized servicing assets for purposes of measuring impairment in accordance with FAS-140 and the resulting stratums change:

   (1) The fact that such change has occurred

   (2) The reasons for such change

e. The activity in any valuation allowance for impairment of recognized servicing assets for each period for which results of operations are presented, including:

   (1) Beginning and ending balances

   (2) Aggregate additions charged to operations

   (3) Aggregate reductions credited to operations

   (4) Aggregate direct write-downs charged against allowances

2. The following disclosures should be made for all servicing assets and servicing liabilities (FAS-140, par. 17e; FAS-156, par. 4h):

a. Management's basis for determining its classes of servicing assets and servicing liabilities

b. A description of the risks inherent in servicing assets and servicing liabilities and, if applicable, the instruments used to mitigate the income statement effect of changes in fair value of the servicing assets and servicing liabilities

c. If instruments are used to mitigate the income statement effect of changes in fair value of the servicing assets and servicing liabilities, quantitative information about the instruments used to manage the risks inherent in those assets and liabilities, including the fair value of those instruments at the beginning and end of the period (**Note:** Entities are *encouraged*, but not required, to disclose this information.)

d. For each period for which results of operations are presented, the following related to contractually specified servicing fees (as defined in the glossary of FAS-140), late fees, and ancillary fees:

   (1) The earned amount

      (2) A description of where each earned amount is reported in the income statement

3. The following disclosures should be made for all servicing assets and servicing liabilities subsequently measured at fair value (FAS-140, par. 17f; FAS-156, par. 4h):

  a. For each class of servicing assets and servicing liabilities, a description of where changes in fair value are reported in the income statement for each period for which results of operations are presented

  b. For each class of servicing assets and servicing liabilities, the activity in the balance of servicing assets and the activity in the balance of servicing liabilities, including, but not limited to, the following:

      (1) The beginning and ending balances

      (2) Additions (through purchases of servicing assets, assumptions of servicing obligations, and servicing obligations that result from transfers of financial assets)

      (3) Disposals

      (4) Changes in fair value during the period resulting from:

         (i) Changes in valuation inputs or assumptions used in the valuation model

        (ii) Other changes in fair value and a description of those changes

      (5) Other changes that affect the balance and a description of those changes

  c. A description of the valuation techniques or other methods used to estimate the fair value of servicing assets and servicing liabilities, which should include the following information if a valuation model is used:

      (1) The methodology

      (2) The model validation procedures

      (3) The quantitative and qualitative information about the assumptions used in the valuation model (e.g., discount rates and prepayment speeds)

  d. If instruments are used to mitigate the income statement effect of changes in fair value of the servicing assets and servicing liabilities and quantitative information about the instruments used to manage the risks inherent in those assets and liabilities, including the fair value of those instruments at the beginning and end of the period, is disclosed (see item 2c above):

   (1)   A description of the valuation techniques

   (2)   The quantitative and qualitative information about the assumptions used to estimate the fair value of those instruments

       (**Note**: Entities are *encouraged*, but not required, to disclose this information.)

4. The following disclosures should be made for all servicing assets and servicing liabilities subsequently amortized in proportion to and over the period of estimated net servicing income or loss and assessed for impairment or increased obligation (FAS-140, par. 17g; FAS-156, par. 4h; FAS-140, Q&A, No. 100):

   a. For each class of servicing assets and servicing liabilities, a description of where changes in the carrying amount are reported in the income statement for each period for which results of operations are presented

   b. For each class of servicing assets and servicing liabilities, the activity in the balance of servicing assets and the activity in the balance of servicing liabilities, including, but not limited to, the following:

      (1)   The beginning and ending balances

      (2)   Additions (through purchases of servicing assets, assumption of servicing obligations, and servicing obligations that result from transfers of financial assets)

      (3)   Disposals

      (4)   Amortization

      (5)   Application of valuation allowance to adjust carrying value of servicing assets

      (6)   Other-than-temporary impairments

      (7)   Other changes that affect the balance and a description of those changes

   c. For each class of servicing assets and servicing liabilities, the fair value of recognized servicing assets and servicing liabilities (if estimation of such value is practicable) at the beginning and end of the period

   d. A description of the valuation techniques or other methods used to estimate fair value of the servicing assets and servicing liabilities, which should include the following information if a valuation model is used:

      (1)   The methodology

    (2)   The model validation procedures

    (3)   The quantitative and qualitative information about the assumptions used in the valuation model (e.g., discount rates and prepayment speeds)

  e. If instruments are used to mitigate the income statement effect of changes in fair value of the servicing assets and servicing liabilities and quantitative information about the instruments used to manage the risks inherent in those assets and liabilities, including the fair value of those instruments at the beginning and end of the period, is disclosed (see item 2c above):

    (1)   A description of the valuation techniques

    (2)   The quantitative and qualitative information about the assumptions used to estimate the fair value of those instruments

    (**Note:** Entities are *encouraged*, but not required, to disclose this information.)

  f. The risk characteristics of the underlying financial assets used to stratify recognized servicing assets for purposes of measuring impairment in accordance with paragraph 63 of FAS-140

  g. If the predominant risk characteristics of the underlying financial assets used to stratify recognized servicing assets for purposes of measuring impairment in accordance with FAS-140 and the resulting stratums change:

    (1)   The fact that such change has occurred

    (2)   The reasons for such change

  h. For each period for which results of operations are presented, the activity by class in any valuation allowance for impairment of recognized servicing assets, including the following:

    (1)   Beginning and ending balances

    (2)   Aggregate additions charged to operations

    (3)   Aggregate recoveries credited to operations

    (4)   Aggregate write-downs charged against the allowance

5. If, upon the initial adoption of FAS-156, an entity irrevocably elects to subsequently measure separately recognized servicing assets and servicing liabilities at fair value in accordance with paragraph 9 of FAS-156, separate disclosures should be made of the difference, as of the beginning of the year, between the fair value and the carrying amount, net of any related valuation allowance, of separately recognized

servicing assets and servicing liabilities existing at the date of initial adoption (FAS-156, par. 9)

6. If, upon the initial adoption of FAS-156, an entity with recognized servicing rights makes an irrevocable election to reclassify available-for-sale securities to trading securities as of the beginning of the year of adoption in accordance with paragraph 10 of FAS-156, separate disclosures should be made of (FAS-156, par. 10):

    a. The carrying amount of reclassified securities

    b. The effect of the reclassification on the related cumulative-effect adjustment

7. If, after the initial adoption of FAS-156, an entity irrevocably elects to subsequently measure a class of separately recognized servicing assets and servicing liabilities at fair value in accordance with paragraph 11 of FAS-156, separate disclosures should be made of the amount of the cumulative-effect adjustment (resulting from the difference between the fair value and the carrying amount, net of any related valuation allowance, of the servicing assets and servicing liabilities that exist at the beginning of the fiscal year in which the entity makes the fair value election) (FAS-156, par. 11)

8. If an entity subsequently measures separately-recognized servicing assets and servicing liabilities using the fair value measurement method and presents the aggregate of (a) those amounts that are subsequently measured at fair value and (b) those other amounts that are separately recognized and subsequently measured using the amortization method, the amount that is subsequently measured at fair value that is included in the aggregate amount should be disclosed parenthetically on the face of the balance sheet (FAS-140, par. 13B; FAS-156, par. 4f)

EXAMPLES OF FINANCIAL STATEMENT DISCLOSURES

 The following sample disclosures are available on the accompanying disc.

Note: The illustrations in Examples 35–1 through 35–7 are substantially the same under both FAS-140, *Accounting for Transfers and Servicing of Financial Assets and Extinguishments of Liabilities,* and FAS-156, *Accounting for Servicing of Financial Assets.* Examples 35–8 and 35–9 are illustrations of disclosures that are applicable only under FAS-156, which is effective on a prospective basis in the first period ending in the first fiscal year that begins after September 15, 2006.

Example 35–1: Summary of Significant Accounting Policies—Receivable Sales

When the Company sells receivables in securitizations of automobile loans, credit card loans, and residential mortgage loans, it may hold interest-only strips, one or more subordinated tranches, and in some cases a cash reserve account, all of which are interests that continue to be held by the transferor in the securitized receivables. In addition, the Company may obtain servicing assets or assume servicing liabilities that are initially measured at fair value. Gain or loss on sale of the receivables depends, in part, on both (1) the previous carrying amount of the financial assets involved in the transfer, allocated between the assets sold and the interests that continue to be held by the transferor based on their relative fair value at the date of transfer and (2) the proceeds received. To obtain fair values, quoted market prices are used, if available. However, quotes generally are not available for interests that continue to be held by the transferor, thus the Company estimates fair value based on the present value of future expected cash flows estimated using management's best estimates of the key assumptions—credit losses, prepayment speeds, forward yield curves, and discount rates commensurate with the risks involved.

Example 35–2: Detailed Disclosures by Major Asset Type about the Characteristics of Securitizations, Related Gains or Losses, Key Assumptions, and Certain Cash Flows

Credit Card Securitizations: The Company enters into securitization transactions, which allow for the sale of credit card receivables to unrelated entities, to finance the consumer revolving credit receivables generated by the Company's finance operation. For transfers of receivables that qualify as sales, the Company recognizes gains or losses as a component of the Company's finance operation. In these securitizations, the Company retains servicing rights and subordinated interests.

At December 31, 20X2, the total principal amount of loans managed was $54 million. Of the total loans, the principal amount of loans securitized was $52 million, and the principal amount of loans held for sale was $2 million. The aggregate amount of loans that were 31 days or more delinquent was $3 million at December 31, 20X2. The principal amount of losses net of recoveries amounted to $1 million and $1.5 million for the years ended December 31, 20X2 and December 31, 20X1, respectively.

The Company receives annual servicing compensation approximating 2% of the outstanding principal loan balance of the receivables and retains the rights to future cash flows arising after the investors in the securitization trusts have received the return for which they contracted. The investors and the securitization trusts have no recourse to the Company's other assets for failure of debtors to pay when due. The Company's retained interests are subordinate to investors' interests. Their value is subject to credit, prepayment, and interest rate risks on the transferred financial assets. The servicing fees specified in the credit card securitization agreements adequately compensate the finance operation for servicing the securitized assets; accordingly, no servicing asset or liability has been recorded.

The Company recognized pretax gains of $3.3 million and $2.6 million on the securitization of credit card loans for the years ended December 31, 20X2 and December 31, 20X1, respectively.

The table below summarizes certain cash flows received from and paid to securitization trusts:

	20X2	20X1
Proceeds from new securitizations	$4,100,000	$3,500,000
Proceeds from collections reinvested in previous credit card securitizations	$9,400,000	$8,300,000
Servicing fees received	$1,250,000	$1,210,000
Other cash flows received on retained interests*	$1,050,000	$1,000,000
Purchases of delinquent or foreclosed assets	$(135,000)	$ (95,000)
Servicing advances	$(295,000)	$(263,000)
Repayment of servicing advances	$ 260,000	$ 225,000

*This amount represents cash flows received from retained interests by the transferor other than servicing fees, including cash flows from interest-only strips and cash above the minimum required level in cash collateral accounts.

In determining the fair value of retained interests, the Company estimates future cash flows using management's best estimates of key assumptions such as finance charge income, default rates, payment rates, forward yield curves, and discount rates. The Company employs a risk-based pricing strategy that increases the stated annual percentage rate for accounts that have a higher predicted risk of default. Accounts with a lower risk profile may qualify for promotional financing.

Rights recorded for future finance income from serviced assets that exceed the contractually specified servicing fees are carried at fair value, amounted to $2.7 million and $2.1 million at December 31, 20X2 and December 31, 20X1, respectively, and are included in net accounts receivable.

Key economic assumptions used in measuring the retained interests at the date of securitization resulting from securitizations completed during the year were as follows:

	20X2	20X1
Prepayment speed	14.0%	13.1%
Weighted-average life (in years)	.5	.4
Expected credit losses	6.2%	5.6%
Discount rate	11.0%	12.2%

The fair value of retained interests at December 31, 20X2, was $6.5 million, with a weighted-average life of 5 months. The following table shows the key economic assumptions used in measuring the fair value of retained interests at December 31, 20X2, and a sensitivity analysis showing the hypothetical effect on the fair value of those interests when there are unfavorable variations from the assumptions used:

	Assumptions Used (Annual)	Impact on Fair Value of 10% Adverse Change	Impact on Fair Value of 20% Adverse Change
Prepayment speed	15.0%	$200,000	$1,375,000
Expected credit losses	6.1%	$550,000	$1,125,000
Discount rate	14.0%	$160,000	$1,170,000

These sensitivities are hypothetical and should be used with caution. In this table, the effect of a variation in a particular assumption on the fair value of the retained interest is calculated without changing any other assumption; in reality, changes in one factor may result in changes in another, which might magnify or counteract the sensitivities.

Automobile Loan Securitizations: The Company also has asset securitization programs, operated through special purpose subsidiaries on behalf of the Automart Group, to finance the consumer installment credit receivables generated by Automart's automobile loan finance operation. For transfers of receivables that qualify as sales, the Company recognizes gains or losses as a component of Automart's finance operation. In these securitizations, the Company retains servicing rights and subordinated interests.

At December 31, 20X2, the total principal amount of loans managed was $30 million. Of the total loans, the principal amount of loans securitized was $29 million, and the principal amount of loans held for sale or investment was $1 million. The principal amount of loans that were delinquent 31 days or more was $400,000 at December 31, 20X2. The principal amount of losses net of recoveries amounted to $175,000 and $120,000 for the years ended December 31, 20X2 and December 31, 20X1, respectively.

The Company receives annual servicing fees approximating 1% of the outstanding principal balance of the securitized automobile loans and retains the rights to future cash flows arising after the investors in the securitization trusts have received the return for which they contracted. The investors and the securitization trusts have no recourse to the Company's other assets for failure of debtors to pay when due. The Company's retained interests are subordinate to investors' interests. Their value is subject to credit, prepayment, and interest rate risks on the transferred financial assets. The servicing fees specified in the automobile loan securitization agreements adequately compensate the finance operation for servicing the accounts; accordingly, no servicing asset or liability has been recorded.

The Company recognized pretax gains of $1.1 million and $1.3 million on the securitization of automobile loans for the years ended December 31, 20X2 and December 31, 20X1, respectively.

The table below summarizes certain cash flows received from and paid to securitization trusts:

	20X2	20X1
Proceeds from new securitizations	$3,800,000	$3,200,000
Proceeds from collections reinvested in previous automobile loan securitizations	$2,600,000	$2,100,000
Servicing fees received	$ 75,000	$ 660,000
Other cash flows received on retained interests*	$ 350,000	$ 300,000
Purchases of delinquent or foreclosed assets	$ (121,000)	$ (82,000)
Servicing advances	$ (274,000)	$ (241,000)
Repayment of servicing advances	$ 241,000	$ 208,000

* This amount represents cash flows received from retained interests by the transferor other than servicing fees, including cash flows from interest-only strips and cash above the minimum required level in cash collateral accounts.

In determining the fair value of retained interests, the Company estimates future cash flows using management's best estimates of key assumptions such as finance charge income, default rates, prepayment rates, and discount rates. The Company employs a risk-based pricing strategy that increases the stated annual percentage rate for accounts that have a higher predicted risk of default. Accounts with a lower risk profile may qualify for promotional financing.

Rights recorded for future finance income from serviced assets that exceed the contractually specified servicing fees are carried at fair value, amounted to $1.4 million and $1.2 million at December 31, 20X2 and December 31, 20X1, respectively, and are included in net accounts receivable.

Key economic assumptions used in measuring the retained interests at the date of securitization resulting from securitizations completed during the year were as follows:

	20X2	20X1
Prepayment speed	1.0%	1.0%
Weighted-average life (in years)	1.8	1.7
Expected credit losses	3.2%	3.4%
Discount rate	12.0%	13.0%

The fair value of retained interests at December 31, 20X2, was $2.5 million, with a weighted-average life of 1.7 years. The following table shows the key economic assumptions used in measuring the fair value of retained interests at December 31, 20X2, and a sensitivity analysis showing the hypothetical effect on the fair value of those interests when there are unfavorable variations from the assumptions used:

	Assumptions Used (Annual)	Impact on Fair Value of 10% Adverse Change	Impact on Fair Value of 20% Adverse Change
Prepayment speed	1.3%	$85,000	$195,000
Expected credit losses	3.0%	$50,000	$100,000
Discount rate	14.0%	$35,000	$165,000

These sensitivities are hypothetical and should be used with caution. In this table, the effect of a variation in a particular assumption on the fair value of the retained interest is calculated without changing any other assumption; in reality, changes in one factor may result in changes in another, which might magnify or counteract the sensitivities.

Expected credit losses for static pools are as follows:

Actual and Projected Credit Losses (%) as of:	Automobile Loans Securitized in	
	20X2	20X1
December 31, 20X2	5.1	5.0
December 31, 20X1	4.5	

Example 35–3: Transfer of Accounts Receivable Does Not Qualify as a Sale

The Company has an asset securitization program with a large financial institution to sell, with recourse, certain eligible trade receivables up to a maximum of $12 million. As receivables transferred to the financial institution are collected, the Company may transfer additional receivables up to the predetermined facility limit. Gross receivables transferred to the financial institution amounted to $9,760,000 and $10,397,000 in 20X2 and 20X1, respectively. The Company has the right, and is obligated, to repurchase transferred receivables under the program and, therefore, the transaction does not qualify as a sale under the terms of FASB Statement of Financial Accounting Standards No. 140, *Accounting for Transfers and Servicing of Financial Assets and Extinguishments of Liabilities*. Included in the Balance Sheets as receivables at December 31, 20X2, and December 31, 20X1, are account balances totaling $2,412,000 and $2,867,000, respectively, of uncollected receivables transferred to the financial institution.

Example 35–4: Transfer of Accounts Receivable Qualifies as a Sale

During 20X2, the Company sold certain receivables ("Receivables") as part of its plan to reduce debt. The net book value of Receivables sold was $12.8 million for which the Company received approximately $13.2 million in cash proceeds. In 20X1, the Company sold similar assets with a net book value of $7.6 million for cash proceeds of $7.9 million. These transactions were accounted for as sales and as a result the related Receivables have been excluded from the accompanying Consolidated Balance Sheets. The agreements underlying the sale of Receivables contain provisions that indicate the Company is responsible for up to 15% of end-user customer payment defaults on sold Receivables. Accordingly, the Company provides reserves for the probable and reasonably estimable portion of these liabilities. Additionally, the Company typically services the sold Receivables whereby it continues collecting payments from the end user customer on the behalf of the purchaser of the Receivables. The Company estimates the fair value of this service arrangement as a percentage of the sold Receivables and amortizes this amount to income over the estimated life of the service period. At December 31, 20X2, and December 31, 20X1, there was $123,000 and $109,000, respectively, of deferred service fees included in accrued liabilities on the Consolidated Balance Sheets. For the years ended December 31, 20X2 and December 31, 20X1, there was $32,000 and $27,000, respectively, of deferred service fees amortized to income.

Example 35–5: Factored Accounts Receivable and Factoring Agreement

Accounts receivable comprise the following at December 31, 20X2, and December 31, 20X1:

	20X2	20X1
Receivables assigned to factor	$ 6,125,000	$3,655,000
Advances to (from) factor	(2,264,000)	616,000
Amounts due from factor	3,861,000	4,271,000
Unfactored accounts receivable	758,000	869,000
Allowances for returns and allowances	(415,000)	(463,000)
	$ 4,204,000	$4,677,000

Pursuant to a factoring agreement, with recourse against the Company in the event of a loss, the Company's principal bank acts as its factor for the majority of its receivables, which are assigned on a preapproved basis. At December 31, 20X2, and December 31, 20X1, the factoring charge amounted to 0.25% of the receivables assigned.

The Company's obligations to the bank are collateralized by all of the Company's accounts receivable, inventories, and equipment. The advances for factored receivables are made pursuant to a revolving credit and security agreement, which expires on March 31, 20X4. Pursuant to the terms of the agreement, the Company is required to maintain specified levels of working capital and tangible net worth, among other covenants.

Example 35–6: Mortgage Servicing Rights

Upon sale or securitization of servicing retained mortgages, the Company capitalizes mortgage servicing rights. The Company determines fair value based on the present value of estimated net future cash flows related to servicing income. In estimating net future cash flows from servicing income, the Company first determines net future servicing income, which is future servicing revenue less future servicing expense over the expected life of the servicing arrangement. Servicing revenue includes contractual servicing fees and other ancillary fees, and prepayment and late fees. Servicing expenses consist of direct servicing costs and allocated indirect expenses relating to the servicing operations. Servicing expenses also include an estimate for the interest cost to carry advances to the securitization trusts, which approximates 20 basis points of the mortgage loans in the securitization trusts. The Company uses a 15% discount rate to calculate the present value of net future cash flows relating to servicing income. The servicing rights are amortized in proportion to and over the period of estimated net future servicing fee income. The Company periodically reviews capitalized servicing rights for valuation impairment. The Company's periodic valuation of its servicing rights considers the amount of advances which have been made and that are expected to be made, an estimate of the cost to carry such advances, and the estimated period of time over which the advances will be outstanding. At December 31, 20X2, and December 31, 20X1, there were no valuation allowances on mortgage servicing rights.

The activity in mortgage servicing rights (net) during the years ended December 31, 20X2, and December 31, 20X1, is summarized as follows:

	20X2	20X1
Mortgage servicing rights, net, at beginning of year	$4,050,000	$6,100,000
Mortgage servicing rights activity during the year:		
Originated	1,200,000	1,500,000
Amortized	(1,900,000)	(2,550,000)
Charged-off	–0–	(1,000,000)
Mortgage servicing rights, net, at end of year	$3,350,000	$4,050,000

The mortgage servicing rights are amortized over the estimated lives of the loans to which they relate. During the year ended December 31, 20X1, the Company reduced the carrying value of its mortgage servicing rights by $1,000,000, reflecting management's estimate of the effects of increased costs associated with the Company's increased early intervention efforts in servicing delinquencies in the servicing portfolio.

Example 35–7: Collateral and Pledged Assets

The Company's policy is to take possession of securities purchased under agreements to resell. The market value of securities to be repurchased and resold is monitored, and additional collateral is obtained where appropriate to protect against credit exposure.

Collateral: At December 31, 20X2, the approximate market value of collateral received by the Company that may be sold or repledged by the Company was $7.2 million. This collateral was received in connection with resale agreements and derivative transactions. At December 31, 20X2, $3.1 million of the collateral received by the Company had been sold or repledged in connection with repurchase agreements, securities sold not yet purchased, and derivative transactions.

Pledged Assets: At December 31, 20X2, certain investment securities and other assets with a carrying value of $9.7 million were pledged as collateral, of which $8.2 million may not be sold or repledged by the secured parties, for borrowings to secure public and trust deposits, and for other purposes.

Example 35–8: Tabular Disclosure under FAS-156 of Changes in Servicing Assets and Servicing Liabilities Subsequently Measured Using the Fair Value Measurement Method

	Class 1		Class 2	
	Servicing Asset	Servicing Liability	Servicing Asset	Servicing Liability
Fair value at January 1, 20X2	$1,800,000	$1,500,000	$1,750,000	$1,300,000
Additions: Purchases of servicing assets	400,000	N/A	300,000	N/A
Assumption of servicing obligations	325,000	470,000	720,000	540,000
Servicing obligations that result from transfers of financial assets	210,000	315,000	460,000	525,000
Subtractions: Disposals	(150,000)	(260,000)	(190,000)	(350,000)
Changes in fair value:				
Due to change in valuation inputs or assumptions used in the valuation model	230,000	(175,000)	(165,000)	280,000
Other changes in fair value	145,000	(60,000)	75,000	100,000
Other changes that affect the balance	90,000	(50,000)	80,000	65,000
Fair value at December 31, 20X2	$3,050,000	$1,740,000	$3,030,000	$2,460,000

Example 35–9: Tabular Disclosure under FAS-156 of Changes in Servicing Assets and Servicing Liabilities Subsequently Measured Using the Amortization Method

	Class 3		Class 4	
	Servicing Asset	Servicing Liability	Servicing Asset	Servicing Liability
Carrying amount at January 1, 20X2	$1,200,000	$1,400,000	$1,310,000	$1,070,000
Additions:				
Purchases of servicing assets	350,000	N/A	200,000	N/A
Assumption of servicing obligations	125,000	170,000	320,000	230,000
Servicing obligations that result from transfers of financial assets	185,000	265,000	390,000	415,000
Subtractions:				
Disposals	(150,000)	(260,000)	(190,000)	(500,000)
Amortization	(60,000)	(80,000)	(90,000)	(70,000)
Application of valuation allowance to adjust carrying values of servicing assets	(80,000)	N/A	(40,000)	N/A
Other-than-temporary impairments	(110,000)	(100,000)	(105,000)	(165,000)
Carrying amount before valuation allowance	1,460,000	1,395,000	1,795,000	980,000
Other changes that affect the balance	125,000	(75,000)	80,000	95,000
Valuation allowance for servicing assets:				
Beginning balance	170,000	N/A	400,000	N/A

Provisions/ recoveries	60,000	N/A	(50,000)	N/A
Application of valuation allowance to adjust carrying values of servicing assets	80,000	N/A	(40,000)	N/A
Other-than-temporary impairments	(50,000)	N/A	(80,000)	N/A
Sales and disposals	(100,000)	N/A	(120,000)	N/A
Ending balance	160,000	N/A	110,000	N/A
Carrying amount at December 31, 20X2	$1,425,000	$1,320,000	$1,765,000	$1,075,000
Fair Value Disclosures:				
Fair value at January 1, 20X2	$1,300,000	$1,350,000	$1,400,000	$1,000,000
Fair value at December 31, 20X2	$1,350,000	$1,300,000	$1,600,000	$1,025,000

PART II—
BALANCE SHEET

CHAPTER 36
ASSETS AND LIABILITIES: GENERAL

CONTENTS

EXECUTIVE SUMMARY

The distinction between current and noncurrent assets and liabilities in a classified balance sheet is an important feature of financial reporting because considerable interest in the liquidity of the reporting enterprise exists. One way to measure a company's liquidity is to have separate classification of current assets and liabilities. Therefore, classified balance sheets should present current assets and current liabilities separately from other assets and liabilities. Resources that are expected to be realized in cash, sold, or consumed during the next year (or operating cycle, if longer) are classified as *current assets*. Assets not expected to be realized within one year (or operating cycle, if longer) should be included as *noncurrent*. Asset valuation allowances (e.g., uncollectible accounts) should be deducted from the assets to which they relate. Also, a description of assets pledged, subject to liens, or otherwise encumbered should be disclosed.

The major assets are generally presented in the following order:

- Cash
- Short-term investments (including marketable securities)
- Trade accounts receivable
- Inventories
- Long-term investments (including marketable securities)
- Property, plant, and equipment
- Intangible assets
- Other noncurrent assets (e.g., deferred charges, deposits)

Current liabilities are obligations that are reasonably expected to be settled by either liquidating current assets or creating other current liabilities. Current liabilities include obligations that, by their terms, are due and payable on demand. This includes long-term obligations that are callable because a violation of an objective acceleration clause in a long-term debt agreement may exist at the date of the debtor's balance sheet. Such callable obligations must be classified as a current liability at the debtor's balance-sheet date unless one of the following conditions is met:

1. The creditor has waived or subsequently lost the right to demand repayment for more than one year (or operating cycle, if longer) from the balance-sheet date.

2. For long-term obligations containing a grace period within which the debtor may cure the violation, it is probable that the violation will be cured within that period, which would prevent the obligation from being callable.

A short-term obligation can be excluded from current liabilities only if the company intends to refinance it on a long-term basis and the intent is supported by the ability to refinance that is demonstrated in one of the following ways:

1. A long-term obligation or equity security whose proceeds are used to retire the short-term obligation is issued after the date of the balance sheet but before the issuance of the financial statements.

2. Before the issuance of the financial statements, the company has entered into an agreement that enables it to refinance a short-term obligation on a long-term basis.

The major liabilities are generally presented in the order of maturity as follows:

- Demand notes and other short-term debt
- Trade accounts payable
- Accrued expenses
- Long-term debt (including capital lease obligations)
- Other long-term liabilities

Offsetting assets and liabilities (i.e., the display of a recognized asset and a recognized liability as one net amount in a financial statement) is improper except where a right of setoff exists.

The following four criteria must be met for the right to offset assets and liabilities to exist:

1. Each party owes the other party specific amounts.

2. The reporting party has the right to set off the amount payable, by contract or other agreement, with the amount receivable from the other party.

3. The reporting party intends to set off.

4. The right of setoff is enforceable by law.

Financial Instruments with Characteristics of Both Liabilities and Equity

FASB Statement of Financial Accounting Standards (FAS) No. 150, *Accounting for Certain Financial Instruments with Characteristics of Both Liabilities and Equity,* establishes standards for issuers of financial instruments with characteristics of both liabilities and equity related to the classification and measurement of those instruments. FAS-150 essentially requires the following three classes of financial instruments previously classified as equity to be classified as liabilities (or assets in some cases):

1. *Mandatorily redeemable financial instruments.* These financial instruments should be classified as liabilities in an entity's financial statements unless the redemption is required to occur only upon the entity's liquidation or termination. A financial instrument issued in the form of shares is mandatorily redeemable if it embodies an unconditional obligation requiring the issuer to redeem the instrument by transferring its assets at a specified or determinable date or upon an event certain to occur. For example, shares that are required to be redeemed by an entity upon the death of a stockholder (an event certain to occur) are mandatorily redeemable shares.

2. *Obligations to repurchase the issuer's equity shares by transferring assets.* Financial instruments other than outstanding shares that, at inception, meet the following criteria should be classified as liabilities (or as assets in some circumstances): (a) the financial instruments embody an obligation to repurchase the issuer's equity shares, or are indexed to such an obligation, *and* (b) they require, or may require, the issuer to settle the obligation by transferring assets. Examples include forward purchase contracts or written put options on an issuer's equity shares that are to be physically settled or net cash settled.

3. *Certain obligations to issue a variable number of shares.* Financial instruments that embody an unconditional obligation or

financial instruments other than outstanding shares that embody a conditional obligation, which the entity must ormay settle by issuing a variable number of equity shares, should be classified as liabilities (or as assets in some circumstances) if, at inception, the monetary value of the obligation is based solely or predominantly on any of the following:

(a) A fixed monetary amount that is known at inception (e.g., a payable to be settled with a variable number of the entity's equity shares).

(b) Variations in something other than the fair value of the entity's equity shares (e.g., a financial instrument indexed to the S&P 500 and to be settled with a variable number of the entity's equity shares).

(c) Variations inversely related to changes in the fair value of the entity's equity shares (e.g., a written put option that could be settled net by delivering a variable number of equity shares).

With limited exceptions, FAS-150 is effective for financial instruments entered into or modified after May 31, 2003; for financial instruments entered into previously, FAS-150 is effective at the beginning of the first interim period beginning after June 15, 2003.

See Chapter 15, "Financial Instruments, Derivatives, and Hedging Activities," for further guidance including effective date, for the disclosure requirements of FAS-150, and for related examples of financial statement disclosures.

Authoritative Literature

ARB-43	Chapter 3A, Current Assets and Current Liabilities
APB-10	Omnibus Opinion—1966
APB-12	Omnibus Opinion—1967
FAS-6	Classification of Short-Term Obligations Expected to Be Refinanced
FAS-78	Classification of Obligations That Are Callable by the Creditor
FAS-150	Accounting for Certain Financial Instruments with Characteristics of Both Liabilities and Equity
FSP FAS 150-3	Effective Date, Disclosures, and Transition for Mandatorily Redeemable Financial Instruments of Certain Nonpublic Entities and

	Certain Mandatorily Redeemable Noncontrolling Interests under FASB Statement No. 150, *Accounting for Certain Financial Instruments with Characteristics of Both Liabilities and Equity*
FIN-8	Classification of a Short-Term Obligation Repaid Prior to Being Replaced by a Long-Term Security
FIN-39	Offsetting of Amounts Related to Certain Contracts
FTB 79-3	Subjective Acceleration Clauses in Long-Term Debt Agreements

DISCLOSURE REQUIREMENTS

Assets and liabilities must be identified clearly in the financial statements, and the basis for determining the stated amounts must be disclosed fully.

For specific disclosure requirements, see individual chapters relating to specific balance sheet accounts.

EXAMPLES OF FINANCIAL STATEMENT DISCLOSURES

See individual chapters relating to specific balance sheet accounts for examples of financial statement disclosures.

CHAPTER 37
CASH AND CASH EQUIVALENTS

CONTENTS

EXECUTIVE SUMMARY

Cash generally consists of cash on hand, available funds on deposit at a financial institution, and negotiable instruments (e.g., money orders, personal checks). Cash equivalents generally consist of highly liquid investments (e.g., certificates of deposit, money market accounts) with initial maturity of three months or less.

The following are common balance sheet captions used to describe cash and cash equivalents on the face of a balance sheet:

- Cash (this is used if there are no cash equivalents)
- Cash and cash equivalents
- Cash and equivalents
- Cash, including certificates of deposit
- Cash and short-term investments

Cash overdrafts not having free cash balances against which they may be offset should be classified as a current liability. The following are common balance sheet captions used to describe the overdraft as a current liability on the face of a balance sheet:

- Overdraft
- Cash overdraft
- Bank overdraft
- Checks drawn in excess of available bank balances

To be classified as a current asset, cash and cash equivalents must be readily available to pay current obligations and free from any contractual restrictions. Cash that is restricted or in escrow should be segregated from the general cash category; the restricted cash is either classified in the current asset or in the noncurrent asset section, depending on the date of availability or disbursement. If the cash is to be used for payment of existing or maturing obligations (within a year or within the operating cycle, whichever is longer), classification as a current asset is appropriate; otherwise, it should be shown as a noncurrent asset.

Authoritative Literature

ARB-43	Chapter 3A, Current Assets and Current Liabilities
FAS-5	Accounting for Contingencies
FAS-95	Statement of Cash Flows

FAS-133   Accounting for Derivative Instruments and Hedging Activities

DISCLOSURE REQUIREMENTS

Restrictions on cash should be properly disclosed and the amount of restricted cash and cash equivalents should be segregated from cash available for current operations (ARB-43, Ch. 3A, par. 6).

Significant concentrations of credit risk should be appropriately disclosed (FAS-133, par. 531). Bank statement balances in excess of FDIC-insured amounts represent a credit risk and, therefore, should be disclosed.

There is no generally accepted accounting principles (GAAP) requirement to disclose compensating balance agreements unless the agreement legally restricts the use of the funds. For legally restrictive compensating balance agreements, the following disclosures should be made:

- The terms of the compensating balance agreement
- The amount of the compensating balance requirement
- The amount required to be maintained to assure future credit availability and the terms of that agreement
- The maintenance of compensating balances for the benefit of a related party

EXAMPLES OF FINANCIAL STATEMENT DISCLOSURES

 The following sample disclosures are available on the accompanying disc.

Example 37–1: Note Discloses the Components of Cash and Cash Equivalents

Cash and cash equivalents consist of the following:

	20X2	20X1
Cash	$1,102,000	$116,000
Certificates of deposit	200,000	250,000
Money market funds	300,000	125,000
Commercial paper	500,000	500,000
Total	$1,102,000	$991,000

Example 37–2: Restricted Cash from Industrial Revenue Bonds Is Shown as a Noncurrent Asset

	20X2	20X1
Noncurrent assets:		
Restricted cash from industrial revenue bonds	$1,200,000	$ -0-
Intangible assets	200,000	220,000
Deposits	125,000	100,000
Total noncurrent assets	$1,525,000	$320,000

At December 31, 20X2, the Company had borrowings under Industrial Revenue and Job Development Authority Bonds available for and restricted for the construction of a new facility and the purchase of certain equipment. The unexpended portion of such funds totaling $1,200,000 have been classified as "Restricted cash from industrial revenue bonds" in the accompanying Balance Sheet.

Example 37–3: Cash Not Available for Use in Operations and Restricted for Capital Expenditures Is Shown as a Noncurrent Asset

	20X2	20X1
Noncurrent assets:		
Cash restricted for capital expenditures	$3,200,000	$ -0-
Intangible assets	200,000	220,000
Deposits	125,000	100,000
Total noncurrent assets	$3,525,000	$320,000

The Company has classified as restricted certain cash and cash equivalents that are not available for use in its operations. At December 31, 20X2, the Company had commitments to construct additional warehouse facilities at an estimated cost of $8,600,000. As December 31, 20X2, the Company expended $5,400,000 on this capital program and had $3,200,000 in cash and cash equivalents on hand restricted for use in completing this project.

Example 37–4: Restricted Cash Has Both a Current and Noncurrent Portion

	20X2	20X1
Current assets:		
Cash	$ 723,000	$1,325,000

Restricted cash for litigation settlement	600,000	-0-
Accounts receivable	4,736,000	4,244,000
Inventory	4,317,000	3,978,000
Total current assets	10,376,000	9,547,000
Property and equipment, net	6,759,000	6,316,000
Noncurrent assets:		
Restricted cash for litigation settlement	900,000	-0-
Deposits	125,000	100,000
Total assets	$18,160,000	$15,963,000

At December 31, 20X2, the Company has $1,500,000 of restricted cash of which $900,000 is classified as a noncurrent asset. The restricted cash serves as collateral for an irrevocable standby letter of credit that provides financial assurance that the Company will fulfill its obligations with respect to certain litigation settlement discussed in Note [X]. The cash is held in custody by the issuing bank, is restricted as to withdrawal or use, and is currently invested in money market funds. Income from these investments is paid to the Company. The current portion of restricted cash of $600,000 represents the amount of current liability for amounts billed to the Company for certain repairs agreed to be made under the settlement agreement.

Example 37–5: Note Discloses Cash Equivalents That Include Securities Purchased under Agreement to Resell

The Company considers all investments purchased with initial maturity of three months or less to be cash equivalents. On December 31, 20X2, and December 31, 20X1, the Company purchased $2,500,000 and $2,000,000, respectively, of U.S. government securities under agreements to resell on January 4, 20X3, and January 5, 20X2, respectively, which are included in cash and cash equivalents in the accompanying Balance Sheets. Due to the short-term nature of the agreements, the Company did not take possession of the securities, which were instead held in the Company's safekeeping account at the bank.

Example 37–6: General Accounting Policy Describes the Components of Cash Equivalents and Indicates There Is No Exposure to Credit Risk

Cash equivalents include money market accounts, certificates of deposit, and commercial paper, all of which have maturities of three months or less. Cash equivalents are stated at cost plus accrued interest, which approximates market value. The maximum amount placed in any one financial institution is limited in order to reduce risk. The Company does not believe it is exposed to any significant credit risk on cash and cash equivalents.

Example 37–7: General Accounting Policy Describes Cash Equivalents and Indicates at Times They May Exceed the FDIC Insurance Limit

Cash and cash equivalents include all cash balances and highly liquid investments with an initial maturity of three months or less. The Company places its temporary cash investments with high credit quality financial institutions. At times such investments may be in excess of the Federal Deposit Insurance Corporation (FDIC) insurance limit.

Example 37–8: Concentration of Credit Risk for Cash Deposits at Banks

Financial instruments that potentially subject the Company to concentrations of credit risk consist principally of cash deposits. Accounts at each institution are insured by the Federal Deposit Insurance Corporation (FDIC) up to $100,000. At December 31, 20X2, and December 31, 20X1, the Company had approximately $2,317,000 and $1,945,000 in excess of FDIC insured limits, respectively.

Example 37–9: Concentration of Credit Risk for Cash Deposits at Brokerage Firms

Financial instruments that potentially subject the Company to concentrations of credit risk consist principally of cash deposits at a brokerage firm. The accounts at the brokerage firm contain cash and securities. Balances are insured up to $500,000, with a limit of $100,000 for cash, by the Securities Investor Protection Corporation (SIPC). At December 31, 20X2, and December 31, 20X1, the Company had approximately $434,000 and $369,000 in excess of SIPC insured limits, respectively.

Example 37–10: Compensating Balance Requirement Is Based on a Percentage of the Available Line of Credit

As part of its line of credit agreement with a bank, the Company is expected to maintain average compensating cash balances that are based on a percentage of the available credit line. The amount of compensating balances required at December 31, 20X2, was $300,000. The compensating balances are held under agreements that do not legally restrict the use of such funds and, therefore, the funds are not segregated on the face of the balance sheet. The compensating cash balances are determined daily by the bank based on cash balances shown by the bank, adjusted for average uncollected funds and Federal Reserve requirements. During the year ended December 31, 20X2, the Company was in substantial compliance with the compensating balance requirements. Funds on deposit with the bank and considered in the compensating balances are subject to withdrawal; however, the availability of the line of credit is dependent on the maintenance of sufficient average compensating balances.

> **Note:** Alternatively, the disclosure of compensating balances may be included in the note disclosure of the related debt agreement.

Example 37–11: Compensating Balance Requirement Is a Fixed Amount

As part of its line of credit agreement with a bank, the Company has agreed to maintain average compensating balances of $150,000. The balances are not legally restricted as to withdrawal and serve as part of the Company's normal operating cash.

> **Note:** Alternatively, the disclosure of compensating balances may be included in the note disclosure of the related debt agreement.

Example 37–12: Change in Method of Classifying Cash Equivalents and Restatement of Prior-Year Balances

During the year ended December 31, 20X2, the Company changed the method of classifying cash equivalents and has restated prior-year balances to reflect the change. All highly liquid investments with original maturities of three months or less at date of purchase are carried at cost, which approximates fair value, and are considered to be cash equivalents. These investments were previously classified as marketable securities. All other investments not considered to be a cash equivalent now are categorized separately as investments.

CHAPTER 38
ACCOUNTS AND NOTES RECEIVABLE

CONTENTS

EXECUTIVE SUMMARY

For financial statement purposes, accounts and notes receivable are generally classified into two categories: (1) trade receivables and (2) nontrade receivables. *Trade receivables* are amounts owed by customers for goods and services sold as part of the normal operations of the business and include open accounts, notes, and installment contracts. *Nontrade receivables,* or other receivables, include items such as advances to officers and employees, interest and dividend receivables, tax refund claims, and receivables from sales of assets. Technically, a great distinction does not exist between accounts and notes receivable, except that typically a note receivable (1) involves a formal promissory note, (2) carries interest, and (3) is of a longer duration.

Valuation allowances for losses on trade receivables should be recorded if a loss is probable and the amount of the loss can be reasonably estimated, and should be deducted from the related receivables. Similarly, a note receivable generally is considered impaired, and a valuation allowance should be recorded, when it is probable that a creditor will be unable to collect all amounts due, including principal and interest, according to the contractual terms and schedules of the loan agreement. If a loan is considered to be impaired, its value generally should be measured based on the present value of expected future cash flows discounted at the note's effective interest rate.

When a note is exchanged for property, goods, or services in an arm's-length transaction, it is generally presumed that the interest stated on the note is fair and adequate. If no interest is stated or if the interest stated appears unreasonable, the transaction should be valued at the fair value of the note or property, goods, or services, whichever is more clearly determinable. If such fair value is not readily determinable, the transaction should be valued at the present value of the note, determined by discounting the future cash payments under the note by an appropriate interest rate.

Unearned finance charges, interest, or discount on installment receivables should be amortized using the interest method, or a method that approximates the interest method, and should be shown as a reduction of the applicable receivables. Installment receivables should be allocated between current and noncurrent assets in the balance sheet, where applicable.

AICPA Statement of Position (SOP) 01-6, *Accounting by Certain Entities, Including Entities with Trade Receivables, That Lend to or Finance the Activities of Others*, provides accounting guidance for *any* entity that lends to or finances the activities of others, including arrangements that may be (a) secured mortgage loans, (b) unsecured commercial loans, or (c) financing arrangements that only involve extending credit to trade customers resulting in trade receivables.

The following is a summary of the SOP's more significant recognition and measurement principles affecting loans and trade receivables:

1. *Loans and trade receivables not held for sale*—Loans and trade receivables that management has the intent and ability to hold for the foreseeable future, or until maturity or payoff, should be reported at outstanding principal adjusted for any of the following:

   a. Chargeoffs

   b. Allowance for doubtful accounts or allowance for loan losses

   c. Deferred fees or costs on originated loans

   d. Unamortized premiums or discounts on purchased loans

2. *Nonmortgage loans held for sale*—Nonmortgage loans held for sale should be reported at the lower of cost or fair value.

3. *Sales of loans not held for sale*—When an entity decides to sell loans not previously classified as held for sale, such loans should be transferred into the "held-for-sale" classification and carried at the lower of cost or fair value. At the time of such transfer, any amount by which cost exceeds fair value should be recorded as a valuation allowance.

4. *Credit losses*—Credit losses for loans and trade receivables should be deducted from the allowance. The related loan or trade receivable balance should be charged off in the period in which the loans or trade receivables are deemed uncollectible. Recoveries of loans and trade receivables previously charged off should be recorded when received.

5. *Credit losses on off-balance-sheet instruments*—An accrual for credit loss on a financial instrument with off-balance-sheet risk should be recorded separate from a valuation account related to a recognized financial instrument. Credit losses for off-balance-sheet financial instruments should be deducted from the liability for credit losses in the period in which the liability is settled.

6. *Delinquency fees*—Delinquency fees should be recognized in income when chargeable and when collectibility is reasonably assured.

7. *Prepayment fees*—Prepayment fees and penalties should not be recognized in income until the related loans or trade receivables are prepaid, except as permitted under FAS-91 (Accounting for Nonrefundable Fees and Costs Associated with Originating or Acquiring Loans and Initial Direct Costs of Leases).

8. *Transfers of receivables or factoring arrangements*—Transfers, sales, and securitizations of receivables should be accounted for pursuant to FAS-140 (Accounting for Transfers and Servicing of Financial Assets and Extinguishments of Liabilities—A Replacement of FASB Statement No. 125), as amended, and is discussed in Chapter 35, "Transfers and Servicing of Financial Assets."

For transfers, sales, and securitizations of receivables, see Chapter 35, "Transfers and Servicing of Financial Assets."

Authoritative Literature

ARB-43	Chapter 1A, Rules Adopted by Membership Chapter 3A, Current Assets and Current Liabilities
APB-10	Omnibus Opinion—1966
APB-12	Omnibus Opinion—1967
APB-21	Interest on Receivables and Payables
FAS-15	Accounting by Debtors and Creditors for Troubled Debt Restructurings
FAS-114	Accounting by Creditors for Impairment of a Loan

FAS-118	Accounting by Creditors for Impairment of a Loan—Income Recognition and Disclosures
FAS-140	Accounting for Transfers and Servicing of Financial Assets and Extinguishments of Liabilities
FAS-156	Accounting for Servicing of Financial Assets
SOP 01-6	Accounting by Certain Entities (Including Entities with Trade Receivables) That Lend to or Finance the Activities of Others

DISCLOSURE REQUIREMENTS

1. The summary of significant accounting policies should include the following (SOP 01-6, pars. 13a–c):

   a. The basis for accounting for loans, trade receivables, and lease financings, including those classified as held for sale

   b. The method used in determining the lower of cost or fair value of nonmortgage loans held for sale (i.e., aggregate or individual asset basis)

   c. The classification and method of accounting for interest-only strips, loans, other receivables, or retained interests in securitizations that can be contractually prepaid or otherwise settled in such a way that the holder would not recover substantially all of its recorded investment

   d. The method for recognizing interest income on loan and trade receivables, including a statement about the entity's policy for treatment of related fees and costs, including the method of amortizing net deferred fees or costs

   e. A description of the accounting policies and methodology the entity used to estimate its (1) allowance for loan losses, (2) allowance for doubtful accounts, and (3) any liability for off-balance-sheet credit losses and related charges for loans, trade receivables, or other credit losses. Such a description should identify the factors that influenced management's judgment (e.g., historical losses and existing economic conditions) and may also include discussion of risk elements relevant to particular categories of financial instruments.

   f. The policy for (1) placing loans, and trade receivables if applicable, on nonaccrual status (or discontinuing accrual of interest), (2) recording payments received on nonaccrual loans, and trade receivables if applicable, and (3) resuming accrual of interest

   g. The policy for charging off uncollectible loans and trade receivables

    h.   The policy for determining past due or delinquency status (i.e., whether past due status is based on how recently payments have been received or contractual terms)

2. For each period for which an income statement is presented, the following disclosures should be made for sales of loans and trade receivables (SOP 01-6, par. 13d):

    a.   The aggregate amount of gains or losses on sales of loans or trade receivables, including adjustments to record loans held for sale at the lower of cost or fair value (*Note:* Alternatively, this information may be presented separately in the financial statements)

3. For each period for which a balance sheet is presented (SOP 01-6, pars. 13e–13i) the following items are required:

    a.   Loans or trade receivables held for sale should be presented as a separate balance-sheet category

    b.   Major categories of loans or trade receivables (other than those held for sale) should be presented separately either in the balance sheet or in the notes to the financial statements

    c.   The following disclosures should be made: (1) the allowance for credit losses, (2) the allowance for doubtful accounts, and (3) any unearned income, any unamortized premiums and discounts, and any net unamortized deferred fees and costs

    d.   Foreclosed and repossessed assets should be classified as a separate balance-sheet amount or included in other assets on the balance sheet with separate disclosures in the notes to the financial statements

    e.   The recorded investment in loans, and trade receivables if applicable, on nonaccrual status should be disclosed

    f.   The recorded investment in loans, and trade receivables if applicable, past due 90 days or more and still accruing should be disclosed

    g.   The carrying amount of loans and trade receivables that serve as collateral for borrowings should be disclosed

4. For impaired loans, the disclosures should include the following (FAS-118, pars. 6 and 24):

    a.   As of the date of each statement of financial position presented, the total recorded investment in the impaired loans at the end of each period and (i) the amount of that recorded investment for which there is a related allowance for credit losses and the amount of that allowance and (ii) the amount of that recorded investment for which there is no related allowance for credit losses

  b. The creditor's policy for recognizing interest income on impaired loans, including how cash receipts are recorded

  c. For each period for which results of operations are presented:

  — The average recorded investment in the impaired loans during each period

  — The related amount of interest income recognized during the time within that period that the loans were impaired

  — The amount of interest income recognized using a cash-basis method of accounting during the time within that period that the loans were impaired, unless not practicable

  d. For each period for which results of operations are presented, disclosures should be made of the activity in the total allowance for credit losses related to loans, including the following:

  — The balance in the allowance at the beginning and end of each period

  — Additions charged to operations

  — Direct write-downs charged against the allowance

  — Recoveries of amounts previously charged off

5. For notes receivable that require the imputation of interest, or that bear interest at an inappropriate rate, the disclosures should include the following (APB-21, par. 16):

  a. A description of the note

  b. The effective interest rate

  c. The face amount of the note

  d. The amount of discount or premium resulting from present value determination

  e. The amortization of the discount or premium, as interest expense

6. For troubled debt restructurings, the creditor should include the disclosures in items 4a through 4d and the following (FAS-15, par. 40):

  a. The amount of commitments, if any, to lend additional funds to debtors who are party to the restructuring

For disclosure requirements of concentrations of credit risk arising from financial instruments (including receivables), see Chapter 15, "Financial Instruments, Derivatives, and Hedging Activities."

For amounts due from related parties, see the disclosure requirements in Chapter 30, "Related-Party Disclosures."

EXAMPLES OF FINANCIAL STATEMENT DISCLOSURES

The following sample disclosures are available on the accompanying disc. For additional information, see:

- Chapter 2, "Accounting Policies," for examples of general accounting policy disclosures relating to accounts receivable

- Chapter 15, "Financial Instruments, Derivatives, and Hedging Activities," for sample disclosures of fair value of financial instruments, including accounts and notes receivable, and concentrations of credit risk

- Chapter 23, "Leases," for sample disclosures of lease receivables

- Chapter 24, "Long-Term Contracts," for sample disclosures of contract receivables and related concentrations in connection with long-term contracts

- Chapter 30, "Related-Party Disclosures," for sample disclosures of accounts receivable due from related parties

- Chapter 35, "Transfers and Servicing of Financial Assets," for additional sample disclosures of sales of receivables

Example 38–1: Accounting Policy for Trade Accounts Receivable and Allowance for Doubtful Accounts

Trade accounts receivable are stated at the amount the Company expects to collect. The Company maintains allowances for doubtful accounts for estimated losses resulting from the inability of its customers to make required payments. Management considers the following factors when determining the collectibility of specific customer accounts: customer credit-worthiness, past transaction history with the customer, current economic industry trends, and changes in customer payment terms. If the financial condition of the Company's customers were to deteriorate, adversely affecting their ability to make payments, additional allowances would be required. Based on management's assessment, the Company provides for estimated uncollectible amounts through a charge to earnings and a credit to a valuation allowance. Balances that remain outstanding after the Company has used reasonable collection efforts are written off through a charge to the valuation allowance and a credit to accounts receivable.

[*If the changes in the valuation allowance for trade accounts receivable are material to the financial statements, disclosure of the changes in the valuation allowance might be appropriate, such as provided below.*]

Changes in the allowance for doubtful accounts are as follows:

	20X2	20X1
Beginning balance	$2,354,000	$1,941,000
Provision for doubtful accounts	456,000	785,000
Write-offs	(219,000)	(372,000)
Ending balance	$2,591,000	$2,354,000

Example 38–2: Accounting Policy for Trade Accounts Receivable and Allowance for Doubtful Accounts—A General Reserve Is Maintained and Past Due Balances Over 90 Days Are Individually Reviewed

Trade accounts receivable are recorded at the invoiced amount and do not bear interest. The allowance for doubtful accounts is the Company's best estimate of the amount of probable credit losses in the Company's existing accounts receivable; however, changes in circumstances relating to accounts receivable may result in a requirement for additional allowances in the future. The Company determines the allowance based on historical write-off experience, current market trends and, for larger accounts, the ability to pay outstanding balances. The Company continually reviews its allowance for doubtful accounts. Past due balances over 90 days and other higher risk amounts are reviewed individually for collectibility. In addition, the Company maintains a general reserve for all invoices by applying a percentage based on the age category. Account balances are charged against the allowance after all collection efforts have been exhausted and the potential for recovery is considered remote.

[*If the changes in the valuation allowance for trade accounts receivable are material to the financial statements, disclosure of the changes in the valuation allowance might be appropriate, such as provided below.*]

Changes in the allowance for doubtful accounts are as follows:

	20X2	20X1
Beginning balance	$2,354,000	$1,941,000
Provision for doubtful accounts	456,000	785,000
Write-offs	(219,000)	(372,000)
Ending balance	$2,591,000	$2,354,000

Example 38–3: Accounting Policy for Loans and Trade Receivables

The allowance for loan losses on small-balance receivables reflects management's best estimate of probable losses determined principally on the basis of historical experience. For larger loans, the allowance for losses is determined primarily on the basis of management's best estimate of probable losses, including specific allowances for known troubled accounts. All accounts or portions thereof deemed to be uncollectible or to require an excessive collection cost are written off to the allowance for losses. Small-balance accounts generally are written off when 6 to 12 months delinquent, although any such balance judged to be uncollectible, such as an account in bankruptcy, is written down immediately to estimated realizable value. Large-balance accounts are reviewed at least quarterly, and those accounts with amounts that are judged to be uncollectible are written down to estimated realizable value.

When collateral is repossessed in satisfaction of a loan, the receivable is written down against the allowance for losses to the estimated fair value of the asset less costs to sell, transferred to other assets, and subsequently carried at the lower of cost or estimated fair value less costs to sell.

For trade receivables, the allowance for doubtful accounts is based on management's assessment of the collectibility of specific customer accounts, the aging of the accounts receivable, historical experience, and other currently available evidence. If there is a deterioration of a major customer's credit worthiness or actual defaults are higher than the historical experience, management's estimates of the recoverability of amounts due the Company could be adversely affected.

Example 38–4: Company Requires No Collateral and Concentrations of Credit Risk Virtually Limited

Concentrations of credit risk with respect to accounts receivable are limited because a large number of geographically diverse customers make up the Company's customer base, thus spreading the trade credit risk. At December 31, 20X2, and December 31, 20X1, no single group or customer represents greater than 10% of total accounts receivable. The Company controls credit risk through credit approvals, credit limits, and monitoring procedures. The Company performs ongoing credit evaluations of its customers but generally does not require collateral to support accounts receivable.

> **Note:** For disclosure requirements of concentrations of credit risk arising from financial instruments (including receivables), see Chapter 15, "Financial Instruments, Derivatives, and Hedging Activities."

Example 38–5: Company Requires Collateral and Has Concentrations in Accounts Receivable

The Company sells its products to distributors and original equipment manufacturers throughout the United States. The Company performs ongoing credit evaluations of its customers' financial condition and, generally, requires collateral, such as letters of credit, whenever deemed necessary. At December 31, 20X2, three customers, each of which accounted for more than 10% of the Company's accounts receivable, accounted for 58% of total accounts receivable in aggregate. At December 31, 20X1, four customers, each of which accounted for more than 10% of the Company's accounts receivable, accounted for 52% of total accounts receivable in aggregate.

> **Note:** For disclosure requirements of concentrations of credit risk arising from financial instruments (including receivables), see Chapter 15, "Financial Instruments, Derivatives, and Hedging Activities."

Example 38–6: Details of Current Accounts Receivable

Accounts receivable consist of the following at December 31, 20X2, and December 31, 20X1:

	20X2	20X1
Trade receivables	$8,659,000	$9,054,000
Income taxes receivable	216,000	192,000
Due from officers and employees	200,000	100,000
Interest and dividend receivable	81,000	73,000
Receivable from affiliate	354,000	297,000
Insurance claim receivable	162,000	175,000
Litigation settlement (received in January 20X3)	314,000	-0-
	9,986,000	9,891,000
Allowance for doubtful accounts	(418,000)	(504,000)
Allowance for returns and discounts	(376,000)	(452,000)
	$9,192,000	$8,935,000

Example 38–7: Allowances for Commitments Regarding Price Concessions and Sales Returns Are Based on Historical Experience

The Company has agreements with distributor customers that, under certain conditions, allow for returns of overstocked inventory and provide protection against price reductions initiated by the Company. Allowances for these commitments are included in the Balance Sheets as reductions in trade accounts receivable. The Company adjusts sales to distributors through the use of allowance accounts based on historical experience. During 20X2 and 20X1, provisions for these commitments were recorded in the amounts of $2,679,000 and $3,182,000, respectively.

Example 38–8: Write-Off of a Significant Account Receivable Balance

The "Special charge" of $513,000 in the 20X2 Statement of Operations relates to the write-off of receivables due from a customer who filed for protection under Chapter 11 of the U.S. Bankruptcy Code during the year. The write-off was necessary because the Company's receivable was unsecured and the amount that the Company may ultimately recover, if any, is not presently determinable.

Example 38–9: Receivable from Sale of Assets

In December 20X2, the Company sold substantially all of the assets of its electrical tools division for a gain of $716,000. The sales price of $4,825,000 consisted of $1,500,000 in cash and a term note of $3,325,000. The term note bears interest at 2% above the prime rate (9% at December 31, 20X2). Interest and principal payments on the note are due monthly until maturity at December 31, 20X6. Certain mandatory prepayments are required upon the occurrence of certain events. The note receivable is collateralized by the assets of the purchaser.

Principal contractual maturities on the note receivable are as follows:

Year	Maturities
20X3	$1,200,000
20X4	850,000
20X5	800,000
20X6	475,000
	$3,325,000

Example 38–10: Notes Receivable Requiring Imputation of Interest Are Received in Payment of Outstanding Trade Receivables from Major Customer Pursuant to a Bankruptcy Decree

In March 20X2, the Company received $50,000 in cash and $2,200,000 in notes in full payment of outstanding trade receivables resulting from the reorganization by a major customer, pursuant to a bankruptcy decree. The notes vary in maturity from six months to five years. They include non-interest bearing notes and notes bearing interest at rates of 4% to 6%. The notes are recorded at the present value of the future cash flows, utilizing an imputed interest of 10%, which equals $2,017,000. During 20X2, the Company received all scheduled payments on a timely basis. In management's opinion, the remaining balance is collectible. Notes receivable are due as follows: $418,000 in 20X3, $536,000 in 20X4, $374,000 in 20X5, $318,000 in 20X6, and $196,000 in 20X7.

The trade receivables balance due from the customer of $3,136,000 exceeded the fair value of the settlement amounts received by $1,069,000 and, accordingly, a loss in that amount has been charged to operations in 20X2.

Example 38–11: Installment Receivables and Disclosure of Changes in the Allowance Account

Installment receivables bear interest at rates ranging from 8% to 13% and have initial terms of three to seven years. Installment receivables were reduced for unearned finance charges of $1,284,000 and $918,000 at December 31, 20X2, and December 31, 20X1, respectively. Unearned finance charges are amortized to interest income using a method that approximates the interest method. The installment receivables are collateralized by security interests in the related machinery and equipment sold to customers.

Details of installment receivables at December 31, 20X2, and December 31, 20X1 are as follows:

	20X2	20X1
Due in:		
20X2	$ -0-	$1,637,000
20X3	1,961,000	1,176,000
20X4	1,381,000	833,000
20X5	1,006,000	522,000
20X6	675,000	420,000
20X7	385,000	382,000
Thereafter	719,000	200,000
Gross installment receivables	6,127,000	5,170,000
Less: unearned finance charges	(1,284,000)	(918,000)
Less: allowance for doubtful receivables	(566,000)	(419,000)

	20X2	20X1
Installment receivables, net	$4,277,000	$3,833,000
Current balance	$1,711,000	$1,039,000
Long-term balance	2,566,000	2,794,000
	$4,277,000	$3,833,000

An analysis of the allowance for doubtful installment receivables for 20X2 and 20X1 follows:

	20X2	20X1
Balance, beginning of the year	$419,000	$390,000
Provision charged to operations	322,000	317,000
Amounts written off	(225,000)	(363,000)
Recoveries	50,000	75,000
Balance, end of the year	$566,000	$419,000

Example 38–12: Impaired Loans and Disclosure of Changes in the Allowance Account

The Company's impaired notes receivable, including current portion, are as follows at December 31, 20X2, and December 31, 20X1:

	20X2	20X1
Impaired notes with related allowances	$3,589,000	$1,743,000
Credit loss allowance on impaired notes	(1,176,000)	(718,000)
	2,413,000	1,025,000
Impaired notes with no related allowances	211,000	763,000
Net impaired notes receivable	$2,624,000	$1,788,000

Average investments in impaired notes were $3,140,000 in 20X2 and $1,413,000 in 20X1.

Activity in the allowance for credit losses is as follows:

	20X2	20X1
Balance, beginning of the year	$ 718,000	$597,000
Provision charged to operations	617,000	269,000
Amounts written off	(224,000)	(241,000)
Recoveries	65,000	93,000
Balance, end of the year	$1,176,000	$718,000

Interest income on impaired loans is recognized only when payments are received and totaled $289,000 in 20X2 and $173,000 in 20X1.

Example 38–13: Noncurrent Receivables from Related Parties

At December 31, 20X2, and December 31, 20X1, "Other noncurrent receivables" in the Balance Sheets consist of accounts and notes receivable from employees and officers that are due on demand and are uncollateralized. The notes receivable carry interest at rates ranging from 6% to 10% per annum. Accrued interest receivable included in these balances totaled $43,000 and $31,000 at December 31, 20X2, and December 31, 20X1, respectively. The aggregate receivable balances have been classified as noncurrent assets because they are not expected to be collected within one year from the Balance Sheet dates.

Example 38–14: Transfer of Accounts Receivable Does Not Qualify as a Sale

The Company has an asset securitization program with a large financial institution to sell, with recourse, certain eligible trade receivables up to a maximum of $12 million. As receivables transferred to the financial institution are collected, the Company may transfer additional receivables up to the predetermined facility limit. Gross receivables transferred to the financial institution amounted to $9,760,000 and $10,397,000 in 20X2 and 20X1, respectively. The Company has the right, and is obligated, to repurchase transferred receivables under the program and, therefore, the transaction does not qualify as a sale under the terms of Financial Accounting Standards Board Statement No. 140 (Accounting for Transfers and Servicing of Financial Assets and Extinguishments of Liabilities—a Replacement of FASB Statement No. 125). Included in the Balance Sheets as receivables at December 31, 20X2, and December 31, 20X1, are account balances totaling $2,412,000 and $2,867,000, respectively, of uncollected receivables transferred to the financial institution.

> **Note:** For disclosure requirements concerning transfers, sales, and securitizations of receivables, see Chapter 35, "Transfers and Servicing of Financial Assets."

Example 38–15: Factored Accounts Receivable and Factoring Agreement

Accounts receivable comprise the following at December 31, 20X2, and December 31, 20X1:

	20X2	*20X1*
Receivables assigned to factor	$6,125,000	$3,655,000
Advances to (from) factor	(2,264,000)	616,000
Amounts due from factor	3,861,000	4,271,000

	20X2	*20X1*
Unfactored accounts receivable	758,000	869,000
Allowances for returns and allowances	(415,000)	(463,000)
	$4,204,000	$4,677,000

Pursuant to a factoring agreement, with recourse against the Company in the event of a loss, the Company's principal bank acts as its factor for the majority of its receivables, which are assigned on a pre-approved basis. At December 31, 20X2, and December 31, 20X1, the factoring charge amounted to 0.25% of the receivables assigned. The Company's obligations to the bank are collateralized by all of the Company's accounts receivable, inventories, and equipment. The advances for factored receivables are made pursuant to a revolving credit and security agreement, which expires on March 31, 20X4. Pursuant to the terms of the agreement, the Company is required to maintain specified levels of working capital and tangible net worth, among other covenants.

Example 38–16: Accounts Receivable Financing Agreement Includes Issuance of Warrants

In 20X2, the Company entered into an Accounts Receivable Financing Agreement (Financing Agreement) with AMC Bank whereby the Company can finance up to a maximum of $25 million of its eligible accounts receivables with an 80% advance rate. Under the Financing Agreement, the Company is required to repay advances upon the earlier of its receipt of payment on the financed accounts receivables from its customers, or the financed accounts receivable being aged greater than 90 days from date of service. The Financing Agreement has a two-year term, expiring in August 20X4, and bears an annual interest rate of prime rate plus 4.0% (9.25% at December 31, 20X2), with a minimum $15,000 monthly finance charge. The Financing Agreement also contains certain affirmative and negative covenants, and is secured by substantially all of the Company's tangible and intangible assets. As part of the Financing Agreement, in 20X2 the Company issued to AMC Bank warrants to purchase up to 200,000 shares of the Company's common stock with an exercise price of $1.50. The warrants were estimated to have a fair value of $425,000 using the Black-Scholes option-pricing model. The value of the warrants is being amortized into interest expense over the term of the Financing Agreement. At December 31, 20X2, the Company had $17,600,000 outstanding under the Financing Agreement, which represented the maximum borrowings under the Financing Agreement at that time. At December 31, 20X2, the outstanding balance is shown as a current liability under the caption "Accounts receivable financing line" in the Company's balance sheet.

Example 38–17: Finance Receivables Income Recognition Policy

Interest income on finance receivables is recorded as earned and is based on the average outstanding daily balance for wholesale and retail receivables. Accrued interest is classified with finance receivables. Loan origination payments made to dealers for certain retail installment sales contracts are deferred and amortized over the estimated life of the contract. Fees earned on revolving charge transactions are recognized upon assessment.

Example 38–18: Finance Receivables Credit Losses Policy

The provision for credit losses on finance receivables is charged to income in amounts sufficient to maintain the allowance for uncollectible accounts at a level management believes is adequate to cover the losses of principal and accrued interest in the existing portfolio. The Company's wholesale and other large loan charge-off policy is based on a loan-by-loan review. Retail revolving charge receivables are charged off at the earlier of 180 days contractually past due or when otherwise deemed to be uncollectible. Retail installment receivables are generally charged off at 120 days contractually past due. Repossessed inventory is recorded at net realizable value at time of repossession and any deficiency is charged off at that time.

Example 38–19: Receivables Used as Collateral

During 20X2, the Company negotiated a new secured $15 million line of credit, of which $3 million is available exclusively for letters of credit. Borrowings under this new credit facility are collateralized by a security interest in the Company's receivables, which had a carrying amount of $23 million at December 31, 20X2. Interest on amounts outstanding under the line of credit is payable at 1% above the prime rate, which was 6.5% at December 31, 20X2. The line of credit matures on April 30, 20X4. The agreement contains certain financial covenants with respect to tangible net worth, liquidity, and other ratios. As of December 31, 20X2, the Company was in compliance with these covenants. Borrowings of $10 million were outstanding under this secured revolving credit facility at December 31, 20X2.

Example 38–20: Unbilled Accounts Receivable—Contracts

Accounts receivable, net consists of the following:

	20X2	20X1
Accounts receivable	$6,723,000	$7,941,000

	20X2	20X1
Unbilled accounts receivable	1,456,000	1,785,000
Allowance for doubtful accounts	(219,000)	(372,000)
	$7,960,000	$9,354,000

In certain of the Company's contracts, contractual billings do not coincide with revenue recognized on the contract. Unbilled accounts receivable represent revenue recorded in excess of amounts billable pursuant to contract provisions and, generally, become billable at contractually specified dates or upon the attainment of milestones. Unbilled amounts are expected to be collected within one year.

Example 38–21: Unbilled Accounts Receivable—Professional Services

Unbilled accounts receivable result from professional services provided to customers that have not yet been formally invoiced as of the reporting date. Such amounts are generally invoiced within 15 business days of the end of the period in which services are provided.

CHAPTER 39
INVENTORY

CONTENTS

EXECUTIVE SUMMARY

Note: In November 2004, the FASB issued Statement of Financial Accounting Standards No. 151 (FAS-151), *Inventory Costs, Chapter 4.* FAS-151 is the result of a broader effort by the FASB to improve financial reporting by eliminating differences between U.S. GAAP and international GAAP. FAS-151 clarifies that abnormal amounts of idle facility expense, freight, handling costs, and spoilage should be recognized as current-period charges and not included as part of inventory cost. In addition, FAS-151 requires that allocation of fixed production overheads to the costs of conversion be based on normal capacity of the production facilities. Further, if an entity has significant changes to its inventory accounting as a result of adopting FAS-151, the effect on income before extraordinary items and on net income (and on related per-share amounts when presented) of the period of the change should be disclosed. FAS-151 is effective for inventory costs incurred during fiscal years beginning after June 15, 2005. Companies must apply the standard prospectively.

Inventory usually is classified as (1) finished goods, (2) work in process, or (3) raw materials. Inventories exclude long-term assets that are subject to depreciation. Inventories are classified as current assets, except when there are excessive quantities that may not reasonably be expected to be used or sold within the normal operating cycle of a business. In this event, the excess inventory is classified as noncurrent.

Generally, inventory should be stated at the *lower of cost or market.* Cost is the sum of the expenditures and charges, direct and indirect, incurred in bringing inventories to their existing condition or location. Cost may be determined by specific identification or by the association of the flow of cost factors, such as first-in, first-out (FIFO); last-in, first-out (LIFO); and average cost.

In the phrase *lower of cost or market,* the term *market* means current replacement cost, whether by purchase or by reproduction, and is limited to the following maximum and minimum amounts:

- *Maximum*—The estimated selling price less any costs of completion and disposal, referred to as net realizable value

- *Minimum*—The net realizable value, less an allowance for normal profit

The write-down of inventory to market usually is reflected in cost of goods sold, unless the amount is unusually material, in which case the loss should be identified separately in the income statement.

Losses on firm purchase commitments for inventory goods are measured in the same manner as inventory losses and, if material, recognized in the accounts and disclosed separately in the income statement.

Inventories used in discontinued segments of a business should be written down to their net realizable value and the amount of writedown included as part of the gain or loss recognized on the disposal of the discontinued segment.

Interim Financial Reporting

Generally, the same principles and methods are used to value inventories for interim financial statements as are used for annual reports. For practical purposes, however, the following exceptions apply:

1. An estimated gross profit frequently is used to determine the cost of goods sold during an interim period. This is acceptable for generally accepted accounting principles (GAAP), as long as periodic physical inventories are taken to adjust the gross profit percentage used.

2. When the LIFO method is used for interim financial statements and a LIFO layer is depleted, in part or in whole, that is expected to be replaced before the end of the fiscal period, the expected cost of replacement for the depleted LIFO inventory can be used in determining cost of goods sold for the interim period.

3. Inventory losses from market declines, other than those expected to be recovered before the end of the fiscal year, are included in the results of operations of the interim period in which the loss occurs. Subsequent gains from market price recovery in later interim periods are included in the results of operation in which the gain occurs, but only to the extent of the previously recognized losses.

4. Standard costs are acceptable in determining inventory valuations for interim financial reporting. Unplanned or unanticipated purchase price, volume, or capacity variances should be included in the results of operations of the interim period in which they occur. Anticipated and planned purchase price, volume, or capacity variances that are expected to be recovered by the end of the fiscal year are deferred at interim dates. In general, the same procedures for standard costs used at the end of the fiscal year should be used for interim financial reporting.

Business Combinations

Inventory acquired in a business combination accounted for by the purchase method is valued as follows:

- *Raw materials*—Current replacement cost
- *Work-in-process*—Estimated selling prices of finished goods, less costs to complete, costs of disposal, and a reasonable profit for the completion and selling effort based on profit for similiar finished goods
- *Finished goods*—Estimated selling prices, less costs of disposal and a reasonable profit for the selling effort

Authoritative Literature

ARB-43	Chapter 3A, Current Assets and Current Liabilities
	Chapter 4, Inventory Pricing
APB-28	Interim Financial Reporting
FAS-141	Business Combinations
FAS-151	Inventory Costs
EITF 04-13	Accounting for Purchases and Sales of Inventory with the Same Counterparty
PB-2	Elimination of Profits Resulting from Intercompany Transfers of LIFO Inventories

DISCLOSURE REQUIREMENTS

The following disclosures about inventories are required to be disclosed in a company's financial statements:

1. The basis for carrying inventories (e.g., cost) (ARB-43, Ch. 3A, par. 9; ARB-43, Ch. 4)
2. The method of determining cost (e.g., FIFO) (ARB-43, Ch. 3A, par. 9; ARB-43, Ch. 4)
3. Any inventories stated above cost (ARB-43, Ch. 4, par. 16)
4. Major categories of inventories (raw materials, work in process, finished goods, and supplies), if practicable (Generally accepted practice)
5. Material losses resulting from the write-down from cost to market (ARB-43, Ch. 4, par. 14)
6. Material net losses on inventory firm purchase commitments (ARB-43, Ch. 4, par. 17)
7. If an entity has significant changes to its inventory accounting as a result of adopting FAS-151, the effect on income before extraordinary items and on net income (and on related

per-share amounts when presented) of the period of the change (FAS-151, par. 4)

8. The amount of revenue and costs (or gains/losses) associated with inventory exchanges recognized at fair value should be disclosed (EITF 04-13, par. 5) **(Note: For an affected entity, this disclosure should be applied to new arrangements that it enters into in reporting periods beginning after March 15, 2006.)**

The following disclosures, although not required by GAAP, are commonly found in practice as they are considered informative:

1. If the LIFO inventory method is used, the difference between the LIFO amount and replacement cost (LIFO reserve)

2. The effect on income due to liquidation of a portion of LIFO inventory

EXAMPLES OF FINANCIAL STATEMENT DISCLOSURES

 The following sample disclosures are available on the accompanying disc.

Example 39–1: Basis of Valuation and Method of Determining Cost Are Included in Summary of Accounting Policies Note

Inventories are stated at the lower of cost (first-in, first-out) or market (net realizable value).

> **Note:** See Chapter 2, "Accounting Policies," for additional examples of inventory disclosures that are typically included as part of the general note describing the company's accounting policies.

Example 39–2: Disclosure of Major Components of Inventory under FIFO

Inventories, consisting of material, material overhead, labor, and manufacturing overhead, are stated at the lower of cost (first-in, first-out) or market and consist of the following at December 31:

	20X2	20X1
Raw materials	$ 9,826,000	$ 6,286,000
Work-in-process	3,061,000	1,167,000
Finished goods	6,188,000	8,501,000
	$19,075,000	$15,954,000

Example 39–3: Disclosure of Major Components of Inventory under LIFO

Inventories consist of the following at December 31:

	20X2	20X1
Finished goods	$ 9,803,000	$ 8,014,000
Work-in-progress	5,047,000	5,386,000
Raw materials	2,003,000	2,042,000
FIFO inventories	16,853,000	15,442,000
Less provision for LIFO method of valuation	(1,230,000)	(1,402,000)
LIFO inventories	$15,623,000	$14,040,000

Example 39–4: Inventories Valued on Both Average Cost and LIFO Methods

At December 31, 20X2, and December 31, 20X1, approximately 59% and 53% of total inventories, respectively, were valued on a LIFO basis; the cost of other inventories is principally determined under the average cost method. If all inventories were valued on an average cost basis, total inventories would have been $951,000 and $873,000 higher at December 31, 20X2, and December 31, 20X1, respectively.

Example 39–5: Reserves for Obsolete Inventories Disclosed

At December 31, 20X2 and December 31, 20X1, the reserve for obsolescence was $1,051,000 and $805,000, respectively. Reserves for obsolescence were increased by $1,782,000 and $1,209,000 for 20X2 and 20X1, respectively. Reserves for obsolescence were reduced, due to inventory written off, by $1,132,000 and $759,000 for 20X2 and 20X1, respectively.

Example 39–6: Material Losses Resulting from the Write-Down of Inventory to Its Net Realizable Value

Due to changing market conditions in the electronics industry, in 20X2 management conducted a thorough review of the inventory in all of its product lines. As a result, a provision for inventory losses of $4,421,000 was charged against operations in 20X2 to write down inventory to its net realizable value. This was based on the

Company's best estimates of product sales prices and customer demand patterns, and its plans to transition its products. It is at least reasonably possible that the estimates used by the Company to determine its provision for inventory losses will be materially different from the actual amounts or results. These differences could result in materially higher than expected inventory provisions, which could have a materially adverse effect on the Company's results of operations and financial condition in the near term.

Example 39–7: Inventory Held as a Noncurrent Asset

In 20X2, the Company purchased inventory quantities in excess of amounts expected to be utilized in the Company's operating cycle at very favorable terms. At December 31, 20X2, inventory of $780,000 shown on the balance sheet as a noncurrent asset represents that portion of the inventory acquired in excess of amounts expected to be sold in the next twelve months.

Example 39–8: Inventories Produced in a "Maquiladora" Operation

The Company operates its Mexican manufacturing facilities under the "Maquiladora" program. Pursuant to this program, materials and components owned by the Company are transferred to the Mexican subsidiaries where they are used to produce finished goods. The finished goods are returned to the United States and the Company reimburses the Mexican subsidiaries for their manufacturing costs without any intended significant profit or loss of consequence.

Example 39–9: Liquidation of LIFO Inventory Quantities

In 20X2 and 20X1, certain inventory quantities were reduced, resulting in liquidations of LIFO inventory quantities carried at lower costs prevailing in prior years. The effect was to increase net income by $676,000 in 20X2 and $493,000 in 20X1.

Example 39–10: Purchase Contracts

In connection with the EFTX transaction in January 20X1, EFTX and the Company entered into a manufacturing agreement whereby the Company committed to purchase minimum amounts of goods and services used in its normal operations during the first 48 months after the transaction. Future annual minimum purchases remaining under the agreement are $19 million and $22 million for 20X3 and 20X4, respectively. During 20X2 and 20X1, the Company's total purchases under the agreement were $17 million and $13 million, respectively.

Example 39–11: Firm Price Commitment Manufacturing and Supply Agreement

The Company entered into a firm price commitment manufacturing and supply agreement in connection with the acquisition of the F&D trademarks purchased in 20X2. The agreement was entered into with the seller of the trademarks upon request by the Company to obtain from the seller tools and other manufacturing resources of the seller for the manufacture of products. The manufacturing and supply agreement has created a firm commitment by the Company for a minimum of $4,500,000. A minimum payment of $500,000 on the agreement was due on December 31, 20X2, with three additional payments of $400,000 and five additional payments of $560,000 to follow thereafter, through December 31, 20X6, which is also the date on which the agreement terminates.

Example 39–12: Commitment to Sell Inventory at a Fixed Price

At December 31, 20X2, the Company has an agreement with a customer to sell a specified minimum number of units of its Eglaze adhesive products over the next thirty months at a fixed price of $10,200,000. The fixed price is equal to approximately 5% above the aggregate selling price at current market prices.

Example 39–13: Materials Prices Are Linked to the Commodity Markets and Are Subject to Change

The principal raw materials purchased by the Company (fabricated aluminum, plastics, metals, and copper) are subject to changes in market price as these materials are linked to the commodity markets. To the extent that the Company is unable to pass on cost increases to customers, the cost increases could have a significant impact on the results of operations of the Company.

CHAPTER 40
INVESTMENTS: DEBT
AND EQUITY SECURITIES

CONTENTS

EXECUTIVE SUMMARY

The topic of this chapter applies to both current and noncurrent investments in debt and equity securities. The primary issue in accounting and reporting for debt and equity investments is the appropriate use of market value. Generally accepted accounting principles (GAAP) require that investments in equity securities that have readily determinable fair values and all investments in debt securities be classified in three categories (held to maturity, trading securities, and available for sale) and be given specific accounting treatments, as follows:

Classification	Accounting Treatment
1. *Available for sale*—Debt and equity securities that do not meet the criteria to be classified as held to maturity or trading.	Fair value, with unrealized holding gains and losses reported in other comprehensive income. Nontemporary losses should be charged to earnings.
2. *Held to maturity*—Debt securities that the entity has the positive intent and ability to hold to maturity.	Amortized cost, reduced for nontemporary losses that are charged to earnings. Other unrealized gains or losses should not be recognized.
3. *Trading securities*—Debt and equity securities bought and held primarily for sale in the near term (e.g., the entity's normal operating cycle).	Fair value, with unrealized holding gains and losses included in earnings.

The following are examples of debt and equity securities:

Debt Securities	Equity Securities
U.S. Treasury securities	Common stock
U.S. government agency securities	Preferred stock
Municipal securities	Warrants
Corporate bonds	Rights
Convertible debt	Call options
Commercial paper	Put options
Collateralized mortgage obligations	
Preferred stock that must be redeemed	
Real estate mortgage investment conduits	
Interest-only and principal-only strips	

Held-to-maturity securities should be classified as noncurrent assets until they are within one year of maturity; at that time, they should be classified as current. Trading securities should always be classified as current assets. Available-for-sale securities are classified as current or noncurrent, as appropriate.

Authoritative Literature

FAS-115	Accounting for Certain Investments in Debt and Equity Securities
FSP FAS 115-1	The Meaning of Other-Than-Temporary Impairment and Its Application to Certain Investments
FAS-130	Reporting Comprehensive Income
FAS-133	Accounting for Derivative Instruments and Hedging Activities
FAS-140	Accounting for Transfers and Servicing of Financial Assets and Extinguishments of Liabilities
FTB 79-19	Investor's Accounting for Unrealized Losses on Marketable Securities Owned by an Equity Method Investee
FTB 94-1	Application of Statement 115 to Debt Securities Restructured in a Troubled Debt Restructuring
SOP 83-1	Reporting by Banks of Investment Securities Gains or Losses
SOP 90-3	Definition of the Term "Substantially the Same" for Holders of Debt Instruments, as Used in Certain Audit Guides and a Statement of Position
SOP 90-11	Disclosure of Certain Information by Financial Institutions about Debt Securities Held as Assets
SOP 93-1	Financial Accounting and Reporting for High-Yield Debt Securities by Investment Companies
SOP 01-6	Accounting by Certain Entities (Including Entities with Trade Receivables) That Lend to or Finance the Activities of Others
EITF 96-11	Accounting for Forward Contracts and Purchased Options to Acquire Securities Covered by FASB Statement No. 115, "Accounting for Certain Investments in Debt and Equity Securities"
EITF 03-1	The Meaning of Other-Than-Temporary Impairment and Its Application to Certain Investments

DISCLOSURE REQUIREMENTS

Note: FASB Statement of Financial Accounting Standards No. 157 (FAS-157), *Fair Value Measurements*, expands disclosures about the use of fair value to measure assets and liabilities in interim and annual periods subsequent to initial recognition. It does not eliminate or modify the fair value disclosure requirements under other accounting pronouncements (e.g., Statement of Financial Accounting Standards No. 107 (FAS-107), *Disclosures about Fair Value of Financial Instruments*); rather, it encourages entities to combine the fair value information disclosed under FAS-157 with the fair value information disclosed under other such accounting pronouncements. See Chapter 14, "Fair Value Measurements," for additional disclosures of fair value that are required under FAS-157.

1. For securities classified as available for sale, the following disclosures should be made, by major security type, as of each date for which a balance sheet is presented (FAS-115, par. 19; FAS-133, par. 534):

   a. The aggregate fair value

   b. Total gains for securities with net gains in accumulated other comprehensive income

   c. Total losses for securities with net losses in accumulated other comprehensive income

2. For securities classified as held to maturity, the following disclosures should be made, by major security type, as of each date for which a balance sheet is presented (FAS-115, par. 19; FAS-133, par. 534):

   a. The aggregate fair value

   b. Gross unrecognized holding gains

   c. Gross unrecognized holding losses

   d. Net carrying amount

   e. Gross gains and losses in accumulated other comprehensive income for any derivatives that hedged the forecasted acquisition of the held-to-maturity securities

Note: Financial institutions should disclose the information in items 1 and 2 above for the following types of securities: (i) equity securities, (ii) debt securities issued by the U.S. Treasury and other U.S. government corporations and agencies, (iii) debt securities issued by states of the United States and political subdivisions of the states, (iv) debt securities issued by foreign governments, (v) corporate debt securities, (vi) mortgage-backed securities, and (vii) other debt securities.

3. For investments in debt securities classified as available for sale and separately for securities classified as held to maturity, the following disclosures should be made (FAS-115, par. 20):

   a. Information about the contractual maturities of the securities as of the date of the most recent balance sheet presented (Maturity information may be combined in appropriate groupings for companies other than financial institutions.)

   b. The basis for allocation of securities not due at a single maturity date, if such securities are allocated over several maturity groupings

   Note: Financial institutions should disclose the fair value and the net carrying amount (if different from fair value) of debt securities based on at least the following four maturity groupings: (i) within one year, (i) after one year and up to the fifth year, (iii) after five years and up to the tenth year, and (iv) after ten years.

4. The following disclosures should be made for each period for which an income statement is presented (FAS-115, par. 21; FAS-133, par. 534):

   a. The proceeds from sales of available-for-sale securities and the gross realized gains and the gross realized losses on those sales

   b. The method used to determine the cost of a security sold or the amount reclassified out of accumulated other comprehensive income into earnings (i.e., specific identification, average cost, or other method used)

   c. The gross gains and gross losses included in earnings from transfers of securities from the available-for-sale category into the trading category (Such transfers should be rare.)

   d. The amount of the net unrealized holding gain or loss on available-for-sale securities that has been included in accumulated other comprehensive income for the period

   e. The amount of gains and losses reclassified out of accumulated other comprehensive income into earnings for the period

   f. The portion of trading gains and losses for the period that relates to trading securities still held at the balance-sheet date

5. For any sales of or transfers from securities classified as held to maturity, the following disclosures should be made for each period for which an income statement is presented (FAS-115, par. 22; FAS-133, par. 534):

  a. The net carrying amount of the sold or transferred security

  b. The net gain or loss in accumulated other comprehensive income for any derivative that hedged the forecasted acquisition of the held-to-maturity security

  c. The related realized or unrealized gain or loss at the date of sale or transfer

  d. The circumstances leading to the decision to sell or transfer the security

6. For each balance sheet presented, the carrying amount of securities that serve as collateral for borrowings should be disclosed (SOP 01-6, par. 13).

7. The policy for accounting for the premium paid to acquire an option classified as held-to-maturity or available for sale should be disclosed (EITF 96-11).

8. For debt and marketable equity securities classified as available for sale or held to maturity that are impaired at the balance-sheet date but for which an other-than-temporary impairment has not been recognized, the following disclosures should be made (EITF 03-1, par. 21; FSP FAS 115-1, par. 17):

  a. As of each date for which a balance sheet is presented, the following *quantitative* information, in tabular form, by each category of investment and segregated by those investments that have been in a continuous unrealized loss position for less than 12 months and those that have been in a continuous unrealized loss position for 12 months or longer:

    (i) The aggregate amount of unrealized losses (i.e., the amount by which cost exceeds fair value)

    (ii) The aggregate fair value of investments with unrealized losses

  b. As of the date of the most recent balance sheet presented, the following *qualitative* information, in narrative form, that provides the information that the entity considered (both positive and negative) in reaching the conclusion that the impairments are not other than temporary:

    (i) The nature of the investment

    (ii) The cause of the impairment

    (iii) The number of investment positions that are in an unrealized loss position

    (iv) The severity and duration of the impairment

    (v) Other evidence considered by the entity in reaching its conclusion that the investment is not other than temporarily impaired, including, for example, industry analyst reports, sector credit ratings, volatility of the security's market price, and/or any other information that the entity considers relevant

EXAMPLES OF FINANCIAL STATEMENT DISCLOSURES

 The following sample disclosures are available on the accompanying disc.

Note: FAS-157, *Fair Value Measurements*, expands disclosures about the use of fair value to measure assets and liabilities in interim and annual periods subsequent to initial recognition. It does not eliminate or modify the fair value disclosure requirements under other accounting pronouncements (e.g., FAS-107, *Disclosures about Fair Value of Financial Instruments*); rather, it encourages entities to combine the fair value information disclosed under FAS-157 with the fair value information disclosed under other such accounting pronouncements. See Chapter 14, "Fair Value Measurements," for additional disclosures of fair value that are required under FAS-157.

Example 40–1: Accounting Policy Note Explains Classification of Marketable Securities as Held to Maturity, Trading, and Available for Sale

The Company determines the appropriate classification of its investments in debt and equity securities at the time of purchase and reevaluates such determinations at each balance-sheet date. Debt securities are classified as held to maturity when the Company has the positive intent and ability to hold the securities to maturity. Debt securities for which the Company does not have the intent or ability to hold to maturity are classified as available for sale. Held-to-maturity securities are recorded as either short term or long term on the Balance Sheet based on contractual maturity date and are stated at amortized cost. Marketable securities that are bought and held principally for the purpose of selling them in the near term are classified as trading securities and are reported at fair value, with unrealized gains and losses recognized in earnings. Debt and marketable equity securities not classified as held to maturity or as trading, are classified as available for sale, and are carried at fair market value, with the unrealized gains and losses, net of tax, included in the determination of comprehensive income and reported in shareholders' equity.

The fair value of substantially all securities is determined by quoted market prices. The estimated fair value of securities for which there are no quoted market prices is based on similar types of securities that are traded in the market.

Example 40–2: Available-for-Sale Securities Are Classified as Debt and Equity Securities

Available-for-sale securities consist of the following:

	December 31, 20X2		
	Estimated Fair Value	*Gains in Accumulated Other Comprehensive Income*	*Losses in Accumulated Other Comprehensive Income*
U.S. government securities	$1,406,000	$ -0-	$ (6,000)
Commercial paper	1,350,000	5,000	(2,000)
Corporate bonds	1,187,000	51,000	(17,000)
Fixed rate notes	100,000	-0-	-0-
Total debt securities	4,043,000	56,000	(25,000)
Common stock	866,000	100,000	(56,000)
Preferred stock	145,000	5,000	-0-
Total equity securities	1,011,000	105,000	(56,000)
Total available-for-sale securities	$5,054,000	$161,000	$(81,000)

	December 31, 20X1		
	Estimated Fair Value	*Gains in Accumulated Other Comprehensive Income*	*Losses in Accumulated Other Comprehensive Income*
U.S. government securities	$1,157,000	$ -0-	$ (4,000)
Commercial paper	1,635,000	9,000	(6,000)
Corporate bonds	1,727,000	12,000	(73,000)
Fixed rate notes	150,000	-0-	-0-
Total debt securities	4,669,000	21,000	(83,000)
Common stock	626,000	37,000	(26,000)
Preferred stock	114,000	4,000	-0-
Total equity securities	740,000	41,000	(26,000)
Total available-for-sale securities	$5,409,000	$62,000	$(109,000)

During the years ended December 31, 20X2, and December 31, 20X1, available-for-sale securities were sold for total proceeds of $823,000 and $617,000, respectively. The gross realized gains on these sales totaled $147,000 and $104,000 in 20X2 and 20X1, respectively. For purpose of determining gross realized gains, the cost of securities sold is based on specific identification. Net unrealized holding gains on available-for-sale securities in the amount of $127,000 and $53,000 for the years ended December 31, 20X2, and December 31, 20X1, respectively, have been included in accumulated other comprehensive income.

Contractual maturities of available-for-sale debt securities at December 31, 20X2, are as follows:

	Estimated Fair Value
Due in one year or less	$2,388,000
Due in 1–2 years	1,161,000
Due in 2–5 years	273,000
Due after 5 years	221,000
Total investments in debt securities	$4,043,000

Actual maturities may differ from contractual maturities because some borrowers have the right to call or prepay obligations with or without call or prepayment penalties.

Example 40–3: Available-for-Sale Securities Are Classified as Current and Noncurrent Assets

Available-for-sale securities consist of the following:

	December 31, 20X2		
	Estimated Fair Value	*Gains in Accumulated Other Comprehensive Income*	*Losses in Accumulated Other Comprehensive Income*
Current:			
Auction rate securities	$2,800,000	-0-	-0-
Municipal bonds and notes	744,000	-0-	(4,000)
Asset-backed securities	306,000	6,000	(2,000)
U.S. government obligations	680,000	12,000	(7,000)
Total current securities	4,530,000	18,000	(13,000)

Noncurrent:

Auction rate securities	1,300,000	-0-	-0-
Municipal bonds	681,000	8,000	(6,000)
Corporate bonds	265,000	-0-	(9,000)
Common stock	434,000	47,000	(26,000)
Preferred stock	290,000	24,000	(13,000)
Total noncurrent securities	2,970,000	79,000	(54,000)
Total available-for-sale securities	$7,500,000	$97,000	$(67,000)

	December 31, 20X1		
	Estimated Fair Value	*Gains in Accumulated Other Comprehensive Income*	*Losses in Accumulated Other Comprehensive Income*
Current:			
Auction rate securities	$4,300,000	$ -0-	$ -0-
Municipal bonds and notes	620,000	-0-	(3,000)
Asset-backed securities	294,000	4,000	(1,000)
U.S. government obligations	604,000	10,000	(6,000)
Total current securities	5,818,000	14,000	(10,000)
Noncurrent:			
Auction rate securities	1,450,000	-0-	-0-
Municipal bonds	612,000	7,000	(5,000)
Corporate bonds	285,000	-0-	(11,000)
Common stock	485,000	43,000	(29,000)
Preferred stock	353,000	28,000	(17,000)
Total noncurrent securities	3,185,000	78,000	(62,000)
Total available-for-sale securities	$9,003,000	$92,000	$(72,000)

Proceeds from the sales of available-for-sale securities were $511,000 and $307,000 during 20X2 and 20X1, respectively. Gross realized gains on those sales during 20X2 and 20X1 were $107,000 and $95,000, respectively. Gross realized losses on those sales during 20X2 and 20X1 were $53,000 and $46,000, respectively. For purpose of determining gross realized gains and losses, the cost of securities sold is based on average cost. Net unrealized holding gains on available-for-sale securities in the amount of $10,000 and $36,000 for the years ended December 31, 20X2, and December 31, 20X1, respectively, have been included in accumulated other comprehensive income.

Contractual maturities of available-for-sale debt securities at December 31, 20X2, are as follows:

	Estimated Fair Value
Within one year	$1,730,000
After 1–5 years	750,000
After 5–10 years	196,000
	$2,676,000

Actual maturities may differ from contractual maturities because some borrowers have the right to call or prepay obligations with or without call or prepayment penalties.

Example 40–4: Trading Securities

The Company's short-term investments comprise equity and debt securities, all of which are classified as trading securities and are carried at their fair value based on the quoted market prices of the securities at December 31, 20X2, and December 31, 20X1. Net realized and unrealized gains and losses on trading securities are included in net earnings. For purpose of determining realized gains and losses, the cost of securities sold is based on specific identification.

The composition of trading securities, classified as current assets, is as follows at December 31, 20X2, and December 31, 20X1:

	December 31, 20X2		December 31, 20X1	
	Cost	Fair Value	Cost	Fair Value
Treasury bills	$2,796,000	$2,796,000	$2,515,000	$2,515,000
Mutual funds	883,000	765,000	691,000	653,000
Common stock	617,000	501,000	574,000	452,000
Preferred stock	311,000	294,000	282,000	258,000
Total trading securities	$4,607,000	$4,356,000	$4,062,000	$3,878,000

Investment income for the years ended December 31, 20X2, and December 31, 20X1, consists of the following:

	20X2	20X1
Gross realized gains from sale of trading securities	$162,000	$129,000
Gross realized losses from sale of trading securities	(71,000)	(46,000)
Dividend and interest income	194,000	123,000
Net unrealized holding losses	(67,000)	(134,000)
Net investment income	$218,000	$ 72,000

Example 40–5: Held-to-Maturity Securities

At December 31, 20X2, and December 31, 20X1, the Company held investments in marketable securities that were classified as held to maturity and consisted of the following:

	December 31, 20X2			
	Net Carrying Amount	Unrecognized Holding Gains	Unrecognized Holding Losses	Estimated Fair Value
U.S. government securities	$4,997,000	$ 8,000	$ (3,000)	$5,002,000
States and municipalities	1,170,000	75,000	(10,000)	1,235,000
Corporate bonds	1,219,000	67,000	(11,000)	1,275,000
Total held-to-maturity securities	$7,386,000	$150,000	$(24,000)	$7,512,000

	December 31, 20X1			
	Net Carrying Amount	Unrecognized Holding Gains	Unrecognized Holding Losses	Estimated Fair Value
U.S. government securities	$3,624,000	$ 9,000	$ (2,000)	$3,631,000
States and municipalities	1,641,000	95,000	(16,000)	1,720,000
Corporate bonds	1,023,000	61,000	(13,000)	1,071,000
Total held-to-maturity securities	$6,288,000	$165,000	$(31,000)	$6,422,000

During the years ended December 31, 20X2, and December 31, 20X1, held-to-maturity securities were sold for total proceeds of $917,000 and $733,000, respectively. The gross realized gains on these sales totaled $58,000 and $64,000 in 20X2 and 20X1, respectively. For purpose of determining gross realized gains, the cost of securities sold is based on specific identification.

Contractual maturities of held-to-maturity securities at December 31, 20X2, are as follows:

	Net Carrying Amount
Due in one year or less	$1,380,000
Due in 2–5 years	5,481,000
Due in 6–10 years	525,000
Total investments in held-to-maturity securities	$7,386,000

Actual maturities may differ from contractual maturities because some borrowers have the right to call or prepay obligations with or without call or prepayment penalties.

Example 40–6: Estimated Fair Value of Held-to-Maturity Securities Approximates Cost

At December 31, 20X2, and December 31, 20X1, the Company had marketable debt securities that were classified as held to maturity and carried at amortized cost. Held-to-maturity securities consisted of the following:

	20X2	20X1
Current:		
U.S. government securities	$ 1,714,000	$ -0-
Commercial paper	1,975,000	1,810,000
Certificates of deposit	1,315,000	600,000
Corporate notes	2,417,000	1,976,000
Total current held-to-maturity securities	7,421,000	4,386,000
Noncurrent:		
U.S. government securities	3,411,000	3,100,000
Corporate notes	3,719,000	2,418,000
Total noncurrent held-to-maturity securities	7,130,000	5,518,000
Total held-to-maturity securities	$14,551,000	$9,904,000

At December 31, 20X2, maturities for noncurrent held-to-maturity securities were between one and two years. At December 31, 20X2, and December 31, 20X1, the estimated fair value of each investment approximated its amortized cost and, therefore, there were no significant unrecognized holding gains or losses.

Example 40–7: Decline in Market Value Is Considered Other Than Temporary

The Company invests in debt and equity securities of technology companies for business and strategic purposes. Investments in public companies are classified as "available for sale" and are carried at fair value based on quoted market prices. The Company reviews its marketable equity holdings in publicly traded companies on a regular basis to determine if any security has experienced an other-than-temporary decline in fair value. The Company considers the investee company's cash position, earnings and revenue outlook, stock price performance, liquidity and management ownership, among other factors, in its review. If it is determined that an other-than-temporary decline exists in a marketable equity security, the Company writes down the investment to its market value and records the related write-down as an investment loss in its Statement of Operations.

At December 31, 20X2, the Company wrote down to fair market value certain equity security investments. The write-down amounted to $157,000 and was due to a decline in the fair value of the equity security which, in the opinion of management, was considered to be other than temporary. The write-down is included in general and administrative expenses in the accompanying Statement of Operations for 20X2.

Exhibit 40–8: Transfer of Held-to-Maturity Investments to Available-for-Sale Category

In March 20X2, the Company transferred all of its held-to-maturity investments to the available-for-sale category. Management determined that it no longer had the positive intent to hold its investment in securities classified as held-to-maturity for an indefinite period of time because of management's desire to have more flexibility in managing the investment portfolio. The securities transferred had a total amortized cost of $3,770,000, fair value of $3,862,000 and unrealized gross gains of $218,000 and unrealized gross losses of $126,000 at the time of the transfer. The net unrealized gain of $92,000 was recorded as other comprehensive income at the time of transfer.

Example 40–9: Pledged Investments

The Company has pledged certain held-to-maturity investments as collateral for payments due under operating leases and for a standby letter of credit related to an operating lease. Total amount of securities pledged at December 31, 20X2, was approximately $736,000, of which $400,000 is classified as a restricted investment. The operating leases expire at various dates through December 31, 20X5. The standby letter of credit expires on March 31, 20X3, but is automatically renewable through the underlying lease expiration date of March 31, 20X5.

Example 40–10: Application of EITF 03-1 and FSP FAS 115-1 on Disclosures of Investments in an Unrealized Loss Position That Are Not Other-Than-Temporarily Impaired

> **Note:** To facilitate the illustration of narrative disclosures and for simplicity, this example presents only the quantitative information as of the date of the latest balance sheet. However, GAAP requires the quantitative information to be presented as of each date for which a balance sheet is presented.

The following table shows the Company's investments' gross unrealized losses and fair value, aggregated by investment category and length of time that individual securities have been in a continuous unrealized loss position, at December 31, 20X2:

Description of Securities	Less than 12 Months		12 Months or More		Total	
	Fair Value	Unrealized Losses	Fair Value	Unrealized Losses	Fair Value	Unrealized Value
U.S. Treasury obligations	$1,000,000	$ 15,000	$1,100,000	$ 20,000	$2,100,000	$ 35,000
Federal agency mortgage-backed securities	750,000	18,000	800,000	14,000	1,550,000	32,000
Corporate bonds	1,540,000	60,000	1,300,000	85,000	2,840,000	145,000
Total debt securities	3,290,000	93,000	3,200,000	119,000	6,490,000	212,000
Common stock	860,000	55,000	920,000	150,000	1,780,000	205,000
Total temporarily impaired securities	$4,150,000	$148,000	$4,120,000	$269,000	$8,270,000	$417,000

The Company has determined that the unrealized losses are deemed to be temporary impairments as of December 31, 20X2. The Company believes that the unrealized losses generally are caused by liquidity discounts and increases in the risk premiums required by market participants rather than an adverse change in cash flows or a fundamental weakness in the credit quality of the issuer or underlying assets.

U.S. Treasury Obligations. The unrealized losses on the Company's investments in U.S. Treasury obligations were caused by interest rate increases. The contractual terms of those investments do not permit the issuer to settle the securities at a price less than the amortized cost of the investment. Because the Company has the ability and intent to hold those investments until a recovery of fair value, which may be maturity, the Company does not consider those investments to be other-than-temporarily impaired at December 31, 20X2.

Federal Agency Mortgage-Backed Securities. The unrealized losses on the Company's investment in federal agency mortgage-backed securities were caused by interest rate increases. The Company purchased those investments at a discount relative to their face amount, and the contractual cash flows of those investments are guaranteed by an agency of the U.S. government. Accordingly, it is expected that the securities would not be settled at a price less than the amortized cost of the Company's investment. Because the decline in market value is attributable to changes in interest rates and not credit quality, and because the Company has the ability and intent to hold those investments until a recovery of fair value, which may be maturity, the Company does not consider those investments to be other-than-temporarily impaired at December 31, 20X2.

Corporate Bonds. The Company's unrealized losses on investments in corporate bonds relate to a $1,540,000 investment in ABC Company's Series B Debentures and a $1,300,000 investment in XYZ Company's Series C Debentures. The unrealized losses were primarily caused by (a) a recent decrease in profitability and near-term profit forecasts by industry analysts resulting from intense competitive pricing pressure in the manufacturing industry and (b) a recent sector downgrade by several industry analysts. The contractual terms of those investments do not permit ABC Company and XYZ Company to settle the security at a price less than the amortized cost of the investment. While the credit ratings of ABC Company and XYZ Company have decreased from A to BBB (S&P), the Company currently does not believe it is probable that it will be unable to collect all amounts due according to the contractual terms of the investments. Therefore, it is expected that the debentures would not be settled at a price less than the amortized cost of the investments. Because the Company has the ability and intent to hold these investments until a recovery of fair value, which may be maturity, it does not consider the investment in the debentures of ABC Company and XYZ Company to be other-than-temporarily impaired at December 31, 20X2.

Common Stock. The Company's investments consist primarily of investments in common stock of companies in the consumer tools and appliances industry ($1,100,000 of the total fair value and $155,000 of the total unrealized losses in common stock investments) and the air courier industry ($680,000 of the total fair value and $50,000 of the total unrealized losses in common stock investments). Within the Company's portfolio of common stocks in the consumer tools and appliances industry (all of which are in an unrealized loss position) approximately 35% of the total fair value and 30% of the Company's total unrealized losses are in ABC Company. The remaining fair value and unrealized losses are distributed in four companies. The severity and duration of the impairment correlate with the weak sales experienced recently within the consumer tools and appliance industry. The Company evaluated the near-term prospects of the issuer in relation to the severity and duration of the impairment. Based on that evaluation and the Company's ability and intent to hold those investments for a reasonable period of time sufficient for a forecasted recovery of fair value, the Company does not consider those investments to be other-than-temporarily impaired at December 31, 20X2. The Company's portfolio of common stocks in the air courier industry consists of investments in 6 companies, 4 of which (or approximately 80% of the total fair value of the investments in the air courier industry) are in an unrealized loss position. The air courier industry and the Company's investees are susceptible to changes in the U.S. economy and the industries of their customers. A substantial number of their principal customers are in the automotive, personal computer, electronics, telecommunications, and related industries, and their businesses have been adversely affected by the slowdown of the U.S. economy, particularly during the first half of 20X2 when the Company's investments became impaired. In addition, the credit ratings of nearly all companies in the portfolio have decreased from A to BBB (S&P or equivalent designation). The severity of the impairments in relation to the carrying amounts of the individual investments is consistent with those market developments. The Company evaluated the near-term prospects of the issuers in relation to the severity and duration of the impairment. Based on that evaluation and the Company's ability and intent to hold those investments for a reasonable period of time sufficient for a forecasted recovery of fair value, the Company does not consider those investments to be other-than-temporarily impaired at December 31, 20X2.

Example 40–11: Auction Rate Securities

At December 31, 20X2 and 20X1, the Company held $2,800,000 and $4,300,000, respectively, of auction rate securities, which are shown as a separately stated current asset in the accompanying financial statements. Also, at December 31, 20X2 and 20X1, the Company held $1,300,000 and $1,450,000, respectively, of auction rate securities related to the Company's standby letters of credit, which collateralize the leases for its Irvine and San Diego offices and are classified as other noncurrent assets. Auction rate securities are variable-rate bonds tied to short-term interest rates with maturities on the face of the securities in excess of 90 days. The Company's investments in these auction rate securities are classified as available-for-sale securities under FAS-115, *Accounting for Certain Investments in Debt and Equity Securities*. The securities are recorded at cost, which approximates fair market value because of their variable interest rates, which typically reset every 7 to 35 days. Despite the long-term nature of their stated contractual maturities, the Company has the intent and ability to quickly liquidate these securities; therefore, the Company had no cumulative gross unrealized holding gains or losses, or gross realized gains or losses from these investments. All income generated from these investments was recorded as interest income.

CHAPTER 41
INVESTMENTS: EQUITY AND COST METHODS

CONTENTS

EXECUTIVE SUMMARY

The equity method of accounting for investments in common stock is appropriate if an investment enables the investor to significantly influence the operating or financial decisions of the investee. Absent evidence to the contrary, an investor is presumed to have the ability to significantly influence an investee if it owns (directly or indirectly) 20% or more of the investee's voting stock. The authoritative literature presumes that significant influence does not exist in an investment of less than 20%. However, this presumption may be overcome by evidence to the contrary. Therefore, significant influence over the operating and financial policies of an investment of less than 20% can occur. The 20% cutoff is intended to be a guideline, subject to individual judgment rather than a rigid rule.

The equity method is not intended as a substitute for consolidated financial statements when the conditions for consolidation are present. Under the equity method, an investment is initially recorded at cost. Thereafter, the carrying amount of the investment is (1) increased for the investor's proportionate share of the investee's earnings or (2) decreased for the investor's proportionate share of the investee's losses or for dividends received from the investee. The effect of this treatment is that net income for the period and stockholders' equity at the end of the period are the same as if the companies had been consolidated.

An investor's share of earnings or losses from its investment usually is shown as a single amount (called a *one-line consolidation*) in the income statement. The following procedures are appropriate in applying the equity method:

1. Intercompany profits and losses are eliminated by reducing the investment balance and the income from investee for the investor's share of the unrealized intercompany profits and losses.

2. Any difference between the underlying equity in net assets of the investee and the cost of the investment is amortized over the period of the remaining lives of the investee assets that give rise to the difference.

3. The investment is shown in the investor's balance sheet as a single amount and earnings or losses are shown as a single amount (one-line consolidation) in the income statement, except for the investor's share of (a) extraordinary items and (b) prior-period adjustments, which are shown separately.

4. Capital transactions of the investee that affect the investor's share of stockholders' equity are accounted for as if the investee were consolidated.

5.   Gain or loss is recognized when an investor sells the common stock investment, equal to the difference between the selling price and the carrying amount of the investment at the time of sale.

6.   If the investee's financial reports are not timely enough for an investor to apply the equity method currently, the investor may use the most recent available financial statements, and the lag in time created should be consistent from period to period.

7.   Other than temporary declines, a loss in value of an investment should be recognized in the books of the investor.

8.   When the investee has losses, applying the equity method decreases the basis of the investment. The investment account generally is not reduced below zero, at which point the use of the equity method is discontinued, unless the investor has guaranteed obligations of the investee or is committed to provide financial support. The investor resumes the equity method when the investee subsequently reports net income and the net income exceeds the investor's share of any net losses not recognized during the period of discontinuance.

9.   Dividends for cumulative preferred stock of the investee are deducted before the investor's share of earnings or losses is computed, whether the dividend was declared or not.

10.   The investor's shares of earnings or losses from an investment accounted for by the equity method are based on the outstanding shares of the investee without regard to common stock equivalents.

Authoritative Literature

APB-18	The Equity Method of Accounting for Investments in Common Stock
FAS-94	Consolidation of All Majority-Owned Subsidiaries
FAS-130	Reporting Comprehensive Income
FIN-35	Criteria for Applying the Equity Method of Accouning for Investments in Common Stock
FTB 79-19	Investor's Accounting for Unrealized Losses on Marketable Securities Owned by an Equity Method Investee

EITF 99-10	Percentage Used to Determine the Amount of Equity Method Losses
EITF 03-1	The Meaning of Other-Than-Temporary Impairment and Its Application to Certain Investments
EITF 06-9	Reporting a Change in (or the Elimination of) a Previously Existing Difference between the Fiscal Year-End of a Parent Company and That of a Consolidated Entity or between the Reporting Period of an Investor and That of an Equity Method Investee
FSP FAS 115-1	The Meaning of Other-Than-Temporary Impairment and Its Application to Certain Investments

DISCLOSURE REQUIREMENTS

Note: FASB Statement of Financial Accounting Standards No. 157 (FAS-157), *Fair Value Measurements,* expands disclosures about the use of fair value to measure assets and liabilities in interim and annual periods subsequent to initial recognition. It does not eliminate or modify the fair value disclosure requirements under other accounting pronouncements (e.g., Statement of Financial Accounting Standards No. 107 (FAS-107), *Disclosures about Fair Value of Financial Instruments*); rather, it encourages entities to combine the fair value information disclosed under FAS-157 with the fair value information disclosed under other such accounting pronouncements. See Chapter 14, "Fair Value Measurements," for additional disclosures of fair value that are required under FAS-157.

1. An entity's financial statements should include the following disclosures about an investment accounted for under the equity method (when determining the extent of the disclosures, the investment's significance to the investor's financial position and results of operations should be considered) (APB-18, par. 20):

   a. The name of the investee

   b. The percentage ownership of the investee's common stock

   c. The accounting policies of the investor with respect to the investment in common stock

   d. The difference, if any, between the amount of the carrying value of the investment and the amount of underlying equity in net assets and the accounting treatment of the difference

   e. The aggregate market value of investments for which quoted market prices are available (not required for investments in common stock of subsidiaries)

   f. When investments in common stock of corporate joint ventures or other investments accounted for under the equity method are, in the aggregate, material, summarized information of assets, liabilities, and results of operations of the investees should be presented in notes or separate statements, either individually or in groups

   g. Material effects of possible conversions of outstanding convertible securities, exercise of outstanding options and warrants, and other contingent issuances that could have a significant effect on the investor's share of reported earnings or losses

2. If the equity method is not used for an investment of 20% or more of the voting stock of the investee company, disclosure of the reason is required. Conversely, if the equity method is used for an investment of less than 20%, disclosure of the reason is required (APB-18, par. 20, footnote 13).

3. Investments accounted for on the equity method should be shown in the balance sheet of the investor as a single amount, and the investor's share of earnings or losses of investees should be shown in the income statement as a single amount, with separate identification of the investor's share of the investee's extraordinary items, the cumulative effect of changes in accounting principles, and gains or losses from the disposition of a business segment (APB-18, par. 19).

4. The investor's proportional share of prior-period adjustments made by the investee company should be presented as part of the retained earnings of the investor company (APB-18, par. 19).

5. If an equity method investment has been reduced to zero as a result of previous losses, the policy for determining the amount of subsequent losses should be disclosed (EITF 99-10, par. 5).

6. For cost method investments (i.e., those equity securities that are not subject to the scope of FAS-115 and not accounted for under the equity method), the following additional disclosures should be made as of each date for which a balance sheet is presented) (EITF 03-1, par. 22; FSP FAS 115-1, par. 18):

   a. The aggregate carrying amount of all cost method investments

b.   The aggregate carrying amount of cost method investments that were not evaluated for impairment

c.   The fact that the fair value of a cost method investment is not estimated if there are no identified events or changes in circumstances that may have a significant adverse effect on the fair value of the investment, and:

(1)   A determination was made in accordance with paragraphs 14 and 15 of FAS-107 that it is not practicable to estimate the fair value of the investment, or

(2)   The investor is exempt from estimating fair value under FAS-126

Note: The disclosure requirements in item 7 below are prescribed by EITF Issue No. 06-9, *Reporting a Change in (or the Elimination of) a Previously Existing Difference between the Fiscal Year-End of a Parent Company and That of a Consolidated Entity or between the Reporting Period of an Investor and That of an Equity Method Investee.* EITF 06-9 is effective for changes in, or eliminations of, a previously existing difference between an entity's reporting period and that of an equity method investee that occur in interim or annual reporting periods beginning after November 29, 2006. Earlier application is only permitted if an entity has not yet issued its financial statements for the period.

7.   If a previously existing difference between the entity's reporting period and that of an equity method investee is changed or eliminated, the disclosures in items 7 through 9 of Part IV, *"Accounting Changes—Changes in Accounting Principle,"* of the Financial Statement Disclosure Checklist should be made (EITF 06-9).

EXAMPLES OF FINANCIAL STATEMENT DISCLOSURES

The following sample disclosures are available on the accompanying disc.

Note: FAS-157, *Fair Value Measurements,* expands disclosures about the use of fair value to measure assets and liabilities in interim and annual periods subsequent to initial recognition. It does not eliminate or modify the fair value disclosure requirements under other accounting pronouncements (e.g., FAS-107, *Disclosures about Fair Value of Financial Instruments*); rather, it encourages entities to combine the fair value information disclosed under FAS-157 with the fair value information disclosed under other such accounting pronouncements. See Chapter 14,

"Fair Value Measurements," for additional disclosures of fair value that are required under FAS-157.

Example 41–1: General Accounting Policy Describes the Equity and Cost Methods of Accounting

Equity Method. Investee companies that are not consolidated, but over which the Company exercises significant influence, are accounted for under the equity method of accounting. Whether or not the Company exercises significant influence with respect to an Investee depends on an evaluation of several factors including, among others, representation on the Investee company's board of directors and ownership level, which is generally a 20% to 50% interest in the voting securities of the Investee company. Under the equity method of accounting, an Investee company's accounts are not reflected within the Company's Consolidated Balance Sheets and Statements of Operations; however, the Company's share of the earnings or losses of the Investee company is reflected in the caption "Equity loss—share of Investee company losses" in the Consolidated Statements of Operations. The Company's carrying value in an equity method Investee company is reflected in the caption "Ownership interests in Investee companies" in the Company's Consolidated Balance Sheets.

When the Company's carrying value in an equity method Investee company is reduced to zero, no further losses are recorded in the Company's consolidated financial statements unless the Company guaranteed obligations of the Investee company or has committed additional funding. When the Investee company subsequently reports income, the Company will not record its share of such income until it equals the amount of its share of losses not previously recognized.

Cost Method. Investee companies not accounted for under the consolidation or the equity method of accounting are accounted for under the cost method of accounting. Under this method, the Company's share of the earnings or losses of such Investee companies is not included in the Consolidated Balance Sheet or Statement of Operations. However, impairment charges are recognized in the Consolidated Statement of Operations. If circumstances suggest that the value of the Investee company has subsequently recovered, such recovery is not recorded.

When a cost method Investee company initially qualifies for use of the equity method, the Company's carrying value is adjusted for the Company's share of the past results of the Investee's operations.

Therefore, prior losses could significantly decrease the Company's carrying value in that Investee company at that time.

Example 41–2: Disclosure of Summarized Information of Assets, Liabilities, and Results of Operations of Investees Accounted for on the Equity Method

The Company's investments in companies that are accounted for on the equity method of accounting consist of the following: (1) 25% interest in Kalass, Inc., which is engaged in the manufacture and sale of automotive replacement radiators; (2) 30% interest in Safir Industries, a manufacturer of water pumps; and (3) 50% interest in Tetera Co., a manufacturer of rubber bearings. The investments in these companies amounted to $5,542,000 and $4,668,000 at December 31, 20X2, and December 31, 20X1, respectively.

The combined results of operations and financial position of the Company's equity basis investments are summarized below:

	20X2	20X1
Condensed income statement information:		
Net sales	$51,173,000	$49,742,000
Gross margin	$17,321,000	$16,235,000
Net income	$ 2,174,000	$ 1,839,000
Company's equity in net income of affiliates	$874,000	$716,000
Condensed balance sheet information:		
Current assets	$29,316,000	$31,067,000
Noncurrent assets	20,011,000	17,374,000
Total assets	$49,327,000	$48,441,000
Current liabilities	$26,851,000	$28,992,000
Noncurrent liabilities	12,787,000	11,603,000
Equity	9,689,000	7,846,000
Total liabilities and equity	$49,327,000	$48,441,000

Note: The following tables illustrate the captions used in the Company's Balance Sheets and Income Statements for its equity basis investments described above.

Balance Sheet Presentation

	20X2	20X1
Total current assets	$36,823,000	$37,015,000
Equity in net assets of and advances to affiliates	5,542,000	4,668,000
Property and equipment	11,610,000	10,539,000
Other assets	411,000	402,000
	$54,386,000	$52,624,000

Income Statement Presentation

	20X2	20X1
Income before income taxes	$8,941,000	$7,916,000
Provision for income taxes	(3,576,000)	(3,287,000)
Income before equity in net income of affiliates	5,365,000	4,629,000
Equity in net income of affiliates	874,000	716,000
Net income	$6,239,000	$5,345,000

Example 41–3: *Investment Accounted for on the Equity Method Is Reduced to Zero—Investor Is Not Obligated to Provide Additional Financial Support to Investee*

The Company has a 40% interest in Shana, Ltd., a manufacturer of medical diagnostic products, which has been accounted for on the equity method since 19X9. The Company's 20X2 operations include a loss of $1,975,000, which represents the Company's share of loss on its investment in Shana, Ltd. The loss resulted largely from Shana, Ltd.'s decision to write-down certain assets, predominantly property and intangibles, in light of current market conditions affecting the medical supplies industry. The loss reduced the Company's investment in Shana, Ltd. to zero and, as a consequence, the Company's future financial results will not be negatively affected by Shana, Ltd.'s ongoing operations. The Company has no obligation to fund future operating losses of Shana, Ltd.

Example 41–4: *Investment Accounted for on the Equity Method Is Reduced to Zero—Investor Is Obligated to Provide Additional Financial Support to Investee*

The Company has a 40% interest in Shana, Ltd., a manufacturer of medical diagnostic products, which has been accounted for on the equity method since 19X9. The Company's 20X2 operations include a loss of $1,975,000, which represents the Company's share of loss on its investment in Shana, Ltd. The loss resulted largely from Shana, Ltd.'s decision to write-down certain assets, predominantly property and intangibles, in light of current market conditions affecting the medical supplies industry. The loss reduced the Company's investment in Shana, Ltd. to zero.

Under the terms of an agreement with Shana, Ltd., the Company is obligated to advance additional funds to Shana, Ltd. through July 20X5. As a result, the Company recorded an additional loss of $2,360,000 in 20X2, which represents the estimated amount of such required future advances under the terms of the agreement.

Example 41–5: Equity Method Used for Less Than 20% Owned Investee because Investor Exercises Significant Influence Over Investee's Operating and Financial Activities

The Company has a 15% interest in Fadar, a producer of chemical-based materials, which is accounted for on the equity method because the Company exercises significant influence over Fadar's operating and financial activities. Therefore, the Company's investment in Fadar, which was initially carried at cost, is adjusted annually for the Company's proportionate share of Fadar's earnings or losses.

Example 41–6: Cost Method Applied to 20% or More Owned Subsidiary Due to Lack of Significant Influence Over Investee's Operating and Financial Activities

At December 31, 20X2, and December 31, 20X1, "Investment in associated company" as shown on the Company's Balance Sheet consists of the cost of an investment in Acker, Inc., in which the Company has a 45% interest. Prior to 20X1, the Company's 45% ownership in this Canadian affiliate was recorded on the equity basis. In 20X1, the Company concluded that it could no longer exert a significant influence over Acker, Inc.'s operating and financial activities; therefore, the Company began accounting for this investment using the cost method effective January 1, 20X1. The carrying value of this investment at December 31, 20X2, and December 31, 20X1, was $725,000, which approximates the Company's pro rata share of Acker, Inc.'s underlying value.

Example 41–7: Company Resumes Applying the Equity Method, Which Was Previously Suspended in Prior Years Due to Losses by Investee

The Company has a 30% interest in Fadar, a producer of chemical-based materials. In 20X0, when the Company's share of losses equaled the carrying value of its investment, the Company suspended the use of the equity method, and no additional losses were recognized since the Company was not obligated to provide further financial support for Fadar. The Company's unrecorded share of Fadar's losses for 20X0 and 20X1 totaled $210,000. In 20X2, Fadar reported earnings of $1,200,000, of which the Company's share was $360,000. Accordingly, the Company has included $150,000 in income in 20X2, which represents the excess of the Company's share of Fadar's earnings for 20X2 over the Company's share of prior unrecorded losses.

Example 41–8: Financial Statements Currently Include on the Equity Basis of Accounting the Accounts of a Previously Consolidated Business

On January 1, 20X2, the Company transferred its medical equipment business segment and contributed certain assets and liabilities, totalling $15 million and $4 million, respectively, to a joint venture named Hope Enterprises (a partnership). The Company's equity interest in the joint venture is 35%. As a result, the 20X1 Income Statement, which included the accounts of the medical equipment business segment on a consolidated basis, has been restated to reflect adjustments of line items for revenue and costs applicable to the medical equipment business segment transferred to the joint venture and to reflect the losses of this business on the equity basis of accounting.

Example 41–9: Change to Equity Method from Cost Method Due to Increasing Stake in Investee

During 20X2, the Company bought an additional 25% interest in Bodair Co., thereby increasing its holdings to 40%. As a result, the Company changed its method of accounting for this investment from the cost method to the equity method. Under the cost method, the investment is recorded at cost and dividends are treated as income when received. Under the equity method, the Company records its proportionate share of the earnings or losses of Bodair Co. The effect of the change was to increase 20X2 net income by $437,000 ($0.23 per share). The financial statements for 20X1 have been restated for the change, which resulted in an increase of net income for 20X1 of $211,000 ($0.12 per share). Retained earnings as of the beginning of 20X1 has been increased by $589,000 for the effect of retroactive application of the new method.

Example 41–10: Nonmarketable Investments Are Impaired and Written Down to Net Realizable Value

At December 31, 20X2, and December 31, 20X1, "Other long term investments" of $2,057,000 and $2,819,000, respectively, consist of nonmarketable investments in private companies and venture capital partnerships, which are carried at the lower of cost or net realizable value. The estimated aggregate fair value of these investments approximated their carrying amount. The fair values of these investments were estimated based on the most recent rounds of financing and securities transactions and on other pertinent information, including financial condition and operating results of the investees. The Company wrote-down certain investments by $762,000 in 20X2 and $604,000 in 20X1 to their estimated net realizable value due to deterioration in the investees' financial condition and the decision by the Company to liquidate its position in investments no longer meeting its overall strategic objectives.

Example 41–11: Company Discloses That It Is Not Practicable to Estimate the Fair Value of Its Nonmarketable Investment

It is not practicable to estimate the fair value of the Company's 11% investment in the common stock of Linkets, Inc., a producer of precision fasteners, because of the lack of quoted market prices and the inability to estimate fair value without incurring excessive costs. However, management believes that the carrying amount (on the cost method) of $1,571,000 at December 31, 20X2, and December 31, 20X1, was not impaired.

Example 41–12: Disclosure of Nature of Transactions between Company and Investee

The Company uses the equity method to account for its 39% investment in Coreson, Inc., a manufacturer of electrical and electronic products and systems. Included in accounts receivable of the Company at December 31, 20X2, and December 31, 20X1, are amounts due from Coreson, Inc. of $298,000 and $357,000, respectively. Included in accounts payable of the Company at December 31, 20X2, and December 31, 20X1, are amounts due to Coreson, Inc. of $481,000 and $517,000, respectively. Transactions with Coreson, Inc. consist of the following:

	20X2	20X1
Sales to Coreson, Inc.	$2,415,000	$2,074,000
Purchases from Coreson, Inc.	$6,712,000	$5,649,000

Example 41–13: Disclosure of Cumulative Unremitted Earnings and Dividends Received

The Company's investment in and advances to joint venture at December 31, 20X2, and December 31, 20X1, consists of its 25%

investment in Keset, Inc., a manufacturer of electronic components. The amount of cumulative unremitted earnings of this joint venture included in the Company's consolidated retained earnings at December 31, 20X2, was $3,892,000. During the years ended December 31, 20X2, and December 31, 20X1, distributions in the amounts of $600,000 and $550,000, respectively, were received from Keset, Inc.

Example 41–14: Company Has an Obligation to Guarantee Debt of Investee

The Company has an obligation to guarantee a pro rata share of debt incurred by Keeler, a joint venture in which the Company has a 45% interest, up to a maximum of $5,000,000. At December 31, 20X2, the Company has guaranteed the payment of $1,710,000 of the affiliate's indebtedness.

Example 41–15: Underlying Net Assets Exceed Investment Accounted for on the Equity Method—Excess Relates to Depreciable Assets

The Company's investment in and advances to joint venture at December 31, 20X2, and December 31, 20X1, consists of its 32% investment in Bisara, Co. a manufacturer of medical instruments, which is accounted for on the equity method. At December 31, 20X2, and December 31, 20X1, the Company's share of the underlying net assets of Bisara, Co. exceeded its investment by $1,543,000 and $1,807,000, respectively. The excess, which relates to certain property, plant, and equipment, is being amortized into income over the estimated remaining lives of the assets.

Example 41–16: Carrying Value of Investment Accounted for on the Equity Method Exceeds Underlying Net Assets—Excess Relates to Depreciable Assets

The Company accounts for its 29% investment in Kamas, Inc., an engineering and construction enterprise, under the equity method. At December 31, 20X2, and December 31, 20X1, the carrying value of the investment in Kamas, Inc. exceeded the Company's share of the underlying net assets of Kamas, Inc. by $1,123,000 and $1,207,000, respectively. The excess, which relates to certain property, plant, and equipment, is being amortized against the Company's share of Kamas, Inc.'s net income over the useful lives of the assets that gave rise to the difference.

Example 41–17: Excess of the Fair Value of the Assets Sold or Transferred to Investee over the Investor's Book Value Is Deferred and Amortized

The Company conducts some of its operations through various joint venture and other partnership forms that are accounted for using the equity method. When the Company sells or transfers assets to an affiliated company that is accounted for using the equity method and the affiliated company records the assets at fair value, the excess of the fair value of the assets over the Company's net book value is deferred and amortized over the expected lives of the assets. Deferred gains included in the Company's other liabilities were $135,000 and $102,000 at December 31, 20X2, and December 31, 20X1, respectively.

Example 41–18: Potential Conversion of Outstanding Convertible Securities and Exercise of Options and Warrants of Investee May Have a Significant Effect on Investor's Share of Reported Earnings

The Company has a 35% interest in Fadar, Inc. a producer of chemical-based materials, which is accounted for on the equity method. At December 31, 20X2, and December 31, 20X1, Fadar, Inc. had outstanding convertible securities, options, and warrants that, if in the aggregate were converted and exercised, would have reduced the Company's interest to 26% and, accordingly, would have reduced the Company's share of earnings in Fadar, Inc. for 20X2 and 20X1 by $195,000 and $167,000, respectively.

Example 41–19: Investor's Proportionate Share of Extraordinary Item Reported by Investee

The extraordinary item of $320,000 represents the Company's proportionate share of a gain realized in connection with [*describe*] by Kametz, Ltd., a manufacturer of electronic parts in which the Company has a 40% interest that is accounted for on the equity method. The Company has not provided any income tax related to its share of the extraordinary gain because it is the Company's intention to reinvest all undistributed earnings of Kametz, Ltd. indefinitely.

Note: The following table illustrates the portion of the Income Statement reflecting the Company's proportionate share of extraordinary item reported by Kametz, Ltd.

Income Statement Presentation

	20X2	20X1
Income before income taxes	$8,941,000	$7,916,000
Provision for income taxes	(3,576,000)	(3,287,000)
Income before equity in net income of affiliate and extraordinary item	5,365,000	4,629,000
Equity in net income of affiliate, excluding extraordinary gain of $320,000 in 20X2	554,000	716,000
Income before extraordinary item	5,919,000	5,345,000
Extraordinary item—equity in undistributed extraordinary gain of affiliate	320,000	-0-
Net income	$6,239,000	$5,345,000

Example 41–20: Gains on Issuance of Stock by Subsidiaries and Affiliates

At the time a subsidiary sells its stock to unrelated parties at a price in excess of its book value, the Company's net investment in that subsidiary increases. If at that time, the subsidiary is not a newly formed or newly acquired, non-operating entity, nor a research and development, start-up or development stage company, nor is there question as to the subsidiary's ability to continue in existence, the Company records the increase in its Consolidated Statement of Operations. Otherwise, the increase is reflected as additional paid-in-capital in the line item "Effect of subsidiaries' equity transactions" in the Company's Consolidated Statement of Stockholders' Equity.

If gains have been recognized on issuances of a subsidiary's stock and shares of the subsidiary are subsequently repurchased by the subsidiary or by the Company, gain recognition does not occur on issuance subsequent to the date of a repurchase until such time as shares have been issued in an amount equivalent to the number of repurchased shares. Such transactions are reflected as equity transactions, and the net effect of these transactions is reflected in the Consolidated Statement of Stockholders' Equity.

Example 41–21: Application of EITF 03-1 and FSP FAS 115-1 on Disclosures of Cost Method Investments in an Unrealized Loss Position That Are Not-Other-Than-Temporarily Impaired

> **Note:** To facilitate the illustration of narrative disclosures and for simplicity, this example presents only the quantitative information as of the date of the latest balance sheet. However,

GAAP requires the quantitative information to be presented as of each date for which a balance sheet is presented.

The following table shows the Company's cost method investments' gross unrealized losses and fair value, aggregated by length of time that individual securities have been in a continuous unrealized loss position, at December 31, 20X2:

Description of Securities	Less Than 12 Months		12 Months or More		Total	
	Fair Value	Unrealized Losses	Fair Value	Unrealized Losses	Fair Value	Unrealized Losses
Investments in equity securities carried at cost	$200,000	$10,000	$ -0-	$ -0-	$200,000	$10,000

The aggregate cost of the Company's cost method investments totaled $450,000 at December 31, 20X2. Investments with an aggregate cost of $100,000 were not evaluated for impairment because (a) the Company did not estimate the fair value of those investments in accordance with paragraphs 14 and 15 of FAS-107, *Disclosures about Fair Value of Financial Instruments,* and (b) the Company did not identify any events or changes in circumstances that may have had a significant adverse effect on the fair value of those investments. Of the remaining $350,000 cost of investments, the Company estimated that the fair value exceeded the cost of investments (i.e., the investments were not impaired) with an aggregate cost of $140,000. The remaining $210,000 of cost method investments consists of one investment in a privately owned company in the consumer tools and appliance industry. That investment was evaluated for impairment because of an adverse change in the market condition of companies in the consumer tools and appliance industry. As a result of that evaluation, the Company identified an unrealized loss of $10,000. The severity of the impairment (fair value is approximately 5% less than cost) and the duration of the impairment (less than 3 months) correlate with the weak 20X2 year-end sales experienced within the consumer tools and appliance industry, as reflected by lower customer transactions and lower-than-expected performance in traditional gift categories, such as hardware and power tools. Based on the Company's evaluation of the near-term prospects of the investee and the Company's ability and intent to hold the investment for a reasonable period of time sufficient for a forecasted recovery of fair value, the Company does not consider that investment to be other-than-temporarily impaired at December 31, 20X2.

CHAPTER 42
PROPERTY, PLANT, AND EQUIPMENT

CONTENTS

EXECUTIVE SUMMARY

Fixed assets (also referred to as *property, plant, and equipment; plant assets; capital assets; or tangible long-lived assets*) are used in production, distribution, and services by all enterprises. Examples include land, buildings, furniture, fixtures, machinery, equipment, and vehicles. The nature of the assets employed by a particular enterprise is determined by the nature of its activities.

Fixed assets have two primary characteristics:

1. They are acquired for use in operations and enter into the revenue-generating stream indirectly. They are held primarily for use, not for sale.

2. They have relatively long lives.

Generally accepted accounting principles (GAAP) generally require a fixed asset to be recorded at its cost, which includes all normal expenditures of readying an asset for its intended use. However, unnecessary expenditures that do not add to the utility of the asset are charged to expense.

The asset's cost, less any salvage value, is charged to expense (i.e., depreciated) over the asset's estimated useful life in a systematic and rational manner. Commonly used depreciation methods include straight-line, units of production, sum-of-the-years'-digits, and declining balance, although other methods may meet the criteria of *systematic* and *rational*.

If an entity constructs an asset for the entity's own use, the entity should capitalize the related interest cost incurred as part of the cost of the asset until the asset is substantially complete and ready for its intended use. Once the interest cost is capitalized, it should be depreciated in the same manner as other costs of the underlying asset.

For impairment and disposal of property, plant, and equipment, see Chapter 20, "Impairment and Disposal of Long-Lived Assets."

For capitalized leased assets, see Chapter 23, "Leases."

Asset Retirement Obligations

An entity may have a legal obligation for the retirement of a tangible long-lived asset. Such a legal obligation generally is the result of an existing or enacted law, statute, ordinance, or written or oral contract. An entity should recognize the fair value of a liability for an asset retirement obligation in the period in which the retirement obligation is incurred, if a reasonable estimate of fair value can be made. If such an estimate cannot be made in the period the asset retirement obligation is incurred, the liability should be recognized when the fair value can be reasonably estimated. Quoted market prices in active markets, if available, should be used to measure fair value. If quoted market prices are not available, fair value may be based on the best information available in the circumstances, including present value techniques.

When a liability is initially recognized for an asset retirement obligation, the entity should capitalize an asset retirement cost by increasing the carrying amount of the related long-lived asset by the same amount as the liability. Such cost should subsequently be charged to expense using a systematic and rational method over the asset's useful life.

After initial measurement, the liability for the asset retirement obligation should be adjusted for changes resulting from (1) the passage of time or (2) revisions to the timing or the amount of the original estimate of undiscounted cash flows. Changes due to the passage of time should first be incorporated into the carrying amount of the liability before adjusting for changes resulting from a revision of either the timing or the amount of estimated cash flows. Changes in the liability due to the passage of time should be measured by applying an interest method of allocation to the liability at the beginning of the period using the credit-adjusted risk-free interest rate that existed when the liability was initially measured. The amount of the change increases the carrying amount of the liability and the expense should be shown as an operating expense in the income statement (called *accretion expense*).

Changes resulting from revisions to the amount and/or timing of the original estimate of undiscounted cash flows should be recognized as an increase or decrease in the carrying amount of the liability and the related asset retirement cost capitalized. Upward revisions should be discounted using the current credit-adjusted risk-free rate. Downward revisions should be discounted using the credit-adjusted risk-free rate that existed when the original liability was recognized. When asset retirement costs change as a result of revisions to estimated cash flows, an entity should adjust the amount of asset retirement cost allocated to expense in the period of change if the change affects that period only, or in the period of change and future periods if the change affects more than one period.

Authoritative Literature

ARB-43   Chapter 9A, Depreciation and High Costs
Chapter 9C, Emergency Facilities—Depreciation, Amortization, and Income Taxes

APB-6	Status of Accounting Research Bulletins
APB-12	Omnibus Opinion—1967
FAS-34	Capitalization of Interest Cost
FAS-92	Regulated Enterprises—Accounting for Phase-in Plans
FAS-93	Recognition of Depreciation by Not-for-Profit Organizations
FAS-109	Accounting for Income Taxes
FAS-143	Accounting for Asset Retirement Obligations
FAS-144	Accounting for the Impairment or Disposal of Long-Lived Assets
FIN-47	Accounting for Conditional Asset Retirement Obligations
EITF 04-2	Whether Mineral Rights Are Tangible or Intangible Assets

DISCLOSURE REQUIREMENTS

Note: FASB Statement of Financial Accounting Standards No. 157 (FAS-157), *Fair Value Measurements*, expands disclosures about the use of fair value to measure assets and liabilities in interim and annual periods subsequent to initial recognition. It does not eliminate or modify the fair value disclosure requirements under other accounting pronouncements (e.g., Statement of Financial Accounting Standards No. 107 (FAS-107), *Disclosures about Fair Value of Financial Instruments*); rather, it encourages entities to combine the fair value information disclosed under FAS-157 with the fair value information disclosed under other such accounting pronouncements. See Chapter 14, "Fair Value Measurements," for additional disclosures of fair value that are required under FAS-157.

Depreciable Assets

1. The following disclosures of depreciable assets and depreciation are required in the financial statements or notes thereto (APB-12, par. 5):

   a. The basis of determining the amounts shown in the balance sheet, such as cost

   b. Balances of major classes of depreciable property presented by nature or function at the balance-sheet date

   c. Accumulated depreciation presented by major classes of assets or in total at the balance-sheet date

    d.   A description of the method(s) used to compute depreciation for major classes of depreciable assets

    e.   The amount of depreciation expense for each year for which an income statement is presented

2.   Property, plant, and equipment that is idle or held for sale should be identified and presented separately from property, plant, and equipment currently used in the business (generally accepted disclosure)

3.   The amount of interest capitalized as part of the cost of property, plant, and equipment should be disclosed (FAS-34, par. 21)

4.   Assets pledged as security for loans should be disclosed (FAS-5, par. 18)

5.   The following disclosures, although not required by GAAP, are in some cases made by companies when they are considered useful:

    a.   The accounting treatment for maintenance and repairs, betterments, and renewals

    b.   The policy for adjusting accumulated depreciation when property and equipment is disposed of, and the treatment of any gain or loss on disposition

    c.   The rates or lives used in computing depreciation

6.   The aggregate carrying amount of mineral rights should be reported as a separate component of property, plant, and equipment either on the face of the balance sheet or in the notes to the financial statements (EITF 04-2, par. 9)

For disclosure requirements relating to impairment of property, plant, and equipment, see Chapter 20, "Impairment and Disposal of Long-Lived Assets."

Asset Retirement Obligations

1.   The following information should be disclosed about an entity's asset retirement obligations (FAS-143, par. 22):

    a.   A general description of the asset retirement obligations and the associated long-lived assets

    b.   The fair value of assets that are legally restricted for purposes of settling asset retirement obligations

    c.   A reconciliation of the beginning and ending aggregate carrying amounts of asset retirement obligations showing separately the following (whenever there is a significant change in one or more of these components during the reporting period):

(1) Liabilities incurred in the current period

(2) Liabilities settled in the current period

(3) Accretion expense

(4) Revisions in estimated cash flows

    d. If the fair value of an asset retirement obligation cannot be reasonably estimated, that fact and the reasons for that should be disclosed

EXAMPLES OF FINANCIAL STATEMENT DISCLOSURES

The following sample disclosures are available on the accompanying disc. For additional information, see:

- Chapter 1, "Accounting Changes and Error Corrections," for disclosures required in connection with a change in depreciation methods or useful lives

- Chapter 2, "Accounting Policies," for additional examples of disclosures of property, plant, and equipment that are typically included as part of the company's general note on significant accounting policies

- Chapter 20, "Impairment and Disposal of Long-Lived Assets," for additional examples of disclosures relating to impairment of property, plant, and equipment

- Chapter 23, "Leases," for disclosures required by lessees and lessors of assets held under capitalized leases

Note: FAS-157, *Fair Value Measurements*, expands disclosures about the use of fair value to measure assets and liabilities in interim and annual periods subsequent to initial recognition. It does not eliminate or modify the fair value disclosure requirements under other accounting pronouncements (e.g., FAS-107, *Disclosures about Fair Value of Financial Instruments*); rather, it encourages entities to combine the fair value information disclosed under FAS-157 with the fair value information disclosed under other such accounting pronouncements. See Chapter 14, "Fair Value Measurements," for additional disclosures of fair value that are required under FAS-157.

Example 42–1: Basis for Recording Assets and Depreciation Methods

Property and equipment are recorded at cost. Depreciation is provided over the estimated useful lives of the related assets using the straight-line method for financial statement purposes. The

Company uses other depreciation methods (generally, accelerated depreciation methods) for tax purposes where appropriate. Amortization of leasehold improvements is computed using the straight-line method over the shorter of the remaining lease term or the estimated useful lives of the improvements.

Example 42–2: Different Methods of Depreciation Used for Depreciable Assets

Property, equipment, and special tools are stated at cost, less accumulated depreciation and amortization. Property and equipment placed in service before January 1, 19X6, are depreciated using an accelerated method that results in accumulated depreciation of approximately two-thirds of the asset cost during the first half of the estimated useful life of the asset. Property and equipment placed in service after December 31, 19X5, are depreciated using the straight-line method of depreciation over the estimated useful life of the asset. Special tools are amortized using an accelerated method over periods of time representing the estimated productive life of those tools.

Example 42–3: Estimated Service Lives of Property and Equipment Disclosed

The estimated service lives of property and equipment are principally as follows:

Buildings and improvements	3–40 years
Machinery and equipment	2–15 years
Computer software	2–5 years
Transportation vehicles	2–6 years

> **Note:** Disclosure of estimated service lives of property and equipment is not required by GAAP. However, in some cases companies disclose the information because it is considered useful.

Example 42–4: Policy for Repairs and Maintenance, Capitalization, and Disposal of Assets Disclosed

Repairs and maintenance are expensed as incurred. Expenditures that increase the value or productive capacity of assets are capitalized. When property and equipment are retired, sold, or otherwise disposed of, the asset's carrying amount and related accumulated depreciation are removed from the accounts and any gain or loss is included in operations.

Note: Disclosure of policy for repairs and maintenance, capitalization, and disposal of assets is not required by GAAP. However, in some cases companies disclose the information because it is considered useful.

Example 42–5: Review of Carrying Value of Property and Equipment for Impairment

The Company reviews the carrying value of property, plant, and equipment for impairment whenever events and circumstances indicate that the carrying value of an asset may not be recoverable from the estimated future cash flows expected to result from its use and eventual disposition. In cases where undiscounted expected future cash flows are less than the carrying value, an impairment loss is recognized equal to an amount by which the carrying value exceeds the fair value of assets. The factors considered by management in performing this assessment include current operating results, trends, and prospects, as well as the effects of obsolescence, demand, competition, and other economic factors.

Note: See Chapter 20, "Impairment and Disposal of Long-Lived Assets," for additional sample disclosures of impairment of property, plant, and equipment.

Example 42–6: Components of Property and Equipment Disclosed in a Note

The following is a summary of property and equipment, at cost less accumulated depreciation, at December 31:

	20X2	20X1
Land	$1,500,000	$1,500,000
Buildings and improvements	5,250,000	5,250,000
Data processing equipment	1,975,000	1,050,000
Furniture and fixtures	725,000	536,000
Purchased software	612,000	590,000
Internally developed software	388,000	410,000
Transportation equipment	347,000	213,000
Leasehold improvements	290,000	230,000
Construction in progress	200,000	100,000
	11,287,000	9,879,000
Less: accumulated depreciation	(2,804,000)	(2,091,000)
	$8,483,000	$7,788,000

Depreciation of property and equipment amounted to $713,000 for 20X2 and $671,000 for 20X1.

> **Note:** Alternatively, the components of property and equipment may be disclosed on the face of the balance sheet.

Example 42–7: Construction in Progress

Construction in progress is stated at cost, which includes the cost of construction and other direct costs attributable to the construction. No provision for depreciation is made on construction in progress until such time as the relevant assets are completed and put into use. Construction in progress at December 31, 20X2, represents machinery under installation.

Example 42–8: Property and Equipment Include Assets Acquired under Capital Leases

Property, plant, and equipment include gross assets acquired under capital leases of $493,000 and $414,0000 at December 31, 20X2, and December 31, 20X1, respectively. Related amortization included in accumulated depreciation was $251,000 and $176,000 at December 31, 20X2, and December 31, 20X1, respectively. Capital leases are included as a component of vehicles and equipment and machinery. Amortization of assets under capital leases is included in depreciation expense.

Example 42–9: Interest Cost Capitalized

The Company capitalizes interest cost incurred on funds used to construct property, plant, and equipment. The capitalized interest is recorded as part of the asset to which it relates and is amortized over the asset's estimated useful life. Interest cost capitalized was $315,000 and $268,000 in 20X2 and 20X1, respectively.

Example 42–10: Property Held for Sale

In July 20X2, the Company signed a letter of intent to sell substantially all its plant assets at its manufacturing facility in Cleveland, Ohio. These assets have been classified as "Property held for sale" in the Company's Balance Sheet.

Example 42–11: Commitment Required under Construction in Progress

The Company is constructing a new facility, which is scheduled to be completed in 20X4. As of December 31, 20X2, the Company incurred and capitalized in "Construction in progress" $1,600,000.

The estimated cost to be incurred in 20X3 and 20X4 to complete construction of the facility is approximately $12 million.

Example 42–12: Write-Down Recognized as a Result of Change in Policy for Replacing Property and Equipment

Effective October 1, 20X2, management approved a revision to the Company's policy of replacing certain transportation equipment and heavy duty machinery and equipment. Under the revised policy, the Company replaces transportation equipment after eight years, and heavy duty machinery and equipment after ten years. The previous policy was to not replace transportation equipment before it was a minimum of ten years old, and heavy duty machinery and equipment before they were a minimum of 12 years old. As a result of this decision, the Company recognized a write-down of $4,736,000 in 20X2 for those transportation equipment and heavy duty machinery and equipment scheduled for replacement in the next two years under the new policy. Depreciable lives were also adjusted effective October 1, 20X2, to reflect the new policy.

Example 42–13: Gain from Sale of Assets

In October 20X2, the Company sold its manufacturing plant building in Boise, Idaho, for $2,374,000. The net pretax gain from the sale was $1,693,000 and is included in "Gain from sale of assets" in the 20X2 Statement of Operations.

Example 42–14: Deferred Revenue on Sale of Plant and Equipment

In March 20X2, the Company sold its Toledo, Ohio, facility for approximately $16 million. The provisions of the contract state that the Company will continue to own and occupy the warehouse portion of the facility for a period of up to ten years (the "Reservation Period"). The contract also contains a buyout clause, at the buyer's option and under certain circumstances, of the remaining Reservation Period. Under the provisions of FASB Statement of Financial Accounting Standards (FAS) No. 66, *Accounting for Sales of Real Estate*, the Company is required to account for this as a financing transaction as the Company continues to have substantial involvement with the facility during the Reservation Period or until the buyout option is exercised. Under this method, the cash received is reflected as non-current deferred revenue, and the assets and the accumulated depreciation remain on the Company's books. Depreciation expense continues to be recorded each period, and imputed interest expense is also recorded and added to deferred revenue. Offsetting this is the imputed fair value lease income on the non-Company occupied portion of the building. A pretax gain, which will be recognized at the earlier of the exercise of the buyout option or the expiration of the Reservation Period, is estimated to be

$10 million to $12 million. The annual cost of operating the ware-house portion of the facility is not material.

Example 42–15: Asset Retirement Obligations

In accordance with Statement of Financial Accounting Standards No. 143 (FAS-143), *Accounting for Asset Retirement Obligations*, as interpreted by FASB Interpretation No. 47 (FIN-47), *Accounting for Conditional Asset Retirement Obligations*, the Company has recognized asset retirement obligations for the following activities: (1) demolition and remediation activities at manufacturing sites in the United States and Germany, and (2) obligations to remove lease-hold improvements at the conclusion of the Company's facility lease.

Asset retirement obligations are recorded in the period in which they are incurred and reasonably estimable, including those obligations for which the timing method of settlement are conditional on a future event that may or may not be within the control of the Company. Retirement of assets may involve such efforts as removal of leasehold improvements, contractually required demolition, and other related activities, depending on the nature and location of the assets. In identifying asset retirement obligations, the Company considers identification of legally enforceable obligations, changes in existing law, estimates of potential settlement dates, and the calculation of an appropriate discount rate to be used in calculating the fair value of the obligations. For those assets where a range of potential settlement dates may be reasonably estimated, obligations are recorded. The Company routinely reviews and reassesses its estimates to determine if an adjustment to the value of the asset retirement obligation is required.

Adoption of FIN-47 on December 31, 20X1 resulted in the recognition of an asset retirement obligation of $5,000,000 and a charge of $3,000,000 (net of tax of $1,050,000), which was included in "Cumulative effect of change in accounting principle." In accordance with FIN-47, the Company has recognized conditional asset retirement obligations related to (e.g., contractual obligation to remove leasehold improvements at the conclusion of the Company's facility lease; the cost of abandoning wells, well-site cleanup, facilities abandonment, and environmental closure and post-closure care). At December 31, 20X2, the aggregate carrying amount of conditional asset retirement obligations recognized by the Company was $7,200,000 ($5,000,000 at December 31, 20X1). The discount rate used to calculate the Company's asset retirement obligations was 5.2%. These obligations are included in the balance sheets as "Other non-current obligations."

If the conditional asset retirement obligation measurement and recognition provisions of FIN-47 had been in effect on January 1, 20X1, the aggregate carrying amount of those obligations on that date would have been $4,500,000. If the amortization of asset retirement cost and accretion of asset retirement obligation provisions of

FIN-47 had been in effect during 20X1, the impact on "Income before cumulative effect of change in accounting principle" and "Net-income" would have been immaterial.

The aggregate carrying amount of asset retirement obligations recognized by the Company was $11,010,000 at December 31, 20X2 and $9,200,000 at December 31, 20X1. The following table shows changes in the aggregate carrying amount of the Company's asset retirement obligations for the year ended December 31, 20X2:

Balance, January 1, 20X2	$ 9,200,000
Additional accruals	2,500,000
Liabilities settled	(1,250,000)
Accretion expense	475,000
Revisions in estimated cash flows	85,000
Balance, December 31, 20X2	$11,010,000

CHAPTER 43
INTANGIBLE ASSETS

CONTENTS

EXECUTIVE SUMMARY

Intangible assets are assets that lack physical substance. Many kinds of intangible assets may be identified and given reasonably descriptive names such as patents, franchises, trademarks, customer lists and the like. Other types of intangible assets are unidentifiable, such as goodwill.

Intangible Assets Other Than Goodwill

Intangible assets that are acquired individually or as part of a group of assets, other than those acquired in a business combination, are initially recorded at their fair value. The cost of a group of assets acquired in a transaction is allocated to the individual assets based on their relative fair values. Goodwill does not arise in such a transaction. Intangible assets that are acquired in a business combination are accounted for in accordance with FASB Statement of Financial Accounting Standards (FAS) No. 141, *Business Combinations*, as discussed in Chapter 4, "Business Combinations." The costs of intangible assets that are developed internally, as well as the costs of maintaining or restoring intangible assets that have indeterminate lives or that are inherent in a continuing business and related to the entity as a whole, are expensed as incurred.

The accounting for intangible assets, other than goodwill, subsequent to acquisition is based on the asset's useful life. The useful life of the intangible asset is the period over which the asset is expected to contribute directly or indirectly to the entity's future cash flows. An asset for which no legal, regulatory, contractual, competitive, economic, or other factors limit its useful life is considered to have an indefinite useful life. The accounting requirements are as follows:

1. *Intangible assets subject to amortization*—The cost of a recognized intangible asset, less its residual value to the reporting entity, should be amortized over its useful life unless that life is determined to be indefinite. If the life is finite, but the precise length of that life is not known, the best estimate of the asset's useful life should be used for amortization purposes. The method of amortization should be the pattern in which

the economic benefits are consumed or otherwise used up. If that pattern cannot be reliably determined, the straight-line method should be used. An intangible asset should not be written down or written off in the period of acquisition unless it becomes impaired during that period. An intangible asset's remaining useful life should be reviewed during each period to determine if the remaining amortization period should be revised. If a revision is deemed necessary, the remaining carrying amount of the intangible asset should be amortized prospectively over the revised remaining useful life. Also, an intangible asset that is subject to amortization should be reviewed for impairment in accordance with FAS-144 (Accounting for the Impairment or Disposal of Long-Lived Assets), as discussed in Chapter 20, "Impairment and Disposal of Long-Lived Assets."

2. *Intangible assets not subject to amortization*—If an intangible asset is determined to have an indefinite useful life, it should not be amortized until its useful life is determined to be no longer indefinite. The asset's remaining useful life should be reviewed each reporting period. If such an asset is later determined to have a finite useful life, the asset should be tested for impairment. That asset should then be amortized prospectively over its estimated remaining useful life and accounted for in the same way as intangible assets subject to amortization. An intangible asset that is not subject to amortization should be tested for impairment at least annually.

Regardless of whether an intangible asset is subject to amortization, if an impairment loss is recognized, the adjusted carrying amount of the intangible asset should become its new accounting basis. Subsequent reversal of a previously recognized impairment loss is prohibited.

Goodwill

Goodwill should not be amortized; rather, it should be tested for impairment at a level of reporting referred to as a *reporting unit*. A reporting unit is an operating segment or one level below an operating segment (referred to as a component), as defined in FAS-131, *Disclosures about Segments of an Enterprise and Related Information*. An entity must test goodwill at the reporting unit level, even if it is not subject to the segment information reporting requirements of FAS-131.

Assessing goodwill for impairment involves the following two steps:

1. Identify potential impairment by comparing the fair value of a reporting unit with its carrying value, including goodwill. If the fair value is less than the recorded amount, impairment exists and the test in step 2 below should be performed. If the fair value is greater than the recorded amount, goodwill is not impaired (and the second step below is not necessary).

2. Measure the amount of the impairment loss by comparing the implied fair value of the reporting unit's goodwill with its carrying amount. The implied fair value of goodwill should be determined in the same way that goodwill is recognized in a business combination; that is, the implied fair value is the excess of the fair value of the reporting unit over the amounts assigned to the reporting unit's assets and liabilities. If the carrying amount of the reporting unit's goodwill is greater than the implied fair value, an impairment loss equal to the difference should be recognized. Subsequent reversals of recognized impairment losses are prohibited.

Once the initial determination of the fair value of a reporting unit is made, that value may be carried forward to the next year if certain criteria are met. Goodwill should be tested for impairment at least annually, or more frequently if events and circumstances change. Goodwill also should be tested for impairment after a portion of goodwill has been allocated to a business to be disposed of.

For purposes of testing goodwill for impairment, all goodwill that is acquired in a business combination must be assigned to one or more reporting units as of the acquisition date. Goodwill may be assigned to reporting units on the basis of expected benefits from the synergies of the combination, even though other assets or liabilities of the acquired entity may not be assigned to those reporting units.

When an entire reporting unit is to be disposed of, that unit's goodwill should be included in the unit's carrying amount in determining any gain or loss on disposal. When a portion of a reporting unit that constitutes a business is to be disposed of, goodwill associated with that business should be included in the business' carrying amount in determining the gain or loss on disposal. The amount of the related goodwill should be allocated based on the relative fair values of the business to be disposed of and the portion of the reporting unit that will be retained.

Authoritative Literature

FAS-109   Accounting for Income Taxes

FAS-141   Business Combinations

FAS-142   Goodwill and Other Intangible Assets

FAS-144   Accounting for the Impairment or Disposal of Long-Lived Assets

DISCLOSURE REQUIREMENTS

Note: FASB Statement of Financial Accounting Standards No. 157 (FAS-157), *Fair Value Measurements*, expands disclosures about the use of fair value to measure assets and liabilities in interim and annual periods subsequent to initial recognition. It does not eliminate or modify the fair value disclosure requirements under other accounting pronouncements (e.g., Statement of Financial Accounting Standards No. 107 (FAS-107), *Disclosures about Fair Value of Financial Instruments*); rather, it encourages entities to combine the fair value information disclosed under FAS-157 with the fair value information disclosed under other such accounting pronouncements. See Chapter 14, "Fair Value Measurements," for additional disclosures of fair value that are required under FAS-157.

1. For intangible assets (other than goodwill) acquired either individually or with a group of assets, the following disclosures should be made in the period of acquisition (FAS-142, par. 44):

   a. For intangible assets subject to amortization:

      (1) The total amount assigned and the amount assigned to any major intangible asset class

      (2) The amount of any significant residual value, in total and by major intangible asset class

      (3) The weighted-average amortization period, in total and by major intangible asset class

   b. For intangible assets *not* subject to amortization, the total amount assigned and the amount assigned to any major intangible asset class

   c. The amount of research and development assets acquired and written off in the period, and the line item in the income statement in which the amounts written off are aggregated

2. The following disclosures should be made for each period for which a balance sheet is presented (FAS-142, par. 45):

   a. For intangible assets subject to amortization:

      (1) The gross carrying amount and accumulated amortization, in total and by major intangible asset class

      (2) The aggregate amortization expense for the period

    (3) The estimated aggregate amortization expense for each of the five succeeding years

  b. For intangible assets (other than goodwill) not subject to amortization, the total carrying amount and the carrying amount for each major intangible asset class

  c. Changes in the carrying amount of goodwill during the period, including:

    (1) The aggregate amount of goodwill acquired

    (2) The aggregate amount of impairment losses recognized

    (3) The amount of goodwill included in the gain or loss on disposal of all or a portion of a reporting unit

    (4) For entities that report segment information in accordance with FAS-131 (Disclosures about Segments of an Enterprise and Related Information), such entities should disclose the above information about goodwill in total and for each reportable segment, and any significant changes in the allocation of goodwill by reportable segment. If any portion of goodwill has not been allocated to a reporting unit at the date the financial statements are issued, that unallocated amount and the reasons for not allocating it should be disclosed.

3. For each impairment loss recognized related to an intangible asset (other than goodwill), the following disclosures should be made in the period in which the impairment loss is recognized (FAS-142, par. 46):

  a. A description of the impaired intangible asset, and the facts and circumstances leading to the impairment

  b. The amount of the impairment loss and the method for determining fair value

  c. The caption in the income statement in which the impairment loss is aggregated

  d. The segment in which the impaired intangible asset is reported under FAS-131, if applicable

4. For each goodwill impairment loss recognized, the following disclosures should be made in the period in which the impairment loss is recognized (FAS-142, par. 47):

  a. A description of the facts and circumstances leading to the impairment

  b. The amount of the impairment loss and the method for determining the fair value of the associated reporting unit (e.g., quoted market prices, prices of comparable businesses, present value, other valuation technique)

c. If a recognized impairment loss is an estimate that has not yet been finalized, that fact and the reasons for using an estimate; and, in subsequent periods, the nature and amount of any significant adjustments made to the initial estimate of the impairment loss

EXAMPLES OF FINANCIAL STATEMENT DISCLOSURES

The following sample disclosures are available on the accompanying disc.

Note: FAS-157, *Fair Value Measurements*, expands disclosures about the use of fair value to measure assets and liabilities in interim and annual periods subsequent to initial recognition. It does not eliminate or modify the fair value disclosure requirements under other accounting pronouncements (e.g., FAS-107, *Disclosures about Fair Value of Financial Instruments*); rather, it encourages entities to combine the fair value information disclosed under FAS-157 with the fair value information disclosed under such other accounting pronouncements. See Chapter 14, "Fair Value Measurements," for additional disclosures of fair value that are required under FAS-157.

Example 43–1: Disclosure of Acquired Intangible Assets in the Period of Acquisition

Note: This example assumes that, in connection with a business combination, the Company allocated $10 million of the purchase price to intangible assets (other than goodwill). For simplicity, background information about the business combination and the related disclosures required for business combinations are not presented in this example. See Chapter 4, "Business Combinations," for detailed illustrative disclosures for business combinations.

In December 20X2, the Company completed the purchase of MBK, Inc. a privately held manufacturer of industrial computer systems and enclosures. The assets acquired included $10 million of intangible assets, other than goodwill. Of the $10 million of acquired intangible assets, $5 million was assigned to registered trademarks that are not subject to amortization and $2 million was assigned to research and development assets that were written off at the date of acquisition in accordance with FASB Interpretation No. 4, *Applicability of FASB Statement No. 2 to Business Combinations Accounted for by the Purchase Method*. Those write-offs are included in general and administrative expenses. The remaining $3 million of acquired intangible assets have a weighted-average useful life of approximately four years. The intangible assets that make up that amount include: computer software of $ 1.6 million (three-year weighted-average useful life), patents of $900,000 (seven-year weighted-average useful life), and other assets of $500,000 (fiveyear weighted-average useful life).

Example 43–2: Disclosure of Acquired Intangible Assets in the Periods Subsequent to a Business Combination

> **Note:** This example assumes that the business combination was completed in 20X0. In accordance with FAS-142, this example illustrates the disclosures for acquired intangible assets that are required to be made in the Company's December 31, 20X2 and 20X1, financial statements (the years subsequent to the business combination).

As of December 31, 20X2 and December 31, 20X1, the Company has the following amounts related to intangible assets:

	December 31, 20X2		December 31, 20X1	
	Gross Carrying Amount	Accumulated Amortization	Gross Carrying Amount	Accumulated Amortization
Amortized intangible assets:				
Trademark	$1,078,000	$ (66,000)	$1,078,000	$ (38,000)
Unpatented technology	475,000	(380,000)	375,000	(220,000)
Other	90,000	(30,000)	90,000	(18,000)
Total	$1,643,000	$(476,000)	$1,543,000	$(276,000)
Unamortized intangible assets:				
Broadcast licenses	$1,400,000		$1,200,000	
Trademark	600,000		450,000	
Total	$2,000,000		$1,650,000	

No significant residual value is estimated for these intangible assets. Aggregate amortization expense for the years ended December 31, 20X2 and December 31, 20X1, totaled $200,000 and $180,000, respectively. The following table represents the total estimated amortization of intangible assets for the five succeeding years:

For the Year Ending December 31	Estimated Amortization Expense
20X3	$199,000
20X4	$ 74,000
20X5	$ 74,000
20X6	$ 64,000
20X7	$ 54,000

Example 43–3: Disclosure of Goodwill Information in the Period Subsequent to a Business Combination

Note: This example assumes that the business combination was completed in 20X1. In accordance with FAS-142, this example illustrates the disclosures for goodwill that are required to be made in the Company's December 31, 20X2, financial statements (the year subsequent to the business combination). Also, this example assumes that the Company has two reporting units with goodwill—Technology and Communications—which are also reportable segments.

The changes in the carrying amount of goodwill for the year ended December 31, 20X2, are as follows:

	Technology Segment	Communications Segment	Total
Balance as of January 1, 20X2	$1,413,000	$904,000	$2,317,000
Goodwill acquired during the year	189,000	115,000	304,000
Impairment losses	-0-	(46,000)	(46,000)
Goodwill written off related to sale of business unit	(484,000)	-0-	(484,000)
Balance as of December 31, 20X2	$1,118,000	$973,000	$2,091,000

The fair value of the Communications segment is tested for impairment in the third quarter, after the annual forecasting process. Due to an increase in competition in the California and Arizona cable industry, operating profits and cash flows were lower than expected in the fourth quarter of 20X1 and the first and second quarters of 20X2. Based on that trend, the earnings forecast for the next five years was revised. In September 20X2, a goodwill impairment loss of $46,000 was recognized in the Communications reporting unit. The fair value of that reporting unit was estimated using the expected present value of future cash flows.

Example 43–4: Components of Intangible Assets Disclosed in a Note

Intangible assets consist of the following at December 31:

	20X2	20X1
Patents	$ 450,000	$ 370,000
Trademarks	300,000	210,000
Trade names	415,000	300,000
Copyrights	175,000	175,000
Intellectual property	420,000	225,000
Customer lists	790,000	620,000
Non-compete agreements	600,000	300,000
	3,150,000	2,200,000
Less: accumulated amortization	(1,440,000)	(1,090,000)
Net intangible assets	$1,710,000	$1,110,000

Amortization of intangible assets amounted to $350,000 for 20X2 and $270,000 for 20X1.

> **Note:** Alternatively, the components of intangible assets may be disclosed on the face of the balance sheet.

Example 43–5: Accounting Policy for Impairment of Goodwill

The Company evaluates the carrying value of goodwill during the fourth quarter of each year and between annual evaluations if events occur or circumstances change that would more likely than not reduce the fair value of the reporting unit below its carrying amount. Such circumstances could include, but are not limited to: (1) a significant adverse change in legal factors or in business climate, (2) unanticipated competition, or (3) an adverse action or assessment by a regulator. When evaluating whether goodwill is impaired, the Company compares the fair value of the reporting unit to which the goodwill is assigned to the reporting unit's carrying amount, including goodwill. The fair value of the reporting unit is estimated using a combination of the income, or discounted cash flows, approach and the market approach, which utilizes comparable companies' data. If the carrying amount of a reporting unit exceeds its fair value, then the amount of the impairment loss must be measured. The impairment loss would be calculated by comparing the implied fair value of reporting unit goodwill to its carrying amount. In calculating the implied fair value of reporting unit goodwill, the fair value of the reporting unit is allocated to all of the other assets and liabilities of that unit based on their fair values. The excess of the fair value of a reporting unit over the amount assigned to its other assets and liabilities is the implied fair value of goodwill. An impairment loss would be recognized when the carrying amount of goodwill exceeds its implied fair value. The Company's evaluation of goodwill completed during the year resulted in no impairment losses.

> **Note:** See Chapter 20, "Impairment and Disposal of Long-Lived Assets" for additional sample disclosures.

Example 43–6: Accounting Policy for Impairment of Intangible Assets

The Company evaluates the recoverability of identifiable intangible assets whenever events or changes in circumstances indicate that an intangible asset's carrying amount may not be recoverable. Such circumstances could include, but are not limited to: (1) a significant decrease in the market value of an asset, (2) a significant adverse change in the extent or manner in which an asset is used, or (3) an accumulation of costs significantly in excess of the amount originally expected for the acquisition of an asset. The Company measures the carrying amount of the asset against the estimated undiscounted future cash flows associated with it. Should the sum of the expected future net cash flows be less than the carrying value of the asset being evaluated, an impairment loss would be recognized. The impairment loss would be calculated as the amount by which the carrying value of the asset exceeds its fair value. The fair value is measured based on quoted market prices, if available. If quoted market prices are not available, the estimate of fair value is based on various valuation techniques, including the discounted value of estimated future cash flows. The evaluation of asset impairment requires the Company to make assumptions about future cash flows over the life of the asset being evaluated. These assumptions require significant judgment and actual results may differ from assumed and estimated amounts. During the year ended December 31, 20X2, the Company recorded an impairment loss of $620,000 related to an intangible asset (see Note X).

> **Note:** See Chapter 20, "Impairment and Disposal of Long-Lived Assets" for additional sample disclosures.

Example 43–7: Accounting Policy for Patents

Patents are initially measured based on their fair values. Patents are being amortized on a straight-line basis over a period of 10 to 25 years and are stated net of accumulated amortization of $195,000 and $173,000 at December 31, 20X2, and 20X1, respectively. Amortization expense charged to operations was $22,000 for 20X2 and $19,000 for 20X1.

Example 43–8: Accounting Policy for Trademarks

Trademarks are initially measured based on their fair values. Trademarks are being amortized on a straight-line basis over a period of 5 to 15 years and are stated at cost net of accumulated amortization of $213,000 and $184,000 at December 31, 20X2, and 20X1, respectively. Amortization expense charged to operations was $29,000 for 20X2 and $24,000 for 20X1.

Example 43–9: Accounting Policy for Organization Costs

Organization costs, including legal fees, are expensed as incurred. Organization costs charged to operations totaled $23,000 and $12,000 for 20X2 and 20X1, respectively.

Example 43–10: Accounting Policy for Deferred Financing Costs

Costs relating to obtaining the mortgage debt and the Industrial Revenue Bond financing are capitalized and amortized over the term of the related debt using the straight-line method. Accumulated amortization at December 31, 20X2, and 20X1, was $38,000 and $29,000, respectively. Amortization of deferred financing costs charged to operations was $9,000 for 20X2 and $7,000 for 20X1. When a loan is paid in full, any unamortized financing costs are removed from the related accounts and charged to operations.

Example 43–11: Amount Initially Assigned to Goodwill in Business Combination Subsequently Revised

In October 20X1, the Company acquired XDEG, Inc., a leading provider of health care information products. The Company issued 3,000,000 shares of common stock and 700,000 common stock options with a total fair value of $35,000,000 in exchange for all outstanding shares of XDEG, Inc. The Company accounted for the acquisition using the purchase method of accounting for business combinations. The purchase price and costs associated with the acquisition exceeded the preliminary estimated fair value of net assets acquired by $10,200,000, which was preliminarily assigned to goodwill.

During 20X2, the Company completed the valuation of the intangible assets acquired in the XDEG, Inc. transaction. Pursuant to the valuation, the Company expensed $4,400,000 of the excess purchase price representing purchased in-process technology that previously had been assigned to goodwill. In management's judgment, this amount reflects the amount the Company would reasonably expect to pay an unrelated party for each project included in the technology. The value of in-process research and development of $4,400,000 represented approximately 37% of the purchase price and was determined by estimating the costs to develop the purchased technology into commercially viable products, then estimating the resulting net cash flows from each project that was incomplete at the acquisition date, and discounting the resulting net cash flows to their present value. The $4,400,000 charge is included as a component of "Other Charges" in the accompanying Consolidated Statements of Operations for the year ended December 31, 20X2. Based on the final valuation, the remaining excess purchase price of $5,800,000 was assigned to existing technologies, trade names and goodwill.

Example 43–12: Covenant Not to Compete Agreements

Covenant not to compete (net) of $623,000 and $823,000 at December 31, 20X2 and 20X1, respectively, represents the portion of the purchase price associated with the 20X1 acquisition of Baysol Co. allocated to noncompetition agreements. Under these agreements, the former stockholders of Baysol Co. agreed not to compete with the Company for a period of five years. The related cost is being amortized on the straight-line method over the terms of the agreements. Accumulated amortization related to the covenant not to compete agreements totaled $377,000 and $177,000 at December 31, 20X2 and 20X1, respectively. Amortization expense charged to operations was $200,000 for 20X2 and $177,000 for 20X1.

Example 43–13: License Agreement

In 20X2, the Company entered into an agreement to license the rights to certain laboratory equipment developed and manufactured by another company. The purchase price paid for the license was $400,000 in cash which represents its fair value. This amount was recorded as an intangible asset and is being amortized over the period of its estimated benefit period of 10 years. At December 31, 20X2, accumulated amortization was $30,000. Under the terms of the agreement, the Company is also required to pay royalties, as defined, to the licensors semiannually.

Example 43–14: Patent Acquisition

In 20X0, the Company acquired certain patents pertaining to technology incorporated into certain of the Company's products. The Company paid approximately $1,975,000 for these patents and related expenses upon entering into the agreement. In April 20X2, this agreement was amended such that the Company paid approximately $1,215,000 for additional patent rights and related expenses.

The fair values of these patents is being amortized over their expected life of 10 years.

Example 43–15: Debt Issuance Costs Written Off Against Additional Paid-in Capital

Specific costs related to the Company's convertible debt offering in September 20X1 were capitalized upon issuance of the debt and are being amortized to interest expense using the effective interest rate method over the five-year term of the debt. Upon conversion of $8.3 million of the convertible debt in April 20X2, approximately $260,000 of debt issuance costs were written off against additional paid-in capital. As of December 31, 20X2, the remaining debt issuance costs of $55,000 are classified in other assets on the Balance Sheet.

Example 43–16: Impairment Charge Related to Trademarks

The Company performed, with the assistance of independent valuation experts, an impairment test of the carrying value of the XYZ Trademarks to determine whether any impairment existed. The Company determined that the sum of the expected undiscounted cash flows attributable to the XYZ Trademarks was less than its carrying value and that an impairment write-down was required. Accordingly, the Company calculated the estimated fair value of the intangible asset by summing the present value of the expected cash flows over its life. The impairment was calculated by deducting the present value of the expected cash flows from the carrying value. This assessment resulted in an impairment write-down of $1,050,000, which was included in "Impairment charges" in the accompanying Statement of Operations for the year ended December 31, 20X2.

CHAPTER 44
OTHER ASSETS: CURRENT AND NONCURRENT

CONTENTS

EXECUTIVE SUMMARY

Rarely is the nature of other assets appearing in the current or noncurrent asset sections of an entity's balance sheet disclosed in the financial statements. This is generally because such assets are not material to the financial statements taken as a whole. Typically, other assets include items such as prepaid expenses, deferred charges, and deposits. However, if several other assets are included as a single line item in the balance sheet, it is generally informative to include the details of such items in a note to the financial statements.

Other assets generally have one main characteristic: They represent costs and expenditures that are expected to benefit future periods. They include payments in advance for services to be rendered to the entity by others in the future. Therefore, if a current expenditure has an economic benefit obtainable in a future period and is quantifiable, the expenditure most likely qualifies to be reported as an other asset in the financial statements.

Some items in the other assets category are sufficiently important in specific financial statement contexts and have already been covered in other chapters. This chapter includes only examples of the most common types of other assets, current and noncurrent, found in practice that have not already been addressed in other chapters.

Authoritative Literature

ARB-43	Chapter 3A, Current Assets and Current Liabilities
APB-10	Omnibus Opinion—1966
APB-12	Omnibus Opinion—1967

DISCLOSURE REQUIREMENTS

If other assets are material to the financial statements, the following generally accepted disclosures should be made: ·

1. A description of the asset and the basis of its valuation
2. If applicable, the method of amortization, the amortization period, the amount of amortization expense, and the accumulated amortization

EXAMPLES OF FINANCIAL STATEMENT DISCLOSURES

 The following sample disclosures are available on the accompanying disc.

Example 44–1: Prepaid Expenses

Prepaid expenses comprise the following at December 31, 20X2, and December 31, 20X1:

	20X2	20X1
Royalty advances	$132,000	$116,000
Prepaid insurance	92,000	85,000
Prepaid advertising costs	74,000	48,000
Prepaid rent	29,000	27,000
Prepaid taxes	20,000	25,000
Other prepaid expenses	14,000	12,000
	$361,000	$313,000

Example 44–2: Deposits

At December 31, 20X2, the Company has deposits with vendors totaling $100,000 for the purchase of machinery and equipment.

Example 44–3: Deferred Advertising Costs

Direct response advertising costs, consisting primarily of catalog book production, printing, and postage costs, are capitalized and amortized over the expected life of the catalog, not to exceed six months. Prepaid expenses at December 31, 20X2, and December 31, 20X1, include deferred advertising costs of $275,000 and $350,000, respectively. Total advertising expenses were $1,900,000 and $1,600,000 in 20X2 and 20X1, respectively.

> **Note:** For additional examples of disclosures relating to advertising costs, see Chapter 3, "Advertising Costs."

Example 44–4: Deferred Financing Costs

Costs relating to obtaining the mortgage debt and the Industrial Revenue Bond financing are capitalized and amortized over the term of the related debt using the straight-line method. Accumulated amortization at December 31, 20X2, and December 31, 20X1, was $38,000 and $29,000, respectively. Amortization of deferred financing costs charged to operations was $9,000 for 20X2 and $7,000 for 20X1. When a loan is paid in full, any unamortized financing costs are removed from the related accounts and charged to operations.

Example 44–5: Organization Costs

Organization costs, including legal fees, are expensed as incurred. Organization costs charged to operations totaled $23,000 and $12,000 for 20X2 and 20X1, respectively.

Example 44–6: Covenant Not to Compete Agreements

Covenant not to compete (net) of $623,000 and $823,000 at December 31, 20X2, and December 31, 20X1, respectively, represents the portion of the purchase price associated with the 20X1 acquisition of Baysol Co. allocated to noncompetition agreements. Under these agreements, the former stockholders of Baysol Co. agreed not to compete with the Company for a period of five years. The related cost is being amortized on the straight-line method over the terms of the agreements. Accumulated amortization related to the covenant not to compete agreements totaled $377,000 and $177,000 at

December 31, 20X2, and December 31, 20X1, respectively. Amortization expense charged to operations was $200,000 for 20X2 and $177,000 for 20X1.

Example 44–7: Cash Surrender Value of Life Insurance, Net of Policy Loans

The Company has purchased insurance on the lives of certain key executive officers. As beneficiary, the Company receives the cash surrender value if the policy is terminated and, upon death of the insured, receives all benefits payable. Cash value of life insurance is reported in the financial statements net of policy loans. The loans carry interest at a rate of 6.5%, require interest only payments annually, and are collateralized by the cash value of the policies. A summary of "Net cash value of life insurance" as reported in the accompanying Balance Sheets at December 31, 20X2, and December 31, 20X1, is as follows:

	20X2	20X1
Cash surrender value of life insurance	$1,156,000	$1,005,000
Policy loans balances outstanding	(418,000)	(329,000)
Net cash value of life insurance	$ 738,000	$ 676,000

Example 44–8: Life Insurance Contracts Used to Fund Deferred Compensation Plan

The Company has a deferred compensation plan that permits management and highly compensated employees to defer portions of their compensation and earn a guaranteed interest rate on the deferred amounts. The salaries that have been deferred since the plan's inception have been accrued and the only expense, other than salaries, related to this plan is the interest on the deferred amounts. Interest expense during 20X2 and 20X1 includes $103,000 and $68,000, respectively, related to this plan. The Company has included in "Deferred employee benefits" $1,150,000 and $935,000 at December 31, 20X2, and December 31, 20X1, respectively, to reflect its liability under this plan. To fund this plan, the Company purchases corporate-owned whole-life insurance contracts on the related employees. The Company has included in "Other assets" $1,200,000 and $967,000 at December 31, 20X2, and December 31, 20X1, respectively, which represents cash surrender value of these policies.

CHAPTER 45
INCOME TAXES

CONTENTS

EXECUTIVE SUMMARY

The tax consequences of many transactions recognized in the financial statements are included when determining income taxes currently payable in the same accounting period. Sometimes, tax laws differ from the recognition and measurement requirements of financial reporting standards. Differences arise between the tax bases of assets or liabilities and their reported amounts in the financial statements. These differences are called *temporary differences* and they give rise to deferred tax assets and liabilities.

Temporary differences ordinarily reverse when the related asset is recovered or the related liability is settled. A *deferred tax liability* or *deferred tax asset* represents the increase or decrease in taxes payable or refundable in future years as a result of temporary differences and carryforwards at the end of the current year.

The objectives of accounting for income taxes are to recognize:

- The amount of taxes payable or refundable for the current year

- The deferred tax liabilities and assets that result from future tax consequences of events that have been recognized in the enterprise's financial statements or tax returns

To implement these objectives, the following basic principles should be observed at the date of the financial statements:

1. Recognize a *tax liability* or *asset* for the amount of taxes currently payable or refundable.

2. Recognize a *deferred tax liability* or *asset* for the estimated future tax effects of temporary differences or carryforwards.

3. Measure *current* and *deferred tax assets* and *liabilities* based on provisions of enacted tax laws.

4. Reduce the amount of any deferred *tax assets* by a valuation allowance, if necessary, based on available evidence.

The following are exceptions to these basic principles:

1. Certain exceptions to the requirements for recognition of deferred tax assets and liabilities for the areas addressed by Accounting Principles Board Opinion No. 23, *Accounting for Income Taxes—Special Areas*, as amended by FASB Statement of Financial Accounting Standards (FAS) No. 109, *Accounting for Income Taxes*, paragraphs 31–34, notably the investments in foreign subsidiaries and joint ventures

2. Special transitional procedures for temporary differences related to deposits in statutory reserve funds by U.S. steamship enterprises

3. Accounting for leveraged leases as required by FAS-13, *Accounting for Leases*, and FASB Interpretation No. 21, *Accounting for Leases in a Business Combination*

4. Prohibition of the recognition of a deferred tax liability or asset related to goodwill for which amortization is not deductible for tax purposes

5. Accounting for income taxes under Accounting Research Bulletin No. 51, *Consolidated Financial Statements*

6. Prohibition of the recognition of a deferred tax liability or asset for differences related to assets and liabilities accounted for under FAS-52, *Foreign Currency Translation*

The emphasis placed on the balance sheet by the asset/liability method of accounting for income taxes is evident from the focus on the recognition of deferred tax liabilities and assets. The change in these liabilities and assets is combined with the income taxes currently payable or refundable to determine income tax expense.

The following five steps are required to complete the annual computation of deferred tax liabilities and assets:

1. Identify the types and amounts of existing temporary differences and the nature and amount of each type of operating loss and tax credit carryforward and the remaining length of the carryforward period.

2. Measure the total deferred tax liability for taxable temporary differences using the applicable tax rate.

3. Measure the total deferred tax asset for deductible temporary differences and operating loss carryforwards using the applicable tax rate.

4. Measure deferred tax assets for each type of tax credit carryforward.

5. Reduce deferred tax assets by a valuation allowance if it is more likely than not that some or all of the deferred tax assets will not be realized.

Determining the need for and calculating the amount of the valuation allowance requires the following steps at the end of each accounting period:

1. Determine the amount of the deferred tax asset recognized on each deductible temporary difference, operating loss, and tax credit carryforward. These are not offset by the deferred tax liability on taxable temporary differences.

2. Assess the sources of future taxable income that may be available to recognize the deductible differences and carryforwards by considering the following:

   a. Future reversals of existing taxable temporary differences

   b. Taxable income in prior carryback year(s) if carryback is permitted under tax law

   c. Future taxable income exclusive of reversing differences and carryforwards

   d. Tax planning strategies that would make income available at appropriate times in the future that would otherwise not be available

3. Based on all available evidence, make a judgment concerning the realizability of the deferred tax asset.

4. Record the amount of the valuation allowance, or change in the valuation allowance.

Accounting for Uncertainty in Income Taxes

The Financial Accounting Standards Board has issued FASB Interpretation No. 48 (FIN-48), *Accounting for Uncertainty in Income Taxes—An Interpretation of FASB Statement No. 109*. FIN-48 recognizes that the ultimate deductibility of positions taken or expected to be taken on tax returns is often uncertain. It provides guidance on when tax positions claimed by an entity can be recognized (*recognition*) and guidance on the dollar amount at which those positions are recorded (*measurement*). In order to recognize the benefits associated with a tax position taken (i.e., generally a deduction on a corporation's tax return), the entity must conclude that the ultimate allowability of the deduction is more likely than not. If the ultimate allowability of the tax position exceeds 50% (i.e., it is more likely than not), the benefit associated with the position is recognized at the largest dollar amount that has more than a 50% likelihood of being realized upon ultimate settlement. Differences between tax positions taken in a tax return and recognized in accordance with FIN-48 will generally result in (1) an increase in income taxes currently payable or a reduction in an income tax refund receivable or (2) an increase in a deferred tax liability or a decrease in a deferred tax asset, or both (1) and (2).

FIN-48 also provides guidance on:

- Derecognizing the benefits associated with a recognized tax position where subsequent events indicate that it is *not* more likely than not that the entity will benefit from the tax position taken
- Classification of financial statement elements that result from recognizing benefits associated with uncertain tax positions
- Treatment of interest and penalties related to uncertain tax positions
- Accounting for uncertain tax positions in interim periods
- Disclosure and transition

FIN-48 is effective for fiscal years beginning after December 15, 2006.

Authoritative Literature

APB-2	Accounting for the "Investment Credit"
APB-4	Accounting for the "Investment Credit" (Amending No. 2)
APB-9	Reporting the Results of Operations

APB-10	Omnibus Opinion—1966
APB-23	Accounting for Income Taxes—Special Areas
FAS-37	Balance Sheet Classification of Deferred Income Taxes
FAS-95	Statement of Cash Flows
FAS-109	Accounting for Income Taxes
FSP FAS 109-1	Application of FASB Statement No. 109, *Accounting for Income Taxes*, to the Tax Deduction on Qualified Production Activities Provided by the American Jobs Creation Act of 2004
FSP FAS 109-2	Accounting and Disclosure Guidance for the Foreign Earnings Repatriation Provision within the American Jobs Creation Act of 2004
FAS-115	Accounting for Certain Investments in Debt and Equity Securities
FAS-123	Accounting for Stock-Based Compensation
FAS-130	Reporting Comprehensive Income
FIN-18	Accounting for Income Taxes in Interim Periods
FIN-48	Accounting for Uncertainty in Income Taxes—An Interpretation of FASB Statement No. 109
FTB 79-9	Accounting in Interim Periods for Changes in Income Tax Rates
FTB 82-1	Disclosure of the Sale or Purchase of Tax Benefits though Tax Leases
EITF 00-15	Classification in the Statement of Cash Flows of the Income Tax Benefit Received by a Company upon Exercise of a Nonqualified Employee Stock Option

DISCLOSURE REQUIREMENTS

1. If a classified balance sheet is presented, the following items should be disclosed (ARB-43, Ch. 3A; FAS-109, par. 41):

   a. Income taxes currently payable or refundable

   b. Current and noncurrent deferred tax assets, including the valuation allowance, if any

   c. Current and noncurrent deferred tax liabilities

2. The following components of the net deferred tax liability or asset recognized in the balance sheet should be disclosed (FAS-109, par. 43):

   a. The total of all deferred tax liabilities for taxable temporary differences

   b. The total of all deferred tax assets for deductible temporary differences, operating loss carryforwards, and tax credit carryforwards

   c. The total valuation allowance recognized for deferred tax assets

3. The net change during the year in the total valuation allowance account should be disclosed (FAS-109, par. 43).

4. The following components (where applicable) of income tax expense related to continuing operations for each year presented should be disclosed (FAS-109, par. 45):

   a. Current tax expense or benefit

   b. Deferred tax expense or benefit (exclusive of items listed below)

   c. Investment tax credits

   d. Government grants (to the extent they have been used to reduce income tax expense)

   e. Benefits arising from operating loss carryforwards

   f. Tax expense arising from allocating tax benefits either directly to contributed capital or to reduce goodwill or other noncurrent intangible assets of an acquired company

   g. Adjustments to a deferred tax liability or asset arising from changes in tax laws, tax rates, or the entity's tax status

   h. Adjustments to the beginning balance in the valuation allowance account related to deferred tax assets that arise due to changes in the amount of assets expected to be realized

5. The amount of income tax expense or benefit should be disclosed for each of the following items for each year for which the items are presented (FAS-109, par. 46; APB-9, par. 26; APB-9, par. 20):

   a. Continuing operations

   b. Discontinued operations

   c. Extraordinary items

   d. The cumulative effect of accounting changes

    e. Prior-period adjustments

    f. Items charged or credited directly to shareholders' equity

    g. Other comprehensive income

6. For a particular tax paying component of an enterprise and within a particular tax jurisdiction (e.g., federal, state, or local), the following items should be disclosed (FAS-109, par. 42):

    a. The amount of current deferred tax liabilities and assets offset and presented as a single amount

    b. The amount of noncurrent deferred tax liabilities and assets offset and presented as a single amount

    c. The net current deferred tax asset or liability and the net noncurrent deferred tax asset or liability within each tax jurisdiction shown separately for each tax paying component

7. If the entity is a member of a group that files a consolidated tax return, the following disclosures should be made in the entity's separately issued financial statements (FAS-109, par. 49):

    a. The amount of current and deferred tax expense for each statement of income presented

    b. The amount of any tax-related balances due to or from affiliates as of the date of each balance sheet presented

    c. The principal provisions of the method by which the consolidated amount of current and deferred tax expense is allocated to members of the group, and the nature and effect of any changes in that method (and in determining related balance to or from affiliates) during the years for which the disclosures in items 7a and 7b are presented

8. In addition to the above, the notes to the financial statements should also disclose:

    a. The types of significant temporary differences and carry-forwards (FAS-109, par. 43)

    b. The nature of significant reconciling items between (i) the reported amount of income tax expense attributable to continuing operations for the year and (ii) the amount of income tax expense that would result from applying domestic federal statutory tax rates to pretax income from continuing operations (FAS-109, par. 47)

    c. The amounts and expiration dates for operating loss and tax credit carryforwards for tax purposes (FAS-109, par. 48)

d. The portion of the valuation allowance for deferred tax assets for which subsequently recognized tax benefits will be allocated to reduce goodwill or other noncurrent intangible assets of an acquired entity or directly to contributed capital (FAS-109, par. 48)

e. The method of accounting for the investment tax credit (deferral method or flow-through method) and related amounts (APB-4, par. 11)

f. The change in an entity's tax status that becomes effective after year end but before the financial statements are issued (FAS-109, QA-11)

g. The nature and effect of any other significant matters affecting comparability of information for all periods presented, if not otherwise evident (FAS-109, par. 47)

9. The following items should be disclosed when a deferred tax liability is not recognized because of the exceptions allowed by APB-23 (i.e., undistributed earnings of subsidiaries or corporate joint ventures, bad debt reserves of savings and loan associations, or policy holders' surplus of life insurance companies) or for deposits in statutory reserve funds by U.S. steamship companies (FAS-109, par. 44):

a. Description of temporary differences that did not create a deferred tax liability and the event(s) that would cause the temporary differences to become taxable

b. Cumulative amount of each type of temporary difference

c. Amount of unrecognized deferred tax liability arising from temporary differences related to investments in foreign subsidiaries and foreign corporate joint ventures that are considered permanent (If it is not practical to compute the amount, then that fact should be stated.)

d. Amount of unrecognized deferred tax liability for temporary differences related to (i) undistributed domestic earnings, (ii) bad-debt reserve for tax purposes of U.S. savings and loan associations or other qualified thrift lenders, (iii) the policyholders' surplus of a life insurance enterprise, and (iv) statutory reserve funds of a U.S. steamship enterprise

10. If an entity has previously recognized the qualified production activities deduction as a tax rate reduction, the following disclosures should be made in conjunction with restatement of its financial statements to reflect the deduction as a special deduction (FSP FAS 109-1, par. 7):

a. For prior years' financial statements:

       (1)   The nature of and justification for a change in accounting principle

       (2)   The effect of the change on income before extraordinary items and net income (and on related per-share amounts when presented) for all periods presented

    b.   If financial information is not separately reported for the fourth quarter, or that information is not presented in the annual report:

       (1)   Extraordinary, unusual, or infrequent transactions or events

       (2)   The aggregate effect of year-end adjustments that are material to the operating results of the fourth quarter

       (3)   Accounting changes presented in the manner required for interim accounting changes

11. For an entity that has not yet completed its evaluation of the repatriation provision in the *American Jobs Creation Act of 2004* (the Act) for purposes of applying FAS-109, the following disclosures should be made for each period for which financial statements covering periods affected by the Act are presented (FSP FAS 109-2, par. 9):

    a.   A summary of the repatriation provision, including the status of the entity's evaluation of the effects of the repatriation provision as well as the entity's expected completion date for the evaluation

    b.   If the entity makes decisions in stages, the effect on income tax expense (or benefit) for any amounts that have been recognized under the repatriation provision

       Note: The effect should be shown separately either on the face of the income statement or in the footnotes, consistent with where the amounts of current and deferred taxes are disclosed for the period.

    c.   The range of reasonably possible amounts of unremitted earnings that is being considered for repatriation as a result of the repatriation provision (excluding any amounts that have been recognized in the financial statements) and the potential range of related income tax effects

       Note: If the potential range of related income tax effects cannot be reasonably estimated, a statement to that effect should be made.

    d.   Pro forma financial data reflecting the effect of the repatriation provision (at a minimum, the effect on income tax expense or benefit), if the entity decides on a plan for reinvestment or repatriation of foreign earnings subsequent to the date of its financial statements but prior to their issuance

12. The financial statements for the period in which an entity completes its evaluation of the repatriation provision in the *American Jobs Creation Act of 2004* should disclose the effect on income tax expense (or benefit) for the period as a result of the repatriation provision (FSP FAS 109-2, par. 10a).

> **Note:** Such effect should be shown separately either on the face of the income statement or in the footnotes, consistent with where the amounts of current and deferred taxes are disclosed for the period.

13. Companies that recognize the tax benefits of prior deductible temporary differences and carryforwards in income rather than contributed capital (i.e., companies that have previously adopted FAS-96 and effected a quasi-reorganization that involved only the elimination of a deficit in retained earnings) should disclose the following (FAS-109, par. 39):

   a. The date of the quasi-reorganization

   b. The manner of reporting the tax benefits and that it differs from present accounting requirements for other entities

   c. The effect of those tax benefits on income from continuing operations, income before extraordinary items, and net income (and on related per-share amounts, if applicable)

14. If the amount of income tax benefit realized from the exercise of employee stock options is credited to equity but is not presented as a separate line item in the statement of changes in stockholders' equity or in the statement of cash flows, the amount of that income tax benefit should be disclosed (EITF 00-15, par. 3).

It should be noted that several distinctions are made in the disclosures required by public entities and those required by nonpublic entities. The two most significant ones are summarized as follows:

	Public/Nonpublic Company Disclosures	
	Public	*Nonpublic*
Temporary differences and carry forwards	Approximation of tax effect of each type	Description of types
Statutory reconciliation	Reconciliation in percentages or dollars	Description of major reconciling items

Accounting for Uncertainty in Income Taxes

The disclosure requirements in items 1 through 3 below are pre-scribed by FIN-48, *Accounting for Uncertainty in Income Taxes—An Interpretation of FASB Statement No. 109*. FIN-48 is effective for fiscal years beginning after December 15, 2006, with early adoption per-mitted as long as (1) the consensus is applied as of the beginning of the fiscal year and (2) financial statements for any period (interim or annual) of the fiscal year have not yet been issued.

1. Disclosure should be made of the entity's policy on classifi-cation of interest and penalties (FIN-48, par. 20).

2. The following should be disclosed for each annual reporting period presented (FIN-48, par. 21):

   a. A tabular reconciliation of the total amounts of unrecog-nized tax benefits at the beginning and end of the period, which should include at a minimum:

      (1) The gross amounts of the increases and decreases in unrecognized tax benefits as a result of tax positions taken during a prior period

      (2) The gross amounts of increases and decreases in unrecognized tax benefits as a result of tax positions taken during the current period

      (3) The amounts of decreases in the unrecognized tax benefits relating to settlements with taxing authori-ties

      (4) Reductions to unrecognized tax benefits as a result of a lapse of the applicable statute of limitations

   b. The total amount of unrecognized tax benefits that, if rec-ognized, would affect the effective tax rate

   c. The total amounts of interest and penalties recognized in the statement of operations and the total amounts of interest and penalties recognized in the statement of financial position

   d. For positions in which it is reasonably possible that the total amounts of unrecognized tax benefits will signifi-cantly increase or decrease within 12 months of the reporting date:

      (1) The nature of the uncertainty

      (2) The nature of the event that could occur in the next 12 months that would cause the change

   (3) An estimate of the range of the reasonably possible change or a statement that an estimate of the range cannot be made

  e. A description of tax years that remain subject to examination by major tax jurisdictions

 3. In the year of adopting FIN-48, the cumulative effect of the change on retained earnings as of the date of adoption should be disclosed in the statement of financial position (FIN-48, par. 24).

EXAMPLES OF FINANCIAL STATEMENT DISCLOSURES

The following sample disclosures are available on the accompanying disc. For examples of income tax disclosures that are typically described in a note summarizing a company's significant accounting policies, see Chapter 2, "Accounting Policies".

Example 45–1: Company's Disclosure of the Provision for Income Taxes, Reconciliation of Statutory Rate to Effective Rate, and Significant Components of Deferred Tax Assets and Liabilities

> **Note:** A nonpublic company may, alternatively, describe in a narrative format the major reconciling items between the statutory tax rate and effective tax rate and the significant components of deferred tax assets and liabilities as shown in Example 45–2.

The federal and state income tax provision (benefit) is summarized as follows:

	Year Ended December 31	
	20X2	20X1
Current:		
Federal	$250,000	$(45,000)
State	50,000	5,000
	300,000	(40,000)
Deferred:		
Federal	(80,000)	(125,000)
State	(20,000)	30,000
	(100,000)	(95,000)
Total provision (benefit) for income taxes	$200,000	$(135,000)

A reconciliation of the provision (benefit) for income taxes with amounts determined by applying the statutory U.S. federal income tax rate to income before income taxes is as follows:

	Year Ended December 31	
	20X2	20X1
Computed tax at the federal statutory rate of 34%	$700,000	$(150,000)
State taxes, net of federal benefit	30,000	20,000
Write-down of asset not deductible	80,000	450,000
Foreign sales corporation benefits	(15,000)	(10,000)
Corporate-owned life insurance	10,000	-0-
Tax exempt interest	(75,000)	(15,000)
Research and development tax credits	(290,000)	-0-
Operating loss carryforwards	(300,000)	(400,000)
Valuation allowance	-0-	(20,000)
Settlement of prior years' audit issues	50,000	-0-
Adjustment of prior years' accruals	15,000	-0-
Other	(5,000)	(10,000)
Provision (benefit) for income taxes	$200,000	$(135,000)
Effective income tax rate	10%	(31%)

Deferred income taxes reflect the net tax effects of temporary differences between the carrying amounts of assets and liabilities for financial reporting purposes and the amounts used for income tax purposes. Significant components of the Company's deferred tax assets and liabilities are as follows:

	As of December 31	
	20X2	20X1
Deferred tax assets:		
Inventory capitalization	$450,000	$675,000
Inventory obsolescence	300,000	125,000
LIFO inventory valuation	200,000	150,000
Intercompany profit in inventory	75,000	50,000
Allowance for doubtful accounts	50,000	100,000
Allowance for sales returns	100,000	150,000
Warranty expense	300,000	400,000

Postretirement benefit obligation	250,000	125,000
Deferred compensation	100,000	50,000
Accrued vacation	125,000	75,000
Deferred revenue	275,000	200,000
Unrealized foreign exchange losses	15,000	10,000
Net operating losses carryforwards	300,000	400,000
Tax credits carryforwards	200,000	100,000
AMT credit	50,000	25,000
Other	5,000	10,000
Total deferred tax assets	2,795,000	2,645,000
Deferred tax liabilities:		
Difference between book and tax depreciation	1,755,000	1,515,000
Unrealized gains on marketable securities	75,000	60,000
Unrealized foreign exchange gains	25,000	40,000
Unremitted earnings of subsidiaries	75,000	50,000
Other	15,000	5,000
Total deferred tax liabilities	1,945,000	1,670,000
Net deferred tax assets before valuation allowance	850,000	975,000
Valuation allowance	(200,000)	(500,000)
Net deferred tax assets	$650,000	$475,000

Example 45–2: Company's Disclosure of the Provision for Income Taxes, Major Reconciling Items between the Statutory Tax Rate and Effective Tax Rate, and the Significant Components of Deferred Tax Assets and Liabilities

Note: This example is applicable only to nonpublic entities. For a sample disclosure that is applicable to a public entity, see Example 45–1.

The federal and state income tax provision (benefit) is summarized as follows:

| | Year Ended December 31 ||
	20X2	20X1
Current:		
Federal	$250,000	$(45,000)
State	50,000	5,000
	300,000	(40,000)
Deferred:		
Federal	(80,000)	(125,000)
State	(20,000)	30,000
	(100,000)	(95,000)
Total provision (benefit) for income taxes	$200,000	$(135,000)

The Company's effective income tax rate is lower than what would be expected if the federal statutory rate were applied to income before income taxes primarily because of certain expenses deductible for financial reporting purposes that are not deductible for tax purposes, tax-exempt interest income, research and development tax credits, and operating loss carryforwards.

Deferred income taxes reflect the net tax effects of temporary differences between the carrying amounts of assets and liabilities for financial reporting purposes and the amounts used for income tax purposes. The major temporary differences that give rise to the deferred tax assets and liabilities are as follows: inventory capitalization, LIFO inventory valuation, provision for doubtful accounts, warranty expense, post-retirement benefit obligation, deferred compensation, depreciation, net operating losses carryforwards, and tax credits carryforwards.

Example 45–3: Disclosure of Net Operating Losses and Tax Credits Carryforwards

At December 31, 20X2, the Company has available unused net operating losses and investment tax credits carryforwards that may be applied against future taxable income and that expire as follows:

Year of Expiration	Net Operating Losses Carryforwards	Investment Tax Credits Carryforwards
20X3	$ 3,000,000	$ 1,000,000
20X4	1,000,000	2,000,000
20X5	6,000,000	4,000,000
20X6	4,000,000	3,000,000

20X7	3,000,000	1,000,000
Thereafter up to 20X9	8,000,000	2,000,000
	$25,000,000	$13,000,000

In addition, the Company has available Alternative Minimum Tax credit carryforwards for tax purposes of approximately $1,800,000, which may be used indefinitely to reduce regular federal income taxes.

Example 45–4: Company Has Substantial Net Operating Loss Carryforwards and a Valuation Allowance Is Recorded

For the years ended December 31, 20X2 and December 31, 20X1, the Company incurred net operating losses and, accordingly, no provision for income taxes has been recorded. In addition, no benefit for income taxes has been recorded due to the uncertainty of the realization of any tax assets. At December 31, 20X2, the Company had approximately $12,500,000 of federal and $8,300,000 of state net operating losses. The net operating loss carryforwards, if not utilized, will begin to expire in 20X9 for federal purposes and in 20X5 for California purposes.

The components of the Company's deferred tax assets/liabilities are as follows:

	As of December 31	
	20X2	20X1
Deferred tax assets:		
Reserves and accruals	$ 613,000	$ 250,000
Credit carryforwards	655,000	367,000
Net operating loss carryforwards	4,700,000	2,645,000
Total deferred tax assets	5,968,000	3,262,000
Deferred tax liabilities:		
Depreciation and amortization	(275,000)	(210,000)
Net deferred tax assets before valuation allowance	5,693,000	3,052,000
Less: Valuation allowance	(5,693,000)	(3,052,000)
Net deferred tax assets	$ -0-	$ -0-

For financial reporting purposes, the Company has incurred a loss in each period since its inception. Based on the available objective evidence, including the Company's history of losses, management believes it is more likely than not that the net deferred tax assets will not be fully realizable. Accordingly, the Company provided for a full valuation allowance against its net deferred tax assets at December 31, 20X2 and December 31, 20X1.

A reconciliation between the amount of income tax benefit determined by applying the applicable U.S. statutory income tax rate to pre-tax loss is as follows:

	Year Ended December 31	
	20X2	20X1
Federal statutory rate	$(1,020,000)	$(850,000)
State tax, net of federal impact	(30,000)	(50,000)
Nondeductible stock compensation	370,000	150,000
Tax credit carryforwards generated	(10,000)	(125,000)
Write-off of acquisition related assets	540,000	50,000
Change in valuation allowance on deferred tax assets	150,000	825,000
	$ -0-	$ -0-

Example 45–5: Company Discloses Its Consideration of Sufficient Positive Evidence to Support Its Conclusion Not to Record a Valuation Allowance

A significant portion of the deferred tax assets recognized relate to net operating loss and credit carryforwards. Because the Company operates in multiple overseas jurisdictions, it considered the need for a valuation allowance on a country-by-country basis, taking into account the effects of local tax law. Where a valuation allowance was not recorded, the Company believes that there was sufficient positive evidence to support its conclusion not to record a valuation allowance. Management believes that the Company will utilize the loss carryforwards in the future because: (1) prior to the restructuring charges, the Company had a history of pre-tax income; (2) a significant portion of the loss carryforwards resulted from restructuring costs; (3) management believes that the restructuring of the Company's businesses will reduce their cost structures and that the Company will be profitable and will generate taxable income in the near term; (4) management is aware of viable tax strategies that could be implemented to accelerate taxable income in order to realize a substantial portion of the recorded deferred tax assets; and (5) a significant portion of the net operating losses have an indefinite life or do not expire in the near term. However, there can be no assurance that the Company will generate taxable income or that all of its loss carryforwards will be utilized.

Example 45–6: Change in Valuation Allowance During the Year Is Described

In 20X2, the valuation allowance increased approximately $1,950,000, composed of increases to allowances due to the uncertainty of realizing research and development tax credits, tax benefits from certain asset impairment write-downs, and net operating loss carryforwards.

Example 45–7: Valuation Allowances Related to Preacquisition NOL Carryforwards of Acquired Business Are Being Applied to Reduce Goodwill Arising from the Acquisition

Valuation allowances related to the preacquisition net operating loss carryforwards of Instarr, Inc., which was acquired by the Company in 19X9, are being applied to reduce goodwill arising from the acquisition as the related tax benefits are realized. During 20X2 and 20X1, reversals of valuation allowances applied to reduce goodwill totaled $4,200,000 and $3,100,000, respectively. Any subsequent decreases in the deferred tax valuation allowance will also be recorded as a reduction to goodwill.

Example 45–8: Reduction in Valuation Allowance Recorded as an Increase in Additional Paid-in Capital in Connection with "Fresh-Start" Accounting

As of December 31, 20X0, the Company had various net deferred tax assets made up primarily of the expected future tax benefit of net operating loss carryforwards, various credit carryforwards, and reserves not yet deductible for tax purposes. A valuation allowance was provided in full against these net deferred tax assets upon the Company's emergence from bankruptcy when "fresh-start" reporting was adopted.

During 20X2 and 20X1, the Company reduced the valuation allowance related to the remaining net tax assets by $2,800,000 and $1,900,000, respectively. The reduction reflects the Company's expectation that it is more likely than not that it will generate future taxable income to utilize this amount of net deferred tax assets. The benefit from this reduction was recorded as an increase in additional paid-in capital in accordance with Statement of Position No. 90-7 (Financial Reporting by Entities in Reorganization Under the Bankruptcy Code).

Example 45–9: Tax Benefits Associated with Stock Options Recorded as an Increase to Additional Paid-in Capital

During 20X2 and 20X1, the Company recognized certain tax benefits related to stock option plans in the amount of $1,200,000 and

$800,000, respectively. Such benefits were recorded as a reduction of income taxes payable and an increase in additional paid-in capital.

Example 45–10: Deferred Taxes Not Provided on Undistributed Earnings of Foreign Subsidiaries—Amount of Deferred Tax Liability Not Disclosed

A provision has not been made at December 31, 20X2, for U.S. or additional foreign withholding taxes on approximately $10 million of undistributed earnings of foreign subsidiaries because it is the present intention of management to reinvest the undistributed earnings indefinitely in foreign operations. Generally, such earnings become subject to U.S. tax upon the remittance of dividends and under certain other circumstances. It is not practicable to estimate the amount of deferred tax liability on such undistributed earnings.

Example 45–11: Deferred Taxes Not Provided on Undistributed Earnings of Foreign Subsidiaries—Amount of Deferred Tax Liability Is Disclosed

The Company has not recorded deferred income taxes applicable to undistributed earnings of foreign subsidiaries that are indefinitely reinvested in foreign operations. Undistributed earnings amounted to approximately $6,000,000 and $5,200,000 at December 31, 20X2, and December 31, 20X1, respectively. If the earnings of such foreign subsidiaries were not definitely reinvested, a deferred tax liability of approximately $1,500,000 and $1,300,000 would have been required at December 31, 20X2, and December 31, 20X1, respectively.

Example 45–12: Deferred Taxes Recorded on Undistributed Earnings of Foreign Subsidiaries

At December 31, 20X2, the accompanying consolidated Balance Sheet includes a deferred tax liability of $300,000 for the estimated income taxes that will be payable upon the anticipated future repatriation of approximately $1,000,000 of undistributed earnings of foreign subsidiaries in the form of dividends.

Example 45–13: Subchapter S Status Terminated

Prior to January 1, 20X2, the Company had operated as a C corporation. Effective January 1, 20X2, the stockholders of the Company elected to be taxed under Subchapter S of the Internal Revenue Code. During such period, federal income taxes were the responsibility of the Company's stockholders, as were certain state income taxes. As of the effective date of the election, the Company was responsible for Federal built-in-gain taxes to the extent applicable. Accordingly, the consolidated Statement of Operations for the year ended December

31, 20X2, provides for such taxes. The S corporation election terminated in connection with the consummation of the initial public offering of the Company's common stock on October 10, 20X2.

Example 45–14: Conversion from an LLC to a C Corporation

From the Company's inception in March 19X7 to February 20X2, the Company was not subject to federal and state income taxes since it was operating as a Limited Liability Company (LLC). On February 2, 20X2, the Company converted from an LLC to a C corporation and, as a result, became subject to corporate federal and state income taxes. The Company's accumulated deficit of $4.3 million at that date was reclassified to additional paid-in capital.

Example 45–15: Conversion from a C Corporation to an S Corporation

Prior to January 1, 20X2, the Company had operated as a C Corporation. Effective January 1, 20X2, the Company has elected S Corporation status. Earnings and losses after that date will be included in the personal income tax returns of the stockholders and taxed depending on their personal tax strategies. As a result, the Company will not incur any additional income tax obligations, and future financial statements will not include a provision for income taxes. Prior to the change to S Corporation status, income taxes currently payable and deferred income taxes were recorded in the Company's financial statements.

The provision for income taxes consists of the following:

	20X2	20X1
Current	$ —	$42,000
Deferred	90,000	(11,000)
	$90,000	$31,000

Substantially all of the deferred income tax provision in 20X2 relates to the elimination of the deferred tax asset of $90,000 at the date the election for the change to Subchapter S Status was filed.

Example 45–16: Conversion from Cash Basis to Accrual Basis for Tax Purposes Results in a Deferred Tax Liability

In the current year, the Company converted from a cash basis to accrual basis for tax purposes in conjunction with its conversion to a C corporation. Due to temporary differences in recognition of revenue and expenses, income for financial reporting purposes exceeded income for income tax purposes. The conversion to the accrual basis along with these temporary differences resulted in the recognition of a net deferred tax liability and a corresponding one-time charge to expense of $3.5 million as of December 31, 20X2.

Example 45–17: Disclosures About Uncertainty in Income Taxes under FIN-48

> **Note:** The disclosure requirements that are prescribed by FIN-48 are effective for fiscal years beginning after December 15, 2006, with early adoption permitted as long as (1) the consensus is applied as of the beginning of the fiscal year and (2) financial statements for any period (interim or annual) of the fiscal year have not yet been issued.
> This example, which is adapted from FIN-48, assumes that the reporting entity has adopted the provisions of FIN-48 for the year ended December 31, 2007.

The Company or one of its subsidiaries files income tax returns in the U.S. federal jurisdiction, and various states and foreign jurisdictions. With few exceptions, the Company is no longer subject to U.S. federal, state, and local or non-U.S. income tax examinations by tax authorities for years before 2001. The Internal Revenue Service (IRS) commenced an examination of the Company's U.S. income tax returns for 2002 through 2004 in the first quarter of 2007 that is anticipated to be completed by the end of 2008. As of December 31, 2007, the IRS has proposed certain significant adjustments to the Company's transfer pricing and research credits tax positions. Management is currently evaluating those proposed adjustments to determine if it agrees; but, if accepted, the Company does not anticipate the adjustments would result in a material change to its financial position. However, the Company anticipates that it is reasonably possible that an additional payment in the range of $800,000 to $1,000,000 will be made by the end of 2008.

The Company adopted the provisions of FASB Interpretation No. 48 (FIN-48), *Accounting for Uncertainty in Income Taxes,* on January 1, 2007. As a result of the implementation of FIN-48, the Company recognized approximately a $2,000,000 increase in the liability for unrecognized tax benefits, which was accounted for as a reduction to the January 1, 2007, balance of retained earnings. A reconciliation of the beginning and ending amount of unrecognized tax benefits is as follows:

Balance at January 1, 2007	$3,700,000
Additions based on tax positions related to the current year	100,000
Additions for tax positions of prior years	300,000
Reductions for tax positions of prior years	(600,000)
Settlements	(400,000)
Balance at December 31, 2007	$3,100,000

Included in the balance at December 31, 2007, are $600,000 of tax positions for which the ultimate deductibility is highly certain but for which there is uncertainty about the timing of such deductibility. Because of the impact of deferred tax accounting, other than interest and penalties, the disallowance of the shorter deductibility period would not affect the annual effective tax rate but would accelerate the payment of cash to the taxing authority to an earlier period.

The Company recognizes interest accrued related to unrecognized tax benefits in interest expense and penalties in operating expenses. During the years ended December 31, 2007, 2006, and 2005, the Company recognized approximately $100,000, $110,000, and $120,000 in interest and penalties. The Company had approximately $600,000 and $500,000 for the payment of interest and penalties accrued at December 31, 2007, and 2006, respectively.

CHAPTER 46
DEBT OBLIGATIONS AND
CREDIT ARRANGEMENTS

CONTENTS

EXECUTIVE SUMMARY

Note: The Financial Accounting Standards Board has issued Statement of Financial Accounting Standards No. 156 (FAS-156), *Accounting for Servicing of Financial Assets,* which amends the guidance in Statement of Financial Accounting Standards No. 140 (FAS-140), *Accounting for Transfers and Servicing of Financial Assets and Extinguishments of Liabilities.* Among other requirements, FAS-156 requires an entity to recognize a servicing asset or servicing liability each time it undertakes an obligation to service a financial asset by entering into a servicing contract in any of the following three situations:

1. A transfer of the servicer's financial assets that meets the requirements for sale accounting

2. A transfer of the servicer's financial assets to a qualifying special-purpose entity in a guaranteed mortgage securitization in which the transferor retains all of the resulting securities and classifies them as either available-for-sale securities or trading securities in accordance with Statement of Financial Accounting Standards No. 115 (FAS-115), *Accounting for Certain Investments in Debt and Equity Securities*

3. An acquisition or assumption of an obligation to service a financial asset that does not relate to financial assets of the servicer or its consolidated affiliates

FAS-156 is effective as of the beginning of an entity's first fiscal year that begins after September 15, 2006. Earlier adoption is permitted as of the beginning of an entity's fiscal year, provided the entity has not issued financial statements.

Debt Obligations and Credit Arrangements

Debt obligations that, by their terms, are due and payable on demand should be presented as a current liability in the balance sheet. Current liabilities include long-term obligations that are callable because a violation of an objective acceleration clause in a long-term debt agreement may exist at the date of the debtor's balance sheet. Such callable obligations must be classified as a current liability at the debtor's balance-sheet date unless one of the following conditions is met:

1. The creditor has waived or subsequently lost the right to demand repayment for more than one year (or operating cycle, if longer) from the balance-sheet date.

2. For long-term obligations containing a grace period within which the debtor may cure the violation, it is probable that the violation will be cured within that period, therefore preventing the obligation from being callable.

A short-term obligation can be excluded from current liabilities only if the company intends to refinance the obligation on a long-term basis and the intent is supported by the ability to refinance in one of the following ways:

1. A long-term obligation or equity security whose proceeds are used to retire the short-term obligation is issued after the date of the balance sheet but before the issuance of the financial statements.

2. Before the issuance of the financial statements, the company has entered into an agreement that enables it to refinance a short-term obligation on a long-term basis.

When a note is exchanged for property, goods, or services in an arm's-length transaction, it is generally presumed that the interest stated on the note is fair and adequate. If no interest is stated or if the interest stated appears unreasonable, the transaction should be valued at the fair value of the note or property, goods, or services, whichever is more clearly determinable. If such fair value is not readily determinable, the transaction should be valued at the present value of the note, determined by discounting the future cash payments under the note by an appropriate interest rate. The difference between the face amount of the note and its present value represents a discount or premium, which should be amortized over the life of the note using the interest method, or a method that approximates the interest method. The discount or premium amount is not an asset or a liability separable from the note that gives rise to it; therefore, the discount or premium should be reported in the balance sheet as a direct deduction from or addition to the face amount of the note.

When convertible debt is issued without an embedded beneficial conversion feature (i.e., a conversion feature that is not in-the-money at the commitment date), no value should be assigned to the conversion feature because it generally is inseparable from the debt.

Consequently, the transaction should be recorded entirely as the issuance of debt. When debt is converted into stock, the debt obligation and unamortized premium or discount should be eliminated; the issuance of the shares should be recorded as outstanding stock and additional paid-in capital.

When debt is issued with detachable stock purchase warrants, a portion of the proceeds should be allocated to the warrants and recorded as additional paid-in capital because the warrants and debt are viewed as separate securities.

Debt Extinguishment

An *extinguishment of debt* is the reacquisition of debt, or removal of debt from the balance sheet, prior to or at the maturity date of that debt. Debt is extinguished and should be de-recognized in the debtor's financial statements only if one of the following conditions is met:

1. The debtor pays the creditor and is relieved of its obligations for the liability. This includes (a) the transfer of cash, other financial assets, goods, or services, or (b) the debtor's reacquisition of its outstanding debt securities, whether the securities are canceled or held as treasury bonds.
2. The debtor is legally released from being the primary obligor under the liability, either judicially or by the creditor. If a third party assumes nonrecourse debt in conjunction with the sale of an asset that serves as sole collateral for that debt, the sale and related assumption effectively accomplish a legal release of the seller-debtor.

Gain or loss on the extinguishment is the difference between the total reacquisition cost of the debt to the debtor and the net carrying amount of the debt on the debtor's books at the date of extinguishment. The gain or loss on the extinguishment of debt is recognized immediately in the period of extinguishment and should be identified as a separate item in the income statement.

Debt Restructuring

The types of debt restructuring include (a) transfer of assets or transfer of an equity interest in full settlement, (b) modification of the terms of the debt, or (c) a combination of the two.

If a debtor satisfies a debt in full by transferring assets, or by granting an equity interest, to a creditor and the fair market value of the assets transferred or equity interest granted is less than the carrying value of the debt, the debtor generally should recognize the difference as gain on the restructuring of debt. In addition, the debtor should recognize a gain or loss for any difference between the carrying value of the assets transferred and their fair value, which should be reported as gain or loss on transfer of assets.

A troubled debt restructuring involving only modification of terms of a payable (i.e., not involving a transfer of assets or grant of an equity interest) should be accounted for prospectively. However, if the carrying amount of the debt exceeds the total future cash payments specified by the new terms, the debtor should reduce the debt's carrying amount to the total future cash payments specified by the new terms and recognize a gain on debt restructuring.

Unconditional Purchase Obligations

An unconditional purchase obligation is an obligation to transfer funds in the future for fixed or minimum amounts or quantities of goods or services at fixed or minimum prices. Such obligations often are in the form of "take-or-pay contracts" or "throughput agreements," which generally require the buyer to pay specified amounts periodically, even if delivery of goods is not taken or the service is not used. Liabilities created by purchase obligations may or may not be recorded under current accounting standards. However, all unconditional purchase obligations should be disclosed in the financial statements regardless of whether they have been recorded as liabilities.

Product Financing Arrangements

A product financing arrangement is a transaction in which an entity sells products to another entity and, in a related transaction, agrees to repurchase the products at a specified price over a specified period. A product financing arrangement should be accounted for as a borrowing rather than as a sale. It should be noted that the accounting for product financing arrangements differs from the accounting for long-term unconditional purchase obligations. In a product financing arrangement, the entity is in substance the owner of the product and, therefore, should report the product as an asset and the related obligation as a liability. In contrast, at the time a contract is entered into under an unconditional purchase obligation arrangement, either the product does not yet exist or the product exists in a form unsuitable to the buyer; in other words, the buyer has a right to receive a future product but is not the substantive owner of an existing product.

Financial Instruments with Characteristics of Both Liabilities and Equity

FASB Statement of Financial Accounting Standards No. 150 (FAS-150), *Accounting for Certain Financial Instruments with Characteristics of Both Liabilities and Equity*, establishes standards for issuers of financial instruments with characteristics of both liabilities and equity related to the classification and measurement of those instruments. FAS-150 essentially requires the following three classes of financial instruments previously classified as equity to be classified as liabilities (or assets in some cases):

1. *Mandatorily redeemable financial instruments.* These financial instruments should be classified as liabilities in an entity's financial statements unless the redemption is required to occur only upon the entity's liquidation or termination. A financial instrument issued in the form of shares is mandatorily redeemable if it embodies an unconditional obligation requiring the issuer to redeem the instrument by transferring its assets at a specified or determinable date or upon an event certain to occur. For example, shares that are required to be redeemed by an entity upon the death of a stockholder (an event certain to occur) are mandatorily redeemable shares.

2. *Obligations to repurchase the issuer's equity shares by transferring assets.* Financial instruments other than outstanding shares that, at inception, meet the following criteria should be classified as liabilities (or as assets in some circumstances): (a) the financial instruments embody an obligation to repurchase the issuer's equity shares, or are indexed to such an obligation, *and* (b) they require, or may require, the issuer to settle the obligation by transferring assets. Examples include forward purchase contracts or written put options on an issuer's equity shares that are to be physically settled or net cash settled.

3. *Certain obligations to issue a variable number of shares.* Financial instruments that embody an unconditional obligation, or financial instruments other than outstanding shares that embody a conditional obligation, that the entity must or may settle by issuing a variable number of equity shares should be classified as liabilities (or as assets in some circumstances) if, at inception, the monetary value of the obligation is based solely or predominantly on any of the following:

    a. A fixed monetary amount that is known at inception (e.g., a payable to be settled with a variable number of the entity's equity shares).

    b. Variations in something other than the fair value of the entity's equity shares (e.g., a financial instrument indexed to the S&P 500 and to be settled with a variable number of the entity's equity shares).

    c. Variations inversely related to changes in the fair value of the entity's equity shares (e.g., a written put option that could be settled net by delivering a variable number of equity shares).

Except for mandatorily redeemable financial instruments of non-public companies, FAS-150 is effective for financial instruments entered into or modified after May 31, 2003; for financial instruments entered into previously, FAS-150 is effective for interim periods beginning after June 15, 2003. For financial instruments of nonpublic companies that are mandatorily redeemable on fixed dates for amounts that either are fixed or are determined by reference to an interest rate index, currency index, or another external index, FAS-150 is effective for fiscal periods beginning after December 15, 2004. For all other mandatorily redeemable financial instruments of nonpublic companies, FAS-150 is deferred indefinitely pending further action by the FASB.

See Chapter 15, "Financial Instruments, Derivatives, and Hedging Activities," for further guidance including effective date, for the disclosure requirements of FAS-150, and for related examples of financial statement disclosures.

Authoritative Literature

ARB-43	Chapter 3A, Current Assets and Current Liabilities
APB-10	Omnibus Opinion—1966
APB-12	Omnibus Opinion—1967
APB-14	Accounting for Convertible Debt and Debt Issued with Stock Purchase Warrants
APB-21	Interest on Receivables and Payables
APB-26	Early Extinguishment of Debt
FAS-6	Classification of Short-Term Obligations Expected to Be Refinanced
FAS-15	Accounting by Debtors and Creditors for Troubled Debt Restructurings
FAS-22	Changes in the Provisions of Lease Agreements Resulting from Refundings of Tax-Exempt Debt
FAS-47	Disclosure of Long-Term Obligations
FAS-49	Accounting for Product Financing Arrangements
FAS-78	Classification of Obligations That Are Callable by the Creditor
FAS-84	Induced Conversions of Convertible Debt
FAS-114	Accounting by Creditors for Impairment of a Loan

FAS-129	Disclosure of Information about Capital Structure
FAS-140	Accounting for Transfers and Servicing of Financial Assets and Extinguishments of Liabilities
FAS-145	Rescission of FASB Statements No. 4, 44, and 64, Amendment of FASB Statement No. 13, and Technical Corrections
FAS-150	Accounting for Certain Financial Instruments with Characteristics of Both Liabilities and Equity
FSP FAS 150-3	Effective Date, Disclosures, and Transition for Mandatorily Redeemable Financial Instruments of Certain Nonpublic Entities and Certain Mandatorily Redeemable Noncontrolling Interests under FASB Statement No. 150, *Accounting for Certain Financial Instruments with Characteristics of Both Liabilities and Equity*
FAS-156	Accounting for Servicing of Financial Assets
FIN-8	Classification of a Short-Term Obligation Repaid Prior to Being Replaced by a Long-Term Security
FIN-39	Offsetting of Amounts Related to Certain Contracts
FTB 79-3	Subjective Acceleration Clauses in Long-Term Debt Agreements
FTB 80-1	Early Extinguishment of Debt through Exchange for Common or Preferred Stock
FTB 80-2	Classification of Debt Restructurings by Debtors and Creditors
FTB 81-6	Applicability of Statement 15 to Debtors in Bankruptcy Situations
EITF 86-30	Classification of Obligations When a Violation Is Waived by the Creditor
EITF 95-22	Balance Sheet Classification of Borrowings Outstanding under Revolving Credit Agreements That Include Both a Subjective Acceleration Clause and a Lockbox Arrangement
EITF 98-5	Accounting for Convertible Securities with Beneficial Conversion Features or Contingently Adjustable Conversion Ratios

EITF 00-19   Accounting for Derivative Financial Instruments Indexed to, and Potentially Settled in, a Company's Own Stock

EITF 00-27   Application of Issue No. 98-5 to Certain Convertible Instruments

DISCLOSURE REQUIREMENTS

Debt Obligations and Credit Arrangements

The following disclosures should be made about debt obligations and credit arrangements:

1. The terms, interest rates, maturity dates, and subordinate features of significant categories of debt (e.g., notes payable to banks, line of credit agreements, related-party notes) (generally accepted disclosure)

2. Any restrictive covenants (e.g., restrictions on additional borrowings, obligations to maintain minimum working capital or restrict dividends) and assets mortgaged, pledged, or otherwise subject to lien (FAS-5, pars. 18–19)

3. If a short-term obligation expected to be refinanced on a long-term basis is excluded from current liabilities (FAS-6, par. 15):

    a. A general description of the financing agreement

    b. The terms of any new obligation incurred or expected to be incurred or equity securities issued or expected to be issued as a result of the refinancing

4. Subjective clauses in long-term debt agreements that may accelerate the due date, unless acceleration is remote (FTB 79-3)

5. For each of the five years following the date of the latest balance sheet presented (FAS-47, par. 10; FAS-129, par. 8):

    a. The combined aggregate amount of maturities and sinking fund requirements for all long-term borrowings

    b. The amount of redemption requirements for all issues of capital stock that are redeemable at fixed or determinable prices on fixed or determinable dates, separately by issue or combined

6. The conversion features and descriptions of convertible debt, including the pertinent rights and privileges of the convertible debt (APB-14, pars. 16–18)

7. For convertible securities with beneficial conversion features or contingently adjustable conversion ratios accounted for in

accordance with EITF 98-5, disclosure should be made of the terms of the transaction, including the excess of the aggregate fair value of the instruments that the holder would receive at conversion over the proceeds received and the period over which the discount is amortized (These disclosures would only be applicable if the intrinsic value of the beneficial conversion feature is greater than the proceeds allocated to the convertible instrument) (EITF 98-5, par. 7)

8. For debt securities that carry an unreasonable interest rate or are non-interest-bearing (APB-21, par. 16):

    a. The unamortized discount or premium that is reported in the balance sheet as a direct deduction from or as an addition to the face amount of the note

    b. The face amount of the note

    c. The effective interest rate

    d. Amortization of discount or premium reported as interest in the income statement

    e. Related debt issue costs that are reported as deferred charges in the balance sheet

9. If the debtor has violated a provision of a long-term debt agreement at the balance-sheet date but classifies the obligation as noncurrent because it is probable (likely) that the violation will be cured within the grace period, the circumstances should be described (FAS-78, par. 5)

10. When events of default under a credit agreement have occurred at any time prior to the date of the accountant's report and have not been cured or waived or a valid waiver has been obtained for only a stated period of time (SAS-1, AU 560) (EITF 86-30):

    a. The nature and amount of the default

    b. The period for which the violation has been waived

11. Significant changes in long-term obligations subsequent to the date of the financial statements (FAS-5, par. 11)

Debt Extinguishment

The following disclosures should be made about debt extinguishment:

1. If debt was considered to be extinguished by in-substance defeasance under the provisions of FAS-76, prior to January 1, 1997 (FAS-140, par. 17b; FAS-156, par. 4h):

    a. A general description of the transaction

    b.   The amount of debt that is considered extinguished at the end of the period so long as that debt remains outstanding

2.   If assets are set aside after January 1, 1997 solely for satisfying scheduled payments of a specific obligation, a description of the nature of restrictions placed on those assets (FAS-140, par. 17c; FAS-156, par. 4h)

Debt Restructuring

The following disclosures should be made about debt restructuring:

1.   For the period in which the debt is restructured (FAS-15, par. 25):

    a.   For each restructuring, a description of the principal changes in terms, the major features of settlement, or both

    b.   Aggregate gain on restructuring of payables

    c.   Aggregate net gain or loss on transfers of assets recognized during the period

    d.   If applicable, the per share amount of the aggregate gain on restructuring

2.   For periods subsequent to the period in which the debt was restructured (FAS-15, par. 26):

    a.   The extent to which amounts contingently payable are included in the carrying amount of restructured payables

    b.   Total amounts that are contingently payable on restructured payables and the conditions under which those amounts would become payable or would be forgiven when there is at least a reasonable possibility that a liability for contingent payments will be incurred

Unconditional Purchase Obligations

The following disclosures should be made about unconditional purchase obligations:

1.   For unconditional purchase obligations that have not been recorded (FAS-47, pars. 6–8):

    a.   The nature and term of the obligation

    b.   The amount of the fixed and determinable portion of the obligation as of the date of the latest balance sheet presented in the aggregate and, if determinable, for each of the five succeeding fiscal years

c. The nature of any variable components of the obligation

d. The amounts purchased under the obligation for each period for which an income statement is presented

e. The amount of imputed interest necessary to reduce the unconditional purchase obligation to its present value (optional)

2. For unconditional purchase obligations that have been recorded, the following disclosures should be made for each of the five years following the date of the latest balance sheet presented (FAS-47, par. 10):

a. The aggregate amounts of payments for unconditional purchase obligations

b. The combined aggregate amount of maturities and sinking fund requirements

c. The amount of redemption requirements for all issues of capital stock that are redeemable at fixed or determinable prices on fixed or determinable dates, separately by issue or combined

Product Financing Arrangements

The disclosure requirements for product financing arrangements are the same as for debt obligations discussed above; there are no additional disclosure requirements that are unique to product financing arrangements.

EXAMPLES OF FINANCIAL STATEMENT DISCLOSURES

 The following sample disclosures are available on the accompanying disc. For examples of disclosures of capital lease obligations, see Chapter 23, "Leases".

Short-Term and Long-Term Debt Obligations

Example 46–1: Borrowings under Revolving Line of Credit and Restrictive Covenants

The Company has available a revolving line of credit with a bank for the lesser of (a) $5,000,000, or (b) the sum of 80% of eligible domestic trade accounts receivable and 55% of eligible inventory, as defined. The line of credit expires in November 20X3, unless extended. Borrowings under the line of credit bear interest (9.25% at December 31, 20X2) at one of the following rates as selected by the Company: LIBOR plus 1% to 2.25%, or the bank's prime rate plus 0.5%. All borrowings are collateralized by substantially all assets of the Company. The outstanding balance on the line of credit was $4,436,000 and $3,879,00 at December 31, 20X2, and December 31, 20X1, respectively. Borrowings under the line are subject to certain financial covenants and restrictions on indebtedness, dividend payments, financial guarantees, business combinations, and other related items. As of December 31, 20X2, the Company is in compliance with all covenants. Retained earnings available for the payment of cash dividends was $657,000 at December 31, 20X2. The carrying amount of receivables that serve as collateral for borrowings totaled $6,300,000 at December 31, 20X2.

Example 46–2: Details of Short-Term Debt

Short-term debt consists of the following at December 31, 20X2, and December 31, 20X1:

	20X2	20X1
Demand note payable to bank, secured by machinery and equipment, interest at 10%	$2,137,000	$1,785,000
Demand notes payable to an entity owned by a majority stockholder, unsecured, interest rates ranging from 8% to 11%	971,000	813,000
Demand note payable to a former stockholder, unsecured, interest at 12%	624,000	674,000
Notes payable to officers with initial maturities of 6 to 12 months, unsecured, interest at 9%	237,000	218,000
	$3,969,000	$3,490,000

Example 46–3: Details of Long-Term Debt

Long-term debt consists of the following at December 31, 20X2, and December 31, 20X1:

	20X2	20X1
Mortgage note payable to bank in monthly installments of $86,000, including interest at 9.25%, due in December 20X9, secured by office building	$7,155,000	$7,514,000

Industrial Revenue Bonds with varying quarterly principal payments due through December 20X9, including interest at 85% of the current prime rate (8.72% at December 31, 20X2), collateralized by property, plant, and equipment	5,767,000	6,158,000
8% convertible subordinated debentures, due in May 20X8 with annual sinking fund requirements of $280,000, convertible into 833,126 shares of common stock at any time prior to maturity	5,160,000	5,440,000
Note payable to bank in quarterly installments of $47,000, including interest at prime plus 1% (9.25% at December 31, 20X2), due in August 20X7, secured by machinery and equipment	922,000	1,013,000
Note payable to an entity owned by a majority stockholder in semi-annual installments of $75,000, plus interest at 10%, due in April 20X7, unsecured	611,000	701,000
Note payable to supplier in monthly installments of $19,000, non-interest bearing (imputed interest of 12%), due in December 20X4, secured by equipment, less unamortized discount of $51,000 at December 31, 20X2, and $112,000 at December 31, 20X1	398,000	565,000
Other	317,000	492,000
Total debt	20,330,000	21,883,000
Less: current portion	(1,636,000)	(1,519,000)
Long-term debt, less current portion	$18,694,000	$20,364,000

Future maturities of long-term debt are as follows as of December 31, 20X2:

20X3	$ 1,636,000
20X4	1,758,000
20X5	1,520,000
20X6	1,619,000
20X7	1,748,000
Thereafter	12,049,000
	$20,330,000

Example 46–4: Issuance of Convertible Subordinated Debt

In February 20X2, the Company issued $10,000,000 of 9% convertible subordinated notes, due on February 1, 20X7. Interest is payable semiannually in February and August. The notes are convertible by the holders into shares of the Company's common stock at any time at a conversion price of $8.50 per share. The notes are subordinated in right of payment to all existing and future senior indebtedness, as defined in the indenture. The notes are redeemable after February 1, 20X5, at the option of the Company at 101.6% of the principal amount, declining to 100.8% of the principal amount on February 1, 20X6, and thereafter until maturity, at which time the notes will be redeemed at par, plus accrued interest. The proceeds were primarily used to repay debt under the Company's bank borrowings and for general corporate purposes.

Example 46–5: Long-Term Debt Classified as a Current Liability Due to Covenant Violations

As a result of operating losses, the Company was unable to remain in compliance with the financial covenants arising under substantially all of its long-term note agreements. The creditors have not waived the financial covenant requirements. The Company has been working with the different creditors to restructure the existing debt; however, an agreement satisfactory to the Company has not been reached. A total of $7,856,000 of long-term debt is subject to accelerated maturity and, as such, the creditors may, at their option, give notice to the Company that amounts owed are immediately due and payable. As a result, the full amount of the related long-term debt has been classified as a current liability in the accompanying Balance Sheet at December 31, 20X2. Regardless of the non-compliance with financial covenants, the Company has made every scheduled payment of principal and interest.

Example 46–6: Long-Term Debt Classified as a Current Liability Due to Company's Likelihood of Missing Its Next Interest Payment

At December 31, 20X2, the long-term portion of the Senior Secured Notes was reclassified to a current liability due to the uncertainty surrounding the Company's ability to make its next interest payment in the approximate amount of $273,000 due in May 20X3.

Example 46–7: Long-Term Debt Classified as a Current Liability Because Company Anticipates to Pay Debt within a Year from the Balance-Sheet Date

The entire outstanding balance of the industrial revenue bond issue, totaling $2,876,000 at December 31, 20X2, has been classified as a current liability as the Company anticipates repaying the entire balance during 20X3 upon the sale of the Company's manufacturing facility in Gary, Indiana.

Example 46–8: Short-Term Debt Classified as Long-Term Because Company Has Both Ability and Intent to Refinance the Debt

Commercial paper debt is due within one year, but has been classified as long-term because the Company has the ability through a $25,000,000 credit agreement to convert this obligation into longer term debt. The credit agreement expires in 20X5 and provides for interest on borrowings at prevailing rates. The Company intends to refinance the commercial paper debt by replacing them with long-term debt.

Example 46–9: Short-Term Debt Classified as Long-Term Because Proceeds of Long-Term Financing Issued Subsequent to Balance-Sheet Date Were Used to Retire the Short-Term Debt

On February 13, 20X3, the Company borrowed $1,000,000 from a financial institution at 1% above the prime rate. The loan is secured by inventory and accounts receivable (with a carrying value of $700,000 at December 31, 20X2), is payable in quarterly installments of principal and interest, and matures in December 20X6. The Company has used a portion of the proceeds to pay off the outstanding balance of the 10% short-term notes payable to a finance company, totaling $473,000 at December 31, 20X2. Accordingly, that balance of $473,000 has been classified as long-term debt at December 31, 20X2.

Example 46–10: Short-Term Debt Classified as Long-Term Because Proceeds from Sale of Stock Subsequent to Balance-Sheet Date Are Expected to Be Used to Retire the Short-Term Debt

On January 28, 20X3, the Company sold 300,000 shares of its $.01 par value common stock for $5 per share. Of the total proceeds of $1,500,000, the Company expects to use $695,000 to refinance on a long-term basis the outstanding principal balance of its 11% short-term notes payable to a vendor. Accordingly, the amount of $695,000 has been classified as long-term debt at December 31, 20X2.

Example 46–11: Bank Waives Noncompliance with Financial Covenants

The Company's credit agreement with the bank contains certain financial covenants that require, among other things, maintenance of minimum amounts and ratios of working capital; minimum amounts of tangible net worth; maximum ratio of indebtedness to tangible net worth; and limits purchases of property, plant and equipment. Certain financial covenants have not been met, and the bank has waived such noncompliance.

Credit Arrangements and Compensating Balances

Example 46–12: Credit Facility Classified as a Current Liability as a Result of a Lockbox Arrangement and Subjective Acceleration Clause

The Company's revolving credit facility requires a lockbox arrangement, which provides for all receipts to be swept daily to reduce borrowings outstanding under the credit facility. This arrangement, combined with the existence of a subjective acceleration clause in the revolving credit facility, necessitates the revolving credit facility be classified a current liability on the balance sheet in accordance with EITF Issue No. 95-22, *Balance Sheet Classification of Borrowings Outstanding under Revolving Credit Agreements That Include Both a Subjective Acceleration Clause and a Lock-Box Arrangement*. The acceleration clause allows the Company's lenders to forgo additional advances should they determine there has been a material adverse change in the Company's financial position or prospects reasonably likely to result in a material adverse effect on its business, condition, operations, performance, or properties. Management believes that no such material adverse change has occurred. In addition, at December 31, 20X2, the Company's lenders had not informed the Company that any such event had occurred. The revolving credit facility expires in March 20X7. Management believes that it will continue to borrow on the line of credit to fund its operations over the term of the revolving credit facility.

Example 46–13: Unused Available Line of Credit

The Company has a demand bank line of credit totalling $6,000,000, including letters of credit, under which the Company may borrow on an unsecured basis at the bank's prime rate. There were no amounts outstanding under this line of credit at December 31, 20X2, and December 31, 20X1. The credit agreement requires compliance with certain financial covenants and expires on April 30, 20X4.

Example 46–14: Borrowings under Line of Credit May Be Converted into a Term Loan

The line of credit agreement allows the Company to convert the borrowing to a term loan for any outstanding amount upon request prior to the expiration of the agreement.

Example 46–15: Factoring Agreement

Pursuant to a factoring agreement, the Company's principal bank acts as its factor for the majority of its receivables, which are assigned on a pre-approved basis. At December 31, 20X2, and December 31, 20X1, the factoring charge amounted to 0.25% of the receivables assigned. The Company's obligations to the bank are collateralized by all of the Company's accounts receivable, inventories, and equipment. The advances for factored receivables are made pursuant to a revolving credit and security agreement, which expires on March 31, 20X4. Pursuant to the terms of the agreement, the Company is required to maintain specified levels of working capital and tangible net worth, among other covenants.

The Company draws down working capital advances and opens letters of credit (up to an aggregate maximum of $10 million) against the facility in amounts determined on a formula that is based on factored receivables, inventory, and cost of imported goods under outstanding letters of credit. Interest is charged at the bank's prime lending rate plus 1% per annum (9.25% at December 31, 20X2) on such advances. As of December 31, 20X2, the Company was in compliance with the covenants under its revolving credit facility.

Example 46–16: Letters of Credit—Inventory

At December 31, 20X2, and December 31, 20X1, the Company has outstanding irrevocable letters of credit in the amount of $1,800,000 and $700,000, respectively. These letters of credit, which have terms from two months to one year, collateralize the Company's obligations to third parties for the purchase of inventory. The fair value of these letters of credit approximates contract values based on the nature of the fee arrangements with the issuing banks.

Example 46–17: Letters of Credit—Contracts and Debt Obligations

At December 31, 20X2, standby letters of credit of approximately $2,400,000 have been issued under an agreement, expiring September 30, 20X3, which is being maintained as security for performance and advances received on long-term contracts and as security for debt service payments under industrial revenue bond loan agreements. The agreement provides a maximum commitment for letters of credit of $3,500,000 and requires an annual commitment fee of $25,000.

Example 46–18: Compensating Balance Requirement Is Based on a Percentage of the Available Line of Credit

As part of its line of credit agreement with a bank, the Company is expected to maintain average compensating cash balances, which are based on a percentage of the available credit line. The amount of compensating balances required at December 31, 20X2, was $300,000. The compensating balances are held under agreements that do not legally restrict the use of such funds and, therefore, the funds are not segregated on the face of the Balance Sheet. The compensating cash balances are determined daily by the bank based upon cash balances shown by the bank, adjusted for average uncollected funds and Federal Reserve requirements. During the year ended December 31, 20X2, the Company was in substantial compliance with the compensating balance requirements. Funds on deposit with the bank and considered in the compensating balances are subject to withdrawal; however, the availability of the line of credit is dependent upon the maintenance of sufficient average compensating balances.

Example 46–19: Compensating Balance Requirement Is a Fixed Amount

As part of its line of credit agreement with a bank, the Company has agreed to maintain average compensating balances of $150,000. The balances are not legally restricted as to withdrawal and serve as part of the Company's normal operating cash.

Debt Issued with Stock Purchase Warrants

Example 46–20: Debt Issued with Stock Purchase Warrants—Fair Value of Warrants Recorded as Additional Paid-in Capital

In May 20X2, the Company sold in a private placement to qualified buyers and accredited investors 10,000 Note Units (the Note Offering). Each Note Unit consisted of $1,000 principal amount of 13.5% unsecured Notes (collectively, the Notes) due May 1, 20X9, and one Common Stock Purchase Warrant (collectively the Warrants) to purchase 85 shares of the Company's common stock, par value $ 0.01 per share (the Common Stock), at an exercise price of $3.09 per share, first exercisable after May 20, 20X3. Total funds received of $10,000,000 were allocated $2,000,000 to the Warrants and $8,000,000 to the Notes. In accordance with EITF No. 00-27, *Application of Issue No. 98-5 to Certain Convertible Instruments*, the values assigned to both the Notes and the Warrants were allocated based on their relative fair values. The relative fair value of the Warrants of $2,000,000 at the time of issuance, which was determined using the Black-Scholes option-pricing model, was recorded as additional paid-in capital and reduced the carrying value of the Notes. The discount on the Notes is being amortized to interest expense over the term of the Notes. At December 31, 20X2, the unamortized discount on the Notes is approximately $1,825,000.

Interest on the Notes is payable semiannually on May 1 and November 1. The Notes will mature on May 1, 20X9. The Notes are not redeemable at the option of the Company prior to May 1, 20X7.

On or after May 1, 20X7, the Notes are redeemable at the option of the Company, in whole or in part, at an initial redemption price of 106.75% of the aggregate principal amount of the Notes until May 1, 20X8, and at par thereafter, plus accrued and unpaid interest, if any, to the date of redemption.

Example 46–21: Debt Issued with Stock Purchase Warrants—Fair Value of Warrants Recorded as a Liability

On January 16, 20X2, the Company issued unsecured promissory notes in the aggregate principal amount of $1,000,000 (the Notes) and warrants to purchase the Company's common stock (the Warrants) to Blue Alliance, Inc. The Notes bear interest at a rate of 11%, mature on July 16, 20X3, and are convertible into 542,000 shares of the Company's common stock at a conversion price of $1.75 per share. The difference between the conversion price and the fair market value of the common stock on the commitment date (transaction date) resulted in a beneficial conversion feature recorded of $590,000. The associated Warrants are exercisable for 270,000 shares of common stock at an exercise price of $1.75 per share. The Warrants, which expire four years after issuance, were assigned a value of $410,000, estimated using the Black-Scholes valuation model. The following assumptions were used to determine the fair value of the Warrants using the Black-Scholes valuation model: a term of four years, risk-free rate of 3.28%, volatility of 100%, and dividend yield of zero. The discounts on the Notes for the beneficial conversion feature and the Warrants are being amortized to interest expense, using the effective interest method, over the term of the Notes. Total interest expense recognized relating to the beneficial conversion feature and the Warrants discount was $673,000 during the year ended December 31, 20X2.

The holders of the Notes and Warrants have registration rights that require the Company to file a registration statement with the Securities and Exchange Commission to register the resale of the common stock issuable upon conversion of the Notes or the exercise of the Warrants. Under EITF No. 00-19, *Accounting for Derivative Financial Instruments Indexed to, and Potentially Settled in, a Company's Own Stock*, the ability to register stock is deemed to be outside of the Company's control. Accordingly, the initial fair value of the Warrants of $410,000 was recorded as an accrued warrant liability in the consolidated balance sheet, and is marked to market at the end of each reporting period. At December 31, 20X2, the warrant liability was adjusted to its new fair value of $217,000 as determined by the Company, resulting in a gain of $193,000, which has been reflected in "Interest income and other, net" on the consolidated statement of operations for the year ended December 31, 20X2.

Redeemable Convertible Preferred Stock Reported as a Liability

Example 46–22: Mandatorily Redeemable Convertible Preferred Stock Reported as a Long-Term Liability

The Company issued 400,000 shares of mandatorily redeemable Series B Convertible Preferred Stock in March 20X1. Each share has a liquidation value of $10 per share. The liquidation value, plus accrued but unpaid dividends, is payable on March 8, 20X9, the mandatory redemption date. The Company has the option to redeem all, but not less than all, of the shares of Series B preferred stock at any time after six years from the date of issuance for a number of shares of the Company's common stock equal to the liquidation value plus accrued and unpaid dividends divided by the current market price of common stock determined in relation to the date of redemption. Under this option, were the redemption to have taken place at December 31, 20X2, each share would have been converted into 1.081 shares of common stock. Also, each share of preferred stock is convertible, at any time, at the option of the holder into the right to receive shares of the Company's common stock. Initially, each share was convertible into .732 shares of common stock, subject to adjustment in the event of certain dividends and distributions, a merger, consolidation or sale of substantially all of the Company's assets, a liquidation or distribution, and certain other events. Were the conversion to have taken place at December 31, 20X2, each share would have been converted into .732 shares of common stock. Holders of preferred stock are entitled to cumulative annual cash dividends of $1 per share, payable quarterly. In any liquidation of the Company, each share of preferred stock is entitled to a liquidation preference before any distribution may be made on the Company's common stock or any series of capital stock that is junior to the Series B preferred stock. In the event of a change in control of the Company, holders of Series B preferred stock also have specified exchange rights into common stock of the Company or into specified securities or property of another entity participating in the change in control transaction.

Effective July 1, 20X2, the Company adopted FASB Statement No. 150, *Accounting for Certain Financial Instruments with Characteristics of Both Liabilities and Equity*. Following adoption of the standard, mandatorily redeemable preferred stock, totaling $4,000,000, is reported as a long-term liability in the balance sheet. As of December 31, 20X2, 1,000,000 preferred stock shares are authorized and 400,000 shares are issued and outstanding.

Balance Sheet Presentation—The following presentation illustrates the reporting of the mandatorily redeemable convertible preferred stock as a long-term liability based on this example.

Liabilities:

Accounts payable	$ 2,350,000
Short-term debt	900,000
Accrued expenses	500,000
Total current liabilities	3,750,000
Long-term debt	2,500,000

Mandatorily redeemable convertible preferred stock	4,000,000
Deferred income taxes	725,000
Total liabilities	$10,975,000

Stockholders' equity:
(Details omitted)

Debt Extinguishment

Example 46–23: Gain from Early Extinguishment of Debt Does Not Meet the Criteria for Classification as an Extraordinary Item

During the year ended December 31, 20X2, in connection with the settlement of obligations involving Hope Enterprises, the Company recognized a gain of $1,200,000 representing the difference between the fair value of the consideration issued in the settlement transaction and the carrying value of the amounts due Hope Enterprises. The Company evaluated the classification of this gain and determined that the gain does not meet the criteria for classification as an extraordinary item. As a result, the gain has been included as "Gain on early extinguishment of debt" under "Other income (expense)" within income from continuing operations in the accompanying Consolidated Statement of Operations for the year ended December 31, 20X2.

Example 46–24: Loss from Early Extinguishment of Debt Meets the Criteria for Classification as an Extraordinary Item

In September 20X2, the Company redeemed various outstanding notes and debentures with an aggregate principal value of $2,769,000. The Company paid a premium to the debenture holders, and the transaction resulted in an extraordinary charge. The extraordinary loss of $452,000, net of a tax benefit of $165,000, principally represents the premium paid in connection with the early extinguishment of the debt and unamortized discount. The payments were made out of available cash.

Debt Restructuring

Example 46–25: Terms of Troubled Debt Modified—Carrying Amount of Troubled Debt Exceeds Future Cash Payments

At December 31, 20X1, the Company had a 12% note payable to its primary bank with an outstanding principal balance of $1,756,000, due in December 20X7. In September 20X2, the Company reached an agreement with the bank to modify the terms of the note, due to cash flow problems experienced by the Company. The bank has agreed to accept a cash payment of $250,000 and installment payments on a note for a total of $900,000 at no interest, due in December 20X7. As a result, the amount of the note to the bank was reduced by $606,000 to reflect the revised terms, and a gain of $352,000 has been included in the Statement of Operations for 20X2.

Example 46–26: Terms of Troubled Debt Modified—Future Cash Payments Exceed Carrying Value of Troubled Debt

At December 31, 20X1, the Company had an 11% note payable to its primary bank with an outstanding principal balance of $1,500,000, due in December 20X3. In September 20X2, the Company reached an agreement with the bank to modify the terms of the note, due to cash flow problems experienced by the Company. The bank has agreed to extend the due date of the note until December 20X6 and to reduce the interest rate to 9%. The modifications have resulted in an effective interest rate of 8.2% to be applied to the carrying amount of the debt prospectively. Interest expense through the revised maturity date of December 20X6 will be reduced accordingly.

Example 46–27: Transfer of Assets and Grant of Equity Interest in Full Settlement of Troubled Debt Restructuring—Ordinary Gain Is Recognized on Transfer of Assets and Extraordinary Gain Is Recognized on Restructured Debt

In March 20X2, the Company reached an agreement with its principal vendor to transfer fixed assets and to grant 50,000 shares of the Company's $0.01 par value common stock to the vendor in full settlement of a 12% note payable to the vendor due in February 20X4. At the date of transfer, the fair market value of the fixed assets and common stock transferred exceeded their carrying value by $179,000; accordingly, an ordinary gain of $179,000 has been included in the Statement of Operations in 20X2. At the date of transfer, the carrying value of the debt payable to the vendor exceeded the fair market value of the fixed assets and common stock transferred by $611,000; accordingly, an extraordinary gain of $397,000, net of income tax of $214,000, has been included in the Statement of Operations in 20X2.

Example 46–28: Modified Terms of Troubled Debt Restructuring Include Future Contingent Payments

Due to significant cash flow problems, in April 20X2 the Company modified the terms of its 10% note payable to a principal vendor with an outstanding balance of $1,618,000, due in quarterly installments through May 20X7. The vendor has agreed to (1) accept 2,000,000 shares of the Company's $0.01 par value common stock,

(2) reduce the required quarterly payments by $35,000 through May 20X7, and (3) receive an additional $50,000 annual payment for each year in which the Company's cash flow from operations exceeds $250,0000. As a result of these modifications, the Company recorded a gain of $315,000 in the Statement of Operations in 20X2.

Unconditional Purchase Obligations

Example 46–29: Unconditional Obligation under a Throughput Agreement—Includes Optional Disclosure of Present Value of Required Payments

To secure access to facilities to process high damping rubber compound, the Company has signed a processing agreement with BJ Rubber allowing the Company to submit 150,000 tons for processing annually for 15 years. Under the terms of the agreement, the Company may be required to advance funds against future processing charges if BJ Rubber is unable to meet its financial obligations. The aggregate amount of required payments at December 31, 20X2, is as follows:

20X3	$ 215,000
20X4	200,000
20X5	185,000
20X6	175,000
20X7	150,000
Thereafter	1,260,000
Total	2,185,000
Less: amount representing interest	(1,487,000)
Present value of required payments	$ 698,000

In addition, the Company is required to pay a proportional share of the variable operating expenses of the plant. The Company's total processing charges under the agreement for 20X2 and 20X1 was $289,000 and $266,000, respectively.

Example 46–30: Unconditional Obligation under Take-or-Pay Agreement—Includes Optional Disclosure of Present Value of Required Payments

To assure a long-term supply, the Company has contracted to purchase 20% of the production of microprocessors of Microteks, Inc. through the year 20X7 and to make minimum annual payments as follows, whether or not it is able to take delivery:

20X3	$ 5,000,000
20X4	5,000,000
20X5	4,500,000
20X6	4,500,000
20X7	4,000,000
Total	23,000,000
Less: amount representing interest	(10,125,000)
Present value of required payments	$12,875,000

In addition, the Company must reimburse Microteks, Inc. for a proportional share of its plant operating expenses. The Company's total purchases under the agreement were $5,769,000 and $5,432,000 in 20X2 and 20X1, respectively.

Example 46–31: Unconditional Purchase Obligation in Connection with Acquisition—Disclosure of Present Value of Minimum Payments Not Made (Present Value Disclosure Is Optional)

In connection with the EFTX acquisition in January 20X1, EFTX and the Company entered into a manufacturing agreement whereby the Company committed to purchase minimum amounts of goods and services used in its normal operations during the first 48 months after the transaction. Future annual minimum purchases remaining under the agreement are $19 million and $22 million for 20X3 and 20X4, respectively. During 20X2 and 20X1, the Company's total purchases under the agreement were $17 million and $13 million, respectively.

Product Financing Arrangements

Example 46–32: Obligations and Commitments under Product Financing Arrangement

In 20X2, the Company entered into a product financing arrangement with a vendor for the purchase of $13 million of electronic connectors. Accordingly, this inventory and the related short-term debt have been included in the Balance Sheet at December 31, 20X2. The vendor has also made commitments, on the Company's behalf, to purchase additional amounts of the electronic connectors for delivery in 20X3. The average interest rate on the product financing arrangement was 7.3% at December 31, 20X2. Interest expense incurred and paid under this product financing arrangement totaled $186,000 for 20X2. The Company is obligated to pay the vendor under this product financing arrangement upon its receipt of the products.

Subsequent Events Involving Debt Obligations and Credit Arrangements

Example 46–33: Subsequent Event—New Financing Arrangement

On January 29, 20X3, the Company entered into a Revolving Loan Agreement (the Loan Agreement) with Ace State Bank. The Loan Agreement provides for borrowings through January 31, 20X8 (the Maturity Date). Borrowings will bear interest at the bank's prime rate. The maximum amount that may be outstanding under the Loan Agreement is $20,000,000 through December 31, 20X4. Thereafter, the maximum amount of borrowings that may be outstanding under the Loan Agreement is reduced by $1,000,000 in calendar 20X5 and by $1,000,000 in each of the following calendar years up to the Maturity Date. Under the terms of the Loan Agreement, the Company will pay Ace State Bank $200,000 plus an unused commitment fee during the term of the Loan Agreement. The Company will also pay legal, accounting, and other fees and expenses in connection with the Loan Agreement.

Example 46–34: Subsequent Event—Issuance of Convertible Subordinated Notes

On January 12, 20X3, the Company executed an agreement with a group of institutional investors whereby the Company issued $12 million in convertible subordinated loan notes. These notes bear an interest rate of 11% per year and mature in 20X5. The Company intends to use the proceeds for general corporate purposes, including working capital and machinery and equipment purchases, and to finance the construction of the Company's new facility in Dayton, Ohio.

Example 46–35: Subsequent Event—Maximum Borrowing under Line of Credit

In February and March 20X3, the Company borrowed $800,000 under its line of credit for working capital purposes. As a result, the Company has borrowed the maximum amount available under the credit line. The Company is negotiating with the bank to increase its credit line limit by $2,000,000. However, there can be no assurance that the Company will be successful in increasing its credit line.

CHAPTER 47
OTHER LIABILITIES: CURRENT
AND NONCURRENT

CONTENTS

EXECUTIVE SUMMARY

The most common types of current and noncurrent liabilities are discussed in numerous chapters throughout this book. For example:

- Capital lease obligations are discussed in Chapter 23.

- Obligations relating to pension plans, postemployment benefits, and postretirement benefits are discussed in Chapters 26–28.

- Current and deferred income tax liabilities are discussed in Chapter 45.

- Debt obligations (short-term and long-term debt) are discussed in Chapter 46.

The discussion and examples in this chapter address both current and noncurrent liabilities that have not been covered in other chapters of this book.

Current liabilities may be listed in the balance sheet in order of maturity, according to amount (largest to smallest), or in order of liquidation preference. However, generally, trade accounts payable or short-term debt is listed first and a catchall caption such as "Other liabilities" or "Accrued expenses" is typically listed last. Current liabilities typically include the following:

- Trade accounts payable

- Short-term debt (e.g., notes and loans, including borrowings under line of credit arrangements)

- Current maturities of long-term debt

- Current maturities of capital lease obligations

- Employee related liabilities (e.g., salaries, wages, bonuses, commissions, and related benefits)

- Taxes (e.g., income taxes payable, deferred income taxes, and sales taxes)

- Dividends payable

- Accrued interest

- Customer deposits and advances

- Deferred income

- Accrued expenses (e.g., product warranties, royalties)

Long-term liabilities primarily consist of debt obligations (e.g., bonds, mortgages, notes, and capital leases), deferred income taxes, and a catchall caption such as "Other long-term liabilities."

If several "Other liabilities" type items (current or noncurrent) are included as a single line item in the balance sheet, and the amount is material, it is generally informative to include the details of such items in a note to the financial statements.

Authoritative Literature

ARB-43	Chapter 3A, Current Assets and Current Liabilities
APB-10	Omnibus Opinion—1966
APB-12	Omnibus Opinion—1967

DISCLOSURE REQUIREMENTS

Detail and supplemental information concerning current and non-current liabilities should be sufficiently included in the financial statements, or notes thereto, to meet the requirement of adequate informative disclosure. If other liabilities, current or noncurrent, are material to the financial statements, disclosures should include a description of the liability, its carrying value, and the basis of its valuation.

EXAMPLES OF FINANCIAL STATEMENT DISCLOSURES

 The following sample disclosures are available on the accompanying disc.

Example 47–1: Details of Other Current Liabilities

> **Note:** This example is a comprehensive example of the details of current liabilities provided in a note to the financial statements. The order in which the items are presented in the note will depend on the individual circumstances, but, generally, the items are presented according to amount (largest to smallest).

Other current liabilities consist of the following at December 31, 20X2, and December 31, 20X1:

	20X2	20X1
Accrued income taxes	$300,000	$250,000
Gift certificate and credit memo liability	153,000	157,000
Sales tax payable	140,000	132,000
Accrued salaries, wages, and related payroll taxes	120,000	115,000
Deferred revenue	102,000	111,000
Customer deposits	93,000	91,000
Accrued warranties	88,000	83,000
Accrued sales returns and discounts	70,000	78,000

	20X2	20X1
Accrued royalties payable	61,000	68,000
Accrued commissions	59,000	53,000
Accrued profit sharing contribution	46,000	42,000
Accrued insurance	37,000	31,000
Accrued rent	26,000	24,000
Accrued interest	19,000	15,000
Dividends payable	16,000	10,000
	$1,330,000	$1,260,000

Example 47–2: Accrued Product Liability and Warranty Claims

The Company's financial statements include accruals for potential product liability and warranty claims based on the Company's claims experience. Such costs are accrued at the time revenue is recognized. At December 31, 20X2, and December 31, 20X1, accrued product warranties totaled $373,000 and $419,000, respectively, and are included in "Other current liabilities" in the accompanying Balance Sheets.

Example 47–3: Deferred Revenue

Revenue under maintenance agreements is deferred and recognized over the term of the agreements (typically two years) on a straight-line basis. At December 31, 20X2, and December 31, 20X1, deferred revenue totaled $556,000 and $471,000, respectively, of which the amount recognizable within one year is included under "Accrued liabilities" in the accompanying Balance Sheets.

Example 47–4: Deferred Rent

The Company has entered into operating lease agreements for its corporate office and warehouse, some of which contain provisions for future rent increases, or periods in which rent payments are reduced (abated). In accordance with generally accepted accounting principles, the Company records monthly rent expense equal to the total of the payments due over the lease term, divided by the number of months of the lease term. The difference between rent expense recorded and the amount paid is credited or charged to "Deferred rent" which is reflected as a separate line item in the accompanying Balance Sheets.

Example 47–5: Accrued Rebates

The Company enters into contractual agreements for rebates on certain products with its customers. These amounts are recorded as a reduction of gross sales to arrive at net sales, and a corresponding accrual is made in the balance sheet. At December 31, 20X2, and December 31, 20X1, "Accrued expenses" include accrued rebates of $298,000 and $347,000, respectively.

Example 47–6: Accrual for Litigation Based on Company's Best Estimate

The Company is a defendant in a lawsuit, filed by a former supplier of electronic components alleging breach of contract, which seeks damages totaling $750,000. The Company proposed a settlement in the amount of $500,000, based on the advice of the Company's legal counsel, and this amount represents the Company's best estimate for which the litigation will settle. Consequently, $500,000 was charged to operations in 20X2 and a corresponding liability has been recorded under "Litigation accrual" as of December 31, 20X2, in the accompanying financial statements. However, if the settlement offer is not accepted by the plaintiff and the case goes to trial, the amount of the ultimate loss to the Company, if any, may equal the entire amount of damages of $750,000 sought by the plaintiff.

Example 47–7: Accrual for Lawsuit Settlement Recorded at Present Value of Amount to Be Paid

In October 20X2, the Company settled a legal action brought by a group of employees alleging certain discriminatory employment practices by the Company. Under the settlement, the Company has agreed to provide monetary relief in the amount of approximately $2,500,000, to be paid in installments over a five-year period. The present value of the cost of the settlement and estimated additional legal fees, totalling $1,900,000, have been included in results of operations for 20X2. At December 31, 20X2, the current portion of the liability recorded is approximately $500,000 and is included in "Other current liabilities"; the remaining amount of $1,400,000 is classified as a noncurrent liability under "Lawsuit settlement liability" in the accompanying Balance Sheets.

Example 47–8: Liability under Self-Insured Group Medical Insurance Plan

The Company sponsors a self-insured group medical insurance plan. The plan is designed to provide a specified level of coverage, with stop-loss coverage provided by a commercial insurer in order to limit the Company's exposure. The Company's maximum claim exposure is limited to $35,000 per person per policy year. At December 31, 20X2, the Company had 244 employees enrolled in the plan. The plan provides non-contributory coverage for employees and contributory coverage for dependents. The Company's contributions totaled $617,000 in 20X2 and $564,000 in 20X1.

The Company provides accruals based on the aggregate amount of the liability for reported claims and an estimated liability for claims incurred but not reported. At December 31, 20X2, and December 31, 20X1, "Other liabilities" include accrued liability related to this plan of $116,000 and $149,000, respectively.

Example 47–9: Accrued Liability for Estimated Environmental Remediation Costs

The Company is involved in environmental remediation and ongoing compliance at several sites. At December 31, 20X2, the Company estimated, based on engineering studies, total remediation and ongoing monitoring costs to be made in the future to be approximately $6,500,000, including the effects of inflation. Accordingly, the Company recorded a liability of approximately $4,000,000, which represents the net present value of the estimated future costs discounted at 6%. This is management's best estimate of these liabilities, although possible actual costs could range up to 50% higher. The Company has not anticipated any third-party payments in arriving at these estimates.

> **Note:** See Chapter 10, "Contingencies, Risks, Uncertainties, and Concentrations," for additional examples regarding accruals for estimated environmental remediation costs.

Example 47–10: Allowances for Contract Losses

Other current liabilities at December 31, 20X2, and December 31, 20X1, include allowances for contract losses aggregating $512,000 and $390,000, respectively.

Example 47–11: Termination Benefit Payable

At December 31, 20X2, the Company has included as a liability the present value, computed with an effective annual rate of 10%, of a death benefit related to the termination of an employment contract as a result of the death of the president in 20X2. This termination death benefit will be paid in 36 equal monthly installments of $30,000 commencing in April 20X3.

Example 47–12: Asset Retirement Obligations

At December 31, 20X2, the Company has recorded an asset retirement obligation and associated long-lived asset of $250,000 for the fair value of a contractual obligation to remove leasehold improvements at the conclusion of the Company's facility lease in Stockton, California. The obligation and asset are classified on the Company's consolidated balance sheet as of December 31, 20X2 as non-current liabilities and property and accreting equipment, respectively. The Company is amortizing the asset and accreting the obligation over the remaining life of the associated leasehold improvements.

Example 47–13: Fair Value of Warrants Recorded as a Liability

In June 20X2, the Company completed a $1,100,000 private placement of its common stock. The Company issued 1,125,000 shares of common stock along with warrants to purchase 410,000 shares of common stock at $1.15 per share, which were valued at $436,000. The Company received approximately $941,000 in net proceeds from this transaction. As the warrants originally included a requirement for net cash settlement if the Company was unable to register the shares to be issued upon exercise of the warrants, these warrants were required to be recorded as a liability until such time as the registration requirements expired. The Company subsequently signed a "Waiver Letter Agreement" with certain warrant holders, which resulted in the warrants being modified to provide for a cashless exercise in the event of a Nonregistration Event, as defined, and the elimination of the net cash settlement provision. In addition, certain penalty provisions were modified to provide that the warrant holders would receive no liquidated damages in the event of a Nonregistration Event. Upon the elimination of the net cash settlement provision, the fair value of the warrants ($311,000) was reclassified from other current liabilities to additional paid-in capital. As of December 31, 20X2, remaining warrants with a fair value of $132,000 are included in other current liabilities in the accompanying consolidated balance sheet.

CHAPTER 48
STOCKHOLDER'S EQUITY

CONTENTS

EXECUTIVE SUMMARY

Stockholders' equity includes the following three broad categories:

1. *Contributed capital*—This represents (a) the amounts paid by common and preferred stockholders when they purchased the company's stock and (b) the amounts arising from subsequent transactions such as treasury stock transactions.

2. *Retained earnings*—This represents the amount of previous income of the company that has not been distributed to owners as dividends or transferred to contributed capital.

3. *Accumulated other comprehensive income*—Under current accounting literature, other comprehensive income includes (a) unrealized gains and losses on available-for-sale marketable securities, (b) minimum pension liability adjustments, (c) foreign currency translation adjustments and gains and losses from certain foreign currency transactions, and (d) the effective portion of gains and losses on certain hedging activities. Components of other comprehensive income are covered in more detail in Chapter 54, "Comprehensive Income," because comprehensive income may be reported in an income statement, in a separate statement of comprehensive income that begins with net income, or in a statement of changes in stockholder's equity.

Generally, the components of stockholders' equity are presented in the following order in the balance sheet:

- Preferred stock
- Common stock

- Additional paid-in capital
- Retained earnings (accumulated deficit)
- Accumulated other comprehensive income (loss)
- Treasury stock

Capital transactions should generally be excluded from the determination of income but should be adequately disclosed in the financial statements.

Capital Stock

Capital stock represents the legal or stated capital provided by stockholders. Capital stock may consist of common or preferred shares. Common stock usually has (1) the right to vote, (2) the right to share in earnings, (3) a preemptive right to a proportionate share of any additional common stock issued, and (4) the right to share in assets on liquidation. Preferred stock carries certain specified preferences or privileges over common stock. For example, preferred shares may be (1) voting or nonvoting, (2) participating or nonparticipating as to the earnings of the corporation, (3) cumulative or noncumulative as to the payment of dividends, (4) callable for redemption at a specified price, or (5) convertible to common stock.

A corporation's charter contains the types and amounts of stock that it can legally issue, which is called the *authorized capital stock*. When part or all of the authorized capital stock is issued, it is called *issued capital stock*. Because a corporation may own issued capital stock in the form of treasury stock, the amount of issued capital stock in the hands of stockholders is called *outstanding capital stock*.

If capital stock is issued for the acquisition of property and it appears that, at about the same time and pursuant to a previous agreement or understanding, some portion of the stock so issued is donated to the corporation, the par value of the stock is not an appropriate basis for valuing the property. Rather, the property should be recorded at its fair value.

Additional Paid-in Capital

Generally, stock is issued with a par value. No-par value stock may or may not have a stated value. *Par* or *stated value* is the amount that is established in the stock account at the time the stock is issued. When stock is issued above or below par value, a premium or discount on the stock is recorded, respectively. A discount reduces paid-in or contributed capital; a premium increases paid-in or contributed capital. A premium on stock is often referred to as "Additional paid-in capital" or "Paid-in capital in excess of par value." Because the issuance of stock at a discount is not legal in many jurisdictions, discounts on stock are not frequently encountered.

Stock Subscriptions Receivable

A corporation may sell its capital stock by subscriptions. An individual subscriber becomes a stockholder upon subscribing to the capital stock, and, upon full payment of the subscription, a stock certificate evidencing ownership in the corporation is issued. When the subscription method is used to sell capital stock, a subscription receivable account is debited and a capital stock subscribed account is credited. On payment of the subscription, the subscription receivable account is credited and cash or other assets are debited. On the actual issuance of the stock certificates, the capital stock subscribed account is debited and the regular capital stock account is credited.

Stock subscriptions receivable generally should be reported as a deduction from stockholders' equity. They should be shown as an asset only in rare circumstances when the receivables mature in a relatively short period of time and there is substantial evidence of ability and intent to pay.

Treasury Stock

Treasury stock is a company's own capital stock that has been issued and subsequently reacquired. It is ordinarily presented as a reduction in the amount of stockholders' equity. Treasury stock is not considered an asset, because it is widely held that a corporation cannot own part of itself. The status of treasury stock is similar to that of authorized but unissued capital stock. Dividends on a company's own stock are not considered a part of income. Gains and losses on sales of treasury stock should be accounted for as adjustments to capital and not as part of income.

Stock Dividends

A *dividend* is a pro rata distribution by a corporation, based on shares of a particular class, and usually represents a distribution based on earnings. Cash dividends are the most common type of dividend distribution and are recorded on the books of the corporation as a liability (dividends payable) on the date of declaration. Stock dividends are distributions of a company's own capital stock to its existing stockholders in lieu of cash. Stock dividends are accounted for by transferring an amount equal to the fair market value of the stock from retained earnings to paid-in capital.

Stock Splits

When a stock distribution is generally more than 20% to 25% of the outstanding shares immediately before the distribution, it is considered a stock split. A stock split increases the number of shares of capital stock outstanding, and a reverse stock split decreases the number of shares of capital stock outstanding. In both straight and reverse stock splits, the total dollar amount of stockholders' equity does not change. The par or stated value per share of capital stock, however, decreases or increases in proportion with the increase or decrease in the number of shares outstanding.

Dividends-in-Kind

Dividends payable in assets of the corporation other than cash (e.g., marketable securities) are commonly referred to as dividends-in-kind. Such dividend distributions of nonmonetary assets to stockholders should be recorded at the fair value of the assets transferred, and a gain or loss should be recognized on the disposition of the asset.

Retained Earnings

If a portion of retained earnings is appropriated for loss contingencies, the appropriation of retained earnings should be shown within the stockholder's equity section of the balance sheet and be clearly identified as an appropriation of retained earnings.

Costs or losses should not be charged to an appropriation of retained earnings, and no part of the appropriation should be transferred to income.

Financial Instruments with Characteristics of Both Liabilities and Equity

FASB Statement of Financial Accounting Standards No. 150 (FAS-150), *Accounting for Certain Financial Instruments with Characteristics of Both Liabilities and Equity*, establishes standards for issuers of financial instruments with characteristics of both liabilities and equity related to the classification and measurement of those instruments. FAS-150 essentially requires the following three classes of financial instruments previously classified as equity to be classified as liabilities (or assets in some cases):

1. *Mandatorily redeemable financial instruments.* These financial instruments should be classified as liabilities in an entity's financial statements unless the redemption is required to occur only upon the entity's liquidation or termination. A financial

instrument issued in the form of shares is mandatorily redeemable if it embodies an unconditional obligation requiring the issuer to redeem the instrument by transferring its assets at a specified or determinable date or upon an event certain to occur. For example, shares that are required to be redeemed by an entity upon the death of a stockholder (an event certain to occur) are mandatorily redeemable shares.

2. *Obligations to repurchase the issuer's equity shares by transferring assets.* Financial instruments other than outstanding shares that, at inception, meet the following criteria should be classified as liabilities (or as assets in some circumstances): (a) the financial instruments embody an obligation to repurchase the issuer's equity shares, or are indexed to such an obligation, and (b) they require, or may require, the issuer to settle the obligation by transferring assets. Examples include forward purchase contracts or written put options on an issuer's equity shares that are to be physically settled or net cash settled.

3. *Certain obligations to issue a variable number of shares.* Financial instruments that embody an unconditional obligation, or financial instruments other than outstanding shares that embody a conditional obligation, which the entity must or may settle by issuing a variable number of equity shares should be classified as liabilities (or as assets in some circumstances) if, at inception, the monetary value of the obligation is based solely or predominantly on any of the following:

   (a) A fixed monetary amount that is known at inception (e.g., a payable to be settled with a variable number of the entity's equity shares).

   (b) Variations in something other than the fair value of the entity's equity shares (e.g., a financial instrument indexed to the S&P 500 and to be settled with a variable number of the entity's equity shares).

   (c) Variations inversely related to changes in the fair value of the entity's equity shares (e.g., a written put option that could be settled net by delivering a variable number of equity shares).

Except for mandatorily redeemable financial instruments of nonpublic companies, FAS-150 is effective for financial instruments entered into or modified after May 31, 2003; for financial instruments entered into previously, FAS-150 is effective for interim periods beginning after June 15, 2003. For financial instruments of nonpublic companies that are mandatorily redeemable on fixed dates for amounts that either are fixed or are determined by reference to an interest rate index, currency index, or another external index, FAS-150 is effective for fiscal periods beginning after December 15, 2004. For all other mandatorily redeemable financial instruments of nonpublic companies, FAS-150 is deferred indefinitely pending further action by the FASB.

See Chapter 15, "Financial Instruments, Derivatives, and Hedging Activities," for further guidance including effective date, for the disclosure requirements of FAS-150, and for related examples of financial statement disclosures.

Authoritative Literature

ARB-43	Chapter 1A, Rules Adopted by Membership
	Chapter 1B, Opinion Issued by Predecessor Committee
	Chapter 7B, Stock Dividends and Stock Split-ups
APB-6	Status of Accounting Research Bulletins
APB-10	Omnibus Opinion—1966
APB-12	Omnibus Opinion—1967
APB-14	Accounting for Convertible Debt and Debt Issued with Stock Purchase Warrants
APB-29	Accounting for Nonmonetary Transactions
FAS-5	Accounting for Contingencies
FAS-129	Disclosure of Information about Capital Structure
FSP FAS 129-1	Disclosure Requirements under FASB Statement No. 129, *Disclosure of Information about Capital Structure*, Relating to Contingently Convertible Securities
FAS-150	Accounting for Certain Financial Instruments with Characteristics of Both Liabilities and Equity
FSP FAS 150-3	Effective Date, Disclosures, and Transition for Mandatorily Redeemable Financial Instruments of Certain Nonpublic Entities and Certain Mandatorily Redeemable Noncontrolling Interests under FASB Statement No. 150, *Accounting for Certain Financial Instruments with Characteristics of Both Liabilities and Equity*
FTB 85-6	Accounting for a Purchase of Treasury Shares at a Price Significantly in Excess of the Current Market Price of the Shares and the Income Statement Classification of Costs Incurred in Defending against a Takeover Attempt

EITF 98-5	Accounting for Convertible Securities with Beneficial Conversion Features or Contingently Adjustable Conversion Ratios
EITF 00-19	Accounting for Derivative Financial Instruments Indexed to, and Potentially Settled in, a Company's Own Stock
EITF 00-27	Application of Issue No. 98-5 to Certain Convertible Instruments

DISCLOSURE REQUIREMENTS

The following disclosures should be made.

1. For each class of capital stock (generally accepted practice):
   a. Shares authorized, issued, and outstanding
   b. Par value or stated value
   c. The number of shares reserved for future issuance and the purpose for such reservation
2. For preferred stock or other senior stock that has a preference in involuntary liquidation considerably in excess of the par or stated values of the shares (FAS-129, pars. 6–7):
   a. The liquidation preference of the stock (the relationship between the preference in liquidation and the par or stated value of the shares) (This disclosure should be made in the equity section on the face of the balance sheet, in the aggregate, rather than the notes.)
   b. The aggregate or per-share amounts at which preferred stock may be called or is subject to redemption through sinking-fund operations or otherwise
   c. The aggregate and per-share amounts of arrearages in cumulative preferred dividends
3. The rights and privileges of the various securities outstanding, including (FAS-129, par. 4):
   a. Dividend, liquidation, or call preferences
   b. Participation rights
   c. Call prices and dates
   d. Conversion or exercise prices or rates and pertinent dates
   e. Sinking fund requirements
   f. Unusual voting rights
   g. Significant terms of contracts to issue additional shares

4. The number of shares issued on conversion, exercise, or otherwise during at least the most recent annual fiscal period and any subsequent interim period presented (FAS-129, par. 5)

5. For each of the five years following the date of the latest balance sheet presented, the amount of redemption requirements for all issues of capital stock redeemable at fixed or determinable prices on fixed or determinable dates (FAS-47, par. 10 and FAS-129, par. 8)

6. For retained earnings:

   a. Appropriations of retained earnings for loss contingencies separately shown in the stockholders' equity section and clearly identified as such (FAS-5, par. 15)

   b. The nature and extent to which retained earnings is restricted (APB-6, par. 13)

7. For each period in which both a balance sheet and statement of income are presented, the changes in stockholders' equity, including (APB-12, par. 10):

   a. Changes in the separate accounts comprising stockholders' equity

   b. Changes in the number of shares of equity securities during at least the most recent annual fiscal period

8. Stock subscriptions receivable presented as a contra-equity account, or if shown as an asset, the receivable should be clearly labeled and segregated from any other type of asset (generally accepted practice)

9. For treasury stock (APB-6, par. 13):

   a. The method used to account for the treasury stock

   b. The number of shares of treasury stock held

   c. Accounting treatment in accordance with state law if it is at variance with GAAP

10. If treasury stock is acquired for purposes other than retirement (formal or constructive), or if the ultimate disposition has not yet been decided (APB-6, par. 12b):

    a. The cost should be shown separately as a deduction from the total of capital stock, additional paid-in capital, and retained earnings; or

    b. The par value of the shares should be charged to the specific stock issue and the excess of purchase price over the par value should be allocated between additional paid-in capital and retained earnings (alternatively, the excess may be charged entirely to retained earnings).

11. If treasury stock of the entity is shown as an asset, the circumstances for such classification should be adequately disclosed (ARB-43, Ch. 1A, par. 4)

12. If treasury shares are purchased at a stated price significantly in excess of the current market price of the shares, disclosure should include the amounts allocated to other elements of the transaction and the related accounting treatment (FTB 85-6)

13. Capital shares reserved for future issuance in connection with a business combination (FAS-141, par. 51)

14. Dividends declared but not yet paid at the balance-sheet date (ARB-43, Ch. 3A, par. 7)

15. Restrictions on dividend payments (FAS-5, pars. 18–19)

16. If nonmonetary assets are distributed as dividends (i.e., dividends-in-kind) (APB-29, par. 28):

    a. The nature of the distribution

    b. The basis of accounting for the assets transferred

    c. The gains and losses recognized

17. If a stock dividend, split, or reverse split occurs after the date of the latest balance sheet presented but before the issuance of the financial statements (generally accepted practice):

    a. An explanation of the stock dividend, split, or reverse split and the date

    b. The retroactive effect provided in the balance sheet

18. For warrants or rights outstanding as of the most recent balance-sheet date (generally accepted practice):

    a. The title and aggregate amount of securities called for by warrants or rights outstanding

    b. The period during which warrants or rights are exercisable

    c. The exercise price

19. For all contingently convertible securities, the significant terms of the conversion features should be disclosed to enable users of the financial statements to understand the circumstances of the contingency and the potential impact of conversion, including (FSP FAS 129-1, pars. 3–5):

    a. Events or changes in circumstances that would cause the contingency to be met and any significant features necessary to understand the conversion rights and the timing of those rights (e.g., the periods in which the contingency might be met and in which the securities may be converted if the contingency is met)

b. The conversion price and the number of shares into which the security is potentially convertible

c. Events or changes in circumstances, if any, that could adjust or change the contingency, conversion price, or number of shares, including significant terms of those changes

d. The manner of settlement upon conversion and any alternative settlement methods (e.g., cash, shares, or a combination)

e. Whether the shares that would be issued if the contingently convertible securities were converted are included in the calculation of diluted EPS, and the reasons why or why not

f. Information about derivative transactions entered into in connection with the issuance of the contingently convertible securities, such as the terms of the derivative transaction, how the transaction relates to the contingently convertible securities, and the number of shares underlying the derivatives

20. For convertible securities with beneficial conversion features or contingently adjustable conversion ratios accounted for in accordance with EITF 98-5, disclosure should be made of the terms of the transaction, including the excess of the aggregate fair value of the instruments that the holder would receive at conversion over the proceeds received and the period over which the discount is amortized (These disclosures would only be applicable if the intrinsic value of the beneficial conversion feature is greater than the proceeds allocated to the convertible instrument) (EITF 98-5, par. 7)

EXAMPLES OF FINANCIAL STATEMENT DISCLOSURES

 The following sample disclosures are available on the accompanying disc.

Presentation of Components of Stockholders' Equity

Example 48–1: Details of Stockholders' Equity on the Face of the Balance Sheet

	20X2	20X1
Stockholders' Equity:		
3% cumulative preferred stock; par value $.10; authorized 1,000,000 shares; issued and outstanding 200,000 shares in 20X2 and 100,000 shares in 20X1; aggregate liquidation preference of $2,400,000 in 20X2 and $1,200,000 in 20X1	$ 20,000	$ 10,000

6% convertible preferred stock; par value $.50; authorized 1,000,000 shares; issued and outstanding 400,000 shares in 20X2 and 300,000 shares in 20X1	200,000	150,000
Class A common stock; par value $.01; authorized 100,000,000 shares; issued and outstanding 15,000,000 shares in 20X2 and 13,000,000 shares in 20X1	150,000	130,000
Class B common stock; par value $.01; authorized 50,000,000 shares; issued and outstanding 10,000,000 shares in 20X2 and 20X1	100,000	100,000
Additional paid-in capital	5,475,000	4,692,000
Retained earnings	1,413,000	1,017,000
Accumulated other comprehensive income 80,000	65,000	
Less: stock subscriptions receivable	(180,000)	-0-
Less: treasury stock, at cost—150,000 shares in 20X2 and 20X1	(675,000)	(675,000)
Total stockholders' equity	$6,583,000	$5,489,000

Example 48–2 Statement of Changes in Stockholders' Equity

Note: The following is a comprehensive presentation of changes in components of stockholders' equity shown as a separate statement in the financial statements.

	Preferred Stock		Common Stock		Additional Paid-in Capital	Retained Earnings	Accumulated Other Comprehensive Income	Stock Subscriptions Receivable	Treasury Stock		Total Stockholders' Equity
	Shares	Amount	Shares	Amount					Shares	Amount	
Balance at December 31, 20X0	100,000	$10,000	250,000	$2,500	$418,000	$111,000	$56,000	$(8,000)	(4,000)	$(40,000)	$549,500
Net income	-0-	-0-	-0-	-0-	-0-	316,000	-0-	-0-	-0-	-0-	316,000
Foreign currency adjustment	-0-	-0-	-0-	-0-	-0-	-0-	(27,000)	-0-	-0-	-0-	(27,000)
Unrealized gain on marketable securities	-0-	-0-	-0-	-0-	-0-	-0-	34,000	-0-	-0-	-0-	34,000
Cash dividends ($.16 per share)	-0-	-0-	-0-	-0-	-0-	(58,000)	-0-	-0-	-0-	-0-	(58,000)
Exercise of stock options	-0-	-0-	150,000	1,500	198,500	-0-	-0-	-0-	-0-	-0-	200,000
Repurchase of preferred stock	(20,000)	(2,000)	-0-	-0-	(48,000)	-0-	-0-	-0-	-0-	-0-	(50,000)
Payment received on stock sale	-0-	-0-	-0-	-0-	-0-	-0-	-0-	6,000	-0-	-0-	6,000
Purchase of 10,000 shares	-0-	-0-	-0-	-0-	-0-	-0-	-0-	-0-	(10,000)	(50,000)	(50,000)
Balance at December 31, 20X1	80,000	8,000	400,000	4,000	568,500	369,000	63,000	(2,000)	(14,000)	(90,000)	920,500
Net income	-0-	-0-	-0-	-0-	-0-	243,000	-0-	-0-	-0-	-0-	243,000
2 for 1 stock split	-0-	-0-	400,000	4,000	(4,000)	-0-	-0-	-0-	-0-	-0-	-0-
Conversion of 8% debentures	-0-	-0-	100,000	1,000	149,000	-0-	-0-	-0-	-0-	-0-	150,000
Stock issued for acquisition	-0-	-0-	50,000	500	199,500	-0-	-0-	-0-	-0-	-0-	200,000
Stock exchanged for services	-0-	-0-	20,000	200	59,800	-0-	-0-	-0-	-0-	-0-	60,000
Foreign currency adjustment	-0-	-0-	-0-	-0-	-0-	-0-	(11,000)	-0-	-0-	-0-	(11,000)
Unrealized gain on marketable securities	-0-	-0-	-0-	-0-	-0-	-0-	17,000	-0-	-0-	-0-	17,000
Dividends	-0-	-0-	-0-	-0-	-0-	(225,000)	-0-	-0-	-0-	-0-	(225,000)
Balance at December 31, 20X2	80,000	$8,000	970,000	$9,700	$972,800	$387,000	$69,000	$(2,000)	(14,000)	$(90,000)	$1,354,500

Capital Stock

Example 48–3: Description of Rights and Privileges of Capital
Stock—Capital Structure Consists of Common Stock

At December 31, 20X2, the authorized capital of the Company consists of 40,000,000 shares of capital stock comprising 30,000,000 shares of no par common stock and 10,000,000 shares of no par Class A common stock. Both classes of stock have a stated value of $0.001 per share. The Class A Common Stock has certain preferential rights with respect to cash dividends and upon liquidation of the Company. In the case of cash dividends, the holders of the Class A Common Stock will be paid one-half cent per share per quarter in addition to any amount payable per share for each share of Common Stock. In the event of liquidation, holders of the Class A Common Stock are entitled to a preference of $1 per share. After such amount is paid, holders of the Common Stock are entitled to receive $1 per share for each share of Common Stock outstanding. Any remaining amount would be distributed to the holders of the Class A Common Stock and the Common Stock on a pro rata basis.

In general, with respect to the election of directors, the holders of Class A Common Stock, voting as a separate class, are entitled to elect that number of directors, which constitutes 25% of the total membership of the board of directors. Holders of Common Stock, voting as a separate class, are entitled to elect the remaining directors. In all other matters not requiring a class vote, the holders of the Common Stock and the holders of Class A Common Stock vote as a single class provided that holders of Class A Common Stock have one-tenth of a vote for each share held and the holders of the Common Stock have one vote for each share held.

Example 48–4: Description of Rights and Privileges of Capital
Stock—Capital Structure Consists of Common and Preferred Stock

The Company has three classes of capital stock: Preferred Stock, Common Stock, and Class B Common Stock. Holders of Common Stock are entitled to one vote for each share held. Holders of Class B Common Stock generally vote as a single class with holders of Common Stock but are entitled to ten votes for each share held. The Common Stock and Class B Common Stock have equal liquidation and dividend rights except that any regular quarterly dividend declared shall be $0.05 per share less for holders of Class B Common Stock. Class B Common Stock is nontransferable, except under certain conditions, but may be converted into Common Stock on a share-for-share basis at any time.

The preferred stock has an annual dividend rate of 6% and is cumulative. Preferred stockholders are not entitled to voting privileges except on matters involving liquidation, dissolution, or merger of the Company, in which case they are entitled to one vote for each ten shares held.

Example 48–5: Redeemable Convertible Preferred Stock with a Beneficial Conversion Feature

On June 15, 20X2, the Company issued 250,000 shares of its Series B Preferred Stock, and six-year warrants to purchase 5,528,000 shares of its common stock, in exchange for $9,700,000 in cash, net of issuance costs of $300,000. The Series B Preferred Stock is initially convertible into approximately 4,000,000 shares of the Company's common stock at a conversion price of $2.50 per share. The exercise price for the warrants is $2.95 per share and they were immediately exercisable upon issuance.

The holders of the Series B Preferred Stock and warrants have registration rights that require the Company to file, to have declared effective, and to maintain the effectiveness of a registration statement with the SEC to register the resale of the common stock issuable upon conversion of the Series B Preferred Stock and the common stock issuable upon exercise of the warrants. In the event the Company is unable to cause the registration statement to be declared effective by March 1, 20X3, cash penalties of $7,500 per day are due to the holders during the period commencing on March 1, 20X3, and ending on the date the registration statement is declared effective by the SEC. Under EITF No. 00-19, *Accounting for Derivative Financial Instruments Indexed to, and Potentially Settled in, a Company's Own Stock*, the ability to register stock is deemed to be outside of the Company's control. Accordingly, the initial fair value of the warrants of $3,100,000 was recorded as an accrued warrant liability in the consolidated balance sheet and is marked to market at the end of each reporting period. At December 31, 20X2, the warrant liability was adjusted to its new fair value of $2,375,000 as determined by the Company, resulting in a gain of $725,000, which has been reflected in "Interest income and other, net" on the consolidated statement of operations.

The initial value attributed to the Series B Preferred Stock of $6,900,000 represents a discount from its initial conversion value of $9,500,000. In accordance with EITF No. 00-27, *Application of Issue No. 98-5 to Certain Convertible Instruments*, which provides guidance on the calculation of a beneficial conversion feature on a convertible instrument, the Company has determined that the Series B Preferred Stock had a beneficial conversion feature of $2,600,000 as of the date of issuance. The Company recorded this beneficial conversion feature as a deemed dividend upon issuance.

The holders of the Series B Preferred Stock may require the Company to redeem its shares upon certain events, including failure to cause a registration statement to be effective by April 1, 20X3, at a redemption price equal to the greater of 120% of the original purchase price plus any accrued and unpaid dividends or the value of the Series B Preferred Stock on an as-converted-to-common-stock basis. Because the Company has not yet been able to cause a registration statement to be declared effective, the Company determined, as of December 31, 20X2, that it was probable that effectiveness would not be obtained prior to the deadline and that the Series B Preferred Stock should be stated at its redemption value at December 31, 20X2. Accordingly, the Company has recorded a deemed dividend charge of $5,350,000 in order to accrete the Series B Preferred Stock to its $12,250,000 redemption value at December 31, 20X2, which includes $325,000 of dividends accrued through December 31, 20X2.

Balance Sheet Presentation—The following presentation illustrates the reporting of the redeemable convertible preferred stock outside of permanent equity ("mezzanine") and the fair value of the warrant as a liability based on this example.

Liabilities:

Accounts payable	$12,650,000
Short-term debt	15,725,000
Accrued expenses	1,210,000
Total current liabilities	29,585,000
Long-term debt	14,500,000
Warrant liability	2,375,000
Deferred income taxes	1,000,000
Total liabilities	47,460,000
Commitments and contingencies	—
Redeemable convertible preferred stock	12,250,000

Stockholders' equity:

(*Details omitted*)

Example 48–6: Redemption of Convertible Preferred Stock during the Reporting Period

In December 20X2, the Company redeemed all 200,000 outstanding shares of 5.75% Series A Convertible Preferred Stock (the Preferred Stock). The Preferred Stock was issued to certain former shareholders of Mederatus, Inc. as a portion of the total consideration of the

Company's 20X0 acquisition of Mederatus, Inc. The redemption price per share of stock was $10.40 per share, or $2,080,000 in the aggregate, which included a redemption premium of $.40 per share, or $80,000 in the aggregate. The redemption premium of $80,000 is deducted from net earnings to arrive at net earnings applicable to common shareholders in the accompanying Statements of Operations.

Example 48–7: Conversion of Subordinated Debentures into Common Stock during the Reporting Period

During 20X2, $4,500,000 of the Company's $5,000,000 of 6% Convertible Subordinated Debentures due in 20X7 were converted into 680,000 shares of the Company's common stock at the conversion price of $10.50 per share. As a result of the conversion, $67,000 of costs associated with the issuance of the debentures was charged against additional paid-in capital.

Example 48–8: Common Stock Reserved for Future Issuance

At December 31, 20X2, and December 31, 20X1, the Company has reserved 1,389,000 and 1,016,000 shares of its authorized but unissued common stock for possible future issuance in connection with the following:

	20X2	20X1
Exercise and future grants of stock options	660,000	404,000
Exercise of stock warrants	394,000	311,000
Conversion of preferred stock	217,000	183,000
Contingently issuable shares in connection with the XYZ business combination	118,000	118,000
	1,389,000	1,016,000

Example 48–9: Change from Stated to Par Value

On May 1, 20X2, the Company was reincorporated in Delaware. As a result, each of the Company's classes of stock was changed from a stated value of $0.05 per share to a par value of $0.01 per share, resulting in a decrease in common stock and an increase in additional paid-in capital of $235,000. At the same time, the authorized number of shares of common stock was increased from 10 million to 25 million.

Example 48–10: Amendment to Certificate of Incorporation

On October 26, 20X2, the Company's stockholders approved an amendment to the Certificate of Incorporation reducing the par value of the Common Stock from $1 to $.01 per share and increasing the number of authorized shares of Common Stock from 1 million to 10 million. As a result of the reduction in par value, the "Common stock" account was reduced by $250,000 and the "Additional paid-in capital" account was increased by the same amount in the accompanying Statement of Stockholders' Equity for 20X2.

Treasury Stock

Example 48–11: Treasury Stock Purchase

In fiscal 20X1, the board of directors authorized the purchase of up to 1,200,000 shares of the Company's common stock, which may be used to meet the Company's common stock requirements for its stock benefit plans. In fiscal 20X2, the board of directors increased the number of shares of common stock that the Company is authorized to repurchase under this plan by 200,000 shares. During fiscal 20X2 and 20X1, the Company repurchased 473,000 and 518,000 shares, respectively, at an aggregate cost of $4,565,000 and $3,238,000, respectively.

Example 48–12: Treasury Stock Sale

In October 20X2, the Company sold 125,000 shares of common stock previously held in the treasury for $625,000. The aggregate purchase price of the treasury shares sold exceeded the aggregate sales price by $156,000 and has been charged to "Additional paid-in capital."

Receivables from Sale of Stock

Example 48–13: Outstanding Receivables from Sale of Stock Reported as a Reduction of Stockholders' Equity

Notes receivable from stock sales resulting from the exercise of stock options for notes totaled $218,000 and $203,000 at December 31, 20X2, and December 31, 20X1, respectively, and are reported as a reduction of stockholders' equity. The notes are full recourse promissory notes bearing interest at variable rates ranging from 6.25% to 8.50% and are collateralized by the stock issued upon exercise of the stock options. Interest is payable semi-annually and principal is due from 20X3 through 20X6.

Options and Warrants

> **Note:** For additional sample disclosures of stock options and warrants, see Chapter 33, "Stock-Based Compensation, Stock Option Plans, and Stock Purchase Plans."

Example 48–14: Accounting Policy for Stock Warrants Issued to Third Parties

The Company accounts for stock warrants issued to third parties, including customers, in accordance with the provisions of the (EITF) Issue No. 96-18, *Accounting for Equity Instruments That Are Issued to Other Than Employees for Acquiring, or in Conjunction with Selling Goods or Services*, and EITF 01-9, *Accounting for Consideration Given by a Vendor to a Customer (Including a Reseller of the Vendor's Products)*. Under the provisions of EITF 96-18, because none of the Company's agreements have a disincentive for nonperformance, the Company records a charge for the fair value of the portion of the warrants earned from the point in time when vesting of the warrants becomes probable. Final determination of fair value of the warrants occurs upon actual vesting. EITF 01-9 requires that the fair value of certain types of warrants issued to customers be recorded as a reduction of revenue to the extent of cumulative revenue recorded from that customer.

Example 48–15: Warrants Activity for the Period and Summary of Outstanding Warrants

During the years ended December 31, 20X2, and December 31, 20X1, the board of directors approved the issuance of warrants to purchase an aggregate of 565,000 shares of the Company's common stock. Such warrants are exercisable at prices ranging from $9.50 to $20.625 per share, vest over periods up to 48 months, and expire at various times through April 20X9.

During the years ended December 31, 20X2, and December 31, 20X1, certain warrant holders exercised warrants to purchase 278,000 and 11,000 shares, respectively, of the Company's common stock for an aggregate of $673,000 and $22,000, respectively.

Included in the issuance of warrants to purchase 565,000 aggregate shares of the Company's common stock is a warrant to purchase 50,000 shares that was issued to a director under the terms of a consulting agreement during fiscal 20X1. Such issuance was accounted for under Financial Accounting Standards Board Statement No. 123 using the Black-Scholes option-pricing model (with the same assumptions as those used for the option), which resulted in the recording of $233,000 and $50,000 in compensation cost during the years ended December 31, 20X2, and December 31, 20X1, respectively.

A summary of warrant activity for 20X2 and 20X1 is as follows:

	Number of Warrants	Weighted-Average Exercise Price	Warrants Exercisable	Weighted-Average Exercise Price
Outstanding, December 31, 20X0	427,000	4.44	409,916	$4.13
Granted	350,000	11.95		
Exercised	(11,000)	2.00		
Outstanding, December 31, 20X1	766,000	7.42	493,082	4.91
Granted	215,000	17.31		
Exercised	(278,000)	2.42		
Outstanding, December 31, 20X2	703,000	12.42	482,166	12.20

At December 31, 20X2, the range of warrant prices for shares under warrants and the weighted-average remaining contractual life is as follows:

	Warrants Outstanding			Warrants Exercisable	
Range of Warrant Exercise Price	Number of Warrants	Weighted-Average Exercise Price	Weighted-Average Remaining Contractual Life	Number of Warrants	Weighted-Average Exercise Price
$6.00–9.50	200,000	$ 7.81	5.83	200,000	$ 7.81
11.78–12.81	288,000	11.96	6.01	92,166	12.11
16.88–20.63	215,000	17.31	9.22	190,000	16.88
	703,000			482,166	

Example 48–16: Warrants Issued in Connection with a Financing Agreement

In connection with the Financing Agreement with ABC State Bank, on March 18, 20X2, the Company issued warrants to ABC State Bank for the purchase of 150,000 shares of common stock at an exercise price of $2.25 per share. The fair value of the warrants of $325,000 was determined using the Black-Scholes option-pricing model. The value of the warrants is being amortized into interest expense over the term of the Financing Agreement. The warrants are exercisable at any time on or after November 1, 20X2.

Example 48–17: Warrants Issued in Connection with a Lease Agreement

In July 20X1, the Company issued a fully vested, non-forfeitable warrant that entitles the holder to purchase 25,000 shares of the Company's common stock at an exercise price of $10.00 per share, in connection with a lease agreement. This warrant is exercisable through July 20X6. The fair value of this warrant, approximately $375,000, is being expensed over the term of the lease. The fair value of this warrant was calculated using the Black-Scholes option-pricing model. As of June 20X2, this warrant was exercised in full.

In addition, in January 20X1, in connection with an equipment lease line, the Company issued a fully vested warrant that entitles the holder to purchase 110,000 shares of the Company's common stock at an exercise price of $1.50 per share. This warrant is exercisable through January 20X8. The fair value of this warrant, approximately $362,000, is being expensed as a cost of financing over the four-year period of the lease line. The fair value of this warrant was calculated using the Black-Scholes option-pricing model. The warrant was exercised in full during 20X2.

Example 48–18: Fair Value of Warrants Reclassified from Liabilities to Additional Paid-in Capital upon Elimination of the Net Cash Settlement Provision

In June 20X2, the Company completed a $1,100,000 private placement of its common stock. The Company issued 1,125,000 shares of common stock along with warrants to purchase 410,000 shares of common stock at $1.15 per share, which were valued at $436,000. The Company received approximately $941,000 in net proceeds from this transaction. As the warrants originally included a requirement for net cash settlement if the Company was unable to register the shares to be issued upon exercise of the warrants, these warrants were required to be recorded as a liability until such time as the registration requirements expired. The Company subsequently signed a "Waiver Letter Agreement" with certain warrant holders, which resulted in the warrants being modified to provide for a cashless exercise in the event of a Nonregistration Event, as defined, and the elimination of the net cash settlement provision. In addition, certain penalty provisions were modified to provide that the warrant holders would receive no liquidated damages in the event of a Nonregistration Event. Upon the elimination of the net cash settlement provision, the fair value of the warrants ($311,000) was reclassified from other current liabilities to additional paid-in capital. As of

December 31, 20X2, remaining warrants with a fair value of $132,000 are included in other current liabilities in the accompanying consolidated balance sheet.

Example 48–19: Reversal of Deferred Stock-Based Compensation and Additional Paid-in Capital Relating to Employees Who Left the Company

As a result of employees who left the Company during the years ended December 31, 20X2, and 20X1, the Company reversed approximately $329,000 and $415,000, respectively, of deferred stock-based compensation and additional paid-in capital, which represented the unamortized balance of deferred stock-based compensation relating to employees who left the Company.

Example 48–20: Tax Benefit Associated with Exercise of Stock Options Is Reflected as an Increase in Additional Paid-in Capital

All options granted under the 20X0 Stock Option Plan were granted at exercise prices not less than the fair market value of the underlying common stock at the date of grant. In the event that shares purchased through the exercise of incentive stock options are sold within one year of exercise, the Company is entitled to a tax deduction. The tax benefit of the deduction is not reflected in the statements of operations, but is reflected as an increase in additional paid-in capital under the caption "Tax benefit associated with exercise of stock options."

Cash and Stock Dividends

Example 48–21: Cash Dividends

On February 16, 20X2, the board of directors approved an annual cash dividend for 20X2 of $0.03 per share payable on April 15, 20X2, to holders of common stock as of close of business on April 1, 20X2. Cash dividends paid in 20X2 totaled $213,000 and have been charged to retained earnings.

Example 48–22: Stock Dividends

On December 1, 20X2, the Company paid a 2% stock dividend to shareholders of record on November 10, 20X2. Based on the number of common shares outstanding on the record date, the Company issued 200,000 new shares. The fair market value of the additional shares issued, aggregating $613,000, was charged to retained earnings, and common stock and additional paid-in capital were increased by $2,000 and $611,000, respectively. All references in the accompanying financial statements to the number of common shares and per share amounts are based on the increased number of shares giving retroactive effect to the stock dividend.

Example 48–23: Dividends in Arrears Deferred

Payments of annual dividends for 20X2 and 20X1 were deferred by the Company's board of directors on the outstanding preferred stocks because of losses sustained by the Company. As of December 31, 20X2, preferred dividends in arrears amounted to $400,000, or $2 per share, on the 5% Cumulative Preferred Stock.

Example 48–24: Dividends in Arrears Paid in Amended New Shares of Preferred Stock

Prior to November 20X1, dividends with respect to the Series A Preferred Stock were in arrearage. Effective November 10, 20X1, the Series A Preferred Stock was amended, reclassified, and converted to Amended Series A Preferred Stock. As a consequence of such consent, all dividend arrearages, and accrued and unpaid dividends were paid in additional shares of Amended Series A Preferred Stock.

Dividends-in-Kind

Example 48–25: Dividend-in-Kind Consists of a Spin-Off of a Business Segment

In May 20X2, the Company announced plans to spin off its electronic connectors business to shareholders in a tax-free distribution. In August 20X2, the Company's board of directors approved the spin-off effective December 31, 20X2, to shareholders of record as of December 17, 20X2, through the issuance of shares in a new legal entity, Electors, Inc. Common shares were distributed on a basis of one share of Electors, Inc. for every five shares of the Company's common stock.

The consolidated financial results of the Company have been restated to reflect the divestiture of Electors, Inc. Accordingly, the revenues, costs, and expenses; assets and liabilities; and cash flows of Electors, Inc. have been excluded from their respective captions in the Consolidated Statements of Income, Consolidated Balance Sheets, and Consolidated Statements of Cash Flows. These items have been reported as "Income from discontinued operations, net of income taxes" in the Consolidated Statements of Income; "Net assets of discontinued operations" in the Consolidated Balance Sheets; and "Net cash flows from discontinued operations" and

"Net investing and financing activities of discontinued operations" in the Consolidated Statements of Cash Flows.

As of December 31, 20X2, the net assets of the discontinued segment of $4,289,000 have been charged against the Company's retained earnings to reflect the spin-off. During 20X2, the Company recorded a pre-tax charge of $615,000 ($483,000 after taxes) for expenses related to the spin-off.

The following table summarizes financial information for the discontinued operations for all periods presented:

	20X2	*20X1*
Net sales	$8,300,000	$8,750,000
Income before income taxes	$ 211,000	$ 273,000
Net income	$ 107,000	$ 182,000
Current assets	$2,436,000	$2,543,000
Total assets	$8,161,000	$8,615,000
Current liabilities	$2,597,000	$1,796,000
Total liabilities	$3,872,000	$3,978,000
Net assets of discontinued operations	$4,289,000	$4,637,000

Stock Splits

Example 48–26: Stock Split During the Reporting Period

On January 30, 20X2, the Company's board of directors declared a two-for-one stock split, effected in the form of a stock dividend, on the shares of the Company's common stock. Each shareholder of record on February 20, 20X2, received an additional share of common stock for each share of common stock then held. The stock was issued March 19, 20X2. The Company retained the current par value of $.01 per share for all shares of common stock. All references in the financial statements to the number of shares outstanding, per share amounts, and stock option data of the Company's common stock have been restated to reflect the effect of the stock split for all periods presented.

Stockholders' equity reflects the stock split by reclassifying from "Additional paid-in capital" to "Common stock" an amount equal to the par value of the additional shares arising from the split.

Example 48–27: Stock Split Subsequent to the Balance-Sheet Date

On February 18, 20X3, the Company's board of directors authorized a two-for-one split of the common stock effected in the form of a 100%

stock dividend to be distributed on or about March 31, 20X3, to holders of record on March 5, 20X3. Accordingly, all references to numbers of common shares and per share data in the accompanying financial statements have been adjusted to reflect the stock split on a retroactive basis. The par value of the additional shares of common stock issued in connection with the stock split will be credited to "Common stock" and a like amount charged to "Additional paid-in-capital" in 20X3.

Other Comprehensive Income

Example 48–28: Components of Other Comprehensive Income and Accumulated Other Comprehensive Income

> **Note:** See Chapter 54, "Comprehensive Income," for additional examples of disclosures regarding comprehensive income.

The pretax, tax, and after-tax effects of the components of other comprehensive income (loss) for 20X2 and 20X1 are as follows:

	Pretax	*Tax*	*After-tax*
20X2			
Unrealized gains on available-for-sale securities	$ 102,000	$ (43,000)	$ 59,000
Foreign currency translation adjustment	(23,000)	-0-	(23,000)
Minimum pension liability adjustment	(193,000)	81,000	(112,000)
Other comprehensive income (loss)	$ (114,000)	$ 38,000	$ (76,000)
20X1			
Unrealized gains on available-for-sale securities	$ 357,000	$ (140,000)	$217,000
Foreign currency translation adjustment	(130,000)	-0-	(130,000)
Minimum pension liability adjustment	(46,000)	18,000	(28,000)
Other comprehensive income (loss)	$ 181,000	$ (122,000)	$ 59,000

Balances of related after-tax components comprising accumulated other comprehensive income (loss), included in stockholders' equity, at December 31, 20X2, and December 31, 20X1, are as follows:

	December 31	
	20X2	*20X1*
Unrealized gains on available-for-sale securities	$ 311,000	$252,000
Foreign currency translation adjustment	(176,000)	(153,000)
Minimum pension liability adjustment	(256,000)	(144,000)
Accumulated other comprehensive income (loss)	$(121,000)	$ (45,000)

PART III—
INCOME STATEMENT

CHAPTER 49
REVENUES AND GAINS

CONTENTS

EXECUTIVE SUMMARY

Generally accepted accounting principles (GAAP), as well as recognized industry practices, generally call for revenue recognition at the point of sale. Revenue usually is recognized when the earning process is complete and an exchange has taken place. The earning process is not complete until collection of the sales price is reasonably assured. The installment method of recognizing revenue is not acceptable unless collection of the sale price is *not* reasonably estimated or assured.

Revenue from sales transactions in which the buyer has a right to return the product should be recognized at time of sale only if *all* of the following conditions are met:

1. The price between the seller and the buyer is substantially fixed or determinable.

2. The seller has received full payment, or the buyer is indebted to the seller and the indebtedness is not contingent on the resale of the merchandise.

3. Physical destruction, damage, or theft of the merchandise would not change the buyer's obligation to the seller.

4. The buyer has economic substance and is not a front or conduit existing for the benefit of the seller.

5. No significant obligations exist for the seller to help the buyer resell the merchandise.

6. A reasonable estimate can be made of the amount of future returns.

If all of the above conditions are met, revenue is recognized on sales for which a right of return exists, provided that an appropriate provision is made for costs or losses that may occur in connection with the return of merchandise from the buyer. If those conditions are not met, revenue recognition should be postponed.

Revenue from the sale of separately priced extended warranty and product maintenance contracts should be deferred and generally recognized in income on a straight-line basis. Costs that are directly related to the acquisition of those contracts are deferred and charged to expense in proportion to the revenue recognized. All other costs are charged to expense as incurred.

Gains are increases in equity (net assets) from peripheral or incidental transactions of an entity and from all other transactions and other events and circumstances affecting the entity during a period, except those that result from revenues or investments by owners. The most common types of gains are discussed in numerous chapters throughout this book. For example:

- Gain contingencies are covered in Chapter 10, "Contingencies, Risks, Uncertainties, and Concentrations."

- Foreign exchange gains are covered in Chapter 17, "Foreign Operations and Currency Translation."

- Gains resulting from marketable securities and other investments are covered in Chapter 40, "Investments: Debt and Equity Securities," and Chapter 41, "Investments: Equity and Cost Methods."

Authoritative Literature

ARB-43	Chapter 1A, Rules Adopted by Membership
APB-10	Omnibus Opinion—1966
FAS-5	Accounting for Contingencies

FAS-48   Revenue Recognition When Right of Return Exists

FTB 90-1   Accounting for Separately Priced Extended Warranty and Product Maintenance Contracts

EITF 00-21 Revenue Arrangements with Multiple Deliverables

DISCLOSURE REQUIREMENTS

There are no specific disclosures about revenues that are prescribed by authoritative literature, except as follows:

1. Significant amounts of discounts, returns, and allowances are generally disclosed (generally accepted practice).

2. Sales with significant rights of return should be excluded from the income statement and disclosed, if significant (FAS-48, pars. 3–7).

3. For revenue arrangements with multiple deliverables, the following disclosures should be made (EITF 00-21, par. 18):

    a. The accounting policy for recognizing revenue from multiple-deliverable arrangements (e.g., whether deliverables are separable into units of accounting)

    b. The description and nature of such arrangements, including performance, cancellation, termination, or refund type provisions

Pronouncements covered in other chapters of this book may require specific disclosures about revenues or gains related to specific types of transactions (e.g., revenues related to long-term contracts, as discussed in Chapter 24, "Long-Term Contracts"; revenues related to computer software, as discussed in Chapter 8, "Computer Software"; and gains on sale of marketable securities, as discussed in Chapter 40, "Investments: Debt and Equity Securities").

EXAMPLES OF FINANCIAL STATEMENT DISCLOSURES

Most of the disclosures that are typically associated with revenues and gains are covered throughout this book. Individual chapters should be consulted for specific disclosure requirements and examples of financial statement disclosures. This chapter provides only examples of disclosures relating to revenues and gains that are not covered elsewhere in this book. For additional information, see the following chapters:

*   Chapter 1, "Accounting Changes and Error Corrections," for changes in revenue recognition methods

- Chapter 2, "Accounting Policies," for revenue recognition policies and concentrations in sources of revenue

- Chapter 8, "Computer Software," for software revenue recognition policies

- Chapter 10, "Contingencies, Risks, Uncertainties, and Concentrations," for concentrations in accounts receivable, concentrations in sources of revenue, and gains from litigation

- Chapter 17, "Foreign Operations and Currency Translation," for revenues and gains resulting from foreign operations

- Chapter 23, "Leases," for revenues from leasing transactions

- Chapter 24, "Long-Term Contracts," for revenues under long-term contracts

- Chapter 30, "Related-Party Disclosures," for revenues and gains resulting from transactions with related parties

- Chapter 32, "Segment Information," for revenues by major business segments

- Chapter 38, "Accounts and Notes Receivable," for balance sheet accounts arising from various revenue sources

- Chapter 40, "Investments: Debt and Equity Securities," for gains on sale of marketable securities

- Chapter 41, "Investments: Equity and Cost Methods," for earnings from investees accounted for under the equity method

- Chapter 51, "Discontinued Operations," for revenues and gains applicable to discontinued operations

- Chapter 52, "Extraordinary Items," for extraordinary gains

 The following sample disclosures are available on the accompanying disc.

Example 49–1: Revenue Recognition Policy for a Manufacturing Company

The Company generally recognizes product revenue when persuasive evidence of an arrangement exists, delivery has occurred, the fee is fixed or determinable, and collectibility is probable. In instances where final acceptance of the product is specified by the customer, revenue is deferred until all acceptance criteria have been met. Cash payments received in advance are recorded as deferred revenue. The Company is generally not contractually obligated to accept returns, except for defective product. However, the Company may permit its customers to return or exchange products and may provide pricing allowances on products unsold by a customer. Revenue is recorded net of an allowance for estimated returns, price concessions, and other discounts. Such allowance is reflected as a reduction to accounts receivable when the Company expects to grant credits for such items; otherwise, it is reflected as a liability.

Example 49–2: Revenue Recognition Policy for Royalties

Royalty revenue is recognized by the Company upon fulfillment of its contractual obligations and determination of a fixed royalty amount or, in the case of ongoing royalties, upon sale by the licensee of royalty-bearing products, as estimated by the Company.

Example 49–3: Revenue Recognition Policy for Individual Membership

The Company generally recognizes membership revenue upon the expiration of the membership period, as memberships are generally cancelable for a full refund of the membership fee during the entire membership period, which is generally one year. Revenues generated from certain memberships, which are subject to a pro rata refund, are recognized ratably over the membership period.

Example 49–4: Components of Other Income Disclosed in a Note to the Financial Statements

The components of other income for the years ended December 31, 20X2, and December 31, 20X1, are as follows:

	20X2	20X1
Interest income	$161,000	$143,000
Gain on sale of fixed assets	78,000	37,000
Royalties	45,000	41,000
Rental income	63,000	58,000
Miscellaneous other income	18,000	22,000
Total other income	$365,000	$301,000

Example 49–5: Other Income Resulting from Termination of License Agreement

Other revenues for the year ended December 31, 20X2, includes a gain of $473,000 related to the termination of a license agreement, net of charges for related equipment write-offs and capacity adjustments, under which the Company had produced plastic multipack carriers for beverage cans.

Example 49–6: Income from Life Insurance Proceeds

Due to the death of the Company's president and chief executive officer in February 20X2, the Company realized non-taxable income from life insurance proceeds in the amount of $1,243,000, which is separately stated in the Statement of Operations for the year ended December 31, 20X2.

Example 49–7: Gain from Sale of Assets

In October 20X2, the Company sold its manufacturing plant building in Boise, Idaho, for $2,374,000. The net pretax gain from the sale was $1,693,000 and is included in "Gain from sale of assets" in the 20X2 Statement of Operations.

CHAPTER 50
EXPENSES AND LOSSES

CONTENTS

EXECUTIVE SUMMARY

Accounting literature recognizes two basic types of expenses: direct and indirect. *Direct expenses* are those that are clearly associated with the production of revenue during a period or with the production of assets held for future sale (e.g., inventories). *Indirect expenses* are all other costs, such as selling and administrative expenses.

Losses are decreases in equity (net assets) from peripheral or incidental transactions of an entity and from all other transactions and other events and circumstances affecting the entity during a period, except those that result from expenses or distributions to owners.

Disclosures that are typically associated with expenses and losses are covered throughout this book. Individual chapters, such as the following, should be consulted for specific disclosure requirements and examples of financial statement disclosures:

- Chapter 1, "Accounting Changes and Error Corrections," for changes in recognition methods for costs and expenses

- Chapter 2, "Accounting Policies," for general accounting policies for expenses

- Chapter 3, "Advertising Costs," for capitalized and expensed advertising costs

- Chapter 7, "Compensated Absences," for vacation pay and sick pay expense

- Chapter 8, "Computer Software," for accounting for the costs of computer software

- Chapter 10, "Contingencies, Risks, Uncertainties, and Concentrations," for concentrations in accounts payable, purchases from vendors, and loss contingencies

- Chapter 17, "Foreign Operations and Currency Translation," for expenses and losses resulting from foreign operations

- Chapter 20, "Impairment and Disposal of Long-Lived Assets," for impairment losses related to fixed assets
- Chapter 21, "Interest Cost," for interest capitalized, expensed, and paid
- Chapter 23, "Leases," for rental expense
- Chapter 24, "Long-Term Contracts," for cost recognition methods under long-term contracts
- Chapter 26, "Pension Plans," Chapter 27, "Postemployment Benefits," and Chapter 28, "Postretirement Benefits Other Than Pensions," for pension and other retirement related costs
- Chapter 30, "Related-Party Disclosures," for expenses and losses resulting from transactions with related parties
- Chapter 31, "Research and Development Costs," for expense and capitalization of research and development costs
- Chapter 32, "Segment Information," for operations by major business segments
- Chapter 33, "Stock-Based Compensation, Stock Option Plans, and Stock Purchase Plans," for compensation expense in connection with such plans
- Chapter 40, "Investments: Debt and Equity Securities," for losses on sale of marketable securities
- Chapter 41, "Investments: Equity and Cost Methods," for losses from investees accounted for under the equity method
- Chapter 42, "Property, Plant, and Equipment," for depreciation expense and impairment losses related to fixed assets
- Chapter 43, "Intangible Assets," for amortization expense and impairment losses related to intangible assets
- Chapter 45, "Income Taxes," for current and deferred income tax expense
- Chapter 51, "Discontinued Operations," for expenses and losses applicable to discontinued operations
- Chapter 52, "Extraordinary Items," for extraordinary losses

CHAPTER 51
DISCONTINUED OPERATIONS

CONTENTS

EXECUTIVE SUMMARY

The results of discontinued operations, less applicable income taxes, should be reported as a separate component of income before extraordinary items and the cumulative effect of accounting changes (if applicable). A gain or loss recognized on the disposal should be disclosed either on the face of the income statement or in the notes to the financial statements.

Adjustments to amounts previously reported in discontinued operations that are directly related to the disposal of a component of an entity in a prior period should be classified separately in the current period in discontinued operations. Also, the nature and amount of such adjustments should be disclosed.

The assets and liabilities of a component of an entity that is classified as held for sale should be presented separately in the asset and liability sections, respectively, of the balance sheet. Those assets and liabilities should not be offset and presented as a single amount. A component of an entity comprises operations and cash flows that can be clearly distinguished, operationally and for financial reporting purposes, from the rest of the entity. A component of an entity that is classified as held for sale or that has been disposed of should be presented as a discontinued operation if both of the following conditions are met:

1. The operations and cash flows of the component will be, or have been, eliminated from the ongoing operations of the entity, *and*

2. The entity will not have any significant continuing involvement in the operations of the component.

Authoritative Literature

APB-9	Reporting the Results of Operations
FAS-16	Prior Period Adjustments
FAS-144	Accounting for the Impairment or Disposal of Long-Lived Assets
EITF 03-13	Applying the Conditions in Paragraph 42 of FASB Statement No. 144 in Determining Whether to Report Discontinued Operations

DISCLOSURE REQUIREMENTS

The following disclosures are required for discontinued operations:

1. For a component of an entity that either has been sold or is classified as held for sale, the following disclosures should be made in financial statements that include the period in which the component has been sold or is classified as held for sale (FAS-144, par. 47):

    a. A description of the facts and circumstances leading to the expected disposal

    b. The expected manner and timing of the disposal

    c. The carrying amount(s) of the major classes of assets and liabilities included as part of a component, if not separately presented on the face of the balance sheet

d. The gain or loss recognized and, if not separately presented on the face of the income statement, the caption in the income statement that includes the gain or loss

e. If applicable, amounts of revenue and pretax profit or loss reported in discontinued operations

f. If applicable, the segment in which the component is reported

2. If an entity decides not to sell a component previously classified as held for sale, or removes an individual asset or liability from a component previously classified as held for sale, the following disclosures should be made in the financial statements that include the period of that decision (FAS-144, par. 48):

a. A description of the facts and circumstances leading to the decision to change the plan to sell the component

b. The effect on the results of operations for the period and any prior periods presented

3. If the criteria for classification of a component of an entity as held for sale are met after the balance-sheet date, but before issuance of the financial statements, the following information should be disclosed (FAS-144, par. 33):

a. A description of the facts and circumstances leading to the expected disposal

b. The expected manner and timing of the disposal

c. The carrying amount(s) of the major classes of assets and liabilities included as part of a component, if not separately presented on the face of the balance sheet

4. The results of discontinued operations, less applicable income taxes, should be reported separately from continuing operations and, if applicable, before extraordinary items and the cumulative effect of accounting changes (FAS-144, par. 43)

5. If adjustments are made in the current period to amounts previously reported in discontinued operations (FAS-144, par. 44):

a. The adjustments should be classified separately in the current period in discontinued operations

b. The nature and amount of such adjustments should be disclosed

6. For each discontinued operation that generates continuing cash flows, the following disclosures should be made (EITF 03-13, par. 17):

    a. The nature of the activities that give rise to continuing cash flows

    b. The period of time continuing cash flows are expected to be generated

    c. The principal factors used to conclude that the expected continuing cash flows are not direct cash flows of the disposed component

7. In the period in which operations are initially classified as discontinued, if there is a continuation of activities between the ongoing entity and the disposed component after the disposal transaction, the following disclosures should be made for all periods presented in the financial statements (EITF 03-13, par. 17):

    a. If the ongoing entity's activities include continuation of revenues and expenses that were previously eliminated intercompany transactions (for purposes of the consolidated financial statements) before the disposal transaction, the intercompany amounts before the disposal transaction

    b. The types of continuing involvement that will exist after the disposal transaction

In addition, the following items should be presented separately in the balance sheet: (1) long-lived assets that are classified as held for sale and (2) the assets and liabilities of a disposal group classified as held for sale—the assets and liabilities should *not* be offset and presented as a single amount (FAS-144, par. 46).

EXAMPLES OF FINANCIAL STATEMENT DISCLOSURES

 The following sample disclosures are available on the accompanying disc.

Example 51–1: Presentation of Discontinued Operations in an Income Statement That Does Not Include Extraordinary Items or Cumulative Effect of Accounting Change

	20X2	20X1
Income from continuing operations before income taxes	$3,117,000	$2,018,000
Provision for income taxes	(1,311,000)	(827,000)
Income from continuing operations	1,806,000	1,191,000

	20X2	20X1
Discontinued operations:		
Loss from operations of discontinued Minimed Component (including loss on disposal of $322,000 in 20X2)	(925,000)	(790,000)
Income tax benefit	375,000	280,000
Loss on discontinued operations	(550,000)	(510,000)
Net income	$1,256,000	$681,000

Example 51–2: Presentation of Discontinued Operations in an Income Statement That Includes Extraordinary Item or Cumulative Effect of Accounting Change

	20X2	20X1
Income from continuing operations before income taxes	$3,117,000	$2,018,000
Provision for income taxes	(1,311,000)	(827,000)
Income from continuing operations	1,806,000	1,191,000
Discontinued operations:		
Loss from operations of discontinued Minimed Component (including loss on disposal of $322,000 in 20X2)	(925,000)	(790,000)
Income tax benefit	375,000	280,000
Loss on discontinued operations	(550,000)	(510,000)
Income before extraordinary item and cumulative effect of accounting change	1,256,000	681,000
Extraordinary item, net of income tax expense of $682,000 (Note X)	1,100,000	-0-
Income before cumulative effect of accounting change	2,356,000	681,000
Cumulative effect on prior years of change in accounting for product maintenance contracts, net of tax effect of $440,000	(678,000)	-0-
Net income	$1,678,000	$681,000

Example 51–3: Disclosure of Discontinued Operations in the Period in Which a Component of an Entity Is Classified as Held for Sale

On September 1, 20X2, the Company determined to discontinue operations at its Paramount division, a manufacturer of electronic power systems, and put the assets and business up for sale. The Company decided to sell this division primarily because it has incurred significant operating losses in each of the last four years and because the division has lost significant market share in the last two years. The expected disposal date is June 1, 20X3. Paramount's sales, reported in discontinued operations, for the years ended December 31, 20X2, and December 31, 20X1, were $7,359,000 and $6,986,000, respectively. Paramount's pretax loss, reported in discontinued operations, for the years ended December 31, 20X2, and December 31, 20X1, were $603,000 and $790,000, respectively. Prior year financial statements for 20X1 have been restated to present the operations of the Paramount division as a discontinued operation.

In conjunction with the discontinuance of operations, the Company recognized a loss of $322,000 in 20X2 to write down the related carrying amounts to their fair values less cost to sell. The assets and liabilities of the discontinued operations are presented separately under the captions "Assets of discontinued division" and "Liabilities of discontinued division," respectively, in the accompanying Balance Sheets at December 31, 20X2 and December 31, 20X1, and consist of the following:

	20X2	20X1
Assets of discontinued division:		
Accounts receivable	$ 403,000	$3,488,000
Inventories	622,000	723,000
Property and equipment, net	1,954,000	1,995,000
Other assets	123,000	100,000
Total assets	$3,102,000	$3,306,000
Liabilities of discontinued division:		
Accounts payable	$ 862,000	$1,156,000
Accrued liabilities	134,000	221,000
Total liabilities	$3,996,000	$1,377,000

Note: The following table illustrates the reporting of the discontinued operations on the face of the Statements of Operations for the years ended December 31, 20X2, and December 31, 20X1.

	20X2	20X1
Income from continuing operations before income taxes	$3,117,000	$2,018,000
Provision for income taxes	(1,311,000)	(827,000)
Income from continuing operations	1,806,000	1,191,000

	20X2	20X1
Discontinued operations:		
Loss from operations of discontinued Minimed Component (including loss on disposal of $322,000 in 20X2)	(925,000)	(790,000)
Income tax benefit	375,000	280,000
Loss on discontinued operations	(550,000)	(510,000)
Net income	$1,256,000	$681,000

Example 51–4: Disclosure of Discontinued Operations in the Period in Which a Component of an Entity Has Been Sold

> **Note:** For this example, assume the same background information as in Example 51–3, but the financial statements presented are for the years ended December 31, 20X3 (the year of disposal), and December 31, 20X2.

On September 1, 20X2, the Company determined to discontinue operations at its Paramount division, a manufacturer of electronic power systems, and put the assets and business up for sale. The Company decided to sell this division primarily because it has incurred significant operating losses in each of the last four years and because the division has lost significant market share in the last two years. On June 1, 20X3, the Company completed the sale of this division for total cash proceeds of $1,730,000. The assets sold consisted primarily of accounts receivable, inventories, property and equipment, and other assets. The buyer also assumed certain accounts payable and accrued liabilities.

In 20X2, the Company recognized a loss on disposal of $322,000 for the initial write-down of the division's carrying amounts to fair value less cost to sell. In 20X3, the actual loss on the sale of net assets totaled $380,000. Accordingly, the accompanying Statement of Operations for 20X3 includes an additional loss of $58,000.

Paramount's sales, reported in discontinued operations, for the five months ended May 31, 20X3, and for the year ended December 31, 20X2, were $2,863,000 and $7,359,000, respectively. Paramount's pretax loss, reported in discontinued operations, for the five months ended May 31, 20X3, and for the year ended December 31, 20X2, were $275,000 and $603,000, respectively.

The following is a summary of the net assets sold as initially determined at December 31, 20X2 and as finally reported on the closing date of June 1, 20X3:

	June 1, 20X3	December 31, 20X2
Accounts receivable	$ 387,000	$ 403,000
Inventories	602,000	622,000

	June 1, 20X3	December 31, 20X2
Property and equipment, net	1,904,000	1,954,000
Other assets	100,000	123,000
Total assets	2,993,000	3,102,000
Accounts payable	858,000	862,000
Accrued liabilities	125,000	134,000
Total liabilities	983,000	996,000
Net assets of discontinued operations	$2,010,000	$2,106,000

Note: The following table illustrates the reporting of the discontinued operations on the face of the Statements of Operations for the years ended December 31, 20X3, and December 31, 20X2.

	20X3	20X2
Income from continuing operations before income taxes	$3,692,000	$3,117,000
Provision for income taxes	(1,552,000)	(1,311,000)
Income from continuing operations	2,140,000	1,806,000
Discontinued operations:		
Loss from operations of discontinued Minimed Component (including loss on disposal of $58,000 in 20X3 and $322,000 in 20X2)	(333,000)	(925,000)
Income tax benefit	135,000	375,000
Loss on discontinued operations	(198,000)	(550,000)
Net income	$1,942,000	$1,256,000

Example 51–5: Adjustment of Loss Reported in a Prior Period on Discontinued Operations

In 20X1, the Company sold all of the assets, net of certain liabilities, associated with its Stretchflex product line. The loss on disposal of this segment recognized in 20X1 was $940,000. In 20X2, the Company revised its loss on disposal of the segment by $200,000 for the estimated loss on a note received in connection with the sale. A tax benefit was not recorded on this loss in 20X2 due to limitations on current tax recognition.

Note: The following table illustrates the reporting of the adjustment of loss on the face of the Statements of Operations.

	20X2	20X1
Income from continuing operations before income taxes	$1,563,000	$1,832,000
Provision for income taxes	(601,000)	(658,000)
Income from continuing operations	962,000	1,174,000
Discontinued operations:		
Income from operations of discontinued segment, net of income tax expense of $382,000	-0-	609,000
Loss on disposal of business segment, net of income tax benefit of $576,000 in 20X1	(200,000)	(940,000)
Loss on discontinued operations	(200,000)	(331,000)
Net income	$ 762,000	$ 843,000

Example 51–6: Subsequent Event—Long-Lived Assets to Be Disposed of by Sale

On January 24, 20X3, the Company signed a definitive agreement to sell its Aquatech retail and wholesale distribution business unit. The Company anticipates the sale to be completed by June 30, 20X3. The asset group involved was tested for recoverability as of the balance-sheet date; accordingly, an impairment loss of $500,000 was recognized which represents the amount by which the carrying amount of the asset group exceeded its fair value at the balance-sheet date.

The assets and liabilities of Aquatech are comprised of the following at December 31, 20X2, and December 31, 20X1:

	20X2	20X1
Assets:		
Accounts receivable	$ 637,000	$ 418,000
Inventories	3,570,000	2,913,000
Other current assets	37,000	22,000
Property, plant and equipment, net	1,322,000	1,174,000
Other assets	62,000	65,000
Total assets	$5,628,000	$4,592,000
Liabilities:		
Accounts payable	$1,698,000	$1,996,000
Accrued liabilities	211,000	678,000
Other noncurrent liabilities	35,000	47,000
Total liabilities	$1,944,000	$2,721,000

CHAPTER 52
EXTRAORDINARY ITEMS

CONTENTS

EXECUTIVE SUMMARY

Extraordinary items are events and transactions that are distinguished by their unusual nature *and* by the infrequency of their occurrence. Therefore, *both* of the following criteria should be met to classify an event or transaction as an extraordinary item:

1. *Unusual nature*—The underlying event or transaction possesses a high degree of abnormality and is of a type clearly unrelated to, or only incidentally related to, the ordinary and typical activities of the enterprise, taking into account the environment in which the enterprise operates.

2. *Infrequency of occurrence*—The underlying event or transaction is of a type that would not reasonably be expected to recur in the foreseeable future, taking into account the environment in which the enterprise operates.

Extraordinary items should be presented separately in the income statement, net of any related income tax effect. If the income statement includes discontinued operations or the cumulative effect of accounting changes, extraordinary items should be presented following discontinued operations and preceding the cumulative effect of accounting changes.

Events or transactions that are *either* unusual or infrequent, but not both (and therefore do not meet the criteria for extraordinary items), should be classified and reported as separate components of income from continuing operations. See Chapter 53, "Unusual or Infrequent Items," for a discussion of unusual or infrequent items.

Authoritative Literature

APB-9	Reporting the Results of Operations
APB-30	Reporting the Results of Operations—Reporting the Effects of Disposal of a Segment of a Business, and Extraordinary, Unusual, and Infrequently Occurring Events and Transactions
FAS-16	Prior Period Adjustments
FAS-144	Accounting for the Impairment or Disposal of Long-Lived Assets

DISCLOSURE REQUIREMENTS

The following disclosures are required for extraordinary items:

1. A description of the nature of an extraordinary event or transaction and the principal items entering into the computation of the gain or loss (APB-30, par. 11)

2. The following captions used on the face of the income statement when there is an extraordinary item (and there are no discontinued operations or changes in accounting principles) (APB-30, pars. 10–12):

    a. Income before extraordinary items

    b. Extraordinary item (less applicable income taxes)

    c. Net income

    d. Earnings per share amounts before extraordinary items and net income, where applicable

3. The following disclosures should be made for each adjustment in the current period of an element of an extraordinary item that was reported in a prior period (APB-30, par. 25; FAS-16, par. 16):

   a. The year of origin, nature, and amount

   b. The adjustment classified separately in the current period as an extraordinary item

EXAMPLES OF FINANCIAL STATEMENT DISCLOSURES

 The following sample disclosures are available on the accompanying disc.

Example 52–1: Presentation of Extraordinary Items in an Income Statement That Does Not Include Discontinued Operations and Cumulative Effect of Accounting Change

	20X2	20X1
Income before income taxes and extraordinary items	$2,078,000	$2,774,000
Provision for income taxes	(874,000)	(1,138,000)
Income before extraordinary items	1,204,000	1,636,000
Extraordinary items:		
Gain on litigation settlement, less income tax of $233,000	-0-	417,000
Insurance settlement for earthquake damage, less income tax expense of $310,000	624,000	-0-
Net income	$1,828,000	$2,053,000

Example 52–2: Presentation of Extraordinary Items in an Income Statement That Includes Discontinued Operations and Cumulative Effect of Accounting Change

	20X2	20X1
Income (loss) from continuing operations before income taxes	$4,914,000	$(1,811,000)
Income taxes	(2,113,000)	652,000
Income (loss) from continuing operations	2,801,000	(1,159,000)

	20X2	20X1
Discontinued operations:		
Loss from operations of discontinued component, net of income tax benefit of $617,000 in 20X2 and $1,515,000 in 20X1	(1,568,000)	(3,726,000)
Gain on disposal of component, net of income tax expense of $986,000	1,347,000	-0-
Loss on discontinued operations	(221,000)	(3,726,000)
Income (loss) before extraordinary item and cumulative effect of accounting change	2,580,000	(4,885,000)
Extraordinary item—Loss on litigation settlement, net of income tax benefit of $165,000	(452,000)	-0-
Income (loss) before cumulative effect of accounting change	2,128,000	(4,885,000)
Cumulative effect on prior years of change in accounting for product maintenance contracts, net of tax effect of $878,000	(1,356,000)	-0-
Net income (loss)	$772,000	$(4,885,000)

Example 52–3: Extraordinary Gain Related to Insurance Settlement for Earthquake Damage

In September 20X2, the Company's headquarters building in Apple Valley, Florida, was severely damaged by an earthquake. After the settlement with the insurer in December 20X2, the Company retired the building and recognized an extraordinary gain of $624,000, net of income taxes of $310,000, during 20X2.

Example 52–4: Adjustment of a Prior-Period Extraordinary Item

In September 20X1, the Company's warehouse in Los Angeles, California, was substantially damaged by fire. As a result, the Company recorded in 20X1 an extraordinary loss of $918,000 (net of income tax benefit of $491,000 and net of insurance proceeds of $1,836,000). Included in the 20X1 extraordinary loss was a provision for estimated inventory damage. During 20X2, the Company determined that actual inventory damage exceeded its original estimate. Therefore, an extraordinary loss of $386,000, net of income tax benefit of $211,000, has been included in the Statement of Operations for 20X2.

Note: The following table illustrates the reporting of the adjustment of loss on the face of the Statements of Operations.

	20X2	20X1
Income before income taxes and extraordinary items	$1,563,000	$1,832,000
Provision for income taxes	(601,000)	(658,000)
Income before extraordinary items	962,000	1,174,000
Extraordinary item:		
Fire loss, net of income tax benefit of $211,000 in 20X2 and $491,000 in 20X1	(386,000)	(918,000)
Net income	$ 576,000	$ 256,000

Example 52–5: Investor's Proportionate Share of Investee's Extraordinary Gain

The extraordinary item of $320,000 represents the Company's proportionate share of a gain realized on the extinguishment of debt by Kametz, Ltd., a manufacturer of electronic parts in which the Company has a 40% interest that is accounted for on the equity method. The Company has not provided any income tax related to its share of the extraordinary gain because it is the Company's intention to reinvest all undistributed earnings of Kametz, Ltd. indefinitely.

Note: The following table illustrates the portion of the income statement reflecting the Company's proportionate share of extraordinary item reported by Kametz, Ltd.

	20X2	20X1
Income before income taxes	$8,941,000	$7,916,000
Provision for income taxes	(3,576,000)	(3,287,000)
Income before equity in net income of affiliate and extraordinary item	5,365,000	4,629,000
Equity in net income of affiliate, excluding extraordinary gain of $320,000 in 20X2	554,000	716,000
Income before extraordinary item	5,919,000	5,345,000
Extraordinary item—Equity in undistributed extraordinary gain of affiliate	320,000	-0-
Net income	$6,239,000	$5,345,000

CHAPTER 53
UNUSUAL OR INFREQUENT ITEMS

CONTENTS

EXECUTIVE SUMMARY

Events or transactions that are *either* unusual or infrequent, but not both (and therefore do not meet the criteria for extraordinary items), should be classified and reported as separate components of income from continuing operations. However, the income statement presentation should *not* imply that the event is an extraordinary item. Therefore, the separately identified item should *not* be reported net of its related tax effect as a separate line item following income from continuing operations. Instead, it should be classified separately as a component of ordinary income or loss.

Authoritative Literature

APB-9   Reporting the Results of Operations

APB-30   Reporting the Results of Operations—Reporting the Effects of Disposal of a Segment of a Business, and Extraordinary, Unusual, and Infrequently Occurring Events and Transactions

DISCLOSURE REQUIREMENTS

The nature and financial effects of material transactions that are either unusual or infrequent (but not both) should be disclosed and presented as a separate component of income from continuing operations (APB-30, par. 26).

EXAMPLES OF FINANCIAL STATEMENT DISCLOSURES

 The following sample disclosures are available on the accompanying disc.

Example 53–1: Unusual/Infrequent Items—Pre-Opening Store Costs and Charges Related to Hiring and Litigation

In September 20X2, the Company recorded unusual expenses of $1,044,000 before taxes. This is presented separately as a component of income from operations in the Statement of Operations. The unusual expenses relate to (1) $712,000 incurred in pre-opening costs for two new company-owned stores opened in Los Angeles, California, and Chicago, Illinois; (2) $217,000 incurred in the hiring of the new chief executive officer; and (3) $115,000 of cost of litigation associated with such hiring.

Note: The following table illustrates the portion of the income statement reflecting an unusual or infrequent item.

	20X2	20X1
Net sales	$82,174,000	$74,311,000
Costs and expenses:		
Cost of sales	50,947,000	46,816,000
Selling expenses	4,142,000	3,268,000
General and administrative expenses	23,743,000	19,492,000
Unusual expenses	1,044,000	-0-
	79,876,000	69,576,000
Income before income taxes	$ 2,298,000	$ 4,735,000

Example 53–2: Unusual/Infrequent Items—Write-Off of Receivables and Inventories of a Former Affiliate

In 20X2, the Company recorded a special charge of $425,000 relating to the write-off of receivables due from a former affiliate, Biznetics Corp., and for inventories that were dedicated to the market, which this former affiliate served. The write-off was necessary because the former affiliate did not, and is not expected to, meet its financial obligations to the Company.

Example 53–3: Unusual/Infrequent Items—Hiring of a New Company President

In 20X2, the Company recorded unusual expenses of $250,000, before taxes, which was incurred in the hiring of the new Company president in June 20X2. This is presented separately as a component of income (loss) from operations in the Statement of Operations.

CHAPTER 54
COMPREHENSIVE INCOME

CONTENTS

EXECUTIVE SUMMARY

Generally accepted accounting principles (GAAP) require comprehensive income and its components to be reported when a company presents a full set of financial statements that report financial position, results of operations, and cash flows. The term *comprehensive income* refers to net income plus other comprehensive income, i.e., certain revenues, expenses, gains, and losses that are reported as separate components of stockholders' equity instead of net income. Under current accounting standards, other comprehensive income includes the following:

1. Unrealized holding gains and losses on available-for-sale securities

2. Unrealized holding gains and losses that result from a debt security being transferred into the available-for-sale category from the held-to-maturity category

3. Subsequent decreases (if not an other-than-temporary impairment) or increases in the fair value of available-for-sale securities previously written down as impaired

4. Foreign currency translation adjustments

5. Gains and losses on foreign currency transactions that are designated as, and are effective as, economic hedges of a net investment in a foreign entity, commencing as of the designation date

6. Gains and losses on intercompany foreign currency transactions that are of a long-term investment nature, when the entities to the transaction are consolidated, combined, or accounted for by the equity method

7. Minimum pension liability adjustments

8. A change in the fair value of a derivative instrument that qualifies as the hedging instrument in a cash flow hedge

An entity is required to (1) present items of other comprehensive income by their nature in a financial statement *and* (2) display the accumulated balance of other comprehensive income separately from retained earnings and additional paid-in capital in the equity section of a balance sheet.

Authoritative Literature

FAS-130   Reporting Comprehensive Income

FAS-133   Accounting for Derivative Instruments and Hedging Activities

DISCLOSURE REQUIREMENTS

The following are the presentation and disclosure requirements for comprehensive income:

1. Comprehensive income should be displayed in one of the following three alternative presentation formats (FAS-130, pars. 14 and 22):

    a. In a single statement of income and comprehensive income that extends a traditional income statement to include (following net income) the elements of other comprehensive income and the total of comprehensive income

    b. In a separate statement of comprehensive income that begins with net income and includes the elements of other comprehensive income and then a total of comprehensive income

    c. In the statement of changes in equity

2. The components of other comprehensive income should be displayed either (i) net of related income tax effects *or* (ii) before related tax effects with one amount shown for the aggregate income tax expense or benefit related to the total of other comprehensive income items (FAS-130, par. 24)

3. The amount of income tax expense or benefit allocated to each component of other comprehensive income, including reclassification adjustments, should be disclosed either (i) on the face of the financial statement in which the components are displayed or (ii) in the notes to the financial statements (FAS 130, par. 25)

4. Reclassification adjustments for each classification of other comprehensive income (other than minimum pension liability adjustments) should be disclosed either (i) on the face of the financial statement in which comprehensive income is reported *or* (ii) in the notes to the financial statements (FAS-130, par. 20)

5. The accumulated balance of other comprehensive income should be reported separately from retained earnings and additional paid-in capital in the equity section of the balance sheet (FAS-130, par. 26)

6. The ending accumulated balances for each item in accumulated other comprehensive income should be disclosed either (i) on the face of the balance sheet, (ii) in a statement of changes in equity, *or* (iii) in the notes to the financial statements (FAS-130, par. 26)

7. For derivative instruments and hedging activities, the following disclosures should be made (FAS-133, pars. 46 and 47):

    a. The net gain or loss on derivative instruments designated as cash flow hedging instruments (including qualifying foreign currency cash flow hedges) should be reported as a separate classification within other comprehensive income

    b. As part of the disclosures of accumulated other comprehensive income:

        — The beginning and ending accumulated derivative gain or loss

        — The related net change associated with current period hedging transactions

        — The net amount of any reclassification into earnings

EXAMPLES OF FINANCIAL STATEMENT DISCLOSURES

The following sample disclosures are available on the accompanying disc.

Example 54–1: Comprehensive Income Reported in a Single Statement of Income and Comprehensive Income

ABC Company
Statement of Income and Comprehensive Income
Years Ended December 31, 20X2, and December 31, 20X1

	20X2	20X1
Revenues	$ 12,760,000	$ 11,312,000
Costs and expenses	(12,663,000)	(11,226,000)
Other income and expenses, net	10,000	5,000
Income from operations before tax	107,000	91,000
Income tax expense	(44,000)	(37,000)
Net income	63,000	54,000
Other comprehensive income, net of tax:		
Unrealized gains on securities:		
Unrealized holding gains arising during the period	13,000	18,000
Less: reclassification adjustment for gains included in net income	(2,000)	(4,000)
	11,000	14,000
Minimum pension liability adjustment	(2,000)	(5,000)
Foreign currency translation adjustment	8,000	3,000
Other comprehensive income, net of tax	17,000	12,000
Comprehensive income	$ 80,000	$ 66,000

Note: Components of other comprehensive income also could be displayed on a before tax basis, with one amount shown for the aggregate income tax effect as follows:

	20X2	20X1
Net income	$63,000	$54,000
Other comprehensive income, before tax:		
Unrealized gains on securities:		
Unrealized holding gains arising during the period	18,000	26,000
Less: reclassification adjustment for gains included in net income	(3,000)	(6,000)
	15,000	20,000
Minimum pension liability adjustment	(4,000)	(9,000)
Foreign currency translation adjustment	11,000	4,000
Other comprehensive income, before tax	22,000	15,000
Income tax expense related to items of other comprehensive income	(5,000)	(3,000)
Other comprehensive income, net of tax	17,000	12,000
Comprehensive income	$80,000	$66,000

Example 54–2: Comprehensive Income Reported in a Separate Statement of Comprehensive Income

ABC Company
Statement of Comprehensive Income
Years Ended December 31, 20X2, and December 31, 20X1

	20X2	20X1
Net income	$63,000	$54,000
Other comprehensive income, net of tax:		
Unrealized gains on securities:		
Unrealized holding gains arising during the period	13,000	18,000
Less: reclassification adjustment for gains included in net income	(2,000)	(4,000)
	11,000	14,000
Minimum pension liability adjustment	(2,000)	(5,000)
Foreign currency translation adjustment	8,000	3,000
Other comprehensive income, net of tax	17,000	12,000
Comprehensive income	$80,000	$66,000

Example 54–3: Comprehensive Income Reported in a Statement of Changes in Equity

ABC Company
Statement of Changes in Stockholders' Equity
Years Ended December 31, 20X2, and December 31, 20X1

	Common Stock Shares	Common Stock Amount	Additional Paid-in Capital	Retained Earnings	Accumulated Other Comprehensive Income	Total
Balance at December 31, 20X0	$1,250,000	$125,000	$250,000	$49,000	$13,000	$437,000
Comprehensive income:						
Net income				54,000		54,000
Unrealized gains on securities, net of reclassification adjustment					14,000	14,000
Minimum pension liability adjustment					(5,000)	(5,000)
Foreign currency translation adjustment					3,000	3,000
Total comprehensive income						66,000
Common stock issued	250,000	25,000	50,000			75,000
Dividends				(15,000)		(15,000)
Balance at December 31, 20X1	1,500,000	150,000	300,000	88,000	25,000	563,000
Comprehensive income:						
Net income				63,000		63,000
Unrealized gains on securities, net of reclassification adjustment					11,000	11,000
Minimum pension liability adjustment					(2,000)	(2,000)
Foreign currency translation adjustment					8,000	8,000
Total comprehensive income						80,000
Common stock issued	500,000	50,000	100,000			150,000
Dividends				(10,000)		(10,000)
Balance at December 31, 20X2	$2,000,000	$200,000	$400,000	$141,000	$42,000	$783,000

Example 54–4: Income Tax Expense or Benefit Allocated to Each Component of Other Comprehensive Income, Including Reclassification Adjustments

The pretax, tax, and after-tax effects of the components of other comprehensive income (loss) for 20X2 and 20X1 are as follows:

	Pre-Tax Amount	Tax (Expense) Benefit	After-tax Amount
20X2			
Unrealized gains on securities:			
Unrealized holding gains arising during the period	$18,000	$(5,000)	$13,000
Less: reclassification adjustment for gains included in net income	(3,000)	1,000	(2,000)
Net unrealized gains	15,000	(4,000)	11,000
Minimum pension liability adjustment	(4,000)	2,000	(2,000)
Foreign currency translation adjustment	11,000	(3,000)	8,000
Other comprehensive income	$22,000	$(5,000)	$17,000
20X1			
Unrealized gains on securities:			
Unrealized holding gains arising during the period	$26,000	$(8,000)	$18,000
Less: reclassification adjustment for gains included in net income	(6,000)	2,000	(4,000)
Net unrealized gains	20,000	(6,000)	14,000
Minimum pension liability adjustment	(9,000)	4,000	(5,000)
Foreign currency translation adjustment	4,000	(1,000)	3,000
Other comprehensive income	$15,000	$(3,000)	$12,000

Note: Alternatively, the tax amounts for each component of other comprehensive income can be displayed parenthetically on the face of the financial statement in which comprehensive income is reported.

Example 54–5: Display of Accumulated Other Comprehensive Income Separately as a Component of Equity in a Balance Sheet

	20X2	20X1
Stockholders' Equity:		
Common stock; par value $.10; authorized 10,000,000 shares; issued and outstanding 2,000,000 shares in 20X2 and 1,500,000 shares in 20X1	$200,000	$150,000
Additional paid-in capital	400,000	300,000
Retained earnings	141,000	88,000
Accumulated other comprehensive income	42,000	25,000
Total stockholders' equity	$783,000	$563,000

Example 54-6: Details of the Accumulated Balances for Each Component Comprising Accumulated Other Comprehensive Income

Balances of related after-tax components comprising accumulated other comprehensive income (loss), included in stockholders' equity, at December 31, 20X2, and December 31, 20X1, are as follows:

	Unrealized Gains on Securities	Minimum Pension Liability Adjustment	Foreign Currency Translation Adjustment	Accumulated Other Comprehensive Income
Balance at December 31, 20X0	$12,000	$5,000	$(4,000)	$13,000
Change for 20X1	14,000	(5,000)	3,000	12,000
Balance at December 31, 20X1	26,000	-0-	(1,000)	25,000
Change for 20X2	11,000	(2,000)	8,000	17,000
Balance at December 31, 20X2	$37,000	$(2,000)	$7,000	$42,000

Note: Alternatively, the balances of each classification within accumulated other comprehensive income can be displayed in a statement of changes in equity or in a balance sheet.

CHAPTER 55
EARNINGS PER SHARE

CONTENTS

EXECUTIVE SUMMARY

Note: The FASB has issued an Exposure Draft of a proposed Statement of Financial Accounting Standards (FAS) entitled *Earnings per Share*. This proposed FAS is a revision of the

December 2003 proposed FAS, *Earnings per Share*, which was issued as part of the FASB's project on short-term international convergence. The proposed FAS would amend FAS-128, *Earnings per Share*, to clarify guidance for mandatorily convertible instruments, the treasury stock method, contracts that may be settled in cash or shares, and contingently issuable shares. In addition, the proposed FAS would (1) amend the computational guidance in FAS-128 for calculating the number of incremental shares included in diluted shares when applying the treasury stock method; (2) eliminate the provisions of FAS-128 that allow an entity to rebut the presumption that contracts with the option of settling in either cash or stock will be settled in stock; and (3) require that shares that will be issued upon conversion of a mandatorily convertible security be included in the weighted-average number of ordinary shares outstanding used in computing basic earnings per share from the date when conversion becomes mandatory.

Readers should be alert to further developments in this area.

Earnings per share (EPS) is an important measure of corporate performance for investors and other users of financial statements. EPS figures must be presented in the income statement of a publicly held company and must be presented in a manner consistent with the captions included in the company's income statement. Certain securities, such as convertible bonds, preferred stock, and stock options, permit their holders to become common stockholders or add to the number of shares of common stock already held. When potential reduction, called *dilution*, of EPS figures is inherent in a company's capital structure, a dual presentation of EPS is required—basic EPS and diluted EPS.

For purposes of presenting earnings per share, a distinction is made between enterprises with a simple capital structure and those with a complex capital structure. *A simple capital structure* is one that consists of capital stock and includes no potential for dilution via conversions, exercise of options, or other arrangements that would increase the number of shares outstanding. For organizations with complex capital structures, two EPS figures are presented with equal prominence on the face of the income statement: basic EPS and diluted EPS. The difference between basic EPS and diluted EPS is that *basic EPS* considers only outstanding common stock, whereas *diluted EPS* incorporates the potential dilution from all potentially dilutive securities that would have reduced EPS.

Basic EPS excludes dilution and is computed by dividing income available to common stockholders by the weighted-average number of common shares outstanding for the period. Diluted EPS reflects the potential dilution that could occur if securities or other contracts to issue common stock were exercised or converted into common stock or resulted in the issuance of common stock that then shared in the earnings of the entity. The computation of diluted EPS should not assume conversion, exercise, or contingent issuance of securities that would have an anti-dilutive effect on earnings per share.

Authoritative Literature

APB-30	Reporting the Results of Operations—Reporting the Effects of Disposal of a Segment of a Business, and Extraordinary, Unusual, and Infrequently Occurring Events and Transactions
FAS-95	Statement of Cash Flows
FAS-128	Earnings per Share
FAS-129	Disclosure of Information about Capital Structure
FSP FAS 129-1	Disclosure Requirements under FASB Statement No. 129, *Disclosure of Information about Capital Structure,* Relating to Contingently Convertible Securities
FAS-150	Accounting for Certain Financial Instruments with Characteristics of Both Liabilities and Equity
FIN-28	Accounting for Stock Appreciation Rights and Other Variable Stock Option or Award Plans
FIN-38	Determining the Measurement Date for Stock Option, Purchase, and Award Plans Involving Junior Stock

DISCLOSURE REQUIREMENTS

The following are the required disclosures relating to earnings per share (Nonpublic companies are not required to present earnings per share):

1. For each period for which an income statement is presented:

    a. A reconciliation of the numerators and denominators of the basic EPS and the diluted EPS computations for income from continuing operations, including the individual income and share amount effects of all securities that affect EPS; insignificant reconciling items need not be itemized as part of the reconciliation and can be aggregated (FAS-128, pars. 40 and 138)

    b. The effect that has been given to preferred dividends in determining the income available to common stockholders in computing basic EPS (FAS-128, par. 40)

    c. Securities (including those issuable pursuant to contingent stock agreements) that could potentially dilute EPS in the future, but which were not included in the calculation of diluted EPS because to do so would have been antidilutive for the periods presented (FAS-128, par. 40)

2. For the latest period for which an income statement is presented, a description of any transaction that occurs after the end of the most recent period but before the issuance of the financial statements that would have changed materially the number of common shares or potential common shares outstanding at the end of the period if the transaction had occurred before the end of the period (FAS-128, par. 41)

3. When prior EPS amounts have been restated in compliance with an accounting standard requiring restatement, the per share effect of the restatement should be disclosed (FAS-128, pars. 57–58)

4. When the number of common shares outstanding increases as a result of a stock dividend or stock split, or decreases as a result of a reverse stock split, the computations of basic EPS and diluted EPS should be adjusted retroactively for all periods presented to reflect such changes in the number of shares, and that fact should be disclosed (FAS-128, par. 54)

5. If changes in common stock resulting from stock dividends, stock splits, or reverse stock splits occur after the close of the period but before the issuance of the financial statements, the per-share computations for all periods presented should be based on the new number of shares, and that fact should be disclosed (FAS-128, par. 54)

6. For shares that would be issued if contingently convertible securities were converted, disclosure should be made of whether the shares are included in the calculation of diluted EPS, and the reasons why or why not (FSP FAS 129-1, par. 4)

EXAMPLES OF FINANCIAL STATEMENT DISCLOSURES

 The following sample disclosures are available on the accompanying disc.

Example 55–1: Earnings-per-Share Calculation Shows Reconciliation of Denominator

Basic net earnings per share is computed using the weighted-average number of common shares outstanding. The dilutive effect of potential common shares outstanding is included in diluted net earnings per share. The computations of basic net earnings per share and diluted net earnings per share for 20X2 and 20X1 are as follows:

	20X2	20X1
Net earnings from continuing operations	$10,174,000	$9,143,000
Basic weighted-average shares	6,119,000	6,625,000
Effect of dilutive securities:		
Common and convertible preferred stock options	90,200	55,400
Convertible preferred stock	70,800	42,600
Dilutive potential common shares	6,280,000	6,723,000
Net earnings per share from continuing operations:		
Basic	$ 1.66	$ 1.38
Diluted	$ 1.62	$ 1.36

Example 55–2: Dilutive Potential Common Shares Are Calculated in Accordance with the Treasury Stock Method That Is Described

Basic earnings per common share for the years ended December 31, 20X2, and December 31, 20X1, are calculated by dividing net income by weighted-average common shares outstanding during the period. Diluted earnings per common share for the years ended December 31, 20X2, and December 31, 20X1, are calculated by dividing net income by weighted-average common shares outstanding during the period plus dilutive potential common shares, which are determined as follows:

	20X2	20X1
Weighted-average common shares	20,745,000	21,881,000
Effect of dilutive securities:		
Warrants	5,550,000	4,734,000
Options to purchase common stock	219,000	241,000
Dilutive potential common shares	26,514,000	26,856,000

Dilutive potential common shares are calculated in accordance with the treasury stock method, which assumes that proceeds from the exercise of all warrants and options are used to repurchase common stock at market value. The amount of shares remaining after the proceeds are exhausted represents the potentially dilutive effect of the securities. The increasing number of warrants used in the calculation is a result of the increasing market value of the Company's common stock.

Example 55–3: Diluted Net Earnings per Share Excludes Securities with Antidilutive Effect

Basic earnings per share is computed by dividing net income by the weighted-average number of common shares outstanding during the period. Diluted earnings per share is computed by dividing net income by the weighted-average number of common shares and dilutive potential common shares outstanding during the period.

The following is a reconciliation of the number of shares used in the calculation of basic earnings per share and diluted earnings per share for the years ended December 31, 20X2, and December 31, 20X1:

	20X2	20X1
Net income	$5,323,000	$10,471,000
Weighted-average number of common shares outstanding	7,419,000	7,699,000
Incremental shares from the assumed exercise of dilutive stock options	198,000	174,000
Dilutive potential common shares	7,617,000	7,873,000
Net earnings per share:		
Basic	$ 0.72	$ 1.36
Diluted	$ 0.70	$ 1.33

The following securities were not included in the computation of diluted net earnings per share as their effect would have been antidilutive:

	20X2	20X1
Options to purchase common stock	1,140,000	1,173,000
Warrants to purchase common stock	227,000	282,000
Unvested shares of common stock subject to repurchase	55,000	-0-
Convertible preferred stock	125,000	110,000
Convertible subordinated notes	1,022,000	1,022,000
	2,569,000	2,587,000

Example 55–4: EPS Calculations Are Adjusted for Tax-Effected Interest Expense to Calculate Diluted Earnings per Share and for Stock Split

In December 20X2, the Company issued a two-for-one stock split effected in the form of a 100% stock dividend. Previously reported share and earnings per share amounts have been restated. Basic earnings per share is computed by dividing net earnings by the weighted-average number of common shares outstanding. Diluted earnings per share is computed by dividing net earnings by the sum of the weighted-average number of common shares outstanding and the weighted-average number of potential common shares outstanding. The calculations of basic and diluted earnings per share for 20X2 and 20X1 are as follows:

	20X2	20X1
Calculation of basic earnings per share:		
Net earnings	$1,614,000	$1,160,000
Weighted-average number of common shares outstanding	1,471,000	1,459,000
Basic earnings per share	$ 1.10	$ 0.80
Calculation of diluted earnings per share:		
Net earnings	$1,614,000	$1,160,000
Tax-effected interest expense attributable to 3% Notes	23,000	23,000
Net earnings assuming dilution	$1,637,000	$1,183,000
Weighted-average number of common shares outstanding	1,471,000	1,459,000
Effect of potentially dilutive securities:		
3% Notes	48,000	48,000
Employee stock plans	28,000	17,000
Weighted-average number of common shares outstanding assuming dilution	1,547,000	1,524,000
Diluted earnings per share	$ 1.06	$ 0.78

Employee stock plans represent shares granted under the Company's employee stock purchase plan and stock option plans. For 20X2 and 20X1, shares issuable upon conversion of the Company's 3% Notes were included in weighted-average shares assuming dilution for purposes of calculating diluted earnings per share. To calculate diluted earnings per share, net earnings are adjusted for tax-effected net interest and issue costs on the 3% Notes and divided by weighted-average shares assuming dilution.

Example 55–5: EPS Calculations Include Cumulative Effect of Change in Accounting Principle

Basic net income per share is computed by dividing net income available to common stockholders by the weighted-average number of common shares outstanding during the period and excludes the dilutive effect of stock options. Diluted net income per share gives effect to all dilutive potential common shares outstanding during a period. A reconciliation of the numerators and denominators of the basic and diluted income per share for 20X2 and 20X1 is presented below:

	20X2	20X1
Basic earnings per share:		
Income before cumulative effect of change in accounting principle	$4,200,000	$3,700,000
Cumulative effect of change in accounting principle	-0-	(400,000)
Net income	$4,200,000	$3,300,000
Weighted shares outstanding—Basic	2,545,000	2,185,000
Per share:		
Income before cumulative effect of change in accounting principle	$ 1.65	$ 1.69
Cumulative effect of change in accounting principle	-0-	(0.18)
Basic earnings per share	$ 1.65	$ 1.51
Diluted earnings per share:		
Income before cumulative effect of change in accounting principle	$4,200,000	$3,700,000
Effect of 5.75% convertible subordinated notes	110,000	170,000
Income before cumulative effect of change in accounting principle including the effect of dilutive securities	4,310,000	3,870,000
Cumulative effect of change in accounting principle	-0-	(400,000)
Net income	$4,310,000	$3,470,000
Weighted shares outstanding—Basic	2,545,000	2,185,000
Effect of dilutive securities:		
Stock options	112,000	125,000
5.75% convertible subordinated notes	115,000	220,000
Weighted shares outstanding—Diluted	2,772,000	2,530,000

	20X2	20X1
Per share:		
Income before cumulative effect of change in accounting principle	$ 1.55	$ 1.53
Cumulative effect of change in accounting principle	-0-	(0.16)
Diluted earnings per share	$ 1.55	$ 1.37

Example 55–6: EPS Calculations Include Discontinued Operations and Extraordinary Items

Note: This example illustrates (1) the presentation of earnings per share on the face of the income statement and (2) the computation of basic earnings per share and diluted earnings per share for income from continuing operations in a note to the financial statements.

Income Statement

	20X2	20X1
Income from continuing operations	$8,750,000	$7,450,000
Discontinued operations:		
Income from discontinued operations, net of taxes	500,000	-0-
Gain on disposition of business, net of taxes	600,000	-0-
Extraordinary items, net of taxes	-0-	(700,000)
Net income	$9,850,000	$6,750,000
Earnings per share—Basic:		
Income from continuing operations	$ 0.51	$ 0.45
Discontinued operations	0.06	-0-
Extraordinary items	-0-	(0.04)
Net income	$ 0.57	$ 0.41
Earnings per share—Diluted:		
Income from continuing operations	$ 0.50	$ 0.44
Discontinued operations	0.06	-0-
Extraordinary items	-0-	(0.04)
Net income	$ 0.56	$ 0.40
Weighted-average number of shares—Basic	17,160,000	16,600,000
Weighted-average number of shares assuming dilution	17,530,000	16,825,000

Note to the Financial Statements

Basic earnings per share is computed by dividing net income by the weighted-average number of common shares outstanding during the period. Diluted earnings per share is computed by dividing net income by the weighted-average number of common shares and dilutive potential common shares outstanding during the period. The computation of basic earnings per share and diluted earnings per share for "Income from continuing operations" is as follows:

	20X2	20X1
Income from continuing operations	$8,750,000	$7,450,000
Weighted-average number of common shares outstanding—Basic	17,160,000	16,600,000
Effect of dilutive securities—Stock options	370,000	225,000
Weighted-average number of common shares outstanding—Diluted	17,530,000	16,825,000
Net earnings per share from continuing operations:		
Basic	$ 0.51	$ 0.45
Diluted	$ 0.50	$ 0.44

Example 55–7: Earnings-per-Share Amounts for Prior Period Have Been Restated to Give Effect to the Adoption of a New Accounting Standard

In 20X2, the Company adopted Financial Accounting Standards Board Statement (FAS) No. [*number*] [*title*], which requires [*describe briefly the requirements of the new standard*]. The effect of this change was to [*increase/decrease*] 20X2 net income by $[*amount*], basic earnings per share by $[*amount*], and diluted earnings per share by $[*amount*]. The financial statements for 20X1 have been retroactively restated for the change, which resulted in an [*increase/decrease*] in net income for 20X1 of $[*amount*]. Earnings per share amounts for 20X1 have been restated to give effect to the application of the new accounting standard. The effect of the restatement was to [*increase/decrease*] 20X1 basic earnings per share by $[*amount*] and diluted earnings per share by $[*amount*]. Retained earnings as of January 1, 20X1, has been adjusted for the effect of retroactive application of the new Statement.

Example 55–8: EPS Calculations Reflect Deemed Dividend Related to Beneficial Conversion Feature on Preferred Stock and Accretion of Preferred Stock to Redemption Value

> **Note:** This example illustrates the presentation of earnings per share on the face of the income statement giving effect to

deemed dividend related to beneficial conversion feature on preferred stock and accretion of preferred stock to redemption value.

Income Statement

	20X2	20X1
Net loss before income taxes	$(6,015,800)	$(6,911,000)
(Benefit) Provision for income taxes	(238,800)	200,000
Net loss	(6,254,600)	(6,711,000)
Deemed dividend related to beneficial conversion feature on Series A Preferred Stock	(332,700)	-0-
Accretion of Series A Preferred Stock to redemption value	(589,500)	-0-
Series A Preferred Stock dividends	(40,000)	-0-
Net loss attributable to common stockholders	$(7,216,800)	$(6,711,000)
Basic and diluted net loss per share attributable to common stockholders	$(1.25)	$(1.29)
Weighted-average number of shares—Basic and diluted	5,760,000	5,202,325

PART IV—
STATEMENT OF CASH FLOWS

CHAPTER 56
STATEMENT OF CASH FLOWS

CONTENTS

EXECUTIVE SUMMARY

A statement of cash flows is required as part of a complete set of financial statements prepared in conformity with generally accepted accounting principles (GAAP) for all business enterprises. A statement of cash flows specifies the amount of net cash provided by or used by an enterprise during a period from (1) operating activities, (2) investing activities, and (3) financing activities. The statement of cash flows indicates the net effect of these cash flows on the enterprise's cash and cash equivalents. A reconciliation of beginning and ending cash and cash equivalents is included in the statement of cash flows. Also, a statement of cash flows should contain separate related disclosures about all investing and financing activities of an enterprise that affect its financial position but do not directly affect its cash flows during the period. Descriptive terms such as "Cash" or "Cash and cash equivalents" are required in the statement of cash flows, whereas ambiguous terms such as "Funds" are inappropriate.

Cash equivalents are short-term, highly liquid investments that are (1) readily convertible to known amounts of cash and (2) so near their maturities that they present insignificant risk of changes in value because of changes in interest rates. As a general rule, only investments with original maturities of three months or less qualify as cash equivalents. Examples of items commonly considered to be cash equivalents include Treasury bills, commercial paper, money market funds, and federal funds sold.

GAAP specifically prohibit reporting cash flow per share.

Authoritative Literature

FAS-95 Statement of Cash Flows

FAS-102 Statement of Cash Flows—Exemption of Certain Enterprises and Classification of Cash Flows from Certain Securities Acquired for Resale

FAS-104 Statement of Cash Flows—Net Reporting of Certain Cash Receipts and Cash Payments and Classification of Cash Flows from Hedging Transactions

FAS-115 Accounting for Certain Investments in Debt and Equity Securities

FAS-117	Financial Statements of Not-for-Profit Organizations
FAS-133	Accounting for Derivative Instruments and Hedging Activities
FAS-145	Rescission of FASB Statements No. 4, 44, and 64, Amendment of FASB Statement No. 13, and Technical Corrections

DISCLOSURE REQUIREMENTS

The following are required disclosures related to statements of cash flows:

1. The accounting policy for determining which items are treated as cash and cash equivalents (FAS-95, par. 10)

2. If the indirect method of reporting cash flows is used, a reconciliation of net income to net cash provided or used by operating activities (presented in notes to the financial statements or on the face of the statement of cash flows) (FAS-95, par. 6)

3. Information about noncash investing and financing activities that affect assets or liabilities (FAS-95, par. 32)

4. If the indirect method of reporting cash flows from operating activities is used, disclosures should include the amounts of interest paid (net of amounts capitalized) and income taxes paid during the period (FAS-95, par. 29)

EXAMPLES OF FINANCIAL STATEMENT DISCLOSURES

 The following sample disclosures are available on the accompanying disc.

Example 56–1: Statement of Cash Flows—Indirect Method

	Year Ended December 31	
	20X2	20X1
Operating activities:		
Net income (loss)	$36,000,000	$19,000,000
Adjustments to reconcile net income (loss) to net cash provided by (used in) operating activities:		

Depreciation and amortization	7,500,000	3,700,000
Amortization of deferred compensation	1,300,000	800,000
Deferred taxes	(1,500,000)	(500,000)
Changes in operating assets and liabilities, net of effects from acquired companies:		
Accounts receivable	(20,000,000)	(8,000,000)
Inventory	(4,500,000)	(1,200,000)
Income taxes receivable	(3,500,000)	(2,400,000)
Prepaid expenses and other assets	(2,000,000)	(500,000)
Accounts payable	14,000,000	7,000,000
Other accrued liabilities	5,500,000	3,500,000
Net cash provided by (used in) operating activities	32,800,000	21,400,000
Investing activities:		
Net assets of acquired companies, net of cash acquired	(16,000,000)	(10,000,000)
Purchases of property and equipment	(11,000,000)	(12,000,000)
Purchases of investments	(2,000,000)	(1,000,000)
Net cash used in investing activities	(29,000,000)	(23,000,000)
Financing activities:		
Proceeds from bank term loan	1,000,000	5,700,000
Payments on bank term loan	(500,000)	(7,000,000)
Payments on capital lease obligations	(700,000)	(800,000)
Proceeds from issuance of common stock	2,000,000	3,000,000
Payments on repurchase of preferred stock	(200,000)	(300,000)
Net cash provided by financing activities	1,600,000	600,000
Effect of exchange rate changes on cash and cash equivalents	(100,000)	200,000
Increase (decrease) in cash and cash equivalents	5,300,000	(800,000)

Cash and cash equivalents at beginning of year	2,300,000	3,100,000
Cash and cash equivalents at end of year	$7,600,000	$2,300,000

Example 56–2: Statement of Cash Flows—Direct Method, Including Reconciliation of Net Income to Net Cash from Operating Activities

	Year Ended December 31	
	20X2	20X1
Cash flows from operating activities:		
Cash received from customers	28,000,000	22,000,000
Cash paid to suppliers and employees	(25,500,000)	(21,700,000)
Interest received	200,000	100,000
Interest paid	(1,000,000)	(1,500,000)
Income tax refunds received	400,000	100,000
Income taxes paid	(1,500,000)	(2,000,000)
Other cash received (paid)	(200,000)	100,000
Net cash provided by (used in) operating activities	400,000	(2,900,000)
Cash flows from investing activities:		
Payments for business acquisitions, net of cash acquired	(1,500,000)	(1,000,000)
Purchases of property and equipment	(500,000)	(500,000)
Proceeds from disposition of capital equipment	400,000	1,700,000
Purchases of short-term investments	(300,000)	(100,000)
Proceeds from short-term investments	200,000	400,000
Net cash provided by (used in) investing activities	(1,700,000)	500,000
Cash flows from financing activities:		
Proceeds from short-term borrowings	3,000,000	100,000
Repayment of long-term debt	(700,000)	(200,000)

Proceeds from issuance of long-term debt	800,000	1,500,000
Proceeds from issuance of common stock	200,000	400,000
Net cash provided by financing activities	3,300,000	1,800,000
Effect of exchange rate changes on cash and cash equivalents	(400,000)	(100,000)
Increase (decrease) in cash and cash equivalents	1,600,000	(700,000)
Cash and cash equivalents at beginning of year	1,200,000	1,900,000
Cash and cash equivalents at end of year	$2,800,000	$1,200,000

Reconciliation of Net Income (Loss) to Net Cash Provided by (Used in) Operating Activities

	Year Ended December 31	
	20X2	20X1
Net income (loss)	$(3,500,000)	$4,700,000
Adjustments to reconcile net income (loss) to net cash provided by (used in) operating activities:		
Depreciation and amortization	1,800,000	1,400,000
Deferred income taxes	(500,000)	200,000
Foreign exchange (gains) losses	(150,000)	100,000
Loss (gain) on sale of equipment	(100,000)	250,000
Inventory write-off	400,000	300,000
Equity in losses of affiliates	100,000	200,000
Minority interest	(200,000)	(100,000)
Changes in operating assets and liabilities, net of effects of business acquisitions:		
Accounts receivable	2,000,000	(3,850,000)
Inventory	(4,000,000)	(2,000,000)
Income taxes receivable	300,000	100,000
Prepaid expenses and other assets	700,000	(600,000)

Accounts payable	1,650,000	(2,500,000)
Other accrued liabilities	1,900,000	(1,100,000)
Net cash provided by (used in) operating activities	$400,000	$(2,900,000)

Example 56–3: Statement of Cash Flows—Discontinued Operations

Note: Statement of Financial Accounting Standards (FAS) No. 95, *Statement of Cash Flows*, does not require discontinued operations to be separately disclosed in the statement of cash flows. This example is provided for entities that nevertheless choose to report such category. It should be noted that, although separate disclosure of cash flows related to discontinued operations is not required, separate disclosure is permitted so long as those separate cash flows are presented in conformity with the basic requirements of FAS-95 and are presented consistently for all periods. If a company chooses to separately present cash flows from discontinued operations, the presentation should discretely report the operating, investing and financing cash flows from discontinued operations by category. It would not be appropriate to aggregate all cash flows from discontinued operations within a single line item, either as a separate category or within an existing category, such as operating cash flows.

	Year Ended December 31	
	20X2	20X1
Cash flows from operating activities:		
Net income	$6,000,000	$9,000,000
Adjustments to reconcile net income to net cash provided by operating activities:		
Depreciation and amortization	2,500,000	1,700,000
Estimated loss on disposal of discontinued operations	2,400,000	-0-
Increase in accounts receivable	(2,000,000)	(6,000,000)
Increase in accounts payable	3,000,000	4,000,000
Net cash provided by operating activities	11,900,000	8,700,000
Cash flows from investing activities:		
Purchases of property and equipment	(7,000,000)	(2,000,000)
Net investing activities of discontinued operations	(3,000,000)	(1,200,000)

Net cash used in investing activities	(10,000,000)	(3,200,000)
Cash flows from financing activities:		
Payments on capital lease obligations	(700,000)	(800,000)
Net financing activities of discontinued operations	(500,000)	(400,000)
Net cash used in financing activities	(1,200,000)	(1,200,000)
Increase in cash and cash equivalents	700,000	4,300,000
Cash and cash equivalents at beginning of year	6,500,000	2,200,000
Cash and cash equivalents at end of year	$7,200,000	$6,500,000

Example 56–4: Statement of Cash Flows—Extraordinary Items

Note: FAS-95 does not require extraordinary items to be separately disclosed in the statement of cash flows. This example is provided for entities that nevertheless choose to report such category.

	Year Ended December 31	
	20X2	*20X1*
Cash flows from operating activities:		
Net income	$36,000,000	$19,000,000
Adjustments to reconcile net income to net cash provided by operating activities:		
Depreciation and amortization	7,500,000	3,700,000
Extraordinary loss on fire damage	2,300,000	-0-
Net cash provided by operating activities	45,800,000	22,700,000

(Remaining details omitted.)

Example 56–5: Statement of Cash Flows—Cumulative Effect of Accounting Changes

Note: FAS-95 does not require the cumulative effect of accounting changes to be separately disclosed in the statement of cash flows. This example is provided for entities that nevertheless choose to report such category.

	Year Ended December 31	
	20X2	*20X1*
Cash flows from operating activities:		
Net income	$6,000,000	$9,000,000
Adjustments to reconcile net income to net cash provided by operating activities:		
Depreciation and amortization	1,500,000	1,700,000
Cumulative effect of changing overhead recorded in inventory	(400,000)	-0-
Net cash provided by operating activities	7,100,000	10,700,000

(Remaining details omitted.)

Example 56–6: Foreign Currency Cash Flows

FASB Statement of Financial Accounting Standards No. 95, *Statement of Cash Flows* specifies that the effect of exchange rate changes on cash balances held in foreign currencies be reported as a separate part of the reconciliation of the change in cash and cash equivalents in the Statement of Cash Flows.

> **Note:** For examples of reporting foreign currency cash flows, see Examples 56–1 and 56–2.

Example 56–7: Cash Overdraft Reported as a Financing Activity

	Year Ended December 31	
	20X2	*20X1*
Cash flows from financing activities:		
Proceeds of long-term borrowings	1,000,000	500,000
Payments on capital lease obligations	(700,000)	(800,000)
Net increase (decrease) in bank overdrafts	500,000	(400,000)
Net cash provided by (used in) financing activities	800,000	(700,000)

(Remaining details omitted.)

Example 56–8: Other Adjustments to Arrive at Net Cash Flows from Operating Activities

Note: This example is a comprehensive illustration of adjustments to arrive at net cash flows from operating activities, other than changes in operating assets and liabilities. The objective of these adjustments is to account for noncash operating activities, by adding noncash expenses to net income and subtracting noncash revenues from net income. For complete examples of statements of cash flows under the direct and indirect methods, see Examples 56–1 and 56–2.

	Year Ended December 31	
	20X2	20X1
Cash flows from operating activities:		
Net income	$4,000,000	$5,000,000
Adjustments to reconcile net income to net cash provided by operating activities:		
Cash value of life insurance	(100,000)	(200,000)
Common stock issued to employees	500,000	100,000
Depreciation and amortization	1,500,000	1,700,000
Foreign currency translation loss (gain)	100,000	(300,000)
Gain on litigation settlement	(600,000)	(100,000)
Imputed interest on debt	300,000	100,000
Inventory write-down	200,000	300,000
LIFO effect	200,000	(250,000)
Loss (gain) on sale of property and equipment	100,000	(200,000)
Minority interest in net income (loss) of consolidated subsidiary	(400,000)	300,000
Provision for environmental remediation	200,000	700,000
Provision for losses on accounts receivable	700,000	500,000
Provision related to early retirement program	1,100,000	900,000
Restructuring charges	900,000	600,000
Undistributed (earnings) losses of affiliate	300,000	(400,000)

Write-down of certain long-lived assets	150,000	200,000
Write-off of advances to affiliates	500,000	200,000
Changes in operating assets and liabilities:		
Accounts receivable	600,000	(400,000)

(Remaining details omitted.)

Net cash provided by operating activities	10,250,000	8,750,000

(Remaining details omitted.)

Example 56–9: Cash Flows from Investing Activities

Note: This example is a comprehensive illustration of cash flows provided by and used in investing activities. For complete examples of statements of cash flows under the direct and indirect methods, see Examples 56–1 and 56–2.

	Year Ended December 31	
	20X2	20X1
Cash flows from investing activities:		
Additions to long-term notes receivable	(600,000)	(900,000)
Collections of loans to officers	250,000	150,000
Deconsolidation of joint ventures	(200,000)	(500,000)
Increase in intangibles	(400,000)	(200,000)
Increase in restricted cash equivalents	(1,000,000)	-0-
Investment in and advances to affiliates	(500,000)	(700,000)
Payment for business acquisitions, net of cash acquired	(1,000,000)	(2,000,000)
Payments on long-term notes receivable	200,000	300,000
Proceeds from property insurance settlement	200,000	400,000
Proceeds from sale of assets held for resale	600,000	150,000

Proceeds from sale of marketable securities and investments	6,000,000	2,000,000
Proceeds from sale of property and equipment	1,000,000	3,000,000
Purchase of marketable securities and investments	(3,000,000)	(6,000,000)
Purchase of minority interests	(150,000)	(100,000)
Purchases of property and equipment	(1,000,000)	(2,000,000)
Release of restricted cash equivalents and investments	(1,000,000)	-0-
Repayments from (loans to) employees	100,000	(50,000)
Restricted funds held in escrow	(1,200,000)	(1,500,000)
Sale (purchase) of available-for-sale securities	1,800,000	(400,000)
Sale (purchase) of investments held-to-maturity	(600,000)	500,000
Net cash provided by (used in) investing activities	1,500,000	(7,850,000)

(Remaining details omitted.)

Example 56–10: Cash Flows from Financing Activities

Note: This example is a comprehensive illustration of cash flows provided by and used in financing activities. For complete examples of statements of cash flows under the direct and indirect methods, see Examples 56–1 and 56–2.

	Year Ended December 31	
	20X2	*20X1*
Cash flows from financing activities:		
Capital contributions from (distributions to) minority interests	(200,000)	150,000
Debt issue costs	(300,000)	(100,000)
Decrease (increase) in funds restricted for payment of long-term debt	600,000	(400,000)
Loans to ESOP	(400,000)	(300,000)

Net borrowings under line-of-credit agreement	1,000,000	2,000,000
Net increase (decrease) in bank overdrafts	400,000	(600,000)
Payment of debt and capital lease obligations	(3,500,000)	(800,000)
Payment of dividends	(100,000)	(200,000)
Premiums paid on early retirement of debt	(500,000)	(300,000)
Proceeds from issuance of common stock	700,000	600,000
Proceeds from issuance of long-term debt	2,000,000	3,000,000
Proceeds from notes receivable—stock	100,000	200,000
Proceeds from stock options exercised	200,000	300,000
Proceeds of preferred stock issued to ESOP	250,000	150,000
Reduction of loan to ESOP	150,000	100,000
Repurchase of common stock	(1,500,000)	(1,300,000)
Treasury stock issued	400,000	500,000
Treasury stock purchased	(600,000)	(700,000)
Net cash provided by (used in) financing activities	(1,300,000)	2,300,000

(Remaining details omitted.)

Noncash Investing and Financing Activities

Example 56–11: Note Receivable Received in Connection with Sale of Business

In 20X2, the Company sold certain assets of its frozen food distribution business. The selling price was $2,800,000, which included a cash payment of $1,000,000 and a note receivable of $1,800,000 payable in three equal annual installments.

Example 56–12: Casualty Results in an Insurance Claim Receivable

On August 13, 20X2, the Company experienced a major fire, which destroyed a significant part of the manufacturing facility. The total amount of the insurance claim was for $8,500,000, which is presented as "Business interruption insurance" in the 20X2 Income Statement. The Company has received $7,000,000 in cash in 20X2 and the balance of $1,500,000 is recorded as an insurance claim receivable due from the insurance company. The receivable was received in January 20X3.

Example 56–13: Forgiveness of Note Receivable

During the year ended December 31, 20X2, the Company forgave a note receivable, including interest, totaling $210,000, in connection with its sales quota agreement with Sarak, Inc.

Example 56–14: Conversion of Accounts Receivable to Notes Receivable

During the year ended December 31, 20X2, the Company converted $350,000 of accounts receivable to notes receivable.

Example 56–15: Note Receivable Balance Reduced for Expenses Incurred

During the year ended December 31, 20X2, the Company reduced its note receivable balance from its affiliate, Sisak Corp., by $125,000 for a management fee charged by the affiliate.

Example 56–16: Property Acquired under Capital Lease Obligations

The Company acquired equipment of $430,000 and $310,000 in 20X2 and 20X1, respectively, under capital lease obligations.

Example 56–17: Note Payable Issued in Connection with Property Acquisition

During the years ended December 31, 20X2, and December 31, 20X1, the Company issued notes payable for $450,000 and $375,000, respectively, in connection with the acquisition of certain property and equipment.

Example 56–18: Property Distributed to Shareholder as Salary

In 20X2, the Company distributed an automobile with a book value of $17,900 to a 5% shareholder as salary.

Example 56–19: Property Acquired in Exchange for Services Rendered

In 20X2, the Company acquired furniture and equipment with a value of $38,500 in exchange for consulting services rendered.

Example 56–20: Issuance of Preferred Stock and Warrants as Payment of Accrued Interest

In 20X2, the Company issued 30,000 shares of Amended Series A Preferred Stock and 150,000 warrants to acquire shares of Common Stock, in respect of approximately $750,000 of accrued interest payable to certain institutional holders of secured subordinated debt.

Example 56–21: Issuance of Warrants Recorded as Stock Dividends

In 20X2, the Company issued warrants to holders of its Series B Preferred Stock at $0.15 per share, which was recorded as a preferred stock dividend of approximately $400,000.

Example 56–22: Issuance of Warrants as Finder's Fee

During May 20X2, the Company issued to a finder 20,000 warrants to purchase 20,000 shares of common stock, as compensation for the placement with its clients of 200,000 units, comprising shares of common stock and warrants to purchase common stock.

Example 56–23: Conversion of Preferred Stock into Common Stock

In April 20X2, the 4,000 shares of 5% redeemable convertible preferred stock with a total stockholders' equity value of $4,800,000 were converted into an aggregate of 100,000 shares of the Company's common stock.

Example 56–24: Common Stock Issued Pursuant to Conversion of Bridge Financing Notes

500,000 shares of common stock were issued in 20X2 pursuant to the conversion of bridge financing promissory notes, which provided net proceeds of $2,000,000.

Example 56–25: Issuance of Stock Dividends

In 20X2, the Company declared and issued a stock dividend of 2,545,000 common shares resulting in a transfer from retained earnings to additional paid-in capital of $725,000.

Example 56–26: Business Combinations

Supplemental cash flow information regarding the Company's acquisitions in 20X2 and 20X1 are as follows:

	20X2	20X1
Fair value of assets acquired	$3,100,000	$2,900,000
Less liabilities assumed	(900,000)	(200,000)
Net assets acquired	2,200,000	2,700,000
Less shares issued	(300,000)	(400,000)
Less cash acquired	(100,000)	(200,000)
Business acquisitions, net of cash acquired	$1,800,000	$2,100,000

Example 56–27: Assets and Liabilities Contributed to Newly Formed Joint Venture

In April 20X2, the Company contributed its medical diagnostics business to a newly formed, equally owned joint venture with Sabak, Inc. This transaction had the following non-cash effect on the Company's 20X2 balance sheet:

Current assets	$(300,000)
Property and equipment	(900,000)
Long-term receivables	500,000
Current liabilities	600,000

Example 56–28: Increase in Goodwill and Payables under Contingent Purchase Price Obligations

During 20X2, the Company recorded a payable to the former owners of Lisba, Inc. and increased goodwill by $325,000 under its contingent purchase price obligations.

Example 56–29: Transfer of Inventory to Property and Equipment

During the years ended December 31, 20X2, and December 31, 20X1, the Company transferred $80,000 and $95,000 of inventory to property and equipment, respectively.

Example 56–30: Refinance of Term Loan

During the year ended December 31, 20X2, the Company refinanced a term loan of $3,500,000 for the same amount.

Example 56–31: Insurance Premiums Financed

During 20X2 and 20X1, the Company financed $75,000 and $63,000, respectively, of insurance premiums relating to general liability and workers' compensation. The liability is recorded as a note payable.

Accounting Policy for Cash Equivalents

Example 56–32: Cash Equivalents Include Money Market Accounts and Short-Term Investments

Cash and cash equivalents include cash on hand, money market accounts, and short-term investments with original maturities of three months or less.

Example 56–33: Cash Equivalents Include Marketable Securities

For purposes of the Statements of Cash Flows, marketable securities purchased with an original maturity of three months or less are considered cash equivalents.

Example 56–34: Cash Equivalents Exclude Securities Held in Trust

The Company considers all short-term debt securities purchased with an initial maturity of three months or less and not held in trust to be cash equivalents.

Example 56–35: Cash Equivalents Include Repurchase Agreements

At December 31, 20X2, cash equivalents include overnight repurchase agreements.

Example 56–36: Negative Book Cash Balances Are Included in Accounts Payable

Cash equivalents consist of all highly liquid investments with an original maturity of three months or less. As a result of the

Company's cash management system, checks issued but not presented to the banks for payment may create negative book cash balances. Such negative balances are included in trade accounts payable and totaled $175,000 and $150,000 as of December 31, 20X2, and December 31, 20X1, respectively.

Disclosure of Interest and Income Taxes Paid (When the Indirect Method Is Used)

Example 56–37: Interest and Income Taxes Paid

Cash paid for interest and income taxes for 20X2 and 20X1 were as follows:

	20X2	20X1
Interest, net of amount capitalized of $113,000 in 20X2	$166,000	$244,000
Income taxes	$100,000	$125,000

FINANCIAL STATEMENT DISCLOSURES CHECKLIST

CLIENT NAME:_____

DATE OF FINANCIAL STATEMENTS:_____

Prepared by_____

Date_____

Reviewed by_____

Date_____

INSTRUCTIONS

This checklist is intended to be used as a guide for determining whether the financial statements of for-profit type entities include the primary disclosures as required by U.S. generally accepted accounting principles (GAAP). It should be noted that this checklist does not address the specialized disclosure requirements of specialized industries, not-for-profit organizations, the Securities and Exchange Commission (SEC), or the Governmental Accounting Standards Board (GASB).

Most of the questions addressed in this checklist refer to specific authoritative literature and use the following acronyms:

- FAS—Financial Accounting Standards Board Statement of Financial Accounting Standards
- FIN—Financial Accounting Standards Board Interpretation
- FSP—Financial Accounting Standards Board Staff Position
- APB—Accounting Principles Board Opinion
- ARB—Accounting Research Bulletin
- FTB—Financial Accounting Standards Board Technical Bulletin
- SOP—AICPA Statement of Position of the Accounting Standards Division
- EITF—Consensus Position of the FASB Emerging Issues Task Force
- PB—Practice Bulletin of the AICPA's Accounting Standards Executive Committee
- Q&A—FASB Question-and-Answer documents

- AU—Statement on Auditing Standards, Professional Standards, published by the AICPA
- CON—Financial Accounting Standards Board Statement of Financial Accounting Concepts

Some of the questions included in the checklist do not refer to any specific authoritative literature. Nevertheless, the disclosure items they address are considered informative disclosures for users of the financial statements and usually are disclosed. These disclosures are generally accepted by accountants and auditors and, accordingly, are referenced as "Generally accepted practice" in this checklist.

This checklist is divided into the following four major financial statement parts:

- Part I—Balance Sheet
- Part II—Income Statement
- Part III—Statement of Cash Flows
- Part IV—Other Financial Statement Topics and Disclosures

Review the topics within each of the four major parts for possible disclosures. For each topic that is applicable, check the "Item Present" column; otherwise, check the "Item Not Present" column. For each topic checked "Item Present," complete the individual checklist items by placing a checkmark in the appropriate "Yes,""No," or "N/A"(not applicable) column. Any item marked "No" should be explained in the checklist or in a separate memorandum. It is not necessary to complete the individual checklist items for topics checked "Item Not Present."

This Financial Statement Disclosures Checklist has been updated through the following authoritative pronouncements:

- FAS-158, "Employers' Accounting for Defined Benefit Pension and Other Postretirement Plans";
- FSP EITF 00-19-2, "Accounting for Registration Payment Arrangements";
- FSP FAS 123(R)-6, "Technical Corrections of FASB Statement No. 123(R)"; and
- EITF 06-9, "Reporting a Change in (or the Elimination of) a Previously Existing Difference between the Fiscal Year-End of a Parent Company and That of a Consolidated Entity or between the Reporting Period of an Investor and That of an Equity Method Investee."

TABLE OF CONTENTS

PART I—BALANCE SHEET

PART II—INCOME STATEMENT

PART III—STATEMENT OF CASH FLOWS

PART IV—OTHER FINANCIAL STATEMENT TC [CS AND DISCLOSURES

	Page No.	*Item Present*	*Item Not Present*
Pension and Postretirement Benefit Plans:		_____	_____
• Pension and Postretirement Defined Benefit Plans—Reduced Disclosure Requirements for Nonpublic Entities (Annual Periods)—Prior to the Adoption of FAS-158		_____	_____
• Pension and Postretirement Defined Benefit Plans—Reduced Disclosure Requirements for Nonpublic Entities (Annual Periods)—After the Adoption of FAS-158		_____	_____
• Pension and Postretirement Defined Benefit Plans—Public Entities and Nonpublic Entities That Elect to Voluntarily Provide Additional Disclosures (Annual Periods)—Prior to the Adoption of FAS-158		_____	_____
• Pension and Postretirement Defined Benefit Plans—Public Entities and Nonpublic Entities That Elect to Voluntarily Provide Additional Disclosures (Annual Periods)—After the Adoption of FAS-158		_____	_____
• Pension and Postretirement Defined Benefit Plans—Disclosure Requirements for Public Entities (Interim Periods)		_____	_____
• Pension and Postretirement Defined Benefit Plans—Disclosure Requirements for Nonpublic Entities (Interim Periods)		_____	_____
• Pension and Postretirement Defined Contribution Plans—All Companies		_____	_____

PART I—BALANCE SHEET

Yes *No* *N/A*

GENERAL DISCLOSURES

1. If a classified balance sheet is used, does the balance sheet contain classifications for:

    a. Total current assets? (Generally accepted practice) ___ ___ ___

    b. Total current liabilities? (FAS-6, par. 15) ___ ___ ___

2. Are items classified as current assets expected to be realized within one year (or within the entity's operating cycle)? (ARB-43, Ch. 3A) ___ ___ ___

3. If a company's normal operating cycle is longer than one year and the balance sheet is classified, has disclosure been made of the practice followed for the classification of current assets and liabilities, including the following: (ARB-43, Ch. 3A)

    a. An estimate of the amounts not realizable or payable within one year, if practicable? ___ ___ ___

    b. The amount of liabilities maturing in each year, if practicable, and applicable interest rates or range of rates? ___ ___ ___

4. Are contra-valuation accounts properly disclosed? (CON-6, par. 34) ___ ___ ___

CASH AND CASH EQUIVALENTS

1. Are cash overdrafts not subject to offset by other cash accounts in the same financial institution classified as current liabilities? (Generally accepted practice) ___ ___ ___

2. Are checks from customers held as of the end of the period accounted for as cash? (Generally accepted practice) ___ ___ ___

3. Are checks payable to vendors held as of the end of the period accounted for as accounts payable? (Generally accepted practice) ___ ___ ___

4. Are the following items excluded from the cash classification: (ARB-43, Ch. 3A, par. 6)

<u>*Yes*</u> <u>*No*</u> <u>*N/A*</u>

    a. Cash amounts restricted as to withdrawal or use for other than current operations? ___ ___ ___

    b. Cash amounts designated for expenditure in the acquisition or construction of noncurrent assets? ___ ___ ___

    c. Cash amounts segregated for the liquidation of long-term debt? ___ ___ ___

5. Are significant concentrations of credit risk arising from cash deposits in excess of federally insured amounts disclosed? (FAS-133, par. 531) ___ ___ ___

6. Have the following disclosures been made for legally restrictive compensating balance agreements: (Generally accepted practice)

    a. The terms of the compensating balance agreement? ___ ___ ___

    b. The amount of the compensating balance requirement? ___ ___ ___

    c. The amount required to be maintained to assure future credit availability and the terms of that agreement? ___ ___ ___

    d. The maintenance of compensating balances for the benefit of a related party? ___ ___ ___

ACCOUNTS AND NOTES RECEIVABLE

1. Are trade notes and accounts receivable reported under a heading separate from other receivables (e.g., tax refunds, receivables from sale of capital assets)? (ARB-43, Ch. 1A, par. 5) ___ ___ ___

2. Are notes and accounts receivable from officers, employees, or affiliated companies reported under separate headings? (ARB-43, Ch. 1A, par. 5) ___ ___ ___

3. Are receivables that are not expected to be collected within twelve months from the balance-sheet date excluded from current assets? (ARB-43, Ch. 3A, par. 6) ___ ___ ___

4. Are valuation allowances (such as uncollectible accounts and returned goods) deducted from the related accounts and notes receivable? (APB-12, par. 3) ___ ___ ___

<u>Yes</u> <u>No</u> <u>N/A</u>

5. Are unearned discounts (other than cash or quantity discounts and the like), interest, and finance charges included in receivables deducted from the face of the related receivables? (APB-6, par. 14; APB-21, par. 16)   ___ ___ ___

6. Is the unamortized balance of loan origination, commitment, other fees and costs, and purchase premiums and discounts recognized as adjustments of yield pursuant to FAS-91 reported on the company's balance sheet as part of the related loan balance? (FAS-91, par. 8)   ___ ___ ___

7. Do notes receivable that require the imputation of interest, or that bear interest at an inappropriate rate, include the following disclosures: (APB-21, par. 16)

   a. A description of the note?   ___ ___ ___

   b. The effective interest rate?   ___ ___ ___

   c. The face amount of the note?   ___ ___ ___

   d. The amount of discount or premium resulting from present value determination?   ___ ___ ___

   e. The amortization of discount or premium classified as part of interest expense?   ___ ___ ___

8. Does the summary of significant accounting policies include the following disclosures: (SOP 01-6, pars. 13a–c)

   a. The basis for accounting for loans, trade receivables, and lease financings, including those classified as held for sale?   ___ ___ ___

   b. The method used in determining the lower of cost or fair value of nonmortgage loans held for sale (i.e., aggregate or individual asset basis)?   ___ ___ ___

   c. The classification and method of accounting for interest-only strips, loans, other receivables, or retained interests in securitizations that can be contractually prepaid or otherwise settled in a way that the holder would not recover substantially all of its recorded investment?   ___ ___ ___

   d. The method for recognizing interest income on loan and trade receivables, including a

<u>*Yes*</u> <u>*No*</u> <u>*N/A*</u>

statement about the entity's policy for treatment of related fees and costs, including the method of amortizing net deferred fees or costs? ___ ___ ___

e. A description of the accounting policies and methodology the entity used to estimate its (1) allowance for loan losses, (2) allowance for doubtful accounts, and (3) any liability for off-balance-sheet credit losses and related charges for loans, trade receivables, or other credit losses? (Such a description should identify the factors that influenced management's judgment (e.g., historical losses and existing economic conditions) and may also include discussion of risk elements relevant to particular categories of financial instruments.) ___ ___ ___

f. The policy for (1) placing loans, and trade receivables if applicable, on nonaccrual status (or discontinuing accrual of interest), (2) recording payments received on nonaccrual loans, and trade receivables if applicable, and (3) resuming accrual of interest? ___ ___ ___

g. The policy for charging off uncollectible loans and trade receivables? ___ ___ ___

h. The policy for determining past due or delinquency status (i.e., whether past due status is based on how recently payments have been received or contractual terms)? ___ ___ ___

9. Has the following disclosure been made for sales of loans and trade receivables for each period for which an income statement is presented: (SOP 01-6, par. 13d)

a. The aggregate amount of gains or losses on sales of loans or trade receivables, including adjustments to record loans held for sale at the lower of cost or fair value? (*Note:* Alternatively, this information may be presented separately in the financial statements.) ___ ___ ___

10. Have the following presentation and disclosure requirements been complied with for each period for which a balance sheet is presented: (SOP 01-6, pars. 13e–i)

	Yes	No	N/A

a. Loans or trade receivables held for sale presented as a separate balance-sheet category?

b. Major categories of loans or trade receivables (other than those held for sale) presented separately either in the balance sheet or in the notes to the financial statements?

c. Disclosures of: (1) the allowance for credit losses, (2) the allowance for doubtful accounts, and (3) any unearned income, any unamortized premiums and discounts, and any net unamortized deferred fees and costs?

d. Foreclosed and repossessed assets classified as a separate balance-sheet amount, or included in other assets on the balance sheet with separate disclosures in the notes to the financial statements?

e. The recorded investment in loans, and trade receivables if applicable, on nonaccrual status?

f. The recorded investment in loans, and trade receivables if applicable, past due 90 days or more and still accruing?

g. The carrying amount of loans and trade receivables that serve as collateral for borrowings?

11. Have disclosures been made for transfers of receivables? (See Part IV, "Transfers and Servicing of Financial Assets")

12. Are disclosures made with respect to guarantees to repurchase receivables or related property that has been sold or otherwise assigned? (FAS-5, par. 12)

13. Are significant concentrations of credit risk arising from receivables disclosed? (See Part IV, "Financial Instruments—Other Disclosures," item 1)

14. Have the applicable fair value disclosures been made? (See Part IV, "Financial Instruments—Other Disclosures," item 2)

15. Have the disclosures required by FAS-118 been made for impaired loans? (See Part IV, "Impairment of Certain Loans")

INVENTORY

1. Are major categories of inventories (raw materials, work in process, finished goods, and supplies) presented, if practicable? (Generally accepted practice)   ___ ___ ___

2. Have the basis for carrying inventories and the method of determining cost been disclosed? (ARB-43, Ch. 3A, par. 9; ARB-43, Ch. 4)   ___ ___ ___

3. Are valuation allowances for inventory losses deducted from related inventory balances? (CON-6, par. 34)   ___ ___ ___

4. If material, are losses resulting from the write-down from cost to market disclosed? (ARB-43, Ch. 4, par. 14)   ___ ___ ___

5. If the LIFO inventory method is used, is the difference between the LIFO amount and replacement cost (LIFO reserve) disclosed? (Generally accepted practice)   ___ ___ ___

6. Are amounts from the liquidation of a LIFO layer disclosed? (Generally accepted practice)   ___ ___ ___

7. Has overhead been allocated to inventory in accordance with GAAP? (ARB-43, Ch. 4, par. 8)   ___ ___ ___

8. Have material losses on inventory purchase commitments been recorded and properly disclosed? (ARB-43, Ch. 4, par. 17)   ___ ___ ___

9. If an entity has significant changes to its inventory accounting as a result of adopting FAS-151, has the effect on income before extraordinary items and on net income (and on related per share amounts when presented) of the period of the change been disclosed? (FAS-151, par. 4)   ___ ___ ___

10. Has the amount of revenue and costs (or gains/losses) associated with inventory exchanges recognized at fair value been disclosed? (*Note:* For an affected entity, this disclosure should be applied to new arrangements that it enters into in reporting periods beginning after March 15, 2006.) (EITF 04-13, par. 5)   ___ ___ ___

Yes *No* *N/A*

INVESTMENTS—DEBT AND EQUITY SECURITIES

Note: Financial institutions should disclose the information in items 1 and 2 below for the following types of securities: (1) equity securities, (2) debt securities issued by the U.S. Treasury and other U.S. government corporations and agencies, (3) debt securities issued by states of the United States and political subdivisions of the states, (4) debt securities issued by foreign governments, (5) corporate debt securities, (6) mortgage-backed securities, and (7) other debt securities.

1. For securities classified as available-for-sale, have the following disclosures been made, by major security type, as of each date for which a balance sheet is presented: (FAS-115, par. 19; FAS-133, par. 534)

    a. The aggregate fair value?   ___ ___ ___

    b. Total gains for securities with net gains in accumulated other comprehensive income?   ___ ___ ___

    c. Total losses for securities with net losses in accumulated other comprehensive income?   ___ ___ ___

2. For securities classified as held-to-maturity, have the following disclosures been made, by major security type, as of each date for which a balance sheet is presented: (FAS-115, par. 19; FAS-133, par. 534)

    a. The aggregate fair value?   ___ ___ ___

    b. Gross unrecognized holding gains?   ___ ___ ___

    c. Gross unrecognized holding losses?   ___ ___ ___

    d. Net carrying amount?   ___ ___ ___

    e. Gross gains and losses in accumulated other comprehensive income for any derivatives that hedged the forecasted acquisition of the held-to-maturity securities?   ___ ___ ___

3. For investments in debt securities classified as available-for-sale and separately for securities classified as held-to-maturity, have the following disclosures been made: (FAS-115, par. 20)

    a. Information about the contractual maturities of the securities as of the date of the most recent balance sheet presented? (*Note*: Maturity information may be combined in appropriate groupings for companies other than financial institutions.) ___ ___ ___

b. The basis for allocation of securities not due at a single maturity date, if such securities are allocated over several maturity groupings? ___ ___ ___

Note: Financial institutions should disclose the fair value and the net carrying amount (if different from fair value) of debt securities based on at least the following four maturity groupings: (1) within one year, (2) after 1 year through 5 years, (3) after 5 years through 10 years, and (4) after 10 years.

4. Have the following disclosures been made for each period for which an income statement is presented: (FAS-115, par. 21; FAS-133, par. 534)

a. The proceeds from sales of available-for-sale securities and the gross realized gains and the gross realized losses on those sales? ___ ___ ___

b. The method used to determine the cost of a security sold or the amount reclassified out of accumulated other comprehensive income into earnings (i.e., specific identification, average cost, or other method used)? ___ ___ ___

c. The gross gains and gross losses included in earnings from transfers of securities from the available-for-sale category into the trading category? (*Note*: Such transfers should be rare.) ___ ___ ___

d. The amount of the net unrealized holding gain or loss on available-for-sale securities that has been included in accumulated other comprehensive income for the period? ___ ___ ___

e. The amount of gains and losses reclassified out of accumulated other comprehensive income into earnings for the period? ___ ___ ___

f. The portion of trading gains and losses for the period that relates to trading securities still held at the balance-sheet date? ___ ___ ___

5. For any sales of or transfers from securities classified as held-to-maturity, have the following disclosures been made for each period for which

<u>Yes</u> <u>No</u> <u>N/A</u>

an income statement is presented: (FAS-115, par. 22; FAS-133, par. 534)

   a. The net carrying amount of the sold or transferred security?   —— —— ——

   b. The net gain or loss in accumulated other comprehensive income for any derivative that hedged the forecasted acquisition of the held-to-maturity security?   —— —— ——

   c. The related realized or unrealized gain or loss at the date of sale or transfer?   —— —— ——

   d. The circumstances leading to the decision to sell or transfer the security?   —— —— ——

6. Has disclosure been made of the carrying amount of securities that serve as collateral for borrowings, for each period for which a balance sheet is presented? (SOP 01-6, par. 13i)   —— —— ——

7. Has the policy for accounting for the premium paid to acquire an option classified as held-to-maturity or available-for-sale been disclosed? (EITF 96-11)   —— —— ——

8. For debt and marketable equity securities that are accounted for under FAS-115 or FAS-124 (and the investor reports a "performance indicator"), and cost method investments (i.e., those equity securities that are not subject to the scope of FAS-115 and not accounted for under the equity method) that are impaired at the balance-sheet date but for which an other-than-temporary impairment has not been recognized, have the following disclosures been made (*Note*: This disclosure is effective for debt and marketable equity securities accounted for under FAS-115 and FAS-124 for annual financial statements with fiscal years ending after December 15, 2003. This disclosure is effective for cost method investments for annual financial statements with fiscal years ending after June 15, 2004.): (EITF 03-1, par. 21; FSP FAS 115-1 and FAS 124-1, par. 17)

   a. As of each date for which a balance sheet is presented, the following *quantitative* information, in tabular form, should be aggregated by each category of investment that the investor disclosed in accordance with Statements 115

and 124 and cost method investments and segregated by those investments that have been
in a continuous unrealized loss position for
less than 12 months and those that have been
in a continuous unrealized loss position for
12 months or longer:

(1) The aggregate amount of unrealized
losses (i.e., the amount by which cost exceeds fair value)? ___ ___ ___

(2) The aggregate related fair value of investments with unrealized losses? ___ ___ ___

b. As of the date of the most recent balance sheet,
the following qualitative information, in narrative form, that provides sufficient information to allow the financial statement users to
understand the quantitative disclosures and
the information that the entity considered
(both positive and negative) in reaching the
conclusion that the impairments are not other-
than-temporary:

(1) The nature of the investment? ___ ___ ___

(2) The cause of the impairment? ___ ___ ___

(3) The number of investment positions that
are in an unrealized loss position? ___ ___ ___

(4) The severity and duration of the impairment? ___ ___ ___

(5) Other evidence considered by the entity
in reaching its conclusions that the investment is not other-than-temporarily impaired, including, for example, industry
analyst reports, sector credit ratings, volatility of the security's fair value, and/or
any other information that the entity considers relevant? ___ ___ ___

9. Have the required disclosures been made for
transfers of financial assets? (See Part IV, "Transfers and Servicing of Financial Assets") ___ ___ ___

<u>Yes</u> <u>No</u> <u>N/A</u>

INVESTMENTS—EQUITY AND COST METHODS

1. Have the following disclosures been made with respect to investments in common stock of 20% or more when the equity method is used: (APB-18, par. 20)

    a. The name of each investee and percentage of ownership of common stock? ____ ____ ____

    b. The accounting policies of the investor with respect to the investment in common stock? ____ ____ ____

    c. The difference, if any, between the amount of the carrying value of the investment and the amount of underlying equity in net assets and the accounting treatment of the difference? ____ ____ ____

    d. The aggregate market value of investments for which quoted market prices are available (not required for investments in common stock of subsidiaries)? ____ ____ ____

    e. When investments in common stock of corporate joint ventures or other investments accounted for under the equity method are in the aggregate material, has summarized information of assets, liabilities, and results of operations of the investees been presented in notes or separate statements, either individually or in groups? ____ ____ ____

    f. Material effects of possible conversions of outstanding convertible securities, exercise of outstanding options and warrants, and other contingent issuances that could have a significant effect on the investor's share of reported earnings or losses? ____ ____ ____

2. Is the reason for not using the equity method when the investor company owns 20% or more of the voting stock of the investee company, and the name of the significant investee, disclosed? (APB-18, par. 20, footnote 13) ____ ____ ____

3. Is the reason for using the equity method when the investor company owns less than 20% of the voting stock of the investee company, and the name of the significant investee, disclosed? (APB-18, par. 20, footnote 13) ____ ____ ____

4. Is the investment presented in the balance sheet as a single amount rather than as proportional amounts of specific assets and liabilities of the investee company? (APB-18, par. 19)   ⎯⎯ ⎯⎯ ⎯⎯

5. Is the equity in the earnings of the investee company presented in the investor company's income statement as a single amount, except for the proportional amount of gains/losses from the disposition of a business segment, extraordinary gains/ losses, and the cumulative effects of changes in accounting principles? (APB-18, par. 19)   ⎯⎯ ⎯⎯ ⎯⎯

6. Is the proportional share of prior period adjustments made by the investee company, if any, presented as part of the retained earnings of the investor company? (APB-18, par. 19)   ⎯⎯ ⎯⎯ ⎯⎯

7. Is the policy disclosed for determining the amount of equity method losses after the common stock investment has been reduced to zero as a result of previous losses? (EITF 99-10, par. 5)   ⎯⎯ ⎯⎯ ⎯⎯

8. For cost method investments (i.e., those equity securities that are not subject to the scope of FAS-115 and not accounted for under the equity method) that are impaired at the balance-sheet date but for which an other-than-temporary impairment has not been recognized, have the impairment disclosures in Part I, "Investments— Debt and Equity Securities," item 8, been made?   ⎯⎯ ⎯⎯ ⎯⎯

9. For cost method investments (i.e., those equity securities that are not subject to the scope of FAS-115 and not accounted for under the equity method), have the following additional disclosures been made as of each date for which a balance sheet is presented in annual financial statements (*Note*: This disclosure is effective for fiscal years ending after June 15, 2004): (EITF 03-1, par. 22; FSP FAS 115-1 and FAS 124-1, par. 18)

   a. The aggregate carrying amount of all cost method investments?   ⎯⎯ ⎯⎯ ⎯⎯

   b. The aggregate carrying amount of cost method investments that were not evaluated for impairment?   ⎯⎯ ⎯⎯ ⎯⎯

   c. The fact that the fair value of a cost method investment is not estimated if there are no

Yes *No* *N/A*

identified events or changes in circumstances that may have a significant adverse effect on the fair value of the investment, and:

(1) A determination was made in accordance with paragraphs 14 and 15 of FAS-107, that it is not practicable to estimate the fair value of the investment, or

___ ___ ___

(2) The investor is exempt from estimating fair value under FAS-126?

___ ___ ___

Note: The disclosure requirements in item 10 below are prescribed by EITF 06-9, *Reporting a Change in (or the Elimination of) a Previously Existing Difference between the Fiscal Year-End of a Parent Company and That of a Consolidated Entity or between the Reporting Period of an Investor and That of an Equity Method Investee.* EITF 06-9 is effective for changes in, or eliminations of, a previously existing difference between an entity's reporting period and that of an equity method investee that occur in interim or annual reporting periods beginning after November 29, 2006. Earlier application is only permitted if an entity has not yet issued its financial statements for the period.

10. If a previously existing difference between the entity's reporting period and that of an equity method investee is changed or eliminated, have the disclosures in items 7 through 9 of Part IV, "Accounting Changes—Changes in Accounting Principle," been made? (EITF 06-9)

___ ___ ___

PROPERTY, PLANT, AND EQUIPMENT

1. Have the following disclosures been made with respect to depreciable assets: (APB-12, par. 5)

a. The basis of determining the amounts shown in the balance sheet, such as cost?

___ ___ ___

b. Balances of major classes of depreciable property presented by nature or function at the balance-sheet date?

___ ___ ___

c. Accumulated depreciation presented by major classes of assets or in total at the balance-sheet date?

___ ___ ___

    d. A general description of the method(s) used to compute depreciation for major classes of depreciable assets?   ___ ___ ___

    e. The amount of depreciation expense for each year for which an income statement is presented?   ___ ___ ___

2. Is property, plant, and equipment that is idle or held for sale identified and presented separately from property, plant, and equipment currently used in the business? (Generally accepted practice)   ___ ___ ___

3. Is the amount of interest capitalized as part of the cost of plant and equipment disclosed? (FAS-34, par. 21)   ___ ___ ___

4. Are property and equipment pledged as security for loans disclosed? (FAS-5, par. 18)   ___ ___ ___

5. Have the following *optional* disclosures been made if they are considered useful: (*Note:* Although not required by GAAP, these disclosures are in some cases made by companies when they are considered useful to a better understanding of the company's accounting policies.):

    a. The accounting treatment for maintenance and repairs, betterments, and renewals?   ___ ___ ___

    b. The policy for adjusting accumulated depreciation when property and equipment is disposed of, and the treatment of any gain or loss on disposition?   ___ ___ ___

    c. The rates or lives used in computing depreciation?   ___ ___ ___

6. If property, plant, and equipment are impaired or are to be disposed of, have the disclosures required by FAS-144 been made? (See Part IV, "Impairment and Disposal of Long-Lived Assets")   ___ ___ ___

7. Have the applicable disclosure requirements with respect to asset retirement obligations been made? (See Part IV, "Asset Retirement Obligations")   ___ ___ ___

8. Has the aggregate carrying amount of mineral rights been disclosed as a separate component of property, plant and equipment either on the

face of the balance sheet or in the notes to the
financial statements? (EITF 04-2, par. 9) ___ ___ ___

INTANGIBLE ASSETS

1. Are intangible assets (other than goodwill), at a
    minimum, aggregated and presented as a sepa-
    rate line item in the balance sheet? (FAS-142,
    par. 42) (*Note*: Presentation of individual intan-
    gible assets or classes of intangible assets as sepa-
    rate line items is also acceptable.) ___ ___ ___

2. Is the aggregate amount of goodwill presented
    as a separate line item in the balance sheet? (FAS-
    142, par. 43) ___ ___ ___

3. Is the aggregate amount of goodwill impairment
    losses presented as a separate line item in the
    income statement, before income from continu-
    ing operations (unless it is associated with a dis-
    continued operation, in which case is it included
    in the results of discontinued operations, net of
    tax)? (FAS-142, par. 43) ___ ___ ___

4. For intangible assets (other than goodwill) ac-
    quired either individually or with a group of as-
    sets, have the following disclosures been made
    in the period of acquisition: (FAS-142, par. 44)

    a. For intangible assets subject to amortization:

        (1) The total amount assigned and the
            amount assigned to any major intangible
            asset class? ___ ___ ___

        (2) The amount of any significant residual
            value, in total and by major intangible
            asset class? ___ ___ ___

        (3) The weighted-average amortization pe-
            riod, in total and by major intangible as-
            set class? ___ ___ ___

    b. For intangible assets *not* subject to amortiza-
        tion, the total amount assigned and the
        amount assigned to any major intangible as-
        set class? ___ ___ ___

    c. The amount of research and development as-
        sets acquired and written off in the period, and

<u>Yes</u> <u>No</u> <u>N/A</u>

    the line item in the income statement in which
the amounts written off are aggregated?   ⎯⎯ ⎯⎯ ⎯⎯

5. Have the following disclosures been made for
each period for which a balance sheet is presented: (FAS-142, par. 45)

  a. For intangible assets subject to amortization:

    (1) The gross carrying amount and accumu-
lated amortization, in total and by major
intangible asset class?   ⎯⎯ ⎯⎯ ⎯⎯

    (2) The aggregate amortization expense for
the period?   ⎯⎯ ⎯⎯ ⎯⎯

    (3) The estimated aggregate amortization
expense for each of the five succeeding
years?   ⎯⎯ ⎯⎯ ⎯⎯

  b. For intangible assets (other than goodwill) *not*
subject to amortization, the total carrying
amount and the carrying amount for each
major intangible asset class?   ⎯⎯ ⎯⎯ ⎯⎯

  c. Changes in the carrying amount of goodwill
during the period, including:

    (1) The aggregate amount of goodwill ac-
quired?   ⎯⎯ ⎯⎯ ⎯⎯

    (2) The aggregate amount of impairment
losses recognized?   ⎯⎯ ⎯⎯ ⎯⎯

    (3) The amount of goodwill included in the
gain or loss on disposal of all or a portion
of a reporting unit?   ⎯⎯ ⎯⎯ ⎯⎯

    (4) For entities that report segment informa-
tion in accordance with FAS-131, *Disclosures about Segments of an Enterprise and
Related Information,* the above information
about goodwill in total and for each reportable segment, and any significant
changes in the allocation of goodwill by
reportable segment? (*Note:* If any portion
of goodwill has not been allocated to a
reporting unit at the date the financial
statements are issued, that unallocated
amount and the reasons for not allocating it should be disclosed.)   ⎯⎯ ⎯⎯ ⎯⎯

6. For each impairment loss recognized related to
an intangible asset (other than goodwill), have

                                                        <u>Yes</u> <u>No</u> <u>N/A</u>

the following disclosures been made in the period in which the impairment loss is recognized: (FAS-142, par. 46)

a. A description of the impaired intangible asset, and the facts and circumstances leading to the impairment?   ___ ___ ___

b. The amount of the impairment loss and the method for determining fair value?   ___ ___ ___

c. The caption in the income statement in which the impairment loss is aggregated?   ___ ___ ___

d. The segment in which the impaired intangible asset is reported under FAS-131, if applicable?   ___ ___ ___

7. For each goodwill impairment loss recognized, have the following disclosures been made in the period in which the impairment loss is recognized: (FAS-142, par. 47)

a. A description of the facts and circumstances leading to the impairment?   ___ ___ ___

b. The amount of the impairment loss and the method for determining the fair value of the associated reporting unit (e.g., quoted market prices, prices of comparable businesses, present value, other valuation technique)?   ___ ___ ___

c. If a recognized impairment loss is an estimate that has not yet been finalized, that fact and the reasons for using an estimate; and, in subsequent periods, the nature and amount of any significant adjustments made to the initial estimate of the impairment loss?   ___ ___ ___

INCOME TAXES

1. If a classified balance sheet is presented, have the following been disclosed: (ARB-43, Ch. 3A; FAS-109, par. 41)   ___ ___ ___

a. Income taxes currently payable or refundable?   ___ ___ ___

b. Current and noncurrent deferred tax assets, including the valuation allowance, if any?   ___ ___ ___

c. Current and noncurrent deferred tax liabilities?   ___ ___ ___

<u>Yes</u> <u>No</u> <u>N/A</u>

2. Have the following components of the net deferred tax liability or asset recognized in the balance sheet been disclosed: (FAS-109, par. 43)

   a. The total of all deferred tax liabilities for taxable temporary differences? ___ ___ ___

   b. The total of all deferred tax assets for deductible temporary differences, operating loss carryforwards, and tax credit carryforwards? ___ ___ ___

   c. The total valuation allowance recognized for deferred tax assets? ___ ___ ___

3. Has the net change during the year in the total valuation allowance account been disclosed? (FAS-109, par. 43) ___ ___ ___

4. Are the following components (where applicable) of income tax expense related to continuing operations for each year presented: (FAS-109, par. 45)

   a. Current tax expense or benefit? ___ ___ ___

   b. Deferred tax expense or benefit (exclusive of items listed below)? ___ ___ ___

   c. Investment tax credits? ___ ___ ___

   d. Government grants (to the extent they have been used to reduce income tax expense)? ___ ___ ___

   e. Benefits arising from operating loss carryforwards? ___ ___ ___

   f. Tax expense arising from allocating tax benefits either directly to contributed capital or to reduce goodwill or other noncurrent intangible assets of an acquired company? ___ ___ ___

   g. Adjustments to a deferred tax liability or asset arising from changes in tax laws, tax rates, or the entity's tax status? ___ ___ ___

   h. Adjustments to the beginning balance in the valuation allowance account related to deferred tax assets that arise due to changes in the amount of assets expected to be realized? ___ ___ ___

5. Is income tax expense or benefit (intra-period income tax allocation) for each of the following disclosed for each year for which the items are

<u>Yes</u> <u>No</u> <u>N/A</u>

presented: (FAS-109, par. 46; APB-9, par. 26; APB-20, par. 20)

a. Continuing operations? ___ ___ ___

b. Discontinued operations? ___ ___ ___

c. Extraordinary items? ___ ___ ___

d. The cumulative effect of accounting changes? ___ ___ ___

e. Prior period adjustments? ___ ___ ___

f. Items charged or credited directly to shareholders' equity? ___ ___ ___

g. Other comprehensive income? ___ ___ ___

6. For a particular tax-paying component of an enterprise and within a particular tax jurisdiction (e.g., federal, state, or local): (FAS-109, par. 42)

a. Have all current deferred tax liabilities and assets been offset and presented as a single amount? ___ ___ ___

b. Have all noncurrent deferred tax liabilities and assets been offset and presented as a single amount? ___ ___ ___

c. Have the net current deferred tax asset or liability and the net noncurrent deferred tax asset or liability within each tax jurisdiction been shown separately for each tax-paying component? ___ ___ ___

7. If the entity is a member of a group that files a consolidated tax return, are the following disclosures made in its separately issued financial statements: (FAS-109, par. 49)

a. The amount of current and deferred tax expense for each statement of income presented? ___ ___ ___

b. The amount of any tax-related balances due to or from affiliates as of the date of each balance sheet presented? ___ ___ ___

c. The principal provisions of the method by which the consolidated amount of current and deferred tax expense is allocated to members of the group, and the nature and effect of any changes in that method (and in determining related balance to or from affiliates) during the years for which the disclosures in a and b above are presented?

8. Have types of significant temporary differences and carryforwards been disclosed? (FAS-109, par. 43)

9. Has the nature of significant reconciling items been disclosed between (a) the reported amount of income tax expense attributable to continuing operations for the year and (b) the amount of income tax expense that would result from applying domestic federal statutory tax rates to pretax income from continuing operations? (*Note*: A numerical reconciliation, such as the one described in 15b below, is not required for nonpublic companies.) (FAS-109, par. 47)

10. Have the amounts and expiration dates for operating loss and tax credit carryforwards for tax purposes been disclosed? (FAS-109, par. 48)

11. Has the portion of the valuation allowance for deferred tax assets for which subsequently recognized tax benefits will be allocated to reduce goodwill or other noncurrent intangible assets of an acquired entity or directly to contributed capital been disclosed? (FAS-109, par. 48)

12. Have the nature and effect of any other significant matters affecting comparability of information for all periods presented been disclosed if not otherwise evident from the disclosures discussed in this section? (FAS-109, par. 47)

13. Is the method of accounting for the investment tax credit (deferral method or flow-through method) and related amount used in the determination of income tax expense disclosed? (APB-4, par. 11)

14. Are proper disclosures made when a change in an entity's tax status becomes effective after year-end but before the financial statements are issued? (FAS-109, Q&A, No. 11)

15. Have the following required disclosures been made for *public* companies (optional for nonpublic companies): (FAS-109, par. 43)

a. The approximate tax effect of each type of temporary difference and carryforward that gives rise to a significant portion of deferred tax liabilities and assets (before allocation of valuation allowance)? (FAS-109, par. 43) ___ ___ ___

b. A reconciliation (using percentages or dollar amounts) of the reported amount of income tax expense attributable to continuing operations for the year to the amount of income tax expense that would result from applying domestic federal statutory tax rates to pretax income from continuing operations? (*Note*: If alternative tax systems exist, such as the U.S. alternative minimum tax, the regular tax rate should be used.) (FAS-109, par. 47) ___ ___ ___

16. Are the following items disclosed when a deferred tax liability is not recognized because of the exceptions allowed by APB-23 (i.e., undistributed earnings of subsidiaries or corporate joint ventures, bad debt reserves of savings and loan associations, or policyholders' surplus of life insurance companies) or for deposits in statutory reserve funds by U.S. steamship companies: (FAS-109, par. 44)

a. Description of temporary differences that did not create a deferred tax liability and the events that would cause the temporary differences to become taxable? ___ ___ ___

b. Cumulative amount of each type of temporary difference? ___ ___ ___

c. Amount of unrecognized deferred tax liability arising from temporary differences related to investments in foreign subsidiaries and foreign corporate joint ventures that are considered permanent? (If it is not practical to compute the amount, then that fact should be stated.) ___ ___ ___

d. Amount of unrecognized deferred tax liability for temporary differences related to (1) undistributed domestic earnings, (2) bad-debt reserve for tax purposes of U.S. savings and loan associations or other qualified thrift lenders, (3) the policyholders' surplus of a life insurance enterprise, and (4) statutory reserve funds of a U.S. steamship enterprise?　____ ____ ____

17. For an entity that has not yet completed its evaluation of the repatriation provision in the *American Jobs Creation Act of 2004* (the Act) for purposes of applying FAS-109, have the following disclosures been made for each period for which financial statements covering periods affected by the Act are presented: (FSP FAS 109-2, par. 9)

a. A summary of the repatriation provision, including the status of the entity's evaluation of the effects of the repatriation provision as well as the entity's expected completion date for the evaluation?　____ ____ ____

b. If the entity makes decisions in stages, the effect on income tax expense (or benefit) for any amounts that have been recognized under the repatriation provision? (*Note*: The effect should be shown separately either on the face of the income statement or in the footnotes, consistent with where the amounts of current and deferred taxes are disclosed for the period.)　____ ____ ____

c. The range of reasonably possible amounts of unremitted earnings that is being considered for repatriation as a result of the repatriation provision, and the potential range of related income tax effects (excluding any amounts that have been recognized in the financial statements)? (*Note*: If the potential range of related income tax effects cannot be reasonably estimated, a statement to that effect should be made.)　____ ____ ____

d. Pro forma financial data reflecting the effect of the repatriation provision (at a minimum, the effect on income tax expense [or benefit]), if the entity decides on a plan for reinvestment or repatriation of foreign earnings subsequent to the date of its financial statements but prior to their issuance?　____ ____ ____

18. Do the financial statements for the period in which an entity completes its evaluation of the

Yes *No* *N/A*

repatriation provision in the *American Jobs Creation Act of 2004* disclose the effect on income tax expense (or benefit) for the period as a result of the repatriation provision? (*Note*: Such effect should be shown separately either on the face of the income statement or in the footnotes, consistent with where the amounts of current and deferred taxes are disclosed for the period) (FSP FAS-109-2, par. 10a.)   ___ ___ ___

19. If an entity has previously recognized the qualified production activities deduction as a tax rate reduction, have the following disclosures been provided in conjunction with restatement of its financial statements to reflect the deduction as a special deduction: (FSP FAS 109-1, par. 7)

    a. For prior years' financial statements: ___ ___ ___

       (1) The nature of and justification for a change in accounting principle?   ___ ___ ___

       (2) The effect of the change on income before extraordinary items and net income (and on related per share amounts when presented) for all periods presented?   ___ ___ ___

    b. If financial information is not separately reported for the fourth quarter, or that information is not presented in the annual report:

       (1) Extraordinary, unusual, or infrequent transactions or events?   ___ ___ ___

       (2) The aggregate effect of year-end adjustments that are material to the operating results of the fourth quarter?   ___ ___ ___

       (3) Accounting changes presented in the manner required for interim accounting changes?   ___ ___ ___

20. For companies that recognize the tax benefits of prior deductible temporary differences and carryforwards in income rather than contributed capital (i.e., companies that have previously adopted FAS-96 and effected a quasi-reorganization that involved only the elimination of a deficit in retained earnings), have the following disclosures been made: (FAS-109, par. 39)

    a. The date of the quasi-reorganization?   —— —— ——

    b. The manner of reporting the tax benefits and that it differs from present accounting requirements for other entities?   —— —— ——

    c. The effect of those tax benefits on income from continuing operations, income before extraordinary items, and net income (and on related per share amounts, if applicable)?   —— —— ——

21. Has disclosure been made of the amount of income tax benefit realized from the exercise of employee stock options, if the amount of that benefit is credited to equity but is not presented as a separate line item in the statement of changes in stockholders' equity or in the statement of cash flows? (EITF 00-15, par. 3)   —— —— ——

Note: The disclosure requirements in items 22 through 24 below are prescribed by FIN-48, *Accounting for Uncertainty in Income Taxes*. FIN-48 is effective for fiscal years beginning after December 15, 2006, with early adoption permitted as long as: (a) the consensus is applied as of the beginning of the fiscal year and (b) financial statements for any period (interim or annual) of the fiscal year have not yet been issued.

22. Has disclosure been made of the entity's policy on classification of interest and penalties? (FIN-48, par. 20)   —— —— ——

23. Have the following been disclosed for each annual reporting period presented (FIN-48, par. 21):

    a. A tabular reconciliation of the total amounts of unrecognized tax benefits at the beginning and end of the period, which shall include at a minimum:

       (1) The gross amounts of the increases and decreases in unrecognized tax benefits as a result of tax positions taken during a prior period?   —— —— ——

       (2) The gross amounts of increases and decreases in unrecognized tax benefits as a result of tax positions taken during the current period?   —— —— ——

       (3) The amounts of decreases in the unrecognized tax benefits relating to settlements with taxing authorities?   —— —— ——

Yes No N/A

    (4) Reductions to unrecognized tax benefits as a result of a lapse of the applicable statute of limitations? _____ _____ _____

  b. The total amount of unrecognized tax benefits that, if recognized, would affect the effective tax rate? _____ _____ _____

  c. The total amounts of interest and penalties recognized in the statement of operations and the total amounts of interest and penalties recognized in the statement of financial position? _____ _____ _____

  d. For positions for which it is reasonably possible that the total amounts of unrecognized tax benefits will significantly increase or decrease within 12 months of the reporting date:

    (1) The nature of the uncertainty? _____ _____ _____

    (2) The nature of the event that could occur in the next 12 months that would cause the change? _____ _____ _____

    (3) An estimate of the range of the reasonably possible change or a statement that an estimate of the range cannot be made? _____ _____ _____

  e. A description of tax years that remain subject to examination by major tax jurisdictions? _____ _____ _____

24. In the year of adopting FIN-48, has the cumulative effect of the change on retained earnings as of the date of adoption been disclosed in the statement of financial position? (FIN-48, par. 24) _____ _____ _____

CURRENT LIABILITIES

1. Are liabilities due on demand or within a year from the balance-sheet date (or operating cycle, if longer), presented as current liabilities and segregated by type? (ARB-43, Ch. 3A, par. 7) _____ _____ _____

2. With respect to accounting for compensated absences: (FAS-43, pars. 6, 7, 15)

  a. Are liabilities appropriately accrued and reported for employees' compensation for future absences? _____ _____ _____

<u>Yes</u> <u>No</u> <u>N/A</u>

    b. If the entity has not accrued a liability for compensated absences because the amount cannot be reasonably estimated, has that fact been disclosed?   —— —— ——

3. With respect to real and personal property taxes: (ARB-43, Ch. 10A, par. 16)

    a. Is an accrued liability, whether estimated or definitely known, included in current liabilities?   —— —— ——

    b. If estimates are used for accrual and are subject to a substantial measure of uncertainty, has the liability been disclosed as estimated?   —— —— ——

DEBT OBLIGATIONS AND CREDIT ARRANGEMENTS

1. Are significant categories of debt (e.g., notes payable to banks, related-party notes, or capital lease obligations) and the terms, interest rates, maturity rates, and subordinate features disclosed? (Generally accepted practice)   —— —— ——

2. Are restrictive covenants (e.g., restrictions on additional borrowings, obligations to maintain minimum working capital or restrict dividends) and pledged assets disclosed? (FAS-5, pars. 18–19)   —— —— ——

3. Are the following disclosures made for debt securities that carry an unreasonable interest rate or are non-interest-bearing: (APB-21, par. 16)

    a. The unamortized discount or premium that is reported in the balance sheet as a direct deduction from or as an addition to the face amount of the note?   —— —— ——

    b. The face amount of the note?   —— —— ——

    c. The effective interest rate?   —— —— ——

    d. Amortization of discount or premium reported as interest in the income statement?   —— —— ——

    e. Related debt issue costs that are reported as deferred charges in the balance sheet?   —— —— ——

4. Are the following disclosures made for each of the five years following the date of the latest bal-

<u>Yes</u> <u>No</u> <u>N/A</u>

ance sheet presented: (FAS-47, par. 10; FAS-129, par. 8)

a. The combined aggregate amount of maturities and sinking fund requirements for all long-term borrowings?   ____ ____ ____

b. The amount of redemption requirements for all issues of capital stock, which are redeemable at fixed or determinable prices on fixed or determinable dates, separately by issue or combined?   ____ ____ ____

5. If a short-term obligation expected to be refinanced on a long-term basis is excluded from current liabilities, are the following disclosures made: (FAS-6, par. 15)

a. A general description of the financing agreement?   ____ ____ ____

b. The terms of any new obligation incurred or expected to be incurred or equity securities issued or expected to be issued as a result of the refinancing?   ____ ____ ____

6. Have disclosures been made of subjective clauses in long-term debt agreements that may accelerate the due date, unless acceleration is remote? (FTB 79-3)   ____ ____ ____

7. Are current maturities of long-term debt presented as current liabilities? (ARB-43, Ch. 3A, par. 7)   ____ ____ ____

8. Are debt obligations that, by their terms, are due on demand or will be due on demand within one year (or operating cycle, if longer) from the balance-sheet date, even though liquidation may not be expected within that period, included in current liabilities? (FAS-78, par. 5)   ____ ____ ____

9. Do current liabilities include long-term obligations that are or will be callable by the creditor either because the debtor's violation of a provision of the debt agreement at the balance-sheet date makes the obligation callable or because the violation, if not cured within a specified grace period, will make the obligation callable unless one of the following conditions is met: (FAS-78, par. 5)

<u>*Yes*</u> <u>*No*</u> <u>*N/A*</u>

    a. The creditor has waived or subsequently lost the right to demand repayment for more than one year (or operating cycle, if longer) from the balance-sheet date?   —— —— ——

    b. For long-term obligations containing a grace period within which the debtor may cure the violation, it is probable that the violation will be cured within that period, thus preventing the obligation from becoming callable?   —— —— ——

    c. If an obligation under b above is classified as a long-term liability, are the circumstances disclosed?   —— —— ——

10. Are the conversion features and descriptions of convertible debt adequately disclosed and do they explain the pertinent rights and privileges of the convertible debt? (APB-14, pars. 16–18)   —— —— ——

11. For convertible securities with beneficial conversion features or contingently adjustable conversion ratios accounted for in accordance with EITF 98-5, are disclosures made of the terms of the transaction, including the excess of the aggregate fair value of the instruments that the holder would receive at conversion over the proceeds received and the period over which the discount is amortized? (EITF 98-5, par. 7) (These disclosures would only be applicable if the intrinsic value of the beneficial conversion feature is greater than the proceeds allocated to the convertible instrument.)   —— —— ——

12. Have the following disclosures been made when events of default under a credit agreement have occurred at any time prior to the date of the accountant's report and have not been cured or waived or a valid waiver has been obtained for only a stated period of time (SAS-1, AU 560) (EITF 86–30):

    a. The nature and amount of the default?   —— —— ——

    b. The period for which the violation has been waived?   —— —— ——

13. Are significant changes in long-term obligations subsequent to the date of the financial statements disclosed? (FAS-5, par. 11)   —— —— ——

Yes *No* *N/A*

14. For unrecorded, unconditional purchase obligations, have the following disclosures been made: (FAS-47, pars. 6–8)

    a. The nature and term of the obligation? ___ ___ ___

    b. The amount of the fixed and determinable portion of the obligation as of the date of the latest balance sheet presented in the aggregate and, if determinable, for each of the five succeeding fiscal years? ___ ___ ___

    c. The nature of any variable components of the obligation? ___ ___ ___

    d. The amounts purchased under the obligation for each period for which an income statement is presented? ___ ___ ___

    e. The amount of imputed interest necessary to reduce the unconditional purchase obligation to its present value (optional disclosure)? ___ ___ ___

15. For recorded, unconditional purchase obligations, have the following disclosures been made for each of the five years following the date of the latest balance sheet presented: (FAS-47, par. 10)

    a. The aggregate amounts of payments for unconditional purchase obligations? ___ ___ ___

    b. The combined aggregate amount of maturities and sinking fund requirements? ___ ___ ___

    c. The amount of redemption requirements for all issues of capital stock that are redeemable at fixed or determinable prices on fixed or determinable dates, separately by issue or combined? ___ ___ ___

16. Have the applicable fair value disclosures been made? (See Part IV, "Financial Instruments—Other Disclosures," item 2) ___ ___ ___

STOCKHOLDERS' EQUITY

1. Are the following disclosures made for each class of capital stock: (Generally accepted practice)

    a. Shares authorized, issued, and outstanding? ___ ___ ___

    b. Par value or stated value? ___ ___ ___

	Yes	No	N/A

c. The number of shares reserved for future issuance and the purpose for such reservation? ___ ___ ___

2. Are the following disclosures made for preferred stock or other senior stock that has a preference in involuntary liquidation considerably in excess of the par or stated values of the shares: (FAS-129, pars. 6–7)

   a. The liquidation preference of the stock (the relationship between the preference in liquidation and the par or stated value of the shares)? (*Note:* That disclosure should be made in the equity section of the balance sheet in the aggregate, rather than the notes.) ___ ___ ___

   b. The aggregate or per share amounts at which preferred stock may be called or is subject to redemption through sinking-fund operations or otherwise? ___ ___ ___

   c. The aggregate and per share amounts of arrearages in cumulative preferred dividends? ___ ___ ___

3. Have the following disclosures been made of the rights and privileges of the various securities outstanding (which includes all contingently convertible securities regardless of whether the contingency has been met or whether the securities have been included in diluted earnings per share): (FAS-129, par. 4 and FSP FAS 129-1, par.2)

   a. Dividend, liquidation, or call preferences? ___ ___ ___

   b. Participation rights? ___ ___ ___

   c. Call prices and dates? ___ ___ ___

   d. Conversion or exercise prices or rates and pertinent dates? ___ ___ ___

   e. Sinking fund requirements? ___ ___ ___

   f. Unusual voting rights? ___ ___ ___

   g. Significant terms of contracts to issue additional shares? ___ ___ ___

4. Have the number of shares issued on conversion, exercise, or otherwise during at least the most recent annual fiscal period and any subsequent interim period presented been disclosed? (FAS-129, par. 5) ___ ___ ___

Yes No N/A

5. Is there a disclosure for each of the five years following the date of the latest balance sheet presented for the amount of redemption requirements for all issues of capital stock redeemable at fixed or determinable prices on fixed or determinable dates? (FAS-47, par. 10 and FAS-129, par. 8) ___ ___ ___

6. Are appropriations for loss contingencies shown in the stockholders' equity section and clearly identified as such? (FAS-5, par. 15) ___ ___ ___

7. Are disclosures made of the nature and extent to which retained earnings is restricted? (APB-6, par. 13) ___ ___ ___

8. Are the following disclosures relative to changes in stockholders' equity made for each period in which both a balance sheet and statement of income are presented (the disclosures may be in the form of a separate statement, in a note to the financial statements, or in the body of the balance sheet): (APB-12, par. 10)

    a. Changes in the separate accounts comprising stockholders' equity? ___ ___ ___

    b. Changes in the number of shares of equity securities during at least the most recent annual fiscal period? ___ ___ ___

9. Are stock subscriptions receivable presented as a contra-equity account (or if shown as an asset, is the receivable clearly labeled and segregated from any other type of asset)? (Generally accepted practice) ___ ___ ___

10. Are the following disclosures made with respect to treasury stock: (APB-6, par. 13)

    a. The method used to account for the treasury stock? ___ ___ ___

    b. The number of shares of treasury stock held? ___ ___ ___

    c. Accounting treatment in accordance with state law if it is at variance with GAAP? ___ ___ ___

11. If treasury stock is acquired for purposes other than retirement (formal or constructive), or if the ultimate disposition has not yet been decided, has it been accounted for in one of the following ways: (APB-6, par. 12b)

   a. Has the cost been shown separately as a deduction from the total of capital stock, additional paid-in capital, and retained earnings? Or   ___ ___ ___

   b. Has the par value of the shares been charged to the specific stock issue and the excess of purchase price over the par value allocated between additional paid-in capital and retained earnings? (Alternatively, the excess may be charged entirely to retained earnings.)   ___ ___ ___

12. If treasury stock of the entity is shown as an asset, have the circumstances for such classification been disclosed? (ARB-43, Ch. 1A, par. 4)   ___ ___ ___

13. If an agreement to purchase treasury shares also involves the receipt or payment of consideration in exchange for stated or unstated rights or privileges, has the purchase price been allocated properly and the accounting treatment disclosed? (FTB 85-6)   ___ ___ ___

14. Is disclosure made of capital shares reserved for future issuance in connection with a business combination (FAS-141, par. 51)?   ___ ___ ___

15. Are dividends declared but not yet paid at the balance-sheet date classified as a current liability? (ARB-43, Ch. 3A, par. 7)   ___ ___ ___

16. Are restrictions on dividend payments disclosed? (FAS-5, pars. 18–19)   ___ ___ ___

17. If nonmonetary assets are distributed as dividends (i.e., dividends-in-kind), have the following disclosures been made: (APB-29, par. 28)

   a. The nature of the distribution?   ___ ___ ___

   b. The basis of accounting for the assets transferred?   ___ ___ ___

   c. The gains and losses recognized?   ___ ___ ___

18. If a stock dividend, split, or reverse split occurs after the date of the latest balance sheet presented, but before the issuance of the financial statements have the following disclosures been made: (Generally accepted practice)

   a. An explanation of the stock dividend, split, or reverse split and the date?   ___ ___ ___

Yes *No* *N/A*

    b. The retroactive effect provided in the balance sheet? ___ ___ ___

19. Have the following disclosures been made for warrants or rights outstanding as of the most recent balance-sheet date: (Generally accepted practice)

    a. The title and aggregate amount of securities called for by warrants or rights outstanding? ___ ___ ___

    b. The period during which warrants or rights are exercisable? ___ ___ ___

    c. The exercise price? ___ ___ ___

20. For all contingently convertible securities, have disclosures been made of the significant terms of the conversion features to enable users of the financial statements to understand the circumstances of the contingency and the potential impact of conversion, including: (FSP 129-1, pars. 3 and 5)

    a. Events or changes in circumstances that would cause the contingency to be met and any significant features necessary to understand the conversion rights and the timing of those rights (e.g., the periods in which the contingency might be met and in which the securities may be converted if the contingency is met)? ___ ___ ___

    b. The conversion price and the number of shares into which the security is potentially convertible? ___ ___ ___

    c. Events or changes in circumstances, if any, that could adjust or change the contingency, conversion price, or number of shares, including significant terms of those changes? ___ ___ ___

    d. The manner of settlement upon conversion and any alternative settlement methods (e.g., cash, shares, or a combination)? ___ ___ ___

    e. Information about derivative transactions entered into in connection with the issuance of the contingently convertible securities, such as the terms of the derivative transaction, how the transaction relates to the contingently convertible securities, and the number of shares

Yes No N/A

underlying the derivatives? (*Note*: This disclosure may be useful in providing the information in items a through d above.) ___ ___ ___

21. For convertible securities with beneficial conversion features or contingently adjustable conversion ratios accounted for in accordance with EITF 98-5, are disclosures made of the terms of the transaction, including the excess of the aggregate fair value of the instruments that the holder would receive at conversion over the proceeds received and the period over which the discount is amortized? (EITF 98-5, par. 7) (These disclosures would only be applicable if the intrinsic value of the beneficial conversion feature is greater than the proceeds allocated to the convertible instrument.) ___ ___ ___

22. Is the accumulated balance of other comprehensive income displayed separately from retained earnings and additional paid-in capital in the equity section of the balance sheet? (FAS-130, par. 26) ___ ___ ___

23. Is each classification of accumulated other comprehensive income presented in one of the following manners: (FAS-130, par. 26)

    a. On the face of the balance sheet as a separate component of equity? ___ ___ ___

    b. On the statement of changes in stockholders' equity? ___ ___ ___

    c. In the notes to the financial statements? ___ ___ ___

24. Have the following been separately disclosed as part of the disclosures of accumulated other comprehensive income: (FAS-133, par. 47)

    a. The beginning and ending accumulated derivative gain or loss? ___ ___ ___

    b. The related net change associated with current period hedging transactions? ___ ___ ___

    c. The net amount of any reclassification into earnings? ___ ___ ___

<u>Yes</u> <u>No</u> <u>N/A</u>

PART II—INCOME STATEMENT

COMPREHENSIVE INCOME

1. Are elements of comprehensive income displayed in one of the following three alternative presentation formats: (FAS-130, pars. 14 and 22)

   a. In a single statement of income and comprehensive income that extends a traditional income statement to include (following net income) the elements of other comprehensive income and the total of comprehensive income?   ___ ___ ___

   b. In a separate statement of comprehensive income, which begins with net income and includes the elements of other comprehensive income and then a total of comprehensive income?   ___ ___ ___

   c. In the statement of changes in stockholders' equity?   ___ ___ ___

2. Are components of other comprehensive income shown either: (a) net of related tax effects or (b) before related tax effects with one amount shown for the aggregate income tax expense or benefit related to the total of other comprehensive income items? (FAS-130, par. 24)   ___ ___ ___

3. Has the amount of income tax expense or benefit allocated to each component of other comprehensive income, including reclassification adjustments, been disclosed either: (a) on the face of the financial statement in which the components are displayed or (b) in the notes to the financial statements? (FAS-130, par. 25)   ___ ___ ___

4. Have reclassification adjustments for each classification of other comprehensive income (other than minimum pension liability adjustments) been disclosed either: (a) on the face of the financial statement in which comprehensive income is reported or (b) in the notes to the financial statements? (FAS-130, par. 20; FAS-158, par. F4c). (*Note*: Upon the adoption of FAS-158, the

Yes *No* *N/A*

reference to "other than minimum pension liability adjustments" is no longer applicable [see Part IV, "Pension and Postretirement Benefit Plans"].) ___ ___ ___

5. Has the accumulated balance of other comprehensive income been reported separately from retained earnings and additional paid-in capital in the equity section of the balance sheet? (FAS-130, par. 26) ___ ___ ___

6. Has the ending accumulated balances for each item in accumulated other comprehensive income been disclosed either: (a) on the face of the balance sheet, (b) in a statement of changes in equity, or (c) in the notes to the financial statements? (FAS-130, par. 26) ___ ___ ___

7. For derivative instruments and hedging activities, have the following disclosures been made: (FAS-133, pars. 46–47)

   a. The net gain or loss on derivative instruments designated as cash flow hedging instruments (including qualifying foreign currency cash flow hedges) reported as a separate classification within other comprehensive income? ___ ___ ___

   b. As part of the disclosures of accumulated other comprehensive income:

      (1) The beginning and ending accumulated derivative gain or loss? ___ ___ ___

      (2) The related net change associated with current period hedging transactions? ___ ___ ___

      (3) The net amount of any reclassification into earnings? ___ ___ ___

EARNINGS PER SHARE

Note: Nonpublic companies are NOT required to present earnings per share.

1. Have the following disclosures been made for each period for which an income statement is presented:

   a. A reconciliation of the numerators and denominators of the basic and diluted EPS computations for income from continuing operations, including the individual income and share amount effects of all securities that affect EPS. Insignificant reconciling items need not be itemized as part of the reconciliation and can be aggregated? (FAS-128, pars. 40 and 138)   ___ ___ ___

b. The effect that has been given to preferred dividends in determining the income available to common stockholders in computing basic EPS? (FAS-128, par. 40)   ___ ___ ___

c. Securities (including those issuable pursuant to contingent stock agreements) that could potentially dilute EPS in the future, but which were not included in the calculation of diluted EPS because to do so would have been antidilutive for the periods presented? (FAS-128, par. 40)   ___ ___ ___

2. For the latest period for which an income statement is presented, have disclosures been made of any transaction that occurs after the end of the most recent period but before the issuance of the financial statements that would have changed materially the number of common shares or potential common shares outstanding at the end of the period if the transaction had occurred before the end of the period? (FAS-128, par. 41)   ___ ___ ___

3. When prior EPS amounts have been restated in compliance with an accounting standard requiring restatement, has disclosure been made of the per share effect of the restatement? (FAS-128, pars. 57–58)   ___ ___ ___

4. When the number of common shares outstanding increases as a result of a stock dividend or stock split, or decreases as a result of a reverse stock split, have the computations of basic and diluted EPS been adjusted retroactively for all periods presented to reflect such changes in the number of shares, and has that fact been disclosed? (FAS-128, par. 54)   ___ ___ ___

5. If changes in common stock resulting from stock dividends, stock splits, or reverse stock splits occur after the close of the period but before the issuance of the financial statements, have the per share computations for all periods presented

been based on the new number of shares, and has that fact been disclosed? (FAS-128, par. 54)   ___ ___ ___

6. For shares that would be issued if contingently convertible securities were converted, has it been disclosed whether the shares are included in the calculation of diluted EPS and the reasons why or why not? (FSP FAS 129-1, par. 4)   ___ ___ ___

INCOME STATEMENT PRESENTATION— DISCONTINUED OPERATIONS

1. Have the results of discontinued operations, less applicable income taxes, been reported separately from continuing operations and, if applicable, before extraordinary items and the cumulative effect of accounting changes? (FAS-144, par. 43)   ___ ___ ___

2. Have the following items been presented separately in the balance sheet: (FAS-144, par. 46)

    a. Long-lived assets that are classified as held for sale?   ___ ___ ___

    b. The assets and liabilities of a disposal group classified as held for sale? (*Note*: The assets and liabilities should *not* be offset and presented as a single amount.)   ___ ___ ___

3. For a component of an entity that either has been sold or is classified as held for sale, have the following disclosures been made in financial statements that include the period in which the component has been sold or is classified as held for sale: (FAS-144, par. 47)

    a. A description of the facts and circumstances leading to the expected disposal?   ___ ___ ___

    b. The expected manner and timing of the disposal?   ___ ___ ___

    c. The carrying amount(s) of the major classes of assets and liabilities included as part of a component, if not separately presented on the face of the balance sheet?   ___ ___ ___

    d. The gain or loss recognized and, if not separately presented on the face of the income

Yes No N/A

statement, the caption in the income statement that includes the gain or loss?   ___ ___ ___

e. If applicable, amounts of revenue and pretax profit or loss reported in discontinued operations?   ___ ___ ___

f. If applicable, the segment in which the component is reported?   ___ ___ ___

4. For each discontinued operation that generates continuing cash flows, have the following disclosures been made: (EITF 03-13, par. 17) (*Note*: This disclosure is applicable to a component of an entity that is either disposed of or classified as held for sale in fiscal periods beginning after December 15, 2004)

    a. The nature of the activities that give rise to continuing cash flows?   ___ ___ ___

    b. The period of time continuing cash flows are expected to be generated?   ___ ___ ___

    c. The principal factors used to conclude that the expected continuing cash flows are not direct cash flows of the disposed component?   ___ ___ ___

5. In the period in which operations are initially classified as discontinued, if there is a continuation of activities between the ongoing entity and the disposed component after the disposal transaction, have the following disclosures been made for all periods presented in the financial statements: (EITF 03-13, par. 17) (*Note*: This disclosure is applicable to a component of an enterprise that is either disposed of or classified as held for sale in fiscal periods beginning after December 15, 2004)

    a. If the ongoing entity's activities include continuation of revenues and expenses that were previously eliminated intercompany transactions (for purposes of the consolidated financial statements) before the disposal transaction, the intercompany amounts before the disposal transaction?   ___ ___ ___

    b. The types of continuing involvement that will exist after the disposal transaction?   ___ ___ ___

6. If an entity decides not to sell a component previously classified as held for sale, or removes an

Yes *No* *N/A*

individual asset or liability from a component previously classified as held for sale, have the following disclosures been made in the financial statements that include the period of that decision: (FAS-144, par. 48):

   a. A description of the facts and circumstances leading to the decision to change the plan to sell the component?   __ __ __

   b. The effect on the results of operations for the period and any prior periods presented?   __ __ __

7. If the criteria for classification of a component of an entity as held for sale are met after the balance-sheet date, but before issuance of the financial statements, has the following information been disclosed: (FAS-144, par. 33)

   a. A description of the facts and circumstances leading to the expected disposal?   __ __ __

   b. The expected manner and timing of the disposal?   __ __ __

   c. The carrying amount(s) of the major classes of assets and liabilities included as part of a component, if not separately presented on the face of the balance sheet?   __ __ __

8. When adjustments are made in the current period to amounts previously reported in discontinued operations: (FAS-144, par. 44)

   a. Are the adjustments classified separately in the current period in discontinued operations?   __ __ __

   b. Are the nature and amount of such adjustments disclosed?   __ __ __

INCOME STATEMENT PRESENTATION— EXTRAORDINARY ITEMS

1. Are items unusual in nature *and* infrequent in occurrence classified as extraordinary items? (APB-30, par. 20)   __ __ __

2. Are the proportional amounts of an investee company's extraordinary items presented on the face of the investor company's income statement as extraordinary if they are material? (APB-18, par. 19)   __ __ __

Yes *No* *N/A*

3. Are descriptive captions and the amounts for individual extraordinary events or transactions presented (preferably) on the face of the income statement or disclosed in related notes? (APB-30, par. 11) ___ ___ ___

4. Are the nature of an extraordinary event or transaction and the principal items entering into the computation of the gain or loss described? (APB-30, par. 11) ___ ___ ___

5. Are the following captions used when there is an extraordinary item (and there are no discontinued operations or changes in accounting principles): (APB-30, pars. 10–12)

   a. Income before extraordinary items? ___ ___ ___

   b. Extraordinary item (less applicable income taxes)? ___ ___ ___

   c. Net income? ___ ___ ___

   d. Earnings per share amounts before extraordinary items and net income, where applicable? ___ ___ ___

   Note: FAS-145 (Rescission of FASB Statements No. 4, 44, and 64, Amendment of FASB Statement No. 13, and Technical Corrections) eliminated the requirement that gains and losses from extinguishments of debt be presented as an extraordinary item on the face of the income statement, effective for fiscal years beginning after May 15, 2002. Therefore, the disclosures in items 6 and 7 below are required only if an entity *has not* yet adopted FAS-145.

6. Are extraordinary gains and losses arising from extinguishments of debt described sufficiently to enable users of financial statements to evaluate their significance? (FAS-4, par. 9) ___ ___ ___

7. Are the following disclosures made on the face of the income statement or in a single note to the financial statements (or adequately cross-referenced if more than one note is used), for extraordinary gains and losses arising from extinguishments of debt: (FAS-4, par. 9)

   a. Description of the transaction, including the sources of any funds used to extinguish debt if it is practicable to identify the sources? ___ ___ ___

    b. Income tax effect in the period of extinguishment?   —— —— ——

    c. Per share amount of the aggregate gain or loss, net of related income tax effect?   —— —— ——

8. Are the following transactions or events *not* reported as extraordinary items: (APB-30, par. 23)

    a. Writedown or writeoff of receivables, inventories, equipment leased to others, or intangible assets?   —— —— ——

    b. Gains or losses from exchange or translation of foreign currencies, including those relating to major devaluations and revaluations?   —— —— ——

    c. Gains or losses on disposal of a component of an entity?   —— —— ——

    d. Other gains or losses from sale or abandonment of property, plant, or equipment used in the business?   —— —— ——

    e. Effects of a strike, including those against competitors and major suppliers?   —— —— ——

    f. Adjustments of accruals on long-term contracts?   —— —— ——

9. Are additional gains or losses arising in the current period but related to transactions or events that were previously reported as extraordinary items presented in the following manner: (APB-30, par. 25; FAS-16, par. 16)

    a. Separately disclosed as to year of origin, nature, and amount?   —— —— ——

    b. Classified separately in the current period as an extraordinary item?   —— —— ——

INCOME STATEMENT PRESENTATION— UNUSUAL OR INFREQUENT ITEMS

1. Are material transactions that are either unusual in nature *or* infrequent in occurrence (but not both and, therefore, not meeting the criteria for extraordinary items) not classified as extraordinary items? (APB-30, par. 26)   —— —— ——

2. Are material transactions that are either unusual in nature or infrequent in occurrence (but not

<u>Yes</u> <u>No</u> <u>N/A</u>

both) presented in the following manner: (APB-30, par. 26)

a. Reported as a separate component of income from continuing operations? ____ ____ ____

b. Nature and financial effects disclosed on the income statement (preferably) or in a note to the financial statements? ____ ____ ____

c. Not reported in a manner that would imply that the item is extraordinary? ____ ____ ____

d. Not reported on an earnings-per share basis? ____ ____ ____

OTHER—REVENUES, GAINS, EXPENSES, AND LOSSES

____ ____ ____

1. Is the statement of operations classified into appropriate functional areas such as sales, costs of goods sold, operating expenses, and other items? (Generally accepted practice) ____ ____ ____

2. Are income before income taxes and net income identified on the income statement? (Generally accepted practice) ____ ____ ____

3. Have significant amounts of discounts, returns, and allowances been disclosed? (Generally accepted practice) ____ ____ ____

4. Are cost of goods sold and expenses shown net of purchase discounts? (Generally accepted practice) ____ ____ ____

5. Have sales with significant rights of return been excluded from the income statement, and disclosed if significant? (FAS-48, pars. 3–7) ____ ____ ____

6. For shipping and handling costs: (EITF 00-10, par. 6) ____ ____ ____

a. Is the accounting policy for classifying shipping and handling costs disclosed? ____ ____ ____

b. If shipping and handling costs are significant and are *not* included in cost of sales, are the amounts of such costs and the line items in which they are included on the income statement disclosed? ____ ____ ____

7. Have the following disclosures been made for revenue arrangements with multiple deliverables: (EITF 00-21, par. 18)

    a. The accounting policy for recognizing revenue from multiple-deliverable arrangements (e.g., whether deliverables are separable into units of accounting)?   ___ ___ ___

    b. The description and nature of such arrangements, including performance, cancellation, termination, or refund type provisions?   ___ ___ ___

Note: The disclosure requirements in item 8 below are prescribed by EITF 06-3, *How Taxes Collected from Customers and Remitted to Governmental Authorities Should Be Presented in the Income Statement (That Is, Gross Versus Net Presentation)*. EITF 06-3 is effective in interim and annual periods beginning after December 15, 2006.

8. For taxes that fall within the scope of EITF 06-3 (e.g., sales tax): (EITF 06-3)

    a. Has the accounting policy that addresses the gross (included in revenues and costs) or net (excluded from revenues) classification of these taxes been disclosed pursuant to APB-22? (See Part IV, "Accounting Policies and Reclassifications")   ___ ___ ___

    b. If those taxes are reported on a gross basis and are significant, have the amounts of those taxes included in annual financial statements been disclosed for each period for which an income statement is presented? (*Note*: This disclosure may be provided on an aggregate basis.)   ___ ___ ___

Note: The disclosure requirements in items 9 and 10 below are prescribed by EITF 06-1, *Accounting for Consideration Given by a Service Provider to a Manufacturer or Reseller of Equipment Necessary for an End-Customer to Receive Service from the Service Provider*. EITF 06-1 is effective for annual periods beginning after June 15, 2007, with early adoption permitted for financial statements that have not yet been issued.

9. Have the following disclosures been made by service providers that have programs in which they provide incentives to third-party manufacturers or resellers of equipment necessary for an end-customer to receive service from the service providers: (EITF 06-1, par. 5)

Yes *No* *N/A*

a. The nature of the incentive programs? ___ ___ ___

b. The amounts recognized in the statement of operations for such programs and their related classification for each period presented? ___ ___ ___

10. Have the following transitional disclosures been made on implementation of EITF 06-1: (EITF 06-1, par. 8)

a. A description of the prior-period information that has been retrospectively adjusted? ___ ___ ___

b. The effect of the change in accounting principle on revenue, cost of sales, income from continuing operations, net income (or other appropriate captions of changes in the applicable net assets or performance indicator), any other affected financial statement caption, and any affected per share amounts for any prior periods retrospectively adjusted? ___ ___ ___

c. The cumulative effect of the change in accounting principle on retained earnings or other components of equity or net assets in the statement of financial position as of the beginning of the earliest period presented? ___ ___ ___

d. If retrospective application to all prior periods is impracticable, the reasons therefor, and a description of the method used to report the change? ___ ___ ___

PART III—STATEMENT OF CASH FLOWS

___ ___ ___

1. Is a statement of cash flows presented as a basic financial statement for each period for which an income statement is presented? (FAS-95, par. 3)

2. Is the statement presented in a manner to reconcile beginning and ending balances of cash (or cash and cash equivalents)? (FAS-95, par. 26) ___ ___ ___

3. Are the beginning and ending balances of cash (or cash and cash equivalents) as shown in the statement of cash flows the same amounts as similarly titled line items or subtotals in the balance sheet? (FAS-95, par. 7) ___ ___ ___

<u>*Yes*</u> <u>*No*</u> <u>*N/A*</u>

4. Is the accounting policy for determining which items are treated as cash equivalents disclosed? (FAS-95, par. 10) ___ ___ ___

5. Are gross amounts of cash receipts and cash payments presented in the statement of cash flows, except for certain items that have a quick turnover, large amounts, or short maturities, which may be presented on a net basis? (FAS-95, pars. 11–13) ___ ___ ___

6. Are cash flows classified as resulting from operating, investing, and financing activities? (FAS-95, pars. 6 and 14) ___ ___ ___

7. Are the following items classified as cash inflows from investing activities: (FAS-95, par. 16)

    a. Receipts from collections or sales of: (1) loans made by the enterprise and (2) other entities' debt instruments (other than cash equivalents, certain debt instruments that are acquired specifically for resale, and securities classified as trading securities) that were purchased by the enterprise? ___ ___ ___

    b. Receipts from sales of equity instruments of other enterprises (other than certain equity instruments carried in a trading account, and securities classified as trading securities) and from returns on investment in those instruments? ___ ___ ___

    c. Receipts from sales of property, plant, and equipment, and other productive assets? ___ ___ ___

8. Are the following items classified as cash outflows from investing activities: (FAS-95, par. 17)

    a. Disbursements for loans made by the enterprise and payments to acquire debt instruments of other entities (other than cash equivalents, certain debt instruments that are acquired specifically for resale, and securities classified as trading securities)? ___ ___ ___

    b. Payments to acquire equity instruments of other enterprises (other than certain equity instruments carried in a trading account, and securities classified as trading securities)? ___ ___ ___

    c. Payments at the time of purchase or soon before or after purchase to acquire property, plant, and equipment and other productive assets? ___ ___ ___

9. Are the following items classified as cash inflows from financing activities: (FAS-95, par. 19)

    a. Proceeds from issuing equity instruments? ___ ___ ___

    b. Proceeds from issuing bonds, mortgages, notes, and from other short-term or long-term borrowings? ___ ___ ___

10. Are the following items classified as cash outflows from financing activities: (FAS-95, par. 20)

    a. Payments of dividends or other distributions to owners, including outlays to reacquire the enterprise's instruments? ___ ___ ___

    b. Repayments of amounts borrowed? ___ ___ ___

    c. Other principal payments to creditors who have extended long-term credit? ___ ___ ___

11. At a minimum, are the following classes of operating cash receipts and payments separately reported when the direct method is used to compute cash flows provided or used by operating activities: (FAS-95, par. 27)

    a. Cash collected from customers, including lessees, licensees, and other customers? ___ ___ ___

    b. Interest and dividends received? ___ ___ ___

    c. Other operating cash receipts, if any? ___ ___ ___

    d. Cash paid to employees and other suppliers of goods or services, including suppliers of insurance, advertising, and the like? ___ ___ ___

    e. Interest paid? ___ ___ ___

    f. Income taxes paid? ___ ___ ___

    g. Other operating cash payments, if any? ___ ___ ___

12. If the indirect method is used to compute cash flows provided or used by operating activities, is a reconciliation of net income to operating cash flows presented on the face of the statement of cash flows or in a separate schedule? (FAS-95, par. 6) ___ ___ ___

Yes No N/A

13. If the direct method is used to compute cash flows provided or used by operating activities, is a reconciliation of net cash flows from operating activities provided in a separate schedule? (FAS-95, par. 29)

____ ____ ____

14. Is information about noncash investing and financing activities presented in a narrative or summarized in a schedule? (FAS-95, par. 32)

____ ____ ____

15. If the indirect method of reporting cash flows from operating activities is used, are amounts of interest paid (net of amounts capitalized) and income taxes paid during the period disclosed? (FAS-95, par. 29)

____ ____ ____

16. If cash flows from derivative instruments that are accounted for as fair value hedges or cash flow hedges are classified in the same category as the cash flows from the items being hedged, is that accounting policy disclosed? (FAS-149, par. 37)

____ ____ ____

PART IV—OTHER FINANCIAL STATEMENT TOPICS AND DISCLOSURES

ACCOUNTING CHANGES—CHANGES IN ACCOUNTING ESTIMATE

Note: The disclosure requirements in items 3 through 5 below are prescribed by FAS-154, *Accounting Changes and Error Corrections*, which is effective for accounting changes and corrections of errors made in fiscal years beginning after December 15, 2005. Early adoption is permitted for accounting changes and corrections of errors made in fiscal years beginning after June 1, 2005. If an entity has not adopted FAS-154, disclosure requirements in items 1 and 2 below apply.

1. For a change in accounting estimate that affects several future periods (e.g., change in service lives of depreciable assets, actuarial assumptions affecting pension costs), has the effect on income before extraordinary items and net income (and on related per share amounts when presented) of the current period been disclosed? (APB-20, par. 33)

____ ____ ____

Yes No N/A

2. For a change in accounting estimate made each period in the ordinary course of accounting for items such as uncollectible accounts or inventory obsolescence, has disclosure been made of the effect, if material, on income before extraordinary items and net income (and on related per share amounts when presented)? (APB-20, par. 33)   ____ ____ ____

3. For a change in accounting estimate that affects several future periods (e.g., change in service lives of depreciable assets), has the effect of the change on the following for the current period been disclosed: (FAS-154, par. 22) (*Note*: Disclosure of these effects is not necessary for estimates made each period in the ordinary course of accounting [e.g., uncollectible accounts, inventory obsolescence] unless the effect of the change in estimate is material.)

   a. Income from continuing operations?   ____ ____ ____

   b. Net income (or other appropriate captions of change in the applicable net assets or performance indicators)?   ____ ____ ____

   c. Related per share amounts?   ____ ____ ____

4. For a change in accounting estimate that has no material effect in the period of change but is reasonably certain to have a material effect in later periods, has a description of the change been disclosed whenever the financial statements of the period of change are presented? (FAS-154, par. 22)   ____ ____ ____

5. If a change in accounting principle effects a change in estimate, have the disclosures detailed in items 7 and 8 of Part IV— "Accounting Changes—Changes in Accounting Principle" and item 26 of Part IV—"Interim Financial Reporting" been made? (FAS-154, par. 22)   ____ ____ ____

ACCOUNTING CHANGES—CHANGES IN ACCOUNTING PRINCIPLE

Note: The disclosure requirements in items 7 through 9 below are prescribed by FAS-154, *Accounting Changes and Error Corrections*, which is effective for accounting changes and corrections of errors made in fiscal years beginning after December 15, 2005. Early adoption is permitted for accounting changes and corrections of errors made in fiscal years beginning after June 1, 2005. If an entity has not adopted FAS-154, disclosure requirements in items 1 through 5 below apply.

1. Are the following disclosures made for a change in accounting principle in the year in which the change occurs: (APB-20, par. 17)

    a. The nature of the change in accounting principle?   —— —— ——

    b. The justification for the change in accounting, including a clear explanation of why the newly adopted accounting principle is preferable?   —— —— ——

    c. The effect of the change in accounting principle on income before extraordinary items and net income (and related per share amounts when presented)?   —— —— ——

2. Have the disclosures detailed in item 1 above been made for the following: (APB-20, pars. 27–28)

    a. A change from the LIFO method of inventory pricing to another method?   —— —— ——

    b. A change in the method of accounting for long-term construction-type contracts?   —— —— ——

    c. A change to or from the full-cost method of accounting that is used in extractive industries?   —— —— ——

    d. A change from retirement-replacement-betterment accounting to depreciation accounting?   —— —— ——

3. For a change in accounting principle that is accounted for as a cumulative effect adjustment: (APB-20, pars. 19–26)

    a. Have the financial statements for prior periods included for comparative purposes been presented as previously reported?   —— —— ——

    b. Has the cumulative effect of change to the new accounting principle on the amount of retained earnings at the beginning of the period in which the change is made been included in net income of the period of the change?   —— —— ——

Yes *No* *N/A*

c. Has the amount of the cumulative effect been shown as a separate item in the income statement between the captions "extraordinary items" and "net income" and the related tax effects (and related per share amounts when presented) been disclosed?   ___ ___ ___

d. Has the effect of adopting the new accounting principle on income before extraordinary items and on net income (and on related per share amounts when presented) of the period of the change been disclosed?   ___ ___ ___

e. Have pro forma amounts of income before extraordinary items and net income been shown on the face of the income statements for all periods presented as if the newly adopted accounting principle had been applied during all periods affected?   ___ ___ ___

f. If the pro forma amounts cannot be computed or reasonably estimated for individual prior periods, although the cumulative effect on retained earnings at the beginning of the period of change can be determined, has the reason for not showing the pro forma amounts by periods been disclosed?   ___ ___ ___

g. If the amount of the cumulative effects of a change in accounting principle on retained earnings at the beginning of the period of change cannot be computed (generally limited to a change from the FIFO inventory method to LIFO), are the following disclosures made: ___ ___ ___

   (1) The effect of the change on the results of operations (and on related per share amounts when presented) for the period of change?   ___ ___ ___

   (2) The reason for omitting (a) accounting for the cumulative effect and (b) disclosures of pro forma amounts for prior years?   ___ ___ ___

4. Are the following disclosures made for a change in the method of depreciation, depletion, or amortization for newly acquired assets while a different method continues to be used for assets of that class acquired in previous years: (APB-20, par. 24)

<u>Yes</u> <u>No</u> <u>N/A</u>

    a. Description of the nature of the change in method? — — —

    b. The effect of the change in method on income before extraordinary items and net income (and on related per share amounts when presented) for the year in which the change in method occurred? — — —

5. If an accounting change is not considered material for the period in which the change occurs, but it is reasonably certain that the change will have a material effect on financial statements of subsequent years, are appropriate disclosures made whenever the financial statements of the year of change are presented? (APB-20, par. 38) — — —

6. When an authoritative accounting pronouncement (e.g., new FASB Statement) has been issued but is not yet effective as of the balance sheet date, and when adopted the company will be required to retroactively restate its financial statements or have a cumulative effect adjustment, has consideration been given to disclosing the following information: (Generally accepted practice and AU 9410.13-.18)

    a. Existence of the authoritative standard? — — —

    b. Date the entity must adopt the new standard or, if early adoption is permitted, the date that it plans to adopt it? — — —

    c. Method of adoption (e.g., retroactive application, cumulative catch-up adjustment)? — — —

    d. Impact of new standard on reported financial position and results of operations? (If the impact has been quantified, indicate amount; if immaterial or not determined, so state.) — — —

7. Have the following been disclosed in the fiscal period in which a change in accounting principle is made: (FAS-154, par. 17)

    a. The nature of and reason for the change in accounting principle, including an explanation of why the newly adopted accounting principle is preferable? — — —

    b. The method of applying the change? — — —

	Yes	No	N/A

c. A description of the prior-period information that has been retrospectively adjusted? ___ ___ ___

d. The effect of the change on the following for the current period and any prior periods retrospectively adjusted:

   (1) Income from continuing operations? ___ ___ ___

   (2) Net income (or other appropriate captions of changes in the applicable net assets or performance indicator)? ___ ___ ___

   (3) Any other affected financial statement line item? ___ ___ ___

   (4) Any affected per share amounts? ___ ___ ___

e. The cumulative effect of the change on retained earnings or other components of equity or net assets in the balance sheet as of the beginning of the earliest period presented? ___ ___ ___

f. If retrospective application to all prior periods is impracticable, the reasons why, and a description of the alternative method used to report the change? ___ ___ ___

g. If indirect effects of the change in accounting principle are recognized:

   (1) A description of the indirect effects of the change in accounting principle, including the amounts that have been recognized in the current period, and the related per share amounts, if applicable? ___ ___ ___

   (2) Unless impracticable, the amount of the total recognized indirect effects of the accounting change and the related per share amounts, if applicable, that are attributable to each prior period presented? ___ ___ ___

8. For a change in accounting principle that has no material effect in the period of change but is reasonably certain to have a material effect in later periods, have disclosures been made of the nature of and reason for the change in accounting principle, including an explanation of why the newly adopted accounting principle is preferable, whenever the financial statements of the

<u>Yes</u> <u>No</u> <u>N/A</u>

period of change are presented? (FAS-154, par. 17) ___ ___ ___

9. If a change in accounting principle effects a change in estimate, have the disclosures detailed in items 7 and 8 above and item 26 of Part IV—"Interim Financial Reporting" been made? (FAS-154, par. 22) ___ ___ ___

ACCOUNTING CHANGES—CHANGES IN REPORTING ENTITY

Note: The disclosure requirements in items 3 through 5 below are prescribed by FAS-154, *Accounting Changes and Error Corrections*, which is effective for accounting changes and corrections of errors made in fiscal years beginning after December 15, 2005. Early adoption is permitted for accounting changes and corrections of errors made in fiscal years beginning after June 1, 2005. If an entity has not adopted FAS-154, disclosure requirements in items 1 and 2 below apply.

1. Are prior years' financial statements restated for a change in the reporting entity, including the following: (APB-20, pars. 12 and 34)

   a. Presenting consolidated or combined statements in place of statements of individual enterprises? ___ ___ ___

   b. Changing specific subsidiaries comprising the group of enterprises for which consolidated financial statements are presented? ___ ___ ___

   c. Changing the enterprises included in combined financial statements? ___ ___ ___

2. Are the following disclosures made for a change in reporting entity for the period in which the change has occurred: (APB-20, par. 35)

   a. A description of the nature of the change? ___ ___ ___

   b. A description of the reason for the change? ___ ___ ___

   c. The effect of the change on income before extraordinary items and net income (and on related per share amounts when presented) for all periods presented? ___ ___ ___

<u>Yes</u> <u>No</u> <u>N/A</u>

3. Has a description of the nature of the change in reporting entity and the reason for it been disclosed in the period of the change? (FAS-154, par. 24)

    ____ ____ ____

4. Has the effect of the change in reporting entity on the following been disclosed for all periods presented: (FAS-154, par. 24)

    a. Income before extraordinary items?

       ____ ____ ____

    b. Net income (or other appropriate captions of change in the applicable net assets or performance indicators)?

       ____ ____ ____

    c. Other comprehensive income?

       ____ ____ ____

    d. Related per share amounts?

       ____ ____ ____

5. For a change in reporting entity that has no material effect in the period of change but is reasonably certain to have a material effect in later periods, has the nature of and reason for the change been disclosed whenever the financial statements of the period of change are presented? (FAS-154, par. 24)

    ____ ____ ____

ACCOUNTING POLICIES AND RECLASSIFICATIONS

1. Is a summary of significant accounting policies presented and does it include important judgments about the appropriateness of principles relating to revenue recognition and asset cost allocation to current and future periods, and in particular include the following: (APB-22, pars. 8–15)

    a. Selection from existing acceptable alternative accounting principles and methods?

       ____ ____ ____

    b. Principles and methods peculiar to the industry (even if the principle or method is predominant in the industry)?

       ____ ____ ____

    c. Unusual or innovative applications of GAAP (including principles and methods peculiar to the industry)?

       ____ ____ ____

Yes No N/A

2. Are material changes in classifications made to previously issued financial statements disclosed? (ARB-43, Ch. 2A, par. 3; AU 420.16) ___ ___ ___

ADVERTISING COSTS

1. Are the following disclosures made for direct-response advertising: (SOP 93-7, par. 49)

   a. A description of the direct-response advertising reported as assets, if any? ___ ___ ___

   b. The accounting policy for it? ___ ___ ___

   c. The amortization period? ___ ___ ___

2. For non-direct response advertising costs, are disclosures made about whether such costs are expensed as incurred for the first time the advertising takes place? (SOP 93-7, par. 49) ___ ___ ___

3. Is the disclosure made of the total amount charged to advertising expense for each income statement presented, with separate disclosure of amounts, if any, representing a writedown to net realizable value? (SOP 93-7, par. 49) ___ ___ ___

4. Is disclosure made of the total amount of advertising costs reported as assets in each balance sheet presented? (SOP 93-7, par. 49) ___ ___ ___

5. Is the amount of revenue and expense recognized from advertising barter transactions disclosed for each income statement period presented? (EITF 99-17, par. 8) (*Note*: Entities providing advertising in barter transactions that do not qualify for recognition at fair value under EITF 99-17 should disclose for each income statement presented the volume and type of advertising provided and received, such as the number of equivalent pages, number of minutes, or the overall percentage of advertising volume.) ___ ___ ___

ASSET RETIREMENT OBLIGATIONS

1. Are the following items disclosed about an entity's asset retirement obligations: (FAS-143, par. 22)

Yes *No* *N/A*

a. A general description of the asset retirement obligations and the associated long-lived assets? ___ ___ ___

b. The fair value of assets, which are legally restricted for purposes of settling asset retirement obligations? ___ ___ ___

c. A reconciliation of the beginning and ending aggregate carrying amounts of asset retirement obligations showing separately the following (whenever there is a significant change in one or more of these components during the reporting period):

    (1) Liabilities incurred in the current period? ___ ___ ___

    (2) Liabilities settled in the current period? ___ ___ ___

    (3) Accretion expense? ___ ___ ___

    (4) Revisions in estimated cash flows? ___ ___ ___

d. If the fair value of an asset retirement obligation cannot be reasonably estimated, has that fact and the reasons therefor been disclosed? ___ ___ ___

BUSINESS COMBINATIONS

1. Are the following disclosures made in the period in which a material business combination is completed: (FAS-141, par. 51)

a. The name and a brief description of the acquired entity? ___ ___ ___

b. The percentage of voting equity interests acquired? ___ ___ ___

c. The primary reasons for the acquisition, including a description of the factors that contributed to a purchase price that result in recognition of goodwill? ___ ___ ___

d. The period for which the results of operations of the acquired entity are included in the combined entity's income statement? ___ ___ ___

e. The cost of the acquired entity and, if applicable, the number of shares of equity interests (e.g., common shares) issued or issuable, the value assigned to those interests, and the basis for determining that value?

f. A condensed balance sheet disclosing the amount assigned to each major asset and liability caption of the acquired entity at the acquisition date?

g. Contingent payments, options, or commitments specified in the acquisition agreement and the accounting treatment that will be followed should any such contingency occur?

h. The amount of purchased research and development assets acquired and written off in the period and the income statement line item in which the amounts written off are aggregated?

i. If the purchase price allocation has not been finalized, that fact and the reasons therefor?

2. If material adjustments are made in the current period to the initial allocation of the purchase price recorded in prior periods, have the nature and amount of such adjustments been disclosed? (FAS-141, par. 51)

3. If the amounts assigned to goodwill or to other intangible assets acquired are significant to the total cost of the acquired entity, are the following disclosures made: (FAS-141, par. 52)

a. For intangible assets subject to amortization: the amount, residual value, and weighted-average amortization period, in total and by major intangible asset class?

b. For intangible assets *not* subject to amortization, the total amount assigned and the amount assigned to any major intangible asset class?

c. The total amount of goodwill and the amount expected to be deductible for tax purposes?

d. The amount of goodwill by reportable segment, if the combined entity is required to disclose segment information in accordance with FAS-131, *Disclosures about Segments of an Enterprise and Related Information?*

4. If a series of individually immaterial business combinations that were completed during the

period are material in the aggregate, are the following disclosures made: (FAS-141, par. 53)

a. The number of entities acquired and a brief description of those entities? ___ ___ ___

b. The aggregate cost of the acquired entities, the number of equity interests (e.g., common shares) issued or issuable, and the value assigned to those interests? ___ ___ ___

c. The aggregate amount of any contingent payments, options, or commitments and the accounting treatment that will be followed should any such contingency occur (if potentially significant to the aggregate cost of the acquired entities)? ___ ___ ___

d. If the aggregate amount assigned to goodwill or to other intangible assets acquired is significant to the aggregate cost of the acquired entities, is the information described in item 3 above disclosed? ___ ___ ___

5. If the combined entity is publicly held (optional for nonpublic companies), is the following supplemental information disclosed for the period in which a material business combination occurs (or if a series of individually immaterial business combinations occur that are material in the aggregate): (FAS-141, pars. 54–55)

a. Pro forma results of operations for the current period as though the companies had combined at the beginning of the period, unless the acquisition was at or near the beginning of the period? ___ ___ ___

b. If comparative statements are presented, pro forma results of operations for the immediately preceding period as though the companies had combined at the beginning of that period? ___ ___ ___

c. On a pro forma basis, at a minimum: revenue; income before extraordinary items and the cumulative effect of accounting changes; net income; and earnings per share? ___ ___ ___

d. The nature and amount of any material, nonrecurring items included in the reported pro forma results of operations? ___ ___ ___

<u>*Yes*</u> <u>*No*</u> <u>*N/A*</u>

6. If an extraordinary gain is recognized related to a business combination, is the information required by paragraph 11 of APB-30 disclosed? (FAS-141, par. 56) (See Part II, "Income Statement Presentation—Extraordinary Items")   ___ ___ ___

7. If a material business combination is completed after the balance-sheet date but before the financial statements are issued, is the information in items 1 through 3 above disclosed, unless not practicable? (FAS-141, par. 57)   ___ ___ ___

8. Are the following disclosures made in the interim financial information of a publicly held entity (optional for nonpublic companies), if a material business combination is completed during the interim period: (FAS-141, par. 58)

    a. The name and a brief description of the acquired entity?   ___ ___ ___

    b. The percentage of voting equity interests acquired?   ___ ___ ___

    c. The primary reasons for the acquisition, including a description of the factors that contributed to a purchase price, which results in recognition of goodwill?   ___ ___ ___

    d. The period for which the results of operations of the acquired entity are included in the combined entity's income statement?   ___ ___ ___

    e. The cost of the acquired entity and, if applicable, the number of shares of equity interests (e.g., common shares) issued or issuable, the value assigned to those interests, and the basis for determining that value?   ___ ___ ___

    f. Supplemental pro forma information that discloses the results of operations for the current interim period and the current year up to the date of the most recent interim balance sheet presented (and for the corresponding periods in the preceding year) as though the business combination had been completed as of the beginning of the period being reported on? (*Note*: That pro forma information should disclose, at a minimum: revenue; income before extraordinary items and the cumulative effect

Yes No N/A

of accounting changes; net income; and earnings per share.)

    ____ ____ ____

g. The nature and amount of any material, nonrecurring items included in the reported pro forma results of operations?

    ____ ____ ____

9. For transfers of net assets or exchanges of shares between entities under common control, have the following disclosures been made: (FAS-141, pars. D16-D18)

a. The nature of and effects on earnings per share of nonrecurring intercompany transactions involving long-term assets and liabilities?

    ____ ____ ____

b. For the period in which the transfer of assets and liabilities or exchange of equity interests occurred:

    ____ ____ ____

(1) The name and brief description of the entity included in the reporting entity as a result of the net asset transfer or exchange of equity interests?

    ____ ____ ____

(2) The method of accounting for the transfer of net assets or exchange of equity interests?

    ____ ____ ____

10. Are the following disclosures made if a combined entity plans to incur costs from exiting an activity of an acquired entity, involuntarily terminating employees of an acquired entity, or relocating employees of an acquired entity and the activities of the acquired entity that will not be continued are significant to the combined entity's revenues or operating results or the cost recognized from those activities as of the consummation date are material to the combined entity: (EITF 95-3, par. 13ab)

a. For the period in which a purchase business combination occurs:

(1) When the plans to exit an activity or involuntarily terminate or relocate employees of the acquired entity are not final as of the balance-sheet date, a description of any unresolved issues, the types of additional liabilities that may result in an

Yes *No* *N/A*

adjustment to the purchase price allocation, and how any adjustment will be reported?   — — —

(2) A description of the type and amount of
liabilities assumed in the purchase price
allocation for costs to exit an activity or
involuntarily terminate or relocate employees?   — — —

(3) A description of the major actions that
make up the plan to exit an activity or
involuntarily terminate or relocate employees of an acquired entity?   — — —

(4) A description of activities of the acquired
entity that will not be continued, including the method of disposition, and the
anticipated date of completion and description of employee groups to be terminated or relocated?   — — —

b. For all periods presented subsequent to the
acquisition date in which a purchase business
combination occurred, until a plan to exit an
activity or involuntarily terminate or relocate
employees of an acquired entity is fully executed:

(1) A description of the type and amount of
exit costs, involuntary employee termination costs, and relocation costs paid and
charged against the liability?   — — —

(2) The amount of any adjustments to the liability account and whether the corresponding entry was an adjustment of the
costs of the acquired entity or included in
the determination of net income for the
period?   — — —

11. For business combinations between parties with
a preexisting relationship, have the following
disclosures been made: (EITF 04-1, par. 8)

a. The nature of the preexisting relationship?   — — —

b. The settlement amount of the preexisting relationship, if any, and the valuation method
used to determine that amount?   — — —

Yes *No* *N/A*

   c. The amount of any settlement gain or loss recognized and its income statement classification? ___ ___ ___

CHANGING PRICES

Note: Disclosure of the effects of changing prices is currently voluntary (*not* required) under GAAP.

1. Have the following disclosures been made for each of the five most recent years: (FAS-89, par. 7)

   a. Net sales and other operating revenues? ___ ___ ___

   b. Income from continuing operations on a current cost basis? ___ ___ ___

   c. Purchasing power gain or loss on net monetary items? ___ ___ ___

   d. Increase or decrease in the current cost or lower recoverable amount of inventory and property, plant, and equipment, net of inflation? ___ ___ ___

   e. The aggregate foreign currency translation adjustment on a current cost basis, if applicable? ___ ___ ___

   f. Net assets at year-end on a current cost basis? ___ ___ ___

   g. Income per common share from continuing operations on a current cost basis? ___ ___ ___

   h. Cash dividends declared per common share? ___ ___ ___

   i. Market price per common share at year-end? ___ ___ ___

   j. The Consumer Price Index—All Urban Consumers (CPI-U) used for each year's current cost/constant purchasing power calculations? ___ ___ ___

   k. If the Company has a significant foreign operation measured in a functional currency other than the U.S. dollar, has disclosure been made of whether adjustments to the current cost information to reflect the effects of general inflation are based on the U.S. general price level index or on a functional currency general price level index? ___ ___ ___

2.   In addition to the disclosures in item 1 above, if income from continuing operations on a current cost/constant purchasing power basis differs significantly from the income from continuing operations reported in the primary financial statements, has the following additional information been disclosed: (FAS-89, pars. 11–13 and 25)

   a. Components of income from continuing operations for the current year on a current cost/constant purchasing power basis?   ____ ____ ____

   b. Separate amounts for the current cost or lower recoverable amount at the end of the current year of inventory and property, plant, and equipment?   ____ ____ ____

   c. The increase or decrease in current cost or lower recoverable amount before and after adjusting for the effects of inflation of inventory and property, plant, and equipment for the current year?   ____ ____ ____

   d. The principal types of information used to calculate the current cost of (1) inventory, (2) property, plant, and equipment, (3) cost of goods sold, and (4) depreciation, depletion, and amortization expense?   ____ ____ ____

   e. Any differences between (1) the depreciation methods, estimates of useful lives, and salvage values of assets used for calculations of current cost/constant purchasing power depreciation and (2) the methods and estimates used for calculations of depreciation in the primary financial statements?   ____ ____ ____

   (*Note*: If an entity has assets [i.e., timberlands and growing timber, income-producing real estate, or motion picture films] that may raise doubts about the applicability of the current cost measurement methods required for other assets, it may disclose historical cost amounts adjusted by an externally generated index of a broad-based measure of general purchasing power as substitutes for current cost amounts for such assets and their related expenses [see items 2b and 2d above].)

<u>Yes</u> <u>No</u> <u>N/A</u>

3. For companies with mineral resource assets (other than oil and gas), such as metal ores and coal, have the following additional disclosures been made: (FAS-89, par. 14)

   a. Estimates of significant quantities of proved mineral reserves or proved and probable mineral reserves (whichever is used for cost amortization purposes) at the end of the year or at the most recent date during the year for which estimates can be made? ___ ___ ___

   b. If the mineral reserves include deposits containing one or more significant mineral products, the estimated quantity, expressed in physical units or in percentages of reserves, of each mineral product that is recoverable in significant commercial quantities? ___ ___ ___

   c. Quantities of each significant mineral produced during the year? ___ ___ ___

   d. Quantity of significant proved, or proved and probable, mineral reserves purchased or sold in place during the year? ___ ___ ___

   e. The average market price of each significant mineral product or, for mineral products transferred within the enterprise, the equivalent market price prior to use in a manufacturing process? ___ ___ ___

4. When determining the quantities of mineral reserves to be reported in item 3 above, have the following been applied: (FAS-89, par. 15)

   a. If consolidated financial statements are issued, 100% of the quantities attributable to the parent company and 100% of the quantities attributable to its consolidated subsidiaries (whether or not wholly owned) should be included? ___ ___ ___

   b. If the company's financial statements include investments that are proportionately consolidated, the company's quantities should include its proportionate share of the investee's quantities? ___ ___ ___

   c. If the company's financial statements include investments that are accounted for by the equity method, the investee's quantities should not be included in the disclosures of the company's quantities. However, the company's share of the investee's quantities of reserves should be reported separately, if significant?   ___ ___ ___

COMMITMENTS

1. Have disclosures included a description of the commitment, the terms of the commitment, and the amount of the commitment, for large or unusual commitments such as the following:

    a. Unused letters of credit? (FAS-5, par. 18)   ___ ___ ___

    b. Obligation to reduce debt? (FAS-5, par. 18)   ___ ___ ___

    c. Obligation to maintain working capital? (FAS-5, par. 18)   ___ ___ ___

    d. Obligation to restrict dividends? (FAS-5, par. 18)   ___ ___ ___

    e. Commitments for major capital expenditures? (FAS-5, par. 18)   ___ ___ ___

    f. Assets pledged as security for loans? (FAS-5, par. 18)   ___ ___ ___

    g. Net losses on inventory purchase commitments? (ARB-43, Ch. 4, par. 17)   ___ ___ ___

    h. Other commitments? (FAS-5, par. 18)   ___ ___ ___

COMPUTER SOFTWARE REVENUES AND COSTS

1. Have the following accounting policies for recognizing computer software revenues and costs been disclosed: (Generally accepted practice)

    a. Revenue recognition for each significant type of revenue (e.g., product sales, maintenance and post-contract customer service (PCS), installation and other services, and barter transactions)?   ___ ___ ___

    b. Amortization of deferred revenues?   ___ ___ ___

Yes *No* *N/A*

  c. Discounts, incentives, and sales returns, and the methods used to develop estimates of significant sales allowances?   ____ ____ ____

2. If an entity has capitalized costs incurred for computer software costs to be sold, leased, or otherwise marketed, have the following disclosures been made: (FAS-86, par. 11)

  a. Unamortized computer software costs included in each balance sheet presented?   ____ ____ ____

  b. The total amount charged to expense in each income statement presented for amortization of capitalized computer software costs and for amounts written down to net realizable value?   ____ ____ ____

3. Have research and development costs incurred for computer software to be sold, leased, or otherwise marketed been disclosed either separately or as part of total research and development costs for each period presented? (FAS-86, par. 12)   ____ ____ ____

CONSOLIDATED AND COMBINED FINANCIAL STATEMENTS

1. Is the consolidation policy followed by the client apparent by the headings on the financial statements, other information in the statements, or disclosed in notes? (ARB-51, par. 5)   ____ ____ ____

2. Are intercompany accounts and intercompany profits or losses on assets eliminated as part of the preparation of consolidated financial statements? (ARB-51, par. 6)   ____ ____ ____

3. If the consolidated financial statements are prepared using the financial statements of a subsidiary that has a different year-end than the parent, are disclosures made for intervening events that materially affect financial position or results of operations? (ARB-51, par. 4)   ____ ____ ____

4. If the entity is a member of a group that files a consolidated tax return, are the following disclosures made in its separately issued financial statements: (FAS-109, par. 49)

  a. The amount of current and deferred tax expense for each statement of income presented?   ____ ____ ____

Yes *No* *N/A*

   b. The amount of any tax-related balances due to or from affiliates as of the date of each balance sheet presented? ___ ___ ___

   c. The principal provisions of the method by which the consolidated amount of current and deferred tax expense is allocated to members of the group, and the nature and effect of any changes in that method (and in determining related balance to or from affiliates) during the years for which the disclosures in items a and b above are presented? ___ ___ ___

Note: The disclosure requirements in item 5 below are prescribed by EITF 06-9, *Reporting a Change in (or the Elimination of) a Previously Existing Difference between the Fiscal Year-End of a Parent Company and That of a Consolidated Entity or between the Reporting Period of an Investor and That of an Equity Method Investee.* EITF 06-9 is effective for changes in, or eliminations of, a previously existing difference between an entity's reporting period and that of a consolidated entity that occurred in interim or annual reporting periods beginning after November 29, 2006. Earlier application is only permitted if an entity has not yet issued its financial statements for the period.

5. If a previously existing difference between the entity's reporting period and that of a consolidated entity is changed or eliminated, have the disclosures in items 7 through 9 of Part IV, "Accounting Changes—Changes in Accounting Prin-
6. ciple," been made? (EITF 06-9) ___ ___ ___

Variable Interest Entities

1. If the entity is the primary beneficiary of a variable interest entity, have the following disclosures been made (unless the primary beneficiary also holds a majority voting interest): (FIN-46R, par. 23)

   a. The nature, purpose, size, and activities of the variable interest entity? ___ ___ ___

   b. The carrying amount and classification of consolidated assets, which are collateral for the variable interest entity's obligations? ___ ___ ___

 c. The lack of recourse if creditors (or beneficial interest holders) of a consolidated variable interest entity have no recourse to the general credit of the primary beneficiary?

2. If the entity holds a significant variable interest in a variable interest entity, but is not the primary beneficiary, have the following disclosures been made: (FIN-46R, par. 24)

 a. The nature of its involvement with the variable interest entity and when that involvement began?

 b. The nature, purpose, size, and activities of the variable interest entity?

 c. The enterprise's maximum exposure to loss as a result of its involvement with the variable interest entity?

3. Are disclosures required by FAS-140, *Accounting for Transfers and Servicing of Financial Assets and Extinguishments of Liabilities—a Replacement of FASB Statement No. 125*, about a variable interest entity included in the same note to the financial statements as the information required above? (FIN-46R, par. 25) (See Part IV, "Transfers and Servicing of Financial Assets")

4. Has information about variable interest entities been reported in the aggregate for similar entities only if separate reporting would not add material information? (FIN-46R, par. 25)

5. If an enterprise with an interest in a variable interest entity, or potential variable interest entity, created before December 31, 2003 is unable to obtain the information necessary to apply FIN-46R and, as a result, does not apply FIN-46R, has the following information been disclosed: (FIN-46R, par. 26)

 a. The number of entities to which FIN-46R is not being applied and the reason why the information required to apply this interpretation is not available?

 b. The nature, purpose, size (if available), and activities of the variable interest entities and

Yes No N/A

the nature of the enterprise's involvement
with those entities?

c. The reporting enterprise's maximum exposure
to loss because of its involvement with the
variable interest entities?

d. The amount of income, expense, purchases,
sales, or other measure of activity between the
reporting enterprise and the variable interest
entities for all periods presented? (*Note:* If it is
not practicable to present that information for
prior periods that are presented in the first set
of financial statements for which this requirement applies, the information for those prior
periods is not required.)

6. If it is reasonably possible that an entity will initially consolidate or disclose information about
a variable interest entity when FIN-46R becomes
effective, has the following information been disclosed in all financial statements initially issued
after December 31, 2003, regardless of the date
on which the variable interest entity was created:
(FIN-46R, par. 27)

a. The nature, purpose, size, and activities of the
variable interest entity?

b. The enterprise's maximum exposure to loss
as a result of its involvement with the variable interest entity?

CONTINGENCIES, RISKS, UNCERTAINTIES, AND CONCENTRATIONS

Loss and Gain Contingencies

1. If loss contingencies have been accrued, has consideration been given to describing the nature
and amount of the accrual for the financial statements not to be misleading? (FAS-5, par. 9)

2. If no accrual is made for a loss contingency, or if
an exposure to loss exists in excess of the amount
accrued, have the following disclosures been
made when there is at least a reasonable possibility that a loss or an additional loss may have
been incurred: (FAS-5, par. 10)

	Yes	*No*	*N/A*

a. The nature of the contingency? ___ ___ ___

b. An estimate of the possible loss or range of loss, or a statement that such an estimate cannot be made? ___ ___ ___

3. Are the following disclosures made (when it is necessary to keep the financial statements from being misleading) for losses and loss contingencies that arise subsequent to the date of the financial statements: (FAS-5, par. 11)

a. The nature of the loss or loss contingency? ___ ___ ___

b. An estimate of the amount or range of loss, or possible loss, or a statement that an estimate cannot be made? ___ ___ ___

4. Are the following disclosures made for certain *remote* loss contingencies relating to guarantees made for outside parties (such as guarantees of indebtedness of others, obligations of commercial banks under stand-by letters of credit, and guarantees to repurchase receivables or other properties that have been sold or assigned): (FAS-5, par. 12)

a. The nature of the loss contingency? ___ ___ ___

b. The nature and amount of the guarantee? ___ ___ ___

c. If subject to estimation, the value of any recovery from other outside parties that could be expected to result? ___ ___ ___

5. Are there adequate disclosures for unasserted claims or assessments if it is considered probable that a claim will be asserted and there is a reasonable possibility that a loss will arise from the matter? (FAS-5, par. 10) ___ ___ ___

6. Have contingencies that might result in gains been adequately disclosed but not reflected in the financial statements since to do so might be to recognize revenue before to its realization? (Care should be exercised to avoid misleading implications about the likelihood of realization.) (FAS-5, par. 17) ___ ___ ___

Note: The disclosure requirements in items 7 and 8 below are prescribed by FSP EITF 00-19-2, *Accounting for Registration Payment Arrangements.*

<u>*Yes*</u> <u>*No*</u> <u>*N/A*</u>

FSP EITF 00-19-2 is effective immediately for registration payment arrangements and the financial instruments subject to those arrangements that are entered into or modified subsequent to December 21, 2006. For registration payment arrangements and financial instruments subject to those arrangements that were entered into prior to December 21, 2006, the guidance in FSP EITF 00-19-2 is effective for financial statements issued for fiscal years beginning after December 15, 2006, and interim periods within those fiscal years. Early adoption is permitted as long as financial statements for any period (interim or annual) of the fiscal year have not yet been issued.

7. Has the following information been disclosed about each registration payment arrangement or each group of similar arrangements, even if the likelihood of the issuer having to make any payments under the arrangement is remote: (FSP EITF 00-19-2, par. 12)

   a. The nature of the registration payment arrangement? ⎯⎯ ⎯⎯ ⎯⎯

   b. The approximate term of the arrangement? ⎯⎯ ⎯⎯ ⎯⎯

   c. The financial instruments subject to the arrangement? ⎯⎯ ⎯⎯ ⎯⎯

   d. The events or circumstances that would require the issuer to transfer consideration under the arrangement? ⎯⎯ ⎯⎯ ⎯⎯

   e. Any settlement alternatives contained in the terms of the registration payment arrangement, including the party that controls the settlement alternatives? ⎯⎯ ⎯⎯ ⎯⎯

   f. The maximum potential amount of consideration, undiscounted, that the issuer could be required to transfer under the registration payment arrangement, including the maximum number of shares that may be required to be issued? ⎯⎯ ⎯⎯ ⎯⎯

   g. The fact that the terms of the arrangement provide for no limitation to the maximum potential consideration (including shares) to be transferred, if the terms of the arrangement include such provision? ⎯⎯ ⎯⎯ ⎯⎯

Yes *No* *N/A*

h. The current carrying amount of the liability representing the issuer's obligations under the registration payment arrangement and the income statement classification of any gains or losses resulting from changes in the carrying amount of that liability?   ___ ___ ___

8. Has the following information been disclosed related to the adoption of FSP EITF 00-19-2? (FSP EITF 00-19-2, par. 21)

   a. The portion of the cumulative-effect adjustment resulting from the recognition and measurement of a contingent liability under FAS-5?   ___ ___ ___

   b. The portion of the cumulative-effect adjustment resulting from the reclassification of a financial instrument subject to the registration payment arrangement to equity, or the recombination of an embedded derivative?   ___ ___ ___

Environmental Remediation Contingencies

1. Has the following information been disclosed about recorded accruals for environmental remediation loss contingencies and related assets for third-party recoveries: (SOP 96-1, pars. 7.11 and 7.20)

   a. Whether the accrual for environmental remediation liabilities is measured on a discounted basis?   ___ ___ ___

   b. The nature and amount of the accrual if necessary for the financial statements not to be misleading?   ___ ___ ___

   c. If any portion of the accrued obligation is discounted, the undiscounted amount of the obligation and the discount rate used?   ___ ___ ___

   d. If it is at least reasonably possible that the accrued obligation or any recognized asset for third-party recoveries will change within one year of the date of the financial statements and the effect is material, an indication that it is at least reasonably possible that a change in the estimate will occur in the near term?   ___ ___ ___

Yes *No* *N/A*

2. Have the following disclosures been made about unaccrued environmental remediation contingencies, including exposures in excess of amounts accrued: (SOP 96-1, par. 7.21)

   a. A description of the reasonably possible loss contingency and an estimate of the possible loss, or the fact that such an estimate cannot be made? ___ ___ ___

   b. If it is at least reasonably possible that the estimated loss (or gain) contingency will change within one year of the date of the financial statements and the effect is material, an indication that it is at least reasonably possible that a change in the estimate will occur in the near term? ___ ___ ___

3. Have the following *optional* disclosures been made by entities that elect to disclose such items: (*Note*: Entities are *encouraged*, but not required, to disclose this information.) (SOP 96-1, par. 7.22)

   a. The estimated time frame of disbursements for recorded amounts if expenditures are expected to continue over the long term? ___ ___ ___

   b. The estimated time frame for realization of recognized probable recoveries, if realization is not expected in the near term? ___ ___ ___

   c. The factors that cause the estimates to be sensitive to change with respect to: (1) the accrued obligation, (2) any recognized asset for third-party recoveries, or (3) reasonably possible loss exposures, or disclosed gain contingencies? ___ ___ ___

   d. If an estimate of the probable or reasonable possible loss or range of loss cannot be made, the reasons why it cannot be made? ___ ___ ___

   e. If information about the reasonably possible loss or the recognized and additional reasonably possible loss for an environmental remediation obligation related to an individual site is relevant to an understanding of the financial position, cash flows, or results of operations of the entity, are the following disclosures made with respect to the site: ___ ___ ___

	Yes	No	N/A

(1) The total amount accrued for the site?

(2) The nature of any reasonably possible loss contingency or additional loss, and an estimate of the possible loss or the fact that an estimate cannot be made and the reasons why it cannot be made?

(3) Whether other potentially responsible parties are involved and the entity's estimated share of the obligation?

(4) The status of regulatory proceedings?

(5) The estimated time frame for resolution of the contingency?

4. If an environmental liability for a specific cleanup site is discounted because it meets the criteria for discounting in SOP 96-1 and the effect of discounting is material, do the financial statements disclose the undiscounted amounts of the liability and any related recovery and the discount rate used? (SOP 96-1, par. 7.20)

Risks, Uncertainties, and Concentrations

1. Are the following disclosures made about the entity's nature of operations, including: (SOP 94-6, par. 10)

   a. A description of the entity's major products or services?

   b. The principal markets (e.g., industries and types of customers) for the entity's products or services?

   c. If the entity operates in more than one business, the relative importance of the entity's operations in each business and the basis for that determination (e.g., based on assets, revenues, or earnings)? (*Note*: Relative importance need not be quantified and could be conveyed by use of terms, such as *predominately, about equally,* or *major*.)

2. Is disclosure made that the preparation of financial statements in conformity with GAAP

<u>*Yes*</u> <u>*No*</u> <u>*N/A*</u>

requires the use of management's estimates? (SOP 94-6, par. 11)

3. Are the following disclosures made regarding significant estimates used in the determination of the carrying amounts of assets or liabilities or in disclosure of gain or loss contingencies, if: (1) it is at least reasonably possible that the effect on the financial statements of the estimates will change within one year of the date of the financial statements due to one or more future confirming events and (2) the effect of the change would be material to the financial statements: (SOP 94-6, pars. 13–15)

a. The nature of the estimate?

b. An indication that it is at least reasonably possible that a change in the estimate will occur in the near term?

c. The factors that cause the estimate to be sensitive to change? (This disclosure is encouraged, but not required.)

d. If the entity uses risk-reduction techniques to mitigate losses or the uncertainty that may result from future events and, as a result, determines that the criteria described above are not met, the disclosures in a, b, and c are encouraged, but not required?

4. Are the following concentrations disclosed if: (1) the concentration exists at the date of the financial statements, (2) the concentration makes the entity vulnerable to the risk of a near-term severe impact, and (3) it is at least reasonably possible that the events that could cause the severe effect will occur in the near term: (SOP 94-6, pars. 21, 22, and 24)

a. Concentrations in the volume of business transacted with a particular customer, supplier, lender, grantor, or contributor? (For purposes of this disclosure, it is always considered at least reasonably possible that any customer, grantor, or contributor will be lost in the near term.)

    b. Concentrations in revenue from particular products, services, or fund-raising events?   ___ ___ ___

    c. Concentrations in the available sources of supply of materials, labor, or services, or of licenses or other rights used in the entity's operations?   ___ ___ ___

    d. Concentrations in the market or geographic area in which the entity conducts its operations? (For purposes of this disclosure, it is always considered at least reasonably possible that operations located outside an entity's home country will be disrupted in the near term.)   ___ ___ ___

    e. For concentrations of labor subject to collective bargaining agreements, the percentage of the labor force covered by a collective bargaining agreement and the percentage of the labor force covered by a collective agreement that will expire within one year?   ___ ___ ___

    f. For concentrations of operations located outside the entity's home country, the carrying amounts of net assets and the geographic areas in which they are located?   ___ ___ ___

5. Have the following disclosures related to risks for publicly held entities and entities with public accountability been included in the financial statements: (*Note*: Entities are *encouraged,* but not required, to disclose this information.) (EITF 03-8, pars. 27-28)

    a. Circumstances in which the entity is exposed to risks of future material loss related to torts; theft of, damage to, expropriation of, or destruction of assets; business interruption; errors or omissions; injuries to employees; or acts of God?

    Note: A standard form of disclosure is not recommended; however, entities might consider disclosing the following:

      (1) The actual and potential effects of losses from such risks on the entity's historical or planned operations, including exposure to losses from claims, curtailment of

research and development or manufacturing, or contraction or cessation of other
activities, such as discontinuance of a
product line.   ⎯⎯ ⎯⎯ ⎯⎯

(2) Comparison of current insurance coverage by major categories of risk to coverage in prior periods, without necessarily
quantifying such coverage or change in
coverage.   ⎯⎯ ⎯⎯ ⎯⎯

(3) Recent claims experience.   ⎯⎯ ⎯⎯ ⎯⎯

(4) A description of the reporting entity's risk
management programs.   ⎯⎯ ⎯⎯ ⎯⎯

b. Circumstances in which the risks in 5(a) have
not been transferred to unrelated third par-
ties through insurance?   ⎯⎯ ⎯⎯ ⎯⎯

CONTRIBUTIONS RECEIVED AND MADE

1. For entities that are recipients of unconditional
promises to give, have the following disclosures
been made: (FAS-116, par. 24)

a. The amounts of promises receivable in less
than one year, in one to five years, and in more
than five years?   ⎯⎯ ⎯⎯ ⎯⎯

b. The amount of the allowance for uncollectible
promises receivable?   ⎯⎯ ⎯⎯ ⎯⎯

2. For entities that are recipients of conditional
promises to give, have the following disclosures
been made: (FAS-116, par. 25)

a. The total of the amounts promised?   ⎯⎯ ⎯⎯ ⎯⎯

b. A description and amounts for each group of
promises having similar characteristics (e.g.,
those conditioned upon the development of
new programs, upon the purchase or construction of new property and equipment, and
upon the raising of matching funds within a
specified time period)?   ⎯⎯ ⎯⎯ ⎯⎯

CORRECTION OF ERRORS

Note: The disclosure requirements in items 1 through 3 and 7 below are prescribed by FAS-154, *Accounting Changes and Error Corrections*, which is effective for accounting changes and corrections of errors made in fiscal years beginning after December 15, 2005. Early adoption is permitted for accounting changes and corrections of errors made in fiscal years beginning after June 1, 2005. If an entity has not adopted FAS-154, disclosure requirements in items 1 through 6 below apply.

1.   Have the resulting effects (both gross and net of applicable income tax) of prior period adjustments on the net income of prior periods been disclosed in the annual report for the year in which the adjustments are made? (APB-9, par. 26; FAS-154, par. 26)   ____ ____ ____

2.   When single-period financial statements are presented, has the effect (both gross and net of applicable income tax) of prior period adjustments on the opening balance of retained earnings and on net income (and on related per share amounts when presented) of the preceding period been disclosed? (APB-9, par. 26; FAS-154, par. 26)   ____ ____ ____

3.   When financial statements for more than one period are presented, has the effect (both gross and net of applicable income tax) of prior period adjustments on the opening balance of retained earnings and on net income (and on related per share amounts when presented) for each of the periods presented been disclosed? (APB-9, par. 26; FAS-154, par. 26)   ____ ____ ____

4.   If a restated historical, statistical-type summary of financial data for a number of periods (commonly 5 or 10 years) is presented and prior period adjustments have been recorded during any of the periods included therein, has disclosure been made of the restatements in the first summary published after the adjustments? (APB-9, par. 27) (*Note*: Entities are *encouraged*, but not required, to disclose this information.)   ____ ____ ____

5.   For a correction of an error in previously issued financial statements, has the nature of the error

<u>Yes</u> <u>No</u> <u>N/A</u>

been disclosed in the period in which the error was discovered and corrected? (APB-20, par. 37) ___ ___ ___

6. For a correction of an error in previously issued financial statements, has the effect of the correction of the error on the following been disclosed in the period in which the error was discovered and corrected: (APB-20, par. 37)

   (1)Income before extraordinary items? ___ ___ ___

   (2)Net income? ___ ___ ___

   (3)Related per share amounts, when presented? ___ ___ ___

7. If the financial statements have been restated to correct an error, have the following been disclosed? (FAS-154, par. 26)

   a. The fact that previously issued financial statements have been restated? ___ ___ ___

   b. A description of the nature of the error? ___ ___ ___

   c. The effect of the correction on each financial statement line item and any per share amounts affected for each prior period presented? ___ ___ ___

   d. The cumulative effect of the change on retained earnings or other appropriate components of equity or net assets in the balance sheet, as of the beginning of the earliest period presented? ___ ___ ___

DEFERRED COMPENSATION

Note: The disclosure requirements in items 1 and 2 below are prescribed by EITF 06-4, *Accounting for Deferred Compensation and Postretirement Benefit Aspects of Endorsement Split-Dollar Life Insurance Arrangements.* EITF 06-4 is effective for fiscal years beginning after December 15, 2007, with early adoption permitted.

1. If the entity applied the consensus in EITF 06-4 as a change in accounting principle through a cumulative-effect adjustment to retained earnings or other components of equity or net assets in the statement of financial position as of the beginning of the year of adoption, has the cumulative effect of the change been disclosed in

Yes *No* *N/A*

the statement of financial position? (EITF 06-4, par. 8)

2. If the entity applied the consensus in EITF 06-4 as a change in accounting principle through retrospective application to all prior periods, have the following been disclosed: (EITF 06-4, par. 10)

   a. A description of the prior-period information that has been retrospectively adjusted?

   b. The effect of the change on income from continuing operations, net income (or other appropriate captions of changes in the applicable net assets or performance indicator), any other affected financial statement caption, and any affected per share amounts for any prior periods retrospectively adjusted?

   c. The cumulative effect of the change on retained earnings or other components of equity or net assets in the statement of financial position as of the beginning of the earliest period presented?

DEVELOPMENT STAGE ENTERPRISES

1. Are the following included in the financial statements issued by a development stage enterprise: (FAS-7, par. 11)

   a. A balance sheet, including any cumulative net losses reported with a descriptive caption, such as "deficit accumulated during the development stage," in the stockholders' equity section?

   b. An income statement showing amounts of revenues and expenses for each period covered by the income statement and, in addition, cumulative amounts from the enterprise's inception?

   c. A statement of cash flows showing the cash inflows and cash outflows for each period for which an income statement is presented and, in addition, cumulative amounts from the enterprise's inception?

    d. A statement of stockholders' equity showing from the enterprise's inception:

      (1) For each issuance, the date and number of shares of stock, warrants, rights, or other equity securities issued for cash and for other consideration?   ___ ___ ___

      (2) For each issuance, the dollar amounts (per share or other equity unit and in total) assigned to the consideration received for shares of stock, warrants, rights, or other equity securities? (Dollar amounts should be assigned to any noncash consideration received.)   ___ ___ ___

      (3) For each issuance involving noncash consideration, the nature of the noncash consideration and the basis for assigning amounts?   ___ ___ ___

2. Are the financial statements identified as those of a development-stage enterprise? (FAS-7, par. 12)   ___ ___ ___

3. Is there a description of the nature of the development-stage activities in which the enterprise is engaged? (FAS-7, par. 12)   ___ ___ ___

4. If this is the first year in which the client is not considered to be a development-stage enterprise, is there a disclosure that in prior years the client had been in the development stage? (FAS-7, par. 12)   ___ ___ ___

5. If the client is no longer a development-stage enterprise and financial statements from the years of the development stage are presented on a comparative basis, are the cumulative amounts and other additional disclosures related to a development-stage enterprise as described in items 1 through 4 above omitted from presentation? (FAS-7, par. 13)   ___ ___ ___

EMPLOYEE STOCK OWNERSHIP PLANS (ESOPS)

1. Do the financial statements of an employer sponsoring an ESOP disclose the following information about the plan: (SOP 93-6, par. 53a)

	Yes	No	N/A

a. A description of the plan?

b. The basis for determining contributions?

c. The employee groups covered?

d. The nature and effects of significant matters affecting comparability of information for all periods presented?

e. For leveraged ESOPs and pension reversion ESOPs, the basis for releasing shares and how dividends on allocated and unallocated shares are used?

2. Are the following accounting policies for blocks of both "old ESOP shares" and "new ESOP shares" disclosed (the following disclosures are required if the employer has both old ESOP shares for which it does not adopt the guidance in SOP 93-6 and new ESOP shares for which the guidance in SOP 93-6 is required; old ESOP shares are those acquired or held by the plan on or before December 31, 1992): (SOP 93-6, par. 53b)

a. The method of measuring compensation?

b. The classification of dividends on ESOP shares?

c. The treatment of ESOP shares for earnings per share computations?

3. Is disclosure made of the amount of plan compensation cost recognized during the period? (SOP 93-6, par. 53c)

4. Are the following disclosures made at the balance-sheet date for both old ESOP shares and new ESOP shares, if the employer does not adopt SOP 93-6 for the old shares: (SOP 93-6, par. 53d)

a. The number of allocated shares?

b. The number of committed-to-be-released shares?

c. The number of suspense shares held by the ESOP?

5. Is disclosure made of the fair value of unearned ESOP shares at the balance-sheet date for shares accounted for under SOP 93-6? (This disclosure need not be made for old ESOP shares for which

       the employer does not apply the guidance in SOP 93-6 for those shares.) (SOP 93-6, par. 53e)   —— —— ——

6. Is disclosure made of the existence and nature of any repurchase obligation, including disclosure of the fair value of the shares allocated as of the balance-sheet date, which are subject to a repurchase obligation? (SOP 93-6, par. 53f)   —— —— ——

7. If an employer has, in substance, guaranteed the debt of an ESOP, have the employer's financial statements disclosed the following: (SOP 76-3, par. 10)

    a. The compensation element and the interest element of annual contributions to the ESOP?   —— —— ——

    b. The interest rate and debt terms?   —— —— ——

EXIT OR DISPOSAL ACTIVITIES

1. Have the following disclosures been made in the period in which an exit or disposal activity is initiated and in any subsequent period until the activity is completed: (FAS-146, par. 20

    a. A description of the exit or disposal activity, including the facts and circumstances leading to the activity and the expected completion date?   —— —— ——

    b. For each major type of costs associated with the activity (e.g., one-time termination benefits, contract termination costs, and other associated costs):

      (1) The total amount expected to be incurred in connection with the activity?   —— —— ——

      (2) The amount incurred in the period?   —— —— ——

      (3) The cumulative amount incurred to date?   —— —— ——

      (4) A reconciliation of the beginning and ending liability balances showing separately the changes during the period attributable to costs incurred and charged to expense, costs paid or otherwise settled, and adjustments to the liability with an explanation of the reasons for those adjustments?   —— —— ——

	Yes	No	N/A

c. The line item in the income statement in which the costs described above are included?

d. For each reportable segments:

    (1) The total amount of costs expected to be incurred in connection with the activity?

    (2) The amount incurred in the period?

    (3) The cumulative amount incurred to date, net of any adjustment to the liability with an explanation of the reasons for the adjustment?

e. If a liability for a cost associated with the activity is not recognized because fair value cannot reasonably be determined, that fact and the reasons for that?

EXTINGUISHMENTS OF LIABILITIES

1. If debt was considered to be extinguished by in-substance defeasance under the provisions of FAS-76, prior to January 1, 1997, have the following disclosures been made: (FAS-140, par. 17b; FAS-156, par. 4h)

   a. A general description of the transaction?

   b. The amount of debt that is considered extinguished at the end of the period so long as that debt remains outstanding?

2. If assets are set aside after January 1, 1997, solely for satisfying scheduled payments of a specific obligation, has a description of the nature of restrictions placed on those assets been disclosed? (FAS-140, par. 17c; FAS-156, par. 4h)

FAIR VALUE MEASUREMENTS

Note: The disclosure requirements in items 1 and 2 below are prescribed by FAS-157, *Fair Value Measurements*. FAS-157 is effective for fiscal years beginning after November 15, 2007 and interim periods within those fiscal years. Early adoption is permitted as long as financial statements for any period (interim or annual) of the fiscal year have not yet been issued.

<u>*Yes*</u> <u>*No*</u> <u>*N/A*</u>

The disclosure requirements of FAS-157 need not be applied for financial statements for periods presented prior to its initial application.

The quantitative disclosures in items 1 and 2 below should be presented in a tabular format (FAS-157, par. 34). In addition, the entity is encouraged, but not required, to combine the fair value information disclosed in accordance with items 1 and 2 with the fair value information disclosed in accordance with other items in this checklist (e.g., the items listed in Part IV, "Financial Instruments—Other Disclosures"). The entity is also encouraged, but not required, to disclose information about other similar measurements (e.g., inventories measured at market value under ARB-43), if practicable. (FAS-157, par. 35)

1. For assets and liabilities that are measured at fair value on a recurring basis subsequent to initial recognition, have the following disclosures been made for each major category of assets and liabilities for each annual period: (FAS-157, par. 32)

    a. The fair value measurements at the reporting date? ___ ___ ___

    b. The level within the fair value hierarchy in which the fair value measurements in their entirety fall, segregating fair value measurements using quoted prices in active markets for identical assets or liabilities (Level 1), significant other observable inputs (Level 2), and significant unobservable inputs (Level 3)? ___ ___ ___

    c. For fair value measurements using significant unobservable inputs (Level 3), a reconciliation of the beginning and ending balances, separately presenting changes during the period attributable to the following:

        (1) Total gains or losses for the period (realized and unrealized), segregating those gains or losses included in earnings (or changes in net assets), and a description of where those gains or losses included in earnings (or changes in net assets) are reported in the statement of income (or activities)? ___ ___ ___

<u>Yes</u> <u>No</u> <u>N/A</u>

(2) Purchases, sales, issuances, and settlements (net)? ___ ___ ___

(3) Transfers in or out of Level 3 (e.g., transfers due to changes in the observability of significant inputs)? ___ ___ ___

(*Note*: This reconciliation disclosure may be presented net for derivative assets and liabilities.)

d. The amount of the total gains or losses for the period in 1c above included in earnings (or changes in net assets) that are attributable to the change in unrealized gains or losses relating to those assets and liabilities still held at the reporting date and a description of where those unrealized gains or losses are reported in the statement of income (or activities)? ___ ___ ___

e. The valuation technique(s) used to measure fair value and a discussion of changes in valuation techniques, if any, during the period? ___ ___ ___

2. For assets and liabilities that are measured at fair value on a nonrecurring basis in periods subsequent to initial recognition, have the following disclosures been made for each major category of assets and liabilities for each annual period: (FAS-157, par. 33)

a. The fair value measurements recorded during the period and the reasons for the measurements? ___ ___ ___

b. The level within the fair value hierarchy in which the fair value measurements in their entirety fall, segregating fair value measurements using quoted prices in active markets for identical assets or liabilities (Level 1), significant other observable inputs (Level 2), and significant unobservable inputs (Level 3)? ___ ___ ___

c. For fair value measurements using significant unobservable inputs (Level 3), a description of the inputs and the information used to develop the inputs? ___ ___ ___

d. The valuation technique(s) used to measure fair value and a discussion of changes, if any, in the valuation technique(s) used to measure similar assets and liabilities in prior periods? ___ ___ ___

FINANCIAL INSTRUMENTS—DERIVATIVES AND HEDGING ACTIVITIES

1. Have the following disclosures been made for all derivative instruments (and for nonderivative instruments designated and qualifying as hedging instruments): (FAS-133, par. 44)

   a. The entity's objectives for holding or issuing the instruments? ___ ___ ___

   b. The context needed to understand the entity's objectives? ___ ___ ___

   c. The entity's strategies for achieving these objectives? ___ ___ ___

   d. The entity's risk management policy for each type of hedge, including a description of the items or transactions for which risks are hedged? ___ ___ ___

   e. For derivative instruments not designated as hedging instruments, the purpose of the derivative activity? ___ ___ ___

   f. Do the disclosures for items 1a through 1e above distinguish between:

      (1) Derivative instruments (and nonderivative instruments) designated as fair value hedging instruments? ___ ___ ___

      (2) Derivative instruments designated as cash flow hedging instruments? ___ ___ ___

      (3) Derivative instruments (and nonderivative instruments) designated as hedging instruments for hedges of the foreign currency exposure of a net investment in a foreign operation? ___ ___ ___

      (4) All other derivatives? ___ ___ ___

Note: The disclosure requirement in item 2 below is prescribed by FAS-133, *Accounting for Derivative Instruments and Hedging Activities*, as amended by FAS-155, *Accounting for Certain Hybrid Financial Instruments*. The disclosure requirement in item 3 below is prescribed by FAS-155. FAS-155 is effective for all financial instruments acquired, issued, or subject to a remeasurement (new basis) event occurring after the beginning of an entity's first fiscal year that begins after September 15, 2006. Early application is permitted only if: (a) it occurs at the beginning of an entity's fiscal year and (b) the entity has not yet issued any interim or annual financial statements for that fiscal year. (FAS-155, par. 6)

2. Have disclosures been made that will provide information to users of the financial statements that will allow such users to understand the effects on earnings (or other performance indicators for entities that do not report earnings) of changes in the fair value of hybrid financial instruments measured at fair value under the election and under the practicability exception in paragraph 16 of FAS-133? (FAS-133, par. 44B; FAS-155, par. 4e)   ___ ___ ___

3. Have separate disclosures been made, upon adoption of FAS-155, of the gross gains and losses that make up the cumulative-effect adjustment (resulting from the difference between the total carrying amount of the individual components of the existing bifurcated hybrid financial instrument and the fair value of the combined hybrid financial instrument), determined on an instrument-by-instrument basis? (FAS-155, par. 7)   ___ ___ ___

4. Have the following disclosures been made for derivative instruments designated and qualifying as fair value hedging instruments (as well as nonderivative instruments that may give rise to foreign currency transaction gains or losses) and for the related hedged items, for each reporting period for which a complete set of financial statements is presented: (FAS-133, par. 45)

    a. The net gain or loss recognized in earnings during the reporting period representing: (a) the amount of the hedges' ineffectiveness, (b) the component of the derivative instruments' gain or loss, if any, excluded from the assessment of hedge effectiveness, and (c) a description of where the net gain or loss is reported in the statement of income or other statement of financial performance?   ___ ___ ___

    b. The amount of net gain or loss recognized in earnings when a hedged firm commitment no longer qualifies as a fair value hedge? ___ ___ ___

5. Have the following disclosures been made for derivative instruments that have been designated and qualifying as cash flow hedging instruments and for the related hedged transactions: (FAS-133, par. 45)

   a. The net gain or loss recognized in earnings during the reporting period representing: (a) the amount of the hedges' ineffectiveness, (b) the component of the derivative instruments' gain or loss, if any, excluded from the assessment of hedge effectiveness, and (c) a description of where the net gain or loss is reported in the statement of income or other statement of financial performance? ___ ___ ___

   b. A description of the transactions or other events that will result in the reclassification into earnings of gains and losses that are reported in accumulated other comprehensive income, and the estimated net amount of the existing gains or losses at the reporting date that is expected to be reclassified into earnings within the next 12 months? ___ ___ ___

   c. The maximum length of time over which the entity is hedging its exposure to the variability in future cash flows for forecasted transactions excluding those forecasted transactions related to the payment of variable interest on existing financial instruments? ___ ___ ___

   d. The amount of gains and losses reclassified into earnings as a result of the discontinuance of cash flow hedges because it is probable that the original forecasted transactions will not occur by the end of the originally specified time period or within the additional period of time discussed in FAS-133, as amended? ___ ___ ___

6. Has the following disclosure been made for derivative instruments designated and qualifying as hedging instruments for hedges of the foreign currency exposure of a net investment in a foreign operation (as well as for nonderivative instruments that may give rise to foreign currency transaction gains or losses): (FAS-133, par. 45)

<u>Yes</u> <u>No</u> <u>N/A</u>

a. The net amount of gains or losses included in the cumulative translation adjustment during the reporting period?   ___ ___ ___

7. Have the following disclosures been made as part of reporting changes in the components of other comprehensive income: (FAS-133, pars. 46–47)

    a. The net gain or loss on derivative instruments designated and qualifying as cash flow hedging instruments that are reported in comprehensive income are displayed as a separate classification within other comprehensive income?   ___ ___ ___

    b. As part of the disclosures of accumulated other comprehensive income, are the following disclosed separately:

      (1) The beginning and ending accumulated derivative gain or loss?   ___ ___ ___

      (2) The related net change associated with current-period hedging transactions?   ___ ___ ___

      (3) The net amount of any reclassification into earnings?   ___ ___ ___

8. For freestanding derivative financial instruments (e.g., forward sale contract, purchase put or call option or written call option) that are indexed to, and potentially settled in, a company's own stock, have the following disclosures been made: (EITF 00-19, pars. 51-53)

    a. The pertinent information about the contract, including:

      (1) The forward rate?   ___ ___ ___

      (2) The option strike price?   ___ ___ ___

      (3) The number of issuer's shares to which the contract is indexed?   ___ ___ ___

      (4) The settlement date(s) of the contract?   ___ ___ ___

      (5) The issuer's accounting for the contract (i.e., as an asset, liability, or equity)?   ___ ___ ___

    b. If the terms of the contract provide settlement alternatives, have those settlement alternatives been disclosed, including who controls the settlement alternatives and the maximum number of shares that could be required to be issued to net share settle a contract, if applicable? (*Note*: Paragraph 5 of FAS-129 requires additional disclosures for actual issuances and settlements that occurred during the accounting period. (See Part I, "Stockholders' Equity," item 4)   —— —— ——

c. The fact that a potentially infinite number of shares could be required to be issued to settle the contract, if a contract does not have a fixed or determinable maximum number of shares that may be required to be issued?   —— —— ——

d. A contract's current fair value for each settlement alternative (denominated, as relevant, in monetary amounts or quantities of shares) and how changes in the price of the issuer's equity instruments affect those settlement amounts (e.g., the issuer is obligated to issue an additional X shares or pay an additional Y dollars for each $1 decrease in stock price)?   —— —— ——

e. If contracts that are classified as assets or liabilities meet the definition of a derivative instrument under the provisions of FAS-133, have the disclosures that are required by paragraphs 44 and 45 of FAS-133 been made? (See Part IV, "Financial Instruments—Derivatives and Hedging Activities," items 1 and 4 through 6)   —— —— ——

f. If contracts have been reclassified into (or out of) equity during the life of the instrument (in whole or in part), have the following disclosures been made:

    (1) Contract reclassifications (including partial reclassifications)?   —— —— ——

    (2) The reason for the reclassification?   —— —— ——

    (3) The impact on the issuer's financial statements?   —— —— ——

    (4) The accounting policy for partial reclassifications?   —— —— ——

g. Are the disclosures required by paragraph 8 of FAS-129 made for any equity instrument in the scope of EITF 00-19 that is (or would be if the issuer were a public company) classified as temporary equity? (See Part I, "Stockholders' Equity," item 5)

Note: The disclosure requirements in item 9 below are prescribed by EITF 06-7, *Issuer's Accounting for a Previously Bifurcated Conversion Option in a Convertible Debt Instrument When the Conversion Option No Longer Meets the Bifurcation Criteria in FASB Statement No. 133, "Accounting for Derivative Instruments and Hedging Activities."* EITF 06-7 is effective for all previously bifurcated conversion options in convertible debt instruments that no longer meet the bifurcation criteria in FAS-133, *Accounting for Derivative Instruments and Hedging Activities,* in annual or interim periods beginning after December 15, 2006, irrespective of when the debt instrument was entered into. Early adoption is permitted only if financial statements for the period have not yet been issued. Retrospective application in accordance with FAS-154, *Accounting Changes and Error Corrections,* is permitted.

9. For previously bifurcated conversion options in convertible debt instruments that no longer meet the bifurcation criteria in FAS-133, have the following disclosures been made: (EITF 06-7)

   a. A description of the principal changes causing the embedded conversion option to no longer require bifurcation under FAS-133?

   b. The amount of the liability for the conversion option reclassified to stockholders' equity?

FINANCIAL INSTRUMENTS— INSTRUMENTS WITH CHARACTERISTICS OF BOTH LIABILITIES AND EQUITY

Note: With limited exceptions, FAS-150, *Accounting for Certain Financial Instruments with Characteristics of both Liabilities and Equity,* is effective for financial instruments entered into or modified after May 31,

Yes *No* *N/A*

2003; for financial instruments entered into previously, FAS-150 is effective at the beginning of the first interim period beginning after June 15, 2003; for certain mandatorily redeemable financial instruments, FSP FAS 150-3 defers the effective date of FAS-150 to fiscal periods beginning after December 15, 2004 and for certain other mandatorily redeemable financial instruments it defers the effective date of FAS-150 indefinitely. For further guidance, see Chapter 15, "Financial Instruments, Derivatives, and Hedging Activities" of the *GAAP Financial Statement Disclosures Manual*.

1. For financial instruments with characteristics of both liabilities and equity, have the following disclosures been made: (FAS-150, par. 26) ___ ___ ___

    a. The nature and terms of the financial instruments? ___ ___ ___

    b. The rights and obligations embodied in those financial instruments? ___ ___ ___

    c. Information about any settlement alternatives in the contract? ___ ___ ___

    d. The identity of the entity that controls the settlement alternatives? ___ ___ ___

2. For all outstanding financial instruments with characteristics of both liabilities and equity, and for each settlement alternative, have the following disclosures been made: (FAS-150, par. 27)

    a. The amount that would be paid or the number of shares that would be issued and their fair value, determined under the conditions specified in the contract if the settlement were to occur at the reporting date? ___ ___ ___

    b. How changes in the fair value of the entity's equity shares would affect those settlement amounts? ___ ___ ___

    c. The maximum amount that the entity could be required to pay to redeem the instrument by physical settlement? ___ ___ ___

    d. The maximum number of shares that could be required to be issued? ___ ___ ___

<u>Yes</u> <u>No</u> <u>N/A</u>

    e. That a contract does not limit the amount that the entity could be required to pay or the number of shares that the entity could be required to issue? ____ ____ ____

    f. For a forward contract or an option indexed to the entity's equity shares:

       (1) The forward price or option strike price? ____ ____ ____

       (2) The number of the entity's shares to which the contract is indexed? ____ ____ ____

       (3) The settlement date(s) of the contract? ____ ____ ____

3. Are financial instruments that are required to be presented as liabilities not being presented between the liabilities section and the equity section of the balance sheet? (FAS-150, par. 18) ____ ____ ____

4. For entities that have no equity instruments outstanding but have financial instruments issued in the form of shares, all of which are mandatorily redeemable financial instruments required to be classified as liabilities:

    a. Are those financial instruments described as "shares subject to mandatory redemption" in the balance sheets to distinguish those instruments from other liabilities? (FAS-150, par. 19) ____ ____ ____

    b. Are payments to holders of such instruments and related accruals presented separately from payments to and interest due to other creditors in the statements of cash flows and operations? (FAS-150, par. 19) ____ ____ ____

    c. Are the components of the liability that would otherwise be related to shareholders' interest and other comprehensive income, if any, subject to the redemption feature disclosed (e.g., par value and other paid-in amounts of mandatorily redeemable instruments should be disclosed separately from the amount of retained earnings or accumulated deficit)? (FAS-150, par. 28) ____ ____ ____

FINANCIAL INSTRUMENTS—OTHER DISCLOSURES

1. Have significant concentrations of credit risk aris-
    ing from all financial instruments been disclosed,
    including the following about each significant
    concentration: (FAS-107, par. 15A; FAS-133,
    par. 531d)

    a. Information about the activity, region, or eco-
        nomic characteristic that identifies the concen-
        tration?   ___ ___ ___

    b. The maximum amount of loss due to credit
        risk that, based on the gross fair value of the
        financial instrument, the entity would incur
        if parties to the financial instruments that
        make up the concentration failed completely
        to perform according to the terms of the con-
        tracts and the collateral or other security, if any,
        for the amount due proved to be of no value
        to the entity?   ___ ___ ___

    c. The entity's policy of requiring collateral or
        other security to support financial instruments
        subject to credit risk?   ___ ___ ___

    d. Information about the entity's access to the
        collateral or other security?   ___ ___ ___

    e. The nature and a brief description of the col-
        lateral or other security supporting those fi-
        nancial instruments?   ___ ___ ___

    f. The entity's policy of entering into master
        netting arrangements to mitigate the credit
        risk of financial instruments, information
        about the arrangements for which the entity
        is a party, and a brief description of the terms
        of those arrangements, including the extent
        to which they would reduce the entity's maxi-
        mum amount of loss due to credit risk?   ___ ___ ___

2. Has the following information about fair value
    of financial instruments been disclosed either in
    the body of the financial statements or in the ac-
    companying notes: (*Note*: These disclosures
    about the fair value of financial instruments are
    optional, not required, for an entity that meets
    all of the following criteria: (1) the entity is a

<u>Yes</u> <u>No</u> <u>N/A</u>

nonpublic entity, (2) the entity's total assets are less than $100 million on the date of the financial statements, and (3) the entity has not held or issued any derivative financial instruments during the reporting period.) (FAS-107, pars. 10 and 14; FAS-133, pars. 531–532)

a. Fair value of financial instruments for which it is practicable to estimate fair value? (For trade receivables and payables, no disclosure is required when the carrying amount approximates fair value). In connection with this item:

   (1) When disclosure is made in the accompanying notes, is the fair value presented together with the related carrying amount in a form that makes it clear whether the fair value and carrying amount represent assets or liabilities and how the carrying amounts relate to what is reported in the balance sheet?   ____ ____ ____

   (2) Has disclosure been made in a single note or, if disclosed in more than a single note, does one of the notes include a summary table that contains the fair value and related carrying amounts and cross-references to the locations of the remaining disclosures?   ____ ____ ____

b. The methods and significant assumptions used to estimate the fair value of financial instruments?   ____ ____ ____

c. In disclosing the fair value of a financial instrument, did the entity *not* net that fair value with the fair value of other financial instruments, except to the extent that the offsetting of carrying amounts in the balance sheet is permitted?   ____ ____ ____

d. For financial instruments for which it is concluded that estimating fair value is not practicable, have disclosures been made of: (1) information related to estimating the fair value of the financial instrument (such as the carrying amount, effective interest rate, and maturity) and (2) the reasons why it is not practicable to estimate fair value?   ____ ____ ____

Yes *No* *N/A*

3. Have existing GAAP disclosures for financial instruments, such as those required in FAS-107, been made for weather derivative instruments within the scope of EITF 99-2? (EITF 99-2, par. 11) ___ ___ ___

4. Has quantitative information about the market risks of financial instruments that is consistent with the way an entity manages or adjusts its market risks (e.g., details of current positions, details of activity during the period, a gap analysis of interest rate repricing or maturity dates, the duration of the financial instruments) been disclosed? (*Note*: Entities are *encouraged*, but not required, to disclose this information.)(FAS-107, pars. 15C and 15D; FAS-133, par. 531d) ___ ___ ___

5. Has information on how underwriting procedures are designed to control the credit risk that may arise from future payment increases been disclosed? (*Note*: Entities are *encouraged*, but not required, to disclose this information.)(FSP SOP 94-6-1, par. 8) ___ ___ ___

6. Have the required disclosures been made for transfers of financial instruments? (See Part IV, "Transfers and Servicing of Financial Assets") ___ ___ ___

FOREIGN OPERATIONS AND CURRENCY TRANSLATION

1. Are significant foreign operations disclosed, including foreign earnings reported in excess of amounts received in the United States? (ARB-43, Ch. 12, pars. 5–6) ___ ___ ___

2. Is the aggregate exchange transaction gain or loss disclosed as follows: (FAS-133, par. 45)

   a. For derivative instruments designated and qualifying as fair value hedging instruments, as well as nonderivative instruments that may give rise to foreign currency transaction gains or losses, and for the related hedged items, for each reporting period for which a complete set of financial statements is presented:

   (1) The net gain or loss recognized in earnings during the reporting period representing: (a) the amount of the hedges' in-

<u>Yes</u> <u>No</u> <u>N/A</u>

effectiveness, (b) the component of the derivative instruments' gain or loss, if any, excluded from the assessment of hedge effectiveness, and (c) a description of where the net gain or loss is reported in the statement of income or other statement of financial performance?   ___ ___ ___

(2) The amount of net gain or loss recognized in earnings when a hedged firm commitment no longer qualifies as a fair value hedge?   ___ ___ ___

b. For derivative instruments that have been designated and qualifying as cash flow hedging instruments and for the related hedged transactions:

(1) The net gain or loss recognized in earnings during the reporting period representing: (a) the amount of the hedges' ineffectiveness, (b) the component of the derivative instruments' gain or loss, if any, excluded from the assessment of hedge effectiveness, and (c) a description of where the net gain or loss is reported in the statement of income or other statement of financial performance?   ___ ___ ___

(2) A description of the transactions or other events that will result in the reclassification into earnings of gains and losses that are reported in accumulated other comprehensive income, and the estimated net amount of the existing gains or losses at the reporting date that is expected to be reclassified into earnings within the next 12 months?   ___ ___ ___

(3) The maximum length of time over which the entity is hedging its exposure to the variability in future cash flows for forecasted transactions excluding those forecasted transactions related to the payment of variable interest on existing financial instruments?   ___ ___ ___

(4) The amount of gains and losses reclassified into earnings as a result of the

Yes No N/A

discontinuance of cash flow hedges because it is probable that the original forecasted transactions will not occur? ___ ___ ___

c. For derivative instruments designated and qualifying as hedging instruments for hedges of the foreign currency exposure of a net investment in a foreign operation (as well as for nonderivative instruments that may give rise to foreign currency transaction gains or losses):

(1) The net amount of gains or losses included in the cumulative translation adjustment during the reporting period? ___ ___ ___

3. Is there an analysis of the change in the cumulative translation adjustments (included as a component of accumulated other comprehensive income), and does the analysis include the following: (FAS-52, par. 31)

a. Beginning and ending amounts of cumulative translation adjustments? ___ ___ ___

b. The aggregate adjustment for the period resulting from translation adjustments and gains and losses from hedges of a net investment in a foreign entity and long-term intercompany balances? ___ ___ ___

c. The amount of income taxes for the period allocated to translation adjustments? ___ ___ ___

d. The amounts transferred from cumulative translation adjustments and included in determining net income for the period as a result of the sale or complete (or substantially complete) liquidation of an investment in a foreign entity? ___ ___ ___

4. Are the following disclosures made for rate changes that occur after the date of the client's financial statements: (FAS-52, pars. 32 and 143)

a. Disclosure for the rate change? ___ ___ ___

b. The effects of rate changes on unsettled balances pertaining to foreign currency transactions? ___ ___ ___

c. If the effects of rate changes cannot be determined, is that fact disclosed? ___ ___ ___

<u>Yes</u> <u>No</u> <u>N/A</u>

5. Are additional (*optional*) disclosures, such as the following, considered to supplement the required disclosures described above: (FAS-52, par. 144)

    a. Mathematical effects of translating revenue and expenses at rates that are different from those used in previous financial statements?   ___ ___ ___

    b. Economic effects (such as selling prices, sales volume, and cost structures) of rate changes?

FOURTH QUARTER INFORMATION

1. If financial information detailed in item 35 of Part IV, "Interim Financial Reporting," is not separately reported for the fourth quarter, or that information is not presented in the annual report, has the following information about the fourth quarter been disclosed in a note to the annual financial statements: (FAS-3, par. 14; APB-28, par. 31; FAS-154, par. 16)

    a. Disposal of a segment of a business?   ___ ___ ___

    b. Extraordinary, unusual, or infrequent transactions or events?   ___ ___ ___

    c. The aggregate effect of year-end adjustments that are material to the operating results of the fourth quarter?   ___ ___ ___

    d. Accounting changes presented in the manner required for interim accounting changes?   ___ ___ ___

GOING-CONCERN DISCLOSURES

1. If the auditor concludes, after considering management's plans, that there is substantial doubt about the entity's ability to continue as a going concern for a period of time not to exceed one year beyond the balance-sheet date, do the financial statements include the following disclosures: (AU 341.10)

    a. Pertinent conditions and events giving rise to the assessment of substantial doubt about the entity's ability to continue as a going concern

Yes No N/A

for a period of time not to exceed one year
beyond the balance-sheet date?

b. The possible effects of such conditions and
events?

c. Management's evaluation of the significance
of those conditions and events and any mitigating factors?

d. Possible discontinuance of operations?

e. Management's plans (including relevant prospective financial information)?

f. Information about the recoverability or classification of recorded asset amounts or the
amounts or classification of liabilities?

2. When, primarily because of the auditor's consideration of management's plans, the auditor
concludes that substantial doubt about the
entity's ability to continue as a going concern for
a period of time not to exceed one year from the
balance-sheet date is alleviated, do the financial
statements include the following disclosures:
(AU 341.11)

a. The principal conditions and events that initially caused the auditor to believe there was
substantial doubt?

b. The possible effects of such conditions and
events, and any mitigating factors, including
management's plans?

GUARANTEES

1. Is the following information disclosed for each
guarantee, or each group of similar guarantees,
even if the likelihood of the entity having to make
any payments under the guarantee is remote:
(FIN-45, pars. 13–14)

a. The nature of the guarantee?

b. The approximate term of the guarantee?

c. How the guarantee arose?

d. The events or circumstances that would require the entity to perform under the guarantee?

<u>Yes</u> <u>No</u> <u>N/A</u>

e. The maximum potential amount of future payments, undiscounted, the entity could be required to make under the guarantee? (This disclosure is not required for product warranties.) With respect to this disclosure item:

   (1) If the maximum potential future payments under the guarantee are unlimited, has that fact been disclosed?   ____ ____ ____

   (2) If the entity is unable to develop an estimate of the maximum potential amount of future payments, has the entity disclosed the reasons why it cannot estimate the maximum potential amount?   ____ ____ ____

f. The current carrying amount of the liability, if any?   ____ ____ ____

g. The nature of any recourse provisions that would enable the entity to recover from third parties any of the amounts paid under the guarantee?   ____ ____ ____

h. The nature of any assets held either as collateral or by third parties that, upon the occurrence of any triggering event or condition under the guarantee, the entity can obtain and liquidate to recover the amounts paid under the guarantee? (Also, if estimable, the entity should indicate the extent to which the proceeds from liquidation of those assets would be expected to cover the maximum potential amount of future payments under the guarantee.)   ____ ____ ____

i. For product warranties or for guarantees related to the functional performance of nonfinancial assets owned by the guaranteed party, have the following additional items been disclosed:

   (1) The entity's (guarantor's) accounting policy and methodology used in determining its liability for such product warranties or guarantees, including any liability (such as deferred revenue) associated with extended warranties?   ____ ____ ____

   (2) A reconciliation of the changes in the entity's aggregate liability for such

<u>Yes</u> <u>No</u> <u>N/A</u>

product warranties or guarantees, showing the following: ___ ___ ___

(i)   The beginning balance of the aggregate liability? ___ ___ ___

(ii) Aggregate reductions in that liability for payments made (in cash or in kind)? ___ ___ ___

(iii) Aggregate changes in the liability for accruals related to such product warranties or guarantees issued during the period? ___ ___ ___

(iv) The aggregate changes in the liability for accruals related to preexisting warranties (including adjustments related to changes in estimates)? ___ ___ ___

(v)   The ending balance of the aggregate liability? ___ ___ ___

Note: The disclosure requirements in item 2 below are prescribed by FSP FIN 45-3, *Application of FASB Interpretation No. 45 to Minimum Revenue Guarantees Granted to a Business or Its Owners*, which is effective for all minimum revenue guarantees in financial statements of annual periods ending after the beginning of the first fiscal quarter following November 10, 2005. Early application is permitted.

2.   Have the disclosure requirements detailed in item 1 above been made for all minimum revenue guarantees, regardless of whether they were recognized and measured under FASB Interpretation No. 45, *Guarantor's Accounting and Disclosure Requirements for Guarantees, Including Indirect Guarantees of Indebtedness of Others*? (FSP FIN 45-3, par. 7) ___ ___ ___

IMPAIRMENT OF CERTAIN LOANS

1.   Have the following disclosures been made, either in the body of the financial statements or in the accompanying notes, about impaired loans as defined in paragraph 8 of FAS-114: (FAS-118, pars. 6 and 24)

	Yes	No	N/A

a. As of the date of each statement of financial position presented, the total recorded investment in the impaired loans at the end of each period and (1) the amount of that recorded investment for which there is a related allowance for credit losses and the amount of that allowance and (2) the amount of that recorded investment for which there is no related allowance for credit losses? ___ ___ ___

b. The creditor's policy for recognizing interest income on impaired loans, including how cash receipts are recorded? ___ ___ ___

c. For each period for which results of operations are presented:

(1) The average recorded investment in the impaired loans during each period? ___ ___ ___

(2) The related amount of interest income recognized during the time within that period that the loans were impaired? ___ ___ ___

(3) The amount of interest income recognized using a cash-basis method of accounting during the time within that period that the loans were impaired, unless not practicable? ___ ___ ___

d. For each period for which results of operations are presented, have disclosures been made of the activity in the total allowance for credit losses related to loans, including the following:

(1) The balance in the allowance at the beginning and end of each period? ___ ___ ___

(2) Additions charged to operations? ___ ___ ___

(3) Direct writedowns charged against the allowance? ___ ___ ___

(4) Recoveries of amounts previously charged off? ___ ___ ___

IMPAIRMENT AND DISPOSAL OF LONG-LIVED ASSETS

1. For impaired assets to be held and used, have the following disclosures been made in financial

statements that include the period of the impairment loss: (FAS-144, par. 26)

a. A description of the impaired assets and the facts and circumstances leading to the impairment? ___ ___ ___

b. If not separately presented on the face of the income statement, the amount of the impairment loss and the caption in the income statement that includes that loss? ___ ___ ___

c. The method(s) for determining fair value (e.g., quoted market price, present value techniques)? ___ ___ ___

d. If applicable, the business segment in which the impaired long-lived asset is reported? ___ ___ ___

2. Have the following items been presented separately in the balance sheet: (FAS-144, par. 46)

a. Long-lived assets that are classified as held for sale? ___ ___ ___

b. The assets and liabilities of a disposal group classified as held for sale? (*Note*: The assets and liabilities should *not* be offset and presented as a single amount.) ___ ___ ___

3. For a long-lived asset (disposal group) that either has been sold or is classified as held for sale, have the following disclosures been made in financial statements that include the period in which the asset (group) has been sold or is classified as held for sale: (FAS-144, par. 47)

a. A description of the facts and circumstances leading to the expected disposal? ___ ___ ___

b. The expected manner and timing of the disposal? ___ ___ ___

c. The carrying amount(s) of the major classes of assets and liabilities included as part of a disposal group, if not separately presented on the face of the balance sheet? ___ ___ ___

d. The gain or loss recognized and, if not separately presented on the face of the income statement, the caption in the income statement that includes the gain or loss? ___ ___ ___

Yes *No* *N/A*

    e. If applicable, amounts of revenue and pretax profit or loss reported in discontinued operations?   —— —— ——

    f. If applicable, the segment in which the long-lived asset (disposal group) is reported?   —— —— ——

4. If an entity decides not to sell a long-lived asset (disposal group) previously classified as held for sale, or removes an individual asset or liability from a disposal group previously classified as held for sale, have the following disclosures been made in the financial statements that include the period of that decision: (FAS-144, par. 48)

    a. A description of the facts and circumstances leading to the decision to change the plan to sell the long-lived asset (disposal group)?   —— —— ——

    b. The effect on the results of operations for the period and any prior periods presented?   —— —— ——

5. If the criteria for classification of a long-lived asset as held for sale are met after the balance-sheet date, but before issuance of the financial statements, has the following information been disclosed: (FAS-144, par. 33)

    a. A description of the facts and circumstances leading to the expected disposal?   —— —— ——

    b. The expected manner and timing of the disposal?   —— —— ——

    c. The carrying amount(s) of the major classes of assets and liabilities included as part of a disposal group, if not separately presented on the face of the balance sheet?   —— —— ——

INSURANCE CONTRACTS AND RECOVERIES

1. Have the following disclosures been made for insurance and reinsurance contracts that are accounted for as deposits: (SOP 98-7, par. 18)

    a. A description of the contracts accounted for as deposits?   —— —— ——

    b. Total deposit assets reported in the balance sheet?   —— —— ——

Yes *No* *N/A*

    c. Total deposit liabilities reported in the balance sheet?

2. If business interruption insurance recoveries were recognized during the period, have the following disclosures been made: (EITF 01-13, par. 7)

    a. The nature of the event resulting in business interruption losses?

    b. The aggregate amount of business interruption insurance recoveries recognized during the period and the income statement line item in which they are classified (including amounts reported as extraordinary items)?

INTEREST COST

1. Have the following disclosures been made with respect to interest costs:

    a. For an accounting period in which no interest cost is capitalized, the amount of interest cost incurred and charged to expense during the period? (FAS-34, par. 21)

    b. For an accounting period in which some interest cost is capitalized, the total amount of interest cost incurred during the period and the amount thereof that has been capitalized? (FAS-34, par. 21)

    c. The amount of interest costs incurred in connection with product financing arrangements? (FAS-34, par. 21; FAS-49, par. 9)

    d. For notes payable or receivable that require the imputation of interest, have disclosures included: (APB-21, par. 16)

        (1) A description of the note?

        (2) The effective interest rate?

        (3) The face amount of the note?

        (4) The amount of discount or premium resulting from present value determination?

        (5) The amortization of the discount or premium to interest?

<u>Yes</u> <u>No</u> <u>N/A</u>

e. The amount of interest paid (net of amounts capitalized) for each period for which a statement of cash flows is presented? (FAS-95, par. 29)

____ ____ ____

INTERIM FINANCIAL REPORTING

1. If the company uses estimated gross profit rates to determine the cost of goods sold during interim periods or uses other methods different from those used at annual inventory dates, have the following disclosures been made: (APB-28, par. 14)

    a. The method used at the interim date?

    ____ ____ ____

    b. Any significant adjustments that result from reconciliations with the annual physical inventory?

    ____ ____ ____

2. When costs and expenses incurred in an interim period cannot be readily identified with the activities or benefits of other interim periods, have disclosures been made about the nature and amount of such costs? (*Note*: Disclosure is not required if items of a comparable nature are included in both the current interim period and the corresponding interim period of the preceding year.) (APB-28, par. 15)

    ____ ____ ____

3. If revenues of the entity are subject to material seasonal variations, have the following disclosures been made to avoid the possibility that interim results may be taken as fairly indicative of the estimated results for a full fiscal year: (APB-28, par. 18)

    a. The seasonal nature of the business activities?

    ____ ____ ____

    b. Information for 12-month periods ended at the interim date for the current and preceding years (*optional*)?

    ____ ____ ____

4. Have disclosures been made of the reasons for significant variations in the customary relationship between income tax expense and pretax accounting income, if they are not otherwise apparent from the financial statements or from the nature of the entity's business? (APB-28, par. 19; FIN-18, par. 25)

    ____ ____ ____

<u>*Yes*</u> <u>*No*</u> <u>*N/A*</u>

5. Are extraordinary items, gains or losses from disposal of a component of an entity, unusual seasonal results, business combinations, unusual and infrequently occurring transactions, and events that are material to the operating results of the interim period reported separately and included in the determination of net income for the interim period in which they occur? (APB-28, par. 21)   ___ ___ ___

6. Have disclosures been made about contingencies and other uncertainties that could be expected to affect the fairness of presentation of the interim financial information? (*Note*: Such disclosures should: (a) include, but not be limited to, those matters that form the basis of a qualification of an independent auditors' report and (b) be repeated in interim and annual reports until the contingencies have been removed or resolved or have become immaterial.) (APB-28, par. 22)   ___ ___ ___

7. Have the number of shares issued on conversion, exercise, or otherwise during at least the most recent annual fiscal period and any subsequent interim period presented been disclosed? (FAS-129, par. 5)   ___ ___ ___

8. Has total comprehensive income been disclosed in condensed financial statements? (FAS-130, par. 27)   ___ ___ ___

9. If there is a significant difference between total comprehensive income and net income, has disclosure of the components of the difference been considered? (FAS-130, par. 125)   ___ ___ ___

10. Have unusual or infrequently occurring items that will be separately disclosed in the financial statements for the fiscal year been separately disclosed as a component of pretax income from continuing operations? (FIN-18, par. 17)   ___ ___ ___

Note: The disclosure requirements in items 11 through 21 below are required for entities that have not adopted FAS-154, *Accounting Changes and Error Corrections*. The disclosure requirements in items 16 through 30 below are required for entities that have adopted FAS-154, which is effective for accounting changes and corrections of errors made in fiscal years beginning after December 15, 2005. Early adoption is permitted for accounting changes and corrections of errors made in fiscal years beginning after June 1, 2005.

11. If there were changes in accounting principles or reporting entity that result in retroactive re-statement of previously issued financial state-ments, have the following been disclosed for all periods presented, if not presented on the income statement: (APB-28, par. 25; APB-20, pars. 28 and 35)

   a. Nature and justification?   ___ ___ ___

   b. Effect on income before extraordinary items, net income, and related per share, if appli-cable, amounts?   ___ ___ ___

12. For corrections of errors that result in the retro-active restatement of previously issued financial statements, have the following been disclosed in the period in which the error was discovered and corrected: (APB-28, par. 25; APB-20, par. 37)

   a. Nature?   ___ ___ ___

   b. Effect on income before extraordinary items, net income, and related per share, if appli-cable, amounts?   ___ ___ ___

13. Has the effect of a change in accounting estimate, including a change in the estimated effective annual tax rate, on income before extraordinary items, net income, and related per share amounts, if applicable, been disclosed if material in rela-tion to any period presented? (*Note*: Disclosure of the effect on income statement amounts is not necessary for estimates made each period in the ordinary course of accounting for certain items [e.g., uncollectible accounts or inventory obso-lescence]. However, if the effects are material, then disclosure of the income statement amounts is recommended but not required.) (*Note*: The effect on earnings of a change in estimate that is made in the current interim period should be reported in the current and subsequent interim periods, if material to any period presented. It should continue to be reported in the interim fi-nancial information of the subsequent year for

as many periods as necessary to avoid misleading comparisons.) (APB-28, par. 26; APB-20,
par. 33)

    ––– ––– –––

14. Have the following disclosures about a cumulative effect-type accounting change, other than
changes to last-in, first-out (LIFO), been made in
interim financial reports: (FAS-3, par. 11; APB-
28, par. 27B)

    ––– ––– –––

a. In financial reports for the interim period in
which the new accounting principle is
adopted, have disclosures been made of:

(1) The nature of and justification for the
change?

    ––– ––– –––

(2) The effect of the change on income from
continuing operations and net income
(and related per share amounts for public companies) for the interim period in
which the change is made? (*Note*: If the
change is made in a period other than the
first interim period of a fiscal year, the
effect of the change on income from continuing operations, net income, and related per share amounts for each pre-
change interim period of the fiscal year
should be disclosed. Also, the restated
income from continuing operations, net
income, and related per share amounts for
each pre-change interim period of the fiscal year should be disclosed.)

    ––– ––– –––

(3) Income from continuing operations and
net income (and related per share
amounts for public companies) computed
on a pro forma basis for: (i) the interim
period in which the change is made and
(ii) any interim periods of prior fiscal
years for which financial information is
being presented? (*Note*: If no financial information for interim periods of prior fiscal years is being presented, disclosure
shall be made, in the period of change, of
the actual and pro forma amounts of income from continuing operations, net income, and related per share amounts for
the interim period of the immediately

<u>Yes</u> <u>No</u> <u>N/A</u>

preceding fiscal year that corresponds to the interim period in which the changes are made.)

   — — —

b. In year-to-date and last-12-months-to-date financial reports that include the interim period in which the new accounting principle is adopted, have disclosures been made of:

(1) The effect of the change on income from continuing operations and net income (and related per share amounts for public companies) for the interim period in which the change is made?

   — — —

(2) Income from continuing operations and net income (and related per share amounts for public companies) computed on a pro forma basis for: (i) the interim period in which the change is made and (ii) any interim periods of prior fiscal years for which financial information is being presented? (*Note*: If no financial information for interim periods of prior fiscal years is being presented, disclosure should be made, in the period of change, of the actual and pro forma amounts of income from continuing operations, net income, and related per share amounts for the interim period of the immediately preceding fiscal year that corresponds to the interim period in which the changes are made.)

   — — —

c. In financial reports for subsequent (postchange) interim periods of the fiscal year in which the new accounting principle is adopted, have disclosures been made of the effect of the change on income from continuing operations and net income (and related per share amounts for public companies) for that postchange interim period?

   — — —

15. For changes in accounting principles when neither the cumulative effect of the change nor the pro forma amounts can be computed (principally a change to the LIFO method of inventory pricing), have the following disclosures been made: (*Note*: If a change of this type has been made in

<u>*Yes*</u> <u>*No*</u> <u>*N/A*</u>

the first or any other interim period of an entity's fiscal year, the disclosures in item 14 above [except the pro forma amounts for interim periods of prior fiscal years included in item 14a(3) above] should be made.) (FAS-3, pars. 12-13; APB-28, pars. 27C-27D)

a. An explanation of the reasons for omitting accounting for the cumulative effect of the change? ___ ___ ___

b. An explanation of the reasons for omitting disclosure of pro forma amounts for prior years? ___ ___ ___

16. Have disclosures been made of any changes in accounting principles or practices from those applied in: (APB-28, par. 23)

a. The comparable interim period of the prior year? ___ ___ ___

b. The preceding interim periods in the current year? ___ ___ ___

c. The prior annual financial statements? ___ ___ ___

17. Have the cumulative effects of an accounting change or correction of an error that are material to an interim period, but not material to the estimated income for the full fiscal year or to the trend of earnings, been disclosed separately in the interim period? (*Note*: The related amount of applicable income taxes may be disclosed but is not required.)(APB-28, par. 29; FIN-18, par. 71) ___ ___ ___

18. Have the following disclosures been made in interim financial statements about an adjustment related to prior interim periods of the current fiscal year: (FAS-16, par. 15)

a. The effect on income from continuing operations and net income for each prior interim period of the current fiscal year? ___ ___ ___

b. Restated income from continuing operations and net income for each prior interim period? ___ ___ ___

19. Have the resulting effects (both gross and net of applicable income tax) of prior period adjustments on the net income of prior periods been disclosed in the annual report for the year in which the adjustments are made? (APB-9, par. 26; FAS-154, par. 26) ___ ___ ___

Yes No N/A

20. When single-period financial statements are presented, has the effect (both gross and net of applicable income tax) of prior period adjustments on the opening balance of retained earnings and on net income (and on related per share amounts when presented) of the preceding period been disclosed? (APB-9, par. 26; FAS-154, par. 26)   ___ ___ ___

21. When financial statements for more than one period are presented, has the effect (both gross and net of applicable income tax) of prior period adjustments on the opening balance of retained earnings and on net income (and on related per share amounts when presented) for each of the periods presented been disclosed? (APB-9, par. 26; FAS-154, par. 26)   ___ ___ ___

22. Are the following disclosures made for a change in accounting principle in the interim period the change occurs: (FAS-154, par. 17)

    a. The nature of and reason for the change in accounting principle, including an explanation of why the newly adopted accounting principle is preferable?   ___ ___ ___

    b. The method of applying the change?   ___ ___ ___

    c. A description of the prior-period information that has been retrospectively adjusted?   ___ ___ ___

    d. The effect of the change on the following for the current period and any prior periods retrospectively adjusted:

    (1) Income from continuing operations?   ___ ___ ___

    (2) Net income (or other appropriate captions of changes in the applicable net assets or performance indicator)?   ___ ___ ___

    (3) Any other affected financial statement line item?   ___ ___ ___

    (4) Any affected per share amounts?   ___ ___ ___

    e. The cumulative effect of the change on retained earnings or other components of equity or net assets in the balance sheet as of the beginning of the earliest period presented?   ___ ___ ___

    f. If retrospective application to all prior periods is impracticable, the reasons why, and a description of the alternative method used to report the change? ___ ___ ___

g. If indirect effects of the change in accounting principle are recognized:

(1) A description of the indirect effects of the change in accounting principle, including the amounts that have been recognized in the current period, and the related per share amounts, if applicable? ___ ___ ___

(2) Unless impracticable, the amount of the total recognized indirect effects of the accounting change and the related per share amounts, if applicable, that are attributable to each prior period presented? ___ ___ ___

23. For a change in accounting principle that has no material effect in the period of change but is reasonably certain to have a material effect in later periods, have disclosures been made of the nature of and reason for the change in accounting principle, including an explanation of why the newly adopted accounting principle is preferable, whenever the financial statements of the period of change are presented? (FAS-154, par. 17) ___ ___ ___

24. In the fiscal year in which a new accounting principle is adopted, for financial information reported in interim periods after the date of adoption of a new accounting principle, has the effect of the change on the following been disclosed for those post-change interim periods: (FAS-154, par. 18)

a. Income from continuing operations? ___ ___ ___

b. Net income (or other appropriate captions of change in the applicable net assets or performance indicators)? ___ ___ ___

c. Related per share amounts, if applicable? ___ ___ ___

25. If a change in accounting principle effects a change in estimate, have the disclosures detailed in items 22 through 24 above been made? (FAS-154, par. 22; APB-28, par. 26) ___ ___ ___

26. For a change in accounting estimate that affects several future periods (e.g., change in service

lives of depreciable assets), has the effect of the change on the following for the current period been disclosed: (FAS-154, par. 22; APB-28, par. 26) (*Note*: Disclosure of these effects is not necessary for estimates made each period in the ordinary course of accounting [e.g., uncollectible accounts, inventory obsolescence] unless the effect of the change in estimate is material.)

a. Income from continuing operations?

b. Net income (or other appropriate captions of change in the applicable net assets or performance indicators)?

c. Related per share amounts?

27. For a change in accounting estimate that has no material effect in the period of change but is reasonably certain to have a material effect in later periods, has a description of the change been disclosed whenever the financial statements of the period of change are presented? (FAS-154, par. 22; APB-28, par. 26)

28. For changes in the reporting entity, have the following been disclosed in the period of the change: (FAS-154, par. 24)

a. Nature and reason for it?

b. Effect on income before extraordinary items, net income (or other appropriate captions of changes in the applicable net assets or performance indicator), other comprehensive income, and any related per share amounts?

29. For a change in reporting entity that has no material effect in the period of change but is reasonably certain to have a material effect in later periods, have disclosures been made of the nature of and reason for the change, whenever the financial statements of the period of change are presented? (FAS-154, par. 24)

30. If the financial statements have been restated to correct an error, have the following been disclosed? (FAS-154, par. 26)

a. The fact that previously issued financial statements have been restated?

b. A description of the nature of the error?

Yes No N/A

c. The effect of the correction on each financial statement line item and any per share amounts affected for each prior period presented? ___ ___ ___

d. The cumulative effect of the change on retained earnings or other appropriate components of equity or net assets in the balance sheet, as of the beginning of the earliest period presented? ___ ___ ___

31. Is the following information disclosed for each guarantee, or each group of similar guarantees, even if the likelihood of the entity having to make any payments under the guarantee is remote: (FIN-45, pars. 13–14)

a. The nature of the guarantee? ___ ___ ___

b. The approximate term of the guarantee? ___ ___ ___

c. How the guarantee arose? ___ ___ ___

d. The events or circumstances that would require the entity to perform under the guarantee? ___ ___ ___

e. The maximum potential amount of future payments, undiscounted, the entity could be required to make under the guarantee? (*Note:* This disclosure is not required for product warranties.) With respect to this disclosure item:

  (1) If the maximum potential future payments under the guarantee are unlimited, has that fact been disclosed? ___ ___ ___

  (2) If the entity is unable to develop an estimate of the maximum potential amount of future payments, has the entity disclosed the reasons why it cannot estimate the maximum potential amount? ___ ___ ___

f. The current carrying amount of the related liability, if any? ___ ___ ___

g. The nature of any recourse provisions that would enable the entity to recover from third parties any of the amounts paid under the guarantee? ___ ___ ___

h. The nature of any assets held either as collateral or by third parties that, on the occurrence of any triggering event or condition under the guarantee, the entity can obtain and liquidate to recover the amounts paid under the guarantee? (Also, if estimable, the entity should indicate the extent to which the proceeds from the liquidation of those assets would be expected to cover the maximum potential amount of future payments under the guarantee.)

  —— —— ——

i. For product warranties or for guarantees related to the functional performance of nonfinancial assets owned by the guaranteed party, have the following additional items been disclosed:

  (1) The entity's (guarantor's) accounting policy and methodology used in determining its liability for such product warranties or guarantees, including any liability (such as deferred revenue) associated with extended warranties?

   —— —— ——

  (2) A reconciliation of the changes in the entity's aggregate liability for such product warranties or guarantees, showing the following:

   (i) The beginning balance of the aggregate liability?

    —— —— ——

   (ii) Aggregate reductions in that liability for payments made (in cash or in kind)?

    —— —— ——

   (iii) Aggregate changes in the liability for accruals related to such product warranties or guarantees issued during the period?

    —— —— ——

   (iv) The aggregate changes in the liability for accruals related to preexisting warranties (including adjustments related to changes in estimates)?

    —— —— ——

   (v) The ending balance of the aggregate liability?

    —— —— ——

Note: The disclosure requirements in item 32 below are prescribed by FSP FIN 45-3, *Application of FASB Interpretation No. 45 to Minimum Revenue Guarantees Granted to a Business or Its Owners*, which is effective for all minimum revenue guarantees in financial statements of interim periods ending after the beginning of the first fiscal quarter following November 10, 2005. Early application is permitted.

32. Have the disclosure requirements detailed in item 31 above been made for all minimum revenue guarantees, regardless of whether they were recognized and measured under FASB Interpretation No. 45, *Guarantor's Accounting and Disclosure Requirements for Guarantees, Including Indirect Guarantees of Indebtedness of Others*? (FSP FIN 45-3, par. 7)   ___ ___ ___

33. Have the following transitional disclosures been made on implementation of FAS-142: (FAS-142, pars. 60–61; FAS-128, par. 6)

    a. On completion of the first step of the transitional goodwill impairment test, the reportable segment(s) in which an impairment loss might have to be recognized and the period in which that potential loss will be measured? ___ ___ ___

    b. In the period of initial application and thereafter, until goodwill and all other intangible assets have been accounted for in accordance with FAS-142, *Goodwill and Other Intangible Assets*, in all periods presented, has the following information been displayed either on the face of the income statement or in the notes to the financial statements:

        (1) Income before extraordinary items and net income for all periods presented adjusted to exclude amortization expense (and any related tax effects) recognized in those periods related to goodwill, including adjustments for:

            (i) Changes in amortization periods for intangible assets that will continue to be amortized? ___ ___ ___

            (ii) Intangible assets that are no longer being amortized? ___ ___ ___

            (iii) Any deferred credit related to an excess over cost (amortized in accordance with APB-16, *Business Combinations*)? ___ ___ ___

<u>Yes</u> <u>No</u> <u>N/A</u>

      (iv) Equity method goodwill?   ___ ___ ___

   (2) A reconciliation of reported net income to the adjusted net income?   ___ ___ ___

   (3) Adjusted earnings per share amounts for all periods presented (required for public entities; optional for nonpublic entities)?   ___ ___ ___

34. For defined benefit pension plans and other defined benefit postretirement plans of nonpublic entities, have disclosures been made of the total amount of the employer's contributions paid, and expected to be paid, during the current fiscal year, if significantly different from amounts previously disclosed? (*Note:* Estimated contributions may be presented in the aggregate for contributions required by funding regulations or laws, discretionary contributions, and noncash contributions.) (*Note:* This disclosure requirement applies only to nonpublic entities; see items 36 through 39, 43 and 44 for disclosures that are applicable to only publicly held companies.) (FAS-132R, par. 10)   ___ ___ ___

Note: Except for certain nonpublic entities, the disclosure requirements in items 35b-e below are effective for the first interim or annual periods beginning after June 15, 2004. For nonpublic entities that sponsor one or more defined benefit postretirement health care plans, which provide prescription drug coverage but of which no plan has more than 100 participants, the disclosure requirements in items 35b-e below are effective for fiscal years beginning after December 15, 2004. Early adoption is encouraged but not required. Prior to applying the accounting guidance in FSP FAS 106-2, *Accounting and Disclosure Requirements Related to the Medicare Prescription Drug, Improvement and Modernization Act of 2003,* the disclosure requirements in 35a below should be provided.

35. For employers that sponsor single-employer defined benefit postretirement health care plans that provide prescription drug coverage, have the following been disclosed: (FSP FAS 106-2, pars. 20–22)   ___ ___ ___

   a. For periods in which the employer has not yet been able to determine the actuarial equivalency to Medicare Part D under the Medicare

<u>Yes</u> <u>No</u> <u>N/A</u>

Prescription Drug, Improvement and Modernization Act of 2003 (the Act):

(1) The existence of the Act? ___ ___ ___

(2) A statement clarifying that measures of the accumulated postretirement benefit obligation (APBO) or net periodic postretirement benefit cost do not reflect any amount associated with the federal subsidy provided by the Act because the employer is unable to conclude whether the benefits provided by the plan are actuarially equivalent to Medicare Part D under the Act? ___ ___ ___

b. For financial statements for the first period in which the employer includes the effects of the federal subsidy provided by the Act in measuring the APBO and net periodic postretirement benefit cost:

(1) The reduction in the APBO for the subsidy related to benefits attributed to past service? ___ ___ ___

(2) The effect of the subsidy on the measurement of net periodic postretirement benefit cost for the current period, including:

(i) Any amortization of the actuarial experience gain in item (1) above as a component of the net amortization called for by paragraph 59 of FAS-106, *Employers' Accounting for Postretirement Benefits Other Than Pensions*? ___ ___ ___

(ii) The reduction in current period service cost and interest cost on the APBO due to the subsidy? ___ ___ ___

c. An explanation of any significant change in the benefit obligation or plan assets not otherwise apparent in the above disclosures? ___ ___ ___

d. Gross benefit payments (paid and expected), including prescription drug benefits? ___ ___ ___

e. Gross amount of the subsidy receipts (received and expected)? ___ ___ ___

Yes No N/A

Items 36 through 39, 43 and 44 below are additional disclosures that are applicable only to publicly held companies   ___ ___ ___

36. For publicly traded companies that report summarized financial information to their security holders at interim dates (including reports on fourth quarters), have the following items, at a minimum, been reported: (APB-28, par. 30)

   a. Sales or gross revenues?   ___ ___ ___

   b. Provision for income taxes?   ___ ___ ___

   c. Extraordinary items (including related income tax effects)?   ___ ___ ___

   d. Cumulative effect of a change in accounting principles or practices?   ___ ___ ___

   e. Net income?   ___ ___ ___

   f. Comprehensive income?   ___ ___ ___

   g. Basic and diluted earnings per share data for each period presented?   ___ ___ ___

   h. Seasonal revenue, costs, or expenses?   ___ ___ ___

   i. Significant changes in estimates or provisions for income taxes?   ___ ___ ___

   j. Disposal of a segment of a business and extraordinary, unusual or infrequently occurring items?   ___ ___ ___

   k. Contingent items?   ___ ___ ___

   l. Changes in accounting principles or estimates?   ___ ___ ___

   m. Significant changes in financial position?   ___ ___ ___

   n. The following information about reportable operating segments (including provisions related to the restatement of segment information in previously issued financial statements):

      (1) Revenues from external customers?   ___ ___ ___

      (2) Intersegment revenues?   ___ ___ ___

      (3) A measure of segment profit or loss?   ___ ___ ___

      (4) Total assets for which there has been a material change from the amount disclosed in the last annual report?   ___ ___ ___

(5) A description of differences from the last annual report in the basis of segmentation or in the measurement of segment profit or loss? ___ ___ ___

(6) A reconciliation of the total of the reportable segments' measures of profit or loss to the enterprise's consolidated income before income taxes, extraordinary items, discontinued operations, and the cumulative effect of changes in accounting principles? (However, if, for example, an enterprise allocates items, such as income taxes and extraordinary items to segments, the enterprise may choose to reconcile the total of the segments' measures of profit or loss to consolidated income after those items. Significant reconciling items shall be separately identified and described in that reconciliation.) ___ ___ ___

o. The effects of significant events on the interim financial results? (*Note*: Entities are *encouraged*, but not required, to disclose this information.) ___ ___ ___

37. If condensed interim balance sheet information or cash flow data is not presented, have significant changes since the last reporting period with respect to liquid assets, net working capital, long-term liabilities, or stockholder's equity been disclosed? (APB-28, par. 33) ___ ___ ___

38. Are the following disclosures made in the interim financial information if a material business combination is completed during the interim period: (FAS-141, par. 58)

a. The name and a brief description of the acquired entity? ___ ___ ___

b. The percentage of voting equity interests acquired? ___ ___ ___

c. The primary reasons for the acquisition, including a description of the factors that contributed to a purchase price, that result in recognition of goodwill? ___ ___ ___

d. The period for which the results of operations of the acquired entity are included in the combined entity's income statement? ___ ___ ___

<u>Yes</u>   <u>No</u>   <u>N/A</u>

e. The cost of the acquired entity and, if applicable, the number of shares of equity interests (e.g., common shares) issued or issuable, the value assigned to those interests, and the basis for determining that value?   ___ ___ ___

f. Supplemental pro forma information that discloses the results of operations for the current interim period and the current year up to the date of the most recent interim balance sheet presented (and for the corresponding periods in the preceding year) as though the business combination had been completed as of the beginning of the period being reported on? (*Note*: That pro forma information should disclose, at a minimum: revenue; income before extraordinary items and the cumulative effect of accounting changes; net income; and earnings per share.)   ___ ___ ___

g. The nature and amount of any material, non-recurring items included in the reported pro forma results of operations?   ___ ___ ___

39. If an entity changes the structure of its internal organization in a manner that causes the composition of its reportable segments to change, has the corresponding information for earlier periods, including interim periods, been restated, unless it is impracticable to do so? (*Note*: The entity should also disclose whether it has restated the segment information for earlier periods. If the segment information for earlier interim periods is not restated to reflect the change, the entity should disclose in the year in which the change occurs segment information for the current period under both the old basis and the new basis of segmentation, unless it is impracticable to do so.) (FAS-131, pars. 34–35)   ___ ___ ___

Note: The disclosure requirement in item 41 below is prescribed by EITF 06-3, *How Taxes Collected from Customers and Remitted to Governmental Authorities Should Be Presented in the Income Statement (That Is, Gross Versus Net Presentation)*. EITF 06-3 is effective in interim and annual periods beginning after December 15, 2006.

Yes *No* *N/A*

40. For taxes that fall within the scope of EITF 06-3 (e.g., sales tax), if those taxes are reported on a gross basis and are significant, have the amounts of those taxes included in interim financial statements been disclosed for each period for which an income statement is presented? (*Note*: This disclosure may be provided on an aggregate basis.) (EITF 06-3)   ___ ___ ___

Note: The disclosure requirements in items 41 and 42 below are prescribed by FAS-157, *Fair Value Measurements*. FAS-157 is effective for fiscal years beginning after November 15, 2007 and interim periods within those fiscal years. Early adoption is permitted as long as financial statements for any period (interim or annual) of the fiscal year have not yet been issued. The disclosure requirements of FAS-157 need not be applied for financial statements for periods presented prior to its initial application.

The quantitative disclosures required in items 41 and 42 below should be presented in a tabular format (FAS-157, par. 34). In addition, the entity is encouraged, but not required, to combine the fair value information disclosed in accordance with items 41 and 42 with the fair value information disclosed in accordance with other items in this checklist. The entity is also encouraged, but not required, to disclose information about other similar measurements (e.g., inventories measured at market value under ARB-43), if practicable. (FAS-157, par. 35)   ___ ___ ___

41. For assets and liabilities that are measured at fair value on a recurring basis subsequent to initial recognition, have the following disclosures been made for each major category of assets and liabilities for each interim period: (FAS-157, par. 32)

a. The fair value measurements at the reporting date?   ___ ___ ___

b. The level within the fair value hierarchy in which the fair value measurements in their entirety fall, segregating fair value measurements using quoted prices in active markets for identical assets or liabilities (Level 1),

Yes *No* *N/A*

significant other observable inputs (Level 2), and significant unobservable inputs (Level 3)? ___ ___ ___

c. For fair value measurements using significant unobservable inputs (Level 3), a reconciliation of the beginning and ending balances, separately presenting changes during the period attributable to the following:

   (1) Total gains or losses for the period (realized and unrealized), segregating those gains or losses included in earnings (or changes in net assets), and a description of where those gains or losses included in earnings (or changes in net assets) are reported in the statement of income (or activities)? ___ ___ ___

   (2) Purchases, sales, issuances, and settlements (net)? ___ ___ ___

   (3) Transfers in or out of Level 3 (e.g., transfers due to changes in the observability of significant inputs)? ___ ___ ___

(*Note*: This reconciliation disclosure may be presented net for derivative assets and liabilities.)

d. The amount of the total gains or losses for the period in 1c above included in earnings (or changes in net assets) that are attributable to the change in unrealized gains or losses relating to those assets and liabilities still held at the reporting date and a description of where those unrealized gains or losses are reported in the statement of income (or activities)? ___ ___ ___

e. In the first interim period in the fiscal year in which FAS-157 is initially applied, the valuation technique(s) used to measure fair value and a discussion of changes in valuation techniques, if any, during the period? ___ ___ ___

42. For assets and liabilities that are measured at fair value on a nonrecurring basis in periods subsequent to initial recognition, have the following disclosures been made for each major category of assets and liabilities for each interim period: (FAS-157, par. 33)

<u>*Yes*</u>   <u>*No*</u>   <u>*N/A*</u>

a. The fair value measurements recorded during the period and the reasons for the measurements?   —— —— ——

b. The level within the fair value hierarchy in
which the fair value measurements in their
entirety fall, segregating fair value measurements using quoted prices in active markets
for identical assets or liabilities (Level 1), significant other observable inputs (Level 2), and
significant unobservable inputs (Level 3)?   —— —— ——

c. For fair value measurements using significant
unobservable inputs (Level 3), a description
of the inputs and the information used to develop them?   —— —— ——

d. In the first interim period in the fiscal year in
which FAS-157 is initially applied, the valuation technique(s) used to measure fair value
and a discussion of changes, if any, in the valuation technique(s) used to measure similar
assets and liabilities in prior periods?   —— —— ——

Note: In September 2006, the FASB issued Statement of Financial Accounting Standards No. 158,
*Employers' Accounting for Defined Benefit Pension
and Other Postretirement Plans*. This standard
amends FAS-87, *Employers' Accounting for Pensions*; FAS-88, *Employers' Accounting for Settlements and Curtailments of Defined Benefit Pension
Plans and for Termination Benefits*; FAS-106, *Employers' Accounting for Postretirement Benefits Other
Than Pensions*; and FAS-132 (Revised 2003), *Employers' Disclosures about Pensions and Other
Postretirement Benefits*.

For an employer with publicly traded equity
securities, FAS-158 is effective for financial statements with fiscal years ending after December
15, 2006.

See item 43 below for the disclosure requirements about defined benefit pension plans and
other defined benefit postretirement plans prior
to the adoption of FAS-158 and item 44 below
for the disclosure requirements after the adoption of FAS-158.

43. If the employer is a publicly traded entity, are
the following disclosures made about defined

benefit pension plans and other defined benefit postretirement plans: (FAS-132R, par. 9; APB-28, par. 30k)

a. For each income statement presented, the amount of net periodic benefit cost recognized, showing separately the following: (1) service cost component, (2) interest cost component, (3) expected return on plan assets for the period, (4) amortization of the unrecognized transition obligation or asset, (5) amount of recognized gains or losses, (6) amount of prior service cost recognized, and (7) amount of gain or loss recognized due to a settlement or curtailment? ___ ___ ___

b. The total amount of the employer's contributions paid, and expected to be paid, during the current fiscal year, if significantly different from amounts previously disclosed? (*Note:* Estimated contributions may be presented in the aggregate for contributions required by funding regulations or laws, discretionary contributions, and noncash contributions.) ___ ___ ___

44. If the employer is a publicly traded entity, are the following disclosures made about defined benefit pension plans and other defined benefit postretirement plans: (APB-28, par. 30k; FAS-132R, par. 9; FAS-158, pars. E1s and F3)

a. For each income statement presented, the amount of net periodic benefit cost recognized, showing separately the following: (1) service cost component, (2) interest cost component, (3) expected return on plan assets for the period, (4) gain or loss component, (5) prior service cost or credit component, (6) transition asset or obligation component, and (7) gain or loss recognized due to a settlement or curtailment? ___ ___ ___

b. The total amount of the employer's contributions paid, and expected to be paid, during the current fiscal year, if significantly different from amounts previously disclosed? (Estimated contributions may be presented in the aggregate for contributions required by funding regulations or laws, discretionary contributions, and noncash contributions.) ___ ___ ___

Note: The disclosure requirements in item 45 below are prescribed by EITF 06-7, *Issuer's Accounting for a Previously Bifurcated Conversion Option in a Convertible Debt Instrument When the Conversion Option No Longer Meets the Bifurcation Criteria in FASB Statement No. 133, "Accounting for Derivative Instruments and Hedging Activities."* EITF 06-7 is effective for all previously bifurcated conversion options in convertible debt instruments that no longer meet the bifurcation criteria in FAS-133, *Accounting for Derivative Instruments and Hedging Activities*, in annual or interim periods beginning after December 15, 2006, irrespective of when the debt instrument was entered into. Early adoption is permitted only if financial statements for the period have not yet been issued. Retrospective application in accordance with FAS-154, *Accounting Changes and Error Corrections*, is permitted.

45. For previously bifurcated conversion options in convertible debt instruments that no longer meet the bifurcation criteria in FAS-133, have the following disclosures been made: (EITF 06-7)

    a. A description of the principal changes causing the embedded conversion option to no longer require bifurcation under FAS-133? ___ ___ ___

    b. The amount of the liability for the conversion option reclassified to stockholders' equity? ___ ___ ___

Note: The disclosure requirements in item 46 below are prescribed by EITF 06-9, *Reporting a Change in (or the Elimination of) a Previously Existing Difference between the Fiscal Year-End of a Parent Company and That of a Consolidated Entity or between the Reporting Period of an Investor and That of an Equity Method Investee.* EITF 06-9 is effective for changes in, or eliminations of, a previously existing difference between an entity's reporting period and that of a consolidated entity or an equity method investee that occur in interim or annual reporting periods beginning after November 29, 2006. Earlier application is only permitted if an entity has not yet issued its financial statements for the period.

46. If a previously existing difference between the entity's reporting period and that of a consolidated entity or an equity method investee is changed or eliminated, have the disclosures in items 22 through 25 of this section been made? (EITF 06-9)

    ____ ____ ____

Note: The disclosure requirements in items 47 and 48 below are prescribed by FSP EITF 00-19-2, *Accounting for Registration Payment Arrangements*. FSP EITF 00-19-2 is effective immediately for registration payment arrangements and the financial instruments subject to those arrangements that are entered into or modified subsequent to December 21, 2006. For registration payment arrangements and financial instruments subject to those arrangements that were entered into prior to December 21, 2006, the guidance in FSP EITF 00-19-2 is effective for financial statements issued for fiscal years beginning after December 15, 2006, and interim periods within those fiscal years. Early adoption is permitted provided that financial statements for any period (interim or annual) of the fiscal year have not yet been issued.

47. Has the following information been disclosed about each registration payment arrangement or each group of similar arrangements, even if the likelihood of the issuer having to make any payments under the arrangement is remote: (FSP EITF 00-19-2, pars. 12 and 16)

  a. The nature of the registration payment arrangement?

    ____ ____ ____

  b. The approximate term of the arrangement?

    ____ ____ ____

  c. The financial instruments subject to the arrangement?

    ____ ____ ____

  d. The events or circumstances that would require the issuer to transfer consideration under the arrangement?

    ____ ____ ____

  e. Any settlement alternatives contained in the terms of the registration payment arrangement, including the party that controls the settlement alternatives?

    ____ ____ ____

  f. The maximum potential amount of consideration, undiscounted, that the issuer could be required to transfer under the registration

Yes No N/A

payment arrangement, including the maximum number of shares that may be required to be issued? ___ ___ ___

g. The fact that the terms of the arrangement provide for no limitation to the maximum potential consideration (including shares) to be transferred, if the terms of the arrangement include such provision? ___ ___ ___

h. The current carrying amount of the liability representing the issuer's obligations under the registration payment arrangement and the income statement classification of any gains or losses resulting from changes in the carrying amount of that liability? ___ ___ ___

48. Has the following information been disclosed related to the adoption of FSP EITF 00-19-2? (FSP EITF 00-19-2, par. 21)

a. The portion of the cumulative-effect adjustment resulting from the recognition and measurement of a contingent liability under FAS-5? ___ ___ ___

b. The portion of the cumulative-effect adjustment resulting from the reclassification of a financial instrument subject to the registration payment arrangement to equity, or the recombination of an embedded derivative? ___ ___ ___

LEASES—LESSEES

1. Is there a general description of leasing arrangements including, but not limited to, the following: (FAS-13, par. 16)

a. The basis on which contingent rental payments are determined? ___ ___ ___

b. The existence and terms of renewal or purchase options and escalation clauses? ___ ___ ___

c. Restrictions imposed by lease agreements such as those concerning dividends, additional debt, and further leasing? ___ ___ ___

Yes *No* *N/A*

2. Has the nature and extent of leasing transactions with related parties been disclosed? (FAS-13, par. 29) _____ _____ _____

3. Are the following disclosures made for capital leases: (FAS-13, pars. 13 and 16)

    a. The gross amount of assets recorded under capital leases as of the date of each balance sheet presented by major classes according to nature or function? (This information may be combined with the comparable information for owned assets.) _____ _____ _____

    b. Capitalized lease obligations separately identified in the balance sheet and appropriately classified as current and noncurrent amounts? _____ _____ _____

    c. Future minimum lease payments as of the date of the latest balance sheet presented, in the aggregate and for each of the five succeeding fiscal years, with separate deductions from the total for the amount representing executory costs (including any profit thereon), that are included in the minimum lease payments, and for the amount of the imputed interest necessary to reduce the net minimum lease payments to present value? _____ _____ _____

    d. The total of minimum sublease rentals to be received in the future under noncancelable subleases as of the date of the latest balance sheet presented? _____ _____ _____

    e. Total contingent rentals actually incurred for each period for which an income statement is presented? _____ _____ _____

    f. Amortization of capitalized leases separately reported on the income statement or presented in a note to the financial statements? (The amortization may be combined with depreciation expense, but that fact must be disclosed.) _____ _____ _____

4. Are the following disclosures made for operating leases having initial or remaining noncancelable lease terms in excess of one year: (FAS-13, par. 16)

Yes *No* *N/A*

    a. Future minimum rental payments required as of the date of the latest balance sheet presented, in the aggregate and for each of the five succeeding fiscal years?   ___ ___ ___

    b. The total amount of minimum rentals to be received in the future under noncancelable subleases as of the date of the latest balance sheet presented?   ___ ___ ___

5. Are the following disclosures made for all operating leases, except for rental payments under leases with terms of a month or less that were not renewed: (FAS-13, par. 16)

    a. Rental expense for each period for which an income statement is presented?   ___ ___ ___

    b. Presentation of separate amounts for minimum rentals, contingent rentals, and sublease rental income?   ___ ___ ___

6. For seller-lessee transactions, is there a description of the terms of the sale-leaseback transaction including future commitments, obligations, provisions, or circumstances that require or result in the seller-lessee's continuing involvement? (FAS-98, par. 17)   ___ ___ ___

7. If a sale-leaseback transaction is accounted for by the deposit method or as a real estate financing arrangement, are the following disclosures made: (FAS-98, par. 18)

    a. The obligation for future minimum lease payments as of the date of the latest balance sheet presented in the aggregate and for each of the five succeeding fiscal years?   ___ ___ ___

    b. The total of minimum sublease rentals, if any, to be received in the future under noncancelable subleases in the aggregate and for each of the five succeeding fiscal years?   ___ ___ ___

LEASES—LESSORS

1. Is there a general description of the lessor's leasing arrangements? (FAS-13, par. 23)   ___ ___ ___

2. Has the nature and extent of leasing transactions

Yes *No* *N/A*

with related parties been disclosed? (FAS-13, par. 29) ___ ___ ___

3. For sales-type and direct-financing leases, are the following components of the net investment in sales-type and direct financing leases disclosed as of the date of each balance sheet presented: (FAS-13, par. 23; FAS-91, par. 25)

a. Future minimum lease payments to be received with separate deductions for: (1) amounts representing executory costs, including any profit thereon, included in the minimum lease payments and (2) the accumulated allowance for uncollectible minimum lease payments receivable? ___ ___ ___

b. The unguaranteed residual values accruing to the benefit of the lessor? ___ ___ ___

c. Initial direct costs for direct financing leases only? ___ ___ ___

d. Unearned income? ___ ___ ___

4. Are the following disclosures made for sales-type and direct financing leases: (FAS-13, par. 23)

a. Future minimum lease payments to be received for each of the five succeeding fiscal years as of the date of the latest balance sheet presented? ___ ___ ___

b. Total contingent rentals included in income for each period for which an income statement is presented? ___ ___ ___

5. Are the following disclosures made for operating leases: (FAS-13, par. 23)

a. The cost and carrying amount, if different, of property on lease or held for leasing, by major classes of property according to nature or function, and the amount of accumulated depreciation in total as of the date of the latest balance sheet presented? ___ ___ ___

b. Minimum future rentals on noncancelable leases as of the date of the latest balance sheet presented, in the aggregate and for each of the five succeeding fiscal years? ___ ___ ___

c. Total contingent rentals included in income for

each period for which an income statement is
presented? ___ ___ ___

6. Are the following disclosures made for leveraged
   leases: (FAS-13, par. 47)

   a. The amount of related deferred taxes pre-
      sented separately from the remainder of the
      net income investment? ___ ___ ___

   b. Separate presentation (in the income state-
      ment or in related notes) of pretax income from
      the leveraged lease, the tax effect of pretax
      income, and the amount of investment tax
      credit recognized as income during the pe-
      riod? ___ ___ ___

7. If leveraged leasing is a significant part of the
   lessor's business activities in terms of revenue,
   net income, or assets, are the following components of the net investment in leveraged leases
   disclosed in notes to the financial statements:
   (FAS-13, par. 47)

   a. Rentals receivable, net of that portion of the
      rental applicable to principal and interest on
      the nonrecourse debt? ___ ___ ___

   b. A receivable for the amount of the investment
      tax credit to be realized on the transaction? ___ ___ ___

   c. The estimated residual value of the leased as-
      sets? (The estimated residual value should not
      exceed the amount estimated at the inception
      of the lease, except as provided in FAS-23.) ___ ___ ___

   d. Unearned and deferred income consisting of:
      (1) the estimated pretax lease income (or loss),
      after deducting initial direct costs, remaining
      to be allocated to income over the lease term
      and (2) the investment tax credit remaining to
      be allocated to income over the lease term? ___ ___ ___

8. For lessors that recognize contingent rental income, have disclosures been made of the following: (EITF 98-9, par. 13)

   a. The accounting policy for recognizing contin-
      gent rental income? ___ ___ ___

   b. If contingent rental income is recognized (ac-
      crued) prior to achieving the specified target
      that triggers the contingent rents, the impact

Yes *No* *N/A*

on net income of accruing such rents prior to achieving the specified target?

Note: The disclosure requirements in item 9 below are prescribed by FSP FAS 13-2, *Accounting for a Change or Projected Change in the Timing of Cash Flows Relating to Income Taxes Generated by a Leveraged Lease Transaction*. FSP FAS 13-2 is effective for fiscal years beginning after December 15, 2006, with early adoption permitted provided that: (a) the consensus is applied as of the beginning of the fiscal year and (b) financial statements for any period (interim or annual) of the fiscal year have not yet been issued.

9. Has the lessor disclosed the following in the fiscal year of adoption of FSP FAS 13-2 as of the most recent statement of financial position or income statement presented: (FSP FAS 13-2, par. 14)

   a. The nature of the change in accounting principle?

   b. The cumulative effect of the change on retained earnings in the statement of financial position as of the date of adoption?

LEASES—TAX LEASES

1. If the entity is involved in the sale or purchase of tax benefits through tax leases, have disclosures been made of the following: (FTB 82-1, par. 4)

   a. The method of recognizing revenue?

   b. The method of allocating the income tax benefits and asset costs to current and future periods?

2. If unusual or infrequent, have disclosures been made of the nature and financial effects of sales or purchases of tax benefits through tax leases on the face of the income statement or in a note to the financial statements? (FTB 82-1, par. 6)

3. Have significant contingencies existing with respect to sales or purchases of tax benefits through tax leases been disclosed? (FTB 82-1, par. 7)

<u>Yes</u>   <u>No</u>   <u>N/A</u>

4. If comparative financial statements are presented, have disclosures been made of any changes in the method of accounting for sales or purchases of tax benefits through tax leases that significantly affect comparability? (FTB 82-1, par. 7)   ___ ___ ___

5. If a significant variation in the customary relationship between income tax expense and pretax accounting income occurs as a result of sales or purchases of tax benefits through tax leases, has the estimated amount and nature of the variation been disclosed? (FAS-109, par. 288)   ___ ___ ___

LENDING ACTIVITIES

1. If the company anticipates prepayments of loan balances, have disclosures been made regarding the policy and the significant assumptions underlying the prepayment estimates? (FAS-91, par. 19)   ___ ___ ___

LIFE SETTLEMENT CONTRACTS

Note: The disclosure requirements in items 1 through 4 below are prescribed by FSP FTB 85-4-1, *Accounting for Life Settlement Contracts by Third-Party Investors*. The disclosure requirements in FSP FTB 85-4-1 should be applied as of the most recent balance sheet or income statement presented in fiscal years beginning after June 15, 2006. Early application is permitted only if: (a) it occurs at the beginning of an entity's fiscal year and (b) the entity has not yet issued its first quarter financial statements for that fiscal year. (FSP FTB 85-4-1, par. 22)

1. If the entity is a third-party investor in life settlement contracts, has it disclosed the following in addition to other disclosures required by GAAP: (FSP FTB 85-4-1, pars. 12, 13, and 17)

    a. The accounting policy for the life settlement contracts?   ___ ___ ___

Yes No N/A

b. The classification of related cash receipts and cash disbursements in the statement of cash flows? ___ ___ ___

c. Separately for those life settlement contracts accounted for under the investment method and those accounted for under the fair value method (as described in FSP FTB 85-4-1), the following based on remaining life expectancy for each of the first five succeeding years from the date of the balance sheet and thereafter, as well as in the aggregate:

   (1) The number of life settlement contracts? ___ ___ ___

   (2) The carrying value of the life settlement contracts? ___ ___ ___

   (3) The face value (death benefits) of the life insurance policies underlying the contracts? ___ ___ ___

2. If the entity is a third-party investor in life settlement contracts and elects to account for such contracts under the fair value method in accordance with FSP FTB 85-4-1, have the following been disclosed in addition to other disclosures required by GAAP: (FSP FTB 85-4-1, pars. 9, 10, 12, 16, 18, and 19)

a. If the entity presents on the balance sheet the aggregate of the carrying amounts of investments in life settlement contracts accounted for under the fair value method and investment method, the carrying amount of those investments accounted for under the fair value method that is included in the aggregate amount, parenthetically on the face of the balance sheet? ___ ___ ___

b. If the entity presents the aggregate investment income in life settlement contracts on the income statement, the investment income from those investments accounted for under the fair value method that is included in the aggregate amount, parenthetically on the face of the income statement? ___ ___ ___

c. The methods and significant assumptions (including any mortality assumptions) used to

      estimate the fair value of investments in life
settlement contracts?   ___ ___ ___

  d. The reasons for changes in the entity's expectation of the timing of the realization of the investments in life settlement contracts, including significant changes to the amounts disclosed in accordance with item 1c above?   ___ ___ ___

  e. For each reporting period presented in the income statement:

    (1) The gains or losses recognized during the period on investments sold during the period?   ___ ___ ___

    (2) The unrealized gains or losses recognized during the period on investments that are still held at the balance-sheet date?   ___ ___ ___

3. If the entity is a third-party investor in life settlement contracts and elects to account for such contracts under the investment method in accordance with FSP FTB 85-4-1, have the following been disclosed in addition to other disclosures required by GAAP: (FSP FTB 85-4-1, pars. 12, 14, and 15)

  a. The life insurance premiums anticipated to be paid for each of the five succeeding fiscal years to keep the life settlement contracts in force as of the date of the most recent balance sheet presented?   ___ ___ ___

  b. If the entity becomes aware of new or updated information that causes it to change its expectations on the timing of the realization of proceeds from the investments in life settlement contracts:

    (1) The nature of the information?   ___ ___ ___

    (2) The effect of the information on the timing of the realization of proceeds from the life settlement contracts?   ___ ___ ___

    (3) Any significant changes to the amounts disclosed in accordance with item 1c above that result from this information?   ___ ___ ___

4. If the entity is a third-party investor in life settlement contracts and records a change in accounting principle in connection with adopting FSP

FTB 85-4-1, have the following been disclosed in the fiscal period of adoption: (FSP FTB 85-4-1, par. 23)

a. The nature of the change in accounting principle?   ___ ___ ___

b. The reason for the change in accounting principle?   ___ ___ ___

c. The cumulative effect of the change on retained earnings in the balance sheet as of the date of adoption?   ___ ___ ___

LIFE INSURANCE

Note: The disclosure requirements in items 1 through 3 below are prescribed by EITF 06-5, *Accounting for Purchases of Life Insurance —Determining the Amount That Could Be Realized in Accordance with FASB Technical Bulletin No. 85-4*. EITF 06-5 is effective for fiscal years beginning after December 15, 2006, with early adoption permitted provided that: (a) the consensus is applied as of the beginning of the fiscal year and (b) financial statements for any period (interim or annual) of the fiscal year have not yet been issued.

1. Have the nature of contractual restrictions on a policyholder's ability to surrender a life insurance policy been disclosed? (EITF 06-5, par. 11)   ___ ___ ___

2. If the entity applied the consensus in EITF 06-5 as a change in accounting principle through a cumulative-effect adjustment to retained earnings or other components of equity or net assets in the statement of financial position as of the beginning of the year of adoption, has the cumulative effect of the change been disclosed in the statement of financial position? (EITF 06-5, par. 13)   ___ ___ ___

3. If the entity applied the consensus in EITF 06-5 as a change in accounting principle through retrospective application to all prior periods, have the following been disclosed: (EITF 06-5, par. 15)

a. A description of the prior-period information that has been retrospectively adjusted?   ___ ___ ___

b. The effect of the change on income from continuing operations, net income (or other appropriate captions of changes in the applicable net assets or performance indicator), any other affected financial statement caption, and any affected per share amounts for any prior periods retrospectively adjusted? ___ ___ ___

c. The cumulative effect of the change on retained earnings or other components of equity or net assets in the statement of financial position as of the beginning of the earliest period presented? ___ ___ ___

LIMITED LIABILITY COMPANIES OR PARTNERSHIPS (LLCS OR LLPS)

1. In addition to all the disclosures that typically apply to any other business entity, are the following additional disclosures made in the financial statements of an LLC or an LLP: (PB-14, pars. 15–16)

   a. A description of any limitation of the LLC or LLP members' liability? ___ ___ ___

   b. The different classes of members' interests and the respective rights, preferences, and privileges of each class? ___ ___ ___

   c. The amount of each class of members' equity either in the equity section of the balance sheet or in the notes to the financial statements? ___ ___ ___

   d. The date the LLC or LLP will cease to exist, if the entity has a finite life? ___ ___ ___

   e. In the year of formation for LLCs and LLPs formed by combining entities under common control or by conversion from another type of entity, the fact that the assets and liabilities were previously held by a predecessor entity or entities? ___ ___ ___

LONG-TERM CONTRACTS

1. Have the following disclosures been made for long-term contracts:

Yes *No* *N/A*

a. The method used to account for long-term contracts (i.e., the percentage-of-completion method or the completed-contract method)? (ARB-45, par. 15)   ___ ___ ___

b. Departure from the basic revenue recognition policy for a single contract or group of contracts? (SOP 81-1, pars. 25 and 31)   ___ ___ ___

c. The policies relating to combining and segmenting contracts, if applicable? (SOP 81-1, par. 21)   ___ ___ ___

d. When the percentage-of-completion method of accounting is used, the method of measuring the extent of progress toward completion (e.g., cost-to-cost, direct labor)? (SOP 81-1, pars. 21 and 45)   ___ ___ ___

e. If the completed-contract method is used, the criteria used to determine substantial completion? (SOP 81-1, par. 52)   ___ ___ ___

f. The amount of revenue from claims recognized in excess of the agreed contract price? (SOP 81-1, pars. 65–67)   ___ ___ ___

g. If the contractor recognizes revenues from claims only when the amounts have been received or awarded, the amounts of such revenues recorded during the period? (SOP 81-1, par. 66)   ___ ___ ___

h. The effect of significant revisions in contract estimates? (SOP 81-1, par. 84)   ___ ___ ___

i. The amount of advances, if any, offset against cost-type contract receivables? (ARB-43, Ch. 11A, par. 22)   ___ ___ ___

j. Provisions for losses on contracts separately shown as liabilities on the face of the balance sheet, if material? (SOP 81-1, par. 89)   ___ ___ ___

k. Provisions for losses on contracts that are material, unusual, or infrequent shown as a separate component of construction costs on the face of the income statement? (SOP 81-1, par. 88)   ___ ___ ___

l. The nature and amount of any large or unusual contract commitments? (FAS-5, par. 18)   ___ ___ ___

m. Unbilled costs and fees under cost-type contracts shown separately from billed accounts receivable? (ARB-43, Ch. 11A, par. 21) ___ ___ ___

NONMONETARY TRANSACTIONS

1. Are the following disclosures made for nonmonetary transactions: (APB-29, par. 28)

    a. The nature of the transactions? ___ ___ ___

    b. The basis of accounting for the assets transferred? ___ ___ ___

    c. Gains or losses, if any, recognized on transfers? ___ ___ ___

2. Are gains and losses resulting from involuntary conversions of nonmonetary assets to monetary assets reported as either an extraordinary item or an unusual or infrequent item, as appropriate? (FIN-30, par. 4) ___ ___ ___

3. Is disclosure made in each period's financial statements of the amount of gross operating revenue recognized as a result of nonmonetary transactions for which the entity provides goods or services in exchange for equity instruments issued by the customer? (EITF 00-8, par. 10) ___ ___ ___

4. Has the amount of revenue and costs (or gains/losses) associated with inventory exchanges recognized at fair value been disclosed? (Note: For an affected entity, this disclosure should be applied to new arrangements that it enters into in reporting periods beginning after March 15, 2006.) (EITF 04-13, par. 5) ___ ___ ___

PENSION AND POSTRETIREMENT BENEFIT PLANS

Note: In December 2003, the FASB issued Statement of Financial Accounting Standards No. 132 (Revised 2003) entitled *Employers' Disclosures about Pensions and Other Postretirement Benefits*. This standard replaces

<u>*Yes*</u> <u>*No*</u> <u>*N/A*</u>

FAS-132 of the same title, which was previously issued in February 1998. The revised FAS-132 was issued in response to concerns expressed by financial statement users about their need for more transparency of pension information. The revised standards increased the existing GAAP disclosures for defined benefit pension plans and other defined benefit postretirement plans.

The revised FAS-132 (FAS-132R) is effective for financial statements with fiscal years ending after December 15, 2003 and for interim periods beginning after December 15, 2003, except as follows:

- Companies with foreign plans may defer certain disclosures associated with those plans until fiscal years ending after June 15, 2004.

- For nonpublic entities, reduced disclosures are permitted (like the original FAS-132) and some of the new additional disclosures may be deferred until fiscal years ending after June 15, 2004.

Note: In September 2006, the FASB issued Statement of Financial Accounting Standards No. 158 entitled *Employers' Accounting for Defined Benefit Pension and Other Postretirement Plans.* This standard amends FAS-87, *Employers' Accounting for Pensions;* FAS-88, *Employers' Accounting for Settlements and Curtailments of Defined Benefit Pension Plans and for Termination Benefits;* FAS-106, *Employers' Accounting for Postretirement Benefits Other Than Pensions;* and FAS-132 (Revised 2003), *Employers' Disclosures about Pensions and Other Postretirement Benefits.*

For an employer with publicly traded equity securities, the disclosure and recognition provisions of FAS-158 are effective for financial statements with fiscal years ending after December 15, 2006. For an employer without publicly traded equity securities, the disclosure and recognition provisions of FAS-158 are effective for financial statements with fiscal years ending after June 15, 2007. Certain additional disclosures are required for employers without publicly traded equity securities until they apply the recognition provisions of FAS-158 (see item 19 under "Pension and Postretirement Defined Benefit Plans— Reduced Disclosure Requirements for Nonpublic

Yes *No* *N/A*

Entities (Annual Periods)—Prior to the Adoption of FAS-158"). For all employers, the measurement provisions of FAS-158 are effective for financial statements with fiscal years ending after December 15, 2008. Until that time, certain measurement-related disclosures continue to be required (see item 10 under "Pension and Postretirement Defined Benefit Plans—Reduced Disclosure Requirements for Nonpublic Entities (Annual Periods)—Prior to the Adoption of FAS-158" and item 12 under "Pension and Postretirement Defined Benefit Plans—Public Entities and Nonpublic Entities That Elect to Voluntarily Provide Additional Disclosures (Annual Periods)—Prior to the Adoption of FAS-158").

For the disclosure requirements applicable prior to the adoption of FAS-158, see the sections below entitled "Pension and Postretirement Defined Benefit Plans—Reduced Disclosure Requirements for Nonpublic Entities (Annual Periods)—Prior to the Adoption of FAS-158" and "Pension and Postretirement Defined Benefit Plans—Public Entities and Nonpublic Entities That Elect to Voluntarily Provide Additional Disclosures (Annual Periods)—Prior to the Adoption of FAS-158." For the disclosure requirements applicable after the adoption of FAS-158, see the sections below entitled "Pension and Postretirement Defined Benefit Plans—Reduced Disclosure Requirements for Nonpublic Entities (Annual Periods)—After the adoption of FAS-158" and "Pension and Postretirement Defined Benefit Plans—Public Entities and Nonpublic Entities That Elect to Voluntarily Provide Additional Disclosures (Annual Periods)—After the Adoption of FAS-158."

Pension and Postretirement Defined Benefit Plans—Reduced Disclosure Requirements for Nonpublic Entities (Annual Periods)— Prior to the Adoption of FAS-158

1. Has the following information about the plan been disclosed, for each balance sheet presented: (FAS-132R, par. 8a)

<u>Yes</u> <u>No</u> <u>N/A</u>

a. The benefit obligation? (This is the *projected benefit obligation* for pension plans and the *accumulated postretirement benefit obligation* for postretirement plans.)   ___ ___ ___

b. The fair value of plan assets?   ___ ___ ___

c. The funded status of the plan?   ___ ___ ___

2. Has the following information about the plan been disclosed, for each income statement presented: (FAS-132R, par. 8b)

   a. Employer contributions?   ___ ___ ___

   b. Participant contributions?   ___ ___ ___

   c. Benefits paid?   ___ ___ ___

3. Has the following information about plan assets been disclosed: (FAS-132R, par. 8c) (*Note:* This disclosure item is effective for fiscal year ending after June 15, 2004)

   a. For each balance sheet presented, the percentage of the fair value of total plan assets held in each major category of plan assets, including at a minimum the following categories: (1) equity securities, (2) debt securities, (3) real estate, and (4) all other assets? (Also, disclosure of additional asset categories, and additional information about specific assets within a category, is encouraged if that information is considered useful.)   ___ ___ ___

   b. As of the latest balance sheet presented, a narrative description of investment policies and strategies, including: (1) target allocation percentages, or range of percentages, for each major category of plan assets presented on a weighted-average basis, and (2) other factors that are pertinent to an understanding of the policies or strategies such as investment goals, risk management practices, permitted and prohibited investments, including the use of derivatives, diversification, and the relationship between plan assets and benefit obligations?   ___ ___ ___

   c. As of the latest balance sheet presented, a narrative description of the basis used to determine the overall expected long-term rate-of-

Yes No N/A

return-on-assets assumption, such as: (1) the general approach used, (2) the extent to which the overall rate-of-return-on-assets assumption was based on historical returns, (3) the extent to which adjustments were made to those historical returns in order to reflect expectations of future returns, and (4) how those adjustments were determined?   ___ ___ ___

4. For defined benefit pension plans, has the accumulated benefit obligation been disclosed for each balance sheet presented? (FAS-132R, par. 8d) (*Note*: This disclosure item is effective for fiscal years ending after June 15, 2004.)   ___ ___ ___

5. As of the latest balance sheet presented, has disclosure been made of the benefits expected to be paid in each of the next five fiscal years and in the aggregate for the five fiscal years thereafter? (FAS-132R, par. 8e) (*Note*: This disclosure item is effective for fiscal years ending after June 15, 2004.)   ___ ___ ___

6. Has disclosure been made of the company's best estimate of contributions expected to be paid during the next fiscal year beginning after the date of the latest balance sheet presented? (FAS-132R, par. 8f) (Estimated contributions may be presented in the aggregate for contributions required by funding regulations or laws, discretionary contributions, and noncash contributions.) (*Note*: This disclosure item is effective for fiscal years ending after June 15, 2004.)   ___ ___ ___

7. Has disclosure been made of the amounts recognized in the balance sheet, including the following for each balance sheet presented: (FAS-132R, par. 8g)

   a. The net pension or net postretirement benefit prepaid assets or accrued liabilities?   ___ ___ ___

   b. The amount of any intangible asset recognized? (*Note*: This is applicable to pension plans only.)   ___ ___ ___

   c. The amount of accumulated other comprehensive income recognized pursuant to FAS-87, paragraph 37, as amended? (*Note*: This is applicable to pension plans only.)   ___ ___ ___

<u>Yes</u> <u>No</u> <u>N/A</u>

8. Has the amount of net periodic benefit cost rec-
    ognized and the amount included within other
    comprehensive income arising from a change in
    the minimum pension liability recognized pur-
    suant to FAS-87, paragraph 37, as amended, been
    disclosed, for each income statement presented?
    (FAS-132R, par. 8h)   ___ ___ ___

9. Have the following assumptions used in the ac-
    counting for the plan been disclosed, for each
    balance sheet presented: (FAS-132R, par. 8i)

    a. The weighted-average assumed discount
       rates?   ___ ___ ___

    b. The weighted-average rates of compensation
       increase (for pay-related plans)?   ___ ___ ___

    c. The weighted average expected long-term
       rates of return on plan assets specifying, in
       tabular format, the assumptions used to de-
       termine the benefit obligation and the net ben-
       efit cost?   ___ ___ ___

10. Has the measurement date used to determine
    benefit information for the plans that make up
    at least the majority of plan assets and benefit
    obligations been disclosed? (FAS-132R, par. 8j)
    (*Note*: This disclosure item is effective for fiscal
    years ending after June 15, 2004.)   ___ ___ ___

11. Has disclosure been made of the assumed
    healthcare cost trend rate(s) for the next year used
    to measure the expected cost of benefits covered
    by the plan (gross eligible charges) and a gen-
    eral description of the direction and pattern of
    change in the assumed trend rates thereafter, to-
    gether with the ultimate trend rate(s) and when
    that rate is expected to be achieved? (FAS-132R,
    par. 8k) (*Note*: This is applicable to healthcare
    postretirement benefit plans only.)   ___ ___ ___

12. Have the following transactions and events been
    disclosed:

    a. The amounts and types of securities of the
       employer and related parties included in plan
       assets? (FAS-132R, par. 8l)   ___ ___ ___

<u>*Yes*</u> <u>*No*</u> <u>*N/A*</u>

  b. The approximate amount of future annual benefits of plan participants covered by insurance contracts issued by the employer or related parties? (FAS-132R, par. 8l)   ___ ___ ___

  c. Any significant transactions between the employer or related parties and the plan during the period? (FAS-132R, 8l)   ___ ___ ___

  d. The nature and effect of significant non-routine events, such as amendments, combinations, divestitures, curtailments, and settlements? (FAS-132R, par. 8m)   ___ ___ ___

13. As a result of applying the provisions of FAS-132R, have the disclosures for prior annual periods that are presented for comparative purposes been restated for: (a) the percentages of each major category of plan assets held, (b) the accumulated benefit obligation, and (c) the assumptions used in the accounting for the plans? (FAS-132R, par. 20) (If this is not practicable, the notes to the financial statements should include all available information and identify the information that is not available.)   ___ ___ ___

14. For employers with two or more defined benefit pension plans, if disclosures for plans that have accumulated benefit obligations in excess of plan assets and plans that have plan assets in excess of accumulated benefit obligations are presented on a combined basis, have the following disclosures been made separately with respect to plans that have *projected* benefit obligations in excess of plan assets: (FAS-132R, par. 6)

  a. The aggregate projected benefit obligations?   ___ ___ ___

  b. The aggregate fair value of plan assets?   ___ ___ ___

15. For employers with two or more defined benefit pension or postretirement plans, if disclosures for plans that have accumulated benefit obligations in excess of plan assets and plans that have plan assets in excess of accumulated benefit obligations are presented on a combined basis, have the following disclosures been made separately with respect to plans that have *accumulated* benefit obligations in excess of plan assets: (FAS-132R, par. 6)

<table>
<tr><td></td><td>Yes</td><td>No</td><td>N/A</td></tr>
</table>

a. The aggregate accumulated benefit obligations? ___ ___ ___

b. The aggregate fair value of plan assets? ___ ___ ___

16. If two or more defined benefit plans are combined, have the amounts recognized as prepaid benefit costs and accrued benefit liabilities been disclosed separately? (FAS-132R, par. 6) ___ ___ ___

17. Have domestic and foreign defined benefit plans been disclosed separately if the benefit obligations of the foreign plans are significant relative to the total benefit obligation and the plans use significantly different assumptions? (FAS-132R, par. 7) ___ ___ ___

18. If a gain or loss from settlement or curtailment has not been recognized in the current year and the employer's financial position or results of operations would have been materially different had it been recognized, have appropriate disclosures been made? (FAS-88 Q&A, No. 28) ___ ___ ___

19. For fiscal years ending after December 15, 2006, but before June 16, 2007, for entities that have not applied the recognition provisions of FAS-158, have the following disclosures been made: (FAS-158, par. 14)

a. A brief description of the provisions of FAS-158? ___ ___ ___

b. The date that the adoption of FAS-158 is required? ___ ___ ___

c. The date the employer plans to adopt the recognition provisions of FAS-158, if earlier? ___ ___ ___

Pension and Postretirement Defined Benefit Plans—Reduced Disclosure Requirements for Nonpublic Entities (Annual Periods)— After the Adoption of FAS-158

Note: For entities that appropriately do not report other comprehensive income (e.g., not-for-profits), the references to results of operations (including items of other comprehensive income) and income statement in the disclosures included in this section correspond to changes in unrestricted net assets and statement of activities, respectively. (FAS-132R, par. 10D; FAS-158, par. E1t)

<u>Yes</u> <u>No</u> <u>N/A</u>

1. Has the following information about the plan been disclosed for each balance sheet presented: (FAS-132R, par. 8a)

   a. The benefit obligation? (This is the *projected benefit obligation* for pension plans and the *accumulated postretirement benefit obligation* for postretirement plans.)   ___ ___ ___

   b. The fair value of plan assets?   ___ ___ ___

   c. The funded status of the plan?   ___ ___ ___

2. Has the following information about the plan been disclosed, for each income statement presented: (FAS-132R, par. 8b)

   a. Employer contributions?   ___ ___ ___

   b. Participant contributions?   ___ ___ ___

   c. Benefits paid?   ___ ___ ___

3. Has the following information about plan assets been disclosed: (FAS-132R, par. 8c) (*Note:* This disclosure item is effective for fiscal year ending after June 15, 2004)

   a. For each balance sheet presented, the percentage of the fair value of total plan assets held in each major category of plan assets, including at a minimum the following categories: (1) equity securities, (2) debt securities, (3) real estate, and (4) all other assets? (Also, disclosure of additional asset categories and additional information about specific assets within a category is encouraged if that information is considered useful.)   ___ ___ ___

   b. As of the latest balance sheet presented, a narrative description of investment policies and strategies, including: (1) target allocation percentages, or range of percentages, for each major category of plan assets presented on a weighted-average basis, and (2) other factors that are pertinent to an understanding of the policies or strategies, such as investment goals, risk management practices, permitted and prohibited investments, including the use of derivatives, diversification, and the relationship between plan assets and benefit obligations?

<u>*Yes*</u> <u>*No*</u> <u>*N/A*</u>

    c. As of the latest balance sheet presented, a narrative description of the basis used to determine the overall expected long-term rate-of-return-on-assets assumption, such as: (1) the general approach used, (2) the extent to which the overall rate-of-return-on-assets assumption was based on historical returns, (3) the extent to which adjustments were made to those historical returns in order to reflect expectations of future returns, and (4) how those adjustments were determined?

    ___ ___ ___

4. For defined benefit pension plans, has the accumulated benefit obligation been disclosed for each balance sheet presented? (FAS-132R, par. 8d) (*Note*: This disclosure item is effective for fiscal years ending after June 15, 2004.)

    ___ ___ ___

5. As of the latest balance sheet presented, has disclosure been made of the benefits expected to be paid in each of the next five fiscal years and in the aggregate for the five fiscal years thereafter? (FAS-132R, par. 8e) (*Note*: This disclosure item is effective for fiscal years ending after June 15, 2004.)

    ___ ___ ___

6. Has disclosure been made of the company's best estimate of contributions expected to be paid during the next fiscal year beginning after the date of the latest balance sheet presented? (FAS-132R, par. 8f) (Estimated contributions may be presented in the aggregate for contributions required by funding regulations or laws, discretionary contributions, and noncash contributions.) (*Note*: This disclosure item is effective for fiscal years ending after June 15, 2004.)

    ___ ___ ___

7. Has disclosure been made of the amounts recognized in the balance sheet, including showing separately the postretirement benefit assets and current and noncurrent postretirement benefit liabilities for each balance sheet presented? (FAS-132R, par. 8g; FAS-158, par. E1m)

    ___ ___ ___

8. Have the following amounts been separately disclosed for each income statement presented as those amounts, which include amortization of the net transition asset or obligation, are recognized

as components of net periodic benefit cost: (FAS-132R, pars. 8h and 10A-B; FAS-158, pars. E1m and E1t) ___ ___ ___

   a. The net gain or loss and net prior service cost or credit recognized in other comprehensive income for the period pursuant to paragraphs 25 and 29 of FAS-87 and paragraphs 52 and 56 of FAS-106, as amended? ___ ___ ___

   b. Reclassification adjustments of other comprehensive income for the period? ___ ___ ___

(*Note:* For entities that appropriately do not report other comprehensive income (e.g., not-for-profits): (a) the references to the net gain or loss, net prior service cost or credit, and net transition asset or obligation recognized in other comprehensive income correspond to such amounts recognized as changes in unrestricted net assets arising from a defined benefit plan but not yet included in net periodic benefit cost and (b) the reference to reclassification adjustments of other comprehensive income corresponds to reclassifications to net periodic benefit cost of amounts previously recognized as changes in unrestricted net assets arising from a defined benefit plan but not included in net periodic benefit cost when they arose.) ___ ___ ___

9. Have the amounts in accumulated other comprehensive income that have not yet been recognized as components of net periodic benefit cost, showing separately the net gain or loss, net prior service cost or credit, and net transition asset or obligation, been disclosed for each income statement presented? (*Note:* For entities that appropriately do not report other comprehensive income (e.g., not-for-profits), the references to the net gain or loss, net prior service cost or credit, and net transition asset or obligation recognized in accumulated other comprehensive income correspond to such amounts recognized as changes in unrestricted net assets arising from a defined benefit plan but not yet reclassified as components of net periodic benefit cost.) (FAS-132R, pars. 8hh and 10C; FAS-158, pars. E1o and E1t) ___ ___ ___

10. Have the following assumptions used in the accounting for the plan been disclosed for each balance sheet presented: (FAS-132R, par. 8i)

   a. The weighted-average assumed discount rates?   ___ ___ ___

   b. The weighted-average rates of compensation increase (for pay-related plans)?   ___ ___ ___

   c. The weighted average expected long-term rates of return on plan assets specifying, in tabular format, the assumptions used to determine the benefit obligation and the net benefit cost?   ___ ___ ___

11. Has disclosure been made of the assumed healthcare cost trend rate(s) for the next year used to measure the expected cost of benefits covered by the plan (gross eligible charges) and a general description of the direction and pattern of change in the assumed trend rates thereafter, together with the ultimate trend rate(s) and when that rate is expected to be achieved? (FAS-132R, par. 8k) (*Note*: This is applicable to healthcare postretirement benefit plans only.)   ___ ___ ___

12. Have the following transactions and events been disclosed:

   a. The amounts and types of securities of the employer and related parties included in plan assets? (FAS-132R, par. 8l)   ___ ___ ___

   b. The approximate amount of future annual benefits of plan participants covered by insurance contracts issued by the employer or related parties? (FAS-132R, par. 8l)   ___ ___ ___

   c. Any significant transactions between the employer or related parties and the plan during the period? (FAS-132R, 8l)   ___ ___ ___

   d. The nature and effect of significant nonroutine events, such as amendments, combinations, divestitures, curtailments, and settlements? (FAS-132R, par. 8m)   ___ ___ ___

   13. Have the amounts in accumulated other comprehensive income expected to be recognized as components of net periodic benefit cost over the fiscal year that follows the most

recent annual balance sheet presented, showing separately the net gain or loss, net prior
service cost or credit, and net transition asset
or obligation, been disclosed for each balance
sheet presented? (*Note*: For entities that appropriately do not report other comprehensive
income (e.g., not-for-profits), the references to
the net gain or loss, net prior service cost or
credit, and net transition asset or obligation
recognized in accumulated other comprehensive income correspond to such amounts recognized as changes in unrestricted net assets
arising from a defined benefit plan but not yet
reclassified as components of net periodic benefit cost.) (FAS-132R, pars. 8n and 10C; FAS-
158, par. E1t)   ___ ___ ___

14. Have the amount and timing of any plan assets
    expected to be returned to the employer during
    the 12-month period, or operating cycle if longer,
    that follows the most recent annual balance sheet
    presented been disclosed? (FAS-132R, par. 8o)   ___ ___ ___

15. As a result of applying the provisions of FAS-
    132R, have the disclosures for prior annual peri-
    ods that are presented for comparative purposes
    been restated for: (a) the percentages of each
    major category of plan assets held, (b) the accu-
    mulated benefit obligation, and (c) the assump-
    tions used in the accounting for the plans? (FAS-
    132R, par. 20) (If this is not practicable, the notes
    to the financial statements should include all
    available information and identify the informa-
    tion that is not available.)   ___ ___ ___

16. For employers with two or more defined benefit
    pension plans, if disclosures for plans that have
    accumulated benefit obligations in excess of plan
    assets and plans that have plan assets in excess
    of accumulated benefit obligations are presented
    on a combined basis, have the following disclo-
    sures been made separately with respect to plans
    that have *projected* benefit obligations in excess
    of plan assets: (FAS-132R, par. 6; FAS-158,
    par. E1k)

    a. The aggregate projected benefit obligations? ___ ___ ___

    b. The aggregate fair value of plan assets?   ___ ___ ___

17. For employers with two or more defined benefit pension or postretirement plans, if disclosures for plans that have accumulated benefit obligations in excess of plan assets and plans that have plan assets in excess of accumulated benefit obligations are presented on a combined basis, have the following disclosures been made separately with respect to plans that have *accumulated* benefit obligations in excess of plan assets: (FAS-132R, par. 6; FAS-158, par. E1k)

   a. The aggregate accumulated benefit obligations?   ___ ___ ___

   b. The aggregate fair value of plan assets?   ___ ___ ___

18. Have domestic and foreign defined benefit plans been disclosed separately if the benefit obligations of the foreign plans are significant relative to the total benefit obligation and the plans use significantly different assumptions? (FAS-132R, par. 7)   ___ ___ ___

19. If a gain or loss from settlement or curtailment has not been recognized in the current year and the employer's financial position or results of operations would have been materially different had it been recognized, have appropriate disclosures been made? (FAS-88 Q&A, No. 28)   ___ ___ ___

20. Has the following information been disclosed separately for pension plans and other postretirement benefit plans: (FAS-158, par. 7)

   a. For each annual statement of income presented, the amounts recognized in other comprehensive income, showing separately the net gain or loss and net prior service cost or credit?   ___ ___ ___

   b. The amounts disclosed in item 20a above separated into amounts arising during the period and reclassification adjustments of other comprehensive income as a result of being recognized as components of net periodic benefit cost for the period?   ___ ___ ___

   c. `For each annual statement of income presented, the net transition asset or obligation

Yes *No* *N/A*

recognized as a reclassification adjustment of other comprehensive income as a result of being recognized as a component of net periodic benefit cost for the period?

d. For each annual statement of financial position presented, the amounts in accumulated other comprehensive income that have not yet been recognized as components of net periodic benefit cost, showing separately the net gain or loss, net prior service cost or credit, and net transition asset or obligation?

e. The amounts in accumulated other comprehensive income expected to be recognized as components of net periodic benefit cost over the fiscal year that follows the most recent annual statement of financial position presented, showing separately the net gain or loss, net prior service cost or credit, and net transition asset or obligation?

f. The amount and timing of any plan assets expected to be returned to the business entity during the 12-month period, or operating cycle if longer, that follows the most recent annual statement of financial position presented?

21. Have the following transitional disclosures been made on implementation of FAS-158:

a. In the year that the recognition provisions of FAS-158 are initially applied, the incremental effect of applying FAS-158 on individual line items in the year-end balance sheet? (FAS-158, par.20)

b. In the year that the measurement date provisions of FAS-158 are initially applied, the separate adjustments of both retained earnings and accumulated other comprehensive income from applying FAS-158? (FAS-158, par. 21)

<u>*Yes*</u> <u>*No*</u> <u>*N/A*</u>

Pension and Postretirement Defined Benefit Plans—Public Entities and Nonpublic Entities That Elect to Voluntarily Provide Additional Disclosures (Annual Periods)—Prior to the Adoption of FAS-158

1. Has disclosure been made of the amount of net periodic cost recognized, for each income statement presented, showing separately the following: (FAS-132R, par. 5h)

    a. Service cost component? ___ ___ ___

    b. Interest cost component? ___ ___ ___

    c. Expected return on plan assets for the period? ___ ___ ___

    d. Amortization of the unrecognized transition obligation or asset? ___ ___ ___

    e. Amount of recognized gains or losses? ___ ___ ___

    f. Amount of prior service cost recognized? ___ ___ ___

    g. Amount of gain or loss recognized due to a settlement or curtailment? ___ ___ ___

2. Has disclosure been made of the funded status of the plan, amounts not recognized in the entity's balance sheet, and amounts recognized in the entity's balance sheet, including the following, for each balance sheet presented: (FAS-132R, par. 5c)

    a. Amount of any unamortized prior service cost? ___ ___ ___

    b. Amount of any unrecognized net gain or loss (including asset gains and losses not yet reflected in market-related value)? ___ ___ ___

    c. Amount of any remaining unamortized, unrecognized net obligation or net asset existing at the date of initial application of FAS-87 or FAS-106? ___ ___ ___

    d. Amount of net pension or net postretirement asset or liability? ___ ___ ___

    e. Any intangible asset and the amount of accumulated other comprehensive income? (*Note*: This is applicable to pension plans only.) ___ ___ ___

3. Has a reconciliation of the beginning and end-
    ing balances of the benefit obligation been dis-
    closed, for each balance sheet presented, with
    separate disclosure of the following: (FAS-132R,
    par. 5a)

    a. Service cost? _____ _____ _____

    b. Interest cost? _____ _____ _____

    c. Contributions by plan participants? _____ _____ _____

    d. Actuarial gains and losses? _____ _____ _____

    e. Foreign currency exchange rate changes? _____ _____ _____

    f. Benefits paid? _____ _____ _____

    g. Plan amendments? _____ _____ _____

    h. Business combinations? _____ _____ _____

    i. Divestitures? _____ _____ _____

    j. Curtailments? _____ _____ _____

    k. Settlements? _____ _____ _____

    l. Special termination benefits? _____ _____ _____

4. Has a reconciliation of the beginning and end-
    ing balances of the fair value of plan assets been
    disclosed, for each balance sheet presented, in-
    cluding the effects of the following: (FAS-132R,
    par. 5b)

    a. Actual return on plan assets? _____ _____ _____

    b. Foreign currency exchange rate changes? _____ _____ _____

    c. Contributions by employer? _____ _____ _____

    d. Contributions by plan participants? _____ _____ _____

    e. Benefits paid? _____ _____ _____

    f. Business combinations? _____ _____ _____

    g. Divestitures? _____ _____ _____

    h. Settlements? _____ _____ _____

5. Has the amount included within other compre-
    hensive income arising from a change in the ad-
    ditional minimum pension liability recognized
    been disclosed, for each income statement pre-
    sented? (FAS-132R, par. 5i) _____ _____ _____

6. Have the following assumptions used in the ac-
    counting for the plan been disclosed, for each
    balance sheet presented: (FAS-132R, par. 5j)

Yes No N/A

    a. The weighted-average assumed discount rates?   —— —— ——

    b. The weighted-average rates of compensation increase (for pay-related plans)?   —— —— ——

    c. The weighted-average expected long-term rates of return on plan assets specifying, in tabular format, the assumptions used to determine the benefit obligation and the net benefit cost?   —— —— ——

7. Has the following information about plan assets been disclosed: (FAS-132R, par. 5d) (*Note*: For foreign plans, this disclosure item is effective for fiscal years ending after June 15, 2004)

    a. For each balance sheet presented, the percentage of the fair value of total plan assets held in each major category of plan assets, including at a minimum the following categories: (1) equity securities, (2) debt securities, (3) real estate, and (4) all other assets? (Also, disclosure of additional asset categories, and additional information about specific assets within a category, is encouraged if that information is considered useful.)   —— —— ——

    b. As of the latest balance sheet presented, a narrative description of investment policies and strategies, including: (1) target allocation percentages, or range of percentages, for each major category of plan assets presented on a weighted-average basis, and (2) other factors that are pertinent to an understanding of the policies or strategies such as investment goals, risk management practices, permitted and prohibited investments, including the use of derivatives, diversification, and the relationship between plan assets and benefit obligations?   —— —— ——

    c. As of the latest balance sheet date presented, a narrative description of the basis used to determine the overall expected long-term rate-of-return-on-assets assumption, such as: (1) the general approach used, (2) the extent to which the overall rate-of-return-on-assets assumption was based on historical returns, (3)

Yes No N/A

the extent to which adjustments were made to those historical returns in order to reflect expectations of future returns, and (4) how those adjustments were determined?

8. For defined benefit pension plans, has the accumulated benefit obligation been disclosed for each balance sheet presented? (FAS-132R, par. 5e) (*Note*: For foreign plans, this disclosure items is effective for fiscal years ending after June 15, 2004)

9. Until the provisions of FAS-132R are adopted in full for domestic and foreign plans, do financial statements that exclude foreign plans from the disclosure requirements of items 7 or 8 above disclose separately for domestic plans the following: (FAS-132R, par. 19)

   a. The total fair value of plan assets as of the date of the latest balance sheet presented?

   b. The overall expected long-term rate of return on assets for the latest period for which an income statement is presented?

10. As of the latest balance sheet presented, have disclosures been made of the benefits expected to be paid in each of the next five fiscal years and in the aggregate for the five fiscal years thereafter? (FAS-132R, par. 5f) (*Note*: For all plans, this disclosure item is effective for fiscal years ending after June 15, 2004)

11. Has disclosure been made of the company's best estimate of contributions expected to be paid to the plan during the next fiscal year beginning after the date of the latest balance sheet presented? (FAS-132R, par. 5g) (Estimated contributions may be presented in the aggregate for contributions required by funding regulations or laws, discretionary contributions, and noncash contributions) (*Note*: For foreign plans, this disclosure item is effective for fiscal years ending after June 15, 2004)

12. Has the measurement date used to determine benefit information for the plans that make up at least the majority of plan assets and benefit obligations been disclosed? (FAS-132R, par. 5k)

<u>Yes</u> <u>No</u> <u>N/A</u>

(*Note*: For foreign plans, this disclosure item is effective for fiscal years ending after June 15, 2004)   ___ ___ ___

13. Has disclosure been made of the assumed healthcare cost trend rate(s) for the next year used to measure the expected cost of benefits covered by the plan (gross eligible charges) and a general description of the direction and pattern of change in the assumed trend rates thereafter, together with the ultimate trend rate(s) and when that rate is expected to be achieved? (FAS-132R, par. 51) (*Note*: This is applicable to healthcare postretirement benefit plans only.)   ___ ___ ___

14. Has disclosure been made of the effect of a one-percentage-point increase and the effect of a one-percentage-point decrease in the assumed healthcare cost trend rates on: (FAS-132R, par. 5m) (*Note*: This is applicable to healthcare postretirement benefit plans only.)

   a. The aggregate of the service and interest cost components of net periodic postretirement healthcare benefit cost of the current period?   ___ ___ ___

   b. The accumulated postretirement benefit obligation for healthcare benefits as of the latest balance sheet presented?   ___ ___ ___

15. Have the following transactions and events been disclosed:

   a. The amounts and types of securities of the employer and related parties included in plan assets? (FAS-132R, par. 5n)   ___ ___ ___

   b. The approximate amount of future annual benefits of plan participants covered by insurance contracts issued by the employer or related parties? (FAS-132R, par. 5n)   ___ ___ ___

   c. Any significant transactions between the employer or related parties and the plan during the period? (FAS-132R, par. 5n)   ___ ___ ___

   d. Any alternative amortization method used to amortize prior service costs or unrecognized net gains and losses? (FAS-87, pars. 26 and 33; FAS-106, par. 60; FAS-132R, par. 5o)   ___ ___ ___

    e. Any substantive commitment, such as past practice or a history of regular benefit increases, used as the basis for accounting for the benefit obligation? (FAS-132R, par. 5p)   ___ ___ ___

    f. The cost of providing special or contractual termination benefits recognized during the period and a description of the nature of the event? (FAS-132R, par. 5q)   ___ ___ ___

    g. An explanation of any significant change in the benefit obligation or plan assets not otherwise apparent in the above disclosures? (FAS-132R, par. 5r)   ___ ___ ___

16. As a result of applying the provisions of FAS-132R, have the disclosures for prior annual periods that are presented for comparative purposes been restated for: (a) the percentages of each major category of plan assets held, (b) the accumulated benefit obligation, and (c) the assumptions used in the accounting for the plans? (FAS-132R, par. 20) (If this is not practicable, the notes to the financial statements should include all available information and identify the information that is not available.)   ___ ___ ___

17. For employers with two or more defined benefit pension plans, if disclosures for plans that have accumulated benefit obligations in excess of plan assets and plans that have plan assets in excess of accumulated benefit obligations are presented on a combined basis, have the following disclosures been made separately with respect to plans that have *projected* benefit obligations in excess of plan assets: (FAS-132R, par. 6)

    a. The aggregate projected benefit obligations?   ___ ___ ___

    b. The aggregate fair value of plan assets?   ___ ___ ___

18. For employers with two or more defined benefit pension or postretirement plans, if disclosures for plans that have accumulated benefit obligations in excess of plan assets and plans that have plan assets in excess of accumulated benefit obligations are presented on a combined basis, have the following disclosures been made separately with respect to plans that have *accumulated* benefit obligations in excess of plan assets: (FAS-132R, par. 6)

<u>Yes</u> <u>No</u> <u>N/A</u>

a. The aggregate accumulated benefit obligations? ___ ___ ___

b. The aggregate fair value of plan assets? ___ ___ ___

19. If two or more defined benefit plans are combined, have the amounts recognized as prepaid benefit costs and accrued benefit liabilities been disclosed separately? (FAS-132R, par. 6) ___ ___ ___

20. Have domestic and foreign defined benefit plans been disclosed separately if the benefit obligations of the foreign plans are significant relative to the total benefit obligation and the plans use significantly different assumptions? (FAS-132R, par. 7) ___ ___ ___

21. If a gain or loss from settlement or curtailment has not been recognized in the current year and the employer's financial position or results of operations would have been materially different had it been recognized, have appropriate disclosures been made? (FAS-88 Q&A, No. 28) ___ ___ ___

Pension and Postretirement Defined Benefit Plans—Public Entities and Nonpublic Entities That Elect to Voluntarily Provide Additional Disclosures (Annual Periods)—After the Adoption of FAS-158

Note: For entities that appropriately do not report other comprehensive income (e.g., not-for-profits), the references to results of operations (including items of other comprehensive income) and income statement in the disclosures included in this section correspond to changes in unrestricted net assets and statement of activities, respectively. (FAS-132R, par. 10D; FAS-158, par. E1t)

1. Has disclosure been made of the amount of net periodic cost recognized, for each income statement presented, showing separately the following: (FAS-132R, par. 5h; FAS-158, par. E1d)

a. Service cost component? ___ ___ ___

b. Interest cost component? ___ ___ ___

c. Expected return on plan assets for the period? ___ ___ ___

	Yes	No	N/A

    d. Gain or loss component?   ___ ___ ___

    e. Prior service cost or credit component? ___ ___ ___

    f. Transition asset or obligation component? ___ ___ ___

    g. Amount of gain or loss recognized due to settlements or curtailments? ___ ___ ___

2. Has disclosure been made of the funded status of the plans and the amounts recognized in the entity's balance sheet, showing separately the assets and current and noncurrent liabilities recognized, for each balance sheet presented? (FAS-132R, par. 5c; FAS-158, par. E1c) ___ ___ ___

3. Has a reconciliation of the beginning and ending balances of the benefit obligation been disclosed, for each balance sheet presented, with separate disclosure of the following: (FAS-132R, par. 5a)

    a. Service cost? ___ ___ ___

    b. Interest cost? ___ ___ ___

    c. Contributions by plan participants? ___ ___ ___

    d. Actuarial gains and losses? ___ ___ ___

    e. Foreign currency exchange rate changes? ___ ___ ___

    f. Benefits paid? ___ ___ ___

    g. Plan amendments? ___ ___ ___

    h. Business combinations? ___ ___ ___

    i. Divestitures? ___ ___ ___

    j. Curtailments? ___ ___ ___

    k. Settlements? ___ ___ ___

    l. Special termination benefits? ___ ___ ___

4. Has a reconciliation of the beginning and ending balances of the fair value of plan assets been disclosed, for each balance sheet presented, including the effects of the following: (FAS-132R, par. 5b)

    a. Actual return on plan assets? ___ ___ ___

    b. Foreign currency exchange rate changes? ___ ___ ___

    c. Contributions by employer? ___ ___ ___

    d. Contributions by plan participants? ___ ___ ___

<u>Yes</u> <u>No</u> <u>N/A</u>

    e. Benefits paid?   —— —— ——

    f. Business combinations?   —— —— ——

    g. Divestitures?   —— —— ——

    h. Settlements?   —— —— ——

5. Have the following amounts been separately disclosed for each income statement presented as those amounts, which include amortization of the net transition asset or obligation, are recognized as components of net periodic benefit cost: (FAS-132R, pars. 5i and 10A-B; FAS-158, pars. E1e and E1t)

    a. The net gain or loss and net prior service cost or credit recognized in other comprehensive income for the period pursuant to paragraphs 25 and 29 of FAS-87 and paragraphs 52 and 56 of FAS-106, as amended?   —— —— ——

    b. Reclassification adjustments of other comprehensive income for the period?   —— —— ——

    (*Note*: For entities that appropriately do not report other comprehensive income (e.g., not-for-profits): (a) the references to the net gain or loss, net prior service cost or credit, and net transition asset or obligation recognized in other comprehensive income correspond to such amounts recognized as changes in unrestricted net assets arising from a defined benefit plan but not yet included in net periodic benefit cost and (b) the reference to reclassification adjustments of other comprehensive income corresponds to reclassifications to net periodic benefit cost of amounts previously recognized as changes in unrestricted net assets arising from a defined benefit plan but not included in net periodic benefit cost when they arose.)

6. Have the amounts in accumulated other comprehensive income that have not yet been recognized as components of net periodic benefit cost, showing separately the net gain or loss, net prior service cost or credit, and net transition asset or obligation, been disclosed for each income statement presented? (*Note*: For entities that appropriately do not report other comprehensive income (e.g., not-for-profits), the references to the

Yes *No* *N/A*

net gain or loss, net prior service cost or credit, and net transition asset or obligation recognized in accumulated other comprehensive income correspond to such amounts recognized as changes in unrestricted net assets arising from a defined benefit plan but not yet reclassified as components of net periodic benefit cost.) (FAS-132R, pars. 5ii and 10C; FAS-158, pars. E1f and E1t)   ___ ___ ___

7. Have the following assumptions used in the accounting for the plan been disclosed for each balance sheet presented: (FAS-132R, par. 5j)

   a. The weighted-average assumed discount rates?   ___ ___ ___

   b. The weighted-average rates of compensation increase (for pay-related plans)?   ___ ___ ___

   c. The weighted-average expected long-term rates of return on plan assets specifying, in tabular format, the assumptions used to determine the benefit obligation and the net benefit cost?   ___ ___ ___

8. Has the following information about plan assets been disclosed: (FAS-132R, par. 5d) (*Note*: For foreign plans, this disclosure item is effective for fiscal years ending after June 15, 2004)

   a. For each balance sheet presented, the percentage of the fair value of total plan assets held in each major category of plan assets, including at a minimum the following categories: (1) equity securities, (2) debt securities, (3) real estate, and (4) all other assets? (Also, disclosure of additional asset categories and additional information about specific assets within a category is encouraged if that information is considered useful.)   ___ ___ ___

   b. As of the latest balance sheet presented, a narrative description of investment policies and strategies, including: (1) target allocation percentages, or range of percentages, for each major category of plan assets presented on a weighted-average basis and (2) other factors that are pertinent to an understanding of the policies or strategies, such as investment goals,

<u>Yes</u> <u>No</u> <u>N/A</u>

     risk management practices, permitted and prohibited investments, including the use of derivatives, diversification, and the relationship between plan assets and benefit obligations?

    c. As of the latest balance sheet date presented, a narrative description of the basis used to determine the overall expected long-term rate-of-return-on-assets assumption, such as: (1) the general approach used, (2) the extent to which the overall rate-of-return-on-assets assumption was based on historical returns, (3) the extent to which adjustments were made to those historical returns in order to reflect expectations of future returns, and (4) how those adjustments were determined?

9.   For defined benefit pension plans, has the accumulated benefit obligation been disclosed for each balance sheet presented? (FAS-132R, par. 5e) (*Note*: For foreign plans, this disclosure item is effective for fiscal years ending after June 15, 2004)

10. Until the provisions of FAS-132R are adopted in full for domestic and foreign plans, do financial statements that exclude foreign plans from the disclosure requirements of items 8 or 9 above disclose separately for domestic plans the following: (FAS-132R, par. 19)

    a. The total fair value of plan assets as of the date of the latest balance sheet presented?

    b. The overall expected long-term rate of return on assets for the latest period for which an income statement is presented?

11. As of the latest balance sheet presented, have disclosures been made of the benefits expected to be paid in each of the next five fiscal years and in the aggregate for the five fiscal years thereafter? (FAS-132R, par. 5f) (*Note*: For all plans, this disclosure item is effective for fiscal years ending after June 15, 2004)

12. Has disclosure been made of the company's best estimate of contributions expected to be paid to the plan during the next fiscal year beginning

after the date of the latest balance sheet presented? (FAS-132R, par. 5g) (Estimated contributions may be presented in the aggregate for contributions required by funding regulations or laws, discretionary contributions, and noncash contributions) (*Note*: For foreign plans, this disclosure item is effective for fiscal years ending after June 15, 2004)   ____ ____ ____

13. Has disclosure been made of the assumed healthcare cost trend rate(s) for the next year used to measure the expected cost of benefits covered by the plan (gross eligible charges) and a general description of the direction and pattern of change in the assumed trend rates thereafter, together with the ultimate trend rate(s) and when that rate is expected to be achieved? (FAS-132R, par. 5l) (*Note*: This is applicable to healthcare postretirement benefit plans only.)   ____ ____ ____

14. Has disclosure been made of the effect of a one-percentage-point increase and the effect of a one-percentage-point decrease in the assumed healthcare cost trend rates on: (FAS-132R, par. 5m) (*Note*: This is applicable to healthcare postretirement benefit plans only.)

    a. The aggregate of the service and interest cost components of net periodic postretirement healthcare benefit cost of the current period?   ____ ____ ____

    b. The accumulated postretirement benefit obligation for healthcare benefits as of the latest balance sheet presented?   ____ ____ ____

15. Have the following transactions and events been disclosed:

    a. The amounts and types of securities of the employer and related parties included in plan assets? (FAS-132R, par. 5n)   ____ ____ ____

    b. The approximate amount of future annual benefits of plan participants covered by insurance contracts issued by the employer or related parties? (FAS-132R, par. 5n)   ____ ____ ____

    c. Any significant transactions between the employer or related parties and the plan during the period? (FAS-132R, par. 5n)   ____ ____ ____

	Yes	No	N/A

d. Any alternative amortization method used to amortize prior service costs or net gains and losses? (FAS-87, pars. 26 and 33; FAS-106, par. 60; FAS-132R, par. 5o; FAS-158, pars. C2d, C2h, D2k, and E1h)

e. Any substantive commitment, such as past practice or a history of regular benefit increases, used as the basis for accounting for the benefit obligation? (FAS-132R, par. 5p)

f. The cost of providing special or contractual termination benefits recognized during the period and a description of the nature of the event? (FAS-132R, par. 5q)

g. An explanation of any significant change in the benefit obligation or plan assets not otherwise apparent in the above disclosures? (FAS-132R, par. 5r)

16. Have the amounts in accumulated other comprehensive income expected to be recognized as components of net periodic benefit cost over the fiscal year that follows the most recent annual balance sheet presented, showing separately the net gain or loss, net prior service cost or credit, and net transition asset or obligation, been disclosed for each balance sheet presented? (*Note:* For entities that appropriately do not report other comprehensive income (e.g., not-for-profits), the references to the net gain or loss, net prior service cost or credit, and net transition asset or obligation recognized in accumulated other comprehensive income correspond to such amounts recognized as changes in unrestricted net assets arising from a defined benefit plan but not yet reclassified as components of net periodic benefit cost.) (FAS-132R, pars. 5s and 10C; FAS-158, pars. E1i and E1t)

17. Have the amount and timing of any plan assets expected to be returned to the employer during the 12-month period, or operating cycle if longer, that follows the most recent annual balance sheet presented been disclosed? (FAS-132R, par. 5t; FAS-158, par. E1j)

Yes No N/A

18. As a result of applying the provisions of FAS-132R, have the disclosures for prior annual periods that are presented for comparative purposes been restated for: (a) the percentages of each major category of plan assets held, (b) the accumulated benefit obligation, and (c) the assumptions used in the accounting for the plans? (FAS-132R, par. 20) (If this is not practicable, the notes to the financial statements should include all available information and identify the information that is not available.)   ___ ___ ___

19. For employers with two or more defined benefit pension plans, if disclosures for plans that have accumulated benefit obligations in excess of plan assets and plans that have plan assets in excess of accumulated benefit obligations are presented on a combined basis, have the following disclosures been made separately with respect to plans that have *projected* benefit obligations in excess of plan assets: (FAS-132R, par. 6)

    a. The aggregate projected benefit obligations?   ___ ___ ___

    b. The aggregate fair value of plan assets?   ___ ___ ___

20. For employers with two or more defined benefit pension or postretirement plans, if disclosures for plans that have accumulated benefit obligations in excess of plan assets and plans that have plan assets in excess of accumulated benefit obligations are presented on a combined basis, have the following disclosures been made separately with respect to plans that have *accumulated* benefit obligations in excess of plan assets: (FAS-132R, par. 6)

    a. The aggregate accumulated benefit obligations?   ___ ___ ___

    b. The aggregate fair value of plan assets?   ___ ___ ___

21. Have domestic and foreign defined benefit plans been disclosed separately if the benefit obligations of the foreign plans are significant relative to the total benefit obligation and the plans use significantly different assumptions? (FAS-132R, par. 7)   ___ ___ ___

22. If a gain or loss from settlement or curtailment has not been recognized in the current year and

the employer's financial position or results of operations would have been materially different had it been recognized, have appropriate disclosures been made? (FAS-88 Q&A, No. 28)   ___ ___ ___

23. Has the following information been disclosed separately for pension plans and other postretirement benefit plans: (FAS-158, par. 7)

   a. For each annual statement of income presented, the amounts recognized in other comprehensive income, showing separately the net gain or loss and net prior service cost or credit?   ___ ___ ___

   b. The amounts disclosed in item 23a above separated into amounts arising during the period and reclassification adjustments of other comprehensive income as a result of being recognized as components of net periodic benefit cost for the period?   ___ ___ ___

   c. For each annual statement of income presented, the net transition asset or obligation recognized as a reclassification adjustment of other comprehensive income as a result of being recognized as a component of net periodic benefit cost for the period?   ___ ___ ___

   d. For each annual statement of financial position presented, the amounts in accumulated other comprehensive income that have not yet been recognized as components of net periodic benefit cost, showing separately the net gain or loss, net prior service cost or credit, and net transition asset or obligation?   ___ ___ ___

   e. The amounts in accumulated other comprehensive income expected to be recognized as components of net periodic benefit cost over the fiscal year that follows the most recent annual statement of financial position presented, showing separately the net gain or loss, net prior service cost or credit, and net transition asset or obligation?   ___ ___ ___

   f. The amount and timing of any plan assets expected to be returned to the business entity during the 12-month period, or operating cycle if longer, that follows the most recent

<u>Yes</u> <u>No</u> <u>N/A</u>

annual statement of financial position presented?   ___ ___ ___

24. Have the following transitional disclosures been made on implementation of FAS-158:

    a. In the year that the recognition provisions of FAS-158 are initially applied, the incremental effect of applying FAS-158 on individual line items in the year-end balance sheet? (FAS-158, par.20)   ___ ___ ___

    b. In the year that the measurement date provisions of FAS-158 are initially applied, the separate adjustments of both retained earnings and accumulated other comprehensive income from applying FAS-158? (FAS-158, par. 21)   ___ ___ ___

Pension and Postretirement Defined Benefit Plans—Disclosure Requirements for Public Entities (Interim Periods)

1. Are disclosures made, for each income statement presented in interim financial statements, of the amount of net periodic benefit cost recognized showing separately the following: (FAS-132R, par. 9)

    a. Service cost component?   ___ ___ ___

    b. Interest cost component?   ___ ___ ___

    c. Expected return on plan assets for the period?   ___ ___ ___

    d. Amortization of the unrecognized transition obligation or asset?   ___ ___ ___

    e. Amount of recognized gains or losses?   ___ ___ ___

    f. Amount of prior service cost recognized?   ___ ___ ___

    g. Amount of gain or loss recognized due to a settlement or curtailment?   ___ ___ ___

2. Is disclosure made of the total amount of the employer's contributions paid, and expected to be paid, during the current fiscal year, if significantly different from amounts previously disclosed? (FAS-132R, par. 9) (Estimated contributions may be presented in the aggregate for contributions required by funding regulations or

Yes *No* *N/A*

laws, discretionary contributions, and noncash contributions.)   ___ ___ ___

Pension and Postretirement Defined Benefit Plans—Disclosure Requirements for Nonpublic Entities (Interim Periods)

1. Is disclosure made of the total amount of the employer's contributions paid, and expected to be paid, during the current fiscal year, if significantly different from amounts previously disclosed? (FAS-132R, par. 10) (Estimated contributions may be presented in the aggregate for contributions required by funding regulations or laws, discretionary contributions, and noncash contributions.)   ___ ___ ___

Pension and Postretirement Defined Contribution Plans—All Companies

1. Is the following information about the entity's defined contribution pension plans disclosed separately from the entity's defined benefit pension plans: (FAS-132R, par. 11)

   a. A brief description of the plan?   ___ ___ ___

   b. The amount of cost recognized during the period?   ___ ___ ___

   c. The nature and effect of significant matters affecting comparability of information for all periods presented such as a change in the rate of employer contributions, a business combination, or a divestiture?   ___ ___ ___

Pension and Postretirement Multiemployer Plans—All Companies

1. For multiemployer plans, has the following been disclosed:

   a. Amount of contributions to such plans during the period? (FAS-132R, par. 12) (Total contributions to multiemployer plans may be

Yes No N/A

disclosed without separating the amounts attributable to pensions and other postretirement benefits.) ___ ___ ___

b. A description of the nature and effect of any changes affecting comparability (such as a change in the rate of employer contributions, a business combination, or a divestiture)? (FAS-132R, par. 12) ___ ___ ___

c. The information required by FAS-5, if it is either probable or reasonably possible that an employer would withdraw from a multiemployer plan under circumstances that would give rise to a withdrawal obligation? (FAS-132R, par. 13) (*Note*: This is applicable to pension plans only.) ___ ___ ___

d. The information required by FAS-5, if it is either probable or reasonably possible that: (a) an employer would withdraw from a multiemployer postretirement benefit plan under circumstances that would give rise to a withdrawal obligation or (b) an employer's contribution to a multiemployer postretirement benefit plan would be increased during the remainder of a contract period in order to maintain a negotiated level of benefit coverage (a "maintenance of benefits" clause)? (FAS-132R, par. 13) (*Note*: This is applicable to pension plans only.) ___ ___ ___

Postretirement Defined Benefit Health Care Plans—All Companies (Interim and Annual Periods)

Note: Except for certain nonpublic entities, the disclosure requirements in 1b-e below are effective for the first interim or annual periods beginning after June 15, 2004. For nonpublic entities that sponsor one or more defined benefit postretirement health care plans, which provide prescription drug coverage but of which no plan has more than 100 participants, the disclosure requirements in 1b-e below are effective for fiscal years beginning after December 15, 2004. Early adoption is encouraged but not required. Prior to applying the accounting guidance in FSP FAS 106-2, *Accounting and Disclosure Requirements*

<u>Yes</u> <u>No</u> <u>N/A</u>

Related to the Medicare Prescription Drug, Improvement and Modernization Act of 2003, the disclosure requirements in 1a below should be provided.

1. For employers who sponsor single-employer defined benefit postretirement health care plans that provide prescription drug coverage, have the following been disclosed: (FSP FAS 106-2, pars. 20–22)

    a. For periods in which the employer has not yet been able to determine the actuarial equivalency to Medicare Part D under the Medicare Prescription Drug, Improvement and Modernization Act of 2003 (the Act):

        (1) The existence of the Act?   ⎯⎯ ⎯⎯ ⎯⎯

        (2) A statement that measures of the accumulated postretirement benefit obligation (APBO) or net periodic postretirement benefit cost do not reflect any amount associated with the federal subsidy provided by the Act because the employer is unable to conclude whether the benefits provided by the plan are actuarially equivalent to Medicare Part D under the Act?   ⎯⎯ ⎯⎯ ⎯⎯

    b. For financial statements for the first period in which the employer includes the effects of the federal subsidy provided by the Act in measuring the APBO and net periodic postretirement benefit cost:

        (1) The reduction in the APBO for the subsidy related to benefits attributed to past service?   ⎯⎯ ⎯⎯ ⎯⎯

        (2) The effect of the subsidy on the measurement of net periodic postretirement benefit cost for the current period, including:

            (i) Any amortization of the actuarial experience gain in (1) as a component of the net amortization called for by paragraph 59 of FAS-106?   ⎯⎯ ⎯⎯ ⎯⎯

            (ii) The reduction in current period service cost and interest cost on the APBO due to the subsidy?   ⎯⎯ ⎯⎯ ⎯⎯

<u>Yes</u> <u>No</u> <u>N/A</u>

    c. An explanation of any significant change in the benefit obligation or plan assets not otherwise apparent in the above disclosures? ___ ___ ___

    d. Gross benefit payments (paid and expected), including prescription drug benefits? ___ ___ ___

    e. Gross amount of the subsidy receipts (received and expected)? ___ ___ ___

Japanese Employee Pension Fund Plans

1. Are the following disclosures made for employers with Japanese Employees' Pension Fund plans (EPFs) that have accounted for the separation of the "substitutional portion" of the benefit obligation of an EPF in Japan from the corporate portion and the transfer of the "substitutional portion" and related assets to the Japanese government: (EITF 03-2, par. 8)

    a. The difference between the obligation settled and the assets transferred to the government, determined in accordance with the government formula and displayed as a subsidy from the government? ___ ___ ___

    b. Separate from the government subsidy, the derecognition of previously accrued salary progression at the time of settlement? ___ ___ ___

PLANNED MAJOR MAINTENANCE ACTIVITIES

Note: The disclosure requirements in items (1) and (2) below are prescribed by FSP AUG AIR-1, *Accounting for Planned Major Maintenance Activities*. FSP AUG AIR-1 is effective for annual periods beginning after December 15, 2006, with early adoption permitted as of the beginning of a fiscal year.

1. Is the method of accounting for planned major maintenance activities disclosed? (FSP AUG AIR-1, par. 11a) ___ ___ ___

2. Have the following transitional disclosures been made on implementation of FSP AUG AIR-1: (FSP AUG AIR-1 pars. 11b-e)

<u>Yes</u> <u>No</u> <u>N/A</u>

a. A description of the prior-period information that has been retrospectively adjusted, if any? ___ ___ ___

b. The effect of the change on income from continuing operations, net income (or other appropriate captions of changes in the applicable net assets or performance indicator), any other affected financial statement line item, and any affected per share amounts for any periods retrospectively adjusted? ___ ___ ___

c. The cumulative effect of the change on retained earnings or other components of equity or net assets in the statement of financial position as of the beginning of the earliest period presented? ___ ___ ___

d. If retrospective application to all prior periods is impracticable, the reasons why it is impracticable and a description of the alternative method used to report the change? ___ ___ ___

POSTEMPLOYMENT BENEFITS

1. If the company has not accrued an obligation for postemployment benefits (e.g., salary continuation, supplemental unemployment benefits, severance benefits, disability related benefits, job training and counseling, and continuation of health and insurance coverage) provided to former or inactive employees, including their beneficiaries and covered dependents, after employment but before retirement, only because the amount cannot be reasonably estimated, has that fact been disclosed? (FAS-112, par. 7) ___ ___ ___

QUASI-REORGANIZATIONS AND REORGANIZATIONS UNDER THE BANKRUPTCY CODE

Quasi-Reorganizations

1. After a quasi-reorganization or corporate re-adjustment: (ARB-43, Ch. 7A, par. 10; ARB-46, par. 2)

Yes No N/A

a. Was the offsetting adjustment charged to retained earnings?   — — —

b. If the adjustment exceeds the balance in the
retained earnings account, was the difference
charged to additional paid-in capital?   — — —

c. Has a new retained earnings account been
established and dated to show that it runs
from the effective date of the readjustment?
(This dating should be disclosed in the financial statements until such time as the effective
date is no longer deemed to possess any special significance, which is generally not more
than ten years.)   — — —

2. Are assets carried forward as of the date of the
readjustment at fair amounts? (ARB-43, Ch. 7A,
par. 4)   — — —

3. If the fair value of any asset is not readily determinable and a conservative estimate was used:
(ARB-43, Ch. 7A, par. 4)

a. Was the amount described as an estimate?   — — —

b. Was any material difference arising through
realization, or otherwise, and not attributable
to events occurring or circumstances arising
after the readjustment date not carried to income or retained earnings?   — — —

4. For companies that recognize the tax benefits of
prior deductible temporary differences and
carryforwards in income rather than contributed capital (i.e., companies that have previously adopted FAS-
96 and effected a quasi-reorganization that involved only the elimination of a deficit in retained
earnings), have the following disclosures been
made: (FAS-109, par. 39)

a. The date of the quasi-reorganization?   — — —

b. The manner of reporting the tax benefits and
that it differs from present accounting requirements for other entities?   — — —

c. The effect of those tax benefits on income from
continuing operations, income before extraordinary items, and net income (and on related
per share amounts, if applicable)?   — — —

Reorganizations under the Bankruptcy Code

1. Have the following disclosures been made for companies that have filed petitions with the Bankruptcy Court and that expect to reorganize as going concerns under Chapter 11: (SOP 90-7, pars. 23–31, 34)

   a. Prepetition liabilities, including claims that become known after a petition is filed, which are not subject to reasonable estimation? ___ ___ ___

   b. Principal categories of claims subject to compromise? ___ ___ ___

   c. The extent to which reported interest expense differs from stated contractual interest? ___ ___ ___

   d. Details of operating cash receipts and payments resulting from the reorganization if the indirect method is used in the statement of cash flows? ___ ___ ___

   e. In the earnings per share calculation whether it is probable that the plan will require the issuance of common stock or common stock equivalents, thereby diluting current equity interests? ___ ___ ___

2. Have the following disclosures been made in consolidated financial statements including one or more entities in reorganization under Chapter 11 and one or more entities not in reorganization proceedings: (SOP 90-7, pars. 32–33)

   a. Condensed combined financial statements of the entities in reorganization proceedings? ___ ___ ___

   b. Intercompany receivables and payables of entities in reorganization? ___ ___ ___

3. Have the following disclosures been made for companies that have emerged from Chapter 11 under confirmed plans that adopt fresh start reporting: (SOP 90-7, par. 39)

   a. Adjustments to the historical amounts of individual assets and liabilities? ___ ___ ___

   b. The amount of debt forgiveness? ___ ___ ___

   c. The amount of prior retained earnings or deficit eliminated? ___ ___ ___

Yes No N/A

d. Significant matters relating to the determination of reorganization value such as:

   (1) The method or methods used to determine reorganization value and factors, such as discount rates, tax rates, number of years for which cash flows are projected and the method of determining terminal value?   ____ ____ ____

   (2) Sensitive assumptions about which there is a reasonable possibility of the occurrence of a variation that would significantly affect the measurement of reorganization value?   ____ ____ ____

   (3) Assumptions about anticipated conditions that are expected to be different from current conditions, unless otherwise apparent?   ____ ____ ____

4. Has the following disclosure been made for companies that have emerged from Chapter 11 under confirmed plans that adopt fresh start reporting and have recorded an adjustment that resulted from a preconfirmation contingency: (PB-11, pars. 8–9)

a. The adjustment in income or loss from continuing operations of the emerged entity?   ____ ____ ____

RELATED-PARTY DISCLOSURES

1. Are the following disclosures made for material related-party transactions (other than compensation arrangements, expense allowances, and other similar items in the ordinary course of business): (FAS-57, par. 2)

a. The nature of the relationship of the parties involved?   ____ ____ ____

b. A description of the transactions, including transactions to which no amounts or nominal amounts were ascribed, for each of the periods for which income statements are presented, and such other information deemed necessary to an understanding of the effects of the transactions on the financial statements?   ____ ____ ____

Yes   No   N/A

   c. The dollar amounts of transactions for each of the periods for which income statements are presented and the effects of any change in the method of establishing the terms from those used in the preceding period?   ____ ____ ____

   d. Amounts due from or to related parties as of the date of each balance sheet presented and, if not otherwise apparent, the terms and manner of settlement?   ____ ____ ____

2. Are disclosures concerning related-party transactions worded in a manner that does not imply that the transactions were consummated on terms equivalent to those that prevail in arm's-length transactions, unless such representations can be substantiated? (FAS-57, par. 3)   ____ ____ ____

3. Is the nature of the control relationship disclosed, even though there are no related-party transactions, when the client and one or more other enterprises are under common ownership or management control and the existence of that control could result in operating results or financial position of the client significantly different from those that would have resulted if the client were autonomous? (FAS-57, par. 4)   ____ ____ ____

4. Are notes or accounts receivable due from officers, employees, or affiliated enterprises shown separately and not included under a general heading, such as notes receivable or accounts receivable? (ARB-43, Ch. 1A, par. 5)   ____ ____ ____

5. Have disclosures been made for guarantees issued for the benefit of related parties such as joint ventures and equity method investees? (See Part IV, "Contingencies, Risk, Uncertainties, and Concentrations")   ____ ____ ____

RESEARCH AND DEVELOPMENT

1. Are the following disclosures made for an entity that accounts for its obligations under a research and development arrangement as a contract to perform research and development for others: (FAS-68, par. 14)

<u>*Yes*</u> <u>*No*</u> <u>*N/A*</u>

    a. The terms of significant agreements under the research and development arrangement (including royalty arrangements, purchase provisions, license agreement, and commitments to provide additional funding) as of the date of each balance sheet presented?   —— —— ——

    b. The amount of compensation earned and costs incurred under such contracts for each period for which an income statement is presented?   —— —— ——

2. Is disclosure made of total research and development costs charged to expense in each period for which an income statement is presented? (FAS-2, par. 13)   —— —— ——

3. For research and development assets acquired in a business combination accounted for as a purchase that have no alternative future use, has disclosure been made of the portion of the purchase price that has been allocated to research and development and charged to expense at the date of consummation of the business combination? (FIN-4, par. 5)   —— —— ——

4. Have research and development costs incurred for computer software to be sold, leased, or otherwise marketed been disclosed either separately or as part of total research and development costs for each period presented? (FAS-86, par. 12)   —— —— ——

SABBATICAL LEAVE AND OTHER SIMILAR BENEFITS

Note: The disclosure requirements in items 1 and 2 below are prescribed by EITF 06-2, *Accounting for Sabbatical Leave and Other Similar Benefits Pursuant to FASB Statement No. 43, "Accounting for Compensated Absences."* EITF 06-2 is effective for fiscal years beginning after December 15, 2006, with early adoption permitted provided that: (a) the consensus is applied as of the beginning of the fiscal year and (b) financial statements for any period (interim or annual) of the fiscal year have not yet been issued.

1. If the entity applied the consensus in EITF 06-2 as a change in accounting principle through a

cumulative-effect adjustment to retained earnings or other components of equity or net assets
in the statement of financial position as of the
beginning of the year of adoption, has the cumulative effect of the change on retained earnings or other components of equity or net assets
in the statement of financial position been disclosed? (EITF 06-2)   ___ ___ ___

2. If the entity applied the consensus in EITF 06-2
as a change in accounting principle through retrospective application to all prior periods, has
the following been disclosed: (EITF 06-2)

    a. A description of the prior period information
that has been retrospectively adjusted?   ___ ___ ___

    b. The effect of the change on income from con-
tinuing operations, net income (or other appropriate captions of changes in the applicable
net assets or performance indicator), any other
affected financial statement line item, and any
affected per share amounts for the current
period and for any prior periods retrospectively adjusted?   ___ ___ ___

    c. The cumulative effect of the change on re-
tained earnings or other components of equity
or net assets in the statement of financial position as of the beginning of the earliest period presented?   ___ ___ ___

SEGMENT INFORMATION

1. Have disclosures been made of the factors used
to identify the entity's reportable segments, including the basis of organization, such as: (FAS-
131, par. 26)

    a. Differences in products and services?   ___ ___ ___

    b. Geographic areas?   ___ ___ ___

    c. Regulatory environments?   ___ ___ ___

    d. A combination of factors?   ___ ___ ___

2. Have the types of products and services from
which each reportable segment derives its rev-
enues been disclosed? (FAS-131, par. 26)   ___ ___ ___

<u>Yes</u> <u>No</u> <u>N/A</u>

3. Have the amount of profit or loss and total assets for each reportable segment been disclosed? (FAS-131, par. 27) — — —

4. Have the following financial information been disclosed about each reportable segment, if the specified amounts are included in the determination of segment profit or loss reviewed by the chief operating decision maker: (FAS-131, par. 27)

   a. Revenues from external customers? — — —

   b. Revenues from transactions with other operating segment? — — —

   c. Interest revenue (this may be reported net of interest expense if a majority of the segment's revenues are from interest and the chief operating decision maker relies primarily on net interest revenue to assess performance)? — — —

   d. Interest expense? — — —

   e. Depreciation, depletion, and amortization? — — —

   f. Unusual items, as described in APB Opinion No. 30? — — —

   g. Equity in the net income of investees accounted for by the equity method? — — —

   h. Income tax expense or benefit? — — —

   i. Extraordinary items? — — —

   j. Significant noncash items other than depreciation, depletion, and amortization? — — —

5. Have the following financial information been disclosed about each reportable segment, if the specified amounts are included in the determination of segment assets reviewed by the chief operating decision maker: (FAS-131, par. 28)

   a. The amount of investment in equity-method investees? — — —

   b. Total expenditures for additions to long-lived assets (other than financial instruments, long-term customer relationships of a financial institution, mortgage and other servicing rights, deferred policy acquisition costs, and deferred tax assets)? — — —

<u>Yes</u> <u>No</u> <u>N/A</u>

6. Have disclosures been made of the measure-
    ments used for segment profit or loss and seg-
    ment assets for each reportable segment, includ-
    ing at a minimum the following information:
    (FAS-131, par. 31)

    a. The basis of accounting for any transactions
       between reportable segments?   ___ ___ ___

    b. The nature of any differences between the
       measurements of the reportable segments'
       profit or loss and the entity's consolidated in-
       come before income taxes, extraordinary
       items, discontinued operations, and cumula-
       tive effect of changes in accounting principles? ___ ___ ___

    c. The nature of any differences between the
       measurements of the reportable segments'
       assets and the entity's consolidated assets?   ___ ___ ___

    d. The nature of any changes from prior periods
       in the measurement methods used to deter-
       mine reported segment profit or loss and the
       effect, if any, of those changes on the amount
       of segment profit or loss?   ___ ___ ___

    e. The nature and effect of any asymmetrical al-
       locations to segments (e.g., an entity might
       allocate depreciation expense to a segment
       without allocating the related depreciable as-
       sets to that segment)?   ___ ___ ___

7. Have reconciliations of all of the following items
    been disclosed: (FAS-131, par. 32)

    a. The total of the reportable segments' revenues
       to the entity's consolidated revenues?   ___ ___ ___

    b. The total of the reportable segments' profit or
       loss to the entity's consolidated income before
       income taxes, extraordinary items, discontin-
       ued operations, and cumulative effect of
       changes in accounting principles? (However,
       if an entity allocates items such as income
       taxes and extraordinary items to segments, the
       entity may choose to reconcile the total of the
       segments' profit or loss to consolidated in-
       come after those items.)   ___ ___ ___

    c. The total of the reportable segments' assets to
       the entity's consolidated assets?   ___ ___ ___

    d. The total of the reportable segments' amounts for every other significant item of information disclosed to the corresponding consolidated amount (e.g., an entity may choose to disclose liabilities for its reportable segments, in which case the entity would reconcile the total of reportable segments' liabilities for each segment to the enterprise's consolidated liabilities if the segment liabilities are significant)?   ___ ___ ___

8. Have the following items been disclosed on an "entity-wide" basis, unless they are disclosed as part of the information about reportable segments (*Note*: Entities that have a single reportable segment are also required to disclose this information.): (FAS-131, pars. 36–39)

    a. Revenues from external customers for each product and service or each group of similar products and services, based on information used to produce the entity's general-purpose financial statements (unless it is impracticable to do so, in which case that fact should be disclosed)?   ___ ___ ___

    b. The following information about geographic areas, based on information used to produce the entity's general-purpose financial statements (unless it is impracticable to do so, in which case that fact should be disclosed):

        (1) Revenues from external sources: (a) attributed to the entity's country of domicile and (b) attributed to all foreign countries in total from which the entity derives revenues? (If revenues from external customers attributed to an individual foreign country are material, those revenues should be disclosed separately; an entity should disclose the basis for attributing revenues from external customers to individual countries.)   ___ ___ ___

        (2) Long-lived assets (other than financial instruments, long-term customer relationships of a financial institution, mortgage and other servicing rights, deferred policy acquisition costs, and deferred tax assets) located in: (a) the entity's country of do-

    micile and (b) all foreign countries in to-
tal in which the entity holds assets? (If
assets in an individual foreign country are
material, those assets should be disclosed
separately.)   ____ ____ ____

  c. The extent of the entity's reliance on a single
external customer from which 10% or more
of revenues are derived, the amount of revenues earned from each such single customer,
and the operating segment reporting the revenue?   ____ ____ ____

9. Has the following information been disclosed
about each reportable segment in condensed financial statements of interim periods: (FAS-131,
par. 33)

  a. Revenues from external customers?   ____ ____ ____

  b. Intersegment revenues?   ____ ____ ____

  c. Segment profit or loss?   ____ ____ ____

  d. Total assets for which there has been a material change from the amount disclosed in the
last annual report?   ____ ____ ____

  e. A description of differences from the last annual report in the basis of segmentation or in
the basis of measurement of segment profit
or loss?   ____ ____ ____

  f. A reconciliation of the total of the reportable
segments' profit or loss to the entity's consolidated income before income taxes, extraordinary items, discontinued operations, and cumulative effect of changes in accounting principles? (However, if an entity allocates items
such as income taxes and extraordinary items
to segments, the entity may choose to reconcile the total of the segments' profit or loss to
consolidated income after those items). ____ ____ ____

10. If an entity changes the structure of its internal
organization in a manner that causes the composition of its reportable segments to change, has
the corresponding information for earlier periods, including interim periods, been restated,
unless it is impracticable to do so? (*Note*: The
entity should also disclose that it has restated the

segment information for earlier periods. If the segment information for earlier periods, including interim periods, is not restated to reflect the change, the entity should disclose in the year in which the change occurs segment information for the current period under both the old basis and the new basis of segmentation, unless it is impracticable to do so.) (FAS-131, pars. 34–35)

____ ____ ____

SHARE-BASED PAYMENT

Note: The disclosure requirements below are prescribed by FAS-123 (Revised 2004), *Share-Based Payment* (FAS-123R), which is effective as of (1) the beginning of the first interim or annual reporting period beginning after June 15, 2005 for public entities that do not file as small business issuers-- however, in Release 33-8568 the SEC adopted a rule that allows public companies that do not file as small business issuers to implement FAS-123R at the beginning of their next fiscal year, instead of the next reporting period, that begins after June 15, 2005; (2) the beginning of the first interim or annual reporting period beginning after December 15, 2005 for public entities that file as small business issuer—however, in Release 33-8568 the SEC adopted a rule that allows small business issuers to implement FAS-123R at the beginning of their next fiscal year, instead of the next reporting period, that begins after December 15, 2005; and (3) the beginning of the first annual period beginning after December 15, 2005 for nonpublic entities. Early adoption is encouraged. If an entity has not adopted FAS-123R, see "Stock-Based Compensation."

1. For an entity with one or more share-based payment arrangements, has the information below been disclosed: (FAS-123R, par. 64 and A240-A242; FSP FAS 123R-6, par. 4)

    a. A description of the share-based payment arrangement(s) that includes the following:

        (1) The general terms of awards under the arrangement(s), such as the requisite service period(s) and any other substantive conditions (including those related to vesting)?

        ____ ____ ____

	Yes	No	N/A

(2) The maximum contractual term of equity (or liability) share options or similar instruments? ___ ___ ___

(3) The number of shares authorized for awards of equity share options or other equity instruments? ___ ___ ___

(4) The method used to measure compensation cost from share-based payment arrangements with employees? ___ ___ ___

b. For the most recent year for which an income statement is presented, the following:

(1) The number and weighted-average exercise prices (or conversion ratios) for each of the following groups of share options (or share units):

(i) Outstanding at the beginning of the year? ___ ___ ___

(ii) Outstanding at the end of the year? ___ ___ ___

(iii) Exercisable or convertible at the end of the year? ___ ___ ___

(iv) Granted during the year? ___ ___ ___

(v) Exercised or converted during the year? ___ ___ ___

(vii) Forfeited during the year? ___ ___ ___

(vii) Expired during the year? ___ ___ ___

(2) The number and weighted-average grant-date fair value (or calculated value for a nonpublic entity that uses that method or intrinsic value for awards measured pursuant to FAS-123R, pars. 24-25) of equity instruments not specified in item 1b(1) above (e.g., shares of nonvested stock), for each of the following groups of equity instruments:

(i) Nonvested at the beginning of the year? ___ ___ ___

(ii) Nonvested at the end of the year? ___ ___ ___

(iii) Granted during the year? ___ ___ ___

(iv) Vested during the year? ___ ___ ___

(v) Forfeited during the year? ___ ___ ___

c. For each year for which an income statement is presented, the following:

   (1) The weighted-average grant-date fair value (or calculated value for a nonpublic entity that uses that method or intrinsic value for awards measured at that value pursuant to FAS-123R, pars. 24-25) of equity options or other equity instruments granted during the year?   ___ ___ ___

   (2) The total intrinsic value of options exercised (or share units converted) during the year?   ___ ___ ___

   (3) Share-based liabilities paid during the year?   ___ ___ ___

   (4) The total fair value of shares vested during the year?   ___ ___ ___

d. For fully vested share options (or share units) and share options expected to vest at the date of the latest balance sheet, the following:

   (1) For options (or share units) outstanding: ___ ___ ___

     (i) The number of options (or share units)?   ___ ___ ___

     (ii) Weighted-average exercise price (or conversion ratio)?   ___ ___ ___

     (iii) Aggregate intrinsic value (except for nonpublic entities)?   ___ ___ ___

     (iv) Weighted-average remaining contractual term?   ___ ___ ___

   (2) For options (or share units) currently exercisable or convertible:

     (i) The number of options (or share units)?   ___ ___ ___

     (ii) Weighted-average exercise price (or conversion ratio)?   ___ ___ ___

     (iii) Aggregate intrinsic value (except for nonpublic entities)?   ___ ___ ___

     (iv) Weighted-average remaining contractual term?   ___ ___ ___

<u>Yes</u> <u>No</u> <u>N/A</u>

e. For each year for which an income statement is presented (not required for entities that use the intrinsic value method pursuant to FAS-123R, pars. 24-25) the following:

(1) A description of the method used during the year to estimate the fair value (or calculated value) of awards under share-based payment arrangements?   ___ ___ ___

(2) A description of the significant assumptions used during the year to estimate the fair value (or calculated value) of share-based compensation awards, including (if applicable):

    (i) Expected term of share options and similar instruments, including a discussion of the method used to incorporate the contractual term of the instruments and employees' expected exercise and post-vesting employment termination behavior into the fair value (or calculated value) of the instrument?   ___ ___ ___

    (ii) Expected volatility of the entity's shares and the method used to estimate expected volatility?   ___ ___ ___

    (iii) If the method used to estimate expected volatility employs different volatilities during the contractual term, the range of expected volatilities used and the weighted-average expected volatility?   ___ ___ ___

    (iv) For nonpublic entities that use the calculated value method: (a) the reasons why it is not practicable to estimate the expected volatility of its share price, (b) the appropriate industry sector index selected, (c) the reasons for selecting the industry sector index, and (d) how historical volatility has been calculated using the industry sector index selected?   ___ ___ ___

    (v) Expected dividends?   ___ ___ ___

    (vi) If the method used to estimate fair value employs different dividend rates during the contractual term, the range of expected dividends used and the weighted-average expected dividends?   ____ ____ ____

    (vii) Risk-free rate(s)?   ____ ____ ____

    (viii) If the method used to estimate fair value employs different risk-free rates, the range of risk-free rates used?   ____ ____ ____

    (ix) Discount for post-vesting restrictions and the method for estimating it?   ____ ____ ____

f. For an entity that grants equity or liability instruments under multiple share-based payment arrangements with employees, the information described in items 1a–e separately for different types of awards to the extent that the differences in the characteristics of the awards are important to an understanding of an entity's use of share-based compensation? Examples of separate disclosures for different types of awards include:

    (1) The weighted exercise prices (or conversion ratios) at the end of the year for options (or share units) with a fixed exercise price (or conversion ratio) and those with an indexed exercise price (or conversion ratio).   ____ ____ ____

    (2) The number of options (or share units) not yet exercisable into those that will become exercisable (or convertible) based solely on fulfilling a service condition and those for which a performance condition must be met for the options (share units) to become exercisable (convertible).   ____ ____ ____

    (3) Awards that are classified as equity and those classified as liabilities.   ____ ____ ____

g. For each year for which an income statement is presented, the following:

    (1) Total compensation cost for share-based payment arrangements recognized in in-

<table>
<tr><td></td><td>Yes</td><td>No</td><td>N/A</td></tr>
</table>

come as well as the total related recognized tax benefit? ____ ____ ____

(2) Total compensation cost for share-based payment arrangements capitalized as part of the cost of an asset? ____ ____ ____

(3) A description of significant modifications, including:

    (i) The terms of the modifications? ____ ____ ____

    (ii) The number of employees affected? ____ ____ ____

    (iii) The total incremental compensation cost resulting from the modifications? ____ ____ ____

h. As of the latest balance sheet date presented, the following:

(1) The total compensation cost related to nonvested awards not yet recognized? ____ ____ ____

(2) The weighted-average period over which the total compensation cost related to nonvested awards not yet recognized is expected to be recognized? ____ ____ ____

i. If not separately disclosed elsewhere, the amount of cash received from exercise of share options and similar instruments granted under share-based payment arrangements? ____ ____ ____

j. If not separately disclosed elsewhere, the tax benefit realized from stock options exercised during the annual period? ____ ____ ____

k. If not separately disclosed elsewhere, the amount of cash used to settle equity instruments granted under share-based payment arrangements? ____ ____ ____

l. A description of the entity's policy, if any, for issuing shares upon share option exercise (or share unit conversion), including the source of those shares (i.e., new shares or treasury shares)? ____ ____ ____

m. If as a result of an entity's policy for issuing shares upon share option exercise (or share unit conversion), an entity expects to repurchase shares in the following annual period, an estimate of the amount (or range, if more

Yes No N/A

appropriate) of shares to be repurchased during that period? ___ ___ ___

n. Any other information necessary to understand:

(1) The nature and terms of share-based payment arrangements that existed during the period and the potential effects of those arrangements on shareholders? ___ ___ ___

(2) The effect of compensation cost arising from share-based payment arrangements on the income statement? ___ ___ ___

(3) The method of estimating the fair value of the goods or services received, or the fair value of the equity instruments granted (or offered to grant), during the period? ___ ___ ___

(4) The cash flow effects resulting from share-based payment arrangements? ___ ___ ___

o. Supplemental information that might be useful to investors and creditors, such as a range of values calculated on the basis of different assumptions? (*Note*: Entities are *encouraged*, but not required, to disclose the supplemental information. Also, the supplemental information should be reasonable and should not lessen the prominence and credibility of the required disclosure information. The alternative assumptions should be described to enable users of the financial statements to understand the basis of the supplemental information.) ___ ___ ___

2. For an entity that acquires goods or services other than employee services in share-based payment transactions, have disclosure requirements similar to those in item 1 above which are important to an understanding of the effects of those transactions on the financial statements been provided? (FAS-123R, par. 65) ___ ___ ___

3. For an entity that applies the modified retrospective application method to all prior years for which FAS-123 was effective and does not present all of those years in comparative financial statements, have the effects of any adjustments to the

beginning balances of paid-in capital, deferred taxes, and retained earnings for the earliest year presented, to reflect the results of modified retrospective application to those prior years not presented, been disclosed in the year FAS-123R is adopted? (*Note:* If an entity applies the modified retrospective application method only to prior interim periods in the year of initial adoption of FAS-123R, there would be no adjustment to the beginning balances of paid-in capital, deferred taxes, or retained earnings for the year of initial adoption.) (FAS-123R, par. 77)   ___ ___ ___

4. In the period that FAS-123R is adopted, has the effect of the change from applying the original provisions of FAS-123 on the following been disclosed: (FAS-123R, par. 84)

a. Income from continuing operations?   ___ ___ ___

b. Income before income taxes?   ___ ___ ___

c. Net income?   ___ ___ ___

d. Cash flow from operations?   ___ ___ ___

e. Cash flow from financing activities?   ___ ___ ___

f. Basic and diluted earnings per share?   ___ ___ ___

5. For a public entity that has awards under share-based payment arrangements with employees that are accounted for under the intrinsic value method of APB-25 for any period for which an income statement is presented, has the following information been disclosed in tabular format: (FAS-123R, par. 84)

a. Net income and basic and diluted earnings per share as reported?   ___ ___ ___

b. The share-based employee compensation cost, net of related tax effects, included in net income as reported?   ___ ___ ___

c. The share-based employee compensation cost, net of related tax effects, which would have been included in net income if the fair value-based method had been applied to all awards?   ___ ___ ___

d. Pro forma net income as if the fair-value-based method had been applied to all awards? (*Note:* Pro forma amounts should reflect the difference in share-based employee compensation cost, if any, included in net income and the total cost measured by the fair-value-based method, as well as additional tax effects, if any, that would have been recognized in the income statement if the fair-value-based method had been applied to all awards.) ___ ___ ___

e. Pro forma basic and diluted earnings per share as if the fair-value-based method had been applied to all awards? (*Note*: Pro forma per share amounts should reflect the change in the denominator of the diluted earnings per share calculation as if the assumed proceeds under the treasury stock method, including measured but unrecognized compensation cost and any excess tax benefits credited to additional paid-in capital, were determined under the fair-value-based method.) ___ ___ ___

6. A nonpublic entity that used the minimum value method for pro forma disclosures under the original provisions of FAS-123 should not continue to provide those pro forma disclosures for outstanding awards accounted for under the intrinsic value method of APB-25. (FAS-123R, par. 85) ___ ___ ___

STOCK-BASED COMPENSATION

Note: The disclosures below are applicable to entities that have not yet adopted FAS-123 (Revised 2004), *Share-Based Payment* (FAS-123R). If an entity has adopted FAS-123R, see "Share-Based Payment."

1. Is the following information prominently disclosed in the "Summary of Significant Accounting Policies," or its equivalent, for all companies regardless of whether they measure compensation cost using FAS-123 or APB-25: (FAS-148, par. 2)

a. The method used (either the intrinsic value method or the fair value based method) to account for stock-based employee compensation in each period? ___ ___ ___

b. If the entity has adopted the fair value method, a description of the method of reporting the

Yes No N/A

change in accounting principle for all financial statements in which the period of adoption is presented?

     ___ ___ ___

c. If awards of stock-based employee compensation were outstanding and accounted for under APB-25's intrinsic value method for any period for which an income statement is presented, is the following information in a tabular format for all periods presented:

    (1) Reported net income, and basic and diluted earnings per share?

     ___ ___ ___

    (2) Stock-based employee compensation cost, net of related tax effects, included in net income as reported?

     ___ ___ ___

    (3) Stock-based employee compensation cost, net of related tax effects, that would have been included in determining net income if the fair-value method had been applied to all awards granted, modified, or settled in fiscal periods beginning after December 15, 1994?

     ___ ___ ___

    (4) Pro forma net income assuming that the fair-value method had been applied to all awards granted, modified, or settled in fiscal periods beginning after December 15, 1994?

     ___ ___ ___

    (5) Pro forma basic and diluted earnings per share assuming that the fair-value method had been applied to all awards granted, modified, or settled in fiscal periods beginning after December 15, 1994?

     ___ ___ ___

2. For those entities adopting the fair-value method, have the following disclosures been made in the year of adoption when using the retroactive restatement or modified prospective transitional approach: (FAS-148, par. 2)

a. The transition adjustment, if any?

     ___ ___ ___

b. The effect of restatement of intervening periods, if any?

     ___ ___ ___

3. Are the following disclosures made regarding the entity's stock-based compensation plans (and separately for each type of award granted to the

Yes No N/A

extent separate disclosure would be useful) for all companies regardless of whether they measure compensation cost using FAS-123 or APB-25: (FAS-123, pars. 46–48) ⎯ ⎯ ⎯

a. A description of the plan, including the general terms of awards, such as vesting requirements, maximum term of options granted, and number of shares authorized for grants of options or other equity instruments? ⎯ ⎯ ⎯

b. The number and weighted-average exercise prices of options that were:

    (1) Outstanding at the beginning of the year? ⎯ ⎯ ⎯

    (2) Outstanding at the end of the year? ⎯ ⎯ ⎯

    (3) Granted during the year? ⎯ ⎯ ⎯

    (4) Exercised during the year? ⎯ ⎯ ⎯

    (5) Exercisable at the end of the year? ⎯ ⎯ ⎯

    (6) Forfeited during the year? ⎯ ⎯ ⎯

    (7) Expired during the year? ⎯ ⎯ ⎯

c. Weighted-average fair value (as of grant date) of options granted during the year? (*Note:* If the exercise price of some options differs from the market price of the stock on the grant date, weighted-average exercise prices and weighted-average fair values of options should be disclosed separately for options whose exercise price (a) equals, (b) exceeds, or (c) is less than the market price of the stock on the date of grant.) ⎯ ⎯ ⎯

d. Number and weighted-average fair value (as of grant date) of equity instruments other than options (e.g., shares of nonvested stock) granted during the year? ⎯ ⎯ ⎯

e. A description of the method and significant assumptions used during the year to estimate the fair values of options, including the risk-free interest rate, expected life, expected volatility, and expected dividends? ⎯ ⎯ ⎯

f. Total compensation cost recognized in the financial statements? ⎯ ⎯ ⎯

g. The terms of significant modifications of outstanding awards? ⎯ ⎯ ⎯

Yes *No* *N/A*

h. The range of exercise prices, the weighted-average exercise price, and the weighted-average remaining contractual life for options outstanding as of the date of the latest balance sheet presented, and for each range: ___ ___ ___

   (1) The number, weighted-average exercise price, and weighted-average remaining contractual life of options outstanding? ___ ___ ___

   (2) The number and weighted-average exercise price of options currently exercisable? ___ ___ ___

4. Is disclosure made of the accounting policy for the method of recognizing compensation cost for fixed awards with graded (pro rata) vesting (i.e., straight-line or the accelerated expense attribution method under FASB Interpretation No. 28)? (EITF 00-23, par. 13) ___ ___ ___

SUBSEQUENT EVENTS

1. Are appropriate adjustments made to the financial statements based on information that became available prior to the issuance of the financial statements (the information provides evidence with respect to conditions that existed at the date of the balance sheet)? (AU 560.03–.04) ___ ___ ___

2. Are appropriate disclosures made in the financial statements based on information that became available prior to the issuance of the financial statements (although the information does not suggest that conditions existed at the date of the balance sheet, it is nonetheless necessary to disclose such conditions in order for the financial statements not to be misleading)? (FAS-5, par. 11; AU 560.05–.07; AU 560.09) ___ ___ ___

TERMINATION CLAIMS

1. If the total of the undeterminable parts of a termination claim is believed to be material, have the essential facts been disclosed? (ARB-43, Ch. 11C, par. 19) ___ ___ ___

Yes No N/A

2. Have material termination claims been separately disclosed in the balance sheet? (ARB-43,
   Ch. 11C, par. 21)   ___ ___ ___

3. Has disclosure been made of the relationship
   between advances or other loans received on terminated contracts and the potential termination
   claim receivable? (ARB-43, Ch. 11C, par. 22)   ___ ___ ___

4. If the amount of termination sales is material, has
   it been separately disclosed in the income statement? (ARB-43, Ch. 11C, par. 23)   ___ ___ ___

TRANSFERS AND SERVICING OF FINANCIAL ASSETS

Transfers of Financial Assets

1. Have the following disclosures been made for
   transfers of financial assets (FAS-140, par. 17a,
   17d, 17h, and 17i; FAS-156, par. 4h):

   a. If the entity has entered into repurchase agree-
      ments or securities lending transactions, has
      the policy for requiring collateral or other se-
      curity been disclosed?   ___ ___ ___

   b. If the entity has pledged any of its assets as
      collateral that are not reclassified and sepa-
      rately reported in the balance sheet, has dis-
      closure been made of the carrying amount and
      classification of those assets as of the date of
      the latest balance sheet presented?   ___ ___ ___

   c. If the entity has accepted collateral that it is
      permitted by contract or custom to sell or re-
      pledge, have the following disclosures been
      made as of the date of each balance sheet pre-
      sented:

      (1) The fair value of the collateral?   ___ ___ ___

      (2) The portion of that collateral that it has
          sold or repledged?   ___ ___ ___

      (3) Information about the sources and uses
          of that collateral?   ___ ___ ___

d. If it is not practicable to estimate the fair value of certain assets obtained or liabilities incurred in transfers of financial assets during the period, has disclosure been made of those items and the reasons why it is not practicable to estimate their fair value? ____ ____ ____

e. If the entity has securitized financial assets during any period presented and accounts for that transfer as a sale, have the following disclosures been made for each major asset type (e.g., credit card receivables, automobile loans, mortgage loans):

   (1) The accounting policies for initially measuring the interests that continue to be held by the transferor, if any, and servicing assets or servicing liabilities, if any, including the methodology (whether quoted market price, prices based on sales of similar assets and liabilities, or prices based on valuation techniques) used in determining their fair value? ____ ____ ____

   (2) The characteristics of securitizations (a description of the transferor's continuing involvement with the transferred assets, including, but not limited to: servicing; recourse, and restrictions on interests that continue to be held by the transferor) and the gain or loss from sale of financial assets in securitizations? ____ ____ ____

   (3) The key assumptions used in measuring the fair value of interests that continue to be held by the transferor and servicing assets or servicing liabilities, if any, at the time of securitization, including, at a minimum: quantitative information about discount rates; expected prepayments including the expected weighted-average life of prepayable financial assets; and anticipated credit losses, if applicable? ____ ____ ____

   (4) Cash flows between the securitization SPE (special purpose entity) and the transferor, unless reported separately elsewhere in the financial statements or notes, including: proceeds from new securitizations; pro-

<u>*Yes*</u> <u>*No*</u> <u>*N/A*</u>

ceeds from collections reinvested in re-
volving-period securitizations; purchases
of delinquent or foreclosed loans; servicing fees; and cash flows received on interests that continue to be held by the
transferor?   —— —— ——

f. If the entity has interests that continue to be
held by the transferor in financial assets that
it has securitized or servicing assets or servicing liabilities relating to assets that it has
securitized, at the date of the latest balance
sheet presented, have the following disclosures been made for each major asset type
(e.g., credit card receivables, automobile loans,
mortgage loans):

  (1) The accounting policies for subsequently
measuring those interests, including the
methodology (whether quoted market
price, prices based on sales of similar assets and liabilities, or prices based on
valuation techniques) used in determining their fair value?   —— —— ——

  (2) The key assumptions used in subsequently measuring the fair value of those
interests, including at a minimum: quantitative information about discount rates;
expected prepayments including the expected weighted-average life of
prepayable financial assets; and anticipated credit losses, including expected
static pool losses if applicable?   —— —— ——

  (3) A sensitivity analysis or stress test showing the hypothetical effect on the fair
value of those interests (including any
servicing assets or servicing liabilities) of
two or more unfavorable variations from
the expected levels for each key assumption that is reported under 2 above independently from any change in another
key assumption, and a description of the
objectives, methodology, and limitations
of the sensitivity analysis or stress test?   —— —— ——

  (4) For the securitized assets and any other
financial assets that it manages together
with them:

Yes *No* *N/A*

(i)   The total principal amount outstanding, the portion that has been derecognized, and the portion that continues to be recognized in each category reported in the balance sheet, at the end of the period?   ___ ___ ___

(ii)   Delinquencies at the end of the period?   ___ ___ ___

(iii)   Credit losses, net of recoveries, during the period?   ___ ___ ___

(iv)   Average balances during the period? (This disclosure item is encouraged, but not required.)   ___ ___ ___

2.   For certain retained beneficial interests in securitization transactions that are accounted for as sales under FAS-140 and certain purchased beneficial interests in securitized financial assets that have unrealized losses that have not been recognized as other-than-temporary in accordance with EITF 99-20 or EITF 03-1, have the disclosures in Part 1, "Investments—Debt and Equity Securities," item 8, been made? (EITF 03-1, par. 21; FSP FAS 115-1 and FAS 124-1, par. 17)   ___ ___ ___

3.   If the condition in either paragraph 16 of FAS-115 or paragraph 8(a) of FAS-5 is met, has information about loans or debt securities ("loans"), with evidence of deterioration of credit quality since origination, acquired by completion of a transfer for which it is probable, at acquisition, that there is an inability to collect all contractually required payments receivable, been included in the impairment disclosures discussed in Part IV, "Impairment of Certain Loans," item 1a and b ? (SOP 03-3, par. 15) (*Note*: This disclosure is applicable to loans acquired in fiscal years beginning after December 15, 2004. Early adoption is encouraged, but not required.)   ___ ___ ___

4.   For loans or debt securities ("loans"), with evidence of deterioration of credit quality since origination, acquired by completion of a transfer for which it is probable, at acquisition, that there is an inability to collect all contractually required payments receivable, have the following been disclosed: (SOP 03-3, pars. 14 and 16)

Yes *No* *N/A*

(*Note*: These disclosure items are applicable to loans acquired in fiscal years beginning after December 15, 2004. Early adoption is encouraged, but not required.)

a. Description of how prepayments are considered in the determination of contractual cash flows and cash flows expected to be collected? ___ ___ ___

b. Separately for both those loans that (i) are accounted for as debt securities and (ii) are not accounted for as debt securities (as of each balance sheet presented):

   (1) Outstanding balance and related carrying amount at the beginning and end of the period? ___ ___ ___

   (2) Amount of accretable yield at the beginning and end of the period, reconciled for additions, accretion, disposals of loans, and reclassifications to or from nonaccretable difference during the period? ___ ___ ___

   (3) For loans acquired during the period: (i) contractually required payments receivable, (ii) cash flows expected to be collected and (iii) fair value at the acquisition date? ___ ___ ___

   (4) For loans for which the income recognition model is not applied in accordance with paragraph 6 of SOP 03-3: (i) carrying amount at the acquisition date for loans acquired during the period and (ii) carrying amount of all loans at the end of the period? ___ ___ ___

c. For loans that are not accounted for as debt securities:

   (1) Amount of expense recognized in accordance with paragraph 8(a) of SOP 03-3, for each period for which an income statement is presented? ___ ___ ___

   (2) Reductions of the allowance recognized in accordance with paragraph 8(b)(1) of SOP 03-3 for each period for which an income statement is presented? ___ ___ ___

Yes No N/A

(3) Amount of allowance for uncollectible accounts at the beginning and end of the period for each balance sheet presented? ___ ___ ___

Servicing of Financial Assets and Liabilities

Note: The disclosure requirements in items 2-4 and 8 below are prescribed by FAS-140, *Accounting for Transfers and Servicing of Financial Assets and Extinguishments of Liabilities*, as amended by FAS-156, *Accounting for Servicing of Financial Assets*. The disclosure requirements in items 5-7 below are prescribed by FAS-156. FAS-156 is effective on a prospective basis in the first period ending in the first fiscal year that begins after September 15, 2006. Early adoption is permitted as of the beginning of an entity's fiscal year, providing the entity has not yet issued annual or interim financial statements for any period of that fiscal year. If an entity has not adopted FAS-156, the disclosure requirements in item 1 below apply.

1. Have the following disclosures been made for all servicing assets and servicing liabilities (FAS-140, par. 17e; FAS-140, Q&A, No. 100):

   a. The amounts of servicing assets or liabilities recognized and amortized during the period? ___ ___ ___

   b. The fair value of recognized servicing assets and liabilities for which it is practicable to estimate that value, and the method and significant assumptions used to estimate the fair value? ___ ___ ___

   c. The risk characteristics of the underlying financial assets used to stratify recognized servicing assets for purposes of measuring impairment in accordance with FAS-140? ___ ___ ___

   d. If the predominant risk characteristics of the underlying financial assets used to stratify recognized servicing assets for purposes of measuring impairment in accordance with FAS-140 and the resulting stratums change:

   (1) The fact that such change(s) has occurred? ___ ___ ___

   (2) The reasons for such change(s)? ___ ___ ___

e. The activity in any valuation allowance for impairment of recognized servicing assets for each period for which results of operations are presented, including:

   (1) Beginning and ending balances? — — —

   (2) Aggregate additions charged to operations? — — —

   (3) Aggregate reductions credited to operations? — — —

   (4) Aggregate direct write-downs charged against the allowances? — — —

2. Have the following disclosures been made for all servicing assets and servicing liabilities (FAS-140, par. 17e; FAS-156, par. 4h):

a. Management's basis for determining its classes of servicing assets and servicing liabilities? — — —

b. A description of the risks inherent in servicing assets and servicing liabilities and, if applicable, the instruments used to mitigate the income statement effect of changes in fair value of the servicing assets and servicing liabilities? — — —

c. If instruments are used to mitigate the income statement effect of changes in fair value of the servicing assets and servicing liabilities, quantitative information about the instruments used to manage the risks inherent in those assets and liabilities, including the fair value of those instruments at the beginning and end of the period? (*Note:* Entities are *encouraged*, but not required, to disclose this information.) — — —

d. For each period for which results of operations are presented, the following related to contractually specified servicing fees (as defined in the glossary of FAS-140), late fees, and ancillary fees:

   (1) The earned amount? — — —

   (2) A description of where each earned amount is reported in the income statement? — — —

Yes No N/A

3. Have the following disclosures been made for all servicing assets and servicing liabilities subsequently measured at fair value (FAS-140, par. 17f; FAS-156, par. 4h):

a. For each class of servicing assets and servicing liabilities, a description of where changes in fair value are reported in the income statement for each period for which results of operations are presented? _____ _____ _____

b. For each class of servicing assets and servicing liabilities, the activity in the balance of servicing assets and the activity in the balance of servicing liabilities, including, but not limited to, the following:

(1) The beginning and ending balances? _____ _____ _____

(2) Additions (through purchases of servicing assets, assumptions of servicing obligations, and servicing obligations that result from transfers of financial assets)? _____ _____ _____

(3) Disposals? _____ _____ _____

(4) Changes in fair value during the period resulting from:

(i) Changes in valuation inputs or assumptions used in the valuation model? _____ _____ _____

(ii) Other changes in fair value and a description of those changes? _____ _____ _____

(5) Other changes that affect the balance and a description of those changes? _____ _____ _____

c. A description of the valuation techniques or other methods used to estimate the fair value of servicing assets and servicing liabilities, which should include the following information if a valuation model is used:

(1) The methodology? _____ _____ _____

(2) The model validation procedures? _____ _____ _____

(3) Quantitative and qualitative information about the assumptions used in the valuation model (e.g., discount rates and prepayment speeds)? _____ _____ _____

d. If instruments are used to mitigate the income statement effect of changes in fair value of the servicing assets and servicing liabilities and quantitative information about the instruments used to manage the risks inherent in those assets and liabilities, including the fair value of those instruments at the beginning and end of the period, is disclosed (see item 2c above):

   (1) A description of the valuation techniques? ___ ___ ___

   (2) The quantitative and qualitative information about the assumptions used to estimate the fair value of those instruments? ___ ___ ___

(*Note*: Entities are *encouraged*, but not required, to disclose this information.)

4. Have the following disclosures been made for all servicing assets and servicing liabilities subsequently amortized in proportion to and over the period of estimated net servicing income or loss and assessed for impairment or increased obligation (FAS-140, par. 17g; FAS-156, par. 4h; FAS-140, Q&A, No. 100): ___ ___ ___

a. For each class of servicing assets and servicing liabilities, a description of where changes in the carrying amount are reported in the income statement for each period for which results of operations are presented? ___ ___ ___

b. For each class of servicing assets and servicing liabilities, the activity in the balance of servicing assets and the activity in the balance of servicing liabilities, including, but not limited to, the following:

   (1) The beginning and ending balances? ___ ___ ___

   (2) Additions (through purchases of servicing assets, assumption of servicing obligations, and servicing obligations that result from transfers of financial assets)? ___ ___ ___

   (3) Disposals? ___ ___ ___

   (4) Amortization? ___ ___ ___

   (5) Application of valuation allowance to adjust carrying value of servicing assets? ___ ___ ___

Yes No N/A

    (6) Other-than-temporary impairments?   —— —— ——

    (7) Other changes that affect the balance and a description of those changes?   —— —— ——

c. For each class of servicing assets and servicing liabilities, the fair value of recognized servicing assets and servicing liabilities (if estimation of such value is practicable) at the beginning and end of the period?   —— —— ——

d. A description of the valuation techniques or other methods used to estimate fair value of the servicing assets and servicing liabilities, which should include the following information if a valuation model is used:

    (1) The methodology?   —— —— ——

    (2) The model validation procedures?   —— —— ——

    (3) Quantitative and qualitative information about the assumptions used in the valuation model (e.g., discount rates and prepayment speeds)?   —— —— ——

e. If instruments are used to mitigate the income statement effect of changes in fair value of the servicing assets and servicing liabilities and quantitative information about the instruments used to manage the risks inherent in those assets and liabilities, including the fair value of those instruments at the beginning and end of the period, is disclosed (see item 2c above):   —— —— ——

    (1) A description of the valuation techniques?   —— —— ——

    (2) The quantitative and qualitative information about the assumptions used to estimate the fair value of those instruments?   —— —— ——

(*Note*: Entities are *encouraged*, but not required, to disclose this information.)

f. The risk characteristics of the underlying financial assets used to stratify recognized servicing assets for purposes of measuring impairment in accordance with paragraph 63 of FAS-140?   —— —— ——

g. If the predominant risk characteristics of the underlying financial assets used to stratify recognized servicing assets for purposes of measuring impairment in accordance with FAS-140 and the resulting stratums change:

(1) The fact that such change(s) has occurred? ___ ___ ___

(2) The reasons for such change(s)? ___ ___ ___

h. For each period for which results of operations are presented, the activity by class in any valuation allowance for impairment of recognized servicing assets, including the following:

(1) Beginning and ending balances? ___ ___ ___

(2) Aggregate additions charged to operations? ___ ___ ___

(3) Aggregate recoveries credited to operations? ___ ___ ___

(4) Aggregate write-downs charged against the allowance? ___ ___ ___

5. If, upon the initial adoption of FAS-156, an entity irrevocably elects to subsequently measure separately recognized servicing assets and servicing liabilities at fair value in accordance with paragraph 9 of FAS-156, have separate disclosures been made of the difference, as of the beginning of the year, between the fair value and the carrying amount, net of any related valuation allowance, of separately recognized servicing assets and servicing liabilities existing at the date of initial adoption? (FAS-156, par. 9) ___ ___ ___

6. If, upon the initial adoption of FAS-156, an entity with recognized servicing rights makes an irrevocable election to reclassify available-for-sale securities to trading securities as of the beginning of the year of adoption in accordance with paragraph 10 of FAS-156, have separate disclosures been made of (FAS-156, par. 10):

a. The carrying amount of reclassified securities? ___ ___ ___

b. The effect of the reclassification on the related cumulative-effect adjustment? ___ ___ ___

7. If, after the initial adoption of FAS-156, an entity irrevocably elects to subsequently measure a class of separately recognized servicing assets and servicing liabilities at fair value in accordance

with paragraph 11 of FAS-156, has separate disclosure been made of the amount of the cumulative-effect adjustment (resulting from the difference between the fair value and the carrying amount, net of any related valuation allowance, of the servicing assets and servicing liabilities that exist at the beginning of the fiscal year in which the entity makes the fair value election)? (FAS-156, par. 11)

8. If an entity subsequently measures separately-recognized servicing assets and servicing liabilities using the fair value measurement method and presents the aggregate of: (a) those amounts that are subsequently measured at fair value and (b) those other amounts that are separately recognized and subsequently measured using the amortization method, has the amount that is subsequently measured at fair value that is included in the aggregate amount been disclosed parenthetically on the face of the balance sheet? (FAS-140, par. 13B; FAS-156, par. 4f)

TROUBLED DEBT RESTRUCTURING— CREDITORS

1. Has the amount of commitments, if any, to lend additional funds to debtors owing receivables whose terms have been modified in troubled debt restructuring been disclosed as of the date of each balance sheet presented? (FAS-15, par. 40)

2. Have the following disclosures been made, either in the body of the financial statements or in the accompanying notes, about impaired loans as defined in paragraph 8 of FAS-114: (FAS-118, pars. 6 and 24)

   a. As of the date of each statement of financial position presented, the total recorded investment in the impaired loans at the end of each period and: (1) the amount of that recorded investment for which there is a related allowance for credit losses and the amount of that allowance and (2) the amount of that recorded investment for which there is no related allowance for credit losses?

<u>Yes</u> <u>No</u> <u>N/A</u>

b. The creditor's policy for recognizing interest income on impaired loans, including how cash receipts are recorded? ___ ___ ___

c. For each period for which results of operations are presented:

   (1) The average recorded investment in the impaired loans during each period? ___ ___ ___

   (2) The related amount of interest income recognized during the time within that period that the loans were impaired? ___ ___ ___

   (3) The amount of interest income recognized using a cash-basis method of accounting during the time within that period that the loans were impaired, unless not practicable? ___ ___ ___

d. For each period for which results of operations are presented, have disclosures been made of the activity in the total allowance for credit losses related to loans, including the following:

   (1) The balance in the allowance at the beginning and end of each period? ___ ___ ___

   (2) Additions charged to operations? ___ ___ ___

   (3) Direct writedowns charged against the allowance? ___ ___ ___

   (4) Recoveries of amounts previously charged off? ___ ___ ___

TROUBLED DEBT RESTRUCTURING— DEBTORS

1. Are the following disclosures made (either in the body of the financial statements or in related notes) for the period in which the troubled debt is restructured: (FAS-15, par. 25)

a. For each restructuring, a description of the principal changes in terms, the major features of settlement, or both? ___ ___ ___

b. Aggregate gain on restructuring of payables? ___ ___ ___

<u>Yes</u> <u>No</u> <u>N/A</u>

    c. Aggregate net gain or loss on transfers of assets recognized during the period?   ——— ——— ———

    d. If applicable, the per share amount of the aggregate gain on restructuring of payables?   ——— ——— ———

2. Are the following disclosures made for periods subsequent to the period in which the debt was restructured: (FAS-15, par. 26)

    a. The extent to which amounts contingently payable are included in the carrying amount of restructured payables?   ——— ——— ———

    b. Total amounts that are contingently payable on restructured payables and the conditions under which those amounts would become payable or would be forgiven when there is at least a reasonable possibility that a liability for contingent payments will be incurred?   ——— ——— ———

Accounting Resources on the Web

The following World Wide Web addresses are just a few of the resources on the Internet that are available to practitioners. Because of the evolving nature of the Internet, some addresses may change. In such a case, refer to one of the many Internet search engines, such as Yahoo (http://www.yahoo.com).

Accounting Research Manager
http://www.accountingresearchmanager.com

AICPA http://www.aicpa.org/

American Accounting Association
http://www.accounting.rutgers.com

CCH Integrated Solutions
http://cchgroup.com/books/default

FASAB http://www.fasab.gov

FASB http://www.fasb.org

Federal Tax Law http://www.taxsites.com/federal.html

Fedworld http://www.fedworld.gov

GASB http://www.gasb.org

Government Accountability Office http://www.gao.gov

House of Representatives http://www.house.gov

International Accounting Standards Board
http://www.iasb.org.uk

IRS Digital Daily http://www.irs.ustreas.gov/prod.cover.html

Learning Center http://cch.learningcenter.com

Library of Congress http://www.loc.gov

Office of Management and Budget http://www.gpo.gov

ProSystem fx Engagement http://www.epacesoftware.com

Public Company Accounting Oversight Board
http://www.pcaobus.org

Securities and Exchange Commission http://www.sec.gov

Thomas Legislative Research http://thomaslocal.gov

Cross-Reference

ORIGINAL PRONOUNCEMENTS TO
2007–2008 *GAAP FINANCIAL STATEMENT*
DISCLOSURES MANUAL CHAPTERS

This locator provides instant cross-reference between an original pronouncement that is in Level A or Level B of the GAAP hierarchy and the chapter(s) in this publication in which a pronouncement is covered. Original pronouncements are listed chronologically on the left and the chapter(s) in which they appear in the 2007–2008 *GAAP Financial Statement Disclosures Manual* on the right. When an original pronouncement has been superseded, cross-reference is made to the succeeding pronouncement.

ACCOUNTING RESEARCH BULLETINS (ARB)

(Accounting Research Bulletins 1-42 were revised, restated, or withdrawn at the time ARB No. 43 was issued.)

ORIGINAL PRONOUNCEMENT	2007–2008 *GAAP FINANCIAL STATEMENT DISCLOSURES MANUAL* REFERENCE
ARB No. 43 Restatement and Revision of Accounting Research Bulletins	

Chapter 1—Prior Opinions
1-A: Rules Adopted by Membership
	Assets and Liabilities: General, ch. **36**
	Consolidated and Combined Financial
	  Statements, ch. **9**
	Revenues and Gains, ch. **49**
	Stockholders' Equity, ch. **48**
	Other Assets: Current and Noncurrent, ch. **44**
	Other Liabilities: Current and Noncurrent,
	  ch. **47**

1-B: Opinion Issued by Predecessor Committee	Stockholders' Equity, ch. **48**
Chapter 2—Form of Statements **2-A:** Comparative Financial Statements	Consolidated and Combined Financial Statements, ch. **9** Financial Statements: Comparative, ch. **16**
2-B: Combined Statement of Income and Earned Surplus	Superseded by APB-9

Chapter 14
Disclosures of Long-Term Leases in
Financial Statements of Lessees   Superseded by APB-5

Chapter 15
Unamortized Discount, Issue Cost, and
Redemption Premium on Bonds Refunded   Superseded by APB-26

ARB No. 44
Declining-Balance Depreciation   Superseded by ARB-44 (Revised)

ARB No. 44 (Revised)
Declining-Balance Depreciation   Superseded by FAS-96 and FAS-109

ARB No. 45
Long-Term Construction-Type Contracts   Long-Term Contracts, ch. **24**

ARB No. 46
Discontinuance of Dating Earned Surplus
under the Bankruptcy Code, ch. **28**   Quasi-Reorganizations and Reorganizations

ARB No. 47
Accounting for Costs of Pension Plans   Superseded by APB-8

ARB No. 48
Business Combinations   Superseded by APB-16 and FAS-141

ARB No. 49
Earnings per Share   Superseded by APB-9

ARB No. 50
Contingencies   Superseded by FAS-5

ARB No. 51
Consolidated Financial Statements   Consolidated and Combined Financial
                                                   Statements, ch. **9**

ACCOUNTING PRINCIPLES BOARD OPINIONS (APB)

	2007–2008 *GAAP* *FINANCIAL STATEMENT*
ORIGINAL PRONOUNCEMENT	*DISCLOSURES MANUAL* REFERENCE

APB Opinion No. 1
New Depreciation Guidelines and Rules   Superseded by FAS-96 and FAS-109

APB Opinion No. 2
Accounting for the "Investment Credit"   Income Taxes, ch. **45**

APB Opinion No. 2—Addendum
Accounting Principles for Regulated
Industries   Superseded by FAS-71

APB Opinion No. 3
The Statement of Source and Application
of Funds   Superseded by APB-19

APB Opinion No. 4
Accounting for the "Investment Credit"   Income Taxes, ch. **45**

APB Opinion No. 5
Reporting of Leases in Financial
Statements of Lessee   Superseded by FAS-13

APB Opinion No. 6
Status of Accounting Research Bulletins   Property, Plant, and Equipment, ch. **42**
                                                  Stockholders' Equity, ch. **43**

APB Opinion No. 7
Accounting for Leases in Financial
Statements of Lessors   Superseded by FAS-13

APB Opinion No. 8
Accounting for the Cost of Pension Plans   Superseded by FAS-87

APB Opinion No. 9
Reporting the Results of Operations   Expenses and Losses, ch. **50**
                                                  Discontinued Operations, ch. **51**
                                                  Extraordinary Items, ch. **52**
                                                  Unusual or Infrequent Items, ch. **53**
                                                  Comprehensive Income, ch. **54**

APB Opinion No. 10
Omnibus Opinion—1966   Assets and Liabilities: General, ch. **36**
                                                  Other Assets: Current and Noncurrent, ch. **44**
                                                  Other Liabilities: Current and Noncurrent,
                                                      ch. **47**
                                                  Income Taxes, ch. **45**
                                                  Revenues and Gains, ch. **49**

APB Opinion No. 11
Accounting for Income Taxes   Superseded by FAS-96 and FAS-109

APB Opinion No. 12
Omnibus Opinion—1967   Deferred Compensation Arrangements, ch. **11**
                                                  Property, Plant, and Equipment, ch. **42**
                                                  Postemployment Benefits, ch. **27**
                                                  Postretirement Benefits Other Than Pensions,
                                                      ch. **28**
                                                  Stockholders' Equity, ch. **48**

APB Opinion No. 13
Amending paragraph 6 of APB Opinion
No. 9, Application to Commercial Banks   Expenses and Losses, ch. **50**
                                                  Discontinued Operations, ch. **51**
                                                  Extraordinary Items, ch. **52**
                                                  Unusual or Infrequent Items, ch. **53**
                                                  Comprehensive Income, ch. **54**

APB Opinion No. 27
Accounting for Lease Transactions by
Manufacturer or Dealer Lessors   Superseded by FAS-13

APB Opinion No. 28
Interim Financial Reporting   Interim Financial Reporting, ch. **21**
                                                   Inventory, ch. **39**

APB Opinion No. 29
Accounting for Nonmonetary Transactions   Nonmonetary Transactions, ch. **25**
                                                   Stockholders' Equity, ch. **48**

APB Opinion No. 30
Reporting the Results of
Operations—Reporting the Effects of
Disposal of a Segment of a Business, and
Extraordinary, Unusual, and Infrequently
Occurring Events and Transactions   Expenses and Losses, ch. **50**
                                                   Extraordinary Items, ch. **52**
                                                   Unusual or Infrequent Items, ch. **53**
                                                   Comprehensive Income, ch. **54**
                                                   Earnings per Share, ch. **55**

APB Opinion No. 31
Disclosure of Lease Commitments by
Lessees   Superseded by FAS-13

FINANCIAL ACCOUNTING STANDARDS BOARD
STATEMENTS (FAS)

	2007–2008 *GAAP* *FINANCIAL STATEMENT*
ORIGINAL PRONOUNCEMENT	*DISCLOSURES MANUAL* REFERENCE

FASB Statement No. 1
Disclosure of Foreign Currency
Translation Information   Superseded by FAS-8 and FAS-52

FASB Statement No. 2
Accounting for Research and
Development Costs   Research and Development Costs, ch. **31**
                                                   Inventory, ch. **39**

FASB Statement No. 3
Reporting Accounting Changes in Interim   Accounting Changes and Error Corrections,
Financial Statements   ch. **1**
                                                   Interim Financial Reporting, ch. **22**

FASB Statement No. 4
Reporting Gains and Losses from
Extinguishment of Debt (superseded by
FAS-145 for fiscal years beginning after
May 15, 2002)   Debt Obligations and Credit Arrangements,
                                                       ch. **46**

FASB Statement No. 5
Accounting for Contingencies — Contingencies, Risks, Uncertainties, and Concentrations, ch. **10**

FASB Statement No. 6
Classification of Short-Term Obligations Expected to Be Refinanced — Assets and Liabilities: General, ch. **36**
Debt Obligations and Credit Arrangements, ch. **46**

FASB Statement No. 7
Accounting and Reporting by Development Stage Enterprises — Development Stage Enterprises, ch. **12**

FASB Statement No. 8
Accounting for the Translation of Foreign Currency Transactions and Foreign Currency Financial Statements — Superseded by FAS-52

FASB Statement No. 9
Accounting for Income Taxes—Oil and Gas Producing Companies — Superseded by FAS-19

FASB Statement No. 10
Extension of "Grandfather" Provisions for Business Combinations — Superseded by FAS-141

FASB Statement No. 11
Accounting for Contingencies—Transition Method — No longer relevant

FASB Statement No. 12
Accounting for Certain Marketable Securities — Superseded by FAS-115

FASB Statement No. 13
Accounting for Leases — Leases, ch. **23**

FASB Statement No. 14
Financial Reporting for Segments of a Business Enterprise — Superseded by FAS-131

FASB Statement No. 15
Accounting by Debtors and Creditors for Troubled Debt Restructurings — Debt Obligations and Credit Arrangements, ch. **46**

FASB Statement No. 16
Prior Period Adjustments — Accounting Changes, ch. **1**
Interim Financial Reporting, ch. **22**

FASB Statement No. 17
Accounting for Leases—Initial Direct Costs — Superseded by FAS-91

FASB Statement No. 18
Financial Reporting for Segments of a
Business Enterprise—Interim Financial
Statements   Superseded by FAS-131

FASB Statement No. 19
Financial Accounting and Reporting by
Oil and Gas Producing Companies   Specialized industry—not discussed

FASB Statement No. 20
Accounting for Forward Exchange
Contracts   Superseded by FAS-52

FASB Statement No. 21
Suspension of the Reporting of Earnings
per Share and Segment Information by
Nonpublic Enterprises   Superseded by FAS-131

FASB Statement No. 22
Changes in the Provisions of Lease
Agreements Resulting from Refundings of
Tax-Exempt Debt   Debt Obligations and Credit Arrangements,
                                                  ch. **46**
                                                  Leases, ch. **23**

FASB Statement No. 23
Inception of the Lease   Leases, ch. **23**

FASB Statement No. 24
Reporting Segment Information in
Financial Statements That Are Presented
in Another Enterprise's Financial Report   Superseded by FAS-131

FASB Statement No. 25
Suspension of Certain Accounting
Requirements for Oil and Gas Producing
Companies   Superseded by FAS-111

FASB Statement No. 26
Profit Recognition on Sales-Type Leases of
Real Estate   Superseded by FAS-98

FASB Statement No. 27
Classification of Renewals or Extensions
of Existing Sales-Type or Direct Financing
Leases   Leases, ch. **23**

FASB Statement No. 28
Accounting for Sales with Leasebacks   Leases, ch. **23**

FASB Statement No. 29
Determining Contingent Rentals   Leases, ch. **23**

FASB Statement No. 30
Disclosure of Information About Major
Customers   Superseded by FAS-131

FASB Statement No. 44
Accounting for Intangible Assets of Motor
Carriers | Rescinded by FAS-145

FASB Statement No. 45
Accounting for Franchise Fee Revenue | Accounting Policies, ch. **2**
Revenues and Gains, ch. **49**

FASB Statement No. 46
Financial Reporting and Changing Prices:
Motion Picture Films | Superseded by FAS-89

FASB Statement No. 47
Disclosure of Long-Term Obligations | Debt Obligations and Credit Arrangements,
ch. **46**

FASB Statement No. 48
Revenue Recognition When Right of
Return Exists | Accounts and Notes Receivables, ch. **38**
Revenues and Gains, ch. **49**

FASB Statement No. 49
Accounting for Product Financing
Arrangements | Commitments, ch. **6**
Contingencies, Risks, Uncertainties, and
Concentrations, ch. **10**
Debt Obligations and Credit Arrangements,
ch. **46**

FASB Statement No. 50
Financial Reporting in the Record and
Music Industry | Specialized industry—not discussed

FASB Statement No. 51
Financial Reporting by Cable Television
Companies | Specialized industry—not discussed

FASB Statement No. 52
Foreign Currency Translation | Portions amended by FAS-96 and 109
Foreign Operations and Currency Translation,
ch. **17**

FASB Statement No. 53
Financial Reporting by Producers and
Distributors of Motion Picture Films | Rescinded by FAS-139

FASB Statement No. 54
Financial Reporting and Changing Prices:
Investment Companies | Superseded by FAS-89

FASB Statement No. 55
Determining Whether a Convertible
Security Is a Common Stock Equivalent | Superseded by FAS-111

FASB Statement No. 56
Designation of AICPA Guide and
Statement of Position (SOP) 81-1 on
Contractor Accounting and SOP 81-2
Concerning Hospital-Related Organiza-
tions as Preferable for Purposes of Applying
APB Opinion No. 20   Superseded by FAS-111

FASB Statement No. 57
Related Party Disclosures   Related Party Disclosures, ch. **30**

FASB Statement No. 58
Capitalization of Interest Cost in Financial
Statements That Include Investments
Accounted For by the Equity Method   Interest Cost, ch. **21**

FASB Statement No. 59
Deferral of the Effective Date of Certain
Accounting Requirements for Pension
Plans of State and Local Governmental
Units   Superseded by FAS-75

FASB Statement No. 60
Accounting and Reporting by Insurance
Enterprises   Specialized industry—not discussed

FASB Statement No. 61
Accounting for Title Plant   Impairment and Disposal of Long-Lived
                                      Assets, ch. **20**

FASB Statement No. 62
Capitalization of Interest Cost in
Situations Involving Certain Tax-Exempt
Borrowings and Certain Gifts and Grants   Interest Cost, ch. **21**

FASB Statement No. 63
Financial Reporting by Broadcasters   Specialized industry—not discussed

FASB Statement No. 64
Extinguishments of Debt Made to Satisfy
Sinking-Fund Requirements (superseded
by FAS-145 for fiscal years beginning after
May 15, 2002)   Debt Obligations and Credit Arrangements,
                                      ch. **46**

FASB Statement No. 65
Accounting for Certain Mortgage Banking
Activities   Specialized industry—not discussed

FASB Statement No. 66
Accounting for Sales of Real Estate   Specialized industry—not discussed

FASB Statement No. 67
Accounting for Costs and Initial Rental
Operations of Real Estate Projects   Specialized industry—not discussed

FASB Statement No. 68
Research and Development Arrangements

Research and Development Costs, ch. **31**

FASB Statement No. 69
Disclosures about Oil and Gas Producing
Activities

Specialized industry—not discussed

FASB Statement No. 70
Financial Reporting and Changing Prices:
Foreign Currency Translation

Superseded by FAS-89

FASB Statement No. 71
Accounting for the Effects of Certain
Types of Regulation

Specialized industry—not discussed

FASB Statement No. 72
Accounting for Certain Acquisitions of
Banking or Thrift Institutions

Superseded by FAS-147

FASB Statement No. 73
Reporting a Change in Accounting for
Railroad Track Structures

Accounting Changes and Error Corrections,
ch. **1**

FASB Statement No. 74
Accounting for Special Termination
Benefits Paid to Employees

Superseded by FAS-88

FASB Statement No. 75
Deferral of the Effective Date of Certain
Accounting Requirements for Pension
Plans of State and Local Governmental
Units

Rescinded by FAS-135

FASB Statement No. 76
Extinguishment of Debt

Superseded by FAS-140

FASB Statement No. 77
Reporting by Transferors for Transfers of
Receivables with Recourse

Superseded by FAS-140

FASB Statement No. 78
Classification of Obligations That Are
Callable by the Creditor

Assets and Liabilities: General, ch. **36**
Debt Obligations and Credit Arrangements,
ch. **46**

FASB Statement No. 79
Elimination of Certain Disclosures for
Business Combinations by Nonpublic
Enterprises

Superseded by FAS-141

FASB Statement No. 80
Accounting for Futures Contracts

Superseded by FAS-133

FASB Statement No. 81
Disclosure of Postretirement Health Care
and Life Insurance Benefits

Superseded by FAS-106

FASB Statement No. 93
Recognition of Depreciation by Not-for-
Profit Organizations

Accounting Policies, ch. **2**
Property, Plant, and Equipment, ch. **42**

FASB Statement No. 94
Consolidation of all Majority-Owned
Subsidiaries

Consolidated and Combined Financial
Statements, ch. **9**

FASB Statement No. 95
Statement of Cash Flows

Statement of Cash Flows, ch. **56**

FASB Statement No. 96
Accounting for Income Taxes

Superseded by FAS-109

FASB Statement No. 97
Accounting and Reporting by Insurance
Enterprises for Certain Long-Duration
Contracts and for Realized Gains and
Losses from the Sale of Investments

Specialized industry—not discussed

FASB Statement No. 98
Accounting for Leases:
• Sale-Leaseback Transactions
  Involving Real Estate
• Sales-Type Leases of Real Estate
• Definition of the Lease Term
• Initial Direct Costs of
  Direct Financing Leases

Accounting Policies, ch. **2**
Leases, ch. **23**

FASB Statement No. 99
Deferral of the Effective Date of
Recognition of Depreciation by Not-for-
Profit Organizations

Property, Plant, and Equipment, ch. **42**

FASB Statement No. 100
Accounting for Income Taxes—Deferral of
the Effective Date of FASB Statement
No. 96

Superseded by FAS-103, FAS-108, and
FAS-109

FASB Statement No. 101
Regulated Enterprises—Accounting for
the Discontinuation of Application of
FASB Statement No. 71

Specialized industry—not discussed

FASB Statement No. 102
Statement of Cash Flows—Exemption of
Certain Enterprises and Classification of
Cash Flows from Certain Securities
Acquired for Resale

Statement of Cash Flows, ch. **56**

FASB Statement No. 103
Accounting for Income Taxes—Deferral
of the Effective Date of FASB Statement
No. 96

Superseded by FAS-108 and FAS-109

FASB Statement No. 104
Statement of Cash Flows-Net Reporting of
Certain Cash Receipts and Cash Payments
and Classification of Cash Flows from
Hedging Transactions

Statement of Cash Flows, ch. **56**

FASB Statement No. 105
Disclosure of Information About Financial
Instruments with Off-Balance-Sheet Risk
and Financial Instruments with
Concentrations of Credit Risk

Superseded by FAS-133

FASB Statement No. 106
Employers' Accounting for Postretirement
Benefits Other Than Pensions

Deferred Compensation Arrangements, ch. **11**
Postemployment Benefits, ch. **27**
Postretirement Benefits Other Than Pensions,
ch. **28**

FASB Statement No. 107
Disclosures about Fair Value of Financial
Instruments

Financial Instruments, Derivatives, and
Hedging Activities, ch. **15**
Transfers and Servicing of Financial Assets,
ch. **35**

FASB Statement No. 108
Accounting for Income Taxes—Deferral of
the Effective Date of FASB Statement
No. 96

Superseded by FAS-109

FASB Statement No. 109
Accounting for Income Taxes

Business Combinations, ch. **4**
Consolidated and Combined Financial
Statements, ch. **9**
Impairment and Disposal of Long-Lived
Assets, ch. **20**
Quasi-Reorganizations and Reorganizations
under the Bankruptcy Code, ch. **29**
Income Taxes, ch. **45**

FASB Statement No. 110
Reporting by Defined Benefit Pension
Plans of Investment Contracts

Specialized industry—not discussed

FASB Statement No. 111
Rescission of FASB Statement No. 32 and
Technical Corrections

Accounting Changes and Error Corrections,
ch. **1**

FASB Statement No. 112
Employers' Accounting for
Postemployment Benefits

Postemployment Benefits, ch. **27**
Postretirement Benefits Other Than Pensions,
ch. **28**

FASB Statement No. 113
Accounting and Reporting for
Reinsurance of Short-Duration and Long-
Duration Contracts

Specialized industry—not discussed

FASB Statement No. 114
Accounting by Creditors for Impairment
of a Loan

Accounts and Notes Receivable, ch. **38**
Intangible Assets, ch. **43**
Debt Obligations and Credit Arrangements,
ch. **46**

FASB Statement No. 115
Accounting for Certain Investments in
Debt and Equity Securities

Investments: Debt and Equity Securities,
ch. 40

FASB Statement No. 116
Accounting for Contributions Received
and Contributions Made

Accounting Policies, ch. **2**

FASB Statement No. 117
Financial Statements of Not-for-Profit
Organizations

Specialized industry—not discussed

FASB Statement No. 118
Accounting by Creditors for Impairment
of a Loan—Income Recognition and
Disclosures

Accounts and Notes Receivable, ch. **38**

FASB Statement No. 119
Disclosure about Derivative Financial
Instruments and Fair Value of Financial
Instruments

Superseded by FAS-133

FASB Statement No. 120
Accounting and Reporting by Mutual Life
Insurance Enterprises and by Insurance
Enterprises for Certain Long-Duration
Participating Contracts

Specialized industry—not discussed

FASB Statement No. 121
Accounting for the Impairment of Long-
Lived Assets and for Long-Lived Assets to
Be Disposed Of

Superseded by FAS-144

FASB Statement No. 122
Accounting for Mortgage Servicing Rights

Superseded by FAS-125 and FAS-140

FASB Statement No. 123
Accounting for Stock-Based Compensation

Stock-Based Compensation, Stock Option
Plans, and Stock Purchase Plans, ch. **33**

FASB Statement No. 123R
Share-Based Payment

Stock-Based Compensation, Stock Option
Plans, and Stock Purchase Plans, ch. **33**

FASB Statement No. 135
Rescission of FASB Statement No. 75 and
Technical Corrections

Segment Information, ch. **32**
Comprehensive Income, ch. **54**

FASB Statement No. 136
Transfers of Assets to a Not-for-Profit
Organization or Charitable Trust That
Raises or Holds Contributions for Others

Transfers and Servicing of Financial Assets,
ch. **35**

FASB Statement No. 137
Accounting for Derivative Instruments
and Hedging Activities—Deferral of the
Effective Date of Statement No. 133

Financial Instruments, Derivatives, and
Hedging Activities, ch. **15**

FASB Statement No. 138
Accounting for Certain Derivative
Instruments and Certain Hedging
Activities

Financial Instruments, Derivatives, and
Hedging Activities, ch. **15**

FASB Statement No. 139
Rescission of FASB Statement No. 53
and amendments to FASB Statements
No. 63, 89, and 121

Accounting Policies, ch. **2**

FASB Statement No. 140
Accounting for Transfers and Servicing of
Financial Assets and Extinguishments of
Liabilities

Transfers and Servicing of Financial Assets,
ch. **35**

FASB Statement No. 141
Business Combinations

Business Combinations, ch. **4**

FASB Statement No. 142
Goodwill and Other Intangible Assets

Intangible Assets, ch. **43**

FASB Statement No. 143
Accounting for Asset Retirement
Obligations

Property, Plant, and Equipment, ch. **42**

FASB Statement No. 144
Accounting for the Impairment or
Disposal of Long-Lived Assets

Impairment and Disposal of Long-Lived
Assets, ch. **20**

FASB Statement No. 153
Exchanges of Nonmonetary Assets—An
Amendment of APB Opinion No. 29

Nonmonetary Transactions, ch. **25**

FASB Statement No. 154
Accounting Changes and Error
Corrections

Accounting Changes and Error Corrections,
ch. **1**
Interim Financial Reporting, ch. **22**

FASB Statement No. 155
Accounting for Certain Hybrid Financial
Instruments—An Amendment of FASB
Statements No. 133 and 140

Financial Instruments, Derivatives, and
Hedging Activities, ch. **15**
Transfers and Servicing of Financial Assets,
ch. **34**

FASB Statement No. 156
Accounting for Servicing of Financial
Assets—An Amendment of FASB
Statement No. 140

Transfers and Servicing of Financial Assets,
ch. **34**

FASB Statement No. 157
Fair Value Measurements

Fair Value Measurements, ch. **14**
Interim Financial Reporting, ch. **21**

FASB Statement No. 158
Employers' Accounting for Defined Benefit
Pension and Other Postretirement
Plans—An Amendment of FASB Statements
No. 87, 88, 106, and 132R

Interim Financial Reporting, ch. **21**
Pension Plans, ch. **26**
Postretirement Benefits Other Than Pensions,
ch. **28**

FINANCIAL ACCOUNTING STANDARDS BOARD
INTERPRETATIONS (FIN)

ORIGINAL PRONOUNCEMENT

2007-2008 *GAAP*
FINANCIAL STATEMENT
DISCLOSURES MANUAL REFERENCE

FASB Interpretation No. 1
Accounting Changes Related to the Cost
of Inventory

Accounting Changes, ch. **1**
Inventory, ch. **39**

FASB Interpretation No. 2
Imputing Interest on Debt Arrangements
Made under the Federal Bankruptcy Act

Superseded by FAS-15

FASB Interpretation No. 13
Consolidation of a Parent and Its
Subsidiaries Having Different Balance
Sheet Dates

Superseded by FAS-115

FASB Interpretation No. 14
Reasonable Estimation of the Amount of a
Loss

Contingencies, Risks, Uncertainties, and
Concentrations, ch. **10**

FASB Interpretation No. 15
Translation of Unamortized Policy
Acquisition Costs by a Stock Life
Insurance Company

Superseded by FAS-52

FASB Interpretation No. 16
Clarification of Definitions and
Accounting for Marketable Equity
Securities That Become Nonmarketable

Superseded by FAS-115

FASB Interpretation No. 17
Applying the Lower of Cost or Market
Rule in Translated Financial Statements

Superseded by FAS-52

FASB Interpretation No. 18
Accounting for Income Taxes in Interim
Periods

Income Taxes, ch. **45**

FASB Interpretation No. 19
Lessee Guarantee of the Residual Value of
Leased Property

Leases, ch. **23**

FASB Interpretation No. 20
Reporting Accounting Changes under
AICPA Statements of Position

Accounting Changes, ch. **1**

FASB Interpretation No. 21
Accounting for Leases in a Business
Combination

Leases, ch. **23**

FASB Interpretation No. 22
Applicability of Indefinite Reversal
Criteria To Timing Differences

Superseded by FAS-96 and FAS-109

FASB Interpretation No. 23
Leases of Certain Property Owned by a
Governmental Unit or Authority

Leases, ch. **23**

FASB Interpretation No. 24
Leases Involving Only Part of a Building

Leases, ch. **23**

FASB Interpretation No. 25
Accounting for an Unused Investment Tax
Credit

Superseded by FAS-96 and FAS-109

FASB TECHNICAL BULLETINS (FTB)

Note: FTBs that have been superseded are not listed herein.

ORIGINAL PRONOUNCEMENT

2007-2008 *GAAP*
FINANCIAL STATEMENT
DISCLOSURES MANUAL REFERENCE

FTB 79-1 (R)
Purpose and Scope of FASB Technical
Bulletins and Procedures for Issuance — Accounting Policies, ch. **2**

FTB 79-3
Subjective Acceleration Clauses in Long-
Term Debt Agreements — Assets and Liabilities: General, ch. **36**
Debt Obligations and Credit Arrangements, ch. **46**

FTB 79-4
Segment Reporting of Puerto Rican
Operations — Segment Information, ch. **32**

FTB 79-5
Meaning of the Term "Customer" as It
Applies to Health Care Facilities under
FASB Statement No. 14 — Segment Information, ch. **32**

FTB 79-9
Accounting in Interim Periods for
Changes in Income Tax Rates — Interim Financial Reporting, ch. **22**
Income Taxes, ch. **45**

FTB 79-10
Fiscal Funding Clauses in Lease Agreements — Leases, ch. **23**

FTB 79-12
Interest Rate Used in Calculating the Present
Value of Minimum Lease Payments — Leases, ch. **23**

FTB 79-13
Applicability of FASB Statement No. 13 to
Current Value Financial Statements — Changing Prices, ch. **5**
Leases, ch. **23**

FTB 79-14
Upward Adjustment of Guaranteed
Residual Values — Leases, ch. **23**

FTB 79-15
Accounting for Loss on a Sublease Not
Involving the Disposal of a Segment — Leases, ch. **23**

FTB 79-16 (R)
Effect of a Change in Income Tax Rate on
the Accounting for Leveraged Leases — Leases, ch. **23**

FTB 79-17
Reporting Cumulative Effect Adjustment
from Retroactive Application of FASB
Statement No. 13   Leases, ch. **23**

FTB 79-18
Transition Requirement of Certain FASB
Amendments and Interpretations of FASB
Statement No. 13   Leases, ch. **23**

FTB 79-19
Investor's Accounting for Unrealized
Losses on Marketable Securities Owned
by an Equity Method Investee   Investments: Debt and Equity Securities,
                                                        ch. 40
                                                     Investments: Equity and Cost Methods, ch. **41**

FTB 80-1
Early Extinguishment of Debt through
Exchange for Common or Preferred Stock   Debt Obligations and Credit Arrangements,
                                                        ch. **46**

FTB 80-2
Classification of Debt Restructurings by
Debtors and Creditors   Debt Obligations and Credit Arrangements,
                                                        ch. **46**

FTB 81-6
Applicability of Statement 15 to Debtors
in Bankruptcy Situations   Quasi-Reorganizations and Reorganizations
                                                        under the Bankruptcy Code, ch. **29**
                                                     Debt Obligations and Credit Arrangements,
                                                        ch. **46**

FTB 82-1
Disclosure of the Sale or Purchase of Tax
Benefits through Tax Leases   Income Taxes, ch. **45**

FTB 84-1
Accounting for Stock Issued to Acquire
the Results of a Research and
Development Arrangement   Research and Development Costs, ch. **31**

FTB 85-1
Accounting for the Receipt of Federal
Home Loan Mortgage Corporation
Participating Preferred Stock   Nonmonetary Transactions, ch. **25**

FTB 85-3
Accounting for Operating Leases with
Scheduled Rent Increases   Leases, ch. **23**

FTB 85-4
Accounting for Purchases of Life
Insurance   Assets and Liabilities: General, ch. **36**
                                                     Other Assets: Current and Noncurrent, ch. **44**

FTB 85-5
Issues Relating to Accounting for Business
Combinations, Including:
• Costs of Closing Duplicate Facilities of an
  Acquirer
• Stock Transactions between Companies
  under Common Control
• Downstream Mergers
• Identical Common Shares for a Pooling of
  Interests
• Pooling of Interests by Mutual and
  Cooperative Enterprises   Business Combinations, ch. **4**

FTB 85-6
Accounting for a Purchase of Treasury
Shares at a Price Significantly in Excess of
the Current Market Price of the Shares
and the Income Statement Classification of
Costs Incurred in Defending against a
Takeover Attempt   Stockholders' Equity, ch. **48**

FTB 86-2
Accounting for an Interest in the Residual
Value of a Leased Asset:
• Acquired by a Third Party or
• Retained by a Lessor That Sells the Related
  Minimum Rental Payments   Leases, ch. **23**

FTB 87-2
Computation of a Loss on an
Abandonment   Specialized industry—not discussed

FTB 87-3
Accounting for Mortgage Servicing Fees
and Rights   Specialized industry—not discussed

FTB 88-1
Issues Related to Accounting for Leases:
• Time Pattern of the Physical Use of the
  Property in an Operating Lease
• Lease Incentives in an Operating Lease
• Applicability of Leveraged Lease
  Accounting to Existing Assets of the
  Lessor
• Money-Over-Money Lease Transactions
• Wrap Lease Transactions   Leases, ch. **23**

FTB 90-1
Accounting for Separately Priced
Extended Warranty and Product
Maintenance Contracts   Accounting Policies, ch. **2**
                                                   Revenues and Gains, ch. **49**

FTB 94-1
Application of Statement 115 to Debt
Securities Restructured in a Troubled Debt
Restructuring   Debt Obligations and Credit Arrangements,
                                                   ch. **46**

FTB 97-1
Accounting under Statement 123 for
Certain Employee Stock Purchase Plans
with a Look-Back Option

Stock-Based Compensation, Stock Option
Plans, and Stock Purchase Plans, ch. **33**

FTB 01-1
Effective Date for Certain Financial
Institutions of Certain Provisions of
Statement 140 Related to the Isolation of
Transferred Financial Assets

Transfers and Servicing of Financial Assets,
ch. **35**

AICPA STATEMENTS OF POSITION (SOP)

Note: SOPs that relate to specialized industries are not listed herein.

ORIGINAL PRONOUNCEMENT

2007-2008 *GAAP*
*FINANCIAL STATEMENT
DISCLOSURES MANUAL* REFERENCE

SOP 76-3
Accounting Practices for Certain
Employee Stock Ownership Plans

Stock-Based Compensation, Stock Option
Plans, and Stock Purchase Plans, ch. **33**

SOP 81-1
Accounting for Performance of
Construction-Type and Certain
Production-Type Contracts

Long-Term Contracts, ch. **24**

SOP 90-3
Definition of the term Substantially the
Same for Holders of Debt Instruments, as
Used in Certain Audit Guides and a
Statement of Position

Investments: Debt and Equity Securities,
ch. **40**

SOP 90-7
Financial Reporting by Entities in
Reorganization Under the Bankruptcy
Code

Quasi-Reorganizations and Reorganizations
under the Bankruptcy Code, ch. **29**

SOP 92-3
Accounting for Foreclosed Assets

Quasi-Reorganizations and Reorganizations
under the Bankruptcy Code, ch. **29**

SOP 93-3
Rescission of Accounting Principles Board
Statements

Accounting Policies, ch. **2**

SOP 93-4
Foreign Currency Accounting and
Financial Statement Presentation for
Investment Companies

Foreign Operations and Currency Translation,
ch. **17**

SOP 93-6
Employers' Accounting for Employee
Stock Ownership Plans

Stock-Based Compensation, Stock Option
Plans, and Stock Purchase Plans, ch. **33**

SOP 93-7
Reporting on Advertising Costs

Advertising Costs, ch. **3**

SOP 94-6
Disclosure of Certain Significant Risks and
Uncertainties

Contingencies, Risks, Uncertainties, and
Concentrations, ch. **10**

SOP 96-1
Environmental Remediation Liabilities

Contingencies, Risks, Uncertainties, and
Concentrations, ch. **10**

SOP 97-2
Software Revenue Recognition

Computer Software, ch. **8**

SOP 98-1
Accounting for Costs of Computer
Software Developed or Obtained for
Internal Use

Computer Software, ch. **8**

SOP 98-5
Reporting on the Costs of Start-Up
Activities

Expenses and Losses, ch. **50**

SOP 98-9
Modification of SOP 97-2, Software
Revenue Recognition, With Respect to
Certain Transactions

Computer Software, ch. **8**

SOP 01-6
Accounting by Certain Entities (Including
Entities With Trade Receivables) That
Lend to or Finance the Activities of
Others

Accounts and Notes Receivable, ch. **38**

SOP 03-3
Accounting for Certain Loans or Debt
Securities Acquired in a Transfer

Transfers and Servicing of Financial Assets,
ch. **35**

Index

CD-ROM Instructions

SYSTEM REQUIREMENTS

- IBM PC or compatible computer with CD-ROM drive
- Windows 95 or higher
- Microsoft Word 7.0 for Windows™ or compatible word processor
- 10 MB available on hard drive

The CD-ROM provided with the *2007–2008 GAAP Financial Statement Disclosures Manual* contains electronic versions of the over 900 separate sample disclosures presented in the book. Disclosures are available as separate pages within files for each chapter. The CD-ROM also includes the complete financial statement disclosures checklist, covering all types of disclosures, including items for special financial statement topics, the balance sheet, the income statement, and the statement of cash flows. Questions addressed in the checklist are keyed to specific authoritative literature to identify their regulatory antecedents.

Subject to the conditions in the license agreement and the limited warranty, which are reproduced at the end of this book, you may duplicate the files on this disc, modify them as necessary, and create your own customized versions. Using the disc in any way indicates that you accept the terms of the license agreement.

USING THE CD-ROM

The data disc is intended for use with your word processing software. Each document is provided in Rich Text Format. These files can be read by all compatible word processors, including Microsoft Word for Windows and WordPerfect 7 or above. Check your owner's manual for information on the conversion of documents as required.

USING THE DOCUMENTS

The list of the Disc Contents is avaiable on your disc in a file called _contents.rtf. You can open this file and view it on your screen and use it to link the documents you're interested in, or print a hard copy to use for reference.

(1)   Open the file _contents.rtf in your word processor.

(2)   Locate the file you wish to access, and click on the hyper-linked file name. Your word processor will then open the file.

(3)   You may copy files from the CD-ROM to your hard disk. To edit files you have copied, remember to clear the read-only attribute from the file. To do this, select the name of the file in My Computer, right-click the filename, then choose Properties, and clear the Read-only checkbox.

SOFTWARE SUPPORT

If you experience any difficulties installing or running the electronic files and cannot resolve the problem using the information presented here, call technical support at 800 835 0105 or visit the web site at http://support.cch.com.

CCH
a Wolters Kluwer business

SOFTWARE LICENSE AGREEMENT FOR ELECTRONIC FILES TO ACCOMPANY
2007–2008 GAAP FINANCIAL STATEMENT DISCLOSURES MANUAL
(THE "BOOK")

READ THE TERMS AND CONDITIONS OF THIS LICENSE AGREEMENT CAREFULLY BEFORE INSTALLING THE SOFTWARE (THE "PROGRAM") TO ACCOMPANY 2007–2008 GAAP FINANCIAL STATEMENT DISCLOSURES MANUAL (THE "BOOK"). THE PROGRAM IS COPYRIGHTED AND LICENSED (NOT SOLD). BY INSTALLING THE PROGRAM, YOU ARE ACCEPTING AND AGREEING TO THE TERMS OF THIS LICENSE AGREEMENT. IF YOU ARE NOT WILLING TO BE BOUND BY THE TERMS OF THIS LICENSE AGREEMENT, YOU SHOULD PROMPTLY RETURN THE PACKAGE IN RE-SELLABLE CONDITION AND YOU WILL RECEIVE A REFUND OF YOUR MONEY. THIS LICENSE AGREEMENT REPRESENTS THE ENTIRE AGREEMENT CONCERNING THE PROGRAM BETWEEN YOU AND CCH (REFERRED TO AS "LICENSOR"), AND IT SUPERSEDES ANY PRIOR PROPOSAL, REPRESENTATION, OR UNDERSTANDING BETWEEN THE PARTIES.

1. License Grant. Licensor hereby grants to you, and you accept, a nonexclusive license to use the Program CD-ROM and the computer programs contained therein in machine-readable, object code form only (collectively referred to as the "Software"), and the accompanying User Documentation, only as authorized in this License Agreement. The Software may be used only on a single computer owned, leased, or otherwise controlled by you; or in the event of the inoperability of that computer, on a backup computer selected by you. Neither concurrent use on two or more computers nor use in a local area network or other network is permitted without separate authorization and the possible payment of other license fees. You agree that you will not assign, sublease, transfer, pledge, lease, rent, or share your rights under the License Agreement. You agree that you may not reverse engineer, decompile, disassemble, or otherwise adapt, modify, or translate the Software.

Upon loading the Software into your computer, you may retain the Program CD-ROM for backup purposes. In addition, you may make one copy of the Software on a set of diskettes (or other storage medium) for the purpose of backup in the event the Program Diskettes are damaged or destroyed. You may make one copy of any additional User Documentation (such as the README.TXT file or the "About the Computer Disc" section of the Book) for backup purposes. Any such copies of the Software or the User Documentation shall include Licensor's copyright and other proprietary notices. Except as authorized under this paragraph, no copies of the program or any portions thereof may be made by you or any person under your authority or control.

2. Licensor's Rights. You acknowledge and agree that the Software and the User Documentation are proprietary products of Licensor protected under U.S. copyright law. You further acknowledge and agree that all right, title, and interest in and to the Program, including associated intellectual property rights, are and shall remain with Licensor. This License Agreement does not convey to you an interest in or to the Program,

including associated intellectual property rights, which are and shall remain with Licensor. This License Agreement does not convey to you an interest in or to the Program, but only a limited right of use revocable in accordance with the terms of the License Agreement.

3. License Fees. The license fees paid by you are paid in consideration of the licenses granted under this License Agreement.

4. Term. This License Agreement is effective upon your installing this software and shall continue until terminated. You may terminate this License Agreement at any time by returning the Program and all copies thereof and extracts therefrom to Licensor. Licensor may terminate this License Agreement upon the breach by you of any term hereof. Upon such termination by Licensor, you agree to return to Licensor the Program and all copies and portions thereof.

5. Limited Warranty. Licensor warrants, for our benefit alone, for a period of 90 days from the date of commencement of this License Agreement (referred to as the "Warranty Period") that the Program CD-ROM in which the Software is contained is free from defects in material and workmanship. If during the Warranty Period, a defect appears in the Program diskettes, you may return the Program to Licensor for either replacement or, at Licensor's option, refund of amounts paid by you under this License Agreement. You agree that the foregoing constitutes your sole and exclusive remedy for breach by Licensor of any warranties made under this Agreement. EXCEPT FOR THE WARRANTIES SET FORTH ABOVE, THE PROGRAM, AND THE SOFTWARE CONTAINED THEREIN, ARE LICENSED "AS IS," AND LICENSOR DISCLAIMS ANY AND ALL OTHER WARRANTIES, WHETHER EXPRESS OR IMPLIED, INCLUDING, WITHOUT LIMITATION, ANY IMPLIED WARRANTIES OF MERCHANTABILITY OR FITNESS FOR A PARTICULAR PURPOSE.

6. Limitation of Liability. Licensor's cumulative liability to you or any other party for any loss or damages resulting from any claims, demands, or actions arising out of or relating to this Agreement shall not exceed the license fee paid to Licensor for the use of the Program. IN NO EVENT SHALL LICENSOR BE LIABLE FOR ANY INDIRECT, INCIDENTAL, CONSEQUENTIAL, SPECIAL, OR EXEMPLARY DAMAGES (INCLUDING, BUT NOT LIMITED TO, LOSS OF DATA, BUSINESS INTERRUPTION, OR LOST PROFITS) EVEN IF LICENSOR HAS BEEN ADVISED OF THE POSSIBILITY OF SUCH DAMAGES.

7. Miscellaneous. This License Agreement shall be construed and governed in accordance with the laws of the State of Delaware. Should any term of this License Agreement be declared void or unenforceable by any court of competent jurisdiction, such declaration shall have no effect on the remaining terms hereof. The failure of either party to enforce any rights granted hereunder or to take action against the other party in the event of any breach hereunder shall not be deemed a waiver by that party as to subsequent enforcement of rights or subsequent actions in the event of future breaches.